THE ROUTLEDGE HANDBOOK OF THE PEOPLES AND PLACES OF ANCIENT WESTERN ASIA

This extensive reference work provides the most comprehensive general treatment yet available of the peoples and places of the regions commonly referred to as the ancient Near and Middle East – covered in this book by the term ancient western Asia – extending from the Aegean coast of Turkey in the west to the Indus river in the east. It contains almost 1,500 entries on the kingdoms, countries, cities, and population groups of Anatolia, Cyprus, Syria–Palestine, Mesopotamia, and Iran and parts of Central Asia, from the Early Bronze Age to the end of the Persian empire.

Trevor Bryce, in collaboration with five international scholars, provides detailed accounts of the Near/Middle Eastern peoples and places known to us from historical records. Each of these entries includes specific references to translated passages from the relevant ancient texts. Numerous entries on archaeological sites contain accounts of their history of excavation, as well as more detailed descriptions of their chief features and their significance within the commercial, cultural, and political contexts of the regions to which they belonged.

Illustrated throughout with 140 images and 20 maps, *The Routledge Handbook of the Peoples and Places of Ancient Western Asia* is a much-needed reference resource for students as well as established scholars of history and archaeology, of both the ancient Near Eastern as well as the Classical civilizations. Including substantial essays on a number of major kingdoms, countries and cities, such as Assyria, Babylon, Persia and Troy, it will also appeal to more general readers who wish to pursue in depth their interest in these civilizations.

Trevor Bryce is an Honorary Research Consultant at the University of Queensland and Fellow of the Australian Academy of the Humanities. He has held positions as Reader in Classics and Ancient History, University of Queensland, Professor of Classics and Ancient History, University of New England (Australia), and Deputy Vice-Chancellor, Lincoln University, New Zealand. He is the author of numerous works on the ancient Near East. His most recent publications are *The Kingdom of the Hittites* (2005), and *The Trojans and their Neighbours* (Routledge, 2006).

THE ROUTLEDGE HANDBOOK OF THE PEOPLES AND PLACES OF ANCIENT WESTERN ASIA

The Near East from the Early Bronze Age to the Fall of the Persian Empire

Trevor Bryce

in consultation with

Heather D. Baker

Daniel T. Potts

Jonathan N. Tubb

Jennifer M. Webb

Paul Zimansky

LONDON AND NEW YORK

First published 2009
First published in paperback 2012
by Routledge
2 Park Square, Milton Park, Abingdon, Oxon OX14 4RN

Simultaneously published in the USA and Canada
by Routledge
711 Third Avenue, New York, NY 10017

Routledge is an imprint of the Taylor & Francis Group, an informa business

British Library Cataloguing in Publication Data
A catalogue record for this book is available from the British Library

Library of Congress Cataloging-in-Publication Data
Bryce, Trevor, 1940–
The Routledge handbook of the peoples and places of ancient Western Asia : the near East from the early Bronze Age to the fall of the Persian Empire / Trevor Bryce in consultation with Heather D. Baker . . . [et al.].
p. cm.
Includes bibliographical references and index.
ISBN 978-0-415-39485-7 (hardback : alk. paper)—
ISBN 978-0-203-87550-6 (e-book) 1. Middle East—Civilization—To 622. 2. Middle East—Antiquities. 3. Excavations (Archaeology)—Middle East. I. Title. II. Title: Handbook of the peoples and places of ancient Western Asia.
DS57.B89 2009
939′.4—dc22
2008054633

ISBN: 978–0–415–39485–7 (hbk)
ISBN: 978–0–415–69261–8 (pbk)
ISBN: 978–0–203–87550–6 (ebk)

Typeset in GaramondThree
by Swales & Willis Ltd, Exeter, Devon

CONTENTS

THE CONSULTANTS

I would like to express my deepest gratitude to the scholars who have contributed to this book. Their contributions have consisted in scrutinizing all the entries relevant to their fields of expertise, and in a large number of cases making amendments and providing additional material. These amendments and additions have often been substantial. In some cases, they have totally rewritten my original entries, and have also provided a number of new entries. In these cases, I have specifically indicated their authorship. But I would stress that their contributions have gone far beyond the entries directly attributed to them. The book as a whole has benefited enormously from the time and expertise which they have devoted to it.

CYPRUS

Jennifer M. Webb received her first degree in Classics and Ancient History from the University of Melbourne. She subsequently worked on a number of excavations in Greece, Cyprus, and Jordan, and completed the degree of Doctor of Philosophy for the University of Melbourne in 1988. Since 1991, she has co-directed three major excavation projects in Cyprus, primarily on settlement and cemetery sites of the Early and Middle Bronze Ages. Her research interests include the material culture of Bronze Age Cyprus, with a particular focus on pottery and glyptic, and the archaeology of households and communities. Her monographs include *Ritual Architecture, Iconography and Practice in the Late Cypriot Bronze Age* (Studies in Mediterranean Archaeology and Literature Pocket-book 75, 1999); *Marki Alonia: An Early and Middle Bronze Age Settlement in Cyprus*, with D. Frankel (Studies in Mediterranean Archaeology CXXIII, 2006), and *The Bronze Age Cemeteries at Deneia in Cyprus*, with D. Frankel (Studies in Mediterranean Archaeology CXXXV, 2007). She is a Fellow of the Australian Academy of the Humanities, and currently a Research Fellow in the Archaeology Program at La Trobe University in Melbourne, Australia.

IRAN AND CENTRAL ASIA

Daniel T. Potts is the Edwin Cuthbert Hall Professor of Middle Eastern Archaeology at the University of Sydney. His research interests cover broadly the archaeology and early history of Iran, the Persian Gulf, Mesopotamia, the Indo-Iranian borderlands, and Central Asia. His publications include *Mesopotamian Civilization: The Material Foundations* (Cornell, 1997), *The Archaeology of Elam* (Cambridge, 1999), *Excavations at Tepe*

Yahya 1967–1975: The Third Millennium (Cambridge, MA, 2001), and edited volumes including *Archaeology of the United Arab Emirates*, with H. Al Naboodah and P. Hellyer (Trident, 2003); *The Mamasani Archaeological Project Stage One: A Report on the First Two Seasons of the ICAR–University of Sydney Expedition to the Mamasani District, Fars Province, Iran*, with K. Roustaei (Tehran, 2006); and *Memory as History: The Legacy of Alexander in Asia*, with H. P. Ray (New Delhi, 2007). He is a Fellow of the Australian Academy of the Humanities.

MESOPOTAMIA

Heather D. Baker, a graduate in Archaeology from the University of Cambridge, has participated in numerous excavations in Britain, Cyprus, Jordan, Turkey, and especially Iraq. At the University of Oxford she gained an MPhil in Cuneiform Studies and a DPhil in Assyriology. Her research interests lie primarily in the social and economic history and material culture of Babylonia and Assyria in the first millennium BCE. Since January 2003, she has been working as a researcher with the START Project on 'The Economic History of Babylonia in the first millennium BC' at the University of Vienna. Her publications include a monograph, *The Archive of the Nappahu Family* (Vienna, 2004), and (as editor) *The Prosopography of the Neo-Assyrian Empire*, Part 2/I (Helsinki, 2000), Part 2/II (Helsinki, 2001), Part 3/I (Helsinki, 2002), and *Approaching the Babylonian Economy*, with M. Jursa (Münster, 2005). She is currently working on a monograph, now nearing completion, on the urban landscape in first millennium BCE Babylonia.

SYRIA AND PALESTINE

Jonathan N. Tubb is Curator of the Ancient Levant in the Department of the Middle East at the British Museum, a post he has held since 1978. He trained in Levantine archaeology at the Institute of Archaeology in London, and began his field career in Syria and Iraq in the 1970s. For ten years he served as Assistant Director of the Institute's excavations in Syria – at Qadesh (Tell Nebi Mend) on the Orontes. In 1984, he excavated the Early Bronze Age site of Tiwal esh-Sharqi in the Jordan valley on behalf of the British Museum, and in 1985 began excavations at the nearby major site of Tell es-Sa'idiyeh, a project which is continuing to this day. An expert on Canaanite civilization, he is the author of many articles and several books on Levantine archaeology, including *Archaeology and the Bible* (London, 1990) and *Canaanites* (London, 2006). He lectures internationally, and for several years was Program Chair of the American Schools of Oriental Research. He is a Fellow of the Society of Antiquaries, and is currently President of the Palestine Exploration Fund, a society founded in 1865 to promote the scientific exploration of the Levant.

URARTU

Paul Zimansky is currently a Professor of Archaeology and Ancient History at the State University of New York, Stony Brook. Since taking his PhD in Near Eastern Languages and Civilizations at the University of Chicago in 1980, he has directed archaeological projects in Syria, Iraq, and Turkey. Much of his research has focused on Urartu, a field in which he began working as a graduate student with the German Archaeological Institute in excavating at Bastam, Iran, in the 1970s. His publications include *Ecology and Empire: The Structure of the Urartian State* (Chicago, 1985), *Ancient Ararat: A Handbook of Urartian Studies* (Delmar, 1998), *The Iron Age Settlement at ʿAin Dara, Syria*, with E. C. Stone (Oxford, 1999), *The Anatomy of a Mesopotamian City: Survey and Soundings at Mashkan-shapir*, with E. C. Stone (Winona Lake, 2004), and *Ancient Turkey*, with A. Sagona (Abingdon, 2009).

LIST OF MAPS

LIST OF FIGURES

ABBREVIATIONS

GENERAL CONVENTIONS

A slash (/) between authors' names indicates separate (not joint) contributions to the article indicated.
An asterisk * indicates that the source referred to contains one or more passages translated from the original texts.
Square brackets [ ] enclose a restored word, part-word, or passage which has been erased from the original text.
Angle brackets < > enclose a word or part-word omitted from original text.

ap. (*apud*) = in the work(s) of

anc. = ancient

mod. = modern

Mt = Mount

q.v. (*quod vide*) = see this (entry)

r. = river

s.v. (*sub verbo*) = under the word

CHRONOLOGY ABBREVIATIONS

(Note that all dates are BCE unless otherwise stated)

BCE = Before the Common Era
CE = Common Era
C + no. = a particular century. Thus C5 = fifth century BCE
M + no. = a particular millennium. Thus M2 = second millennium BCE
M1 BCE–M1 CE = a period extending from the first millennium BCE to the first millennium CE.

BIBLIOGRAPHICAL ABBREVIATIONS

ABC – Grayson, A. K. (1975), *Assyrian and Babylonian Chronicles*, New York: J. J. Augustin (cited by page nos)

AfO – *Archiv für Orientforschung*

ÄHK – Edel, E. (1994), *Die Ägyptisch-hethitische Korrespondenz aus Boghazköy*, vol. I, Opladen: Westdeutscher Verlag

AJA – *American Journal of Archaeology*

AJNEAS – *Armenian Journal of Near Eastern Studies*

AM – Goetze, A. (1933), *Die Annalen des Mursilis, MVAG* 38, Leipzig (repr. Darmstadt, 1967)

AMI – *Archäologische Mitteilungen aus Iran*

An Ant – *Anatolia Antiqua*

ANE I – Pritchard, J. B. (1958), *The Ancient Near East*, vol. I, Princeton: Princeton University Press

ANE II – Pritchard, J. B. (1975), *The Ancient Near East*, vol. II, Princeton: Princeton University Press

ANES – *Ancient Near Eastern Studies*

ANET – Pritchard, J. B. (1969), *Ancient Near Eastern Texts relating to the Old Testament* (3rd edn), Princeton: Princeton University Press

AOAT – *Alter Orient und Altes Testament*

AoF – *Altorientalische Forschungen*

AP – Nassouhi, E. (1924–5), 'Prisme d'Assurbânipal daté de sa trentième année, provenant du temple de Gula à Babylone', *Archiv für Keilschriftforschung* 2: 97–106

ARAB – Luckenbill, D. D. (1928), *Ancient Records of Assyria and Babylonia*, vols I and II, Chicago: University of Chicago Press (repr. Greenwood Press, New York, 1968) (cited by page nos)

ARE III and *IV* – Breasted, J. H. (1906), *Ancient Records of Egypt*, vols III and IV, Chicago: University of Chicago Press (cited by section nos)

ARM – *Archives Royales de Mari*

ARM I: Dossin, G. (1950), *Correspondance de Šamšī-Addu et de ses fils*, Paris: Imprimerie National

ARM XXVI 1/1 – Durand, J.-M. (ed.) (1988), *Archives Épistolaires de Mari* 1/1, Paris: Éditions Recherche sur les Civilisations

ARM XXVI 1/2 – Charpin, D. *et al.* (eds) (1988), *Archives Épistolaires de Mari* 1/2, Paris: Éditions Recherche sur les Civilisations

AS – *Anatolian Studies*

AU – Sommer, F. (1932), *Die Ahhijavā Urkunden*, Munich: Bayerischen Akademie der Wissenschaften (repr. Hildesheim, 1975) (cited by page nos)

BA – *Biblical Archaeologist*

BAGRW – Talbot, R. J. A. (ed.) (2000), *Barrington Atlas of the Greek and Roman World*, Princeton: Princeton University Press

BAR – *Biblical Archaeological Review*

BASOR – *Bulletin of the American Schools of Oriental Research*

BCH – *Bulletin de Correspondance Hellénique*

BiOr – *Bibliotheca Orientalis*

BNP – *Brill's Encyclopedia of the Ancient World. New Pauly (Antiquity)*, Leiden and Boston: Brill (2002–)

BMD – Bienkowski, P. and Millard, A. (eds) (2000), *British Museum Dictionary of the Ancient Near East*, London: British Museum

BSA – *Annual of the British School at Athens*

CAH – *The Cambridge Ancient History*

CANE – Sasson, J. M. (ed.) (1995), *Civilizations of the Ancient Near East* (4 vols), New York: Charles Scribner's Sons

CC – Sigrist, M. and Gomi, T. (1991), *The Comprehensive Catalogue of Published Ur III Tablets*, Bethesda: CDL Press

Chav. – Chavalas, M. W. (ed.) (2006), *The Ancient Near East: Historical Sources in Translation*, Oxford: Blackwell (cited by page nos)

CHI 2 – *The Cambridge Ancient History of Iran*, vol.2, ed. I. Gershevitch (1985), Cambridge: Cambridge University Press

CHLI I – Hawkins, J. D. (2000), *Corpus of Hieroglyphic Luwian Inscriptions*, vol. I: *Inscriptions of the Iron Age*, Berlin and New York: de Gruyter

CHLI II – Çambel, H. (1999), *Corpus of Hieroglyphic Luwian Inscriptions*, vol. II: *Karatepe-Aslantaş: The Inscriptions*, Berlin and New York: de Gruyter

CMK – Michel, C. (2001), *Correspondance des marchands de Kanish au début du IIe millénaire avant J.-C.*, Paris: Les éditions du Cerf (cited by page nos)

CRAI – *Comptes-rendus de l'Académie des Inscriptions et Belles Lettres*

CS I, II, III – Hallo, W. W. and Younger, K. L. (eds) (1997, 2000, 2002), *The Context of Scripture* (3 vols), Leiden, New York, and Cologne: Brill (cited by page nos)

CTH – Laroche, E. (1971), *Catalogue des textes hittites*, Paris: Klincksieck (cited by catalogue nos)

CTN – *Cuneiform Texts from Nimrud*, London: British School of Archaeology in Iraq (1972 onwards)

DaK – Gelb, I. J. and Kienast, B. (1990), *Die altakkadischen Königsinschriften des dritten Jahrtausends v. Chr.*, Stuttgart: Freiburger altorientalische Studien 6

DB – Inscription of Darius I at Bisitun; for translations of Old Persian version, see Schmitt (1991), Brosius (2000: 27–40), Kuhrt, 2007a (= *PE*), 141–51

DCM – Joannès, F. (ed.) (2001), *Dictionnaire de la civilisation mésopotamienne*, Paris: Éditions Robert Laffont

DS – Güterbock, H. G. (1956), 'The deeds of Suppiluliuma as told by his son, Mursili II', *JCS* 10: 41–68, 75–98, 101–30

DSe – Darius inscription from Susa (e) (Susa's fortifications) (cited by sect. nos), transl. Brosius (2000: 41–2, no. 46), *PE* 491, no. 12

DSf – Darius inscription from Susa (f) (Susa foundation charter) (cited by sect. nos), transl. Brosius (2000: 40–1, no. 45), *PE* 492, no. 13 (i)

DSz – Darius inscription from Susa (foundation charter from the Apadana terrace) (cited by sect. nos.), transl. *PE* 495–7, no. 13 (ii) (a)

DZc – Darius inscription from the Red Sea Canal (c) (cited by sect. nos), transl. Brosius (2000: 47, no. 52), *PE* 486–7, no. 6

EA – *The El-Amarna Letters*, most recently ed. and transl. by Moran, W. (1992), *The Amarna Letters*, Baltimore, London: Johns Hopkins University Press (cited by document nos)

FGrH – Jacoby, F. (ed.), (1923–), *Fragmente der Griechischen Historiker*, Leiden, Berlin: Brill

FHG – Müller, C. (1841–1870), *Fragmenta Historicorum Graecorum*, vols. I–IV, Paris: Ambrosio Firmin-Diodot

Fs Alp – Otten, H., Akurgal, E., Ertem, H., and Süel, A. (eds) (1992), *Hittite and Other Anatolian and Near Eastern Studies in Honour of Sedat Alp*, Ankara: Türk Tarih Kurumu

Fs B. and A. Dinçol – Alparslan, M., Doğan-Alparslan, M., and Peker, H. (eds) (2007), *Festschrift in Honor of Belkıs and Ali Dinçol*, Istanbul: Ege Yayınları

Fs Burney – Sagona, A. (ed.) (2004), *A View from the Highlands: Archaeological Studies in Honour of Charles Burney*, Ancient Near Eastern Studies Supplement 12, Herent: Peeters

HCBD – Achtemeier, P. J. (ed.) (1996), *The HarperCollins Bible Dictionary*, New York: HarperCollins

HcI – König, F. W. (1955), *Handbuch der chaldischen Inschriften, AfO*, Beiheft 8, Graz (cited by document nos)

HDT – Beckman, G. (1999), *Hittite Diplomatic Texts* (2nd edn), Atlanta: Scholars Press (cited by page nos)

IEJ – *Israel Exploration Journal*

Ir An – *Iranica Antiqua*

IstMitt – *Istanbuler Mitteilungen*

JAC – *Journal of Ancient Civilizations*

JCS – *Journal of Cuneiform Studies*

JEOL – *Jaarbericht ex Oriente Lux*

JIES – *Journal of Indo-European Studies*

JNES – *Journal of Near Eastern Studies*

KatHet – Katalog der Ausstellung: *Die Hethiter und ihr Reich. Das Volk der 1000 Götter* (Kunst- und Ausstellungshalle der Bundesrepublik Deutschland, Bonn, 2002), Stuttgart: Theiss

KP – *Der Kleine Pauly*, Munich: Alfred Druckenmüller

KST – *Kazı Sonuçları Toplantısı*

LAAA – *Liverpool Annals of Archaeology and Anthropology*

LAPO – *Littératures anciennes du Proche Orient*

LAPO 16–18 – Durand, J.-M. (1998–2002), *Documents épistolaires du palais de Mari, Tomes I–III*, Paris: Les éditions du Cerf (cited by page and letter nos)

LKM – Heimpel, W. (2003), *Letters to the King of Mari*, Winona Lake: Eisenbrauns (cited by page nos, and also by document nos in cases where more specific references are appropriate)

LKM (refs) – List of references to relevant letters translated in *LKM*

MARI – *Mari. Annales de Recherches Interdisciplinaires*

MDOG – *Mitteilungen der Deutschen Orient-Gesellschaft zu Berlin*

Mesop. – Charpin, D., Edzard, D. O., and Stol, M. (2004), *Mesopotamien. Die altbabylonische Zeit*, Göttingen: Vandenhoeck & Ruprecht

MVAG – *Mitteilungen der vorderasiatisch-ägyptischen Gesellschaft*

N – Neumann, G. (1979), *Neufunde lykischer Inschriften seit 1901*, Vienna: Österreichischen Akademie der Wissenschaften (cited by document nos)

NABU – *Nouvelles Assyriologiques Brèves et Utilitaires*

ND – Inventory Numbers of the Nimrud Excavations

NEAEHL – Stern, E. (ed.) (1993), *The New Encyclopedia of Archaeological Excavations in the Holy Land* (4 vols), New York, London, Toronto, Sydney, Tokyo, and Singapore: Simon and Schuster

Nippur IV – Cole, S. W. (1996), *Nippur IV: The Early Neo-Babylonian Governor's Archive from Nippur*, Chicago: Oriental Institute Publications (OIP) 114, University of Chicago

NP – Der Neue Pauly Enzyklopädie der Antike, Stuttgart: J. B. Metzler

OA – Oriens Antiquus

OCD – Hornblower, S. and Spawforth, A. (eds) (1996), *The Oxford Classical Dictionary* (3rd edn), Oxford: Oxford University Press

OEAE – Redford, D. B. (ed.) (2001), *Oxford Encyclopedia of Ancient Egypt* (3 vols), Oxford: Oxford University Press

OEANE – Meyers, E. M. (ed.) (1997), *The Oxford Encyclopedia of Archaeology in the Near East* (5 vols), Oxford: Oxford University Press

OIP – Oriental Institute Publications, University of Chicago

Or – Orientalia

OT – Old Testament

PE – Kuhrt, A. (2007), *The Persian Empire: A Corpus of Sources from the Achaemenid Period* (2 vols), Abingdon: Routledge (cited by page and document nos)

PECS – Stillwell, R. (ed.) (1976), *The Princeton Encyclopedia of Classical Sites*, Princeton: Princeton University Press

PEQ – Palestine Exploration Quarterly

PRU IV – Nougayrol, J. (1956), *Le Palais Royal d'Ugarit IV* (Mission de Ras Shamra Tome IX), Paris: Klincksieck

RA – Revue d'assyriologie et d'archéologie orientale

RDAC – Report of the Dept of Antiquities, Cyprus

RE – Paulys Realencyclopädie der Classischen Altertumswissenschaft, Stuttgart: Alfred Druckenmüller

RGTC – Répertoire Géographique des Textes Cunéiformes, Wiesbaden: Ludwig Reichert

- *RGTC* 2 – Edzard, D. O. and Farber, G. (1974), *Die Orts- und Gewässernamen der Zeit der 3. Dynastie von Ur*
- *RGTC* 3 – Groneborg, B. (1980), *Die Orts- und Gewässernamen der altbabylonischen Zeit*
- *RGTC* 5 – Nashef, K. (1982), *Die Orts- und Gewässernamen der mittelbabylonischen und mittelassyrischen Zeit*
- *RGTC* 6 – Del Monte, G. F. and Tischler, J. (1978), *Die Orts- und Gewässernamen der hethitischen Texte*
- *RGTC* 8 – Zadok, R. (1985), *Geographical Names According to New- and Late- Babylonian Texts*
- *RGTC* 11 – Vallat, F. (1993), *Les noms géographiques des sources suso-élamites*

RHA – Revue hittite et asianique

RIMA – The Royal Inscriptions of Mesopotamia: Assyrian Periods, Toronto, Buffalo, and London: University of Toronto Press (cited by vol. and page nos)

- *RIMA* 1 – Grayson, A. K. (1987), *Assyrian Rulers of the Third and Second Millennium BC (to 1115 BC)*

RIMA 2 – Grayson, A. K. (1991), *Assyrian Rulers of the Early First Millennium BC I (1114–859 BC)*

RIMA 3 – Grayson, A. K. (1996), *Assyrian Rulers of the Early First Millennium BC II (858–745 BC)*

RIMB – *The Royal Inscriptions of Mesopotamia: Babylonian Periods*, Toronto, Buffalo, and London: University of Toronto Press (cited by vol. and page nos)

RIMB 2 – Frame, G. (1995), *Rulers of Babylonia From the Second Dynasty of Isin to the End of Assyrian Domination (1157–612)*

RIME – *The Royal Inscriptions of Mesopotamia: Early Periods*, Toronto, Buffalo, and London: University of Toronto Press (cited by vol. and page nos)

RIME 2 – Frayne, D. R. (1993), *Sargonic and Gutian Periods (2334–2113 BC)*

RIME 3/1 – Edzard, D. O. (1997), *Gudea and His Dynasty*

RIME 3/2 – Frayne, D. R. (1997), *Ur III Period (2112–2004 BC)*

RIME 4 – Frayne, D. R. (1990), *Old Babylonian Period (2003–1595 BC)*

RlA – *Reallexikon der Assyriologie und Vorderasiatischen Archäologie*, Berlin and New York: de Gruyter: *RlA* 1 (1928/32), *RlA* 2 (1938), *RlA* 3 (1957–71), *RlA* 4 (1972–5), *RlA* 5 (1976–80), *RlA* 6 (1980–3), *RlA* 7 (1987–90), *RlA* 8 (1993–7), *RlA* 9 (1998–2001), *RlA* 10 (2003–5), *RlA* 11 (2006–)

RS – Tablets from Ras Shamra (*RS* 34.165 is ed. by Lackenbacher, 1982)

SAA – *State Archives of Assyria*, Helsinki: Helsinki University Press (cited by page and document nos)

SAA I – Parpola, S. (1987), *The Correspondence of Sargon II, Part I*

SAA II – Parpola, S. and Watanabe, K. (1988), *Neo-Assyrian Treaties and Loyalty Oaths*

SAA V – Lanfranchi, G. B. and Parpola, S. (1990), *The Correspondence of Sargon II, Part II*

SAA VIII – Fuchs, A. (1998), *Die Annalen des Jahres 711 v. Chr.*

SAA XI – Fales, F. M. and Postgate, J. N. (1995), *Imperial Administrative Records, Part II*

SAA XII – Katala, L. and Whiting, R. (1995), *Grants, Decrees and Gifts of the Neo-Assyrian Period*

SAA XV – Fuchs, A. and Parpola, S. (2001), *The Correspondence of Sargon II, Part III*

SAA XVII – Dietrich, M. (2003), *The Babylonian Correspondence of Sargon and Sennacherib*

SAA XVIII – Reynolds, F. (2003), *The Babylonian Correspondence of Esarhaddon*

SAIO II – Lipiński, E. (1975), *Studies in Aramaic Inscriptions and Onomastics II*, Leuven: Leuven University Press

Sargon II – Fuchs, A. (1994), *Die Inschriften Sargons II. aus Khorsabad*, Göttingen: Cuvillier

SCE – Gjerstad, E. *et al.* (1934–48), *The Swedish Cyprus Expedition: Finds and Results of the Excavations in Cyprus, 1927–1931* (4 vols), Stockholm: Swedish Cyprus Expedition

Sennach. – Luckenbill, D. D. (1924), *The Annals of Sennacherib*, Chicago: University of Chicago Press (repr. Wipf & Stock Publishers, Eugene, OR, 2005) (cited by page nos)

SMEA – *Studi Micenei ed Egeo-Anatolici*

StBoT – *Studien zu den Boğazköy-Texten*

TAM I – *Tituli Asiae Minoris. Tituli Lyciae lingua Lycia conscripti* (cited by document nos)
TAM II – *Tituli Asiae Minoris. Tituli Lyciae linguis Graeca et Latina conscripti* (cited by document nos)
Tigl. III – Tadmor, H. (1994), *The Inscriptions of Tiglath-Pileser III, King of Assyria: Critical Edition with Introduction, Translation, and Commentary*, Jerusalem: The Israel Academy of Sciences and Humanities (cited by page nos)
TSSI II – Gibson, J. C. L. (1975), *Textbook of Syrian Semitic Inscriptions, II: Aramaic Inscriptions*, Oxford: Clarendon Press
TTKY – *Türk Tarih Kurumu Yayinlarından*
TÜBA-AR – *Türkiye Bilimler Akademisi Arkeoloji Dergisi*
UF – *Ugarit-Forschungen*
WO – *Die Welt des Orients*
XPa – Xerxes inscription from Persepolis (a), transl. Brosius (2000: 51, no. 63), *PE* 581, no. 4
XPh – Xerxes inscription from Persepolis (h) (*daiva* inscription; see glossary); transl. Brosius (2000: 89, no. 191), *PE* 304–5, no. 88
ZA – *Zeitschrift für Assyriologie und vorderasiatische Archäologie*

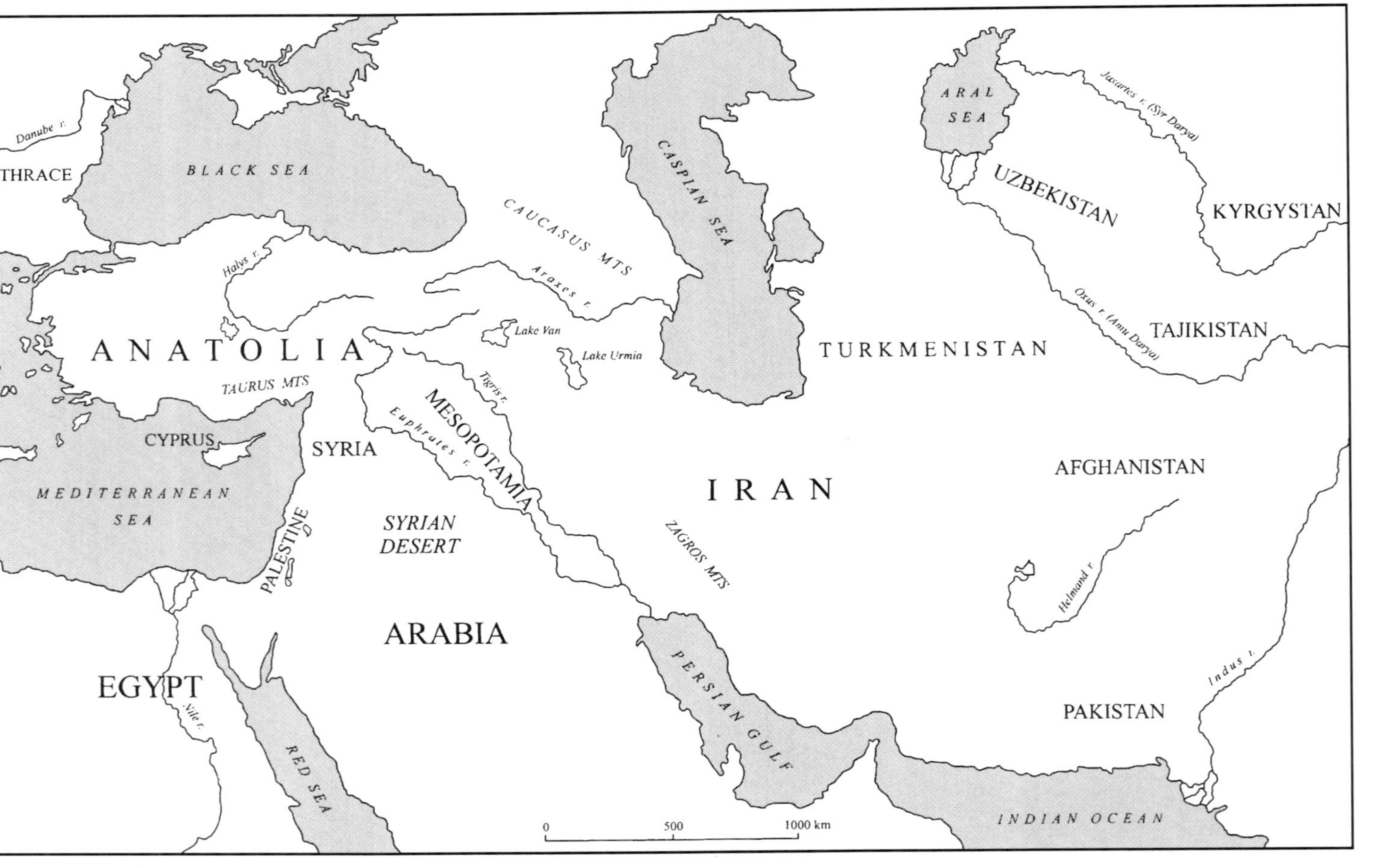

Map 1 Ancient western Asia.

Map 2 Anatolia, northern Syria, and northern Mesopotamia: modern names.

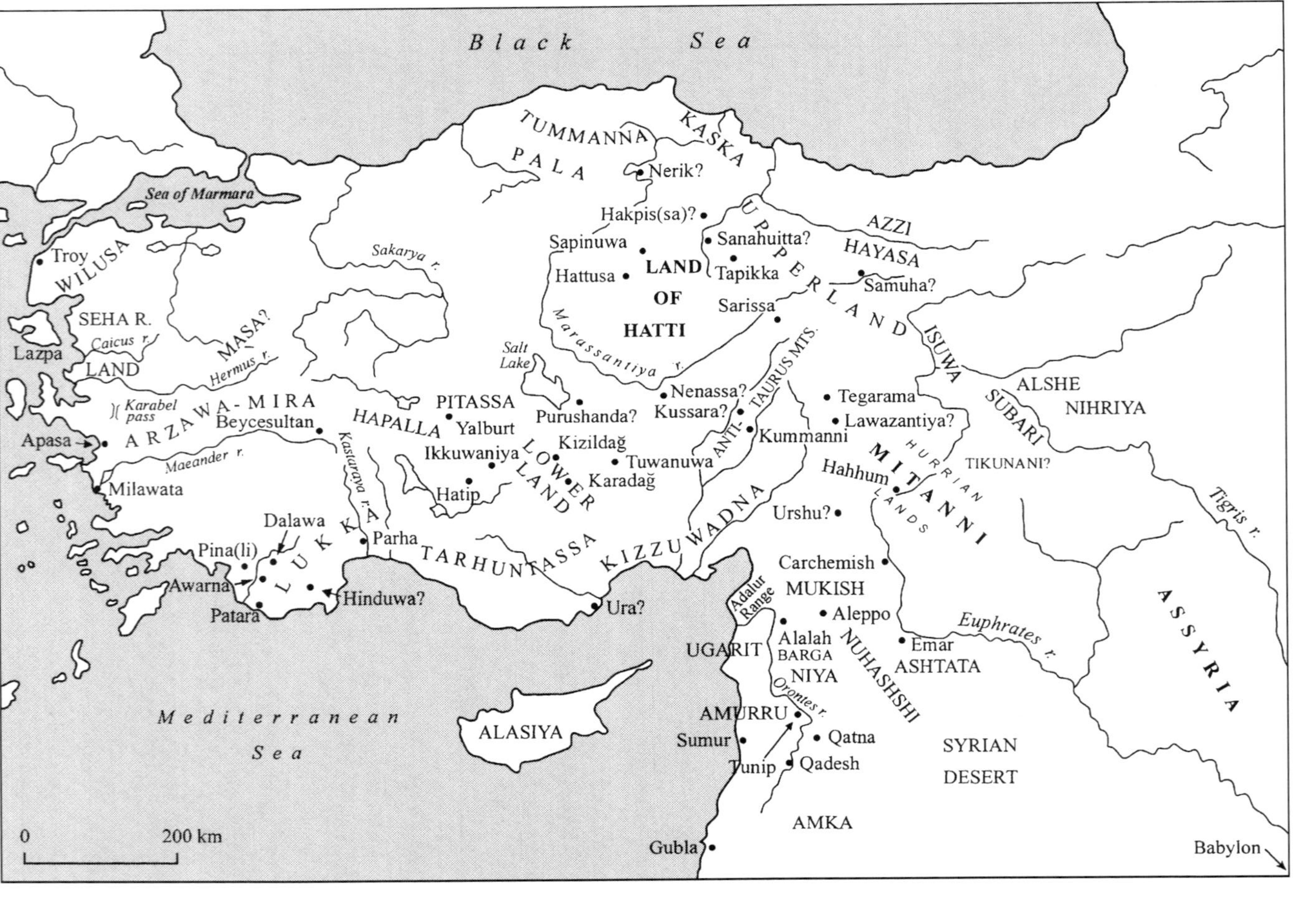

Map 3 Late Bronze Age Anatolia, northern Syria, and northern Mesopotamia.

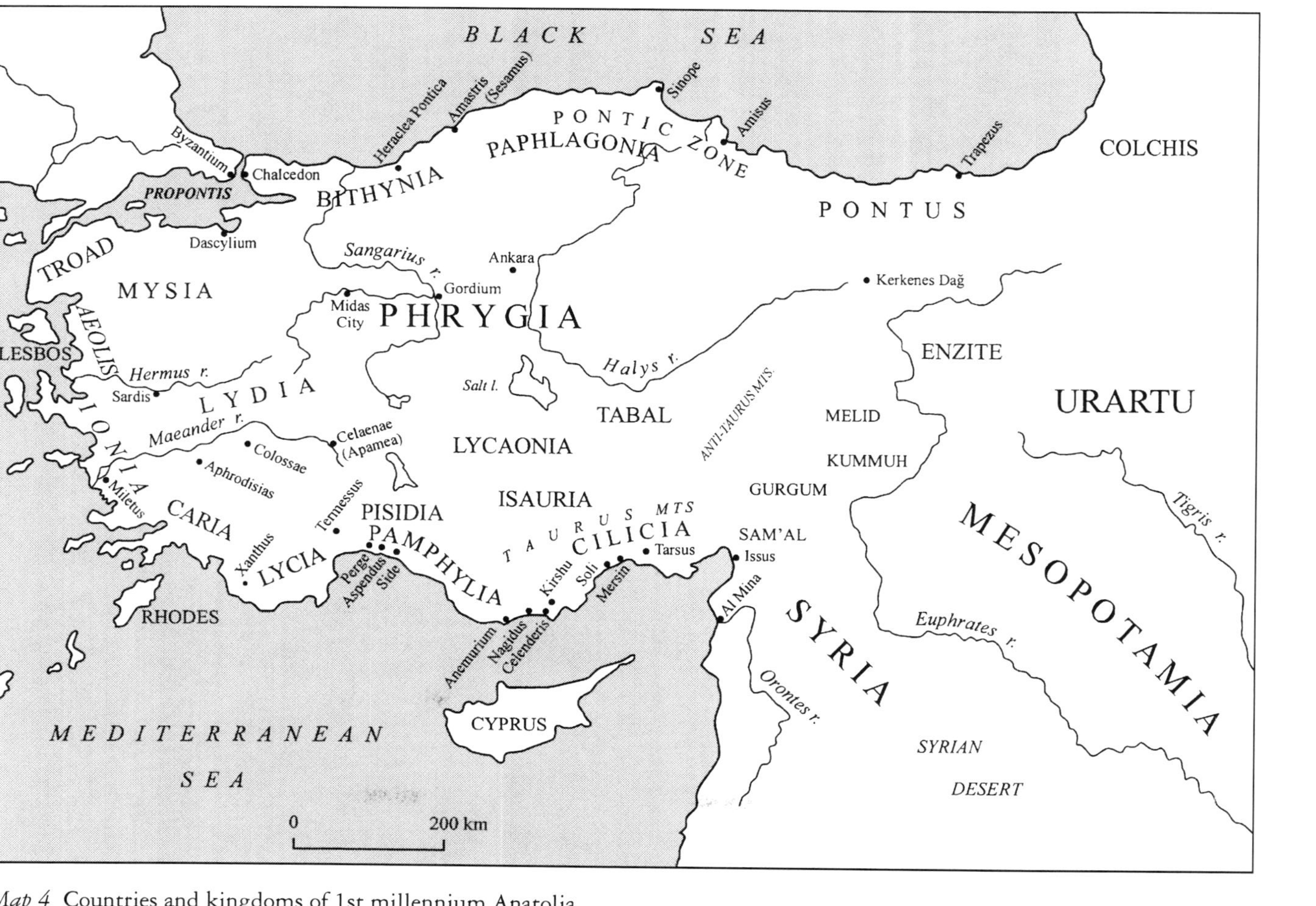

Map 4 Countries and kingdoms of 1st millennium Anatolia.

Map 5 Greek and Roman cities of western Anatolia.

Map 6 The Late Bronze Age Syrian principalities.

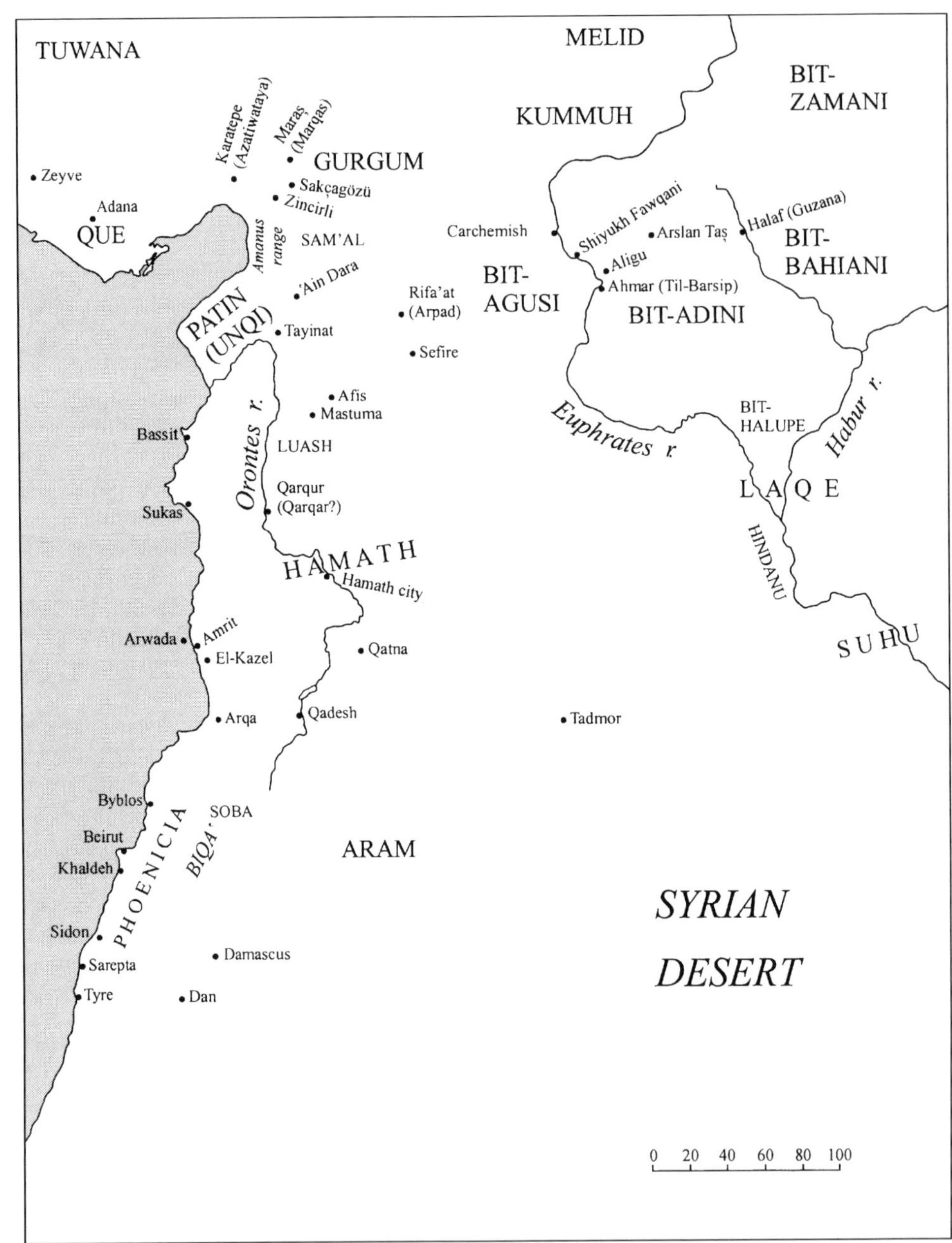

Map 7 Iron Age cities and countries in northern Syria.

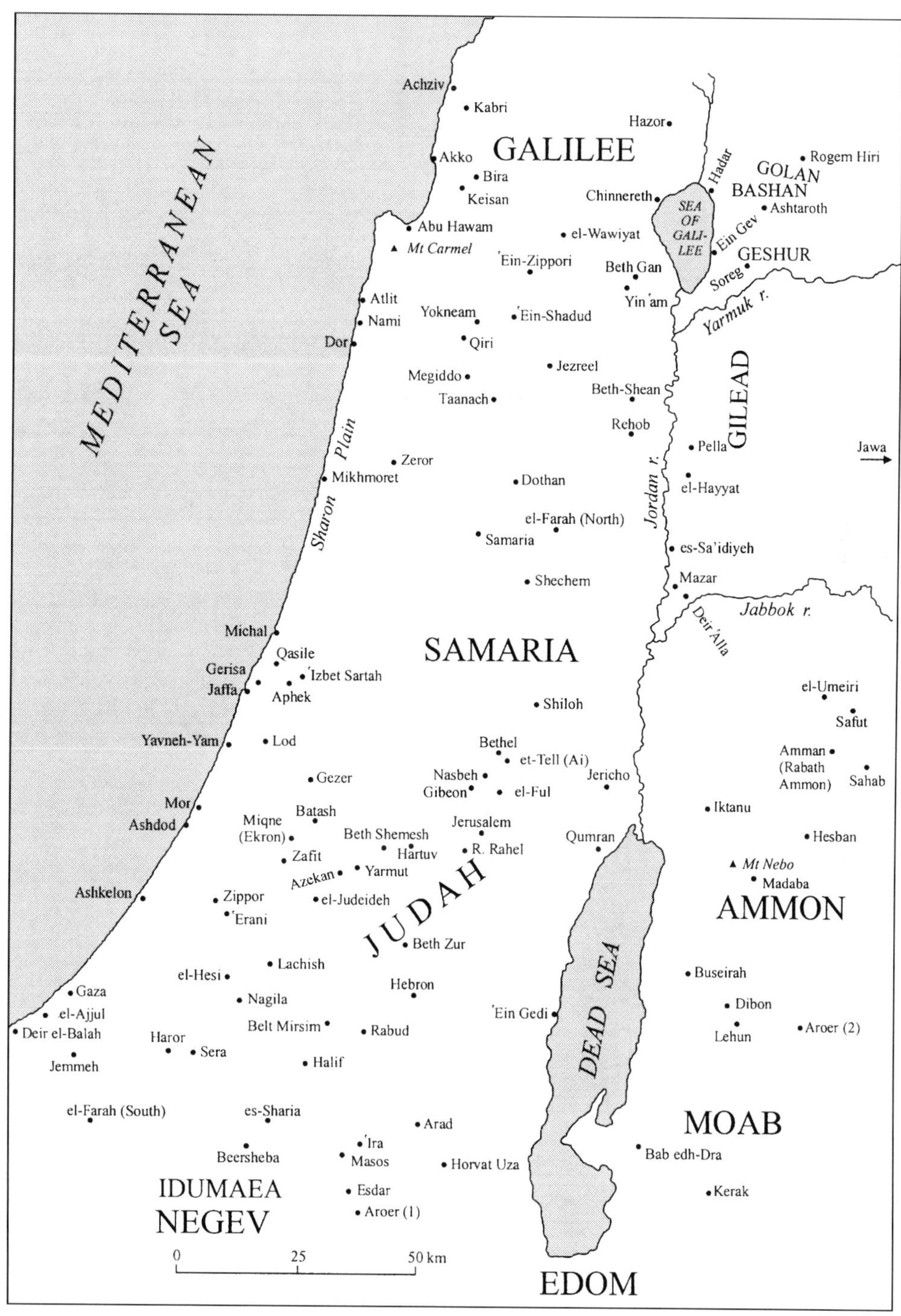

Map 8 Iron Age Palestine and Transjordan.

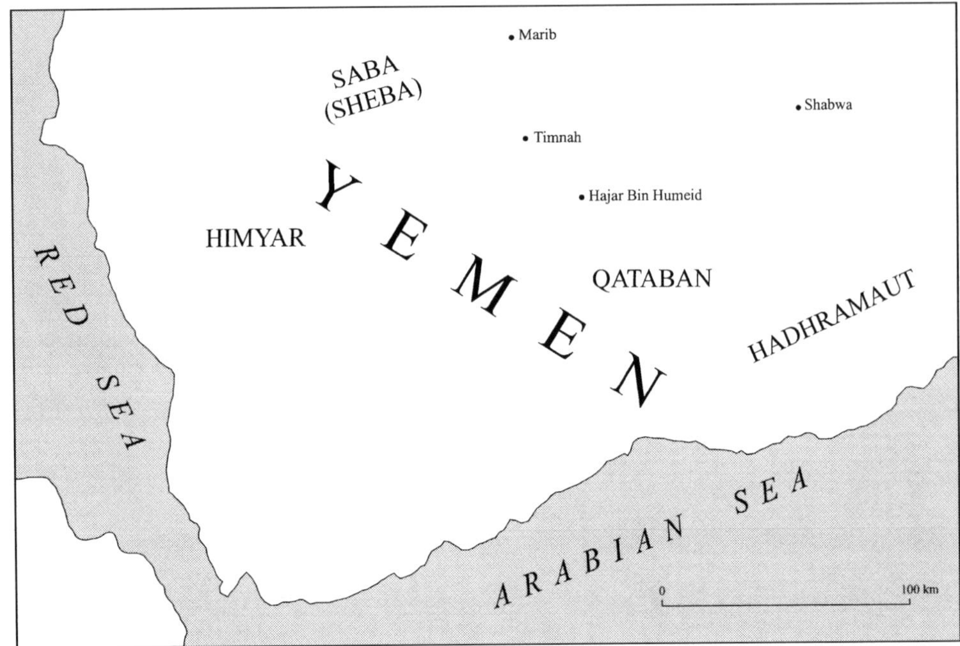

Map 9 Southern Arabia.

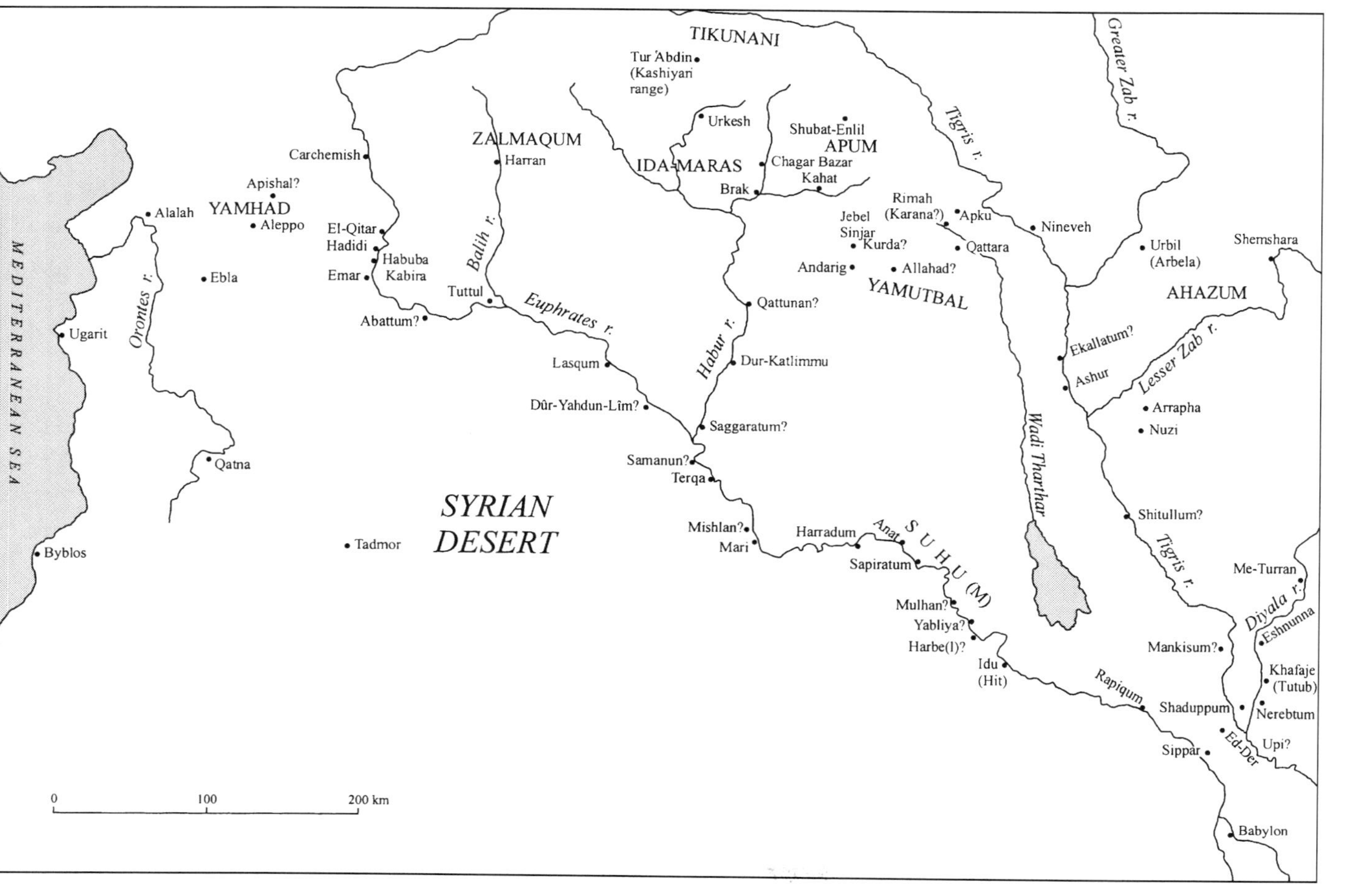

Map 10 Northern Syria and northern Mesopotamia in the Middle Bronze Age.

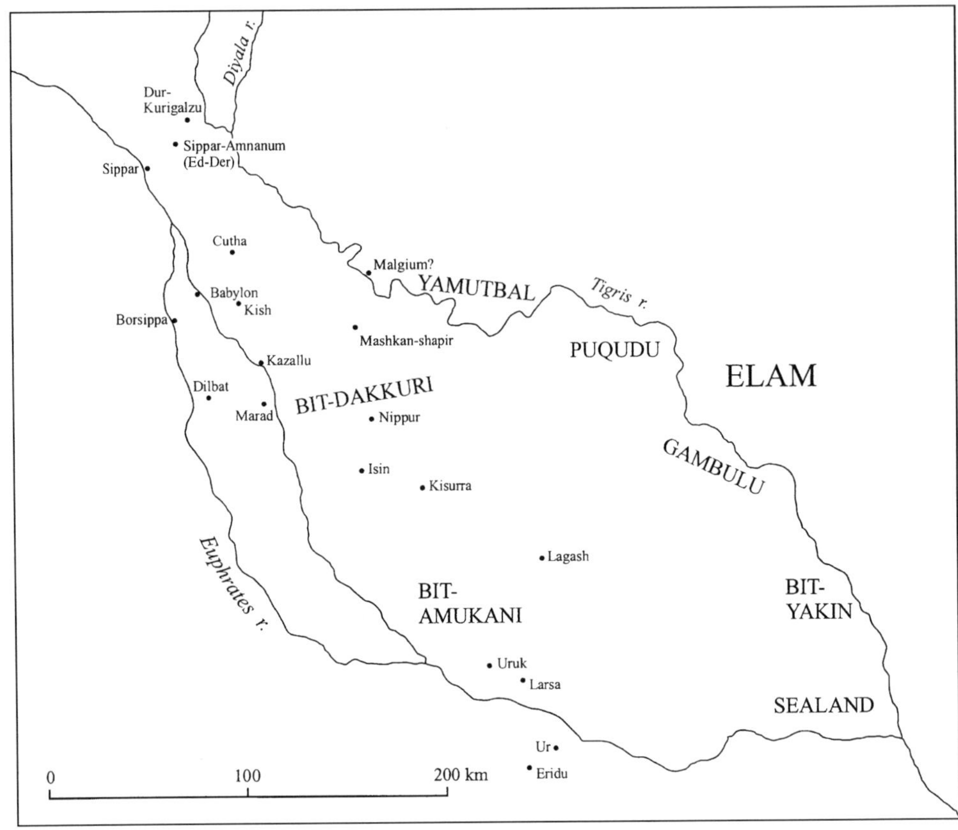

Map 11 Babylonia in the 2nd and 1st millennia BCE.

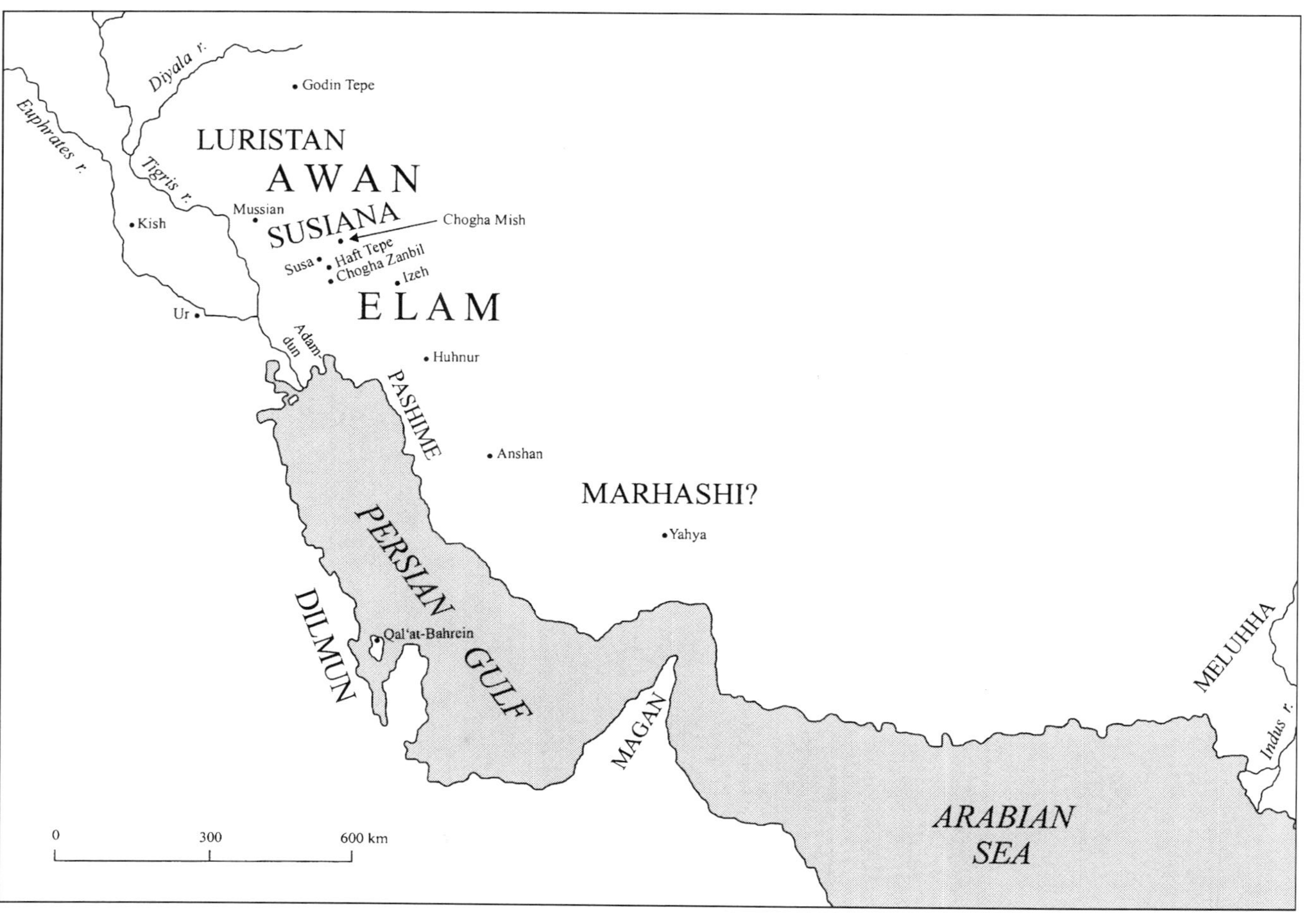

Map 12 Iran in the 3rd and 2nd millennia BCE.

INTRODUCTION

The evolution of writing in southern Mesopotamia towards the end of the fourth millennium BCE marked the beginning of the so-called 'historical era' in western Asia. Documents, produced from that time onwards, have provided scholars with an invaluable complement to archaeological data, in the task of reconstructing the various civilizations which emerged in the western Asian regions, and in identifying the cultural features and affinities of these civilizations, and the political and social structures which they developed.

My aim in writing this book is to provide a comprehensive reference work on the peoples, kingdoms, countries, cities, towns, and other sites of western Asia from the Early Bronze Age to the end of the Persian empire, i.e. from the late fourth millennium to 330 BCE. For the purposes of continuity, a number of entries contain brief discussions of periods before and after this time-frame. The main regions covered are Anatolia, Cyprus, Syria–Palestine, Mesopotamia, and Iran and territories lying to its east. I have generally used the designation 'western Asia' in reference to these regions, rather than the more common term 'Near East', the definition of which varies from one scholar to another, and rarely encompasses any territories east of Iran. There are, however, some contexts where Near East remains an appropriate designation, e.g. in discussions of the Sea Peoples and their constituent groups, and I have retained the term in these contexts. Frequent references are made to Egypt, because of its close cultural, political, and military involvement in the affairs of the lands which lay to the north, east, and northeast of it. But specific treatments of the peoples and places of the Nile valley lie beyond the scope of the present work.

The book contains approximately 1,500 entries, ranging from descriptions of major cities and kingdoms to brief sketches of small villages, sanctuaries, and in a few cases, the sites of apparently isolated monuments. It also includes entries on population groups which were often spread over a number of regions. Generally, cities are listed in alphabetical order under their ancient names, if known, with modern names (italicized) appended in brackets where applicable – thus **Tushpa** (***Van Kale***). They appear alphabetically under their modern names if the ancient names are not known – e.g. **Agrab, Tell** – or if their names changed in different periods of their history – e.g. **Ahmar, Tell (Masuwari, Til-Barsip/Tarbusiba, Kar-Shalmaneser)**. As in many ancient sources, the term 'city' is used in a very broad sense to refer to settlements ranging from royal capitals and major urban centres to small townships.

Most entries have bibliographies attached. These have been kept short, generally between one and four items per entry, arranged in order of publication. In a few cases, all the bibliographical information is included within the entry itself. Full publication details appear in the Bibliography. Wherever appropriate, the bibliographies cite articles appearing in standard reference works, such as *The New Encyclopedia of Archaeological Excavations in the Holy Land* (*NEAEHL*), *The Oxford Classical Dictionary* (*OCD*), *The Oxford Encyclopedia of Archaeology in the Near East* (*OEANE*), *The Princeton Encyclopedia of Classical Sites* (*PECS*), and the *Reallexikon der Assyriologie und Vorderasiatischen Archäologie* (*RlA*). Of course, much new material has come to light since many of these articles were published, and the information they contain needs constant updating. Nevertheless, they provide useful basic information – e.g. about the history of excavation of an archaeological site, the history of the site itself, and the chief features of its layout and architecture – which can be supplemented and amended in the light of more recent investigations and discoveries.

In many entries where our information is based wholly or partly on ancient written sources, a select number of these sources have been cited. Asterisks are used to indicate translated passages, sometimes incorporated into discussions by modern authors. In most cases, the selection has been largely determined by what is relatively accessible to the reader, as illustrated, for example, by the frequent references made to the Toronto *Royal Inscriptions of Mesopotamia* series (*RIMA*, *RIMB*, *RIME*). (When citing passages in this series, I have given only the relevant page numbers, not the full reference: e.g. the citation under **Baqanu** simply reads **RIMA* 3: 31 rather than **RIMA* 3: A.0.102.5 vi 6, p. 31.) Occasionally, I have included references to more obscure editions and translations of the ancient texts, generally in cases where there are no more readily available sources.

Different scholars have different views on the chronologies of many of the ancient western Asian civilizations. This is particularly evident in discussions of the Bronze Age cities and kingdoms. High, Middle, and Low chronologies have been devised, which differ substantially from one another in the time-frames assigned to them by their proponents. Some scholars adopt one chronology, others another. There is a higher degree of consensus in the chronological schemes applied to the cities and kingdoms of the first millennium BCE – except for the regnal dates of the kings of Urartu, which still remain very problematic (see Appendix III). For the most part, the chronologies I have used are similar to those adopted in the *Dictionnaire de la civilisation mesopotamienne*, ed. F. Joannès (*DCM*). I should stress that, like Joannès (*et al.*), I have not drawn a distinction between dates we can be reasonably certain about, and those which are little more than calculated guesses. The regnal years of most of the Neo-Assyrian kings fall into the former category, those of the Late Bronze Age Hittite kings into the latter. (Note that in Neo-Assyrian and various other royal chronologies, the year designated as a king's accession year runs to the end of the calendar year in which the king took the throne. The numbering of his regnal years begins with the following year. Thus his accession year was counted as the last regnal year of his predecessor.) Cryer (1995) provides a useful overview of the issues and problems associated with ancient western Asian chronology. All dates refer to the period 'Before the Common Era' (BCE) unless otherwise indicated.

Classical writers cited in this book are listed in Appendix IV. The titles of their works are not specified in the citations unless two or more works known to have been written by a particular author have survived. For example, all references to the Roman writer Pliny the Elder come from his only surviving work, *Naturalis Historia*. On the other hand, four works of Xenophon are cited – *Agesilaus*, *Anabasis*, *Cyropedia*, and *Hellenica* – so that the relevant work needs to be specified on each occasion. Place-names attested in the Classical sources are generally represented by their Latin rather than their Greek forms, in accordance with the convention used in the *Oxford Classical Dictionary* – e.g. Curium rather than Kourion, Lycia rather than Lykia, Miletus rather than Miletos. There are a few cases where the Greek form is the preferred one – e.g. Assos, Lesbos.

Some variations will be found in the representation of names occurring in a Mesopotamian context. This frequently applies to names ending in 'um' in the Old Babylonian period. In later M2 and M1 contexts, the final 'm' is commonly dropped: thus Old Babylonian Suhum later becomes Suhu, Hiritum becomes Hiritu, etc.

Twenty maps provide locations for many of the cities and kingdoms dealt with in this book. (My sincere thanks to Dr G. D. Tully for drawing these maps from my drafts.) For more precise and more detailed maps, the reader should consult such works as Roaf (1996) (Near Eastern sites), and Talbot (2000; cited as *BAGRW*) (Classical Greek sites). Note that there is some variation in the forms of names appearing in the maps – thus Qadesh in maps 3 and 7, but Kadesh in map 6. The form Qadesh is used in the text. In map 15, the Greek forms of the place-names are generally used – thus Korydalla, Letoon, and Xanthos, which appear in the text as Corydalla, Letoum, and Xanthus. These variations reflect the fact that though most of the maps were drawn specifically for this project, a few of them had been prepared prior to the project, and reflect slightly different spelling conventions. Maps 1–12 appear at the beginning of the book. They are general maps of their regions, and their order reflects a rough progression from west to east. Maps 13–20 are more country- or kingdom-specific, and are located near entries in the text directly relevant to them.

What I hope will be a particular merit of this book is its much more comprehensive coverage of ancient western Asian peoples and places, attested in archaeological and/or written sources, than the reader would normally find in general reference works on the Near East. Of course, the list of entries which it contains is far from exhaustive. And I often found it difficult to decide what to include and what to leave out, in order to stay within the contracted word limit, particularly when it came to making selections from among the less well-known archaeological sites and the more obscure cities attested in written records. Other scholars might well have made other choices.

My work on this project has been helped by a number of people, in addition to the consultants whom I acknowledge separately. Here, I would like to express my sincere thanks, for their assistance, to Mr Charles Burney, Mr Caillan Davenport, Em. Prof. Bob Milns, Ms Paola Mior, and Dr Sonia Puttock. My sincere thanks are due also to the School of History, Philosophy, Classics, and Religion, University of Queensland, for its valuable infrastructural support.

It has been a pleasure to work with Routledge staff throughout this project, Richard Stoneman in the project's early stages, and subsequently Matthew Gibbons and Lalle Pursglove. I would also like to express my sincere appreciation to Katy Carter for her meticulous work in copy-editing the text. Her contribution has been invaluable.

Trevor Bryce
University of Queensland

November 2008

HISTORICAL OVERVIEW

EARLY BRONZE AGE

The Sumerians are the earliest peoples in western Asia with whom written records can be firmly associated. Scholars still debate whether they were a race of newcomers who arrived in southern Mesopotamia at the end of M4, or whether they belonged to the indigenous peoples of the region. But probably from the time of their first appearance in history, they intermingled with population groups of Semitic origin. Out of this ethnic mix, the Early Bronze Age Sumerian civilization evolved. The most important administrative unit within the Sumerian world was the city-state, consisting of an urban centre with peripheral areas where villages and farmlands were located. Fourteen such city-states are known to us from written sources. They were largely independent of one another, although according to the Sumerian King List, some degree of hegemony was exercised by one state over the others on a kind of rotational basis.

Scholars refer to the period of the Sumerian city-states as the Early Dynastic period (c. 2990–2334). It came to an end with the rise of the Semitic kingdom of Akkad, in the northern part of southern Mesopotamia. The kingdom was founded by Sargon (Sharrum-kin) c. 2334, in Agade, a city whose site has yet to be located. Here, Sargon established the seat of a royal dynasty which held sway over what many scholars regard as the first 'empire' in western Asian history. During the reign of its founder's grandson Naram-Sin (2254–2218), the Akkadian empire attained its greatest limits. Extending over the whole of Mesopotamia, it reached as far north as modern Kurdistan (and perhaps even Armenia), as far east as the Zagros mountains, and as far west as eastern Anatolia and the Mediterranean Sea. In the south, Naram-Sin's campaigns took his armies to Magan. But after his death, the empire rapidly disintegrated, coming abruptly to an end in the reign of his son Shar-kali-sharri (2217–2193). Various factors may have contributed to its destruction, including incessant revolts by subject peoples, internal political instability, and a period of sustained, severe drought. But the immediate agent of its fall, according to Mesopotamian literary tradition, was a group of raiders from the Zagros mountain region called the Gutians. They were eventually driven from Mesopotamia by a man called Utu-hegal, ruler of the southern Mesopotamian city of Uruk (2123–2113). Despite its relatively short existence and violent end, the kingdom of Akkad left a number of important cultural legacies to the western Asian world. The most notable of these was its language, later to become the international language of diplomacy throughout western Asia.

After his expulsion of the Gutians, Utu-hegal established his dominance throughout southern Mesopotamia until his reign was ended by a new royal dynasty which arose in the city of Ur – the so-called Ur III dynasty. Ur lay to the northwest of Utu-hegal's capital, Uruk. Founded by Ur-Nammu c. 2112, the Ur III dynasty held power through the last century of the Early Bronze Age. Under its rule, Ur enjoyed the status of capital of an empire which extended over much of Mesopotamia and the neighbouring Zagros mountain region to the east. The Ur III administration's official language was Sumerian. Many tens of thousands of administrative documents of the period, inscribed on clay tablets found in Ur, indicate an extensive and complex bureaucracy used in the governance of the empire. But this empire too had a short existence. It came under serious pressure from a people called the Amorites during the reign of its penultimate ruler Shu-Sin. Its final destruction was due to the Elamites, who captured and sacked the empire's capital Ur, and took its last ruler Ibbi-Sin (2028–2004) back to their homeland.

Located in western Iran, Elam became one of the most enduring powers of the ancient western Asian world, with a history extending over 2,000 years, from M3 until mid M1. Elam is the Sumerian name for the country, which at its greatest extent stretched across the Zagros mountains from modern Khuzestan to Fars. (The Elamites themselves referred to their country as Haltamti or Hatamti.) Mesopotamian texts dating to mid and late M3 indicate frequent conflicts between Elam and its neighbours in southern Mesopotamia. The kings of both the Akkadian and the Ur III dynasties conducted military campaigns into Elamite territory. Sargon claimed to have conquered it and to have incorporated it into his empire. But after the collapse of Akkad, Elam regained and retained its independence through the period of the Ur III regime, despite a number of attacks upon it by members of this regime. Finally, under the leadership of the so-called Shimashki dynasty, an Elamite alliance destroyed the Ur III empire. Susa, which had originally been separate from Elam and had come under the control of Ur, was a member of the victorious alliance, and thenceforth became an integral part of the kingdom of Elam. Under the successive regimes of the Shimashki and the *sukkalmah* (Epartid) dynasties (c. 2100–1600), Elam became one of the largest and most powerful of the western Asian kingdoms, with extensive diplomatic, commercial, and military interests both in Mesopotamia and Syria. Its territories extended north to the Caspian Sea, south to the Persian Gulf, eastwards to the desert regions of Kavir and Lut, and westwards into Mesopotamia.

MIDDLE BRONZE AGE

After the fall of the Ur III empire, Ur itself remained under Elamite control for the next twenty-one years. It was subsequently rebuilt by the kings of Isin, who regarded themselves as the legitimate successors of the Ur III dynasts. Isin first rose to prominence in the last years of M3, when Ishbi-Erra, high-ranking official of the last Ur III king, Ibbi-Sin, established his authority over much of the region formerly controlled by the Ur III administration, and shifted the seat of his own administration to the southern Mesopotamian city Isin. He was the founder of the First Isin dynasty, which lasted for more than two centuries (c. 2017–1794). During this period, it became one of the major powers of southern Mesopotamia. But throughout its existence, its rulers were constantly threatened by rival kings, notably those of Larsa and Babylon. In 1794 Larsa's last king, Rim-Sin, conquered Isin and incorporated it into his kingdom. This triumph marked the high point of Rim-Sin's reign. The second half of the reign was characterized by increasingly strained relations with Babylon, then ruled by Hammurabi, who like his father and grandfather had been a vassal of Rim-Sin. When Rim-Sin refused to join Hammurabi in a war against the Elamites, the Babylonian king used this as a pretext for attacking Larsa. He succeeded in capturing the city after a six-month siege, and took Rim-Sin and his son prisoner (1763). Isin was incorporated into the Babylonian empire, along with Larsa's subject cities Isin, Ur, and Uruk.

Hammurabi belonged to a dynastic line of Amorite stock. The Amorites were a Semitic-speaking population who may originally have lived a nomadic existence in the Syrian desert. During M3, they settled in Mesopotamia, and spread both east and west from there in late M3 and early M2. In Mesopotamia, they came into conflict with the kings of Akkad. Subsequently, the Ur III kings attempted to keep Amorite groups out of their homeland territories by building a chain of fortifications or watchtowers across northern Babylonia, somewhere between Mari and Ur. Despite these defences, Amorite chieftains overran southern Babylonia, and shortly before the fall of the Ur III kingdom, an Amorite had set himself up as ruler of the city-state of Larsa, 40 km to the north of Ur. Other Babylonian cities, including Babylon, also came under Amorite control.

The first of the great Amorite kings was Shamshi-Addu, the most important ruler of Middle Bronze Age Assyria. He is commonly referred to by the Akkadian form of his name, Shamshi-Adad, and will henceforth be referred to by this name. This period in Assyria's history is commonly referred to by scholars as the Old Assyrian kingdom (c. 2000 to 1760). (Note that some scholars prefer to call Shamshi-Adad's kingdom the kingdom of Upper Mesopotamia rather than Assyria, because it was not centred on Ashur – see below; they consider the application of the concept of Assyria to this period anachronistic.) It began with the rise of a small independent state based at Ashur on the west bank of the Tigris, following the collapse of the Ur III empire. It reached its peak when Shamshi-Adad seized the throne from his brother in Ashur in 1796, and embarked on a series of military campaigns which took him as far west as the Mediterranean coast in the Levantine region. Most importantly, he gained control of the kingdom of Mari on the Euphrates. The territories which he conquered between the Tigris and the Euphrates were consolidated into 'the kingdom of Upper Mesopotamia'. Shamshi-Adad established his residence at Shubat-Enlil (formerly Shehna, modern Tell Leilan) in the Habur plains of northern Mesopotamia. He appointed his sons Yasmah-Addu and Ishme-Dagan as viceroys in Mari and Ekallatum respectively. The conflicts and the politics of the period, before and after as well as during his reign, are documented in the voluminous archives unearthed at Mari.

Shortly after Shamshi-Adad's death in 1775, the Old Assyrian kingdom began to disintegrate. Mari fell to the Amorite ruler Zimri-Lim in 1774, and Shamshi-Adad's capital Shubat-Enlil was seized by a dynasty from the nearby land of Apum. The disintegrating kingdom survived an invasion by the rival kingdom of Eshnunna, but fell, finally, to the Babylonian king Hammurabi c. 1763.

Other major powers of the age were, in Mesopotamia, the kingdoms of Larsa and Eshnunna; in the west, the kingdoms of Yamhad and Qatna; and in the southeast, the kingdom of Elam. We have referred to Larsa and Elam above. Yamhad was a Middle and (early) Late Bronze Age Amorite kingdom in northern Syria. Its royal seat was located at Aleppo. By the beginning of C18, Yamhad had replaced Ebla (Tell Mardikh), which lay 70 km southeast of Aleppo, as the dominant power in the region, exercising sovereignty over a number of cities and petty kingdoms between the Euphrates and Orontes rivers. Its first known ruler, Sumu-epuh, had a long history of conflict with Mari, extending back to the period before Mari was seized by Shamshi-Adad. Sumu-epuh subsequently became embroiled in hostilities with Shamshi-Adad, who formed an alliance with Qatna against him. Qatna (Mishrifeh) was another of the kingdoms ruled by an Amorite dynasty. It was located in central Syria, east of the Orontes river and 18 km northeast of modern Homs. In the course of his hostilities with Shamshi-Adad, Sumu-epuh was killed, and his throne passed to his son Yarim-Lim I. The disintegration of the Old Assyrian kingdom and the seizure of Mari by Zimri-Lim paved the way for a period of sustained peace and cooperation between Yamhad and Mari. Yamhad's relations also improved with Qatna in this period, and Yarim-Lim concluded an alliance with Babylon. His successor Hammurabi sent troops to the Babylonian king, also called Hammurabi, to assist in the latter's capture of the kingdom of Larsa. Yamhad became one of the great political and military powers of the Middle Bronze Age, holding sway over some twenty subject-rulers.

Eshnunna (Tel Asmar) was located in the Diyala river basin of southern Mesopotamia, 81 km northeast of Baghdad. During Shamshi-Adad's reign, it frequently clashed with Assyria over control of territories in the middle Euphrates region. Mari itself came under direct threat from Eshnunnite forces. But hostilities between the Assyrian and Eshnunnite kingdoms ended when Dadusha, king of Eshnunna, concluded a peace with Shamshi-Adad c. 1781. Four years later, Dadusha's successor Ibal-pi-El II supplied the Assyrians with military forces for an attack on the land of Malgium, which lay on the Tigris south of its confluence with the Diyala. But after Shamshi-Adad's death, Eshnunna embarked on an aggressive new programme of expansion in the territories over which the Assyrian king had held sway. Ibal-pi-El's forces occupied the city of Shubat-Enlil, and a second Eshnunnite army seized the Assyrian cities Ashur and Ekallatum. But in 1765 Eshnunna fell to the Elamites, who brought Ibal-pi-El's reign to an abrupt end. In 1762 his successor Silli-Sin was conquered by the Babylonian king Hammurabi. With this conquest, Eshunna's power in the region was effectively terminated.

Babylon's rise to power had begun in 1894, when the Amorite chieftain Sumu-abum founded the first royal dynasty there. The city reached its first peak in the reign of the dynasty's sixth king, Hammurabi (1792–1750), when it became the centre of the first great Babylonian empire, the Old Babylonian kingdom, whose sway extended through the whole of Mesopotamia. But Hammurabi's successes were offset by constant Elamite incursions into his territories. The task of driving out the Elamites was made more difficult by the support they received from a number of Mesopotamian rulers who were supposedly subject to Hammurabi. Other rulers remained firm in their allegiance to Hammurabi, who eventually succeeded in curbing, if not eliminating, Elamite aggression against his kingdom.

Soon after his death, the empire which he had built began to contract. This was due in part to the emergence of a new rival dynasty called the Sealand, which arose in the marshlands of southern Mesopotamia and won control over Babylonia as far north as the city of Nippur. Elam also remained a serious threat. Early in the reign of Hammurabi's successor-but-one Abi-eshuh (1711–1684), an Elamite campaign which Kutir-Nahhunte I, prince of Susa, conducted into Babylonia allegedly resulted in the conquest of thirty Babylonian cities. Despite both internal and external threats to its survival, the Old Babylonian kingdom continued for almost one hundred years after Abi-eshuh's death. It came to an end in 1595, in the reign of Samsu-ditana, last ruler of Hammurabi's dynasty, when Babylon was destroyed by the Hittite king Mursili I.

LATE BRONZE AGE

The Late Bronze Age kingdom of the Hittites arose in north-central Anatolia, probably during the first half of C17, in the region that had already long been known as the land of Hatti. This was the name of one of a number of kingdoms that emerged in eastern Anatolia in the second half of the Early Bronze Age. In texts of the Middle Bronze Age Assyrian Colony period, these kingdoms are attested in the letters which Assyrian merchants based in Anatolia exchanged with their home offices in Ashur. The Anatolian headquarters of the merchant operations in Anatolia were located at Kanesh (Nesa), near modern Kayseri. In the Late Bronze Age, 'Hatti' was regularly used as a general term to designate the kingdom of the people we call the Hittites, and more specifically, the homeland of the Hittites within the Halys river basin (modern Kızıl Irmak, Hittite Marassantiya). The population of Late Bronze Age Hatti consisted of a number of ethnic groups, including elements of both the early Hattic population of the region as well as later Indo-European groups who had begun settling in central Anatolia by the end of M3. The capital of the Hittite kingdom was located at Hattusa, modern Boğazköy/Boğazkale. Hittite history is generally divided into two periods – the Hittite Old and New Kingdoms. Though the distinction is a somewhat arbitrary one, and scholars have different views on when one period ended and the other began, we can for convenience' sake regard the Old Kingdom as extending from early C17 to c. 1400, and the New Kingdom from c. 1400 to early C12. The kingdom reached the peak of its development in the second half of C14, when it controlled an empire which extended from the Aegean coast of Anatolia in the west to the western fringes of Mesopotamia in the east, and south through Syria as far as the region of Damascus.

During the first half of the Late Bronze Age, Hatti became locked in bitter rivalry with the kingdom of Mitanni. The latter had been formed by the end of C16 from a number of small Hurrian states in northern Mesopotamia and northern Syria. Mitanni's royal capital, Washshukkanni, has yet to be located with certainty, but is commonly identified with the site of modern Tell Feheriye in the Habur river triangle of northern Mesopotamia. In the course of their expansion west of the Euphrates, the Mitannians frequently clashed with the Hittites, but also with Egypt, which similarly sought to extend its subject territories through the Syro-Palestinian regions. Agreement was reached early in C14 between the Mitannian king Artatama and his Egyptian counterpart Tuthmosis IV over a division of these regions between them. Virtually the whole of northern Syria was conceded to Mitanni. But Hatti also sought to extend its territories into northern Syria.

In the first centuries of M2, much of this region had belonged to the kingdom of Yamhad, until the reign of Yarim-Lim III in the second half of C17. At that time, the Hittite king Hattusili I embarked on a series of campaigns in Syria which seriously weakened Yamhad. His grandson and successor Mursili I brought the kingdom to an end by capturing and destroying its capital Aleppo, shortly before his conquest of

Babylon. It was Mitanni's move to fill the power vacuum in northern Syria left by the fall of Yamhad, and its attempts to extend its sovereignty over parts of eastern Anatolia, that generated its ongoing conflicts with Hatti. These came to a head when the Hittite king Suppiluliuma I (1350–1322) crushed the Mitannian empire, and put to flight its last ruler, Tushratta. To consolidate Hittite authority in northern Syria, Suppiluliuma established viceregal seats at Aleppo and at Carchemish, the last Mitannian stronghold to fall to him, and appointed two of his sons, Telipinu and Sharri-Kushuh (Piyassili), as the first viceroys. Other parts of the Hittite empire outside the core homeland territory consisted largely of vassal states, whose rulers were bound by treaty to the Hittite king.

Much information about Hittite policy towards its vassal states and the obligations which Hittite kings imposed upon their subject rulers is contained in the copies of vassal treaties found in the Hittite capital. Archives unearthed from Ugarit, a Hittite vassal state in northwestern Syria, also provide important information about relations between the Hittites and their Syrian subjects as well as about the history of the Syrian region as a whole. Of great importance too is the information contained in the so-called Amarna letters discovered on the site of the pharaoh Akhenaten's capital Akhetaten (modern Tell el-Amarna) in Egypt. The Amarna correspondence, dating to mid C14, sheds considerable light on the international politics of the age as well as on the pharaoh's relations with his Syro-Palestinian vassals and the relations of these vassals with one another.

In the wake of the Hittite destruction of Babylon in 1595, a population group called the Kassites, who had settled in Babylonia several hundred years earlier, provided a royal line which established its sovereignty over the country after conquering the 'Sealanders' in the south. First attested in C18 Babylonian texts, the Kassites may have come from a homeland in the Zagros mountain region in western Iran. But other places of origin have also been proposed. The Kassite royal dynasty ruled Babylonia almost without interruption until the final years of the Late Bronze Age. This period in Babylonian history is commonly referred to by scholars as the Middle Babylonian kingdom. Under Kassite rule, Babylonia became once more a major international power, achieving the status of one of the Great Kingdoms of the Late Bronze Age. The other Great Kingdoms were, initially, Egypt, Hatti, and Mitanni, with Assyria replacing Mitanni after the latter's destruction by the Hittites.

Assyria had sunk into insignificance in the period following the collapse of the Old Assyrian kingdom. It reached its lowest point when its traditional capital, Ashur, was sacked and looted by the Mitannian king Saushtatar, and the former Great Kingdom was reduced to Mitannian vassal status. But when Mitanni was destroyed by the Hittites, Assyria once more rose to prominence, in the reign of Ashur-uballit (1365–1330), who became in effect the first king of the Middle Assyrian kingdom. Ashur-uballit rapidly began to fill the power vacuum in northern Mesopotamia created by the fall of Mitanni, by taking over parts of former Mitannian territory. His and his successors' expansion of their boundaries seemed to pose an ever-increasing threat to the Hittites' subject states west of the Euphrates, including the viceregal kingdom Carchemish. And a resounding military victory won by the Assyrian king Tukulti-Ninurta I over the Hittite king Tudhaliya IV c. 1230 at Nihriya in the region of modern Kurdistan could well have paved the way for an Assyrian invasion of Hittite territory. But Assyria had also become caught up in conflicts with its southern neighbour Babylonia, and Tukulti-Ninurta now moved south against the Babylonians instead of west across the Euphrates against the Hittites.

A peace treaty concluded in 1259 between Hattusili III and Ramesses II, respective rulers of Hatti and Egypt, put an end to the tensions between the two Great Kingdoms which had erupted into open conflict on several occasions, most notably in 1274 in the battle of Qadesh on the Orontes river in Syria. Fear of an aggressive Assyria may have been one of a number of factors prompting the treaty partners to negotiate what was called 'the Eternal Peace'. But the Assyrian threat never materialized, and in other respects the Hittite–Egyptian alliance appears to have had little more than symbolical value.

The Hittite empire had in fact only a few more decades to run before it disintegrated, early in C12, during the course of widespread upheavals throughout much of the western Asian world. A number of other centres of Bronze Age civilization also came to an end in the same period. Their collapse and disappearance are generally associated with the so-called Sea Peoples attested in Egyptian texts, though the activities of marauding populations looking for new lands to settle may have been but one of many (perhaps interconnected) factors responsible for the apparently chaotic events of the age. Assyria seems to have been largely unaffected by the upheavals affecting other parts of the western Asian world. It was to prove one of the most resilient of the Bronze Age Great Kingdoms. Decades after the kingdom of Hatti had disappeared, when Egypt had lost its status as a major international power, and Babylon was being ruled by a succession of insignificant dynasties, Assyria remained a formidable power in western Asia. In the reign of Tiglath-pileser I (1114–1076) it still retained control over a substantial part of northern Mesopotamia. Indeed, Tiglath-pileser extended considerably the earlier boundaries of Assyrian enterprise by leading an expedition across the Euphrates to the Mediterranean coast.

IRON AGE

A number of the urban centres of the Late Bronze Age survived into the succeeding Iron Age, and indeed sometimes enjoyed greater prosperity than they had in their earlier existence. But the overall geopolitical structure of western Asia, especially west of the Euphrates, changed substantially in the last two centuries of M2 and the early centuries of M1. In eastern Anatolia and northern Syria, a number of small states now known as the Neo-Hittite kingdoms emerged. For the most part, these states were located within Hatti's former subject-territories, particularly in the Taurus region and northern Syria, where the name Hatti continued to be used throughout the Iron Age, as attested in Neo-Assyrian, Urartian, and Hebrew texts. Some of the Neo-Hittite centres had their origins in Bronze Age cities and states; others appear to have been new foundations. All of them, however, preserved in modified form many Hittite cultural traditions, albeit intermixed with Assyrian and other cultural elements, for a period of half a millennium after Late Bronze Age Hatti's disappearance. Carchemish was probably, at least to begin with, the most important of these kingdoms, and seems initially to have been ruled by direct descendants of the former Hittite royal dynasty.

Along the Syro-Palestinian coast lay the region called Phoenicia in Classical sources. It consisted of a number of principalities or city-states, the most prominent of which were Byblos, Sidon, and Tyre. The Phoenicians are generally regarded as the Iron Age successors of the Canaanites, attested in biblical and Bronze Age texts, though the precise nature of the relationship between Phoenicians and Canaanites is still unclear. On the Orontes in northern Syria, the city of Hamath had become, by the early years of M1, the capital of a large and important Iron Age kingdom of the same name, thenceforth frequently attested in both biblical and Assyrian sources. During the first part of its Iron Age phase, Hamath was ruled by a Neo-Hittite dynasty, which was replaced in early C8 by a line of Aramaean rulers. In southern Syria, Damascus became, probably in C10, the capital of one of the most important Aramaean states in the Levant, called Aram or Aram-Damascus.

First attested in C11 Assyrian texts, the Aramaeans were probably tribal pastoral groups in origin, inhabiting the fringes of the Syrian desert. By the early Iron Age, they had spread through many parts of western Asia, especially Syria, Mesopotamia, and eastern Anatolia. They spoke a West Semitic language called Aramaic. From C11 onwards, a number of small Aramaean states had begun to emerge. Some of the more important of these were Bit-Zamani, Bit-Bahiani, Bit-Adini, Bit-Agusi, Aram-Damascus, and Sam'al (Zincirli). In spite of the constant threat posed by Assyria to their independence, and indeed to their very survival, the Aramaean states failed to form any lasting union among themselves, though some of them occasionally joined forces to meet a specific military threat. In an Assyrian-dominated world, the Aramaean states enjoyed, by and large, a relatively prosperous existence, until their destruction by the Assyrians in late C8. The breakup of the Aramaean states and the dispersal of their populations increased substantially the spread of Aramaean settlers throughout western Asia. By this process, Aramaic became the main language of communication in much of western Asia, replacing Akkadian as the international language of diplomacy. The script in which the language was written was an alphabetic script, taken over from the Phoenicians.

The kingdom of Israel is generally given a prominent role in histories of the ancient Near East, particularly those dealing with Syria–Palestine in the region's Iron Age phase. But much of the material relating to Israel's history is derived solely from biblical tradition. To judge from *OT* sources, the kingdom reached its peak in C10, during the reign of King David, who allegedly exercised control over a large expanse of territory extending from the Palestinian coastlands and plains northwards to the region of Damascus, and eastwards to the Euphrates. The united monarchy over which he ruled had allegedly been established in the reign of his predecessor Saul, and fractured during the reign of his son and successor Solomon into two kingdoms, Israel to the north and Judah to the south. There is ongoing debate about the historicity of the biblical account of Israel, particularly in view of significant discrepancies between the *OT* narratives on the one hand and archaeological and contemporary written sources on the other. And many scholars do not believe that there was ever a united monarchy (or that if there was, it should be assigned to the period of the C9 Omride dynasty), preferring to see David and Solomon as literary rather than as historical figures. There are, none the less, numerous matters of detail in *OT* sources which can be corroborated from historical sources belonging to the periods to which the *OT* passages refer. The composers of the books of the *OT* undoubtedly had access to many of these sources, and incorporated information from them in their narratives. That would not, however, constitute proof that their narratives as a whole can be regarded as historically valid in a strictly literal sense.

We have seen that Assyria largely escaped the devastation to which other kingdoms, notably Hatti, succumbed at the end of the Late Bronze Age, and remained a formidable power in western Asia during C12 and early C11, particularly in the reign of its king Tiglath-pileser I. But after Tiglath-pileser's death, Assyria entered upon almost two centuries of decline, perhaps due in some measure to an increasing Aramaean presence in many of the regions where it had exercised control. In the last decades of C10, however, the Assyrian king Ashur-dan II (934–912) began the process of winning back Assyria's lost territories and restoring its status as a major international power. His reign effectively marked the beginning of the Neo-Assyrian kingdom. He was succeeded by his son Adad-nirari II (911–891), who shortly after his accession embarked upon a vigorous new programme of territorial expansion.

Adad-nirari's successful campaigns against the Aramaeans in the Tigris valley and the Babylonian king Shamash-mudammiq, part of whose territory he incorporated into his own rapidly expanding empire, laid the foundations for further campaigns beyond Assyria's frontiers in the reigns of his successors. Shalmaneser III (858–824) focused his attention particularly on the lands lying west of the Euphrates. Nineteen of his thirty-four campaigns were conducted into these lands. The rich booty which they provided, in the form of precious and commodity metals, horses and chariots, prisoners for resettlement, linen garments, timber from the forests of Lebanon and the Amanus mountains, and a range of exotic and luxury items, added substantially to the revenue flowing into Assyria's royal coffers. Initially, the conquered cities and kingdoms of the west had the status of client kingdoms, which paid an annual tribute to the Assyrian king but were otherwise left to manage their own affairs. Eventually they were absorbed within the Assyrian provincial system, under the direct authority of governors appointed by the Assyrian king. The ethnic composition of the conquered territories was in a constant state of flux, because of the Assyrians' practice of deporting large numbers of a conquered kingdom's inhabitants to other parts of their realm and resettling the depopulated areas with deportees brought from the Assyrian homeland or elsewhere.

Assyria's military enterprises inevitably brought it into conflict with another great power which lay beyond its northern borders, in the highlands of eastern Anatolia – the kingdom of Urartu. The name Urartu is first attested, in the form Uruatri, in the inscriptions of the C13 Assyrian king Shalmaneser I. (Urartu's own inhabitants called their country Bianili, from which the modern name Van is derived.) However, it was not until the second half of C9 that Urartu's lands and cities were consolidated into a united kingdom. This was the achievement of a king called Sarduri I (832–825), who founded a royal dynasty in the city of Tushpa (modern Van). Sarduri and his successors embarked on a programme of territorial expansion which extended Urartu's frontiers northwards into Armenia, eastwards to the Araxes river, southeastwards to the shores of Lake Urmia, and southwestwards to the western bend of the Euphrates. The greatest period of expansion occurred in the reign of King Minua (805–788), grandson of Sarduri I, and son and (for a time) co-regent of Ishpuini. Minua's expansionist programme, continued by his successor Argishti I (787–766), led to an intensification of Urartu's ongoing conflicts with Assyria. The contests between the kingdoms culminated in a military showdown in 714 between the Assyrian king Sargon II and his Urartian counterpart Rusa I while Sargon was campaigning in the northern Zagros region. Sargon won a decisive victory, which he followed up by invading and plundering Rusa's kingdom. During the following century, tensions and sporadic conflicts appear to have continued between Assyria and Urartu, though there is no evidence of any further major military confrontation.

The Urartian kingdom came to a violent end in the last decades of C7, when almost all Urartian sites were destroyed by fire. We have no clear indication of who their destroyers were. But despite the devastation inflicted upon it at this time, Urartu has left us relatively substantial remains of its material civilization. Most impressive among these remains are the massive fortresses which its kings built on great outcrops of rock. The fortresses were strategically located to control the plains and valleys which lay among the rugged highland mountains. They contained palaces and administrative centres, temples to the state gods, and great warehouses to store the produce of the plains. Our knowledge of Urartian history is based on written records, which began with the reign of Sarduri I. At that time, Urartian scribes used the Assyrian language and cuneiform script. But in the reigns of subsequent Urartian kings, all surviving inscriptions were written in the Urartian language, which was closely related to Hurrian.

One of the regions which became caught up in the Urartian–Assyrian conflicts was called Mannaea, the general name for what was originally a number of small Iron Age kingdoms located south of Lake Urmia in modern Iranian Kurdistan. Mannaea was plundered by the Assyrians in 828, during the reign of the Assyrian king Shalmaneser III. But Shalmaneser apparently made no attempt to establish permanent authority there. The Urartians, however, did impose their sovereignty over the land, probably in 802/801 after repeated attacks upon its territory, when Urartu's throne was occupied by Minua. Mannaea subsequently broke twice from Urartian sovereignty and became for a time, on both occasions, an independent united kingdom. During the last decades of C8 its king, Iranzu, had aligned himself with the Assyrian king Sargon II against Urartu. The outcome proved disastrous for Mannaea, whose governors were split into pro-Urartian and pro-Assyrian factions. Iranzu's son and Assyrian-appointed successor Aza was assassinated by pro-Urartian rebels, and a Urartian appointee, Ullusunu, brother of Aza, was installed on the throne. Sargon responded by invading Mannaea, destroying its royal capital, and devastating other parts of the land. Ullusunu had fled at the approach of the Assyrian army. But Sargon was subsequently reconciled with him, and restored him to the throne. None the less, in the years that followed hostilities between Mannaea and Assyria, generally at the expense of the former, were much more characteristic of the relations between the two kingdoms, until peace was concluded between the Mannaean king Ualli and the Assyrian king Ashurbanipal (668–630/627). The Assyrian–Mannaean alliance which was thus established appears to have remained in force until late C7, when the Babylonian king Nabopolassar (626–605) launched a series of campaigns into Assyrian territory, and inflicted a defeat on Assyria's Mannaean allies.

ANATOLIA AND CYPRUS IN THE FIRST MILLENNIUM

To the west of the Euphrates, in central Anatolia, another great power, comparable to Assyria and Urartu, had emerged in the early centuries of the Iron Age – the kingdom of Phrygia. According to Greek legendary tradition, the earliest Phrygians were emigrants from Macedon and Thrace. At some point in their history, they became associated with a people called the Mushki in Assyrian sources. The latter, first mentioned in C12 Assyrian texts, may originally have been tribal groups from the Armenian highlands. An amalgamation between the Phrygians and Mushki has been credited to a C8 Mushki king called Mita, better known by his Greek name Midas. From his capital at Gordium, Mita/Midas ruled a kingdom which stretched eastwards towards the Euphrates, southwards into the region later known as Cappadocia, and westwards as far as the Aegean Sea. The extent of his territories, and especially the contacts which he established with other states in southeastern Anatolia, as far afield as the Neo-Hittite kingdom of Carchemish on the Euphrates, brought him into conflict with Assyria. In particular, Midas threatened the security of Assyria's western frontiers. He seized border territories of the kingdom of Que, which lay to the southeast of the Phrygian kingdom, and subsequently sought to win local rulers in the country of Tabal away from their allegiance to the Assyrian king Sargon II. Despite this provocation, Sargon was anxious to reach an accommodation with Midas, very probably in order to offset the danger of an alliance formed by Midas with Assyria's other great rival in the region, Urartu. A diplomatic initiative taken by Midas was welcomed by Sargon, and provided the basis for the establishment of a permanent peace between them.

Midas' peace initiative may have been prompted by the threat posed to his kingdom by the Cimmerians, a people of perhaps Thraco-Phrygian or Indo-Iranian stock, who had descended upon the western Asian world from a homeland in southern Russia. In fact, within a few years of Midas' *détente* with Sargon, Phrygia fell victim, c. 695, to an invasion from the north by the Cimmerians, who occupied large areas of Anatolia, and in the process destroyed Midas' kingdom. Sargon himself may have been killed during a campaign which he conducted against the Cimmerians in eastern Anatolia in 705.

The Cimmerians also posed a severe threat to Phrygia's successor in Anatolia, the kingdom of Lydia. Lydia's rise to power began with a man called Gyges, who established a ruling line called the Mermnad dynasty, c. 685. From his royal capital, Sardis, Gyges embarked on a programme of territorial expansion, continued by his successors, which made Lydia the dominant power in western Anatolia. But his reign was abruptly ended when he was killed in an attack by the Cimmerians c. 644. Lydia's conflicts with the Cimmerians continued into the reign of the fourth ruler of the Mermnad dynasty, Alyattes (c. 609–560), who eventually drove the invaders from his kingdom. Alyattes also had to deal with another formidable enemy which threatened the eastern frontiers of his land – the Medes from the Zagros region (see below). According to Greek sources, a five-year conflict between the Lydians and the Medians culminated in the so-called 'battle of the eclipse', fought between Alyattes and the Median king Cyaxares on the banks of the Halys in north-central Anatolia; the outcome was a treaty between the two kings, which established the border between their kingdoms along the banks of the river.

Lydia reached the peak of its development under Croesus (560–546), the last member of the Mermnad dynasty. But the kingdom was now entering its final phase. Alarmed by the rapid expansion of Persian power westwards, Croesus led his troops across the Halys in an attempt to forestall a Persian invasion of his own territory. After an inconclusive encounter with Cyrus in the so-called 'battle of Pteria' (spring 546), Croesus was pursued by Cyrus' army and defeated in a pitched battle outside his capital, Sardis. The city fell to the Persians after a siege, and Lydia was incorporated into the Persian empire. Sardis became Persia's chief administrative centre in the west.

The Persian king Cyrus also inherited the sovereignty imposed by Lydia upon the

Greek Ionian cities in the west. The region called Ionia in Greek sources extended along Anatolia's Aegean coast between the bays of Izmir and Bargylia and included the offshore islands Samos and Chios. It was settled by waves of refugee colonists, called Ionians, from the Greek mainland in the last two centuries of M2. The largest and most important of the cities of the region, Miletus, played a leading role in an ultimately unsuccessful rebellion against Persian rule at the beginning of C5. Miletus' Late Bronze Age predecessor was called Milawata (Millawanda) in Hittite texts. Archaeological evidence indicates that in late C14 or early C13 the city had become a substantially Mycenaean Greek settlement. This accords with Hittite textual evidence which indicates that Milawata came under the control of a king of Ahhiyawa (the Hittite name for the Mycenaean world) in the same period. North of Ionia lay the region called Aeolis in Greek texts, extending from the Hellespont to the mouth of the Hermus river Like the Ionians, the Aeolians were late M2 immigrants from the Greek mainland. They settled first on the islands of Lesbos and Tenedos before occupying the coastal part of the Troad and the region to its south.

The region called Caria by the Greeks lay to the south of Ionia. According to the Greek historian Herodotus, the Carians were immigrants to western Anatolia from the Aegean islands, displaced from their original homelands by Ionian and Dorian Greeks. If this tradition is historically valid, the Carians may have participated in the general migratory movements to the coastlands of western Anatolia in late M2. But Herodotus notes that the Carians themselves claimed that they were native Anatolians, and had always been called Carians. The name may in fact be etymologically linked with Karkisa, a Late Bronze Age country in western Anatolia attested frequently in Hittite texts. It is possible that at least part of the population of M1 Caria was of indigenous origin. So too, without doubt, was at least part of the population of the country on the southwestern coast of Anatolia called Lycia by the Greeks. Lycia belonged to the region known as Lukka or the Lukka Lands in Hittite texts. Its native language, preserved mainly in rock-cut inscriptions dating to C5 and C4, is closely related to the Indo-European Luwian language, which was widely spoken throughout Anatolia during M2. According to one Classical tradition preserved by Herodotus, Lycia was settled by refugee immigrants from Crete. From C4 onwards, Greeks settled in the country in increasing numbers, to the extent that during the Hellenistic Age, Lycia had become a substantially Greek region.

Greek cities also appeared in increasing numbers along Anatolia's southern coast in the regions which the Greeks called Pamphylia and Cilicia. The latter name is probably derived from Hilakku, one of the kingdoms to emerge in southeastern Anatolia in the centuries following the collapse of the Late Bronze Age kingdom of Hatti. It occupied the region called Rough Cilicia (Cilicia Tracheia/Aspera) in Classical sources. To its east lay the kingdom of Que, in the region of Smooth Cilicia (Cilicia Pedias/Campestris). Hilakku and Que are attested in both Assyrian and Babylonian sources as well as in a small number of Luwian hieroglyphic inscriptions. In Babylonian sources, Hilakku is referred to as Pirindu, and Que as Hume.

The island of Cyprus lies 69 km off Anatolia's southeastern coast, directly south of Cilicia. It occupied an excellent strategic position within the ancient international trading network which linked Egypt and the Aegean and western Asian worlds. Almost all scholars now accept the identification of Cyprus with the Bronze Age land called Alasiya, attested first in a Middle Bronze Age text from Mari, and frequently mentioned in Late Bronze Age Egyptian and Hittite texts. Cyprus was among the victims of the upheavals which brought many of the Late Bronze Age civilizations in the western Asian and Aegean worlds to an end. But the island seems to have suffered less destruction than other areas. In the aftermath of the upheavals, between 1100 and 800, there was a significant degree of continuity and contact between Cyprus and the Aegean and Levantine regions. But major changes were taking place in the island's geopolitical organization. A C7 Assyrian inscription reports that Cyprus was in this period dominated by ten separate kingdoms. The fact that some of the island's rulers had Greek names and some Semitic names is seen as an indication of the ethnic diversity of its population during its Iron Age phase.

After a period of apparent independence in C7, Cyprus became subject to Egypt in C6, but was under Egyptian control for only a few decades before the Persian king Cyrus II established his sovereignty over the island c. 545. Cyprus remained under Persian rule for much of C5 and C4, up to its conquest by Alexander the Great in 330, though during this period a number of battles were fought on its territory between Greek and Persian forces. Cyprus' system of individual kingdoms was left largely undisturbed, until Ptolemy I Soter conquered the island in 294 and abolished all but one of its monarchies.

THE NEO-BABYLONIAN AND PERSIAN PERIODS

Following the death of Sargon II in 705, Assyria maintained its position as the dominant power in western Asia through the reigns of Sargon's successors Sennacherib, Esarhaddon, and Ashurbanipal. Indeed, under Ashurbanipal (668–630/627) the empire reached its greatest territorial limits. It extended from Elam in the east to eastern Anatolia in the west, and from Armenia in the north to Egypt in the southwest and the Persian Gulf in the southeast. But after Ashurbanipal's death the empire went into irreversible decline. The final blow was delivered by a combined force of Chaldaeans (from Babylonia) and Medes (from western Iran). In 615, the Medes invaded the Assyrian homeland, and in the following year captured the city of Ashur. Then in 612 Chaldaean and Median forces captured and destroyed Assyria's administrative capital Nineveh. By the end of the year, all the chief cities of the Assyrian homeland had been destroyed, and the empire was at an end.

For the next few decades, the mantle of leadership in western Asia was assumed by the rulers of what is now referred to as the Neo-Babylonian empire. In the centuries which followed the fall of the Kassite dynasty at the end of the Late Bronze Age, Babylonia had enjoyed several brief periods when it could claim once more the status of a major international power, notably under Nebuchadnezzar I (1126–1105), who invaded Elam and sacked the city of Susa, and Nabu-apla-iddina (888–855), whose reign was marked by a peace treaty with the Assyrian king Shalmaneser III and a decisive victory over the Sutaeans, Amorite tribal groups which had been making constant incursions into Babylonian territory. But for longer periods, Babylonia had been overshadowed by its northern neighbour Assyria, and the latter generally emerged as victor in the frequent wars between the two kingdoms. A number of Assyrian kings claimed to have conquered the whole of Babylonia and to have established their sovereignty over it. In 729 one of these kings, Tiglath-pileser III, instituted a period of 'double monarchy' in the land, where kingship was in theory shared by the Assyrian Great King and a Babylonian appointee.

But Assyrian overlordship in Babylonia was vigorously challenged by a series of local leaders of Chaldaean origin. By C8, Chaldaean tribal groups, which had apparently entered Babylonia from the northwest some time during C11 or C10, had become a major political force in Babylonia. In the course of C8, three of their leaders had occupied the Babylonian throne. The most notable of them was a man called Marduk-apla-iddina II (biblical Merodach-baladan) who became king in 721 and united Babylonia under his leadership for a protracted struggle with Assyria, during the reigns of Sargon II and his successor Sennacherib. He was finally defeated by Sennacherib's forces. But subsequent Chaldaean leaders continued to attack Assyrian garrisons stationed in Babylonia. It was one of these leaders, Nabopolassar, who brought the Assyrian kingdom to an end, in partnership with the Medes (see below), some years after he had seized the Babylonian throne in 626. Nabopolassar became the founder of the Neo-Babylonian empire (626–539).

The empire reached its height in the reign of Nabopolassar's son and successor Nebuchadnezzar II (604–562). Campaigns conducted by Nebuchadnezzar in the Syro-Palestinian regions extended Babylonian power westwards to the Levant, over territories formerly controlled by both Assyria and Egypt. Jerusalem was captured in 597, and after an uprising there in 586 was totally destroyed. The deportation of its population to Babylon marked the beginning of the period of the Jewish exile. A Babylonian army may also have invaded Egypt. In the east, the old Elamite capital Susa came for a time under Nebuchadnezzar's sovereignty (c. 595). But in spite of these impressive, far-flung conquests, the empire built by Nebuchadnezzar began to crumble soon after his death. In 539, when its throne was occupied by a man called Nabonidus, the empire fell to the Persians, and it remained under Persian sovereignty until this empire in its turn fell to Alexander the Great, who conquered Babylon in 331.

The Persian empire was founded in mid C6 by Cyrus II, a member of a local ruling dynasty based originally, according to tradition, in the city of Anshan in southwestern Iran (modern province of Fars). The dynasty was later to be called the Achaemenid dynasty, after its alleged founder Achaemenes. Anshan had long played an important role in Iranian history as one of Elam's royal capitals. First attested in texts dating to c. 2500, Elam had been a major power in western Iran for much of M2. But in the final phase of its existence, the so-called Neo-Elamite period (1100–539), its role in western Asian affairs was a greatly diminished one. A brief resurgence of power in late C8 in the reign of its king Shutruk-Nahhunte II (716–699) did little to interrupt Elam's progressive decline, hastened by the Assyrian sack of its royal capital Susa in 646. A fragmentary Elamite kingdom survived for a time after this, and managed to secure an alliance with Babylon. But after the fall of the Neo-Babylonian empire to the Persians in mid C6, the Persian king Cyrus II established his sovereignty over all territories formerly belonging to Elam. Some scholars believe that Anshan no longer existed at this time, and that the adoption of the title 'King of Anshan' by Cyrus and his successors was 'an act of political symbolism with which the Persians gave weight to their role as successors of the Elamite kings' (thus M. Brosius, 2006: 6).

According to both Classical and Babylonian sources, Cyrus laid the foundations of his empire by conquering his Median overlord Astyages, alleged by Herodotus, probably wrongly, to have been Cyrus' maternal grandfather. The Medes were subsequently absorbed into the fledgling Persian empire, and played an important role within it as its second most important ethnic group. This in effect marks the final phase in the history of Media. The Medes were, like the Persians, an Indo-European-speaking people whose homeland lay in the central Zagros mountains. They are first attested in mid C9 Assyrian texts. Fragments of their history can be pieced together from Assyrian and Babylonian sources. But they are best known from Herodotus' account of them in his so-called *Medikos Logikos* (*Histories* 1.95–106).

According to Herodotus, the Medes originally comprised a number of independent tribal groups, who were eventually united (apparently in C7) into a single kingdom by a man called Deioces. Media's royal capital was established at Ecbatana (modern Hamadan). The kingdom allegedly reached the height of its power in the reign of Cyaxares, commonly regarded as the true founder of the Median empire. Acceding to his country's throne c. 625, Cyaxares ruled for forty years, during which time he conquered Assyria's traditional capital Ashur, and subsequently formed an alliance with the Babylonian king Nabopolassar. This Median–Babylonian partnership brought the Neo-Assyrian empire to an end, by its conquest and destruction of the Assyrian capital Nineveh in 612. In the latter years of his reign Cyaxares expanded his territories progressively westwards, eventually into the eastern half of Anatolia, which brought the Medians into conflict with the Lydian empire (see above). Peaceful relations between Media and Lydia were subsequently consolidated by a royal marriage alliance, when Alyattes wed his daughter to Cyaxares' successor Astyages. After thirty-five years of despotic rule, Astyages was attacked and overthrown by his 'grandson', the Persian Cyrus II.

In recent years, a number of scholars have cast considerable doubt on the historicity of a Median empire as presented in Classical sources, particularly Herodotus. They have emphasized the absence of any archaeological evidence for the Herodotean account of Media, and a perceived lack of consistency between this account and contemporary treatments of the Medes in Assyrian and Neo-Babylonian documentary sources. A conference held in Padua in 2001 provided the opportunity for a comprehensive review of the sources on which modern reconstructions of the Median kingdom have been based. In their summing up of the proceedings, the editors (Lanfranchi *et al.*, 2003: 397–406) noted that recent re-examinations of the sources relating to Media have led to a radical reduction of the extent of the 'Median empire' before it was incorporated into the Persian empire. But they observed that opinions still vary between two extremes – a 'maximalist' and a 'minimalist' view. The former 'might extend Median power from the west of the former kingdom of Urartu to the borders of Fars and from the western outliers of the Zagros mountains on the plains of eastern Assyria to the fringes of the central Iranian desert beyond Rayy', while the latter 'would abandon the whole of the north, east and central western Iran to bands of nomads roaming freely over an extensive territory, and consider Median influence to be negligible'. The 'truth', the editors say, may well lie between these extremes.

Under Cyrus, the process began of building Persia into the greatest empire western Asia had ever seen. In the west, Cyrus extended Persian power through Anatolia to the Aegean coast, by destroying the Lydian empire. He subsequently turned his attention to Babylonia, already on the verge of disintegration under its last king, Nabonidus, and occupied the royal capital Babylon without a battle (539). Some time after this, he probably conducted a campaign into Central Asia, which resulted in the incorporation of a number of eastern lands into his empire. He may now have set his sights on the conquest of Egypt. But he was diverted by uprisings on the eastern frontiers of his kingdom and was killed during a campaign against rebel forces in the region of the Oxus and Jaxartes rivers. His son and successor Cambyses II (530–522) conquered Cyprus, and resumed his father's plans for the conquest of Egypt, leading a campaign there in 525. He defeated the pharaoh Psammetichus III in a battle outside Memphis, and incorporated the whole of Egypt into the Persian empire.

In 522, the Persian throne was seized by Darius I, a member of the Persian aristocracy but probably not of the royal dynasty. After crushing a number of rebellions which broke out among his subject states at the beginning of his reign, Darius set his sights on expanding the empire's territories yet further. Indeed, the empire reached its greatest extent during his reign, with new campaigns in the east, the conquest of parts of northern India, and the addition to its realm of Hindush or Sind along the banks of the Indus. The empire was divided into twenty provinces, called satrapies, which were placed under the authority of governors, or satraps, who were in most cases rulers of local origin.

Darius now prepared to move westwards into Europe. A campaign across the Bosporus in 516 against the Scythian tribes paved the way for further expeditions on European soil, and the establishment of a Persian presence in Thrace and the northern Aegean. This in turn paved the way for a Persian invasion of the Greek mainland in 490, which ended with the rout of Darius' forces on the plain of Marathon outside Athens and the abandonment of the campaign. A fresh campaign launched against Greece by Darius' son and successor Xerxes I in 481 similarly ended in decisive Greek victories over Persia's land and sea forces. As a result of these victories, the Greek city-states, at least on the mainland, were secured against any further foreseeable threat from Persia.

Xerxes was assassinated in a palace conspiracy in 465. A number of his successors met a similar fate, sometimes after only a short reign. But other occupants of the Persian throne managed to remain there for many years. And their reigns were sometimes marked by significant achievements. In early C4, Artaxerxes II (404–359) re-established Persian control over Cyprus and the Greek states in western Anatolia. His successor Artaxerxes III (359–338) reconquered Egypt, which had rebelled against Persian rule in 405, and put down revolts in Cyprus and a number of Phoenician cities. But the Persian empire was to survive Artaxerxes III's death by only eight years. In 330 it fell to Alexander the Great under its last king, Darius III.

A

Aba see **Upi (2)**.

Abattum (map 10) Middle Bronze Age city in the middle Euphrates region, probably to be located on the river's right bank between Tuttul and Emar. Its king, Ayalum, referred to as ruler of the land of the Rabbu, one of the five main Yaminite tribal groups (see **Yaminites**), participated in a Yaminite revolt against Yahdun-Lim (1810–1794), king of Mari. Yahdun-Lim claimed a decisive victory in the contest, in a battle fought at Samanum which lay on the Euphrates in the north part of the district of Terqa.

LKM 605 (refs), *Mesop.* 140–1.

Abdadanu Iron Age city in the central-western Zagros region. It was among the cities conquered by the Assyrian king Shalmaneser III in his sixteenth regnal year (843) (**RIMA* 3: 40). Haban was another city in the region which fell to the Assyrians at this time. Abdadanu later appears among the conquests of the Assyrian king Adad-nirari III (810–783) (**RIMA* 3: 212).

Abu Hawam, Tell (biblical **Shihor-Libnah**?) (map 8) 4 ha settlement-mound on the coast of Israel, located within the limits of mod. Haifa. Its history of occupation extends from the Middle Bronze Age (C16–15) to the Persian period (C6–4). Excavations, carried out by archaeological teams from Britain (1922–33), Israel (1952, 1963), and France and Israel (1984–9), have identified six major occupation levels. Founded at the end of the Middle Bronze Age (level VI), Tell Abu Hawam became an important trading entrepôt during the Late Bronze Age (V) when a sanctuary and citadel were constructed on the site. The end of this phase of its existence has been associated with the arrival of the Sea Peoples in the region during C12. Reoccupation took place in C11, the Iron Age I period (IV), but ended in destruction the following century. The succeeding Iron Age II settlement (III; C10–8) indicates significant Phoenician influence, if not an actual Phoenician presence, and provides evidence in its ceramic ware of trading contacts with Cyprus and the Aegean world. The end of this level has been associated either with a steady decline due to the silting up of the city's harbour, or with the Assyrian invasions of the region in C8. During the Persian period, a strongly fortified settlement was built on the site (II; C5–4). Overseas trading contacts are again evident in this level. At the end of the Persian period, the site was largely abandoned.

Balensi, Herrera, Artzy (*NEAEHL* 1: 7–14), Dever (*OEANE* 1: 9).

Abu Salima, Tell (map 13) Settlement-mound in the northern Sinai, southern Palestine, with a history of occupation extending from the Late Bronze Age to the early Roman imperial period (late C14–1). The site was excavated in 1935 and 1936 by

W. M. F. Petrie on behalf of the British School of Archaeology in Egypt. Petrie identified twelve levels of buildings and floors, the entire sequence illustrated by the pottery unearthed from the site. Other small finds included amulets and scarabs, incense altars from the Persian period (C6–4), and sherds with Aramaic inscriptions from the Hellenistic period (C4–1). Petrie also uncovered the remains of a large fortified structure in the level designated Stratum G, identifying in this level what he believed to be a temple of the Neo-Babylonian period (C6). On the basis of its Assyrian features, R. Reich subsequently proposed redating the building to C8. He believed the site to be that of an Assyrian fortress, established here, near the Egyptian border, to ensure the region's military and political stability. He has suggested that in the Hellenistic period Abu Salima may have served as a commercial centre. All trace of the settlement has now disappeared.

Reich (*NEAEHL* 1: 15).

Abydus (map 5) M1 BCE–M1 CE harbour-city belonging to the country of Mysia in northwestern Anatolia, 6 km north of mod. Çannakale. It is first attested in Homer's *Iliad* (2.836). Strabo (13.1.22) reports that the city was occupied by Thracians after the Trojan War, but was refounded by colonists from Miletus who were granted permission to settle there by the Lydian king Gyges (c. 700). Abydus came under Persian control in 514, and in 481, the Persian emperor Xerxes used it as the starting-point for his bridge across the Hellespont (Herodotus 7.33–4). Later in C5, after the allied Greek victory over the Persians in 479, the city became a member of the Athenian Confederacy. But it revolted against Athens in 411 (Thucydides 8.62), and became an ally of Sparta until 394. In 386 it fell to Persia by the terms of the King's Peace (see glossary), and remained under Persian sovereignty until its liberation by Alexander the Great in 334. In the Hellenistic period, it was noted for its courageous but ultimately unsuccessful resistance to Philip V of Macedon (200), and in the Roman and Byzantine periods it was an important toll-station on the Hellespont. The city minted coins from early C5 to mid C3 CE. Goldmines provided one of the sources of its wealth, probably until C1 when the mines had been largely worked out. There were still, apparently, significant remains of Abydus up to C19 CE. But virtually no trace of the city survives today.

Bean (*PECS* 5).

Abzuya Late Bronze Age Syrian city within the land of Qadesh on the Orontes r. Shutatarra, ruler of Qadesh, sought refuge here, along with his son Aitakkama and his chariot contingent, following his defeat in battle by the Hittite king Suppiluliuma I during the latter's one-year Syrian war, c. 1340 (**HDT* 44). Suppiluliuma laid siege to the city, captured it, and deported the refugees to Hatti.

Acem Höyük (map 2) Settlement-mound in central Anatolia, located 18 km northwest of mod. Aksaray on the southern bank of the Salt Lake (Tuz Gölü). Its history of occupation extends from the Chalcolithic period (M4) to the Middle Bronze Age (C20–18), with some reoccupation in Hellenistic and Roman times. Excavations were conducted from 1962 onwards by N. Özgüç on behalf of the University of Ankara and the Turkish Historical Foundation. The most recent excavations date to 1988 and 1989 (the latter under the direction of A. Özten).

Acem Höyük reached the peak of its development during the Middle Bronze Age, the period of the Assyrian merchant-colonies in eastern and central Anatolia (C20–18). Remains of this period include a substantial mudbrick palace on stone foundations, private houses, and a wide range of small finds unearthed in various rooms of the palace. These finds include bronze and ivory artefacts, vases of crystal and obsidian, and large numbers of seal impressions on clay bullae. A number of rooms contained large pithos vessels, used for storage. All this is indicative of Acem's extensive commercial activities, with the establishment and operation of trading links reaching to Syria, Mesopotamia, and the Persian Gulf.

It has proved surprisingly difficult to identify this major site with a city known from contemporary written records. Though long thought to be the important city of Purushattum (Hittite Purushanda) attested in Middle Bronze Age texts (see **Purushanda**), this city is now commonly identified with the site of Karahöyük near Konya.

With the disappearance of the Assyrian colonies from Anatolia in C18 at the end of the Middle Bronze Age, Acem was abandoned for many centuries, with some resettlement taking place in the Hellenistic and Roman periods on the southwestern part of the mound.

N. Özgüç (1966; 1980), Burney (2004: 2–5).

Achshaph Biblically attested Canaanite city, thought to have been situated near mod. Akko. An identification with Tell Keisan (see ***Keisan, Tell***) has been proposed. According to Joshua 11:1, Achshaph's king was a member of the military coalition summoned by Jabin, ruler of Hazor, to fight against the Israelites, led by Joshua. The coalition's forces were defeated, and Achshaph was among the many cities which fell to the victors (Joshua 12:20).

Achtemeier (*HCBD* 10).

Achziv (*OT* **Achzib**, Assyrian **Accipu**, Classical **Ekdippa**, ***Ez-Zib, Tel Akhziv***) (map 8) Double-mound settlement located in northern Canaan, on the coast of Israel, 25 km south of Tyre. In *OT* tradition, Achzib is attested as one of the Canaanite cities allocated to the tribe of Asher (Joshua 19:29). Located in a highly valuable strategic position on the Via Maris (q.v.), the site has a long history of settlement, from the Middle Bronze Age to the mediaeval period. Excavations were conducted in 1963 and 1964 by M. W. Prausnitz for the Istituto di Vicino Oriente, University of Rome, in collaboration with the Israel Dept of Antiquities. Later excavations of the eastern and southern of the city's four cemeteries (see below) were conducted from 1988 to 1990 by A. Mazar for the Institute of Archaeology at the Hebrew University of Jerusalem and the Israel Antiquities Authority.

The city was first fortified, with rampart and glacis (see glossary) earthworks, in the Middle Bronze IIB period (mid C18). Its fortifications were destroyed and rebuilt on two occasions in the Late Bronze Age. Following its recovery in C11, Achziv reached the peak of its development in C8, when it also attained its maximum size, extending over some 8 ha. In 701, it fell to the invading army of the Assyrian king Sennacherib during his third campaign to Phoenicia and Palestine. It was subsequently rebuilt and refortified in the Persian period (C6–4), and continued to prosper through Hellenistic and Roman times. Human occupation continued until the Middle Ages.

Excavations of the city's four cemeteries – central (on the eastern slope of the mound), northern, eastern, and southern – brought to light a large number of rock-cut and built tombs, including pit- and cist-graves, and a number of shaft tombs which were accessed by vertical shafts leading to square openings in the burial chambers. The cemeteries are primarily of Iron Age date, but the central and southern ones also contained evidence of use in the Middle Bronze II period. In their totality, the cemeteries spanned the entire period of the site's existence. Many tombs were used for family burials and still housed their occupants when they were excavated, along with rich assemblages of tomb-goods, including cylinder seals, a wide range of ceramic wares, jewellery, ivories, scarabs, weapons, and figurines. It seems that certain rituals were performed in the cemeteries, presumably cultic rites in honour of the dead, by surviving members of their families. The grave goods reflect ties with Sidon, which lies to the north, and cultural and commercial contacts with the wider Mediterranean world.

Prausnitz and Mazar (*NEAEHL* 1: 32–6), Prausnitz (*OEANE* 1: 13–14).

Acco see Akko.

Adab (*Bismaya*) (map 17) Bronze Age city in southern Mesopotamia, 30 km southeast of Nippur, excavated by J. E. Banks in 1903 and 1904. The site, which occupies a number of mounds, is roughly rectangular in shape, c. 1.5 km long by 0.5 km wide, and surrounded by a double wall. On one of its mounds a sacred precinct was identified, containing a ziggurat and a temple. Other mounds contain the remains of a residential area and 'palace'.

Adab is one of the fourteen city-states of Early Bronze Age Sumer and Akkad listed in Early Dynastic sources (c. 2900–2334). According to the Sumerian King List, it had a royal dynasty which consisted of only one king, Lugal-anne-mundu, who reigned for ninety years (*sic*) before kingship was carried off to the city of Mari (**Chav* 83). A long inscription proclaiming Lugal-anne-mundu's exploits attests to the king's supremacy over Sumer, and relates his victory over thirteen princes from neighbouring lands who had risen against him, among them the land of Marhashi (q.v.) (*Güterbock, 1934: 40–7). However, the text is apocryphal, having been composed several centuries after the late Early Dynastic III period when Lugal-anne-mundu probably reigned. Adab retained its independence until conquered by Lugal-zage-si of Uruk, who confirmed Mes-kigal as its ruler (**RIME* 2: 252). It was apparently destroyed during the reign of the Akkadian king Rimush (2278–2270), who reports that he fought a battle with it and the nearby city Zabala(m), killing 15,718 of the enemy's troops and taking 14,576 people prisoner, including the cities' governors; he demolished the walls of both cities (**DaK* 200–1, **RIME* 2: 41–2).

However, Adab (like Zabala) was rebuilt and was clearly a city of some importance in the last centuries of M3, as reflected in the cuneiform tablets discovered in the so-called palace and residential area of the city, and the bricks found in the city's sacred precinct. The bricks were stamped with the names of Sumerian and Akkadian kings. Artefacts from this period include many fragments of finely made stone bowls, inscribed and decorated. It has been suggested that Adab may have served as a distribution centre for a range of stone vessels brought from Iran and Arabia as well as from various Mesopotamian cities.

Adab's continuing existence in the Middle Bronze Age is indicated by a reference to it in the prologue to the law code of the Babylonian king Hammurabi (1792–1750), who claims to have built (i.e. rebuilt) the temple and the city. It was still occupied in the Late Bronze Age, when southern Mesopotamia was ruled by a Kassite dynasty. A small number of bricks from the site bear the name of the C14 Kassite king Kurigalzu.

Banks (1912), Unger (*RlA* 1: 21–2), Crawford (*OEANE* 1: 14–15).

Adallaya (Adalle) Middle Bronze Age city in the Jebel Sinjar region of northern Mesopotamia, attested in texts from Mari dating to the reign of Zimri-Lim (1774–1762). It lay near the territories of the royal cities Andarig and Kurda, both of whose kings sought to gain control over it. Andarig's king Atamrum laid siege to it, and Hammurabi, king of Kurda, used it as a base for his military operations, and as a repository for the prisoners-of-war and grain which he had taken from the nearby villages.

LKM 605 (refs).

Adalur (Atalur) **range** (map 3) Offshoot of the Amanus range in southeastern Anatolia, cited in both Late Bronze Age Hittite and Iron Age Assyrian texts. The Hittite king Hattusili I defeated there an army from the city of Hassuwa, which was supported by troops from Aleppo, early in his second Syrian campaign (mid C17) (**RGTC* 6: 54). The Assyrian king Shalmaneser III marched to Mt Adalur, after reaching the Mediterranean Sea during his first western campaign (858), and erected a statue of himself there alongside the statue of a certain Anum-hirbe (**RIMA* 3: 17).

Adamdun (Adamshah) (map 12) Small Early Bronze Age city and region in Susiana, southwestern Iran, attested in Mesopotamian texts of the Ur III period (C21). A location at mod. Tepe Surkehgan, near Shushtar, has been suggested (Lafont, 1996; Steve, 2001) but remains hypothetical (Michalowski, 2007). Adamdun was subject to the Ur III administration, and paid tax to it as one of its peripheral territories. But during the reign of Ibbi-Sin, last ruler of the Ur III dynasty (2028–2004), it joined with other states in Susiana in rebellions against Ur's overlordship. This prompted a campaign by Ibbi-Sin, in the fourteenth year of his reign, against Susa, Adamdun, and Awan. The three states had apparently united forces for a showdown with Ibbi-Sin, who claims that in a single day he subdued them and captured their leaders.

*Sigrist and Gomi (*CC* 329), Lafont (1996), D. T. Potts (1999: 135, 136, 138, 143, 145), Steve (2001), Michalowski (2007).

Adana/Adaniya/Adanawa (probably = *Adana*) (map 7) Late Bronze and early Iron Age country in southern Anatolia. Subject to Hatti early in the Hittite Old Kingdom, Adaniya was among the hostile countries which rebelled against the Hittite king Ammuna in mid C15 (**Chav.* 231). It subsequently became part of the kingdom of Kizzuwadna, newly created in the second half of C15. Early in C14, the Hittite king Arnuwanda I conducted a campaign into the region of Adana, according to a fragmentary passage in his Annals (*Carruba, 1977: 167). Adana may have played a role in the Sea Peoples' onslaught on Egypt during the reign of the pharaoh Ramesses III (1184–1153); but this depends on the questionable identification of the group called the *Dnyn* in the list of Sea Peoples as the 'people of Adana' (see **Denyen**). In the early Iron Age, Adana(wa) was very likely the capital of the kingdom also called Adanawa in Luwian hieroglyphic texts but known as Que in Assyrian texts. (For the kingdom's history, see under **Que**.) It encompassed much of the territory formerly occupied by Late Bronze Age Kizzuwadna. From the well-known C8 Karatepe (q.v.) bilingual inscription, we learn that a local ruler called Azatiwatas fortified and extended the land of Adanawa, whose inhabitants are called the Danunians in the Phoenician version of the text, and established the family of his overlord Awarikus (Warikas) (the C8 king of Que called Urikki in Assyrian texts) as its royal dynasty. Awarikus is himself the author of another Luwian–Phoenician bilingual inscribed on a statue discovered at Çineköy, 30 km south of Adana. In the Phoenician version, the Danunians are again named as his subjects, though in the Luwian version of this inscription, Awarikus' land is called Hiyawa (see ***Çineköy***, and also **Hivites**).

**CS* II: 125–6, *CHLI* I: 41, 42–4, **CHLI* II, *Tekoğlu and Lemaire (2000), Bryce (2005: 102–4, 351).

Adaush (and nearby lands) One of the countries in northeastern Mesopotamia conquered by the Assyrian king Tiglath-pileser I in the second year of his reign (1113). Its inhabitants initially fled to mountain refuges on the approach of the Assyrian army, but eventually returned and submitted without resistance. The lands of Ammaush and Saraush, on the other hand, made a stand against the invaders, in defence of their long tradition of freedom from foreign rule. But in a confrontation at Mt Aruma, Tiglath-pileser routed their armies, and followed up his victory by plundering and razing their cities (**RIMA* 2: 18–19). He then proceeded to the conquest of the 'rebellious and insubmissive' lands Isua and Daria. Thenceforth all these lands became subject territories of the Assyrian kingdom.

Adaush was among the lands which made payments of tribute to the Assyrian king Ashurnasirpal II when he was in Mt Kirruru, during the northeastern campaign which he conducted in his accession year (884) (**RIMA* 2: 197).

Adennu Iron Age city in northern Syria belonging to the kingdom of Hamath. It was one of the three 'royal cities' captured by the Assyrian king Shalmaneser III in 853 during his campaign against Hamath, then ruled by Irhuleni (**RIMA* 3: 23). Parga (Parqa) and Argana were the other two cities (on the latter, see Lipiński, 2000: 262). The capture of Adennu (Ada) and Parga is depicted on the gates at Balawat (see **Imgur-Enlil**). The city has been tentatively identified as Ad-Dana, 30 km west of Aleppo (Lipiński, 2000: 259).

Adilcevaz (*Kef Kalesi*) (map 20) Iron Age city of the Urartian god Haldi in the land of Ziuquni (q.v.) in eastern Anatolia, on the northern shore of Lake Van. It was founded by the Urartian king Rusa II in the second quarter of C7. The site was first mapped by C. Burney in the 1950s and excavated in the 1960s and 1970s by Turkish teams under the direction of E. Bilgiç and B. Öğün. Their excavations revealed a palace complex with reception halls and storage magazines, and a lower town. Kef Kalesi itself is on high ground several km northwest of the mod. town Adilcevaz, which lies on the shore of Lake Van. A lengthy inscription of Rusa II, which gives the putative anc. name of Kef Kalesi ('City of Haldi in the land of Ziuquni'), and blocks bearing the most elaborate relief sculptures known in Urartu, have been found in secondary contexts in Adilcevaz. These are assumed to be from Kef Kalesi since no Urartian establishment has been found in the mod. town.

Zimansky (1998: 241).

Figure 1 Relief sculpture from Adilcevaz, now in Van Museum.

Aegae (*Nemrud Kalesi*) (map 5) M1 city in northwestern Anatolia, located 35 km south of Pergamum in the region of Aeolis. According to Herodotus (1.149), it was one of originally twelve Aeolian cities on the Anatolian mainland. In 218, the city was incorporated into the Pergamene empire by Attalus I. Its impressive remains, yet to be fully investigated, date to the Hellenistic period (C4–1). They indicate construction in the style of the buildings at Pergamum, and include a well-preserved three-storeyed market hall over 75 m in length, three temples, a theatre, and a stadium.

Bean (*PECS* 19).

Aegean Sea (map 5) The island-dotted expanse of water separating mainland Greece from Anatolia, and bounded on the south by the island of Crete. The name is of Classical origin. Greek tradition has several explanations for it, the most common of which derives it from Aegeus, a legendary king of Athens. Aegeus allegedly threw himself to his death in the sea after believing, falsely, that his son Theseus had failed in the mission he undertook to Crete to kill the bull-man monster called the Minotaur.

Warmington (*OCD* 16).

Aeolis (map 4) Classical designation for the Aegean coastal region of northwestern Anatolia, extending from the Hellespont to the mouth of the Hermus r. The name was derived from a Greek population group called the Aeolians, who in the last two centuries of M2 migrated eastwards from their homelands which lay in the regions later called Boeotia and Thessaly on the Greek mainland. They settled first on the islands of Lesbos and Tenedos before occupying the coastal part of the Troad and the region to its south. Strictly, 'Aeolis' and 'Aeolian' are purely ethno-linguistic terms. They reflect neither a political nor a clearly definable geographical entity. However, the southern Aeolian settlements may have formed a league which had a religious centre in the temple of Apollo at Grynium (q.v.). Cyme was the most important city in the southern Aeolian region, and perhaps the chief city of the league. In the Troad, Aeolian settlers occupied the abandoned site on the mound at Hisarlık, reputedly the site of Bronze Age Troy, and thenceforth called Ilion. According to Herodotus (1.149), there were in his day eleven remaining original Aeolian communities: Cyme, Lerisae, Neoteichos ('New Walls'), Temnus, Cilla, Notium, Aegiroessa, Pitane, Aegae, Myrina, and Grynium; a twelfth community, Smyrna, had once belonged to this group but had been taken over by the Ionians.

Schwertheim (*BNP* I: 226–31).

Afis, Tell (map 7) 32 ha settlement-mound consisting of acropolis and lower town, located in northwestern Syria c. 40 km southwest of Aleppo, with a continuous series of occupational levels extending from late M2 through early M1. Remains of the Chalcolithic period have also been uncovered. Architectural and other forms of cultural continuity spanning the end of the Late Bronze Age and the early Iron Age indicate the lack of any significant break between these two periods. By C9, Afis had developed and increased in size from a village community to a well-planned and fortified urban centre, with a number of public buildings erected on its acropolis and a lower town surrounded by a mudbrick casemate wall. A stele with an Aramaic inscription, authored by Zak(k)ur, king of Hamath, was discovered here in 1903 (*Lipiński, 2000: 254–5, **CS* II: 155, **Chav.* 307–11). It records Zakur's victory over a coalition of seventeen northern enemy states, after their forces had blockaded him in the city of Hatarikka. Zakur then goes on to describe his building achievements. Suggested dates for the composition of the inscription range from 805 to 775. Afis may in fact be the city Hatarikka/Hazrek (biblical Hadrach), capital of the Iron Age country of Lugath (Luash), which Zakur united with the kingdom of Hamath. If Afis is Hatarikka, then the city may have become the royal seat of the new Aramaean dynasty which ruled Hamath. An objection to the Afis–Hatarikka equation is that the inscription appears to refer to the city as Apish, of which Afis is the later Arabic form. Lipiński, however, argues that Apish was not the name of the city as a whole, but designated the sacred precinct, probably on the acropolis, where the temple of the god Il-Wer was located.

Cecchini and Mazzoni (1998), Lipiński (2000: 255–8).

Afrasiab see **Marakanda**.

Agade (Akkad) (map 17) City of uncertain location, probably near the confluence of the Tigris and Diyala rivers in the northern part of southern Mesopotamia. Its history of occupation extends from mid M3 until (at least) early C5. Around 2334, it came under the control of a leader of Semitic origin called Sharrum-kin (Sharrukin), more commonly known as Sargon, who established there the seat of a royal dynasty which lasted almost 150 years (c. 2334–2193). (For the legend of Sargon's birth, see **CS* I: 461, **Chav.* 22–5.) The city was probably founded a generation or so before

Sargon adopted it as his capital. He then bestowed its name, in the Semiticized form Akkad, upon the kingdom which eventually held sway over the whole of Mesopotamia, and a number of regions beyond (see **Akkad**). Both contemporary and later written sources create a picture of a busy, cosmopolitan centre, which contained a number of temples, palaces, and a large quayside area, and whose population included the personnel of an extensive civil service bureaucracy, merchants who travelled to and from distant parts of the western Asian world, and large numbers of troops. A well known literary lament commonly known as 'The Curse of Agade', composed within a century or so of the fall of the Akkadian empire, describes in graphic detail the collapse and abandonment of its capital (*Cooper, 1983). According to this text, the city, and especially the Akkadian king Naram-Sin, had grievously offended its deities who brought about its destruction, through a combination of drought, famine, and outside invaders, notably the Gutians (q.v.).

As a historical source, the text is of limited value. In fact, Agade was to survive for many centuries after its alleged fall. A provincial governor was installed there under the Ur III dynasty (c. 2112–2004), and the city is attested several hundred years later in the prologue to the law code of the C18 Babylonian king Hammurabi. Further references to it occur in Late Bronze Age Kassite and post-Kassite sources and in M1 Neo-Assyrian, Neo-Babylonian, and Persian texts. It was, for example, probably one of the Babylonian cities affected by the Sutaean invasions of southern Mesopotamia during the reign of the C11 Babylonian king Adad-apla-iddina (who is attested in **ABC* 180–1).

The city's survival and preservation may have been due in no small measure to its association with Sargon, one of the greatest figures in Mesopotamian legendary tradition. Rebuilding programmes were undertaken in the city by the Assyrian king Esarhaddon (680–669), and by the Neo-Babylonian kings in C6. The terms of a treaty between Esarhaddon and the newly enthroned Elamite king Urtaku may also have prompted the Elamite decision to return the statues of Agade's gods (*Borger, 1956: 123, 674/3), probably seized from the city in an Elamite raid. 'Excavations' were conducted in Akkad on the instructions of King Nabonidus (556–539), who undertook a three-year campaign to discover the anc. foundations of the Eulmash temple so that he might rebuild it on its original site. His scribes carefully copied anc. inscriptions which were found among the earlier remains. The Persian conqueror Cyrus II also claimed to have restored the Eulmash temple. Occupation of the settlement must have persisted until at least early C5, when the final known reference to the city occurs.

*Cooper (1983), Weiss (*OEANE* 1: 41–4), Lion (*DCM* 490–1).

Agrab, Tell (map 17) M5–early M2 settlement-mound located in the Diyala region of eastern Mesopotamia. It was one of four major sites in the region investigated by a team from the Oriental Institute, University of Chicago, under the direction of H. Frankfort between 1929 and 1938 (see **Diyala**). The other three sites are Tell Asmar (anc. Eshnunna), Khafaje (Tutub), and Ishchali (Nerebtum). Unlike these, Tell Agrab's anc. name is unknown. Survey has indicated that the earliest occupation dates from the Ubaid period (see glossary). After its M3 heyday, the site was almost entirely abandoned late in the Early Dynastic period (c. 2900–2334), with brief and limited reoccupation in the Ur III and Larsa periods (late C22–18). Excavations uncovered the remains of a rectangular temple (84 × 62 m) with five building phases attributed to the Early Dynastic period, and perhaps dedicated to the god Shara as suggested by the dedicatory inscription on a stone vase fragment. Surrounding the temple were found successive housing phases of later periods which never encroached upon its site. Further material remains from the site include a rampart of the Early Dynastic period, and two buildings of unknown purpose adjoining the city wall on the west side of the settlement. The bricks of these buildings indicate a dating to the Isin-Larsa period (late C21–18).

Delougaz and Lloyd (1942: 218–288), Adams (1965: 155), Sauvage (*DCM* 244).

Ahazum (map 10) Middle Bronze Age vassal state of the Old Assyrian kingdom, attested in texts from Mari and Shemshara. It was located in northern Mesopotamia in the region of the Lesser Zab r., between the countries of Qabra and Shusharra (Shemshara) within the area between the Rania plain and mod. Arbil. In early C18, its ruler Yashub-Addu had allied himself with the Assyrian king Shamshi-Adad I (1796–1775), fearful of the latter's growing power and influence in the region. However, within a few months Yashub-Addu had broken his ties with Shamshi-Adad and formed a series of other alliances, with the Turukkeans who were located to the northeast, with Shimurrum and finally with Kakmum to the southeast. Shamshi-Adad retaliated by dispatching an expeditionary force against Ahazum, as he reports in his correspondence with his ally Kuwari, ruler of Shusharra. Ahazum's capital, Shikshabbum, was placed under siege, and despite the support of a troop of Gutians who were in the city at that time, and some Turukkean refugees, the city fell to the besiegers led by Ishme-Dagan. Yashub-Addu was removed from power and replaced by a new king called Halun-pi-umu.

*Laessøe and Jacobsen (1990), Eidem and Laessøe (2001: 22–3, *44–52, *70–6), *Mesop.* 170–1.

Ahhiyawa Late Bronze Age region and kingdom referred to in Hittite texts. Its widely accepted identification with the Mycenaean Greek world dates back to the 1920s when the Swiss scholar E. Forrer argued that Ahhiyawa was the Hittite form of the Greek name *Achaiwia*, an archaic form of *Achaia.* Forrer drew attention to the fact that the Greeks are frequently called Achaeans in the epic poems of Homer. On the basis of its Mycenaean identification, the term Ahhiyawa appears to be used in Hittite texts (a) as a general ethno-geographical designation encompassing all areas of Mycenaean settlement, both in mainland Greece and overseas; (b) to designate a specific Mycenaean kingdom, at least one of whose rulers corresponded with his counterpart in Hatti; (c) to designate this kingdom in a broader sense, including the territories attached to it as political and military dependencies. Mycenae, Thebes, and other prominent Mycenaean centres are all possible candidates for the nucleus of the kingdom of Ahhiyawa. The German scholar F. Starke has recently proposed that one of the fragmentary Ahhiyawan texts in the archives at Hattusa (**AU* 268–74) is a letter written by a king of Thebes called Cadmus to the king of Hatti. A Theban king called Cadmus is well known from Greek legendary tradition. Most scholars have reacted sceptically to Starke's proposal (cited Latacz, 2004: 243–4), which has yet to be published in detail in an academic context.

Hittite texts indicate political and military as well as commercial involvement by Ahhiyawans in western Anatolian affairs, already in early C15, and most intensively in C13. By the early years of C13, an Ahhiyawan king had established sovereignty over

Milawata (Classical Miletus), from which he sought to extend his influence further afield in western Anatolia. This posed a threat to the Hittites' western vassal states, and was a major source of tension between Ahhiyawa and Hatti. In a well-known letter, commonly (and misleadingly) called the Tawagalawa letter (**AU* 2–19) (see glossary), a Hittite king, probably Hattusili III (1273–1237), complained of Ahhiyawan support for anti-Hittite insurrectionists in the region, and sought his Ahhiyawan counterpart's cooperation in terminating these activities. Ahhiyawa's presence and influence in western Anatolia came to an end in the last decades of C13, during the reign of the Hittite king Tudhaliya IV. This is probably reflected in the erasure of the king of Ahhiyawa from the list of Great Kings of the Near East itemized by Tudhaliya in a treaty which he drew up with his vassal Shaushgamuwa, ruler of the Syrian coastal state of Amurru (**HDT* 103–7, **CS* II: 99).

Shortly afterwards, in the reign of the last Hittite king Suppiluliuma II (1207–), references to 'Hiyawa-men' appear in two parallel letters from the so-called 'house of Urtenu' archive in Ugarit (*Lackenbacher and Malbran-Labat, 2005). 'Hiyawa' is undoubtedly an aphaeresized form of the name Ahhiyawa. The letters indicate that the Hiyawa-men were located in Lukka, in southwestern Anatolia, where they were to receive a consignment of goods to be conveyed to them in ships from Ugarit on the orders of the Hittite king. It is possible that the Hiyawa-men had agreed to serve as mercenaries in the Hittite army, and that the consignment of goods, consisting perhaps of metal ingots, was payment for their services. However, the nature of the goods and the purpose of the mission to the Hiyawa-men are matters for debate (see Singer, 2006). In this same period, Ahhiyawans were very likely among the Sea Peoples who descended upon the coast of Egypt in the reign of the pharaoh Merneptah (1213–1203). This depends on their identification with the group whose name *Ikwš*, attested in Merneptah's Karnak inscription (**ARE III*: §579), is commonly vocalized as Ekwesh (q.v.) or Aqaiwasha (or similar).

The name Hiyawa appears, finally, in an Iron Age context. In the Luwian version of a Luwian–Phoenician bilingual inscription discovered at Çineköy, 30 km south of the Turkish city Adana (*Tekoğlu and Lemaire, 2000), Hiyawa is the name of a kingdom in southern Anatolia ruled by a certain Awarikus (Assyrian Urikki) in late C8. It was part of the region called Cilicia by the Greeks. In the Phoenician version of the bilingual, Awarikus' kingdom is referred to as the land of the Danunians (see also **Adana**). The Assyrians called it Que. However, its 'alternative' name Hiyawa would accord well with Herodotus' statement (7.91) that the Cilicians were originally known as Hypachaeans ('sub-Achaeans') – if Ahhiyawa was in fact the Hittite term for Achaean or Mycenaean Greeks. For the suggestion that Hiyawa provides the origin of the Hebrew name *hiwwi*, see **Hivites**.

**AU*, Bryce (1989).

Ahlamu The term used for nomadic or semi-nomadic tribal groups in Syria and Mesopotamia, first attested in a C18 Mesopotamian text and applied to some immigrants into Babylonia in C17. Like the Habiru (q.v.), the Ahlamu lived on or outside the fringes of settled societies, as farm labourers and as marauding tribespeople who often posed a threat to the security of these societies. In late C14, they are listed with the Sutu and Iuru as allies of the land of Kadmuhu in northeastern Mesopotamia, who were conquered (together with Kadmuhu) by the Assyrian king Arik-den-ili, according to an inscription of his son Adad-nirari I (*RIMA 1: 132). Shalmaneser I (1274–1245) claims that together with the Hittites they supported Shattuara II, king of Hanigalbat, in his rebellion against Assyrian rule (*RIMA 1: 184). The Ahlamu threatened and sometimes disrupted communications between the great western Asian kingdoms. Their attacks on messengers dispatched from the Babylonian royal court were cited by the Babylonian king Kadashman-Enlil II (1263–1255) as the reason for his termination of diplomatic communications with the Hittite king Hattusili III; but the latter responded to this pretext with scorn (*HDT 140).

The Ahlamu are often closely associated, in Babylonian and Assyrian texts of late M2 and M1, with the Aramaeans. For example, the Assyrian king Tiglath-pileser I (1114–1076) makes reference in his Annals to the Ahlamu-Aramaeans, claiming that he crossed the Euphrates r. twenty-eight times in pursuit of them, defeating them in the lands of Amurru in western Syria, Suhu in the middle Euphrates region, and Babylonia, and plundering their possessions (*RIMA 2: 43, *Chav. 156). Similarly, the Assyrian king Adad-nirari II (911–891) refers to his conquest of the Ahlamu-Aramaeans (*RIMA 2: 149). But from the time of Tiglath-pileser I on, the Aramaeans are often referred to without the appellation Ahlamu, and the exact relationship between the two groups, and their names, remains uncertain. Lipiński suggests that the term 'Ahlamu' may not in fact have applied to a particular ethnic or linguistic group, but was rather a nomadic designation of the raiding forces that were making forays or razzias to capture flocks, slaves, and food supplies etc. His view is that sedentary populations used the term to refer to members of nomadic clans making these raids, and towards the end of M2 the Aramaeans were the most conspicuous representatives of this category of roaming tribes. By the later Neo-Assyrian period, the term 'Ahlamu' seems to have become largely synonymous with 'Aramaean'.

Lipínski (2000: 35–9).

Ahmar, Tell (Masuwari, Til-Barsip/Tarbusiba, Kar-Shalmaneser) (map 7) 60 ha tell in northeastern Syria, located on the east bank of the Euphrates r., 22 km south of Carchemish, with principal (acropolis) and lower mounds. The former rises 20 m above the surrounding plain, and has a semicircular fortified lower settlement (Neo-Assyrian period), 1200 m in diameter, at its base. The lower mound lies to the west of the acropolis and rises 10–15 m above the plain. The site's history of occupation includes Ubaid, Early and Middle Bronze Age, Iron Age, Persian, Hellenistic, and Islamic levels. Excavations were conducted by a French mission under the direction of F. Thureau-Dangin and M. Dunand from 1929 to 1931, and were resumed in 1988 by G. Bunnens, initially for the University of Melbourne, and from 2000 for the University of Liège. The earliest levels are represented by ceramic ware, dating to the Ubaid (possibly also to the Uruk) and Early Bronze I periods. An Early Bronze Age temple or palace has also been found on the principal mound. The most significant of the Early Bronze Age finds dates to the end of Early Bronze III (late M3). It is a corbelled stone tomb, known as the hypogeum (see glossary), whose contents included two human skeletons and a substantial quantity of grave goods – 1,045 intact vases and thirty-five bronze weapons, utensils, and ornaments. The number and various styles of the artefacts indicate continual use of the tomb over several centuries. The hypogeum was discovered and first investigated by Thureau-Dangin, who believed it to be an independent structure. Subsequent examination by the

Melbourne University team revealed that it was part of a large above-ground building complex.

The apparent dearth of Middle and Late Bronze Age remains has led to the assumption that the site was unoccupied through most of M2. However, the Melbourne University excavations have brought to light buildings and tombs of Middle Bronze Age date. And there is a possibility that the city in this period is attested in the Middle Bronze Age Mari archives, under the name Yabuhum. D. Charpin (*Mesop.* 174, n. 818) suggests an identification with Shubat-Shamash (q.v.). The region where it was located came under Mitannian control in C16, and was attached to the Hittite viceregal kingdom of Carchemish following the fall of the Mitannian empire in the third quarter of C14. Very likely it became subject to Assyria in the reign of Adad-nirari I (1307–1275).

But Tell Ahmar's main period of occupation began in the early Iron Age (C10). The first Iron Age settlement appears to have been the centre of a small kingdom. Luwian hieroglyphic inscriptions found at or near Tell Ahmar indicate that in this, and perhaps even in an earlier phase of its existence, the kingdom was known by the Luwian name Masuwari. This was probably also the name of the settlement itself in this period. Bunnens (2006: 88–96) makes a case for identifying Masuwari with the country called Musri (see **Musri (2)**) in Late Bronze and Iron Age Assyrian texts.

The author of five of the hieroglyphic inscriptions, carved on stelae which are dated by style to the end of C10 or early C9 (for the most recently published see Bunnens, 2006), was a king of Masuwari called Hamiyatas. He was one of six of Masuwari's attested rulers, who collectively spanned four generations. The names of only three of these kings are known to us: Hapatilas (first generation), and Ariyahinas and Hamiyatas (third generation). (Sons of Ariyahinas and Hamiyatas are attested but not named in the inscriptions.)

The generations run thus (cf. *CHLI* I: 226; Lipiński, 2000: 187):

Original dynasty	*Usurping dynasty*
Hapatilas	unattested
(son, father of Ariyahinas)	father of Hamiyatas
Ariyahinas	Hamiyatas
son of Ariyahinas	son of Hamiyatas

Hawkins suggests, on the basis of the narrative content of the inscription designated as TELL AHMAR 1 (**CHLI* I: 239–43), that power in Masuwari alternated between two competing lines; Hapatilas and Ariyahinas belonged to one, Hamiyatas to the other. The latter's father had apparently seized power in a coup from Ariyahinas, and though Hamiyatas succeeded him, it seems that he restored some of the powers of the displaced dynastic line to Ariyahinas' son (**CHLI* I: 240–1). This was probably intended to pave the way for the succession of Ariyahinas' son and the reinstatement of his family as the kingdom's ruling dynasty. But after Hamiyatas' death, the king's own son apparently rescinded these powers. The legitimate heir rose up against him, defeated him, and regained the throne (cf. Bunnens, 2006: 85–7, 103). Beneath the later Assyrian palace at Tell Ahmar are the remains of two monumental buildings which very likely belong to the period when the city was ruled by these kings. They were perhaps built by Hamiyatas, who claims credit for major construction projects in Masuwari as well as in at least one other settlement belonging to his domain. Both the architecture and the sculpture of this period have close parallels with the material remains of contemporary Carchemish.

The contest for power between the two dynasties in Masuwari has been seen as ethnically based, with a former Luwian-speaking Neo-Hittite regime in the city being replaced in late C10 or early C9 by one of Aramaean origin. Perhaps the city's two names in this period – Masuwari and Til-Barsip – reflect this: Masuwari was almost certainly a Luwian name, and Til-Barsip an Aramaean name, first attested in the records of the C9 Assyrian king Shalmaneser III. On the assumption that Hapatilas and his successors belonged to a Neo-Hittite dynasty, Lipiński (2000: 186–7) proposes that a line of Aramaean tribal leaders in the service of this dynasty seized power in the city after Hapatilas' death (c. 925). Bunnens (2006: 87) believes that the situation in the city was more complex than a contest between rival dynasties of different ethnic origins. While Hamiyatas' origins were almost certainly Aramaean, he suggests that the regime which his father displaced could also have come from one of the Aramaean tribes in the region. He argues that some of the personal names in the Luwian inscriptions from Tell Ahmar may be Semitic in origin.

None the less, the material remains of the city through the period of assumed Aramaean domination continue to be Neo-Hittite. This apparent discrepancy in the evidence has generated much inconclusive debate. But it may simply illustrate the fact that a site's cultural affinities and characteristics need not reflect its regime's ethnic origins. As Bunnens (2006: 97) has argued, the use of the Luwian language and script in inscriptions does not necessarily imply that the authors of the inscriptions were themselves Luwians. It is not unlikely, however, that the city's Neo-Hittite character does in fact reflect both its origins and the continuing ethnicity of a significant component of its population under an Aramaean regime – which in the first half of C9 may have competed with, or replaced, one of primarily Luwian origin.

In mid C9, Masuwari came under the control of a certain Ahuni, ruler of the Aramaean tribe Bit-Adini. Bunnens speculates that Hamiyatas was himself a member of this tribe, and ruled Masuwari as Ahuni's subordinate. It was in Masuwari/Til-Barsip that Ahuni, a longstanding enemy of the Assyrians, made his last stand against the Assyrian king Shalmaneser III (856). The city fell to the Assyrians after a siege. Ahuni managed to escape, but was captured by Shalmaneser the following year and deported to Ashur (**RIMA* 3: 21–2). Subsequent to his seizure of Til-Barsip, Shalmaneser renamed the city Kar-Shalmaneser (Port Shalmaneser), and allocated to it settlers from Assyria (**RIMA* 3: 19). He claims that he founded a palace in the city, to serve as one of his royal residences. An Assyrian palace was in fact built on the city's principal mound over part of the remains of the earlier settlement. Measuring 130 m × 70 m, it consisted of two main parts – a public administrative quarter and a private residential sector, with a large court as the focus of each. In the throne-room, which linked both sectors, the remains of splendid polychrome frescoes came to light, with scenes depicting the king's hunting exploits, soldiers, executions, tribute-bearers, processions, and rituals. Sculptures of lions guarding the city gates and two large stelae of the Assyrian king Esarhaddon (680–669) are further features of a provincial centre under Assyrian rule. Settlement now extended to include a lower town at the base of the tell. Here, a large Assyrian residential building dating to C7 was uncovered during the University of Melbourne's excavations. Its contents included a number of Syrian-style ivories, Akkadian legal and administrative texts, and two tablets in Aramaic.

Kar-Shalmaneser became the administrative centre of a region, perhaps largely coextensive with the former kingdom of Bit-Adini, which was first attached to the Assyrian province of Harran. Later, in the reign of Tiglath-pileser III (745–727), the region became a province of the Assyrian empire in its own right, with the old name Til-Barsip restored. In C8 the administrative seat in Kar-Shalmaneser was occupied by an important official, an Assyrian governor (*turtenu*) and commander-in-chief called Shamshi-ilu (*regn.* c. 796–752 or longer). He inscribed here, on two colossal stone lions, a record of his titles and exploits, the latter including a military defeat of the Urartian king Argishti I (**RIMA* 3: 231–3). Immediate authority in the city was exercised by a certain Ninurta-bel-usur, perhaps to be regarded as a 'traditional ruler' (thus Bunnens), but subject to the authority of Shamshi-ilu as regional overlord. Though Masuwari/Kar-Shalmaneser/Til-Barsip lost some of its strategic importance after the Assyrian annexation of Carchemish (717), it still remained a valuable river port, and in 703 the Assyrian king Sennacherib had a number of ships built there for a campaign against the Chaldaeans in the south.

Following the fall of the Assyrian empire at the end of C7, the city seems to have been only intermittently occupied. Tombs of the Persian period (C6–4) have been uncovered, as have the remains of a small sanctuary of Hellenistic date. In the Roman imperial (and perhaps already in the Hellenistic) period, the settlement occupying the site was known as Bersiba.

Bunnens (1990; 1993–4; 1995; 2006), Dornemann (*OEANE* 5: 209–10), Roobaert and Bunnens (1999), **CHLI* I: 224–48, Lipiński (2000: 183–93).

Ahuna (1) (*Tell es-Seman?*) Middle Bronze Age city in northwestern Mesopotamia, probably to be located east of the Balih r. in the land of Zalmaqum, to the northwest of the city of Tuttul (Tell Bia). It was apparently allied with the Assyrian king Shamshi-Adad I (1796–1775), and probably for this reason was attacked c. 1779 by Larim-Numaha, king of Aparha, with a force of 3,000 troops. The attack and seizure are reported by the Assyrian viceroy Yasmah-Addu in a letter to his mother Akatiya (**LAPO* 18: 268, no. 1085). For the Assyrian response to Larim-Numaha's seizure of the city, and also of the city Zihlalum, see **Aparha**.

Córdoba (1990), *Mesop.* 174.

Ahuna (2) Late Bronze Age city located on the west bank of the middle Euphrates within the land of Ashtata. Formerly a subject territory of Mitanni, it came under Hittite control when the Mitannian empire was destroyed by the Hittite king Suppiluliuma I during the third quarter of C14 (**HDT* 45–6).

Ai see *et-Tell*

'Ain Dara (map 7) Large settlement in the Afrin valley, northern Syria, 67 km northwest of Aleppo. It has two components: a citadel and a 24 ha lower city. The former was occupied from the Chalcolithic to the Ottoman periods (excluding the Roman period), the latter from the end of the Late Bronze Age (C13–early C12) until Iron Age II (c. 740). Excavations were conducted by the Dept of Antiquities of Aleppo, under the direction of F. Sairafe in 1956, 1962, and 1964, and A. Abou Assaf in 1976, 1978, and 1980–5. The most significant discovery on the citadel mound was a temple, apparently constructed in three phases between c. 1300 and 740. Features of the

Figure 2 Temple, ʿAin Dara.

temple noted by its excavator Abou Assaf include: a paved courtyard with well, an entry portico flanked by two sphinxes and four colossal lions, a façade decorated with lion- and sphinx-reliefs, and a raised corridor which surrounded the temple in its third phase, with exterior orthostats of opposing lions and sphinxes and flanking lions at its entrance. There are a total of 168 reliefs and sculptures in protome, though the repertoire is limited to lions and sphinxes. Abou Assaf concluded that the temple was dedicated to the worship of the goddess Ishtar, on the basis of her known association with both these creatures. But the identity of the temple's deity remains uncertain. Similarities were noted by Abou Assaf between the temple's plan and features of temples at Tell Chuera, Munbaqa, Emar, Ebla, Hazor, and Tell Tayinat. The great majority of the reliefs date to C9 and C8 and are in the Neo-Hittite style. They bear some similarities to the lions and sphinxes of the Late Bronze Age Hittite royal city Hattusa and the nearby Hittite rock sanctuary at Yazılıkaya.

In its Iron Age phase, ʿAin Dara belonged to the Neo-Hittite kingdom called Pat(t)in (Unqi in Assyrian texts). Possibly it is to be identified with Patin's capital city Kinulua. But Kinulua has more plausibly been identified with the site of Tell Tayinat (q.v.). An alternative identification of ʿAin Dara with the Assyrian-attested city Muru (q.v.) has been proposed.

Abou Assaf (1990; *OEANE* 1: 33–5).

Ajjul, Tell el- (map 8) Canaanite settlement-mound, roughly rectangular and covering an area of c. 13 ha, located in the Gaza strip 6 km southwest of Gaza city. Its history of occupation extends from the Early Bronze to the early Iron Age. The site was originally excavated between 1930 and 1934 by W. M. Petrie for the British School of Egyptian Archaeology, with a further short season by E. H. Mackay and M. A. Murray in 1938. New excavations began in 1999, under the direction of P. M. Fischer and M. Sadeq. Though Petrie originally identified the site with anc. Gaza, it was subsequently equated with a coastal village called Beth Eglayim, and more recently, by A. Kempinski, with biblical Sharuhen (Joshua 19:6). Remains of a cemetery and small village date to the end of the Early Bronze Age (EB III). By the Middle Bronze Age, Tell el-Ajjul achieved the proportions of a significant Canaanite city ('City III'), due no doubt to its location at the junction of important trade routes and its accessibility to the sea. The dominant building on the site, called a palace by Petrie, was originally constructed in the Middle Bronze IIB and C periods, and subsequently reconstructed four times. In its last three reconstructions (the final one dating to the early Iron Age), it may have functioned as a fortress rather than as a ruler's residence.

The wealth Tell el-Ajjul acquired through trading operations, which brought to it a range of goods from a number of foreign locations, including Cyprus, Egypt, and the Mycenaean world, is reflected in the rich finds of jewellery dating to Middle and Late Bronze Age levels. Of particular note are the gold hoards unearthed in 'City II', which was founded in C17, during the period of Egypt's fifteenth (Hyksos) dynasty. A century later, the city was destroyed, probably by Ahmose (1550–1525), first king of Egypt's eighteenth dynasty, in the course of his Asiatic campaigns which followed his expulsion of the Hyksos from Egypt. Though it was subsequently rebuilt, the city was now entering its final phase ('City I'). Decline and almost total abandonment are evident by the end of C15. However, some continuity of occupation is indicated by the remains of a fort whose last phase dates to the early Iron Age.

Tufnell and Kempinski (*NEAEHL* 1: 49–53).

Akkad (map 17) Early Bronze Age kingdom in the northern part of southern Mesopotamia, founded by Sargon (Sharrum-kin in Akkadian) c. 2334. In the city of Agade, Sargon established the seat of a royal dynasty – which lasted through five reigns until c. 2193 – and built and held sway over the first 'empire' in western Asian history. For the record of his conquests, achieved with the help of a substantial standing army, see **CS* II: 243, **Chav.* 18. He bestowed the name of his capital, in the Semiticized form Akkad, upon the whole of his newly created kingdom. Strong resistance to Akkadian imperialism provoked uprisings in the subject territories during the reigns of Sargon's successors. His first son and successor, Rimush (2278–2270), put down numerous rebellions throughout the kingdom, as well as conducting a campaign of conquest into the lands of Elam and Marhashi (**Chav.* 19–20). Following Rimush's assassination, his brother and successor Manishtushu (2269–2255) was confronted with, and crushed, widespread rebellions in the subject territories. His reign was also characterized by trade expeditions to the regions of Anshan and Magan (the latter located in the Persian Gulf), whence ivory, gold, timber, and semi-precious stones were imported. Already in his father's time, ships from Magan, Meluhha, and Dilmun docked at the royal capital Agade.

During the reign of Sargon's grandson Naram-Sin (2254–2218), son of Manishtushu, the Akkadian empire attained its greatest limits. Extending over the whole of

Mesopotamia, it reached as far north as mod. Kurdistan (and perhaps even Armenia), as far east as the Zagros mountains, and as far west as southeastern Anatolia (Cilicia) and the Mediterranean Sea. In the south and southeast, Naram-Sin's campaigns took his armies to Magan and Susa. Like his predecessors, Naram-Sin encountered widespread resistance to his rule. A number of versions of a text commonly known as the Great Revolt record a massive uprising against him involving all the major cities of his realm, including those of its Mesopotamian heartland (*J. G. Westenholz, 1997: 221–61, **Chav.* 31–2). Though the text contains some admixture of legendary elements, there is no doubt that it preserves a genuine historical tradition which reflects the ongoing hostility towards and rejection of centralized rule which Sargon and his successors had forced upon Mesopotamia and neighbouring regions. Like his predecessors, Naram-Sin succeeded in suppressing the rebellion.

But military force proved no lasting solution to the problems faced by the Akkadian kings in administering their empire. Like many later conquerors and empire-builders, they lacked the organizational capacity and the resources in manpower which were essential for controlling and governing effectively the vast, unwieldy complex of territories which had fallen to them by the sword. The fact that the Akkadian empire lasted as long as it did was probably due largely to the formidable reputations and the lengthy reigns of its two most important rulers, Sargon and Naram-Sin. Naram-Sin further tried to bolster his reputation by declaring himself a god – the first known assumption of divinity by a living king. But after his death, the empire rapidly disintegrated, coming abruptly to an end in the reign of his son Shar-kali-sharri (2217–2193). Various factors may have contributed to its destruction, including the incessant revolts by subject peoples, internal political instability, and a period of sustained, severe drought. But the immediate agents of its fall, according to Mesopotamian literary tradition, were the Gutians, raiders from the Zagros mountain region who destroyed the capital and thus brought the empire and the royal dynasty to an end. (In fact, the capital itself recovered from its alleged destruction and was to survive for at least another 1,700 years; see **Agade**.) But the name Akkad, like Sumer, continued to be used down to the period of the M1 Neo-Assyrian and Neo-Babylonian kingdoms, as a geographical designation for Babylonia (e.g. **ABC* 181, **RIMB* 2: 137). And like Sumer, the name also became part of the Assyrian royal titulary. A number of kings of the Neo-Assyrian empire proclaimed themselves 'king of Sumer and Akkad' (e.g. Esarhaddon; see **RIMB* 2: 173).

Though the Akkadian empire was relatively shortlived, it left a lasting cultural legacy to successor kingdoms and civilizations. The spread of Akkadian political and military power through large parts of the western Asian world provided the initial means and stimulus for the extension of many aspects of southern Mesopotamian civilization, particularly the civilization of the Sumerians, throughout this world for the next two millennia. And for well over a thousand years, the Semitic Akkadian language was widely used in western Asia as the international language of diplomacy.

History and culture: Foster (*OEANE* 1: 49–54), *J. G. Westenholz (1997), A. Westenholz (1999), Lafont and Lion (*DCM* 22–6). Language: Huehnergard (*OEANE* 1: 44–9), Joannès (*DCM* 26–8).

Akko (Acco, *Tell Akko, Tell el-Fukhar*) (map 8) 20 ha Canaanite settlement-mound on the coast of Israel, 12 km north of Haifa. Its history of occupation extends from the Middle Bronze Age (c. 2000) until the Ottoman period, with evidence also of a Late Chalcolithic–Early Bronze Age agricultural community in the southwestern area of the mound. The site was excavated over twelve campaigns, between 1973 and 1989, by M. Dothan with the support of Haifa University, the University of Marburg, the Israel Dept of Antiquities and Museums, and the Israel Exploration Society. Akko was a well-fortified city during the Middle Bronze Age, its defence system based on a beaten earth (*terre pisée*) rampart which was progressively strengthened and augmented. The city appears to have been a major port on the Mediterranean in this period, though by Middle Bronze Age III there are indications that it was in decline. To this last period belong a number of pit-graves and built tombs, including a stone-vaulted tomb. Akko's Late Bronze Age I phase, during which some reconstruction of the fortifications was carried out, apparently ended in destruction by fire. But this was followed by the prosperous Late Bronze II phase, characterized by large, well-planned buildings and evidence of international trade contacts, notably with Cyprus, the Aegean world, and Egypt (as reflected in finds of Cypriot and Mycenaean pottery, and eighteenth and nineteenth dynasty Egyptian scarabs). Deposits of murex shells suggest that Akko was a centre for the production of purple dye in this period, and stone silos indicate that it served also as a grain storage centre.

There are a number of references to Akko in Egyptian sources, beginning with a possible mention of it in the Middle Bronze Age Egyptian Execration texts. The pharaoh Tuthmosis III (1479–1425) lists the city among his Asiatic conquests, and it appears a number of times in the mid C14 Amarna letters, which indicate its involvement in the squabbles and conflicts of the Canaanite cities during the reigns of the pharaohs Amenhotep III and Akhenaten (Amenhotep IV). Though its rulers in this latter period (Surata and Satatna) clearly acknowledged the pharaoh as their overlord (**EA* 232–4), the city apparently rebelled against Egyptian rule in later times, since the C13 pharaohs Seti I and his son and successor Ramesses II both claim to have conquered it. In a relief on one of the walls of the temple of Karnak in Luxor, Ramesses is depicted destroying one of its city gates. Particularly in Late Bronze Age II, and despite its involvement in local conflicts, Akko seems to have flourished as a Canaanite port-city, and is attested as such in documents from the city of Ugarit. However, it never seems to have achieved the importance of other Mediterranean port-cities like Ugarit, Sidon, and Tyre. Nor does the city appear to have been fortified during its Late Bronze II phase.

New settlers apparently arrived on the site early in C12 (Iron Age I). Dothan suggests that they may have been Sherdens (q.v.), one of the groups of Sea Peoples. His suggestion is based on the archaeological finds of this period, which include workshop installations, pottery kilns, and incised drawings of ships on a stone vessel shaped like a mortar and apparently serving as a portable altar. A scarab found on the site bearing the name of the Egyptian queen Tausret (1188–1186), principal consort of Seti II and regent after his death, provides useful information on the date of the new settlement. On the basis of biblical references, Dothan believes that at least during David's time and the early part of Solomon's reign (C10) Akko belonged to the 'united monarchy' (but on the so-called united kingdom, see under **Israel**). But there is no archaeological evidence to support this. Present indications, based on a recent survey, suggest that Akko served as a major urban centre in its region from the Late Bronze Age onwards, continuing to exercise this role in the Iron Age, except during a period of decline in Iron Age IB and Iron Age IIA (C11–10), quite independently of Israel. From C9 onwards (Iron Age IIB), the remains of several large public buildings in the city indicate significant urban development. But this phase of its existence ended in destruction by fire, probably at the hands of the Assyrians. Assyrian records report assaults upon the city by the Assyrian kings Sennacherib (701) and Ashurbanipal (mid C7). The latter claimed to have killed those inhabitants of Akko who refused to submit to him, and to have hanged their corpses on poles around the city.

Akko continued to be occupied, but remained in a depressed state, during the Neo-Babylonian period, to judge from the meagre remains of this period. However, it recovered substantially under Persian rule when it appears to have served once more as an international port as well as an administrative centre of the Persian empire (C6–4). Greek sources indicate that it served also as a military centre, playing an important strategic role in Persia's ongoing conflicts with Egypt. A number of Greeks settled in the city during the period of Persian sovereignty, their presence reflected in the fact that from mid C4 onwards Akko was referred to by its Greek name, Ake. Its prosperity continued into the Hellenistic period, following its voluntary surrender to Alexander the Great in 332. In the time of Ptolemy II Philadelphus (285–246), it was given the status of a polis, and thenceforth named Ptolemais. At the end of C3, it was incorporated into the Seleucid empire. It continued to play a significant role in Syro-Palestinian affairs during the Roman imperial period.

Dothan and Goldmann (*NEAEHL* 1: 16–23), Lehmann (2001), Laughlin (2006: 9–13).

Akshak (map 17) Early Bronze Age Sumerian city-state in southern Mesopotamia, one of fourteen such states attested, in written sources, for the regions of Sumer and Akkad. According to the Sumerian King List, in the period after the great flood six rulers of Akshak reigned between the third and fourth dynasties of Kish. The city-state's location has yet to be determined, though attention has been drawn to inscriptions of kings of Akshak discovered at Tell Umar (Hellenistic Seleucia-on-the-Tigris, near Ctesiphon); note also Akshak's connection with Upi/Opis (Brinkman, 1968: 111, n. 608; see **Upi (1)**). Around the middle of M3, Akshak's king Zuzu (or Unzi) led a coalition of forces from Kish and Mari against Eannatum, king of Lagash. Eannatum claimed victory in the battle (**Chav.* 83–4).

Alabanda (*Araphisar*) (map 5) M1 BCE–M1 CE city in Caria, southwestern Anatolia, 11 km west of mod. Çine. It is first attested in C5 by Herodotus (7.195) in the context of the campaign undertaken by the Persian king Xerxes against Greece in 481–479. Aridolis, tyrant of Alabanda, was on one of the fifteen Persian ships captured by the Greeks off Cape Artemisium on the western coast of mainland Greece (480). The city Alabanda, which Herodotus locates in Phrygia (8.136), is almost certainly the Carian Alabanda. All material remains of the city, including two temples, a theatre, and a colonnaded stoa, date to the Hellenistic and Roman periods.

Bean (1971: 180–9).

Alaca Höyük (map 2) City in north-central Anatolia, 180 km east of Ankara and 40 km northeast of the Late Bronze Age Hittite capital Hattusa. Covering an area of c. 7 ha, the site was occupied from late M4, at the end of the Chalcolithic Age, until the Ottoman period. It was first excavated over several decades, beginning in 1935, by Turkish teams under the successive direction of R. O. Arık and H. Koşay. New excavations conducted in the last decade, and currently under the direction of A. Çınaroğlu, have uncovered a district of large, circular, stone-paved silos, like those found on Büyükkaya at Boğazköy (Boğazkale)/Hattusa, overlaid by a Phrygian megaron (see glossary).

The first of the two most important phases in Alaca's history dates to the Early Bronze II period (from mid to late M3), as reflected in the thirteen 'royal' shaft graves of this period and their rich funerary goods. The rectangular stone- and wood-lined shafts were used for both single and double burials, and the goods which accompanied the bodies included jewellery and cosmetics items for women, and tools and weapons for men. Among the finds of jewellery were bronze and copper mirrors, silver combs, gold necklaces, pins, bracelets, ear-pendants, and diadems. The graves also contained an assortment of domestic utensils and vessels (long-stemmed gold cups, gold jugs, and gold 'fruit-stands'), ritual implements, and wooden furniture. Most impressive of all the grave goods are the ritual disk and arc standards. Each of these incorporated a stylized bull or stag, usually made of bronze inlaid with silver or gold. They appear to have been fitted to the tops of funerary biers or cult furniture, and in some cases were mounted on poles, presumably to be carried in ritual processions. There is a theory that the occupants of the tombs were not from the native Hattian population of central Anatolia, but were Kurgan immigrants (see glossary) from the region of Maikop in southern Russia, who spoke an Indo-European language and perhaps became rulers of the local Hattian population. The theory is based primarily on the nature of the tombs and burials, and the solar disks and theriomorphic standards.

In the Late Bronze Age, Alaca Höyük became a fortified Hittite city containing a palace, residential quarters, and several temples. There are well-preserved remains of the city's monumental entranceway, and the sphinxes which flank it. Sculptured blocks

Figure 3 Festival scene, Alaca Höyük.

which form part of the gateway complex portray a religious festival in progress. There are depictions of the king and queen standing before an altar of the storm god, zoomorphically represented as a bull, a seated goddess (almost certainly the sun goddess of Arinna), cult officials, animals for sacrifice, a sword-swallower, acrobats, a lute-player and perhaps a bagpiper. Other reliefs, now out of context but probably belonging to the same composition, depict hunting scenes. All scenes almost certainly represent festival celebrations, and their prominence at the very entrance of the city, along with the temple complex within, provide strong support for the view that Alaca Höyuk was one of the holy cities of the Hittite realm. It is commonly identified with the city Arinna, sacred to the sun goddess (*contra* the alternative proposed identification with Zippalanda; see **Zippalanda**).

Hittite Alaca was supplied with water from a dam at Gölpınar, 1 km to the southeast of the city. First identified in the 1930s, the entire dam was exposed in the course of the 2002–4 seasons at Alaca. Covering an area of 130 m × 15 m, the dam was coated with lime and revetted with small stones. While it was being excavated, a stele-base set into the top of it was discovered, along with some stele fragments which bore the remains of a Luwian hieroglyphic inscription. A certain Tudhaliya named in the inscription is probably to be identified with the Hittite king Tudhaliya IV (1237–1209).

Koşay and Akok (1966; 1973), Bittel (1976: 30–46, 186–201), Çınaroğlu and Çelik (2006), Yıldırım and Gates (2007: 296–7).

Alalah (*Tell Atchana*) (maps 3, 6) Oval settlement-mound (750 m × 300 m), located in the Amuq plain of southeastern Turkey near the northernmost bend of the Orontes r. It has seventeen designated occupation levels, extending through the Middle and Late Bronze Ages, with evidence also of Chalcolithic and Early Bronze Age settlement. The site was excavated by C. L. Woolley on behalf of the Society of Antiquaries of London from 1937 to 1939, and from 1946 to 1949. His excavations revealed palace, temple, and residential areas, protected by a circuit wall and accessed by a city gate. The earliest temple building dates to level XIV; the palace, whose location changed from temple to city gate area in mid M2, to level XII. Both levels belong within the Middle Bronze IIA phase (levels XVII–X). Excavations were resumed in 2003 by the Oriental Institute, University of Chicago, under the direction of K. A. Yener.

The most important periods of Alalah's history are represented archaeologically by levels VII and IV, belonging respectively to the Middle Bronze IIB phase (levels IX–VII) and the Middle Bronze IIC–Late Bronze I phase (levels VI–IV). Both these levels have produced tablet archives. Most of the tablets are inscribed in Akkadian cuneiform. Their contents, which cover legal, diplomatic, and administrative topics, provide valuable insights into the life, economy, and social structure of Alalah in the periods to which they belong. We have almost 200 tablets from level VII, discovered mainly in the palace and the temple. From historical information contained in these, we learn that Alalah was for part of that period ruled by a certain Ammitaqum, nominally the vassal of Yarim-Lim III who occupied the throne of Aleppo, seat of the powerful northern Syrian kingdom of Yamhad. (In the previous century, a namesake of Yarim-Lim had been given the throne of Alalah by his brother Abba-il/Abban, king of Yamhad, in exchange for the city of Irridu, which Abba-il had seized and apparently destroyed after it had rebelled against him; **RIME* 4: 799–800). In his first campaign against Aleppo, the Hittite king Hattusili I (1650–1620) led his troops against Alalah, then an imposing fortified city, for their first military operation in Syrian territory. Alalah's forces were routed, and the city reduced to ruins (**Chav.* 220). The destruction of level VII, whose timespan was probably no more than fifty or seventy-five years, can be tentatively dated early in the second half of C17, during the first part of Hattusili's reign. But the absolute chronology of the period is much disputed.

After Alalah was rebuilt, it came under the sovereignty of the kingdom of Mitanni, during Mitanni's westward expansion in the reign of its king Parrattarna (second half of C15). Parrattarna's first main objective in Syria was to establish his sovereignty over the territories controlled by Aleppo. A rebellion had broken out in the kingdom following the death of its king Ilim-ilimma, which led to the flight of Ilim-ilimma's son Idrimi to the city of Emar on the Euphrates. His flight is recorded in the inscription on his famous statue, discovered by Woolley in 1939 (*Greenstein, 1995: 2423–8, **CS* I: 479–80). After seven years in exile, Idrimi was installed as one of Parrattarna's vassal rulers in what remained of his father's kingdom. The royal seat of this kingdom, now reduced to only the western parts of the former kingdom of Aleppo, had its royal seat at Alalah. Idrimi later drew up a treaty with Pilliya, ruler of the southern Anatolian kingdom Kizzuwadna (**CS* II: 331–2, **Chav.* 174–5). At this time both Idrimi and Pilliya were tributaries of Parrattarna.

Figure 4 Idrimi, ruler of Alalah.

These events belong within the context of level IV at Alalah. Again, the absolute dates of this level are open to question. It may have begun within the last decades of C15. The level IV palace, which has produced an archive of some 300 tablets, can be assigned to Idrimi's son Niqmepa. The end of the level is now generally associated with the Syrian campaigns of the Hittite king Suppiluliuma I (1350–1322). These campaigns resulted in the establishment of Hittite authority over much of northern Syria, consequent upon Suppiluliuma's destruction of the Mitannian empire in the third quarter of C14. Following their destruction of Alalah IV, the Hittites rebuilt the fortress and temple complex on an imposing scale. Further destruction occurred at the end of level III. Once more the complex was rebuilt, this time on a more modest scale. In early C12, the city was again destroyed, probably during the upheavals associated with the so-called Sea Peoples. It was never reoccupied.

Woolley (1955), Stein (*OEANE* 1: 55–9); on the Alalah texts, Greenstein (*OEANE* 1: 59–61).

Alambra (map 14) Early and Middle Bronze Age settlement and cemetery in central Cyprus, c. 15 km south of Nicosia. Early investigations at the site in C19 are reported to have opened some one hundred tombs. E. Gjerstad excavated a house here for the Swedish Cyprus Expedition in 1924, and an expedition from Cornell University, directed by J. E. Coleman, uncovered remains of seven houses and six tombs between 1974 and 1982. Several of the tombs date to the Early Bronze Age while the excavated domestic buildings belong to the Middle Bronze Age. The latter produced evidence of food storage, food preparation, cooking, and many other domestic tasks as well as ores, crucibles, and slags, indicating the small-scale processing of copper ores.

(J. M. Webb)
Coleman *et al.* (1996).

Alana Late Bronze Age frontier settlement in southern Anatolia, located at the foot of Mt Arlanda in the border zone between Hatti and the Hulaya River Land. The latter had become part of the kingdom of Tarhuntassa in early C13. A treaty drawn up by the Hittite king Hattusili III (1267–1237) with Ulmi-Teshub (probably Kurunta), ruler of the Hittite appanage kingdom of Tarhuntassa, confirmed Alana as part of the Hulaya River Land. Other cities in the border zone also confirmed as part of this land include Allupatra, Huhhura, Ninainta, Santimma, and Zarata.

**HDT* 110.

Alasiya (map 3) Late Bronze Age country and kingdom in the eastern Mediterranean region, generally identified with the island of Cyprus, or part thereof. R. S. Merrillees continues to maintain his long-held belief that the country should be sought near Ras Shamra (Ugarit) on the Syrian coast, or near Al Mina at the mouth of the Orontes r. But the majority of scholars now accept an identification with Cyprus, and all available evidence seems to point strongly if not conclusively to this identification.

Alasiya is first attested in the Middle Bronze Age archives at Mari (Charpin, 1990), but the most frequent references to it are found in texts from the Hittite capital Hattusa. The earliest of these references date to early C14 when the Hittite king Arnuwanda I, who claimed that Alasiya was a tribute-paying subject state of Hatti, complained that his renegade vassal Madduwatta had seized it, in concert with two other men, Attarssiya and Piggaya, both apparently rulers of independent territories in Anatolia (**HDT* 160). Though Madduwatta relinquished his hold over Alasiya under pressure from

Arnuwanda, Hittite control of it must have been extremely tenuous, given that the Hittites had no seagoing capacity beyond that provided by their coastal vassal states. It was sufficiently remote from the Hittite homeland to be considered a suitable place of exile, in the early decades of C13, for disgraced members of the extended Hittite royal family (**CS* I: 202), and possibly also for an unseated Hittite king (Urhi-Teshub).

By this time, Alasiya may long have enjoyed the status of an independent kingdom. In C14, its ruler corresponded with the pharaoh Akhenaten (1352–1336) on virtually equal terms (**EA* 33–9), calling him 'My Brother', a form of address generally confined to peer relationships. In one of his letters to the pharaoh, the Alasiyan king sought tax exemptions for his merchants while they were in Egyptian territory. Alasiya seems to have enjoyed particularly close relations with Egypt during Akhenaten's reign, when trade links flourished between the two kingdoms. Of special importance among the items traded, under the guise of gift-exchange, was Alasiyan copper sent to Egypt in exchange for silver. Alasiya had commercial dealings with a number of western Asian kingdoms as well, but with none of these were its ties as close as with Egypt. On the other hand, relations with the pharaoh sometimes became strained, particularly when Akhenaten accused his fellow king of complicity in pirate raids on the Egyptian coast (**EA* 38). The latter indignantly denied the accusation, protesting that his land too had been plagued by pirates.

In the final decades of the Late Bronze Age (late C13–early C12), Alasiya figured in military operations which the last Hittite kings conducted in the Mediterranean, presumably using ships from coastal subject states like Ugarit. These operations very likely belong within the context of the Hittites' attempts to protect grain shipments brought by sea to the southern Anatolian coast, for overland transport from there to the Hittite homeland. The third last Hittite king Tudhaliya IV (1237–1209) reports a conquest of Alasiya, the deportation of the Alasiyan king and his family to Hattusa, and the imposition of Hittite control over the land (**CS* I: 192–3, *Bryce, 2005: 321). Nevertheless, his son and second successor Suppiluliuma II (1207–) was obliged to conduct further naval campaigns in the region, and reports both land and sea engagements, fought either against native Alasiyans or against foreigners who had occupied their land (**CS* I: 193, *Bryce, 2005: 332).

While Suppiluliuma may have succeeded in re-establishing temporary control over Alasiya, the land remained vulnerable to external aggression. In one of the last known documents of the Late Bronze Age, Ammurapi, the last king of Ugarit, responded to a desperate appeal for assistance from the Alasiyan king (perhaps appointed by Suppiluliuma following his conquest of the land), by declaring that his own kingdom was in serious danger, having been attacked by enemy ships. He declared that Alasiya would have to fend for itself (*Bryce, 2005: 333–4). We have no further references to the land of Alasiya.

Bryce (2005: 135–7, 321–3, 332–4).

Alassa (map 14) Late Bronze Age settlement 15 km northwest of Limassol in the lower foothills of the Troodos range, so called after the nearby mod. village of Alassa. Two areas within the settlement were excavated by S. Hadjisavvas from the Dept of Antiquities, Cyprus, in the 1980s and 1990s, ahead of the construction of the Kouris r. dam. Burials at the site date from Late Cypriot IB, but the surviving architecture belongs exclusively to Late Cypriot IIC and IIIA (1250–1150). Houses, a street, and a square were found in the lower area, known as Pano Mandilaris, which produced evidence for both agricultural and metallurgical activity (pot bellows and slag). Burials were located in open spaces.

In the upper area, known as Paliotaverna, a 4.3 m wide street flanked by monumental ashlar-built structures (see glossary) was uncovered to a length of 43 m. Building I, to the south, had been badly destroyed. Building II, to the north, occupies an area of 1,394 sq. m. It is a Π-shaped square building constructed of ashlar blocks with drafted margins, some of which are up to 5 m long and weigh almost 3 tons. It has an inner courtyard, a hearth-room, a portico, and spacious storerooms containing enormous storage jars, a number of which have seal impressions on the shoulder, depicting chariot and hunting scenes, lions, griffins, bulls, and plants.

Indications of town planning and the segregation of industrial, administrative, and domestic quarters suggest that Alassa was a major urban settlement in C13 and C12. It has been proposed that it was a regional administrative centre responsible for managing the transportation, production, and trade in copper from the mines of the Troodos via a chain of settlements stretching to a harbour town in the vicinity of Curium (Kourion).

(J. M. Webb)

Hadjisavvas (1996).

Alatru Middle Bronze Age city in or near the land of Zalmaqum, northern Mesopotamia. It was one of the cities involved in the anti-Assyrian uprising in Zalmaqum in 1778. The Assyrian king Shamshi-Adad I instructed his son Yasmah-Addu, viceroy in Mari, to seize and destroy the city. Alatru did in fact fall to and was occupied by Yasmah-Addu. But contrary to his father's orders, he refortified the city, whose

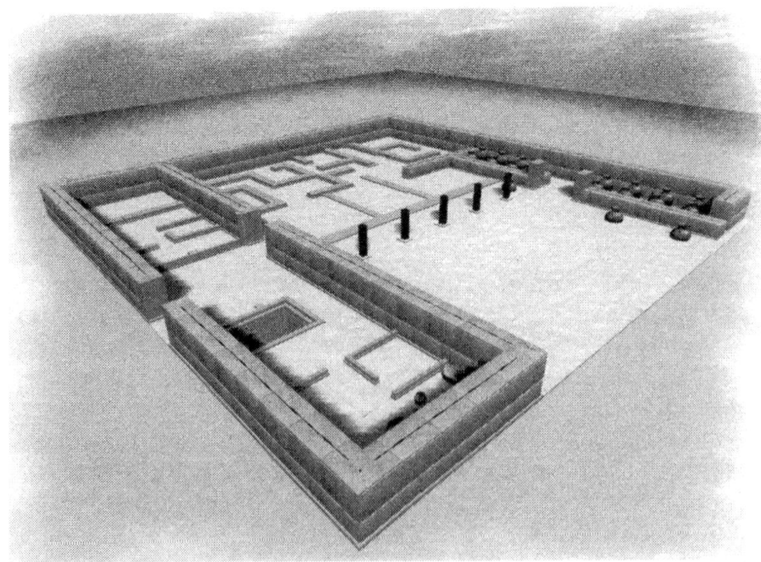

Figure 5 Plan of Alassa.

walls were in poor condition, and used it as a base for his troops. For this he was commended by his brother Ishme-Dagan, viceroy at Mari, who encouraged him to maintain his hold upon the city and place it under his administration.

**LAPO* 17: 47–9, nos 471–2, *Mesop.* 182.

Aleppo (maps 2, 3) City in northwestern Syria, whose origins probably extend back at least to the Early Bronze Age. In the Middle and early Late Bronze Ages, it was the capital of the northern Syrian kingdom of Yamhad. This was one of the great political and military powers of the western Asian world until its conflicts with the Hittites in the second half of C17 and early C16 led to its decline and disintegration. Yarim-Lim III was the ruler of the kingdom when the Hittite king Hattusili I (1650–1620) embarked upon the first of his campaigns against the northern Syrian city-states which were subject to or allied with Yamhad (Bryce, 2005: 70–2). Though his forces destroyed a number of the cities in the region, Hattusili never succeeded in breaching the defences of Aleppo, called Halab, Halap, and Halpa in Hittite texts. The city remained unconquered at the time of his death. It fell finally to Hattusili's grandson and successor Mursili I c. 1595 (*Bryce, 2005: 97–9), shortly before Mursili's expedition to Babylon (see under **Babylon**).

After the Hittite conquest, there are no further references to Yamhad. But probably not long after its destruction by the Hittites, its former capital Aleppo was rebuilt and regained its independence. It maintained this into the following century under a series of kings – Sarra-el, Abba-el, and Ilim-ilimma – and in fact expanded its territory to include a number of nearby states, notably Niya (Nii), Ama'u (Amae), and Mukish.

Figure 6 Aleppo, citadel.

But after the death of Ilim-ilimma, a rebellion broke out in the kingdom. By this time the Hurrian kingdom of Mitanni was on the rise, and its ruler Parrattarna took advantage of the volatile situation in the region to establish his sovereignty over Aleppo and the lands it controlled. He placed the remnants of the kingdom under the immediate authority of Idrimi, son of Ilim-ilimma, now installed as a Mitannian vassal ruler in the city of Alalah. In the following century, Aleppo was among the Mitannian dependencies that fell to the Hittite king Suppiluliuma I during his one-year Syrian campaign against Mitanni and its subjects and allies, c. 1340. Breaking with precedent, Suppiluliuma did not install or reinstate a local ruler in the city under Hittite sovereignty. Instead, he made it one of the two viceregal centres which he set up in Syria (the other was Carchemish), under the direct command of his son Telipinu (Bryce, 1992). Thenceforth, it continued as the seat of a Hittite viceroy until the collapse of the Hittite kingdom at the end of the Bronze Age.

In M1, Aleppo was a politically insignificant city, becoming part of the Aramaean kingdom of Bit-Agusi. However, it remained an important cult centre (as it had been in the Bronze Age), where the storm god Adad was worshipped. The Assyrian king Shalmaneser III made sacrifice to the god there (he called the city Halman) during his western Syrian campaign in 853, after the city had voluntarily submitted to him (*RIMA* 3: 23). A large Iron Age temple recently discovered on the citadel of Aleppo may have been dedicated to Adad. It is decorated with orthostats which feature reliefs of gods and mythological creatures.

Under Seleucid and Roman rule, Aleppo seems to have prospered, though it never regained the status it had once enjoyed, more than a millennium earlier, as one of Syria's most important cities. The material remains of its anc. phases are meagre, due largely to its continuous occupation up to the present day.

Klengel/Hawkins (*RlA* 4: 50–3, s.v. Halab), Klengel (1992: 44–83, 128–30), Lion (*DCM* 30–3).

Al-gabbari-bani (*Sur-Jar'a*) Iron Age Mesopotamian city in the middle Euphrates region built in early C8 by Shamash-resha-usur, ruler of the Aramaean state Suhu on the middle Euphrates, and provided by him with statues of the gods Adad, Apla-Adad, Shala, and Madanu. Shamash-resha-usur also claims to have established an apiculture industry in the city, with honey bees brought from one of the regions called Habhu (see **Habhu (4)**) (*RIMB* 2: 281–2). In mid C8, Suhu's ruler Ninurta-kudurri-usur, son and successor of Shamash-resha-usur, built a wall and moat around the city. He defeated a force of 2,000 marauding Aramaeans from the Hatallu tribe, who had plundered the land of Laqe, and draped the skin of their leader Shama-gamni over Al-gabbari-bani's city gate (*RIMB* 2: 297). Note that the city name is sometimes represented as Gabbari-ibni.

Aliabad, Tepe M3 cemetery mound, located on the Deh Luran plain in southwestern Iran, 90 km northwest of Susa, and 1.5 km from Tepe Mussian, the largest site on the plain. The name Tepe Mussian is also applied generically to a group of sites which include Tepe Aliabad and Tepe Khazineh as well as Tepe Mussian proper. The cemetery at Tepe Aliabad comprised rectangular vaulted and unroofed cist-tombs lined with mudbrick and used for single or double burials. The tombs were excavated by J. E. Gautier and G. Lampre on behalf of a French mission to Iran in 1905. Items found in them included both plain and polychrome painted jars, alabaster vessels, and metal weapons. The ceramic ware contributes to evidence for contact in M3 between the Deh Luran plain and the Diyala, Hamrin, and Pusht-i Kuh.

D. T. Potts (1999: 93–6).

Aligu (*Iliğak, Al-Liğa*) (map 7) Iron Age city in northwestern Mesopotamia near the confluence of the Euphrates and Sajur rivers, 7 km northeast of Tell Ahmar. It was one of the cities belonging to the kingdom of Bit-Adini, which in 856 (when the kingdom was ruled by Ahuni) were attacked and conquered by the Assyrian king Shalmaneser III during his military operations in the Euphrates region (**RIMA* 3: 19). The conquered towns (which included Nappigu, Rugulitu, Pitru, and Mutkinu) were assigned new Assyrian names. Aligu was thenceforth called Asbat-la-kunu, and a palace was established there as a royal residence. The military campaigns conducted by Shalmaneser in this year resulted in the total conquest of Bit-Adini and its absorption into the Assyrian empire. I[al]igu, an older form of the city's name, is attested in an inscription of Ashurnasirpal II (883–859) on a bronze band from Balawat (see **Imgur-Enlil**) (**RIMA* 2: 348).

Lipiński (2000: 168–9, 189).

Alilanum Middle Bronze Age royal city in northern Mesopotamia, attested in the Mari letters from the reign of Zimri-Lim (1774–1762). During this period, it was ruled by a king called Masum-Atal, who was a vassal (along with Hazip-Ulme, king of Ashihum) of Sharraya, king of Razama (in the land of Yussan) (see **Razama (2)**).

LKM 117, *435–6.

Aliler Early Iron Age hilltop fortress in eastern Anatolia, 52 km north of mod. Van. The site has most recently been investigated by O. Belli, who noted its strategic location in the midst of fertile pastures and mountain meadows watered by freshwater springs, and understood it to be the home of a typical regional early Iron Age dynasty. In C9, it came under the control of the kingdom of Urartu. New buildings were constructed during its Urartian phase, of which the most imposing was a seven-room rectangular complex covering 2,700 sq. m. It lay to the west of the fortress and was apparently the residence of an Urartian ruler. A fragmentary inscription found on a column-base on the site identifies its builder as the Urartian king Minua (805–788). Near the complex are the remains of a civilian settlement, mostly now below ground level.

Belli (2004).

Alimush (or **Alishir**) Iron Age city belonging to the Neo-Hittite kingdom of Pat(t)in (Assyrian Unqi) in northern Syria, mentioned in the texts of the Assyrian king Shalmaneser III (858–24). It was used as a stronghold by the Patinite king Sapalulme when Shalmaneser launched a campaign against the cities of northern Syria during the first year of his reign. At Alimush, Shalmaneser was confronted by a military coalition assembled from a number of northern Syrian and southern Anatolian kingdoms (Bit-Adini, Carchemish, Sam'al, Que, and Hilakku). After defeating the coalition forces, he captured Alimush, and then proceeded to the conquest of other Patinite cities (**RIMA* 3: 10, 16).

CHLI I: 362.

Alinda (*Karpuzlu*) (map 5) City in Caria, southwestern Anatolia, 60 km east of

Miletus. Its origins are obscure, though an identification has been suggested with the Late Bronze Age city called Iyalanda (q.v.) in Hittite texts. Very little is known of Alinda's history. In C5, it belonged for a brief period to the Athenian Confederacy (see glossary), and in C4 it provided a place of exile for Ada, a member of Caria's ruling Hecatomnid dynasty, after her expulsion from Halicarnassus by her brother Pixodarus. Ada voluntarily surrendered the city to Alexander the Great on his arrival in the region in 334, and was then appointed by him as queen of Caria (Strabo 14.2.17, Arrian, *Anab.* 1.23.8). Alinda may subsequently have been renamed Alexandria-by-Latmus; the Byzantine scholar Stephanus of Byzantium refers to a city of this name in Caria, which has not otherwise been identified.

A well-preserved city wall, perhaps of C4 date and built by the Carian satrap Mausolus, is one of Alinda's earliest material remains. Almost all the other remains date to the Hellenistic and Roman periods. The most outstanding of these is a well-preserved Hellenistic three-storey market building, 90 m long and 15 m high, fronting upon the city's agora. There are also substantial remains of a theatre, built in the Hellenistic period and redeveloped in Roman times. Large numbers of tombs can be found on the site, some of traditional Carian type. But none bears inscriptions.

Bean (1971: 190–8).

Alişar (map 2) Settlement-mound, c. 400 m in diameter, in north-central Anatolia, 170 km southeast of mod. Boghazköy (Hittite Hattusa). The site was excavated by E. Schmidt and H. H. von der Osten for the Oriental Institute, University of Chicago, from 1927 to 1932. Its numerous occupation levels, extending from the Chalcolithic period (c. 4000) through the first half of M1, enabled the excavators to make a detailed investigation of its stratigraphy. This was the first investigation of its kind in central Anatolia, and provided an important basis for reconstructing the sequence of civilizations in the region. Unfortunately, confusion in the stratigraphy of different parts of the site led to some anomalies in the numbering of the levels. Thus the level designated as Alişar II belongs to the Middle Bronze Age (early M2), but *succeeds* the level designated as Alişar III, which belongs to the second half of M3 – i.e. to the Early Bronze Age.

During the Middle Bronze Age, an Assyrian merchant-colony was located at Alişar. It is one of only three places where tablets of the Assyrian merchants have been found (the other two are Kanesh and Hattus). The settlement was enclosed by a casemate fortification wall, 5–6 m thick. Its fortifications were constructed in a steplike formation, without towers, and included a corbelled postern tunnel similar to that of the Late Bronze Age Hittite capital Hattusa (located on the site of Middle Bronze Age Hattus). Handmade painted pottery, or 'Cappadocian ware', was a feature of the material culture of the period. Though commonly identified with Hittite Ankuwa, Alişar may have been abandoned at the end of the Assyrian Colony period (mid C18), and left unoccupied through the Late Bronze Age. But some time after the collapse of the Bronze Age civilizations, a fortified Phrygian settlement was built on the site (perhaps in early M1). One of its features was a distinctive painted pottery, similar to the so-called Phrygian grey ware which was widely distributed through parts of western and southern Anatolia. Alişar's Iron Age settlement may have survived for a century or more after the fall of the Phrygian empire, c. 695, before it was destroyed by fire.

von der Osten (1937).

Allabria (map 13) Iron Age country located in the northeastern Mesopotamian–northwestern Iranian borderlands, between Mannaea and Parsua. It was one of the countries attacked and plundered by the Assyrian king Shalmaneser III during his campaign in 843 in the upper Diyala and Zagros region (**RIMA* 3: 40). Allabria subsequently appears among the conquests of Adad-nirari III (810–783) in this region (**RIMA* 3: 212). It was still under Assyrian sovereignty at the beginning of Sargon II's reign (721). But shortly afterwards, its ruler Itti was persuaded by the Mannaean king Ullusunu to defect from Assyria and join him in an alliance with Urartu. In 716 Sargon retaliated, with a campaign directed primarily against Ullusunu. The Mannaean king was defeated, along with Itti and other members of the alliance, and his capital Izirtu destroyed. Ullusunu, however, was subsequently restored to his throne by Sargon, as an Assyrian vassal. Itti did not fare so well. He was deported either to Assyria or to Amatti (depending on which Assyrian source is followed), along with Ashur-le'i, ruler of Karalla, another partner in the anti-Assyrian alliance (**ARAB* II: 5, 29). Two years later, in the course of his eighth campaign (714), Sargon passed through Allabria on his way to Parsua and received tribute from its governor Bel-aplu-iddina (**ARAB* II: 76).

Allabsia Iron Age city in the Kashiyari range (mod Tur ʿAbdin) of northern Mesopotamia. The Assyrian king Ashurnasirpal II reports that he entered the pass of Mt Kashiyari at the city of Allabsia during his campaign in 866, and was the first Assyrian king ever to set foot in the city (**RIMA* 2: 220). Lipiński suggests an identification with mod. Epşi, on the road from Diyarbakır to Midyat.

Lipiński (2000: 140, with map, 139).

Allahad (map 10) Middle Bronze Age city in the land of Yamutbal in northern Mesopotamia, attested in the Mari correspondence in the period when Mari's throne was occupied by Zimri-Lim (1774–1762). For part of this period, Allahad was ruled by a king called Atamrum, who eventually lost his throne, in unknown circumstances, and sought refuge in Eshnunna. He later became ruler of the city of Andarig, which lay to the northwest of Allahad. His elevation to Andarig's throne followed in the wake of the flight and murder of his predecessor, the (pro-Assyrian) king Qarni-Lim, who had annexed Allahad to Andarig. Allahad appears a number of times in the Mari correspondence as a place used by Atamrum for mustering troops, including allied forces from Babylon and Eshnunna. An Eshnunnite army based itself in the city during a campaign which culminated in its capture of Shubat-Enlil (Shehna), formerly the capital of the Assyrian king Shamshi-Adad I. Two letters sent to Zimri-Lim by his protégé Ashkur-Adad, king of Karana, report Babylonian intervention in the succession at Allahad after the death of Atamrum. Ashkur-Adad informed Zimri-Lim that troops from Babylon had been dispatched to the city (doubtless on the orders of Hammurabi) as an escort for a man called Hulalum, who was to be installed there as the city's new king, successor to Atamrum.

Mesop. 213, 325, *LKM* 605–6 (refs).

Al Mina (map 4) M1 settlement, founded probably in C8, on the coast of Syria at the mouth of the Orontes r. Excavated by C. L. Woolley in 1936–7, the site was long thought to have been established as a Greek colony by settlers from the island of Euboea. This conclusion was based exclusively on the presence of large quantities of

Greek ceramic ware on the site; no other evidence for Greek settlement, such as Greek architectural remains or burials, ever came to light. Al Mina is now regarded as a Syrian trading-post. Visited by Cypriots and Greeks from Euboea and other Greek islands, it served as an emporium where pottery from the Greek world was imported, for sale in the markets of Syria. Ten archaeological levels were identified by Woolley, the earliest of which are now dated to C8 (levels X–VII) and contained large quantities of sub-Protogeometric and Geometric pottery. East Greek and Corinthian ware become predominant in C7 (levels VI–V). Under Neo-Babylonian rule in C6 (level IV), Al Mina went into decline. But its fortunes revived in the period of Persian domination, C5 to C4 (level III), and it continued as a flourishing commercial settlement until the end of C4. Material remains of this period include a number of courtyard buildings which have been interpreted as merchants' warehouses.

Boardman (1980: 38–54; 2002), Akkermans and Schwartz (2003: 388).

Altıntepe (map 20) 4 ha Iron Age Urartian fortress settlement in eastern Anatolia, 20 km east of mod. Erzincan. It was excavated by a Turkish team in 1959 and the 1960s under the direction of T. Özgüç. Investigation of the site was resumed in 2003 by M. Karaosmanoğlu. Two levels of occupation have been identified. The main features of level I, the Urartian level, dating from C8, are a well-preserved tower-temple surrounded by a portico, and adjacent to it a columned hall, presumably the reception area of the local palace. Both buildings were decorated with wall paintings, surviving fragments of which depict ceremonial religious court scenes, indicative of strong Assyrian influence (divine figure with bucket sprinkling water, genii with sacred trees, etc.). Large numbers of iron and bronze weapons, bronze helmets and shields, an elaborately decorated bronze door-chain, a finely carved ivory lion, and ivories thought to be from a throne appear among the finds made in the temple. These finds suggest that Altıntepe may have escaped the plundering suffered by other Urartian sites at the end of their existence. Storage areas and a burial complex also belong to this phase. Several major tombs were discovered on the site, one cut from the rock on the hillside, the others built of well-dressed stone. Two of the tombs contained three rooms; in another, the burial chamber contained stone sarcophagi, and its outer chamber a bronze cauldron, silver-plated stools, and a dismantled chariot. An open-air shrine was constructed on a platform outside the tombs. It featured four basalt stelae with a small basin in front, apparently for libations. This mortuary complex was obviously intended for the local elite and their families. The settlement's general cemetery lay 2 km north of the citadel. Its accidental discovery in 1965 was due to highway construction. The small portion of the cemetery so far investigated includes rock-tombs, urn-burials, and simple earth-graves. The rock-tombs, approached by a dromos-type entrance, were single-room structures with niches carved into the walls for the interments. The urn- and earth-burials indicate that both cremation and inhumation were practised here – perhaps, it has been suggested, by two different ethnic groups.

On the basis of these remains, together with inscriptional evidence, level I appears to have been established in mid C8 at the latest, probably during the reign of the Urartian king Sarduri II (765–733). Burials and other inscriptional evidence appear to date to Sarduri's first two successors, Rusa I (732–714) and Argishti II (713–679). The phase II occupation at Altıntepe, once also considered to be Urartian, has now

Figure 7 Altıntepe, general view.

Figure 8 Altıntepe, temple.

been dated to the Persian period (C6–4), on the basis of its architectural remains and ceramic ware.

Burney and Lang (1971: 158–60), T. Özgüç (1966; 1969), Sevin and Özfırat (2001a).

Alzu Late Bronze and Iron Age country in northern Mesopotamia, to the north of the Kashiyari mountain range (mod. Tur ʿAbdin). Alzu joined a rebellion in the region against Assyrian rule at the beginning of Tukulti-Ninurta I's reign (1244–1208). Shubaru and Amadanu were also among the principal rebel lands. In the course of his retaliatory campaign against the rebels, Tukulti-Ninurta captured four strongholds of the land of Alzu, then ruled by a certain Ehli-Teshub. Tukulti-Ninurta plundered his kingdom, and conveyed its booty and prisoners-of-war to Ashur. But Ehli-Teshub himself escaped capture, and fled with a number of his sons and courtiers to an unknown land near the country of Nairi. Tukulti-Ninurta claims to have destroyed a total of 180 fortified cities of the rebels. Assyrian sovereignty was imposed upon Alzu, as upon the other rebel lands, and hostages were taken from these lands to ensure their future obedience. Other states which he subdued during this campaign, and over which he established or restored Assyrian sovereignty, included Alaia, Bushshu, Madanu, Mummu, Nihanu, Paphu, and Tepurzu (**RIMA* 1: 236–7, 244, 272).

Subsequently Alzu, along with the land of Purulumzu, was occupied by settlers from Mushki (for details, see **Purulumzu**). In the context of his campaign of conquest against the Shubarian peoples, the Assyrian king Tiglath-pileser I (1114–1076) reports that he reimposed Assyrian control over the lands of Alzu and Purulumzu, forcing them once more to pay tribute, a practice which they had apparently abandoned, probably at the instigation of the Mushki, at (if not before) the time of Tiglath-pileser's accession (**RIMA* 2: 17). The Assyrian king Adad-nirari II (911–891) claims to have destroyed the entire land during his fourth campaign against the Nairi lands (**RIMA* 2: 149).

Amadanu (Madanu) Late Bronze and Iron Age mountain country in northern Mesopotamia, to the northwest of the Kashiyari mountain range (mod. Tur ʿAbdin). The land of Amadanu joined a rebellion in the region against Assyrian rule at the beginning of Tukulti-Ninurta I's reign (1244–1208) (**RIMA* 1: 236–7). Shubaru and Alzu were also among the principal rebel countries. During his retaliatory campaign against the rebels, Tukulti-Ninurta captured six cities of Amadanu, and conveyed its booty and prisoners-of-war to Ashur. Assyrian sovereignty was imposed upon Amadanu, as upon the other rebel lands (see **Alzu**), and hostages were taken from these lands to ensure their future obedience.

The land of Amadanu may be identical with the Mt Amadanu through which Tiglath-pileser I (1114–1076) passed during his campaign against the Nairi lands (**RIMA* 2: 21), and which was later traversed by Ashurnasirpal II (883–859) (**RIMA* 2: 219–20). It may also be identical with Mt Amadinu, mentioned in the Annals of Tiglath-pileser III (745–727) (*Tigl. III* 54–5, 184–5). According to Kessler, if all of these toponyms belong together, then Amadanu is to be located north of the Karacadağ mountains and cannot be identified with the Karacadağ itself, as others have proposed.

Kessler (1980: 61–2).

Amalekites Iron Age tribal, nomadic or semi-nomadic people, attested in *OT* tradition as the descendants of Amalek, a grandson of Esau (Genesis 36:15–16). They feature in the *OT* as fringe-dwellers and desert wanderers, and like the Habiru (q.v.)

were notorious for their raids on villages and farming communities. Their presence in territories allotted to the Israelites in Israel, Judah, and Transjordan led to frequent conflicts between the two peoples. According to *OT* tradition, they were already attacking the Israelites during the period of the Exodus (Exodus 17:8–16). However, by the reign of King David in C10, they seem no longer to have constituted a serious threat to Israelite communities, and after David's reign they disappear from *OT* records altogether, except for a passing reference in 1 Chronicles 4:43. They are not attested in extra-biblical sources.

Dearman (*HCBD* 28).

Amanus (map 7) Mountain range in southern Anatolia. In the Late Bronze Age, its passes provided one of the chief means of land access between Hittite Anatolia and Syria, and were frequently used by Hittite armies, beginning with those of the C17 king Hattusili I, for their campaigns in Syria. Mt Adalur (Atalur), the setting of one of Hattusili's early military confrontations with a coalition of Syrian forces (see **Adalur**), is probably to be identified with the southern offshoot of the Amanus range. At the source of the Saluara r., which lay at the foot of the range, the Assyrian king Shalmaneser III erected a colossal statue of himself, inscribed with his military exploits, following his victory over a coalition of northern Syrian states – Sam'al, Carchemish, and Patin, together with the northwestern Mesopotamian state Bit-Adini – in his accession year (859) (**RIMA* 3: 10, 16). On a number of occasions, Shalmaneser crossed the Amanus for military expeditions against the land of Que (q.v.) in southern Anatolia. On his return from (at least) one of these expeditions, he ascended the range and cut cedars from it, for transport back to Ashur (**RIMA* 3: 69).

RGTC 6: 11–12.

Amasaku (Masaku) City in northern Mesopotamia attested in Late Bronze Age and early Iron Age Assyrian texts. In the Late Bronze Age, it belonged to the kingdom of Hanigalbat. When the Hanigalbatean king Wasashatta rebelled against Assyrian sovereignty, Amasaku was among the cities which Adad-nirari I (1307–1275) conquered while crushing the rebellion (**RIMA* 1: 131, 136). It is later attested in the reign of the Assyrian king Tiglath-pileser I (1114–1076), and is to be located in the area of mod. Nusaybin; in the Neo-Assyrian era, Amasa(k)ku formed part of the province of Nasibina (see **Nisibis**) (Kessler, 1980: 209). The city is perhaps identical with Old Babylonian Amurzakkum, which was also situated in the Nusaybin area.

Ebeling (*RlA* 1: 93), Lipiński (2000: 113 (map), 139 (map), 143–4).

Amastris (*Amasra*) (map 4) M1 Greek city located on a small peninsula and adjacent island on Anatolia's Black Sea coast in the region of Paphlagonia. Originally called Sesamus, it was renamed at the end of C4 in honour of Amastris, widow and successor of Dionysius, the former tyrant of Heraclea Pontica, when she made it the nucleus of a synoecism (see glossary). The synoecism included three other Greek settlements on the coast east of Heraclea: Tios, Cromna, and Cytorus. In mid C3 Eumenes, tyrant of Amastris, handed over Amastris to Ariobazarnes, king of Pontus, and it remained part of the Pontic kingdom until captured and destroyed by the Roman commander Lucullus in 70. Material remains of the city, notably a temple and a warehouse, date to the Roman period.

Wilson (*PECS* 47).

Amathus (map 14) City and kingdom on the south coast of Cyprus; 10 km east of mod. Limassol, consisting of an acropolis and lower city, and surrounded by large cemeteries. A Phoenician sanctuary may have occupied the summit of the hill called Viklaes, located to the east of the acropolis. According to Greek tradition, the city was founded by Cinyras, who named it after his mother Amathus. In a tradition recorded by the C4 Greek historian Theopompus, the inhabitants of Amathus were descendants of the companions of Cinyras, whom Agamemnon's Greeks had put to flight at the time of the Trojan War. In another tradition, the Amathite population was of indigenous stock. In any case, the city was a post Bronze Age foundation, whose origins date no earlier than C11. A number of excavations have been conducted on various parts of the site, beginning with those of a British team in 1893 and 1894, followed by a Swedish expedition in 1930, and from 1975 by the French School of Archaeology in Athens. The Dept of Antiquities of Cyprus has conducted excavations in the lower city.

The earliest C11 community is attested by no more than a few pottery remains. More substantial evidence of settlement is found in the Cypro-Geometric II–III period (late C10–8), when Amathus had commercial and cultural contacts with Phoenicia and the Aegean world. In C8, there is evidence of a significant Phoenician presence in the city, reflected in strong Phoenician influence on the city's material culture and religion. A large quantity of vase-burials discovered in 1992 in the western part of the necropolis, containing the remains of both children and adults, are thought to indicate a Phoenician cemetery at Amathus. The burials date probably between the end of the Cypro-Geometric and the Cypro-Archaic periods. A large building located halfway up the acropolis is very likely the palace of the kings of Amathus. Its earliest levels date to C8, the end of the Cypro-Geometric and Cypro-Archaic periods. The city was rebuilt at the end of C6, and finally destroyed c. 300, probably at the time of the war between Ptolemy I and Demetrius Poliorcetes. On the summit of the acropolis lie the remains of the famous sanctuary of Aphrodite, whose origins also date back to C8. Tacitus (*Annals* 3.62) includes it among Cyprus' most important temples. We know that the city also contained sanctuaries dedicated to Zeus, Hera, Hermes, and Adonis, but no trace of any of these has come to light.

Amathus is perhaps to be identified with the capital of the kingdom of Qartihadasht (q.v.), the Cypriot Carthage. This possibility arises partly from the mention of Qartihadasht on a bronze bowl discovered near Amathus. The bowl is inscribed with a dedication to the god Baal of Lebanon by a governor of Qartihadasht called 'the servant of Hiram', a C8 king of Sidon. Qartihadasht is also mentioned in the list of Cypriot rulers subject in C7 to the Assyrian kings Esarhaddon and Ashurbanipal. Whether or not the Amathus–Qartihadasht identification is valid, the population of Amathus remained predominantly an indigenous one. Inscriptions from the city indicate the use by its literate inhabitants of the Cypro-Minoan syllabary down to C4, for writing their own non-Greek language.

Amathus along with the rest of Cyprus was under Persian control for much of C5 and C4. In 498 it refused the request of Onesilus, king of Cyprus' largest city Salamis, to join all the other Cypriot cities in the anti-Persian Ionian revolt. This prompted Onesilus to lay siege to it, a siege which he was eventually forced to abandon because of more pressing matters. He was later killed in the land battle before Salamis, which resulted in a decisive victory for the Persian forces and their allies. According to Herodotus (5.114), the people of Amathus now took their final revenge on Onesilus by carrying his head back to their city and hanging it above the main entrance – until it was filled with honeycomb by a swarm of bees. When they consulted an oracle about the meaning of this, the oracle advised them to take the head down, bury it, and institute a hero-cult for Onesilus. They followed this advice and continued to practise the cult in Herodotus' own day. A later king of Salamis, Evagoras I (411–374/373), conquered Amathus as he was attempting to liberate Cyprus from Persian control. But its ruler Rhoicus, who had been taken prisoner, was released and returned to his kingdom at the instigation of Evagoras' Athenian allies. The last of the kings of Amathus, Androcles, fought on the side of Alexander the Great in his siege of the Levantine city of Tyre in 334.

Amathus continued to prosper through the Hellenistic, Roman, and Byzantine periods until its abandonment in C7 CE at the time of the first Arab invasions.

Nicolaou (*PECS* 47–8), Hermary (*OEANE* 1: 87–8), Iacovou (2002).

Amatu M1 Aramaean tribe in southern Babylonia, first attested in the inscriptions of Ninurta-kudurri-usur, mid C8 ruler of the Aramaean kingdom of Suhu on the middle Euphrates. At this time, it joined with the Hatallu tribe (q.v.) for a plundering expedition against the land of Laqe. After they had lain waste the land, the raiders were confronted and crushed by an army from Suhu led by Ninurta-kudurri-usur, in response to an appeal for assistance from the governor of Laqe. Following their defeat, the Amatu tribesmen apparently migrated east across the Tigris. They are among the Aramaean states said to have been conquered by Tiglath-pileser III, probably in his accession year (745), in an area stretching as far south as the Uqnu r. (**Tigl. III* 160–1); their land is to be distinguished from the land of Amatu (Amate) in western Media, also referred to in Tiglath-pileser's inscriptions (**Tigl. III* 72–3). The city of Amatu was among fourteen cities located on the Uqnu r. which submitted to Sargon II during the campaign of his twelfth regnal year (710) (*Fuchs, 1994: 149); this settlement is surely associated with the tribal group of the same name.

Lipiński (2000: 468–70).

Amaz Middle Bronze Age city in the Ida-maras region (q.v.) of northern Mesopotamia. Control of it was contested by Zimri-Lim, king of Mari (1774–1762) and Himdiya, king of Andarig.

LKM 606 (refs).

Amazons Race of female warriors in Greek legendary tradition, whose homeland lay in a remote region on the southern shores of the Black Sea. Popular etymology assigned to their name the meaning 'without breast', in the belief that they cauterized their right breasts to enable them to take surer aim with their bows and javelins. They appear twice in Homer's *Iliad* (3.189, 6.186), the first time when they attack a Phrygian encampment on the Sangarius river, the second time when the Greek hero Bellerophon does battle with and slaughters them in Lycia in the far southwest of Anatolia. Despite the location of their homeland in a remote, far-off region, Greek tradition associates the Amazons with many places in western Anatolia, making them the founders of cities such as Priene, Ephesus, and Smyrna, and also with cities in mainland Greece – for example, Chalcis and Athens, where cults were established in their honour. They have sometimes been linked to the Hittites, partly on the grounds of the representation of a Hittite warrior on one of the gates of the Hittite capital

Hattusa. The warrior's smooth, unbearded cheeks, contoured chest, and enlarged nipples have given rise to the fanciful hypothesis that it is intended to portray an Amazon.
Dowden (*OCD* 69–70), Ley (*BNP* 1: 563–5).

Amidu (Assyrian **Amedu**, ***Diyarbakır***) (maps 2, 13) Iron Age city in northern Mesopotamia on the right bank of the Tigris r., capital of the Aramaean state Bit-Zamani. Lipiński argues that prior to the Aramaean occupation in late M2, the city was called Eluhat or Elahut (q.v.) in Late Bronze Age texts, retaining that name until it was conquered by the Aramaeans. Amidu was captured by the Assyrian king Ashurnasirpal II during his campaign in the region in 866 (**RIMA* 2: 220). It joined in a widespread revolt against the Assyrian king Shalmaneser III (858–824), initiated by the king's son Ashur-da'in-apla. The rebellion continued into the early regnal years of Shalmaneser's son and successor Shamshi-Adad V before it was finally crushed (**RIMA* 3: 183).
Lipiński (2000: 153, 159–61).

Amisus (***Samsun***) (map 4) M1 BCE–M1 CE city founded by Ionian colonists from Miletus or Phocaea in C6, on a peninsula on the southern coast of the Black Sea within the region of Pontus. It was the terminus of a route leading north to the Black Sea coast from Cappadocia. In mid C5 Athenians from Peiraeus, the port of Athens, settled in Amisus and had it renamed Peiraeus. In C4 the city came under Persian rule and was forced to abandon the democratic constitution which the Athenians had brought with them. When Alexander the Great liberated Amisus from the Persians in 334, he restored its democratic constitution along with the city's former name. In mid C3, Amisus was incorporated into the kingdom of Pontus, becoming a royal seat of the Pontic king Mithradates VI (120–63). Later in C1, the Roman emperor Augustus conferred upon it the status of a free city within the province of Pontus and Bithynia.
Wilson (*PECS* 49), Olshausen (*BNP* 1: 582).

Amka (**Amqa, Amki**) (maps 3, 6) Late Bronze Age country located in the Biqaʿ valley of central Syria, on the frontier of Egyptian subject territory. It became embroiled in the contests between Egypt and Hatti for the control of states to which both kingdoms laid claim, notably the kingdoms of Amurru and Qadesh. During the reign of the pharaoh Akhenaten (1352–1336), word was brought to Egypt that Hittite troops had captured cities in the land of Amka. Subsequently, in the death year of Akhenaten's successor Tutankhamun (1327), a Hittite force attacked the land, allegedly in retaliation for an Egyptian attack on Qadesh, now under Hittite control (**DS* 94, **CS* I: 190, **Chav.* 237). The Hittite assault on Amka violated an earlier treaty drawn up between Hatti and Egypt (see **Kurustama**), and was seen to be one of the causes of a god-inflicted plague which devastated the Hittite homeland for twenty years, beginning in the final year of the Hittite king Suppiluliuma I (1322) (**CS* I: 158, *Singer 2002: 58).
Bryce (2005: 172–3, 178, 181, 206).

Ammali Fortified Iron Age city in the land of Zamua, located in the borderlands between northeastern Mesopotamia and northwestern Iran. It was apparently the chief city of Arashtua, one of the kings of Zamua. The withholding of tribute from Assyria by Arashtua and another Zamuite king Ameka prompted, in 880, the third campaign against Zamua undertaken by the Assyrian king Ashurnasirpal II (**RIMA* 2: 205–6).

Ammali was besieged, captured, and destroyed by the Assyrians, along with many other cities ruled by Arashtua, including Hudun and allegedly thirty other cities in its environs.

Ammash Iron Age city in northern Mesopotamia, within or near the land of Bit-Zamani. In 832, the Assyrian king Shalmaneser III dispatched an army against Urartu under the leadership of the commander-in-chief Dayyan-Ashur (**RIMA* 3: 69). He reports that Dayyan-Ashur engaged with, and defeated, the Urartian king Sarduri I, after previously entering the pass of the city of Ammash, and crossing the Arsanias r. (Murat Su) (q.v.).

Ammiya Late Bronze Age city on or near the Levantine coast, first attested in the C15 Idrimi inscription (see **Alalah**) (**CS* I: 479), and perhaps to be identified with Amyun, near (Lebanese) Tripoli. It was one of several small Levantine cities located within the kingdom of Rib-Hadda, mid C14 king of Gubla (Byblos), an Egyptian vassal state. Abdi-Ashirta, ruler of Byblos' northern neighbour Amurru, sought to gain control of Ammiya (along with other cities in Rib-Hadda's territory), by attempting to intimidate its citizens into assassinating their ruler and joining forces with him (*EA 73, 74). He appears not to have succeeded in this attempt before he was captured by Egyptian troops (see **Amurru**). But subsequently, Ammiya was seized by his son and successor Aziru, who promptly executed its ruler, as he did the rulers of other cities which he had captured in the region (**EA* 140).

Ammon (maps 8, 13) Iron Age kingdom in Transjordan, located on the plateau east of the Dead Sea between the countries of Gilead to the north and Moab to the south. Its chief city was Rabbath-Ammon, on the site of the mod. Jordanian capital Amman, where settlement dates back to the Neolithic period. In *OT* tradition, the Ammonites figure a number of times as the enemies and sometimes as the subjects of the Israelites. According to Genesis 19:38, they were descended from Ben-Ammi, the son of Abraham's nephew Lot. Ammon is not attested in texts of the Late Bronze Age or earlier periods. However, archaeological evidence indicates that towards the end of the Late Bronze Age, a number of settlements began to appear in the region, which hitherto was only sparsely populated, providing the material foundations for the emergence of a small politically and culturally coherent kingdom. This kingdom reached its full development in Iron Age II, between C8 and C6, as illustrated both by the remains of the capital Rabbath-Ammon, and by those of the walled cities Hesban and Tell el Umeiri which lay not far distant.

M1 Assyrian records provide the names of a number of Ammonite kings, and attest to the presence of Ammonites in the coalition of Syro-Palestinian states that confronted the army of the Assyrian king Shalmaneser III at Qarqar on the Orontes r. in 853 (e.g. **RIMA* 3: 23). However, through much of the Neo-Assyrian period the Ammonite kingdom was a vassal state of the Assyrian empire. It subsequently became subject to the Neo-Babylonian empire which emerged in the wake of Assyria's collapse in late C7. During the Neo-Babylonian period (C6), Ammon maintained some degree of autonomy under its own kings. But when Babylon fell to the Persians c. 539, the Ammonite monarchy disappeared as the country was absorbed into the Persian provincial administrative system.

Ammonite culture reached its peak in the Late Iron Age II and Persian periods. The region's characteristic ceramic ware and figurines help emphasize the Ammonites' distinctive identity and strong sense of cultural coherence. None the less, loyalties to family and clan seem always to have prev iled over any sense of national identity. Though Ammonite religion was polytheistic, worship was strongly focused on the chief deity Milkom. Unlike most other southern Levantine peoples, the Ammonites made images of their gods. Many Ammonite personal names include elements from the names of these gods. The Ammonites spoke a Semitic dialect, related to other contemporary dialects in the broader region, including Hebrew, Moabite, and Edomite. A number of Ammonite texts have survived, written in a script derived from Aramaic, and inscribed on stone (notably the so-called fragmentary Amman Citadel inscription assigned to early C8 and of uncertain purpose), metal, pottery, and clay. The largest number of inscriptions appears on seal-stones, dating to the period C8 to C6.

Labianca and Younker (1995), Herr (*OEANE* 1: 103–5); for Ammonite inscriptions, Felice (*OEANE* 1: 105–7).

Amorites A branch of the Semitic-speaking peoples, representing the indigenous population of northwestern Syria. In M3 the Amorites developed a highly accomplished and sophisticated culture, based on urban centres such as Ebla, Hamath, and Qatna. During late M3, Amorites moved eastwards along the Euphrates and migrated into Mesopotamia. 'Amorite' is derived from the Akkadian term *Amurrum*, corresponding to Sumerian *mar.du* (MAR.TU), which means 'west'. (See also Edzard, *RlA* 7: 438–40.) Sumerian (and Eblaite) sources indicate that there was a place called Martu to the west of Sumer; it is clearly from this land that the use of the term to designate 'west' derived. The precise relationship between Sumerian and Eblaite Martu and Akkadian Ammurum is rather unclear. Amurru(m) was also the name of the Amorites' chief deity. The Amorites have left behind no written texts of their own but are attested primarily through their personal names (over 4,000 attestations) and through references to Amorite people(s) in texts written in other languages, especially Akkadian and Sumerian. Moreover, their material culture cannot be distinguished from that of other, contemporary population groups. The Amorite language belongs to the northwest Semitic language family, which includes the M2 languages Ugaritic and Canaanite, and the M1 languages Phoenician, Aramaic, and Hebrew.

The names of persons designated as Amorite are first attested in Sumerian texts from Fara (c. 2600–2500). In some Sumerian literary compositions, the MAR.TU are regarded with considerable contempt: 'The MAR.TU who know no grain . . . no house nor town, the boors of the mountains. The MAR.TU who digs up truffles . . . who does not bend his knees (to cultivate the land), who eats raw meat, who has no house during his lifetime, who is not buried after his death . . .' (transl. by E. Chiera, cited Roux, 1980: 166). Amorite names also appear in the archives from Ebla in northwestern Syria (c. 2400–2350). The number of such names greatly increases in texts of the Ur III period (2112–2004), no doubt reflecting a substantial increase in the Amorite population in the regions with which the Ur III texts are concerned.

Initially, the Amorites may have entered the Mesopotamian plain in search of suitable pastureland for their flocks. But as their numbers increased, they adopted a more settled existence, posing an ever-increasing threat to the security of the kingdoms and city-states of the region. The Akkadian king Sargon (2334–2279) engaged in conflicts with Amorites west of the Euphrates, and the final, decisive battle fought by his grandson Naram-Sin (2254–2218), when he quashed the 'Great Revolt', took place at Basar (Jebel Bishri), called 'the mountain of (the land) Martu'. Kings of the Ur III dynasty tried unsuccessfully to keep Amorite groups at bay by building a chain of fortifications or watchtowers across northern Babylonia. Despite these defences, Amorite chieftains overran Babylonia, and shortly before the fall of the Ur III kingdom, an Amorite had set himself up as ruler of the city-state of Larsa, 40 km north of Ur. Other Babylonian cities, including Babylon, Kish, Marad, and Sippar, also came under Amorite control, indicating that by this time the Amorites – whatever their origins – had completely assimilated into urban society. The first great king of Assyria, Shamshi-Adad I (1796–1775), who brought the Old Assyrian kingdom to the height of its military power and commercial prosperity, was also the first of the great Amorite rulers. The second was Hammurabi. In Babylon, a dynasty of Amorite kings was established c. 1894. Hammurabi was the sixth member of this dynasty. Yarim-Lim I, ruler of the kingdom of Yamhad in northern Syria, was a third powerful king of Amorite descent.

By mid M2, the Amorites had merged with other population groups to the extent that they were often not explicitly designated as MAR.TU, and only their personal names betray their background. However, their name lived on in the designation *Amurru*. In M3 and early M2, this term applied to a large expanse of territory extending through much of what is now Syria. But from C14 onwards, its use was restricted to the territory lying between the Orontes r. and the central Levantine coast. The territory so designated achieved some degree of political coherence when in mid C14 it came under the control of a local chieftain called Abdi-Ashirta who gave token allegiance to the pharaoh. Subsequently, it became a Hittite vassal state (see **Amurru**).

In M1 Babylonian texts, Amurru is used as a general, old-fashioned way of referring to lands to the west (Syria–Palestine and North Arabia). The term 'Amorite' recurs many times in the later *OT* sources. These sources identify the Amorites as tribal groups occupying parts of Canaan before the arrival of the Israelites. In Ezekiel 16:3, they figure alongside the Hittites and the Canaanites as pre-Israelite peoples.

Roux (1980: 169–83), Whiting (1995), Buccellati (*OEANE* 1: 107–11), Goddeeris (2005).

Amrit see **Marathus**.

Amuq plain Marshy fertile plain, covering c. 14,000 sq. km, in the southeastern Turkish–northwestern Syrian border region, near the northern bend of the Orontes r. Human occupation, evidenced by numerous tells in the region, dates back before the Neolithic period, with continuous archaeological sequences from that period to the present day. One of its most significant anc. sites is the Middle–Late Bronze Age city Alalah (mod. Tell Atchana). The later Iron Age Neo-Hittite kingdom Pat(t)in, called Unqi in Assyrian records, was also located in the Amuq plain, in roughly the same territory once occupied by the kingdom of Alalah. The name Unqi may have been the origin of the mod. name Amuq (Aramaic Amq).

Dornemann (*OEANE* 1: 115–17).

Amurru (maps 3, 6) (see also **Amorites**) Bronze Age country in Syria. In M3 and early M2, the term applied to a large expanse of territory extending through much of mod. Syria. In the Late Bronze Age, its use was restricted to the territory lying between the Orontes and the central Levantine coast. This territory was incorporated into the Egyptian empire in C15 during Tuthmosis III's Syrian campaigns. But its attachment to Egypt remained very tenuous. Prior to the second half of C14, it was a wild and anarchic region, inhabited by semi-nomadic groups called the Habiru (q.v.) who attacked merchants and other travellers passing through it as well as the more settled communities that lay within their striking range. In mid C14, a local leader called Abdi-Ashirta united the Habiru as a highly effective fighting force under his command. Though he claimed allegiance to the pharaoh Amenhotep III, he plundered many of Egypt's subject territories in the region, before his career ended in capture by the Egyptian authorities (**EA* 117: 21–8). However, his son Aziru inherited his *de facto* leadership of the country and followed a course similar to that of his father. He terrorized, plundered, and occupied neighbouring states, while maintaining a semblance of loyalty to the pharaoh, now Amenhotep IV/Akhenaten. (For the Amurru letters in the Amarna correspondence, see refs in Moran, 1992: 388.) But eventually he switched allegiance to the Hittite king Suppiluliuma I.

Thenceforth, Amurru became a subject ally of Hatti, as reflected in a treaty drawn up between Suppiluliuma and Aziru (**HDT* 36–41, **CS* II: 93–5). There is also an extant treaty between Suppiluliuma's son and (second) successor Mursili II and Aziru's grandson Duppi-Teshub (**HDT* 59–64, *CS II: 96–8). Amurru remained Hittite subject territory until the reign of Mursili's son and successor Muwattalli II, when the nineteenth dynasty pharaoh Seti I wrested it back (along with Qadesh) from the Hittites by winning a resounding victory over Muwattalli in a military engagement at Qadesh (c. 1290). Control over Amurru and Qadesh continued to be a major source of dispute between Egypt and Hatti, and provided a direct cause for a second military confrontation at Qadesh fought in 1274 between Muwattalli and Seti's son and successor Ramesses II.

Though the battle itself ended in a stalemate, one of its outcomes was that both Amurru and Qadesh were firmly established as Hittite vassal states, and remained so until the end of the Hittite kingdom. Treaties survive between the Hittite king Hattusili III and the Amurrite ruler Benteshina (son of Duppi-Teshub), whose family was linked by marriage to the Hittite ruling dynasty (**HDT* 100–3), and between Hattusili's son and successor Tudhaliya IV and Benteshina's son(?) and successor Shaushgamuwa (**HDT* 103–7, **CS* II: 98–100). The Assyrian king Tiglath-pileser I (1114–1076) claims to have conquered the entire land of Amurru during a campaign which he conducted to the Syro-Palestinian coast (**RIMA* 2: 37, 53). 'Amurru' seems to be used here in reference to the region occupied by the Phoenician cities, including Byblos, Sidon, and the island-city Arwad, along the Levantine coast. But the term must have had a much broader application, since elsewhere Tiglath-pileser includes within it the city of Tadmor (*RIMA* 2: 43), which was located in the Syrian desert 235 km northeast of Damascus. It was presumably to this broader region that Adad-nirari III (810–783) also referred in his record of conquests in the lands of Hatti and Amurru (e.g. **RIMA* 3: 211).

Singer (1991), Bryce (2003b: 145–68).

Amurzakkum Middle Bronze Age city in northern Mesopotamia, located to the northwest of the Old Assyrian capital Shubat-Enlil (Shehna, *Tell Leilan*) in the vicinity of mod. Nusaybin. In the autumn of 1779, the Turukkaean forces who had occupied the city were placed under siege by an army of the Assyrian viceroy Ishme-Dagan. With their capture imminent, the Turukkaeans were forced to abandon the city and flee northwards towards the Tigris r., with the Assyrians in hot pursuit (see **Turukkum**). Amurzakkum is perhaps identical with later Amasaku/Masaku.

Eidem (1985: 104–5), *Mesop.* 177.

Ana-Ashur-uter-asbat see **Pitru**.

Anafa, Tel Small settlement in northeastern Israel, with a history of occupation extending from the Early Bronze Age through C1. The site was excavated by teams from the Museum of Art and Archaeology, University of Missouri, between 1968 and 1973 under the direction of S. Weinberg, and subsequently between 1978 and 1986 by a joint expedition of the Missouri Museum and the Kelsey Museum, University of Michigan, with S. Weinberg and S. Herbert as co-directors. Attention was focused on the remains of the late Hellenistic period, the best-preserved phase in the sites' history. Large numbers of imported luxury products are a feature of this phase. At this time, Tel Anafa may have belonged within the administrative orbit of the city of Tyre.

Herbert (*NEAEHL* 1: 58–61; *OEANE* 1: 117–18).

Ana(t) (Hanat, *ʿAna*) (map 10) Bronze and Iron Age city on an island in the middle Euphrates. Earlier M2 Hanat is very likely identical with later M2 and M1 Ana(t), and with mod. ʿAna, where excavations on the island have uncovered remains of the Neo-Assyrian period (Northedge, Bamber, and Roaf, 1988). Hanat is first attested in Middle Bronze Age texts as the chief city of Upper Suhu(m). The region of Suhum lay south of the kingdom of Mari and was subject to Mari, first under the Assyrian viceroy Yasmah-Addu (1782–1775) and subsequently under King Zimri-Lim (1774–1762). Hanat figures in a number of letters from the Mari archive, particularly in association with troop movements in the area (*LKM* 611, refs).

Ana(t) is subsequently attested as an Iron Age settlement of the Aramaean kingdom of Suhu. In this phase of its existence, it appears first in the Annals of Tiglath-pileser I (1114–1076), in the context of the Assyrian king's campaigns against the Ahlamu-Aramaeans (**RIMA* 2: 38, 43). Tiglath-pileser's successor-but-one Ashur-bel-kala (1073–1056) also refers to the city in his account of his extensive campaigns against the Aramaeans, from Anat in the land of Suhu to Rapiqu in Babylonia (**RIMA* 2: 98).The Assyrian king Tukulti-Ninurta II encamped his forces near the city in the course of his last recorded campaign (885), which took him through the middle Tigris and Euphrates regions during his progress around the western and southern limits of his kingdom. He received there from Ilu-Ibni, Suhu's governor, a payment of tribute, in the form of provisions and costly gifts (**RIMA* 2: 174–5). Seven years later, Tukulti-Ninurta's son and successor Ashurnasirpal II pitched camp outside Anat, the night before laying siege to the city of Suru where Kudurru, the rebel governor of Suhu, was preparing to confront the Assyrian army (**RIMA* 2: 213). Under the Assyrian king Adad-nirari III (810–783), Anat was among the cities and lands assigned to the governorship of a certain Nergal-erish (Palil-erish) (**RIMA* 3: 209, 211). During this period, the Assyrians were obliged to conduct a number of campaigns in the region to maintain their authority there. The country is also referred to in Luwian hieroglyphic inscriptions from Tell Ahmar (see Bunnens, 2006: 95–6).

The inscriptions of Ninurta-kudurri-usur, governor of Suhu in mid C8, indicate that prior to the period when governorship of the land was exercised by his father Shamash-resha-usur, Anat had been under Assyrian rule for fifty years. This rule had extended into the first three years of his father's governorship. Ninurta-kudurri-usur claims that Assyrian sovereignty had come about when Suhu's governor Tabnea went to Assyria to render tribute and have an audience (with the Assyrian king?), but was assassinated there. The circumstances of the assassination are not recorded. But it caused the people of Anat to revolt against Suhu and deliver themselves up to Assyria. Subsequently, they were harshly treated by the Assyrians. The Assyrian king (unnamed) demolished part of their city, desecrated and removed the statues of its gods, and evacuated its population, resettling the city with people of his own. We may assume his actions were in response to anti-Assyrian activities by Anat, which must have regretted its links with Assyria and sought to break them. It apparently succeeded in doing so, returning its allegiance to Suhu during the period of Shamash-resha-usur's governorship. The latter's son Ninurta-kudurri-usur claims credit for restoring to Anat the statues of its gods and the treasures associated with them, all of which had been removed by the Assyrians. They were now returned to their original dwellings. For Ninurta-kudurri-usur's account of all these events, see **RIMB* 2: 307–8, 315–16, 318.

In late C7, although the land of Suhu had paid tribute to the Babylonian king Nabopolassar in 616, it subsequently rebelled against him and took the side of Assyria in its final struggle for survival. Nabopolassar besieged Anat during a campaign to subdue Suhu in 613 (**ABC* 93).

Na'aman (2007: 115–17).

Anatolia (maps 1, 2, 3, 4) The name first adopted by the Classical Greeks as a general term to refer to the land-mass lying to their east – where, from a European perspective, the 'rising' (Greek *anatolē*) of the sun takes place. 'Anatolia' is now commonly used as a designation for mod. Turkey (sometimes more specifically for Turkey's central highlands), represented as *Anadolu* in its Turkish form. Less commonly, Turkey is sometimes referred to as Asia Minor. This name goes back to mid M1 CE, when it was first used in reference to the westernmost part of the Asian continent, between the Aegean Sea and the Euphrates r. The Anatolian highland plateau rises 1000 m above sea level. It is bounded by the Pontic mountains in the north, the Taurus mountains in the south, and the Armenian mountains in the east. These mountain ranges sharply differentiate the plateau from the rest of the Anatolian region. In the west, the plateau slopes down more gently to the Aegean coast. From the Early Bronze Age onwards, Anatolia has served as an important land-bridge between the peoples and civilizations of Europe and Asia. It was the homeland of several great anc. kingdoms, most notably the Late Bronze Age kingdom of Hatti, and the Iron Age kingdoms of Phrygia, Lydia, and Urartu.

Lloyd (1989), Gorny/Gunter/Scott (*OEANE* 1: 127–35).

Ancyra (*Ankara*) (map 2) M1 BCE–M1 CE city in central Anatolia. According to tradition, it was founded by the C8 Phrygian king Midas. However, the city is not attested in historical sources prior to the conquests of Alexander the Great in 334–333. It achieved high prominence early in the Roman imperial period as the capital of Galatia, which became a Roman province in 25, and was a flourishing city during both

the Roman and the Byzantine periods. Most of its anc. remains have been obliterated by the mod. city Ankara. Those that survive are of Roman and Byzantine date.
Mitchell (*PECS* 54–5).

Andarig (probably = ***Tell Koshi***) (map 10) Middle Bronze Age city and kingdom in northern Mesopotamia, located between the Habur and Tigris rivers, to the south of the Jebel Sinjar. It was apparently the most important city of the (northern) Amorite Yamutbal tribe (see **Yamutbal**). Andarig is first attested as a subject state of the Assyrian king Shamshi-Adad I (1796–1775). When the Old Assyrian kingdom fragmented after Shamshi-Adad's death, a palace revolution in Andarig led to the overthrow, flight, and assassination of the city's pro-Assyrian ruler Qarni-Lim. Andarig now became independent under its new king Atamrum (who had previously ruled in Allahad, but had lost his throne in unknown circumstances), and went on to play a politically and militarily prominent role in its region as it aligned itself with one or other of the major powers of the day (e.g. Mari and Eshnunna). Hostilities with Mari early in the reign of the Mariote king Zimri-Lim (c. 1771) resulted in a siege and conquest of the city by Zimri-Lim's forces.

For an undetermined period from c. 1765 onwards, during the reigns of Atamrum and his successor Himdiya, Andarig exercised control over Shamshi-Adad's former capital Shubat-Enlil, and the city of Kurda. For part of this time its king, Atamrum, aligned himself with the Elamite king, who had launched a major offensive in Mesopotamia in 1765, against the anti-Elamite alliance of Babylon and Mari (*Charpin, 2003: 77). The Elamite troops were forced by the alliance to withdraw from Mesopotamia the following year. Around this time, Atamrum formed an alliance with his former enemy Zimri-Lim, in response to aggression by Ishme-Dagan, king of Ekallatum. But the threats posed by Ishme-Dagan to Andarig and other cities in the region came to an end when Ishme-Dagan, under pressure from enemy forces, fled from Ekallatum and sought refuge (for a second time) in Babylon.

In the period following the fall of Mari in 1762, a king of Andarig called Buriya established an alliance with Hazi-Teshub, king of Razama (in the land of Yussan), in opposition to a bloc formed by Mutiya and Ashtamar-Adad, the kings of Apum (capital Shubat-Enlil/Shehna) and Kurda respectively, and a third king, Shepallu (country unknown). Subsequently, Andarig may have been incorporated into the nearby kingdom of Karana, when the latter was ruled by Aqba-Hammu, vassal of the Babylonian king Hammurabi (1792–1750).
LKM 114–20, 606 (refs), *Mesop.* 350.

Anemurium (***Eski Anamur***) (map 4) M1 BCE–M1 CE city located in Rough Cilicia (Cilicia Tracheia/Aspera) on the southernmost tip of Turkey, 64 km north of Cyprus. Its antiquity is uncertain, since the earliest attestation of it, in the C1 Roman historian Livy (33.20), belongs to the Hellenistic period. Its material remains are of Hellenistic, Roman, and Byzantine date. They include an impressive necropolis (C1–C4 CE) containing some 350 individual numbered tombs.
Russell (*PECS* 58).

Ankuwa (Amkuwa) Middle and Late Bronze Age city in north-central Anatolia, three days' journey (in anc. terms) from the Hittite capital Hattusa. It is first attested in the Middle Bronze Age Assyrian Colony period (C20–18) as one of several cities which rebelled against Hattus (Late Bronze Age Hattusa) (*Larsen, 1972). In the Late Bronze Age, Hittite kings used Ankuwa as a winter residence. Though it appears to have been of no political importance in the Hittite world, it figures frequently in cultic contexts and in the celebration of religious festivals. The city is commonly but not conclusively identified with the site at mod. Alişar (q.v.).

**RGTC* 6: 19–23.

Anshan (*Tal-e Malyan*) (maps 12, 16) City in southwestern Iran, located on the Marv Dasht plain, in the mod. province of Fars, 50 km northwest of Shiraz and 43 km west of Persepolis. Its history of occupation extends from M6 until the Islamic period, with a number of intervals in between when the site was abandoned or only sparsely populated. Excavations were conducted by F. Tavaloli in 1961 for the Archaeological Dept in Fars, and subsequently by W. M. Sumner for the University Museum of the University of Pennsylvania between 1971 and 1978 (five seasons).

The first substantial settlement on the site dates to the (inappropriately named) Proto-Elamite period (see under **Elam**), late M4–early M3. At this time, the site was fortified by a wall enclosing 200 ha, though human occupation covered only two-thirds of the enclosed area. Polychrome wall-paintings, with rosette, swirl, and nested-step motifs (thus Sumner) featured in one of the five building levels of the period. The site appears to have been abandoned at the end of its so-called Proto-Elamite phase, then reoccupied, and refortified, in the second half of M3. This reoccupation marked the beginning of the site's history as part of the Elamite world. Its identification with the city of Anshan, attested in historical texts from late M3 until the Persian Achaemenid period (C6–4), was confirmed by the appearance of this name in cuneiform tablets unearthed on the site and dating to the so-called Middle Elamite phase (c. 1600–1100).

The city's importance is indicated by its repeated appearance in the royal Elamite titulary from the sukkalmah dynasty (early M2; see glossary) onwards. Already in C23 it was the Elamite capital of its region, when it was attacked and conquered by the Akkadian king Manishtushu. Perhaps the silver mines which lay nearby provided an incentive for Akkadian aggression. It suffered a further conquest the following century by Gudea, ruler of the Sumerian city-state Lagash. Yet despite these and no doubt other conquests by its Babylonian neighbours, it succeeded in maintaining its status as a centre of Elamite power, and was considered sufficiently important by Shu-Sin (2037-2029), the penultimate ruler of the Ur III empire, for him to form a marriage alliance with its king. Anshan no doubt prospered along with the rest of the Elamite kingdom during the peak period of Elamite power, under the Shimashki and sukkalmah dynasties, in the first half of M2 (though it suffered a major setback c. 1928 when it was attacked and destroyed by Gungunum, fifth king of the Larsa dynasty). Inscriptional evidence indicates that it maintained its importance as a royal seat of Elamite power down to the final years of the Middle Elamite period.

The city appears to have been destroyed by fire at the end of this period, with some modest resettlement shortly after. However, there is a complete absence of any material remains of the Persian period. This is all the more surprising since in historical tradition Teispes, great-grandfather of Cyrus II, founder of the Persian empire, styled himself 'King of Anshan', as did his successors including Cyrus. Brosius (2006: 6) sees this as 'an act of political symbolism with which the Persians gave weight to their role as successors of the Elamite kings', at a time when Anshan itself had ceased to function as a major city. It is, however, possible that the Persian royal dynasty established its base in Anshan following the campaigns which the Assyrian king Ashurbanipal conducted into the region in mid C7. (D. T. Potts, 2005a, suggests that Cyrus and his Teispid line were in fact Anshanite, as distinct from Darius and the Achaemenid line; for the two apparently separate royal lines, see under **Persians**. Note too the report in the Nabonidus Chronicle – see glossary – that Cyrus carried off to Anshan the spoils of Ecbatana after his defeat and capture of the Median king Astyages in 550: **ABC* 106, **Chav.* 419, **PE* 50, no. 1.) These campaigns no doubt hastened the disintegration of the already declining Elamite empire. Cyrus re-established his royal capital at the new site of Pasargadae. But there is no known reason why Anshan should have been totally abandoned at this time. In any case, despite the lack of archaeological evidence for Anshan's existence during the Persian period, it continued to be referred to in the tablets unearthed at Persepolis, another new Persian city, founded by the emperor Darius I in late C6. There is some scattered evidence of occupation of Anshan in the centuries following the Persian period, up to the time of Islamic occupation.

The name Anshan may also have been used of the region in which Anshan, the city, was located, until it was perhaps replaced by the name Parsa when the Persians established control over the region in mid C6.

Briant (1984a: 80–8), Sumner (*RlA* 7: 306–20; *OEANE* 3: 406–9), Young (1988: 24–6), D. T. Potts (2005a).

Antiphellus (*Kaş*, formerly ***Andifili***) (map 15) M1 BCE–M1 CE harbour-city in Lycia in southwestern Anatolia, first attested in C4 coins and inscriptions. 'Antiphellus' is the Greek form of the name. The city originally served as the port of Phellus (which means 'stony' in Greek), which lay inland to its northwest. According to Pliny the Elder (5.100), Antiphellus' original name was Habesus. Up to the Hellenistic period, it remained a relatively small and insignificant city, essentially a coastal appendage to Phellus. But with the decline of Phellus in the Hellenistic period, Antiphellus increased rapidly in importance, and by the Roman imperial period had become the chief city in its region. Its wealth no doubt derived largely from its having one of the few good harbours along Anatolia's southwestern coast. And Pliny (5.131) refers to the fine quality of its sponges.

Remains of the first attested period of its existence include a number of tombs, located on the hill-slopes to the west and north of the city. The most notable of these is a well-preserved Lycian sarcophagus erected on a high base and bearing a long inscription in the more obscure of the two known native Lycian dialects (the so-called Lycian B dialect) (**TAM* I 55), now almost entirely unintelligible. Several other funerary monuments in the vicinity can be dated to C4 by the native Lycian inscriptions carved on them. Many other tombs date to the Hellenistic and Roman periods, as do most of Antiphellus' other remains, including a beautiful, well-preserved Hellenistic theatre overlooking the sea.

Bean (*PECS* 64–5; 1978: 92–6).

Anzaf Kale (map 20) Two neighbouring Iron Age Urartian fortress-sites in eastern Anatolia, located 11 km northeast of the Urartian capital Tushpa (mod. Van). The lower fortress was built by the Urartian king Ishpuini (824–806). The upper fortress, 900 m to its south, was built by Ishpuini's son, co-regent, and successor Minua

(805–788) and is associated with a lower-lying settlement area. It was to undergo a number of developments and restorations throughout the Urartian kingdom's history.

Ishpuini's lower fortress, covering c. 6,000 sq. m, was strategically positioned along a major route approaching the Urartian capital at Tushpa from Iran and the Transcaucasus region. The upper fortress covered an area of c. 6 ha, ten times the size of the lower fortress, and was sited 1995 m above sea level. A temple dedicated by Minua to the kingdom's chief god Haldi stands at its summit in the south part of the fortress. It is 13.4 m square, with 2.5 m thick walls, and displays a number of distinctive architectural features not evident in later Urartian temples. A series of twenty-two monumental carvings discovered on rock surfaces in the eastern and northwestern part of the fortress, and the unique representation of Urartian deities on votive shields found in the temple, reflect the importance of the site as a cult-centre. On a practical level, the upper fortress provided storage facilities for the agricultural produce collected from surrounding farmlands, which were supplied with water from a dam built by Minua to the east of the fortress.

The lower city extended over an area of c. 14 ha lying to the south of the upper fortress. Both city and fortress were enclosed within a wall, 2 m thick. The wall provides a good example of the curtain-bastion fortification technique, and more generally is one of the finest surviving examples of early Urartian defensive architecture. Several gates gave access to the lower city and fortress complex: an eastern gate, 4.3 m thick, which provides important information on eastern Anatolian gate construction techniques, and monumental northern and southern gates, protected by a tower made of carved limestone blocks. The tower still rises to a height of 7 m above ground level.

Belli (1999; 2001b; 2003).

Figure 9 Anzaf Kale.

Aparha Middle Bronze Age royal city located in northwestern Mesopotamia between the Euphrates and Balih rivers, in or near the land of Zalmaqum. During the reign of the Assyrian king Shamshi-Adad I (1796–1775), its ruler Larim-Numaha seized the cities Zihlalum and Ahuna in the Zalmaqum region, prompting a military response by Yasmah-Addu, Assyrian viceroy at Mari. At the city of Shubat-Shamash he was joined by an army under the command of his brother Ishme-Dagan, viceroy at Ekallatum. The combined Assyrian forces conquered Aparha, thus bringing Larim-Numaha's military adventure to an end, though Larim-Numaha himself appears to have escaped capture (**LAPO* 17: 68–9, no. 488). Aparha's inhabitants were deported, some of them being handed over to Eshnunna, which had provided support for the Assyrian forces.

Mesop. 174–6.

Aparytae Central Asian people attested by Herodotus (3.91) who includes them in the populations constituting, according to him, the Persian empire's seventh province, located in its eastern frontier region (but see glossary under **satrapy**). The Aparytae do not appear in the Bisitun inscription (q.v.) of the Persian king Darius I, or in any other Persian inscriptions for that matter. But it is possible that they were among the eastern peoples incorporated into the Persian empire prior to Darius' accession in 522, probably by the empire's founder Cyrus II some time after 539. Along with other peoples included by Herodotus in the seventh Persian province, they were very likely located in the mountainous northern border region of Afghanistan and Pakistan. An identification has been suggested with the mod. Afridis who continue to live in this region. Alternatively, their name has been linked with Parvata, a mountain in central Afghanistan.

Bivar (1988: 203).

Apasa (map 3) Late Bronze Age city in western Anatolia, on or near the site of Ephesus, and capital of the kingdom of Arzawa 'Minor'. Around 1320, the Hittite king Mursili II conducted an expedition against its ruler Uhhaziti, who had refused to return refugee Hittite subjects seeking asylum with him. Uhhaziti escaped from Apasa before the Hittites invaded and occupied it (**AM* 46–51, **CS* II: 85). Late Bronze Age pottery and parts of what is probably a Late Bronze Age fortification wall have recently been unearthed on the hill now called Ayasuluk near the Classical site of Ephesus. These very probably mark part of the location of Apasa. For the fate of the city and Uhhaziti's kingdom, see **Arzawa 'Minor'**.

Büyükkolanci (2000).

Aperlae (map 15) M1 BCE–M1 CE coastal city in Lycia, southwestern Anatolia, located 15 km southeast of mod. Kaş. Though the site has produced no tombs or inscriptions of the indigenous Lycian civilization, the discovery of a number of C5 silver coins inscribed with the letters APR or PRL in the Lycian script indicate, if they are attributable to Aperlae, that the city's origins extend back at least to mid M1. But its material remains, including a fortification wall and sarcophagi, are of Roman date. During the Roman imperial period, Aperlae was the head of a Lycian tetrapolis (league of four cities), whose other members were Apollonia, Simena, and Isinda.

Bean (*PECS* 67–8; 1978: 101–3).

Aphek ('river-bed'; **Greek Antipatris,** ***Tell Ras el-ʿAin***) (map 8) 12 ha settlement-mound in Israel (four other places of this name are known from *OT* sources), located on the Sharon plain at an important junction on the Via Maris (q.v.) between Beth Shean and Damascus. It has a history of almost continuous occupation from the Chalcolithic to the Ottoman period. Following upon two earlier rescue operations, the site was extensively excavated by P. Beck and M. Kochavi for Tel Aviv University over thirteen seasons from 1972 to 1985.

In the Early Bronze Age, settlement already extended over the entire mound. Remains of a fortification wall of this period were unearthed in the site's northern sector. At the end of the Early Bronze Age the mound was abandoned, and it was then resettled shortly afterwards at the beginning of the Middle Bronze Age. Six phases of Middle Bronze Age occupation have been identified by the excavators. Constructions during these phases included three successive palaces: the largest (phases 5–6) covered 4,000 sq. m. Remains of residential quarters and numerous burials were found in most of the phases. The palace was destroyed at the end of the Middle Bronze Age, c. mid C16, but was followed by three successors in the Late Bronze Age, dating from C15 to C13. The last of these has been identified as a fortified Egyptian governor's residence, which was destroyed by fire.

The first (possible but not certain) written attestation of Aphek occurs in the Egyptian Execration texts (C19–18). Subsequently, the city appears among the places listed by the pharaoh Tuthmosis III (1479–1425) on the Via Maris (q.v.). Tuthmosis' co-regent and successor Amenhotep II (1427–1400) reports that he conquered the city during his expedition to northern Syria via the Sharon plain. From the debris of the

Figure 10 Aphek.

Late Bronze Age Egyptian residence at Aphek, a number of Egyptian, Hittite, and Akkadian documents have come to light. These include two cuneiform lexical tablets in Sumerian and Akkadian, a Hittite royal seal impression, three administrative documents and a letter written in Akkadian, another letter from a high official in Ugarit to the Egyptian high commissioner of Canaan (*CS III: 243–4), and an inscribed Egyptian faience ring.

The Late Bronze Age settlement was destroyed by fire c. 1240, and the site was again abandoned for a brief period before resettlement in C12, at the beginning of the Iron Age. At this time it was occupied by the Philistines, as indicated by ceramic ware and figurines of the Philistine goddess Ashdoda. In *OT* tradition, the Philistines used Aphek as a base in their war with the Israelites (1 Samuel 4:1; 29:1). The new city appears to have been divided into two main sectors on a class basis. The more elite sector contained well-built square houses with large front halls and paved courtyards. The poorer sector contained haphazardly built oblong structures crowded together. The discovery of fish-hooks, lead net-weights, and turtle-shells in the houses of this area suggest that the inhabitants were chiefly fishermen. From the discovery of stone-lined silos typical of C10 Israelite sites, the excavators further concluded that there was an Israelite occupation of the site early in M1. The violent destruction of the city towards the end of C10 is generally attributed to the pharaoh Sheshonq I (biblical Shishak) (945-924) who conducted a campaign in Palestine in this period.

Excavations of later levels revealed houses and a fort dating to the Hellenistic period. Herod the Great rebuilt the city in 9 BCE, and named it after his father Antipater. It was greatly enlarged in C2–3 CE.

Kochavi (1981), Beck and Kochavi (*NEAEHL* 1: 62–72), Kochavi (*OEANE* 1: 147–51), Laughlin (2006: 20–4).

Aphrodisias (map 5) City in the region of Caria, southwestern Anatolia, 200 km southeast of Izmir. From M1 BCE through C6 CE, Aphrodisias was an important cult-centre of the goddess Aphrodite, who may have been a descendant of an earlier nature or fertility deity. According to Stephanus of Byzantium, the city was originally called Ninoe after its reputed founder, a Babylonian king called Ninos (*sic*).

The site was first excavated by P. Gaudin in 1914, subsequently by G. Jacopi in 1937, and on a much more extensive scale by K. Erim for New York University from 1961 to 1990. Excavations by New York University continue to the present day, currently under the direction of R. R. R. Smith and C. Ratté. Aphrodisias' best-preserved remains date to the Roman imperial period. But occupation of the site dates back at least to the end of the Chalcolithic Age (late M4). Settlement continued through the succeeding Bronze Ages, during which the city may have been the centre for a mother-goddess cult, as indicated by significant Bronze Age remains on the site. Aphrodisias' Bronze Age name is unknown, though it may appear among the western Anatolian place-names attested in Late Bronze Age Hittite texts.

E. Akurgal (1973: 171–5), Erim (*PECS* 68–70; 1986), Kaletsch (*BNP* 1: 828–9), Smith and Ratté (2006).

Apina see Upi (2).

Apishal Early and Middle Bronze Age city in northern Mesopotamia, probably to be located to the west of the Euphrates, in the region between Carchemish and Aleppo. It is to be distinguished from the southern Mesopotamian city Apishal which lay

Figure 11 Aphrodisias, temple of Aphrodite, Roman period.

within the Sumerian city-state Umma. Later literary compositions and a Babylonian chronicle text (**ABC* 154) mention Apishal under its ruler Rish-Adad as one of the places defeated by the Akkadian king Naram-Sin (2254–2218) in the 'Great Revolt' (see also **Chav.* 30–2). But the episode is not mentioned (or not preserved) in inscriptions of Naram-Sin himself. (The city of Armanum, perhaps to be identified with Aleppo, was also ruled by a man called Rish-Adad at this time.) Naram-Sin's conquest of Apishal by breaching its walls, and his capture of Rish-Adad, are reported in later omen texts where a word-play is evident: the Akkadian word for 'breach' and the place-name Apishal have the same root consonants. The city is subsequently attested in the reign of the Assyrian king Shamshi-Adad I (1796–1775), when a king of Apishal called Mekum received a consignment of tin from Yasmah-Addu, Assyrian viceroy at Mari. Mekum refused to send wine in exchange, despite the urgings of Aplahanda, king of Carchemish.

Gadd (1971: 429, 442), *Charpin and Ziegler (1997).

Apku (*Tell Abu Marya*) (map 10) Early Iron Age city in northern Mesopotamia, northwest of mod. Mosul. The origins of the city are unknown, but a palace was built there by the late M2 Assyrian king Ashur-resh-ishi I (**RIMA* 1: 319). An inscription of the Assyrian king Ashur-bel-kala (1073–1056) mentions work on the palace which Ashur-resh-ishi had begun but not, apparently, completed (**RIMA* 2: 105). The city subsequently fell into ruins but was rebuilt c. 900 by Adad-nirari II (911–891), who also had a palace constructed there as a royal residence (**RIMA* 2: 149). Ashurnasirpal II (883–859) followed suit, laying the foundations of a palace of his own in the city, with tablets of silver and gold (**RIMA* 2: 342). During the reign of Adad-nirari III (810–783), Apku was among the cities and lands which the king assigned to the authority of his governor Nergal-erish (Palil-erish) (**RIMA* 3: 209).

Apollonia (map 15) M1 BCE–M1 CE inland hilltop city in Lycia, southwestern Anatolia, near the mod. village Siçak. Its material remains, including sections of town walls, a theatre, a vaulted reservoir, and a number of cisterns, are predominantly of Roman date. Inscriptions naming the city also date to the Roman period. Among Apollonia's many funerary monuments, six are pillar-tombs of the type found elsewhere in Lycia, most notably at Xanthus. The tombs are uninscribed, but their architectural features suggest an early C4 date.

Bean (*PECS* 72; 1978: 104), Wirbelauer (*BNP* 1: 866).

Appan Middle Bronze Age city located in the district of Mari on the middle Euphrates, adjacent to the city of Mishlan. It is frequently attested in the Mari archives during the reign of Zimri-Lim (1774–1762), to whom it was subject.

LKM 606 (refs).

Ap(p)arazu (***Tell al Barša?***) Iron Age city in northern Syria belonging to the Aramaean kingdom of Bit-Agusi. It was captured by the Assyrian king Shalmaneser III during his campaign in the region in 848 (**RIMA* 3: 38, 47), when Bit Agusi was ruled by Arame (858–834). Arne and Muru were other cities of Bit-Agusi which fell to the Assyrians on this campaign.

CHLI I: 389, Lipiński (2000: 207, 281).

Apum (map 10) Middle Bronze Age kingdom in the eastern part of the Habur triangle, northern Mesopotamia, first attested in the Mari archives during the reign of Zimri-Lim (1774–1762). It lay close to, and perhaps bordered upon, the territory of the city originally called Shehna, renamed Shubat-Enlil by the Assyrian king Shamshi-Adad I when he established it as his royal capital (c. 1785) (see ***Leilan, Tell***). Following Shamshi-Adad's death in 1775, a dynasty from Apum won control over Shubat-Enlil, and made it Apum's capital. From then on the city was commonly referred to by its original name Shehna. Apum's and Shehna's fluctuating fortunes, as reflected in the Mari archives, illustrate the complex and constantly changing power structures and political relationships of the period throughout the Habur triangle. Around 1771, Apum's ruler Turum-natki was one of seventeen northern Mesopotamian kings who received warning from Zimri-Lim, via an intermediary, of an imminent invasion of the region by the forces of Ibal-pi-El II, king of Eshnunna. Ibal-pi-El succeeded in occupying Shehna/Shubat-Enlil, and while his kingdom was under Eshnunnite occupation, Turum-natki died. When the Eshnunnite army departed the capital, they left behind a force of several thousand men, who were assigned to the responsibility of Turum-nakti's son Zuzu, now installed as ruler of the country. On another occasion, an Elamite force under the command of Kunnam entered Apum and occupied its capital. The king of Apum at this time was a man called Haya-Abum, whom Kunnam referred to rhetorically as a 'son of Zimri-Lim' (**LKM* 495, no.

14.102). By 1761, when the Mari archives came to an end, Shehna/Shubat-Enlil and presumably the kingdom of which it was the capital were controlled by Himdiya, king of Andarig.

Apum's last three kings – Mutiya, Till-Abnu, and Yakun-ashar – are known to us from information contained in texts discovered in the royal archives of Shehna/ Shubat-Enlil, dating to the period 1750–1728. These kings maintained their power through alliances which they made with various other kings in the region (see ***Leilan, Tell***) until their capital was conquered and destroyed by the Babylonian king Samsu-iluna in 1728. With the destruction and abandonment of Shubat-Enlil, the kingdom of Apum came abruptly to an end.

Mesop. 203, 348–51.

Aqarbani (Naqarabani) Iron Age city in the middle Euphrates region, belonging to the land of Laqe and located north of the city of Nagiate. During the course of his last recorded campaign in 885, the Assyrian king Tukulti-Ninurta II approached the city, received tribute from its ruler Mudad(da), and encamped his army in its fields, on his progress up the Euphrates (**RIMA* 2: 175). In 878 Tukulti-Ninurta's son and successor Ashurnasirpal II, conducting a similar expedition along the middle Euphrates (though in the opposite direction), also received tribute from the city and set up camp for the night there (**RIMA* 2: 213). In this latter case, the Assyrian text refers to the city as Naqarabani.

Lipiński (2000: 94).

Arachosia (Old Persian **Harauvatish**) (map 16) Country attested in Iranian and Classical sources, and located in mod. Afghanistan. Its chief city is perhaps to be identified with the site of Old Kandahar (Vogelsang, 1992: 48–9), where excavations indicate occupation during the Persian period (C6–4). Arachosia was among the eastern lands of the Persian empire listed in the inscriptions of Darius I (522–486), e.g. in his Bisitun inscription (**DB* 6), and also in the *daiva* inscription (see glossary) of his son and successor Xerxes (**XPh* 3). These lands had been incorporated into the empire by Cyrus II, probably during a campaign which he conducted into Central Asia some time after his conquest of Babylon in 539. No contemporary record of such a campaign survives, but a later reference to it may be contained in Pliny the Elder's account (6.92) of Persia's eastern satrapies, including Arachosia. Elsewhere, Pliny refers to a city of the Arachosians (6.61). A tradition recorded by Pliny and subsequently by Stephanus of Byzantium relates that the legendary Assyrian queen Semiramis had visited Arachosia and founded a city there.

In the uprisings which confronted Darius I at the beginning of his reign (522), the Arachosian satrap Vivana declared his support for Darius. In response, Vahyazdata, a pretender to the Persian throne (he claimed that he was Bardiya, brother of Cyrus' successor Cambyses), dispatched an expedition to Arachosia in an attempt to win it over to his side. But the province remained loyal to Darius, and under Vivana's command inflicted a series of defeats on the rebel force, notably in the battle of Kapishakanish fought in 521. The rebels' commanding officer was captured and executed. These events are reported in the Bisitun inscription (**DB* 45–7).

Representatives from Arachosia may be depicted as the seventh delegation on the east staircase of the Audience Hall (Apadana) at Persepolis, bringing tribute to Darius in the form of stone mortars and pestles, ivory, camels, and feline animal pelts. But the identification is uncertain. (The representatives have also been thought to be Drangians.) Other information about Arachosia is very meagre. Serpentine and alabaster were mined there, and ivory was brought from the country for use in the construction of Darius I's palace at Susa (**DSf* 11, **DSz* 10). Arachosia apparently played an important role in the history of Zoroastrianism.

According to Arrian (*Anabasis* 3.28.1), Alexander the Great conquered Arachosia on his way to Bactria (327), and appointed Menon as its governor.

Vogelsang (1992: 335, refs).

Arad (map 8) 10 ha settlement-mound in the northeastern Negev desert region, mod. Israel, 35 km northeast of Beersheba. The first phase of its history extends through five main occupation strata, dating from the beginning of M4 (Chalcolithic Age) to mid M3 (Early Bronze Age), followed by a long period of abandonment. The site was inhabited once more in the early Iron Age and continued to be occupied until C1 CE when it was again abandoned until reoccupied by the Arabs in C7–8 CE. The period extending from the early Iron Age to the Roman imperial period is represented by ten archaeological strata (XII–III), with the two final strata (II–I) dating to the periods of Arab and Bedouin occupation respectively.

Eighteen seasons of excavation were carried out on the Early Bronze Age city, between 1962 and 1984, by Israeli teams under the direction of R. Amiran. From c. 3200 to 3000 (Stratum IV), a small unfortified village occupied the site. Egyptian ceramic ware from this level indicates that trading links with Egypt were already in operation at this time. Subsequently in Stratum III, the settlement took on an urban character, with the construction of a city wall (with gates, posterns, and towers), a religious precinct, a 'palace', a reservoir, and a number of public buildings surrounding the reservoir. Domestic and public buildings featured a rectangular 'broadroom' structure, with an entrance on the long side, access by several stone steps leading down from street level, benches along the walls, a central pillar for supporting a flat roof, a courtyard, and one or two smaller rooms which may have been used for storage purposes. The 'palace' was a substantial complex consisting of a network of rooms, courtyards, and passageways. Its nucleus was a large room with antechamber and two adjoining courtyards. This first urban phase of the settlement's existence ended in destruction by enemy attack c. 2800. However, its material culture continued in the succeeding (Stratum II) phase. Excavation of this phase brought to light within the religious precinct two twin-temple structures, one large and one small, and another single-roomed building apparently used for cultic purposes.

The excavators of these early phases of the site have commented that despite its arid location, Early Bronze Age Arad had a highly diversified economy, with evidence of a thriving agricultural base, as illustrated both by palaeobotanical evidence (barley, wheat, peas, lentils, chickpeas, olives) and animal bones (sheep, cattle, and goats). The settlement also engaged in long-distance trade with Sinai, Egypt, and northern Canaan. Finds of jewellery, along with copper and flint awls and drills, indicate the existence of local specialized craft industries. Stamp and cylinder seals made of chalk were also unearthed by the excavators. Small rural settlements surrounding the main settlement are thought to have been economically and politically associated with it. Ilan and Amiran note that Arad was in fact the only urban entity in the Negev during

Early Bronze Age II, and probably functioned as the focal point for much of the region's commercial and political activity. This apparently flourishing settlement was followed after its destruction (environmental and political factors have been suggested as possible reasons for the destruction) by a much smaller settlement whose inhabitants, the excavators suggest, may have been squatters who occupied the ruined city before its final abandonment c. 2650.

Settlement resumed in C11, in the Iron Age I period, on the northeastern hill of the site. Excavations in this second major phase of the site's history were conducted by Israeli teams from 1962 onwards under the direction of Y. Aharoni, jointly with R. Amiran in 1962. The excavations brought to light a series of six Israelite citadels, extending from C10 to early C6 (Iron Age Strata XI to VI), all of which were apparently destroyed in sudden attacks. Typically, the citadels were surrounded by casemate walls with projecting towers on the corners and two towers on each side. Within them were located storerooms, industrial installations, and residential areas, and the first Israelite temple to be discovered in an archaeological excavation. Excavations conducted on the site by Z. Herzog between 1976 and 1977, and subsequently between 1995 and 1996, established that the temple existed through only two strata (X and IX) rather than five as concluded by the earlier excavators. It was probably built in C10 or C9 and abandoned towards the end of C8. Some 223 inscribed pottery sherds (ostraca) are among the most important finds to come from the site during its Iron Age II phase (Strata IX–VI) (**CS* III: 81–5). They include 131 Hebrew inscriptions, which are primarily administrative in character, and contain records of tax payments and letters dealing with the delivery of food supplies to troops and Phoenician merchants, the latter apparently in Arad's employ. Many of the ostraca appear to date to the first years of C6, when Judah was invaded by the Babylonian king Nebuchadnezzar II (c. 597).

Following the destruction of the sixth citadel, the site was again abandoned, marking the end of Israelite settlement there, with a new occupation in C5 during the Persian period. The most important find of this period is an assemblage of eighty-five Aramaic ostraca. This Stratum V level was again probably a citadel, built on a smaller scale than its predecessors and destroyed during the Hellenistic period. Later fortified structures were built in C3 (Stratum IV), in C1 during the Roman period (Stratum III), and in C7 CE under Arab occupation, when the Roman structure was restored and enlarged. Some time after destruction of the fortress' buildings in C8 CE, the mound was used as a Bedouin cemetery.

Arad is frequently attested in *OT* tradition, e.g. as one of the conquered Canaanite cities (Joshua 12:14). However, Canaanite Arad cannot refer to the site being discussed here since the latter has no Middle or Late Bronze Age remains. Scholars have made various attempts to explain this apparent anomaly – e.g. by suggesting that Canaanite Arad was not a city but the name of the entire district (thus B. Mazar).

Y. Aharoni/Amiran/Ilan/M. Aharoni (*NEAEHL* 1: 75–87), Ilan/Amiran/Herzog/Lemaire (the last on the Arad inscriptions) (*OEANE* 1: 169–77), Herzog (2002), Laughlin (2006: 25–9).

Aradus see Arwad.

Aram Name used in association with other names in Iron Age texts to indicate cities and lands which came under the control of the Aramaeans. The name is sometimes used in *OT* sources on its own as a designation for the kingdom of (Aram-)Damascus (e.g. 2 Kings 8:28–9), one of the most important and powerful states in the Levant. Aram is attested also as a personal name in the *OT*. It was first so used as the name of the fifth son of Shem, grandson of Noah (Genesis 10:22). In historical sources, a toponym *Aramu* is first attested in M3 texts from Ebla.

Lipiński (2000: 25–40).

Aramaeans Iron Age population groups inhabiting large areas of the western Asian world, especially Syria and Mesopotamia, and speaking a West Semitic language called Aramaic. They are first explicitly attested in Assyrian texts of early C11, in conflict with the Assyrian king Tiglath-pileser I (1114–1076), who claims to have confronted the Ahlamu-Aramaeans on twenty-eight campaigns across the Euphrates (**RIMA* 2: 43). Tiglath-pileser's successor-but-one, Ashur-bel-kala (1073–1056), reports numerous campaigns against them (**RIMA* 2: 93, 94, 98, 101, 102). Their relatively extensive spread through the middle Euphrates region at this time is indicated by Ashur-bel-kala's claim that he brought about their defeat from the city of Anat in the land of Suhu to the city of Rapiqu in Babylonia. He also reports a military confrontation with them at the city of Shasiru (**RIMA* 2: 101). The Babylonian king Adad-apla-iddina (1069–1048) reports desecration of the sanctuaries of his land (including Akkad, Der (3), Nippur, Sippar, and Dur-Kurigalzu) by Aramaean and Sutaean invaders (**ABC* 180–1, **RIMB* 2: 50).

Scholarly opinion is divided as to whether the Aramaeans were in origin tribal pastoral groups who migrated into Syria and northern Mesopotamia from the fringes of the Syrian desert, or were the descendants of the West Semitic populations, like the Amorites, who already occupied parts of Syria in M2. Lack of any evidence for the former makes the latter more likely. From C11 onwards a number of Aramaean states emerged in Syria, Mesopotamia, and eastern Anatolia in the wake of the collapse and disappearance of the Late Bronze Age kingdoms in the region. Some of the more important of these were Bit-Zamani, Bit-Bahiani, Bit-Adini, Bit-Agusi, Aram-Damascus, and Sam'al (Zincirli). The prefix 'Bit' ('House [of]') reflects the likely tribal origins of these states. As discussed under the separate entries on these states, some submitted to Assyrian domination already in C9, but others fiercely maintained their independence – the Assyrian king Adad-nirari II (911–891) conducted no fewer than eight campaigns against them – in some cases until the second half of C8. In 814 an Aramaean contingent was among the enemy forces assembled against the Assyrian king Shamshi-Adad V when he confronted the Babylonian king Marduk-balassu-iqbi at the eastern Babylonian city of Dur-Papsukkal (q.v.) (**RIMA* 3: 188). The Assyrian king Tiglath-pileser III (745–727) claimed widespread conquests and annexations of the lands inhabited by the Aramaeans (**Tigl. III* 130–1, 160–1).

Despite the constant menace of Assyria, the Aramaean states failed to form any durable union amongst themselves, though some of them occasionally joined forces to meet a specific military threat, as in the alliance formed to confront Shalmaneser III at Qarqar (q.v.) on the Orontes in 853. Aramaean military coalitions could present formidable opposition to Assyrian aggression. But such coalitions ultimately lacked the cohesion or the persistence to keep the Assyrians permanently at bay. There was a clear incentive for submitting to Assyrian overlordship, for those Aramaean rulers who did so were left in power in their states, and allowed a relatively large measure of autonomy, provided they remained loyal to their overlord. In an Assyrian-dominated world, the Aramaean states enjoyed, by and large, a relatively prosperous existence, and a generally peaceful coexistence with their neighbours, the Neo-Hittite kingdoms, until their eventual destruction by the Assyrians in late C8. A consequence of this destruction was the widespread dispersal of their populations throughout the regions that constituted the Neo-Assyrian empire.

The Aramaeans never developed a distinctive culture of their own. Rather, what might be called Aramaean culture was largely a composite of elements drawn from the civilizations of their neighbours, most notably the Neo-Hittites, the Assyrians, and the Phoenicians. This is evident, for example, in the relief sculptures in Neo-Hittite and subsequently Assyrian style which decorated the palaces of Aramaean cities. Aramaean religion had its origins in M2 West Semitic religious traditions. The weather god Hadad (Adad), also a god of fertility, appears to have been the chief deity of the Aramaean world. Other important deities included Shamash, Resheph, and the moon god Sin/Shanar.

Ironically, the demolition of the Aramaean states by the Assyrians helped contribute to the substantial expansion of Aramaean influence in the Near and Middle East. The Aramaeans were the most populous of all the Iron Age ethnic groups, and their dispersal by the Assyrians led to large numbers of Aramaean settlers being distributed through many parts of Assyria and Babylonia as well as Syria–Palestine. By this process, Aramaic became the main language of communication throughout the Near and Middle East, replacing Akkadian as the international language of diplomacy. The script in which the language was written was an alphabetic script, taken over from the Phoenicians. It was normally written on perishable materials such as parchment which have not survived to the present day in the Mesopotamian region, in contrast to the significantly more durable clay tablets bearing writing in cuneiform script.

Despite the widespread adoption of the Aramaic language, the information we have about the Aramaeans themselves from their own written sources remains very limited. Most of our knowledge about their history is derived from Assyrian and biblical texts. And while a combination of written and archaeological sources provides a significant amount of information about the more important Aramaean states, we know very little about the many Aramaean tribes who must have lived outside an urban context, or, more generally, about Aramaean tribal structures and the *mores* and ethos which underpinned Aramaean society.

Dion (1995), Cook (*OEANE* 1: 178–84, s.v. Aramaic language and literature), Lipiński (2000).

Aramale (Armarili) Iron Age Urartian city in eastern Anatolia, centre of a province close to the Urartian royal city Arzashkun. It is probably to be located to the southwest of Lake Urmia, though a location near the shores of Lake Van has also been proposed. The city was destroyed by the Assyrian king Shalmaneser III during his campaign into Urartian territory in his third regnal year (856). He advanced upon the city after capturing and destroying Arzashkun, stronghold of the Urartian king Arame (**RIMA* 3: 21). The province, but not the city, of Armarili, is also mentioned as the third of five Urartian lands traversed by Sargon II during his eighth campaign (714) (**ARAB* II: 90–1).

Salvini (1995b: 46–8).

Aram-Damascus see Damascus.

Aram-Zobah see Zobah.

Aratta Legendary city of great wealth and power, referred to in M3 Sumerian literary and lexical texts, and often sought, on the basis of the literary references to it, in the highlands of Iran east or northeast of Anshan. Aratta may have been a real city, but this cannot be confirmed. Its fabled wealth was due to the vast quantities of precious stones and metals which the local population extracted from their mines. According to the literary tradition, seven mountains had to be crossed within or beyond Anshan in order to reach Aratta. The city's conquest was the greatest achievement of Enmerkar, a legendary early Sumerian king of Uruk known from several Sumerian poems. In two of these poems, the king is supported in his attack upon Aratta by his son, and by the hero Lugalbanda and his seven brothers. A city named Aratta is supposedly attested also in M1 texts, and there has been some debate as to whether it should be identified with Sumerian Aratta; however, the M1 attested city is clearly located in Babylonia, and in any case the cuneiform signs which represent its name should be read 'Bas' (a town near Sippar) rather than 'Aratta'.

Cohen (1973), Berlin (1979), T. Potts (1994: 12–14), **CS* I: 547–50, Joannès (*DCM* 285–7, s.v. Enmerkar), Majidzadeh (2003), D. T. Potts (2005b).

Arawa see **Urua**.

Araxa (map 15) M1 BCE–M1 CE city at the northern end of the Xanthus valley in Lycia, southwestern Anatolia, near the mod. village of Ören. Tombs of Lycian house-type may indicate that the city's origins date back at least to mid M1. However, there are no known inscriptions of this period. Among the town's earliest written records is a C2 decree of the citizens of Araxa honouring one of their fellow citizens, Orthagoras, and referring to wars in which Araxa had engaged with the cities of Bubon and Cibyra. Araxa was a member of the Lycian League, formed in early C2, and had appealed to other member cities for assistance in these wars.

Bean (1978: 70–2).

Arbakku Iron Age city in northern Mesopotamia, in the westernmost of the regions called Habhu in Assyrian texts (see **Habhu (5)**). The Assyrian king Ashurnasirpal II conquered it during a campaign which he conducted in the region in his fifth regnal year (879) (**RIMA* 2: 210–11, 260). He also conquered and plundered on this campaign the fortress-settlements Iiaia and Salaniba which belonged to Arbakku.

Arbatu Iron Age city in the middle Euphrates region, belonging to the land of Laqe. During his last recorded campaign in 885, the Assyrian king Tukulti-Ninurta II encamped his forces overnight in the city, and received tribute from its ruler Haranu (**RIMA* 2: 176).

Arbela (Urbil(um), ***Arbil/Erbil***) (map 10) City in northern Mesopotamia, located in the plain lying east of the Tigris between the Greater and Lesser Zab rivers. Its history of occupation extends from (at least) the last centuries of the Early Bronze Age to the Roman period. There has been no significant excavation of the anc. site because it is overlain by the mod. city. First attested, under the form Urbilum, in sources of the Ur III period, the region in which it lay was devastated by the Ur III king Shulgi (2094–2047), and annexed to the Ur III empire by Shulgi's successor Amar-Sin in the second year of his reign. During the period of the Old Assyrian kingdom, Urbil(um) was among the cities conquered by Shamshi-Adad I (1796–1775) while he was campaigning against the country of Qabra in 1781 (**RIMA* 1: 64). Shamshi-Adad's victory stele, said to have come from Sinjar or Mardin, reports the king's capture of the cities of the land of Urbil and the installation of his garrisons there.

Early in M1, the city, now called Arbela (Assyrian Arbail), became part of the Neo-Assyrian empire. Under Assyrian sovereignty, it served on several occasions as the starting-point for Assyrian campaigns to the east. However in 826, near the end of Shalmaneser III's reign, it participated in a rebellion against Assyrian rule, along with Ashur, Nineveh, and twenty-four smaller Assyrian cities. The rebellion was crushed several years later by Shalmaneser's son and successor Shamshi-Adad V (**RIMA* 3: 183). The name Arbela, which means 'four gods', seems to have been due to a false interpretation by the Assyrians of the original form of the city's name. The new form was obviously intended to highlight the sacred character of the city. Among the deities worshipped in the city, the goddess Ishtar assumed particular significance, and indeed Ishtar of Arbela became one of the most important deities of the Assyrian empire.

Arbela reached the height of its prosperity in the reign of the Assyrian king Ashurbanipal (668–630/627), who established one of his principal residences in the city. Here he received ambassadors from the Urartian king, doubtless Rusa II (see Appendix III), after a victory over the Elamites in mid C7. In 615, the city fell to the Median king Cyaxares, but thenceforth played an important role in the history of the Persian empire (C6–4). It was near Arbela, at the small town of Gaugamela, that Alexander the Great inflicted a decisive defeat on the Persian emperor Darius III in October 331. Darius used Arbela itself as a base for his military operations.

Villard (*DCM* 68–9).

Ardata (map 6) Late Bronze Age city in Amurru (Syria), south of Sumur. Subject to Egypt, it was captured, in mid C14, by a neighbouring king called Miya, an agent or ally of the Amurrite warlord Abdi-Ashirta (**EA* 75). Ardata was no doubt among the cities liberated by Egyptian troops following their capture of Abdi-Ashirta (see under **Amurru**). But it was reoccupied soon after by Abdi-Ashirta's sons (**EA* 104). One of these sons, Aziru, killed Ardata's ruler (name unknown) (**EA* 140).

Ardini see **Musasir.**

Argana see **Adennu.**

Argishtihinili (Armavir) (map 20) Iron Age Urartian fortress and administrative centre consisting of two citadels and areas of lower settlement, located on the Araxes r. in the plain of Ararat, eastern Anatolia. It was founded in early C8 by the Urartian king Argishti I as part of a series of fortress-settlements designed to control and administer the surrounding territories. The site was excavated over a period of two decades, beginning in 1962, by a team from the Institute of Archaeology and Ethnography of the

Armenian SSR Academy of Sciences, under the direction of A. Martirosjan. It is considered particularly important for the information it provides about Urartian domestic architecture. Several centuries after the demise of the Urartian kingdom, Argishtihinili, now named Armavir, became the capital of Armenia under the Orontid dynasty, founded by Orontes I in early C4. Towards the end of C3, Orontes IV shifted his administration to a new city, but Armavir remained the kingdom's religious centre.

Zimansky (1998: 249–50).

Aria (map 16) M1 Central Asian country attested in Iranian and Greek sources, and located in the region of eastern Iran–western Afghanistan, perhaps in the vicinity of mod. Herat (Afghanistan). It was among the eastern lands of the Persian empire listed several times in the inscriptions of Darius I (522–486), e.g. in his Bisitun inscription (**DB* 6), and also in the *daiva* inscription (see glossary) of his son and successor Xerxes (**XPh* 3). Herodotus (3.93) includes Arians in the peoples making up what he called the sixteenth Persian province (but see glossary under **satrapy**), and he lists a contingent of Arians under the command of Sisamnes, son of Hydarnes, among the forces assembled by Xerxes for his invasion of Greece in 481 (7.66). He reports that the Arian troops were equipped like the Bactrians, but carried Median-style bows. On the east staircase of the Audience Hall (Apadana) at Persepolis, representatives from Aria are depicted as Delegation IV, bringing tribute to Darius in the form of a camel with two humps, garments, various vessels, and (apparently) a leopard skin.

Vogelsang (1992: 193).

Ariaspae An Iranian tribal group encountered by Alexander the Great on the Helmand r. in his progress through the land of the Sarangians/Zarangians (Persian Drangiana). The tribe had once provided food and shelter for the army of the Persian king Cyrus II (559–530) in his war with the Scythians. Cyrus had apparently rewarded them by granting them their freedom. From then on they were known as the Benefactors (Greek *Euergetae*). Further rewards were bestowed upon them by Alexander. In recognition of their services to Cyrus, and impressed by their political institutions and good character, Alexander not only confirmed their freedom, but also allegedly offered them as much of their neighbours' lands as they wanted. The tribe was later incorporated into Parthian territory.

Arrian, *Anab.* 3.27.4, Curtius 7.3.1.

Aribua Fortified Iron Age city located near the middle Orontes r. in northern Syria. It belonged to the Neo-Hittite kingdom Pat(t)in (Assyrian Unqi). In 870, the Assyrian king Ashurnasirpal II had invaded Patin and received the submission of its king, Lubarna, in Lubarna's royal capital Kinalua. Ashurnasirpal then led his troops south to Aribua, which he occupied and used as a base for his military operations against Luhutu. Luhutu was the northern province of the kingdom of Hamath, which lay to the south of Patin.

**RIMA* 2: 218.

Aridu (1) Iron Age city in the Habur r. region of northwestern Mesopotamia, belonging originally to the Aramaean kingdom Guzana but later annexed to Assyria. Guzana was first conquered by the Assyrian king Ashurnasirpal II (883–859), and reconquered in 808 by Adad-nirari III after a period of rule by a local dynasty of governors. References to Aridu occur in a royal grant of Adad-nirari III, and in a letter which Sargon II (721–705) received from one of his officials. Lipiński proposes an identification with Tell ʿArada, which lies on the Gümüs r., one of the tributaries of the Habur.

Lipiński (2000: 126, with refs).

Aridu (2) Iron Age fortified city in the borderlands between northeastern Mesopotamia and northwestern Iran, near the southwestern frontier of the country of Hubushkia. The Assyrian king Shalmaneser III captured it early in the northern campaign which he conducted in his accession year (859) (**RIMA* 3: 8, 14). He claims to have burnt ten cities in the district around Aridu, but to have used Aridu itself as a base where he received tribute from the nearby lands Hargu, Harmasa, Simerra, Simesi, Sirishu, and Ulmanu.

Arimatta Late Bronze Age city or frontier-post in southern Anatolia. It lay in the border zone between the country of Pitassa, to which it belonged, and the Hulaya River Land, which became part of the kingdom of Tarhuntassa in early C13 (**HDT* 110).

Arin-berd see **Erebuni**.

Arinu (Arinnu, Arini) City attested in late M2 and early M1 Assyrian texts, probably to be located in northeastern Mesopotamia, in the country of Musri (see **Musri (1)**) at the foot of Mt Aisa. In response to a rebellion by Musri against Assyrian rule, the Assyrian king Shalmaneser I (1274–1245) invaded the country, laid siege to and captured Arinu, called a 'holy city', and razed it to the ground (**RIMA* 1: 183). The city was rebuilt, and was again placed under siege by the Assyrians in the reign of Tiglath-pileser I (1114–1076), apparently in response to another anti-Assyrian uprising. The siege was lifted with the voluntary surrender of the city to the Assyrians and the promise thenceforth of regular tribute payments (**RIMA* 2: 23). Arinu was one of three cities lost by the Assyrians to the land of Shubru (= Shubria), but recaptured by the Assyrian king Adad-nirari II (911–891) (**RIMA* 2: 149). The other two cities were Turhu and Zaduru.

Arinna The name of several cities located in Late Bronze Age Anatolia and attested in Hittite texts. One of these cities was among the western lands against which the Hittite king Tudhaliya I campaigned early in C14 (*Garstang and Gurney, 1959: 121); another lay near Kaska territory in northern Anatolia, and a third may have been located in southern Anatolia. But the most important city so called lay in the Hittite homeland and was dedicated to the worship of the sun goddess, consort of the storm god of Hatti. It was one of the major cult-centres of the Hittite world. The Hittite king had a palace there, where he resided while visiting the city during his annual religious pilgrimages. A number of religious festivals were celebrated in the city, notably the AN.TAH.SUM or 'crocus' festival, which took place in spring. Information from the texts indicates that Arinna, city of the sun goddess, lay one day's journey from the Hittite capital Hattusa. It is commonly, though not conclusively, identified with the site now called Alaca Höyük, located 40 km north of Hattusa.

RGTC 6: 32–6.

Arinnanda Late Bronze Age mountain stronghold in Arzawa, western Anatolia, perhaps to be identified with Classical Mt Mycale (mod. Samsun Dağ) between Ephesus and Miletus. Hittite deportees, taken as booty by the Hittites during Mursili II's Arzawa campaigns, sought refuge there (as also in Puranda) in an attempt to escape Hittite custody (c. 1318) (see **Arzawa**). Mursili's troops ascended the mountain on foot, placed the stronghold under siege, and starved the deportees into submission.

**AM* 54–7, **CS* II: 85; on identification, Hawkins in Easton *et al.* (2002: 97–8).

Aripsa Late Bronze Age fortified city located in northeastern Anatolia on the shore of the Black Sea, in the country of Azzi. The Hittite king Mursili II captured and sacked it while campaigning in the region during his tenth regnal year (c. 1312) (**AM* 132–5, **CS* II 90). Much of the city's population had taken refuge in the nearby mountains on the approach of the Hittite army, leaving its troops behind to defend it. On its fall, the city's defenders were among the spoils of war conveyed, along with cattle, sheep, and other booty, back to the Hittite homeland.

Arkania Iron Age mountain land located northwest of the Kashiyari range (mod. Tur ʿAbdin) in northern Mesopotamia, on the east bank of the Tigris, in the vicinity of the westernmost region called Habhu in Assyrian texts (see **Habhu (5)**). The Assyrian king Ashurnasirpal II includes it in his report of the devastation he inflicted on the cities on both sides of the Tigris during his 866 campaign (**RIMA* 2: 220). It should be distinguished from Mt Arqania (q.v.), which features in the same account.

Arman Iron Age city in northeastern Mesopotamia to the east of the upper Diyala, in the district of Ugar-sallu. It is first attested among the conquests of the Assyrian king Tiglath-pileser I (1114–1076). These occurred in the context of Tiglath-pileser's struggle with the Babylonians over control of the Diyala region (**RIMA* 2: 53). Lubdan and Turshan were other cities in the immediate locality which fell to Tiglath-pileser. In 850 Arman became a final refuge for Marduk-bel-usati, who had rebelled against his brother, the Babylonian king Marduk-zakir-shumi I. The rebel's forces were subsequently defeated by the Assyrian Shalmaneser III in a battle outside the city of Gannanate (q.v.). Shalmaneser had come to Marduk-zakir-shumi's aid at the latter's request. He now marched upon Arman, laid siege to it, and captured and plundered it. Marduk-bel-usati was taken prisoner and put to the sword (**RIMA* 3: 30).

Armanum Bronze Age city, perhaps to be located in northern Syria. It is attested in an inscription of the Akkadian king Naram-Sin (2254–2218), who records his conquest of the city, and the chaining of its king Rish-Adad to the city's entrance gate (**DaK* 255–7, **RIME* 2: 132–4, **CS* II: 244–6). (Coincidentally, another king called Rish-Adad, ruler of the city of Apishal in northwestern Mesopotamia, is attested in Naram-Sim's reign, and in later legends.) In the same inscription, Naram-Sin also claims a military victory over Ebla, and boasts that he was the first king to conquer both cities. The linking of Armanum and Ebla in this way suggests that they probably lay relatively close to each other; this and the obvious pride Naram-Sin takes in his achievement, which he refers to several times, indicates that Armanum had a status, at least in this period, commensurate with that of Ebla, which was then at the height of its political and economic development. It is very likely that Armanum was known more commonly by another name. An identification with Aleppo, which lay c. 60 km northeast of Ebla, has been suggested.

Drower (1971: 325–7).

Armavir see **Argishtihinili**.

Armid An important stronghold of the M1 kingdom of Mannaea in mod. Iranian Kurdistan. It was one of the fortresses captured by the Assyrian king Sargon II in 716, during his campaign against the Mannaean king Ullusunu (**ARAB* II: 28).

Arne Iron Age city in north-central Syria belonging to the Aramaean kingdom of Bit-Agusi. It is attested in Assyrian records as the royal city of Arame, son of the kingdom's founder Gusi, during the reign of Shalmaneser III (858–824). In 849 it was captured and destroyed by Shalmaneser in the course of the western campaign which he conducted in his tenth regnal year (**RIMA* 3: 37). The city's capture is also recorded on one of the bronze bands discovered at Balawat (see **Imgur-Enlil**) (**RIMA* 3: 146). Arpad subsequently became the capital of Bit-Agusi.

Lipiński proposes an identification of Arne with Tell Aran, a large fortified settlement-mound northwest of Lake Ğabbul.

CHLI I: 389, Lipiński (2000: 198, 201 map).

Arneae (***Ernes***) (map 15) Small M1 BCE–M1CE city in central Lycia, southwestern Anatolia, 25 km northwest of mod. Finike. Its origins date back at least to C4, since one of its tombs bears a text in the native Lycian language whose attested use on sepulchral and other monuments dates to C5 and C4. Most of the site's remains date to the Byzantine period, when Arneae became the seat of a bishop.

Bean (1978: 134–5).

Arnuna Late Bronze Age city in the land of Nigimhu, central Zagros region. During his second campaign against Nigimhu, the Assyrian king Arik-den-ili (1319–1308) laid siege to and captured the city after destroying its fortifications, forcing the submission of the country's ruler Esini (**RIMA* 1: 126).

Aroer (1) (in Judaea) (map 8) Israelite settlement in the Negev desert, southern Judaea, c. 20 km southeast of Beersheba, with Iron Age and Herodian levels of occupation. There were seven excavation seasons on the site, between 1975 and 1982. The excavations were carried out by the Nelson Glueck School of Biblical Archaeology at the Hebrew Union College in Jerusalem and the Israel Dept of Antiquities and Museums, under the directorships of A. Biran and R. Cohen. Three Iron Age strata were identified (IV–II), spanning the Iron Age II–III periods, and *originally* dated from early–mid C7 to late C7–early C6, the city apparently being founded in the first half of C7 and fortified at that time with a city wall. Stratum IV, representing the site's first occupation phase, seems to have lasted only a few decades before it was succeeded by the Stratum III settlement, which continued the material culture of its predecessor. Its inhabitants used the same buildings, though making a number of modifications to them. But in contrast to its predecessor, the new settlement was unfortified, and in fact extended its boundaries – both signs that it enjoyed a peaceful and prosperous existence. Assyrian influence upon its culture, already evident in Stratum IV, becomes increasingly marked in this level, which also reflects Edomite influence. Recent studies of the ceramic assemblage from Stratum III has suggested that the date of this level should be raised to C8 (Thareani-Sussely, 2007: 71 for refs). The chronology of its Stratum IV predecessor remains unclear.

In Stratum II, now assigned a starting-point in early C7, a tower or fortress was built on the highest point of the mound. The continuing prosperity of the site is reflected in its large pottery assemblage, which has parallels with the ceramic ware found at a number of other contemporaneous sites, including Lachish, 'Ein-Gedi, Ashdod, and Arad, and has helped date this level. Substantial quantities of Edomite pottery also date to this level. Israelite settlement at Aroer came to an end with the Babylonian conquest in early C6. From then on the site was abandoned for half a millennium until reoccupation occurred (Stratum I) in the Herodian or early Roman period (C1 BCE–C1 CE). The city in this period was small, c. 2.5 ha in extent, and was confined to the summit of the mound. It was apparently unwalled, but protected by a fortress, which may have been intended to guard the southern border of Herod the Great's kingdom against the Nabataeans.

Biran (*NEAEHL* 1: 89–92).

Aroer (2) (in Moab) (***Khirbet Ar'air***) (map 8) Israelite fortress built on the King's Highway (q.v.) apparently to control its crossing at the Arnon r. In *OT* tradition, the tribe of Reuben settled there after the Israelite conquest (1 Chronicles 5:8), and it remained an Israelite possession, along with all the other towns along the Arnon, for 300 years (Judges 11:26). However, Mesha, king of Moab, conquered it c. 850 and incorporated it into his own kingdom, rebuilding and substantially strengthening the fortress (Mesha inscription, line 26; **CS* II: 138, **Chav.* 313). He also built a reservoir in front of the fortress' northwest wall, in order to store rainwater. Within a few years, the settlement fell to Hazael, an Aramaean king of Damascus (2 Kings 10:33), and may have remained under Aramaean control until Damascus was conquered by the Assyrian king Tiglath-pileser III in 732. But it suffered its greatest devastation at the hands of the Babylonian king Nebuchadnezzar II in 582, to judge from the C1 CE Jewish writer Josephus (*Jewish Antiquities* 10.181), and was thenceforth only spasmodically occupied during the Hellenistic and Nabataean periods.

Excavations of the site conducted between 1964 and 1966 by E. Olávarri on behalf of the Casa Santiago of Jerusalem uncovered six occupation levels, the first, in two sub-phases, spanning the last three centuries of M3 and the first century of M2. Semi-nomadic occupation and agricultural activity characterized the first sub-phase, rudimentary stone houses the second. The site was then abandoned and not reoccupied until mid C13, in the last century of the Late Bronze Age and the beginning of the Iron Age, when the Israelite fortress was constructed.

Olávarri-Goicoechea (*NEAEHL* 1: 92–3).

Aroer (3) Attested in Joshua 13:25 as an (Iron Age) Ammonite settlement near Rabbah (Rabbath Ammon) in Transjordan.

Arpad (map 7) Iron Age Aramaean city in north-central Syria, belonging to the kingdom of Bit-Agusi. It is perhaps to be identified with mod. Tell Rifa'at (q.v.), located 35 km north of Aleppo. By late C9 Arpad had become the capital of Bit-Agusi, probably during the reign of Attar-shumki (I), son of Adramu and grandson(?) of the kingdom's founder Gusi. In 805 Attar-shumki led a military coalition against the Assyrian king Adad-nirari III, confronting him at the city of Paqarahubunu on the west bank of the middle Euphrates (**RIMA* 3: 205). Though he defeated the coalition on this occasion, Adad-nirari failed to break it up, and it continued to challenge Assyrian sovereignty in the region for at least the next ten years.

In 754 the Assyrian king Ashur-nirari V conducted a campaign against Arpad, following a military operation by his predecessor Ashur-dan III against the city of Hatarikka in the previous year. Lipiński (2000: 216) believes that these campaigns may indicate that a new anti-Assyrian alliance was taking shape in northern Syria at this time. In the aftermath of his Arpad campaign, Ashur-nirari drew up a treaty with Arpad's ruler Mati'ilu, son and successor of Attar-shumki II. Mati'ilu was the inferior partner in the compact, as also in the Assyrian-imposed treaty (or treaties), recorded on the stelae discovered at Sefire (q.v.), which Mati'ilu concluded with his northern neighbour Bar-Ga'yah, king of Ktk (**CS* II: 213–17).

In 743 Arpad played a leading role in a coalition of northern Syrian and eastern Anatolian states, formed against the Assyrian king Tiglath-pileser III. In the ensuing military confrontation, the coalition was soundly defeated, and Arpad was placed under siege by Tiglath-pileser's forces. The siege lasted three years before the city finally fell (see *CHLI* 1: 390, nn. 28–9). From then on, the kingdom of which it had been the capital was converted into an Assyrian province, called Arpad. During the period 722–720 Arpad rose in revolt against its Assyrian overlord Sargon II (**ARAB* II: 70), but after the revolt was put down the province seems to have remained peaceful through the remaining years of the Assyrian empire. Arpad appears in a number of biblical passages, on two occasions in association with the kingdom of Hamath, which lay to its south (2 Kings 18:34, Isaiah 36:19).

CHLI I: 389–90, Lipiński (2000: 195–219), Kahn (2007).

Arqa (Bronze Age **Irqata**, Classical **Arka**, ***Tell ʿArqa***) (maps 6, 7) M2 and M1 city on the coast of northern Lebanon. First attested in the Middle Bronze Age Egyptian Execration texts (see glossary), it lay within the land of Amurru in the Late Bronze Age, south of the city of Sumur. Subject to Egypt, it was captured and occupied by the Habiru forces of the mid C14 Amurrite leader Abdi-Ashirta, who killed its king Aduna. One of the Amarna letters, written by the people of Irqata to the pharaoh (Amenhotep III or Akhenaten), highlights the city's plight and reaffirms its loyalty to its Egyptian overlord (**EA* 100). In mid C9 the Assyrian king Shalmaneser III reports that ten chariots and 10,000 troops from Irqata (Irqanatu) fought in the Syrian military coalition against him at the battle of Qarqar (853) (**RIMA* 3: 23–4). The city is later attested, in the form Arqa, in texts from the reign of the Assyrian king Tiglath-pileser III (745–727) (e.g. **Tigl. III* 152–3). It was one of the places where Tiglath-pileser resettled deportees from other parts of his kingdom (**Tigl. III* 66–7). At that time, it appears to have belonged to the land of Hamath.

Excavations at Tell ʿArqa have been undertaken since 1972 by J.-P. Thalmann on behalf of the French Institute. Occupation dating back to the Pre-pottery Neolithic (c. 8500–6000) has been revealed, but it was during M2 that the city came into prominence. An important 'warrior' grave, dating to early M2, has been discovered, and studies of the Middle Bronze Age ceramics have demonstrated strong connections between the Akkar plain and the Hyksos capital of Avaris (Tell ed-Daba) in the Egyptian Delta.

Hawkins (*RlA* 5: 164–6), Thalmann (2006).

Arqania Iron Age mountain region located in the western part of the Kashiyari range (mod. Tur ʿAbdin) of northern Mesopotamia. During his campaign in the region in 866, the Assyrian king Ashurnasirpal II entered the land and took possession of the district of Mallanu which lay within it; he also claimed to have burned the cities between Mts Amadanu and Arqania (**RIMA* 2: 220).

Lipiński (2000: 146).

Arrapha (*Kirkuk*) (map 10) City and kingdom in northeastern Mesopotamia in the region east of the Tigris, on the Adhaim r., and serving as the western terminus of an important trade route from Mesopotamia to Iran. Excavation of the anc. city has not proved possible since its remains lie beneath mod. Kirkuk. Its recorded history extends from the Early Bronze Age to the Hellenistic period.

Arrapha is first attested in written records of the Ur III empire. Subsequently it appears in texts of the Old Assyrian and Old Babylonian kingdoms (Middle Bronze Age). The Assyrian king Shamshi-Adad I (1796–1775) records his capture of the city during his expedition in the Lesser Zab region against the kingdom of Qabra (**RIMA* 1: 64), and the sacrifices he made there to the sun god and the storm god. A business letter from Arrapha's neighbour Nuzi, which lay 10 km to the southwest, makes it clear that the city was a base for merchant operations in the Old Assyrian period. Arrapha also appears in correspondence from Mari dating to the reign of Zimri-Lim (1774–1762), as one of the states with which Zimri-Lim had diplomatic dealings. In this period, the city was subject to the Babylonian king Hammurabi, but was lost to Babylonian rule during the reign of Hammurabi's son and successor Samsu-iluna (1749–1712). Subsequently, it came under strong Hurrian influence, and by C14 had become the capital of a small principality with a largely Hurrian population, subject to the Hurrian kingdom of Mitanni. Its territory included the city of Nuzi. Texts from Nuzi refer to Arrapha's royal family, and to its principal temples, dedicated to the storm god, the god Nergal, and the goddess Ishtar of Nineveh.

Following the destruction of the Mitannian empire by the Hittite king Suppiluliuma I (1350–1322), Arrapha was incorporated into the Middle Assyrian kingdom, which arose in the wake of Mitanni's fall. Later it came under the control of the Babylonian Kassite dynasty, but was regained by the Assyrian king Tukulti-Ninurta I following his conquest of Babylonia in 1235. In a group of administrative documents excavated at Ashur, it is listed among the places which sent agricultural produce to Ashur in the brief reign of the Assyrian king Ninurta-tukulti-Ashur (1133). But Assyrian overlordship could not guarantee the city's protection against external aggressors, and in this same period, the region in which it lay was invaded by the Elamite king Shilhak-Inshushinak (1150–1120), who temporarily occupied a number of Assyrian territories. In the following centuries, control over Arrapha and other states in its region was contested by a number of Assyrian and Babylonian kings who sought to establish their dominance over the borderlands which lay between their kingdoms. In late C10 the Assyrian king Adad-nirari II seized it from his Babylonian counterpart

Shamash-mudammiq in the course of his conquest and annexation of large parts of Babylonian territory (**RIMA* 2: 148). But a few years later, Shamash-mudammiq's successor Nabu-shum-ukin I probably restored the city to Babylonian control.

Subsequently Arrapha came once more under Assyrian sovereignty, but rebelled against its overlord on at least two occasions. On the first of these, it joined a widespread revolt against the Assyrian king Shalmaneser III (858–824), initiated by the king's son Ashur-da'in-apla. The rebellion continued into the early regnal years of Shalmaneser's son and successor Shamshi-Adad V before it was finally crushed (**RIMA* 3: 183). The second recorded uprising occurred in 761, according to the Eponym Chronicle entry for that year (Millard 1994: 41), during another of the Assyrian empire's unstable periods, when the throne was occupied by Ashur-dan III (772–755). Once more, Arrapha was firmly restored to Assyrian control. In the ongoing contest with Babylon, the Assyrian king Tiglath-pileser III (745–727) detached a number of Aramaean groups from Babylonian control and incorporated them into Arrapha's territory.

Assyrian sovereignty over Arrapha during Sargon II's reign (721–705) is reflected in a number of letters written to the Assyrian king by Arraphan officials (**SAA* XV: 4–15). Under Sennacherib (704–681), Arrapha's governor was assigned authority over the cities Hardishpi and Bit-Kilamzah, where Sennacherib had settled deportees from other areas of his conquests. The city played a significant role in the security of Assyria's eastern territories, and during the reign of the Assyrian king Ashurbanipal (668–630/627) its governor exercised an important military command in the region. (He was especially active in Babylonia during the revolt instigated by Ashurbanipal's brother Shamash-shum-ukin, ruler of Babylon.) But this did little to keep Assyria's enemies at bay in the final years of the empire. In 616 the Babylonian king Nabopolassar won a victory over a combined Assyrian–Egyptian force near Arrapha (**ABC* 91, **PE* 30, no. 10). In the following year, Arrapha was the target of an expedition led by the Median king Cyaxares (**ABC* 92, **PE* 30, no. 10). Unfortunately, the text which provides this information breaks off before the outcome of the campaign is revealed. In any case it was but a prelude to the destruction of Nineveh by combined Median–Babylonian forces in 612.

During the Hellenistic period, Arrapha, now part of the Seleucid empire, was refounded under the name Karka.

Gadd (1926), Unger (*RlA* 1: 154), Lion (*DCM* 79).

Arsada (map 15) M1 BCE–M1 CE city located on Mt Massicytus (mod. Akdağ) on the eastern side of the Xanthus valley in Lycia, southwestern Anatolia. Unattested in either literary sources or coin legends, the town is named in a Greek inscription (**TAM* II 539) discovered on the site and dated to the Roman imperial period. Lycian house-type tombs also discovered on the site indicate that Arsada was founded at least by C5. The C18 CE explorer T. A. B. Spratt claimed to have read upon the tombs texts written in the Lycian language, whose use in inscriptions dates to C5 and C4. No trace of these texts survives. Remains of the town's defences include a rubble fortification wall, partly preserved, and a small tower or fortress made of large polygonal blocks. The latter is tentatively dated to the early Hellenistic period. Freestanding Lycian tombs are scattered around the nearby village of Arsaköy, a name apparently derived from Arsada.

Bean (1949: 40–9; 1978: 68–70).

Arsanias r. (*Murat Su*) (map 20) River in northern Mesopotamia, so named in Neo-Assyrian texts, located in the region of the Nairi lands. It may have formed the southern frontier of one of these lands, Dayenu. The Assyrian king Shalmaneser III records crossing the river, after passing through the land of Bit-Zamani, for the campaign which he conducted against Urartu and neighbouring lands in his third regnal year (856) (**RIMA* 3: 20). Twenty-four years later, in 832, Shalmaneser reports a victory his commander-in-chief Dayyan-Ashur won over the forces of the Urartian king Sarduri I after crossing the river (**RIMA* 3: 69). The mod. town Palu on the river, where an inscribed stele of the Urartian king Minua (805–788) was found, is probably the site of anc. Shebeteria (q.v.), used by Minua as a base for a western campaign to and beyond the Euphrates r. Further to the east along the river, the shortlived Urartian fortress now called Kayalıdere (anc. name unknown) was built, probably by the Urartian king Rusa I (730–714). West of Palu on the south bank of the river lay the site of Korucutepe (q.v.) whose history of occupation extends from the Chalcolithic Age to c. 800.

Arshada M1 city in the country of Arachosia, a subject state of the Persian empire located in the empire's eastern frontier region in mod. Afghanistan. In the uprisings at the beginning of Darius I's reign (522), Arshada was the site of one of the battles fought between Vivana, satrap of Arachosia and supporter of Darius, and the rebel army sent to take possession of the region by Vahyazdata (the false Bardiya), a pretender to the Persian throne (**DB* 47).

Arslan Taş see **Hadatu**.

Arslantepe (**Melid**, **Meliteia**, Assyrian **Milidia**, Classical **Melitene**) (maps 2, 7) Settlement-mound in eastern Anatolia, 6 km northeast of mod. Malatya, with occupation levels extending from late M5 (Chalcolithic period) to mid M1 CE. Arslantepe's importance was due primarily to its valuable strategic location at a major river-crossing on the Euphrates. The most significant of its levels (III) dates to the Neo-Hittite period, from late M2 until late C8. This and the preceding Late Bronze Age Hittite level (IV) were brought to light by the French archaeologist L. Delaporte in excavations conducted between 1932 and 1939. Delaporte's most notable find was a C10 palace whose entry was flanked by two lions – the so-called Lion Gate. The name Arslan(tepe) comes from the Turkish word for lion. The gate-entrance which Delaporte uncovered, and the paved courtyard within, are decorated with limestone bas-reliefs, providing some of the earliest known examples of Neo-Hittite sculpture. C. F.-A. Schaeffer made a number of soundings on the site in the 1950s, and from 1961 onwards excavations have been carried out by a series of Italian teams.

The excavated area of the earliest level to be identified (VIII), dating to the last centuries of M5, has produced a number of domestic structures. By early M4, Arslantepe had become a settlement of considerable significance, as attested by large public buildings in level VII, and a well-developed residential quarter. The public buildings were forerunners to the impressive temples and administrative structures which were erected on the mound (level VIA) in the Late Uruk period (second half of M4). The rich iconography of this period, as illustrated by the stylized human and animal figures which decorated the temple walls, indicates a relatively high level of cultural sophistication amongst its inhabitants. And the thousands of clay sealings found in the temples provide evidence of a relatively advanced level of economic activity, enhanced no doubt by contacts with urban communities in southern Mesopotamia. The settlement declined and finally collapsed, with evidence of violent destruction, around the end of M4. But shortly after, in early M3, the site was reoccupied by an eastern Anatolian/Transcaucasian population (level VIB), who built a village of mudbrick huts over the ruins of the public buildings of the previous level. The most significant find of this period is an impressive tomb, dated to c. 2900, whose chief occupant, probably a king or prince, was buried with a number of attendants and a large quantity of finely wrought metal artefacts.

From c. 2700 onwards, in Early Bronze II and III, Arslantepe had only tenuous cultural contacts with the urban societies of Mesopotamia and Syria. Instead, material remains from the site in this period (levels VIC–D) reflect the development of a new northeastern Anatolian culture in the Malatya–Elaziğ region, as evidenced by new types of pottery, which persisted well into M2 (level V). In the second half of M3, a well-planned fortified town was built. The Anatolian urban structure which it reflects clearly indicates Arslantepe's Early and Middle Bronze Age cultural orientation in this period.

The earliest attestation of the anc. name of the site appears in the form Maldiya or Malitiya in an early C14 Hittite text commonly known as the Indictment of Mita, who was ruler of the city of Pahhuwa (see **Pahhuwa**). As yet, no reference to the city has been identified in the Middle Bronze Age Assyrian Colony texts, dating to the first three centuries of M2 (see glossary). This is surprising, particularly in view of the city's location on the most important crossing of the Euphrates r. north of the Taurus mountains. Perhaps it does appear in the colony texts, but under a different, earlier name. It may be that Malitiya was a new name devised by the Hittites, and probably derived from the Hittite-Luwian word *melit-/mallit-*, 'honey'.

The resurgence of Assyrian power in the final decades of C14 posed a threat to Malitiya, at that time subject to Hatti, if we can so interpret references to it and Assyria in Hittite texts contemporary with the Assyrian kings Adad-nirari I (1307–1275) and his son Shalmaneser I (1274–1245) (see e.g. **RGTC* 6: 257, *CHLI* I: 283 with refs). However, the first Assyrian king to mention the city (under the name Milidia) is Tiglath-pileser I (1114–1076), some decades after the fall of the Hittite empire. He refers to it in two texts, once as a 'rebellious and insubmissive' city of the land of Hanigalbat (**RIMA* 2: 22), and a second time as a city of the land of Hatti (**RIMA* 2: 43). (The name Hanigalbat continued to be used in Assyrian texts long after the Late Bronze Age land so designated had ceased to exist as a political entity.) Both these texts apparently refer to the same episode, which followed upon Tiglath-pileser's campaign against the Nairi lands in his third regnal year. Tiglath-pileser reports that he spared the city since it had surrendered voluntarily to him on his approach, but took hostages from it and imposed an annual tribute in the form of quantities of lead ore. Its king at the time was a man called Allumari.

The city became the centre of one of the Neo-Hittite kingdoms of the same name, which emerged, after the collapse of the Late Bronze Age civilizations, in the last two centuries of M2. Luwian hieroglyphic inscriptions dating to this period have established for us the names of two kings of Malatya (called Malizi in these inscriptions), Runtiyas and Arnuwantis, who were brothers; they were also the grandsons of Ku(n)zi-

Teshub, king of Carchemish (**CHLI* I: 295–304). Arnuwantis probably succeeded his brother on his kingdom's throne. Since Kuzi-Teshub was a direct descendant of the line of Late Bronze Age Hittite kings, then the kings of Neo-Hittite Malatya extended further the Hittite royal dynastic line, whose origins dated back to C17. We do not know whether the brothers ruled Malatya as viceregal representatives of the Great King of Carchemish, or whether Malatya gained independent status, within the context of an ongoing process of political fragmentation which began with the fall of the Late Bronze Age kingdom of Hatti. At Malatya the Hittite dynastic line continued for at least two more generations, since the inscriptions attest to a second Arnuwantis, grandson of the first (**CHLI* I: 305). Hawkins (*CHLI* I: 283, 284) notes that the discovery of inscribed stelae and rock-inscriptions, connected with the Arslantepe material, from areas outside the plain of Malatya, provides evidence that Malatya's control extended over the plain to the west bank of the Euphrates, up the routes to the northwest at least as far as mod. Hekmihan and Gürün, and into the plain of Elbistan.

We have further information about the kingdom of Malatya for a period of about two centuries, c. 850 to 650, from Assyrian and Urartian inscriptions, in which the kingdom's name appears in the form Melid and Meliteia respectively. These inscriptions have produced the names of a number of Malatyan/Melidite kings who reigned within this period, including Lalli, Hilaruada, Sulumal, Gunzinanu, Tarhunazi, and Mugallu. Very likely the rulers so named had different origins from the old Hittite dynasty, which by C9 may well have become defunct.

From Assyrian and Urartian sources, it is clear that Melid was regularly caught up in the conflicts of the period. Shalmaneser III (858–824) conducted a number of campaigns against it, to secure the submission of its king, Lalli. The latter is listed among the rulers in eastern Anatolia and northern Syria who paid tribute to Shalmaneser early in the campaign he conducted in the west in his sixth regnal year (853) (**RIMA* 3: 23), and again in his fifteenth regnal year, 844. In his twenty-third regnal year, 836, Shalmaneser entered Lalli's land again, and captured his fortified city Uetash (**RIMA* 3: 67). In the following century, Melid was the victim of aggression by three successive Urartian kings, Minua, Argishti I, and Sarduri II (in the latter two cases, the Melidite ruler was a certain Hilaruada, son of Shahu), and was forced to accept Urartian overlordship. This ended abruptly in 743 when a Urartian–Arpad alliance, of which Melid was a member, was decisively defeated by the Assyrian king Tiglath-pileser III (**ARAB* I: 272–3, 287; **Tigl. III* 100–1). At that time, Melid's ruler was a man called Sulumal. Henceforth, Melid became a tributary of the Assyrian empire (**Tigl. III* 68–9, 108–9). From Tiglath-pileser's reign through the reigns of his son Shalmaneser V and his grandson Sargon II, it probably remained under Assyrian sovereignty, though further Assyrian campaigns, e.g. by Sargon, were apparently necessary to keep it in subjection. Sargon records a campaign which he undertook against it in 712, when its then king Tarhunazi (Sargon's own appointee, in place of his predecessor Gunzinanu who had succeeded Sulumal) switched his support to the Phrygian king Midas (Assyrian Mita). In retaliation, Sargon marched against, occupied, and ravaged the kingdom, capturing Tarhunazi, who had taken refuge in Til-garimmu, one of his royal cities. Tarhunazi, his family, and many of his subjects were deported to Assyria. Sargon assigned part of his kingdom, the land of Kammanu with the city of Til-garimmu, to a provincial governor, while the city of Melid was placed under the control of Mutallu, king of Kummuh and a loyal supporter of Assyria.

After Sargon's death in 705, Melid may have regained its independence, and perhaps retained it, despite further Assyrian attempts (e.g. by the Assyrian king Esarhaddon, c. 675) to reconquer it, until early in the reign of Ashurbanipal (668–630/627). Babylonian and Assyrian chronicles record an Assyrian campaign in 675 against Melid and its king Mugallu, who had apparently formed an anti-Assyrian alliance with a certain ruler(?) of Tabal called Ishkallu. The Mugallu who is attested as a king of Tabal in Ashurbanipal's reign is almost certainly the same man as the king of Melid. His association with two countries very likely indicates an extension of his power from Melid to Tabal by the beginning of Ashurbanipal's reign. But Mugallu apparently now sought to make his peace with Assyria. Like Sandasarme, king of Hilakku, he sent an embassy to Ashurbanipal and paid him a yearly tribute. But his approach to Ashurbanipal was probably due much less to pressure from Assyria than to fear of the Cimmerian hordes who were soon to sweep through large parts of Anatolia, in the process bringing to an end the kingdom of Phrygia.

Melid probably fell victim to the Cimmerian invasions in late C7. Its site was abandoned, but there was resettlement in the Roman imperial period on a nearby site called Melite (mod. Eski Malatya). As late as mid M1 CE, a small rural community existed there.

Palmieri (1981), Hawkins/Frangipane (*RlA* 8: 35–52), Frangipane (*OEANE* 1: 212–5), Hawkins (1998a; **CHLI* I: 282–329).

Artulu Iron Age city in the country of Tabal, eastern Anatolia, within the Kululu-Sultanhan-Kültepe region according to Hawkins (*CLHI* I: 427). It appears to have been the centre of a small kingdom which incorporated a number of towns and villages. In 836, it was the capital of a Tabalite king called Tuwatis (Assyrian Tuatti), who was forced to take refuge there when the Assyrian king Shalmaneser III descended upon his land while campaigning in Tabal (**RIMA* 3: 79). When Shalmaneser's troops surrounded his city, Tuwatis submitted without resistance. He was very likely an ancestor of a later king of Tabal also called Tuwatis, who is attested in Luwian inscriptions dating to mid C8. The inscriptions were found at the site now called Kululu (q.v.), perhaps the anc. Artulu, but alternatively identified with Tuna (q.v.).

Aruar see Zaruar.

Arwad (**Arwada**, biblical **Arvad**, Classical **Aradus**, ***Ruad***) (map 6) Small Canaanite-Phoenician island-city (c. 400 ha) located 3 km off the Levantine coast. In *OT* tradition, its inhabitants were included among the descendants of the patriarch Canaan (Genesis 10:18), and are mentioned as rowers in the service of Tyre (Ezekiel 27:8). Arwad is attested in M3 texts from Ebla, and in M2 texts from Alalah and Amarna. From the letters written by Rib-Hadda, king of Gubla (Byblos), to the pharaoh Akhenaten during the mid C14 Amarna period, we learn that Arwad joined forces with the leaders of the country of Amurru for combined sea and land assaults on the coastal cities of Sumur and Tyre (**EA* 98; 101; 104; 105; 149). It also prevented food supplies from reaching Gubla by sea when the city's farmlands were raided by Habiru bands from Amurru.

In late M2 Arwad was a tributary of Assyria, along with Byblos and Sidon, under Tiglath-pileser I (1114–1076) (**RIMA* 2: 37), who was the first Assyrian king to reach

Figure 12 Arwad.

the Mediterranean coast. In 853 it figured among the forces which fought against the Assyrian king Shalmaneser III in the battle of Qarqar (**RIMA* 3: 23). Its ruler at this time was a man called Matinu-ba'al. In 701 its king, Abdil'ti, was a tributary of the Assyrian king Sennacherib, and in C6 Arwad paid tribute to the Babylonian king Nebuchadnezzar II (604–562). During the Persian period (C6–4) a Persian royal residence was located on the island. In 481, an Arwadian naval commander, Merbalus, son of Agbalus, joined the armada of the Persian king Xerxes for the invasion of Greece (Herodotus 7.98). In 333/332 Alexander the Great received the surrender of the island from its king, Straton, along with the city of Marathus (mod. Amrit) (Arrian, *Anabasis* 2.13.7–8), which served as Arwad's continental port. Aradus/Arwad also appears in records of the Roman imperial period. The only anc. remains currently visible on the site date to this period.

Badre (*OEANE* 1: 218–9), Elayi (2000).

Arycanda (map 15) M1 BCE–M1 CE hillside city in eastern Lycia, southwestern Anatolia. It has been suggested, on the basis of the '-anda' ending of the city's name, that Arycanda's origins may date back to the Bronze Age. But as yet there is no hard evidence to support this. So far, the earliest evidence we have for the city's existence is provided by coins bearing the name Pericle (Greek Pericles), a local ruler based at Limyra who extended his sway over much of Lycia during the first half of C4. Arycanda's substantial remains, which include well-preserved fortifications, a theatre, baths, and a number of sarcophagi, date almost entirely to the Hellenistic and Roman periods. A number of its rock-cut tombs may have been built in C4. But no inscriptions in the native language (whose use on sepulchral and other monuments dates to C5 and C4) have been found on any of the tombs (or anywhere else on the site) to provide confirmation of their dates. The tombs were still being used in the Byzantine period.

Bean (1978: 135–9).

Arzashkun (Arzashkunu, Arsashku) M1 royal Urartian city in eastern Anatolia, one of the strongholds of the Urartian king Arame (c. 860–850). (His other stronghold was called Suguniya.) It lay beneath a mountain called Mt Eritia (not yet identified) and was probably located to the southwest of Lake Urmia, though locations north, east, and west of the lake have also been proposed. The city was destroyed by the Assyrian king Shalmaneser III during his campaign in Urartian territory in his third regnal year (856). Arame fled the city on his approach, and Shalmaneser captured it and burnt it (*RIMA 3: 20, 29). Its destruction is depicted on one of the bronze bands from the gates at Balawat (see **Imgur-Enlil**), where the fortress is shown as a two-level structure with projecting towers.

Lambert (1961), Salvini (1995b: 46–8).

Arzawa (early variant **Arzawiya**) (map 3) Late Bronze Age region in western Anatolia, attested in Hittite texts. It first appears in the reign of the Hittite king Hattusili I (1650–1620), who conducted a brief raid into Arzawan territory, probably during his third regnal year (**Chav.* 220). In C16 Arzawiya was among the cities and countries which rose up against the Hittites during the reign of King Ammuna (**Chav.* 231). Subsequently, in early C14, Arzawa figured prominently among the western countries which fought against and were conquered by the Hittite king Tudhaliya I/II (*Garstang and Gurney, 1959: 121). In later Hittite documents the name Arzawa is sometimes used in a broad, generic sense, and sometimes more specifically to refer to up to five states or kingdoms constituting the 'Arzawa Lands': Arzawa 'Minor', Mira-Kuwaliya, Seha River Land, Wilusa, and Hapalla. (See separate entries for each of these.) Arzawa and Hatti were frequently in conflict, and during the first half of C14, in the reign of the Hittite king Tudhaliya III, Arzawan forces invaded Hittite subject territory and occupied it up to the northern limits of the southwestern Hittite buffer zone called the Lower Land (q.v.) (*Bryce, 2005: 146). But in the penultimate decade of the century, the Arzawa Lands were reduced to Hittite vassal status by the Hittite king Mursili II (1321–1295), who bound their rulers to him in a series of vassal treaties.

Most scholars believe that Arzawa was inhabited by Luwian-speaking population groups, and ruled by kings of Luwian origin. This view has recently been challenged by I. Yakubovich (2008), according to whom the political unification of Arzawa was the achievement of 'Proto-Carian groups' who provided the ruling aristocracies in the region. Luwian and 'Proto-Carian' both belong to the Indo-European family of languages. In whatever way we explain the Indo-European presence in Arzawa during the Late Bronze Age, the region almost certainly contained a substantial non-Indo-European population, which may well have occupied it long before the arrival of the first Indo-European speakers.

Heinhold-Krahmer (1977), Bryce (2003a: 35–84), Yakubovich (2008).

Arzawa 'Minor' Late Bronze Age kingdom in western Anatolia, perhaps the original nucleus of the Arzawa Lands. (The appendage 'Minor' is a mod. convention used by some scholars to distinguish the kingdom from Arzawa in the broader sense.) Its capital was Apasa. The kingdom posed a serious threat to Hittite authority in western Anatolia, until it was eventually conquered and dismantled by the Hittite king Mursili II c. 1319. Large numbers of its population were deported to Hatti – 65,000 or 66,000 according to Mursili's own statement (**AM* 76–7, **CS* II: 85–6), and Mursili reassigned much if not all of its territory to the neighbouring kingdom of Mira. Uhhaziti had been ruler of Arzawa 'Minor' at the time of its conquest. He had provoked Hittite action against him by refusing to give up refugees from Hittite authority who had sought asylum with him, and by forming anti-Hittite alliances with other Arzawan states and with the king of Ahhiyawa. He fled at the approach of Mursili's army, and took refuge in islands off the Anatolian coast (*AM 46–53, *CS II: 85), where he later died.

Bryce (2005: 93–7)

Arziya Late Bronze Age country in northeastern Syria, near Carchemish. During the Hittite king Suppiluliuma I's war with Mitanni, Telipinu, son of Suppiluliuma and Hittite viceroy at Aleppo, led an expedition against and conquered both Arziya and the country (but not the city) of Carchemish. This was in response to a final attempt, c. 1340, by the Mitannian king Tushratta to re-establish his power west of the Euphrates (**DS* 92, **CS* I: 189).

Arzizu Iron Age city in the land of Zamua, which was located in the borderlands between northeastern Mesopotamia and northwestern Iran. In early C9 it was ruled, along with the city of Arsindu, by a man called Ata. The Assyrian king Ashurnasirpal II reports his conquest of both cities during his third campaign against Zamua in 880 (**RIMA* 2: 207).

Ashdod (map 8) Settlement-mound consisting of acropolis and lower city covering a total of 36 ha, located on the coast of Palestine, mod. Israel, north of Ashkelon. Its history of occupation, represented by twenty-three archaeological strata, extends from the Middle Bronze Age to the Byzantine period. Excavations were conducted from 1962 to 1972 by M. Dothan for the Israel Dept of Antiquities. In its earliest phase (Middle Bronze III), Ashdod was a fortified city, which continued without apparent interruption through a number of Late Bronze Age levels, the most important of which are represented by Strata XVII–XIV (Late Bronze IIA–B). In this period, the city was subject to Egyptian sovereignty, and a large, multi-roomed building with courtyard reflecting Egyptian influence may have been the residence of an Egyptian governor. C14 texts from Ugarit indicate commercial contacts between Ashdod and Ugarit; the former was apparently noted for its tin and textile merchants. Ashdod's violent destruction around the end of C13 was probably connected with the so-called Sea Peoples.

In the wake of the Sea Peoples' movements along the Syro-Palestinian coast, Ashdod became a Philistine settlement, one of the five cities of the Philistine Pentapolis (see glossary) referred to in *OT* sources. A large fortress was a dominant architectural feature of the new Philistine city, and ceramic ware found in what were apparently potters' workshops highlights the Aegean origins of the Philistine settlers. This first Iron Age phase of Ashdod's existence may have ended with an Israelite destruction of the city in C10, and the *OT* sources (e.g. 2 Chronicles 26:6) probably paint a fairly realistic picture of the turbulent period of conflict between the Israelites and the Philistines throughout C10 and C9.

But already by the end of C9, the Philistines were paying tribute to Assyria. And subsequently, a number of Philistine cities were destroyed by the Assyrians, as reported in both *OT* and Assyrian sources. In 712 Ashdod's king, Azuri, rebelled against the Assyrian king Sargon II (**CS* II: 294, 296). Sargon crushed the rebellion, deposed Azuri, and replaced him on Ashdod's throne with his brother Ahimiti. But Ahimiti was unpopular with his subjects, who rose in rebellion again the following year and put their own man Yadna (Yamani) on the throne (**CS* II: 296–7). Sargon responded promptly. After besieging and conquering Ashdod, he placed it under direct Assyrian control, appointing one of his own governors to administer it. Some 3,000 intramural, sub-floor burials probably dating to this phase of the city's existence may be linked to this event. Sargon's capture of the city is also reported in Isaiah 20:1. Following the collapse of the Assyrian empire, Ashdod was attacked by the Egyptian king Psamtik (I) (664–610) (Greek Psammetichus), according to Herodotus (2.157), who claims that the pharaoh had to invest the city (called Azotus in Greek sources) for twenty-nine years before it finally fell to him. Ashdod subsequently came under Babylonian and then Persian sovereignty before submitting to Alexander the Great in 332.

M. Dothan *et al.* (1967; 1971; 1982), M. Dothan (*NEAHL* 1: 93–102), Dever (*OEANE* 1: 219–20).

Ashdubba City in southern Mesopotamia, attested in early M2 as an appanage of the kingdom of Larsa. It was governed by the prince Sin-iddinam before his accession to Larsa's throne in 1849.

Mesop. 256.

Ashihum Middle Bronze Age royal city north of the eastern part of the Jebel Sinjar in northern Mesopotamia, attested in the Mari archives from the reign of Zimri-Lim (1774–1762). In this period it was ruled by a king Hazip-Ulme (a Hurrian name), who was a vassal of Sharraya, king of Razama (in the land of Yussan). Subsequently the city came under the control of Hammurabi, king of Kurda, at which time Atamrum, king of Andarig, laid siege to it, with the (perhaps reluctant) support of Yasim-El, known elsewhere as Zimri-Lim's agent in Karana. It seems that Ashihum was vigorously defended by Saggar-Abum, a general of Hammurabi, who had been sent by his king to fortify the city with 1,000 troops. We do not know whether or not the besieging army succeeded in taking the city. But if it did, its victory was shortlived, since soon after, the city was in Hammurabi's hands again (*LKM* 119).

LKM 117–19, *346–7, *360–1.

Ashkelon (map 8) 60 ha settlement-mound located in the southern Palestinian coastal region between Ashdod and Gaza, mod. Israel, 63 km south of Tel Aviv. Its history of occupation extends from the Early Bronze Age to the mediaeval period. Some pottery of the Chalcolithic period and a small Neolithic settlement on the nearby beach have also been found. The first official excavation of the site was conducted by J. Garstang for the Palestine Dept of Antiquities and the Palestine Exploration Fund from 1920 to 1921. More extensive excavations were begun in 1985 by the Leon Levy Expedition under the direction of L. E. Stager, with sponsorship by the Semitic Museum of Harvard University, and continue to this day.

The site's earliest significant remains are substantial fortifications of a Caananite city dating to the Middle Bronze Age. These were unearthed at the north end of the mound. The discovery of pottery of the same period at the south end suggests that already in this period, in the early centuries of M2, the Canaanite city had reached its maximum size. Also in this period, Ashkelon is first attested in written records, appearing in the form Ascanu in the C19–18 Egyptian Execration texts (see glossary). During the Late Bronze Age, the city became a vassal state of the Egyptian empire. Small finds from this phase of its existence indicate close links with Cyprus and the

Aegean world. One of the most interesting of the small finds was a silver-plated calf which came to light in a room cut into the city's rampart. The mid C14 Amarna archive contains several exchanges of correspondence between the pharaoh Akhenaten and Yidya/Idiya, king of Ashkelon (Ashqaluna) (**EA* 320–2, 370). A temple to the Egyptian god Ptah is attested in the written records. But it seems that Egyptian overlordship did not sit well upon the city, to judge from the fact that in C13 both Ramesses II and his son and successor Merneptah were obliged to conquer it, apparently in response to rebellions by its inhabitants.

Early in C12 the city was occupied by the Philistines, and became one of the five cities constituting the Philistine Pentapolis (see glossary). Whether it ever fell to the Israelites, as reported in Judges 1:18, remains doubtful. To judge from Assyrian sources, the substantial amount of territory over which it exercised control in early M1 (stretching northwards towards Jaffa) was considerably reduced by Assyrian intervention in the region in C8. In the reign of the Assyrian king Tiglath-pileser III (745–727), it became a tribute-paying state of the Assyrian empire. Severe reprisals were inflicted upon Ashkelon when its king joined in a rebellion against Assyrian rule in 732. Uprisings by the city later in the century resulted in its king Sidka being deported to Assyria. The C7 Assyrian kings Esarhaddon and Ashurbanipal used Ashkelon as a base for their campaigns against Egypt.

Subsequently under Neo-Babylonian rule, the city once more rebelled against its overlord, prompting its seizure by the Babylonian king Nebuchadnezzar II (604–562) during his western campaigns, and the deportation of large numbers of its inhabitants. An interesting feature of the city during the subsequent period of Persian domination (C6–4) is a large dog cemetery, containing the skeletal remains of hundreds of separately buried dogs, all of whom apparently died of natural causes. Other remains of this period indicate strong Aegean and Phoenician influence upon Ashkelon's material culture. The city was finally granted independence by the Ptolemies in the early Hellenistic period. It apparently suffered a major destruction c. 300, but well-preserved remains survive from the Hellenistic, Roman, Byzantine, and Islamic periods.

Stager (*NEAEHL* 1: 103–12), Schloen (*OEANE* 1: 220–3), Laughlin (2006: 37–42).

Ashlakka Middle Bronze Age royal city, located within Ida-maras, the name in the Mari archives for the western sector of the Habur triangle, northern Mesopotamia. Shortly after crushing a Yaminite uprising along the Euphrates, Zimri-Lim, king of Mari (1774–1762), conducted a campaign in the Habur region, seizing Ashlakka and removing its king, Shadum-Alal. Zimri-Lim spent more than two months in the city. During this time, he installed on its throne Ibal-Adda, who had already declared his loyalty to Zimri-Lim on the latter's accession to power in Mari, and apparently complained that he had not been placed on the throne of his father's (i.e. ancestral) house in Ashlakka at that time. Shadum-Alal's apparent refusal to accept the new Mariote king as his overlord was no doubt the reason for Zimri-Lim's campaign against him.

Ashlakka seems also to have provided Zimri-Lim with a place for regrouping his armies and joining forces with the Babylonians in preparation for military operations against Eshnunna. At this time, too, the Habur region was becoming seriously destabilized by divisions among the local rulers into pro- and anti-Elamite groups. Those who had pledged allegiance to Zimri-Lim were being persecuted because of this. Fearing for his own safety, Ibal-Adda wrote in alarm to Mari, informing Zimri-Lim of the assassinations of his loyal vassal rulers at the instigation of the Elamites. Ibal-Adda sought his overlord's protection against a similar fate. Whether or not this particular appeal was answered, Ibal-Adda managed to stay on his throne in Ashlakka for ten years as Zimri-Lim's protégé. He boasted that he had prevented the Ida-maras region from delivering troops to Elam and to Atamrum, king of Andarig. His bonds with Zimri-Lim were also strengthened when the latter married him to one of his daughters. But eventually, for some undocumented reason, he rebelled against his overlord, an act which led to the seizure of his city, his harem, and his official archives, and the abrupt end of his career.

Mesop. 195–6, 201, 220–1.

Ashnakkum City attested in Middle Bronze Age and perhaps also in early Iron Age texts, located within the Ida-maras region of the Habur triangle, northern Mesopotamia. An equation with Chagar Bazar (q.v.) has been suggested. In late C19 the city was captured, along with the city of Tarnip, by the Eshnunnite king Naram-Sin during his campaign of conquest in the Habur triangle. Ashnakkum was the seat of one of four known petty kingdoms in upper Ida-maras (the others were Qirdahat/Kirdahat, Tarmanni, and Shuduhum), whose rulers visited Zimri-Lim, king of Mari (1774–1762), apparently on a joint diplomatic mission (**LKM* 418, no. 27.20). Ashnakkum's king at this time was a man called Sammetar. But his throne was seized by a usurper, Ishme-Adad, who handed him over to the Elamites. Ishme-Adad's collaboration with the Elamites provoked unrest in the kingdom, leading to his assassination by a certain Shadum-Labua, who now seized kingship and sought to renew his kingdom's ties with Zimri-Lim (**LKM* 479–80 = **LAPO* 17: 216–17, no. 583). A number of letters in the Mari archive addressed to Zimri-Lim reflect the volatility of the region at this time, with various local rulers seeking to break their ties with Ashnakkum, from the reign of Sammetar onwards. Divisions among the local states and cities on the matter of whether they should align themselves with Mari or with Elam were probably the root cause of this volatility.

Ashnakkum may appear in an inscription of the Assyrian king Adad-nirari II (911–891) (**RIMA* 2: 149); however, the reading of the place-name is uncertain.

LKM 607 (refs), *Mesop.* 131, 220.

Ashshu Iron Age petty kingdom in northern Mesopotamia. In 866 its ruler, Gir-Dadi, paid a tribute of gold, silver, oxen, and sheep to the Assyrian king Ashurnasirpal II in the city of Huzirina (Sultantepe) (**RIMA* 2: 219). Lipiński locates the country west of the Aramaean state of Bit-Zamani, and suggests that it corresponds to the area between mod. Hilvan and Siverek.

Lipiński (2000: 137).

Ashtam(m)aku Fortified Iron Age city in northern Syria, belonging to the kingdom of Hamath. It was captured by the Assyrian king Shalmaneser III (together, allegedly, with eighty-nine other Hamathite cities) during his campaign against Hamath in 848 (**RIMA* 3: 38), when the Hamathite throne was occupied by Irhuleni. Shalmaneser's capture of Ashtammaku is also recorded on one of the bronze bands from Balawat (**RIMA* 3: 147) (see **Imgur-Enlil**). The city is perhaps to be identified with the site of Tell Mastuma (q.v.), 60 km southwest of Aleppo.

Lipiński (2000: 280–1).

Ashtaroth (map 8) Iron Age city in southern Syria, probably to be identified with the site of Tell Ashtara, which lies 20 km east of the Sea of Galilee. In *OT* tradition it was the royal seat of Og, king of Bashan, who was defeated in battle by the Israelites under Moses (Deuteronomy 1:4). A relief now housed in the British Museum from the Assyrian palace at Nimrud (biblical Calah) depicts the plunder of the city by the troops of the Assyrian king Tiglath-pileser III (745–727). The city's double crenellated wall as depicted in the relief reflects the double-wall fortifications of Tell Ashtara during its Iron Age phase (two levels). A. Abou Assaf directed two excavation seasons on this site, in 1966 and 1967, in which he demonstrated the importance of the city, not only in the Iron Age, but also in the Middle and Late Bronze Ages, finding evidence in the latter period for a metallurgical industry.

Abou Assaf (1968; 1969), Lipiński (2000: 365).

Ashtata (map 3) Late Bronze Age kingdom located in northern Syria along the west bank of the middle course of the Euphrates. It shared frontiers with the kingdoms of Nuhashshi and Aleppo, which lay respectively to its west and northwest. Following the conquest of the Mitannian empire by the Hittite king Suppiluliuma I (1350–1322), Ashtata, previously subject to Mitanni, came under Hittite control. Suppiluliuma placed it under the immediate authority of his son Sharri-Kushuh (Piyassili), whom he had appointed to the newly established viceregal seat at Carchemish. Suppiluliuma's son and (second) successor Mursili II visited Ashtata in his ninth regnal year (c. 1313), following his liberation of the land of Carchemish from Assyrian occupation, and strengthened the city's defences by providing it with a garrison and building a fortress in its chief city (doubtless Emar) (**AM* 120–1, **CS* II: 89). Ashtata was allowed a relatively high degree of autonomy under the governance of its own local ruler and council of elders. The centre of its administration was the recently excavated city of Emar, built from scratch under Hittite direction over the remains of its Early and Middle Bronze Age predecessors. A treaty which Suppiluliuma drew up with Shattiwaza, son of the defeated Mitannian king Tushratta, lists a number of towns which belonged to Ashtata (**HDT* 45–6). These included Ekalte, Ahuna, and Terqa.

**RGTC* 6: 48–9, Bryce (2005: 141, 185–6).

Ashur (*Qal'at Sherqat*) (maps 10, 13) Bronze and Iron Age city (and later a Parthian settlement) located in northern Mesopotamia on the west bank of the Tigris, 110 km south of Mosul. Its main history of occupation extends from mid M3 until the fall of the Assyrian empire in late C7. Following a series of C19 preliminary explorations, beginning with those of A. H. Layard, the first major excavations on the site were conducted by W. Andrae on behalf of the Deutsche Orient-Gesellschaft between 1903 and 1914. From 1978 to 1982 periodic work was carried out by the Iraqi Dept of Antiquities, primarily for restoration purposes. Renewed German excavations were undertaken in 1988 and 1989 by R. Dittmann for the Free University of Berlin, and in 1989 and 1990 by B. Hrouda for Munich University. More recently, excavations have been conducted by the Iraqi Dept of Antiquities (1999–2001) and by German archaeologists led by P. Miglus (2000–1).

The city occupies an excellent defensive position, situated as it is on a lofty, rocky, and roughly triangular promontory between the Tigris and a northern tributary, 40 m above the Sherqat plain. It is protected by natural defences on its northern and eastern sides, which were complemented as the city developed by massive curving double walls erected on the south-southwestern side. The settlement within these fortifications, covering c. 65 ha, consisted of two parts, now referred to as the Old and New Cities. The former, occupying c. two-thirds of the total area, contained temples and palaces as well as a number of other buildings; the latter, which lay in the southeastern part of the site and has yet to be fully explored, is thought to have been primarily a residential area.

In addition to enjoying the advantages of its defensive location, the city was well located on communication routes to Anatolia, Syria, southern Mesopotamia, and Iran. Archaeological evidence dates its foundation to the Early Dynastic period, c. 2500, the period to which the earliest excavated remains of the Ishtar temple sounding belong. In the last centuries of M3, the city came successively under the sovereignty of the Akkadian and Ur III empires. After the fall of the latter, Assyria became an independent state, with Ashur its religious and administrative capital. There is some debate as to whether the city was named after a local god who became its patron deity, or whether the god Ashur was essentially a personification of the city itself. Under Shamshi-Adad I (1796–1775), the Old Assyrian kingdom reached the peak of its development, and Ashur the first high point in its history. During this period it was the headquarters of the great Assyrian international trading network, the home base of a string of Assyrian merchant-colonies established through northern Syria and eastern and central Anatolia. Shamshi-Adad had originally been a local ruler of the city of Ekallatum, but had gained the Assyrian throne by seizing power in Ashur from his brother. Though he built a new capital for himself at Shubat-Enlil (Shehna), Ashur continued to be the kingdom's spiritual and commercial centre, and Shamshi-Adad commissioned an extensive building programme in the city, including the construction of a ziggurat (originally associated with the god Enlil, later with the god Ashur as well), the rebuilding of the Ashur temple in a form which endured until the city's demise, and the first great palace, the so-called 'Old Palace', covering 1.2 ha and constructed in the northern part of the city over earlier remains. To this period also date the first great fortification walls of Ashur, perhaps already constructed before Shamshi-Adad's accession.

Following the decline and fall of the Old Assyrian kingdom not long after Shamshi-Adad's death, Ashur came under the influence of Babylon, after being occupied for a brief period by an army from Eshnunna, and then of the kingdom of Mitanni. It was captured and looted by the C15 Mitannian king Saushtatar, whose booty from the city reportedly included a door of silver and gold which he carried back as a trophy for his palace in the Mitannian capital Washshukkanni. Only one significant building is known from Ashur in this period – a temple dedicated to the gods Sin and Shamash, built in the reign of Ashur-nirari I (early C15), some of whose building inscriptions have been discovered in the city.

Ashur gained a new lease of life when Suppiluliuma I, king of Hatti (1350–1322), destroyed the Mitannian empire. This left a power vacuum east of the Euphrates which was rapidly filled by Assyria, now released from its bondage to Mitanni. The reign of Ashur-uballit I (1365–1330) effectively marks the beginning of the Middle Assyrian period. Ashur now became the centre of one of the four Great Kingdoms of the age – Assyria, Babylon, Egypt, and Hatti. Its status is reflected in major building programmes, undertaken particularly in C13 and C12 and associated in the main with three Assyrian kings: (a) in the reign of Adad-nirari I (1307–1275), the Old Palace was rebuilt, the temple of Sin and Shamash was restored, and quays were constructed on the Tigris; (b) in the reign of Tukulti-Ninurta I (1244–1208), a 'New Palace' was built, and the temple of Ishtar was completely reconstructed; (c) the reign of Tiglath-pileser I (1114–1076) saw the construction of a great double temple dedicated to the gods Anu and Adad. Public building projects in this period were complemented by the development and expansion of the city's residential areas.

In the dying years of the Late Bronze Age, Assyria entered into a period of decline which was to last for several centuries. But it gained a new lease of life in the final years of C10, when King Adad-nirari II (911–891) embarked upon a programme of aggressive territorial expansion, which inaugurated the last and greatest phase in Assyria's history, the Neo-Assyrian empire. Initially, Ashur was the administrative centre of this empire. But from the reign of Ashurnasirpal II (883–859) onwards, it lost its status as the kingdom's royal capital, which was shifted in succession to Kalhu (Nimrud), Ninua (Nineveh), Dur-Sharrukin (Khorsabad), and then back to Ninua. None the less, Ashur retained its importance as the religious and ceremonial centre of the empire. Its revered traditional status is indicated by the fact that Assyrian kings continued to be crowned and buried there. The city's continuing importance is also reflected in the extensive restoration programmes carried out there at various times during the Neo-Assyrian empire. For example, Shalmaneser III (858–824) rebuilt the temple of Ishtar, the double temple of Anu and Adad, and the 'Old Palace' (which had by now been converted into a royal mausoleum); and Sennacherib (704–681) restored the temple of Ashur, the double temple of Sin and Shamash, and the 'New Palace'. A document from his reign records the existence of no fewer than thirty-four temples in the city in this period. Sennacherib also strengthened the city's natural defences on its north side with a series of buttressed walls and a circular watchtower, and built the *Akitu*-house, where the New Year festival was celebrated, outside the city on the west side.

But Ashur's imposing defences failed to protect the city against Assyria's enemies in the kingdom's final years. In 614 Ashur was attacked and destroyed by an army of Medes, just two years before the Babylonian–Median sack of the royal capital Nineveh. In C1 a settlement of unknown name on Ashur's site became a regional centre of the Parthian empire down to mid C3 CE.

Lamprichs (*OEANE* 1: 225–8), Battini and Villard (*DCM* 99–102).

Asia Minor see under **Anatolia**.

Aspendus (map 4) M1 BCE–M1 CE city in Pamphylia, southern Anatolia, located on the Eurymedon r. (mod. Köprüçayi), 13 km upstream, and 30 km east of Antalya. According to Strabo (14.4.2), the city was founded by Argive Greeks. This may tie in, to some extent, with Greek legendary tradition, according to which Pamphylia was settled by Greeks of mixed origin under the leadership of Amphilochus, Calchas, and Mopsus some time after the Trojan War. On the basis of linguistic evidence, however, the population of the city seems to have been predominantly of native Anatolian origin, and Greek settlement may date back no earlier than C7 or C6. The city's Anatolian name, Estwediys, appears on C5 coin issues. This name is almost certainly derived from Azatiwatas, the C8 founder of the settlement now known as Karatepe (anc. Azatiwataya) in Cilicia. In a famous bilingual inscription from Karatepe (q.v.), Azatiwatas refers to himself as a descendant of Mopsus, which suggests that the abovementioned Greek legendary tradition may have some historical basis.

In the early 460s, Aspendus was the assembly-point of the Persian army and fleet which were decisively defeated by the Athenian commander Cimon in the land and sea battle fought at the mouth of the Eurymedon (Thucydides 1.100.1, Diodorus 11.61.1). Subsequently, Aspendus became a member of the Athenian Confederacy, as indicated by its appearance in the Athenian Tribute List of 425. It had, however, reverted to a Persian allegiance by 411 at the latest, and probably remained firm in this allegiance until its surrender to Alexander the Great in 333. It was subject later to Ptolemaic, Seleucid, and Roman rule. The most prominent feature of the site today is a well-preserved Roman theatre, built in C2 CE.

Bean (1968: 67–77; *PECS* 101–3).

Assos (map 5) Graeco-Roman city located on a steep hill, rising 234 m above sea level, on the southern coast of the Troad in northwestern Anatolia. Though a number of scholars have proposed a Bronze Age origin for the city, the earliest remains so far recovered are those of an Archaic Doric temple (c. 530) on the city's acropolis. It was probably dedicated to the goddess Athena. According to Greek literary evidence, the city was founded in C7 by Aeolian colonists from Methymna on the nearby island of Lesbos (thus Strabo 13.1.58, citing Hellanicus and Myrsilus, C5 and C3 writers respectively on the history of Lesbos). Pliny the Elder (5.123) states that the city was also called Apollonia. Following a brief investigation of the site by C. Texier in 1835, the first major excavations were conducted by the Archaeological Institute of America from 1881 to 1883. While their attention was focused primarily on the temple, the archaeological team also carried out some investigation of the lower city's public buildings. Work on the site was resumed in 1980 by an international archaeological team under the direction of the Turkish archaeologist Ü. Serdaroğlu, who concentrated on both the acropolis and the city's western Hellenistic and Roman necropolis.

In C6 Assos was among the western Greek states which became subject to Lydia, and after the destruction of the Lydian kingdom by the Persian king Cyrus II (c. 546) were incorporated into the Persian empire. According to Herodotus (3.90), the city became part of the third Persian province, consisting of Phrygia and the Hellespont (but see glossary under **satrapy**). In C5, it became a member of the Athenian Confederacy, but presumably reverted to Persian control in early C4, under the terms of the King's Peace (386) (see glossary). Two decades later it was caught up in the anti-Persian uprisings in the west, the so-called Satrap Revolt, when its governor Ariobazarnes rebelled against the Persian king Artaxerxes II (366). Assos was subjected to a land and sea investment by the combined forces of the Persian commander Autophradates and the Carian satrap Mausolus, but successfully withstood the besieging forces (Xenophon, *Agesilaus* 2.26, Polyaenus 7.26).

In mid C4 Assos came under the control of a eunuch called Hermias who ruled over the Troad (including the city of Atarneus, 70 km southwest of Assos) and the island of Lesbos. Hermias planned the establishment of a new philosophical school at Assos (he had formerly been a student in Plato's Academy). To bolster this enterprise, he invited the participation of a number of philosophers and natural scientists, including his former fellow students Aristotle and Xenocrates, who spent several years in the city following Plato's death in 347. Aristotle subsequently married Hermias' niece Pythia. In 345 Assos came once more under Persian control, where it remained until its liberation by Alexander the Great in 334. (Hermias had been captured by the Persians, and died under torture.) After Alexander's death, the city was subject to Seleucid rule, and subsequently became part of the kingdom of Pergamum, before passing finally to Roman control in 133.

With the main exception of the Doric temple on the acropolis, most of the city's remains, including an agora with north and south stoas, gymnasium, theatre, bouleuterion (council house), and a large necropolis, date mostly to the Hellenistic period and (to a lesser extent) to the Roman and Byzantine periods. The acropolis and the lower city were strongly and separately fortified. The walls of the lower city are among the finest and best preserved fortifications of the anc. Greek world, still reaching in parts a height of 14 m. Extending for more than 3 km, they enclosed a total area of just over 55 ha, and incorporated along their length a number of towers and nine entrance gates, all of different style. These fortifications are of Hellenistic date, but there are traces of an older polygonal wall, indicating that the city was also fortified during earlier phases of its existence. Work on the site under the current director N. Aslan of Çanakkale Onsekiz Mart University includes ongoing restoration of the city walls.

E. Akurgal (1973: 64–9), Robinson (*PECS* 104–5), Serdaroğlu (1995).

Assuwa Late Bronze Age region in western Anatolia. Its name may provide the origin of the Classical name 'Asia'. In the so-called Annals of the Hittite king Tudhaliya I/II, early C14, Assuwa appears as a collective term embracing twenty-two countries which formed a coalition against Hatti and was defeated by Tudhaliya. The list begins with .]ukka (Lukka?) and ends with Wilusiya and Taruisa (*Bryce, 2005: 124–7). (The latter two names are generally considered the predecessors of Ilios and Troia in Greek epic tradition; see **Wilusa**). The first and last names in the list *may* indicate that the coalition extended from southwestern Anatolia to the Classical Troad (though the first name has alternatively been read as Ard]ukka). In the aftermath of his victory, Tudhaliya transported back to Hatti for resettlement 10,000 infantry from the conquered countries, along with 600 teams of horse and the elite chariot contingent called the 'lords of the bridle'. A longsword discovered in the Hittite capital Hattusa in 1991 may have been part of the spoils of battle. Probably produced in a western Anatolian/ Aegean workshop, it bears the inscription 'As Tudhaliya the Great King shattered the Assuwan country, he dedicated these swords to the storm god, his lord.' It is possible that Assuwa appears in the Linear A and Linear B tablets of Minoan Crete and Mycenaean Greece, as *a-su-ja* in the former case, and *a-si-wi-jo*, *a-si-wi-ja*, *a-si-ja-ti-ja* in the latter.

**RGTC* 6: 52–3, Cline (1996).

Assyria (maps 3, 13) Major western Asian power based in northern Mesopotamia, with a history spanning the Middle Bronze, Late Bronze, and Iron Ages, from the beginning of M2 until late C7. In the first centuries of M2 its population was primarily an admixture of semi-nomadic Amorite groups who had occupied Mesopotamia in M3, and an earlier Akkadian population. Both groups spoke a Semitic language.

Scholars commonly divide Assyria's history into three main phases: Old Assyrian (c. 2000–1763), Middle Assyrian (c. 1365–1076) and Neo-Assyrian (c. 911–607). It

Figure 13 Ashurnasirpal II, from Nimrud.

began with the rise of a small independent state based at Ashur on the west bank of the Tigris, following the collapse of the Ur III empire c. 2004. A ruler of Akkadian stock called Puzur-Ashur I established a dynasty there lasting several generations. Members of this dynasty conducted military campaigns north and south of Ashur, in the process probably incorporating into their kingdom the city of Nineveh, which lay 100 km to Ashur's north.

But the full development of the Old Assyrian kingdom was due to a ruler of Amorite stock called Shamshi-Adad. (Shamshi-Adad represents the Akkadian form of his name, Shamshi-Addu the Amorite form.) After seizing power from his brother in Ashur in 1796, Shamshi-Adad embarked on a series of military campaigns which took him as far west as the Mediterranean coast in the Levantine region. Most importantly, he gained control of the strategically valuable kingdom of Mari on the Euphrates. This followed the assassination of Sumu-Yamam, its previous ruler. Sumu-Yamam had succeeded his father Yahdun-Lim on Mari's throne but occupied it for only two years before his murder in a palace conspiracy, which *may* have been instigated by Shamshi-Adad. The territories between the Tigris and the Euphrates which had been subjugated by Shamshi-Adad were consolidated into 'the kingdom of Upper Mesopotamia'. Other major contemporary powers were: in southern Mesopotamia, the kingdoms of Babylonia, Larsa, and Eshnunna; in the west, the kingdoms of Yamhad and Qatna; and in the southeast, the kingdom of Elam.

In Mari, the Assyrian king installed (after an interval of some years) one of his sons, Yasmah-Addu, as viceroy. His other son, Ishme-Dagan, was appointed viceroy in the city of Ekallatum, which had served as Shamshi-Adad's first capital and his base for the conquest of northern Mesopotamia. (For a sample of the correspondence which passed between the king and his sons, see **Chav.* 111–21.) Shamshi-Adad himself took up residence in his newly established capital Shubat-Enlil (formerly Shehna, mod. Tell Leilan). Commercial considerations were probably one of the incentives for Shamshi-Adad's campaigns of conquest, for by these campaigns he gained control over the major trade routes linking Ashur with Syria and eastern and central Anatolia. In the process, he set up a victory stele on the Mediterranean coast. Before his reign, Assyria had already established a number of highly successful merchant-colonies in eastern and central Anatolia, which lasted from C20 until mid C18. In the final years of his reign, Shamshi-Adad also established trading links with the land of Dilmun, now identified with the islands of the Bahrain archipelago. The Old Assyrian kingdom began to disintegrate shortly after Shamshi-Adad's death in 1775. The viceregal kingdom Mari fell to the Amorite ruler Zimri-Lim in 1774, presumably shortly after Yasmah-Addu's hasty departure from it, and Shamshi-Adad's capital, Shubat-Enlil, was seized by a dynasty from the nearby land of Apum. The disintegrating kingdom survived an invasion by the rival kingdom of Eshnunna, but fell, finally, to the Babylonian king Hammurabi c. 1763.

After the Hittite destruction of Babylon c. 1595, northern Mesopotamia was dominated by the Hurrian kingdom of Mitanni. Assyria's traditional capital Ashur was sacked and looted by the Mitannian king Saushtatar, and the former Great Kingdom was reduced to Mitannian vassal status. But with the destruction of the Mitannian kingdom by the Hittite king Suppiluliuma I (1350–1322), Assyria once more rose to prominence, in the reign of Ashur-uballit (1365–1330), ushering in the Middle Assyrian era. Ashur-uballit rapidly began to fill the power vacuum in northern Mesopotamia created by the fall of Mitanni, by taking over parts of former Mitannian territory. He further sought to bolster his international standing by entering into correspondence with the pharaoh Akhenaten (**EA* 15, 16). The other great western Asian kingdoms, Hatti and Babylon, viewed the Assyrian resurgence with some alarm – particularly Babylon, whose southern Mesopotamian kingdom lay directly south of Assyria. In Ashur-uballit's reign the Assyrians invaded Babylonian territory and captured Babylon itself, in the wake of an abortive marriage alliance between the Assyrian and Babylonian royal families (see Bryce, 2003b: 14). Tensions between the two kingdoms subsequently eased in the reign of the Assyrian king Adad-nirari I (1307–1275), but never fully disappeared. Adad-nirari in the meantime set about consolidating his hold over former Mitannian territory up to the east bank of the Euphrates, a matter of no small concern to the Hittites whose own subject territory began immediately west of the river. Tensions between Hatti and Assyria erupted into conflict when the Assyrian king Tukulti-Ninurta I (1244–1208) confronted and decisively defeated a large Hittite army under the command of the Hittite king Tudhaliya IV at the battle of Nihriya in northern Mesopotamia (see Singer, 1985). Tukulti-Ninurta then engaged in a series of campaigns against Babylonia, which ended with the conquest of Babylon and its incorporation into the Assyrian empire. Tukulti-Ninurta was later assassinated, after suffering a series of military defeats elsewhere in his realm, and from this time on the empire went into decline.

Yet Assyria was to prove one of the most resilient of the Bronze Age Great Kingdoms. Decades after the kingdom of Hatti had disappeared, Egypt had lost its status as a major international power, and Babylon, which had regained its independence some fifteen years after Tukulti-Ninurta's death, was being ruled by a succession of insignificant dynasties, Assyria remained a formidable power in western Asia. In the reign of Tiglath-pileser I (1114–1076) it still retained control over a substantial part of northern Mesopotamia. Indeed, Tiglath-pileser extended considerably the earlier boundaries of Assyrian enterprise by leading an expedition across the Euphrates to the Mediterranean coast. He claims to have conquered the entire land of Amurru (which included the Phoenician cities along the Levantine coast and extended inland as far as the city of Tadmor in the Syrian desert), and to have received tribute from the cities Arwad, Byblos, and Sidon (**RIMA* 2: 37, 53). He also received tribute from a king of Hatti called Ini-Teshub. In this context, Hatti is probably to be understood as the kingdom of Carchemish. Subsequently, Tiglath-pileser reports that he crossed the Euphrates twenty-eight times in pursuit of Aramaean tribal groups, whom he defeated (**RIMA* 2: 53). In another campaign east of the Euphrates, he carried out extensive conquests in the land of Babylonia (**RIMA* 2: 53–4).

Following Tiglath-pileser's reign, Assyria entered upon one-and-a-half centuries of relative weakness, perhaps in some measure the result of an increasing Aramaean presence in many of the regions where it had exercised control. By the beginning of M1, its territory had been reduced to a narrow strip of land extending c. 150 km along the Tigris. But in the last decades of C10, the Assyrian king Ashur-dan II (934–912) began the process of winning back Assyria's lost territories and restoring its status as a major international power. His reign effectively marked the beginning of the Neo-Assyrian era. He was succeeded by his son Adad-nirari II (911–891), who shortly after his accession embarked upon a vigorous new programme of territorial expansion (**Chav.* 280–5). His successful campaigns against the Aramaeans in the Tigris valley and the Babylonian king Shamash-mudammiq, part of whose territory he incorporated into his own rapidly expanding empire, laid the foundations for further campaigns beyond Assyria's frontiers in the reigns of his successors. The countries lying to the west provided a particular focus of attention. Expansion in this direction began with Adad-nirari's grandson, Ashurnasirpal II (883–859), who undertook at least fourteen major military campaigns during his years on the throne. After successful expeditions to the north and northeast, into the regions of Habhu, Kadmuhu, Nairi, and Urartu, Ashurnasirpal turned his attention westwards. Around 870 he led his troops across the Euphrates, and first approached the city of Carchemish. The city was left unmolested after its ruler, Sangara, paid him a substantial tribute (**RIMA* 2: 217). Ashurnasirpal then proceeded to Mt Lebanon, and from there to the principalities of Syria (though some scholars believe that his Syrian expedition should be assigned to a later campaign). Here again the local rulers maintained the peace by voluntarily submitting to him and by paying him large amounts of tribute (**RIMA* 2: 217–19).

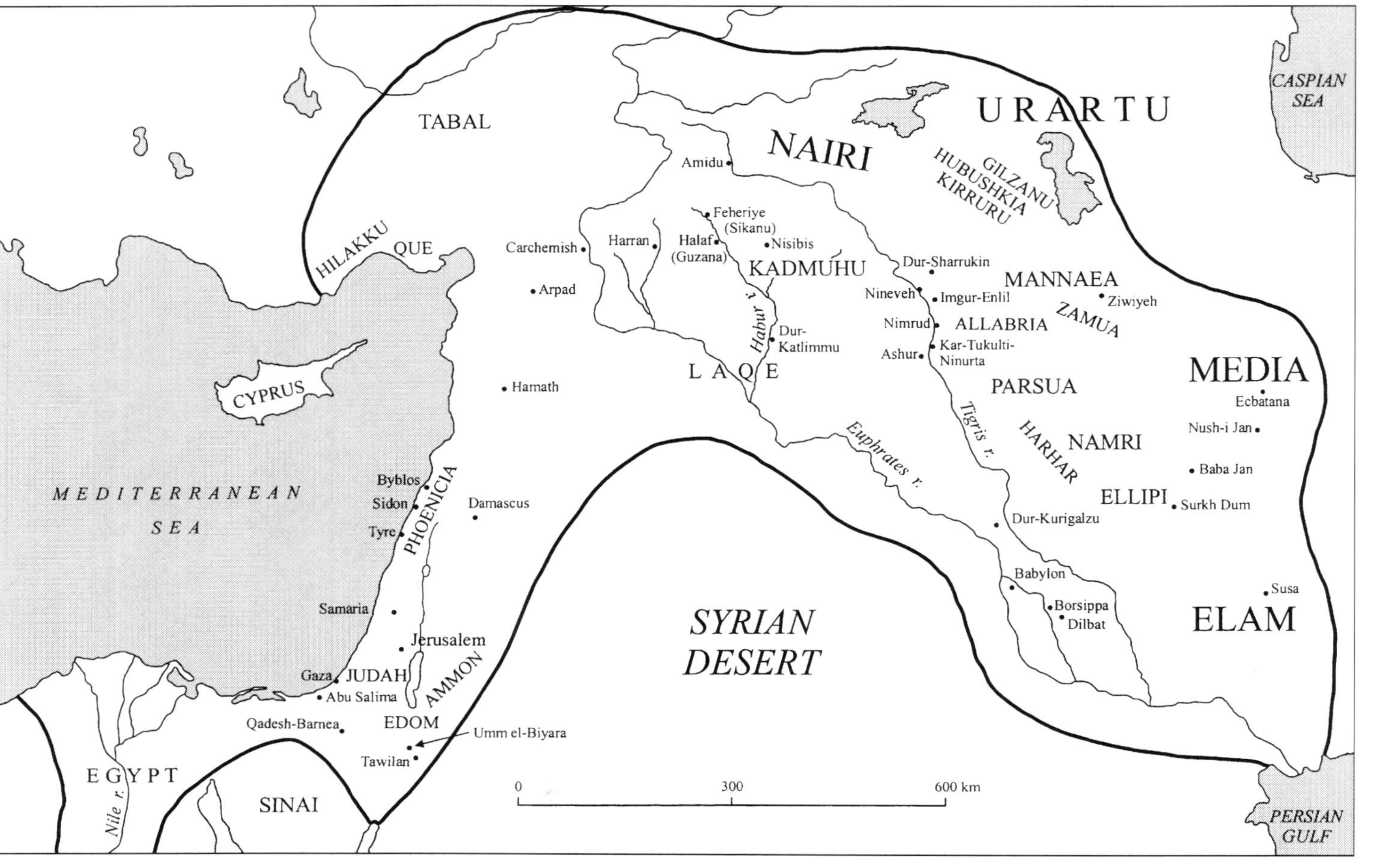

Map 13 The Neo-Assyrian empire.

Syria was to provide one of the most important bases for the future development of the empire. But foreign overlordship was not readily accepted by the Syro-Palestinian states, and the Assyrians had constantly to campaign in the region to suppress uprisings. Ashurnasirpal's son and successor Shalmaneser III (858–824) conducted a number of expeditions against a coalition of Syro-Palestinian states led first by Ahunu, ruler of Bit-Adini, and later by the rulers of Hamath and Damascus (e.g. **RIMA* 3: 23–4). Shalmaneser claimed victory in a battle against this latter coalition fought at Qarqar on the Orontes r. in 853. The outcome was rather less decisive than he reports, for in later years he was obliged to engage in further conflicts with the same alliance. In the wake of his victories, he made no attempt to impose direct rule over the conquered territories, but contented himself with the imposition of tribute upon their kings. But elsewhere, on the northern frontiers, Shalmaneser annexed conquered lands and integrated them into the provincial system, which he reorganized.

Political upheavals within Assyria, which marked the end of Shalmaneser's reign and continued through that of his son and successor Shamshi-Adad V (823–811),

Figure 14 Detail of obelisk of Shalmaneser III, from Nimrud.

ensured that Syria–Palestine was for the time being spared any further Assyrian military intervention – until Adad-nirari III (810–783) resumed campaigns in the region. These campaigns were directed particularly against a group of northern Syrian kings described as the 'eight kings of Hatti', under the leadership of one, Attar-shumki, ruler of the Aramaean north-central Syrian city Arpad. A military showdown fought at Paqarahubunu on the west bank of the middle Euphrates (**RIMA* 3: 205), while apparently resulting in an Assyrian victory, failed to destroy the enemy coalition, which continued its resistance to Assyrian authority. Subsequent western campaigns by Assyria were no more than sporadic, in a period when Assyria was again weakened by internal political disputes and political fragmentation. A symptom of this weakness was the rise of a number of powerful governors who enjoyed *de facto* independent status. The Assyrians had also to contend with the increasing threats posed by their powerful, territorially ambitious neighbour to their north – the kingdom of Urartu.

But with the seizure of the Assyrian throne by Tiglath-pileser III in 745, Assyria entered a major new phase in its development. After securing his frontiers against the Urartians for the time being, Tiglath-pileser embarked on a much more ruthless and more comprehensive programme of conquest in the west. In the wake of his western campaigns, the populations of the defeated states and cities who escaped massacre were deported from their homelands and resettled in many distant regions of the Assyrian realm. Their own cities were now occupied by settlers brought from Assyria. The former independent kingdoms in the region were now dismantled, absorbed into the Assyrian provincial administration, and placed under the direct authority of Assyrian governors. This policy of 'Assyrianization' was vigorously pursued for the remainder of C8.

During Sargon II's reign (721–705), Assyrian–Urartian rivalry culminated in a military showdown between Sargon and his Urartian counterpart, Rusa I (732–714), while Sargon was campaigning in the northern Zagros mountain region. After defeating Rusa's forces, Sargon invaded and plundered part of his kingdom. A detailed account of his campaign against Urartu in 714, Sargon's eighth military campaign, is recorded in the king's well-known 'Letter to Ashur' (**Chav.* 334–40). Subsequently, relations between the two kingdoms appear to have remained fairly amicable. Elsewhere, Assyrian expansion proceeded apace. Sargon also conducted campaigns into eastern-central Anatolia, as Shalmaneser III and Tiglath-pileser III had done. Hieroglyphic inscriptions indicate likely Assyrian sovereignty over a number of cities in the region called Tabal, from Tiglath-pileser's reign onwards. Five kings of the region are included among Tiglath-pileser's tributaries (see **Tabal**). Assyrian intervention in the region during Sargon's reign led to a contest with Midas/Mita, king of the Phrygian/Mushki people, whose territorial ambitions also extended into eastern Anatolia. But a major military showdown between Assyria and Phrygia was avoided when a *détente* was established between their rulers (see **Phrygia**). Sargon continued to campaign in Tabal right up to the last year of his life, when he was killed in the region probably while fighting the Cimmerians there.

Sargon's son and successor Sennacherib (704–681) was faced on his accession with uprisings throughout the empire. In response to these, he undertook campaigns to the Zagros mountain region and Iran in the east, to the Syro-Palestinian region in the west, and to Babylonia in the south, crushing the rebellions in these regions with ruthless efficiency. A record of his campaigns in the latter two regions appears on a prism now

Figure 15 Tiglath-pileser III, from Nimrud.

housed in the Oriental Institute, University of Chicago (**Chav.* 345–9). See also the 'Bavian inscription' (**Chav.* 349), and **Babylonia** for Sennacherib's attacks upon and destruction of Babylon. In the reign of Sennacherib's son and successor Esarhaddon (680–669), Assyrian sovereignty extended to Egypt, conquered by Esarhaddon after a short campaign. In the reign of Ashurbanipal (668–630/627), the last significant Assyrian king (for Esarhaddon's treaty formalizing his son's succession, see *SAA* II: XXIX–XXXI, *28–58), the empire reached its greatest territorial limits. It extended from Elam in the east to central-eastern Anatolia in the west, and from Armenia (Urartu) in the north to Egypt in the southwest and the Persian Gulf in the southeast (**Chav.* 360–8).

During the Neo-Assyrian period, the kingdom's administrative centre changed several times, firstly from Ashur to Nimrud, later to Nineveh, then for a brief period to Sargon II's new city Dur-Sharrukin (mod. Khorsabad), and finally back to Nineveh, where it remained until the fall of the kingdom. Ashur, however, continued to be Assyria's religious centre, the city where Assyrian kings were crowned and buried. Throughout the Neo-Assyrian era, periods of prosperity and great military achievement alternated with stagnation, major rebellions among the subject states, and serious political upheavals within the homeland itself. The narrow militaristic policy of the Assyrians has been held largely responsible for this. Many of the Assyrian kings looked upon their subject territories essentially as revenue-producing areas, and used brute force and mass deportations of conquered populations to maintain their hold over these

Figure 16 Assyrian attack on an enemy city, from Nimrud.

territories. By Ashurbanipal's reign, the empire had far outgrown the Assyrians' ability to maintain it and hold it in subjection. The problems faced by the last Assyrian kings of an ever-widening circle of enemies abroad were almost certainly compounded by fresh outbreaks of political unrest within the homeland itself.

The final blow was delivered by a coalition formed between Nabopolassar, king of Babylonia, and the Medes (from western Iran). In 615, the Medes invaded the Assyrian homeland, and in the following year captured the city of Ashur. Then in 612 Babylonian and Median forces laid siege to Assyria's administrative capital, Nineveh. Nineveh was captured and destroyed. With its fall, the backbone of Assyrian resistance to the invaders was broken. By the end of the year, all the chief cities of the Assyrian homeland had been destroyed. The Assyrians' long lease of power in western Asia was at an end.

Saggs (1984), Grayson (1995; *OEANE* 1: 228–33), relevant chapters in *CAH* II.1, II.2, III.1, III.2, Parpola and Whiting (1997).

Asusu Iron Age city on or near the west bank of the Tigris in central Mesopotamia, near the city of Dur-Kurigalzu. It is attested in the texts of the Assyrian king Tukulti-Ninurta II (890–884), who pitched camp there in the course of his last recorded campaign (885) after his conquests in the land of Utu on the Tigris and before marching his troops to Dur-Kurigalzu (**RIMA* 2: 173).

Athymbra M1 city in Caria (or Lydia?), western Anatolia, 30 km east of mod. Aydın (*BAGRW* 61 G2). According to Strabo (14.1.46; cf. Stephanus of Byzantium s.v. Athymbra), the city was founded by a Spartan called Athymbrus, from an amalgamation of two earlier cities, Athymbrada and Hydreia, on the site where the Hellenistic city Nysa was later built. The new city was founded by the Seleucid king Antiochus I (324–261), and named after his wife, Nysa, though the original name Athymbra appears to have been used until late C3.

Bean (*PECS* 636–7, s.v. Nysa).

Atkun Iron Age city in northeastern Mesopotamia, conquered by the Assyrian king Ashurnasirpal II in a campaign which he launched from Nineveh against the cities at the foot of Mts Nipur and Pasate in his first regnal year (883) (**RIMA* 2: 198). He names Ushhu and Pilazi among these cities, and refers to twenty others in their environs.

Atlila Iron Age city in the land of Zamua, which was located in the borderlands between northeastern Mesopotamia and northwestern Iran. The Assyrian king Ashurnasirpal II refers to it in the record of his campaign against Zamua in 880 (**RIMA* 2: 208). He reports that he undertook the renovation and refortification of the city which had previously been captured by the Babylonian king Sibir and had fallen into a state of ruin. He built a palace there, to serve as a royal residence, and renamed the city Dur-Ashur.

Atlit (map 8) Settlement located on the coast of mod. Israel, 30 km south of Haifa. Occupation levels have been dated to the Middle/Late Bronze Age, Iron Age, Persian, Hellenistic, and mediaeval periods. The site was first excavated from 1930 to 1935 by C. N. Johns of the Dept of Antiquities in Palestine. Johns brought to light remains of Phoenician settlement and an Iron Age/Persian period necropolis, though his investigations were concentrated primarily on the remains of a C13 CE Crusader settlement and fortress. The necropolis contained cremation burials dating to Iron Age II, with a shift to inhumation in C6.

Renewed excavations at the site, conducted by A. Haggi and A. Raban of Haifa University, focused primarily on the artificial harbour of the Phoenician settlement at Atlit. On the basis of Carbon 14 testing, the excavators have dated the harbour to the first half of Iron Age II, probably C9. They note that it replaced the old port at the southern bay of Dor, which had served as the main port of the area from Middle Bronze Age II, commenting that the new location on the northern bay at Atlit was a much more suitable location for an artificial harbour, able to serve and shelter larger vessels.

Johns (*NEAHL* 1: 112–17), Raban and Linder (*NEAHL* 1: 117–20), Haggi (2006).

Atriya Late Bronze Age fortress in the land of Iyalanda (= Classical Alinda?), western Anatolia. It was the only fortified settlement left intact by the Hittite king Hattusili III (1267–1237) during a campaign which he conducted against rebellious vassals in the region. Hattusili reports this in a letter he wrote to the king of Ahhiyawa, often (though misleadingly) referred to as the 'Tawagalawa' letter (see glossary) (*Garstang and Gurney, 1959: 112). Subsequently Atriya came under, or was restored to, Hittite control. A document commonly known as the 'Milawata letter' reports negotiations over a hostage exchange between Hattusili's son and successor Tudhaliya IV (1237–1209), if he is the author of the letter, and the letter's addressee – very likely a king of Mira (q.v.) called Tarkasnawa – to secure the return of prisoners taken by the latter's father from Atriya and the nearby town of Utima (**HDT* 145–6).

Attarimma Late Bronze Age city and country in western Anatolia, within or near the territory of the Lukka Lands. It was one of the lands captured by the renegade Hittite vassal Madduwatta during his campaigns in the region in early C14 (**HDT* 158). At the beginning of the Hittite king Mursili II's reign (1321), Attarimma had apparently joined a general anti-Hittite uprising in the west, for when Mursili campaigned there in his third year, troops from Huwarsanassa, Attarimma, and Suruta fled before him and sought refuge in the land of Arzawa 'Minor' (**AM* 39–40, **CS* II: 85). In mid C13, during the reign of Hattusili III, the city of Attarimma was destroyed in a further anti-Hittite uprising, on this occasion stirred up by a certain Piyamaradu, an agent of the king of Ahhiyawa (*Garstang and Gurney, 1959: 111).

Atuna (Tun(n)a) (map 18) Iron Age city in southern Anatolia in the region of Tabal, attested in Assyrian records from the reigns of Tiglath-pileser III (745–727) and Sargon II (721–705). Atuna's king, Ushhitti, was one of five kings of Tabal who made tribute payments to Tiglath-pileser (**Tigl. III* 68–9, 108–9), no doubt as a form of insurance against Assyrian aggression. The benefits of compliance with Assyria were demonstrated when Sargon handed over to one of Ushhitti's successors, a man called Kurti (name formerly read as Matti), the city of Shinuhtu. He did this in the fourth year of his reign after storming Shinuhtu and deposing its king Kiakki (Luwian Kiyakiya). The latter had broken his oath to Sargon by discontinuing his tribute-payments (**ARAB* II: 4, 27). But Kurti could not be relied upon to maintain his allegiance to Assyria. For a time, he aligned himself with the Phrygian king Mita/Midas, until exemplary action taken by Sargon against another Tabalic king Ambaris (see **Tabal**) persuaded him to switch back to Sargon, sending an envoy to the Assyrian king, at that time in Media, to renew his homage and his tribute payments (**ARAB* II: 111). Around 710, Atuna joined with its neighbour Ishtuanda for an attack on the cities of Bit-Paruta (Bit-Burutash) (**SAA* I: 6, no. 1), the largest of the kingdoms in the Tabal region, perhaps newly constituted under Sargon (see under **Tabal**).

There has been some debate about where precisely Atuna lay, and whether or not it was connected with 'Mt Tunni, the silver-mountain' referred to by the Assyrian king Shalmaneser III. The city has been identified with Classical Tynna (Hittite Dunna) and located at Zeyve Höyük (map 7). However, it is more likely to have lain further to the north, in the vicinity of mod. Aksaray. This is suggested by the probability that Aksaray was the centre of the kingdom of Shinuhtu, whose territory was reassigned to Atuna's king Kurti following Sargon's conquest of Shinuhtu in 718. The Kurti of Assyrian records is almost certainly to be identified with the king called Kurtis in a Luwian hieroglyphic inscription found on a stele near the mod. Turkish village Bohça, located on the southernmost bend of the Kızıl Irmak r. (*CHLI* I: 479). This may well have been the capital of the kingdom of Atuna, whose territory was extended to Aksaray when Sargon assigned to it the capital of the former kingdom of Shinuhtu.

CLHI I: 431–2.

Awan (map 12) City and kingdom in southwestern Iran, attested in Early Bronze Age Mesopotamian and Elamite texts. Located either in the region of Susiana or in the highlands lying to its north, Awan was closely associated with the kingdom of Elam, and is sometimes represented in the texts as part of this kingdom. To judge from the

Sumerian King List, it was already taking an active and aggressive role in southern Mesopotamia by mid M3. The King List reports that it conquered the city-state of Ur, which then exercised hegemony in southern Mesopotamia, and thenceforth ruled over the region for 356 years before it in turn was attacked and deprived of its hegemonic status by the northern Sumerian city-state Kish (*Chav. 83). As far as this account has any basis in fact (the 356-year rule is obviously a gross exaggeration), the events which it records can be attributed to a so-called 'First Dynasty' of Awan. But it should be noted that we have no confirmation from other sources of a period of foreign rule over southern Mesopotamia in this phase (Early Dynastic I) of its history.

In the early years of the Akkadian empire, Awan was one of the states, which included Elam, Parahshum (Sumerian Marhashi), and Susa, attacked and plundered by the Akkadian king Sargon (2334–2279). Following Sargon's death, an anti-Akkadian alliance consisting of Elam, Parahshum, and Zahara was decisively defeated by Sargon's son and successor Rimush (2278–2270) (*Chav. 19–20). Awan is not mentioned in this campaign, beyond a passing reference to the capture of Zahara's ruler and military commander Sargapi between Awan and Susa by the river Qablitum (*DaK 207). Akkadian control was firmly re-established over Elam and other parts of western Iran, including Susa. This control was consolidated during the reign of Rimush's brother and successor Manishtushu (2269–2255), who campaigned east of the Tigris and claimed to have captured the Elamite capital Anshan. A document dating to the reign of his son and successor Naram-Sin (2254–2218) is commonly considered to be a treaty which Naram-Sin drew up with Awan's king Hita (who appears as no. 11 in the Old Babylonian list of kings of Awan and Shimashki; on this list, see below). However, neither Hita nor Awan is actually named in the document, which imposes upon the unidentified ruler obligations similar to those specified in a vassal treaty (*Hinz, 1967). The document survives in an Elamite version discovered at Susa. It has the distinction of being the longest of all the Old Elamite inscriptions.

The most important and best attested of all the kings of Awan was Puzur-Inshushinak, twelfth and last king of Awan's second royal line. (Information about this line, sometimes inappropriately called a dynasty, is provided by an early M2 Old Babylonian school-text from Susa. Of dubious reliability, the text records two lists of rulers, twelve in each list, referred to respectively as 'kings of Awan' and 'kings of Shimashki'. For the lists, see *DaK 317.) Puzur-Inshushinak appears in a total of twelve inscriptions, some written in Elamite, some in Akkadian. One of the latter enables us to synchronize him with Ur-Nammu (2112–2095), founder of the Ur III dynasty, thus dating his reign to early C21. The fact that Puzur-Inshushinak's titulature varies in his inscriptions, from *ensi* (mayor, city-ruler) of Susa to GÌR.NÍTA (viceroy? military governor?) of Elam, to *lugal* (king) of Awan, has raised questions about his actual ethnic origins. Was he in fact of Awanite blood? Or was he of Susianite blood? Did his kingship in Awan represent the culmination of a career progression, from governor of Susa to king of Awan? Whatever the answers to these questions, Puzur-Inshushinak apparently had very high aspirations, if not delusions of grandeur. In one of his Akkadian inscriptions, he claims that his god Inshushinak had given him dominion over the four quarters of the world, an indication that he entertained ambitions of establishing himself as ruler of a large empire, perhaps with Awan as his base. On his way towards achieving this, he claims to have conquered eighty-one cities or regions. These were probably all located east of the Tigris, but an inscription of

Ur-Nammu indicates that he also had control over a number of cities and lands within central Mesopotamia.

His imperial aspirations were abruptly ended when Ur-Nammu confronted him in battle and inflicted a resounding defeat upon him. We do not know whether Ur-Nammu now totally deprived him of power. It has been suggested that he may have set him up as ruler of a much reduced kingdom subject to the overlordship of the Ur III administration. From then on, Awan and other Elamite states were incorporated into the Ur III empire. Ibbi-Sin (2028–2004), last of the Ur III rulers, records a campaign which he undertook against Awan, and also against Susa and Adamdun, presumably in response to a rebellion by these states. He claims to have subdued them and captured their leaders in a single day. But it was perhaps the Gutians who were responsible for delivering to Awan the final *coup de grâce*.

D. T. Potts (1999: 85–129).

Awarna Late Bronze Age city in southwestern Anatolia, attested in both a cuneiform inscription and a hieroglyphic inscription, in each case together with the city of Pina(li). The former, commonly known as the 'Milawata letter' (**HDT* 144–6) and generally assigned to the Hittite king Tudhaliya IV (1237–1209), refers to hostages taken from Awarna and Pina, though the fragmentary nature of the relevant passage leaves it unclear who took the hostages, and in what circumstances. Subsequently, the hostages were involved in hostage exchange negotiations between Tudhaliya and the addressee of the letter. (The latter's name has not survived, but he is very likely to be identified with Tarkasnawa, ruler of the Hittite vassal kingdom of Mira.) In the hieroglyphic, so-called Yalburt (q.v.), inscription, Awarna and Pina(li) appear among the lands conquered by Tudhaliya during a campaign against the Lukka Lands (*Hawkins, 1995: 70–1). Both inscriptions may refer to the same episode. An identification has been suggested between Awarna and the city of Xanthus in Classical Lycia, though as yet there is no evidence of Bronze Age settlement at Xanthus.

Ayanis see **Rusahinili (Eidurukai).**

Ayapir Iron Age Elamite town or sub-kingdom in southwestern Iran in the plain of Izeh (Malamir). In C6 (or perhaps C7) its chief was a man called Hanni, son of Tahhi, who was subordinate to a king Shutur-Nahhunte, son of Indada. This information is provided by the inscriptions which Hanni had carved on two rock-monuments at the sites of Kul-e Farah and Shikaft-e Salman on the Izeh plain (see ***Izeh***).

de Waele (1976), Stolper (*RlA* 7: 276–81).

Ayasuluk see **Apasa.**

Azalla (1) Oasis in the Syrian desert, within reach of Damascus. Azalla is mentioned in accounts of the ninth campaign of the Assyrian king Ashurbanipal (668–630/627) which he directed against the Arabs. It is described as a settlement 'in the desert, a remote place where there are no field animals, nor do the birds nest there'.

(H. D. Baker)
Radner (2006: 298–9).

Azalla (2) see Izalla.

Azallu see Zallu.

Azatiwataya see *Karatepe*.

Azekah (*Tell Zakariyah*) (map 8) Small fortress-settlement located in the Judaean foothills, southern Palestine, to the northeast of Lachish. It is frequently attested in *OT* sources. The site was excavated for three seasons, from 1898 to 1899, by F. J. Bliss and R. A. S. Macalister for the Palestine Exploration Fund. They concluded that there were four main periods of occupation, the first beginning before 1500, the last extending to the Byzantine era. In a number of respects, their stratigraphy and proposed chronology have been questioned. For example, it now seems likely that the fortress which they dated to the late C10 Israelite king Rehoboam (who in *OT* tradition fortified a number of cities, including Azekah, for the defence of Judah; 2 Chronicles 11:5–10), was first constructed in C8. This conclusion is based partly on a comparison with similar C9 and C8 fortresses now excavated elsewhere in the region, and partly on synchronistic data provided by a number of *lamelekh* seal impressions (see glossary) belonging to the end of C8. Around this time, the Assyrian king Sargon II conducted an expedition against the city of Ashdod which had rebelled against him. An Assyrian inscription referring to Azekah (Azaqa) has been dated by Tadmor (1958: 80–4) to this campaign. In early C6, according to a report in Jeremiah 34:7, Lachish and Azekah held out against the Babylonian king Nebuchadnezzar II as the last fortified cities in Judah. Azekah eventually fell to Nebuchadnezzar not long before his conquest of Jerusalem in 586. An inscribed ostracon of this period, found in a guardhouse at Lachish and mentioning both Azekah and Lachish, has been interpreted by some scholars as a letter referring to this event (**ANET* 322).

Nehemiah 11:30 reports that Azekah was one of a number of towns resettled by families from the tribe of Judah in the post-exilic period. Written sources indicate that the city still existed in Roman times, following the destruction of the Second Temple.

Stern (*NEAEHL* 1: 123–4), Laughlin (2006: 43–5).

Aznavurtepe (*Anzavurtepe*) (map 20) Urartian fortress located to the north of Lake Van, eastern Anatolia, near Patnos. Its fortified enclosure contained a military camp and temple, built by the Urartian king Ishpuini and his son and co-regent Minua in late C9. The temple was dedicated to Haldi, chief god of the Urartian pantheon. It was constructed on the standard square plan of Urartian temples, and has extremely thick walls faced with dressed basalt ashlar (see glossary). Fragments of mural decoration were found in the temple's interior. Burney notes the regularity of the enclosure's towers, with each built as a unit and then joined to the others by a screen wall. Aznavurtepe was one of several fortresses built by Ishpuini and Minua around Lake Van. These fortresses are thought to have been intended as much for offensive as for defensive purposes, providing a base for troops prior to campaigns against their enemies in neighbouring regions to the north. The fortress may also have served as an enclosure for livestock taken as booty in the course of these campaigns. An inscription found at Aznavurtepe contains a record of Minua's exploits, which include the suppression of a rebellion probably early in the king's reign in the land of Sharitu, located in Parsua to the south of Lake Urmia.

*Balkan (1960), Burney and Lang (1971: 140–1; 1998: 150).

Azu see *Hadidi, Tell*.

Azzi-Hayasa (map 3) Late Bronze Age country in northeastern Anatolia, between the Hittite Upper Land (q.v.) and the Euphrates. Azzi-Hayasa participated in the comprehensive invasions of the Hittite homeland during the first half of C14, in the reign of the Hittite king Tudhaliya III, sacking the Upper Land and establishing a frontier at Samuha, which probably lay on the upper course of the Marassantiya (Halys) r. (*Bryce, 2005: 146). In the context of the Hittite campaigns of reconquest, Tudhaliya's son Suppiluliuma invaded Azzi-Hayasa and forced a showdown with its king Karanni (or Lanni) (**DS* 66, **CS* I 187). Almost certainly, the confrontation resulted in a Hittite victory, though the passage recording its outcome is not extant. Subsequently, Azzi-Hayasa was reduced to Hittite vassal status, and when Suppiluliuma became king, he drew up a treaty with Hukkana, its ruler, now linked to the Hittite royal family by his marriage to Suppiluliuma's sister (**HDT* 26–34). A unique feature of the treaty is the strict ban which Suppiluliuma imposed on brother–sister marriages, which had apparently been common in the country.

Azzi-Hayasa did not long remain submissive to Hittite overlordship. During the reign of Suppiluliuma's son and successor Mursili II (1321–1295), it broke its ties with Hatti, and in 1315 once more invaded the Upper Land, under its king Anniya. Anniya's forces occupied the land, taking people and livestock from it as booty (**AM* 96–107, **CS* II: 87–8). Mursili demanded their return, but Anniya refused, prompting a Hittite attack on his fortress-settlement Ura on Azzi-Hayasa's frontier. This may have been intended as a prelude to a more extensive campaign against Anniya's kingdom. But Mursili's military commitments elsewhere prevented him from undertaking such a campaign. Anniya's forces continued to occupy the Upper Land for another two years, until 1313 when a Hittite expeditionary force under the command of Mursili's general Nuwanza drove them from it (**AM* 116–19, 130–3). The following year Mursili reconquered Azzi-Hayasa itself, but another year was to elapse before he received its formal submission. Azzi-Hayasa again figures among rebel states which rose up against Hatti during the reign of the Hittite king Tudhaliya IV (1237–1209), in the period when the Hittite empire was beginning to disintegrate (Bryce, 2005: 304). Aripsa and Dukkama were fortified cities of Azzi.

**RGTC* 6: 59–60.

B

Baba Jan Tepe (map 13) Iron Age (Median?) settlement in western Iran, located in the province of Luristan, 170 km northwest of mod. Khorramabad. The site was excavated by C. Goff for the Institute of Archaeology, University of London, between 1966 and 1969. Settlement, which began in C9 and extended over several mounds, continued through three phases until the site was abandoned, probably in the first half of C6, after a period of 'squatter occupation'. Baba Jan Tepe's most prominent features were a so-called 'manor', 33 m × 34 m, which was fortified with seven towers and had a central courtyard flanked by long rectangular rooms, and a 'fort' with a large square hall also flanked by long rectangular rooms. The fort's destruction by fire in the site's second occupation phase may have been connected with an Assyrian campaign in this region during the reign of the Assyrian king Sennacherib (704–681).

Goff (1968–85), Dandamaev and Lukonin (1989: 62–4).

Bab edh-Dhra (map 8) 5 ha Early Bronze Age site in Jordan, on the plain southeast of the Dead Sea. It comprised a walled town, an area of settlement beyond it, and a large cemetery. Following a village existence in its earliest phase (c. 3150–3000), the settlement developed a flourishing urban culture between 3000 and 2300. It was fortified by a 7 m wide stone wall, within which lay a sanctuary with 'broadroom', a courtyard with a circular stone altar, and domestic and industrial areas. The assemblage of artefacts from the site, including weapons, jewellery, and a large number of cylinder-seal impressions, indicates widespread trading contacts, extending as far as Egypt and Mesopotamia. Following its destruction c. 2300, the settlement reverted to a village existence before it was finally abandoned c. 2000. Several scholars have suggested an identification with Sodom in *OT* tradition.

Schaub (*NEAEHL* 1: 130–6).

Babitu Iron Age frontier city of the land of Zamua, located in a mountain pass near the upper reaches of the Lesser Zab r., northeastern Mesopotamia. Liverani suggests identifying it with the mod. Bazian pass. The pass of Babitu provided access from the Assyrian plain into Zamua, which lay in the borderlands between northeastern Mesopotamia and northwestern Iran. Zamua was converted into an Assyrian province by the Assyrian king Adad-nirari II (911–891). In 881 and 880, the third and fourth regnal years of Ashurnasirpal II, grandson of Adad-nirari, Zamua rebelled three times against Assyrian overlordship. On the first occasion, the rebels tried to block Ashurnasirpal's advance by building a wall across the pass at Babitu. But neither this nor the stand made by the combined forces of the rebels prevented the Assyrian conquest and plunder of their cities. On his two subsequent campaigns against Zamua, Ashurnasirpal also entered the land via the passes of Mt Babitu.

**RIMA* 2: 203–5, Liverani (1992: 46).

Babylon (maps 10, 11, 13, 16) Southern Mesopotamian city located on a branch of the Euphrates r., c. 90 km southwest of Baghdad. The name Babili is of unknown linguistic origin, but it came to be interpreted by the Babylonians themselves as Akkadian *Bab-ili(m)* meaning 'gate of God'. 'Babylon' is the Greek form of the name. The biblical form is *Babel*. According to Genesis 11:9, the name was derived from the Hebrew verb *balal*, 'to confuse'. The tradition reported by Genesis is that human beings originally spoke a single common language, but when they were building a city and tower on the site which became known as Babel, God decided to 'confuse their language', making it impossible for them to understand one another. He replaced the one language with many separate languages, whose speakers were thenceforth scattered over all the earth (Genesis 11:1–9). Until mod. times, a hill on the northern part of the site has retained the name Babil.

The site of Babylon is spread over a number of mounds, within a roughly rectangular walled area extending over an area of c. 450 ha. The city is bisected by the Euphrates r. running roughly north–south, though the settlement-mounds are concentrated on the side lying on the eastern bank, and this is the area which has been investigated by archaeologists. The western part of the city remains poorly known, and in fact some of it now lies under the mod. river course, which has shifted somewhat to the west since antiquity. The city's history of occupation extends from mid M3 until C2 CE, with subsequent Arab occupation in late M1 CE. Particularly because of its biblical associations, the site attracted many early European travellers, one of the first being the C12 CE Spanish rabbi Benjamin of Tudela, who wrote a still extant description of the ruins. A survey of the site by C. J. Rich in 1811 served as a prelude to a number of minor excavations carried out there by a succession of C19 proto-archaeologists, including A. H. Layard and H. C. Rawlinson. Major excavations were conducted between 1899 and 1914 by German teams under the direction of R. Koldewey. The main focus of these excavations was the city of the Neo-Babylonian period (626–539). In the 1970s and 1980s further excavations and some substantial restoration work were undertaken by the Iraqi Dept of Antiquities.

Babylon is first attested in written records of the Akkadian and Ur III periods. In C24 it was destroyed by the Akkadian king Sargon, but was probably rebuilt soon after. In the reign of the last Akkadian king, Shar-kali-sharri (2217–2193), it contained at least two temples. Subsequently, it was attacked and captured by the Ur III king Shulgi (2094–2047), who plundered it, taking booty removed from the Esagila, the temple precinct of the god Marduk (see below). For a time, Babylon was a provincial centre of the Ur III administration, but its rise to high prominence did not begin until 1894 when it became the seat of an Amorite ruling dynasty, founded by Sumu-Abum. This was the starting point of its development into one of the greatest of the cities of western Asia. Under the first five kings of the Amorite dynasty (1894–1793), it was the capital of one of a number of petty kingdoms in Mesopotamia. But in the reign of the dynasty's sixth king, Hammurabi (1792–1750), it became the centre of the first great Babylonian empire, whose sway extended through the whole of Mesopotamia. Material remains of Babylon in this period include several residential buildings in the walled inner city, from which clay tablets have been recovered. Information provided by these indicates the existence of a large number of temples built or rebuilt within the inner city at this time, including the temple precinct Esagila, and temples to a number of other deities, including Enlil, Ishtar, and Shamash. In general, though, knowledge of the Old Babylonian city remains limited because the high water table has mostly prevented the excavators from reaching those levels.

The Old Babylonian empire began to contract almost immediately after Hammurabi's death. Nevertheless, the succeeding members of his dynasty managed to maintain their power-base in Babylon for the next 150 years, until the city was captured and sacked by the Hittite king Mursili I c. 1595, ending the reign of its last king, Samsu-ditana. The Hittite victory paved the way for the establishment of a Kassite dynasty in Babylonia, under whose regime Babylon gained a new lease of life as a great centre of culture, commerce, and learning. If we can judge from tablets dating to late C12, which refer to the city's eight gates, its many temples, and its division into ten districts, Babylon may have had many of the same basic features and much the same layout under Kassite rule as it did in the later Neo-Babylonian period. But in late C15 or early C14, it lost its status as the administrative capital of the kingdom when the royal seat was shifted to a new site, the city of Dur-Kurigalzu (mod. Aqar Quf), founded by the Kassite king Kurigalzu I.

In the final centuries of the Late Bronze Age, the Kassites became embroiled in disputes and conflicts with their northern neighbour Assyria, and towards the end of C13 the Assyrian king Tukulti-Ninurta I swept across Babylonia's frontiers, and captured Babylon. But the Assyrian occupation was shortlived. Fifteen years after Tukulti-Ninurta's death in 1208, Babylonia regained its independence, and the Kassite dynasty managed to hold out against foreign aggressors for another seven decades, before its final collapse in mid C12. Babylon survived its fall, but remained relatively insignificant for several centuries before experiencing a resurgence in its fortunes,

Figure 17 Hammurabi and part of law code.

firstly in the reign of Nabu-apla-iddina (888–855) and subsequently in that of Nabonassar (Nabu-nasir; 747–734). The Babylonian Chronicles (see glossary) and the 'Ptolemaic Canon' begin their accounts of Babylonian history from the date of the latter's accession. They saw it as the dawn of a new era in Babylonian history. Nabonassar appears to have enjoyed the patronage of the Assyrian king Tiglath-pileser III, on whose support he relied for securing his kingdom against hostile action by Aramaean and Chaldaean tribes.

Subsequently, after Nabonassar's death, Babylon along with the rest of Babylonia came under Tiglath-pileser's direct rule. But resistance against Assyria was stirred afresh by the Chaldaean leader Marduk-apla-iddina II (721–710) (see **Babylonia**). When Marduk-apla-iddina was finally forced to flee to the south c. 700, the Assyrian king Sennacherib descended upon Babylon, plundered it, and carried off the fugitive's wives and members of his retinue to Assyria. When Babylonia again rose up against Assyria ten years later (689), under the leadership of another Chaldaean tribal chief, Mushezib-Marduk, Sennacherib once again attacked the city. It held out against his besieging forces for fifteen months before finally falling to him. Furious at its resistance, Sennacherib plundered Babylon of its treasures, and either carried off or smashed the statues of its gods. He claimed that he totally destroyed the city, flooding it with the waters of specially dug canals, and turning it into a wasteland (**CS* II: 305, **Chav.* 349). Whether or not Babylon was as thoroughly devastated as Sennacherib would have us believe, it was extensively restored under his first two successors, Esarhaddon and Ashurbanipal, who ordered that its temples be rebuilt, and that the cult-statues and sacred furniture taken from these temples be returned (for Esarhaddon's contribution to the city's reconstruction, see **Chav.* 354–5). In 652, Babylon and other Babylonian cities were caught up in the disputes between Ashurbanipal and his elder brother Shamash-shum-ukin, whom Ashurbanipal had placed on the throne of Babylon. Shamash-shum-ukin developed a number of grievances against Ashurbanipal, and mounting tensions between the brothers eventually erupted into open conflict, in the course of which Ashurbanipal's forces besieged and captured Babylon, where Shamash-shum-ukin had apparently made a final stand. Parts of the city were put to the torch, and it is thought that Shamash-shum-ukin may have died in the royal palace at this time (648). (For a treaty made by Ashurbanipal with a group of Babylonian allies who had initially joined the rebellion but subsequently switched their allegiance to Ashurbanipal, see *SAA* II: XXXII–XXXIII, *64–8.) It is suggested that the Sealanders may have been the group in question.

After the fall of the Assyrian empire in late C7, Babylon entered the most illustrious phase of its history, as the capital of the Neo-Babylonian empire. Drawing on the enormous resources in human labour, booty, and tribute gathered from all parts of the empire, the first two Neo-Babylonian kings, Nabopolassar (626–605) and Nebuchadnezzar II (604–562), reconstructed the city and its temples on a massive scale. The Euphrates flowed through the city and divided it into two sectors of unequal size, the bigger and better known one on the river's east bank. A large bridge, supported on boat-shaped piers, was built across the river to link both sectors of the city. Fortifications were provided by outer and inner baked-brick walls (which we know from inscriptional evidence were initially built in the Neo-Assyrian period), pierced by eight gates and extending over a distance of c. 18 km. The fortifications were strengthened by an embankment and a moat. Herodotus (1.179) claims that the walls were wide enough at the top to provide passage for a four-horse chariot. (He allegedly visited the city a century after the end of Nebuchadnezzar's reign, and provides a detailed description of it, though his account contains some gross exaggerations and is inconsistent with what is known of Babylon from its archaeological remains.)

The most famous of the city's gates is the 15 m high Ishtar Gate, decorated with blue-glazed dragon figures and moulded animal reliefs. A reconstruction of the gate is housed in the Vorderasiatisches Museum in Berlin. Beneath the gate's arched entrance passed the 250 m long Processional Way, which was laid out on a north–south axis, and linked the quay where the king embarked for his journey to the Temple of the New Year festival in the north with the Esagila, the temple precinct of Marduk, in the south. On the way, it passed by the Etemenanki complex (see below). The city's main palace, the so-called 'Southern Palace' (the 'Südburg', as the excavators dubbed it), was located in the northwestern corner of the eastern sector of the inner city. Built by Nabopolassar and rebuilt by Nebuchadnezzar, the complex encompassed five courtyards and numerous apartments and reception rooms. The third and most important courtyard gave access to what has been identified as the king's throne-room, imagined by some to be the place where Belshazzar's feast was held and Alexander the Great breathed his last. The throne-room (73 m × 10.4 m) has been compared in size to the Gallery of Mirrors at Versailles.

Towards the end of his reign, Nebuchadnezzar built a second palace immediately to the north of his principal palace. He and his successors may have used part of it as a 'museum', since assorted antiquities were discovered there; however, there is now some doubt as to whether these items were deliberately collected and kept there out of antiquarian interest. The contents of the so-called museum, some of which date back to M3, included a famous basalt statue of a lion, and statues and stelae of gods, kings, and governors. Both palaces were provided with huge fortification systems. At the extreme north end of the city, within Nebuchadnezzar's outer defensive wall, lay the 'summer palace', so called because of the remains of what were originally thought to be ventilation shafts, but which turned out to be the remains of the substructure of the massive fort built on the site during the Parthian era. The palace as a whole is poorly preserved. Within the centre of the city lay the temple precinct Esagila. This comprised the main shrine of the god Marduk, head of the Babylonian pantheon at this time. Within the Marduk temple and the precinct which enclosed it were cellas dedicated to other deities, including the principal gods Ea and Nabu. To the north of this complex lay another cultic precinct, Etemenanki, which housed the ziggurat dedicated to Marduk. This consisted of six stepped platforms, on the top of which was a shrine to Marduk. It may first have been built in the Late Bronze Age. In addition to these two great religious precincts, other temples were scattered around the city and were more intimately integrated into the urban fabric; they lacked enclosing precincts but simply nestled within the areas of residential housing. Various unsuccessful attempts have been made to locate the famous 'Hanging Gardens of Babylon' (as attested, e.g., in Berossus, *FGrH* 680 F9a = **PE* 44, no. 18ii). S. Dalley has argued that the structures that inspired this tradition were in fact located in Nineveh.

After the Neo-Babylonian empire fell to the Persian Cyrus II, who entered Babylon in triumph in 539 (Nabonidus Chronicle: **ABC* 110, **CS* I: 468, **Chav.* 420, **PE* 51, no. 1; Cyrus Cylinder: **Chav.* 428–9, **CS* II: 315, **PE* 71, no. 21; cf. Herodotus 1.189–92), Babylon continued to be used as a royal residence by the Persian kings, and indeed a number of new building or rebuilding projects were carried out by these kings, especially Cyrus (*PE 78, no. 23) and Artaxerxes II. In 331 Alexander the Great entered the city (Curtius 5.1.17–23; cf. Arrian, *Anabasis* 3.16.3). His vision was to make it the capital of his new world empire. But this vision was never realized, and after Alexander's death in Babylon in 323, the city declined into insignificance, especially with the foundation of a new city, Seleucia, on the Tigris. The city enjoyed a period of renewal during the Parthian era, but was eventually abandoned, probably in C2 CE, until the Arabs resettled the site some seven centuries later.

In *OT* tradition, Babylon was the main place of exile for large numbers of Jews deported by Nebuchadnezzar from their homeland during the reign of the Judaean king Jehoiachin (609–598) (2 Kings 24:12–16). Records from Nebuchadnezzar's palace, which list rations to be provided to Jehoiachin and his family, provide contemporary historical evidence of this event. The deportees and their descendants remained in Babylon until they were liberated by Cyrus, following his conquest of the city in 539. Cyrus allowed them return to Jerusalem. It was this which led the Hebrew prophet Isaiah to refer to Cyrus as the anointed of God (Isaiah 45:1). However, a large Jewish community continued to reside in Babylon, becoming increasingly integrated into the life and activities of their adoptive homeland. Biblical literature presents conflicting views on Babylon, though the most prominent image is that of a city which became a byword for luxury and decadence. Thus the book of Revelation (17:5) refers to Rome as 'Babylon, the Great, the Mother of Prostitutes and of the Abominations of the Earth'.

J. Oates (1986), J. G. Westenholz (1996a), Klengel-Brandt (*OEANE* 1: 251–6).

Babylonia (map 11) A modern term adopted from the city name Babylon and applied to southern Mesopotamia, the region extending roughly from Baghdad southwards to the Persian Gulf. Human settlement in the region dates back at least to M6. From at least the time of the earliest written records, this region was inhabited by a mixture of population groups speaking, variously, the Sumerian and Akkadian languages, with the latter becoming increasingly predominant during M3. However, for these early periods 'Babylonia' is an anachronism, since the term is used primarily to refer to the kingdom of which Babylon was the centre through much of M2 and the first half of M1. (For the same region in M3 see the entries **Akkad** and ***Sumer(ians)***.)

The political history of Babylonia is closely linked with fluctuations in the fortunes of its chief city, Babylon, which first emerged as a small village on the banks of the Euphrates in the Early Dynastic period (c. 2900–2334), and came under the control of the Akkadian and Ur III empires in the final centuries of M3. Babylon's rise to power began with the establishment of an Amorite (q.v.) ruling house in the city in 1894, when the Amorite chieftain Sumu-abum founded the first royal dynasty at Babylon. The city reached its first peak in the reign of Hammurabi (1792–1750), the sixth king of the dynasty, when it became the centre of the first great Babylonian empire, whose sway extended through the whole of Mesopotamia. Hammurabi conquered in succession Larsa (1763), Eshnunna (1762), and Mari (1762). The last of these, after regaining its independence from Assyrian rule under its energetic ruler Zimri-Lim (1774–1762), had become one of western Asia's most powerful kingdoms before it fell to Hammurabi. In his thirty-sixth regnal year, Hammurabi gained control of the final remnants of the Old Assyrian kingdom, which had reached its peak only a few decades before under its king Shamshi-Adad I (1796–1775). There was, however, another formidable power which confronted Hammurabi – the kingdom of Elam which lay to the southeast of Babylonia. Its conflicts with Babylon during Hammurabi's reign are reported in letters from the Mari archives (e.g. **LKM* 320–1). To counter Elamite aggression and expansion east of the Tigris, Hammurabi formed an alliance, and engaged in an exchange of troops, with the Mariote king Zimri-Lim (1765). Yarim-Lim, king of Aleppo, also became a member of the alliance. But the task of driving out the Elamite occupation forces was made more difficult by the fact that the local northern Mesopotamian rulers were divided in their loyalties into pro- and anti-Elamite factions. Eventually, however, the western alliance began gaining the upper hand, and the Elamite king was forced to withdraw his forces along the Tigris, in the process ravaging the territory of Eshnunna before returning to Susa. (For this whole episode, see Charpin, 2003: 69–81.)

By and large, Hammurabi was successful in halting the westward advance of the Elamite forces. Soon after his death, however, the empire which he had built began to contract. This was due in part to the emergence of a new rival dynasty called the Sealand (q.v.), which arose in the marshlands of southern Mesopotamia and won control over Babylonia as far north as the city of Nippur. Hammurabi's successor Samsu-iluna (1749–1712) had to deal with rebellions by a number of Babylonian cities in his ninth

Figure 18 Mesopotamian goddess (C18), probably from Babylon.

Figure 19 Stele of Nabonidus, from Babylon?.

regnal year, but allegedly restored order throughout the region in the following year, claiming to have killed twenty-six rebel kings (**RIME* 4: 387). Elam also remained a serious threat. Early in the reign of Hammurabi's successor-but-one Abi-eshuh (1711–1684), an Elamite campaign which Kutir-Nahhunte I, prince of Susa, conducted into Babylonia allegedly resulted in the conquest of thirty Babylonian cities. But this conquest seems to have made no lasting impact on the Mesopotamian scene, and the Old Babylonian kingdom continued for almost a century after Abi-eshuh's death. It came to an abrupt end c. 1595, in the reign of Samsu-ditana, last ruler of Hammurabi's dynasty, when Babylon was destroyed by the Hittite king Mursili I (**Chav.* 230; cf. **ABC* 156). These were troubled times, and it seems likely that the Hittites were not the only foe Babylon had to contend with in this period (*Mesop.* 382–3).

The Hittite victory facilitated the rise of a Kassite dynasty in Babylonia (see **Kassites**) under whose rulers the Babylonian kingdom once again achieved the status of a major international power. It retained this status until the Kassite dynasty came to an end c. 1155, with the fall of the kingdom to the Elamites. For almost two centuries prior to its fall, Babylonia had become embroiled in a series of disputes and conflicts with its northern neighbour Assyria. These culminated in the invasion and conquest of Babylonia by the Assyrian king Tukulti-Ninurta I (1244–1208), who hauled the

Kassite king Kashtiliash IV back to Assyria in chains (*Chav. 145–52). But fifteen years after Tukulti-Ninurta's death, a Babylonian king called Adad-shuma-usur (1216–1187), son of Kashtiliash, who had come to power in the south of the kingdom, liberated the whole of his country from Assyrian rule.

Babylonia thus regained its independence from Assyria, and the Kassite dynasty continued to hold power for another seven decades. During this time it was not entirely free of foreign interference, suffering particularly from aggression by the Elamites. None the less, during the dynasty's declining years Babylonia seems to have enjoyed brief periods of stability and prosperity, though it had by now ceased to rank as a major international power. The Kassite regime ended with the short reign of Enlil-nadin-ahi (1157–1155). A Babylonian King List then records a line of rulers referred to as the Second Dynasty of Isin (**RIMB* 2: 5–69), which lasted from 1154 until 1026 and consisted of eleven kings (not all of whom seem to have been related to each other). The dynasty's name suggests that the new political and administrative centre of Babylonia may have shifted south from Babylon to Isin for a time. But there is no actual evidence for such a shift, and it seems that most of the members of the 'dynasty' ruled from Babylon. The most famous of these rulers was the fourth king Nebuchadnezzar I (1126–1105), who invaded Elam and sacked the city of Susa, retrieving from it the statue of the god Marduk, which the Elamites had taken during their invasion of Babylonia in mid C12. Following the brief reign of Nebuchadnezzar's successor Enlil-nadin-apli (1104–1101), Babylon's throne was assumed by Marduk-nadin-ahhe (1100–1083) who soon became involved in conflicts with his Assyrian counterpart Tiglath-pileser I. His campaigns into Assyrian territory, during which he captured the royal city Ekallatum near Ashur and carried off from it statues of the gods Adad and Shala (according to a later inscription, of the Assyrian king Sennacherib; **Sennach.* 83), eventually provoked retaliation from Tiglath-pileser. The delay of ten years or more before this happened has been attributed to the king's preoccupation with his interests in the west. When he did finally move against his southern neighbour, he struck deep into Babylonian territory, capturing a number of its important cities, including Dur-Kurigalzu, Sippar, Opis, and Babylon itself (**RIMA* 2: 43).

Following the Second Isin Dynasty, Babylonia was ruled initially by the three kings of the so-called Second Sealand Dynasty (1026–1006) (see under **Sealand**), and then for the next three centuries by a succession of generally insignificant kings – with two notable exceptions (see below). It reached a particularly low point in late C10, when the Assyrian king Adad-nirari II (911–891) defeated his Babylonian counterpart Shamash-mudammiq and conquered his entire land (**RIMA* 2: 148). There was, however, some resurgence of Babylonia's fortunes under its king Nabu-apla-iddina, who succeeded to the throne in 888 and occupied it for thirty-three years. Nabu-apla-iddina was a member of the 'Dynasty of E' (so called in the Babylonian King List), founded by Nabu-mukin-apli in 979 and lasting until 732. During his long reign, Babylonia enjoyed once more a relatively high degree of peace, stability, and prosperity. This was due partly to the fact that the Aramaeans had ceased to be a threat, and partly to Nabu-apla-iddina's decisive victory over the Sutaeans (see **Sutu**), which ended their incursions into Babylonian territory. Nabu-apla-iddina's reign saw a great cultural renaissance in the land, which included the restoration of traditional cult-centres and sacred rites that had fallen into disuse.

But with the breakdown of relations between Babylonia and Assyria in the reign of the Assyrian king Shamshi-Adad V (823–811), who as crown prince had concluded a treaty with the Babylonian king Marduk-zakir-shumi (*SAA* II: XXVI–XXVII, *4–5), the relatively long period of peace and stability which Babylonia had enjoyed came to an end. Shamshi-Adad launched four campaigns against the country: the first two, in 814 and 813, were against Marduk-balassu-iqbi, successor of Marduk-zakir-shumi, and the third was against the next king, Baba-aha-iddina (812), whom Shamshi-Adad defeated and deported to Nineveh. Chaos and anarchy followed, with another resurgence in the country's fortunes in the reign of a king called Nabonassar (Nabu-nasir; 747–734). Two sets of historiographic texts, the Babylonian Chronicles and the 'Ptolemaic Canon', begin with his reign. After Nabonassar's death, Babylonia was again divided by struggles between competing power groups, including the Chaldaeans (see below), until the Assyrian king Tiglath-pileser III intervened in 729. Tiglath-pileser overthrew (Nabu-)Mukin-zeri, a usurper from the clan Bit-Amukani who happened to be occupying the throne at the time, and declared himself king of Babylonia. This instituted a period of 'double monarchy', where kingship in Babylonia was in theory shared by the Assyrian king and a Babylonian appointee. But Assyrian overlordship in Babylonia was constantly challenged, particularly by a series of Chaldaean leaders.

By C8, Chaldaean tribal groups (see **Chaldaeans**), who had apparently entered Babylonia from the northwest some time during C11 or C10 and are attested in Assyrian records from C9 onwards, had become a major political force in Babylonia. Three Chaldaean tribal leaders occupied the Babylonian throne in the course of C8, beginning with Eriba-Marduk (769–761). The most notable of them was a man called Marduk-apla-iddina II (who figures in the Bible as Merodach-baladan), a man of the Bit-Yakin tribe and a former ruler of the Sealand, who assumed kingship in 721 (he was twice king in the country: in 721–710 and 703). Marduk-apla-iddina united Babylonia under his leadership for a protracted struggle with Assyria, in alliance with the Elamites, during the reigns of Sargon II and his successor Sennacherib. He claimed to have re-established the independence of Babylonia after many years of Subarian (i.e. Assyrian) control (**RIMB* 2: 137). However, the Assyrians inflicted a number of defeats on him, and at the end of 710 he was forced to abandon his throne in Babylon and flee for his life as Sargon advanced upon the city. Babylon surrendered to Sargon, who formally became the occupant of the vacant throne at the New Year festival of 709. But Marduk-apla-iddina stirred up fresh resistance against the Assyrians (after unsuccessfully seeking asylum in Elam), first of all using his tribal capital Dur-Yakin as his base. Once again he was defeated, in a battle outside the city. However, he still managed to avoid capture by the Assyrians and to rally troops for further operations against them, until a final campaign conducted by Sennacherib in southern Babylonia, c. 703 (**CS* II: 300–2), forced him to seek refuge once more in Elam, this time successfully. He died there soon afterwards. (For a recent treatment of the Assyrian wars against Marduk-apla-iddina during Sargon's reign, see *SAA* XV: XIII–XXIII, and for reports to Sargon from his officials on Marduk-apla-iddina's movements and activities, **SAA* XV: 119 ff., nos 177 ff.)

Sennacherib now abolished the double monarchy, appointing to Babylonia's throne first an Assyrian puppet ruler, Bel-ibni, and then his own son Ashur-nadin-shumi. But Ashur-nadin-shumi was captured by the Elamite king Hallushu-Inshushinak during an Elamite attack on the northern Babylonian city Sippar, and replaced on Babylonia's throne by the Elamites' own appointee, the Babylonian Nergal-ushezib (693) (**ABC* 78).

Hallushu-Inshushinak's triumph was shortlived. In the following year, Sennacherib won a victory over Elamite and Babylonian forces near the city of Nippur, which had been captured by Nergal-ushezib. Nergal-ushezib was taken prisoner, deported to Nineveh, and executed. Hallushu-Inshushinak escaped back to Susa, where he was killed by his own people. Almost immediately after Sennacherib's victory, resistance against Assyrian rule broke out afresh, firstly under a Chaldaean tribal chief Mushezib-Marduk (Shuzubu) of the Bit-Dakkuri tribe, who secured Elamite support for his military enterprises. For several years he defied the Assyrians, though he may have suffered a military defeat at their hands, until a determined campaign launched by Sennacherib in 689 ended with the Assyrian capture and destruction of Babylon (see **Babylon**) and the deportation of Mushezib-Marduk to Assyria.

Subsequent Chaldaean leaders continued to attack Assyrian garrisons stationed in Babylonia. But the decisive blow against Assyria was delivered by Nabopolassar, a Chaldaean leader who seized the throne in Babylon in 626, founding there a dynasty which ruled over the illustrious Neo-Babylonian kingdom (626–539). In partnership with the Median ruler Cyaxares, Nabopolassar destroyed the Assyrian empire, its death throes ending with the capture and sack of the Assyrian capital Nineveh by Babylonian and Median forces in 612. The kingdom founded by Nabopolassar reached its height in the reign of his son and successor Nebuchadnezzar II (604–562). Campaigns conducted by Nebuchadnezzar in the Syro-Palestinian regions extended Babylonian power westwards to the Levant, over territories formerly controlled by both Assyria and Egypt. Sidon and Tyre were among the cities that fell to Nebuchadnezzar on the Levantine coast, the latter, according to Greek sources, after a thirteen-year siege. Jerusalem was captured in 597, and after an uprising there in 586 was totally destroyed. The deportation of its population to Babylon marked the beginning of the period of the Jewish exile. A Babylonian army may also have invaded Egypt. At this time Egypt, then ruled by the Saite (twenty-sixth) dynasty, was Babylon's chief rival for supremacy over the territories of the Syro-Palestinian region. Several Babylonian campaigns were conducted into the kingdom of Que (Classical Cilicia Pedias/Campestris, called Hume by the Babylonians) in southern Anatolia, and possibly also into the neighbouring country of Hilakku (Classical Cilicia Tracheia/Aspera). Nebuchadnezzar claimed Hume amongst his conquests, and does seem to have exercised some control over the region. In the east, the old Elamite capital Susa came for a time under Nebuchadnezzar's sovereignty (c. 595). But in spite of these impressive, far-flung conquests, the empire built by Nebuchadnezzar began to crumble soon after his death. In 539, when its throne was occupied by a man called Nabonidus, the empire fell to the Persian king Cyrus II (see **Upi (1)**), and remained under Persian sovereignty until this empire in its turn fell to Alexander the Great, who conquered Babylon in 331.

Sumerian was the predominant language of Babylonia for much of M3, but towards the end of the millennium it was gradually replaced as a spoken language by the Semitic Akkadian language. By early M2 Sumerian had died out altogether as a spoken language. It survived, however, in literary and religious texts for many centuries to come, in fact until the demise of the cuneiform written tradition. The Akkadian language is conventionally divided into a number of dialects. During M2 it underwent progressive change, passing through stages now designated as Old Babylonian and Middle Babylonian, covering respectively the first and second half of M2. Later dialects include Standard Babylonian, the literary language used in Babylonia and Assyria in later M2 and M1, and Neo- and Late Babylonian, the vernacular language of M1 Babylonia, covering the Neo-Babylonian, Achaemenid, Hellenistic, and Parthian eras. Already in earlier M1 Aramaic was gaining currency as a spoken language throughout much of the western Asian world, including Babylonia. The Aramaic script was essentially alphabetic, whereas Akkadian, following the tradition first established by the Sumerians, was written in a cuneiform script.

J. Oates (1986), Grayson (1992), Beaulieu (1995), Saggs (1995), Weisberg (1996), Leick (2003; 2007).

Bactria (map 16) Central Asian country located in Afghanistan, north of the Hindu Kush and extending roughly to the Oxus (Amu-Darya) r. It is attested in both Iranian and Classical sources, though for the pre-Hellenistic phase of its history, information provided by Iranian sources is sparse, and the Classical sources, principally Herodotus, Xenophon, and Ctesias, are considered by many scholars to have little historical value. On the basis of what we *can* glean, from both documentary and archaeological records, it seems that Bactria had developed during the early centuries of M1 into a wealthy and populous kingdom, perhaps the most powerful in Central Asia. Its wealth was derived partly from its precious metal resources, and partly from its thriving agriculture, the latter supported by large irrigation networks for which the country was noted throughout its history. According to the Bactrians, Zoroastrianism had its origins in their country. They claimed that Zoroaster's protector, Kavi Vishraspa, was one of their early kings. In a tradition recorded by the C2–3 CE Roman writer Justin (*Epitome* 5.1), Zoroaster himself was a king of Bactria.

According to Classical sources, Bactria clashed a number of times with the Assyrians. Greek writers report several expeditions which the Assyrians mounted against the country. One of these was conducted by an Assyrian king called Ninus (*sic*), who besieged the Bactrian king Oxyartes in his capital Bactra. The city finally fell to an assault by Ninus' queen Semiramis. A Semiramis is attested in Assyrian records as the wife of the C9 king Shamshi-Adad V (**RIMA* 3: 205), though Ninus has also been identified with the C9 Assyrian king Tukulti-Ninurta II. Xenophon (*Cyropaedia* 1.5.2) reports an Assyrian campaign against Bactria during the reign of the Median king Cyaxares (c. 625–585). Greek tradition may also have included Bactrians in the siege and destruction of the Assyrian capital Nineveh c. 612, if we can judge from what appears to be a garbled version of this event in Diodorus (2.26–7). But a number of scholars dispute the historical validity of all these episodes (see e.g. Briant, 1984b: 23–33).

Classical sources also report that the Bactrians, along with other Central Asian groups (Hyrcanians, Parthians, Sacae), paid homage to the Persian king Cyrus II after his victory over the Median ruler Astyages and his capture of the Median capital Ecbatana (c. 550). Yet resentment at the prospect of permanent subjection to Persian overlordship may eventually have led to rebellion by the Bactrians, prompting the expedition which, according to Herodotus (1.153), Cyrus planned against them (and also against the Sacae). He may have conducted such an expedition in the course of his eastern campaigns which ended with his death on the battlefield in 530. Bactria was, however, one of the lands which supported Darius I during the uprisings against him at the beginning of his reign (522), and it appears in Darius' Bisitun inscription (**DB* 6) among Persia's eastern possessions. Its satrap at this time was a Persian official called Dadarshish. Bactria is listed several other times in Darius' inscriptions among the eastern lands of the Persian empire (e.g. **DSe* 3), and also in the *daiva* inscription (see glossary) of his son and successor Xerxes (**XPh* 3).

According to Herodotus (3.92), Bactria constituted on its own the twelfth Persian province (but see glossary under **satrap**), called Baxtrish in the Persepolis tablets. Herodotus (7.64) lists a contingent of Bactrians under the command of Hystaspes, brother of the Persian king Xerxes, among the forces assembled by Xerxes for his invasion of Greece in 481. Later (9.113) he tells of another of Xerxes' brothers, Masistes, who had been appointed governor of Bactria, where he fled after quarrelling with Xerxes with the intention of stirring up a rebellion in the country against the king; Xerxes discovered his plans and sent an army to kill him, along with his sons and troops, before he reached Bactria. According to Ctesias (*FGrH* 688 F14), Bactria did rise up in rebellion against Xerxes' son and successor Artaxerxes I, under the leadership of its satrap Artabanus. Artaxerxes eventually reimposed his authority over the country after fighting two battles against the rebel forces.

Bactria's proverbial wealth in precious metals is reflected in a number of sources. In Classical tradition, when the Assyrian king 'Ninus' sacked the Bactrian treasury, he found enormous quantities of gold and silver there. According to Herodotus (3.92), Bactria was obliged to pay its Persian overlord, by way of tribute, the substantial annual sum of 300 talents of silver. On the reliefs from the Audience Hall (Apadana) at Persepolis, representatives from Bactria are depicted as the thirteenth delegation, bringing tribute to Darius in the form of gold, camels, and metal vessels fashioned by goldsmiths. This is perhaps indicative of a strong goldworking tradition in the country, at least during the Persian period if not also earlier. Darius (**DSz* 9) reports that gold was brought from Bactria for use in the construction of his palace at Susa.

Bactria became a place for the resettlement of peoples deported from the western parts of the Persian empire. Members of the Ionian rebel alliance in Darius I's reign were threatened with exile and enslavement there, according to Herodotus (6.9), who also reports that Barcaeans from Libya were sent to Bactria, and resettled in a village which was thenceforth called Barca (4.204). Following Alexander the Great's conquests, a Hellenistic city was built on the site of Ai Khanoum in Bactria (possibly founded by Alexander himself), and extensive colonization of the country took place under Seleucid rule.

Briant (1984a; 1984b), Holt (1988), Treidler and Brentjes (*BNP* 2: 455–7).

Bad-tibira (*Al-Mada'in/Madina*) (map 17) Early Bronze Age Sumerian city-state in southern Mesopotamia, between Uruk and Lagash. According to the Sumerian King List, Bad-tibira was the second of five Sumerian cities to be granted kingship in Sumer before the great flood, after heaven had first bestowed this honour upon Eridu (**Chav* 82). The King List reports that during Bad-tibira's period of sovereignty, some three kings (one of whom was the shepherd god Dumuzi) reigned for a period of 108,000 years (*sic*), before kingship passed in turn to the cities of Larak, Sippar, and Shuruppak. During the Early Dynastic period (c. 2900–2334), Bad-tibira was one of fourteen major city-states attested in written sources for the regions of Sumer and Akkad. The city is subsequently attested in C19, when Sin-iddinam, king of Larsa (1849–1843), claims to have (re)built its wall (**RIME* 4: 176).

Bahrain see **Dilmun**.

Bala see **Sukkia**.

Balawat see **Imgur-Enlil**.

Balihu Iron Age city located in the Balih r. valley of northwestern Mesopotamia. Its exact location is uncertain, though Lipiński suggests an identification with Tell Abyad near the source of the Balih r. The existence of an Aramaean state called Balihu has been proposed but is far from certain, since it relies on the disputed reading of a toponym in an inscription of Kapara, a C10–9 king of Guzana (Tell Halaf); at any rate, no such state is referred to in Neo-Assyrian sources. The Assyrian eponym official for the year 814 (see glossary under **Eponym Lists**) was a governor of the city Balihu, among others (Millard, 1994: 90). In 853 the Assyrian king Shalmaneser III claims to have advanced upon the cities on the Balih r. and that, fearful at his approach, they seized and assassinated their overlord Giammu. Shalmaneser entered two of these cities, Sahlala and Til-sha-turahi, where he plundered Giammu's palaces and set up his gods (**RIMA* 3: 22, 36 etc.). The city is also mentioned in tablets of the so-called 'Harran Census' (**SAA* XI: 122–45). In 616 it was among the cities captured and plundered by the Babylonian king Nabopolassar (**ABC* 91, **PE* 30, no. 10).

Lipiński (2000: 119–33).

Banat, Tell (map 2) Early Bronze Age urban centre (second half of M3), 25 ha in extent, located on the Middle Euphrates in the Tishrin dam region. Excavations have brought to light in the middle of the site a massive artificial gravel platform 3.5 m or more deep, with a number of large buildings constructed on terraces cut into the platform. Also cut into the platform is a monumental five-chambered tomb made of dressed stone blocks and roofed by nine enormous stone slabs, each measuring 3 m × 2 m. The tomb was apparently used a number of times through the Early Bronze IV (2600–2450) and III (2450–2300) periods. Though it was robbed of most of its contents in antiquity, the surviving grave goods, including gold and lapis lazuli pendants and beads, indicate that it was the burial place of members of an elite class, probably the local ruler and his family. The most prominent architectural feature of the site is a conical mound, 100 m in diameter and 20 m high, identified as a single structure and known as the 'White Monument', because of the whitish gravel used in its construction. A stepped layer of mud encased the original structure. Skeletal remains within suggest that this building too was used for funerary purposes, probably for privileged members of the local society. On the western side of the site an industrial area was identified, containing numerous pottery kilns. The reconstruction of a pottery sequence from Tell Banat IV and III has provided important information on the relative chronology of the region's settlement and culture in its Early Bronze phase. Akkermans and Schwartz comment that the excavations at Tell Banat 'have provided striking evidence of an economically prosperous centre dominated by a powerful and ostentatious elite in mid M3' (2003: 247–8).

McClellan and Porter (1997; 1999), Akkermans and Schwartz (2003: 246–9).

Baqanu Iron Age fortified city of the Chaldaean tribe Bit-Dakkuri in southern

Mesopotamia. It was besieged and destroyed by the Assyrian king Shalmaneser III in his second Babylonian campaign (850) (**RIMA* 3: 31). The battle is also recorded on one of the bronze bands from Balawat (**RIMA* 3: 148) (see **Imgur-Enlil**).

Bara Iron Age population group, and also the name of its chief city, located in the land of Zamua on the fringes of the Zagros mountains, east of the Assyrian plain. Bara was conquered, plundered, and destroyed by the Assyrian king Ashurnasirpal II in 881 while he was campaigning against Zamua, and again in the following year during a further campaign against Zamua (**RIMA* 2: 204–5, 206). In this context, Ashurnasirpal also reports the conquest, plunder, and destruction of the cities of several other population groups – the Larbusu, Dur-Lullumu, and Bunisu.

Liverani (1992: 47).

Barga (Parga) Late Bronze Age city and kingdom in northern Syria, probably lying south of Aleppo and east of the Orontes r., attested in Egyptian and Hittite texts. It is first mentioned in a fragmentary letter from the mid C14 Amarna archive, where reference is made to a king of Barga (**EA* 57). In the seventh year of his reign, the Hittite king Mursili II (1321–1295) wrote to Abiradda, who ruled Barga as a loyal Hittite vassal, concerning a dispute over the possession of a town called Yaruwatta, which lay in the border region between Barga and the Nuhashshi lands. The king of the Nuhashshi lands, Tette, had rebelled against Hittite rule. Secret negotiations led to the overthrow of Tette, and the installation of a pro-Hittite regime in Nuhashshi. Mursili took the field against a minor Nuhashshi rebel king called EN-urta, defeated him, and handed over his land to Abiradda. A peace accord concluded by Mursili between the new Nuhashshi king Shummittara and Abiradda confirmed Shummitara's control over Yaruwatta. There is a possible connection between Barga and the Iron Age city Parga (Parqa), which lay in the same region.

*Klengel (1963), Lipiński (2000: 259–62), Radner (*RlA* 10: 336–7), Bryce (2005: 199–200).

Bargylia (map 5) M1 BCE–M1 CE city in Caria in southwestern Anatolia, built on a low hill with two summits. According to one Greek legendary tradition, the city was founded by the Greek hero Bellerophon, and named after his friend Bargylus, who had been killed by a blow from Bellerophon's horse, Pegasus. But the C6 CE scholar Stephanus of Byzantium states that in Carian tradition Bargylia was founded by Achilles, and that the Carians had called the city Andanus. In C5 Bargylia was overshadowed by its close neighbour Cindya. Both cities were members of the Athenian Confederacy, but Bargylia's assessed tribute was only a small fraction of that payable by Cindya. By C4, however, Bargylia was becoming the more important city, perhaps because of its location near the Gulf of Mandalya (Mendelia?), control of which it came to share with Iasus. By C3, it had apparently absorbed Cindya, which no longer appears in the records. Also by C3, Bargylia had become a thoroughly Hellenized city. The meagre material remains of the site date to the Hellenistic, Roman, and Byzantine periods.

Bean (1971: 82–7, 143), Kaletsch (*BNP* 2: 510).

Barzanishta Iron Age city in the land of Izalla (q.v.), located on the southeastern side of the Kashiyari mountain range (mod. Tur ʿAbdin). Some vineyards in Barzanishta are among those in Izalla which are listed in an inventory of estates probably written in the reign of the Assyrian king Ashurbanipal (668–630/627) (*SAA XII: 52).

(H. D. Baker)

Radner (2006: 296).

Barzanishtun Iron Age city located in the Nairi lands in the western reaches of the upper Tigris region, to the northwest of the Kashiyari mountain range (mod. Tur ʿAbdin). Its location in Nairi is indicated in an inscription of the Assyrian king Ashurnasirpal II (883–859) (**RIMA* 2: 267). Ashurnasirpal reached the city during his campaign in the region in 866 after exiting the pass of Mt Amadanu (**RIMA* 2: 220); his next stop was Damdammusa, a fortified city of Ilanu, a ruler of Bit-Zamani.

Bashan (map 8) Fertile, grain-producing and pastureland region in Transjordan, northeast of the Jordan r. Bashan is a Hebrew name meaning 'smooth, soft earth'. To the north, the region borders on Mt Hermon. To the south, the Yarmuk r. forms the boundary between Bashan and the land of Gilead. In *OT* tradition, Bashan was ruled by a king called Og prior to the Israelite conquest (Joshua 9:10). After the Israelites had defeated Og at Edrei, a Bashanite city (Numbers 21:33–5), the region was allotted to Jair of the tribe of Manasseh (Deuteronomy 3:14). *OT* tradition relates that on the division of the 'United Monarchy' after the death of Solomon (C10), Bashan became part of the kingdom of Israel, but in the latter part of C9, its territory fell to Hazael, king of Damascus, when Israel's throne was occupied by Jehu (2 Kings 10:32–3). (On the so-called United Monarchy, see under **Israel**.) Though it was presumably among the territories regained by Israel in the reign of the late C9–early C8 king Jehoash (2 Kings 13:25), Bashan was also presumably included in the lands conquered by the Assyrian king Tiglath-pileser III during his campaign in the region in 732 (2 Kings 15:29). But there are no sources independent of biblical tradition to confirm the historicity of any of the above events.

Negev and Gibson (2001: 68).

Bassit, Ras el (Greek **Posideion**) (map 7) Small town on the coast of northern Syria, 40 km north of Latakia. Its history of occupation extends from the Late Bronze Age (c. 1600, to which the remains of a 'palace' date) until the Arab conquest in C7. Excavation of the site was conducted by P. Courbin between 1971 and 1984, and since then by J. Y. Perreault, both on behalf of the University of Montreal. Perreault's excavations have concentrated on an early Christian basilica, where the most recent work has been carried out primarily by N. Beaudry, University of Quebec. The Late Bronze Age town was considered by Courbin to have been an outpost of the kingdom of Ugarit. Following destruction of the site in the upheavals at the end of the Late Bronze Age, resettlement took place almost immediately at the beginning of the Iron Age, with the town subsequently becoming subject to the Aramaean kingdom Hamath. Iron Age remains include a number of grain silos and a necropolis of C8–7 date with mainly cremation burials. The cemetery provides evidence of contacts with Phoenicia and Cyprus. Courbin concluded that in this phase of its existence, the town was small and poor, and its society egalitarian.

Bassit's coastal location enabled it to establish contacts with the Greek world from C10 onwards, illustrated by finds of Euboean Protogeometric pottery (c. 1000–950).

But actual Greek settlement seems not to have occurred before the last quarter of C7. It was then that the site was called Posideion. Its former name or names remain unknown. Greek settlement led to closer contacts with the Greek world – on Anatolia's western coast, the Aegean islands, and mainland Greece – as reflected in finds of east Greek pottery (C7) and Attic pottery (C6). These contacts seem not to have been disrupted by the Persian conquest of the town in 539, though there may have been some reduction in trade for a time in C5, during the periods of conflicts between the Greek and Persian worlds. Subsequently Posideion appears to have minted its own coinage, before the arrival of Alexander the Great in the region. Following Alexander's death, it became part of the Seleucid empire. It was conquered by Rome in 64.

Courbin (1986; *OEANE* 1: 278–9).

Bastam see **Rusai-URU.TUR**.

Batash, Tel (biblical **Timnah**) (map 8) Settlement-mound located in the Sorek valley, on the northern border of Judah, southern Palestine, 5 km northeast of Ekron (Tel Miqne). Its history of occupation extends from the Middle Bronze Age (C17–16) to the Persian period (C6–4). The site was excavated over twelve seasons, between 1977 and 1989, as a joint venture of the Southwestern Baptist Seminary and the Institute of Archaeology of the Hebrew University in Jerusalem, under the direction of G. L. Kelm and A. Mazar. Twelve occupation levels were identified, beginning with the foundation of a Middle Bronze IIB fortified settlement on the site c. 1700. The settlement suffered a number of destructions by fire during its Middle and Late Bronze Age phases (levels XII–X and IX–VI respectively). Despite these destructions, Tel Batash developed into a prosperous Canaanite city in the Late Bronze Age. At that time it was probably part of the kingdom of Gezer, which dominated the Sorek valley. Its prosperity is reflected in its substantial two-storeyed public buildings with large pillared halls, and its rich assemblages of artefacts. The city was unfortified in this period. The outer walls of its houses, Mazar comments, apparently served as a defence line. After its destruction in C14, the settlement was rebuilt, but its final Late Bronze Age phase (C13) reflects none of the prosperity of its former existence.

During its Iron Age phases (levels V–II), Tel Batash is generally identified with the Judaean-Philistine city of Timnah (3) attested in *OT* sources. (In Judges 14:1–10, for example, Samson is reported to have married a Philistine woman from the city.) It was probably built by the Philistines in the second half of C12, to serve as a border town in the territory of Ekron (thus Mazar). Its destruction c. 1000 has been associated with the expansion of the Israelites. The city was abandoned for a short period following this destruction. Its rebuilding on a new plan with new structures (level IV) probably reflects Israelite occupation. This level was destroyed in late C10, almost certainly by the pharaoh Sheshonq I (biblical Shishak) during his campaigns in the region. The succeeding level III city was built on a substantial scale and was heavily fortified. A noteworthy feature of the architecture of this period is an impressive city gate, providing the main access to the city. But this level also ended violently, in the campaign conducted by the Assyrian king Sennacherib in 701. Some time prior to this, to judge from 2 Chronicles 28:18, Timnah was one of the cities subject to the Judaean king Ahaz (735–715) which were attacked and captured by the Philistines. In C7 the city once again rose from its ashes. It was rebuilt and refortified. An impressive, well-planned, and densely populated settlement grew up within its walls, which also enclosed a large industrial and commercial complex. The substantial quantities of artefacts found within the houses indicate contacts with Phoenicia and the east Greek world as well as with Transjordan and other Judaean cities. Mazar believes that the export of olive oil was a major factor in the city's prosperity.

Once more, at the end of its level II phase, the city was devastated by fire, in the course of the Babylonian conquests of the region at the end of C7. It was now largely abandoned, except perhaps for a few squatters. During the Persian period (C6–4) a small settlement was built atop the mound (level I).

Mazar and Kelm (*NEAEHL* 1: 152–7), A. Mazar (1997b), Mazar and Panitz-Cohen (2001), Bunimovitz and Lederman (2006: 407–9, 420–4).

Behistun see Bisitun.

Beersheba (*Tell es-Seba'*) (map 8) Iron Age city in southern Palestine (southern Judah), 4 km east of mod. Beersheba in the Negev desert. Its history of occupation extends through nine designated strata, covering the period from C12 to early C7 (with reoccupation occurring, after a period of abandonment, in C4 and continuing through the Hellenistic and Roman periods). Strata IX–VI belong to Iron Age I (C12–10), and V–I to Iron Age II (C10–early C7). The small 1–ha site was excavated for the Institute of Archaeology, Tel Aviv University, by Y. Aharoni from 1969 to 1975, and by Z. Herzog in 1976 and from 1990 onwards. Stratum IX, dated by Philistine pottery and Egyptian scarabs to the second half of C12 and the first half of C11, and probably inhabited by a semi-nomadic community, contained a number of pits cut into the bedrock. Some of them apparently served as dwelling-places. Stratum IX was followed, after its destruction, by a settlement which contained the site's first houses (Stratum VIII). When this level was destroyed at the end of C11, a new settlement was built, encircled by four-roomed houses on stone foundations, whose back walls collectively formed an enclosure wall for the community (Stratum VII). A large number of small finds, including ceramic ware, jewellery, weapons, and figurines, date to this period of the community's existence. Its abandonment in early C10 was followed by brief reoccupation (VI), which ended in destruction in mid C10. One of the most noteworthy features of the settlement's Iron Age I phase is a well, 69 m deep, dug into the slope of the mound.

Beersheba reached the height of its development in the Iron Age II phase (V–I), when it became an important administrative centre in an outlying region of Judah. Its features included a well-planned street layout with drainage channels beneath the streets; a number of storehouses and other public buildings – one of which was perhaps a governor's residence – near the town gate; and a large town square. During its Iron Age II phase, Beersheba was an oval-shaped settlement, fortified firstly by a solid wall (V–IV), and subsequently by a casemate wall (III–II). In both cases access to the interior was provided by a four-chambered gate. The Iron Age II town suffered four destructions. Stratum V was possibly destroyed by the pharaoh Sheshonq I (biblical Shishak) in late C10. The violent conflagration which ended Stratum II has been attributed to the Assyrian king Sennacherib, during his campaign in the region in 701, to a later date in C7, or even later, to the campaign of the Babylonian king Nebuchadnezzar II in 586.

Following its destruction Beersheba was once more reoccupied (Stratum I), but now only on a very modest scale. It never again achieved the status it had previously enjoyed as an important urban administrative centre in the region of Judah. Subsequently the site was abandoned for up to three centuries (depending on the date of the destruction of Stratum II). Reoccupation took place in C4 during the Persian period, and continued through the Hellenistic and Roman periods. In these final phases of its existence, Beersheba appears to have supported little more than a modest fort.

The city is frequently attested in *OT* sources, primarily in connection with the patriarchal narratives.

Herzog (*NEAEHL* 1: 167–73; *OEANE* 1: 287–91), Laughlin (2006: 46–51).

Beirut (Berytus) see **Biruta**.

Beit Mirsim, Tell (map 8) 3 ha Canaanite site in Palestine's hill country, c. 20 km southwest of Hebron. Its history of occupation extends through the Bronze and Iron Ages. The site was excavated over four seasons, between 1926 and 1932, by a joint expedition from Xenia Theological Seminary and the American Schools of Oriental Research, under the direction of W. F. Albright. Ten major strata were identified, extending from the Early Bronze Age until Iron Age II. The identification of the site with biblical Debir, as proposed by Albright, is no longer accepted; the latter is probably to be identified, as M. Kochavi has demonstrated, with Khirbet Rabud. A necropolis was discovered during looting of the site in the 1970s. Some thirty tombs were subsequently investigated between 1978 and 1982, by D. Alon and E. Braun on behalf of the Israel Antiquities Authority.

Only meagre remains survive from the city's Early Bronze Age (M3) phase, covering the first three strata. There are, however, more substantial remains of the four Middle Bronze Age strata (early M2), which indicate that the city was fortified in the second of these strata, had a number of large houses, presumably the residences of a social elite, and displayed some attention to urban planning. The city reached the height of its development as a Canaanite urban centre in the last two of its Middle Bronze Age strata. In the last stratum a large courtyard building, identified as a 'palace', was unearthed. The many storage jars which it contained indicate that part of the building was used as a storage magazine. The city's Middle Bronze Age phase came to an end with its destruction in mid C16, followed by a period of abandonment. When it was resettled during the Late Bronze Age, its earlier predominantly urban aspect was now more attenuated, reflected by open spaces, between houses, occupied by grain silos. However, imported Mycenaean and Cypriot ware found in the city indicates some trading links, albeit indirect, with the world beyond the Levantine coast. Around 1225, in the final decades of the Late Bronze Age, the city was destroyed by fire.

The final two strata of its existence belong to the Iron Age. Again, grain silos are a feature of the site. Ceramic ware recovered from these suggest a continuation of Canaanite culture – at least until early C10, when the city may have come under Israelite occupation. A new casemate fortification wall was erected where the old Middle Bronze Age fortifications had once stood. Destruction of the city, probably in late C10, is associated with the campaign which the pharaoh Sheshonq I (biblical

Shishak) conducted into the region in late C10. This destruction in fact paved the way for a new era of prosperity in Beit Mirsim's history, characterized by a planned urban layout, three- and four-roomed pillared houses, a monumental building near the city centre, a tower structure built over part of the casemate fortifications, and rock-cut cisterns and oil presses. The destruction of this city by the Assyrian king Sennacherib in his campaign of 701 effectively marked the end of Beit Mirsim as a prosperous urban centre. There may, however, have been some reoccupation of the site during C7 or early C6.

Albright and Greenberg (*NEAEHL* 1: 177–80), Greenberg (*OEANE* 1: 295–7).

Bellapais (map 14) Early and Middle Bronze Age cemetery at the locality of Vounous, near the mod. village Bellapais in north-central Cyprus on the north slopes of the Kyrenia range. The Swedish excavator E. Gjerstad noted burial chambers here in 1926. Following reports of extensive looting of the tombs, excavations were undertaken in 1931 and 1932 by P. Dikaios for the Cyprus Museum. Further tombs were excavated in 1933 by C. F.-A. Schaeffer on behalf of the Museums of France in collaboration with Dikaios. In 1937 J. R. Stewart undertook final excavations on the site, sponsored by the British School of Archaeology at Athens. The settlement associated with the cemetery has not been located.

A total of 164 tomb complexes were uncovered, some of them multi-chambered. Over 107 of these appeared intact, producing more than 200 burials. These were accompanied by a wide range of ornaments, tools and weapons, and ceramic vessels. Clay models of animal and human figures, sometimes applied to pots, are seen as valuable indicators of the material culture of the Early and Middle Bronze Ages. Swiny comments that the cultural material from the cemetery belongs near the beginning of an artistic tradition that lasted 700 years.

Swiny (*OEANE* 5: 322–3).

Benjaminites and **Bensimalites** see Yaminites.

Bethel (*Tell Beitin*) (map 8) Settlement in southern Palestine, located on the West Bank on the border between Israel and Judah, 16 km north of Jerusalem. Well known from biblical sources, Bethel was first identified with the site of Beitin by the American explorer E. Robinson in 1838. Following a brief settlement in the late Chalcolithic period (c. 3200), Beitin was apparently abandoned and left unoccupied for c. 800 years. It was resettled in the Early Bronze III period, c. 2400, and thenceforth occupied, with several further intervals of abandonment, until the Byzantine age. Excavations on the site were carried out, on behalf of the American Schools of Oriental Research, by W. F. Albright and J. L. Kelso in 1934, and subsequently by Kelso in 1954, 1957, and 1960. Bethel is one of the most frequently attested towns in *OT* sources. Its importance must have been due at least in part to its strategic location on the border between Israel and Judah, and at the junction of major north–south and east–west routes of communication.

Early Bronze Age remains on the site are meagre. However, by the Middle Bronze II period (c. 1800–1650) Bethel had become a prosperous town with impressive Cyclopean fortifications (see glossary) and well-built private houses. It continued to flourish in its Middle Bronze Age III phase (c. 1650–1500), but may have been destroyed at the end of this phase. It was abandoned for about a century, before being reoccupied in the Late Bronze II period (c. 1400–1200). Well laid out houses with courtyards and drains typify the new settlement. The excavators divided this period into two phases, observing that the earlier C14 phase was superior in quality to its C13 successor.

We have no hard evidence to indicate what brought this level to an end, though attempts have been made to link it with the Israelites' alleged conquest of Canaan. From the beginning of the Iron Age, early C12, Beitin/Bethel was again occupied, possibly by a new population group, presumably the Israelites. Unfortunately, archaeological reports provide little detailed information about the site in its Iron Age phases. It was apparently unfortified during the first two centuries of the Iron Age. To judge from *OT* references, it was an important Israelite city at this time, particularly in the last two centuries of M2, corresponding in biblical terms to the period of the judges. According to the biblical stories, it was used as an assembly point for the Israelite tribal confederacy (Judges 20:18), and for a time it became the repository of the Ark of the Covenant (Judges 20:26–8). Samuel's regular visits to it as a judge is further testimony to its importance in *OT* tradition. By C10 it had again become a strongly fortified, apparently prosperous town.

In *OT* tradition, Bethel appears to have lost much of its importance during the reigns of David and Solomon (C10), if we can so judge from the absence of any biblical references to it in this period. But with the emergence of the divided monarchy following Solomon's reign, it came once more into prominence. It was established as a major sanctuary by Jeroboam I, first ruler of the Northern Kingdom, in late C10, and is referred to as a royal sanctuary at the time of the C8 prophet Amos (Amos 7:12–13). In late C7 the Judaean king Josiah reportedly destroyed this sanctuary (2 Kings 23:15). (None of the above events is attested in extra-biblical sources.) The city's fortifications were rebuilt several times in the following centuries, until it presumably fell victim to the Babylonians in early C6. (The archaeological reports do not provide any clear indications of this.) The Babylonians may have destroyed the town, but there is evidence of later settlement during the Persian period (C6–4). In the Hellenistic and Roman periods, the town may once again have enjoyed some of its former importance and prosperity. It is still attested in Byzantine times.

Kelso (1968; *NEAEHL* 1: 192–4), Dever (*OEANE* 1: 300–1).

Beth Gan (map 8) Site located in northern Palestine, to the west of the Sea of Galilee. Its history of occupation extends from the Late Bronze Age until the Byzantine and Mamluk periods. The site was excavated by H. Leibowitz for the University of Texas at Austin in 1992, 1994, and 1995. According to the excavator, evidence of Beth Gan's Late Bronze Age occupation lends support to the idea of a significant population in the eastern Lower Galilee at that time. Pottery and domestic dwellings represent Iron Age settlement, a storage jar represents settlement in the Persian period (C6–4), and architectural fragments and domestic ware reflect settlement in the Roman period.

Leibowitz (*OEANE* 1: 301–2).

Beth-Shean (Beth Shan, *Tell el-Husn*) (map 8) 4 ha settlement-mound located in the Jezreel valley in northern Palestine at the intersection of two major routes running north–south (through the Jordan valley) and west–east (through the Jezreel and

Beth-Shean valleys). An extensive lower settlement at the base of the mound dates from the Hellenistic period onwards. The site's history of occupation extends from the Late Neolithic to the mediaeval period, with a number of breaks in between. Excavations were conducted by C. S. Fisher, A. Rowe, and subsequently G. M. FitzGerald, on behalf of the University Museum of the University of Pennsylvania, from 1921 to 1933, by Y. Yadin for the Institute of Archaeology, the Hebrew University in Jerusalem, in 1983, and by A. Mazar for the Hebrew University and the Tourism Administration of Beth-Shean, from 1989 to 1996. Following continuous settlement on the mound through the Neolithic, Chalcolithic, Early Bronze, and Middle Bronze Age I levels, there was an occupation gap during Middle Bronze IIA (early M2) before resettlement in the Middle Bronze IIB–C period. Throughout its Middle Bronze Age phases the city was unfortified. The fine quality of its ceramic ware and other artefacts in this period indicates a relatively advanced, sophisticated society.

For the Late Bronze Age, five settlement phases have been identified. During the last four of these, Beth-Shean was under Egyptian sovereignty, becoming one of the most important centres of the pharaoh's administration in Syria–Palestine. It was a garrison city, under the direct authority of a resident Egyptian governor. References to it occur in the texts of the pharaohs Tuthmosis III, Seti I, and Ramesses II. Seti was perhaps responsible for rebuilding the city after it was destroyed by fire in late C14 or early C13. Two basalt stelae from his reign indicate the city's importance as a bulwark of Egyptian authority in the region against rebellious subject states and marauding Habiru (q.v.) groups. One of the major archaeological features of the site during this period is a sequence of five temples extending through the Late Bronze and Iron Age I levels. The plan and layout of one of these (Stratum IX) display a number of unique

Figure 20 Beth-Shean.

architectural characteristics. One of the most notable finds of the transitional period between the Late Bronze Age and the Early Iron Age is a cemetery containing more than fifty anthropoid coffins, most of whose lids depict human faces. Mazar believes that the coffins belonged to Egyptian officials and military personnel, though some of them may have contained the bodies of mercenaries from among the Sea Peoples who served in the Egyptian army.

The two Iron Age I strata at Beth-Shean (C12–11) reflect the final period of Egyptian authority in Syria–Palestine. At this time, Egypt was ruled by the pharaohs of the twentieth dynasty. In the reign of one of these (Ramesses VI or Ramesses VIII, according to Mazar), Beth-Shean was again destroyed by fire. By C11 it had been rebuilt, and was now probably occupied by Canaanites, and perhaps also, Mazar suggests, by some of the Sea Peoples. Its material culture was Canaanite, and it now featured twin temples. According to *OT* sources, Beth-Shean was one of the cities whose Canaanite occupants resisted the Israelites' attempts to drive them out (Joshua 17:11–12; Judges 1:27). And it was to the walls of Beth-Shean that the Philistines are alleged to have attached the body of Saul, after stripping him of his armour and cutting off his head (1 Samuel 31:10). Excavations have failed, however, to find any hint of Philistine occupation at the site. The Canaanite city was destroyed at the end of C11 or early in C10, concluding its Iron Age I phase. It was subsequently rebuilt in Iron Age II. Not long after, it appears among the cities conquered by the pharaoh Sheshonq I (biblical Shishak) during his campaign in the region in late C10. Evidence of further violent destruction by fire at the end of the Iron Age II phase is probably to be associated with the campaign which the Assyrian king Tiglath-pileser III conducted in the region c. 732.

A small community subsequently arose on the mound, which may have continued to function as a cultic site through the Persian period (C6–4). But there was no significant reoccupation of the site until the Hellenistic period, from which time the city became known as Nysa or Scythopolis.

A. Mazar (1997a; *NEAEHL* 1: 214–23; *OEANE* 1: 305–9; 2006).

Beth-Shemesh (map 8) 3 ha settlement-mound located in the northeastern Shephelah hill region of western Palestine. Its name was identified by E. Robinson in 1838. The city is frequently attested in biblical sources: for example, in the allocation of lands to the Israelite tribes, it is assigned to the tribe of Dan (Joshua 19:31). But it occurs in no written sources outside the Bible. Beth-Shemesh's history extends through six major occupation levels, from Early Bronze IV to the mediaeval period. The first excavations were undertaken by D. Mackenzie in 1911–12 for the Palestine Exploration Fund, and subsequently by E. Grant from 1923 to 1928 for Haverford College, Pennsylvania. Work on the site was resumed in 1990 by S. Bunimovitz and Z. Lederman on behalf of Bar-Ilan and Ben-Gurion Universities (1990–6), and from 1997 onwards under the auspices of the Institute of Archaeology, Tel Aviv University. The earliest of the six occupation levels identified on the site, Stratum VI, spanning Early Bronze IV to Middle Bronze II (C22–18), is represented only by pottery sherds. Stratum V (Middle Bronze II–III) was the first significant phase in the site's development, when the city was strongly fortified and accessed by a triple-entry gate. The prosperity of this period, as indicated by residences of an elite upper class, continued into the following Late Bronze Age phase (Stratum IV), from which a number of well-built houses were unearthed, along with numerous cisterns, a smelting furnace, and a hoard of jewellery. Tombs dating to both this and the preceding period were also brought to light. The cause of the destruction of the Late Bronze Age city c. 1200 remains unknown.

The large Iron Age I settlement (Stratum III) showed some degree of continuity with its predecessor, though with little evidence of town planning. Its destruction early in C11 is generally attributed to the Philistines. The successor Iron Age II settlement (Stratum II), extending from C10 to C8 (which included three sub-phases), was a well-planned, prosperous city. One of its most noteworthy features is a rock-hewn, cross-shaped water reservoir, discovered in 1994, with a capacity of c. 200 cubic metres. Other features of the city in this period include a number of pillared courtyard houses, a large grain silo, a tripartite storehouse, and some structures identified as industrial installations. All lay within a casemate city wall, built c. mid C10. Bunimovitz and Lederman (2001: 145) observe that at approximately this time, the large and unfenced Iron Age I village of Beth-Shemesh was transformed by a central authority into a fortified town with an impressive array of public buildings. It has been suggested, by scholars who accept the historicity of an Israelite United Monarchy, that Beth-Shemesh now became an administrative centre of the monarchy. The destruction of this phase of the city's existence was attributed by the earlier excavators to the Babylonians in 586. But since no C7 remains have been revealed by the recent excavations, this destruction is now thought to belong within the context of the Judaean campaigns conducted in 701 by the Assyrian king Sennacherib. Some years earlier the city was, according to 2 Chronicles 28:18, seized by the Philistines from Judah, along with other cities in the region, during the reign of the Judaean king Ahaz (735–715). Through the Iron Age, and particularly in C8, Beth-Shemesh served as a frontier post on Judah's northern border.

Following its destruction at the end of the Iron Age, Beth-Shemesh was apparently abandoned for several centuries before it was reoccupied in the Hellenistic period. Hellenistic, Roman, and Byzantine remains are represented in Stratum I.

Bunimovitz and Lederman (*NEAEHL* 1: 249–53; 2000; 2001; 2006: 409–24), Dever (*OEANE* 1: 311–12), Laughlin (2006: 68–72).

Beth-Zur (*Khirbet el-Tubeiqa*) (map 8) Settlement-mound, 1000 m above sea level, located in the hill country of Judah, southern Palestine, 30 km southwest of Jerusalem. It has a commanding position overlooking routes passing north to Jerusalem and west towards the Shephelah, on Judah's northern frontier. The site was excavated by O. R. Sellers, sponsored by the Presbyterian (McCormick) Theological Seminary, Chicago, and the American Schools of Oriental Research, in 1931, and again in 1957. Five main occupation strata were identified, extending from the Early Bronze Age through Middle Bronze Age, Iron Age I and II levels, and terminating with a 'Second Temple' level spanning the period from C5 to the end of C1.

After sporadic occupation in M3 (Stratum V), Beth-Zur was resettled in mid C17 (Stratum IV, Middle Bronze II), and fortified the following century. Its massive 2.5 m thick city wall, consisting partly of huge polygonal stones, is considered to be a typical 'Hyksos' (q.v.) construction. The city appears to have suffered destruction by fire c. 1550, and its site was abandoned for almost half a millennium before resettlement occurred in the early Iron Age, C11. The new 'Israelite' settlement, Stratum III, appears to have been a relatively poor one, smaller in size than its Middle Bronze Age predecessor. However, a new city wall was built, using in part materials from the Middle Bronze Age fortifications. (The identification of this settlement as Israelite is based on biblical, not archaeological information.) Stratum III was destroyed by fire towards the end of C11, and the site was almost entirely abandoned at that time. The only indications of any habitation there for the next three centuries are provided by a few pottery sherds. Israelite occupation resumed in Iron Age II, as attested by the material remains of Stratum II, dated to the period c. 700–587. Despite the claim made in 2 Chronicles 11:7 that Beth-Zur was one of the towns built up by Rehoboam for the defence of Judah, no evidence has been found to indicate that the city was fortified in this period. However, the discovery of a number of *lamelekh* (see glossary) handles have led to the suggestion that a military garrison was stationed in the city, perhaps in the reign of Hezekiah (c. 715–687). Stratum II probably came to a violent end c. 587, and if so, it was presumably a victim of the Babylonian invasions of Palestine at this time – though the evidence for such a destruction is not conclusive.

Once again the site may have been abandoned, until C5, when there is some sparse evidence for reoccupation, marking the beginning of Stratum I. The city grew in importance during the Hellenistic period, with the construction of the first stage of a citadel in C3, and appears to have enjoyed a period of peace and prosperity under Seleucid rule. Its value as a Judaean garrison-city was no doubt at least partly responsible for this. In the Hellenistic period, the city came to be known as Bethsura. It was finally, and permanently, abandoned c. 100.

Our knowledge of Beth-Zur's history is almost entirely dependent on archaeological evidence. There are only four references to the city in the *OT*, and none in extra-biblical written sources prior to the Hellenistic period. Information about the city during the Hellenistic period is provided by the first and second book of the Maccabees, and by the Jewish historian Josephus.

Funk (*NEAEHL* 1: 259–61).

Beycesultan (map 2) Large double-mound settlement in western Anatolia, 600 m × 400 m in extent, located on a former course of the Maeander r., 5 km south of mod. Çivril (Denizli province). Its history of occupation extends from the Chalcolithic to the Late Bronze Age, with subsequent resettlement on the flat-topped southern part of the site during the Byzantine period. The site was excavated between 1954 and 1959 by S. Lloyd and J. Mellaart for the British Institute of Archaeology at Ankara. Forty occupation levels were identified, extending from the Chalcolithic to the Late Bronze Age. Twenty-one of these levels are of Chalcolithic date (XL–XX), when the site was characterized by rectangular mudbrick houses, sometimes with stone foundations, equipped with benches, hearths, and ovens. In the Early Bronze I period, perhaps after a gap in occupation, megaron-type structures (see glossary) were built on the site. The characteristic feature of these structures was a main room entered through a portico and containing hearths and so-called 'horns of consecration', with another room at the back. Though the excavators believed that buildings of this kind were shrines, it is now thought more likely that they were domestic dwellings. The excavators interpreted the presence of northwestern handmade Anatolian pottery in Beycesultan's Early Bronze II period (mid M3) as indicating the arrival of new elements on the site. By the end of Early Bronze II, wheel-made pottery was also being produced. After this phase of the city's existence ended in destruction, another hiatus in occupation may have occurred, as reflected in a gap in the pottery sequence, before the third and final phase of the Early Bronze Age settlement (Early Bronze III). In total, the Early Bronze Age at Beycesultan was spanned by fourteen occupation levels (XIX–VI).

The most important phase in Beycesultan's development occurred during the succeeding Middle Bronze Age – levels V–III. Excavation of the first of these levels brought to light the remains of a burnt 'palace', dating to the first centuries of M2 and contemporaneous with the Assyrian Colony period (see glossary). The building complex, measuring 85 m × 55 m, was at least two storeys high, made of timber and mudbrick, and when excavated still contained traces of painted murals. Its presence on the site suggests that by this time Beycesultan had become the seat of a local ruler. A temple and parts of the city's fortifications were also discovered in this level. Beycesultan's apparent prosperity in this period was probably due in large part to its strategically advantageous position at the headwaters of the Maeander r. It is very likely that it lay on major routes of communication which linked it with the Troad as well as with the central Aegean coast, and perhaps also with places lying to its east. In the Late Bronze Age, another palace was built, on the city's eastern summit. This was smaller than its predecessor, measuring c. 60 m × 60 m. Its reduced size suggested to Lloyd that Beycesultan had by this time suffered a decline in importance. However, much of the city remained unexplored at the close of excavations, making it difficult to form any clear notions as to its size and significance at the time Anatolia was dominated by the Hittites.

Beycesultan lay in the region where scholars believe the complex of countries called the Arzawa Lands was located. These are attested in numerous Hittite records. Mellaart had hoped that Lloyd's and his excavations might confirm Beycesultan as one of Arzawa's cities. Unfortunately, this hope was not realized, partly because of the failure to find any trace of written records on the site. Nevertheless, Beycesultan was almost certainly a part of the Arzawa geopolitical complex. In the light of recent research on the political geography of Late Bronze Age Anatolia, J. D. Hawkins (1998b: 24) has suggested that it may have been the chief city of the land called Kuwaliya in Hittite texts, which was attached to the Arzawan kingdom of Mira as frontier territory probably in mid or late C14.

Mellaart (1998).

Beydar, Tell (Nabada?) (map 2) M3 settlement located on a tributary of the Habur r. in northern Mesopotamia. The site is circular, covering c. 28 ha, with a walled citadel at the centre and a lower town around it surrounded by an outer circular wall (in other words, a typical 'Kranzhügel'). It has been excavated since 1992 by a joint European and Syrian expedition, under the direction of M. Lebeau and, in succession, H. Hammade, A. Suleiman, and A. Baghdo. The excavations have so far brought to light over 200 clay tablets written in Akkadian cuneiform and dating to the late Early Dynastic III period, contemporary with the tablets from the Ebla archive (C24). The texts are administrative documents, dealing with such matters as workers from different parts of the town and from different villages, and the distribution of animal products. The majority of the tablets came from what appear to have been private dwellings, but four were unearthed in a building on top of the mound interpreted as a palace, and two others from what was apparently a large official building. The excavators have concluded that the site was probably a regional administrative centre, called Nabada, belonging to the kingdom of Nagar (see **Brak, Tell**).

Lebeau and Suleiman (2003; 2007), Milano *et al.* (2004).

Biʿa, Tell see **Tuttul**.

Biqaʿ (map 7) Narrow plain and valley in central Lebanon located between the Lebanon range in the west and the anti-Lebanon in the east. The Greeks called the region Coele-Syria ('Hollow Syria'). Throughout its history, it was the home of numerous small countries and cities which became embroiled in the political and military upheavals of their ages.

Dever (*OEANE* 1: 41).

Bira, Tel (map 8) Settlement-mound in northern Palestine, 9 km southeast of Akko, bordering on the Akko plain. It is probably to be identified with Rehob (see **Rehob** (2)), which in *OT* tradition was one of the Canaanite cities assigned to the tribe of Asher (Joshua 19:30, Judges 1:31). The site consists of an acropolis, a lower city, and several cemeteries located near the mound. Its history of occupation extends from the Middle Bronze Age to the Hellenistic period. Excavations were conducted on the site by M. Prausnitz for the Israel Dept of Antiquities and Museums between 1957 and 1980. Attention was focused primarily on the lower city and the cemeteries. In the Middle Bronze Age, the settlement was fortified by a city wall and a glacis (see glossary), the wall enclosing a total area of some 20 ha, encompassing both citadel and lower city. Excavation of the Middle and Late Bronze Age cemeteries revealed numerous burials in rock-cut pit-graves, the bodies surrounded by funerary goods, including weapons and ceramic ware. Iron Age burials were also made in rock-cut tombs, for both single and double interments. Some of the tombs were cut to fit the size of the bodies, with hewn niches for the accompanying funerary goods. Tombs dating to the Hellenistic period indicate that the settlement was still in existence at that time, but was probably abandoned shortly after.

Prausnitz (*NEAEHL* 1: 362–3).

Biruta (Classical **Berytus**, ***Beirut***) (maps 6, 7) City on the Levantine coast, the capital of mod. Lebanon, located between Byblos and Sidon. Though we have evidence of human settlement in the area from the Palaeolithic period onwards, there are only meagre material remains of the anc. city prior to the Roman imperial period. Historical records are also sparse before this period. The earliest significant documents are six letters found in the mid C14 Amarna archive, addressed to the pharaoh Akhenaten. Three are written by Ammunira, king of Biruta (**EA* 141–3), and three by Rib-Hadda, king of Gubla (Byblos) (**EA* 136–8). Both writers are vassals of the pharaoh. Rib-Hadda had formed an alliance with Ammunira in an attempt to counter the threat which Gubla's aggressive northern neighbour Amurru posed to a number of cities along the Levantine coast and its hinterland. After losing power in a coup in his own kingdom, Rib-Hadda sought refuge with Ammunira while vainly awaiting support from Egypt in his bid to regain his throne. Ammunira was sympathetic to his cause, but apparently unwilling or unable to provide him with any material assistance.

The M1 Phoenician city is briefly attested in the Persian period (C6–4), but it remained relatively insignificant until the end of the Hellenistic period. Around 14 BCE, Berytus became a Roman colony.

Khalifeh (*OEANE* 1: 292–5), Vidal (2005).

Bisitun (*Behistun*) (map 16) Site located in a mountain pass in western Iran, 30 km east of Bactaran (formerly Kermanshah). It is best known for its famous rock-cut relief and trilingual inscription, carved at the command of the Persian king Darius I in 520–519 on the site's southeast cliff-face, 70 m above the highway leading from Mesopotamia into the highlands of Media.

The inscription appears in three versions – Old Persian, Babylonian, and Elamite. It records Darius' seizure of his throne and the military triumphs he won during his accession year and first regnal year. The inscription was carved in three stages. The Elamite text was the earliest version, followed by the Babylonian and finally the Old Persian texts. All three texts are inscribed in the cuneiform script. Differing from one another in a number of matters of detail, they provide the only historical account we have of Persian history from Persian sources during the Achaemenid period (see glossary). Copies of the inscription were distributed throughout the Persian empire, as illustrated by remains of it discovered at Elephantine in Egypt (written in Aramaic) and Babylon. The three versions partly frame a 3 m high relief panel, which depicts Darius placing his foot on Gaumata, a defeated pretender to his throne, and nine other captive rebel leaders from different parts of the empire. Roped together at the neck, they are proceeding from the right towards Darius. Between 1835 and 1847, H. C. Rawlinson, a British officer stationed in the region, copied the trilingual inscription and undertook the decipherment of the Old Persian version. His success in so doing provided the foundation for all subsequent investigations and translations of the cuneiform languages.

Other anc. remains found at Bisitun date back to the Palaeolithic period, and extend through the pre-Achaemenid, Achaemenid, Parthian, Sasanian, and Islamic periods.

Schmitt (1987), Kleiss and Calmeyer (1996), Stronach and Zournatzi (*OEANE* 1: 330–1).

Bit-Adini (1) (map 7) Early Iron Age Aramaean tribal area and people, located in the middle Euphrates region between the Balih and the Euphrates rivers but also extending westwards across the Euphrates into northeastern Syria. In mid C9, the region came under the control of a certain Ahuni, and included the Neo-Hittite city-state Masuwari (called by the Aramaean name Til-Barsip in Assyrian records), which was probably the centre of a small kingdom or principality of the same name (see ***Ahmar, Tell***). Other cities of Bit-Adini included Asmu/Azmu, Dabigu, Dummetu, Kaprabu, and La'la'tu. Bit-Adini's commanding strategic location, astride important routes which linked Anatolia and the Syro-Palestinian coastlands with Mesopotamia, made it an obvious target of the westward expanding Neo-Assyrian kingdom. Conflict with the Assyrians began in the reign of Ashurnasirpal II (883–859). It may have been precipitated by support which Bit-Adini, along with Babylonia, apparently gave to an unsuccessful rebellion by the states Suhu, Hindanu, and Laqe (which lay between Bit-Adini and Babylonia) against Assyrian rule. Ashurnasirpal followed up his victory over the rebel states by launching an attack upon Dummetu and Azmu, cities of Bit-Adini (**RIMA* 2: 215). One of the rebel leaders, Azi-ilu of Laqe, had headed towards them, accompanied by the remnants of his troops, after the rebel alliance's defeat. Ashurnasirpal retaliated by storming Dummetu and Azmu and putting them to the torch. His subsequent military operations in Bit-Adini in 878 resulted in the capture and destruction of its fortified city Kaprabu, whose population he deported (*RIMA* 2: 216). Yet he apparently made no attempt t· annex Bit-Adini's territory. Instead, he contented himself with receiving a substantial payment of tribute from Ahuni.

Bit-Adini remained independent of Assyrian rule until the reign of Ashurnasirpal's son and successor Shalmaneser III (858–824). In his first regnal year, Shalmaneser took the field against a coalition of northern Syrian and southern Anatolian states. Bit-Adini, under the leadership of Ahuni, played a leading role in the coalition, which suffered two defeats by the Assyrians (**RIMA* 3: 9–10, 15, 16–17) (see **Pat(t)in**). Shalmaneser conducted further campaigns in Bit-Adini, subduing many of its cities both east and west of the Euphrates. Ahuni made his last stand against Shalmaneser in Til-Barsip (856) (**RIMA* 3: 10–11, 19, 21), which fell to the Assyrians after a siege. Ahuni managed to escape, but was captured the following year and deported to Assyria (**RIMA* 3: 22, 29–30). In the aftermath of Shalmaneser's conquests, Bit-Adini was absorbed into the Assyrian empire, forming part of the Province of the Commander-in-Chief (see glossary). Its elimination as an independent state paved the way for the consolidation of Assyrian power in the middle Euphrates region, and provided the Assyrians with an important bridgehead across the Euphrates for their campaigns in the west.

CHLI 1: 224–5, Lipiński (2000: 163–93).

Bit-Adini (2) M1 Chaldaean state in southern Babylonia, whose population was apparently a clan of the Bit-Dakkuri tribe. The Assyrian king Shalmaneser V (726–722) deported captives from there, according to a later letter written in Aramaic which refers to the king by his other name, Ululaiu. In 691 troops from Bit-Adini were among the forces which fought the army of the Assyrian king Sennacherib at the battle of Halule (q.v.) on the Tigris r.

Lipiński (2000: 163).

Bit-Agusi (map 7) Iron Age Aramaean state located in north-central Syria, occupying much of the territory between the kingdoms of Carchemish and Pat(t)in (Assyrian Unqi). To the south, it shared a frontier with the kingdom of Hamath. It is attested in Assyrian sources from the reign of Ashurnasirpal II (883–859) onwards. Named after its eponymous founder Gusi, Bit-Agusi is closely associated, in the record of Ashurnasirpal's western campaign (c. 870), with a land called Yahan, to the north of which Ashurnasirpal passed in his march from Carchemish to Patin. During the course of this campaign, we are told that Ashurnasirpal received tribute from Gusi, who is referred to as 'the Yahanite'. An Aramaean land called Yahan is first attested in the reign of the Assyrian king Ashur-dan II (934–912), who reports his conquest of it during his third campaign. He notes that the land was already in existence at the time his kingdom's throne was occupied by Ashurabi II (1013–973). As attested in these periods, Yahan appears to have been located east of the Tigris, in the vicinity of Lake Šari (thus Lipiński; see his map, 2000: 197). The apparent existence of another western Aramaean tribe bearing the name Yahan and first attested in Ashurnasirpal's reign probably reflects a westwards migration by the tribe or some of its clans in late C10 or early C9.

In 858 and 857, Gusi's son and successor Arame paid a substantial tribute to Ashurnasirpal's son and successor Shalmaneser III, during the western campaigns which the latter conducted in his first and second regnal years (**RIMA* 3: 17, 18), and again as he was embarking on another western campaign in his sixth year (853). One of the versions of the 858 campaign contains a reference to a man called Adanu the Yahanite, who appears among the local rulers who opposed Shalmaneser (**RIMA* 3: 10, 17). This may imply that Gusi's kingdom was divided between Arame and Adanu, or that at this time Yahan was not yet part of the kingdom of Bit-Agusi – though we have no other evidence that there was ever any distinction between Bit-Agusi and Yahan. Possibly Adanu was assigned rule over part of the kingdom's territory, under Arame's overall authority.

Arame reigned for at least twenty-five years, from 858 to 834 or later. During his reign there were further conflicts with Assyria, in the course of which Arame lost to the Assyrians the city of Arne, apparently his royal seat, and the cities Apparazu and Muru. But resistance to Assyria continued under Arame's son(?) and successor Attar-shumki (I). The latter is actually identified in the texts as 'son of Adramu', but it is likely that Adramu is simply a variant form of Arame's name. The city of Arpad (which has been identified with Tell Rifaʿat, 35 km north of Aleppo) is now attested as Bit-Agusi's capital. Attar-shumki led a coalition of northern Syrian states against the Assyrian king Adad-nirari III (810–783), who claimed victory in the ensuing battle fought at Paqarahubunu on the upper Euphrates (**RIMA* 3: 205). But the outcome of the conflict may have been inconclusive (see under **Paqar(a)hubunu**). Later, Attar-shumki participated in another coalition of forces against his kingdom's southern neighbour Hamath, now attached as a client-kingdom to Assyria. Subsequent intervention by Adad-nirari led to terms of peace being settled between Attar-shumki and Hamath's king Zakur. In accordance with these terms, the boundary between the two kingdoms was redrawn (**RIMA* 3: 203–4), resulting in territorial gains for Attar-shumki at Hamath's expense. Treaties were also concluded by a later ruler of Bit-Agusi, Matiʾilu (son and successor of a second Attar-shumki who was grandson of the first), with the Assyrian king Ashur-nirari V (754–746) (**ARAB* I: 265–7) and with a man called Bar-gaʾya, king of Ktk (**CS* II: 213–17).

In spite of these treaties, Bit-Agusi continued to stir up opposition to Assyria among the northern Syrian and eastern Anatolian states, no doubt encouraged by its alliance with the kingdom of Urartu, Assyria's most formidable enemy. But the anti-Assyrian forces suffered a major defeat in 743 at the hands of the Assyrian king Tiglath-pileser III. Arpad, Bit-Agusi's capital, had played a leading role in the confrontations with Assyria, and now became a specific target of Assyrian retaliation (**Tigl. III* 186–7). After a three-year siege, the city finally fell to the Assyrians. Bit-Agusi now became Assyria's first fully fledged province in Syria, and was renamed Arpad after its capital. From then on it appears to have remained submissive to Assyrian overlordship, except for one (known) occasion when it joined Hamath in a revolt against the Assyrian king Sargon in 721–720.

Hawkins (*RlA* 5: 238–9, s.v. Jahan), *CHLI* I: 388–90, Lipiński (2000: 195–219), Kahn (2007).

Bit-Amukani (map 11) M1 Aramaean tribe in southern Mesopotamia. It was probably located not far north of the city of Uruk, with which it had close ties. The Assyrian king Shalmaneser III reports that it paid tribute to him while he was residing in Huradu, royal city of the Bit-Dakkuri tribe, during his second Babylonian campaign

(850) (*RIMA 3: 31–2). A scene, with inscription, carved on the throne-base of Shalmaneser excavated at Fort Shalmaneser in Kalhu (Nimrud), depicts tribute being brought to Shalmaneser by Mushallim-Marduk, ruler of Bit-Amukani, and Adinu, ruler of Bit-Dakkuri (*RIMA 3: 139). In 729 Bit-Amukani was conquered by the Assyrian king Tiglath-pileser III (*Tigl. III 122–3), who had blockaded the tribe's leader (Nabu-)Mukin-zeri in his city Sapiya (Babylonian Shapiya) in a siege begun in 731 (*Tigl. III 163–4, 196–7). The Assyrian king Sennacherib includes thirty-nine walled cities of Bit-Amukani in his lists of conquests in Chaldaea during his first military campaign against Marduk-apla-iddina II (some time between 704 and 702; see under **Babylonia**) (*CS II: 301).

Though once allied with the Aramaean tribe Puqudu, whose territories lay near the Elamite frontier, Bit-Amukani subsequently came into conflict with it, particularly in mid C7 at the time of, or shortly after, the rebellion against the Assyrian king Ashurbanipal by his brother Shamash-shum-ukin (see **Babylon**). At least some of the Puqudu clans had supported the rebel, while Bit-Amukani remained loyal to Ashurbanipal. We learn this from a letter written to Ashurbanipal by Uruk's governor, Kudurru (c. 647), which reports that the Puqudu had carried out a raid against Bit-Amukani and had even settled in its territory (*Waterman, 1930: 189, no. 275). The most famous of Bit-Amukani's chiefs was the aforementioned (Nabu-)Mukin-zeri, who seized the throne of Babylon in 731 and occupied it until 729.

Lipiński (2000: 419–22).

Bit-Bahiani (Bet-Bagyan) (map 7) Iron Age Aramaean state in the Habur valley, northern Mesopotamia, first attested in the records of the Assyrian king Adad-nirari II (911–891). Ashurnasirpal II, Adad-nirari's successor-but-one, received tribute from it during his campaign in the region in his second regnal year (882) (*RIMA 2: 203), and also on a later campaign in northern Syria (*RIMA 2: 216). The name of the state is derived from its founder, a C10 Aramaean chieftain called Bagyan. Its capital was the city of Guzana (*OT* Gozan, mod. Tell Halaf; see ***Halaf, Tell***) near the source of the Habur r. By the end of C9 Bit-Bahiani had been absorbed into the Assyrian empire, and thenceforth its capital was administered by governors acting on behalf of the Assyrian king.

Lipiński (2000: 119–33).

Bit-Burutash (Bit-Paruta) see **Tabal**.

Bit-Dakkuri (map 11) M1 Chaldaean tribe located to the southeast of Babylon in southern Mesopotamia, mentioned in texts of the Assyrian king Shalmaneser III (858–824). It is one of five Chaldaean tribal groups known from written sources (for the others, see **Chaldaeans**). In 850, during the course of his second Babylonian campaign, Shalmaneser invaded Bit-Dakkuri and destroyed its fortified city Baqanu. This action was apparently sufficient to discourage any further resistance in the land, and when Shalmaneser approached the royal city Huradu, Bit-Dakkuri's ruler Adinu submitted voluntarily to him, paying a handsome tribute in the form of gold, silver, and other metals, special wood, ivory, and elephant hides (*RIMA 3: 31). A scene, with inscription, carved on the throne-base of Shalmaneser found in Fort Shalmaneser at Kalhu (Nimrud), depicts tribute being brought to Shalmaneser by Mushallim-Marduk, ruler of Bit-Amukani, and Adinu, ruler of Bit-Dakkuri (**RIMA* 3: 139). A Chaldaean called Nabu-shuma-ishkun, a member of the Bit-Dakkuri tribe, occupied the throne of Babylon from c. 760 to 748 (**RIMB* 2: 117–26), and another member of this tribe, Mushezib-Marduk, occupied it from 692 to 689 (for this king, see under **Babylonia**). The Assyrian king Sennacherib includes thirty-three walled cities of Bit-Dakkuri in his lists of conquests in Chaldaea during his first military campaign, against Marduk-apla-iddina II (some time between 704 and 702; see under **Babylonia**) (**CS* II: 301). Later on, following the fall of Babylon to Sennacherib in 689, its ruler Mushezib-Marduk was deported to Assyria with his family. In 678, during the reign of the Assyrian king Esarhaddon, the Bit-Dakkuri tribe under the leadership of a certain Shamash-ibni came into conflict with Assyrian troops after it had seized territory belonging to the cities Babylon and Borsippa. The Assyrians were victorious, the seized land was restored to its original owners, and Shamash-ibni was executed (*ABC* *83, *126, 218).

Lipiński (2000: 419–22).

Bit-Gabbari see Sam'al.

Bit-Halupe M1 Aramaean tribal state in northern Mesopotamia, located within the triangular region formed by the confluence of the Euphrates and Habur rivers. It was one of four Aramaean states on Assyria's western frontier which by C9 had come under Assyrian control (the other three states were Bit-Zamani, Bit-Bahiani, and Laqe). While in the city of Sur(u) in Bit-Halupe, the Assyrian king Tukulti-Ninurta II received tribute from Hamataya, the ruler of Laqe (**RIMA* 2: 176). Suru also figured in an unsuccessful rebellion against the Assyrian king Ashurnasirpal II in 883 (**RIMA* 2: 198–200) (see **Suru (2)**).

Lipiński (2000: 78–82).

Bithynia (map 4) Classical name for the region in northern Anatolia between Mysia to the west and Paphlagonia to the east. Through it ran major routes linking the Anatolian plateau with the Pontic region. Its rugged mountain terrain was complemented by fertile plains, watered by the Sangarius r. (mod. Sakarya) and its tributaries. Its inhabitants, whose ancestors came originally from Thrace, enjoyed a prosperous existence, their wealth deriving in large measure from the region's abundant timber stands and rich agricultural resources. During the period of the Persian empire (C6–4), Bithynia enjoyed a relatively high degree of independence, as it also did in the Hellenistic period when its kings formed alliances with the Galatians against the Seleucid kings (C3). In 75/74 the Bithynian king Nicomedes IV bequeathed his kingdom to Rome, and under Roman rule, the province of Bithynia and Pontus was created by Pompey the Great in 63.

Broughton/Mitchell (*OCD* 244–5).

Bitik (map 2) Findspot in north-central Anatolia, 25 km northwest of Ankara, of a large fragmentary vase, dating to the Hittite Old Kingdom (C17–15) and notable for its polychrome relief scenes. These appear in three registers. The top register depicts a standing man lifting a seated woman's veil and holding a cup to her lips. The lower registers may depict worshippers or other persons engaged in ritual activities. The ensemble is generally interpreted as a depiction of a sacred marriage. It is possible, however, that the apparently ritual elements portrayed in the relief scenes were normally associated with Hittite weddings, at least at the higher social levels. The vase is often compared with the famous polychrome vessel found at İnandıktepe (q.v.). Here too the reliefs are generally assumed to represent a sacred marriage.

Bittel (1976: 142–5).

Bit-Kilamzah Iron Age city in the Zagros region of northeastern Mesopotamia. It was attacked and captured by the Assyrian king Sennacherib during the first of his campaigns in the mountains east of Assyria (702) (**Sennach.* 26–7). Sennacherib garrisoned the city and settled deportees there taken from other areas of his conquests.

Bit-Rehob see Soba.

Bit-Shilani M1 Chaldaean tribe in southern Mesopotamia. It was conquered by the Assyrian king Tiglath-pileser III (745–727), along with other Chaldaean groups, during the king's Babylonian campaign of 731. Tiglath-pileser reports defeating Bit-Shilani's chieftain Nabu-ushabshi in a battle outside his city Sarrabanu. Nabu-ushabshi was impaled before the city gate, and the city itself was captured by the Assyrians after a siege. Tiglath-pileser looted it, allegedly taking prisoner 55,000 of its inhabitants, then destroyed it along with other cities in its vicinity (**Tigl. III* 160–3, 272).

Bit-Yahiri Iron Age Aramaean tribal state located in northern Mesopotamia, to the southwest of the Kashiyari range (mod. Tur ʿAbdin) and occupying at least part of the land called Zallu (Azallu) (q.v.). In 882 the Assyrian king Ashurnasirpal II received tribute from its ruler Ahi-ramu, described as 'belonging to the house of Yahiru, of the Zallean land' (**RIMA* 2: 203, 346).

Liverani (1992: 43).

Bit-Yakin (map 11) The wealthiest and most powerful of the five Chaldaean tribes attested in Iron Age sources. Located in southern Mesopotamia in the Sealand, it exercised extensive control over the region of Ur and the marshland areas to the east. The Assyrian king Shalmaneser III reports receiving tribute from it while he was residing in Huradu, royal city of the Bit-Dakkuri tribe, during his second Babylonian campaign (850) (**RIMA* 3: 31). The Babylonian king Eriba-Marduk (769–761) was a member of the Bit-Yakin tribe. Its tribal capital Dur-Yakin was the original seat of the Chaldaean leader Marduk-apla-iddina II (the biblical Merodach-baladan) who was twice king of Babylonia (721–710, 703; see under **Babylonia**) (**RIMB* 2: 135–42). Particularly during the reign of Marduk-apla-iddina, Bit-Yakin's resistance to the Assyrians was strengthened by its close alliance with Elam. But by the end of C8 the once powerful tribe had become greatly weakened, due both to heavy losses in military conflicts with the Assyrians, and to the deportation of large numbers of its population (to Kummuh in eastern Anatolia) in the aftermath of Assyrian conquest. Sennacherib includes eight walled cities of Bit-Yakin in his list of conquests in Chaldaea during his first military campaign (some time between 704 and 702) (**CS* II: 301).

However, Bit-Yakin's hostilities with Assyria continued in the reign of Sennacherib's son Esarhaddon (680–669), when Nabu-zer-kitti-lishir, the Bit-Yakinite governor of the Sealand and a son of Marduk-apla-iddina, rebelled against Assyrian rule and in 680 laid siege to Ur, which remained loyal to its Assyrian allegiance. Troops sent by Esarhaddon forced Nabu-zer-kitti-lishir to abandon the siege and flee to Elam, where he was executed by the Elamite king (*ABC 82). Some time before 651 Bit-Yakin's leader, Nabu-bel-shumati, grandson of Marduk-apla-iddina and ruler of the Sealand, supported Shamash-shum-ukin in his revolt against his brother, the Assyrian king Ashurbanipal (see under **Babylon**). Like his grandfather, Nabu-bel-shumati was closely allied with the Elamites. Perhaps with their support, he had some successes in his anti-Assyrian operations until he was forced, like his father, to flee to Elam, where he committed suicide. His corpse was packed in salt and dispatched to Assyria, where the king mutilated it.

Lipiński (2000: 419–20, 422, 433–4, 479).

Bit-Zamani (map 7) Aramaean state located northwest of the Kashiyari range (mod. Tur ʿAbdin) of northern Mesopotamia, to the north of the kingdom of Bit-Bahiani. Its capital was the city of Amidu (Assyrian Amedu, mod. Diyarbakır). It is first attested in an early C13 Assyrian cuneiform text from Shibaniba (mod. Tell Billa), which names Ashur-kashid as governor of the province of Bit-Zamani. The next reference to the land occurs in early C9, when its king Ammi-Ba'al suffered a defeat at the hands of the Assyrian king Tukulti-Ninurta II (890–884) (*RIMA 2: 171–2). Subsequently, Tukulti-Ninurta concluded a pact with Ammi-Ba'al, which secured the latter's continuing occupancy of his kingdom's throne, as an ally, in effect a vassal, of Assyria. Lipiński (2000: 154) notes that Bit-Zamani appears in Tukulti-Ninurta's Annals as an ally of the Assyrians in their fight against the Hurrian and Urartian principalities around the upper Tigris, the so-called Nairi lands (*RIMA 2: 171). But Ammi-Ba'al's rule came abruptly to an end in 879, in the reign of Tukulti-Ninurta's son and successor Ashurnasirpal II, when he was assassinated in a rebellion by the elders of Bit-Zamani, under the leadership of a man called Bur-Ramman. Ashurnasirpal responded promptly, crushing the rebels, and flaying alive their ringleader (*RIMA 2: 211, 261). He was, however, content to leave the kingdom under the immediate authority of a local ruler, appointing Bur-Ramman's brother Ilan to this position, and taking a number of steps to ensure that the region remained submissive to Assyrian control. For a while, he may have succeeded. But eventually Ilan broke his allegiance to his Assyrian overlord, prompting retaliatory action by Ashurnasirpal in 866. The Assyrian king led his troops into Bit-Zamani, captured Ilan's stronghold Damdammusa, and attacked his capital city Amedu (*RIMA 2: 220).

The final outcome of this campaign is not known, nor do we know of any other military operations later conducted by Ashurnasirpal in the region. Bit-Zamani probably maintained a relatively high degree of independence, albeit as a nominal vassal state of the Assyrians. In 856, however, the Assyrian king Shalmaneser III conquered the region as he passed through it (*RIMA 3: 19), and added it to the province governed by his chief cupbearer. In 830, Shalmaneser's commander-in-chief Dayyan-Ashur led an army from Bit-Zamani to the Arsanias r. (mod. Murat Su) where he met and defeated the Urartian king Se-duri (Sarduri I) (*RIMA 3: 69). The Assyrian province which Shalmaneser created in the region was subsequently known by various appellations: the province of Bit-Zamani (after the former Aramaean state), the province of (the city) Amedu, of Nairi, of (the city) Sinabu, and of (the city) Tushhan (see

Radner, *RlA* 11: 49–50, for details). In late C7, for example, the eponym official Bel-iqbi was known variously as governor of Bit-Zamani or governor of Tushhan (Millard, 1994: 90).

Lipiński (2000: 135–61).

Borsippa (Barsipa, Parsipa, ***Birs Nimrud***) (maps 11, 13) City in southern Babylonia, c. 20 km southwest of Babylon. Its history of occupation extends from late M3 until the Islamic period. Birs Nimrud has been excavated on a number of occasions, from mid C19 CE onwards, most notably by H. Rassam (1879–82), R. Koldewey (1902), and E. Trenkwalder (beginning in 1980). The site has long attracted attention because its ziggurat, still imposing in its ruins, was mistakenly identified by early travellers with the biblical 'tower of Babel'. In fact, this structure and the temple associated with it are all that remain of the precinct, known as the Ezida, of the city's chief deity Nabu and his consort Tashmetum. Its earliest phase dates back to the Old Babylonian period (Middle Bronze Age), when it is mentioned in the prologue to Hammurabi's laws.

From at least the reign of Hammurabi (1792–1750), Borsippa was one of the great cult-centres of the Babylonian world. But virtually nothing is known of its history before the early centuries of M1, when it was subject to incursions by the Aramaeans. A number of privileges were granted to the city, especially exemption from certain taxes, by the Babylonian king Marduk-zakir-shumi I (854–819). In 850, during the course of his second Babylonian campaign, the Assyrian king Shalmaneser III visited the city and made sacrifices to the gods there (**RIMA* 3: 31). Around 769, the Babylonian king Eriba-Marduk restored to the city land taken from it by the Aramaeans (**ABC* 182–3), but a few years later, members of the Chaldaean Bit-Dakkuri tribe settled in its territory. In spite of the insecurity which these encroachments must have caused, Borsippa enjoyed high prestige as a holy city, especially from mid C8 onwards, becoming a place of pilgrimage for both Assyrian and Babylonian kings. Nabu-shuma-imbi, a governor of the city when the Babylonian throne was occupied by Nabu-shuma-ishkun (760–748), describes Borsippa as 'the city of truth and justice'. But during Nabu-shuma-ishkun's reign, it suffered from severe political turmoil, and from conflicts with outside groups, including Chaldaeans and Aramaeans and the people of the city of Dilbat (**RIMB* 2: 124). These conflicts arose from disputes over Borsippa's territory. Hostilities between Borsippa and Babylon are reported during the reign of Nabu-shuma-ishkun's successor Nabu-nasir (Nabonassar; 747–734), who conducted a campaign against the city (**RIMB* 2: 127).

As noted above, Assyrian kings who campaigned in Babylonia acknowledged Borsippa's sacred character, and they sometimes bestowed material benefits on it. Tiglath-pileser III (745–727) offered sacrifices to the gods there (**Tigl. III* 160–1). Sargon II (721–705) repaired the canal which linked it to Babylon (*Sargon II* 332), and restored to the city the land taken from it by a tribal group called the Sutaeans (see **Sutu**) (*Sargon II* 335). Yet Borsippa's relations with Assyria remained volatile. The city supported the Chaldaean tribal leader Marduk-apla-iddina II (biblical Merodach-baladan) in his struggle with the Assyrians during the reigns of Sargon II and his successor Sennacherib. But part of its population held fast to Assyria, prompting Marduk-apla-iddina to take hostages from among them, whom he dispatched to his capital Dur-Yakin (for further details, see under **Babylonia**). The Assyrian king

Esarhaddon (680–669) granted a number of benefits to the city, repairing its sacred precinct and restoring its traditional administrative institutions which had been abolished by his father Sennacherib. He also restored to the city land seized from it by the Bit-Dakkuri tribe, after defeating the tribe in battle and capturing and executing its leader Shamash-ibni (678) (**RIMB* 2: 164, *173–4). However, in the conflict between Esarhaddon's son and successor Ashurbanipal (668–630/627) and Ashurbanipal's brother Shamash-shum-ukin, Borsippa made the mistake of supporting the rebel. (The latter had carried out some restoration work on the enclosure wall of the Ezida temple in the city while he occupied the Babylonian throne; **RIMB* 2: 252–3.) Ashurbanipal retaliated by attacking Borsippa. It fell after a two-year siege, and was plundered by the Assyrian troops. Ashurbanipal confiscated its important collection of literary and scientific texts and added them to his library in Nineveh. But at some time in his reign he also rebuilt the city's walls, which had fallen into ruin, in order to increase the security of its sanctuaries, and restored the temple of the god Nabu (**RIMB* 2: 216, 217–9).

In the Assyrian empire's declining years, Borsippa allied itself with the Babylonian king Nabopolassar. His successor Nebuchadnezzar II (604–562) carried out extensive restoration works in the city – to the walls, and to many of its sacred buildings, most notably the Ezida and the ziggurat Eurmeiminanki (**CS* II: 309–10). Further restoration work in the city was carried out by Nabonidus (556–539), the last of the Babylonian kings before Babylon fell to the Persians. According to Berossus (**FGrH* 680 F10 = **PE* 81–2, no. 25), Nabonidus sought refuge in Borsippa after being defeated in battle by Cyrus II (for more on the battle and its aftermath, see **Upi (1)**). Following his capture of Babylon, Cyrus proceeded to Borsippa to place it under siege, when Nabonidus voluntarily surrendered to him. The Babylonian king's life was spared, and he was sent to Carmania, southern Iran, where he spent his remaining days in exile. Under Persian rule Borsippa continued to flourish as a religious centre, and more restoration work was carried out on the Ezida during the Hellenistic period by the Seleucid king Antiochus I (280–261). The cult of the god Nabu persisted for many centuries, and was still being celebrated in Assyria in C3 CE.

Borsippa's basic layout was rectangular in plan, covering an area of c. 240 ha. Access through its walls was provided by at least eight gates. The Ezida precinct lay at the centre of the city and had its own enclosing wall. A number of other temples were located elsewhere in the city.

Unger (*RlA* 1: 402–29), Joannès and Sauvage (*DCM* 140–1).

Bosporus Narrow strait connecting the Propontis (mod. Sea of Marmara) with the Euxine Sea (Black Sea), 27 km in length. The Bosporus, Propontis, and the Hellespont (mod. Dardanelles) constitute the waterway between the Aegean and Black Seas. Counter-currents and strong counter-winds made navigation of this route from the Aegean end difficult for Bronze Age sailing ships: the daily average speed of the winds is 16.2 km per hour, and the current in the Bosporus has an average maximum of 4 to 5 knots, which can climb to 7 knots. But the introduction of the powerful fifty-oared Greek penteconters in C8 overcame the problems of wind and current, and from then on the waterway was regularly used by ships for both commercial and military purposes. It provided the chief route taken by Greek colonists, particularly from Miletus, who travelled to the northern shores of the Black Sea to found new settlements.

Figure 21 Bosporus today.

In C5 control of the waterway became vital in protecting the shipments of grain brought from Black Sea regions to provision Greek cities of the Aegean world. The most important city located on the Bosporus was Byzantium, founded in 668 by Greek colonists from Megara. Seventeen years earlier, on the opposite shore, the city of Chalcedon had been founded by settlers from the same mother city. The later Constantinople, mod. Istanbul, encompassed both cities, and is thus situated partly in Europe and partly in Asia, the Bosporus (along with the Hellespont) providing the narrow dividing strip between the two continents.

von Bredow and Toktas'ev (*BNP* 2: 733–4).

Bozrah The name (meaning 'fortress', 'enclosure' in Hebrew) of several cities in Syria and Palestine. The most important of these was a city belonging to the kingdom of Edom, according to *OT* sources (e.g. 1 Chronicles 1:44), and perhaps the Edomite capital. This Bozrah has been identified with mod. Buseirah (q.v.). Another city called Bozrah, attested in Jeremiah 48:24, lay in the land of Moab, and may be mod. Bezer. A third, near Syria's southern frontier, is mod. Busra eski-Sham. It became the northernmost stronghold of the Nabataean empire.

Baly (*HCBD* 153).

Brak, Tell (Nagar/Nawar) (map 10) Settlement-mound on the upper Habur plains in northeastern Syria, covering an area of 43 ha, with a history of occupation extending from the Ubaid period (M6–5) to the end of the Bronze Age (c. 1200). It is now generally believed to be the site of the M3–2 city Nagar/Nawar (q.v.). Excavations were conducted by M. Mallowan for the British School of Archaeology in Iraq, from 1937 to 1938, and by D. and J. Oates for the Institute of Archaeology, London University, between 1976 and 1993. Subsequently excavations have been conducted by a number of field directors under the general direction of D. Oates (1994–2004) and J. Oates (1994–present): by R. Matthews for the British School of Archaeology in Iraq and the McDonald Institute of Cambridge University (1994–6); by G. Emberling (1998–2002) and H. McDonald (2000–4), with sponsorship by the Metropolitan Museum of Art and the British School of Archaeology in Iraq; and by A. McMahon of the University of Cambridge, sponsored by the British School of Archaeology in Iraq and other bodies (2006 on).

During the Uruk period (M4), the site became a major urban centre, 'as large and complex as cities in southern Iraq during early M4' (Emberling and McDonald, 2001: 21), and in the second half of the period developed extensive cultural and commercial contacts with the cities of southern Mesopotamia, as reflected in the strongly southern Mesopotamian character of its culture. Its most prominent architectural feature in this period was a tripartite 'Eye Temple', so called from the discovery in it of a number of small stone plaques with eye symbols.

After a period of apparent decline during the early centuries of the Early Bronze Age (M3), reflected in a reduction in the size of the settlement, Tell Brak had once more grown to its maximum size by the middle of M3, when it was almost certainly the most important political and economic centre in the Habur region. Its strategic location on the Jaghjagh r., at the entrance to the Habur plains from southern Mesopotamia and astride the route to the Ergani Maden copper mines in eastern Anatolia, is considered to be a major factor in the prominence which it achieved. Rich hoards of artefacts and precious metals testify to its wealth. Recent excavations have uncovered what Emberling and McDonald (2001) call the 'Brak Oval' dating to this period. Its excavated portion contains a large bakery with facilities for storing and grinding grain and a series of rooms arranged around an inner courtyard. Around 250 seal impressions were recovered from the building.

This phase of the city's existence ended violently c. 2300 when large parts of it were put to the torch, almost certainly by the forces of the newly emerging Akkadian empire. It was restored under Akkadian domination, probably in the reign of the Akkadian king Naram-Sin (2254–2218), who used it as a centre for the administration of the Habur region. The focal point of the administration was a 'palace' (probably, rather, a fortified storehouse), discovered by Mallowan and attributed to Naram-Sin because of inscriptions bearing his name stamped on mudbricks used in the building's construction. It was a massive square structure covering an area of c. 1 ha. An apparent destruction of this building during Naram-Sin's reign has been associated with a supposed attack upon the city by the warlike Lullubu peoples (q.v.) who were allegedly responsible for widespread devastation throughout Naram-Sin's kingdom. Other monumental buildings of the period, including one adjacent to the palace, were unearthed by D. and J. Oates. Around the time of the collapse of the Akkadian empire, c. 2193, the city was again destroyed by fire, perhaps at the hands of the Gutians. It was reoccupied very soon after, at the end of M3, when it probably became a capital of one of the Hurrian principalities of northern Mesopotamia, most likely the kingdom of Urkesh and Nagar/Nawar. But by early M2 the southern half of the site had been abandoned.

Tell Brak gained new prominence in the Late Bronze Age when it became a major centre of the kingdom of Mitanni. A palace-fortress dating to this period has produced the earliest known Hurrian text of the Mitannian empire, as well as texts dating to the reigns of the C14 Mitannian kings Artashumara and his brother and successor Tushratta. The latter was the last ruler of the Mitannian empire, which was conquered by the Hittite king Suppiluliuma I in the third quarter of C14. Brak itself apparently survived the Hittite conquest, but its palace was destroyed the following century by the Assyrians. The site continued to be occupied until it was abandoned, finally, at the end of the Late Bronze Age, in the early years of C12. There is also some evidence for later settlement, in the Neo-Assyrian and Roman periods.

D. Oates (1982b), T. J. Matthews *et al.* (1994), Oates and Oates (1997), Oates *et al.* (1997), Emberling and McDonald (2001; 2003).

Branchidae see **Didyma**.

Buliiana Iron Age city located in northern Mesopotamia in the eastern part of the Kashiyari mountain range (mod. Tur ʿAbdin). On his return from Tushhan in 882, after conquering the city of Ishpilibria, the Assyrian king Ashurnasirpal II entered the pass of Buliiana and followed the Luqia r. as far as the Tigris (**RIMA* 2: 203, 244). The settlements in this part of the Kashiyari, which the king conquered en route, reportedly belonged to one of the regions called Habhu (q.v.).

Radner (2006: 290).

Bunashi Fortified Iron Age city located in northeastern Mesopotamia or northwestern Iran near the land of Zamua. It was conquered by the Assyrian king Ashurnasirpal II, allegedly along with thirty other cities in its environs, during his campaign in the region in his third regnal year (881) (**RIMA* 2: 204–5). A man called Musasina was ruler of Bunashi at that time.

Burgaz see **Uranium**.

Burmarina (*Tell Shiyukh/Shioukh/Šuyuh Fawqani/Faouqani*) (map 7) M1 city in northwestern Mesopotamia, located on the east bank of the Euphrates r. near Carchemish, within the Aramaean state Bit-Adini. In 858, when Bit-Adini was ruled by Ahuni, Burmarina was one of the cities conquered by the Assyrian king Shalmaneser III during his first western campaign (**RIMA* 3: 15). It has been identified with Tell Shiyukh Fawqani, a 35 m high mound to the northwest of Tell Ahmar (Ahuni's capital, Til-Barsip). This identification is based on several documents belonging to a C7 Neo-Assyrian archive (which contained tablets written in Aramaic) discovered in a house on the site. Excavations carried out at Shiyukh Fawqani in the course of the Tishrin dam salvage project, which encompassed a number of cities on the upper Euphrates, have indicated that the site was already occupied in the Late Bronze Age. It is likely that the Late Bronze Age city Marina (q.v.), first attested in a C13 Assyrian text, was located there.

*Fales, Bachelot, and Attardo (1996), Bachelot (1999), Fales (1999), Lipiński (2000: 175–6).

Buruncuk Site of M1 city in the region of Aeolis, northwestern Anatolia, 28 km north of Izmir. It is often identified, though inconclusively, with one of the places called Larisa in Classical sources, in particular, the legendary Larisa of the Pelasgians in Homeric tradition (*Iliad* 2.840–1). Remains of the city, located on the hill above the mod. village, have been assigned to three periods: pre-Greek (early M1), late Archaic (c. 500), and late Classical–early Hellenistic (C4). They include fortifications dating to each of these periods, and within them the foundations of two temples, a palace, megaron- and subsequently peristyle-type houses (see glossary for both terms), and the remains of an aqueduct dated to c. 500. From a necropolis of C6 date lying to the east of the city, more than one hundred tombs have been recovered. These are tumulus tombs for the most part, consisting of stone circular structures surmounted by cones of earth. The graves themselves are made of stone slabs and are located in the middle of the tumuli.

Bean (*PECS* 174).

Burunkaya see under **Kızıldağ**.

Buseirah (map 8) Iron Age city located in mod. Jordan 10 km south of Tafila. It was identified with the Edomite city called Bozrah in *OT* sources (e.g. Genesis 36:33, 1 Chronicles 1:44) by U. J. Seetzen in 1806. There is, however, no inscriptional evidence to confirm his proposal. The uncertainty of the identification was one of the reasons prompting C.-M. Bennett to begin excavating the site in 1971. She conducted five seasons there, from 1971 to 1974 and in 1980, first on behalf of the British School of Archaeology in Jerusalem, and subsequently for the British Institute at Amman for Archaeology and History. Her excavations brought to light a major Edomite city of Iron Age II date (early M1), with possible continuity into the Persian period (C6–4), and perhaps reoccupation in the Nabataean and Roman periods. The Iron Age settlement, which was fortified by a city wall, featured several large buildings, apparently used for administrative purposes. It appears to have been a major regional centre of the kingdom of Edom, perhaps even the capital. The fact that in prophetic oracles Bozrah seems to be synonymous with the whole land of Edom (Isaiah 34:6, Jeremiah 49:13, 22, Amos 1:12) may provide some support for the conjecture that it was indeed Edom's capital.

The date of the city's foundation is at present uncertain. Ceramic evidence suggests that it was no earlier than C7, though a foundation date in C8 or even C9 has not been ruled out. At all events, it is clear that the city did not exist in Iron Age I, thus excluding a foundation before 1000. This would virtually rule out the historical validity of the Edomite list of kings, recorded in Genesis 36:31–9 and 1 Chronicles 1:43–51, 'who reigned in Edom before any Israelite king reigned' – on the assumption, of course, that Bozrah's identification with Buseirah is correct.

Bienkowski (1990: 101–3; *OEANE* 1: 387–90), Reich (*NEAEHL* 1: 264–6).

Butamu Iron Age city belonging to the Neo-Hittite kingdom of Pat(t)in (Assyrian Unqi) in northwestern Syria. It was captured by the Assyrian king Shalmaneser III during his campaign west of the Euphrates in his first regnal year (858) (**RIMA* 3: 17).

CHLI I: 362.

Byblos (Gubla, Gebal, *Jebail*) (maps 3, 6, 7, 10, 13) Port-city located on the coast of Lebanon, 60 km north of Beirut, with a history of occupation extending from the

Pre-pottery Neolithic period (M6 or earlier) to the present day, with a gap in occupation after the mediaeval period. The anc. city was rediscovered in 1860, and identified as Byblos by the end of C19. Excavations were conducted initially by the French archaeologist P. Montet between 1921 and 1924, and subsequently by M. Dunand, on behalf of the Lebanese government and the French Academy of Inscriptions, from 1928 until 1975. The name Byblos derives from the Greek word *bublos* meaning 'papyrus scroll', reflecting the city's importance as an intermediary in the papyrus trade between Egypt and the Aegean world. In Bronze Age Akkadian texts, the city is called Gubla. In Hebrew texts, it is called Gebal.

By the Early Bronze Age, Byblos had become a thriving commercial centre, enjoying trade links with Anatolia and Mesopotamia, and particularly with Old Kingdom Egypt. It was the chief port on the Lebanese coast for the export of cedar, in high demand in Egypt for construction projects, including the building of palaces and ships. Already in the first centuries of M3, Byblos was defended by massive fortifications, which enclosed a well-planned urban centre with solidly built houses. Access to the city was via two gates in the walls, a 'Sea Gate' and a 'Land Gate'. The most important building of this period was the temple of the goddess Baalat Gebal, 'lady of Byblos'. Erected c. 2800, it was one of the first monumental structures of the Syro-Palestinian region. About 200 years later, a second temple was built opposite it, called the L-shaped temple by Dunand because the two units and courtyard of which it was composed were so arranged. Though destroyed in an Amorite invasion towards the end of M3, Byblos was rebuilt and resettled by early M2. In the Middle Bronze Age (c. 1900–1600), it was again one of the most important commercial centres along the Syro-Palestinian coast. Trade was resumed with Egypt, and trade links were also

Figure 22 Byblos.

established with Crete, as attested by finds of the famous Minoan Kamares ceramic ware in the city, dating to Crete's First Palace period (c. 1900–1650). During Byblos' Middle Bronze phase, the 'Obelisk temple' (so named because of twenty-six obelisks discovered in its courtyard) was constructed over the remains of the Early Bronze Age temple of Baalat Gebal. Dunand had the building relocated a short distance away so that he could excavate the earlier temple.

Through the Middle and Late Bronze Ages, Byblos retained its close ties with Egypt, ties of both a commercial and a political nature (its commercial dealings with Egypt are mentioned by the C15 pharaoh Tuthmosis III) – in the face of threats posed by the other major powers which sought to establish their dominance in the region, notably the kingdoms of Hatti and Mitanni. In mid C14, Byblos under its Akkadian name Gubla figured prominently in the Amarna letters (see glossary). The ruler of the city at the time was a man called Rib-Hadda, whose kingdom incorporated a number of small coastal towns, including Ammiya, Batruna, and Shigata. Rib-Hadda's letters to the pharaoh Akhenaten constitute the most voluminous body of correspondence exchanged between vassal and overlord in the Amarna archive (**EA* 68–140). For the most part, the letters deal with the aggression and depredations of Abdi-Ashirta and his son Aziru, successive rulers of Gubla's northern neighbour Amurru, and are full of complaints about the pharaoh's alleged failure to respond to Rib-Hadda's appeals for assistance.

The fate of Byblos at the end of the Bronze Age is uncertain. However, during the Iron Age, from C12 onwards, it ranked as one of the wealthiest and most important of the Phoenician cities. Unfortunately, remains of the Iron Age city have not yet been uncovered, and may lie beyond the limits of the French excavations. The Assyrian king

Figure 23 Obelisks temple, Byblos.

Tiglath-pileser I (1114–1076) reports receiving tribute from it – and also from Sidon and the island-city Arvad (Arwada) – during his campaign in the west against the land of Amurru (**RIMA* 2: 37, 53). In early C11, Byblos figured in the well-known *Tale of Wenamun* (**CS* I: 89–93); the merchant Wenamun had been sent to obtain cedar from the king of Byblos, but suffered a hostile reception from him before he managed to secure his consignment of timber. A noteworthy find of this late M2 period is the so-called Ahiram sarcophagus (Ahiram was a king of Byblos), now in the Beirut Museum. In addition to the artistic motifs on its lid, which display a range of Egyptian, Hittite, and Syrian influences, it exhibits the earliest surviving example of a Phoenician alphabetic inscription.

During its Iron Age phase, Byblos owed much of its importance to the role it played as a centre for the papyrus trade, and the export of Lebanese timber. It was noted also for the skills of its stonemasons and carpenters, who according to 1 Kings 5:18 assisted in the construction of Solomon's temple. Like other Phoenician city-states, Byblos succumbed to Assyrian domination, beginning in C9 with the reign of the Assyrian king Ashurnasirpal II (883–859), who conquered the city. Following its participation in the ultimately unsuccessful anti-Assyrian coalition which confronted Ashurnasirpal's son and successor Shalmaneser III at the battle of Qarqar in 853 (**RIMA* 3: 23), it remained under Assyrian domination until the fall of the Assyrian empire in late C7. But like the other Phoenician cities, it was allowed a high degree of independence, and continued to prosper, so long as it remained submissive to Assyrian overlordship and continued to pay the tribute demanded of it, as illustrated by the appearance of its king Sibittibi'il among the tributaries of the Assyrian king Tiglath-pileser III (745–727) (**Tigl. III* 68–9).

Byblos subsequently came under Babylonian and then Persian domination. Herodotus (3.91) included it in what he called the fifth Persian province (but see glossary under **satrapy**), the seat of whose administration was located in Sidon. A limestone stele discovered in 1869 contains an inscription, datable to C5 or C4, of a king of Byblos called Yehawmilk (**CS* II: 151–2). A relief carving on the stele depicts the king, bearded and dressed in Persian-type attire, receiving a blessing from the goddess Baalat. In general, there is little surviving evidence of Persian influence in the city, though the Persians were responsible for reinforcing the city's walls. Byblos submitted without resistance to Alexander the Great when he came to the region in 332 (Arrian, *Anabasis* 15.6), and subsequently became part of the Seleucid empire. During the Hellenistic and Roman periods, it was thoroughly Hellenized and then Romanized. Almost all traces of its Phoenician character were obscured. In the Roman period it became a centre of the cult of Adonis.

Jidejian (1971), Joukowsky (*NEAEHL* 1: 390–3). The primary work is the account of M. Dunand's excavations (Dunand, 1937–73).

Byzantium (map 4) City founded on the western side of the Bosporus on the site of European Istanbul. Its location on the eastern end of the triangular peninsula, bounded by the Propontis (Sea of Marmara) to the south and the Golden Horn to the north, provided it with an excellent defensive position, as well as enabling it to control all sea traffic passing between the Aegean and the Black Seas. Though evidence of occupation of the site dates back to prehistoric times, the city proper was founded opposite the city of Chalcedon (Herodotus 4.144) in 688 by colonists from the mainland Greek city

Megara, who were probably joined by settlers from central and southern Greece. In 516 the city became subject to the Persian emperor Darius I during his campaign against the Scythians, and remained under Persian control except for the period of the Ionian revolt (499–494) until the Persian retreat from the Greek world in 479. Subsequently, it became a member of the Athenian Confederacy, but rebelled twice against Athens, in 440–439 and 411–408. Later it allied itself with Athens on two occasions, between c. 378 and 357, and in its opposition to Philip II of Macedon in 340–339.

It was during the Byzantine period that the city reached the height of its power and splendour under the name Constantinople, as the capital of a vast empire extending over the eastern half of the world formerly ruled by Rome. There is little remaining material evidence of the Greek, Hellenistic, and Roman phases of the city's existence.
MacDonald (*PECS* 177–9).

C

Cadyanda (map 15) M1 BCE–M1 CE city in Lycia, southwestern Anatolia, located on a steep mountainside 19 km northeast of Fethiye and c. 400 m above the mod. village Üzümlü. The Lycians themselves called the city Khadawanti. Tombs and inscriptions in the native Lycian language date its origins back to at least C5. A fragmentary bilingual inscription (in Lycian and Greek versions) found at Xanthus records grants made by the C4 Carian dynast Pixodarus to four Lycian cities – Xanthus, Tlos, Pinara, and Cadyanda (**TAM* I: 45). Many tombs have been found on and near the site of Cadyanda. Those of specifically Lycian type include a pillar-tomb similar to the pillar-tombs erected at Xanthus (but with its surmounting grave chamber now missing), and a freestanding house-type tomb embellished with relief carvings of human figures (warriors and other men and women seated or reclining) and animals. Some of the human figures have their names carved next to them in Lycian and Greek. These tombs are probably to be dated to the second half of C4. The most substantial material remains of the anc. city date to the Roman period, and include a stadium, gymnasium, baths, and a theatre.

Bean (1978: 42–5, *PECS* 429–30), Wörrle (*BNP* 2: 870).

Figure 24 Tomb with relief, Cadyanda.

Çadır Höyük see Zippalanda.

Cadytis see Gaza.

Calah see Nimrud.

Calynda (*Kozpınar*) (map 5) M1 BCE–M1 CE city in Caria or Lycia in southwestern Anatolia, 4 km east of Dalaman. It is first attested in C5 by Herodotus (8.87–8), who reports that a ship from Calynda, with the Calyndian king Damasithymus on board, participated on the Persian side in the sea battle between the Greeks and the Persians off the Greek island of Salamis in the Saronic Gulf (480). In later years, after the Greek repulse of Persia, Calynda became a member of the Athenian Confederacy (see glossary). Calynda apparently shared a border with the Carian city Caunus (Herodotus 1.172). During the first half of the Hellenistic period, it was under the control of the Ptolemies, but in 164 the Roman Senate handed it over to Rhodes. In C2 CE it became a member of the Lycian League.

The earliest remains of the hilltop site at Kozpınar are those of the anc. city's fortifications, dating back to the early Hellenistic period. Calynda appears to have been of no great importance during the Roman and Byzantine periods. There are remains of a wall of mediaeval date.

Roos (1969: 72–4), Bean (*PECS* 434).

Canaan(ites) A term applicable in its broadest sense to the anc. peoples and cultures of the Levant, up to the last decades of C4. But it is clear from Bronze Age and M1 written sources (the latter including the Bible) that the term was used with much more limited application in the periods in which these texts were composed. Many of the peoples we might now designate as Canaanites would not have identified themselves as such, nor would they have been so identified by others. Their common ethnic origin was obscured by their divisions into a number of tribal groups, city-states, and kingdoms, each of which developed its own political and social structures, and a number of its own distinctive cultural traits. But archaeological evidence makes clear that throughout the region encompassing the territories covered today by Israel, Lebanon, coastal Syria, southern inland Syria, and Transjordan there was a high degree of ethnic and cultural continuity, beginning in the Neolithic period and extending through the Bronze and Iron Ages up to the early Hellenistic period. We should, however, be careful not to assign too precise a definition to the territory we have called Canaanite. There were marked fluctuations in the cultural and ethnic boundaries of this territory through Canaanite history, coinciding to some extent with the changing political and military fortunes of the Syro-Palestinian region as a whole.

The first clearly attested written reference to Canaan, or rather to Canaanites, appears in the C18 archives of Mari. A possible earlier reference found in the Early Bronze Age archive at Ebla, which dates to C24, depends on the disputed reading of the term *ga-na-na* as 'Canaanite'. In any case, the Ebla archive contains the first attestation of the Canaanite language, a member of the Semitic language group. The Canaanites used the cuneiform script at that time. But several centuries later, at the beginning of M2, they were the first people to devise an alphabetic system for their written records. The derivation of the name 'Canaan' remains uncertain. It may in fact have had a non-Semitic, Hurrian origin – *kinahhu*, meaning 'blue cloth'. An alternative possibility is that it derives from the Semitic word *k-n-'* meaning to 'be subdued'.

Canaan's strategic location at an important meeting place between the western Asian, Egyptian, and Mediterranean worlds gave it excellent access to trade contacts with these worlds. Already in the Early Bronze Age a number of flourishing urban centres had emerged throughout Canaanite territory, the forerunners of the kingdoms and city-states of the Middle and Late Bronze Ages, whose prosperity no doubt depended much on the region's commercial links with Egypt. Indeed throughout its history, Canaan's fortunes, both political and economic, were closely tied to the fluctuating fortunes of the kingdom of the Nile. The collapse of the Egyptian Old Kingdom saw a corresponding decline in the material civilization of the Canaanite region and the abandonment of a number of settlements, in the period designated as Early Bronze Age IV (c. 2400–2000).

The Middle Bronze Age in Canaan (c. 2000–1550) witnessed the development of fully fledged city-states and kingdoms, which became important centres for commercial activity as well as for the development of arts and crafts to a high level of sophistication. The major centres were protected by massive fortifications, like those of Akko, Ashkelon, Dan, Dor, Gezer, Hazor, Lachish, Megiddo, and Shechem. The gold hoards unearthed in Tell el-Ajjul ('City II') provide some of the finest examples of Canaanite craftsmanship in the Middle Bronze IIB–C period (c. 1750–1550), the period that has been called the golden age of Canaanite culture. The re-establishment of links with Egypt was no doubt a major factor in Canaan's Middle Bronze Age resurgence, but important links were also established with Anatolia, Cyprus, and the Aegean world, as well as with other parts of Syria. The Canaanite city-states, each of whose urban centres controlled a peripheral area occupied by small towns and villages, remained independent of one other, competed with one other, and no doubt frequently squabbled and fought with one other.

References to Canaan in Middle and Late Bronze Age texts are few and far between. One of the most notable of these references is contained in the famous inscription of Idrimi, a C15 king of Alalah, who reports that he spent part of his exile in the land of Canaan (*Greenstein, 1995: 2426, **CS* I: 479) before returning to his kingdom to claim its throne. In another C15 text, from Egypt, the pharaoh Amenhotep II (1427–1400) includes in a booty list Canaanites for deportation to Egypt. There are also several references to Canaan in the mid C14 Amarna letters (in the form *Kinahhi*). But in general, the very rarity of Bronze Age text references to Canaan is in itself a reflection of the fact that there was no perception, either by the Canaanites themselves or by others, of a common identity which linked all Canaanites together. They did form coalitions from time to time, for *ad hoc* military purposes against a common enemy. But such military coalitions involved non-Canaanite states as well, and were clearly not based on ethnic considerations.

The Egyptian campaigns conducted through Syria–Palestine to the Euphrates, beginning with the military enterprises of Tuthmosis I (1504–1492), effectively brought to an end the Canaanite Middle Bronze Age. The climax of these campaigns was the decisive victory which Tuthmosis III (1479–1425) won over a coalition of Canaanite and Syrian forces at the battle of Megiddo (**ANET* 234–8). Many of the Canaanite states were now reduced to Egyptian vassal status, though sovereignty in the Canaanite territories as well as in other Syro-Palestinian territories fluctuated between Egypt and the other superpowers of the day – Mitanni (up to its destruction by the Hittite king Suppiluliuma I c. 1340) and Hatti. The pharaoh's Canaanite vassals continued to thrive, for the most part, under Egyptian sovereignty, due to their continuing close cultural and commercial contacts with Egypt. Moreover, the relative stability which Egyptian rule brought to the region (despite the stream of complaints directed to the pharaoh Akhenaten by his vassal rulers in the Amarna correspondence) increased the opportunities for the expansion of Canaanite commercial contacts beyond the shores of the Levant, to Cyprus and the Aegean world in particular.

The upheavals which accompanied the end of the Bronze Age paved the way for major changes in the nature and patterns of settlement in the Canaanite region. By the end of C13, as Egypt was reducing its presence in Syria–Palestine, a number of the Canaanite settlements were abandoned. Other major centres continued to survive and prosper for a time, but these centres too disappeared around mid C12, many of the inhabitants taking to the hills, when Egypt withdrew completely from Syro-Palestinian territory. This was a pivotal time in the history of the region – marking as it did the transition between the Bronze and Iron Ages. By this time, a Philistine presence was becoming firmly established in the coastal plains, and in *OT* tradition the Israelites, very likely a Canaanite sub-group, now appear more distinctly on the scene, after making a first brief and much debated appearance in the well-known stele-inscription of the pharaoh Merneptah (1213–1203) (**ANET* 376–8) (see under **Israel**). *OT* tradition clearly distinguishes three major groups at this time – Philistines along Palestine's southern coast, Canaanites on the plains, and Israelites in the hills. To begin with, these groups may have coexisted relatively peacefully, for as much as one hundred years. But then, according to *OT* sources, the Philistines took on a more aggressive aspect, seeking to expand into the interior. At the same time the Israelites sought to extend their territory westwards, onto the plains and towards the coast. In the process, they absorbed Canaanite territory on the plains. The scene was now set for the series of bitter conflicts, recorded in the *OT*, between the Philistines and the Israelites, conflicts which continued from late M2 into the first decades of M1 when the Philistines were, according to biblical tradition, defeated by King David.

It is to the Israelites that we should now turn for the remaining episodes of Canaanite history. We should also look to the Phoenicians, the Canaanites' most visible Iron Age descendants, for a continuation of the mercantile and artistic traditions which had brought prosperity and distinction to many Canaanite towns in their Middle and Late Bronze Age phases.

Redford (1992), Hackett (*OEANE* 1: 408–14), Tubb (1998).

Candyba (*Gendive*) (map 15) M1 mountaintop city in Lycia, southwestern Anatolia, perhaps to be identified with Late Bronze Age Hinduwa. According to Greek literary tradition, it was founded by the legendary hero Candybus. Two inscriptions in the Lycian language (*TAM* I: 81, 82) and several house-tombs and sarcophagi of Lycian type reflect the indigenous civilization of the region, which flourished in the first half of M1. Candyba is generally equated with the Lycian town called Khãkbi; but numismatic evidence appears to cast doubt on this identification (see **Khãkbi**).

Bean (*PECS* 435).

Capisa M1 city attested in Pliny the Elder (6.92) who locates it in Central Asia north of the country of Arachosia (which lay in Afghanistan) within a region called Capisene. According to Pliny, Capisa was destroyed by the Persian king Cyrus II during his campaign in the east, probably some time after his capture of Babylon in 539. Capisa is commonly equated with the Arachosian city Kapishakanish (q.v.), attested in texts of Darius' reign (e.g. **DB* 45), despite the fact that Pliny clearly distinguishes Capisa from Arachosia. To accommodate the inconsistency, it has been suggested that the city may originally have belonged to Arachosia, but was subsequently partitioned off, becoming the capital of a new province Paropanisadae (q.v.), also referred to by Pliny. An identification has been suggested between Capisa and the archaeological site at Begram, near the Hindu Kush.

Bivar (1988: 200).

Carbasyanda by Caunus see **Kızıltepe**.

Carchemish (Karkamish, ***Jerablus***) (maps 6, 7, 10, 13) Bronze and Iron Age city located on the upper Euphrates r. near Turkey's border with Syria. First identified by the Assyriologist George Smith in 1876, Carchemish was excavated for the British Museum by P. Henderson (1878–81), by D. G. Hogarth, C. Thompson, and C. L. Woolley successively (1911–14), and again by Woolley (1920). Political developments in the region brought the last excavation period abruptly and prematurely to an end. Evidence of settlement on the site goes back to M5 (Halaf period). The earliest significant material remains are those of a number of stone cist tombs, dating to the beginning of M3, in which were found large quantities of vases often decorated with red geometric motifs. But the most important periods in the city's history fall within the Late Bronze and Iron Ages.

In written records, Carchemish is first mentioned among the cities subject to the king of Ebla at the end of M3. It subsequently appears in the C18 Mari archives. At this time, as later, it was an important political and commercial centre, no doubt because of its excellent strategic location on the Euphrates at the junction of major trade routes. In early C18 it was ruled by a local dynasty which enjoyed peaceful trading relations with Mari. Wood, wine, and cereals were among the goods it dispatched to Mari when the latter was ruled by Yasmah-Addu, viceroy and son of the Assyrian king Shamshi-Adad I (1796–1775). At that time, the ruler of Carchemish was a man called Aplahanda. Close links with Mari continued when the Mariote throne was occupied by Zimri-Lim (1774–1762), who may have been, at least nominally, overlord of Carchemish.

Subsequently, Carchemish became a subject state of Aleppo, capital of the kingdom of Yamhad. Following the final conquest of this kingdom by the Hittites in early C16, Carchemish was incorporated into the Hurrian kingdom of Mitanni, and remained subject to Mitanni until the Hittite king Suppiluliuma I captured it after a six-day siege in 1327. It was the last remaining Mitannian stronghold to fall to the Hittites. It then became a viceregal seat of the Hittite empire, with its territory expanded both east and west of the Euphrates, under the rule of a member of the Hittite royal family (the first viceroy was Suppiluliuma's son Sharri-Kushuh/Piyassili), and remained so until the end of the Late Bronze Age. The viceroy's prominence in Syrian affairs in this period is clearly attested in the archives of Ugarit and Emar. Suppiluliuma established another of his sons, Telipinu, as viceroy in Aleppo, but the Carchemish viceroy appears

Figure 25 Environs of Carchemish.

to have played the more important military, political, and judicial roles in the Syro-Palestinian region, virtually with the status of a regional overlord. The death of Sharri-Kushuh c. 1313, when the Hittite throne was occupied by the viceroy's brother Mursili II, prompted the Assyrians to invade and occupy Carchemish, until they were driven from the land by a Hittite military force under Mursili's personal command (**AM* 116–19). Before returning home from Syria, Mursili installed Sharri-Kushuh's son Shahurunuwa on the throne of Carchemish (**AM* 124–5). Two decades later, the Assyrian king Adad-nirari I (1307–1275) claimed Carchemish amongst his extensive conquests (**RIMA* 1: 131). But the Assyrians failed to make any lasting impact on the city or its associated territories, which appear to have remained fairly firmly under Hittite control until the end of the Bronze Age.

Carchemish figures among the cities and countries devastated by the so-called Sea Peoples' invasions in early C12, according to the account of the pharaoh Ramesses III (**ARE IV*: §§65–6, **ANET* 262). But there is nothing in the archaeological or epigraphic record to indicate that the city suffered significantly, if at all, from these invasions. (Hawkins, *CHLI* I:73, suggests that in this context 'Carchemish' probably refers to the Hittite empire in Syria.) Indeed at Carchemish a branch of the Hittite royal dynasty continued for at least several more generations after the disappearance of the central dynasty at Hattusa. From royal seal impressions discovered in 1985 at Lidar Höyük (q.v.) on the east bank of the Euphrates, we know that Talmi-Teshub, the great-great-grandson of Suppiluliuma I and the viceroy at Carchemish during the reign of Suppiluliuma II, was succeeded by his son Ku(n)zi-Teshub. The fact that the latter styled himself 'Great King' suggests that the central dynasty at Hattusa was now defunct and that he saw himself as the one true heir to the line of Suppiluliuma. However, the kingdom over which he held sway extended through only part of the eastern territories of the former Late Bronze Age Hittite kingdom, along the west bank of the Euphrates from Malatya through Carchemish to Emar. And his kingdom soon fragmented, perhaps even in his own lifetime, into a number of small principalities – e.g. Melid (Classical Melitene, mod. Malatya), where his grandsons later ruled.

Like its fellow Neo-Hittite states and other Syro-Palestinian principalities, Carchemish came under increasing pressure from the aggressively expansionist Assyrian empire. Already in late C12, its ruler Ini-Teshub was made a tributary of the Assyrian king Tiglath-pileser I (on the assumption that the king of Hatti called Ini-Teshub by Tiglath-pileser was in fact a king of Carchemish) (**RIMA* 2: 37; cf **RIMA* 2: 23). In C9 Sangara, a king of Carchemish attested in Assyrian records, was forced to accept the overlordship of the Assyrian king Ashurnasirpal II (c. 870), and pay him an enormous tribute (**RIMA* 2: 217). Sangara's reign was preceded by a four-member dynasty at Carchemish, attested in a group of sculptures with accompanying inscriptions. The names of the dynasts, in succession, were Suhis I, Astuwatamanzas, Suhis II, and Katuwas. Unfortunately, as Hawkins (1982: 383–4) points out, none of these can be directly linked with Assyrian chronology. On the other hand, Assyrian records indicate that in 858 Sangara joined the military coalition of kings, from southern Anatolia, northern Syria, and northern Mesopotamia, which confronted Ashurnasirpal's successor Shalmaneser III twice on the campaign he conducted into the region in his first regnal year. (The coalition was made up of the kingdoms of Bit-Adini, Sam'al, Patin, and Carchemish in the first confrontation, joined by Que and Hilakku in the second.) The coalition was defeated, and Sangara like other kings in the region was forced into submission (**RIMA* 3: 9–10, 16–17). Shalmaneser's second western campaign, conducted in 857, led to further Assyrian conquests in Carchemishite territory, forcing once more the submission of Sangara and payment of a substantial tribute to the Assyrian king (**RIMA* 3: 18). Again in 853, Sangara was among the rulers west of the Euphrates who paid tribute to Shalmaneser early in the western campaign of his sixth regnal year (**RIMA* 3: 23). But Sangara apparently rose up against Shalmaneser on at least two further occasions, since the latter carried out attacks on Carchemish (and Bit-Agusi) in 849 and 848 (**RIMA* 3: 37, 38).

For the next century or so, the Assyrian records are silent on Carchemish, up to the first attested year, 738, of the reign of Pisiris, Carchemish's last king. Possibly the small kingdom regained some measure of independence during the period when the Assyrian kingdom was afflicted with internal upheavals, and involved in military confrontations with Urartu. Three Carchemishite rulers are attested in the interval between Sangara and Pisiris: Astiruwas, Yariris (regent), and Kamanis (successor of Yariris and son of Astiruwas). Inscriptions and sculptures of fine quality have survived from the reigns of Yariris and Kamanis, which can be dated to the first half of C8 (for the inscriptions, see **CHLI* I: 123–64). Yariris claimed to be well known internationally, and was in contact with at least one of the Assyrian kings of the period, perhaps Ashur-dan III (772–755). Hawkins (1982: 407) suggests that Carchemish enjoyed peaceful relations, and very likely close commercial and cultural contacts, with Assyria in this period.

But Assyrian control was firmly re-established over Carchemish by Tiglath-pileser III, following his victory over a coalition of forces from Urartu and the Aramaean city

Figure 26 Inscription of Katuwas, Neo-Hittite king of Carchemish.

of Arpad in 743. Pisiris thenceforth became a tributary of Tiglath-pileser (**Tigl. III* 68–9, 108–9). But in 717, during the reign of Sargon II, he was accused by his Assyrian overlord of communicating, presumably with a view to forming an alliance, with the Phrygian king Mita (Greek Midas). Sargon attacked and captured Carchemish, took Pisiris and his family and leading courtiers back to Assyria as captives, and stripped the land of its wealth (**ARAB* II: 4, **CS* II: 293). Carchemish then came under the direct control of the Assyrian administration, as a province ruled by an Assyrian governor.

Subsequently, in the period 612–610, the city provided a base of operations for an army of Assyria's Egyptian allies, led by the pharaoh Necho II, against a Median–Babylonian alliance. And here, in 605, the Babylonian crown prince Nebuchadnezzar inflicted a resounding defeat upon the Egyptian forces (**CS* I: 467–8). From then on, Carchemish was abandoned. It was partly reoccupied in the Hellenistic period, under the name Europos.

Three main areas of the city were uncovered during the 1911–14 excavations. These were a citadel mound, an outer fortified city, and an inner fortified city. Very little of

Figure 27 Lion head, Carchemish (C9).

the pre-Iron Age city survives, apart from some fortifications of the inner town. Of Iron Age date are the meagre remains of a building on the citadel mound, conjecturally identified, without evidence, as those of the temple of Kubaba, the city's chief deity. More substantial remains of the Neo-Hittite city were uncovered within the inner city wall – most notably, the sculpted and inscribed exterior façades (mainly relief orthostats and dedicatory inscriptions) of the temple of the storm god, the gatehouse and great staircase leading up to the citadel, the so-called herald's wall, the processional entry (later modified by an addition called the royal buttress), and the king's gate. These monuments all date within the period from early M1 to the Assyrian takeover in 717. Both the sculptures and the inscriptions (in Luwian hieroglyphs) provide information about two successive ruling dynasties in this period, founded respectively by Suhis I (c. 950) and Astiruwas (c. 850).

Hawkins (*RlA* 5: 426–46; 1995: 1295–1307; **CHLI* I: 73–223).

Carduchians M1 people of eastern Anatolia occupying a mountainous region on the northernmost spurs of the Zagros mountains bordering the land of Armenia. They may have been descendants of the Urartians, whose kingdom had ended violently in late C7. In the winter of 400–399 the Greek force led by Xenophon had a hostile encounter with the Carduchians while it was crossing into Armenia on its march home after its abortive expedition to Persia in support of the Persian pretender Cyrus the Younger (Xenophon, *Anabasis* 4.3).

Caria (maps 4, 5) Region in southwestern Anatolia, first settled in the Neolithic

Figure 28 Storm god, Carchemish.

period. The name Caria, attested in Classical sources, may be etymologically linked with Karkisa, the name of a Late Bronze Age country in western Anatolia (whose precise location is uncertain), attested in Hittite texts. According to a tradition recorded by Herodotus (1.171), the Carians were immigrants to western Anatolia from the Aegean islands, displaced from their original homelands by Ionian and Dorian Greeks. If so, they may have participated in the general migratory movements to the coastlands of western Anatolia in late M2. But Herodotus notes that the Carians themselves claimed that they were native Anatolians, and had always been called Carians. This claim would be compatible with the proposed etymological link between the names Caria and Late Bronze Age Karkisa. It might also be supported by Homer's description of the Carians in the *Iliad* (2.867) as 'speakers of a barbarian language' – a description which clearly distinguishes them from immigrant Greeks. I. Yakubovich (2008) has recently proposed that the political unification of the region in western and southwestern Anatolia called Arzawa in Late Bronze Age Hittite texts was the achievement of Proto-Carian groups who provided the ruling aristocracies in the region. He argues against the common assumption that Arzawa was inhabited and ruled by Luwian-speaking peoples.

Until C4, many of the Carians lived in hilltop communities in independent tribal groups, each of which was subject to its own ruling dynasty. Caria had, however, been incorporated into the Lydian empire in C6 by the Lydian king Croesus, and after the fall of Croesus' empire in 546, the Carians became subjects of the Persian king Cyrus II. They subsequently joined the Ionians in their revolt against Persian rule (499–494), and also served alongside Ionians as mercenaries, especially in Egypt where a significant number of Carians appear to have settled. Urbanization of the Carian homeland

Figure 29 Mausolus and his sister/wife, Artemisia.

progressed substantially in C4, under the Persian-backed Hecatomnid dynasty, most notably during the rule of Mausolus (377–353), who styled himself Persian satrap in his inscriptions. Mausolus played an important role in the spread of Greek influence through Caria, but was also concerned to preserve elements of the indigenous culture of the region.

The Carian language has survived in a number of alphabetic inscriptions (the alphabet is largely of Greek origin), in Caria itself but mainly in Egypt, where Carian mercenaries had settled. It appears to have been an Indo-European language, but has yet to be fully deciphered (see Giannotta *et al.*, 1994).

The following cities of Caria are separately listed: Alabanda, Alinda, Aphrodisias, Athymbra (in Caria or Lydia?), Bargylia, Calynda (in Caria or Lycia?), Castabus, Caunus, Cedreae, Ceramus, Chalcetor, Cindya, Cnidus, Crya (in Caria or Lycia?), Euromus, Halicarnassus, Heraclea under Latmus, Hydae, Hydissus, Iasus, Idyma, Labraunda, Loryma, Madnasa, Mylasa, Myndus, Olymus, Pasanda, Pedasa, Physcus, Pyrnus, Side (2), Syangela, Syrna, Telmessus (1), Termera, Uranium.

Schmitt (*RlA* 5: 423–5), Mellink (1991: 662–5), Masson (1991: 674–6).

Carmania (map 16) Central Asian country, attested in Persian and Classical texts, located north of the Strait of Hormuz in the Persian Gulf. It first appears in inscriptions of the Persian king Darius I (522–486) from Susa (**DSf* 9, **DSz* 8) as a source of a special timber, called sissoo-wood (yaka-wood), used in the construction of Darius' palace at Susa. Though the country is largely mountainous, with tracts of desert in the north, it had a number of fertile valleys which from ancient to mediaeval times produced vines and fruit crops. Strabo (15.2.14) refers to its production of all kinds of fruits and an abundance of large trees, except for the olive. He notes, however, that the country is subject to crop failures, prompting its inhabitants to store sufficient produce to last several years. He cites the C4 Greek writer Onescritus who refers to a gold-bearing river in the country and mines of silver and copper. Herodotus (1.125) lists its population, under the name Germanioi, among the Persian tribes who were workers of the soil, in contrast to other Persian tribes who led a nomadic existence. The Carmanians are said to have lived and fought like the Persians, but Strabo (15.2.14) comments that even in war they rode asses rather than horses, because of the scarcity of the latter. He observes too that no man in the country marries until he has cut off the head of an enemy and brought it to the king. Allegedly, the king stored the skull of the severed head in the palace, minced the tongue, mixed it with flour, then after tasting the mixture himself handed it over to the man who had brought the head to him, to be eaten by the man and his family.

Following his conquest of the Babylonian empire in 539, the Persian king Cyrus II deported the last Babylonian king Nabonidus to Carmania, where he spent his remaining years until his death (Berossus, *FGrH* 680 F10a = **PE* 81–2, no. 25). It was not an unpleasant place of exile. Alexander the Great found its environment a relatively benevolent one when he passed through it on his campaign in the region in 325. At this time, he established, or re-established, the land as a separate satrapy (it had previously had this status under Persian rule), extending south of Persis along the Persian Gulf. The name Carmania survives in that of the mod. Iranian city Kerman.

D. T. Potts (1989; 2006), Schmitt (1990), Wiesehöfer (*BNP* 2: 1107–8).

Carpasia (***Haghios Philon***) (map 14) City on the peninsula of the same name at the northeastern end of the coast of Cyprus. It was founded, according to Greek tradition, by a legendary king of Cyprus called Pygmalion. Archaeological evidence suggests a foundation date no earlier than C7. In historical sources the city is first attested in 399, when one of its citizens led a mutiny at Caunus (in Caria, southwestern Anatolia) of Cypriot mercenary forces employed by the Athenian commander Conon for his military operations against the Spartans. The Macedonian Demetrius I Poliorcetes used Carpasia as a launching-point for his Cypriot campaign in 306.

Material remains of the city include a number of rock-cut tombs from its necropolis, fragments of marble columns and sculptures dating probably to C4 (the former perhaps belonging to a temple), and traces of a city wall, church, and 'palace' dating to the early Byzantine period. The city was finally abandoned in C7 CE following the first Arab invasions. Most of it is now covered by sand dunes.

Nicolaou (*PECS* 436–7), Taylor *et al.* (1980), Megaw (1981).

Caryanda M1 island settlement in Caria, southwestern Anatolia. See ***Salıhadası***.

Castabus (***Pazarlık***) (map 5) M1 BCE–M1 CE city in Caria, southwestern Anatolia. The well-known sanctuary of the healing goddess Hemithea was established there – by Apollo, according to a tradition recorded by Diodorus (5.62–3). Diodorus reports that the sanctuary achieved high renown, attracting large numbers of pilgrims from near and far. He comments that though it was filled with rich offerings, and was not protected by walls or by custodians, neither Persians nor robbers molested it, out of respect for its reputation. During the Persian period (C6–4), the sanctuary was no more than a small hilltop shrine, c. 5 m square. But in late C4, this modest structure was succeeded by an imposing Ionic temple, built on a platform 53 m × 34 m in area. The cult of Hemithea seems to have reached its peak in C2 when the city came under the domination of the island of Rhodes. We learn from an inscription (the so-called Gölenye inscription) that in the first half of C2 major improvements were made to the sanctuary, to reflect the goddess' status and importance, and also to cope with the apparently ever-increasing numbers of visitors. Perhaps not long after this the sanctuary went into decline, its lessening importance thought to be connected with the decline of its overlord Rhodes. By the Roman period, the cult of the goddess may have ceased.

Cook and Plommer (1966), Bean (*PECS* 440–1, s. v. Kastabos), Kaletsch (*BNP* 2: 1176).

Cauconians A legendary people located by Greek tradition in various parts of mainland Greece, and in northern Anatolia near the Black Sea coast in the region of Bithynia and Paphlagonia (*BAGRW* 58 B3, 86 C2). In Homer, the Cauconians appear among the allies of the Trojans (*Iliad* 10.429, 20.329).

Lafond (*BNP* 2: 38).

Caunus (map 5) M1 BCE–M1 CE city in Caria in southwestern Anatolia. According to Herodotus (1.172), the Caunians were of indigenous stock, though they themselves believed that their ancestors came from Crete. Herodotus comments that their lifestyle and customs were different from those of all other peoples, including their fellow Carians. His claim that their language was similar but not identical to the Carian language is to some extent borne out by the surviving remnants of the language preserved in inscriptions. It is still almost entirely unintelligible.

Caunus is first attested in history when it was captured by the Persian general Harpagus during his campaign through southwestern Anatolia c. 540 (Herodotus 1.171, 176). Some time after the withdrawal of the Persian forces from Greece in 479, the city became a member of the Athenian Confederacy, but during the Peloponnesian War (431–404; see glossary), it provided a port for both sides in the conflict. In mid C4 it came under the control of the Carian satrap Mausolus (377–353), and thenceforth became increasingly Greek in its culture and ethnic composition. In the Hellenistic age, almost all trace of the indigenous population and culture disappeared. Control over Caunus fluctuated between the various Hellenistic kingdoms, until 167, when the Roman Senate declared it a free city. In 129 it was incorporated into the Roman province of Asia.

Despite the fact that the city was notorious for its unhealthy climate (the marshlands which surrounded it made its population highly prone to malaria), it appears to have prospered for much of its history. This was no doubt largely due to its harbour facilities and lively export trade, in goods such as figs (for which it was famous), salt, fish, and slaves. But the city needed to acquire other sources of wealth as its harbour began silting up – already a serious problem by C1 CE. Caunus now lies 3 km from the sea.

Notable among the city's material remains are its well-preserved walls, fortified with towers, to the northwest and north of the city. Parts of them date back to the reign

Figure 30 Temple tombs, Caunus.

of Mausolus. Other features of the site include an impressive Greek-style theatre, a nymphaeum (fountain-house), Roman baths, and a palaestra. In the centre of the palaestra, a large Byzantine church was later built. But the most spectacular remains of Caunus are the rock-cut Ionic-style temple-tombs carved into the cliff-face between the city and the mod. village of Dalyan. There are about twenty of these structures. Some have passageways hollowed out around them so that their walls are completely disengaged from the parent rock. They are part of a necropolis complex consisting of more than 150 tombs (the majority are simple chambers cut into the rock below the temple-tombs). Pottery found in the temple-tombs helps date their construction to mid C4.

Bean (1971: 166–79; *PECS* 443–4), Kaletsch (*BNP* 3: 39–41).

Çavuştepe see **Sardurihinili**.

Cedreae (map 5) M1 BCE–M1 CE city in Caria, southwestern Anatolia, on the island of Sedir Ada (Şehir Ada, Şehiroğlu) in the Cedreatic Gulf, 16 km north of mod. Marmaris. A purely Carian foundation in origin, the city is first attested in C5 as a member of the Athenian Confederacy (see glossary). In 405, when it was still allied to Athens, it was attacked by the Spartan commander Lysander and its population enslaved. Xenophon (*Hellenica* 2.1.15) describes this event, referring to the city's inhabitants as semi-barbarians. During the Hellenistic period, Cedreae became part of the Rhodian Peraea (see glossary).

Among the city's remains, which lie on the eastern half of the island, are a theatre, an agora, and the foundations of a Doric temple (no doubt dedicated to Apollo, the city's chief deity in Graeco-Roman times). A necropolis consisting mainly of sarcophagi and built tombs is located on the mainland opposite the island.

Bean (1971: 156–7; *PECS* 444–5).

Celaenae (***Dinar***) (map 4) M1 BCE–M1 CE city in southern Phrygia, south-central Anatolia, strategically located, on the Maeander r., at the junction of major east–west and north–south routes. Xenophon (*Anabasis* 1.2.7–9) claims that the Persian king Xerxes built a strongly fortified palace in Celaenae, allegedly above the sources of the Maeander, while making his withdrawal from his abortive invasion of the Greek mainland in 480. Alexander the Great gained control over the city during his campaign through Phrygia in 333, and appointed there his general Antigonus as satrap of Phrygia. In the Hellenistic period, Celaenae came under Seleucid control and was shifted to a new site by Antiochus I Soter (324–261), who renamed the city Apamea after his mother, the Bactrian princess Apame.

Bayburtluoğlu (*PECS* 444), Drew-Bear (*BNP* 3: 66).

Celenderis (map 4) M1 BCE–M1 CE city on the coast of Rough Cilicia (Cilicia Tracheia/Aspera), southern Anatolia, 46 km west of mod. Anamur (anc. Anemurium). Recent excavations on the city's acropolis conducted by a Turkish team under the direction of K. L. Zoroğlu have shown that settlement there dates back at least to the Late Chalcolithic period. But evidence for Bronze Age occupation is sparse, and the site may have been unoccupied for many centuries before it was colonized, probably in C8, by settlers from the island of Samos. In C5 Celenderis became a member of the Athenian Confederacy (see glossary), and apparently played an important role at this time as a station on the route to Egypt. Also in mid C5 it began issuing its own coinage. There are no further historical references to the city after this time, though its survival into the Byzantine period is indicated by its appearance in the list of cities of the eastern Roman empire attested in the *Synekdemos* of Hierocles (dating probably to C5 CE).

Mitford (*PECS* 445), Zoroğlu (2006).

Ceramus (map 5) M1 BCE–M1 CE city in Caria in southwestern Anatolia on the Ceramic Gulf, 40 km southeast of mod. Milas. Virtually nothing is known of the city's pre-Hellenistic history, beyond the fact that in C5 it was a member of the Athenian Confederacy (see glossary). There is no information on its foundation, though its origins are generally thought to have been Carian rather than Greek. Scholars agree that the resemblance of its name to the Greek word for pottery is purely coincidental. However, the appearance on the site of Greek-type archaic statuary suggests that by C6 the city was coming under Greek influence. Other material remains of the site, dating to the Hellenistic and Roman periods, include stretches of a city wall, the remains of two temples, and outside the city gates a number of tombs on either side of the road – both sarcophagi and tombs of alleged Carian type sunk into the ground.

Bean (1971: 53–7).

Chagar Bazar (map 10) Settlement located in the Habur r. basin, northwestern Mesopotamia, with a history of occupation extending from the Halaf period (c. 6000–4500) to the final abandonment of the site in the first half of the Late Bronze Age (c. mid M2). Excavations were carried out by M. Mallowan in the 1930s, and subsequently by joint British–Belgian and Spanish teams from 1999 onwards.

McMahon *et al.* (2001: 201) report that the new research programme focuses on two related diachronic questions: (1) the site's internal cycle of occupation, abandonment, and reoccupation, and its internal diversity; (2) its changing role within settlement trends in the upper Habur r. valley, focusing on its status as a relatively small site in the Mesopotamian context.

The site was first occupied, as noted, in the Halaf period, and recently evidence has been found for occupation during the Late Chalcolithic (Northern Uruk) period in early M4. Chagar Bazar was then abandoned until the Early Bronze Age (M3), its first major occupation phase. Material remains from the Early Bronze settlement include painted and incised pottery, bullae with seal impressions, and short Akkadian cuneiform inscriptions. The inscribed pieces date to the Early Dynastic and Akkadian periods. The early post-Akkadian era saw a reduced occupation, and around 2000 the site was abandoned for two centuries, but it came into prominence again during the reign of the Assyrian king Shamshi-Adad I (1796–1775). In this period, a large 'palace' (if not a storehouse) was constructed, presumably the residence of a local governor of the Assyrian administration. An archive of about 100 cuneiform tablets also came to light. The tablets were administrative in nature, containing records of barley used for making bread and beer, animal fodder, and food rations for palace personnel. The mixed population of the settlement at this time is reflected in the Hurrian, Akkadian, and Amorite personal names attested in the tablets. Houses and graves appear to have been built on the settlement-mound some time after the destruction of the palace, before the settlement was finally abandoned c. 1500. Identifications have been suggested with anc. Ashnakkum and Qirdahat (Kirdahat).

J. E. Curtis (1982b), Matthews (*BMD* 69–70), McMahon *et al.* (2001), McMahon *et al.* (2005).

Chalcedon (*Kadıköy*) (map 4) M1 BCE–M1 CE city in Bithynia, northwestern Anatolia, located on the Asiatic side of the Bosporus. Though its site was perhaps originally occupied by settlers from Phoenicia and Thrace, it was established as a Greek colony in 685 by colonists from the mainland Greek city of Megara, under the leadership of Archias. According to Herodotus (4.144), the Persian commander Megabazus referred to Chalcedon as 'the city of the blind', because its first settlers failed to realize the superior qualities of a location directly across the Bosporus, where Byzantium was settled seventeen years later (cf. Pliny the Elder 5.149). Subsequently, Chalcedon and Byzantium were closely linked. In the aftermath of the Greek Ionian rebellion against Persian rule (499–494), both cities were put to the torch by the Persians in 494 after their populations had abandoned them (Herodotus 6.33). They were later rebuilt, and in mid C5 Chalcedon became a member of the Athenian Confederacy (see glossary). It had, however, established its independence by 416, when together with Byzantine and Thracian forces it inflicted a resounding military defeat on the Bithynians (thus Diodorus 12.82.2), whose land lay to the east. Thirty years later, in 387, Chalcedon came under Persian control, where it remained until its liberation by Alexander the Great in 334. Virtually nothing of the city survives today.

Bean (*PECS* 216), Aune (*OEANE* 1: 481–2).

Chalcetor (map 5) M1 BCE–M1 CE city in Caria in southwestern Anatolia, 10 km northwest of Mylasa (mod. Milas). Almost nothing is known of the city's pre-Hellenistic history beyond the fact that in C5, it was a member of the Athenian

Confederacy (see glossary). Material remains of the site include a ring wall which fortified the city's acropolis and was 'well built of squared blocks in the Lelegian manner' (Bean), a temple of Apollo, and a number of tombs – sarcophagi, shallow graves, and underground chambers. Among several inscriptions found in the temple was a three-line text in the Carian language.

Bean (1971: 48–9; *PECS* 216).

Chaldaeans Tribal groups probably speaking a West Semitic language, first clearly attested in southern Mesopotamia (Babylonia) in an inscription of the C9 Assyrian king Ashurnasirpal II (c. 878). The Chaldaeans appear to have entered Babylonia from the northwest some time in C11 or C10, settling along the lower Euphrates and the Sealand marshlands at the head of the Persian Gulf. 'Chaldaean' is derived from the Greek *Chaldaioi* which comes from the Akkadian word *kaldu*, used to designate both a people and a land. Though the Chaldaeans had a number of features in common with the Aramaeans, they are clearly distinguished from them in the anc. sources. Lipiński (2000: 417) concludes that the distinction is basically cultural and social-economic (rather than ethnic). Five Chaldaean tribes are identified in the anc. sources. As listed by Lipiński (419), they are: Bit-Dakkuri (southeast of Borsippa), Bit-Amukani (north of Uruk), Bit-Yakin (around Ur and the marshes to the east), Bit-Sha'alli (near the Persian Gulf), and Bit-Shilani (to the east of Bit-Dakkuri). (The compound name in each case consists of Bit, i.e. 'House' + the name of its eponymous founder.)

A significant number of the Chaldaean immigrants may have continued to pursue a nomadic or semi-nomadic existence in their new homeland, and many grazed horses and cattle. But Lipiński comments that others appear to have adapted quickly to a settled way of life. They built towns and villages of their own – though the eighty-eight walled cities and 820 villages which the Assyrian king Sennacherib claims to have conquered (see below) may exaggerate the number of Chaldaean settlements – became agriculturalists, or settled in the large urban centres of southern Mesopotamia. In many cases they assumed Babylonian names and became closely involved in Babylonian social and political life, while still maintaining their traditional tribal structure and distinct identity. A number of them appear to have become extremely wealthy, through their large herds of livestock and the income resulting from the excellent strategic location of a number of their settlements on major trade routes.

Political instability and economic weakness in Babylonia during the early centuries of M1 are seen as factors promoting the rise to prominence within the region of a number of Chaldaean tribal leaders. Several of these leaders, beginning with Eriba-Marduk (769–761), occupied the Babylonian throne and became embroiled in the constant warfare in the country, sometimes against its central administration, but more often against the Assyrians. Most notable in this respect was the Chaldaean Marduk-apla-iddina II (biblical Merodach-baladan), leader of the tribe Bit-Yakin. To judge from Assyrian records, Marduk-apla-iddina had already been prominent in Babylonia for a decade before coming to the throne c. 721. He held the kingship twice (721–710, 703). In alliance with the Elamites, he united Babylonia under his leadership, for what proved to be a protracted but ultimately unsuccessful struggle with Assyria, during the reigns of Sargon II and his successor Sennacherib (see under **Babylonia**). The Chaldaeans had already been in conflict with Assyria in the reign of Tiglath-pileser III (745–727), who records his conquest of a number of their tribes in 731 and the imposition of tribute on their chieftains (**Tigl. III* 122–5, 130–3). Marduk-apla-iddina also appears in *OT* sources, which record his dispatch of a diplomatic mission to the Judaean king Hezekiah, bearing letters and a gift, after he had received news of the king's illness (2 Kings 20:12, Isaiah 39:1). It is very likely that he took this initiative as a first step towards securing an anti-Assyrian alliance with Judah, in addition to the alliance he probably already had with the Elamites. Sennacherib won a conclusive, final victory over Marduk-apla-iddina in his first military campaign, conducted in Babylonia some time between 704 and 702; he claimed that in the course of this campaign he conquered eighty-eight walled cities of Chaldaea (**CS* II: 301). But despite the ultimate failure of Marduk-apla-iddina's resistance to Assyria, he had succeeded for a time in uniting the Babylonians in a common cause. Fifty years later, his grandson Nabu-bel-shumate, a Chaldaean leader, ruler of the Sealand, rallied Babylonian support for Shamash-shum-ukin, the Assyrian ruler of Babylon, in his rebellion against the Assyrian king Ashurbanipal, his brother.

The fact that in both Classical and *OT* sources the terms 'Chaldaean' and 'Babylonian' seem to be virtually synonymous may well be an indication of how significant and integral a role Chaldaeans played in Babylonian society. It appears that a number of them had reputations as magicians, diviners, astrologers, priests, and scholars, for the term 'Chaldaean' is often applied to such persons in both Classical and biblical texts (for the latter, see esp. Daniel 2:5, 10; 5:7, 11). It is, however, difficult to determine whether the persons so specified in these texts were actually Chaldaeans, or whether the term was being used in a generic sense to apply to all Babylonians.

Our information about the Chaldaeans is derived almost entirely from non-Chaldaean sources. No Chaldaean inscriptions have survived, and virtually nothing is known of the Chaldaean language, beyond the fact that Chaldaean names indicate that it was a form of West Semitic. The Chaldaeans' M1 history is known to us mainly from Assyrian records, particularly in the period from mid C9 to mid C7. These records report the conflicts in which the Chaldaeans were involved, particularly against Assyria, and the punishments they suffered as a consequence, including the destruction of their towns and villages and the mass deportation of their populations, for resettlement in the Assyrian homeland or other parts of the empire. Chaldaeans are also attested as serving in the Assyrian army.

Edzard (*RlA* 5: 291–7 s.v. Kaldu), J. Oates (1986: 111–35), Frame (*OEANE* 1: 482–4), Lipiński (2000: esp. 416–22).

Chalybe Legendary country attested in Classical tradition, apparently located on the southern coast of the Black Sea (thus Strabo 12.3.19–20), and perhaps in the mountains south of Trapezus (mod. Trabzon). Its inhabitants, the Chalybes, were famous in legend as workers of iron. See also **Halizones**.

Chinnereth, Tel (Arabic *Tell el-ʿOreimeh*) (map 8) Bronze and Iron Age Canaanite city, consisting of a small tell and lower city, located in northern Palestine on the western shore of the Sea of Galilee. In 1922 it was identified by G. Dalman and W. F. Albright with biblical Kinnereth, attested in Joshua 19:35 as one of the fortified cities allotted to the Israelite tribe of Naphtali. Its history of (significant) occupation extends from the Early Bronze Age through the Iron Age. After earlier investigations in 1932, 1939, 1963, and 1982 and 1983, the site was systematically excavated by V. Fritz from 1982 to 1985, and from 1994 to 1999, on behalf of the Johannes Gutenberg University in Mainz, Germany.

The first significant settlement was built during Early Bronze II (mid M3). But it was abandoned, for reasons unknown, at the end of this period, and resettlement did not occur until the end of Middle Bronze II (C16), when a new township was built, lasting through at least the first phase of the Late Bronze Age (C15). But remains for this period are very meagre. In written records, the city appears among the Syro-Palestinian conquests of the pharaoh Tuthmosis III (1479–1425), and is also listed with ten major Canaanite cities, including Megiddo, Ashkelon, and Hazor, in the so-called Papyrus Leningrad (1116A). Its inclusion with these cities is an indication of its importance in this period. The site may again have been abandoned before the end of the Late Bronze Age, with reoccupation occurring some time during Iron Age I (late M2).

In C10 a new, strongly fortified 4 ha city was built, one of whose buildings may have been a palace. The city was destroyed by the end of C10, or in early C9, probably too late to be associated with the pharaoh Sheshonq I's campaign in the region. Squatters apparently now occupied the site, and during C9 the only evidence of rebuilding is provided by a small fortress or watchtower, overlooking the important road that passed by the site. At the beginning of C8, a small, new, apparently Israelite settlement was constructed on part of the mound, but it was destroyed during the second half of C8, probably by the Assyrian king Tiglath-pileser III during his campaign in the region in 733. A further small settlement rose up almost immediately after. It was less than half a hectare in area, and had been abandoned by the end of C8. This was effectively the last settlement on the site, though the remains of a few houses dating to the Hellenistic period have been unearthed, perhaps dwellings built by local farmers.

Fritz (*NEAEHL* I: 299–301).

Chogha Mish (map 12) Settlement-mound in southwestern Iran, located on the Karun r. in the region of Susiana (mod. Khuzestan), 27 km east of Susa. Evidence of human occupation on the mound dates back to M7. From M6 until its abandonment in late M5, Chogha Mish was Susiana's dominant site. In this phase of its existence, it covered c. 20 ha, and was apparently an important centre for pottery production. Its abandonment c. 4200, about the same time that Susa makes its first appearance in the archaeological record, may have been due to population upheavals within the region. During the second half of M4, corresponding to the Late Uruk period in Mesopotamia, Chogha Mish appeared again, as one of several major centres of Susiana – along with Abu Fanduweh and Susa (the Susa II period; see under **Susa**) – at a time when Susiana appears to have experienced an overall decline in its population. Notable among the artefacts dating to this period from Chogha Mish, as well as from Susa and Uruk, are tablets with cylinder seal impressions. A number of these depict a male figure whom scholars refer to as a 'priest-king'. There has been much speculation about who this figure was, and what authority he exercised. Another of the sealings depicts a musician and a singer. There is also evidence for occupation at Chogha Mish during the Persian and Parthian periods.

Delougaz and Kantor (1996–).

Chogha Zanbil (Al-Untash-Napirisha) (map 12) Late Bronze Age Elamite city in southwestern Iran, in the region of Susiana, 40 km southeast of Susa. Covering an area of c. 100 ha, the city was built in C13 as a religious and ceremonial centre by the Elamite king Untash-napirisha (1275–1240). Though apparently intended as an alternative royal seat to Susa, the city was never completed, and was abandoned soon after Untash-napirisha's death. The site was discovered in 1935, and initially investigated by R. de Mecquenem, who made limited soundings in 1936 and 1939, and again in 1946. It was excavated on a more extensive scale by R. Ghirshmann during nine seasons between 1951 and 1962 on behalf of the French Archaeological Mission in Iran.

There are two main sections of the site. The first consists of a temenos, or sacred walled precinct, containing a number of temples, and in the centre of the complex a square-based ziggurat made of baked and sun-dried bricks, and enclosed within a wall of its own. Originally, the building was a single-level structure with rooms surrounding an open sunken courtyard, which was accessed by monumental gateways in the middle of each of three of its 100 m long sides. The gateways were guarded by bulls and winged griffins made of glazed terracotta. The building was transformed into a ziggurat (see glossary) in a subsequent building phase when a tower consisting of three concentric levels was erected in the central courtyard, to a total estimated height of c. 12 m. On top of the uppermost level, a high temple was constructed. It had a facing of blue-, green-, gold- and silver-coloured glazed bricks, and was accessed from ground level by a series of staircases. Called the *kukunnum*, it was dedicated to two deities – Inshushinak and Napirisha, originally the chief gods of Susa and Anshan respectively. The other temples within the precinct were dedicated to a wide range of Elamite, Susian, and Mesopotamian deities, as attested in the inscriptions found on the site. Up

Figure 31 Chogha Zanbil.

to 6,500 inscribed bricks have come to light, along with other texts. A few of these texts are in Akkadian, but the great majority (some fifty-two texts) are written in the Elamite language, thus providing us with an invaluable source of information on this language. The texts make clear that the city was a new foundation, built by Untash-napirisha, and that it was primarily sacred and ceremonial in character and function.

The second section of the site, designated as the royal city, covers an area of c. 85 ha, lying to the east of the temenos, and protected by a rampart. A double gate and inner courtyard complex, dubbed the Royal Entrance (it is referred to in inscriptions as the 'Great Gate'), provides access through the fortifications to the northeastern sector of the city, referred to as the 'royal quarter'. It contains the remains of three large buildings which Ghirshmann labelled as palaces (a fourth building, poorly preserved, was also designated by Ghirshmann as a palace). The most complex of these – Palace I, also called the *palais hypogée* ('underground palace') – is particularly noteworthy because of a number of tombs built beneath the building's private and domestic apartments. The tombs were spacious, architecturally elaborate vaulted chambers, up to 4 m high and 5–6 m long. Each was accessed by a steep staircase. The tombs were used for multiple burials, and with only one exception all the bodies, together with their funerary goods, were cremated. The single exception was a female, forty to fifty years of age, whose skeleton was found intact. Ghirshmann stresses the significance of these cremation burials, observing that not one single instance of cremation has been discovered at nearby Susa. On the assumption that all those interred were members of royalty, he speculates that the uncremated female may have come from a foreign land where cremation was not practised (presumably because it was inconsistent with notions of an afterlife). Conceivably, she was a princess sent from abroad to wed an Elamite prince, in order to consolidate an international alliance between two royal houses.

Artefacts unearthed from various locations on the site include the glazed terracotta

Figure 32 Chogha Zanbil, inscription on baked brick.

bull and griffin sculptures referred to above, c. 160 cylinder seals, a range of stone and metal tools and weapons, a large number of votive offerings (animal figurines, beads, and maceheads), the cremated remains of grave goods (weapons and jewellery) in the Palace I tombs, a cache of alabaster jugs, and an ivory panel depicting a winged goddess and a frieze of wild goats.

The building of Al-Untash-Napirisha on virgin soil has been seen as reflecting its founder's vision of a new centre for the Elamite empire, one which all members of the empire could claim equally as their capital, and which in its sacred precinct united the major gods of the empire's main cities and provinces (thus de Miroschedji). But the enterprise was shortlived, abandoned before completion on the death of its founder. The final destruction and pillaging of the site may have been due to Nebuchadnezzar I, fourth king of the Second Dynasty of Isin (see under **Babylonia**), during his campaign of devastation in Susiana c. 1110.

Ghirshman (1966–8), de Miroschedji (*OEANE* 1: 487–90), D. T. Potts (1999: 222–30).

Choma M1 BCE–M1 CE city in northern Lycia, southwestern Anatolia, 15 km southwest of mod. Elmalı (*BAGRW* 65 C4). It is not attested in written sources before C1 CE, when Pliny the Elder (5.101) refers to it. No trace of the anc. city remains, its existence indicated only by scattered sherds and inscriptions, and anc. dressed building stones reused in the nearby villages. However, a rock-cut tomb located c. 5 km to the northwest of the site, and bearing an inscription in the native Lycian language, indicates that settlement in the area dates back at least to C5 or C4, the period when inscriptions in this language were carved on sepulchral and other monuments. The inscription is the most northerly of all known inscriptions in the native Lycian language. Another similar but uninscribed tomb is located close by. These tombs probably have no connection with Choma, but rather belong to a Lycian settlement which existed perhaps some centuries before Choma was established.

Bean (*PECS* 223; 1978: 156–7).

Chorasmia (map 16) Central Asian country attested in M1 Greek and Iranian texts (the latter consisting of Persian inscriptions and Avestan literature), located to the south of the Aral Sea. It may have played an important role, in early M1, in the beginnings of the Zoroastrian cult. Its population consisted of both nomadic and sedentary elements. The latter apparently lived mainly in villages – some 285 of these have been identified – which appear to have engaged primarily in agricultural activities and the raising of livestock, including cattle, sheep, goats, pigs, donkeys, horses, and camels. A typical simple Chorasmian dwelling consisted of two to three rooms, sometimes with courtyards and gardens attached. A farming establishment discovered at Dingil'dže consists of six rooms and has been interpreted as a small manor house (Russian ref. cited by Francfort, 1988: 187, n. 116). Fortress-complexes dating to the so-called Archaic period (C6–4) have come to light at Kyuzeli Gyr and Kalaly Gyr. For a brief summary of excavations conducted in the region from the 1930s onwards, see Vogelsang (1992: 289–91).

Chorasmia was among the eastern lands of the Persian empire listed several times in the inscriptions of Darius I (522–486), e.g. in his Bisitun inscription (**DB* 6), and also in the *daiva* inscription (see glossary) of his son and successor Xerxes (**XPh* 3). These lands had been incorporated into the empire by Cyrus II, probably during a campaign which he conducted into Central Asia some time after his conquest of Babylon in 539. Herodotus (3.117) reports the devastation caused to Chorasmian farmlands when the Persians converted a large, mountain-locked plateau in the region into a lake by damming the surrounding river, thereby cutting off the water supply to these farmlands. Chorasmians are listed by Herodotus (3.93) among the peoples making up what he calls the sixteenth Persian province (but see glossary under **satrapy**). They appear among the tributaries of the Persian empire in the foundation documents of the palace at Susa (reign of Darius I), where they are recorded bringing a tribute of turquoise (**DSf* 10, **DSz* 9). (Carnelian may also have been mined in Chorasmia.) A palace with hypostyle hall, excavated at the large site of Kalaly Gyr in Chorasmia, is thought to have been the residence of a Persian official, possibly a satrap (see Francfort, 1988: 181, fig. 6). A contingent of Chorasmians under the command of Artabazus, son of Pharnaces, is listed by Herodotus (7.66) among the forces assembled by the Persian king Xerxes for his invasion of Greece in 481.

Francfort (1988).

Chuera, Tell (Assyrian **Harbe (3)/Hurbe**) Bronze Age settlement, consisting of citadel-mound and lower city, in northeastern Syria, between the Balih and Habur river valleys. The site, covering c. 65 ha, was excavated on behalf of the Max von Oppenheim Foundation by A. Moortgat between 1958 and 1976, U. Moortgat-Correns between 1982 and 1985, and W. Orthmann from 1986 onwards.

The earliest settlement on the site dates from the Halaf period (M5); it was abandoned in M4. The site was then reoccupied during much of M3, when Tell Chuera reached its maximum development. The entire settlement was surrounded by a mudbrick fortification wall, with a second inner fortification wall surrounding at least part of the citadel-mound. On the citadel, a number of major buildings were constructed, including several temples, a large palace, and a residential quarter. The 22 ha lower city appears to have consisted entirely of private houses. The site was abandoned in late M3, following its Akkadian-period occupation. After a long hiatus it was reoccupied in the second half of M2, in the period when the region came first under Mitannian and subsequently under Assyrian control. The few material remains from this phase include a small shrine of the Mitannian period, and a well-fortified governor's residence of the Middle Assyrian period. A small cuneiform archive dating to C13 was unearthed in one of the rooms of this residence, enabling Tell Chuera to be identified with the city of Harbe (Hurbe) referred to in Middle Assyrian texts from Dur Katlimmu. (There were several Bronze Age cities of this name; see **Harbe (1)** and **(2)**.) The site was finally abandoned in C12.

Moortgat-Correns (*RlA* 4: 480–7), Orthmann (*OEANE* 1: 491–2).

Chytroi (*Kythrea*) (map 14) City-kingdom in northeastern Cyprus, listed as Kitrusi among the ten kingdoms of the island in an inscription of the Assyrian king Esarhaddon dated to 673/672, the so-called Esarhaddon prism (*Borger, 1956: 60 §27, Heidel, 1956). In Greek tradition, its eponymous founder Chythrus was the grandson of Acamus, son of the Athenian hero Theseus. Evidence provided by tombs indicates that settlement on the site extends back at least to the last century of M2. The M1 city consisted of both acropolis and lower town, with a large necropolis extending to the south and southeast of the city. Its king at the time of the Esarhaddon prism was called Pilagura

(Greek Pylagoras or Philagoras). The city is not attested in Greek sources until early C4, when reference to it is made in one of the speeches of the Athenian orator Lysias. Thenceforth it is mentioned by numerous Greek and Roman writers. It apparently flourished during the Hellenistic, Roman, and Byzantine periods, becoming a bishopric in the last of these. The Arab sack of the city in 912 CE resulted in its final abandonment.

Chytroi remains virtually unexcavated. However, inscriptions indicate a number of buildings of Graeco-Roman date, including a gymnasium and shrines to Hermes, Artemis, and Hercules. The remains of a sanctuary on a hill northwest of the city have been attributed to the goddess Paphian Aphrodite on the basis of inscriptions. The sanctuary's origins appear to date back to the Archaic period (C7–6).

Nicolaou (*PECS* 223–4), Iacovou (2002).

Cilicia (map 4) M1 BCE–M1 CE country in southern Anatolia. Its name is probably derived from Hilakku, the term used in Assyrian texts to designate the western part of the region called Cilicia in Graeco-Roman times. In Classical tradition, the name originates from a legendary Greek people called the Cilices, who according to Homer (*Iliad* 6.397) were one of the population groups of the Troad (q.v.). It is in any case conceivable that the ancestors of one of M1 Cilicia's population groups did in fact come from the Troad, migrating to southern Anatolia during the upheavals which accompanied and followed the collapse of the Late Bronze Age civilizations. Graeco-Roman Cilicia consisted primarily of two distinct parts, known by the terms Cilicia Tracheia (Latin Aspera) or 'Rough Cilicia', and Cilicia Pedias (Latin Campestris) or 'Cilicia of the Plain'. Cilicia Tracheia was the rugged, mountainous western part of the region, Cilicia Pedias the 'smoother', fertile eastern part. These regions roughly corresponded to the countries respectively called Hilakku and Que in Assyrian texts. Jones (1971: 192) noted that the contrast in physical conditions corresponded to a contrast in civilization: 'In Cilicia Pedias, trade and industry fostered the growth of towns. In Cilicia Tracheia, a primitive tribal life prevailed; only along the coast did a few small towns manage to subsist, as ports of call for the coastal trade and export depots for the timber from the mountains inland.'

In the earliest historical reference to Cilicia in Classical sources, Herodotus (1.28) observes that the Cilicians and the Lycians were the only peoples whom the Lydian king Croesus (560–546) failed to subdue during his campaigns west of the Halys r.; we do not know whether this means that they successfully resisted any attempts he made to conquer them, or whether he simply decided that the rewards to be won did not warrant the risks entailed in campaigning against them. Subsequently, from the last decades of C6 onwards, both peoples were subject, at least nominally, to Persian rule. During the first period of Persian sovereignty, from c. 542 to 401, the Cilicians appear to have enjoyed a relatively high degree of autonomy under a line of local kings who went by the title Syennesis. The title was probably adopted from the name of the founder of the dynasty, who was, according to Herodotus (1.74), one of the mediators in the conflict between the Medes and the Lydians in 585. The dynasty's seat of power may have been located at Tarsus. In the following period, from 401 to the conquests of Alexander the Great in 333, Cilicia was directly governed by a Persian satrap. Throughout the period of Persian domination, as in other periods, it is likely that Cilicia Tracheia remained effectively independent, except perhaps for a narrow strip along the coast.

An important feature of M1 Cilicia, particularly Cilicia Tracheia, is the persistence of Luwian (q.v.) elements in the region down to and including the Hellenistic and Roman periods. Southern Anatolia had been one of the major areas of Luwian settlement in M2. And an ongoing M1 Luwian presence throughout southern Anatolia is reflected in a number of Luwian onomastic elements found in the inscriptions of Lycia, Pisidia, Pamphylia, Isauria, Lycaonia, and Cilicia. The greatest concentrations of these elements occur in Lycia and Cilicia Tracheia. From this, it seems likely that Lycia and Cilicia Tracheia had significant numbers of Luwian speakers in their populations in M1 BCE and early M1 CE, and that these countries became the most important centres of Luwian settlement in Anatolia in the centuries which followed the collapse of the Late Bronze Age civilizations.

*Houwink ten Cate (1965), Magness-Gardiner (*OEANE* 2: 8–11).

Cimmerians An Iron Age people, perhaps of Thraco-Phrygian or Indo-Iranian stock, originating in southern Russia. According to Herodotus (1.15), they descended upon Asia when they were driven from their homeland by nomadic Scythians. The earliest references to them occur in Assyrian letters, from the reign of Sargon II (721–705), which record their rout of an army from the kingdom of Urartu and the slaughter of a number of the kingdom's provincial governors (*Ivantchik, 1993: 161–80, **SAA* I: 29–32, nos 30–2, **SAA* V: 109–10, no. 145). In Assyrian records the Cimmerians are called the Gumurru, from the land of Gamir. Their wars with Assyria arose out of their attempts, from Sargon's reign onwards, to expand their territorial holdings southwards, partly at Assyria's expense. But they appear to have had little success against the Assyrians. In 679 the Assyrian king Esarhaddon defeated their leader Teushpa in a battle in the land of Hubushna (see **Hupis(h)na**), southern Anatolia (**ARAB* II: 206; cf. *Ivantchik, 1993: 180–5). In 652 the Cimmerian leader Lygdamis (Tugdammu in Assyrian records) suffered a defeat at the hands of Esarhaddon's son and successor Ashurbanipal. According to Strabo (1.3.21), Lygdamis was later killed in Cilicia (some time between 637 and 626).

The Cimmerians' onslaught upon Anatolia also brought them into conflict with the Phrygians, whose empire they destroyed c. 695 under its last king Midas (Assyrian Mita). Subsequently they engaged in a prolonged struggle with the kingdom of Lydia, Phrygia's successor as the dominant power in western Anatolia. One of the principal victims of this struggle was the Lydian king Gyges (Guggu in Assyrian texts), founder of Lydia's Mermnad dynasty, who in 644 was killed in a Cimmerian attack upon his kingdom. He had previously secured assistance against the invaders from Ashurbanipal, but had forfeited this when he supported Egypt's rebellion against Assyria. The Cimmerians' attacks upon Lydia lasted for about 100 years until late C7 or early C6, when the invaders were finally driven from Lydian territory by Alyattes, fourth ruler of the Mermnad dynasty.

Kammenhuber (*RlA* 5: 594–6), Ivantchik (1993), Bouzek (*OEANE* 2: 11–12), Hellmuth (2008).

Cindya (map 5) M1 hilltop city in Caria in southwestern Anatolia, with remains of a citadel and enclosing fortification wall. The goddess Artemis was worshipped here, as Artemis Cindyas. A man called Pixodarus (son of a certain Mausolus) who lived in Cindya in early C5 was almost certainly one of the ancestors of the Hecatomnid dynasty which ruled Caria in C4 on behalf of the Persian administration. Later in C5,

Cindya became a member of the Athenian Confederacy (see glossary). In 425 its annual contribution to the Confederacy's treasury was assessed at the substantial sum of four talents. From C3 onwards the city is no longer attested in written records. It had now apparently been amalgamated into the neighbouring city of Bargylia.

Bean (1971: 82–7; *PECS* 455).

Çineköy Site in southern Anatolia of a C8 statue of the storm god Tarhunza, discovered in 1997 and inscribed with a hieroglyphic Luwian–Phoenician bilingual text. The site (which is not where the monument was originally located) lies 30 km south of Adana, in the region called Cilicia in Classical texts. In the early centuries of M1, it belonged to the kingdom called Que by the Assyrians. The statue is mounted on a base, and sculptured in high relief, depicting a chariot pulled by a pair of bulls. Its hair, beard, and clothing reflect Assyrian influence. The author of the inscription is identified as Warikas (Awarikus) in the Luwian version, Urikki in the Phoenician. This man is well known from Assyrian texts as the king of Que, who occupied his country's throne from c. 738 to 709 (see under **Que**). In the Luwian text, Warikas states that he belongs to the line of Muk(a)sas, a name corresponding to MPŠ – i.e. Mopsus – in the Phoenician text. This ancestral reference provides a further example of the association of Que's royal line with the legendary Greek seer and city-founder Mopsus (see ***Karatepe***). The kingdom of Awarikus/Urikki is called Adanawa in the Luwian version of the Karatepe bilingual, and its inhabitants the Danunians in the Phoenician version. The latter name is used also in the Phoenician version of the Çineköy bilingual.

In the Luwian version, Awarikus' kingdom is called Hiyawa. This name undoubtedly represents an aphaeresized form of Ahhiyawa (q.v.), a name well known from Hittite Late Bronze Age texts, and generally believed to refer to the Achaean or Mycenaean Greek world. If so, its appearance in the Çineköy inscription may well reflect a migration of populations from western Anatolia or the Aegean to Cilicia at the beginning of the Iron Age, as Tekoğlu and Lemaire suggest (2000: 1006). Such a hypothesis would fit neatly with Herodotus' statement (7.91) that the Cilicians were originally known as Hypachaeans ('sub-Achaeans') – provided that Ahhiyawa was in fact the Hittite term for Achaean or Mycenaean Greeks. We have yet to explain satisfactorily why the kingdom of Awarikus/Urikki is called Adanawa in the Luwian version of the Karatepe bilingual, but Hiyawa in the Luwian version of the Çineköy bilingual.

*Tekoğlu and Lemaire (2000), Lebrun and De Vos (2006).

Citium (Kition, ***Larnaka***) (map 14) City and M1 kingdom on the southeast coast of Cyprus. Its history of occupation extends from the Early Bronze Age to the Roman period. Excavations on the Bamboula hill (i.e. the city's acropolis) conducted in 1929 and 1930 by E. Gjerstad for the Swedish Cyprus Expedition brought to light a sanctuary dedicated to the god Heracles–Melqart. There is some evidence to suggest that a temple to Aphrodite–Astarte had once stood beside it. (Melqart and Astarte were deities figuring prominently in Phoenician cult.) In 1959, excavations were begun at Kathari at the northern end of the site by V. Karageorghis for the Cypriot Dept of Antiquities. These uncovered a number of Late Bronze Age sanctuaries within a fortified settlement, and also produced evidence of a bronze metallurgical industry. Further excavations at Bamboula from 1976 onwards by a French team under the direction of M. Yon brought to light C9–8 sanctuaries of Melqart and Astarte, and a number of naval installations. Included among the sanctuaries was an imposing temple of Astarte, built towards the end of C9. It lasted for five centuries, undergoing a number of changes throughout this period, until its final destruction by Ptolemy I Soter in 312 (see below). The city's port lay on the east side of the site, below the acropolis.

Though Early Bronze Age tombs in various parts of Larnaka attest to some form of human occupation in this period, the earliest archaeological evidence for actual settlement dates to C13, the last century of the Late Bronze Age. In this period, a fortified city was built on the site. Substantial remains of its wall, as also of the later Classical wall, are still visible at the northern end of the anc. city. The old view that Citium's Late Bronze Age founders came from the Mycenaean world is now seriously questioned. While Mycenaean products certainly reached Cyprus in large numbers, there is no firm evidence that Mycenaeans themselves ever occupied the site or indeed settled anywhere in Cyprus. There is, however, no doubt that Phoenicians from Tyre had arrived in Citium by late C9, with merchants and traders paving the way for permanent settlers to establish a colony there. But despite a significant Phoenician presence in the city from this time onward, Citium's population was predominantly Greek, the city's culture reflecting a blend of both Phoenician and Greek elements.

Circumstantial evidence suggests that up to the time of the Ionian revolt against Persia in 499–494, Citium may have been ruled by Greek kings, probably under the last of whom Citium participated in the revolt. But following Persia's crushing victory over the rebels, Phoenicians gained dominance in Citium, with Persian support. In C5 and C4 the city and kingdom were ruled by a line of Phoenician kings, who in mid C5 captured and annexed their kingdom's northern neighbour, Idalium. A number of Citium's Phoenician kings are attested in Phoenician inscriptions and coin legends – e.g. Baalmilk I, Azibaal, Baalmilk II (C5), and Milkyaton and Pumayyaton (C4). These kings owed their dominance, at least in part, to Persian support. Their powerful navy enabled them to play a significant role in the contests between Greeks and Persians in the eastern Mediterranean as well as providing a major source of the city's wealth. Except for a brief period in early C4, when a Greek called Demonicus was installed on the kingdom's throne (388–387), the Phoenician dynasty held uninterrupted sway until Citium fell to Ptolemy I Soter in 312. He executed its last Phoenician king, Pumiathon, and destroyed its Phoenician temples. In 50 CE Citium was incorporated into the Roman provincial system.

Citium's most famous inhabitant was the philosopher Zeno, founder of the Stoic school of philosophy, who was born in the city in C4. His contemporaries believed that he was a Phoenician.

Gjerstad (*SCE* III: 1–75), Karageorghis (1976), Nicolaou (*PECS* 456–8), Iacovou (2002).

Clarus (map 5) M1 BCE–M1 CE sanctuary and oracular centre of the god Apollo, located on Anatolia's western coast in the region called Ionia in M1. From its foundation, probably in C8, it was under the control of the city of Colophon, whence came all the sanctuary's officials. The earliest of the many literary references we have to Clarus occur in the Greek poet Hesiod (late C8–early C7), and in the Homeric Hymn to Delian Apollo (C7?). The sanctuary first came to light in 1907, when the Turkish archaeologist T. Makridy discovered a number of columns and inscriptions there, which provided the site's identification. In 1913, further investigations by Makridy and C. Picard showed that the columns belonged to the propylaea (dated to C2), i.e.

the monumental entrance to the sanctuary. The Doric temple of Apollo, focal point of the sanctuary, was excavated by L. Robert from 1950 to 1960. In the course of these excavations, a well-preserved two-roomed oracular complex was discovered beneath the temple floor, along with a number of inscriptions. The latter have provided much valuable information on the procedures and rituals associated with oracular consultation in the sanctuary. By C3 Clarus was becoming one of Anatolia's most important oracular centres, reaching its peak in C2 and C3 CE. Its clients came from a wide variety of places in Anatolia and regions beyond. Throughout its long history, the temple underwent a number of substantial changes. In the Roman imperial period, its cella (inner sanctuary) was enlarged to accommodate three colossal statues – of Apollo, his mother Leto, and his sister Artemis. Further excavations of the sanctuary, beginning in 1988, were undertaken by J. de la Genière.

E. Akurgal (1973: 136–9), L. Robert (*PECS* 226), Robert and Robert (1989; 1992), de la Genière (1996).

Clazomenae (map 5) Greek city on the central Aegean coast of Anatolia, in the region called Ionia in M1. Mycenaean sherds found on the site provide evidence of Late Bronze Age settlement there. But the settlement was probably of indigenous origin. In the absence of other evidence, the Mycenaean pottery fragments very likely indicate no more than trading contacts between the settlement and the Mycenaean world, and not actual Mycenaean occupation. Clazomenae was one of the twelve members of the Ionian League (see **Panionium**). In C5 it was moved to a new location on an island in the Gulf of Smyrna, and linked by a causeway to the mainland where the original settlement had been built. According to Pausanias (7.3.9), the population shifted to the island in order to protect themselves against the Persians during the Ionian revolt against Persian rule, 499–494. Half a century earlier the city had fallen to the Lydian king Croesus (560–546), after having successfully resisted an attack by Croesus' father and predecessor Alyattes.

Clazomenae was liberated from Persian control when the Persian forces were driven from the Greek world in 479, and subsequently became a member of the Athenian Confederacy (see glossary). But it reverted to Persian control in 386 when it was added, as an island (along with Cyprus), to the 'cities in Asia' ceded by the Greeks to Persia under the terms of the 'King's Peace' (see glossary; Xenophon, *Hellenica* 5.1.31). Some years later, according to the Greek writer Diodorus (15.18), it gained control by means of a stratagem of the city of Leucae (see under **Leucae**), founded in 383 by the Persian Tachos. However, it remained a subject of Persia until its liberation by Alexander the Great in 334.

Recent excavations at Clazomenae under the direction of G. Bakır, Ege University, have provided more information about the prehistoric settlement on the site and the transition there from Bronze to Iron Age. The finds brought to light by these excavations include structures of early Protogeometric (C10–9) date (built directly above Bronze Age layers), apsidal, single-room houses whose pottery dates them to late C6, an olive oil production plant dating to mid C6, and above it a 'mansion' of the second quarter of C4 (Bakır in Yıldırım and Gates, 2007: 322).

Bean (*PECS* 458, s.v. Klazomenai), Moustaka *et al.* (2004).

Cnidus (map 5) City located in the southwestern corner of Anatolia, at the tip of Cape Crio on the Reşadiye peninsula. The site was occupied from the Bronze Age through the Greek, Hellenistic, Roman, and Byzantine periods until C7 CE. Bronze Age remains include sherds of Mycenaean type, and, pre-dating the Mycenaean period, a number of tombs which contained marble figurines of Early Cycladic type. From Linear B tablets (see glossary) found at the Mycenaean palace at Pylos in western Greece, we know that Cnidus was one of the eastern Aegean–western Anatolian recruiting grounds for women employed in the palace's textile workforce. Following the collapse of the Bronze Age civilizations in C12, Cnidus was occupied by Greek colonists. Greek legendary traditions attribute its settlement to immigrants from the Peloponnese (southern mainland Greece) – Dorian Greeks in one tradition, Argive Greeks in another. The original Greek settlement was located near mod. Datça. But the city was relocated on the peninsula's tip c. 360, no doubt for commercial and strategic reasons connected with its maritime enterprises.

M1 Cnidus was one of the six cities constituting the Dorian hexapolis; the other five were Lindus, Camirus, and Ialysus on the island of Rhodes, the island of Cos, and the city of Halicarnassus (mod. Bodrum) on the Anatolian mainland (Herodotus 1.144). Every four years, the federation celebrated Dorian Games at Cnidus. The remains of a Doric temple dedicated to Apollo may indicate the site where the common sanctuary of the hexapolis was located. In C7 and C6 Cnidus established colonies in the western Mediterranean and participated in Greek trading activies in Egypt, through the Greek trading settlement established at Naucratis in the Nile Delta. Trade and commerce provided the basis for the city's considerable wealth. The Cnidians allocated some of this wealth to the treasury which they built and dedicated to the god Apollo at Delphi in mid C6.

Around this time, the Lydian empire fell to the Persian king Cyrus II. Cnidus acknowledged the new overlord of the region by surrendering to the Persian general Harpagus, during his campaign along Anatolia's western and southern coasts c. 540 (Herodotus 1.174). In the years following the Greek victory over the Persian forces in 479, Cnidus became a member of the Athenian Confederacy (see glossary). The Athenian commander Cimon used the city as a base for his fleet prior to his decisive campaign against the Persians at the Eurymedon r. in Pamphylia c. 468. In 412, in the final decade of the Peloponnesian War (see glossary), Cnidus shifted its allegiance to Sparta. In 386 it was handed over to Persia under the terms of the so-called 'King's Peace' (see glossary). It remained subject to Persia until liberated by Alexander the Great in 334.

The 'double city' of Cnidus, to which Strabo refers (14.2.15), consisted of a mainland settlement linked by causeway to the island where the main residential area was located. Two harbours were formed, one on each side of the causeway, the larger being used as a naval station which could accommodate twenty triremes (Greek warships). The city's material remains date predominantly to the Hellenistic and Roman periods. They include domestic dwellings, a gridlike street layout, a theatre, a bouleuterion (council house), a stadium, and several temples. A large necropolis, containing sarcophagi and rock-cut and chamber tombs, lies to the east of the city. Cnidus was a centre of great cultural activity. Its temple of Aphrodite housed the famous statue of the goddess sculpted by Praxiteles (C4). By the end of C4 an important medical school was established in the city. And c. 279, Sostratus, a native of Cnidus, designed and built the great lighthouse of Alexandria.

E. Akurgal (1973: 252–3), Love (*PECS* 459), Jenkins (1999–).

Colchis (Kulhai in Urartian texts) (map 4) Region on the east coast of the Black Sea, occupied by a number of population groups, though Herodotus (2.104) claims that the Colchians were Egyptian in origin. In Classical tradition the kingdom of Colchis, ruled by Aeëtes, father of Medea, was the land to which Phrixus fled on the golden ram, whose fleece inspired the quest of Jason and the Argonauts. Colchis had abundant iron deposits, and already in C12 the metal was being extracted from its soil. Trade access to this rich metalliferous region *may* have been one of the reasons for campaigns beyond Urartu's northwestern frontier by the Urartian kings Minua, Argishti I, and Sarduri II in late C9 and C8 – though there is no actual evidence for Urartian trade with the Black Sea region. In mid C8, Sarduri conducted a campaign against Colchis, with a further campaign in the region six or seven years later. On the latter occasion, he burnt the kingdom's royal city Ildamusha.

In C6 the Colchian coast was colonized by Greek settlers, probably from Miletus. In C5, according to Herodotus (3.97), the Colchians and neighbouring tribes were the northernmost subjects of the Persian empire. Herodotus reports that every fourth year they were required to pay a tribute of 100 boys and 100 girls to their overlord. During the Hellenistic period, Colchis became an outlying territory of the Seleucid empire. It appears to have lost much of its former prosperity at this time. In 64 CE Nero annexed the region to the Roman empire.

CAH III.1: 1034 (index refs, s.v. Kulkhai), Braund (*OCD* 361), von Bredow (*BNP* 3: 527–8).

Colophon (map 5) M2–1 city located near Anatolia's Aegean coast, in the region called Ionia in M1, 40 km south of Izmir. In the Classical period, Notium served as its harbour (Thucydides 3.34). Colophon may have been a Minoan settlement in origin, though later Greek tradition ascribed its foundation to settlers from Pylos in the western Peloponnese (Strabo 14.1.3). This would suggest a Mycenaean origin. But there is no evidence that Colophon was ever a Mycenaean settlement, as once believed, though its population may have contained some Mycenaean elements. A small Mycenaean tholos tomb (see glossary), discovered in 1922, has been attributed to local builders working outside the mainstream of the tholos tradition. Mycenaean sherds were also found on the site, but these have since been lost.

We cannot be sure whether the city was abandoned at the end of the Late Bronze Age. If so, it had been reoccupied by early M1, and was to become, perhaps by the end of C9, one of the chief cities of the Ionian League (see **Panionium**). It was famous for its horses and the skill of its horsemen, and was also noted for the fertility of its soil. Strabo (14.1.28) observes that it was once renowned for its naval and cavalry forces, who proved highly effective as allies in bringing wars to an end. In C7, the city was incorporated into the Lydian empire after its capture by the Lydian king Gyges (680–652). After the fall of Lydia to the Persians in 546, Colophon became subject to Persian overlordship. By this time, it had lost much of the importance and affluence it had earlier enjoyed. In C5 it became for a time a member of the Athenian Confederacy (see glossary), but factional strife within the city led to its rejoining Persia in 430 (Thucydides 3.34). In 409, it again allied itself with Athens (Xenophon, *Hellenica* 1.2.4), but once more submitted to Persian overlordship after the fall of Athens in 404. From then on it remained subject to Persia until the Persian empire fell to Alexander the Great in 330. Following Alexander's death, Colophon came into conflict with Lysimachus, one of his successors, who transplanted its population to his newly founded city of Ephesus. Lysimachus left Colophon largely derelict. It was rebuilt and resettled after his death, but never regained its former status. It was subsequently incorporated into the Seleucid and Attalid empires.

Most of Colophon's remains, excavated by teams from the Fogg Art Museum of Harvard University and the American School of Classical Studies in Athens, date to C4. These include a number of houses, a stoa, and a temple of the goddess Demeter. The remains are spread over a roughly triangular site, covering c. 1 sq. km and confined within a defensive wall which was fortified by twelve semicircular towers.

E. Akurgal (1973: 133–4), Bridges (1974), MacDonald (*PECS* 233), Ziegler (*BNP* 3: 578–9).

Colossae (map 5) M1 BCE–M1 CE city in the Lycus valley, western Anatolia, 20 km east of mod. Denizli. Herodotus (7.30) refers to it, during his account of the Persian king Xerxes' progress through the region in 481, as a large Phrygian city where the Lycus r. disappears underground for five stades (c. 900 m) before becoming a tributary of the Maeander. (The Lycus does in fact run underground for much of its course, but not at Colossae.) In early C4, at the time of the ill-fated expedition of the 10,000-strong Greek mercenary force to Persia to fight for the Persian pretender Cyrus the Younger (see **Cunaxa**), Colossae was apparently a populous and prosperous city, its wealth due partly to its flourishing trade in high quality wool and its cloth-dyeing industry. According to Pliny the Elder, it was once one of Phrygia's most famous cities. But it was eclipsed in C1 by Laodicea, a city founded in mid C3 by the Seleucid king Antiochus II (and named after his wife Laodice). Though its decline continued during the Roman period, it gained an important place in Christian tradition as the home of a Christian community, recipient of the famous letter from Paul.

The city's name, with its double-s infix, is of Anatolian origin, which may indicate that its beginnings date back before the period of M1 Greek settlement in Anatolia. But the few meagre material remains of the site all date to the Roman and Byzantine periods.

Bean (1971: 257–9).

Corydalla (map 15) M1 BCE–M1 CE city in eastern Lycia, southwestern Anatolia, 1 km west of mod. Kumluca. Like the nearby cities of Rhodiapolis, Gagae, and Phaselis, Corydalla was probably founded by settlers from the island of Rhodes, perhaps in early C7 when Phaselis was allegedly settled. A bilingual inscription in Lycian and Greek, discovered on a block of stone reused for building a house at Kumluca but apparently originating from Corydalla, indicates an indigenous Lycian presence at the site, at least within the period of the inscriptions written in the Lycian language (C5–4). The relatively substantial remains of the city which T. A. B. Spratt saw when he visited it in 1842 have now almost totally disappeared, due to constant quarrying of these remains for building materials.

Bean (*PECS* 464).

Crya M1 BCE–M1 CE town in either Caria or Lycia in southwestern Anatolia, probably to be identified with mod. Taşyaka on the western side of the Gulf of Fethiye (*BAGRW* 65 A4). In C5 the city was a member of the Athenian Confederacy (see glossary). Its continuing existence in Roman times is indicated by references to it in the C1 CE Roman writers Pomponius Mela and Pliny the Elder. Taşyaka is a small site, with a fortified acropolis accessed by a rock-cut stairway. An Ionic temple with a Carian inscription is located on the shore.

Bean (*PECS* 886).

Cunaxa M1 Mesopotamian town on the Euphrates r. near Baghdad. It was the scene of a battle in 401 between the Persian king Artaxerxes II (404–359) and his younger brother Cyrus the Younger, a pretender to the throne. Cyrus' army was swelled by a force of over 10,000 Greek mercenaries, among whom was Xenophon. Though the Greek force easily defeated Artaxerxes' left flank troops, the rebellion was crushed and Cyrus was killed. Even so, the Greeks routed Artaxerxes' troops in a second encounter. But after the satrap Tissaphernes inveigled the Greek generals into a meeting and had them murdered, Xenophon was one of those elected to command the surviving Greek forces and lead them back to Greece.

Xenophon, *Anabasis* 1.8, Plutarch, *Artaxerxes* 7–13.

Curium (Kourion) (map 14) City and M1 kingdom on the southwest coast of Cyprus, 16 km west of mod. Limassol. Its history of occupation extends from the Late Bronze Age through the Byzantine period. Excavations have been carried out on various parts and levels of the site since 1934. According to Classical tradition, Curium was founded by immigrants from Argos in southern Greece (Herodotus 5.113, Strabo 14.6.3). Cemeteries at localities Bamboula and Kaloriziki date back to the Late Bronze Age and provide the first material evidence of occupation. The Kaloriziki burial ground continued to be used into the Cypro-Classical period, apparently by settlers of Greek origin. The most notable small find from the cemetery is a falcon-headed gold and enamel royal sceptre, dating to C11.

It is possible that the first written attestation of the city appears in an Egyptian inscription of the pharaoh Ramesses III (1184–1153), but this depends on the identification with it of the name read as *Kir* in this inscription. A further possible reference to the city as Kuri occurs in the prism text of the Assyrian king Esarhaddon, dated to 673/672 (*Borger, 1956: 60 §27, Heidel, 1956), which would indicate that Curium was in C7 subject to Assyrian sovereignty. When Onesilus, king of Salamis, stirred other Cypriot principalities to enter the Ionian rebellion which broke out against Persia in 499, Curium's king Stasanor first joined the rebels, but subsequently, in the battle fought outside Salamis, defected to Persia and made a significant contribution to the Persians' victory. In mid C4 Curium was one of nine attested kingdoms of Cyprus. Diodorus (16.42, 46) reports a rebellion by these kingdoms against the Persian king Artaxerxes III. Curium's last known king, Pasicrates, joined Alexander the Great against the Persians in Alexander's siege of the Levantine city of Tyre in 332 (Arrian, *Anabasis* 2.22).

Curium seems to have had a relatively flourishing existence in the Hellenistic period, and also under Roman domination, until an earthquake destroyed much of it in 365 CE. Cultural continuity throughout this period is reflected in the continuous use from C7 (or earlier) to C4 CE of a sanctuary dedicated to Apollo Hylates. The sanctuary was excavated by G. McFadden for the University of Pennsylvania Museum between 1934 and 1953. The earthquake of 365 CE led to the abandonment of the site for eighteen or more years. In C7 CE it was again abandoned, this time permanently, during the early Arab invasions.

Nicolaou (*PECS* 467–8), Soren (*OEANE* 3: 304–6), Iacovou (2002).

Cutha (map 11) Bronze and Iron Age city and cult-centre, especially of the deities of the netherworld, in northern Babylonia. It is almost certainly to be identified with the site of Tall Ibrahim, which is located 30 km northeast of Babylon. A brief, partial excavation of the site was conducted by H. Rassam in 1881–2. Cutha is first attested in C23, in an inscription of the Akkadian king Naram-Sin (2254–2218). During the period of the Ur III empire (C21) it was ruled by a series of governors (*ensis*) on behalf of the Ur administration.

There are only scant references to Cutha in Middle and Late Bronze Age texts (M2). More information about the city is available for its Iron Age phase, from references to it in M1 Assyrian and Babylonian texts. In C9 and early C8, a number of Assyrian kings visited Cutha and offered up sacrifices to the gods there (e.g. Shalmaneser III, Shamshi-Adad V, Adad-nirari III, and Tiglath-pileser III). The city also played a significant role in the military history of the period. Around 703, the Babylonian king Marduk-apla-iddina II (biblical Merodach-baladan) used it as a military base for assembling a coalition force, consisting of Babylonians, Chaldaeans, Aramaeans, Elamites, and Arabs, against the new Assyrian king Sennacherib (**CS* II: 301) (see under **Babylonia**). Sennacherib responded by leading his troops to the city to confront Marduk-apla-iddina's army. In the ensuing conflict, the coalition was crushed, and its leader was forced to flee for his life. Sennacherib followed up his victory by systematically exterminating the rebel factions in Cutha and other major cities of the region. This paved the way for the reassertion of Assyrian authority over Babylonia, and marked the beginning of an apparently stable period in Cutha's history. During this period, restoration work was carried out on Emeslam, the temple of the city god Nergal, by Sennacherib's grandson and second successor Ashurbanipal (668–630/627).

In 651 Cutha was among the cities captured by the Assyrian prince Shamash-shum-ukin in his rebellion against his brother, the Assyrian king Ashurbanipal (**ABC* 129). Sixteen years earlier, Ashurbanipal had installed Shamash-shum-ukin on Babylon's throne as his subject-ruler. But growing tensions between the brothers had erupted into war, and Cutha and other Babylonian cities were lost by Ashurbanipal to Shamash-shum-ukin. Yet within a month of Cutha's fall to Shamash-shum-ukin, the tide of conflict began to turn in favour of Ashurbanipal. His troops laid siege to Cutha and other cities seized by the rebel (including Borsippa, Sippar, and Babylon itself). These sieges took an increasing toll upon the cities affected, through disease and starvation as well as enemy-inflicted casualties. Within two years the rebellion had been crushed, and Ashurbanipal had re-established his control over Babylonia. The surviving inhabitants of Cutha's (and Sippar's) urban population were deported to the Assyrian capital.

In the late 620s Cutha, along with other north-central Babylonian cities including Dilbat and Borsippa, came under the control of the Babylonian king Nabopolassar. It enjoyed a fresh lease of life as a cult-centre under Nabopolassar's son and successor Nebuchadnezzar II (604–562). Archival tablets written in Cutha show that the city was occupied down to at least the late Persian (Achaemenid) period (C4), and in fact a Seleucid chronicle mentions a temple administrator of Emeslam, the temple of Nergal in Cutha (**ABC* 117).

Edzard and Gallery (*RlA* 6: 384–7).

Cyaneae (map 15) M1 BCE–M1 CE hill town in Lycia, southwestern Anatolia, situated 5 km from the coast. It was the most important Lycian settlement in the region lying between the cities Myra and Antiphellus. A circuit wall and most of the remains within it, including a theatre, baths, library, cisterns, and numerous sarcophagi, are of Roman date. However, there are also a number of traditional Lycian tombs, freestanding or cut into the cliff-face, built as stone replicas of the Lycians' wooden houses. Several of the tombs bear inscriptions in the Lycian language, thus dating them to the period C5–4. A well-preserved temple-tomb of Ionic type probably dates to C3. Cyaneae was the site of one of Apollo's Lycian oracles. Here, according to Pausanias (7.21.13), the method of divination was for the enquirer to gaze into the sacred pool, to see there 'everything he wants to behold'.

Bean (1978: 108–11).

Cyme (map 5) Greek city on the Aegean coast of Anatolia, in the region of Aeolis. It was the most important of the Aeolian cities, and perhaps the chief city of an Aeolian League. The father of the Greek poet Hesiod (late C8–early C7) was a citizen of Cyme before migrating to Boeotia in mainland Greece. Ephorus, the C4 Greek historian, also came from Cyme. The city was subject to a succession of overlords. It fell to Persia in mid C6, became a member of the Athenian Confederacy (see glossary) in C5, and from late C4 onwards was successively subject to Seleucid, Attalid, and Roman rule.

For the episode in which emissaries from Cyme sought advice from the oracle at Didyma (Branchidae) on how they should respond to an ultimatum from the Persian king Cyrus II, see Herodotus 1.157–60.

Wormell/Mitchell (*OCD* 418).

Cyprus (map 14) Island in the eastern Mediterranean Sea, 9,251 sq. km in area, located 69 km south of Turkey's southern coast and 122 km west of the coast of Syria. Its most prominent topographical features include the Troodos mountain massif in the central-western region, the fertile Mesaoria plain lying to its northeast, and the Kyrenia mountain range which dominates the island's northern littoral.

The beginning of the Early Bronze Age (known as the Philia phase) is marked by major innovations in technology, economy, and society. These include the first systematic exploitation of the island's copper resources and the introduction of cattle, donkeys, the plough, rectilinear architecture, extra-mural burial, new ceramic wares, and a range of domestic technologies and practices. Most scholars accept that southwestern Anatolia and/or Cilicia are the source of most, if not all, of these innovations. Intermittent contacts between Cyprus and Anatolia during the Late Chalcolithic period appear to have been followed by intensive interaction, culminating in significant population movement and the arrival of settlers at the beginning of the Philia period.

Cyprus occupied an excellent strategic position within the anc. international trading network which linked Egypt and the Aegean and western Asian worlds. Its close cultural and commercial ties with the civilizations of these worlds, from the end of the Middle Bronze Age onwards, are attested by the large deposits of Cypriot imports found in numerous overseas sites, and by the many imported products, e.g. from the Late Bronze Age Mycenaean world, found at Cypriot sites. The island was noted for its substantial copper ore deposits, located principally in the foothills of the Troodos mountains. The ore began to be exploited and exported from the island around the middle of M3 (Early Cypriot period), and was a principal component, in the form of ingots, of the cargoes of Late Bronze Age merchant vessels which took on and

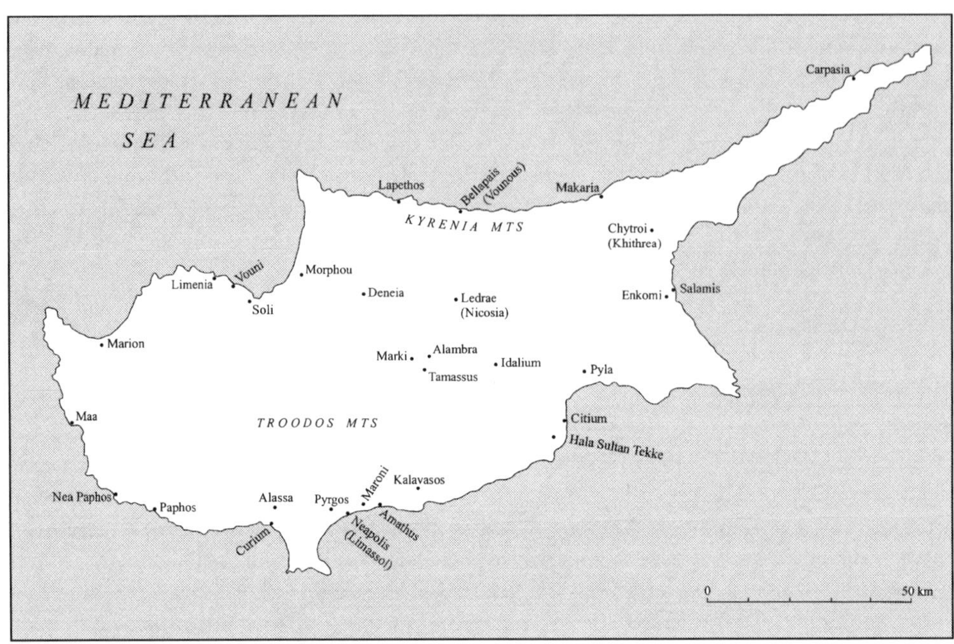

Map 14 Cyprus.

discharged their merchandise at many trading emporia along the Egyptian, Anatolian, Levantine, and Aegean littorals. Timber also played an important role in the island's economy, both for local building activities and for export.

In recent years, a number of Early and Middle Bronze Age settlements have been excavated on Cyprus (see **Alambra, Marki, Pyrgos, Sotira**). There are also numerous cemeteries dating back to the Early and Middle Cypriot periods. The gradual progression from isolated rural communities to hierarchies of urban settlements over a period of a thousand or more years has been closely connected with the development of metal technology on the island, beginning in M3. Almost all scholars now accept the identification of Cyprus (or at least part of Cyprus) with the Bronze Age land called Alasiya, attested first in a Middle Bronze Age text from Mari on the Euphrates, and frequently mentioned in Late Bronze Age Egyptian and Hittite texts. The latter make clear the island's vulnerability to attacks and subjugation by external enemies throughout its history, no doubt primarily because of its strategic location near the main sea routes linking Egypt, Syria–Palestine, and Anatolia. Correspondence passing between the king of Alasiya and the pharaoh of Egypt during the mid C14 Amarna age seems to indicate a special relationship between the two rulers (see **Alasiya**). Alasiya supplied Egypt with copper, under the guise of 'gifts' from the Alasiyan king, in exchange for silver. The Alasiyan–Egyptian letters (**EA* 33–9) are written in Akkadian, the Late Bronze Age international language of diplomacy. However, we know that at this time the Cypriots had their own writing system, the so-called Cypro-Minoan script. Many scholars now dispute the longstanding assumption that substantial numbers of Mycenaean Greeks settled on Cyprus during the Late Bronze Age. There is no clear evidence for any Mycenaean settlement on the island, or even for direct contacts between Cyprus and the Mycenaean world. The presence of Mycenaean goods on the island may have been due to the latter's inclusion on the international sea-trading route in this period, with third-party merchantmen acting as commercial intermediaries.

Cyprus was among the victims of the upheavals which brought many of the Late Bronze Age civilizations in the western Asian and Aegean worlds to an end. These upheavals are commonly associated with the so-called Sea Peoples attested in Egyptian records. In fact, if Cyprus is Alasiya, the island is specifically mentioned in the account by the pharaoh Ramesses III of the devastations inflicted by these peoples on the western Asian world in the first half of C12 (**ARE IV*: §§65–6, **ANET* 262). Even so, Cyprus seems to have suffered less destruction than other areas, perhaps, in J. D. Muhly's view, because Bronze Age Cyprus had never developed the highly centralized palace economy of other contemporary cultures. In any case, there was a significant degree of continuity and contact, in the aftermath of these upheavals, between Cyprus and the Aegean and Levantine worlds, in the period from 1100 to 800. But significant changes were also taking place. An inscription from the reign of the Assyrian king Esarhaddon, dated to 673/672, the so-called Esarhaddon prism (*Borger, 1956: 60 §27, Heidel, 1956), reports that Cyprus at this time was dominated by ten separate kingdoms. In Assyrian records, Cyprus is referred to as Yadnana, the land 'in the midst of the sea'. The fact that some of its rulers had Greek names and some Semitic names is seen as an indication of the ethnic diversity of Cyprus' population during its Iron Age phase. The ten attested kingdoms of Iron Age Cyprus are: Amathus, Chytroi, Citium, Curium, Idalium, Marion, Paphos, Salamis (perhaps the earliest), Soli, and Tamassus. Most if not all of these kingdoms may have originated in the early post-Bronze Age period.

Unfortunately, we have only scattered scraps of information about the history of Iron Age Cyprus and its kingdoms. In an inscription engraved on a stele discovered apparently near Citium in late C19 CE, the Assyrian king Sargon II claims to have conquered the seven kings of the island (707) (**CS* II: 297). But this claim is viewed with some scepticism by scholars, particularly since the alleged conquest has left no trace in the archaeological record. There is, however, clear evidence of a Phoenician presence on the island from late C9 onwards, when Phoenician settlers arrived in the city of Citium. Thenceforth the city's culture reflected a blend of both Phoenician and Greek elements. In C5 and C4 Citium was ruled by a line of Phoenician kings. We also have evidence of a significant Phoenician presence in the city of Amathus in C8, reflected in strong Phoenician influence on the city's material culture and religion. It has been suggested that Amathus is to be identified with the capital of the kingdom called Qartihadasht (Cypriot Carthage) in C8 inscriptions. (Citium has also been proposed as a candidate for Qartihadasht.) Phoenician cultural influence and political control may have been closely associated. Na'aman (1998) has argued that the Phoenician city of Tyre, while a vassal state of Assyria, enjoyed a hegemonic position in Cyprus at least until the end of C8.

After a period of apparent independence in C7, Cyprus was dominated by Egypt in C6 until the Persian king Cyrus II established sovereignty over the island c. 545. Under Persian overlordship the local kings seem to have enjoyed a relatively high degree of autonomy, being allowed (among other things) to mint their own coinage. When the Persian king Darius I (522–486) reorganized the administration of his empire, Cyprus was incorporated into what Herodotus (3.91) called the fifth province (but see glossary under **satrapy**), along with Phoenicia and Syria–Palestine. At the

Figure 33 Cypriot *oinochoe* (C7).

beginning of C5, Darius firmly reasserted his control over the island after the abortive attempt by all but one of its kingdoms to throw off the Persian yoke by joining the Ionian revolt in 499 under the leadership of Onesilus, king of Salamis. Amathus alone remained loyal to the Persians. (Muhly suggests that the island was divided between pro-Greek and pro-Persian camps.) Though Cyprus remained under Persian rule for much of C5 and C4, up to its conquest by Alexander the Great in 330, the island became a battleground several times in this period between Greek and Persian forces. Diodorus (16.42, 46) also reports an island-wide and ultimately unsuccessful rebellion against the Persian king Artaxerxes III (359–338). Yet in spite of Persian political and military dominance, Cyprus demonstrated an increasingly Greek cultural orientation from mid M1 onwards. And the island's system of individual monarchies remained largely undisturbed until Ptolemy I Soter conquered the island in 294 and abolished all its monarchies, except for the one installed at Soli.

Karageorghis (1982; 1985), Reyes (1994), Muhly (*OEANE* 2: 89–96), Steel (2004).

Cyropolis (Cyreschata, ***Leninabad***) (map 16) City founded in mid C6 by the Persian king Cyrus II, on the Jaxartes r. (mod. Syr Darya) in the country of Sogdiana, Khazakstan–Uzbekistan region. It was one of a series of defence settlements established by Cyrus for the protection of his empire's northeastern frontier against incursions by nomadic tribes, including the Saka (q.v.). Two centuries later, it was among the cities in the region destroyed by Alexander the Great (Arrian, *Anabasis* 4.3.1, Strabo 11.11.4).

Benveniste (1943–5).

Cyzicus (*Belkis, Balkız*) (map 5) City on the southwest coast of the Propontis (Sea of Marmara), northwestern Anatolia. In Greek tradition, it was the earliest colony founded on the Propontis by settlers from Miletus (Strabo 14.1.6, Pliny the Elder 5.142). According to Pliny, the city was formerly called Arctonessus, the name of the peninsula on which it lay; the peninsula was originally an island joined to the mainland by two parallel dykes. A statement by Eusebius (2.81.87) that Cyzicus was founded first in 756 (and then again in 679), is considered unlikely, since a C8 date seems too early for a Milesian settlement anywhere. The earliest feasible date for the city's foundation is believed to be c. 700. Cyzicus' location on the busy trade route between the Black Sea regions and the Aegean was well chosen, and was no doubt a major reason for its wealth. Its splendid gold coinage was the most important currency of the eastern Greek world between C6 and C4.

At the beginning of C5, Cyzicus participated in the abortive Ionian rebellion (499–494) against the Persian king Darius I. Some years later, after the final Greek repulse of Persia in 479, it became a member of the Athenian Confederacy. During the Peloponnesian War (433–404) (see glossary), domination of Cyzicus fluctuated between Athens and Sparta. In 411 the Athenians under Alcibiades won a major battle against the Spartans off the coast at Cyzicus. Under the arrangements of the so-called 'King's Peace' in 386 (see glossary), the city fell to Persian overlordship until liberated by Alexander the Great in 334. In the Hellenistic period, it became part of the kingdom of Pergamum (c. 190), but in 133 was incorporated into the Roman empire.

Little of the city survives today beyond the remains of a temple of the early C2 CE Roman emperor Hadrian.

E. Akurgal (*PECS* 473–4), Drew-Bear (*BNP* 4: 26–7).

D

Dabigu (*Tell Dabiq*) Iron Age fortified city located in northeastern Syria on the west bank of the Quwaiq r. (Lipiński, 2000: 167, map). In C9, Dabigu was among the territories west of the Euphrates belonging to the Aramaean kingdom Bit-Adini, then ruled by Ahuni. It was one of six fortified cities of the kingdom which the Assyrian king Shalmaneser III placed under siege during his campaign against Ahuni in his second regnal year (857) (**RIMA* 3: 11, 18, 35, 51, 64). (Shalmaneser's reference to Dabigu as 'a fortress-city of Hatti' reflects the M1 Assyrian, Urartian, and Hebrew practice of designating the Taurus region and Syria as 'the Land of Hatti'.) The cities were captured and their inhabitants either massacred or carried off as booty. Dabigu's conquest is also recorded on one of the bronze bands from Balawat (**RIMA* 3: 142) (see **Imgur-Enlil**). The reliefs on the band show the city defended by a crenellated double wall with flanking towers. Following his conquest of it, Shalmaneser may have used Dabigu as a military base for his later campaigns west of the Euphrates.

Lipiński (2000: 192–3).

Dadicae Central Asian people incorporated into the Persian empire, probably by Cyrus II some time after 539. Herodotus (3.91) includes them among the peoples constituting what he calls the empire's seventh province (but see glossary under **satrapy**). He lists (7.66) a contingent of Dadicae under the command of Artyphius, son of Artabanus (probably a cousin of the king), among the forces assembled by Xerxes for his invasion of Greece in 481. Along with other peoples in their region, the Dadicae are probably to be located in the mountainous northern border area of Afghanistan and Pakistan. A suggested identification with the Daradas, a people of mediaeval and mod. times, is fairly widely accepted.

Bivar (1988: 203).

Dagara Iron Age petty kingdom belonging to the land of Zamua, located in the Zagros mountains in the borderlands between northeastern Mesopotamia and northwestern Iran. In 881, its ruler Nur-Adad led Zamua in rebellion against the Assyrian king Ashurnasirpal II (**RIMA* 2: 203–4). The rebellion was crushed, and Nur-Adad was forced to flee for his life. In 880 Ashurnasirpal went on a third campaign against Zamua, at which time he received tribute from Dagara, in the form of oxen, sheep, and wine (**RIMA* 2: 205).

Liverani (1992: 46).

Daiashetu Iron Age city in northern Babylonia, located on the middle Euphrates r., between Kabsitu to the south and Idu to the north. The Assyrian king Tukulti-Ninurta II encamped his forces there during the course of his last recorded campaign (885) which took him through the middle Tigris and Euphrates regions (**RIMA* 2: 174).

Daistipassa Late Bronze Age Kaska land in northern Anatolia. Early in C13, when the Hittite king Muwattalli II shifted his capital south from Hattusa to Tarhuntassa, Daistipassa joined with another Kaska land, Pishuru, in an invasion of Hittite territory and the destruction of a number of northern Hittite cities (**CS* I: 200).

Dalawa Late Bronze Age city located in southwestern Anatolia, in or near the Lukka lands. It may be the ancestor of Classical Tlos (Lycian Tlawa) in Lycia. Early in C14, Dalawa joined the nearby city of Hinduwa in a rebellion against Hittite rule during the reign of the Hittite king Tudhaliya I/II. Hatti's renegade vassal Madduwatta proposed to the Hittite commander Kisnapili a joint military operation against the rebel cities. But he subsequently formed an alliance with the rebels, and under his leadership their combined forces ambushed the Hittite army and killed its commander and his deputy (**HDT* 156–7).

Damascus (Aram-Damascus) (maps 6, 7, 13) City located in southern Syria, east of the Anti-Lebanon range, with a history of continuous occupation from at least the Middle Bronze Age to the present day. Because of its many successor cities, including the capital of mod. Syria, archaeological work on the site has been extremely limited, with almost no material remains known from any period prior to that of the Roman empire. The earliest attested reference to the city (its beginnings may date back to a much earlier period) occurs in written records dating to the reign of the pharaoh Tuthmosis III, where it appears as one of the cities and principalities whose kings were captured by Tuthmosis at the battle of Megiddo during his first Asiatic campaign (1479) (**ANET* 234–8). Thenceforth, it remained under Egyptian control for the rest of the Late Bronze Age. In other Late Bronze Age texts, it appears as the centre of a region called Aba/Apa/Apina/Upi/Upu. A number of letters in the mid C14 Amarna archive (see Moran, 1992: 381, index refs) indicate that it became caught up, under its king, Biryawaza, in the disputes and conflicts among Egypt's Syro-Palestinian vassals during the reign of the pharaoh Akhenaten (1352–1336). In the aftermath of the battle of Qadesh, fought between the Hittite king Muwattalli II and the pharaoh Ramesses II in 1274, the Egyptian army was forced to retreat to Aba, the region around Damascus. Aba fell to the Hittites, and remained under the command of Muwattalli's brother Hattusili (*Beal, 1992b: 307) until Hattusili was granted permission to return home. From then on, Damascus and its surrounding region marked part of Egypt's northern frontier, beyond which lay Hittite-controlled territory.

Probably in C10, Damascus became the capital of one of the most important Aramaean states in the Levant, called Aram or Aram-Damascus. *OT* sources report a number of conflicts in which it engaged with the Israelites from C10 onwards. According to 2 Samuel 8:5–6, the Israelite king David occupied the city and placed garrisons in it. But it was subsequently lost to the Israelites in the reign of David's son and successor Solomon (1 Kings 11:23–4). Around 900 its king, Bar-Hadad (I) (Hebrew Ben-Hadad), made a treaty with Israel, which he treacherously broke, attacking the kingdom after receiving a bribe from Asa, king of Judah (1 Kings 15:16–22). In 853 Bar-Hadad's successor Hadadezer (Assyrian Adad-idri) played a leading role in the anti-Assyrian coalition which confronted the forces of the Assyrian king Shalmaneser III at the battle of Qarqar on the Orontes r. (**RIMA* 3: 23). Hadadezer led several more confrontations with the Assyrians (e.g. in Shalmaneser's tenth and eleventh regnal years, 849, 848, *RIMA 3: 37–8) before Shalmaneser finally crushed the coalition forces in 845 (*RIMA 3: 39).

Some time between 845 and 841, Hadadezer died and was replaced on the throne by one of his officers, Hazael, 'the son of a nobody' (an expression indicating that he was illegitimate) (*RIMA 3: 118). (2 Kings 8:7–15 reports that Hazael had seized the throne after murdering his predecessor, wrongly identified as Ben-Hadad). Hazael too suffered a military defeat at the hands of Shalmaneser, in 841, Shalmaneser's eighteenth regnal year (*RIMA 3: 48, 60). Again in 838, Shalmaneser marched into the territory controlled by Damascus and seized four of its cities (and during this same campaign received tribute from the coastal cities Tyre, Sidon, and Byblos; *RIMA 3: 67). Nevertheless, Hazael managed to retain his kingdom's independence, and went on to build it into an empire which incorporated large parts of Palestine, including Judah, Israel, and Philistia, and perhaps also parts of northern Syria (for the extent of his kingdom, see map in Liverani, 2005: 115). Hazael was the author of a fragmentary Aramaic royal inscription recently discovered in the city of Dan (Tell el-Qadi). The inscription contains, among other things, a report of Hazael's victory over the kings of Israel and Judah, and the deaths of these kings at his hands (*Chav. 307). Hazael's death can perhaps be dated to the year 803, the same year as the Assyrian king Adad-nirari III attacked and conquered Damascus, and received a substantial tribute from it (*RIMA 3: 213). Adad-nirari refers to its king at the time by the name Mari', which in Aramaic means 'lord'. Thus the name conceals the king's identity, and there is uncertainty as to whether he is Hazael or his son and successor Bar-Hadad II. Lipiński (2000: 390–3) favours the former, and suggests that Hazael may have died while his city was under siege by the Assyrians, or shortly after its capture. But whether Mari was Hazael or Bar-Hadad, the Assyrian capture of Damascus almost certainly marked the beginning of the city's and the kingdom's decline. Within a few years of his accession, Bar-Hadad led a coalition of northern allies against the Hamathite city Hatarikka, but the besieging army was driven off by Zakur, king of Hamath (*Lipiński, 2000: 254–5, *CS II: 155, *Chav. 307–11).

Probably in 773, the last year of the Assyrian king Shalmaneser IV, the Assyrian commander-in-chief Shamshi-ilu attacked Damascus again, and took extensive tribute from the battle-field, which was then ruled by Hadyan II (Hezyon, Assyrian Hadiiani). Hadyan's daughter and her extensive dowry were included in the tribute-list, which is recorded on a stele found near Maraş (*RIMA 3: 239–40). Subsequently, to judge from 2 Kings 14:28, Damascus may have become for a time a subject state of the Israelite king Jeroboam II (c. 770). If so, it later regained its independence. And c. 732, Damascus' last independent king Rasyan (Rahianu, *OT* Rezin) led another anti-Assyrian coalition, which included Israel, Tyre, and Philistia. The coalition's forces were decisively defeated by the Assyrian king Tiglath-pileser III c. 732 (*ARAB I: 278–9). Damascus fell to the Assyrians, though initially its king, Rasyan, avoided capture by fleeing the city (*Tigl. III 78–81). He was eventually taken prisoner and executed by Tiglath-pileser, according to 2 Kings 16:5–9, which also records the Assyrian capture of Damascus. The city was now absorbed into the Assyrian provincial system.

Because of its valuable strategic location on the major trade routes of the region, Damascus continued to play an important role in the commercial activities of the Levant through the Assyrian, Babylonian, and Persian periods. After Alexander the Great's conquests in 333, it enjoyed a new lease of life as the site of a Macedonian colony. During the Hellenistic and Roman periods the city was greatly expanded and substantially redeveloped.

Pitard (1987), *CAH* III.1: 1022 (index refs), Lipiński (2000: 347–407), Kahn (2007).

Damdam(m)usa Iron Age fortress-settlement in northern Mesopotamia, belonging to the Aramaean kingdom of Bit-Zamani, in the region of Amidu (mod. Diyarbakır). Lipiński (2000: 148) suggests an identification with mod. Pornak. The city probably first came under Assyrian sovereignty, at least nominally, in early C9 when the Assyrian king Tukulti-Ninurta II concluded his pact with Bit-Zamani's ruler Ammi-Ba'al in 886, having captured his city Damdammusa (see **Bit-Zamani**). Tukulti-Ninurta's son and successor Ashurnasirpal II refers to Damdammusa as his 'royal city'. In 882, a certain Hulaya, ruler of the nearby land of Halziluha, rebelled against Ashurnasirpal and attempted to seize Damdammusa (**RIMA* 2: 200–1). Ashurnasirpal led an expeditionary force against the rebels, capturing Hulaya and destroying his chief city Kinabu. The rebel leader was flayed alive, and his skin draped over Damdammusa's walls. In 879 Ashurnasirpal installed grain-storage facilities in the city following his punitive expedition against the elders of Bit-Zamani who had rebelled against and assassinated Ammi-Ba'al (**RIMA* 2: 261–2). He subsequently received tribute there from the land of Shubru (Shubria). He also appointed a man called Ilanu as the new ruler of Bit-Zamani. Ilanu later broke his allegiance to Assyria, and used Damdammusa as his stronghold when Ashurnasirpal led an expedition into his land in 866. Ashurnasirpal took the city after a siege before moving on to attack Ilanu's royal capital Amidu (**RIMA* 2: 220).

Lipiński (2000: 145, 148, 159).

Damrum City and kingdom near Kish in Babylonia, first attested in late C20 or early C19 as a subject state like Kish of Sumu-ditana, king of Kazallu and Marad. After establishing its independence under its first known king, Haliyum, Damrum was subsequently ruled by Abdi-Erah, who had seized power at Tutub, and then by Manana who occupied the throne for at least fourteen years. Both kings also held sway over Kish. Manana's achievements included the construction of fortifications for the nearby city Akusum, where his successor Naqimum built a gate in honour of the goddess Ishtar. Naqimum had three known successors: Ahi-maras, Sumu-Yamutbal, who promulgated a decree jointly with the Babylonian king Sumu-la-El (1880–1845), and Manium. The last of these was still alive in Sumu-la-El's thirty-second year. Probably at the end of his reign, Damrum was incorporated into the kingdom of Babylon.

Mesop. 89–91.

Damunu M1 tribe, probably of North Arabian origin, located in southeastern Babylonia. The Damunu are first attested in the list of thirty-five so-called Aramaean tribes which the Assyrian king Tiglath-pileser III claims to have conquered, probably in his accession year (746) (**Tigl. III* 160–1). The tribe's capital was Amlatu, from which Tiglath-pileser deported 600 captives to the cities of the land of Unqi (Pat(t)in) in Syria. The Damunu were among the peoples in Tiglath-pileser's list who subsequently supported the Chaldaean tribal leader Marduk-apla-iddina II (biblical Merodach-baladan; see under **Babylonia**) in his conflict with the Assyrian king Sargon II (721–705) (**Sargon II* 350). In the records of Sargon's reign, the Damunu are frequently mentioned in the same context as the Puqudu and Gambulu tribes. During the reign of Sargon's successor, Sennacherib (704–681), they were allied with the Elamites, Babylonians, and Chaldaeans in further military confrontations with Assyria (*Sennach.* 43, 49). Sennacherib conquered the enemy forces and deported large numbers of their populations to other parts of his kingdom (*Sennach.* 25, 54, 57). But the Damunu survived the Assyrian purge and were still attested in the reign of the Assyrian king Ashurbanipal (668–630/627).

Lipiński (2000: 463–4).

Dan (biblical **Laish**, ***Tell el-Qadi***) (map 7) 20 ha settlement-mound located on the northern border of mod. Israel near the source of the Jordan r. Its history of occupation is represented by sixteen archaeological levels extending from the Neolithic period (M5) through the Bronze and Iron Ages, and by the remains of settlement in the Persian, Hellenistic, Roman, and mediaeval periods. Excavations were begun in 1966 by A. Biran for the Israel Dept of Antiquities. Biran also initially led the expeditions undertaken by the Hebrew Union College in Jerusalem from 1974 onwards. Already in 1838 Dan had been identified with the site of Tell el-Qadi by the discovery there of a Greek–Aramaic bilingual inscription, containing a dedication 'to the God who is in Dan'. In Judges 18:29, Dan is equated with the city formerly called Laish, which is also attested in the C18 Mari texts and appears among the Syro-Palestinian cities conquered in C15 by the pharaoh Tuthmosis III.

Up until Early Bronze I (early M3),Tell el-Qadi seems to have been only sparsely occupied. But by the middle of M3 there is evidence of a strongly fortified, prosperous settlement on the mound, which may have spread over the mound's entire surface. During Middle Bronze II (c. 1900–1700), the city's fortifications were further developed when the settlement was surrounded by a rampart, incorporating a triple-arched mudbrick gate flanked by two towers, which are preserved to a height of over 6 m. Evidence of the site's prosperity in the Late Bronze Age is provided by the remains of public buildings bordering a paved street, the appurtenances of a flourishing metallurgical industry, and a large, C14 corbelled stone tomb commonly known as the 'Mycenaean tomb'. The tomb contained over forty burials. Its rich assemblage of funerary goods included vessels of alabaster and basalt, bronze tools and weapons, ivory ornaments, and gold and silver jewellery. Twenty-eight of the items have been identified as imports from the Aegean world and/or Cyprus. The tomb's ceramic ware included an almost complete charioteer vase.

Semi-nomadic elements are reflected in an apparent change in the city's material culture in the early Iron Age, towards the end of C12. This has been seen as a possible indication of the arrival of the biblically attested people of Dan, one of the twelve tribes of Israel. According to Judges 18:27–9, the Danites torched the city after slaughtering its original inhabitants, then rebuilt it, naming it after their forefather, Dan. The city's 'new' inhabitants quickly assumed the character of a settled, sedentary population. Dan continued to flourish through its Iron Age phases, perhaps due largely to its role as an important cultic centre of the kingdom of Israel. According to 1 Kings 12:29–30, the Israelite king Jeroboam I (931–910) set up a golden calf in Dan, so that the city would become an alternative to Jerusalem as a centre of worship for the Israelites. This may be related to the discovery of a cultic complex in the city, perhaps a *bamah* (Hebrew 'high place'), first built in C10 and altered a number of times over the next two centuries.

Dan continued to prosper under Assyrian rule from C8 onwards, when the city was densely populated and had widespread trading contacts. Its importance as a cult-centre seems also to have continued throughout the period of the Assyrian empire, which fell in late C7. Subsequently, under Persian rule, there was an apparent decline in the city's size and status. However, its role as a cult-centre continued through the Persian and succeeding Hellenistic and Roman periods, when the sacred precinct was substantially redeveloped. The precinct may have continued in use until the reign of Constantine the Great in C4 CE.

In 1993, three fragments of an Aramaic royal inscription dated to mid C9 were discovered in Dan. The information they contain has much importance for the history of Israel. Its author (not identified but generally thought to be Hazael, king of Damascus) records his victory over Israel and Judah, and the deaths of their kings at his hands. He refers to a Judaean king [Ahaz?]iahu as belonging to the House of David (**Chav.* 305–7, **CS* II: 161–2). This is the first reference to an Israelite leader called David outside biblical sources. The account can in part be correlated with the biblical passage in 2 Kings 8:28–9.

Biran (*NEAEHL* 1: 323–32), Ilan (*OEANE* 2: 107–12), Negev and Gibson (2001: 131–2), Laughlin (2006: 103–10).

Danabu Iron Age city in southern Syria belonging to the kingdom of Aram-Damascus. The Assyrian king Shalmaneser III refers to it in the course of his campaigns against Damascus in 838, when the throne of Damascus was occupied by Hazael (**RIMA* 3: 62). Identifications have been proposed with mod. Saydnaya, 20 km north of Damascus, and the village of Ad-Dunaybah, 70 km south of Damascus.

Lipiński (2000: 352–3).

Dankuwa Late Bronze Age Hittite city in north-central Anatolia, in the region called the Upper Land (q.v.) in Hittite texts, close to the kingdom of Azzi-Hayasa. During the seventh regnal year of the Hittite king Mursili II (c. 1315), Anniya, king of Azzi-Hayasa, formerly a Hittite vassal state, attacked Dankuwa and deported part of its population to his own kingdom. This occurred in the context of his occupation of the Upper Land (see **Azzi-Hayasa**). His refusal to return the deportees prompted a Hittite attack on his border fortress Ura (*CS II: 87–8). But Anniya's forces continued to occupy the Upper Land for another two years before being expelled by the Hittites. Mursili reconquered Azzi-Hayasa itself the following year (1312). We do not know if at that time he restored Dankuwa's deported population to its home-city. During the reign of Mursili's son and successor Muwattalli II, Dankuwa suffered further devastation when it was sacked, along with the land of Saddupa, by invaders from the Kaska lands (**CS* I: 201).

Danuna see **Denyen**.

Dardanelles see **Hellespont**.

Dardania Late Bronze Age Anatolian country? The name, which is a vocalized form of Egyptian *Drdnjj*, is attested in Egyptian texts possibly as early as the reign of the pharaoh Amenhotep III (1390–1352), and certainly in the reigns of Horemheb (1323–1295) and Ramesses II (1279–1213). Troops from this land figure among the Hittites' allies in Ramesses' account of the battle of Qadesh, fought in 1274

(*Gardiner, 1960: 8). The similarity of the name to the Dardanoi (q.v.), who are closely linked with the Trojans in Homeric tradition, has led to the suggestion that Dardania was the Late Bronze Age designation for the Troad region in northwestern Anatolia where Troy was located. If so, then Late Bronze Age Wilusa, commonly identified with Homeric Troy/Ilios, must have lain somewhere else – unless Dardania and Wilusa were alternative names for the same land. But Dardania is never mentioned in Hittite texts, our most important source for Anatolian history in the Late Bronze Age. Our only evidence for its existence comes from Egyptian texts – and these provide no information about its location. The name similarity to Dardanoi is not on its own a sufficient basis for placing the Egyptian-attested country in the Troad.

Haider (1997: 117–19).

Dardanoi Legendary Troad people, descendants of Dardanus. In Homer's *Iliad* (2.819–20) a contingent of Dardanians from Mt Ida figures among Troy's allies in the Trojan War, under the leadership of Aeneas, cousin of Hector and Paris. Though Trojans and Dardanians are listed consecutively in a number of passages in the *Iliad*, implying that they are separately identifiable, the Trojans are also referred to as 'Dardanidae' ('children of Dardanus'), and in some cases 'Trojan' and 'Dardanian' appear to be synonymous terms.

Dascylium According to Stephanus of Byzantium, there were five cities called Dascylium in western Anatolia. The following two are the best attested:

Dascylium (1) (map 4) M1 city in northwestern Anatolia on the shore of the Propontis (mod. Sea of Marmara). In C5, it became a member of the Athenian Confederacy (see glossary), as indicated by its appearance in the Athenian Tribute Lists for the year 453. It is later attested by Pliny the Elder (5.143) in the form Dascylos.

Drew-Bear and Bakır-Akbaşoğlu (*BNP* 4 : 99).

Dascylium (2) (map 5) M1 city in northwestern Anatolia, on the shore of Lake Dascylitis which lay just south of the Propontis. From at least the reign of the Persian king Xerxes (486–465) it was the seat of a Persian satrapy, Hellespontine Phrygia, and had a famous hunting park (Xenophon, *Hellenica* 4.1.15). Its best-known satrap was Pharnabazus II (late C5–early C4).

Dascylium has been identified with the site of Hisar Tepe near mod. Ergili. Excavations conducted here in 1954, and recommenced in 1989, have brought to light more than 400 clay bullae with seal impressions reflecting both Greek and Persian artistic traditions. Some of the sealings bear inscriptions of Xerxes and one of the four Persian kings called Artaxerxes. Other discoveries include a number of funerary stelae, also in the Graeco-Persian tradition and embellished with scenes from daily life. One has an inscription in Aramaic. Recent excavations at Hisar Tepe, conducted by T. Bakır and A. Erdoğan for Ege University-Izmir, have concentrated on the sanctuary located there. Under Persian rule it became a centre for Zoroastrian worship. Bakır and Erdoğan report (*ap.* Yıldırım and Gates, 2007: 308) that the Persian sanctuary can be dated to C5 (it had a Phrygian predecessor), and that it was abandoned in the so-called Middle Achaemenid period, most likely in the eighteenth year of the satrap Pharnabazus, when it was deliberately sealed under a layer of fill.

The remains of settlement on the site prior to the Persian period include a 2.2 m wide stone wall and Greek pottery dating to C7–early C6. A Babylonian seal of M2 date has also been discovered.

Drew-Bear and Bakır-Akbaşoğlu (*BNP* 4: 99–100), Bakır (2006).

Datebir Iron Age city in the eastern part of the upper Diyala region, conquered by the Assyrian king Shamshi-Adad V (823–811) during the campaign, his fourth (814), which he conducted into Babylonian territory (**RIMA* 3: 187). Datebir and its neighbour Izduia, which also fell to the Assyrians, lay close to the city of Gannanate (q.v.). Shamshi-Adad claims the conquest and destruction of 200 other cities in their environs. Their inhabitants sought refuge in the fortified city of Qerebti-alani. Shamshi-Adad laid siege to the city, captured it, and plundered it. Those of its people who escaped slaughter were deported along with other booty to Assyria.

Dayenu (Daienu) (map 20) Country in eastern Anatolia attested in Iron Age Assyrian texts, and probably to be located within the region of the Arsanias r. (mod. Murat Su). It is first attested in the reign of the Assyrian king Tiglath-pileser I (1114–1076) (**RIMA* 2: 21, 34, 37, 52) among the Nairi lands whose twenty-three kings (thirty in another account) did battle with Tiglath-pileser in the third year of his reign, under the leadership of Dayenu's king Senu. Tiglath-pileser defeated the coalition and plundered and destroyed its lands and cities. Senu was captured and deported to Ashur. But Tiglath-pileser later released him, as he did all the other defeated kings of Nairi whom he had taken prisoner (**RIMA* 2: 22). Two centuries later, in 856, Dayenu fell victim to the Assyrian king Shalmaneser III during his advance to the heartland of the Urartian kingdom (**RIMA* 3: 20, 29). But on his 844 campaign in the region, Shalmaneser left the country intact, since on this occasion its king, Asia, voluntarily submitted to him, paying him a tax and a tribute of horses (**RIMA* 3: 39). Shalmaneser set up a statue of himself in Asia's royal city. By the reign of the Urartian king Rusa I (730–714), Dayenu had been incorporated into the Urartian kingdom, and the Urartian fortress now called Kayalıdere (anc. name unknown) on the Arsanias r. may have been built within its territory.

Debir (map 8) Canaanite city in Judah, frequently attested in *OT* sources. According to Joshua 15:49 and Judges 1:11, its original name was Kiriath-Sepher, 'city of the scribe'. Almost certainly the city is to be identified with the site of Khirbet Rabud (see ***Rabud, Khirbet***), as M. Kochavi has demonstrated, *contra* the identification with Beit Mirsim once proposed by W. F. Albright.

This Debir should be distinguished from two other places of the same name attested in *OT* sources: (1) a city on the northern boundary of Judah (Joshua 15:7), for which an identification with Thoghret ed-Debr ('pass of Debir'), 16 km east of Jerusalem, has been suggested; (2) a city allocated to the tribe of Gad (Joshua 13:26), for which an identification has been proposed with Umm el-Dabar, which lay 20 km north of Pella in Transjordan.

Boraas (*HCBD* 233).

Dedan (***al-Khuraybah***) (map 16) Northwestern Arabian caravan-centre in the al-ʿUla oasis in Saudi Arabia, 80 km southwest of Tayma (biblical Tema). Rock inscriptions in various Arabian scripts confirm the site's identity as the centre of the land of the Dedanites, an Arabian people whose origins are obscure. Dedan appears to have come into prominence in mid C6 as a trading centre on the route to and from southern Arabia. It is listed in Ezekiel 27:20 as one of Tyre's commercial contacts, reportedly trading with the city in saddle-blankets. For a time, it seems to have been under the control of the kingdom of Edom. This is implied in *OT* references to it in the context of the prophetic oracles uttered against Edom (e.g. Jeremiah 49:8, Ezekiel 25:13). An inscription from Harran lists it (in the form Dadanu) among the cities conquered by the Babylonian king Nabonidus (556–539) while he was living in Tayma. In late C6, following the collapse of the Neo-Babylonian empire, the city may have enjoyed a brief period as the centre of an independent Dedanite kingdom prior to the extension of Persian control over the region. Dedan appears to have prospered under Persian rule, and in the early Hellenistic period, c. 400, became the centre of what was called the Lihyanite kingdom. Around this time, a colony of Minaean merchants from southwest Arabia was established in the city. Dedan was later eclipsed, in C1, by the Nabataean city Hegra, perhaps in the wake of the overthrow of the Lihyanite dynasty in late C2 or early C1 by a Nabataean called Masudu. But the city survived for many centuries after this, as indicated by the establishment of a Jewish colony there in the Byzantine period, attested in Aramaic inscriptions.

Dedan's material remains include a number of tomb-chambers cut into sandstone cliffs (and in two cases flanked by pairs of lions), an underground water system for irrigating the fields, and traces of a city wall and monumental public building.

Parr (*OEANE* 2: 133–4).

Deh Luran Small, fertile plain in southwestern Iran, located west of the foothills of the Zagros mountains and c. 60 km northwest of Susa. A series of surveys was conducted there, beginning with those carried out by J. Gautier and G. Lampre in 1903 on behalf of the French Mission to Iran. Gautier and Lampre also excavated a number of sites, including Tepe Mussian (see ***Mussian, Tepe***), the largest settlement in the plain, Ali Kosh (formerly known as Tepe Mohammed Jaffir), and Tepes Khazineh and Aliabad. Further surveys were conducted by American teams in 1961, 1963, and 1969, under the direction of F. Hole and K. V. Flannery, with the collaboration of J. Neely in the latter two years. The American surveys concentrated on the prehistoric sites in the plain, covering the period from M7 to mid M3. In these surveys, the emphasis was on the recovery of plant and animal remains and other small finds, in the hope that these would provide important environmental and ecological information, as well throw light on the region's agricultural and trade activities.

In general, the excavations carried out in the Deh Luran region have been relatively limited, and as yet no written records have come to light at any of the sites investigated. As a result, we have little knowledge of the region's history during the periods for which we have written records elsewhere in the western Asian world (from M3 onwards). It is possible, however, that Tepe Mussian is the historically attested Elamite city Urua (Arawa) (q.v.). During the so-called Proto-Elamite period (late M4–early M3), Tepe Mussian and its subsidiary Tepe Farukhabad were both substantial settlements, and other settlements in the plain probably also enjoyed a relatively flourishing existence. In the last centuries of M3, there was a substantial decline in the population of the plain, as indicated by the archaeological surveys – though in C21 the rulers of the Ur III dynasty established a route through the region for the shipment from the highlands of much sought-after commodities like silver and timber. Population decline continued in the early centuries of M2, and may have become even more marked then to judge from Tepe Mussian, which was finally abandoned around mid M2. New settlements arose during the second half of M2, e.g. at Tepe Patak and Tepe Goughan. But these, too, were abandoned by the end of the millennium. It has been suggested that they were victims of the incessant conflicts between Middle Elamite kings and the Kassite rulers of Babylonia.

The construction of irrigation canals in the plain during the Persian period (C6–4) enabled new settlements to be built there, sometimes on the sites of former Elamite settlements. The establishment by the Persian kings of a route through the region between the former Elamite capital Susa and the former Median capital Ecbatana may have been largely responsible for settlement revival. During the Sasanian period (C3–7 CE) major new irrigation techniques provided the basis for a substantial increase in the number of settlements in the plain. It is believed that the plain's population reached its maximum size in this period, before decline once more set in during the later Islamic periods.

Hole (*OEANE* 2: 134–7).

Deir ʿAlla, Tell (map 8) Settlement-mound in Jordan, 12 km northeast of the confluence of the Jordan and Jabbok rivers. Its history of occupation extends from the Chalcolithic Age (M4) until the end of the Persian period (C4). The site was excavated first in 1960 by H. J. Franken for the University of Leiden, and subsequently, from 1978 onwards, by teams from the same university in collaboration with Yarmouk University in Jordan. A village was built on the site in the Chalcolithic period, but little else is known of its history before the Late Bronze Age. At that time, a large open-air sanctuary was constructed, with associated workshops, storerooms, and residences. The excavator believes that evidence for strong Egyptian influence indicates the sanctuary's use as an administrative centre for trade between Egypt and Gilead. In early C12 the sanctuary was destroyed by earthquake. Subsequently, in the early Iron Age, the site was reoccupied for a time by a community of metalworkers. Settlement continued after their departure, and by C8 the continuing tradition of the site as a sacred place is reflected in the construction of a new sanctuary, with which a large complex of workrooms and storerooms was associated, as in the Late Bronze Age. A residential quarter was located to the east of the complex.

Within the Iron Age sanctuary a number of so-called proto-Aramaic texts were discovered, on a wall within the workroom and storeroom complex. They include the longest Old Aramaic inscription so far discovered. The non-Israelite prophet Balaam, referred to in a number of *OT* sources (e.g. in the legend recorded in Numbers 22–4), figures in this text. A study of it has led scholars to conclude that the cult practised there in C8 was in the nature of a primitive 'mystery' religion. The architectural layout of the complex resembles, according to Franken, 'what is described in myths as a labyrinth, although a small one – a place of death and victory over death'.

Tell Deir ʿAlla is commonly identified with the place called Succoth in the Bible; the name in Hebrew means 'huts', 'tents', 'temporary dwellings'. Franken comments that 'Succoth may not have been the name used by the local people, but rather was a biblical indication of a place of pagan religion in the Bronze and Iron Ages: the site's sanctuary may have been known as a holy place belonging to certain deities with local names like Beth Sharʿa.'

Baly (*HCBD* 1068–9), Franken (1992; *OEANE* 2: 137–8); for the inscriptions, Lemaire (*OEANE* 2: 138–40).

Deir el-Balah (map 8) Settlement in southern Palestine, 12 km southwest of Gaza. In antiquity, it was the last of the way-stations before Gaza on the so-called Ways of Horus (the main route across Sinai connecting Egypt to Canaan). Its history of occupation extends from the Late Bronze Age to the Byzantine period. The site was excavated from 1972 to 1982 by T. Dothan for the Hebrew University of Jerusalem and the Israel Exploration Society. Nine main occupation strata were identified. The period when the settlement began life is indicated by similarities between its material remains (architectural layout and small finds) and those of Egypt's Amarna age (mid C14). In their totality, Strata IX to IV spanned the second half of the Late Bronze Age, from mid C14 to late C13. The most prominent architectural features of this period are an L-shaped three-unit residential complex of mudbrick built around an artificial lake (IX), a square monumental fourteen-room fortress or tower at least two storeys high (VII), and an artisans' quarter and industrial area replacing the residential complex and fortress of the earlier levels (VI–IV). The industrial area contained a water installation and several kilns. Domestic dwellings of unbaked bricks probably housed the artisans and their families.

Both the kilns and the water installation are thought to have been connected with the preparation of clay to make coffins for a cemetery to the west of the settlement, which was in use through C14 and C13. The cylinder-shaped coffins, which were, perhaps, the burial containers for pre-Philistine Sea People mercenaries serving in the Egyptian garrison, were laid out in graves, and each contained between two and four bodies. The coffins were closed by a lid decorated with anthropoid facial features, wig, arms, and hands. A total of fifty anthropoid coffins, along with their funerary goods, have come to light. Simple inhumation burials were made between the coffins. All burials had a storage jar placed at the deceased's head. The Iron Age I level (Stratum III, C12–11) has produced no architectural remains. However, four pits containing Philistine pottery dug into the Late Bronze Age remains, and large quantities of this pottery found in the valley where Byzantine remains were uncovered, indicate the existence of a substantial Philistine settlement on the site in this period. Pottery sherds are all that are left of the subsequent Iron Age II settlement (Stratum II, C10–9). The site then appears to have been abandoned, and not reoccupied until the Byzantine period (M4 CE onwards).

Dothan (*NEAEHL* 1: 343–7).

Deneia (map 14) Bronze and Iron Age site in the Ovgos valley in west-central Cyprus. Extensive burial grounds at Kafkalla in the immediate vicinity of the mod. village of Deneia and at Mali, several km to the east, were noted by E. Gjerstad, J. R. Stewart, and H. Catling. The site has been subject to intensive looting: vast quantities of pottery vessels and other objects have been removed over the years and sold on the illegal market. Until recently, few tombs had been formally excavated. In 2003 and 2004, D. Frankel and J. M. Webb from La Trobe University (Australia) and M. Iacovou from the University of Cyprus undertook an extensive survey and excavation of a number of looted tombs. Some 1,300 visible tomb entrances were documented, and over 1,000 fragmentary vessels recovered. These suggest a very substantial associated settlement, as yet unlocated, which reached its peak during the Middle Bronze Age, and bear witness to a rich and regionally distinctive material culture. One tomb produced skeletal remains from a minimum of forty-six individuals, over half of whom died in early infancy. Settlement at Deneia may have been established to exploit local agricultural resources and facilitate the transmission of raw copper from the mines of the Troodos to towns such as Bellapais-Vounous and Lapethos on the north coast.

The Kafkalla and Mali cemeteries went out of use some time after 1200. New burial grounds, however, were established in C10, and use of the area continued thereafter, apparently without interruption, until the Hellenistic period. The only other settlement on the island with a comparable occupation record is that of Nicosia-Ayia Paraskevi, the mod. capital of Cyprus.

(J. M. Webb)
Frankel and Webb (2007).

Denyen Late Bronze Age population group listed among the so-called Sea Peoples who swept through large parts of the western Asian world and attacked Egypt by land and sea in the reign of the pharaoh Ramesses III (1184–1153). Their name is represented as *Dnyn* in the Egyptian record (**ARE IV*: §§65–6, **ANET* 262, *Gertzen, 2008: 89, 91). Links have been proposed between them and one or more of the following: (a) The land of Danuna, mentioned in the mid C14 Amarna correspondence (**EA* 151: 50), and for this reason sometimes located in Canaan. (b) The land of Adana, located in the region called Cilicia in the Graeco-Roman period. Adana is first attested in Late Bronze Age Hittite texts, and subsequently in two Luwian–Phoenician bilingual inscriptions from the region, the so-called Karatepe and Çineköy bilinguals (q.v.), dating to C8. The Phoenician versions of these inscriptions refer to the

Figure 34 Tomb, Deneia.

inhabitants of the land as Danunians. (c) The biblical tribe of Dan. (d) A Greek population group called the *Danaoi*. Of these possibilities, a Cilician origin for the Denyen seems the most plausible.

Sandars (1985: 161–4), Bryce (2003a: 103–4), *CHLI* 1: 39–40.

Der (1) Middle Bronze Age city in northwestern Mesopotamia located on the Balih r., near the city of Tuttul and within the territory subject to Mari. During the reign of the Mariote king Zimri-Lim (1774–1762) Der's mayor, Hamman, reported a threatened attack upon his city by the kings of Zalmaqum (**LKM* 189–90).

Der (2) Middle Bronze Age city on the Euphrates downstream from Mari and serving as one of Mari's two southwestern frontier posts. The other, called Hiddan, lay on the opposite bank of the river. The Mari texts refer to the construction of a palace at Der during the reign of Zimri-Lim (1774–1762), and to rites associated with the town's goddess, Deritum.

**LAPO* 3: 124, 281, **LKM* 376, no. 26.455.

Der (3) Iron Age city in the Diyala region, eastern Babylonia. Located on the caravan route which linked the trading city of Lahiru with Elam, it has been equated with the site of Tell Aqar, near Badrah. It was among the Babylonian cities afflicted by the Aramaean and Sutaean invasions of southern Mesopotamia during the reign of the Babylonian king Adad-apla-iddina (1069–1048) (**ABC* 180–1; cf. **RIMB* 2: 50). The Assyrian king Adad-nirari II (911–891) conquered it during the campaign in which he claimed to have subdued the entire land of Babylonia, then ruled by Shamash-mudammiq (**RIMA* 2: 148). Subsequently, Der was one of several cities in the Diyala region which were seized and destroyed by the Assyrian king Shamshi-Adad V in 813, during the second of his four campaigns into Babylonian territory (**ABC* 168, **RIMA* 3: 190–1). (The other cities were Lahiru, Gannanate, Dur-Papsukkal, Bit-reduti, and Me-Turan.) He captured there the Babylonian king Marduk-balassu-iqbi and deported him to Assyria. In 720 Der was the scene of a battle between the army of the recently enthroned Assyrian king Sargon II and the forces of the Elamite king Humban-nikash (**ABC* 73–4, **CS* II: 296) (see under **Elam**).

Brinkman (1968: 205–10), **Nippur* IV: 116–17, no. 43, Lipiński (2000: 432–3), *SAA* XV: XXXII–XXXV.

Der, Tell ed- (maps 10, 11) Settlement in southern Mesopotamia covering an area of c. 50 ha, located at the northern end of Babylonia, 25 km south of Baghdad. Its history of occupation probably began in late M3 and continued until the Persian period (C6–4). Investigation of the site started in 1891, when E. A. W. Budge unearthed many thousands of clay tablets from the mounds of which the site was composed. However, the first official excavations were undertaken in 1941 by T. Baqir and M. A. Mustafa on an Iraqi government-sponsored mission. Further excavations were carried out by a Belgian team, beginning in 1970, under the direction of L. De Meyer and H. Gasche.

During the Old Babylonian period (Middle Bronze Age) the city was called Sippar-Amnanum, as attested in written records from the reign of the Babylonian king Sin-muballit (1812–1793). It was also known as Sippar-rabum ('Great Sippar') and Sippar-durum. Whether or not Sippar-Amnanum was also the city's Early Bronze Age name is unknown. The name is sometimes written simply as Sippar, which has led to some confusion with the well-known, identically named city lying a few km to the southwest. Sippar-Amnanum's chief deity was the goddess Annunitu. From the house of a man called Ur-Utu, a high-ranking official in her service in the final decades of C17, more than 2,000 tablets have come to light. These provide valuable information about many aspects of the city's life – social, religious, and economic – in late C17, as the Old Babylonian empire was entering its final years. In this phase of Sippar-Amnanum's existence, an earthen dyke, revealed by excavations, was intended to protect the city against flooding. Unusually, there were no breaks in the wall for gates, and access must have been gained by going over the wall. It was apparently built to replace an earlier, conventional city wall, referred to in a letter of the Babylonian king Samsu-iluna (1749–1712), which was destroyed by floods.

The city was reoccupied in later M2 (c. 1400). It appears among the conquests of the Assyrian king Tiglath-pileser I (1114–1076) in the form Sippar-(of-)Anunnitu, meaning 'Sippar-of-(the goddess) Anunnitu' (**RIMA* 2: 43), apparently one of several names used to designate it. The city is also attested in this form in records of the Neo-Babylonian and Persian periods. A temple dedicated to Anunnitu still stood, or was built or rebuilt, in the city when it was under Neo-Babylonian rule, as indicated by an inscription of the Babylonian king Nabonidus (556–539). Excavations have failed to reveal any trace of this temple.

De Meyer (*OEANE* 2: 145–6).

Derbices M1 central Asian tribe, probably to be located to the east of Hyrcania, in the region southeast of the Caspian Sea, and perhaps not far from the land of the Massagetae. In a tradition recorded by Ctesias (*FGrH* 688 F9.7–8 = **PE* 101, no. 35), they were the object of the eastern campaign undertaken by the Persian king Cyrus II in 530, which resulted in his death. According to this tradition the Derbices and their Indian allies were defeated, but Cyrus died of a spear wound which he suffered during the conflict. In Herodotus' version of this campaign (1.214) it was the Massagetae, under their queen Tomyris, who were responsible for Cyrus' death. Strabo (11.11.8) gives a description of the Derbices' customs. Allegedly these included their refusal to eat or sacrifice anything female, and the slaughter of their menfolk on reaching seventy and the consumption of their flesh by their nearest relatives.

Tomaschek (*RE* V, 1905: 237–8).

Dhibai, Tell al- see Zaralulu.

Diaue(khi) (map 20) Wealthy Iron Age kingdom in eastern Anatolia, sometime vassal state of the kingdom of Urartu, probably to be located in the vicinity of mod. Erzurum. It should be distinguished from the nearby country of Dayenu, with which it has sometimes been identified. Within the context of securing his northwestern frontier in the Arasa valley region, the Urartian king Minua (805–788) campaigned against Diauekhi, forcing its king, Utupurshi, to hand over several of his cities, Shashilu, Zua, and Utu, to Urartian control, and to pay a tribute of gold and silver (**HcI* 23–4). But Diauekhi was only temporarily pacified, and Minua's son and successor Argishti I was obliged to conduct another campaign against it in the second year of his reign. This resulted in the imposition of a further, much more substantial tribute on the country, in the form of gold, silver, copper, cattle, and horses. Anti-Urartian sentiment remained strong in Diauekhi, and towards the end of his reign Argishti had yet again to campaign against it to quell an uprising led by Utupurshi, who was still its king.

CAH III.1: 1022 (index refs).

Dibina Iron Age city east of the upper Diyala. The Assyrian king Shamshi-Adad V (823–811) reports its submission to him after he had placed it under siege (**RIMA* 3: 187). The booty he took from the city included 3,000 troops. This occurred during his fourth campaign (814), which he conducted into Babylonian territory.

Dibon (***Dhiban***) (map 8) City in Jordan, located on the anc. King's Highway (q.v.), 20 km east of the Dead Sea. Its archaeological remains indicate settlement during the Early Bronze Age, Iron Age, Nabataean, Roman, Byzantine, and Arab periods. The site was excavated periodically between 1950 and 1965 under a series of directors – F. V. Winnett, W. L. Reed, A. D. Tushingham, and W. H. Morton – on behalf of the American School of Oriental Research in Jerusalem. Excavations are currently being conducted (2009) by B. W. Porter, University of Pennsylvania, B. E. Routledge, University of Liverpool, and D. Steen, Stanford University. Their re-examination of the site has been prompted by increasing knowledge of central Jordan's cultural history. (A summary report of their 2004 season appears in *AJA* 109, 2005: 542–4.) Early Bronze Age remains include part of a curved and sloping wall, possibly a gate, and some pottery sherds dating mainly to Early Bronze III. However, Dibon is particularly noted for its Iron Age II levels (early M1), when it was the capital of the kingdom of Moab. It is first attested in *OT* tradition as part of the region of northern Moab captured by the Israelites from the Amorite king Sihon (Numbers 21:21–31); the city was subsequently assigned to the tribes of Reuben and Gad (Joshua 13:9, Numbers 32:3–5).

Of considerable importance for Moabite history was the discovery at Dibon in 1868 of a black basalt stele, commonly referred to as the Moabite Stone, on which appears a 34-line inscription in the Moabite language celebrating the achievements of a Moabite king called Mesha (**CS* II: 137–8, **Chav.* 311–13). This king was already known from 2 Kings 3:4. The inscription informs us that Dibon was Mesha's birthplace, and became his capital. It is possible that the remains of his royal palace have been unearthed in the southeast sector of the site. The dominant feature of these remains is a large rectangular stone building, with perhaps an adjoining sanctuary. From Mesha's inscription, we know that the king did in fact build a new royal quarter in his city next to, but apparently separate from, the old city. The inscription records that in addition to the palace, this new area contained a sanctuary for the god Kemosh, a royal acropolis with gates and towers (perhaps the place referred to as the *Qaroh* – 'the eminent' – in Mesha's inscription), and a residential quarter. But the most significant event of Mesha's reign was his establishment of his kingdom's independence from Israel, c. 835, as recorded in his inscription, following his conflict with Ahab, second Israelite king of the Omride dynasty. Mesha now extended his kingdom as far north as the Jordanian Mt Nebo.

Dibon continued to be important after Mesha's reign, but whether or not it reverted to Israelite control remains uncertain. In 731 it was subjected along with the rest of Moab to the overlordship of the Assyrian king Tiglath-pileser III. Its submission to Assyria probably ensured its peaceful existence down to the end of the Assyrian empire in late C7. But after the fall of Assyria, it joined in a Moabite rebellion against

Babylonian rule, and was destroyed by the Babylonian king Nebuchadnezzar II c. 582. It apparently remained deserted for half a millennium until it gained a new lease of life in late M1 under Nabataean rule.

Tushingham (*NEAEHL* 1: 350–2; *OEANE* 2: 156–8).

Didyma (Branchidae) (***Didim***, formerly ***Yenihisar***) (map 5) Oracular sanctuary of the god Apollo, located on the Milesian peninsula in southwestern Anatolia. It lay 16.4 km south of Miletus, and was linked to it by a sacred way adorned with sculptures and shrines. Its origins are uncertain. According to a tradition recorded by Pausanias (7.2.6), a fountain-oracle of the god was already known on the site prior to Ionian colonization of the region, i.e. by the end of M2. Occupation may in fact have begun in the Late Bronze Age, to judge from the discovery there of a fragment of a Mycenaean kylix (drinking-cup) dating to C14. Of course, Didyma's cultic associations may have been a later development in the site's history. Excavations of the site are currently being conducted by A. Furtwängler, of Martin Luther University, Halle-Wittenberg-Universität.

The earliest surviving architectural remains are those of a late C8 or C7 mudbrick structure where the oracle *may* first have been located. (According to Greek tradition, the oracle was administered in the Archaic period by a clan of priests called the Branchidae.) To the south of this building a roofed portico was constructed, previously dated to late C7, but now to C6. These constructions were followed in the second half of C6 by the first great temple of Apollo. Its meagre remains were found beneath the Hellenistic temple. The oracle's widespread reputation in this period is indicated by the fact that dedications to it were made by the pharaoh Necho II (610–595) and the Lydian king Croesus (560–546). Herodotus (1.157) informs us that it was frequently consulted by Aeolian and Ionian Greeks. (For the episode in which emissaries from Cyme in Aeolis sought advice from the oracle on how they should respond to an ultimatum from the Persian king Cyrus II, see Herodotus 1.157–60.) The sanctuary was plundered and destroyed by the Persians, probably in 494 in the aftermath of the Ionian rebellion (see **Ionia**). Thereafter it remained in a ruined state, while still maintaining its cultic significance, until the early Hellenistic period. Alexander the Great visited the site in 334 after capturing Miletus. Thenceforth, and at his instigation, the oracle, which had ceased to function after the Persian destruction, was revived, and construction was begun on a new temple of the god. Conceived on a vast and elaborate scale, it took some six centuries to complete.

E. Akurgal (1973: 222–31), Tuchelt (*PECS* 272–3), Greaves (2002: 109–36), Furtwängler (2006).

Dilbat (*Tell ed-Deylam*) (map 11) M3–1 city in northwestern Babylonia, first attested as one of the rebel cities which fought against the Akkadian king Naram-Sin (2254–2218) in the so-called Great Revolt (**RIME* 2: 106). In late C19 CE ed-Deylam was excavated by H. Rassam on behalf of the British Museum, but was subsequently unexplored until it was briefly surveyed and excavated in 1989–90 by a team from the Oriental Institute of the University of Chicago led by J. A. Armstrong. The early excavations recovered many cuneiform tablets, and many more came to light through unofficial excavations conducted around the same time. These documents point strongly to an identification of the site with Dilbat. They cover the three centuries of Old Babylonian history (Middle Bronze Age), and also include several hundred economic, legal, and administrative texts dating to the Neo-Babylonian period, especially C7.

Dilbat was one of the most important cities of the Old Babylonian kingdom. When it was seized in 1878 by Halum-pi-umu, king of Kazallu and Marad, the Babylonian king Sumu-la-El promptly regained it by attacking Halum-pi-umu and soundly defeating him. He achieved this success in his third regnal year. The city thenceforth remained firmly under Babylonian control. In Hammurabi's reign (1792–1750) its population was swelled by Hurrian settlers, whom Hammurabi had deported from the Zagros mountain region.

In the Late Bronze Age (when it was under Kassite rule), and in the Neo-Babylonian period (especially C6), Dilbat continued to be one of Babylonia's most important cities and a major religious centre of the kingdom. In the latter period it was under the authority of a local governor, who initially appears to have enjoyed a relatively independent existence. During the reign of the Chaldaean king Nabu-shuma-ishkun (760–748), the governor of Borsippa reported confrontations with marauders from Babylon, Dilbat, and elsewhere, who had attempted to raid his city's fields (*RIMB* 2: 124). In 731 Dilbat was one of a small number of Babylonian cities which supported the Assyrian king Tiglath-pileser III in his attempt to remove the Chaldaean king Nabu-mukin-zeri from the throne of Babylon (see under **Babylonia**). When the throne was occupied by the Assyrian prince Shamash-shum-ukin (667–648), who rebelled against his brother, the Assyrian king Ashurbanipal, Dilbat's governor, Shulaya, was one of the local rulers who clearly supported the rebel. (Another was Sin-sharra-usur, governor of Ur, at the very beginning of the revolt.)

In the contest between Nabopolassar (626–605) and the Assyrian king Sin-sharra-ishkun for control of Babylonia during the Assyrian empire's declining years, Nabopolassar first gained control of the north of the country. Dilbat was one of a number of cities in the region (others were Borsippa, Cutha, and Babylon itself) which he secured. It was subsequently among the cities which benefited from the extensive building and restoration programmes undertaken throughout Babylonia by Nabopolassar's son and successor Nebuchadnezzar II (604–562), no doubt partly because of its continuing status as one of Babylonia's major religious centres. Its temple E-imbi-anu, shrine of the city god Urash, was one of the kingdom's most important religious sanctuaries.

Klengel (1976), Armstrong (1995), *Mesop.* 1013 (index refs). For the city's M1 history, see index refs in *CAH* III.1: 1022 and III.2: 879.

Dildaba Small Middle Bronze Age town in southern Mesopotamia near Larsa. The Babylonian king Hammurabi (1792–1750) used it as his military base for his six-month siege of Larsa in 1763 (*LKM* 152–3, *331–3).

Dilkaya Höyük Settlement-mound in eastern Anatolia, 34 km southwest of mod. Van, with a history of occupation extending back to the Early Bronze Age. A later building phase has been dated to the early Urartian period (early M1). Located 200 m north of the mound was a large cemetery (3 ha or more) of (probable) C9–8 date. It contained both inhumation and cremation burials, including cremation urns and two stone-built chamber-tombs. Funerary goods included a number of bronze bracelets which have helped date the cemetery on stylistic grounds. The site's anc. name (or names) is unknown.

McConchie (2004: 119–21).

Dilmun (map 12) Land in the Persian Gulf attested in Bronze and Iron Age Mesopotamian texts, and now identified with the islands of the Bahrain archipelago, with an extension north to the island of Failaka off the coast of Kuwait. To begin with, Dilmun may have been located in the eastern and continental part of the Arabian peninsula, up to and including the time of the earliest written sources which refer to it (mid M3).

The land is well known for its mythological associations in Mesopotamian literature. It was one of the three countries which in Mesopotamian tradition lay alongside the 'Lower Sea', i.e. south of Babylonia. The other two countries were Magan and Meluhha. In the Sumerian poem *Enki and Ninhursag*, the god Enki carries sweet water, the source of life, to Dilmun, and in the Sumerian version of the flood narrative, Ziusudra and his wife, the sole survivors of the flood, are settled there by the gods for eternity. In Mesopotamian tradition, mythological Dilmun embodied the concept of Paradise.

On the mundane level, Dilmun is noted chiefly for its trading activities with the cities and kingdoms of Mesopotamia. The first evidence of commercial contacts are provided by the presence of M4 Mesopotamian Ubaid ceramic ware at several sites on the main island of Bahrain. By mid M3 at the latest, Dilmun was supplying Mesopotamia with wood and copper. We know this from textual evidence, which indicates that consignments of these commodities were dispatched from Dilmun to the city-state of Lagash in southern Mesopotamia during the reigns of the Lagashite kings Ur-Nanshe (C25) and Lugalbanda and Urukagina (C24). Wool, silver, cereal, and dairy products were used as payment for the imported goods, the latter brought by boats from Dilmun to the quays of the southern Mesopotamian river cities. Towards the end of M3, texts from Ebla, Akkad, Ur (Ur III dynasty), and Lagash (under its king Gudea) provide further evidence of trade with Dilmun, as do early M2 (Middle Bronze Age) texts from Isin, Ur, and Mari. Diplomatic contacts with Dilmun were established by the Assyrian king Shamshi-Adad I in the winter of 1777–6, and maintained over the next two years until his death in 1775.

Wood, ivory, gold, silver, and semi-precious stones figure among the items exported by Dilmun. But the most important of its exports was copper. The metal was not mined in Dilmun itself, but came from sources further afield, probably from Magan (mod. Oman) in the southeast of the Arabian peninsula. Similarly other export items were first shipped to Dilmun from their places of origin, e.g. ebony(?) wood, ivory, gold, silver, and carnelian from the land of Meluhha (Indus valley), before being dispatched to their final destinations. Dilmun thus became an important centre of an international trading network, serving as a redistribution point for goods passing between Mesopotamia and the countries of the Persian Gulf, Iran, Bactria, and the Indus valley. In return for the goods which it shipped to Mesopotamia, Dilmun received silver, textiles, grain products, and sesame oil. It thrived on its role as an international emporium, particularly in late M3 and early M2, the most affluent period in its history. However, its substantial population, as reflected in the 175,000 tumulus tombs of this period, must have put considerable pressure on the land's food resources. Undoubtedly, Dilmun's lack of good agricultural areas limited its food-producing capacity, and large consignments of grain, like the barley imports recorded in Mesopotamian texts, probably had to be imported on a regular basis to feed its population.

Dilmun's chief settlement was located at the site now called Qalʿat al-Bahrain (q.v.), whose origins date back to C24. Cult-centres were located at (mod.) Barbar, Diraz, and

Saar (q.v.), where temples have been found. Barbar contained the most important temple, a stone building, dating back to 2200, surrounded by an oval enclosure wall, and probably dedicated to the Sumerian god Enki. The remains of Dilmun's material culture include large numbers of round cylinder seals found mainly in the tombs and often featuring human and animal motifs (gazelles in particular). Hundreds of seals of local origin, along with ceramics, tablets, and seals of Mesopotamian (Old Babylonian) origin have come to light on the island of Failaka. These finds indicate Failaka's cultural affinities with Dilmun, and probably also its role as a commercial intermediary between Mesopotamia and Dilmun. A settlement of colonists from Dilmun was established at Failaka in early M2.

From mid C18, Dilmun's role as a commercial entrepôt diminished in importance, with the reduction of trading links between Mesopotamia and the Gulf. However, Qalʿat al-Bahrain continued to be a city of some significance. In the Late Bronze Age, Dilmun probably came under the control of the Babylonian Kassite dynasty, to judge from a cylinder seal found there of a man with the Babylonian name Uballissu-Marduk, designated as *šakkanaku* (governor) of Dilmun. Subsequently, the land may have been subject for a time to the Assyrian king Tukulti-Ninurta I, following his conquest of the Babylonian kingdom and the capture of its king, Kashtiliash IV, in 1225. Tukulti-Ninurta referred to himself as king of both Dilmun and Meluhha (**RIMA* 1: 275).

In the Iron Age, Dilmun appears again as an Assyrian subject state. One of its kings, Uperi, became a tributary of Sargon II following the latter's campaign in Babylonia in 710–709. Several decades later, the Assyrian king Ashurbanipal (668–630/627) claims to have 'imposed his yoke' upon Dilmun (**RIMB* 2: 226), and to have received tribute from Hundaru, its king at the time. Remains from the Neo-Babylonian period (C6) have been found on both Bahrain and Failaka. Inscriptions from Failaka indicate that a palace of Nebuchadnezzar II (604–562) and a temple dedicated to the god Shamash were built there during this period. Virtually nothing is known of Dilmun in the Persian period (C6–4). And apart from numerous burials of the Hellenistic age and building levels at Qalʿat al-Bahrain, our knowledge of Dilmun's history in this period, when its main island was called Tylos, is also almost non-existent. Bahrain later became part of the Sasanian empire (C3 CE onwards) with the name Mešmahik.

D. T. Potts (1983; 1990: vol. I, 409–10, index refs; 1995: 1452–5), Lion (*DCM* 233–5).

Diniktum Middle Bronze Age city in the Diyala valley, northern Mesopotamia. Though its precise location is uncertain, it lay on the Tigris r. downstream from Upi (see **Upi (1)**), not far from the Elamite border. The independence it enjoyed in the first half of C19 is typical of a number of cities in the Diyala region, reflecting the political fragmentation of the period. At that time it was ruled by a man called Itur-sharrum, designated as an Amorite chief of Diniktum (**RIME* 4: 683). It was later attached to the kingdom of Eshnunna, and became involved in Eshnunna's confrontations with Elam during the reigns of the Eshnunnite kings Ibal-pi-El II (1779–1765) and Silli-Sin (1764–1762) (**LKM* 328, no. 26.377; 460–1, nos 27.149–50).

Mesop. 96–7.

Dirru Iron Age land in northern Mesopotamia, whose cities lay to the north of the

Kashiyari mountain range (mod. Tur ʿAbdin) on the east bank of the Tigris. The Assyrian king Ashurnasirpal II reports his conquest and destruction of fifty of these cities, and gives a detailed description of his siege and capture of what was probably the chief city, Pitura (q.v.), in 879 (**RIMA* 2: 210, 260). He reports further attacks upon the cities of Dirru in 866, after moving on from the city of Karania (q.v.) and entering the pass of Mt Amadanu (**RIMA* 2: 219–20).

Liverani (1992: 60–1).

Diyala (map 10) Region in eastern Mesopotamia watered by the Diyala r., a tributary of the Tigris which it joins several km downstream from Baghdad. Traversing the northeastern part of the Mesopotamian alluvium, the river is fed by headwaters from the Zagros mountains northeast of Baghdad. The region which it waters consists of three parts: the upper, middle, and lower Diyala. The third of these, which is watered by the river via irrigation canals, is particularly rich in archaeological finds, and the simple term Diyala is traditionally used to refer to this region. It lies southwest of the Hamrin range. Excavations in the Diyala conducted by the Oriental Institute of the University of Chicago between 1930 and 1938, under the direction of H. Frankfort, focused on four major sites: Tell Asmar (Eshnunna), Khafajeh (Tutub, Dur Samsu-iluna), Ishchali (Nerebtum), and Tell Agrab. These sites spanned a total of seventeen centuries, from c. 3500 to 1800 – i.e. from the Late Uruk to the Old Babylonian period. Their excavation enabled the development of a long-range chronology for the lower Diyala region, based especially on its ceramic sequence. Architectural remains of the sites from M3, especially temple remains, provided the basis for the definition of three phases: Early Dynastic I, II, and III. However, scholars point out that this periodization reflects a local evolution and should not be applied too systematically to other regions.

In 1957 and 1958, T. Jacobsen, R. McC. Adams, and F. Safar carried out extensive surveys of the lower Diyala plain for the Diyala Basin Archaeological Project. The purpose of this project was to investigate the region's history of agriculture and irrigation over a period of more than 6,000 years. The surveys provided much important information about settlement patterns and canal systems in the region from the Ubaid period through C19. Increases in the number and size of settlements during the Jemdet Nasr and Early Dynastic periods (c. 3100–2334) point to steady population growth in these periods. Khafajeh, Tell Asmar, and Tell Agrab developed as major urban centres, around which many other sites clustered in a hierarchical settlement pattern. The surveyors noted that of ninety-six sites examined, ten were large towns (more than 10 ha), nineteen were small towns (4–10 ha), and sixty-seven were villages (less than 4 ha). Settlement in the Akkadian period (c. 2334–2193) continued to develop along similar lines. The region is considered to have reached its political peak during the so-called Isin-Larsa period (c. 2000–1736), when Eshnunna, previously subject to the C21 Ur III dynasty, established its independence and became the major centre of the region. The Diyala prospered through the period of Eshnunna's dominance, but its *floruit* came to an end with the rise of the Old Babylonian kingdom under Hammurabi (1792–1750). Adams' surveys showed that the important towns of the region then went into decline. It was not until the Hellenistic period that a major regeneration of the settlement pattern occurred.

Adams (1965), Thuesen (*OEANE* 2: 163–6), Sauvage (*DCM* 242–4).

Djahi (Zahi) Egyptian name for the Late Bronze Age region on the Syro-Palestinian coast where Egypt's northern frontier lay in C13 and early C12. In M1 it was called Phoenicia. Here the army of Ramesses III (1184–1153) confronted and defeated the land forces of the Sea Peoples, thus preventing their movement further southward into Egypt proper (**ARE IV*: §65). The confrontation is recorded in both word and picture on the walls of Ramesses' temple at Medinet Habu.

Dor (***Khirbet el-Buri***) (map 8) Site consisting of a settlement-mound, covering c. 12 ha, and lower city, located on the Carmel coast of northern Palestine, 21 km south of Haifa. Its history of occupation extends from the Middle and Late Bronze Ages, through the Iron Age, Persian, Hellenistic, Roman, and Byzantine periods. The site was first excavated by J. Garstang from 1923 to 1924, on behalf of the British School of Archaeology in Jerusalem. Further excavations, north of the mound in the lower city, were conducted by J. Leibowitz for the Israel Dept of Antiquities in 1950 and 1952. The most recent and most comprehensive excavations on the tell of Dor began in 1980 under the direction of E. Stern for the Hebrew University of Jerusalem and the Israel Exploration Society.

Evidence of settlement in the Middle Bronze Age (early centuries of M2) is provided by building remains and a range of local and imported ceramic ware. For the Late Bronze Age, the only material evidence that has so far come to light are pottery fragments and a few scarabs. However, it is in this period that the city is first historically attested, in an Egyptian inscription discovered in Nubia. The inscription, which dates to the reign of Ramesses II (1279–1213), lists Dor among a number of Syro-Palestinian coastal cities. In early C12, Dor appears to have been taken over by the Tjekker (q.v.), one of the Sea Peoples. In a well-known Egyptian tale of early C11, the sea merchant Wenamun incurs the wrath of the Tjekker prince Beder, ruler of Dor, during a trading expedition along the Syro-Palestinian coast (*Lichtheim, 1976: 224–5, **CS* I: 90). Archaeological evidence indicates that in this period Dor was fortified by a massive mudbrick wall.

OT tradition places Dor among the Canaanite cities conquered by the Israelites in C10, during the reign of King David. It subsequently became the capital of one of the administrative districts into which David's successor Solomon divided Israel (1 Kings 4:11). Later, in 732, the city fell to the Assyrian king Tiglath-pileser III. Its fortifications were destroyed in the attack, but were rebuilt under Assyrian rule, when Dor (Duru in Assyrian records) became the administrative centre of an Assyrian province. Under Persian rule (C6–4), when a high degree of autonomy was granted to former Assyrian subject states, Dor became a dependency of the city of Sidon. It probably now reached the peak of its material development and prosperity. Excavations have revealed a carefully planned residential quarter of this period, occupying the entire eastern part of the mound and laid out on an intersecting grid pattern in accordance with Hippodamian principles (see glossary). Large quantities of pottery unearthed in the Persian levels include ware imported from mainland Greece, most notably Attic ware. Numerous statuettes, figurines, seals, and Phoenician cult objects figure among the small finds of the period. A number of installations of this period indicate that Dor had a significant purple-dye industry.

The city's urban layout remained largely unchanged in the Hellenistic period, when the Ptolemies gained control of Dor and substantially refortified it. The great walls of this period, which today still reach 7 m in height, were apparent built by Ptolemy II Philadelphus (285–246). In 63 the city was granted independence by the Roman commander Pompey the Great, after he had conquered it.

Stern (*NEAEHL* 1: 357–68).

Dorak (map 2) Village in northwestern Anatolia, located just south of the Sea of Marmara (anc. Propontis). It was allegedly the site of a small cemetery dating to the last half of the Early Bronze Age and belonging to the so-called Yortan culture of the region. The British archaeologist James Mellaart claims to have rediscovered the cemetery after its graves were illegally excavated in the early 1920s. As reported by Mellaart, the cemetery contained two cist-graves with royal burials, and two pithos-burials for servants. The grave goods in the royal tombs included a number of figurines, utensils, weapons, and ornaments fashioned from a variety of precious and semi-precious materials. They also included, according to Mellaart, the remains of a wooden throne – apparently a gift from Egypt, because its surviving gold overlay bore an inscription in Egyptian hieroglyphs with the name of Sahure, a king of Egypt's fifth dynasty (2494–2487). It was this discovery that enabled the cemetery and its contents to be dated to the late Early Bronze Age, making its grave goods roughly contemporary with the so-called 'treasures' of Troy IIg.

The 'Dorak treasure' was allegedly spirited away to a house in Izmir by its clandestine excavators. However, no trace of it has ever come to light. The only indications of its existence are Mellaart's report and some sketches of the various items making up the treasure, redrawn from original sketches made by Mellaart, who claims to have seen the items in Izmir before their final disappearance. The sketches were published in the *Illustrated London News* (28 November 1959). There is no independent corroboration of any of Mellaart's claims, and the authenticity of the Dorak treasure has been almost universally rejected.

Lloyd (1967: 29–33).

Dothan (map 8) 10 ha settlement-mound located in Palestine (West Bank), in the northern Samaria hills, 22 km north of Shechem. Its history of occupation extends from the late Chalcolithic Age (c. 3200) through the Byzantine period, with later mediaeval settlement on the site. Excavation was conducted by a team from Wheaton College, Illinois, under the direction of J. P. Free, from 1953 to 1964. The remains of a massive fortification wall on the south side of the mound's summit indicate that already in the Early Bronze Age a large fortified city occupied the site. Continuity of settlement is indicated by fortifications of Middle and Late Bronze Age date. However, the Iron Age II period (early centuries of M1) has produced the most substantial evidence of the city's existence. Four Iron Age II levels were identified in the area designated as L, on the western summit of the mound. The finds from these include a large public building, probably dating back to C10 and used for administration purposes, and perhaps several storeys high. It contained a number of storerooms with storage bins, and rooms with ovens. The area designated as A in the central section of the summit of the mound revealed streets, one more than 30 m long, lined with houses, some of which also contained storerooms and ovens.

The settlement's destruction by fire in late C9 is perhaps to be associated with the Aramaean invasions of the region. Rebuilding occurred in early C8, with several structures reflecting Assyrian influence in their open-court plans. This settlement survived for only a few decades before its destruction by the Assyrians, either during Tiglath-pileser III's campaign in 732, or in the course of the final Assyrian conquest of Israel in 721. The site was then abandoned for several centuries before a small settlement was built on the mound's summit during the Hellenistic period. Occupation remained sparse through the Roman period.

Investigation of the settlement's western cemetery, designated as Area K and located on the western side of the mound, was carried out under the direction of R. E. Cooley between 1959 and 1964. The most notable find was a multiple burial tomb, designated as Tomb 1, apparently used as a family tomb for a period of 200 to 300 years, from Late Bronze Age II to the early Iron Age. The excavators distinguished five levels of stratification and a total of 300 to 500 burials. More than 3,400 grave goods were unearthed, including a wide range of ceramic ware, bronze vessels and weapons, scarabs, beads, bone artefacts, and a figurine lamp. The tomb was accessed by a vertical shaft and stepped entryway.

Dothan can be firmly identified with the biblical city of the same name. In *OT* tradition it is best known for the story in Genesis 37:17–36, where it provides the setting for Joseph's meeting with his brothers after his departure from Shechem. The brothers stripped Joseph of his clothing and threw him into an empty water cistern, from which he was rescued by Midianite merchants, taken to Egypt, and sold to Potiphar, the captain of the pharaoh's guard.

Ussishkin, Cooley, Pratico (*NEAEHL* 1: 372–4).

Drangiana (map 16) M1 Central Asian country located in the region of eastern Iran–Afghanistan, west of the land of Arachosia and attested in both Persian and Classical sources. According to Strabo (15.2.10), the country was a source of tin. Drangiana was among the eastern lands of the Persian empire listed several times in the inscriptions of Darius I (522–486), e.g. in his Bisitun inscription (**DB* 6), and also in the *daiva* inscription (see glossary) of his son and successor Xerxes (**XPh* 3). The sites of Dahan-i Ghulaman and Nad-i Ali can probably be identified as Drangian settlements (see, respectively, Scerrato, 1966, and Dales, 1977). Scerrato suggests that Dahan-i Ghulaman (where an Iron Age settlement with fire-cult temple was discovered) was both the political and the administrative centre of Drangiana.

In Classical sources, the people of Drangiana are referred to as Sarangians or Zarangians, though Pliny the Elder (6.94) lists Drangians and Zarangians separately in his account of Persia's eastern provinces. Herodotus (3.93) includes Sarangians among the members of what was according to him the fourteenth Persian province (but see glossary under **satrapy**), and lists a Sarangian contingent under the command of Pherendates, son of Megabazus, among the forces assembled by the Persian king Xerxes for his invasion of Greece in 481; the Sarangians were armed with bows and Median-style spears, wore knee-high boots, and were conspicuous for their coloured clothing (Herodotus, 7.67). Roaf (1974: 149) has suggested that the boots worn by members of the seventh delegation on the east staircase of the Audience Hall (Apadana) at Persepolis, generally thought to be from Arachosia, may in fact identify the delegates as Drangians/Sarangians. Alternatively, Drangians may constitute the fourteenth delegation, whose four members bring lances, a circular shield, and a spear. According to Arrian (*Anabasis* 3.27.4), Alexander the Great encountered a people called the Ariaspae (q.v.), during his campaigns in the east, in the land of the Zarangians.

Schmitt (1995), Wiesehöfer (*BNP* 4: 713).

Dubrum (*Tell Jidr*) M3 city in southern Mesopotamia, perhaps located north of Umma on the Iturungal canal (*RGTC* 1: 31). The Gutian king Tirigan sought refuge in Dubrum after his defeat by Utuhegal, ruler of the Sumerian city of Uruk (2123–2113), in a battle fought north of the city of Adab (**RIME* 2: 287). On hearing of Utuhegal's victory, the citizens of Dubrum handed the fugitive and his family over to him.

Dukkama Late Bronze Age fortified city located in northeastern Anatolia in the country of Azzi. When the Hittite king Mursili II campaigned in Azzi during the tenth year of his reign (1312), Dukkama, unlike its neighbour Aripsa, surrendered without resistance to his forces (**AM* 134–7). Mursili did not plunder the city, but he deported to Hattusa a number of its able-bodied men for service in the Hittite army.

Dummetu Iron Age city belonging to the middle Euphrates kingdom of Bit-Adini. During an anti-Assyrian uprising by the lands of Laqe and Suhu c. 877, a Laqean ruler, Azi-ilu, fled north and took refuge in Dummetu and Azmu, cities of Bit-Adini. He was pursued there by the Assyrian king Ashurnasirpal II, but escaped (**RIMA* 2: 215). Lipiński suggests that Dummetu should be linked to the land of Dumatum, mentioned in an early C18 letter from the Mari archive (**LAPO* 17: 23, no. 450).

Lipiński (2000: 181–2).

Dunanu M1 Aramaean tribe in northeastern Babylonia, first attested in letters from the mid C8 Nippur archive (**Nippur* IV: 141–4, nos 60–1) and included in the list of thirty-five so-called Aramaean tribes which the Assyrian king Tiglath-pileser III claims to have conquered, probably in his accession year (745) (**Tigl. III* 160–1). A place called Pasitu is attested as one of its cities (**Tigl. III* 122–3). The tribe was perhaps located to the north of Nippur.

Lipiński (2000: 458–9).

Dunnum In Akkadian the name simply means 'fort' or 'fortified house/area', which explains why it was so common. At least three places called Dunnum located on the Euphrates are attested in Old Babylonian (Middle Bronze Age) texts. So far as these cities can be identified, they appear to have been located, proceeding from north to south: (1) On the site of Classical Birtha, on the west bank of the Euphrates, to the southeast of mod. Halebiye and the anc. town Lasqum. The city was fortified by Yadih-abu, king of Terqa (c. 1725). It fell victim to an epidemic, causing its population to seek refuge in Lasqum. (2) Near Mishlan, in the district of Mari, located between Mari and Terqa. (3) In the land of Suhu(m), which bordered the kingdom of Mari to the south. Two more settlements called Dunnum are located in southern Mesopotamia, one near Larsa, the other near Isin (*RGTC* 3: 57).

Mesop. 358, *LKM* 608 (refs).

Dur-Abi-hara (sometimes incorrectly rendered 'Dur-Athara') M1 city of the Aramaean tribe Gambulu in southern Babylonia near the Elamite border. The Assyrian king Sargon II plundered Dur-Abi-hara in the course of his conquest of the tribe,

c. 710, and deported 18,400 of its inhabitants. Gambulu's territory was converted into an Assyrian province, and Dur-Abi-hara became its chief city under the new name Dur-Nabu (*Sargon II* *328, 430, 431).

Lipiński (2000: 472–3).

Dur-Adad-nirari Iron Age city in the middle Euphrates land of Laqe, western Mesopotamia, founded in early C8 by Nergal-erish (Palil-erish), governor of the region under the Assyrian king Adad-nirari III (**RIMA* 3: 211). Fifteen villages were attached to it.

Duranki see **Nippur**.

Dur-Ashur see **Atlila**.

Dur-balati Iron Age city in northern Babylonia, located on the west bank of the Euphrates within two days' march of the city of Sippar. The Assyrian king Tukulti-Ninurta II encamped his forces there during his last recorded campaign (885) which took him through the middle Tigris and Euphrates regions (**RIMA* 2: 174). Dur-balati joined in a widespread revolt against the Assyrian king Shalmaneser III (858–824) towards the end of his reign, initiated by the king's son Ashur-da'in-apla. The rebellion continued into the early regnal years of Shalmaneser's son and successor Shamshi-Adad V (823–811) before it was finally crushed (**RIMA* 3: 183).

Dur-Bel-Harran-belu-usur (*Tell Abta*?) M1 Assyrian city southeast of the Jebel Sinjar, founded by the Assyrian official Bel-Harran-belu-usur, who calls himself 'palace herald of the Assyrian king'. Bel-Harran-belu-usur records in an inscription on a stele found at Tell Abta, located on the Wadi Tharthar in northern Mesopotamia, that he was instructed to build the city in the desert (**RIMA* 3: 241–2). He claims to have completed it 'from top to bottom' and to have built therein a temple and a shrine for the great gods. The original inscription named Shalmaneser IV (782–773) as the Assyrian king at the time it was carved, but his name was later replaced by that of Tiglath-pileser III (745–727). The discovery of the stele at Tell Abta suggests that this was the site of the Assyrian city.

Dur-Ishtar Iron Age city in the middle Euphrates region subject to Assyrian rule. It was among the lands and cities assigned by the Assyrian king Adad-nirari III (810–783) to the governorship of a man called Nergal-erish (Palil-erish) (**RIMA* 3: 211). Twelve villages lay within its territory. Other cities assigned to Nergal-erish included Kar-Sin (with its ten villages), Dur-duklimmu (thirty-three villages), Dur-Ashur (twenty villages), Dur-Nergal-erish (thirty-three villages), Dur-Marduk (forty villages), Kar-Adad-nirari (126 villages), and Dur-Adad-nirari (fifteen villages). Nergal-erish undertook to rebuild all these settlements. See also **Nemed-Ishtar**.

Dur-Katlimmu (**Dur-aduklimmu** (also called **Magdalu** in M1), ***Tell Šayh (Sheikh) Hamad***) (maps 10, 13) City in northwestern Mesopotamia located on the east bank of the Habur, with a history of settlement from the Late Chalcolithic Age (late M4) to the early Islamic period. Preliminary investigations of the site by H. Rassam in 1879 were followed a century later by systematic excavations conducted by H. Kühne from 1978 onwards (and still under way) on behalf of the Free University of Berlin. During the Middle Bronze Age, the site was expanded from a small village to an urban settlement of relatively large proportions (c. 15 ha), which included a citadel and lower city. In the Late Bronze Age, the city fell first under Mitannian and subsequently under Assyrian control. In C13 it became one of the regional centres of the Assyrian empire, probably during the reign of Shalmaneser I (1274–1245). Important information about its administration in this period is provided by an archive of some 500 cuneiform tablets, unearthed in one of the wings of the governor's palace. From this archive the city's Assyrian name, Dur-Katlimmu, was identified. This name was already known from other Assyrian texts, though prior to the discovery of the archive, Dur-Katlimmu's location was unknown.

In the reign of the Assyrian king Ashur-bel-kala (1073–1056), the city provided the setting for a battle fought between Assyrian and Aramaean forces (**RIMA* 2: 102). Assyrian control was again imposed over Dur-Katlimmu in C9, early in the Neo-Assyrian period, when it was one of the cities of the land of Laqe. The Assyrian king Adad-nirari II visited it, claiming it as his own territory, during his campaign in the Habur region in 896 (**RIMA* 2: 153). His successor Tukulti-Ninurta II approached Dur-Katlimmu in the course of his last recorded campaign (885), which took him through the middle Euphrates region, and received a substantial tribute from it (**RIMA* 2: 177). In 878 Tukulti-Ninurta's son and successor Ashurnasirpal II encamped his forces for the night in Dur-Katlimmu during his campaign in the Habur region (**RIMA* 2: 213).

By late C8 the city had grown substantially in size, with the addition of almost 40 ha to the lower town. A new city wall, some 4 km in length, enclosed an area of c. 55 ha. Beyond the city walls a peripheral urban settlement contributed to the city's overall area of 110–120 ha. Dur-Katlimmu's total population at this time is estimated to have been c. 7,000. Broad streets and public open spaces were features of the newly expanded city, along with a palace, built in several stages and presumably housing the local governor, and impressive residences for high officials, with suites of rooms arranged around central courtyards. Dur-Katlimmu once more had the status of an important regional centre of the Assyrian empire. Excavations in the lower town have produced over 200 cuneiform tablets, including the C7 archive of a military official in the service of King Ashurbanipal called Shulmu-sharri. Also in the lower town, some 140 clay dockets bearing Aramaic inscriptions have been found, providing evidence of the growing use of Aramaic in the Neo-Assyrian administration. The city was connected to the Assyrian capital Ashur by a direct east–west route across dry steppe-land. Its relative proximity to Ashur has been suggested as one of the reasons for its choice as a regional centre of the Assyrian administration. Whatever the reasons were, they clearly outweighed the site's natural disadvantages. Because of the harsh, dry environment in which it was located, Dur-Katlimmu could not have existed, certainly not on the scale it achieved under the Assyrians, without a comprehensive and highly effective irrigation system. Traces of such an irrigation system have in fact been found not far from the city.

With the collapse of the Assyrian empire in 612, Dur-Katlimmu was among the Assyrian centres in Syria which were plundered and put to the torch by the Babylonian conquerors. But it was not totally destroyed. The site has produced vitally important documentary evidence for the immediate post-Assyrian era, in the form of cuneiform tablets written in Assyrian but dated to 602–600, early in the reign of the Babylonian king Nebuchadnezzar II. The city continued to flourish under Neo-Babylonian rule. Some of the former buildings of the Assyrian administration were reused, and another 'palace' was constructed, presumably as the residence of a Babylonian governor. The city continued to be occupied during the Persian empire (C6–4), and in the succeeding Hellenistic and Roman periods. But after the collapse of the Neo-Babylonian kingdom, the area occupied by Dur-Katlimmu's inhabitants reverted to what it had been prior to the city's expansion in late C8.

Röllig (1978), Kühne (1983–4; 1989–90; 1993–4; *OEANE* 5: 25–6, under *Sheikh Hamad, Tell*).

Dur-Kurigalzu (Parsa, *ʿAqar Quf*) (maps 11, 13) M2 and M1 city in central Mesopotamia, 30 km west of Baghdad. The site, which consists of several mounds covering an area of c. 225 ha, was identified as Dur-Kurigalzu by H. C. Rawlinson in 1861. It was excavated between 1942 and 1945 by an Iraqi–British team under the direction of S. Lloyd and T. Baqir, for the British School of Archaeology in Iraq and the Iraqi Directorate-General of Antiquities.

Though there are traces of an older settlement of C15 date, the city as such was built in early C14 or late C15 by the Kassite king Kurigalzu I to serve as the new administrative capital of the Kassite-ruled Middle Babylonian kingdom. The former capital Babylon continued to be the kingdom's most important cultural and religious centre. Material features of the site include a temple quarter dedicated to the god Enlil and containing a ziggurat, and a palace with large central hall, a throne-room, a room with wall-paintings depicting a procession of officials, and a treasury. The small finds from the palace include cuneiform tablets, gold jewellery and ornaments, glass inlays, and terracotta sculptures of a bearded man.

On the basis of archaeological evidence, the site is said not to have been reoccupied after its abandonment in C12. There are, however, a number of references to Dur-Kurigalzu in Iron Age texts. The Assyrian king Tiglath-pileser I (1114–1076) lists it among the places he conquered during a campaign in Babylonia (**RIMA* 2: 43). It was one of the Babylonian cities which fell victim to the Aramaean and Sutaean invasions of southern Mesopotamia during the reign of the Babylonian king Adad-apla-iddina (1069–1048) (**ABC* 180–1, where it is called Parsa; cf **RIMB* 2: 73 for the later account given by King Simbar-Shipak, 1026–1009). And it appears on the itinerary of the Assyrian king Tukulti-Ninurta II's last recorded campaign in 885; Tukulti-Ninurta is reported to have camped there for the night during his progress around the western and southern limits of his kingdom (**RIMA* 2: 173–4). The city was known in M1 Babylonian sources as Dur-Galzu (*RGTC* 8: 121).

Kühne (*OEANE* 1: 156–7, s.v. ʿAqar Quf).

Dur-Nabu see Dur-Abi-hara.

Dur-Ninurta-kudurri-usur Iron Age fortress in the land of Suhu, middle Euphrates region. It was built in mid C8 as a frontier post of Suhu by Ninurta-kudurri-usur, ruler of the land, who provided it with a garrison of mounted troops (**RIMB* 2: 298).

Dur-Papsukkal M1 city in the Diyala region, eastern Babylonia. In 814 the Assyrian king Shamshi-Adad V fought a battle there against a coalition of Chaldaean, Babylonian, Elamite, Namrite (see **Namri**), and Aramaean forces, who supported the Babylonian king Marduk-balassu-iqbi (**RIMA* 3: 188). Though Shamshi-Adad claimed victory in the conflict, the outcome was inconclusive. Nevertheless, Marduk-balassu-iqbi's days on the Babylonian throne were numbered. The following year, Shamshi-Adad led another campaign against him in the same region, on this occasion decisively defeating his army, capturing him, and deporting him to Assyria. Again in 812 Shamshi-Adad campaigned in eastern Babylonia, against the new Babylonian king Baba-aha-iddina. Dur-Papsukkal was conquered along with a number of other cities, including Der, Gannanate, Bit-reduti, and Me-Turan (**ABC* 168). Baba-aha-iddina, like his predecessor, was seized and deported to Assyria.

Dur-Shamshi-Adad One of two Middle Bronze Age Assyrian fortresses built on the Euphrates in 1786/1785 by the Assyrian king Shamshi-Adad I, probably in the region of Tell Ahmar. The other fortress was Dur-Adad. Both served as fortified frontier-posts facing the kingdom of Yamhad, and both had apparently been captured in an enemy assault by Sumu-epuh, king of Aleppo.

**LAPO* 17: 79–80, no. 492, *Mesop.* 160, 179.

Dur-Sharrukin (***Khorsabad***) (map 13) Iron Age Assyrian city located on the east bank of the Khosr., a tributary of the Tigris, 20 km northeast of Mosul. Dur-Sharrukin literally means 'Fortress of Sharrukin'. The city was named after its founder, the Assyrian king Sargon (Sharrukin) II (721–705), who began work on it c. 717. It was inaugurated as the Assyrian royal capital in place of Nimrud no later than 706. Over 100 official letters from the time of Sargon, preserved in the State Archives of Assyria, concern the administration of the massive construction project involved in building Khorsabad.

Excavations at Khorsabad were undertaken by P. É. Botta, French consul at Mosul, from 1843 to 1845, and continued by V. Place, Botta's successor in Mosul, from 1852 to 1854. Then followed a long interval before the Oriental Institute of the University of Chicago began new excavations in 1928. These continued until 1935, the most important being conducted from 1932 to 1935 under the direction of G. Loud. Further investigations were carried out in 1957 by the Iraqi Directorate-General of Antiquities.

Dur-Sharrukin is roughly square in shape and covers an area of c. 300 ha. It is enclosed within a wall, with access to the city provided by seven monumental gates, each named after a deity. The city's official government quarter occupied c. 23 ha in the northwestern sector of the site. It was walled off from the rest of the city, with its outer wall forming a projection jutting beyond the main line of the city's northwestern fortifications. The chief buildings in this quarter were the royal palace and a temple to the god Nabu, both raised on artificial platforms above the other buildings in the quarter. The palace was a large, multi-function complex, covering an area of c. 10 ha. It was laid out around three courtyards and contained c. 240 rooms, comprising the residential, religious, administrative, and ceremonial components of the palace. The palace's main entrance consisted of three monumental gateways, each guarded by a pair of colossal winged bulls. Inscriptions found in many parts of the palace and on the winged bulls at the entrance gates have provided much important information about

Figure 35 Courtier, palace of Sargon II, from Dur-Sharrukin.

Sargon's military and building achievements. The temple of Nabu was a 45-room complex incorporating five courtyards. One of the most important finds in the temple was the so-called Khorsabad King List, which provides a record of the names of Assyrian kings from early times down to the reign of Ashur-nirari V (754–746). Four other buildings uncovered within the official compound had extensive mural decorations. Similar in layout to the main palace, these buildings appear to have been residences for the elite elements of the city's population. On the basis of inscriptional evidence, the largest of them, which appears to have contained c. 200 rooms, has been identified as the residence of Sargon's brother, the vizier Sin-aha-usur. A temple to the Sebettu gods is among the building remains which came to light during the limited excavations carried out in the lower city.

Within a little more than a year of declaring Dur-Sharrukin the new Assyrian capital, Sargon was killed while fighting in Tabal in southern Anatolia. His city remained unfinished on his death, and the royal seat was promptly transferred to Nineveh by his son and successor Sennacherib. Dur-Sharrukin probably then continued to be an important centre of the Assyrian administration, under the immediate authority of a local governor, until the end of the Assyrian empire in late C7.

Frame (*OEANE* 3: 295–8), Battini and Villard (*DCM* 248–51).

Durum (*Umm al-Wawiya*?) Southern Mesopotamian city near Uruk, attested in Early and Middle Bronze Age texts. In late M3 it had the status of an appanage of the Ur III dynasty, when it seems to have served a military function, and subsequently, in early M2, of the kingdom of Isin. In this latter period it was governed by heirs to Isin's throne. For example, one of its governors was Ishme-Dagan, son and subsequently successor of Isin's king Iddin-Dagan (1974–1954). Some time after Ishme-Dagan's own reign, Durum was lost by Isin to the rival kingdom Larsa. We conclude this from bricks found on the site of Umm al-Wawiya inscribed with the name of Larsa's king, Gungunum (1932–1906). Later again, it came under the control of Uruk. This happened when a man called Sin-kashid (1865/1860–1833?) regained Uruk's independence from Larsa. Sin-kashid established a new dynasty in Uruk which held sway over a small kingdom, including Durum, until Uruk once more fell to Larsa in 1802. (Larsa's throne was at that time occupied by Rim-Sin.) In the same year, Larsa regained control over Durum.

Michalowski (1977), *Mesop.* 63, 72, 108, 109.

Dur-Yahdun-Lim (map 10) Middle Bronze Age city in the middle Euphrates region, in the district of Saggaratum, founded by Yahdun-Lim, king of Mari (1810–1794) (**RIME* 4: 603). Frequent references to the city in the Mari archives reflect its importance (it provided a central meeting point for representatives from the towns around it) and attest to a palace there. The city was known as Dur-Yasmah-Addu during the period when Yasmah-Addu, son of the Assyrian king Shamshi-Adad I (1796–1775), was viceroy in Mari. Lipiński suggests an identification with the site Tell Muhaisan on the right bank of the Euphrates just north of its confluence with the Habur.

Lipiński (2000: 89, 92), *LKM* 609 (refs).

Dur-Yakin ('Fortress of Yakin') Iron Age city in the marshlands of southern Mesopotamia, tribal capital of the Chaldaean tribe Bit-Yakin. The tribe was so named after Yakin (Iakin), its eponymous ancestor. In the last decades of C8, its ruler was a man called Marduk-apla-iddina (biblical Merodach-baladan), the most famous of several Chaldaean tribal leaders who became king of Babylonia. Marduk-apla-iddina gained the Babylonian throne in 721, and occupied it twice between this year and 710. He led Babylonia in a series of conflicts with Assyria, but at the end of 710 was forced to abandon his throne in Babylon at the approach of the Assyrian army under the command of Sargon II, and flee for his life. After unsuccessfully seeking asylum in Elam, his former ally, Marduk-apla-iddina returned to his tribal capital Dur-Yakin, which he used as his base for further resistance against Assyria. But he was defeated by Sargon's forces in a battle outside the city, and once more forced to flee for his life. He continued to rally fresh troops against the Assyrians (see under **Babylonia**), prompting Sargon to conduct further military operations in the area between 709 and 707. In this last year, Sargon laid siege to Dur-Yakin, and captured and plundered it (**ARAB II* 34–5, **ABC* 75). The city's fortifications were demolished, and its population deported and eventually resettled in Kummuh.

van der Spek (1977–8), Lipiński (2000: 434, 488, 532).

Duteti Iron Age city in Babylonia on the Euphrates. It became caught up in the conflicts in which the city of Borsippa was involved during the period when the Babylonian throne was occupied by the Chaldaean Nabu-shuma-ishkun (760–748) (**RIMB* 2: 124).

E

Ebenezer Early Iron Age city in northern Palestine, attested in *OT* tradition as the site where the Israelites pitched camp before their battle with the Philistines, reported in 1 Samuel 4:1–11. The Philistines, whose encampment was at Aphek, twice defeated the Israelites, and followed up their success by seizing the Ark of the Covenant; the Israelites had brought this from Shiloh in an attempt to secure victory after their first defeat. The site of Ebenezer, not yet identified, must have lain close to Tel Aphek, where the Philistines camped before the battle. An equation with ʿIzbet Sartah (q.v.) has been suggested.

Ebla (*Tell Mardikh*) (map 10) City in northern Syria, located 60 km southwest of Aleppo, with a history of occupation extending from the Early Bronze Age until the early Roman period (C2). It consists of a tell and surrounding lower city, fortified by a large earth-and-stone rampart penetrated by four gates. Excavation of the site was begun in 1964 by the Italian Archaeological Expedition of the University 'La Sapienza', under the direction of P. Matthiae. Prior to excavation, the city was already known from M3 Mesopotamian texts, which included records of its conquest by the Akkadian kings Sargon (2334–2279) and his grandson Naram-Sin (2254–2218) (for the latter, **DaK* 255–7, **CS* II: 244–5, **RIME* 2: 132–3), and economic texts from the Ur III dynasty (c. 2112–2004). Later references to it occur in texts from Alalah in northern Syria, dating to C17 and C15 (Alalah VII and IV respectively), and in the list of the C15 pharaoh Tuthmosis III's Syro-Palestinian conquests.

The city reached the height of its political and economic development in C24, during Early Bronze IV. Archaeologically, this phase of its history is designated as Mardikh IIB1. Its dominant architectural feature was a large, mudbrick palace, now called Palace G. Remains of two sides of the palace and part of a courtyard have been unearthed. Of particular importance was the discovery in this level, between 1974 and 1976, of the city's archives, consisting of c. 2,500 documents, written in cuneiform in the Sumerian and Eblaite languages (the latter is the earliest documented Semitic language). The contents of the archives include a wide range of economic, administrative, legal, lexical, literary, diplomatic, and epistolary texts. These provide valuable insights into the administration and daily life of Ebla and its relations with its surrounding region, during a period of about half a century towards the end of M3. Offering lists included in the texts provide the names of many kings of Ebla, members of a royal dynasty extending back as far as C27. The earliest of these kings is called Kulbanu, the latest Ishar-Damu. They ruled over a prosperous kingdom, part of whose wealth was derived from sheep and textile production.

After the destruction of Mardikh IIB1, presumably by Sargon or Naram-Sin (the latter boasts in one of his inscriptions to have been the first to conquer it; see **Armanum**), a settlement of much reduced proportions, designated as Mardikh IIB2,

Figure 36 Palace G, Ebla.

was built in the northern part of the site. The new city's most significant building was apparently another royal edifice, now referred to as the 'Archaic Palace', which probably dates to the period of the Ur III dynasty (Early Bronze IV). Ebla appears to have been destroyed once more c. 2000, but in the ensuing Middle Bronze Age it gained a new lease of life in the so-called Mardikh IIIA phase (c. 2000–1800) (see espec. Pinnock, 2001). The well-planned urban layout was defended by a double fortification wall, within which a number of sacred and secular buildings were constructed in the lower city, and large public buildings on the tell. There was some reconstruction of these buildings in the Mardikh IIIB phase, which extended into the early centuries of the Late Bronze Age (c. 1800–1600). The destruction of the city at the end of this phase has been associated with Hittite conquests in the region, probably those of King Mursili I (1620–1590).

Thenceforth, the city was largely abandoned. However, evidence of continuing, limited occupation is provided by the scattered remains which constitute the Mardikh IVA–B settlement of the final centuries of the Late Bronze Age (c. 1600–1200), and by the rural-type early Iron Age settlement of the Mardikh VA phase (c. 1200–900). The settlement grew in size in the following Mardikh VB–C phases, extending through the Neo-Assyrian, Neo-Babylonian, and early Persian periods (c. 900–535), with more substantial development in the Mardikh VIA–B phases, covering the later Persian, Hellenistic, and early Roman periods. But the tell appears to have been completely abandoned sometime during C2. Other parts of the site continued to be sparsely occupied until at least C3 CE, and perhaps through much of M1 CE.

Pettinato/Matthiae (*RlA* 5: 9–20), Matthiae (1980; 1985), Archi (1986), Pinnock (2001).

Ecbatana (*Hamadan*; Old Persian **Hagmatana**, Elamite **Agmadana**, Babylonian **Agmatanu**) (map 16) Western Iranian city, located in a commanding position on a major east–west route passing through the central Zagros mountains. Ecbatana is the Greek form of the city's name, first attested in C5 by Herodotus (1.98). The site has a known history of occupation from the second half of M1 down to the present day. The first excavations there were carried out by C. Fossey in 1913 on behalf of the French Archaeological Mission in Iran. Two large treasures uncovered in 1920 and 1923 (their precise findspot is not known) have been dated to the reign of the Persian king Artaxerxes II (404–359). In 1971, S. Swiny conducted an archaeological survey for the British Institute of Persian Studies, and excavations by M. Azarnoush in the same year brought to light part of a Parthian cemetery dating to C1 BCE–C1 CE. More substantial excavations were undertaken on the mound called Tepe Ecbatana in the northern part of Hamadan, under the auspices of the Archaeological Centre of Iran, beginning in 1983 under the direction of M. R. Sarraf. Eleven seasons were conducted between 1983 and 1999. Nine parallel streets with adjoining house units and two water channels, two massive towers, and a 9 m thick mudbrick outer wall were uncovered. The excavators have concluded from its strong fortifications that the site had important political and military functions. They were unable, however, to determine whether the excavated remains represent the anc. city of Ecbatana, in the absence of inscriptions to confirm this proposal. A comparison with the archaeological evidence from sites such as Sialk, Baba Jan, Godin Tepe, and Nush-i Jan has produced no similarities which might point to a definite dating of the remains on Tepe Ecbatana. Though it is clear that the mound was occupied in different periods, perhaps beginning in the Median period (first half of M1; see **Medes**), further excavation will be needed to indicate whether the buildings that have so far come to light on this site are actually remains of the Median city Ecbatana.

The earliest attestation of this city in western Asian sources is provided by the chronicle of the last Babylonian king Nabonidus, which reports that the Persian king Cyrus II, after his defeat of the Median forces led by Astyages in 550, marched upon the Median royal city Ecbatana; he carried off from it silver, gold, and other booty which he took to his city Anshan (**ABC* 106, **PE* 50, no. 1). Ecbatana thenceforth became a summer residence of the Persian royal dynasty. It later appears in the Persian king Darius I's Bisitun inscription (**DB* 32) as the place where the rebel Median leader Phraortes was impaled after his capture in a district of Media called Raga (c. 520), and his most prominent followers executed. The fortress from which they were hanged has been tentatively identified by Stronach (2003: 242) with the Masallah hill, a large outcrop of rock rising to a height of 80 m towards the eastern limits of mod. Hamadan. Stronach notes that the first hard evidence for the city's occupation comes from inscribed stone column bases of the late Achaemenid period, which appear to indicate the construction of an apadana (see glossary) at Hamadan by Artaxerxes II.

Herodotus (1.98) provides a fanciful description of Ecbatana, reporting that it was founded by a Median king called Deioces as an impregnable stronghold consisting of seven concentric circles of defensive walls, each higher than the one below. According to Herodotus, the bastions of the five outermost walls were painted in various colours, while those of the two innermost were covered respectively with silver and gold; the seventh wall enclosed the royal palace and the treasuries. A description of the palace itself was provided several centuries later by the Greek historian Polybius (10.27.1–13), who claims that it was 7 stades (c. 1.5 km) in circumference, contained a number of separate buildings, was constructed from cedar and cypress, and was embellished with tiles of silver and columns plated with silver or gold. Both Greek writers have contributed much to the semi-legendary image of Ecbatana as a city of great opulence and splendour. Polybius also notes that it was famous for its horses and its grain production.

In general, references to Ecbatana in Classical sources are now regarded by many scholars as having little historical value. Nor is there clear evidence in either archaeological or contemporary western Asian documentary sources to support the notion that Ecbatana was the anc. capital of Media. It has been suggested that if there had in fact been a chief city of the Medes in the first half of C6, 'it might well have been moved, either retaining its own name or having been given a new name' (Lanfranchi *et al.*, 2003: 400, n. 15).

Ecbatana fell to Alexander the Great in 330, and subsequently to the Seleucid king Seleucus I in 305. In C7 CE it came under Muslim control, since when it has fulfilled the role of a regional capital. Its continuous occupation has severely limited opportunities for further archaeological investigation, since much of the anc. city lies beneath later levels of settlement. Structures recently unearthed in the area accessible to archaeologists appear to date to after the Achaemenid period. The remains of a rectangular citadel constructed on an 80 m high outcrop of rock are apparently of C3 Parthian date.

Calmeyer (*RlA* 4: 64–7), Brown (*OEANE* 2: 186–7), Sarraf (2003).

Edom(ites) (map 8) A Semitic population group inhabiting, from C14 onwards (if not earlier), the land called Edom, which lay in southern Transjordan south of the Dead Sea and east of the Wadi ʿArabah. The Edomites also settled west of the Wadi ʿArabah, in the region called Seir. 'Edom' is derived from a Semitic word meaning 'red' or 'ruddy', reflecting the colour of the sandstone mountains in the region. The Edomites are first attested in the reign of the pharaoh Merneptah (1213–1203), who granted Edomite nomadic groups access to the pasturelands of the eastern Egyptian Delta. According to *OT* tradition, Edom was conquered by David (early C10; 2 Samuel 8:11–14); in the following century, it re-established its independence by staging a successful revolt against the Judaean king Jehoram (849–842; 2 Kings 8:20–2). Assyrian sources indicate that it was subject to Assyrian rule in C8 and C7, beginning with the reign of the Assyrian king Adad-nirari III (810–783) (**RIMA* 3: 213). The Assyrian king Tiglath-pileser III lists a certain Qaushmalaka of Edom among his tributaries (**Tigl. III* 170–1). Edom apparently enjoyed a flourishing existence in this period, due partly, perhaps, to the wealth it derived from its copper resources. The kingdom was finally destroyed by the Babylonians c. 550.

Bienkowski (1992), Labianca and Younker (1995), Bartlett (*OEANE* 2: 189–91).

Edrei (*Dar'a*) City in Transjordan, attested in *OT* tradition as the royal seat of Og, king of Bashan prior to the Israelite conquest. Og's defeat in a battle fought there with the Israelites (Numbers 21:33–5) resulted in the loss of his kingdom to the victors. In the Roman period, the city became a *polis* with the name Adraene.

It is to be distinguished from another city called Edrei in the territory of Naphtali near the Sea of Galilee, attested in Joshua 19:37 and in the list of Asiatic conquests of the C15 pharaoh Tuthmosis III.

Achtemeier (*HCBD* 270).

Eflatun (Iflatun) Pinar (map 2) Late Bronze Age (water-)spring sanctuary in southwestern Anatolia, to the east of Lake Beyşehir, 70 km west of mod. Konya. Stone blocks form a façade on the sanctuary's north side, 7 m long and decorated with reliefs. The central figures of the reliefs are two seated deities, a god on the right wearing a conical cap, and a goddess on the left. They have been conjecturally interpreted as a mountain god and a goddess of the spring. Above them are two winged sun-disks supported by six demons. The whole composition is surmounted by another sun-disk, now much worn, supported by two more pairs of demons – one in each pair standing upon the other. The lower part of the façade, recently exposed after the draining of the pool, depicts five more figures, identical in appearance, and possibly to be identified as mountain gods in view of the scaly lower halves of their bodies. There is no trace of any inscription. It has been suggested that the whole façade may have been crowned with two colossal divine statues – a god on the left, a goddess on the right – though this has been disputed. A likely date for the complex is late C13, during the reign of the Hittite king Tudhaliya IV, though the composition may have been commissioned by a local ruler rather than by the king. A number of scholars believe that the deities on the façade may derive from pre-Indo-European Hattian tradition, representing respectively a god of rivers and the underworld, and a chthonic fertility goddess.

Bittel (1976: 222; *RlA* 5: 33–6), Burney (2004: 78–9).

ʿEin Gedi (map 8) Oasis located on the western shore of the Dead Sea, southern Palestine. Its history of occupation begins in the Chalcolithic Age (M4), and is represented in later periods by settlements dating to the late Iron Age (late C7–early C6), Persian, Hellenistic, Roman, and Byzantine periods. Following several preliminary surveys, excavations were carried out for the Hebrew University in Jerusalem by B. Mazar, I. Dunayevsky, and T. Dothan from 1961 to 1965. The focus of their investigations was the mound called Tel Goren, the most prominent part of the oasis. Here, a number of barrel-shaped pithoi were found in the late Iron Age settlement on the mound, which was possibly, the excavators suggest, a centre of perfume production. The settlement was destroyed by fire, perhaps during the Babylonian king Nebuchadnezzar II's conquest of Judah in 582–581. It was rebuilt in the Persian period (C6–4), from which there are remains of a large building (550 sq. m), possibly an official's residence, with twenty-three rooms, enclosed courtyards, and storage areas. Occupation during the Hellenistic and Roman periods is indicated by the remains of citadels dating to these periods.

But ʿEin Gedi is probably best known for the important Chalcolithic (M4) sanctuary discovered on the terrace overlooking the spring. Revealed during one of the preliminary surveys by B. Mazar and J. Naveh, it was fully excavated in 1957. The sanctuary consists of a walled enclosure or courtyard, in the centre of which stands a circular structure about 3 m in diameter. The stone enclosure wall contains within its circuit

two rectangular buildings and two gateways. The larger of the two rooms, on the north side and opposite one of the gateways giving access to the spring, was identified by the excavators as a shrine. Consisting of a single broadroom with access on the long southern wall, the building contained an altar, around which were found many animal bones, pottery, and ashes. Benches lined the remaining wall spaces, and a number of pits were found containing burnt bones, horns, and pottery.
Stern (*OEANE* 2: 222).

ʿEin Gev (Arabic ***Khirbet el-ʿAsheq***) (map 8) Iron Age Aramaean city, consisting of acropolis and lower tell, located in Transjordan on the eastern shore of the Sea of Galilee. As part of Tel Aviv University's Land of Geshur Project, the site was excavated between 1990 and 1992 by a Japanese team under the direction of H. Kanaseki and H. Ogawa. A number of Iron Age strata were identified on both the lower tell and the acropolis, with two subsequent occupation levels dating to the Persian (C6–4) and Hellenistic (C4–1) periods. The city appears to have reached its peak in Iron Age II (early M1), when it was strongly fortified and contained a number of major public buildings. Kochavi comments that these buildings were probably connected with the trade in goods on the main road from Bashan to Akko and to the Via Maris (q.v.). The last Iron Age town was probably destroyed by the Assyrian king Tiglath-pileser III during his campaigns in northern Israel in 732. In the final Hellenistic phase of its existence, ʿEin-Gev served as the port for the nearby new city of Hippos/Susita.
Kochavi (*OEANE* 2: 223–4).

ʿEin-Shadud (map 8) Site in Israel on the northwest edge of the Jezreel plain, whose existence, first recognized in 1979, is indicated by Early Bronze Age remains. Most of the anc. site has been destroyed by modern construction. Salvage excavations were carried out by E. Braun and S. Gibson for the Israel Dept of Antiquities and Museums. They concentrated on two areas, which yielded two successive occupation levels. The earlier (Stratum II) built on virgin soil contained a number of stone wall foundations, and a rectangular broadroom with pebble floor and bench-lined interior. Stone pillar-bases indicated the roof supports. Stratum I, which was built directly above the earlier level, contained a number of buildings, mostly rectilinear in shape. Of particular note was a structure described by the excavators as a sausage-shaped house with parallel walls ending in two opposing curvilinear apses, but with otherwise typical broadroom features (internal benches and stone pillar bases). Among the other buildings of this level was a double broadroom with flagstone floor and several curvilinear walls. Grain-growing is indicated by sickle blades and grinding stones. And quantities of animal bones – of sheep, cattle, pig, goat, and ass – provide evidence of animal husbandry, for meat and other animal products. Ceramic finds from the site indicate that both occupation levels were of brief duration and are probably to be dated early in the Early Bronze I period. Cultural and trade contacts appear to have been limited to the Jezreel plain.
Braun (*OEANE* 2: 224).

ʿEin-Zippori, Tel (map 8) 1.5 ha village in the Lower Galilee region of Israel, 5 km north of Nazareth. Excavations have revealed five occupation levels, extending from Late Bronze Age I (c. 1550) through part of Iron Age II (C9). After the apparently sudden end of the first Late Bronze Age village, a second (Late Bronze II; Stratum IV) settlement was built on the site with a different layout, which continued in the succeeding Iron Age I period (Stratum III). The main feature of these two levels was a large building complex, which underwent some modification in its Iron Age phase. Adjoining it was an open courtyard containing several large storage jars and a quantity of imported Cypriot ware. In C10, the settlement was again rebuilt on a different plan (Stratum II). Its main feature was another multi-roomed complex, built in two stages. Also in this level were the remains of a rectangular building containing several large column bases. The site was apparently abandoned for a time in C10 before reoccupation occurred in C9 (Stratum I). A pillared hall on the western slope of the mound featured in this last settlement.

Dessel (*OEANE* 2: 227–8).

Ekallatum (Ekallate) (map 10) Mesopotamian city attested in M2 and M1 Assyrian texts. Its exact location is unknown, but it apparently lay west of the Tigris r., not very far from Ashur. Shamshi-Adad, son of an Amorite chief, seized the city c. 1796 (it may previously have been captured by Naram-Sin, king of Eshnunna), and used it as his base for the conquest of Upper Mesopotamia. This marked the beginning of Shamshi-Adad's career as the greatest ruler of the Old Assyrian kingdom. He subsequently took up residence in his newly established capital Shubat-Enlil (formerly Shehna, mod. Tell Leilan), but in his inscriptions he continued to designate himself as king of Ekallatum. To highlight the city's continuing importance within his realm, Shamshi-Adad made it a viceregal seat, occupied by his son Ishme-Dagan, heir to the Assyrian throne. He appointed his second son Yasmah-Addu as viceroy in the city of Mari on the Euphrates. It was essential to the security of Shamshi-Adad's kingdom that these two cities on the kingdom's most sensitive borders be firmly controlled. Ishme-Dagan had the particular responsibility of using Ekallatum as a base for protecting his father's realm against its most dangerous enemy, the kingdom of Eshnunna, which lay to the southeast.

Even after Shamshi-Adad's death, which marked the beginning of the disintegration of the Old Assyrian kingdom, Ishme-Dagan ensured that Ekallatum was strongly guarded and continued to serve, for a time, as an effective barrier against an invasion of Upper Mesopotamia from the south. Ishme-Dagan was an ally of the Babylonian king Hammurabi, and provided Hammurabi with troops for his war with the Elamites. His city was eventually seized and occupied by an army of Ibal-pi-El II, king of Eshnunna. However, the fall of Eshnunna to the Elamites in 1765 paved the way for Ishme-Dagan, who had spent several years in exile in Babylon, to re-establish himself in Ekallatum. But he became embroiled in further conflicts in the region, notably with Zimri-Lim, king of Mari, and Atamrum, king of Andarig. Hammurabi refused his request for military assistance; an alliance which he concluded with the Eshnunnite king Silli-Sin proved ineffective; and at the end of 1763 attacks on his city by his enemies forced him once more to seek refuge in Babylon. Hammurabi must have restored him to his throne once more, probably after the Babylonian conquest of Eshnunna in 1762, for in Assyrian records he is credited with a reign of forty years. We know that he was eventually succeeded by his son Mut-Askur. But after his second restoration to Ekallatum's throne, we do not know how he fared in Ekallatum, or in his dealings with his neighbours or his Babylonian overlord. The letters from Mari, which inform us about his activities, end abruptly with Mari's fall to Hammurabi in 1761.

During the Middle Assyrian era (c. 1353–1076), Ekallatum was once more under Assyrian control. In C12, however, it was captured by the Babylonian king Nebuchadnezzar I (1126–1105), and again by his successor-but-one Marduk-nadin-ahhe (1100–1083), who carried off the statues of its gods Adad and Shala. For some time it remained in Babylonian hands before the Assyrian king Tiglath-pileser I (1114–1076) managed to regain it, prior to launching attacks of his own on the northern cities of Babylonia. But according to the Assyrian king Sennacherib (704–681), the statues of Adad and Shala remained in Babylon until he himself brought them out of the city, 418 years later, and restored them to their place in Ekallate (**Sennach.* 83).

Unger (*RlA* 2: 319–20), *LKM* 609 (refs), van de Mieroop (2005: 56–61).

Ekal-pi-nari M1 Aramaean city in northern Mesopotamia, tentatively located by Lipiński at the confluence of the Tigris and Lesser Zab rivers. It was among the settlements of the Aramaean Yaush (Iasu) tribe plundered by the Assyrian king Ashur-dan II in his accession and first regnal year (934–933), after Yaushite tribesmen had travelled upstream along the Tigris, and presumably threatened Assyrian cities in the region (**RIMA* 2: 132–3).

Lipiński (2000: 412).

Ekalte (Yakaltum, ***Tall Munbaqa***) (map 2) Middle and Late Bronze Age site located in the Tabqa dam area in northeastern Syria on the west bank of the middle Euphrates r. Following its Middle Bronze Age origins, Ekalte grew substantially in the Late Bronze Age, developing into an important urban centre which extended over an area of c. 15 ha. It lay within the kingdom of Ashtata, and had been subject to Mitanni before the Mitannian empire was destroyed by the Hittite king Suppiluliuma I in the third quarter of C14 (**HDT* 45–6). The city had inner and outer areas of settlement, each enclosed within fortifications of gravel and brick on stone foundations. Cuneiform business and legal texts found in a number of the houses, which typically consisted of large central halls flanked by smaller rooms, indicate that the administration of the city lay in the hands of a group of elders, and another group called the 'Brothers' with their own official cylinder seal. These texts also refer to the important role of Ekalte's chief god Baalaka (Baal). One or more of the city's three known temples were presumably dedicated to his worship. In noting the economic importance of communal, non-royal authorities at Ekalte as well as at Emar and Hadid, Akkermans and Schwartz suggest that this may indicate a middle Euphrates tradition of strong communal authorities alongside or in competition with royal establishments.

Mayer/Machule (*RlA* 8: 417–19), Werner (1998), Akkermans and Schwartz (2003: 341–2, 345).

Ekron (Assyrian **Amqarruna**, ***Tel Miqne***) (map 8) Predominantly Iron Age site consisting of upper and lower tells, covering a total of c. 30 ha at its greatest extent (the upper tell occupied c. 4 ha). It is located in southern Palestine, 18 km east of Ashdod and 37 km southwest of Jerusalem, at the point where the Judaean hills meet the coastal plain; i.e. it lay on the frontier separating Philistia from Judah. The site was excavated by S. Gitin and T. Dothan from 1981 to 1996. Eleven archaeological strata were identified, beginning with the Middle Bronze Age, though pottery remains indicate habitation in M4 and M3 (Chalcolithic and Early Bronze Age) as well. Evidence of Middle Bronze Age occupation (Stratum XI) is provided by Middle Bronze II ceramic ware and the remains of fortifications surrounding both upper and lower settlements. The Canaanite city in its Late Bronze phases (Strata X–VIII) appears to have been unfortified, and confined to the upper tell. There is evidence of trading links with Anatolia, Cyprus, and the Aegean world. Egyptian influence is also reflected in a number of small finds. Ekron was destroyed by fire at the end of the Late Bronze Age, probably in the context of the Sea Peoples' movements through Syria and Palestine.

In its Iron Age I phase (Strata VII–IV), the city was rebuilt and occupied by the Philistines. Refortified and encompassing both tells, it became one of the five cities of the Philistine Pentapolis (see glossary). One of its most significant architectural features was a building complex, either a temple or a palace, with a megaron layout and central hearth, reminiscent of Mycenaean palace architecture, and suggestive to some scholars of an Aegean origin of the Philistines. The complex belongs to Stratum VI. At the end of Iron Age I, c. 1000, the lower city was destroyed and abandoned. In its Iron Age II phase (Strata III–II), which lasted c. 300 years until late C8, Ekron was confined to the small upper tell. Its destruction and subsequent modest reoccupation have been associated with a period of Israelite supremacy, interrupted by the pharaoh Sheshonq I's conquests (*OT* Shishak) in the region in the second half of C10.

This phase of Ekron's existence was abruptly ended in late C8 by the arrival of the Assyrians. Sargon II's siege of Ekron c. 712 was followed by the city's conquest in 701 by Sargon's successor Sennacherib. Ekron's citizens had previously removed their (apparently pro-Assyrian) king Padi from his throne and delivered him in chains to the Judaean king Hezekiah, to be held captive in Jerusalem, calling on Egypt for assistance against Assyria. In his campaign of retaliation against the allied forces, Sennacherib slew the governors and nobles of Ekron, hung their bodies on stakes around the city, and restored Padi to his city's throne (**Sennach.* 31–2). Ekron was now incorporated into the Assyrian empire. Under its king Ikausu (Akhayus) (son and successor of Padi), it was among the cities which supplied building materials to Sennacherib's successor Esarhaddon for his palace in Nineveh (*Borger, 1956: 60). Ikausu subsequently provided Esarhaddon's successor Ashurbanipal with reinforcements for his campaign against Egypt (c. 667). Ikausu appears also in a recently discovered five-line dedicatory inscription, in the Phoenician alphabetic script, as a member of a dynasty of five kings who ruled Ekron.

Under Assyrian sovereignty, Ekron was substantially redeveloped, now reaching its maximum size with the rebuilding of both the upper and the lower cities. During this phase of its history (represented archaeologically by Stratum IC), it became a major centre for the production of olive oil. Indeed, Ekron became the largest producer of olive oil in western Asia. This is reflected in the remains of the city's large olive oil industrial quarter, located along the interior of the city wall. Some 115 olive oil presses have come to light, with a production capacity of 500 tons.

In the last decades of C7, the waning years of the Assyrian empire, Ekron came under Egyptian sovereignty (Stratum IB), and was destroyed by the Babylonians in 603, during a campaign by the Babylonian king Nebuchadnezzar II against Philistia. A long period of abandonment was followed by occasional occupation in the Roman, Byzantine, and mediaeval periods.

Dothan and Gitin (*OEANE* 4: 30–5, s.v. Miqne, Tel), Laughlin (2006: 111–15).

Ekwesh (vocalization of Egyptian *Ikwš*) Late Bronze Age population group, listed in the inscription of the pharaoh Merneptah (1213–1203) on the east wall of the temple of Karnak among the so-called Sea Peoples who joined the Libyans in their attack on Egypt's frontiers during Merneptah's reign (**ARE III*: §579). The Ekwesh are also referred to in a contemporary inscription on the so-called Arthribis stele as belonging to 'the Countries of the Sea'. They probably formed the largest contingent among the allies of the Libyan chief Meryre in his ultimately unsuccessful onslaught on Egypt. It is possible that they were connected with the Ahhiyawans of the Hittite texts, whom most scholars now equate with Mycenaean Greeks. Ahhiyawa had enjoyed a significant presence and influence in western Anatolia through at least the latter part of C14 and for much of C13 (see **Ahhiyawa**). The connection between Ahhiyawa and Ekwesh remains speculative. But if it is valid, then the Ekwesh may represent remnants of Achaean/Mycenaean settlement along the western and southern Anatolian coast and offshore islands after Ahhiyawa's presence as a political power in western Anatolia came to an end in the last decades of C13, during the reign of the Hittite king Tudhaliya IV.

Sandars (1985: 221, index refs).

Elaea (*Kazıkbağları*) (map 5) M1 Greek city on the Aegean coast of northwestern Anatolia, located 24 km southwest of Pergamum in the region of Aeolis. According to Strabo (13.3.5), it was founded by Mnestheus of Athens at the time of the Trojan War. However, the city does not appear in Herodotus' list (1.149) of the eleven original Aeolian communities. In C5 it was a member of the Athenian Confederacy (see glossary), paying to the Confederacy's treasury the small sum of one-sixth of a talent per year, an indication of its relative unimportance at that time. It achieved greater prominence in the Hellenistic period when it served as a port-city for the kings of Pergamum. But the shoreline has long since receded. The meagre surviving material remains of the city include a few blocks from the city wall, and the remnants of the city's harbour works.

Bean (1966: 112–14; *PECS* 295).

Elam (maps 13, 16, 17) Located in western Iran, one of the most important powers of the anc. western Asian world, with a history extending over 2,000 years, from M3 until mid M1. 'Elam' is the Sumerian name for the country, which at its greatest extent stretched across the Zagros mountains from mod. Khuzestan to Fars. The Babylonians called it Elamtu, and the Elamites themselves referred to their country as Haltamti or Hatamti. In the inscriptions of the Persian king Darius I (522–486) it is called Uja. At the peak of its development in M2, the kingdom of Elam incorporated both highland and lowland regions of southern and western Iran. Throughout its history Elam was closely linked with the polities and kingdoms of Mesopotamia. Its earliest known contacts were with the Sumerian city-states in southern Mesopotamia. With these it enjoyed a certain measure of peaceful interaction, diplomatic and commercial, though militaristic ambitions and the desire for territorial expansion frequently brought the Elamites and their western neighbours into open conflict.

It was long assumed that writing developed around the same time, though probably independently, in Sumer and Elam. The basis for this assumption was an assemblage of c. 1,550 texts which were discovered in Susa (Susa III period), the lowland city in mod. Khuzestan which later became one of the royal capitals of Elam (the other main centre of Elam was Anshan in Persis). Scholars once believed that these texts, which were written in a pictographic script and are datable within the period c. 3100 to

2900, were the ancestors of the later 'Old Elamite' inscriptions, dating to later M3 and early M2. Hence they were dubbed 'Proto-Elamite'. In fact, it is now clear that the inscriptions so designated have no connection with the later Elamite inscriptions. The Susa III inscriptions clearly pre-dated the arrival of the Elamites upon the western Asian scene, and therefore the term 'Proto-Elamite' is inappropriate and misleading.

While Elam may first be referred to as early as 3000, in texts from Uruk, the kingdom is not clearly attested before mid M3. The first genuine Elamite tablets, written in the Mesopotamian cuneiform script, appeared about this time. However, these tablets are small in number (five inscribed pottery sherds, eleven inscriptions on stone), and the language which they record is related to no other known language, and is still imperfectly understood. As a result, the information we have from them is largely confined to the names of kings and their royal capitals, and a few indications of ongoing conflicts with Mesopotamian peoples and kingdoms. The most extensive of the Old Elamite inscriptions was found, in a damaged state, at Susa, in the temple of the god Inshushinak. It is commonly considered to be a treaty which the Akkadian king Naram-Sin drew up with a king of Awan (q.v.) called Hita (who appears as no. 11 in the Old Babylonian list of kings of Awan and Shimashki) (*Hinz, 1967). But neither Hita nor Awan is actually named in the document, which imposes upon the unidentified ruler obligations similar to those specified in a vassal treaty. Most of the information we have about the first thousand years of Elamite history comes from Mesopotamian sources. In theory, the earliest recorded events in this history date to c. 2500 and occur in the Sumerian King List. This document reports an attack by Enmebaragesi (Enishibbaragesi), king of the Sumerian city-state Kish, upon Elam, and subsequently an attack by Awan on the city of Ur, which resulted in kingship, or hegemony over southern Mesopotamia, being carried off to Awan, until it was regained by Kish (**Chav.* 83). We should, however, remember that the King List is an early M2 composition (c. 1800), of very limited value as a source of historical information. On the other hand, a number of Mesopotamian texts which do date to mid and late M3 indicate frequent conflicts between Elam and its neighbours in southern Mesopotamia. And Elam was the object of a number of military campaigns by kings of both the Akkadian and Ur III dynasties.

In the first of these, the Akkadian king Sargon (2334–2279) led a major expedition into the highland regions of western Iran, where he conquered Elam (along with other states, including Parahshum, Awan, and Susa) (**DaK* C7: 178–81) and added it to his empire. His son and successor Rimush (2278–2270) conducted another major campaign in the east, against a military coalition made up of Elam, Parahshum, and Zahara (**RIME* 2: 52–67). The coalition forces were crushed, with 16,212 of their troops killed, according to the Akkadian report, and another 4,216 taken prisoner, including the Elamite king Emahsini. Elam was restored firmly to Akkadian control, where it remained through at least the reign of Rimush's brother and successor Manishtushu (2269–2255). Manishtushu's successor Naram-Sin (2254–2218) may have conducted further campaigns against Elam, but the chronology of these is unclear.

Until M2, Elam was probably essentially a highland confederacy, perhaps comprising a core Elamite kingdom centred on Anshan, now identified with Tal-e Malyan (Tepe Malyan) in the region of mod. Fars, and a broader Elamite confederacy of fluctuating composition, made up of a number of highland polities. It has been suggested that Elam resembles what political anthropologists define as a segmentary state: 'Both temporary and longer-lasting alliances seem to have been forged between the constituent members of the greater Elamite segmentary federation which benefited all parties and drew them together in opposition to a common enemy' (D. T. Potts, 1999: 157). Whatever the nature of its composition, the Elamite confederacy appears to have withstood a number of attacks by the aggressive, expansionist Ur III dynasty in the last century of M3 (though it may have suffered a brief conquest in this period), and to have retained its independence, while Susa and its surrounding lowland region succumbed to the invaders and were incorporated into the Ur III empire. It is clear from Mesopotamian texts of late M3 and early M2 that Elam and Susa were up to this time separate political and geographical entities, contrary to a longstanding assumption (based e.g. on *OT* sources) that Susa had always been a centre or stronghold of the Elamite kingdom.

Resistance to the Ur III empire came to a head with the emergence from the Elamite confederacy of the Shimashki dynasty which led an alliance against Ibbi-Sin (2028–2004), the last of the Ur III kings. The forces of Ibbi-Sin were routed, his kingdom was destroyed, and his capital Ur was looted and placed for the next twenty-one years under Elamite military occupation. Susa had been a member of the victorious alliance. It thenceforth became an integral part of the kingdom of Elam, and one of the kingdom's royal seats was established there. Under the successive regimes of the Shimashki and the sukkalmah (Epartid) dynasties (c. 2100–1600), Elam became one of the largest and most powerful of the western Asian kingdoms with extensive diplomatic, commercial, and military interests both in Mesopotamia and Syria. Its territories extended north to the Caspian Sea, south to the Persian Gulf, eastwards to the desert regions of Kavir and Lut, and westwards into Mesopotamia. In this last region, its expansion was halted in mid C18 by the Babylonian king Hammurabi. Letters from the C18 Mari archives report conflicts between Elam and Babylon during Hammurabi's reign (e.g. **LKM* 320–1). To counter Elamite aggression and expansion west of the Tigris, Hammurabi formed an alliance, and engaged in an exchange of troops, with the Mariote king Zimri-Lim (1765). Yarim-Lim, king of Aleppo, also became a member of the alliance. But the task of driving out the Elamite occupation forces was made more difficult by the fact that the local northern Mesopotamian rulers were divided in their loyalties into pro- and anti-Elamite factions. Eventually, however, the western alliance began gaining the upper hand, and the Elamite king was forced to withdraw his forces along the Tigris, in the process ravaging the territory of Eshnunna before returning to Susa. (For this whole episode, see Charpin, 2003: 69–81.)

Early in the reign of Hammurabi's successor-but-one Abi-eshuh (1711–1684), an Elamite campaign which Kutir-Nahhunte, prince of Susa, conducted into Babylonia allegedly resulted in the conquest of thirty Babylonian cities. But this conquest seems to have left no lasting impact on the Mesopotamian scene, and during the Babylonian empire's declining years Elam was itself to enter into several centuries of relative weakness and insignificance. In late C14 the Babylonians, now under Kassite rule, carried out a devastating campaign in Susiana, led by their king Kurigalzu II (1332–1308), who captured Susa and set up his statue in one of its temples, proclaiming himself the conqueror of Susa and Elam. By C13, however, Elam was again emerging as a major power. Ambitious construction projects were undertaken, for example by King Untash-napirisha who built a new religious and ceremonial royal city called Al-Untash-Napirisha (mod. Chogha Zanbil; q.v.). Renewed conflicts broke out with Mesopotamian states, most notàbly the Kassite kingdom of Babylon. The Elamite king Shutruk-Nahhunte I (1185–1155), second (known) ruler of the so-called Shutrukid dynasty, invaded Babylonia, capturing many of its cities, and installing his son Kutir-Nahhunte on the throne of Babylon. A Kassite king, Enlil-nadin-ahi (1157–1155), was subsequently put on the throne by the Elamites as a subject-vassal, but his rule was abruptly terminated when he rebelled against his overlords, was defeated in battle by Kutir-Nahhunte, and sent as an exile to Susa. This brought Kassite rule over Babylonia to an end. Babylon's conflict with Elam was inherited by the rulers of the Second Dynasty of Isin (see under **Babylonia**). Elam suffered a defeat, c. 1110, at the hands of Nebuchadnezzar I (1126–1105), fourth king of the dynasty, who went on to sack the city of Susa. Conflict between the two kingdoms continued sporadically and inconclusively for many years.

In the final phase of its existence, the so-called Neo-Elamite period (1100–539), Elam's role in western Asian affairs seems to have been a greatly diminished one. Indeed, we have no written sources of information about Elamite history during the first 350 years of this period, except for an Assyrian reference to its participation in

Figure 37 Elamite figurine (c. C15), perhaps goddess Ishtar/Ashtarte.

a military alliance which supported the Babylonian king Marduk-balassu-iqbi against the Assyrian king Shamshi-Adad V in their military confrontation at Dur-Papsukkal in 814 (*RIMA 3: 188). In 720, the recently enthroned Assyrian king Sargon II claimed to have won a victory over the Elamite king Humban-nikash (743–717) at the city of Der, in the Diyala region of eastern Babylonia (*CS II: 296). But according to a report of the battle in a Babylonian chronicle, it was Humban-nikash who won the engagement (*ABC 73–4). Brinkman (1984: 48) points out that the immediate result of the battle was a stalemate: 'The Elamites bested the Assyrian army in the field and gained territory south of Der, but the Assyrians retained control of the city.' In late C8, Babylonian sources indicate a resurgence of Elamite power in the reigns of Shutruk-Nahhunte II (716–699), who ascended the throne after the death of Humban-nikash (*ABC 74), and his brother and successor Hallushu (699–693). The latter had seized the throne in a palace coup (*ABC 77). (On the question of Hallushu's identity, see D. T. Potts, 1999: 268–9.)

At this time, Assyria's aggressive expansionism prompted Babylonia and Elam to form an alliance against it. Both Shutruk-Nahhunte and his brother had sought to weaken Assyria's control of territories east of the Tigris by supporting a Chaldaean tribal leader called Marduk-apla-iddina II (the Merodach-baladan of Assyrian records), who gained kingship in Babylonia c. 721 and united the country against Assyrian rule. Marduk-apla-iddina's protracted struggle with the Assyrians ultimately proved unsuccessful. But when the Assyrian king Sennacherib was attempting to hunt him down in the marshlands of southern Babylonia, and then pursued him from there into Elamite coastal territory (c. 700), Hallushu countered by launching an attack on the northern Babylonian city of Sippar, where he captured the Assyrian crown prince Ashur-nadin-shumi, who had been appointed king of Babylonia by his father Sennacherib (*ABC 78). The Assyrian prince was taken to Elam, where he was probably executed, and the Elamites put their own appointee, the Babylonian Nergal-Ushezib, on the Babylonian throne in his place, c. 694.

The following year, Sennacherib did battle with the Elamite and Babylonian forces near Nippur, which had been captured by Nergal-Ushezib. Sennacherib's victory in the confrontation firmly re-established his authority over Babylonia. Nergal-Ushezib was captured, taken to Nineveh, and executed. Hallushu managed to escape back to Susa, but was killed there by his own people (*ABC 79). He was succeeded by a certain Kudur, identified with the Kudur-nahundu of Sennacherib's Annals (*Sennach. 40–1) and thus designated now as Kutir-Nahhunte II (see further D. T. Potts, 1999: 271). In 680, the governor of the Sealand, Nabu-zer-kitti-lisir, sought refuge in Elam after the Assyrian king Esarhaddon foiled his attempt to capture the city of Ur. But he was executed by the newly enthroned Elamite king Humban-haltash II (*ABC 82), who had succeeded his father Humban-haltash I in the preceding year (*ABC 81). This execution may well have been intended by Humban-haltash as an act of goodwill towards his Assyrian counterpart. None the less, relations between Elam and Assyria remained hostile during his brief reign, very likely because of Elam's continuing territorial ambitions in Babylonia. In 675 an Elamite army invaded the country and entered the city of Sippar. But the death of Humban-haltash in this year, Esarhaddon's sixth regnal year, and the withdrawal of the Elamite army from Babylonian territory marked the beginning of an improvement in relations with Assyria (*ABC 83–4), as reflected in the decision by the new king, Urtak(u), brother of

Humban-haltash II, to return to Agade statues of the gods probably taken from the city in an Elamite raid.

This gesture was perhaps associated with a treaty which Urtaku drew up with Esarhaddon. Urtaku appears to have maintained good relations with Assyria during Esarhaddon's remaining years and the early years of his son and successor Ashurbanipal (668–630/627). But hostilities with Assyria erupted afresh when Urtaku joined forces with Bel-iqisha, chief of the Aramaean Gambulu tribe, and Nabu-shum-eresh, governor of Nippur, for an attack on Assyrian subject territories in Babylonia (refs in Lipiński, 2000: 474, nn. 541–5). Ashurbanipal's ensuing conflict with Elam and Gambulu seems not to have been finally resolved until some years after the death of Urtaku c. 664 and the seizure of his throne by a usurper called Te-Umman. In his Elamite campaign of 653, Ashurbanipal defeated and killed Te-Umman in a battle at the Ulaya r. (Classical Eulaeus; *BAGRW* 93 E2).

From this time onwards, the pattern of decline in Elam becomes increasingly marked. The steady decrease in the numbers of towns and cities, evident from the beginning of M1, continued, particularly in the kingdom's lowland areas, as more and more places were abandoned. The greatest single blow to the kingdom was struck in 646, when the Assyrians sacked the Elamite capital Susa. The last known Elamite king, Humban-haltash III, fled the city and took refuge in the mountains, but was captured by local tribesmen and handed over to the Assyrians. Nevertheless, a fragmentary Elamite kingdom survived, and managed to secure an alliance with Babylon. W. Henkelman (2003: 183) argues that there may in fact have been a significant revival of Elamite power after the fall of Assyria, noting the first Neo-Babylonian king Nabopolassar's claim that he returned to Susa the statues of its gods which the Assyrians had carried off and relocated in Uruk (**ABC* 88).

But after the fall of the last Neo-Babylonian king, Nabonidus, to the Persian Cyrus II in mid C6, the Persian dynasty established its control over all territories formerly belonging to the Elamite kingdom. Elam was among the lands of the Persian empire listed several times in the inscriptions of Darius I (522–486), e.g. in his Bisitun inscription (**DB* 6), and also in the *daiva* inscription (see glossary) of his son and successor Xerxes I (**XPh* 3). Elamite resistance to Persian rule continued to surface for some years, culminating in three Elamite uprisings at the beginning of Darius I's reign (**DB* 16, 22, 71). But the rebellions were crushed, and Elam had by this time effectively ceased to exist as a political entity (though a delegation of six Elamites is depicted on the east staircase of the Audience Hall or Apadana at Persepolis, bringing tribute to Darius in the form of bows, daggers, and a lioness with cubs). For a time, the Persian kings ensured the survival of the Elamite language by using it in their monumental inscriptions, as in Darius' trilingual inscription at Bisitun (q.v.) (whose Elamite version is the longest known Elamite text), and as a chancellery language in administrative documents. But it probably rapidly died out as a spoken language, along with all other traces of the Elamite civilization, except for a few references in documents of the Hellenistic period.

De Meyer *et al.* (1986), Zadok (1991), Brentjes (1995), Henrickson (*OEANE* 2: 228–34), D. T. Potts (1999).

Elenzash M1 city in the kingdom of Ellipi (q.v.), located in the central Zagros highlands. After his conquest of Ellipi in 702, the Assyrian king Sennacherib annexed part of its territory and made Elenzash its capital, under the new name Kar-Sennacherib (**Sennach.* 28–9). He placed the city under the authority of the governor of Harhar (q.v.).

Elhunia Country attested in the texts of the Assyrian king Tukulti-Ninurta I (1244–1208), located in northeastern Mesopotamia. It is listed among the lands in the region over which Tukulti-Ninurta established or restored Assyrian sovereignty at the beginning of his reign (**RIMA* 1: 240, 244).

El-Khalil see **Hebron**.

Ellipi (map 13) Iron Age kingdom of western Iran, located in Luristan in the central Zagros highlands to the north of Elam. The kingdom had been established by C9 or earlier, and is attested in Assyrian texts from the time of Shalmaneser III (858–824). Shalmaneser reports that he received tribute from its king, Baru, during his campaign in the western Zagros region in 843 (**RIMA* 3: 40). The Assyrian king Adad-nirari III (810–783) lists the kingdom among his conquests in northeastern Mesopotamia and northwestern Iran (**RIMA* 3: 212). During the reign of Tiglath-pileser III (745–727), Ellipi's king Dalta is listed among Assyria's tributaries (**Tigl. III* 98–99, 108–9, **PE* 22, no. 1(i)). Dalta continued to occupy his country's throne into the reign of the Assyrian king Sargon II (721–705). But in Sargon's early regnal years, he appears to have broken his ties with Assyria, to judge from the fact that the country of Harhar, which bordered Ellipi to the northwest, declared its allegiance to him after expelling its own ruler who had remained loyal to Assyria. Sargon eventually took action against Harhar in 716 (see **Harhar**), and Dalta apparently reaffirmed his loyalty to Assyria. But his renewed Assyrian allegiance caused unrest among the pro-Elamite local aristocracy, prompting the intervention of Sargon himself in the kingdom during his expedition into Median territory in 713.

Sargon made Dalta's position secure on Ellipi's throne. But within a few years his protégé died, and a power struggle broke out between the pro-Assyrian Aspabara and his half-brother Nib'e, who supported Elam. Again Sargon intervened, during his final Median campaign in 706. He defeated and captured Nib'e, who had taken refuge in a stronghold called Mar'ubishtu, and installed Aspabara on Ellipi's throne. Because of Aspabara's loyalty to Assyria, Ellipi retained its independence, though with diminished importance. However, in the reign of Sargon's son Sennacherib (704–681), Aspabara switched his support to Elam. Sennacherib retaliated by invading Ellipi in 702, in the course of his war with Elam, and crushed all resistance there. The defeated kingdom was further weakened when Sennacherib deprived it of one of its provinces which he annexed to his own kingdom, to be used for the settlement of deportees from his conquests in other lands. Sennacherib made Elenzash the capital of the reduced kingdom, under its new name Kar-Sennacherib, and placed it under the authority of the governor of Harhar (**Sennach.* 28–9). However, anti-Assyrian feelings remained strong in the kingdom, and it subsequently joined a coalition against Assyria led by Elam and Babylon in 691, which confronted the Assyrian forces in an indecisive battle at Halule (q.v.) on the Tigris.

Diakonoff (1985: 86–8), Grayson (1991a: 112; 1991b: 93–5, 97), *SAA* XV: XXIX–XXXI.

Ellipu M1 northern Mesopotamian(?) city attested in an inscription on a bronze band from Balawat (see **Imgur-Enlil**), dating to the reign of the Assyrian king Ashurnasirpal II (883–859) (**RIMA* 2: 346). The inscription labels a pictorial depiction of plunder deposited in the palace of Ashurnasirpal from the city of Ellipu, which is otherwise unknown. It almost certainly had no connection with the Iranian kingdom called Ellipi.

Elmalı (map 15) Mod. town in inland Lycia, southwestern Anatolia, and a plain of the same name where two tumuli with built and painted tomb chambers were discovered in 1969–70. One of these, at the site of Kızılbel, 3 km southwest of the town of Elmalı, is a gabled chamber with friezes dating to c. 530. The friezes depict mythological and ceremonial scenes, a warrior departing by chariot apparently for war, hunting scenes, and a sea voyage. The other tumulus, located at Karaburun, 5 km northeast of Elmalı, has a single frieze, dated to c. 480 on the basis of the Graeco-Persian style of its paintings. The deceased tomb owner is portrayed on the main wall of this tomb, reclining on a couch and attended by his wife and servants. The scenes on the side walls depict his funerary rites with accompanying chariot procession, and a battle scene in which the deceased also appears, fighting against Greeks. At this time Lycia was under Persian control, and the deceased was evidently an official in the pro-Persian administration of the region. Greek artistic styles and motifs are a common feature of Lycian art and architecture during the period of Persian political dominance in C5 and early C4.

Mellink (1998).

el-Qadi, Tell see **Dan**.

El-Qitar (map 10) Late Bronze Age fortress-settlement (= anc. Til-Abni?), covering 6 ha, located 9 km south of mod. Bazi in northeastern Syria. The settlement, which consisted of upper and lower sections, was enclosed within stone walls with towers built at intervals along them. The site probably reached the peak of its development in C15, though the only firm dating for it is provided by a C13 Assyrian tablet with a sealing inscribed with Luwian hieroglyphs.

McClellan (1987), Akkermans and Schwartz (2003: 344).

Eluhat (Eluhut) Middle and Late Bronze Age city located in the southern foothills of the Kashiyari range (mod Tur ʿAbdin), northern Mesopotamia, probably in the region known as Ida-maras in the Middle Bronze Age. Eluhut is first attested in the C18 Mari archives as an ally of the cities of Tushhum (Tushha, Tushhan) and Shinamum (*LAPO* 17: 50, n. a). It was the capital of Sharraya, a vassal of the Mariote king Zimri-lim (1774–1762), later replaced by Shukru-Teshub. In the Late Bronze Age it belonged to the kingdom of Hanigalbat, following the Hittite destruction of the Mitannian kingdom in the third quarter of C14. When the Hanigalbatean king Wasashatta rebelled against Assyrian sovereignty, Eluhat was among the cities conquered by the Assyrian king Adad-nirari I (1307–1275) in the course of crushing the rebellion (**RIMA* 1: 131).

LAPO 18: 454.

Elymais Derived from Elam, the name assigned in Greek and Roman sources to the western part of Elam (roughly the mod. province of Khuzestan). Its inhabitants were called Elymaeans. In late Akkadian cuneiform sources, the names Elam and Elamites continued to be used alongside these Classicized forms. The Elymaeans are first attested, in the role of raiders and plunderers, in the memoirs of the C4 writer Nearchus, cited by Strabo (11.13.6). Elsewhere, Strabo refers to the Elymaeans as brigands living in the mountainous regions close to Susiana (15.3.12; 16.1.17). He mentions three provinces of Elymais: Gabiane, Massabatene, and Korbiane. The Elymaeans' territory was larger and more diverse than that of their neighbours, the Paraetaceni (who are first attested in Herodotus 1.101). Farmers inhabited Elymais' fertile areas, while its mountainous regions served as a nursery for soldiers (Strabo 16.1.18). Noted for their warlike qualities, and particularly for their skill with the bow, the Elymaeans frequently conducted raids into Babylonia. During the Hellenistic period, their land seems to have been loosely controlled by the Seleucid kings. Elymaean archers fought in the army of the Seleucid Antiochus III in his disastrous encounter with the Romans at the battle of Magnesia in 190. With the decline and disappearance of the Seleucid empire, Elymais appears to have regained its independence for a time, until the Parthians became dominant in the region, from C1 BCE until C3 CE.

D. T. Potts (1999: 354–409).

Emar (*Meskene*) (maps 3, 10) Bronze Age city, 70 ha in extent, in northeastern Syria, built on top of a large artificial terrace on the west bank of the middle Euphrates, at the junction of major land and river routes. The site of the known city is now partially covered by Lake Assad, which was created by the construction of the Tabqa Dam in the 1970s. Excavations were carried out by J.-C. Margueron on behalf of the French Commission of Excavations of the Ministry of Foreign Affairs between 1972 and 1978. In 1996, following the development of the dam and lake, a new campaign of excavations was begun, to examine those areas of the site left clear of the water. This project has been undertaken jointly by the Syrian Dept of Antiquities and the University of Tübingen, under the direction of J. Massou and U. Finkbeiner.

Prior to the excavations, the name Emar was known from M3 texts found at Ebla, and from M2 texts unearthed in Mari, Nuzi, and Ugarit. It is clear from these texts that Emar had, by early M2, become a major commercial centre within its region, providing an important focus for the economic and commercial activities of Mesopotamia and northern Syria. Parts of this early city have begun to be revealed by the Syrian/German mission, including an area of Early Bronze Age houses and a stretch of the Middle Bronze Age defensive wall. But the most extensively excavated phase of the city's history belongs to the Late Bronze Age, as revealed by the earlier French team. This new city was built by the Hittites, its founder being either the Hittite king Suppiluliuma I (1350–1322) or his son and second successor Mursili II (1321–1295). It became the capital of the Hittite subject kingdom Ashtata, which extended along the Euphrates to the borders of Carchemish on the north and Aleppo on the west. Immediate jurisdiction over the city was in the hands of the Hittite viceroy at Carchemish.

The Late Bronze Age site had been levelled and terraced to accommodate a palace, residential quarters, and four temples. The city's main religious precinct incorporated two temples, dedicated to the worship of Baal and Astarte. The palace, residence of the local ruler, was of the *bit hilani* type (see glossary). It is the earliest example so far discovered in Syria of this kind of building, which became a feature of later northern Syrian residential architecture. During the excavations, approximately 800 cuneiform tablets and fragments were brought to light, dating from C14 to C12. A small number of these are written in Hittite and Hurrian, but the great majority are in Akkadian and

Figure 38 Emar-Meskene.

Sumerian. Many of the tablets cover a range of economic activities and legal transactions. Other tablets contain lexical, omen, and literary texts (the last of these including fragments of the Gilgamesh epic), and there are some 200 texts describing festivals and ritual practices. Much valuable information is provided by these texts about life and society in Late Bronze Age Emar. More generally, they constitute our second most important source of contemporary written information (after the archives of Ugarit) on Late Bronze Age Syria. It is clear that although the Hittites were actively involved in the daily affairs of the kingdom, administrative responsibilities were divided between the Hittite viceroy and the local ruler. The latter was supported by a council of elders. This group, based apparently on a clan system, seems to have exercised an important consultative role, which in effect considerably circumscribed the local ruler's powers. The Hittite king and his viceroy reserved the right to intervene directly in Emar's judicial affairs. Thus a dispute over property and taxes between a priest of Emar and the local Hittite garrison commander was referred, on appeal by the priest, to the Hittite king for arbitration (*Singer, 1999b). The viceroy at Carchemish also became involved in the case. Judgment was given in the priest's favour.

Emar was destroyed, c. 1187, during the upheavals associated with the collapse of many centres of power at the end of the Late Bronze Age, including the kingdom of Hatti. There was some reoccupation of the site in late M1 during the Roman period. The settlement established there was called Barbalissus. Occupation continued on a modest scale through the Byzantine and mediaeval periods.

Beyer (1982), *Arnaud (1986), Huehnergard/Margueron (*RlA* 8: 93), Margueron (1995), Zaccagnini (1995), *J. G. Westenholz (2000), Faist and Finkbeiner (2002), D'Alfonso *et al.* (2008).

Emirgazi (map 2) Late Bronze Age site, probably a sanctuary, located in south-central Anatolia in the Konya plain. Six stones inscribed with Luwian hieroglyphic inscriptions were discovered there, five by W. M. Ramsay in 1904 and 1908, and a sixth fragmentary block by S. Alp in 1957. All are now housed in the Ancient Oriental Museum in Istanbul. Four of the stones, which range in height from 44 to 106 cm, are roughly cylindrical in shape and can be identified as altars, designated as A, B, C, and D. The inscriptions on them were first published by B. Hrozný in 1936, and subsequently by P. Meriggi in 1975 and E. Masson in 1979. The most recent and most authoritative edition of the texts is that of J. D. Hawkins, published in 1995. The inscriptions, which were commissioned by the Hittite king Tudhaliya IV (1237–1209), contain regulations concerning sacrificial offerings and the protection of the altars, with strict prohibitions against damaging or removing them. The remaining two stones are rectangular blocks whose inscriptions, though extremely fragmentary, almost certainly record a military campaign undertaken by Tudhaliya IV. Very likely this is the same campaign as the one recorded in the Yalburt (q.v.) inscription, which was launched by Tudhaliya against the Lukka lands in southwestern Anatolia.

*Masson (1979), *Hawkins (1995: 86–102).

Emutbal(um) see **Yamutbal(um)**.

Enkomi (map 14) Late Bronze Age city near the east coast of Cyprus, so called after the nearby mod. village Enkomi, 8 km northwest of Famagusta. Numerous excavations have been conducted on the site, beginning with those of A. S. Murray for the British Museum in 1896, and ending in 1973 with the final season of French excavations under the direction of O. Pelon. The possibility has been suggested, though not generally accepted, that the city's anc. name was Alasiya, capital of the kingdom of Alasiya (q.v.) attested in a number of Late Bronze Age texts.

Enkomi's history has been divided into three phases, corresponding with the generally accepted phases of the Late Cypriot Bronze Age. The settlement may have been first fortified in Phase I (c. 1600–1450/1400). A long rectangular building belonging to this phase was identified by its excavator P. Dikaios as a fortress containing a metallurgical workshop. Much of the city's wealth in this and the succeeding period may have derived from its copper industry. It is thought to have dominated Cypriot copper production in these periods. Following the destruction of this phase, probably by earthquake, Enkomi in its second phase (c. 1450/1400–1200) developed into a significant urban centre, with a well-planned layout based on a grid plan which divided the city into large rectangular blocks, and a flourishing metallurgical industry, as indicated by many copper-smelting installations. Rich funerary furniture and grave goods (including gold jewellery and items of ivory) testify to the city's wealth, at least among its elite classes, in this phase. It has been suggested that four chamber tombs of ashlar masonry may indicate that some aristocratic families from Ugarit settled in Enkomi during this period. An abundance of Mycenaean pottery indicates regular direct or indirect trading contacts with the Mycenaean world.

The destruction of Phase II is commonly associated with the incursions of the Sea Peoples, a group of whom may have occupied the city in its third phase (c. 1200–1050). The material culture of this period, particularly Mycenaean-style pottery, *may* indicate a Mycenaean element among the new settlers, though there is no clear evidence for Mycenaean settlement. Some features of the former phase continued into this phase, including its geometric grid street plan, and the city again became the centre of an active metallurgical industry. But differences between its current and former inhabitants are also evident, as illustrated by new funerary practices. The rock-cut chamber tombs of the earlier phases were now replaced with shaft graves. Phase III is also associated with the sanctuaries of the so-called Horned-God and Ingot-God. Lagarce notes that the rituals of both deities show great similarities – libations and offerings of bucrania (oxen skulls) – that reflect Aegean, western Asian, and local traditions.

The abandonment of Enkomi in mid C11 may have been due to an earthquake, or to the silting up of its harbour. It was never resettled. At least some of its population probably moved to the newly founded city of Salamis, which lay 2 km to the northeast. Salamis quickly became the dominant city of its region, and subsequently the whole island.

Courtois *et al.* (1986), J. Lagarce (*OEANE* 2: 241–4).

Enzite (**Enzatu, Enzi**) (map 4) City and region within the land of Ishua (Late Bronze Age Isuwa), northern Mesopotamia, attested in late M2 and early M1 Assyrian texts. The Assyrian king Tiglath-pileser I (1114–1076) reports his conquest of the city of Enzatu belonging to the land of Ishua following a campaign in the land of Hatti (**RIMA* 2: 43) (Iron Age texts designate northern Syria and the Taurus region as the land of Hatti). Three centuries later, Shalmaneser III conquered, plundered, and burnt the cities of Enzite early in the campaign which he conducted in his third regnal year (856) against the kingdom of Urartu and other lands in its region (**RIMA* 3: 19–20). In 844, the land of Enzi suffered further devastation from Shalmaneser during another of his campaigns into Urartian territory (**RIMA* 3: 39). In 736–735 Enzi, one of the 'fortresses of Urartu', was among the lands captured and annexed to Assyria by Tiglath-pileser III (**Tigl. III* 126–7).

Ephesus (map 5) City located on the Aegean coast of western Anatolia, with a history of occupation extending from the Late Bronze Age until the Byzantine period. Excavations, concentrating primarily on the Roman city, have been undertaken since 1895 by Austrian archaeological teams, and continue to the present day. Late Bronze Age remains on the hill at Ayasuluk near Classical Ephesus are almost certainly those of the city of Apasa, capital of the kingdom of Arzawa 'Minor' (q.v.) during the Hittite period. Apasa would thus have been the Late Bronze Age forerunner of Ephesus, which according to Classical tradition was an Ionian foundation (probably dating to the end of M2), established on the site of an earlier Carian and Lelegian settlement. Greek legend attributes the city's foundation to Androclus, a son of the Athenian king Codrus.

In the first half of C7, Ephesus fell victim to the Cimmerian invasions, from which it seems to have recovered fairly quickly, and in the following century it was incorporated into the Lydian empire. After Lydia's fall to the Persian king Cyrus II in 546, Ephesus along with the rest of the Ionian cities became subject to Persia, forming part of the first Persian satrapy (see glossary under **satrapy**). In C5, after the Greek liberation of the Ionian states from Persian control, the city became for a time a member of the Athenian Confederacy. But in 386, in accordance with the terms of the 'King's Peace' (see glossary), it reverted to Persian sovereignty, where it remained until liberated by Alexander the Great in 334.

Figure 39 Ephesus, temple of Artemis, Hellenistic period.

Ephesus is best known for its later Hellenistic and especially its Roman remains. These reflect the foundation of a new city, laid out on a rectangular grid plan between the hills Panayirdağ and Bülbüldağ by Alexander's general Lysimachus. But the famous temple of Artemis (Artemisium), traditionally included among the seven wonders of the ancient world, had its origins many centuries earlier. The temple was built on a plain outside the Roman city, east of Ayasuluk, and probably within the sacred area formerly dedicated to the Anatolian mother goddess Cybele. The earliest forerunner to the temple, no more than a shrine, has been dated to C8. A number of building phases followed, interrupted for a brief time by the Cimmerian invasions. They reflect the progressive enlargement and elaboration of the structures on the site, which culminated in the great marble Ionic temple to the goddess, built by the Cretan architects Chersiphron and Metagenes c. 560. The cult of Artemis now became supreme in the region. In 356 the Artemisium was burnt to the ground by a man called Herostratus, allegedly on the night of Alexander the Great's birth. The Ephesians rebuilt the temple (refusing Alexander's offer of assistance), on a higher level but retaining the original dimensions. A number of the new column bases and drums were sculpturally embellished, like their predecessors. Famous artists like Scopas and Apelles, and perhaps Praxiteles, were employed for this purpose. The new temple was completed in mid C3.

Mitsopoulou-Leon (*PECS* 306–10), Bammer (1988), Höcker (*BNP* 4: 1024–32).

'Erani, Tel (map 8) Large settlement-mound (25–36 ha) in the southeastern coastal plain of Israel, 10 km northwest of Lachish, consisting of an acropolis (largely) surrounded by a high and a lower terrace. Its history of occupation extends from the Chalcolithic Age to the Hellenistic period. The site was first excavated from 1956 to 1961 by S. Yeivin for the Israel Dept of Antiquities and Museums, the fourth season being conducted jointly with the Italian Centro per le Antichità e la Storia dell'Arte del Vicino Oriento of the Istituto per l'Oriente of Rome. In 1985, 1987, and 1988, A. Kempinski and I. Gilead of Tel Aviv University and Ben-Gurion University of the Negev (respectively) extended the area of the earlier excavations and re-examined the stratigraphic sequence. Subsequent excavations were carried out by E. Braun and E. C. M. van den Brink in 1994 and 1995.

Early Bronze Age I was the most important period in the site's history. In this period, it appears to have been the centre of Egyptian colonization in the Canaanite coastlands and plain. Both Egyptian and Canaanite elements are reflected in its material culture. The Early Bronze II settlement was smaller than its predecessor, which *may* reflect the departure of the Egyptians. Certainly, the material culture of Early Bronze III, when the city was fortified with a massive wall, was purely Canaanite. Then followed a long period of abandonment before the site was reoccupied in the Late Bronze II period. The new settlement was large, covering the whole of the acropolis and perhaps extending beyond it. It had contacts with Cyprus, and seems once again to have been colonized by Egyptians during the reign of the C13 pharaoh Ramesses II. Traces of a very large building complex, possibly a palace, date to this period. During the succeeding Iron Age I period (C12–11), a Philistine presence is indicated by Philistine ceramic ware and figurines. Under Israelite occupation in Iron Age II, when settlement was confined largely to the fortified acropolis, the city may have had the character of a fortress-establishment on the border of Judah.

Destruction of the settlement at the end of its Iron Age II phase is associated with the Assyrian king Sargon II's campaign in the region in 710. The acropolis was rebuilt and refortified in the aftermath of Assyrian conquest, but may have suffered another destruction at the hands of the Babylonians in early C6. This appears to have led to a partial abandonment, as happened elsewhere in Palestine, in the Persian period (C6–4). Many silos were now erected on the summit of the mound. There are few architectural remains from this period, though the discovery of a favissa containing fragments of stone statuettes and clay figurines suggested to the excavators the existence of a temple on the high terrace. There was a small settlement on the site in the Hellenistic period. Some remains from the Byzantine and Mameluke periods (notably graves) were also uncovered.

Yeivin (*NEAEHL* 2: 417–22), Brandl (*OEANE* 2: 256–8).

Erebuni (Arin-berd, *Erevan*) (map 20) Iron Age fortified Urartian settlement in eastern Anatolia, founded by the Urartian king Argishti I in early C8. The site was excavated by a team from the Academy of Sciences, Armenian SSR, in the 1950s. Its relatively well-preserved remains on the fully excavated citadel include a temple to Urartu's chief deity Haldi, another smaller 'tower' temple, a columned hall, with both residential and storage areas, and fragments of wall-paintings. It was a royal capital and served as an important centre of government in its region until early C7, when the Urartian king Rusa II (678–654) founded the city of Teisheba (mod. Karmir Blur) 7 km to the southwest. Materials dedicated in Erebuni were found in the storerooms of this later site, so it is likely that these were transferred along with administrative functions as part of Rusa's reorganization of the area. They include fourteen bronze shields elaborately decorated with concentric rings of lions and bulls, and are also inscribed with dedicatory cuneiform texts, of Argishti I and his son Sarduri II. A settlement area lies beside the citadel and is currently the subject of archaeological investigation. After the fall of the kingdom of Urartu, there was a reoccupation of Erebuni in the Persian period (C6–4), and many of the Urartian buildings were modified.

Zimansky (1998).

Eresh (*Tell Abu-Salabikh?*) Early and Middle Bronze Age city in southern Mesopotamia, on the Euphrates, not far from and probably north of the city of Nippur. A tentative identification has been suggested with the site of Tell Abu-Salabikh. In C23, Eresh was among the cities that appeared on the side of Kish in the general rebellion against the Akkadian king Naram-Sin (**RIME* 2: 105–6). In the Middle Bronze Age the city became part of the Old Babylonian kingdom. Fortified in 1799, during the reign of the Babylonian king Sin-muballit, it provided the kingdom with a frontier post on the Euphrates.

Mesop. 122.

Erganı Maden (map 2) Site of rich copper mines in northern Mesopotamia, northwest of mod. Diyarbakır in the upper Tigris basin. The mines were worked through the Bronze Ages and succeeding periods, and are still in use today. In the Late Bronze Age, the region in which they lay belonged to the country of Isuwa, which occupied the border territory between Hatti and Mitanni. Their location may have been a factor in the conflicts between the two kingdoms. The mines may also have provided an incentive for an Assyrian military campaign in the region during the reign of Tukulti-Ninurta I (1244–1208). This enterprise resulted in a military showdown with the Hittite king Tudhaliya IV (see **Nairi**).

Bryce (2005: 315, with refs in n. 99).

Eridu (*Abu Shahrain*) (maps 11, 17) Site consisting of seven mounds, located 24 km southwest of Ur on the southwestern edge of the southern Mesopotamian floodplain. Its history of occupation extends from the Ubaid period (mid M6) to the Persian period (C6–4). The earliest excavations were carried out by J. E. Taylor for the British Museum in 1854. Further single-season investigations of the site were conducted by R. C. Thompson and H. R. Hall for the British Museum in 1918 and 1919 respectively. However, the most comprehensive excavations were undertaken by F. Safar, M. A. Mustafa, and S. Lloyd from 1946 to 1949, on behalf of the Iraqi Directorate-General of Antiquities. A large Ubaid-period cemetery was excavated, and Eridu was the site for which the ceramic sequence of the Ubaid period was established. The excavations there brought to light a sequence of eighteen superimposed mudbrick temples, in successive layers extending from the Early Ubaid to the Late Uruk period (M4). The temples, which became increasingly more complex and elaborate with each building phase, were constructed on mudbrick platforms. All were probably dedicated to the worship of Enki (Ea), the Mesopotamian god of the underworld freshwater ocean. The long, unbroken cultural sequence at Eridu from prehistoric times through to M3 has been cited as evidence against the theory that the Sumerians migrated into southern Mesopotamia from elsewhere.

In the Early Bronze Age (M3) Eridu was an important Sumerian city-state and cult-centre of Enki. According to the Sumerian King List, it was the first of the five cities upon which heaven bestowed kingship in the period before the great flood. Architectural remains of the Sumerian phase of its existence include palaces of the Early Dynastic period (c. 2900–2334). An impressive ziggurat was built on the main mound in the Ur III period (c. 2112–2004); it was begun in the reign of the first Ur III ruler Ur-Nammu, and completed under his successors. Ur-Nammu also rebuilt the temple of Enki. The buildings within the sacred precinct of the city in its Ur III phase indicate the continuity of a temple-building tradition which extended back to the beginning of the Ubaid period. The ziggurat has been seen as the culminating point of this tradition.

Occupation of Eridu continued sporadically in later times, up to the end of the Persian period (C6–4). The Larsa king Nur-Adad (1865–1850) and the Babylonian king Nebuchadnezzar II (604–562) apparently carried out a number of restoration projects in the city. In C7 it was governed, along with nearby Ur and the Gurasimmu tribe, by a certain Sin-balassu-iqbi on behalf of the Assyrian king Ashurbanipal (*RIMB* 2: 245).

Safar *et al.* (1981), Danti and Zettler (*OEANE* 2: 258–60).

Erishu (Irsia) City in the Kashiyari mountain range (mod. Tur ʿAbdin) of northern Mesopotamia, attested in the records of the Assyrian king Ashur-bel-kala (1073–1056) as belonging to one of the regions called Habhu in Assyrian texts (see **Habhu (4)**). Ashur-bel-kala conquered it during one of his campaigns against the Aramaeans (**RIMA* 2: 102). The city is probably to be identified with Irsia, where Ashurnasirpal II camped for the night during his passage through the Kashiyari range to reach the land of Nairi in 879 (**RIMA* 2: 209). While there, he received tribute from the city of Shuru, and then went on to burn Irsia, presumably because its inhabitants had not been submissive.

Radner (2006: 287–9).

Eritia, Mt Mountain in Urartian territory, near which lay the stronghold of the C9 Urartian king Arame. Though the mountain has not yet been identified, it may have lain to the southwest of Lake Urmia, if the most recently proposed location for Arzashkun (q.v.) in this area is correct. In the course of his campaign into Urartian territory during his third regnal year (856), the Assyrian king Shalmaneser III set up a monumental victory statue of himself on Mt Eritia following his destruction of Arzashkun and before he moved on to destroy the city of Aramale (**RIMA* 3: 20–1).

Erythrae (map 5) Classical Greek city located on the Aegean coast of Anatolia in the region called Ionia in M1, 20 km northeast of mod. Çeşme. It was one of the twelve members of the Ionian League (see **Panionium**). According to a Greek tradition recorded by Pausanias (7.3.7), Erythrae was founded by settlers from Crete, led by Erythrus, son of the Cretan king Rhadamanthys. Its population was swelled by immigrants from Lycia, Caria, and Pamphylia, and later by Ionian colonists (Strabo 14.1.3) who came allegedly under the leadership of Cnopus, son of the legendary

Athenian king Codrus. In C6 Erythrae was subject in turn to the Lydian and the Persian empires. In C5, it became a member of the Athenian Confederacy (see glossary), paying as its dues the comparatively large sum of seven talents per year. But it fluctuated in its allegiances, abandoning the Confederacy perhaps in 453, shortly after the transference of the Confederacy's funds from Delos to Athens. In 412 it joined Athens' Peloponnesian enemies, and provided a base for their forces. Subsequently, it aligned itself with Persia, and in C4 established friendly relations with Mausolus, ruler of Caria under Persian patronage (377–353). Inscriptional evidence indicates that Mausolus became one of Erythrae's benefactors. The most notable of the city's remains is a relatively well-preserved city wall, dating to late C4 or early C3. The wall is built of ashlar masonry, has several gateways, and is over 3 km long. Remains of the Hellenistic and Roman periods include a theatre, now in a poorly preserved state. New excavations of the site began in 2003 under the direction of C. Özgünel, Ankara University.

E. Akurgal (1973: 231–3).

Esdar, Tel (map 8) 2 ha settlement-mound located in the Negev desert in the southern part of Judah. Discovered by N. Glueck in 1956, the site was excavated in 1963 and 1964 by M. Kochavi for the Israel Dept of Antiquities and Museums. Four main occupation strata were identified, extending from the Chalcolithic (M4) to the Roman–Byzantine period. Remains from the Chalcolithic period (Stratum IVB), notably beaten-earth living-surfaces with fireplaces and ash-pits, identify this first phase of the site's existence with the so-called Beersheba culture. It was followed by a gap in occupation lasting several centuries. Pebbled living-floors and stone silos feature in Stratum IVB, which dates to Early Bronze II (mid M3). Then followed a long period of abandonment before the site was reoccupied in Iron Age I (Stratum III; late M2). In this level, a complex of eight three-room houses came to light. Kochavi suggests that its destruction in late C11 is to be attributed to a raid by the Amalekites, against whom, according to biblical tradition, Saul fought to protect the Israelites' southernmost settlements. Excavation of the Stratum II settlement, dating to C10 and found only on the southern slope of the mound, produced the remains of a three-room house with stone floors, silos, and two associated buildings. The totality has been identified as a farm complex. Stratum I, consisting of agricultural terrace walls, has been dated to the Roman–Byzantine period on the basis of pottery sherds.

Kochavi (*NEAEHL* 2: 423).

Eshnunna (*Tell Asmar*; see also ***Diyala***) (map 10) Early and Middle Bronze Age city (also a city-state in earlier M2) situated in the Diyala r. basin of central Mesopotamia, 81 km northeast of Baghdad. Following discovery of the site in 1930, excavations were conducted there during the 1930s by the Oriental Institute, University of Chicago, under the direction of H. Frankfort. From its origins in late M4 or at the beginning of M3, Eshnunna developed into a major regional urban centre during the Early Dynastic period (c. 2900–2334), with habitation mainly on the northwest area of the mound, where a large residential area was located. The city continued to flourish through the period of the Akkadian empire (c. 2334–2193). It reached the peak of its development and its maximum size under the rule of the Ur III kings (C21) and in the following Isin-Larsa period (C20–18).

A sequence of superimposed temples unearthed on the site, and possibly dedicated to the god Abu, has provided a basis for Mesopotamian chronology in the Early Bronze Age, leading to the division of the Early Dynastic period into three phases – ED I, II, and III. However, Eshnunna's perceived 'provincial' character has led scholars to question the extent to which these divisions are applicable to the core areas of southern Mesopotamian civilization, where the Sumerian city-states were located. The city's alleged provincialism is seen to be reflected in the collection of eleven male and female human sculptures which were discovered in one of the three shrines of the ED II temple, the so-called 'Square Temple'. (Whether these figures were made as a group or assembled over a period of time remains uncertain.) Though they are undoubtedly some of the best-known examples of Early Dynastic art, their alleged naivety is considered to be atypical of mainstream Mesopotamian artistic achievement.

During the Akkadian period, a large building complex designated as the Northern Palace was constructed close to the Abu temple. It may have been connected with the temple, functioning perhaps as a residential compound for those in the god's service. Craft workshops may also have been accommodated within the complex. An elaborate drainage system was one of its most impressive features. This feature continued when the complex was rebuilt, its new layout incorporating a main block of rooms constructed around a large, central courtyard. The new complex is thought to have been devoted entirely to manufacturing purposes, with evidence of a dyeing industry, textile and pottery production, and ornamental craft work in stone and shell. A hoard of objects made of silver and lapis lazuli came to light beneath the floor of the workshops.

During the Ur III period, the hitherto sparsely inhabited southern part of the city-mound became the chief centre of Eshnunna's population. Here a temple was built by the city's ruler Ituriya for the worship of his deified overlord Shu-Sin, penultimate member of the Ur III dynasty. This is the only known Mesopotamian temple which was dedicated to a living king. Adjacent to it, a building called by the excavators the 'Palace of the Rulers' was constructed at the end of the Ur III period or early in the Isin-Larsa period. It was used essentially for administrative purposes rather than as a royal residence. Large numbers of administrative texts were found within it. The building underwent numerous alterations, in the course of which the former temple of Shu-Sin, now divested of its sacred functions, was incorporated into it. Note that the temple is generally referred to in the older literature as the 'Gimilsin Temple', reflecting an earlier reading of the king's name.

Under the Ur III dynasty, Eshnunna was administered by an *ensi* (here meaning 'local governor'). After the collapse of this dynasty, it was the seat of local rulers of the land of Warum. For a time the city was subject to the Isin dynasty, and it was perhaps under Isin's domination that a marriage alliance was contracted between its ruler Bilalama and the daughter of an Amorite leader, Abda-El, when Isin's throne was occupied by Shu-ilishu (1984–1975). Possibly Eshnunna was for a time under Elamite control. But in the volatile conditions which marked the Isin-Larsa period, it enjoyed periods of independence from any of the major powers.

In C19, Eshnunna's king Ipiq-Adad II (1862–1818) extended his country's control over the cities of the Diyala valley, and within the capital rebuilt the royal palace on a grand scale. In early C18, Ipiq-Adad's son and eventual successor Dadusha (*d.* 1780) dispatched two successive armies to the middle Euphrates region, which resulted in

Eshnunna's conquest of the land of Suhum. It was in fact a reconquest. Suhum had been annexed, in late C19, by the Eshnunnite king Naram-Sin, but had subsequently come under the control of the Assyrian king Shamshi-Adad I (1796–1775). Dadusha's forces recaptured it. (Much information about Dadusha's exploits appears in an Akkadian inscription on a stone stele of his found near Tell Asmar; **Chav.* 98–102.) Eshnunna now posed a direct threat to the Assyrian viceregal kingdom Mari, whose territory lay immediately to the north of Suhum. To relieve the pressure on Mari, then ruled by Shamshi-Adad's son Yasmah-Addu as viceroy, Ishme-Dagan, Yasmah-Addu's brother and Assyrian viceroy at Ekallatum, launched a counter-offensive against Eshnunna, perhaps in the upper Diyala region. But hostilities between the Assyrian and Eshnunnite kingdoms came to an end when Dadusha concluded a peace with Shamshi-Adad (1781), and provided him with military assistance during an Assyrian campaign east of the Tigris. Four years later, Shamshi-Adad joined forces with the new Eshnunnite king Ibal-pi-El II and the Babylonian king Hammurabi for an attack on the land of Malgium, which bought off the invaders with a substantial payment of silver (**LAPO* 17: 143, no. 544).

However, Shamshi-Adad's death in 1775 helped pave the way for an aggressive programme of expansion by Eshnunna in the territories over which the Assyrian king had held sway, i.e. the kingdom of Upper Mesopotamia. Ibal-pi-El's forces occupied the city of Shubat-Enlil (c. 1771), and a second Eshnunnite army marched along the Tigris and seized the former Assyrian cities Ashur and Ekallatum. Throughout this period, Eshnunna retained its status as an important regional kingdom. But in 1765 it fell to the Elamites, who brought Ibal-pi-El's reign to an end. In 1762 his successor Silli-Sin was defeated by the Babylonian king Hammurabi. With these conquests, Eshunna's power in the region was effectively terminated. It did, however, make a brief bid for independence, along with other Babylonian cities, when it rebelled against Hammurabi's successor Samsu-iluna in the tenth year of his reign (c. 1738). Samsu-iluna crushed the rebellion the following year, and listed Eshnunna's king Iluni among the rebels whom he killed (**RIME* 4: 387).

After the Old Babylonian era, Eshnunna drops out of the historical record. However, following his conquest of Babylonia in 539, the Persian king Cyrus II claimed to have returned the statues of the gods to their long-abandoned shrines in the sacred centres on the other side (i.e. east) of the Tigris, including those in the land of Eshnunna.

Auerbach (*OEANE* 2: 261–5), Charpin (*DCM* 314–18), *Mesop.* (*passim*, see index).

Eskiyapar Urban settlement in north-central Anatolia, 160 km east of Ankara, with occupation levels dating from the Early Bronze Age to the Roman imperial period. The site was excavated by a Turkish team under the direction of R. Temizer from 1968 to 1983. Two treasure hoards unearthed from it date to the last two centuries of the Early Bronze Age (i.e. late M3). They include, in the larger hoard, silver goblets and a ceremonial electrum axe, and in the smaller one, a range of items of personal jewellery (earrings, bracelet, beads etc.). The strongly fortified M2 settlement became a production centre for pottery in the Hittite period, as illustrated by the remains of two round kilns of this period, built in an open courtyard.

Özgüç and Temizer (1993), Burney (2004: 83).

es-Sarem, Tell see ***Rehob, Tell.***

et-Tell (biblical Ai?) (map 8) 11 ha Bronze and Iron Age settlement-mound in southern Palestine, West Bank, located 20 km northeast of Jerusalem. The site was excavated successively by J. Garstang (1928), J. Marquet-Krause (1933–5), and J. A. Callaway (during several seasons between 1964 and 1976). Ten occupation strata were identified, which the excavators divided between two main periods of occupation – Early Bronze Age (3100–2400) (eight strata) and Iron Age I (1200–1050) (two strata). In its earliest level, et-Tell was an unwalled village, dating to c. 3250–3100, followed in its next Early Bronze phase (c. 3100–2950) by a strongly fortified settlement, with four city gate complexes protected by towers. Within the fortifications, excavations brought to light a large building, commonly referred to as a palace-temple, on the summit ('acropolis') of the mound, a citadel, religious sanctuary, market-place, and residential area. Callaway suggests that the transition from village to urban centre may reflect the arrival of newcomers, perhaps from Anatolia or Syria.

Two further Early Bronze Age phases followed (c. 2950–2775 and 2775–2400, phases 3 and 4 respectively), in each case after the violent destruction of its predecessor. Phase 4, belonging to Early Bronze III, shows evidence of Egyptian influence, reinforced by the discovery in the palace-temple complex of imported Egyptian alabaster and stone vessels. After the destruction of this level, perhaps by earthquake, the site was abandoned. It remained deserted until the early Iron Age, when a small, unwalled agricultural village was built on it (c. 1200). Features of the new settlement included pillared houses with common walls, water cisterns dug into the house courtyards, cobblestone streets, and terraced hill-slopes for crop planting. Early Israelites have been suggested as the new settlers. But whoever occupied the site in this period did so only briefly, for it was abandoned in the course of C11 and never resettled. There is no evidence that the village ended in violent destruction. However, the presence of slingshots on the floors of some of the houses has been seen as an indication that the village was abandoned after a minor battle.

Et-Tell is commonly identified with biblical Ai, a Canaanite town frequently attested in *OT* sources. The identification was first proposed by E. Robinson in 1838. According to Genesis 12:8 and 13:3, Ai lay just to the east of Bethel. Joshua 8 reports its capture and destruction by Joshua during the Israelite conquest of Canaan. But it is difficult to accommodate the biblical references to Ai, particularly the alleged Israelite destruction of it apparently in C13, to the archaeological evidence for et-Tell's history, which indicates that that site had been abandoned c. 2400 and was not finally reoccupied until c. 1200. Various attempts have been made to explain the apparent discrepancy between biblical and archaeological sources, e.g. by suggesting that Ai was some other place, such as nearby Khirbet Heiyan or Khirbet Khudriya. However, the geographical description of Ai in the Bible fits the topography of et-Tell far better than any other site. If in fact the identification is maintained, then in the opinion of a number of scholars this reinforces doubts about the historical validity of the Bible's account of the Israelite conquest of Canaan.

Callaway (1972; 1980), Zevit (1985), Drinkard (*HCBD* 21), Cooley (*NEAEHL* 1: 39–45; *OEANE* 1: 32–3, s.v. Ai), Laughlin (2006: 16–19).

Euromus (*Ayaklı*) (map 5) M1 BCE–M1 CE city in Caria in southwestern Anatolia, 13 km northwest of Mylasa (mod. Milas). In C5 the city was a member of the Athenian Confederacy (see glossary). At this time it was known as Kyromus or Hyromus. Its name was later changed to the Greek form Euromus, probably by the Carian ruler Mausolus (377–353) who played an important role in the spread of Greek influence through Caria. The city is also attested in the form Europus. It is mentioned in literary sources dating to the Hellenistic and Roman periods which refer to various local alliances and conflicts in which it was involved. In 129 Euromus, along with other Carian cities, was incorporated into the Roman province of Asia.

The city was enclosed by a wall, still relatively well-preserved in parts, fortified by towers and dating back to C5 or C4. Other material remains, of Hellenistic and/or Roman date, include a theatre, an agora, and a very well-preserved temple in the Corinthian order just outside the walls. Of C2 CE date (though it had at least one predecessor), the temple was dedicated to the god Zeus Lepsynus.

Bean (1971: 45–8; *PECS* 320–1).

Eurymedon Classical name for the river (mod. Köprüçayi) which drains into the Gulf of Antalya on Anatolia's south-central coast from a source in the mountains of Pisidia (*BAGRW* 65 F3–4). It is best known as the site of a decisive battle between the Athenian commander Cimon and the Persian forces, firstly by land and then by sea, at the mouth of the river c. 466 (Thucydides 1.100, Plutarch, *Cimon* 12–13). Cimon's victory ended any further prospect of comprehensive military action by Persia against the Greek world.

Ezion-geber Iron Age Edomite city apparently situated at the northern tip of the Gulf of Aqabah. It is attested only in *OT* sources. Several of these sources report that King Solomon built ships there for an expedition to Ophir (e.g. 1 Kings 10:26–8), a place of uncertain location but accessible by ship and famous for its gold. Ezion-Geber is perhaps to be identified with the site of Tell el-Kheleifeh, which is in fact located at the northern end of the Gulf (see further under ***Kheleifeh, Tell el-***).

Baly (*HCBD* 323).

F

Failaka see Dilmun.

Fara see Shuruppak.

Farah, Tell el- (*North*) (map 8) 10 ha settlement-mound located in the Samaria hills of Palestine, 10 km northeast of mod. Nablus on the west bank of the Jordan. Its history of occupation extends from the Neolithic period to the Iron Age. Excavations were conducted from 1946 to 1960 by R. de Vaux on behalf of the École Biblique et Archéologique Française in Jerusalem. Though the excavator apparently gave little attention to the site's stratigraphy, and died before producing final excavation reports, Tell el-Farah is none the less ranked alongside Megiddo and Hazor in terms of the importance of the information it provides about northern Canaan and the hill country.

The earliest evidence for human habitation on the site dates to the Pre-Pottery Neolithic period (M7–6), followed by settlement in the Chalcolithic period (M5–4). A number of tombs, from which was unearthed an important collection of ceramic ware and other goods, date to the latter. In the Early Bronze Age, the site was in part protected by a fortification wall of mudbrick on stone foundations, and in part by its own natural defences, consisting of steep slopes to its east and south. The main evidence for its first Early Bronze phase (there were at least five such phases) is provided by several large cemeteries, located to the south, north, and northeast of the mound. Through the succeeding phases, the settlement on the mound itself developed from a village community into a relatively highly urbanized township, which included kilns and pottery workshops, and a number of rectangular houses (typically, single-room structures with courtyards and common walls) divided into blocks by streets. Occupation of the site appears to have come to an end around mid M3, at the end of the Early Bronze II period. There is no sign of violent destruction at this time, which suggests that its abandonment was not due to enemy action.

Resettlement occurred in Middle Bronze IIA, c. 1900, as indicated by the construction of a large village above the remains of the Early Bronze II town. The settlement reached its full development in Middle Bronze IIC. It was apparently refortified in this period, with a large gateway incorporated into its wall. Two structures assigned to the IIC period have been interpreted as cultic installations. One of them, a subterranean chamber with plastered walls and floor, was originally thought to have been an underground shrine, but may in fact have been a granary. Occupation of the settlement continued into the Late Bronze Age, for which there are only meagre remains. By the end of the Late Bronze Age the site was again abandoned, but the date of the abandonment and the reasons for it remain uncertain. There was, however, further resettlement in C12. Though the site's Iron Age strata are better preserved than their Late Bronze Age predecessor, the stratigraphy is highly problematical. In what has been defined as the period VIIb level (C10), Tell el-Farah's urban features have suggested a period of renewal under a central authority. This has provided part of the reasoning for identifying the site with biblical Tirzah (q.v.), which according to *OT* sources was for a brief period the capital of the northern kingdom of Israel (late C10–early C9), initially in the reign of Jeroboam I (c. 922–901). The identification is commonly accepted, but remains uncertain.

Tell el-Farah was destroyed during the Assyrian campaign of 723. After it was apparently partially restored under Assyrian rule, the city was finally abandoned at the end of C7, and never resettled.

de Miroschedji (*NEAEHL* 2: 433–8), Chambon (*NEAEHL* 2: 439–40), Joffe (*OEANE* 2: 303–4).

Farah, Tell el- (*South*) (map 8) 6 ha settlement-mound in the northwestern Negev region of southern Palestine, 29 km southeast of Gaza. Its history of occupation begins in the Middle Bronze IIB period, early M2, and continues until at least C1 CE, the first century of the Roman imperial period. There were intervals in between when the site appears to have been abandoned or only sparsely populated. The site was excavated by W. Flinders Petrie in 1928 and 1929 for the British School of Archaeology in Egypt. Excavations were renewed in 1999 under the direction of G. Lehmann, Ben-Gurion University of the Negev, and T. J. Schneider, Claremont Graduate University, USA.

The site was first occupied by a Middle Bronze Age walled Hyksos settlement, whose defences contained a triple-entry gateway with flanking towers. The Hyksos link is indicated by an Egyptian scarab bearing the name of the Hyksos ruler Maaibre. It was found in one of the tombs dating to this period, which belonged to a cemetery located to the northwest of the mound.

An Egyptian campaign by an early eighteenth dynasty pharaoh may have been the cause of the city's abandonment during the second half of C16. Reoccupation took place in C14. The most prominent survival of this phase of the city's history is a large Egyptian-style brick building, dating to C13, with external staircase and front and central courtyards. At this time the region was subject to Egyptian sovereignty, and the building was probably the residence of a local Egyptian official, perhaps a military governor. A jar bearing cartouches of the pharaoh Seti II (1200–1194) was found in the central courtyard. Philistines had apparently settled in the city while it was still under Egyptian control, and they continued to occupy it when the Egyptians withdrew from southern Palestine during the second half of C12. The Philistine presence is indicated by funerary goods contained in several rock-cut tombs, from which two anthropoid coffins of Philistine type were also unearthed. The site may have been only sparsely inhabited in C10 and C9, to judge from the meagre evidence available to us from this period, and then perhaps was abandoned for two or more centuries before resettlement in C7 and C6. It continued to be inhabited in the Persian period (C6–4), as attested by burials of this time. The most noteworthy of the funerary goods were a silver dipper and fluted bowl. After the Persian period, there was apparently another lengthy interval of abandonment. In the Roman imperial period a small fort was constructed at the north end of the mound.

The site's anc. identity is unknown. It is one of several possible candidates for biblical Sharuhen, which is, however, most likely to be the site of Tell el-Ajjul.

Yisraeli (*NEAEHL* 2: 441–4), Weinstein (*OEANE* 2: 304–5), Lehmann and Schneider (2000).

Farukhabad, Tepe Settlement-mound c. 25 m high and 200 m in diameter, located near the Mehmeh r. in the Deh Luran plain of southwestern Iran, 100 km northwest of Susa. Excavations were carried out on the site in 1968 by the Museum of Anthropology, University of Michigan, in collaboration with the Iranian Archaeological Service. The primary purpose of the excavations was to study trade, craft, and town growth. They revealed a history of occupation dating back to early M6. Like other sites in the Deh Luran plain, Farukhabad was abandoned in late M5. It was resettled in M4, during the so-called Uruk period, and occupation continued into M3. In both this and its earlier period of occupation, Farukhabad appears to have been a subsidiary settlement to the larger site at Tepe Mussian. There are remains of domestic dwellings from this period and evidence of trading activities, which included the export of bitumen, chert, and perhaps cloth, and the import of metal and decorative items. The site was abandoned again in mid M3. There was limited reoccupation in C21, during the Ur III period, and in early M2. In this period, a small settlement was built on the summit of the mound, and c. 1900, the site was occupied by a small fort. The fort has been explained as a military outpost guarding a crossing on the Mehmeh r. at the time of conflicts between the Old Babylonian kings of Mesopotamia and the sukkalmah rulers (see glossary) of Susa. By c. 1300 the site was again abandoned, with brief reoccupation in the first half of M1 CE during the Parthian or Sasanian period. We do not know the site's anc. name.

Wright (1981; *OEANE* 5: 181–3), D. T. Potts (1999: 93–6).

Fasillar (map 2) Site of an unfinished colossal stele, 7.4 m high and of Late Bronze Age date (probably late C13), just to the south of Lake Beyşehir in southwestern Anatolia. The stele depicts a god with conical cap, standing on a mountain god who is flanked by two lions. It has been suggested that this stele when completed was intended for the spring sanctuary now called Eflatun Pinar (q.v.), which lies a few km to the north. A replica of the monument can be seen in the precincts of the Museum of Anatolian Civilizations in Ankara.

Bittel (1976: 228, 230), Burney (2004: 85).

Feheriye, Tell (Sikanu, Sikkan) (maps 2, 13) Site located in the Habur r. triangle, northern Mesopotamia, with eight occupation levels, extending from the Middle and Late Bronze Ages through the Iron Age, Hellenistic, Roman, and mediaeval periods. The site was excavated by C. McEwan in 1940 for the Oriental Institute, University of Chicago, followed by German soundings in 1955 and 1956 on behalf of the Oppenheim Foundation. The earliest identified level (VIII) yielded ceramic ware dating to early M2, the period of the Old Assyrian colonies (Middle Bronze Age). Level VII revealed painted pottery designated as Nuzi ware and belonging to the period of the Late Bronze Age Mitannian kingdom (C15–14). Level VI, dating to C13, contained ivories, sealings, and tablets written in Assyrian cuneiform, indicating that by this time the city had become part of the Middle Assyrian kingdom. Assyrian control of the region appears to have ended in the second half of C11, due to the expansion of Aramaean settlement through the Balih and Habur valleys.

The city's anc. name, Sikanu, appears to date back to c. 2000, when reference is made on a tablet of the Ur III period to 'the Haburite (goddess) of Sikanu', whom Lipiński (2000: 120) equates with the feminine genius of ʿAyn Malha, the source of the

Habur. In the Iron Age, the name Sikanu is firmly linked to the site by its appearance in an Aramaic–Assyrian bilingual inscription dated to the third quarter of C9 (level IV) (*SAIO II: 19–81, *CS II: 153–4; see also Bordreuil, *OEANE* 2: 301). The inscription was carved on the statue of a bearded male, which was erected in honour of the god Hadad – identified with the city of Sikkan in the Aramaic version, and Guzana in the Assyrian. The author of the inscription was Hadd-yitʿi (Assyrian Adda-itʾi), governor of Guzana (*OT* Gozan; see ***Halaf, Tell***), the capital of the Aramaean state called Bit-Bahiani. (The other version of the text calls him 'governor of Guzanu, Sikanu, and Zaranu'.) An earlier reference to Sikanu and Guzana occurs in the context of the 894 campaign conducted in the Habur region by the Assyrian king Adad-nirari II (**RIMA* 2: 153). After marching upon Guzana, then ruled by Abi-salamu, Adad-nirari entered the city of Sikanu. Here he received from Abi-salamu a substantial tribute, of chariots, teams of horse, precious metals, and treasures from the palace.

In the past, it has been suggested that Sikkan/Sikanu is a later form of the name Washshukkanni – thus providing one of the arguments for identifying Washshukkanni, the Mitannian capital, with Tell Feheriye. An objection to the identification is that the clay on which the letters of Tushratta, the last of the Great Kings of Mitanni, were inscribed, does not match the clay from the Middle Assyrian tablets found on the site. It is assumed that Tushratta's letters would have been written in the Mitannian capital on clay obtained locally. Further, as noted above, the name Sikkan existed long before the emergence of the Mitannian kingdom.

Abou Assaf *et al.* (1982), Abou Assaf (*OEANE* 2: 300–1), Lipiński (2000: 683, index refs s.v. Tell Fahariya).

Ferghana (map 16) Central Asian country in the region of mod. Kyrgyzstan. It was probably among the lands incorporated into the Persian empire by Cyrus II, during a campaign which Cyrus conducted into Central Asia some time after his conquest of Babylon in 539. The Saka *para Sugdam*, or alternatively the Saka *haumavarga* (see **Saka**), have been located in this region. The necropolises of the region are suggestive of a nomadic population. For a brief summary of excavations conducted in Ferghana, see Vogelsang (1992: 289–91).

Francfort (1988: 184, 188).

Fertile Crescent Term first coined by the Egyptologist J. H. Breasted to refer to a horseshoe-shaped region (as he delineated it) extending from the Persian Gulf northwards through southern Mesopotamia to northeastern Assyria, east of the Tigris, then westwards across southeastern Anatolia and northern Syria, and southwards along the Syro-Palestinian coast. Breasted likened the Crescent to the shores of a desert bay, upon which mountains look down. He saw the history of western Asia as a struggle for possession of the Crescent between the mountain peoples of the north and the wanderers of the northern desert grasslands lying south of the Crescent's curve. He linked the region's relative fertility (i.e. relative to the wastelands of the desert bay), which was due to its watering by a number of rivers, to the development of civilization within it – from Sumer in southern Mesopotamia at the Crescent's southeastern end to the communities, towns, and petty kingdoms of Palestine at its southwestern end. The term Fertile Crescent is still used today, though less frequently than in the past, and is considered by a number of scholars to be misleading.

Breasted (1944: 135–41, with map between pp. 146 and 147).

Fraktin (map 2) Site of C13 Hittite rock relief, with human and divine figures and accompanying Luwian hieroglyphic inscriptions, located in the region of Cappadocia, southern Anatolia, 50 km southeast of mod. Kayseri. It was first noted by W. M. Ramsay and D. G. Hogarth in August 1890. The figures, 1.3 m in height and carved in low relief, are depicted in two groups. In the left-hand group, the Hittite king Hattusili III (1267–1237) pours a libation on an altar to the storm god. The king wears a conical cap, which may indicate that the sculpture was carved posthumously; in the Hittite world, this form of headgear is a symbol of divinity, and Hittite kings were deified only after their death. In the right-hand group, Hattusili's queen Puduhepa – who is called 'daughter of Kazzuwana (Kizzuwadna), beloved by the god(s)' – makes a similar libation on an altar to the goddess Hepat (Hurrian equivalent of the sun goddess of Arinna). The carving of this latter group was left unfinished.

Bittel (1976: figs 194, 196, 198), Börker-Klähn (1982: 260–2), Rossner (1988: 159–67).

Ful, Tell el- (map 8) Settlement in southern Palestine, mod. Israel, 8 km north of Jerusalem. It has five levels of occupation, extending from the early Iron Age to the Roman imperial period (from c. 1200 BCE to c. 70 CE). The first major excavations on the site were carried out by W. F. Albright in 1922 and 1923 for the American Schools of Oriental Research. Salvage operations were subsequently conducted in 1964 over a six-week period by P. W. Lapp for the American Schools of Oriental Research and the Pittsburgh Theological Seminary. Albright identified the site with Saul's home in Gibeah (1 Samuel 10:26). Lapp believed that his own excavations supported the identification, but a number of scholars remain doubtful. The site's first period of settlement was in Iron Age IA (c. 1200–1150), and, on the assumption that the identification with Gibeah was correct, biblical archaeologists claimed it was associated with an occupation by the *OT* tribe of Benjamin (Judges 19–21) (see also **Yaminites**). After its destruction by fire, a second more extensive settlement was built, dating to Iron Age IC (c. 1025–950), whose main surviving building the excavators have identified with 'Saul's fortress'. It has a casemate wall and a tower at one corner. The fortress was rebuilt in late Iron Age II, and possibly destroyed by the

Figure 40 Fraktin relief.

Babylonian king Nebuchadnezzar II during his campaign in the region in 588/587. But occupation continued on the site up to its abandonment c. 538. Resettlement took place in the late Hellenistic period (c. 175–163), with a final brief period of Roman occupation in C1 CE.

P. W. Lapp (1965), N. L. Lapp (*NEAEHL* 2: 445–8; *OEANE* 2: 346–7).

G

Gagae (map 15) M1 BCE–M1 CE city in eastern Lycia, southwestern Anatolia, 11 km southwest of mod. Kumluca. Like the nearby cities of Rhodiapolis, Corydalla, and Phaselis, Gagae was probably founded by settlers from the island of Rhodes, perhaps in early C7 when Phaselis was allegedly settled. According to a legendary tradition relating to its foundation, the city received its name from the appeal *ga, ga* (the Doric Greek dialect form used on Rhodes for *ge* – 'land') made by Rhodian settlers seeking land in Lycia from the native Lycians for their new settlement. An alternative explanation for the name was that *ga ga* was the cry uttered by the crew of a Rhodian ship who sighted a safe landfall on the Lycian coast after being caught in a storm following their battle with sea-pirates. When the English explorer T. A. B. Spratt visited Gagae in 1842, there were still relatively substantial remains of the anc. city, mainly of Roman and mediaeval date. But these have now almost totally disappeared, due to the constant quarrying of them for building materials.

Bean (*PECS* 342; 1978: 148–50).

Galilee (map 8) Region in northern Palestine located between Lebanon to the north and the Jezreel valley to the south. It is first attested, as an area of relatively dense Canaanite settlement, during one of the Asiatic campaigns conducted by the C15 pharaoh Tuthmosis III, who captured twenty-three Canaanite cities in the region. According to biblical tradition, the Israelites first settled in this region in late C13–early C12. In *OT* sources, the name Galilee is first attested in Joshua 20:7, where reference is made to Kedesh in Galilee, used as a place of refuge in the hill country of the Naphtali tribe. Biblical tradition relates that (in C10) King David strengthened the Israelite presence in Galilee when he organized the united kingdom into a number of administrative districts; during the reign of his son and successor Solomon, Galilee comprised four of these districts. Solomon is further said to have handed over twenty of Galilee's cities to Hiram, King of Tyre, as payment for building materials supplied by Hiram for the construction of the temple in Jerusalem. (On the whole question of the historicity of the tradition of a united Israelite kingdom, see under **Israel**.) In early C9, Bar-Hadad (I) (Hebrew Ben-Hadad), king of Damascus, captured several of Galilee's cities, and in 732 the Assyrian king Tiglath-pileser III carried out further conquests in the region. According to 2 Kings 15:29, Tiglath-pileser captured the cities Ijon, Abel Beth Maacah, Janoah, Kedesh, and Hazor, and deported their populations to Assyria. Thenceforth, Galilee was incorporated into the Assyrian empire, under the authority of an Assyrian governor based in Megiddo. We have little further information about the region until its conquest by Alexander the Great in 323.

Meyers (*HCBD* 359–60).

Gambulu (map 11) Important M1 Aramaean tribal land in the eastern Tigris region of southern Babylonia, near the Elamite border. First attested in inscriptions of the Assyrian king Sargon II referring to a campaign which he conducted in the land c. 710, the tribe is frequently mentioned in the texts of his successors Sennacherib, Esarhaddon, and Ashurbanipal (Parpola, 1970: 128–9, *Sargon II* 433–5). After Sargon's conquest of it in 710, Gambulu was converted into an Assyrian province composed of six districts (in addition to Iadburu): Hubaqanu, Tarbugati, Timassunu (Tibarsunu), Pashur, Hiritu, and Hilmu (**Sargon II* 328). The administration of Babylonia was now shared between the governor of Gambulu and the governor of Babylon. In the following year, part of Bit-Yakin (q.v.) was annexed and divided between Gambulu and Babylon provinces. The fortified city of Dur-Abi-hara (sometimes mistakenly read 'Dur-Athara') became the province's chief city under the new name Dur-Nabu (*Sargon II* *328, 430, 431). Sargon also extended his control over the neighbouring Gambulean sheikhdoms, imposing a large tribute upon them and annexing their lands to his new province. Gambulu's traditional capital was another fortified city called Sha-pi-Bel (also known as Shapiya, Assyrian Sapiya). Esarhaddon regarded it as the gateway to Elam (*Borger, 1956: 53, Episode 13, line 83). Undoubtedly, Gambulu's location bordering upon Elam made it a valuable strategic acquisition for the Assyrian empire. (For the substantial dossier of letters sent from Gambulu by Assyrian officials to either Sargon or Sennacherib, see **SAA* XVII: 84–111, nos 92–128.)

Yet its population resented their subjection to Assyrian overlordship, and already by the second year of Sennacherib's reign (703/702) Gambulu was listed among the insubmissive Aramaean lands which he conquered (**Sennach.* 25, 49, 54, 57). In 691 it joined a coalition of Elamite, Chaldaean, Aramaean, and Babylonian forces which engaged in battle with Sennacherib at Halule (q.v.) on the Tigris r. The Assyrians claimed victory, but the outcome of the conflict was inconclusive, and Gambulu appears to have regained its independence. Around 676, its chief Bel-iqisha paid tribute to Sennacherib's son and successor Esarhaddon. But he must have done so with great reluctance and under much pressure. Gambulu remained strongly anti-Assyrian under his rule and that of his son Dunanu, and sometimes formed an alliance with Elam, Assyria's long-term enemy. Hostilies broke out afresh early in the reign of Esarhaddon's successor Ashurbanipal (668–630/627) when Bel-iqisha joined forces with Nabu-shum-eresh, governor of Nippur, and Urtak(u), king of Elam, for an attack on Assyrian subject territories in Babylonia (refs in Lipiński, 2000: 474, nn. 541–5). Ashurbanipal's ensuing conflict with Gambulu and Elam seems not to have been finally resolved until some years after the death of Urtaku c. 664 and the seizure of his throne by a usurper called Te-Umman. In his Elamite campaign of 653, Ashurbanipal defeated and killed Te-Umman in a battle at the Ulaya r. (Classical Eulaeus; *BAGRW* 93 E2), and then followed up his victory by marching into Gambulu territory and laying siege to Sha-pi-Bel. Though Dunanu, now chief of the Gambulu, surrendered without resistance, the Assyrian king ordered that his land be plundered, and the city of Sha-pi-Bel razed to the ground. Ashurbanipal claims also to have evacuated the land's entire population – an event depicted in a relief dating to Ashurbanipal's reign on the walls of the palace of Sennacherib at Nineveh – seizing along with them countless cattle, sheep, and horses and much other treasure. Gambulu's chief Dunanu and members of his family, including his brother Samgunu, were taken as prisoners to Nineveh. The heads of the conquered Elamite rulers were hung around their necks.

In spite of Ashurbanipal's assertion that he had thoroughly destroyed and totally depopulated the land of the Gambulu, in the year 658 it once more joined Elam in an anti-Assyrian alliance. Retaliatory action was considered by Ashurbanipal, but apparently not put into effect. Subsequently, in 652, Gambuleans (principally from the district of Hilmu) supported Shamash-shum-ukin, the Assyrian prince appointed as ruler of Babylon, in his rebellion against Ashurbanipal, his brother (see **Babylon**), a rebellion which had the support of the then Elamite king (probably Humban-nikash II). But Gambulean participation may have been cut short when early in the rebellion Hilmu's leader Paru was killed in military action with Assyrian forces, and a contingent from Hilmu hired by the Bit-Yakin tribe, which also supported Shamash-shum-ukin, was defeated and many of its members taken prisoner. The Gambulean capital Sha-pi-Bel seems also to have been involved in military action, despite Ashurbanipal's claim a few years earlier that he had wiped it out of existence. But Gambulu appears to have lost its taste for further participation in the rebellion. Along with other cities and tribal groups in the Assyrian–Elamite border region, it submitted without resistance when Ashurbanipal launched a retaliatory campaign against Elam in 647, the year after he had brought the rebellion to an end.

After the fall of the Assyrian empire at the end of C7, Gambulu is finally attested in inscriptions from the reign of the Babylonian king Nebuchadnezzar II (604–562), which mention a governor of the province, Marduk-shar-usur.

Frame (1992: 335, index s.v. Gambulu), Lipiński (2000: 472–9).

Gand(h)ara (map 16) Central Asian country (west of the Indus r. in northwestern Pakistan), attested in M1 Iranian and Greek sources. It was among the eastern lands of the Persian empire listed several times in the inscriptions of Darius I (522–486), e.g. in his Bisitun inscription (**DB* 6), and also in the *daiva* inscription (see glossary) of his son and successor Xerxes (**XPh* 3). Its ruler at this time was a man called Bimbisara. According to Herodotus (3.91), Gandara was one of the countries constituting the Persian empire's seventh province, which paid a total annual tribute of 170 talents of silver to its overlord (but see glossary under **satrapy**). This was a relatively low amount, which has suggested to scholars that the countries in question were inhabited largely by tribal groups. A contingent of Gandarans under the command of Artyphius, son of Artabanus, is listed by Herodotus (7.66) among the forces assembled by the Persian king Xerxes for his invasion of Greece in 481. Darius reports that a special timber called sissoo-wood (yaka-wood) was brought from Gandara (and also from the land of Carmania) for use in the construction of his palace at Susa (**DSf* 9, **DSz* 8).

Unger (*RlA* 3: 138), Brentjes and Duchesne-Guilleman (*BNP* 5: 687).

Ganduvata M1 Central Asian city in the country of Sattagydia, a subject state of the Persian empire located in the empire's eastern frontier region. It is perhaps to be identified with mod. Gandava in Baluchistan. (Alternatively, but less convincingly, it has been identified with Gandamak in Afghanistan.) In the uprisings at the beginning of Darius I's reign, Ganduvata was the site of one of the battles fought in 522 between Vivana, satrap of the neighbouring country of Arachosia and supporter of Darius, and the rebel army sent to take possession of the region by Vahyazdata (who falsely claimed to be Cyrus' son Bardiya), a pretender to the Persian throne (**DB* 46).

Ganibatum Middle Bronze Age city, attested in the Mari archives, in the middle Euphrates region. An identification has been proposed with mod. Abu Saʿid, which lies

15 km downstream from the Balih r.'s confluence with the Euphrates. Though attached to the kingdom of Mari, Ganibatum was apparently subject to Yaminite (q.v.) attacks. The Yaminite presence in Ganibatum's territory was sufficient to dissuade the governor of Saggaratum (one of the most important cities of the kingdom of Mari) from sending a wedding party through it.

Burke (1961), *LKM* 610 (refs).

Gannanate M1 city located in eastern Babylonia on the Diyala r. northeast of the Jebel Hamrin. In 851 the Assyrian king Shalmaneser III laid siege to the city during his campaign in this region in support of the Babylonian king Marduk-zakir-shumi I, whose brother Marduk-bel-usati had rebelled against him. The latter had made a stand in Gannanate. Shalmaneser defeated his forces in a battle outside the city, but was unable to take the city itself, where Marduk-bel-usati withdrew after his defeat, and had to content himself with ravaging its surrounding orchard- and crop-lands. The following year Shalmaneser returned for a fresh assault upon the city, and this time succeeded in capturing it. He then pursued Marduk-bel-usati, who had fled at the approach of the Assyrian army with some of his military officers, and tracked down and killed the fugitives in the city of Arman (**RIMA* 3: 30). In 813 Gannanate was among several important cities in the Diyala region seized by the Assyrian king Shamshi-Adad V, during the second of his four campaigns into Babylonian territory (**ABC* 168, **RIMA* 3: 190). The Babylonian king Marduk-balassu-iqbi, who was in Gannanate at the time, fled the city before it fell to the Assyrians, but was pursued by Shamshi-Adad and finally captured in Der (see **Der (3)**). In 771 and 767 Gannanate was the target of two further Assyrian campaigns, conducted by Ashur-dan III (Millard, 1994: 39, 40). The city is perhaps to be identified with Ganata, one of the towns of the Hamaranu tribe (q.v.).

Unger (*RlA* 3: 139–40).

Gassiya see **Kassiya**.

Gath (Assyrian **Gimtu**) Iron Age city, one of the members of the Philistine Pentapolis (see glossary) in southwestern Palestine. It is frequently referred to in *OT* sources – e.g. as the home of the Philistine champion Goliath (1 Samuel 17:4, 23), and as the city to which the Ark of the Covenant was sent (1 Samuel 5:8 etc.). According to 2 Kings 12:17 Gath was attacked and captured by Hazael, king of Aram-Damascus in the second half of C9, prior to his attack upon Jerusalem. A century later, around 712, the city was conquered by the Assyrian king Sargon II (*CS II: 297). Gath's location has not yet been firmly established, though most scholars now favour the proposal by Y. Aharoni and A. Rainey to equate it with mod. Tel Zafit/Tell es-Safi (see ***Zafit, Tel***).

Schniedewind (1998), Maeir and Ehrlich (2001), Laughlin (2006: 123–6).

Gath-rimmon Late Bronze Age city in Palestine, attested among the Asiatic conquests of the C15 pharaoh Tuthmosis III. It is probably to be equated with the city of Gittirimmunim, which appears in the mid C14 Amarna archive as the object of an attack by Lab'ayu, ruler of Shechem (Shakmu) (**EA* 250:46). In *OT* tradition, Gath-rimmon was a city of the Levites, handed over to them after being originally allocated to the territory of Dan (Joshua 19:25, 21:24). The city is probably to be located near and to the northeast of Jaffa. An identification with Tel Gerisa (q.v.) has been proposed.

Bratcher (*HCBD* 263).

Gaugamela (= *Tell Gomal*?) M1 village in northern Mesopotamia, located between the Tigris and the Greater Zab (Greek Lycus) rivers, to the northwest of Arbela and northeast of Nineveh (*BAGRW* 89 F4). It was the site of Alexander the Great's decisive victory over the Persian king Darius III in 331.

Diodorus 17.56–61, Arrian, *Anabasis* 3.11–15, Plutarch, *Alexander* 31–3, **PE* 447, no. 27.

Gaurahi (Yaurahi) Iron Age fortress-settlement belonging to the kingdom of Melid/Malatya in eastern Anatolia. It was one of the many Melidian fortresses and cities which the Urartian king Sarduri II claimed to have captured and plundered in the second year of his reign (c. 764), and among the nine fortresses which Sarduri added to his own country (*Kuhrt, 1995a: 556–7). Subsequently, it remained under Urartian control until the Assyrian king Tiglath-pileser III defeated an Urartian–Arpad military coalition in 743, and established his sovereignty over the kingdom of Melid and those of its former possessions which it had lost to Urartu.

CHLI I: 284–5.

Gavurkalesi (map 2) Late Bronze Age Hittite sanctuary, probably dating to C13, in north-central Anatolia, 60 km southwest of Ankara. It was discovered in 1862 by G. Perrot, and excavated in 1930 by H. H. van der Osten for the Oriental Institute, University of Chicago. Gavurkalesi is a mod. Turkish name meaning 'castle of the infidels'. Its anc. name is unknown. The site, enclosed by Cyclopean walls (see glossary), is located on a plateau whose surface was levelled to provide an area 35 m × 37 m on which the sanctuary, containing a stone-built chamber, was constructed. The chamber has been interpreted as either a tomb or a shrine. It is possible that the whole sanctuary served as a mausoleum, known as a *hekur*-house in Hittite texts, permanently staffed by attendants. A relief carved into the rock-face below the fortified area depicts two gods wearing horned, conical caps and facing a seated goddess. The three deities may depict a divine triad: father, son, and mother. The composition has been compared with the relief scene in the main chamber at Yazılıkaya (q.v.). This comparison provides the basis for dating the sanctuary to C13, and probably to the reign of the Hittite king Hattusili III. (There may well have been earlier periods of occupation which have left no visible traces.) Other buildings, including housing for cult-personnel, may also have been constructed within the fortified area, but were destroyed during or before the period when the Phrygians occupied the site in early M1. This occupation is reflected in pottery sherds and the remains of limestone walls of Phrygian date.

E. Akurgal (1973: 288–9), Bittel (1976: 114, 179, figs 105, 106, 199, 200), Lumsden (2002), Burney (2004: 92).

Gaza (Akkadian **Hazzatu, Azzatu**) (map 8) Canaanite and subsequently Philistine city located in the mod. Gaza strip on the southern coastal plain of Palestine, c. 5 km from the Mediterranean Sea. Its history of occupation extends from the Late Bronze Age until the present day. Excavations were carried out on the site in 1922 by W. J. Phythian-Adams on behalf of the Palestine Exploration Fund, providing evidence, relatively meagre, for settlement in the Late Bronze Age and in subsequent periods. Investigations of the remains of the anc. city have been extremely restricted, both because of the site's continuous occupation to the present day, and because of the region's ongoing political turbulence. In written records, Gaza is first attested in C15 among the Asiatic conquests of the pharaoh Tuthmosis III. The region in which it lay was later subjected to numerous Egyptian campaigns, a reflection of its vital strategic position linking Egypt with its Asiatic territories. In the mid C14 Amarna texts, the city appears as an Egyptian administrative centre, under the name Hazzatu or Azzatu (e.g. **EA* 289, 296).

At the beginning of C12, Gaza was the southernmost city of the Philistine Pentapolis (see glossary) (Joshua 13:3), and a cult-centre of the Philistine god Dagon. In M1, written records indicate that it fell to three conquerors: (a) the Assyrian king Tiglath-pileser III in 734 (**Tigl. III* 138–40), when it was ruled by a certain Hanunu (who fled to Egypt, but returned and was reinstated by Tiglath-pileser; he subsequently rebelled against and was defeated by the Assyrian king Sargon II at the battle of Raphia, q.v.); (b) the Judaean king Hezekiah several decades later (2 Kings 18:8), but only for a brief period; (c) the pharaoh Necho II in 609, again only briefly. During the Persian period (C6–4), Gaza was an important royal fortress (Herodotus 2.159 calls it Cadytis). When Alexander the Great marched into Palestine in 332, it was the only city in its region that refused to submit to him (Arrian, *Anabasis* 2.25–7). As a consequence, Alexander placed it under siege, captured it, and then sold its population into slavery. Following his death, Gaza first came under the control of the Ptolemies, serving as the northern outpost of their empire, but was captured by the Seleucid king Antiochus III in 198. It was a flourishing city under Roman rule and continued to be so in the Byzantine period.

Ovadiah (*NEAEHL* 2: 464–7), Weinstein (*OEAE* 2: 5–7).

Gaz(z)iura Late Bronze Age country in north-central Anatolia, subject to the kingdom of Hatti. Early in C13, it rebelled against Hatti and participated in the attacks on cities in the northern part of the Hittite homeland when King Muwattalli II shifted the Hittite royal seat south from Hattusa to Tarhuntassa. It is probably to be identified with the Classical city also called Gaziura. Based on information provided by Strabo (12.3.13), this city was located at mod. Turhal on the Yeşil Irmak r. (Classical Iris) (*BAGRW* 87 B4).

Garstang and Gurney (1959: 14–16), **CS* I: 200.

Gedrosia (map 16) Central Asian country with a largely nomadic population, located in mod. Baluchistan on the north coast of the Indian Ocean, and attested in M1 Persian and Greek texts among the eastern lands of the Persian empire. It was probably incorporated into the empire during a campaign which Cyrus II conducted in the east some time after his conquest of Babylon in 539 (though no account of such a campaign survives). Gedrosia was conquered by Alexander the Great during his eastern campaign (Arrian, *Anabasis* 6.22–6), and following his death in 321 was one of the eastern countries which came under the control of the Seleucid empire. However, Seleucus I included it among the countries which he yielded in treaty negotiations with the Indian Maurya ruler Chandragupta.

Kiessling (*RE* VII: 895–903), Brentjes (*BNP* 5: 717).

Gelidonya (map 2) Cape on Anatolia's southern coast in the country of anc. Lycia at the western end of the Bay of Antalya. It is attested in Pliny the Elder (5.97) as the Chelidonian Promontory. At least four ships are known to have sunk in antiquity off the cape. The oldest and best known of these dates to the end of C13, within the final decades of the Late Bronze Age. Discovered in 1954 by a sponge diver, the wreck was excavated by G. Bass in 1960. Further visits to the site in the 1980s by a team led by Bass from the Institute of Nautical Archaeology at Texas A&M University recovered more artefacts and determined how the ship had sunk. Its hull had apparently been torn open on a pinnacle of rock just below the surface of the water. The ship's cargo consisted principally of copper and tin ingots, and scrap bronze tools from Cyprus which were apparently intended for recycling. From the large quantitites of copper and tin being carried by this vessel when disaster struck, as well as by the ship wrecked one hundred years earlier off the Lycian coast at Uluburun (q.v.), we can conclude that consignments of these metals were the largest and most regular components of the cargoes of merchant ships during the Late Bronze Age. These basic cargoes were supplemented by other items, including luxury goods, from all parts of the eastern Mediterranean and Aegean worlds, taken on board at the various ports of call.

The origin of the Gelidonya wreck (as also the Uluburun wreck) remains uncertain. The vessel may have been of Syro-Canaanite origin, though a Cypriot origin is also possible. The discovery in 1994 of the ship's anchor, which proved to be of Syro-Canaanite or Cypriot type, strengthened the case for assigning a Near Eastern origin to the vessel. Its crews, however, were very likely multinational in composition, recruited from many parts of the Near Eastern and Aegean worlds.

Bass (1967; *OEANE* 1: 414–16).

Gergis (Gergithus) (map 5) Small M1 city in the northern Troad, northwestern Anatolia, not far from Ilion (Troy). Its name appears to have been derived from a pre-Greek Troad population of the region called the Gergithes, some of whom may subsequently have been carried off to Miletus. A sanctuary of Apollo was located in the city. In C5, Gergis was subject to Persian overlordship, but in 399 was among the cities captured from the Persians by the Spartan military commander Derkylidas during his Asia Minor campaign. In 188, in the treaty drawn up between Rome and the Seleucid king Antiochus III (the Peace of Apamea), Gergis was declared a free city.

Bürchner (*RE* VII: 1248–9), Danoff (*KNP* 2: 761).

Gerisa, Tel (map 8) 2.6 ha settlement-mound, located in the Yarkon r. valley on the coast of Palestine 8 km northeast of Jaffa. Its history of occupation extends from the Early Bronze Age III (late M3) period through Iron Age IIA (early M1). Excavations have been conducted periodically on the site since 1927, initially under the direction of E. L. Sukenik on behalf of the Hebrew University of Jerusalem, and more recently by teams from Tel Aviv University under the direction of Z. Herzog. The site was first occupied in the Early Bronze Age by an unwalled agricultural settlement. This was replaced during the Middle Bronze Age IIA–B periods by a fortified city whose defence system is indicated by the remains of three sets of city walls built in successive phases. Adjoining the third of these walls, which dates to the IIB period, are the remains of a substantial brick building, perhaps a local ruler's residence. A large water system was another feature of the Middle Bronze Age city. Its remains consist of a circular shaft, 6 m in diameter, and stairs cut into the side of the shaft, leading down to the water source 22 m below.

The dominant feature of the city's Late Bronze Age and most prosperous phase, when settlement expanded to cover the whole mound, was a large square building in the centre of the mound. Assumed to be a palace, its layout consists of three rows of rooms and a stone-paved courtyard. An extensive, white-plastered open space to the west of building has been interpreted as a market-place, on the basis of large quantities of Mycenaean, Cypriot, and Egyptian pottery found within the area (also Egyptian scarabs). These discoveries support the view that Tel Gerisa was a port of some significance on the eastern Mediterranean coast, especially during the Late Bronze Age.

The transition between the end of the Late Bronze Age, when the city was destroyed (c. 1200), and the beginning of the Iron Age is not clear because of the lack of stratigraphical evidence. However, Iron Age occupation of the site appears to have been on a much reduced scale. Settlement was now confined to the northern and southern ends of the mound, predominating on the latter. Herzog suggests that the centre of the mound, which was not occupied, may have been used for horticultural purposes. Pottery from the Iron Age I strata indicates Philistine occupation. But Tell Qasile, which lay only 1.5 km away across the Yarkon r., was a larger and more important Philistine centre. Tel Gerisa must have been no more than a satellite to Tell Qasile.

The Philistine settlement at Tel Gerisa was destroyed by fire some time during the first half of C10. Sukenik assigned this destruction to the conflicts between the Philistines and the Israelite king David. The site was reoccupied soon after, by Israelite settlers according to Sukenik. But it was smaller than its predecessor and had only a short existence. Its destruction before the end of C10 may have been brought about by the pharaoh Sheshonq I (*OT* Shishak) (945–924) during his campaign in Israel. The site was then abandoned until Arab reoccupation of part of it in C9 CE.

An identification has been suggested with the biblical city Gath-rimmon (q.v.), attested in C15 and C14 Egyptian texts.

Herzog (*NEAEHL* 2: 480–4).

Geshur, Land of (map 8) Region in the southern Golan Heights in northern Palestine, located along the Yarmuk r. in the south and extending eastwards into mod. Syria from the Sea of Galilee. Its history of occupation extends from the Early Bronze Age through the Iron Age. A number of Israeli teams have carried out excavations at various sites in the region, within the context of Tel Aviv University's Land of Geshur Project, including the Leviah Enclosure, Tel Soreg, Tel Hadar, and Rogem Hiri. In documentary sources, Geshur may first be attested in one of the mid C14 Amarna letters – **EA* 256: 23, which contains a list of cities belonging to the land of Gari (Garu) (**EA* 256: 23). B. Mazar suggests that *Ga-ri* (*Ga-ru*) should be read as *Ga-<su>-ri*. Later *OT* tradition records the failure of the Israelites to conquer the people of Geshur and Maacah, both of whom maintained their independence at the time of the Israelite occupation of Palestine (Joshua 13:13). According to 2 Samuel 3:3, the Israelite king David married Maacah, daughter of Geshur's king Talmai, and became by her the father of Absalom; this was one of several political marriage alliances which David contracted in order to consolidate his power in his war with the house of Saul. In C9 Geshur was probably incorporated, along with Maacah, into the Aramaean kingdom of Damascus.

B. Mazar (1986).

Gezer (*Tell el-Jezer*) (map 8) 13 ha settlement-mound in Palestine, 8 km southeast of mod. Ramla. Its history of occupation extends from the Late Chalcolithic (mid M4) to the Roman period. Identified with biblical Gezer by C. Claremont-Ganneau in 1871, the site was first excavated by R. A. S. Macalister between 1902 and 1909 for the Palestine Exploration Fund. Later excavations were undertaken by the Hebrew Union College Biblical and Archaeological School in Jerusalem (HUC) from 1964 to 1974, under the direction, successively, of G. E. Wright, W. G. Dever, and J. D. Seger. Dever carried out further excavations in 1984 and 1990. A total of twenty-six occupation strata were identified.

The following account of Gezer's history is based primarily on the information provided by the HUC teams working at Gezer. It should be said that their findings have been criticized, particularly by I. Finkelstein (2002), for a number of alleged methodological and disciplinary deficiencies. Dever (2003a) has responded to these criticisms with a defence of the HUC teams' work on the site.

The Early Bronze II period, represented by Strata XXIV–XXIII (c. 3100–2600), saw a considerable expansion in the size of the settlement, though as yet it was unfortified. At the end of this period the site was abandoned, not to be occupied again until the early Middle Bronze I period, represented by Stratum XXII (c. 1900). By Middle Bronze II (XXI–XX; c. 1750–1650) it had developed into a relatively large urban centre. However, it was not fortified until late Middle Bronze II or early Middle Bronze III (Stratum XIX; c. 1650). The city was now encircled by a wall system (identified by Macalister as the 'Inner Wall') which incorporated many rectangular towers and was some 1,200 m in length. Entry to the city was provided by a monumental triple gateway. The violent destruction of the Middle Bronze Age city in Stratum XVIII may have been due to the pharaoh Tuthmosis III who lists it among the cities he conquered on his first Asiatic campaign (c. 1468). This is the earliest written reference we have to the city. Its destruction was followed by almost total abandonment, with only a few burials and sherds to mark this period (Stratum XVII). However, the settlement gained a major new lease of life in C14 (Stratum XVI), when an impressive multi-storeyed building was constructed, in the style of an Egyptian governor's establishment. Gezer's involvement in the politics and military conflicts of the Syro-Palestinian kingdoms in this period is reflected in frequent references to it (as Gazru) in letters from the mid C14 Amarna archive. Several of its kings corresponded with the pharaoh Akhenaten (e.g. **EA* 298). To this period is now dated the city's 'Outer Wall' as identified by Macalister. Strata XV–XIV, which belong to the last century of the Late Bronze Age (C13–12) reflect a city once more in decline. Dever suggests that this phase of its existence may have been ended c. 1207 by the pharaoh Merneptah who lists Gezer on his 'Israel Stele' among the Canaanite cities and peoples whom he conquered (**ANET* 378).

There was, none the less, some degree of continuity into the transitional period between Bronze and Iron Ages (Strata XIII–XII), as illustrated both by the ceramic ware and by similarities between the buildings of these levels and their predecessors. However, a new multi-roomed public granary now made its appearance, and a Philistine presence is indicated by the finds of Philistine bichrome pottery. This represents the first of five Philistine phases in the city's occupation. The Philistine period seems to have been characterized by considerable disruption, and several destructions. Stratum XII ended in a massive destruction around mid C12. In Stratum XI, which followed in late C12, two large courtyard houses replaced the granary. Both were eventually abandoned after being twice destroyed by fire and twice rebuilt. The decline and disappearance of Philistine wares in this period probably reflects the end of the Philistine presence in the city. The archaeologically impoverished Strata X–IX (late C11–early C10) are seen as representing a post-Philistine, pre-Israelite transitional phase.

The C9 Stratum VIII (Iron Age II) represents a period of major new development in Gezer, in what has commonly been seen as the first Israelite level. The city was now fortified with a casemate wall, through which the main access to the city was provided by a four-entrance gateway. Once seen as testament to Solomon's monumental building programme, this gateway should probably be attributed to Omri or Ahab. Following a destruction, the site continued to be occupied through Stratum VII (C9), when a new palace was built and the four-entrance gate was restored as a three-entrance structure. There is evidence of decline in this period, which continued through Stratum VI, until the site was once again destroyed, almost certainly by the Assyrian king Tiglath-pileser III during his campaigns in the region in 733/732. An Assyrian relief from Tiglath-pileser's reign depicts the siege of Gezer (Gazru in Assyrian texts). Though the city once again recovered, as indicated by two Assyrian texts and royal stamped jar handles found in Stratum V, it was no longer a place of great importance. According to *OT* sources, it was in C7 part of the kingdom of Judah, when the Judaean throne was occupied by Josiah (c. 640–609). The end of Stratum V came with destruction by the Babylonians during their 587/586 campaign There are only meagre remains of the succeeding Persian and Hellenistic periods (Strata IV and III–II respectively). However, a few rich tombs with silver vessels have been dated to the former, and the city seems to have experienced a modest growth in the latter. After Stratum I, which dates to the Roman period (late C1 BCE–C1 CE), Gezer was largely abandoned, though there are Byzantine tombs and mediaeval remains close by.

J. Schwartz (1990), Dever (*NEAEHL* 2: 496–506; *OEANE* 2: 396–400), I. Finkelstein (2002), Dever (2003a).

Gibeah City in southern Palestine, attested in *OT* sources as the home of Saul (1 Samuel 10:26). *OT* tradition associates it with several important episodes in Saul's career (e.g. 1 Samuel 10:1–10; 11:1–11; 14:2), including the event which led to his appointment as king of Israel. W. F. Albright proposed identifying Gibeah with the site of Tell el-Ful (see ***Ful, Tell el-***), which he excavated in 1922–3. This identification has been fairly widely accepted, though a number of scholars remain doubtful.

Coats (*HCBD* 376), Laughlin (2006: 132–4).

Gibeon (*el-Jib*) (map 8) Fortified city in southern Palestine, West Bank, 9 km north of Jerusalem. Its history of occupation extends from the Early Bronze Age to the end of the Iron Age, with reoccupation during the Roman period. Identification of el-Jib with biblical Gibeon was proposed by E. Robinson in 1838, though it had already been suggested by visitors to the site as early as C17 CE. The identification was finally confirmed by epigraphic evidence in the course of the University of Pennsylvania's excavations carried out over five seasons between 1956 and 1962. These excavations, directed by J. B. Pritchard, brought to light a number of jar handles, of C7 and C6 date, inscribed with the name Gibeon. Early Bronze Age occupation of el-Jib is best represented by a number of Early Bronze IV tombs, consisting of shafts which were cut into the limestone on the slope of the mound, leading to circular chambers. The tombs were reused in the Middle and Late Bronze Ages. Features of Iron Age occupation of the site include an impressive water system, built in two stages, with spiral staircase (stage 1) and stepped tunnel (stage 2) leading to underground water sources, and a large winery containing numerous wine presses and sixty-three vats cut into the limestone.

Gibeon appears frequently in *OT* sources. The most famous of the biblical stories associated with it relates Joshua's alliance with the city, and his defeat near Gibeon of the king of Jerusalem and his allies – the occasion on which he reputedly made the sun stand still (Joshua 9–10). Although Joshua is conventionally dated to C13, and Gibeon figures frequently in the period of his leadership of the Israelites, no evidence has been found to indicate that el-Jib was occupied at that time. Similarly, very little evidence has been found for occupation in the centuries following the Iron Age, between C6 and C1. In the Roman period, however, a new unfortified town was built on the site.

Pritchard (*NEAEHL* 2: 511–14), Hallotte (*OEANE* 2: 403–4).

Gidara Iron Age city located in the upper Habur region of northern Mesopotamia, west of Nusaybin and north of Guzana. It had apparently been seized from the Assyrians by an Aramaean tribe called the Temanites (q.v.) after the reign of the Assyrian king Tiglath-pileser II (967–935), and renamed Raqamatu by them. This information is provided by Adad-nirari II (911–891), Tiglath-pileser's successor-but-one, who marched upon the city during his campaign in the region in 898, captured it after a siege, plundered it of its most valuable possessions, and deported its Temanite ruler Muquru and his family to Assyria (**RIMA* 2: 150). A provincial governor of Raqamatu is attested in 773 at the latest; subsequently, the city may have been incorporated into the Province of the Commander-in-Chief (see glossary). Lipiński notes that Gidara is a West Semitic name, and suggests that the dual name of the city (Gidara, Raqamatu), recorded by the Assyrians, implies the coexistence of two population groups in Gidara: the anc. urban population and the Aramaeans who seized the city in Tiglath-pileser's reign.

Lipiński (2000: 114–16).

Giddan see **Hindanu**.

Gilead (map 8) Mountainous region in Transjordan. Its location was strategically important, since through it passed the major road from Damascus to the Gulf of Aqabah, called the King's Highway (q.v.). In *OT* tradition Gilead's territory was divided, following the Israelite conquest, between the tribes of Reuben and Gad and the half-tribe of Manasseh (Deuteronomy 3:12–13). *OT* sources also report that it was rich in pastureland and famous for its balm. Gilead apparently remained under Israelite control until its conquest by the Assyrian king Tiglath-pileser III c. 732, who deported many of its inhabitants to Assyria. Under Persian rule (C6–4) it became a separate province. It was also a separate region in the Hellenistic period, when it was called Galaaditis.

Negev and Gibson (2001: 202–3).

Gilead (**Mizpah of**) An Israelite cult-centre in the land of Gilead, Transjordan, probably to be located north of the Jabbok r. According to *OT* tradition, it was the place where Jacob and Laban made their covenant after the latter's return to Palestine (Genesis 31:49). Here the Israelite forces assembled, facing the encampment of Ammonites (Judges 10:17), and appointed the Gileadite Jephthah as their military leader (Judges 11:11) to free them from Ammonite domination. This city (rather than Ramoth Gilead; q.v.) may be the Gilead included in the list of lands annexed by the Assyrian king Tiglath-pileser III c. 733 (**Tigl III* 138–9). Its precise location remains uncertain, but identifications have been proposed with the settlement-mounds at Tell Hisn, south of Irbid, and Tell Masfa, northwest of Ğeraš (see Lipiński's map, 2000: 357).

Lipiński (2000: 355–6).

Gilzanu (map 13) M1 country lying to the west or southwest of Lake Urmia (in northwestern Iran). Its population was made up of, or included, semi-nomadic tribes. Gilzanu was one of the regular tributaries of the Assyrian king Tukulti-Ninurta II (890–884) (**RIMA* 2: 178), who lists the land among his northeastern conquests (**RIMA* 2: 180). Tukulti-Ninurta's son and successor Ashurnasirpal II also received tribute from Gilzanu, while he was in the land of Mt Kirruru, during the campaign which he conducted to the northeast of his kingdom in his accession year and first regnal year (884–883) (**RIMA* 2: 197). Representatives from Gilzanu were among the guests invited to attend the great banquet celebrating Ashurnasirpal II's building programme at Nimrud (Assyrian Kalhu, biblical Calah), c. 866 (**RIMA* 2: 293). When Ashurnasirpal was succeeded by his son Shalmaneser III, Gilzanu promptly reaffirmed its status as an Assyrian tributary by making a tribute payment to Shalmaneser while he was campaigning in the regions of Hubushkia, Urartu, and Nairi in his accession year (859). Shalmaneser received another payment of tribute from Gilzanu's king Asau following his campaign against Nairi in his third regnal year (**RIMA* 3: 9, 21). Again a tribute payment from Gilzanu is recorded for Shalmaneser's thirty-first regnal year, on this occasion during a campaign conducted by the king's commander-in-chief Dayyan-Ashur (**RIMA* 3: 70). The payment was received by Dayyan-Ashur on Shalmaneser's behalf from Gilzanu's king, Upu.

Girsu (*Telloh*) (map 17) Predominantly Early Bronze Age city in southern Mesopotamia, capital of the city-state Lagash. Ceramic ware and other artefacts indicate that the earliest human occupation dates to the Ubaid and Uruk periods. The first excavations of the site, which consists of a series of mounds covering an area of over 100 ha, were conducted by E. de Sarzec, the French vice-consul at Basra, between 1877 and 1900. These excavations provided important early evidence of Sumerian art and culture. Subsequent excavations were carried out by French teams under the direction of G. Cros (1903 to 1909), H. de Genouillac (1929 to 1931), and A. Parrot (1931 to 1933). Girsu reached the peak of its development in mid M3 during the Early Dynastic III period. Large quantities of clay tablets dating to this period have been unearthed on the site, including 120 royal inscriptions, and almost 2,000 tablets, relating to the administration of an institution/estate belonging to the goddess Ba'u. The royal inscriptions provide important information about Lagash's history and conquests during the period of its first royal dynasty (c. 2520–2330), especially in the reign of its third king, Eannatum. The most famous monument to be unearthed from this phase of the city's existence was the so-called Stele of the Vultures, which records in both bas-relief and text Eannatum's victory over the rival state Umma (see under **Lagash**). Lagash's tutelary deity, Ningirsu, is given much credit for the victory. A temple dedicated to his worship, built in several stages through the Early Bronze Age, was located in the centre of the city.

Girsu was captured and destroyed by Lugal-zage-si, king of Umma, c. 2330. But following the period when Lagash was subject to the Akkadian empire (c. 2334–2193) Girsu enjoyed a new lease of life, as capital (probably) of an independent Lagash, flourishing particularly in the reign of Gudea (c. 2120), the seventh king of Lagash's second 'dynasty'. Numerous steles and statues were carved in his honour. To judge from his commemorative inscriptions, he was a great builder – projects of his include the Ningirsu Temple – and presided over a state which was at the forefront of a great renaissance of Sumerian art and culture. Girsu continued to be a city of some importance during Lagash's subjection to the Ur III dynasty (c. 2112–2004), as attested by the numerous administrative tablets from the site dating to this period. It subsequently began a long period of decline before finally being abandoned in C17, after the reign of the Babylonian king Samsu-iluna (1749–1712). There was, however, some reoccupation of the site in C2, when the chief of a local principality built a palace there which continued in use until C2 CE.

Parrot (1948), Matthews (*OEANE* 2: 406–9), Sauvage (*DCM* 349–51).

Gisha (Kissa, *Tell Jokha*) Early Bronze Age Sumerian city, southern Mesopotamia, belonging to the city-state Umma. It is now identified with the site of Tell Jokha, previously identified with Umma city. Iraqi excavations at Tell Jokha unearthed a temple dating to the Old Babylonian kingdom (Middle Bronze Age), indicating that the city still existed in early M2. The temple was probably dedicated to the worship of Umma's tutelary deity Shara. During the Ur III period (C21), the city-state Umma was divided into two districts for administrative purposes, one centred upon the cities of Gisha and Umma, the other upon the city of Apishal.

Lafont (*DCM* 870–2, s.v. Umma).

Gizilbunda Iron Age country in the Zagros mountain region of Iran, between Parsua and Media. The Assyrian king Shamshi-Adad V (823–811) marched into it during his third campaign in Nairi. He conquered and destroyed there the city of Kinaki, received tribute from the cities of Sassiashu and Karsibuta, besieged and captured the fortified city of Urash, massacring 6,000 of its population and taking prisoner the king Pirishati together with 1,200 of his troops, and received tribute from Bel-ali, ruler of the city of Sibira (**RIMA* 3: 185). Shamshi-Adad erected a colossal statue of himself in Sibira, inscribing it with a record of his achievements in the Nairi lands. His son and successor Adad-nirari III (810–783) lists Gizilbunda among his conquests in northeastern Mesopotamia and northwestern Iran (**RIMA* 3: 212).

Godin Tepe (map 12) Settlement-mound, covering 15 ha, in the Kangavar valley of central western Iran. Discovered in 1961, the settlement was strategically located on a major east–west route passing through the Zagros mountains. It contains eleven occupation phases (designated by the excavator as Periods XI to I), extending from the Neolithic to the Islamic period. Four seasons of excavations, sponsored by the Royal

Ontario Museum, Toronto, were conducted by T. Cuyler Young Jr between 1967 and 1973.

In Period V (c. 3500–3200), there was a Late Chalcolithic settlement on the summit of the mound, sometimes misleadingly referred to as a 'proto-Elamite colony'. It was surrounded by an oval defensive wall, within which lay a central courtyard, gatehouse, storage magazine, and several major buildings of unknown function. The settlement at this time may have been essentially a trading community. Ceramic ware and other small finds indicate possible trading links with southern Mesopotamia (Uruk IV culture) and the Susiana region of southwestern Iran. In Period IV (c. 3100–2650) there was an intrusion into the central western Zagros region of the Early Bronze Age I Transcaucasian culture from the north, which apparently caused the abandonment of the oval enclosure on the mound. The excavator records the appearance in this period of village houses, elaborate open-air structures on the mound's summit, and an industrial area, perhaps for metalworking.

Period III (c. 2600–1500/1400) saw an expansion of the settlement, from 500 to 700 sq. m. Six sub-periods have been identified. Godin Tepe had now assumed the proportions of an important urban centre. It is in fact the largest known settlement of its time in the Kangavar valley. The plain and painted ceramic ware (the latter displaying geometric and bird motifs) produced from its pottery workshops suggests cultural and commercial connections with the Luristan and Susiana regions of western Iran, and the settlement may have been politically connected with a confederacy of Elamite states. However, Godin Tepe was abandoned some time after 1400 and not reoccupied until the second half of C8, represented by Period II on the site. A fortified mansion was built there after 750. At the peak of its development, this palatial structure contained three large columned halls, storage magazines, and an upper floor for living quarters. It appears to have served as the residence of a local Median ruler. Occupation of it continued after the Persian conquest of Media c. 550, until it was abandoned in late C6 or early C5. The final phase of Godin Tepe's existence, Period I, the Islamic phase, dates to C15 CE.

Young and Devine (1974), Young (*OEANE* 2: 416–17).

Golan (map 8) Region in mod. Israel located to the east and northeast of the Sea of Galilee, first attested in *OT* sources as a city in the land of Bashan belonging to the territory of the Manasseh tribe (Deuteronomy 4:43). The region is divided into three sub-units: (a) in the south, a fertile plain with good agricultural land – this was the most densely populated part of the Golan in anc. times; (b) in the centre, an area suited mostly to grazing purposes; (c) in the north, a thickly forested area, which was only sparsely populated during the Early Bronze and Iron Age I periods.

The earliest evidence of human activity in the region dates back to the Upper Palaeolithic period. The Chalcolithic Age saw relatively extensive settlement, as indicated by the remains of more than thirty village sites of this period, with fifteen to forty houses in each. Settlement seems to have been extremely sparse at the beginning of the Early Bronze Age (EBI), but to have grown during the EB II phase, for which some forty-two sites have been identified. These were located throughout the region. By the end of the Early Bronze Age (EB IV) in late M3, settlement seems to have been confined to the southern Golan, as also in Middle Bronze I – i.e. for a period extending from c. 2350 to 1950. Surveyors of the region believe that there was then a gap in occupation lasting c. 150 years before settlement resumed in the Middle Bronze II period, for which c. forty-five sites have been identified. Once again, settlement was concentrated mainly in the south. It is believed that this may have been due in part to the sedimentary rock in the south, in which it was easier to cut water-tight cisterns for storing water than in hard basalt. The surveys suggested that many of the sites were built for strategic reasons, to control the main routes which passed through the region.

There was a sharp decrease in the number of sites in the Late Bronze Age, followed by a renewal and expansion of settlement in the Iron Age (c. 1200–732). A total of fifty-two Iron Age sites have been identified, distributed fairly evenly throughout the region (south, centre, and north). In a number of cases, abandoned Middle Bronze II sites were reoccupied. Strategically located fortresses figure among the Iron Age settlements. The region was annexed by the Assyrian king Tiglath-pileser III, along with the rest of northern Israel, in the aftermath of his campaign in 732. There is no evidence of settlement during the Babylonian, Persian, and early Hellenistic periods (C6–3). However, the Seleucid conquest of Palestine in 200 was a catalyst for substantial resettlement in the later Hellenistic period, and the number of occupied sites grew in the succeeding centuries, reaching a total of c. 173 settlements by C6 CE.

Ma'oz (*NEAEHL* 2: 525–7; *OEANE* 2: 417–24), Goren-Inbar and Epstein (*NEAEHL* 2: 527–34).

Gordium (Gordion) (map 4) Central Anatolian city located on the Sakarya (Classical Sangarius) r., 100 km southwest of Ankara. Its history of occupation extends from the Early Bronze Age (mid M3) to the Roman imperial period. But the most important phase of its existence dates to the Iron Age (especially C9–8), when it was the capital of the Phrygian empire. The site was discovered and identified in 1893 by the German scholar Alfred Körte, who in 1900 began excavations with his brother Gustav on the citadel. More extensive excavations were carried out, from 1950 to 1973, by R. S. Young for the University of Pennsylvania Museum's Gordium Project. Further excavations were conducted by M. M. Voigt in collaboration with K. Sams, beginning in 1988.

The architectural and artefactual remains of the Late Bronze Age settlement make clear that the city in this period belonged to the Hittite empire, no doubt as a component of one of the empire's subject states. But its Late Bronze Age name is unknown. The earliest Iron Age level is built directly over and into the final Late Bronze Age settlement, suggesting that there was no significant time gap between the two. This has led to the conclusion, based partly on ceramic evidence, that shortly after the site was abandoned, probably during the upheavals accompanying the collapse of the Late Bronze Age kingdoms in C12, it was reoccupied by an immigrant group very likely of Thracian or Macedonian origin. The last decades of M2 probably witnessed the formative stages of a Phrygian state, centred on the city which came to be called Gordium.

The Phrygian city at the height of its development in C8 consisted of three parts: a flat-topped mound now called Yassıhöyük, 17.5 ha in area and generally referred to as the Citadel Mound; a walled lower city located immediately to the south and west of the mound; and an unwalled settlement lying to the north and northwest. The palace complex was located on the citadel in a strongly fortified area which separated it from the rest of the city. It contained a number of rectangular buildings laid out on the megaron plan (see glossary), with roofed columned porch and large inner chamber. The largest and apparently the most important of these buildings, designated as Megaron 3, may have been the palace of King Midas (see under **Phrygia**). To the west of the palace area was a high terrace on which two long buildings were erected. These were evidently service buildings for the palace, for they contained food preparation and storage areas, rooms for the production of textiles, and repositories for a range of valuable items, including gold and electrum jewellery, bronze vessels, animal figurines, and imported horse trappings. The city's massive fortifications incorporated gates in its eastern, northern, and western sides. The most imposing and best preserved of these is the eastern gateway, with central ramp and flanking courts, which still reaches a height of 9 m.

Outside the settled areas, and principally to the east, were the city's burial grounds. Phrygian graves were typically wooden, flat-roofed chambers built into rectangular pits sunk into the ground, and then covered with mounds (tumuli) of rocks and earth. Gordium's cemetery contained c. 140 of these burial structures, which range in date from C8 to the Hellenistic period. They varied greatly in size, no doubt a reflection of the status of their occupants, the more important being built for members of the Phrygian royal family. Generally, the tombs were intended for single burials. The largest is still 53 m high (even after erosion) and almost 300 m in diameter. It covers a wooden burial chamber which in this case has a gabled roof. Still in excellent condition, it can be dated to C8 on the basis of its grave goods, which included nine tables and other wooden furniture, inlaid and elaborately decorated, three bronze cauldrons of Urartian origin, many smaller bronze vessels, pottery, 154 fibulae, and studded leather belts. These goods were buried with the deceased, a man in his sixties, whose body was found *in situ*, laid out on a bier. He has commonly been identified either with Midas, or with his father Gordius. Recent recalibration of the tomb's juniper logs has provided a dating of c. 740 for the tomb, which indicates that the tomb was more likely to have been built for Midas' father than for Midas himself.

The destruction of Gordium has in the past been dated early in C7 and attributed to the Cimmerians. However, radiocarbon tests made in 2001 and a re-examination of artefacts from the Citadel Mound have led to a higher dating for the destruction, probably by fire, to c. 800, too early to be associated with the Cimmerian invasions (see DeVries, 2008: 31–3). The city seems to have recovered quickly from this destruction, and probably by mid C8, if not earlier, had been completely rebuilt. By early C6, after the final withdrawal of the Cimmerians, it was incorporated into the Lydian empire, under whose influence it regained much of its former prosperity. In 547, however, it was captured by the Persian king Cyrus II, while Cyrus was in the process of destroying the Lydian empire. Under Persian rule Gordium was no longer a major political centre, but it may have continued to thrive as a centre within its region for trade and commerce. In 333 Alexander the Great wintered in Gordium, after liberating it from Persian rule. Here, according to tradition, he famously cut the Gordian knot, tied by Midas' father Gordius. (No archaeological evidence has yet been found for the temple where this event allegedly took place.) Subsequently Gordium became part of the Seleucid empire. It was abandoned during the latter part of the Hellenistic age, but later reoccupied by Roman settlers, and thenceforth called by its Roman name, Gordium. New information about Gordium's Hellenistic, Roman, and mediaeval phases has come from recent excavations carried out on various parts of the Citadel Mound.

Sams (1994–5; 1995), Voigt (*OEANE* 2: 426–31), Kealhofer (2005), Sams and Goldman (2006), DeVries (2008).

Gozan see *Halaf, Tell.*

Granicus r. (map 5) River in northwestern Anatolia, the site, in 334, of Alexander the Great's first major encounter with and victory over the forces of the Persian emperor Darius III (Arrian, *Anabasis* 1.13–16, Diodorus 17.19–21, Plutarch, *Alexander* 16). Recent surveys have identified more than forty anc. sites, mostly tumuli (burial mounds) in the vicinity of the Granicus and Aesepus rivers. The sites date to the Persian period (C6–4) and can be associated with satrapal estates of this period. Investigations of them, within the context of the Granicus River Project, were undertaken in 2004 by C. B. Rose, University of Pennsylvania, in collaboration with R. Körpe, Çannakale Onsekiz Mart University.

Rose and Körpe (2006); summary of project by Rose *ap*. Yıldırım and Gates (2007: 328).

Grynium (*Temaşalık Burnu*) (map 5) Graeco-Roman city located on the coast of northwestern Anatolia, 30 km south of Pergamum. According to Herodotus (1.149), it was one of the original eleven Aeolian communities surviving to his day (see **Aeolis**). In C5 it became a member of the Athenian Confederacy. According to Xenophon (*Hellenica* 3.1.6), the Persian king (doubtless Xerxes) handed the cities Grynium and Myrina over to a Greek called Gongylus from the city of Eretria on the island of Euboea, as a reward for Gongylus' support of Xerxes' campaign against Greece in 481. (Gongylus had been exiled from his homeland for his treachery.) Well known as the site of a temple and oracle of the god Apollo, Grynium served as the religious centre of a league of southern Aeolian cities. The oracle, which may well have been of considerable antiquity, continued to function through the Hellenistic and Roman periods, to judge from occasional references to it in written sources of these periods (e.g. in the Roman period, Virgil, *Aeneid* 4.345, Strabo 13.3.5). There are, however, no clearly identifiable remains of the temple where consultations of the oracle took place, nor indeed of Grynium itself.

Bean (*PECS* 368).

Gubla (1) see **Byblos**.

Gubla (2) Iron Age city in the kingdom of Hamath, attested in a list of Hamathite cities and districts recorded by the Assyrian king Tiglath-pileser III (745–727) (**Tigl. III* 148–9). An identification has been proposed with Ǧabla, 20 km south of Latakia.

Lipiński (2000: 286–7).

Gulgulu Iron Age land in northern Mesopotamia, in the Habur valley. The Assyrian king Ashur-bel-kala (1073–1056) engaged in conflict there with the Aramaeans (**RIMA* 2: 103). Lipiński suggests it may have lain in the area of Tell Kawkab.

Lipiński (2000: 99).

Gunilaha Early Bronze Age Iranian city or region. Its location is uncertain, beyond the likelihood that it lay somewhere on the Iranian plateau. The Akkadian king Sargon (2334–2279) lists it among the cities and lands against which he campaigned in the east. The fact that it was the seat of a local ruler (*ensi*) at the time indicates that it was a place of some importance, perhaps a member of what was then a loose confederacy of Elamite states. Other cities and regions against which Sargon campaigned and from which he obtained booty in the region included Parahshum (Sumerian Marhashi), Shali'amu, Kardede, Heni, Bunban, Sapum, Awan, Susa, and Shirihum (**DaK* 178–81).

Zadok (1991: 227), D. T. Potts (1999: 102–3).

Gupin Early Bronze Age city in western Iran. It was among the cities and lands conquered by the Akkadian king Rimush (2278–2270) during the eastern campaign which he conducted early in his reign against a coalition of forces from Elam, Parahshum (Sumerian Marhashi), and Zahara (**DaK* 217).

D. T. Potts (1999: 103, 105).

Gurasimmu M1 Aramaean(?) tribe located in southern Babylonia not far from Ur. The earliest surviving references to it may date to the reign of the Assyrian king Esarhaddon (680–669), but it is not clearly attested until the reign of his son and successor Ashurbanipal (668–630/627). A letter written by Ur's governor, Sin-balassu-iqbi, probably to Ashurbanipal, refers to the governor's capture of 500 fugitives after they had found refuge with the Gurasimmu.

RGTC 8: 142–3, Lipiński (2000: 482–3).

Guretu Iron Age city in northern Mesopotamia, in the lower Habur triangle. The Assyrian king Tukulti-Ninurta II encamped his forces there for the night during his progress up the middle Euphrates and Habur region on his last recorded campaign (885) (**RIMA* 2: 177).

Gurgum (map 7) Iron Age Neo-Hittite kingdom located in the plain of mod. Maraş, southern Anatolia, bordering the kingdoms of Sam'al (Zincirli) to the south and Kummuh to the east. Its capital, attested in the reign of the Assyrian king Sargon II (721–705), was Marqas (mod. Maraş). From information provided by the Luwian hieroglyphic inscriptions found at or in the vicinity of Maraş (**CLHI* I: 252–81), a dynasty of Gurgumite kings can be established, four of whose members have been equated with rulers of Gurgum attested in Assyrian records (*CLHI* I: 250–1):

Astuwaramanzas
Muwatalis (I)
Laramas (I)
Muwizis
Halparuntiyas (I)
Muwatalis (II) = Assyrian-attested Mutallu (II)
Halparuntiyas (II) = Assyrian-attested Qalparunda (II)
Laramas (II) = Assyrian-attested Palalam (*CHLI* I: 251)
Halparuntiyas (III) = Assyrian-attested Qalparunda (III)
gap?
Assyrian-attested Tarhulara
Assyrian-attested Mutallu (III).

The earliest of these rulers, Astuwaramanzas, must date back to C11. He was presumably the founder of the Gurgumite dynasty, but not necessarily the founder of the kingdom, whose origins remain obscure. The last two members of the dynasty are known only from Assyrian records, and the dynasty's end can be dated to c. 711, the year in which Mutallu (III) was deported to Assyria by the Assyrian king Sargon II (see below).

Gurgum first appears in Assyrian records when envoys from the kingdom are listed among the 5,000 foreign representatives present at the inauguration of the C9 Assyrian king Ashurnasirpal II's new palace in Nimrud (Kalhu, Calah) (*RIMA 2: 293). As far as we know, the kingdom remained submissive to Assyria through Ashurnasirpal's reign and that of his successor Shalmaneser III. In his first regnal year, 858, Shalmaneser received tribute from Gurgum's king Mutallu (II), which included Mutallu's daughter and a rich dowry (*RIMA 3: 16). Gurgum apparently took no part in the widespread anti-Assyrian movements which came to a head in Shalmaneser's confrontation, in 853, with a coalition of Syro-Palestinian states at Qarqar (q.v.). Prior to the battle, a Gurgumite king called Qalparunda was one of a number of rulers of eastern Anatolia and northern Syria who paid tribute to Shalmaneser (*RIMA 3: 23). Hawkins (*CLHI* I: 251) believes that this Qalparunda can be identified with Mutallu's son and successor Halparuntiyas (II) in Gurgum. (A contemporary ruler of the northern Syrian kingdom Pat(t)in/Unqi – see **Pat(t)in** – was also called Qalparu(n)da; *RIMA 3: 23). We have a surviving fragment of a colossal statue of Halparuntiyas, which showed the king deified after death. Only the feet of the statue remain, but a record of Halparuntiyas' military exploits has been preserved in an accompanying funerary inscription written in Luwian hieroglyphs (*CHLI I: 256–7, *CS II: 126–7).

In 805, the Assyrian king Adad-nirari III ordered a boundary stone to be erected between the kingdoms of Kummuh and Gurgum, ruled respectively by Ushpilulume and Qalparunda (III), son of Palalam. (For the inscription on the boundary stone, the so-called Pazarcık stele, see *RIMA 3: 205; see also Lipiński, 2000: 283–4.) This followed in the wake of Adad-nirari's conflict with and defeat of an anti-Assyrian coalition of kings under the leadership of the Aramaean Attar-shumki, ruler of Arpad (Bit-Agusi). Qalparunda may have been a member of the coalition, and in a subsequent redefinition of his kingdom's border with Kummuh, which had remained loyal to Assyria, he appears to have lost some of his territory to Kummuh. Gurgum was certainly a member of the Arpad-led alliance which later besieged the Hamathite king Zakur in the city of Hatarikka c. 796 (*Lipiński, 2000: 254–5, *CS II: 155, *Chav. 307–11), and a member of the Urartian–Arpad alliance which confronted Tiglath-pileser III in 743 (*ARAB I: 272–3, 287; *Tigl. III 100–1). Its king on the latter occasion was a man called Tarhulara. When Tiglath-pileser invaded Gurgum, Tarhulara submitted without further resistance (*Tigl. III 102–3) and was allowed to retain his throne, which he continued to occupy for another three decades as a tributary of the Assyrian king (*Tigl. III 108–9). He was, however, forced to cede some of his cities to his southern neighbour Panamuwa II, king of Sam'al (*TSSI II: 14, 15, *CS II: 160). He is still attested as an Assyrian tributary in 732. But c. 711 his son Mutallu assassinated him and seized his throne. The Assyrian king at that time, Sargon II, responded promptly, removing Mutallu (III) from the throne, deporting him to Assyria, and annexing his kingdom as a province of the Assyrian empire. It was now called Marqas, the name of the former kingdom's capital, and apparently retained its provincial status until the fall of the Assyrian empire in late C7.

Röllig (*RlA* 3: 703–4), Hawkins (*RlA* 7: 352–3, s.v. Maraş; **CLHI* I: 249–52).

Gutians (Gutium) People of obscure origins and ethnic affinities, regarded in anc. Mesopotamian tradition as mountain-dwellers in the central Zagros region of western Iran, north of Elam. Steinkeller locates the Gutian homeland in the triangular region defined by mod. Kermanshah, Suleimaniyeh, and Kirkuk (see also *CAH* IV map 2, p. 11). Gutium is first attested in an inscription of Lugal-anne-mundu, ruler in the Early Dynastic period (c. 2902–2334) of the Sumerian city-state Adab. The inscription, surviving in copies from the Old Babylonian period (early M2), refers to tribute paid to Lugal-anne-mundu by a number of lands east of the Tigris including Gutium. The earliest contemporary references to Gutium are found in texts of the Akkadian king Shar-kali-sharri (2217–2193); two of his year-names record, respectively, the capture of the Gutian king Sharlak and the defeat of Gutium. Later literary compositions tell of attacks launched by the Gutians against Naram-Sin, father of Shar-kali-sharri (J. G. Westenholz, 1997: 246). One of these, the famous 'Curse of Akkad' (*Kuhrt, 1995a: 56), is a poetical composition in the form of a letter, in which the Gutians appear as the agents of divine wrath against Naram-Sin for sacking the holy city of Nippur and defiling there the sanctuary of the god Enlil. In this account, written by a Sumerian poet several centuries after the events it records, the Gutians attack and defeat Naram-Sin and sack his royal capital Agade. But in the absence of any references in Naram-Sin's own texts to depredations by the Gutians during his reign, a number of scholars think it likely that these events should be assigned to the reigns of his successors. For a time, Akkadian defences in southern Mesopotamia probably kept the region relatively free of Gutian encroachment. There is, however, some evidence that Gutian rulers may have established themselves in Umma and possibly also Sippar relatively early in the Akkadian period. Whatever the extent of their presence in Mesopotamia at this time, tradition assigns to them responsibility for the destruction of the Akkadian empire. In fact, they may have been but one of a number of external as well as internal forces that brought about its decline and collapse.

A Gutian royal line appears in the Sumerian King List among the dynasties which exercised, allegedly in chronological sequence, authority over southern Babylonia during M3. The best preserved exemplar of this list indicates a Gutian dynasty consisting of twenty-one kings who ruled for a total of 91 years and 40 days between the Uruk V and VI dynasties; in other versions of the King List, the dynasty rules for 99, or 124–5 years (**Chav.* 84). However, only three of these twenty-one Gutian kings are known from other, contemporary sources: La-arabum, Iarlagand and Tiriga(n). A fourth Gutian king, Erridu-pizir, does not figure in the Sumerian King List, but is the subject of a long inscription, excavated at Nippur, which is apparently an Old Babylonian copy of an original Akkadian text. It is one of the most important of the small surviving corpus of Gutian inscriptions. However, a precise date for Erridu-pizir cannot be determined.

Various proposals have been made regarding the chronology of a Gutian regime in Mesopotamia and its relationship to the interval between the end of the Akkadian dynasty and the rise of the Ur III dynasty c. 2112. This interval is generally calculated to have been in excess of a century. But Hallo (*RlA* 3: 714) notes 'a remarkable unanimity in the records of the major city-states of the region, all indicating an interval of c. forty years between the death of Shar-kali-sharri and the emergence of Ur-Nammu (founder of the Ur III dynasty)'. He accommodates within this timespan the last dozen Gutian kings who according to the Sumerian King List reigned for a total of thirty-eight years (cf. Hallo, 2005: 153). The extent of their authority in Mesopotamia is unknown, though they were probably only one of a number of powers and local dynasties who exercised control in the region, including perhaps a couple of obscure successors of the Akkadian dynasty.

Though the 'Curse of Akkad' text describes the Gutians as 'a people who know no inhibitions, with human instincts, but canine intelligence, and monkeys' features' (lines 155–6, transl. *Cooper, 1983; cf. *Jacobsen 1987: 368), it seems that they quickly adapted to Mesopotamian customs and lifestyles, wrote their royal inscriptions in Akkadian, and in many cases assumed Akkadian names. But tradition records that they fell as they had risen, through an act of divine vengeance. In this case, the agent of divine wrath (the god Enlil in particular) was a king of Uruk called Utu-hegal (2123–2113), who expelled the Gutians from the land of Sumer during the reign of their king Tirigan, after defeating Tirigan in battle at a place called Ennigi (**RIME* 2: 284–7). Even so, Gutians continue to appear in later sources dealing with the Ur III period, prompting Hallo to comment that Utu-hegal's rout and expulsion of their forces may not have been as dramatic or as comprehensive as tradition indicates.

During the Old Babylonian period (early M2), references to the Gutians are found in northern Mesopotamian texts, from Shemshara, Chagar-Bazar, and Mari. A Gutian king called Indashshu (variant I/Endushshe) is attested in letters from Shemshara during the reign of the Assyrian king Shamshi-Adad I (1796–1775). According to J. Eidem (cited in Hallo, *RlA* 3: 716), the Gutians may have been located in northern Luristan at this time, though in a Mesopotamian context the term 'Gutian', referring to individuals and groups, may simply have meant 'highlander(s)'. It was in this period that references are made to an army of Gutians supporting an Elamite campaign in Mesopotamia, and to Gutians serving in the Elamite garrison in the city of Shubat-Enlil (Shehna), located in the Habur plain of northern Mesopotamia. A Gutian 'queen' called Nawaritum, attested in letters from the Mari archives, was allegedly captured and later released by Elamite troops (**LAPO* 17: 230, no. 589). Another of the Mari texts records her dispatch of a force of 10,000 Gutians against the city of Larsa (**LAPO* 16: 618, no. 424). Eidem and Laessøe (2001: 31) suggest that references to Gutians in early M2 should be separated into two basic categories – those referring to individuals or smaller groups of people called Gutians and serving various functions in Mesopotamia proper, and those that provide evidence for independent action of an actual Gutian polity.

In the Late Bronze Age a Kassite king of Babylonia, Agum II Kakrime, included the designation 'king of the land of Gutium' in his titulary. By then, however, the name Gutium probably had no more than vague geographical connotations. In this sense, it was applied to some of the peoples who occupied the regions where Gutians had once dwelt – like the Qutu or Quti (q.v.) – but had no ethnic or political connections with them. And it was in this sense alone that the name survived in western Asian literature for another thousand years, as indicated by its appearance in Neo-Assyrian, Neo-Babylonian, and Persian texts, long after the disappearance of the Gutians themselves as an ethnic or political entity. At this time, it was simply an archaic designation for the regions northeast of Babylonia (*RGTC* 8: 144). Memories of the Gutians lived on until well into the Hellenistic period, as reflected in a text of the Seleucid era which refers to their destruction of the cities of Sumer and Akkad. Hallo (*RlA* 3: 714) sums them up with the comment: 'After their brief span in the limelight, they became the victim of ethnic stereotyping, serving in M2 and M1 as little more than a derogatory code-word for barbarian or mountaineer.'

The attempt to link the Gutians with the Indo-European Tokharian speakers of M1 CE in Chinese Turkestan (Henning, 1978) has not found much favour amongst anc. western Asian specialists.

Hallo (*RlA* 3: 708–20; 2005), Gadd (1971: 545–63), Eidem and Laessøe (2001: 31–2).

Guzana see *Halaf, Tell*.

H

Habhu (map: Fuchs, 2000: 94) Habhu, attested in Iron Age Assyrian texts, did not refer to a specific land as such but was rather a term used for certain distant, particularly rough and inaccessible mountain regions. According to Fuchs (2000), five distinct Habhu regions can be identified, based on the accounts of military campaigns attested in the Assyrian royal inscriptions from the reign of Tiglath-pileser I (1114–1076) onwards. (Fuchs, however, notes that people and sheep from Habhu are attested in administrative documents already in C13.) The five Habhu regions will be described in turn, progressing from southeast to northwest.

(1) The easternmost Habhu region bordered on Karalla to the north, Namri to the south, Zamua/Lullumi to the west, and (presumably) Parsua to the east. It is mentioned in the inscriptions of Adad-nirari II (**RIMA* 2: 148), Ashurnasirpal II (**RIMA* 2: 340), and Sargon II (Fuchs, 1998: 66–7).

(2) A mountain area (or areas) directly east of Assyria, associated with the upper (Greater) and lower (Lesser) Zab rivers and with the lands Kirruru and Musasir. Campaigns to this Habhu region were led by Tiglath-pileser I (**RIMA* 2: 19–20), Ashur-bel-kala (**RIMA* 2: 89), Ashurnasirpal II (**RIMA* 2: 197), and Sargon II (Mayer, 1983: 100). Sargon remarks that the peoples of the lands of Nairi and Habhu called the upper Zab river by the name 'river Elamunia'.

(3) A region to the north in the Assyrian–Urartian borderlands, associated with the lands Ullubu, Ukku, and Kumme/Qummeni. This area was the target of expeditions by Tiglath-pileser I (**RIMA* 2: 58) and Adad-nirari II. The latter marched there during his operations in the land of Mehru and in defence of the city of Kummu (**RIMA* 2: 144, 152). Shalmaneser III (**RIMA* 3: 69) and Tiglath-pileser III (*Tigl. III* 134–5, 166–7, 182–3) also campaigned in this region, the latter claiming to have annexed Ullubu and Habhu. Finally, a letter addressed to Sargon II from the Treasurer reports that he has been informed that the city of Birate and the whole of the land of Habhu are well (**SAA* I: 45–6, no. 45).

(4) In the Kashiyari (mod. Tur ʿAbdin) mountain region. A campaign was conducted in this region by Ashur-bel-kala (1073–1056), who engaged with the Aramaeans (**RIMA* 2: 102). Ashurnasirpal II received tribute from Habhu in 879 while he was stationed in the city of Zazabuha within the Kashiyari mountain range (**RIMA* 2: 209, 249, 259). In a summary of his achievements, Ashurnasirpal claimed to have subdued the lands of Nairi and Habhu, the Shubaru, and the land of Nirbu (**RIMA* 2: 221, 275, 323); by these exploits he helped secure the northern borders of Assyria. Perhaps it was from the inhabitants of this region that Shamash-resha-usur, governor of the land of Suhu in the middle Euphrates region in the first half of C8, brought the honey bees with which he set up an apiculture industry in his city Al-gabbari-bani (**RIMB* 2: 281).

(5) The westernmost Habhu region, also known as 'Inner Habhu', was associated

with the lands Alzu and Nairi, the city of Tushhan on the upper Tigris, and the Euphrates bank 'opposite Hatti' (i.e. the eastern bank). Campaigns in this direction were undertaken by Adad-nirari II (*RIMA 2: 148–9) and Ashurnasirpal II (*RIMA 2: 210–11, 219, 251, 260).

(H. D. Baker)
Fuchs (2000)

Habiru An Akkadian term (= Sumerian SA.GAZ or SAG.GAZ) meaning 'dust-makers'. It is used in a number of later M3 and M2 western Asian texts to refer to nomadic or semi-nomadic groups of stateless people, comprising refugees, fugitives, social outcasts, and those seeking a life of adventure, living on or outside the fringes of settled societies, and often posing a serious threat to the security of these societies. The term is first attested in C19 texts of the Old Assyrian period, and last appears c. 1200. A connection with the word 'Hebrew' (ʿibri in Hebrew) is often assumed. However, 'Habiru' is clearly not an ethnic designation, but rather one which covers a large assortment of persons and groups from a variety of ethnic backgrounds, living for the most part a gypsy-like existence outside organized society. It is possible that the peoples later identified as Hebrews arose out of the Habiru groups, or at least had some indirect connection with them.

The Habiru often appear in the role of mercenaries, and brigands who preyed upon travellers, farmsteads, villages, and small cities. Generally, they seem to have operated in small bands. The motley nature of these bands is indicated by a text from Alalah which refers to the inclusion within a particular Habiru group of a thief, two charioteers, two beggars, and a priest of Ishtar. Even in small bands they could terrorize the areas in which they operated. Whole communities were persuaded or forced to join their ranks – the only alternative to being slaughtered or compelled to live in constant terror and impoverishment as their townships and crops were repeatedly plundered and destroyed.

If these bands were united under a common leader, they could constitute a very formidable fighting force. This happened in mid C14 when Abdi-Ashirta, a warlord of the Syrian coastal country called Amurru, succeeded in joining the local Habiru groups into a single force which he used to extend his power over a number of cities and small kingdoms through the Syro-Palestinian coastlands (Bryce, 2003b: 145–53). They frequently appear in the mid C14 Amarna letters as a major threat to the Syro-Palestinian cities and kingdoms which were subject to Egypt (see Moran, 1992: 392, index refs s.v. ʿApiru). Sometimes Habiru groups hired themselves out as mercenaries. In the land of Hatti, a number of them formed auxiliary units which fought in the service of the Hittite king. Sometimes they were employed by a king as labourers on a public works project. The best example of this is provided by an inscription on a prism from the reign of the C17 king Tunip-Teshub (Tuniya), ruler of the northern Mesopotamian kingdom called Tikunani (*Salvini, 1996). The inscription records the employment of 438 Habiru workers, divided into three groups, as a royal labour force. By their very nature the Habiru were of a highly anarchic disposition, and whether serving as auxiliary forces in a king's army or as workers in his labour force, they must have required constant and strict supervision.

*Greenberg (1955), Bottéro (*RlA* 4: 142–7), Loretz (1984).

Habuba Kabira (map 10) Middle Euphrates site in Syria, on the western edge of the Tabqa dam reservoir, consisting of two anc. settlements: (a) the mound Tell Habuba Kabira; (b) the settlement known as Habuba Kabira South, which included a smaller mound now known as Tell Qannas. The site was investigated from 1969 to 1975 by E. Heinrich and E. Strommenger for the Deutsche Orient-Gesellschaft.

Tell Habuba Kabira is an irregular oval mound, c. 230 m in diameter, with a history of occupation extending from the Late Uruk period through the Middle Bronze Age (M4 to early M2). The walled settlement's most notable material remains are those of a temple with open porch, dated on the basis of radiocarbon analysis to the period 2290–2040. The small finds suggest that stone and metal processing were the settlement's main industrial activities. Animal remains indicate that the inhabitants kept cattle, sheep, and goats, and hunted onagers and gazelles. Horses were apparently present during the Middle Bronze Age phase.

Tell Qannas was excavated by a Belgian team under the direction of A. Finet, and was identified as the administrative-religious centre of Habuba Kabira South. The settlement was strategically located on major routes linking Anatolia and northern Syria with Mesopotamia. Its history of occupation is relatively short, spanning the Late Uruk period (M4) and the beginning of the Early Bronze Age (late M4–early M3). Its archaeological significance lies in the fact that it has provided the only large-scale example of Late Uruk residential architecture. Its buildings include houses with large halls flanked by smaller rooms, and in some cases opening onto inner courtyards. The wide range of small finds includes stone vessels, cylinder seals, clay tablets, bullae, pins, and fish-hooks. Industries included stone- and metalworking, lead processing, and pottery production. Originally unfortified, the settlement was later enclosed by a city wall which incorporated numerous towers. Its abandonment early in M3 has been attributed to a blockade of trade routes to the south.

Kohlmeyer (*OEANE* 2: 446–8).

Habur r. (*Khabur*) (maps 2, 7, 10, 13) Tributary of the Euphrates with a large catchment area in northern Syria and northern Mesopotamia. It is generally referred to in two parts, the upper Habur (Habur triangle) and the lower Habur. With its own tributaries and the Balih r. to the west, it converts the northern part of the large grassland and semi-desert region known as the Jezireh into productive agricultural land. The region is archaeologically significant because of the concentration within it of a number of important sites, including Tell Beydar, Tell Brak, Chagar Bazar, Tell Feheriyeh, Tell Halaf, Tell Hamoukar, Tell Leilan, and Tell Mozan. In the Habur triangle, the fertility of the soil combined with good annual rainfall facilitated a marked growth in the urbanization of the region in mid M3, and a relatively high level of prosperity in a number of centres like Tell Leilan and Tell Brak.

The end of M3 is thought to have witnessed a major collapse in settlement in the region, perhaps linked to the demise of the Akkadian empire. The cause of this collapse is hotly disputed – climate change (drought) is one suggestion – as is its extent, since some sites, such as Tell Brak, were continuously occupied throughout the relevant centuries. Other sites, such as Tell Leilan, were resettled early in M2, with a period of decline in later M2. However, major settlements continued to develop and prosper there in the early Iron Age, including the city of Guzana (Tell Halaf), capital of the Aramaean kingdom Bit-Bahiani. In C8 and C7 the Habur region was incorporated into the Assyrian empire, and various major Assyrian settlements were established there, including the Assyrian fortress and administrative centre at Dur-Katlimmu (Tell Sheikh Hamad) on the lower Habur. The western part of the Habur triangle formed part of the province of Guzana, while the eastern part belonged to the province of Nasibina (Nusaybin) (Radner, *RlA* 11: 51–2).

Postgate (*RlA* 4: 28–9), McLellan (*OEANE* 3: 286–8), Akkermans and Schwartz (2003: 259–62, 309–313, 346–50).

Hadar, Tell (map 8) 2.5 ha fortified settlement-mound in the land of Geshur, strategically located on the northeastern shore of the Sea of Galilee, near the main ascent to the Golan Heights, and on the main route from the land of Bashan. Occupation extended through the Late Bronze I and Iron Age I and II periods. Following its discovery and initial survey in 1968, the site was excavated between 1987 and 1995 as part of the Land of Geshur Project conducted by the Institute of Archaeology, Tel Aviv University. Its field director was E. Yadin. The earliest settlement (Stratum VI), protected by a fortification wall made up of large boulders, was founded in Late Bronze Age I (C15). Before the end of this period, the settlement was destroyed and abandoned. It was reoccupied in Iron Age I (C12), archaeologically represented by Stratum V. The material remains of this level include a number of stone-lined silos. Stratum IV, dated to C11, marks the highest point in Tell Hadar's development. From this level were unearthed the remains of two large buildings constructed on two terraces. On the upper terrace, a storehouse with three long narrow halls was built, and on the lower terrace there was a tripartite pillared building with a six-roomed granary. A large quantity of pottery was found in the latter, including locally made egg-shaped jars, cooking pots, bowls, and jugs, and imported Phoenician ceramic ware. Destruction of this level was followed by another period of abandonment until a new settlement was built, represented by Strata III to I and extending through C9 and much of C8. Only private dwellings, surrounded by an outer wall, have been unearthed from these strata. This final phase of Tell Hadar's existence ended with its destruction during the Assyrian campaign in Israel conducted by Tiglath-pileser III in 732.

Kochavi (*OEANE* 2: 450–2).

Hadatu (*Arslan Taş*) (map 7) Assyrian Iron Age settlement, covering c. 31 ha, located in the Saruj plain of northern Syria, and consisting of a citadel surrounded by a lower town. The site was excavated in 1928 by a French team led by F. Thureau-Dangin, M. Dunand, and G. Dossin. Hadatu was probably founded by the Assyrians in C9, as a provincial administrative centre of the rapidly developing Neo-Assyrian empire. Excavations revealed the remains of a governor's palace, consisting of three mudbrick building complexes and tiled courtyards. To the east of these, the French team uncovered a basalt and mudbrick building known as the *Bâtiment aux ivoires* ('Building of the Ivories'). It has a black-and-white pebble courtyard, of a kind known also from Til Barsip, and is particularly notable for its rich collection of C8 ivories of various styles, Syrian, Phoenician, and Assyrian among them. The ivories apparently represent tribute paid by Assyrian subject states to the local administration in Hadatu. Basalt lions guarded the city's gate building, which was embellished with relief sculptures depicting hunting scenes and military parades. Another pair of stone lions guarded the entrance to a temple complex, and stone bulls flanked the entrance to the temple itself. Six statues of gods were further important additions to the assemblage of sculptures unearthed on the site. Inscriptions in Akkadian, Luwian, and Aramaic were carved on the lions guarding the gate building. These inscriptions enabled the site to be identified as Hadatu. Their author was a man called Ninurta-belu-usur, apparently an early C8 governor of the city. He appears to have been subordinate to Shamshi-ilu, a well-known governor of Til Barsip (Masuwari, Kar-Shalmaneser, mod. Tell Ahmar). Til Barsip lay to the southwest of Hadatu, and may have exercised some sort of regional authority over it.

Later occupation of the site is indicated by a Hellenistic temple built over the remains of the Assyrian palace.

Thureau-Dangin (1931).

Hadhramaut (map 9) One of the six pre-Islamic kingdoms of South Arabia. The other five were Saba (biblical Sheba), Qataban, Ausin, Himyar, and Ma'in. Its rulers are attested by name from C5 onwards, when Hadhramaut was one of the dominant powers in South Arabia, along with Qataban and Ma'in. Its capital was the city of Shabwa. Probably late in C1 CE Qataban was conquered, and subsequently incorporated into the kingdom of Hadhramaut. As in other South Arabian states, Hadhramaut's principal deity was the moon god, here referred to by the name Sin.

van Beek (*OEANE* 2: 452–3).

Hadidi, Tell (Azu) (map 10) Semicircular settlement-mound, 500 m in diameter, located in Syria on the west bank of the middle Euphrates, 110 km east of Aleppo. It lies within the region which was affected by the Tabqa Dam Project and the creation of Lake Assad. Tell Hadidi is predominantly a Bronze Age site, with areas of occupation also in the Roman and early Islamic periods. The site was excavated in 1973 and 1974 by H. Franken for the University of Leiden, and from 1974 to 1978 by R. H. Dornemann for the Milwaukee Public Museum in collaboration with the Universities of Wisconsin and Michigan. First occupied at the beginning of the Early Bronze Age, the settlement reached the peak of its development in Early Bronze III and IV, in the second half of M3. Among the Early Bronze Age remains are a number of tombs, including both stone-built chambers and simple shaft-graves. The settlement was fortified by a mudbrick wall. Though occupation continued without apparent interruption into the Middle Bronze Age, the settlement was now much reduced in size and relocated on the western part of the mound. Remains of fortifications and domestic buildings date to this period. Beneath the floors of a number of houses, infant burials were brought to light. The settlement's fortifications were rebuilt in the Late Bronze Age, when occupation again continued without apparent interruption from the preceding Middle Bronze phase. There was some rebuilding and expansion of the settlement during the Late Bronze Age. One of its houses contained a small collection of clay tablets, which provide the city's anc. name, Azu. During the Late Bronze Age the settlement was part of the Mitannian empire. It apparently did not survive the destruction of this empire by the Hittites in the third quarter of C14, and was not occupied again until the Roman period.

Dornemann (1985; *OEANE* 2: 453–4).

Hadnum Middle Bronze Age land in northern Mesopotamia, perhaps to be located on the west bank of the Tigris. Originally allied to Zimri-Lim, king of Mari

(1774–1762), and Ashkur-Adad, king of Karana, it realigned itself with the city of Kurda, which lay in the Jebel Sinjar region of northern Mesopotamia. Apparently in response to this switch of alliance, Haqba-Hammu, adviser to and successor of Ashkur-Adad in Karana, invaded Hadnum with 2,000 troops and captured five of its cities. He also defeated a force from the city of Mardaman, which had come to Hadnum's assistance.

LKM 139, 610 (refs).

Haft Tepe (map 12) Late Bronze Age Elamite site located in southwestern Iran in the region of anc. Susiana (mod. Khuzestan), 10 km southeast of Susa. Its anc. name was probably Kabnak (see below). The site consists of fourteen mounds, extending over an area of more than 30 ha. Excavated by E. O. Negahban between 1965 and 1978, it is largely confined to one level, covering a period of no more than two to three centuries in mid M2. The excavations focused almost entirely on (a) an area designated by Negahban as a tomb-temple complex, which was surrounded by a massive sun-dried brick wall, and (b) to the southeast of it, two terrace-complexes. D. T. Potts believes there is no evidence to indicate that the former served as both a tomb and a temple, and prefers to regard it purely as a royal tomb complex. It is associated with the C14 Elamite king Tepti-ahar, because his name appears in an Akkadian cuneiform text which was inscribed on a stele fragment discovered in the central courtyard. The inscription refers to sacrifices to be made before the chariot of the god Inshushinak and the *saparru*-wagon of King Tepti-ahar. The structure within the walled enclosure is made partly of baked brick (sun-dried brick was generally used elsewhere on the site for less important buildings), and is roughly H-shaped in plan. Its courtyard contains a platform where the stele may originally have been erected. Two large chambers located to the north of the courtyard, and designated as Halls 1 and 2, contained vaulted burial areas where numerous human skeletal remains were discovered. Whether or not the king ever lived in Haft Tepe, or was himself buried in the funerary complex there, remains a matter for speculation.

Of the two complexes lying to the southeast of the tomb complex and built on huge brick terraces, the first (Terrace-Complex I) was the more completely excavated. The excavator suggests that its many-sided brick terrace may have provided a foundation for a ziggurat, palace, or temple. It was surrounded by a number of rooms whose walls were decorated with polychrome paintings on gypsum surfaces. The complex included a craft workshop and pottery kiln, the almost complete skeletal remains of an elephant, and a range of artefacts – figures of ivory, sculpted painted human heads (an Elamite king and queen?), mosaic fragments, and bronze weapons. Potts suggests that the terrace area may have been a temple precinct 'where, on analogy with the great temples of southern Mesopotamia, a wide range of craft activities were concentrated, including pottery, statuary, and other craft production destined to manufacture goods for the gods, the priesthood, and a large number of dependents attached to the temple'. Potts notes that on the mound designated as Haft Tepe B, which lies to the east of the main site, a massive construction was partly revealed in 1976 where an unspecified number of tablets were recovered. Virtually nothing else is known about this mound.

Written records unearthed from what Potts calls the temple complex include cylinder-seals, several hundred seal impressions, and almost 4,000 complete and fragmentary clay tablets. The contents of the tablets, inscribed in Akkadian cuneiform, range from letters to administrative accounts, texts dealing with omens and extispicy (see glossary), and inventories of sacrificial offerings and precious metals for the manufacture of chariot parts and jewellery. These documents may reflect the activities of a scribal school associated with the temple complex. In one c ˉ the seal impressions, a man called Athibu, confidant of the king Tepti-ahar, is called 'great governor of Kabnak' – which makes it likely that Kabnak was Haft Tepe's anc. name.

The city appears to have been destroyed by fire after an occupation lasting no more than two to three centuries. The destruction perhaps occurred in C14, during the course of a devastating campaign conducted in Susiana by the Babylonian king Kurigalzu II (1332–1308). The reappearance of the name Kabnak (as Kabinak) in the record of the Assyrian king Ashurbanipal's conquests in Susiana in 646 may indicate a subsequent Iron Age phase in Haft Tepe's history.

Calmeyer (*RlA* 4: 39–40), Neghaban (*OEANE* 2: 454–7), D. T. Potts (1999: 196–205).

Haftavan Tepe (map 20) 25 m high mound (500 m in diameter), located in the Salmas plain of northwestern Iran, near mod. Shahpur. Excavations on the site conducted between 1968 and 1975 by C. A. Burney for the University of Manchester revealed M2 and M1 periods of occupation. During the latter period (Iron Age II), Haftavan was incorporated into the Urartian kingdom as part of a network of Urartian settlements which grew up around the northwest corner of Lake Urmia. It became an important administrative centre of the Urartian towns and strongholds in the region. Burney reports that burials at Haftavan during this phase included the bodies of young girls variously wearing an elaborate headdress of coiled bronze tassels, a skull-cap adorned with bronze discs, and a bronze headband. A large range of bronze jewellery was included among the grave goods.

Burney (1970; 1972; 1973; 1975), Zimansky (1998: 263).

Hahhum (Hahha) Late Bronze Age city on the upper Euphrates. It was attacked by the Hittite king Hattusili I (1650–1620) during his second Syrian campaign (**Chav.* 221). After encountering fierce resistance from its defenders, Hattusili captured, plundered, and torched the city, then harnessed its king, along with the king of Hassuwa (another city conquered by Hattusili), to a transport wagon.

In a recently published letter addressed to Tuniya (Tunip-Teshub), ruler of the northern Mesopotamian kingdom Tikunani, Hattusili called upon Tuniya to support his attack on Hahhum (*Salvini, 1996: 112–14). This is undoubtedly the same military operation referred to above. Tikunani and Hahhum very likely shared borders, and may well have been hostile to each other. Referring to an earlier era, Hattusili claims that the (C24) Akkadian king Sargon had fought a battle against troops from Hahhum when he crossed the Euphrates; but he had done no harm to the city itself.

A number of identifications have been proposed for Hahhum, including mod. Samsat and Lidar Höyük. In suggesting the latter, Liverani (1988) sought to link the archaeologically attested destruction of the site around this time with Hattusili's destruction of Hahhum (but see Gurney, 1992: 217).

**RGTC* 6: 61–2, *Bryce (2005: 76–80).

Hajar Bin Humeid (map 9) 4 ha oval-shaped settlement-mound located 255 km northeast of Aden on a major caravan route leading northwards to Gaza. Excavations directed by W. F. Albright for the American Foundation for the Study of Man in 1950 and 1951 revealed eighteen occupation strata extending from C11 to C2–4 CE. Hajar Bin Humeid was a small farming community, with a population estimated at between 600 and 1,200. The community's income was no doubt partly derived from tolls imposed on the caravans passing through it. Small finds on the site, including imports from Egypt, Anatolia, and Mesopotamia, provide material evidence of its involvement in international trading activities. The excavators concluded that its existence was a peaceful one, since there is no trace of fortifications or of violent destruction at any stage in the site's history. An important result of the excavations was the development by G. W. van Beek (one of the site's excavators) of the first pottery chronology for pre-Islamic South Arabia. The period covered by this chronology extends from c. 1100 to 200 CE.

van Beek (*OEANE* 2: 457–8).

Hakpis(sa)/Hakmis(sa) (map 3) Late Bronze Age Hittite city in north-central Anatolia, perhaps near mod. Çorum. The city's importance was greatly enhanced in C15 when the cults of the holy city of Nerik, then under Kaska occupation, were transferred there. In early C13, the Hittite king Muwattalli II made Hakpis the capital of the northern part of the Hittite homeland. He installed his brother Hattusili (later King Hattusili III) as ruler of the region, using Hapkis as his base, with the intention of strengthening the kingdom's northern defences, and recovering the territories lost to the Kaska peoples (**CS* I: 201). Hattusili apparently fulfilled all his objectives. He subsequently commanded a contingent from Hakpis in the battle of Qadesh (1274), and on his return from Syria resumed kingship in the city, installing as queen there his new wife, Puduhepa (**CS* I: 202). After Muwattalli's death, the growing tensions between Hattusili and the new king, Urhi-Teshub, his nephew, erupted into open conflict when Urhi-Teshub removed from his uncle control of Hakpis and Nerik (**CS* I: 203). The conflict ended when Hattusili overthrew Urhi-Teshub and seized his throne. Some time after assuming kingship, Hattusili appointed his son, the future King Tudhaliya IV, as governor of Hakpis.

Haas (*RlA* 4: 48–50), **RGTC* 6: 65–7.

Halab (**Halap, Halpa**) see **Aleppo**.

Halaf, Tell (**Guzana**, biblical **Gozan**) (maps 7, 13) Settlement-mound located in northwestern Mesopotamia at the headwaters of the Habur r., with two main periods of occupation – the Pottery Neolithic period (M6–5), and the Iron Age (late M2 through the early centuries of M1). Following his preliminary survey of the site in 1899, M. von Oppenheim directed German excavations there from 1911 to 1913, and again in 1927 and 1931. In 2006, a new joint Syrian–German campaign was initiated under the direction of Lutz Martin (Vorderasiatisches Museum, Berlin), Mirko Novák (University of Tübingen), Joerg Becker (University of Halle), and Abd al-Masih Bagdo (Directorate of Antiquities, Hassake) (see www.smb.spk-berlin.de/smb/sammlungen/details.php?lang=en&objID=23&p=7). The site's rich assemblage of decorated polychrome ceramic ware dating from mid M6 to M5, as well as other distinctive features such as its architecture, has led to the definition of the 'Halaf period'. Remains of this cultural/chronological assemblage have been unearthed on many contemporary northern

Mesopotamian sites. It followed on from the Samarra period and was succeeded by the Ubaid.

The Iron Age settlement consisted of several levels extending from C12 to C7. By the end of M2 it had become a substantial city, dominated by its square, fortified citadel, on which a number of large public buildings were erected. Inscriptions from the site, and elsewhere, indicate that the city was called Guzana (*OT* Gozan), and was the capital of the Aramaean state Bit-Bahiani. It reached its peak during the reign of King Kapara (probably second half of C9), son of Handianu, who resided in an impressive palace in the city's northwestern sector. The palace was of the *bit hilani* type (see glossary). Inscriptions indicate that it served also as a temple. It was accessed by a monumental gateway embellished by three monumental caryatid statues with guardian sphinxes. The palace's outer wall featured a number of carved orthostats, depicting hunting and ritual scenes, warriors, a wide range of animals including lions, a panther, bulls, gazelles, and various hybrid mythological creatures. Many if not all of the orthostats were reused from an earlier building phase. The assortment of treasures which came to light in the ruins of Kapara's palace, including gold, silver, and ivory artefacts, give an indication of Guzana's power and prosperity in this period.

The rise of the Neo-Assyrian kingdom early in M1 ensured that the status which Guzana enjoyed as the seat of an independent Aramaean state would soon come to an end. In 894 the Assyrian king Adad-nirari II marched upon Guzana, seat of Bit-Bahiani's then ruler Abi-salamu, and entered the nearby city of Sikanu. He received there a substantial tribute from Abi-salamu (**RIMA* 2: 153). The region was annexed to Assyria by Ashurnasirpal II (883–859), though even after that it continued to be governed by a local dynasty and to enjoy a relatively high degree of independence. This is evident from the bilingual inscription of its governor, Hadd-yitʿi (Assyrian Adad-itʾi), found at Tell Feheriye (q.v.). Hadd-yitʿi's father Shamash-nuri is thought to be the man who was Assyrian eponym official for the year 866.

Figure 41 Tell Halaf.

In 808, the Assyrian king Adad-nirari III had to conquer Guzana anew. From then on, the names of a number of Assyrian governors of Guzana appear in the Assyrian eponym lists (see glossary) down to the end of the reign of Sargon II in late C8. A so-called northern palace apparently built during the period of Assyrian domination probably served as the governor's residence. In fact, an archive belonging to a governor called Mannu-ki-mat-Ashur, Assyrian eponym official for the year 793, was excavated at the site. It contained letters to him from the Assyrian king, and from a number of high officials.

In *OT* tradition, Gozan was one of the cities to which the Israelites were deported after the capture of Samaria (2 Kings 17:6 etc.). Occupation of the site during the Hellenistic, Roman, and Islamic periods is indicated by a small number of excavated remains from these periods.

von Oppenheim (1933), Lipiński (1994; 2000: 119–33), Kuhrt (1995a: 397–8), Dornemann (*OEANE* 2: 460–2). Re the bilingual inscription referred to above, see Abou Assaf *et al.* (1982), Kuhrt (1995a: 397–8), Bordreuil (*OEANE* 2: 301), Radner (*RlA* 11: 51).

Hala Sultan Tekke (map 14) Bronze Age city near the southeast coast of Cyprus in the region of mod. Larnaca. Although it is today located on the shores of the Larnaca Salt Lake, in antiquity it was probably accessible via a navigable inlet from the sea, providing a sheltered harbour. Founded c. 1600 in the Middle Cypriot III/Late Cypriot I period, the town was one of the largest in Late Bronze Age Cyprus, and appears to have had a flourishing existence until its destruction, probably twice in C12 (c. 1190 and 1175). There was some reoccupation in the remaining decades of C12, at the end of which the site was abandoned until the Hellenistic period when partial resettlement took place. Originally excavated by a team from the British Museum in 1897 and 1898, the site was most recently investigated by P. Åström for Göteborg University, Sweden, from 1971 to 1983.

The city's prosperity had already been demonstrated by the British excavations, which brought to light Late Bronze Age tombs, dating before 1200, containing imported pottery and a wealth of gold, silver, bronze, ivory, and faience grave goods. These finds pre-date the C12 settlement uncovered by the Swedish excavations. Features of this later settlement include a broad main street, 4–5 m wide, and housing complexes consisting of rooms surrounding a central courtyard. A large rectangular building has been identified as a shrine. Hala Sultan Tekke's wealth was no doubt largely due to its copper-producing activities, reflected in the finds of copper-working installations and tools. Part of its wealth seems also to have been due to its craft industries in precious and semi-precious materials, as reflected in the production of gold and silver jewellery and in evidence for ivory-working. Quantities of fish bones, and lead and stone weights apparently used in fishing-nets, suggest a local fishing industry as well. The city's involvement in international trading activities is indicated by finds of pottery from the Aegean (Mycenaean and Minoan), Anatolian, and Syro-Palestinian regions. Of particular interest from the last of these regions is a silver bowl bearing a West Semitic cuneiform inscription. Dried Nile perch, amulets, and scarabs were imported from Egypt.

Åström (1986; *OEANE* 2: 462–3).

Halicarnassus (*Bodrum*) (map 5) M1 BCE–M1 CE city in Caria on the southwestern coast of Anatolia, founded c. 900 by settlers from the city of Troezen in the Argolic peninsula of the Peloponnese (southern mainland Greece). Though a Doric city in origin, Halicarnassus had a substantial Carian population, to judge from the names of many of its citizens. By C5 its culture had become strongly Ionian in character, reflected in the Ionic dialect used in the city's inscriptions and also by the Greek historian Herodotus, who was a native of Halicarnassus. Along with the rest of Caria, the city became subject to Persia c. 540, but was under the immediate authority of a local Carian dynasty. One of the rulers of this dynasty, Queen Artemisia I, personally commanded a Carian contingent which joined the Persian king Xerxes in his invasion of Greece in 481, and participated in the battle of Salamis the following year (Herodotus 8.68–9, 87–8). Following the repulse of Persia, Halicarnassus became a member of the Athenian Confederacy (see glossary). Towards the middle of C5, the city was ruled by a grandson of Artemisia, the tyrant Lygdamis II, who was later expelled by his subjects.

Halicarnassus experienced its greatest development in C4 when the Carian satrap Mausolus (377–353) shifted the seat of his administration there from Mylasa. The city was substantially rebuilt under his regime, and protected by a wall almost 7 km in length. This wall encompassed a number of villages inhabited by people of Carian ('Lelegian') stock, thus significantly increasing the indigenous element in the city's population. Great public buildings now adorned the city, the most spectacular of which was the so-called Mausoleum, later to be ranked among the seven wonders of the anc. world. It was begun by Mausolus himself and completed after his death by his sister-wife and successor, Artemisia II. Artemisia proved an effective ruler of the city, repelling a Rhodian attack on it, and following up her success by attacking and capturing the city of Rhodes (Vitruvius 2.8.14–15). Other members of Mausolus' family line continued to rule in Halicarnassus after Artemisia's death until the city fell to Alexander the Great in 334, after a long siege (Arrian, *Anabasis* 1.20.2–3, 23.1–5). Following Alexander's death it was subject to a succession of rulers, beginning with Ada, youngest sister of Mausolus (she was reinstated by Alexander who was 'adopted' by her), until it was declared a free city by the Romans in 190. In 129 it came under direct Roman rule.

Very little of the anc. city survives, apart from a substantial section of the city walls and a few remains of the theatre (in early C19, it was still relatively well preserved) on the slope of the acropolis. This was because the mod. city of Bodrum was built over the top of it. However, a fairly detailed picture of the city is presented by Vitruvius in his ten-volume treatise on architecture. Unfortunately, of the buildings described by Vitruvius, which include a shrine and colossal statue to the god Ares, a temple of Aphrodite and Hermes, and the palace of Mausolus, the only surviving material belongs to the Mausoleum. Some of the Mausoleum's sculptures, notably the statues of Mausolus and Artemisia II, are now in the British Museum. The site of the Mausoleum was the object of a number of campaigns conducted by Danish teams, from 1966 onwards, under the direction of K. Jeppesen. Subsequent excavations on the site have been conducted by the Museum of Bodrum, sometimes in collaboration with the Danish Halicarnassus Expedition. Though the Mausoleum was demolished by the Crusaders, a description by Pliny the Elder (36.30–1) enabled Jeppesen to make a reconstruction of it, probably with a high degree of accuracy. Measuring

38.25 m × 32.5 m at its base, the funerary structure was built on a 25 m high podium surrounded by two bands of sculptures and supporting a colonnade of 9 × 11 Ionic columns. On top of this was a pyramid-shaped roof consisting of twenty-four marble steps surmounted by a chariot drawn by four horses (a *quadriga*). The tomb-chamber was cut into the rock below the building. The total height of the building, including the *quadriga*, is estimated to have been almost 49.6 m. For a recent study of its reliefs, see B. F. Cook (2005).

Bean (1971: 101–14), Pedersen (*OEANE* 2: 463–5), Berg Briese and Pedersen (2005).

Halif, Tel (Arabic *Tell Khuweilifeh*) (map 8) 3 ha settlement-mound located in the Judaean hills of southern Palestine, midway between the Dead Sea and the Mediterranean coast, to the east of the plain of Philistia and bordering on the Negev desert to the south. Halif has long been equated with biblical Ziklag, but more recently an identification with the biblical Judaean city of Rimmon has been suggested. The site is strategically located on a major route passing from Egypt through Gaza to Hebron via the Judaean hills. Its history of occupation, on the mound and its lower eastern terrace, extends from the Late Chalcolithic Age through succeeding habitation levels to the period of Arab occupation, with intervals of abandonment especially from the end of the Early Bronze Age through the Middle Bronze Age. Exploration and excavation of the site began in the 1950s and continued periodically until 1989. Sponsoring bodies have included the Israel Dept of Antiquities and the Hebrew Union College in Jerusalem. From 1976 until 1993 the study of the site and its surrounding region, in what was called the Lahav Research Project, was undertaken by a consortium of American scholars and institutions under the direction of J. D. Seger of Mississippi State University.

Seventeen archaeological strata have been identified. The earliest of these, dating to the Late Chalcolithic and Early Bronze I periods (c. 3500–2900, represented by Strata XVII–XVI), indicate various stages in Halif's development into a prosperous and important village-centre. The earliest stratified remains were found on a terrace to the northeast of the mound, where evidence emerged of cave-dwellings (which ended when their roofs collapsed). Stratum XVI featured well-built rectangular houses with mud-brick walls. The site was apparently abandoned at the end of Early Bronze I, and then reoccupied in Early Bronze III (represented by Strata XV–XII), when a fortified settlement was built on the mound. Following violent destruction of this settlement c. 2500, three successive unfortified towns were built, each of which appears to have ended in destruction. The site was then apparently abandoned until resettlement took place in the Late Bronze Age, beginning in late C16. Several substantial settlements and several destructions are reflected in the archaeological strata (XI–VIII) of this period. Correlations between these levels and the history of the period remain matters for speculation, though almost certainly they are linked with the waxing and waning of Egyptian authority in the Syro-Palestinian region. Surprisingly, Halif appears to have remained unwalled throughout its Late Bronze Age phase. For at least part of this phase, it probably served as a trading station on the route between the coast and the Judaean hills. In Stratum VIII the site was substantially redeveloped, so that it now functioned, through C13, as a large storage complex, very likely as a local grain collection and redistribution centre for the Egyptian administration.

Halif's Iron Age I (Stratum VII) culture evolved, without any apparent break, from its final Late Bronze Age phase. Iron Age II was a period of significant growth and development on the site, beginning in early C9 and represented archaeologically by Stratum VI. The city was now defended by a casemate wall system and stone-covered glacis (see glossary). An Iron Age cemetery, with rows of tombs cut into the limestone, was discovered on the slope of a hill facing the mound's southwest side. Despite its fortifications, the Iron Age II settlement came to a violent end in the final years of C8, its destruction very likely due to the campaigns of the Assyrian king Sennacherib in 701. There was some immediate reoccupation of part of the site, but probably only briefly, by squatters who had survived the settlement's destruction and escaped deportation by the Assyrians. Further evidence of reoccupation is found in Stratum V, dating to the Persian period (C6–4), and also in Stratum IV, which belongs to the Hellenistic period. Strata III–II provide indications of a prosperous settlement in the Roman and Byzantine periods, with occupation continuing into the Arab era (Strata II–I).

Seger (*NEAEHL* 2: 553–9).

Halizones Legendary northern Anatolian people, first appearing in Homer's *Iliad* as the easternmost of Troy's allies (*Iliad* 2.856–7). According to Homer, who refers to their land as 'the birthplace of silver', they came from a distant place called Alybe, unknown outside Classical legendary tradition. For some scholars, the names Halizones and Alybe call to mind the river Halys and a people called the Chalybes. In a tradition recorded by Strabo (12.3.19–20), Alybe is directly linked with Chalybe (q.v.), the land of the Chalybes. Strabo appears to locate this land on the southern coast of the Black Sea, but to the east of the Halys r. A link is sometimes suggested, implausibly, between the Halizones of Classical tradition and the Late Bronze Age Hittites.

Halpa (1) see **Aleppo**.

Halpa (2) Iron Age city and district of the Neo-Hittite kingdom Kummuh in southeastern Anatolia. The Urartian king Sarduri II refers to Halpa in his Annals as one of the royal cities which he captured from Kushtashpi, king of Kummuh, c. 750 (**HcI* 123–4, no. 103 §9). A few years later, Tiglath-pileser III, king of Assyria, claims to have won a victory over an Urartian–Arpad military coalition between Halpa and the neighbouring district of Kishtan (743). The coalition was led by Sarduri and Mati'ilu, ruler of the Aramaean kingdom of Bit-Agusi, and included Kushtashpi among its members (**ARAB* I: 272–3, 276, 281, 287, 292; **Tigl. III* 100–1). Kushtashpi apparently offered his submission to Tiglath-pileser, and later appears among the Assyrian king's tributaries.

CHLI I: 332.

Halule Site on the Tigris r., perhaps near Baghdad, where the Assyrian king Sennacherib fought a battle in 691 against a coalition of Zagros peoples, Elamites, Chaldaeans, Aramaeans, and Babylonians (**Sennach.* 42–7, 88–92). There were heavy casualties on both sides, and the outcome of the battle is uncertain. Although the Assyrians claimed to have won a resounding victory, a Babylonian Chronicle states that the Elamite and Babylonian armies forced the Assyrians to retreat (**ABC* 80). But any success the coalition forces may have achieved was of short duration. In the following year, the Assyrians returned to the site and erected a stele there before advancing upon

Babylon and placing it under siege. By this time, the Babylonians had lost the support of their Elamite allies. Babylon was captured in 689 and its king, Mushezib-Marduk, was taken prisoner and deported to Assyria.

Levine (1982: 48–51).

Halys r. (*Kızıl Irmak*, 'Red River') (maps 2, 3, 4) Classical name for Anatolia's longest river (c. 1050 km). Its source is near the Turkish border with Armenia, and it empties into the Black Sea northwest of mod. Samsun after describing a great southward curve through the north-central region of the Anatolian plateau. The Classical name means 'Salt River'. According to Herodotus (1.74), the Lydian king Alyattes fought a battle with the Median king Cyaxares (the so-called 'battle of the eclipse') on the banks of the river (585); the battle was followed by a treaty which established the Halys as the boundary between Lydian and Median territory (but see under **Medes**). Subsequently, the river formed the dividing line between the Lydian and the Persian empires, respectively ruled by Croesus and Cyrus II. Croesus led his forces across the river and fought a battle with Cyrus (the 'battle of Pteria', spring of 546; Herodotus 1.76), which ended inconclusively but marked the beginning of Cyrus' onslaught upon and destruction of Croesus' kingdom.

In the Late Bronze Age the Halys r. defined what was effectively the core territory of the kingdom of Hatti. In Hittite texts the river is called the Marassantiya.

Halziluha M1 country in northern Mesopotamia, in the vicinity of the Aramaean state of Bit-Zamani. (Lipiński's interpretation of the name as Hals-Eluha, 'District of Eluha(t)' (2000: 150) is unlikely since Eluha(t) (q.v.) was not located in the region.) Halziluha was subject to Assyrian overlordship, and had apparently first been settled with an Assyrian population by the C13 Assyrian king Shalmaneser I. This is mentioned by a later Assyrian king, Ashurnasirpal II, in his report of a rebellion staged against him in 882 by the country's ruler, Hulaya, who attempted to capture the nearby Assyrian stronghold, Damdammusa (**RIMA* 2: 200–1). An expeditionary force led by Ashurnasirpal crushed the rebellion and destroyed Hulaya's chief city, Kinabu. The rebel leader was captured and flayed alive, and his skin was draped over Damdammusa's walls.

Hamadan see **Ecbatana**.

Ham(a)ranu M1 tribe and city in Babylonia, located east of the Tigris r. and perhaps in the environs of the Diyala r. Its population was a disruptive force in its region, conducting raids into northern Babylonia, attacking caravans, and on one occasion capturing a messenger in the service of the Assyrian king Sargon II (721–705) while he was accompanying one of the caravans on a royal mission. A number of Hamaranu tribespeople were surrounded and massacred by Sargon's eunuchs and provincial governors after they had sought refuge in the city of Sippar; they had been robbing the caravans of the Babylonians (**Sargon II* 332). References are made in Assyrian texts to at least two cities of the Hamaranu, including Ganata, perhaps the city of Gannanate (q.v.) in the Diyala region. Hamaranu was also the name of what was probably the tribe's chief city. It was plundered, along with the city of Rabbilu, by the Assyrian king Tiglath-pileser III (745–727) (**ABC* 71), and later conquered and destroyed by Sennacherib during his campaign against Elam in 693/692 (*Sennach.* 40).

Lipiński (2000: 442–4).

Hamath (1) (*Hama*) (map 7) City located on the Orontes r. in central Syria, 146 km south of Aleppo, dominated by a 45 m high tell, 400 m × 300 m in area, which in M1 constituted the citadel of a more extended settlement. Its history of occupation extends from the Neolithic period (M6 or earlier) to the present day. Thirteen archaeological phases have been identified (from phase M in the Neolithic period to phase A in the mediaeval period), divided into forty-two levels. The site was excavated by a Danish team, sponsored by the Danish Carlsberg Foundation, between 1931 and 1938. Its Bronze Age phases, J, H, and G, reflect the development of a relatively densely populated urban society, which produced a wide range of artefacts, including distinctive ceramic vessels and figurines, metal and stone artefacts, cylinder and stamp seals, and ivory and bone inlays. Texts from the mid M3 archive discovered at Ebla contain the earliest written references to Hamath, whose name in these texts appears in the form Amatu. In the Late Bronze Age (in phase G), the narrow streets of the city's earlier phases gave way to more spacious living conditions. Imported goods from Cyprus and the Mycenaean world attest to the city's involvement in international trading activity in this period. However, J. D. Hawkins observes that the name Hamath does not occur in M2 sources (*contra* the suggestion that it is attested in the Middle Bronze Age Egyptian Execration texts and the records of the C15 pharaoh Tuthmosis III), which may indicate that 'it was not one of the main urban centres but rather lay in the territory of another state, perhaps that of Tunip' (*CHLI* I: 399).

By the early years of M1, Hamath had become the capital of a large and important Iron Age kingdom of the same name, thenceforth frequently attested in both biblical and Assyrian sources. In biblical tradition, its earliest known king is Toi (Tou), who sent his son Joram to King David to congratulate him on his victory over a common enemy, Hadadezer, ruler of the Aramaean kingdom of Zobah (2 Samuel 8:9). If historically valid, this event can be dated to c. 980. During the first part of its Iron Age existence, Hamath was under Neo-Hittite rule. In Assyrian sources, the earliest reference to the kingdom dates to the reign of the Assyrian king Tukulti-Ninurta II (890–884). Tukulti-Ninurta's successor-but-one, Shalmaneser III (858–824), names a number of towns belonging to Hamath (**RIMA* 3: 23), only one of which, Qarqar on the Orontes r. (see below), can be confidently located. The Levantine kingdom probably reached its greatest extent during the reign of the Assyrian king Tiglath-pileser III (745–727) who lists nineteen districts belonging to it (**Tigl. III* 60–3). Lipiński (2000: 298) describes its territory as extending from the Syrian steppe to the Mediterranean, and from the lower Orontes r. and the region southwest of Aleppo to a line running from Batrun to Ǧebel al-Garbi, with the addition of the Biqaʿ valley. Hawkins (1982: 389) suggests that the land of Luash (Lugath, Luhuti) (q.v.) may already have formed the northern province of Hamath by the reign of Shalmaneser III, or even earlier.

Material remains of the capital in this period, phases F and E in archaeological terms, include cemeteries (featuring cremation burials) lying to the south and west of the citadel, a complex of large, apparently public buildings surrounding an open courtyard and accessed via a fortified monumental gateway, and a temple to the

Figure 42 Hama.

goddess Baʿalat. The temple is attested in several Luwian hieroglyphic inscriptions, referred to below. The excavators have dated the building complex to C10–9. Lion sculptures of Hittite type flanked the entrances and staircases of several buildings, but apart from these, sculptural remains dating to this period are relatively meagre. Smaller finds include stamp and cylinder seals, carved ivories, a gold-plated statuette of a seated god, about twenty cuneiform tablets and fragments, and a number of graffiti written in Aramaic. The remains of what was once an imposing building with buttressed façade are probably those of a royal palace. The building's ground-floor remains include an entrance court and a large number of storage rooms, with jars for grain, wine, and oil. Though the structures and sculptures of phases F and E are clearly of Hittite type, the complex on the mound is sometimes misleadingly referred to as the 'Aramaean citadel'.

We know from Assyrian texts of a king of Hamath called Irhuleni (853–845), one of the leaders of an anti-Assyrian coalition of states which confronted the Assyrian army led by Shalmaneser III at Qarqar on the Orontes r. in 853 (**RIMA* 3: 23). The outcome of the confrontation was apparently inconclusive, for in later years (849, 848, 845) Shalmaneser III had to engage in further conflicts with the same coalition. He seems eventually to have won over Irhuleni to an Assyrian alliance, by diplomacy rather than by brute force. Irhuleni can be equated with the Hamathite king Urhilina, who identifies himself in several of his Luwian hieroglyphic inscriptions as the son of Paritas, and the builder of a city (perhaps, Hawkins suggests, the Neo-Hittite predecessor of Apamea on the Orontes) and a temple of the goddess Baʿalat (**CHLI* I: 405). In another of his inscriptions Urhilina records his dedication of a granary to the goddess (*CHLI I: 410). In a slightly later inscription, dated to c. 830, Urhilina's son Ur(a)tamis (Rudamu) claims credit for building a fortress, which may indicate a refortification of Hamath city during Uratamis' reign (*CHLI I: 413). Uratamis is also the addressee of a letter which was amongst the cuneiform tablets found on the Hamath citadel. The letter's author was Marduk-aplar-usur, ruler of the middle Euphrates state of Suhu (*Parpola, 1990).

The next attested Hamathite king is Zak(k)ur, who features in an early C8 Aramaic inscription carved on a stele and discovered at Tell Afis, c. 110 km to the north of Hamath (*Lipiński, 2000: 254–5, *CS II: 155, *Chav. 307–11). The stele records Zakur's victory over a coalition of enemy forces, led by Bar-Hadad II, king of Damascus, after these forces had blockaded him in the city of Hatarikka, capital of the province of Luash. The king claims that divine intervention rescued him from the siege, though very likely the gods had Assyrian support! By this time, Neo-Hittite rule had come to an end in Hamath. Zakur, who acceded to the kingdom's throne c. 796, was one of the first, if not the first, of a line of Aramaean rulers who now held sway in the kingdom. It is possible that the seat of their dynasty was located not in Hamath city but in Hatarikka. In any case, their rule was comparatively shortlived. Hamath's last known king, Yaubidi (Ilubidi), led a rebellion involving a number of Syrian kingdoms against the Assyrian king Sargon II soon after his accession (721) (*CS II: 293, 295, 296). Sargon crushed the rebellion, and Yaubidi was captured and flayed alive. The kingdom of Hamath now became a province of the Assyrian empire. In the aftermath of its conquest, a number of Assyrians and other colonists were settled there (*CS II: 294), and a number of Hamath's former subjects were deported to other parts of the Assyrian realm (including Samaria, according to 2 Kings 17:24, to replace the Israelites). Hamath city was probably sacked and put to the torch, an event which is almost certainly reflected in the conflagration which brought phase E of the site to an end. Thenceforth, written information about the land of Hamath is confined to a few literary sources, and to a reference in a Neo-Babylonian chronicle (no. 5) to the conquest of the whole of Hamath by the Babylonian crown prince Nebuchadnezzar (*ABC 99, *CS I: 468); this followed Nebuchadnezzar's crushing victory over the Egyptian forces at Carchemish (605). The new administrative capital was now very likely located elsewhere, perhaps in the city of Hatarikka.

After its destruction, Hamath city apparently remained unoccupied for the next few centuries, until the Hellenistic period when Syria came under the rule of the Seleucid dynasty. A new, well-planned settlement (phase D), rectangular in layout with streets running north–south and east–west, was built on top of the Iron Age city. Credit for building the new city seems to belong to the Seleucid king Antiochus IV Ephiphanes (175–164), whose name is reflected in the city's new name, Epiphaneia. During the Roman imperial period habitation gradually spread from the mound to the valley below. The site was conquered by the Arabs in C7 CE, but continued to be occupied until its destruction by the Mongols during their invasion of Syria in 1260.

Levine (*RlA* 4: 67–71), Klengel (1992: 212–13), Dornemann (*OEANE* 2: 466–8), *CHLI* I: 398–423), Lipiński (2000: 249–318).

Hamath (2) Late Bronze Age city, probably to be located in Transjordan not far from Pella. During the reign of the pharaoh Seti I (1294–1279), it joined forces with

Pella for an attack upon the Egyptian subject cities Beth Shean and Rehob. On a stele discovered in Beth Shean, Seti records the relief of the city (presumably Rehob was also relieved) by an Egyptian army which he dispatched against the attackers (*Faulkner, 1947: 36).

Hamidiya, Tell (map 2) Settlement-mound in northwestern Mespotamia, covering an area of c. 20 ha., with evidence of Late Bronze Age and Iron Age occupation. Excavations which began here in 1938 were continued by M. Wäfler from 1984 onwards. Wäfler explored a massive three-level palace, 250 sq. m in area, with walls preserved up to a height of 14 m. The earliest palace phase belongs to the Late Bronze Age, with evidence also of a later Neo-Assyrian phase. A large number of ivories dating to the reign of Shalmaneser III (858–824) were discovered in this phase. Following its Assyrian occupation, Tell Hamidiya was again settled in the Hellenistic and Parthian eras.

Wäfler's proposed identification of the site with Taidu (1) (q.v.) has been rejected by Guichard (1994) in favour of an identification of the latter with Tell Farfara. An identification between Hamidiya and the city of Kahat (q.v.), attested in Middle and Late Bronze and Iron Age texts, has also been proposed.

Eichler and Wäfler (1989–90; 1985–2003).

Hamoukar, Tell Large settlement-mound at the eastern end of the Habur triangle of Upper Mesopotamia, in what is now the far northeastern part of Syria. Excavations were initiated in 1999 by M. Gibson of the Oriental Institute, University of Chicago, as co-director in partnership with the Syrian Directorate General of Antiquities, with further seasons in 2000 and 2001. The excavations were resumed in 2005 with C. Reichel of the Oriental Institute and S. al-Quntar of the Syrian Dept of Antiquities as American and Syrian co-directors respectively (see http://www-news.uchicago.edu/releases/05/051216.hamoukar.shtml). Tell Hamoukar covered c. 15 ha in the Late Chalcolithic (= Northern Middle Uruk, c. 4000–3500) and the Late Uruk phases (c. 3500–3000), and subsequently expanded following a break in occupation to reach c. 105 ha in the late Ninevite 5 period (see under **Nineveh**). Throughout much of M3, the settlement maintained (or perhaps even exceeded) this size until its abandonment around early M2. Subsequent, limited occupation is attested only for early M1, and then again in the Seleucid and also in the early Islamic era (c. C7 CE).

The excavators have suggested that Late Uruk period Hamoukar was the site of a colony founded by a southern Mesopotamian or southwestern Iranian city-state, comparable to contemporary settlements such as Tell Brak and Habuba Kabira South. During the 2005 excavation season, evidence was recovered of a great battle which took place c. 3500; over 1,200 sling bullets were found *in situ* in association with collapsed walls, as were large clay balls probably used as missiles. Large quantities of southern Uruk pottery were found in pits dug into the destruction levels, supporting the excavators' idea that southerners gained control of the settlement following the battle.

(H. D. Baker)
Gibson *et al.* (2002).

Hamsha Middle Bronze Age city within the land of Zalmaqum in northern Mesopotamia, near mod. Harran. Asdi-takim, an anti-Assyrian rebel in the region, launched an attack upon the city in the spring of 1778. But he called it off after receiving news that a relief force dispatched by Ishme-Dagan, the Assyrian viceroy at Ekallatum, was coming to Hamsha's relief (*LAPO 16: 129, no. 31). Charpin suggests that Asdi-takim's assault on the city may have been the first indication of the general uprising in Zalmaqum which prompted the campaign undertaken there by the Assyrian king Shamshi-Adad I, probably in the summer and autumn of 1778 (see under **Zalmaqum**).

Mesop. 180–1.

Hana Name attested in Middle and Late Bronze Age texts, and used originally to designate a semi-nomadic Amorite tribal population in the middle Euphrates region. The people or peoples so called were already settled in this region before the reign of Yahdun-Lim, king of Mari (1810–1794), who reports conquering seven kings of Hana and annexing their lands (**RIME* 4: 603). These lands became part of the kingdom of Mari, and the title 'king of the land of Hana' was incorporated into the titulature of the Mariote king. From letters in the Mari archives, particularly those dating to the reign of Zimri-Lim (1774–1762), it is clear that Haneans played an important role in Mari's military forces, taking part in the Mariote king's campaigns both in Babylonia and northern Mesopotamia, as well as providing personnel for surveillance operations, military escorts, and garrison duties. However, the majority of the Hanean population appear to have lived a traditional pastoral lifestyle, maintaining their tribal organization under local sheikhs.

The kingdom of Mari came to an end with its destruction by the Babylonian king Hammurabi in 1762. Following Hammurabi's death in 1750 and the loss of Babylonian control over Mari and its surrounding territory, a small kingdom arose around the city of Terqa (mod. Tell Ashara), located 70 km north of Mari. It is today referred to as the kingdom of Hana since two of its rulers designated themselves in their titulature as 'king of Hana'. The royal seat and administrative centre of the kingdom was located either in Terqa, or alternatively in a city called Biddah. The territory over which it held sway was much the same as that formerly controlled by Mari, particularly the region lying between the Habur and middle Euphrates rivers. Its history was apparently a brief one, belonging to the second quarter of M2 and spanning the last part of the Middle and the first part of the Late Bronze Age. Scholars commonly refer to this as the 'Hana period'. The names of ten kings of Hana are attested in this period (**RIME* 4: 723–34). It has been concluded that they were eventually subject to Mitannian sovereignty, on the basis of references to the Mitannian kings Parrattarna and Saushtatar in the Terqa texts. But it is very likely that the kingdom of Hana was originally independent of any foreign control.

After the fall of Mitanni to the Hittites in the third quarter of C14, the land of Hana came under Assyrian sovereignty. In C13 it is listed among the thirty-eight districts and cities which the Assyrian king Tukulti-Ninurta I (1244–1208) brought under Assyrian control (**RIMA* 1: 273). A C11 king of Hana called Tukulti-Mer is known to us from a dedicatory inscription discovered at Sippar (**RIMA* 2: 111). He is thought to be identical with the Tukulti-Mer who was king of Mari in the same period and was defeated by the Assyrian king Ashur-bel-kala (1073–1056) (**RIMA* 2: 89).

Though originally used in Middle Bronze Age texts to designate an Amorite tribal population, the term Hana appears to have lost its ethnic significance, at least in textual attestations, by the end of the Middle Bronze Age. It came to be used as a generic term for any nomadic or pastoralist group and also, to judge from references to Hanean soldiers in texts from Alalah and Larsa, for a particular type of soldier. 'Hanean soldiers' are also mentioned many centuries later in a fragmentary Babylonian chronicle text (no. 8) of the Persian period (**ABC* 112); at this time the term perhaps designated regions west of Babylonia in general (*RGTC* 8: 151).

Kupper (*RlA* 4: 74–6), Rouault (1984), Buccellati (1988), Lion (*DCM* 365), *LKM* 29–36, 582–4 (refs).

Hanat see **Ana(t)**.

Hanhana Late Bronze Age Hittite city in north-central Anatolia, identified by some scholars with İnandıktepe (q.v.). Hanhana was a regional administrative centre of the Hittite Old Kingdom, and a cult centre for the worship of the god Telipinu and the storm god. It was among the northern homeland cities and countries depopulated by Kaska incursions during the Old Kingdom, and later resettled, in C13, by the Hittite prince Hattusili (later King Hattusili III) when he was given sovereignty over the region by his brother King Muwattalli II (1295–1272) (**CS* I: 201). See also **Hakpis(sa)** and **Turmitta**.

**RGTC* 6: 76–7.

Hanigalbat (Haligalbat, Habi(n)galbat) A partly political, partly geographical term, attested as one of the names by which the Hurrian Late Bronze Age kingdom of Mitanni, whose homeland lay in northern Mesopotamia, was known. To judge from a Neo-Assyrian copy of an Old Babylonian oracular tablet, Hanigalbateans were among the enemies of the last Old Babylonian king, Samsu-ditana, at the end of his reign (c. 1595) (**CTN* IV 63, cited *Mesop.* 382). The Hittite king Muwattalli II (1295–1272) refers to the conquest of Hanigalbat, along with the land of Aleppo, by one of his ancestors, Tudhaliya I/II (late C15 or early C14) (*Bryce, 2005: 140). Hanigalbat was also the name by which the C14 Mitannian king Tushratta referred to his kingdom in his correspondence with the pharaoh Amenhotep III (e.g. **EA* 20:17).

Following Tushratta's defeat by the Hittite king Suppiluliuma I, c. 1340, the Mitannian empire was dismembered; much of it was absorbed into Hatti, and what was left of it was subsequently known as the kingdom of Hanigalbat. The territory which it covered extended through northern Mesopotamia westwards from the Tur ʿAbdin to the Euphrates r., across the upper reaches of the Habur and Balih rivers. Initially, this rump kingdom was ruled by Tushratta's son Shattiwaza, who was allied by treaty to Suppiluliuma and his son Sharri-Kushuh (Piyassili), viceroy at Carchemish (**HDT* 42–54). Though nominally an independent ruler, Shattiwaza was in fact a puppet of the Hittite king, whose backing had ensured his succession in Hanigalbat as a close partner of Sharri-Kushuh.

Probably some time after Hanigalbat provided troops for the Hittite army in the battle of Qadesh (1274) its king, Shattuara I, made an attack upon the re-emerging kingdom of Assyria, which was rapidly filling the power vacuum east of the Euphrates left by the Hittite destruction of the Mitannian empire. The attack appears to have been unprovoked, but it may in fact have been a pre-emptive strike by Shattuara designed to forestall Assyrian aggression against his kingdom. If so, his initiative backfired. The Assyrian king at the time, Adad-nirari I (1307–1275), retaliated by seizing Shattuara and taking him to Ashur. After extracting a promise of allegiance from him, Adad-nirari reinstated him on his throne, as his vassal (*RIMA 1: 136, *Chav. 143–4). Despite Hanigalbat's previously close relationship with Hatti, the Hittites apparently did not challenge this action by Assyria. However, increasing tensions between Hatti and Assyria in the reign of the Hittite king Urhi-Teshub (1272–1267) may have encouraged Shattuara's son and successor Wasashatta to establish his independence from Assyrian sovereignty by rebelling against Adad-nirari. He may well have hoped for support from Hatti in this enterprise. But if so, the Hittites again failed to respond, and Wasashatta's rebellion was ruthlessly crushed by Adad-nirari, who captured his royal city Taidu and ravaged his land (*RIMA 1: 136, *Chav. 143–4). Thereupon Adad-nirari withdrew Hanigalbat's vassal status, annexed it to Assyrian territory, and established a royal residence in Taidu. None the less the spirit of resistance continued to smoulder in Hanigalbat, and Wasashatta's son and successor Shattuara II staged a further rebellion, against Adad-nirari's son and successor Shalmaneser I (1274–1245). Once more the Assyrians were victorious. Shalmaneser made a concerted attack upon the rebel kingdom, and firmly re-established his rule over Hanigalbat and all other territories in northern Mesopotamia to the east bank of the Euphrates (*RIMA I: 183–4).

This effectively ended Hanigalbat's existence as a coherent political entity. But the region over which it had held sway was to preserve the name Hanigalbat for some centuries to come. In the first of two references he makes to Milidia (see ***Arslantepe***), the Assyrian king Tiglath-pileser I (1114–1076) calls it a city of the land of Hanigalbat (*RIMA 2: 22). (He later refers to it as a city of the land of Hatti, a general name applied to northern Syria and the Taurus region during the Iron Age; *RIMA 2: 43.) In Assyrian texts from late M2 onwards, Hanigalbat appears as a land occupied by Aramaean peoples. It is referred to as such by the Assyrian king Ashur-bel-kala (1073–1056) (*RIMA 2: 102). Adad-nirari II conducted six campaigns in the land of Hanigalbat between 901 and 894 (*RIMA 2: 149–51, 153), and his successor-but-one Ashurnasirpal II received tribute from the rulers of Hatti and from the kings of Hanigalbat during his campaign in the same region in 882 (*RIMA 2: 203). Hanigalbat again appears in records relating to the Assyrian king Esarhaddon's accession year (681). Rebel forces who had gathered in Hanigalbat subsequently joined Esarhaddon as he returned from his place of refuge to claim the Assyrian throne (*Borger, 1956: 44).

von Weiher (*RlA* 5: 105–7), *RGTC* 5: 117–18.

Hanusa see **Hunusu**.

Hanzat Middle Bronze Age royal city in northern Mesopotamia, in the vicinity of Harran, attested in the Mari texts from the reign of Zimri-Lim (1774–1762). It was at this time part of the land of Zalmaqum (which consisted of a number of principalities), and was ruled by a king called Yarkab-Addu. Qattunan's governor, Zakira-Hammu, reports that 2,000 Zalmaqean troops belonging to Yarkab-Addu had arrived in his city, apparently en route to Mari for service with Zimri-Lim (*LKM* 96, *438).

Hapalla (map 3) One of the Late Bronze Age Arzawa Lands, located in central-western Anatolia close to the Hittite buffer zone called the Lower Land. It is first attested c. 1400 among the Hittites' enemies in the west (**HDT* 158–9), and though the Hittites subsequently claimed it as subject territory, their hold on it remained tenuous. It continued to defy Hittite authority until a campaign by the Hittite commander Hannutti (c. 1350) left it in ruins and largely depopulated (*Bryce, 2005: 151). The country survived this devastation, and subsequently became a Hittite vassal kingdom. Its vassal status is attested in a treaty which its ruler Targasnalli concluded with the Hittite king Mursili II (1321–1295) in the early years of Mursili's reign (**HDT* 69–73).

Otten (*RlA* 4: 111), **RGTC* 6: 79–80.

Hapisna see **Hupisna**.

Harada see **Har(r)adum**.

Harana The name of a mountain and at least two western or southwestern Anatolian cities attested in Late Bronze Age Hittite texts.

Otten (*RlA* 4: 113), *RGTC* 6: 83–4.

Harbe (1) (Harbu) (map 10) City attested in Middle Bronze and Iron Age texts, located in the middle Euphrates region called Suhu(m), south of the kingdom of Mari and a day's march north of the city of Idu (mod. Hit). It lay in Lower Suhum, whose capital was Yabliya.

The city is first attested in the period of heightened tensions between the Assyrian king Shamshi-Adad I (1796–1775) and the Babylonian king Hammurabi (1792–1750), when persons originating from Harbe became involved in hostilities with Babylonian troops near Idu. In 1782, Harbe threw its gates open to 8,000 troops belonging to Dadusha, ruler of Eshnunna, when he invaded Suhum, apparently for a second time. Dadusha went on to conquer all of Lower Suhum, but subsequently made peace with Shamshi-Adad. Later on, Suhum was subject to Zimri-Lim, king of Mari (1774–1762), though Hammurabi disputed with him possession of the cities Harbe, Yabliya, and Idu (**ARM XXVI/2*: 366–7, 449), which lay in the frontier region between Babylonia and Mari. Hammurabi eventually conceded control of the first two cities, but not Idu, to Zimri-Lim when he shared out with him the territories of Suhum following the retreat of the Eshnunnite forces from the region in 1770.

The Assyrian king Tukulti-Ninurta II encamped his forces at Harbu during the course of his last recorded campaign (885) which took him through the middle Tigris and Euphrates regions (**RIMA* 2: 174).

LKM 611–12 (refs; cited there as Harbe 2), *Mesop.* 162–3.

Harbe (2) Middle Bronze Age city in the land of (northern) Yamutbal, attested in correspondence from the reign of Zimri-Lim, king of Mari (1774–1762). Possession of the city was apparently contested by Atamrum, king of Andarig, and Hammurabi, king of Kurda. At Zimri-Lim's instigation, a peace was negotiated between Atamrum and Hammurabi, in accordance with which Hammurabi conceded Harbe and its surrounding territory to Atamrum, after removing its inhabitants and resettling them in Kurda.

LKM 120, 611 (refs; cited there as Harbe 1).

Harbe (3) see ***Chuera, Tell***.

Harbu see **Harbe (1)**.

Harhar (map 13) M1 city and region located in the upper reaches of the Ulaya r. in the central western Zagros highlands. It is first attested in Assyrian record, in the reign of the Assyrian king Shalmaneser III, who in 835 captured and looted the city and set up a stele there, during a campaign against the kingdom of Namri and other cities and countries in the region (**RIMA* 3: 68). Harhar subsequently became subject territory of the Assyrian empire, though probably on more than one occasion it joined other states and cities in defying Assyrian authority. This is implied by its appearance in the list of conquests of Adad-nirari III (810–783) (**RIMA* 3: 212). Whether or not it remained submissive to Assyrian overlordship after this remains unknown. But early in the reign of the Assyrian king Sargon II (721–705), Harhar declared its allegiance to Dalta, ruler of the kingdom of Ellipi which bordered Harhar to the southeast, after expelling its own ruler who had remained loyal to Assyria. Sargon eventually took action in 716, in the course of his sixth campaign, which had taken him to Mannaea and the land of Nairi. He marched upon the city of Harhar, laid siege to it, and captured it. Its ruler Kibaba was removed from power and replaced by Sargon's own appointee. Sargon renamed the city Kar-Sharrukin (the 'quay' of Sargon), and increased the size of its territory by adding to it six border regions which he had conquered, probably to serve as a buffer against Ellipi (**ARAB* II: 29). The city thenceforth became an important centre of the Assyrian administration in the Zagros region. (For letters to Sargon from his officials in Kar-Sharrukin, see **SAA* XV: 56–73, nos 83–110). Sargon's son and successor Sennacherib consolidated its position with his conquest of Ellipi. After annexing part of Ellipi's territory, Sennacherib made Elenzash the capital of the reduced kingdom, under its new name Kar-Sennacherib, and placed it under the immediate authority of the governor of Harhar (**Sennach.* 28–9).

Levine (*RlA* 4: 120–1).

Haria Mountain land to the southwest of Lake Van, near the country of Paphu, attested in the records of the Assyrian king Tiglath-pileser I (1114–1076). Tiglath-pileser reports a campaign against Haria in the second year of his reign, in conjunction with a second campaign which he conducted against Paphu (**RIMA* 2: 18). He claims to have conquered, plundered, and burnt twenty-five of Haria's cities.

Haridi see **Har(r)adum**.

Harna (or **Hir/Kin/Murna** – thus Grayson) Iron Age country bordering on the land of Mannaea in mod. Iranian Kurdistan. Its capital was Masashuru. In 829 Dayyan-Ashur, commander-in-chief of the Assyrian king Shalmaneser III, invaded the country following his conquest of Mannaea (**RIMA* 3: 70). At that time Harna was ruled by a certain Shulusunu. Dayyan-Ashur captured Masashuru, along with other cities in its environs, but spared the lives of the king and his sons. He restored Shulusunu to his land, and imposed upon him a tax and tribute payment of teams of horse.

Haror, Tel (map 8) 16 ha settlement-mound in the western Negev desert, 25 km northwest of Beersheba. A 1 ha upper tell rose 10 m above the mound. Excavation of the site was carried out by a team from Ben-Gurion University of the Negev under the direction of E. D. Oren, from 1982 to 1992. Human occupation dates back to the Chalcolithic–Early Bronze I period (late M4–early M3), followed after a gap of c. 1,000 years by continuous occupation from the Middle Bronze Age (early M2) to the Persian period (C6–4). The main architectural features of the Middle Bronze Age town are (a) a defence system, consisting of earthen ramparts and deep fosse; (b) a large temple complex, whose courtyard favissae (see glossary) contained the bones of sacrificial animals, including sheep, goats, birds, and puppies; and (c) a large public building, thought to be a courtyard-style palace. Cult-vessels, including cylindrical stands with large bowls on top, and votive objects from the temple, the latter including horned animals and snakes and incense stands, reflect Canaanite cult and religion. The Late Bronze Age city (Late Bronze I–III) seems to have been much smaller than its predecessor, its most significant remains being those of what, according to the excavator, may have been a large patrician house. The layout of this building included large pebbled courtyards, a plaster-layered square water reservoir, and a number of rooms for storage and other domestic purposes, while the contents included a rich assemblage of imported Cypriot and Mycenaean pottery, and Egyptian-style cups and bowls.

During the Iron Age the site was heavily fortified, as indicated by its well preserved Iron Age II–III citadel. Also well preserved is a series of storehouses, with long-halled magazines erected on mudbrick platforms. The citadel and the buildings within it have been dated to mid or late C8. Oren suggests that the citadel was built under Assyrian authority, perhaps in late C8 by Sargon II, as part of Assyria's overall military and political organization in southern Philistia and on the border with Egypt. Its destruction a century or so later is perhaps to be attributed to an Egyptian military expedition to Philistia under Egypt's Saite kings. There was much re-levelling of the Iron Age site to make way for reoccupation in the Persian period, on the site's upper tell. Imported Greek and Cypriot wares figure among the finds from this level.

Oren (*NEAEHL* 2: 580–4; *OEANE* 2: 474–6).

Har(r)adum (Harada/Haridi, ***Khirbet ed-Diniye***) (map 10) Middle Bronze and Iron Age city located on the middle Euphrates r., 90 km downstream from Mari, in the upper part of Suhu(m) between Ana(t) and Hindanu(m). The site was excavated between 1981 and 1988 by a team of French archaeologists led by C. Kepinski-Lecomte. The small, square (c. 100 m × 100 m) city, enclosed by a mudbrick wall with corner bastions, was densely occupied with streets laid out according to a regular grid (for a plan of its layout in this period, see *DCM* 740).

Harradum is first attested in the reign of the Assyrian king Shamshi-Adad I (1796–1775). Following Shamshi-Adad's death and the seizure of the Assyrian viceregal throne at Mari by Zimri-Lim (1774–1762), Ibal-pi-El II, king of Eshnnuna, proposed to the new Mariote king that Harradum should mark the boundary between their territories. Zimri-Lim rejected the proposal – primarily, it seems, because it gave the Eshnunnites access to the land of Suhum. Control of Suhum's territory was contested by both kings. Following Zimri-Lim's death, the region in which Harradum lay was seized by the Babylonian king Hammurabi (1792–1750). Within the context of consolidating his control over the middle Euphrates region, Hammurabi's successor Samsu-iluna (1749–1712) rebuilt Harradum as a small fortified city and installed his son as its ruler. The excavators of the site believe that its chief role may have been that of a merchant-colony, fortified by a military garrison, which controlled the route between Babylonia and Syria. Charpin, however, suggests that Samsu-iluna actually moved Harradum to this site, noting that no earlier levels have been excavated that might be attributed to the city's occupation during the times of Shamshi-Adad and Zimri-Lim (*Mesop*. 354–5). He believes that the city's role had more to do with military strategy, and that Samsu-iluna's rapid rebuilding of it was part of the preparations he undertook for his campaign against Terqa (1723). Terqa lay north of Mari, and was the capital or one of the major centres of the kingdom of Hana. Harradum remained part of the Babylonian kingdom until its destruction by enemy forces in 1629, during the reign of the Babylonian king Ammi-saduqa.

Harradum is identical with the Neo-Assyrian city Harada/Haridi in the land of Suhu. The Assyrian king Tukulti-Ninurta II encamped his forces there during his progress up the Euphrates on his last recorded campaign (885) (**RIMA* 2: 175). During a campaign in 878 to put down an uprising by the peoples of Suhu, the land of Laqe, and the city of Hindanu, the Assyrian king Ashurnasirpal II crossed the Euphrates at Haridi, on rafts made of goatskins (**RIMA* 2: 214).

Joannès (1992), Kepinski-Lecomte (1992), *Mesop*. 354–5 (with refs).

Harran (maps 10, 13) Settlement-mound in northwestern Mesopotamia, located 44 km southeast of mod. Urfa on one of the major east–west commercial and military routes linking northern Mesopotamia with Syria. Its name means 'journey', 'caravan' in Akkadian. Harran's history of occupation extends from the Early Bronze Age (M3) to the mediaeval period. Archaeological soundings have produced material remains from the Early Bronze Age and Neo-Babylonian period, but excavations have concentrated mainly on the site's Islamic levels.

First attested in tablets from Ebla (C24), Harran appears in a number of C18 texts found in the city of Mari. During the reign of the Assyrian king Shamshi-Adad I (1796–1775), it was the capital of a large province extending westwards across the Euphrates to the frontiers of the kingdom of Yamhad in northern Syria. In the reign of the Mariote king Zimri-Lim (1774–1762), it was the seat of a small principality, ruled by a king called Asdi-takim, within the land of Zalmaqum (**LKM* 438–9). In C16 it came under the domination of the Hurrian kingdom of Mitanni, and subsequently fell to the Hittites when they destroyed the Mitannian empire in the third quarter of C14. According to the treaty which the Hittite king Suppiluliuma I drew up with Shattiwaza, son of the former Mitannian king Tushratta, Harran surrendered to a joint expeditionary force led by Shattiwaza and the Hittite viceroy Sharri-Kushuh (Piyassili) on their way to the Mitannian capital Washshukkanni (**HDT* 50). But when a renascent Assyria began rapidly filling the political vacuum east of the Euphrates left by the destruction of the Mitannian empire, Harran faced the prospect of a new overlord. The Assyrian king Adad-nirari I (1307–1275) and his son and successor Shalmaneser I (1274–1245) both claimed to have conquered the city and its region (the former in his campaign against Wasashatta, king of Hanigalbat, who rose up against him; **RIMA* 1: 131). In fact, Harran appears to have remained relatively independent of Assyrian rule, though Tiglath-pileser I (1114–1076) and his son and successor-but-one Ashur-bel-kala (1073–1056) conducted raids and hunts in its territory. The former reports killing ten elephants in the land of Harran and the Habur r. region, and capturing four alive (**RIMA* 2: 26). At this time Harran may already have been occupied by large numbers of Aramaeans. Ashur-bel-kala records a campaign against the Aramaeans in the region, claiming to have plundered their territories from the land of Mahiranu to the city of Shuppu (Rupu) of the land of Harran (**RIMA* 2: 102).

There is no doubt that by early M1 Harran had come under firm Aramaean control, before being annexed to the Neo-Assyrian empire in the reign of Shalmaneser III (858–824). At this time, following the conquest of Bit-Adini, Harran was incorporated into the newly formed Province of the Commander-in-Chief (see glossary) which had its capital at Til-Barsip. In C8, however, the province was probably divided into the provinces of Til-Barsip and Harran. Radner (*RlA* 11: 46, 54) has suggested that this reorganization may lie behind the drawing up of the so-called 'Harran Census', a group of tablets listing rural estates and their dependent peoples which may be dated to the reign of Sargon II (**SAA* XI: 122–45, nos 201–20).

In the last years of the Assyrian empire, late C7, and after the fall of the Assyrian capital Nineveh, Harran provided a final place of refuge for the Assyrian court, during the brief reign of Ashur-uballit II (612–610). The city was abandoned when news came of the approach of the Median and Babylonian armies, who thoroughly pillaged it. With the failure of Ashur-uballit's attempt, assisted by the pharaoh Necho II, to regain the city in 609, the Neo-Assyrian kingdom was effectively at an end. Harran was captured by the Babylonian king Nabopolassar, and occupied by one of his garrisons (**ABC* 95, **PE* 31, no. 10). But a few years later, when relations between the Babylonians and the Medes deteriorated, the city came under Median control. In mid C6 the Babylonian king Nabonidus re-established Babylonian authority over it, and rebuilt there the temple of the moon god Sin (**CS* II: 311, **PE* 56, no. 6, **PE* 76, no. 23), at a time when the Medes were distracted by a revolt against their king, Astyages, staged by the up-and-coming Persian king Cyrus II. Harran continued to exist under Persian sovereignty, but its importance was now greatly diminished, and it remained relatively insignificant until the Islamic period.

The important role played by Harran in western Asian affairs for much of its history, particularly in the Old Assyrian and Neo-Assyrian periods, must have been due very largely to its important strategic location, providing as it did a major route of access for northern Mesopotamian merchants and military forces into northern Syria. But it also achieved great significance as a centre of worship for the moon god Sin. During the reign of the C18 Mariote king Zimri-Lim, Sin's temple had the status of a confederate sanctuary for the Yaminite tribes living in the region. Four centuries later, the god was among the deities invoked in the treaty which the Hittite king Suppiluliuma drew up with Shattiwaza of Mitanni, and he continued to feature prominently in the religious life of the city during the period of Neo-Assyrian rule. His temple was restored by the Assyrian king Ashurbanipal (668–630/627) – its ruins may lie below the later mosque – and even in the Babylonian period, the god continued to be revered, despite the opposition of the priesthood of the Babylonian god Marduk. The mother of Nabonidus was a devotee of the god.

In *OT* tradition Abraham's father, Terah, settled his family in Harran after they had left Ur, originally with the intention of going to Canaan (Genesis 11:30–1). Abraham lived there until he was seventy-five (Genesis 12:4). His name is still commemorated in the region by a spring called the lake of Abraham.

The name Harran reappears in the Hellenized form Carrhae, the city near which a

Roman army under the command of M. Licinius Crassus was annihilated by the Parthians in 53.

Postgate (*RlA* 4: 122–5), Villard (*DCM* 367–9).

Harrania Iron Age country located in the region of southeastern Anatolia–northwestern Iran. It was one of the lands from which Dayyan-Ashur, commander-in-chief of the Assyrian king Shalmaneser III, received tribute during his campaign in the region in 828 (**RIMA* 3: 70). Other lands which paid him tribute at this time included Shashganu and Andia, and the city of Gaburisu.

Harrua Iron Age city in southern Anatolia belonging to the kingdom of Que. The Assyrian king Sargon II reports that it was among the cities of Que which he captured in his seventh regnal year (715), after they had previously fallen into the hands of the Mushkian-Phrygian king Mita (Greek Midas) (**ARAB* II: 7).

Hartuv (map 8) Early Bronze I site in the northern Shephelah, Israel, extending over c. 3 ha. Excavations were carried out in 1985 and 1988 by P. Miroschedji and A. Mazar for the French Research Centre in Jerusalem and the Hebrew University of Jerusalem. The site's main architectural feature was a public building complex, which included a central courtyard with rooms on at least three sides, and a broad hall whose monumental entrance had two monolithic door jambs made of stone blocks. The excavators noted the uniqueness of this latter structure, and in general the rarity of such a complex in the Early Bronze Age. They suggested that it served as the community's joint religious and secular centre. The abandonment of the site may, in their view, be related to the emergence of urban life in Canaan during Early Bronze I.

Mazar and Miroschedji (*NEAEHL* 2: 584–5).

Haruha Iron Age city located in the middle Euphrates kingdom of Masuwari (see ***Ahmar, Tell***). It was built by Hamiyatas, one of the attested C9 kings of Masuwari.

Bunnens (2006: 94).

Hasanlu (map 20) Settlement located immediately south of Lake Urmia in the Solduz plain of northwestern Iran (Azerbaijan province). It consists of a central 'Citadel Mound', and an 'Outer Town' located on a flanking low terraced mound. Ten levels of occupation have been identified, the earliest dating back to the Late Neolithic period, the latest to the Islamic period. The most important levels are those of the Iron Age – V to IIIB. V covers the period c. 1450–1250 (Iron Age I in western Iran); IV, with three sub-levels (C–A), extends from c. 1250 to 750 (Iron Age II); IIIB (Iron Age III) ends c. 600.

The most substantial excavations on the site were those carried out by R. H. Dyson Jr from 1956 to 1978 for the University Museum of the University of Pennsylvania. They concentrated on level IVB, dating to C9, when Hasanlu was an important city of the Mannaean civilization (see **Mannaea**). The principal architectural feature of this level was an assemblage of apparently two-storeyed public buildings with columned halls. Of the surviving artefacts from IVB, the most outstanding is a large gold bowl, which is decorated with mythological scenes featuring heroes in battle and gods riding in chariots. Other small finds included weapons and armour, horse-trappings (e.g. bits and bridles), personal ornaments, tools, cylinder seals and sealings, and thousands of objects made of a wide range of materials including glass, amber, ivory, shell, wood, ceramic, and precious and commodity metals. Though no tablets were found, the excavators unearthed some fragments of stone artefacts with names indicating contacts with both the Assyrian and the Elamite worlds. The unfortified Mannaean settlement was destroyed by the Urartians c. 800. It was subsequently rebuilt by the Urartian king Minua (805–788), who transformed it into an Urartian fortress defended by substantial walls. The Urartian phase of the site's existence (IIIB) ended with the fall of the Urartian kingdom c. 600. There are remains of reoccupation in the Persian (IIIA) and Hellenistic (II) periods, followed by a long period of abandonment before the site was recoccupied in Islamic times (I).

Heimpel (*RlA* 4: 128–31), Dyson and Voigt (1989), Dyson (*OEANE* 2: 478–80).

Hashabu Late Bronze Age city in the Biqaʿ valley, Lebanon, attested in the records of the C15 pharaoh Tuthmosis III's Syro-Palestinian campaigns and also in the mid C14 Amarna correspondence (**EA* 174). An identification has been proposed with the large settlement-mound called Tell Hašba, whose remains indicate that it was a relatively important city in the Late Bronze Age, with occupation continuing into the Iron Age.

Lipiński (2000: 321 map, 329 with refs).

Hassuwa Late Bronze Age city in northern Syria, probably to be located in the region north of Carchemish. An army from Hassuwa supported by troops from Aleppo confronted and was destroyed by the Hittite king Hattusili I in a battle at Mt Atalur (Adalur) during the king's second Syrian campaign (mid C17); subsequently Hattusili marched on the city, plundered it, and put it to the torch (**Chav.* 220–1). The city of Hahhum (Hahha) suffered a similar fate, and the kings of both cities were harnessed to a transport wagon, used presumably to convey the spoils of conquest back to Hattusa. In the following century, the Hittite king Telipinu (1525–1500) conducted against the cities of Hassuwa, Zizzilippa, and Lawazantiya the first of a number of campaigns in his bid to regain Hittite territories lost in the reigns of his predecessors. Hassuwa was conquered and destroyed (**Chav.* 231).

Güterbock (*RlA* 4: 137).

Hatallu Iron Age Aramaean tribe in southern Mesopotamia. The earliest reference to it dates to the reign of the Assyrian king Adad-nirari III (810–783) when the king's commander-in-chief Shamshi-ilu laid waste a number of tribal lands, including that of the Hatallu (**RIMA* 3: 232). (The other tribal lands listed here are those of the Utu, the Rupu, and the Labdudu.) In mid C8 Ninurta-kudurri-usur, governor of the land of Suhu on the middle Euphrates, received an appeal from Adad-daʾanu, governor of the neighbouring land of Laqe, for assistance against a force of 2,000 Hatallu tribesmen from the Sarugu and Luhuaiia clans (q.v.), who were at that time plundering Laqe (**RIMB* 2: 292). When he heard reports that the Hatallu were planning to set upon his own land as well, Ninurta-kudurri-usur attacked and annihilated the enemy force while it was still in Laqe territory. He captured and killed their leader, Shamaʾgamni, then stripped off his skin and displayed it in front of the gate of Al-gabbari-bani, one of Suhu's cities (**RIMB* 2: 292–302).

Lipiński locates Hatallu's territory in the steppe to the southwest of Assyria proper, noting that a governor of Ashur province complains in a letter to the governor of Nimrud that the latter's subjects have set fire to the steppe, destroying grazing in his own area as far as the lands of Sutu and Hatallu. The letter is probably to be dated to the reign of the Assyrian king Tiglath-pileser III (745–727), who included the Hatallu in his account of the Aramaean tribes which he conquered (**Tigl. III* 158–9, Lipiński, 2000: 441–2).

Lipiński (2000: 425–8).

Hatarikka (Hadarik, Aramaic Hazrek, *OT* Hadrach, *Tell Afis*?) Iron Age city in northwestern Syria, capital of the region called Luash, which was incorporated into the kingdom of Hamath by the Hamathite king Zak(k)ur c. 796. On a stele with Aramaic inscription discovered at Tell Afis in 1903, Zakur records his victory over a coalition of enemy forces, led by Bar-Hadad, king of Damascus, after these forces had blockaded him in Hatarikka (**CS* II: 155, **Chav.* 307–11). Afis may in fact be the site of Hatarikka (see ***Afis, Tell***). Zakur was one of the first, if not the first, of a line of Aramaean rulers who held sway in the kingdom of Hamath, and it is possible that the seat of their dynasty was located in Hatarikka. Following the suppression of a rebellion in northern Syria by the Assyrian king Tiglath-pileser III c. 737, Hatarikka was organized as an Assyrian province (**Tigl. III* 186–7). A letter dating to the reign of Sargon II (721–705) refers to the king's installation there of a certain Ilu-mushezib, a baker of Bel-emuranni (**SAA* I: 134, no. 171). Assyrian texts record campaigns against Hatarikka by the Assyrian king Shalmaneser IV (782–773), and by his successor Ashur-dan III in 765 and 755. For further information on the city, see **Hamath**.

Hawkins (*RlA* 7: 160–1).

Hatatirra Iron Age city belonging to the Neo-Hittite kingdom of Pat(t)in (Assyrian Unqi) in northwestern Syria. It is mentioned in the Annals of the Assyrian king Tiglath-pileser III (745–727) as one of the cities where Tiglath-pileser resettled deportees from other parts of his kingdom (**ARAB* I: 276, **Tigl. III* 66–7). Other cities in Patin to which Tiglath-pileser assigned deportees included Huzarra, Irgillu, Kulmadara, Kunalia, Tae, and Tarmanazi.

CHLI 1: 362.

Hatenzuwa (Hatinzuwa) Late Bronze Age country in northern Anatolia, in the region of the Kaska lands. It apparently lay a considerable distance north of Hittite territory, for the Hittite king Mursili II (1321–1295) claimed not only to have conquered it, but to have been the first king of Hatti to have reached it since the Old Kingdom ruler Telipinu a century earlier (**AM* 164–5). Mursili's son Hattusili III also credited his own son, the future king Tudhaliya IV, with its conquest during Tudhaliya's extensive campaigns, while still a youth, in Kaska territory (**RGTC* 6: 102–3).

Hatip (map 3) Fortified Late Bronze Age Hittite site, located 17 km southwest of mod. Konya in southern Anatolia. It is best known for the discovery there, in 1993, of a late C13 rock-cut relief and hieroglyphic Luwian inscription. The relief depicts a striding god wearing a horned peak cap and short tunic, and armed with bow, dagger, and lance. The accompanying inscription reads *Kurunta, the Great King,* [*the Hero*]*, the* *son of [Mu]watalli, the Great King, the Hero.* It is possible that the monument is a northern boundary-marker of the kingdom of Tarhuntassa, where Hattusili III had installed Kurunta as local ruler. For the possible significance of the title 'Great King' as applied to Kurunta in this inscription, see Bryce (2007).

Dinçol (1998).

Hattena (**Hatina**) Late Bronze Age Hittite city in northern Anatolia, located not far from the holy city of Nerik, and a centre for the worship of the storm god. It is perhaps to be identified with Classical Sebastopolis (*BAGRW* 87 B4), mod. Sulu Saray (thus Garstang and Gurney, 1959: 14). The city contained a royal residence, which the king may have used fairly regularly in the course of his religious pilgrimages. In C13 Hattena was among the cities and lands, depopulated by enemy incursions, which the Hittite king Muwattalli II assigned to his brother Hattusili (later King Hattusili III) when he appointed Hattusili ruler of the northern part of the Hittite homeland (**CS* I: 201; see also **Hakpis(sa)** and **Turmitta**).

**RGTC* 6: 101–2.

Hatti (map 3) The name initially used of the north-central region of Bronze Age Anatolia thought to be the homeland of the pre-Indo-European Hattic people. A kingdom called Hatti may first have arisen in the region during the second half of the Early Bronze Age (M3). Evidence for its existence comes from a well-known text which records a rebellion of seventeen rulers against the Akkadian king Naram-Sin (c. 2380–2325), including a king of Hatti called Pamba (Bryce, 2005: n. 7, refs). But the tradition is a late attested one (c. 1400), and its historical authenticity has been questioned. In the Middle Bronze Age, Hatti was one of several kingdoms, sometimes called *mātu* in the Assyrian merchant texts, which dominated the central Anatolian region during the Assyrian Colony period (C20–18) (see glossary). Its capital, Hattus (on the site of the later Hittite capital Hattusa), held sway over a number of cities and communities. A fragmentary text records a rebellion which some of them staged against Hattus (*Larsen, 1972). Subsequently, a king of Hatti called Piyusti joined in a military alliance against Anitta, king of the city of Nesa, which lay just south of the Halys r. (mod. Kızıl Irmak, Hittite Marassantiya) (**Chav.* 217). Seeking to extend his power through north-central Anatolia, Anitta conquered the lands lying within the Halys basin, and in the process destroyed Hatti's capital Hattus and declared its site accursed (**Chav.* 218).

In the Late Bronze Age, 'Hatti' was regularly used as a general term to designate the kingdom of the people we call the Hittites, and more specifically, the homeland of the Hittites within the Halys r. basin. The population of Late Bronze Age Hatti consisted of a number of ethnic groups, including elements of both the early Hattic population of the region as well as later Indo-European groups who had begun settling in central Anatolia by the end of M3. The 'Hittites' always referred to themselves as the 'people of the Land of Hatti'. That is, they identified themselves not by an ethnic term but by the region in which they lived, using a name which may already have been in currency for many centuries, or even millennia. Contemporary foreign rulers also referred to the great Anatolian-based power as the kingdom of Hatti. Even after the kingdom's fall in C12, the name Hatti survived through the early centuries of M1, during the period of the so-called Neo-Hittite kingdoms. Assyrians,

Urartians, and Hebrews continued to refer to Syria and the Taurus region as 'the Land of Hatti'.

Singer (1981), Cogan (2002), Bryce (2005: 12–15).

Hattusa (*Boğazköy/Boğazkale*) (map 3) Middle and Late Bronze Age city in north-central Anatolia, 160 km east of Ankara. Originally called Hattus, the city was founded by an indigenous north-central Anatolian people called the Hattians, c. 2000. In the Assyrian Colony Period (Middle Bronze Age; C20–18) (see glossary), Hattus is attested as the seat of a kingdom which traded with the Assyrian merchants. It was destroyed in mid C18 by Anitta, king of Nesa, who declared the site accursed (**Chav.* 218), and thus never again to be resettled. But early in C17 it was rebuilt, and called Hattusa, by one of the first Hittite kings, probably Hattusili I (1650–1620). Thenceforth, it was the royal capital of the fledgling kingdom of Hatti. Dominated by its acropolis (mod. Büyükkale) where the royal palace was built, Hattusa in its first Hittite phase was small (approx. 62 ha) and vulnerable to attack, for it lacked adequate defences. Indeed it was fortunate to survive the century that followed the reign of Hattusili I. In this period, the kingdom became seriously weakened by internal struggles over the royal succession and was almost annihilated by outside forces, especially the Hurrians. King Telipinu (1525–1500) brought new stability to Hatti (**Chav.* 231–4), and in the reign of one of his C15 successors, Hantili II, a wall 8 m thick was built around the capital. It included many of the features of later Hittite fortification architecture, including postern gates and corbelled tunnels through the walls.

But these fortifications failed to save Hattusa from invaders, very likely the Kaska tribes, who captured, sacked, and burned it during the reign of Tudhaliya III

Figure 43 Hattusa, citadel.

Figure 44 Hattusa, postern gate.

(1370?–1350) (*Bryce, 2005: 146). The city was rebuilt after the repulse of the invaders, probably by Tudhaliya's son and successor Suppiluliuma I (1350–1322), who made it the centre of the most powerful kingdom in western Asia. For a brief period, however, Hattusa lost its capital-city status. This was due to Suppiluliuma's grandson and third successor, Muwattalli II (1295–1272), opponent of Ramesses II in the battle of Qadesh, who shifted the capital south to a land called Tarhuntassa. Hattusa was now assigned to the authority of the king's chief scribe, Mittannamuwa (**CS* I: 200, *Bryce, 2005: 231–2). But Muwattalli's son and successor Urhi-Teshub (1272–1267) re-established it as the capital, and so it remained until the kingdom's fall early in C12.

The German Archaeological Institute has conducted excavations at Hattusa since 1907. The earliest campaigns were directed by H. Winckler, who identified the site as the Hittite capital from information contained in one of the tablets unearthed there. (It was part of the text of a treaty between the kings of Hatti and Egypt.) Subsequent campaigns have been carried out by K. Bittel, P. Neve, J. Seeher, and currently A. Schachner. One of the city's remarkable features was its substantial redevelopment during the last two centuries of its existence. The area which it encompassed was increased to 185 ha by a massive expansion to the south, more than doubling Hattusa's original size. It was protected by impressive fortifications, extending over a total distance of 5 km. The main casemate wall reared up on an earth rampart to a height of 10 m, punctuated by towers at 20 m intervals along its entire length. Before it was a second curtain wall, also with towers built in the intervals between those of the main wall. The fortifications extended to the northeast, spanning a deep gorge and enclosing within the city limits a mountain outcrop now called Büyükkaya. Access to the city was provided by a number of gateways, the most impressive of which were decorated by monumental relief sculptures – the so-called Sphinx, Lion, and 'King's' (or 'Warrior-God's') gates.

The original city, containing the royal acropolis and Great Temple (which was dedicated to the storm god and the sun goddess of Arinna), is now commonly referred to as the Lower City, and the later extension as the Upper City. Neve's excavations of the latter brought to light the foundations of twenty-six temples, increasing to thirty-one the city's known temples. This makes it clear, Neve claims, that Hattusa had the character of a sacred and ceremonial city. He sees the layout of the whole city as symbolizing the cosmic world-form of the Hittites, with the palace as the earthly world, the temple-city as the godly world, and the cult-district lying in between as providing the passage from the transient to the eternal.

Neve attributed Hattusa's substantial redevelopment to its third last king Tudhaliya IV (1237–1209), though the inspiration for this grand new city may have come from his father, Hattusili III. But Neve's successor Seeher argued against this attribution. On the basis of radiocarbon dating, analysis of pottery and other stratified finds, and the dating of *in situ* inscriptions by stylistic criteria, Seeher believes that parts of the Upper City were already occupied, and fortified, by late C16 or early C15, and that

Figure 45 Hattusa, lion gate.

Figure 46 Hattusa, 'King's' gate.

many of the finds in the Upper City should be dated no later than C14. Yet he concedes that Tudhaliya may well have contributed significantly to the city's final development. And given the strong emphasis Tudhaliya placed on religious reforms throughout his realm, it is not unlikely that many, perhaps the majority, of the temples in the Upper City were constructed on his orders.

Tens of thousands of tablet fragments, from the capital's palace and temple archives, provide our chief source of written information on the history and civilization of the Hittite world. In 1986 an intact bronze tablet was unearthed near the city's so-called Sphinx Gate. Its 352 lines of text throw important new light on both the political geography and the history of the kingdom in the last decades of its existence (**HDT* 114–24, **CS* II: 100–6). Other recent finds in the capital include an archive of over 3,500 seal impressions (discovered in 1990 and 1991), which provide much important information about the genealogy of members of the royal dynasty, and a cult complex (discovered 1988) on the city's so-called Südburg, just south of the royal acropolis

(*Hawkins, 1995). The complex consists of two chambers, one of which is embellished with reliefs of a deity and a king called Suppiluliuma, and inscribed with a text in the hieroglyphic script. It dates to the reign of the last known king, Suppiluliuma II (1207–). More recently, Seeher's excavations brought to light eleven underground grain-pits on Büyükkaya on the city's northeastern extremity, and behind the so-called 'postern wall' on the southwest of the Lower City, an above-ground storage complex with mudbrick walls, consisting of two parallel rows of sixteen chambers each (Seeher, 2000). On the basis of radiocarbon and pottery analysis the former have been dated to C14–13, the latter to late C16–early C15. The granaries had a total capacity of almost 8,000 tonnes of grain, mostly barley, enough to feed annually tens of thousands of people, both within and beyond the capital. Seeher also discovered five water reservoirs, the 'southern ponds', on the plateau in the Upper City. Up to 8 m deep, four of these were rectangular in shape, one circular. Built in C15, and probably fed by springs located on higher ground nearby, they must have provided the city with a large part of its water supply – but only for a relatively short period. Due to silt accumulation, the reservoirs were abandoned by the end of C15, as indicated by the discovery of numerous pottery sherds in the fill of Pool 1 dating to c. 1400. The sherds include what appear to have been broken cult-containers, among which were a number of long, thin, spindle-shaped bottles – probably libation vessels.

Hattusa along with much else of the empire over which it ruled collapsed in the early decades of the C12. But its end may not have been as abrupt as was once believed. Though there is evidence of violent destruction by fire, at least part of which can be attributed to enemy attack, Seeher believes that such an attack occurred only after the city had been partly abandoned. Evidence from the last period of Hattusa's existence

Figure 47 Hattusa, granaries.

indicates that most of its valuable possessions, at least anything that was portable, were systematically removed before the city fell (Seeher, 2001). The king, his family, and the royal court may well have escaped to a safe place of refuge, taking their most important items, including official records, with them. The rest of the population were left to fend for themselves. When Hattusa was finally taken over and scavenged by bands of marauders, it may already have been in an advanced state of decay.

From early in the Iron Age, the site was reoccupied by native Anatolian 'squatters', and by C9 (beginning of the middle Iron Age) a significant settlement had been established there. Fortification of Büyükkale in the the first half of C7, accompanied by a decrease in the population of the 'Lower City', has been interpreted as a possible response to a Cimmerian invasion. The culture of the middle and late Iron Age settlement displays a number of Phrygian characteristics, including the cult of the Phrygian mother-goddess Cybele. The name of the Iron Age city is unknown. The former generally accepted identification with the M1 Cappadocian city Pteria would be excluded by the more recent identification of this city with Kerkenes Dağ, which lay 40 km to the southeast (but for the most recent argument against the identification of Pteria with Kerkenes Dağ, see Rollinger, 2003a: 322–6). The site continued to be inhabited through the Persian, Hellenistic, and Roman periods.

A major project in recent years has been the reconstruction of part of the fortifications in the Hittite Lower City. A full-scale replica of 65 m of the inner wall,

Figure 48 Hattusa, reconstructed wall.

incorporating two towers up to 12 m high, has been completed in the vicinity of the Great Temple.

Neve (1993), Bryce (2002: 230–56), Seeher (2002; 2006a; 2006b).

Haurani M1 city belonging to the western Aramaean kingdom of Bit-Agusi in north-central Syria. It is attested in a list of cities conquered by the Assyrian king Tiglath-pileser III (745–727) (**Tigl. III* 146–7), and is perhaps to be identified with mod. Hawwar, 15 km west of Aleppo.

Lipiński (2000: 203).

Hayasa see Azzi.

Hayyat, Tell el- (map 8) Bronze Age village located in Transjordan 2 km east of the Jordan r., with four settlement phases extending through the Early and Middle Bronze Ages. Following three preliminary surveys of the site between 1939 and 1976, excavations were carried out by S. Falconer and B. Magness-Gardiner from 1982 to 1985. Their identification of the settlement as a sedentary Canaanite farming hamlet in its Middle Bronze Age IIA–C phase is supported by skeletal remains of domesticated farm animals, and evidence of a range of fruit-bearing orchards and grain crops. The focal point of the settlement was a mudbrick temple surrounded by an enclosure wall. Four stratified layers of the temple were brought to light, corresponding to the four phases of the settlement's history. There is also evidence of pottery and metal workshops, the latter producing a range of tools, weapons, and figurines.

The preliminary surface surveys indicated the possibility of some reoccupation of the site during the Iron Age and Persian periods.

Falconer and Magness-Gardiner (1989).

Hazazu (*ʿAzaz*) Iron Age city belonging to the Neo-Hittite kingdom of Pat(t)in (Assyrian Unqi) in northern Syria, first mentioned in the texts of the Assyrian kings Ashurnasirpal II (883–859) and his son and successor Shalmaneser III (858–824). When Ashurnasirpal invaded the kingdom during his western campaign in 870, he led his troops to Hazazu, and after receiving tribute from the city (gold and linen garments), crossed the Apre r. (mod. Afrin), and advanced upon Patin's capital, Kinalua (Kunulua), where its ruler, Lubarna, submitted to him without resistance (**RIMA* 2: 217). Shalmaneser captured Hazazu in his first regnal year, during his campaign against the cities of northern Syria (**RIMA* 3: 17, 25, 141). Patin's throne was then occupied by a successor of Lubarna called Sapalulme. Hazazu may have been the first Patinite city encountered by an enemy crossing the kingdom's frontiers from the north. The Eponym Chronicle entry (see glossary) for the year 804 records an attack on Hazazu in that year, during the reign of Adad-nirari III. Hazazu was subsequently incorporated into the neighbouring kingdom of Bit-Agusi, appearing in a list of Bit-Agusi's cities conquered by Tiglath-pileser III (745–727) (*Tigl. III* 146–7).

Hawkins (*RlA* 4: 240).

Hazor (*Tell el-Qedah*) (map 8) Urban settlement in Palestine, mod. Israel, located 14 km north of the Sea of Galilee. It consists of a 12 ha upper city built on a mound (the acropolis), and a 70 ha lower city; the former has a history of occupation from the Early Bronze Age to the Hellenistic period, the latter was occupied during the Middle and Late Bronze Ages. Written references to Hazor appear in the Mari archives (C18), and in various later Egyptian sources, including Tuthmosis III's list of conquests (C15), the Amarna letters (mid C14) (see glossary), and the so-called Papyrus Anastasi I text, attributed to the pharaoh Ramesses II (C13). Hazor also appears in numerous *OT* sources, in the context of the Israelite conquest and occupation of Canaan (e.g. Joshua 11:10–13, Judges 4–5). After preliminary soundings by J. Garstang in 1928, the site was excavated by Y. Yadin as director of the James A. de Rothschild Expedition, from 1955 to 1958 and from 1968 to 1972, on behalf of the Hebrew University of Jerusalem, the Palestine Jewish Colonization Association, and the Anglo-Israel Exploration Society. Excavations were resumed in 1990 by A. Ben-Tor on behalf of the Hebrew University of Jerusalem, Complutense University (Madrid), and the Israel Exploration Society, and continue to the present day (see http://unixware.mscc.huji.ac.il/~hatsor/).

Little is yet known of the Early Bronze Age settlement on the mound, though Yadin observed that the ceramic ware recovered from its various levels points to close connections with Syria. Hazor remained a relatively insignificant city at the beginning of the Middle Bronze Age, but with the spread of settlement to a new lower city in Middle Bronze Age II, it grew to become one of the most important cities of Canaan. Yadin dated the development of what he called 'greater Hazor' to mid C18. (There is, however, some disagreement about the precise chronology of Hazor's Middle Bronze Age development.) The remains of residential dwellings, a series of temples, and part of a huge building complex, probably a palace, were unearthed within the city of this period, which was protected by a moat and by a huge earthen rampart penetrated by two city gates. Strong Syrian influence is reflected in a number of the city's architectural features.

After suffering violent destruction at the end of the Middle Bronze Age, Hazor was rebuilt in the Late Bronze Age, and during this period reached the highest point of its development. By mid C14 it had become the largest city in Canaan. But it also suffered several catastrophic reverses during its Late Bronze Age phase. Its destruction by the pharaoh Seti I early in C13 marked the second occasion on which it had been devastated by enemy onslaught during this phase. And within a century of Seti's conquest, the city was again destroyed – on this occasion, according to Yadin, by the Israelites, as recorded in the book of Joshua. Yadin believed that the meagre remains of the first Iron Age occupation of the site (C12–11) reflects Israelite settlement, which was at that time still semi-nomadic in character.

Subsequently, in C10, Hazor once again achieved the status of a major urban centre, which reached its peak in C9. Lipiński (2000: 350–1) proposes that Malaha (q.v.), referred to as 'a royal city of Hazael (king of Damascus)' by the C9 Assyrian king Shalmaneser III, is the early Aramaic name of Hazor. Hazor's initial development in early M1 used commonly to be attributed to the Israelite king Solomon, but with revised thinking putting the status of the so-called 'United Monarchy' in doubt, it is possible that it should be more correctly attributed to Omri or Ahab, and would be a development of C9 rather than C10. Once again, the city was fortified, by casemate walls penetrated by a six-chambered gate. But at its greatest extent it was still much smaller than its Middle and Late Bronze Age predecessors, since it did not go beyond the limits of the original upper city on the mound. Settlement throughout the Iron Age seems to have been confined to the mound.

Aramaean kings were allegedly responsible for the destruction of Hazor on two later occasions, before the city fell victim to an earthquake in mid C8. It was once more rebuilt, but enjoyed only a brief new lease of life before it was again destroyed in 732, on this occasion by the Assyrians. Subsequently, a series of citadels was built on the acropolis over a period of several centuries, before the site was permanently abandoned during the Hellenistic period.

Yadin/Ben-Tor (*NEAEHL* 2: 594–606), Ben-Tor (*OEANE* 3: 1–5; reports in *IEJ* from 1992, vol. 42 onwards), Ben-Ami (2001).

Hazrek see Hatarikka.

Hebron (map 8) Canaanite city located on the West Bank in the southern hill country of Judah, southern Palestine. It is frequently attested in *OT* sources, according to which its original name was Kiriath Arba (Genesis 23:2, Joshua 20:7), probably meaning 'fourfold city'. There is no certain attestation of the city outside biblical sources, though there may be a reference to it in the Medinet Habu inscription of the C12 pharaoh Ramesses III. Its importance in *OT* tradition stems partly from its association with the Hebrew patriarchs, but is due in large measure to its close links with King David, who settled in the city with his two wives after Saul's death, and was anointed king there (2 Samuel 2:1–4). For seven years and six months, Hebron was the capital of his kingdom (2 Samuel 5:5, 1 Chronicles 3:4). It was here too that David's son Absalom began his revolt against his father (2 Samuel 15:7–10).

The biblically attested city is now commonly identified with the site called by the Arabic name El-Khalil, which lies 30 km southwest of Jerusalem. Excavations were conducted from 1964 to 1966 by an American expedition under the direction of P. C. Hammond, and subsequently from 1983 to 1986 by a team from Tel Aviv University under the direction of A. Ofer. Further excavations, on the northern side of the mound, were begun in 1999, by E. Eisenberg. According to Numbers 13:22, Hebron was founded seven years before Zoan (Greek Tanis) in Egypt, which was settled in the Middle Bronze Age (early M2). But El-Khalil's archaeological history extends back to the Chalcolithic period (M5–4), and continues through the Bronze and Iron Ages, Hellenistic, Roman, Byzantine, and Islamic periods. The city was destroyed by fire in Early Bronze III, resettled for a time, and then abandoned until Middle Bronze IIB. The substantial fortified city of this later period may have been a Hyksos settlement. A clay tablet inscribed with Akkadian cuneiform, which records animals (probably for sacrifice), and contains what may be the name of a king, has been seen as an indication of Hebron's role as an administrative centre of its region, perhaps the region's capital.

The city was abandoned during the Late Bronze Age, of which there are only meagre remains, and resettled in the Iron Age. According to Ofer, it reached the peak of its development between C11 and the end of C10. Five *lamelekh* seal impressions (see glossary) on storage jar handles are among the most significant finds of the Iron Age phase. The city subsequently declined in importance, and was apparently completely abandoned during the Persian period (C6–4). There was a Hellenistic settlement on the site, in the valley at the foot of the mound, which appears to have had a relatively flourishing existence under subsequent Roman domination – initially, at least. On two occasions during the Roman period, there is evidence of violent destruction.

Occupation continued through the Byzantine period, before the site was finally abandoned under the Ottomans.

Ofer (*NEAEHL* 2: 606–9), Negev and Gibson (2001: 223–4).

Hellespont (map 19) Narrow strait separating the Troad region of northwestern Anatolia from the southeastern edge of the European continent. According to Greek mythology, the name, which literally means 'Helle's sea', came about when Helle, the daughter of the Theban king Athamas, fell to her death in the strait while fleeing from her stepmother on the back of a winged, golden-fleeced ram. The strait is now known as the Dardanelles. This name also derives from Greek mythology. Dardanus was the son of Zeus and the ancestor of the kings of Troy.

Because of its highly important strategic location, providing as it does a sea passage from the Aegean Sea to the Black Sea via the Propontis (mod. Sea of Marmara), the Hellespont has figured prominently in both military and commercial operations in anc. as well as in more recent times. However, its strong counter-winds and counter-currents make it unlikely that it was used by large sailing vessels before M1, when the Greeks began building fifty-oared ships called penteconters.

Gschnitzer (*BNP* 6: 110).

Heraclea Pontica (*Ereğli*) (map 4) M1 BCE–M1 CE Greek city in northern Anatolia, located on the south coast of the Black Sea in the region of Bithynia. It was founded c. 558 by colonists from Megara and Boeotia in mainland Greece. The territory they occupied formerly belonged to a people called the Mariandyni, whom they reduced to serfdom. Heraclea became the most important city on the Black Sea coast between Byzantium and Sinope. In late C6 it founded colonies of its own, at Callatis and Chersonnesus on the western and northern coasts (respectively) of the Black Sea, as well as a number of trading-posts westwards along the Black Sea's southern coast. It became very active in sea-trading enterprises, particularly in the Black Sea region. In 364, a certain Clearchus established a tyranny in the city, which continued after his assassination in 353/352 through three male successors of his family line. The third of these, his son Dionysius, expanded his territories, as did his wife Amastris, who became ruler of the city after her husband's death in 305. In particular, she extended her control eastwards, in the process amalgamating four cities – Sesamos, Tios, Kromna, and Kytoros – into a single polity with its nucleus at Sesamos, now renamed Amastris. (For these cities, see *BAGRW* 86 C2.) After Amastris was assassinated by her sons, the city came under the control of Lysimachus, one of Alexander the Great's generals (to whom Amastris had been briefly married after Dionysius' death). Following his death in 281, a democratic government was instituted in the city.

Strabo 12.3.1–6, Wilson (*PECS* 383), Broughton/Mitchell (*OCD* 684), Strobel (*BNP* 6: 151–2).

Heraclea under Latmus Carian city in origin, located on the slope of Mt Latmus, in the Aegean coastal area of southwestern Anatolia, 25 km west of Miletus (see *BAGRW* 61 F2). According to Strabo (14.1.8), the city was originally called Latmus. Though lying within the region settled by Ionian colonists in late M2, it seems to have maintained a strong indigenous element in its population and culture, which only gradually gave way to Greek influence. In C5 the city became a member of the Athenian Confederacy (see glossary). In mid C4 it was captured by the Carian ruler

Mausolus, who changed its name from Latmus to Heraclea, and was probably responsible for the relocation of the city on a new site to the west. At least part of the reason for the shift may have been the silting up of the gulf, by the Maeander r., on which Heraclea originally lay. Virtually nothing of the original city survives. The new city was endowed with splendid (and still well-preserved) fortifications over a distance of 6.5 km. Sixty-five towers were incorporated into the walls. There is some uncertainty as to whether these walls were built by Mausolus, or some decades later by Lysimachus, one of Alexander the Great's successors. Laid out in part on a Hippodamian grid plan (see glossary), new Heraclea enjoyed a flourishing existence, probably because of its maritime trading activities, through the Hellenistic, Roman, and Byzantine periods. Remains of all three periods are still visible on the site. In Greek mythological tradition the city is associated with the story of Endymion, a handsome young shepherd who was seduced by the moon goddess Selene.

MacDonald (*PECS* 384–5).

Hesban, Tell (biblical **Heshbon**) (map 8) Iron Age, Hellenistic, Roman, and Byzantine town located on the Transjordanian plateau 19 km southwest of Amman. Excavations were carried out by Andrews University, Michigan, for five seasons between 1968 and 1976 under the direction of S. H. Horn and L. T. Geraty successively, and for a sixth season, in 1978, by the Baptist Bible College, Clarks Summit, Pennsylvania, under the direction of J. Lawlor. The most recent excavations have been those directed by B. J. Walker, Grand Valley State University, and Ø. S. LaBianca, Andrews University. Archaeologists who had previously visited the site identified it with biblical Heshbon, frequently attested in *OT* sources. According to Numbers 21:26–30, Heshbon was captured from the Moabites by the Amorite king Sihon, who made the city his capital. But this information is difficult to square with current archaeological evidence. In *OT* tradition, Sihon belongs to the period of the Israelite conquests (Numbers 21:21, Joshua 12:2), which, if they have any historical basis, date to C12. Hesban has revealed only a few scattered remains belonging to or before this period. At best, the site was at that time occupied by no more than a small village. Nineteen occupation levels were identified, the first four spanning the Iron Age (c. 1200–500).

Remains from the Iron Age site are very fragmentary, though the settlement's growth can be traced through four archaeological strata from a small unfortified agrarian village (level 19: C12–11) to a relatively prosperous town, probably built around a fort (level 16: C7–6) (thus Geraty). Ostraca found in a reservoir (probably built in level 17: C9–8) and bearing inscriptions in the Ammonite language and script suggest that the town was at this time firmly (back?) under Ammonite control. Before the end of C6 it was violently destroyed, and then abandoned until its reoccupation in the late Hellenistic period. In this and the Roman period, it was called Esbus. In C1 it came under Herod the Great's control, and may have been used by him (Geraty suggests) as a border fort against the Nabataeans.

LaBianca (1989), Geraty (*NEAEHL* 2: 626–30).

Hesi, Tell el- (map 8) Settlement in Israel, located near the border of the Shephelah and the Negev desert, consisting of a 10 ha terrace and 1.5 ha mound at its northeast corner. Its history of occupation extends from the Chalcolithic to the Hellenistic period, except for a period of abandonment in the Middle Bronze Age. Excavation of the site was first undertaken by the Palestine Exploration Fund under the direction initially of W. F. M. Petrie, in 1890, and subsequently of F. J. Bliss in 1891 and 1892. Subsequent excavation was conducted from 1970 to 1983 by the Joint Archaeological Expedition affiliated with the American Schools of Oriental Research. The first major period of occupation occurred during the Early Bronze Age when the settlement extended across the entire terrace and was surrounded by a mudbrick wall, within which were discovered the remains of domestic and industrial installations. Meagre results were obtained from the Middle and Late Bronze Age levels. During C9, in Iron Age II, the city was confined to the mound and fortified by a casemate wall system. A 7 m high platform was constructed on the summit of the acropolis to enhance the settlement's defence capabilities. On top of the platform, a large courtyard building was constructed, and subsequently, above this building, several smaller residential structures. In the first half of C5, during the Persian period, another large platform was built. This provided the base for the construction of a small citadel, which consisted of casemate walls surrounding a central courtyard. Fargo suggests that in this period Hesi may have served as a depot and storehouse for the Persian military while they were engaged in raids into Egypt.

Fargo (*NEAEHL* 2: 630–4).

Hilakku (maps 13, 18) M1 kingdom in southern Anatolia (the name is attested in Assyrian texts), bordering upon the kingdom of Que (called Hume in Neo-Babylonian texts), which lay to its east, and the kingdoms of the Tabal region which lay to its north. It extended over much of the territory of Classical Cilicia Tracheia/Aspera ('Rough Cilicia'). Hilakku constantly resisted attempts by Assyrian kings to impose their sovereignty upon it. In 858, under their respective kings Pihirim and Kate, Hilakku and Que sent contingents to join an alliance of northern Syrian states against the new Assyrian king Shalmaneser III during the first of his nineteen campaigns west of the Euphrates. The alliance proved no match for Shalmaneser's army, and was decisively defeated (**RIMA* 3: 10, 16–17). Shalmaneser conducted a campaign against Que in 839 (**RIMA* 3: 55, 58, 67), and two further campaigns into its territory in 834 and 833 (**RIMA* 3: 67–8). He apparently made no attempt during these campaigns to invade Que's western neighbour Hilakku, which lay in a more remote and much less accessible region.

Nevertheless, in the reign of the Assyrian king Shalmaneser V (726–722) or his successor Sargon II (721–705), both Hilakku and Que became Assyrian provinces. Hilakku was assigned by Sargon to Ambaris (son of the former king of Tabal), who after a period of exile in Assyria had been repatriated by Sargon, installed as ruler of the Tabalic kingdom Bit-Burutash, married to Sargon's daughter, and given Hilakku as a dowry (**ARAB* II: 11). When Ambaris was deposed by Sargon in 713 (for the circumstances, see **Tabal**), Hilakku, along with Bit-Burutash, was placed under direct Assyrian rule. Rebellions against Assyria under Sargon's successors, beginning with his son Sennacherib (704–681), ensured that the spirit of anti-Assyrian resistance remained strong in the Anatolian kingdoms. Sennacherib probably succeeded in reasserting Assyrian authority over Que, but Hilakku repeatedly resisted Assyrian attempts to dominate it, even though Sennacherib's successor Esarhaddon claimed to have subdued its rebellious population (**ARAB* II: 206–7). Certainly by the reign of Ashurbanipal (668–630/627) Hilakku had regained its independence from any form of

Assyrian control, though early in his reign Ashurbanipal received an embassy from its king, Sandasarme (Houwink ten Cate, 1965: 26).

In Neo-Babylonian texts, the country attested as Pirindu (Piriddu) corresponded largely, if not entirely, to the kingdom of Hilakku. Its capital was probably Ura (see **Ura (1)**). Kirshu, another royal city of Pirindu, lay 'six double-hours' from Ura. It appears to have been an important base of Pirindu's ruling dynasty. A text from Nebuchadnezzar II's reign refers to prisoners taken from Pirindu in the king's thirteenth year (592/591). Several years after the death of Nebuchadnezzar in 562, his successor-but-one, Neriglissar (560–556), conducted a campaign against a king of Pirindu called Appuashu (557/556) (**ABC* 103–4, **Chav.* 417–18). Hostilities between Pirindu and Babylon may have arisen over control of Hume (Que in Assyrian texts). Neriglissar advanced to Hume, where he inflicted a defeat on Appuashu's troops after a failed attempt by the latter to ambush him. He then pursued Appuashu into his own kingdom, capturing his royal cities Ura and Kirshu, and also the island fortress of Pitusu where 6,000 troops were stationed. He proceeded next to Sallune (Classical Selinus; *BAGRW* 66 A4), the westernmost city on the Cilician coast. From there he marched to the borders of Lydia before returning home.

Houwink ten Cate (1965: 17–18, 28, 43), Hawkins (*RlA* 4: 402–3; *CHLI* I: 43–4), Streck (*RlA* 10: 572–3).

Him(m)e (Himu) Late Bronze and Iron Age country located in the borderlands between northeastern Mesopotamia and northwestern Iran, within the territories inhabited by the Lullubi (Lullumu) tribal groups. It is first attested in the record of the Assyrian king Shalmaneser I's accession year (1275), as one of eight lands belonging to the country Uruatri (var. Uratri; see under **Urartu**) which Shalmaneser conquered, allegedly destroying fifty-one of their cities and carrying off their population and property (**RIMA* 1: 183). The other lands were Bargun (or Mashgun), Halila, Luha, Nilipahru, Salua, Uatqun, and Zingun. Shalmaneser's claim that Uruatri had rebelled against him at the beginning of his reign implies that these lands had previously been subject to Assyrian overlordship. In a campaign against one of the regions called Habhu in Assyrian texts (see **Habhu (2)**), Tiglath-pileser I (1114–1076) fought troops from several countries, including Himme (**RIMA* 2: 19). His successor-but-one Ashur-bel-kala (1073–1056) conducted at least two campaigns against the country (**RIMA* 2: 88, 92–3, 94). On the second of these he used his infantry to lay siege to, capture, and destroy the city of Uruniash, which was in the heart of the mountains and inaccessible to his chariots. Bargun (Mashgun) is also mentioned within the context of these campaigns.

Him(m)e/Himu is perhaps to be identified with Himua (q.v.), attested in Late Bronze Age Hittite and Assyrian texts.

Klengel (*RlA* 4: 411).

Himua Northern Mesopotamian country first attested in the reign of the Hittite king Arnuwanda I (early C14) among the lands whose temples had been sacked by the Kaskan peoples from the Pontic region (*Bryce, 2005: 142). The Assyrian king Tiglath-pileser I (1114–1076) lists it among the Nairi lands which he conquered during his campaigns against Nairi beginning in his third regnal year (**RIMA* 2: 21, 37, 52). Himua is perhaps to be identified with Him(m)e/Himu (q.v.), a Late Bronze and Iron Age country attested in Assyrian texts from the reigns of Shalmaneser I, Tiglath-pileser I, and Ashur-bel-kala.

Hindanu (Hinzanu, Giddan) (map 7) Iron Age city and state located on the west bank of the middle Euphrates between Laqe to the north and Suhu to the south. Hindanu is first mentioned in the context of a campaign conducted by the Assyrian king Tiglath-pileser I (1114–1076) against the land of Suhu (**RIMA* 2: 43). The Assyrian king Adad-nirari II (911–891) received tribute from it on his progress through the middle Euphrates region, as did his son and successor Tukulti-Ninurta II (890–884) during his last recorded campaign in 885 (**RIMA* 2: 154, 175). Tukulti-Ninurta's son and successor Ashurnasirpal II also received tribute payments from the city on a campaign which he conducted in the Habur r. region in his first regnal year (883), and on a second expedition four years later when he encamped his troops near the city (**RIMA* 2: 200, 213). Subsequently Hindanu and Laqe joined with Suhu in an anti-Assyrian coalition, probably with the encouragement of Bit-Adini and Babylonia (c. 877). Ashurnasirpal crushed the coalition's forces, then set about destroying their cities and deporting large numbers of their populations (**RIMA* 2: 214–15).

Several decades later, Hindanu joined in a widespread revolt against Shalmaneser III (858–824), initiated by the king's son Ashur-da'in-apla. The rebellion continued into the early regnal years of Shalmaneser's son and successor Shamshi-Adad V (823–811) before it was finally crushed (**RIMA* 3: 183). Hindanu now apparently remained submissive to Assyrian rule. In the reign of Shamshi-Adad's son and successor Adad-nirari III (810–783), it was among the lands in the middle Euphrates region assigned to Nergal-erish (Palil-erish), governor of the province of Rasappa (**RIMA* 3: 209, 211). The Assyrian king Sargon II (721–705) sought to curb raiding activities by nomadic Arab groups in the middle Euphrates region by assigning them grazing rights in Hindanu, between the Wadi Tharthar and the land of Suhu (**SAA* I: 74, no. 82). In 648, during the reign of Ashurbanipal, Hindanu was governed by a certain Belshunu, the Assyrian eponym (see glossary) for the year. The people of Hindanu and Suhu are attested as paying tribute to the Babylonian king Nabopolassar as he marched up the Euphrates in his tenth year (616) on his way to Assyria, though later in that year he took the people and gods of Hindanu to Babylon (**ABC* 91, **PE* 30, no. 10). For further attestations of Hindanu among Assyrian toponyms, see Parpola (1970: 163–4). Hindanu is mentioned in Neo-Babylonian and Persian tablets (its governor is attested in a tablet from the reign of Darius II).

Postgate (*RlA* 4: 415–16).

Hindaru M1 Aramaean tribe in southeastern Babylonia, first attested in a letter from Nippur, mid C8 (**Nippur* IV: 62–3, no. 13, line 6), and included in the list of thirty-five so-called Aramaean tribes conquered by the Assyrian king Tiglath-pileser III, probably in his first regnal year (745) (**Tigl. III* 158). Four sheikhs of the land of Hindaru are said to have submitted at Dur-Abi-hara to the Assyrian king Sargon II (721–705), who imposed tax and tribute payments upon them (*Sargon II* 329). The Hindaru were among the tribes subjugated by Sargon's son and successor Sennacherib (**Sennach.* 25, 43, 49, 54, 57). Further references to them are found in letters from Sargon's reign (**SAA* XVII: 84, no. 92, 127, no. 146).

Lipiński (2000: 455–8).

Hinduwa Late Bronze Age city in southwestern Anatolia, nominally subject to Hatti; = Classical Candyba in Lycia? For its rebellion against Hittite rule, see **Dalawa**.

**HDT* 156–7.

Hiranu see **Umalia**.

Hirim(m)u Iron Age fortress-city east of the Tigris r., originally belonging to Babylonia, but incorporated, along with the fortress-city Harutu (Hararatu), into the northeastern frontier territory of the Neo-Assyrian kingdom by King Tukulti-Ninurta II (890–884) (**RIMA* 2: 180). His achievement was emulated by his son and successor Ashurnasirpal II (883–859) (**RIMA* 2: 309). Both cities were later attacked and destroyed by the Assyrian king Sennacherib (704–681) (**ABC* 77).

Röllig (*RlA* 4: 418).

Hiritu(m) Southern Mesopotamian city attested in the Middle Bronze Age Mari archives. It was located on the east bank of the Irnina r., a tributary of the Euphrates, not far from Sippar. After being incorporated into the Babylonian empire by Hammurabi (1792–1750), the city was caught up in the conflicts between Elam and Babylon, and was for a time besieged by an Elamite army (1764). But the Elamites abandoned their siege without taking the city when they were defeated in a battle with the forces of a Babylonian–Mariote coalition (Zimri-Lim, king of Mari, was at that time Hammurabi's ally). Their defeat at Hiritum effectively brought to an end the Elamites' offensive in the region, and marked the beginning of their withdrawal from Babylonia.

The city is very probably identical with M1 Hiritu 'in the province of Sippar', the site of a battle between the Assyrian army of Ashurbanipal and the rebel forces of his brother Shamash-shum-ukin in the latter's sixteenth year as ruler of Babylon (652) (Frame, 1992: 289–92; Cole and Gasche, 1998: 16–23).

*Lacambre (1997), *LKM* 103–8, *459–61, *478–9, *Mesop.* 223–4.

Hishamta Mesopotamian city attested in the Middle Bronze Age Mari archives, located in the middle Euphrates region in the district of Terqa. It was one of the cities from which Terqa's governor Kibri-Dagan recruited troops for his army during the reign of the Mariote king Zimri-Lim (1774–1762), who was overlord of the region. Zimri-Lim appointed the city's chief officials, including its mayor. Though formerly enjoying a status equivalent to that of Terqa – at the time Mari's throne was occupied by Yahdun-Lim (1810–1794) – Hishamta had by Zimri-Lim's reign greatly declined in importance. Its palace had now but one inhabitant, an old woman; it was proposed to relocate her to Terqa or Suprum.

LKM 612 (refs), *Mesop.* 267.

Hissashapa Late Bronze Age country in northern Anatolia, and a centre for the worship of the storm god. The Hittite king Mursili II (1321–1295) held a review of his troops in the city prior to one of his campaigns into Kaska territory (**AM* 172–5). Subsequently, Hissashapa must have been among the northern Hittite cities and countries ravaged by enemy incursions, for it was one of the depopulated lands which Mursili's son and successor Muwattalli II assigned to his brother Hattusili (later King

Hattusili III) when he appointed him ruler of the northern part of the Hittite homeland (*CS I: 201). See also **Hakpis(sa)** and **Turmitta**.

Otten (*RlA* 4: 428–9), **RGTC* 6: 111–12.

Hit (Id(u), Itu) (map 10) Middle Bronze and Iron Age city located in the Middle Euphrates region on the west bank of the Euphrates in the region called Suhu(m). The anc. settlement probably lies beneath the mod. city of Hit, and has yet to be excavated. First attested in the C18 archives from Mari, Hit was famous as a source of bitumen. It also had important religious associations, and was particularly noted as a place where river ordeals were carried out (**ARM XXVI/1*: 527–8, no. 249). Located as it was on the frontier between the territories of the Babylonian king Hammurabi (1792–1750) and the Mariote king Zimri-Lim (1774–1762), it was a cause of contention between the two rulers. Both claimed possession of it, along with two other cities in the region, Yabliya and Harbe (**ARM XXVI/2*: 364–7, no. 449). In the interests of maintaining peace with Babylon, Zimri-Lim consulted with his officials as to whether he should cede Hit to Hammurabi, and also sought advice from the gods by means of divination (**ARM XXVI/1*: 326–7, no. 160). The gods' advice, provided by oracles, was clear: he should not give up the city to the Babylonian. But Hammurabi remained adamant, declaring that he needed possession of Hit for its bitumen and pitch, which he used to caulk his ships (**ARM XXVI/2*: 390–3, no. 468). The Babylonian and Mariote kings failed to reach agreement on who had the right to Hit, and control of the city was to resurface as a contentious issue five years later. For the time being, however, the kings maintained their uneasy alliance, and it seems that Hammurabi finally conceded Hit along with Yabliya and Harbe to Zimri-Lim while Rapiqum, downstream from Hit, was confirmed as a Babylonian possession.

Hit re-emerged in late C12 as a fortified city on Assyria's southern frontier. The Assyrian king Ashur-resh-ishi I (1132–1115) won a military victory there over the Babylonian king Nebuchadnezzar I (1126–1105). During the reign of Tiglath-pileser I (1114–1076), Idu is attested as one of the provinces sending contributions to Ashur. Following the Aramaean incursions, the Assyrian king Adad-nirari II (911–891) re-established Idu and nearby Zanqu as Assyrian frontier-posts (**RIMA* 2: 149). His son and successor Tukulti-Ninurta II encamped his forces there during his last recorded campaign (885) which took him through the middle Tigris and Euphrates regions, near one of the bitumen sources (**RIMA* 2: 174). According to Herodotus (1.179), bitumen was transported from the river near the city (he calls both the city and the river Is) to Babylon, a journey of eight days, where it was used in the construction of Babylon's walls; he was, however, writing long after the event. Under the name Itu, the city is occasionally mentioned in Neo-Babylonian sources (*RGTC* 8: 184).

Postgate (*RlA* 5: 33), Lackenbacher (1988), Michel (*DCM* 388–9), *LKM* 613 (refs), van de Mieroop (2005: 69–72).

Hittites (map 3) Mod. name assigned to the peoples of the Late Bronze Age kingdom of Hatti, whose homeland lay in north-central Anatolia. These peoples consisted of a number of ethnic groups from different parts of the western Asian world, speaking a range of languages. However, the official chancellery language of the kingdom was of Indo-European origin, and was called Nesite. Indo-European Nesite may not have been the most widely spoken language in the Hittite homeland, let alone the kingdom at large. But its use may reflect the ethnic origins of the royal dynasty which established the foundations of the Hittite kingdom in the first half of C17. This dynasty maintained its control over Late Bronze Age Hatti, with several brief interruptions, throughout the 500 years of the kingdom's existence. Its ancestral home appears to have been a city called Kussara, probably located in the anti-Taurus region of southeastern Anatolia. But by mid C17 the city of Hattusa, destroyed in the previous century, was rebuilt and became the dynasty's new capital. Hattusili I (1650–1620), one of the first Hittite kings, is generally credited with this achievement.

The Hattians were another of the ethnic components of the Hittite population. Hattians are the earliest identifiable occupants of north-central Anatolia, their association with the region perhaps extending back thousands of years. Their language, which survives in a few passages in Hittite texts, may have died out early in the Hittite period, but many of their traditions and customs became integral features of Hittite society. The Hittite population probably also included a significant Luwian component; the Luwians were another Indo-European group, which spread over large areas of western and southern Anatolia during the Middle and Late Bronze Ages. Hatti's homeland population was constantly swelled by thousands of deportees brought back from many parts of the western Asian world in the aftermath of military conquest. The deportees were rapidly absorbed within the Hittite population, and seem to have enjoyed significant legal rights. At no stage in Hittite history is there any sense of ethnic discrimination. All those who lived within the core region of the Hittite kingdom called themselves, without distinction, the people of the land of Hatti.

Hittite history is generally divided into two periods. Though the distinction is a somewhat arbitrary one, and scholars disagree on when one period ended and the next began, we can for convenience' sake regard the Old Kingdom as extending from early

Figure 49 Double-headed eagle, symbol of Hittite military power, from Alaca Höyük.

C17 to c. 1400, and the New Kingdom from c. 1400 to early C12. The peak of the Old Kingdom period occurred during the reigns of Hattusili I and his grandson and successor Mursili I (1620–1590). These kings conducted extensive military campaigns in Syria (*Chav. 219–22) and (in the case of Hattusili) Mesopotamia. Mursili's crowning military achievement was the conquest, in a single campaign, of both Aleppo and Babylon (*Chav. 230). But his assassination a few years later plunged Hatti into a period of turmoil, characterized by numerous struggles for the royal succession. These left the kingdom in a weak and divided state, exposing it to invasions by its enemies and indeed bringing it close to extinction, until a king called Telipinu (1525–1500) managed to reunify the kingdom under his authority. In an attempt to prevent further contests for the Hittite throne, Telipinu laid down formal rules for the royal succession, and established a set of procedures for enforcing them. The measures he took are recorded in a document commonly known as the 'Proclamation of Telipinu' (*Chav. 228–35), which also reports Telipinu's military successes in regaining a number of the territories lost to Hatti in the reigns of his predecessors. But it was not until the early C14, when King Tudhaliya I/II embarked on a series of campaigns both in western Anatolia and northern Syria, that Hatti could once more claim the status of one of the Great Kingdoms of the western Asian world.

Its chief rival at this time was the Hurrian kingdom of Mitanni, whose rulers had been building a formidable empire of subject states stretching through northern Mesopotamia and northern Syria into eastern Anatolia. Both Hatti and Mitanni sought to establish their control over the regions which lay between their homelands. But before Hittite–Mitannian rivalry came to a head, the Hittite kingdom was once more plunged into crisis, in the reign of Tudhaliya III, when the homeland was invaded and occupied by enemy forces attacking from all directions (*Bryce, 2005: 146). The Hittite capital was captured and destroyed. Its royal family managed to escape and set up residence-in-exile in a city called Samuha, which lay to the east. From there, Tudhaliya and his son Suppiluliuma staged a comeback, dislodging the enemies from the homeland and in some cases pursuing them into their own countries, destroying their forces there, and laying waste their territories.

With the death of Tudhaliya c. 1350, Suppiluliuma (I) became the new ruler of the Hittite world, after the assassination of the rightful heir, his brother Tudhaliya the Younger. Once on the throne, Suppiluliuma set his sights upon destroying the kingdom of Mitanni. By achieving this objective (*Chav. 241–4) he made Hatti the most powerful kingdom in western Asia. Hittite subject territory in Syria–Palestine now abutted that of Egypt, and tensions began mounting between the two Great Kingdoms. Already Hittite and Egyptian armies had clashed in the region of Qadesh on the Orontes r. during the reign of the boy-pharaoh Tutankhamun, while Suppiluliuma still occupied the Hittite throne (*Chav. 237). Shortly afterwards Tutankhamun died (1327), and when a Hittite prince sent to Egypt to marry his widow was killed on the journey, Suppiluliuma, holding the Egyptians responsible, retaliated by attacking Egyptian subject territory in southern Syria. Large numbers of prisoners-of-war were taken back to the homeland. They brought with them a plague which ravaged the Hittite homeland for the next twenty years (*Chav. 259–66). One of its victims was Suppiluliuma himself.

The showdown between Hatti and Egypt came in 1274, when their armies clashed in a major battle near Qadesh, under their respective commanders Muwattalli II and

Figure 50 Hittite axe.

Ramesses II. (For an earlier engagement at Qadesh between Muwattalli and Ramesses' father Seti I, see under **Qadesh**.) The battle itself ended in a stalemate, but the Hittites were the ultimate victors in terms of their territorial gains at Egypt's expense. Hittite territory now extended well into Syria–Palestine, to the region north of Damascus. Tensions between the two kingdoms continued in the years which followed the battle, until a treaty was drawn up, in 1259, between Ramesses and the then Hittite king Hattusili III, brother of Muwattalli (**Chav.* 244–8). The treaty, which was cemented thirteen years later by a royal marriage alliance, marked the end of any further (known) hostilities between Egypt and Hatti.

The treaty may have been prompted in part by an ominous new development east of the Euphrates – the re-emergence of Assyria in the wake of the destruction of Mitanni. A military confrontation between a Hittite army led by Hattusili's son and successor Tudhaliya IV and the forces of the Assyrian king Tukulti-Ninurta I resulted in a devastating defeat for the former, c. 1230 (see **Nihriya**). Tudhaliya's kingdom was also being plagued by unrest in a number of his subject territories, as well as by threats posed by pretenders to the throne from rival factions within his own family. His father and predecessor Hattusili III had seized the throne from his nephew

Urhi-Teshub, son of Muwattalli (*CS I: 202–3). The deposed king had been sent into exile in Syria, but constantly sought assistance from foreign powers, especially from the pharaoh Ramesses II, to get his throne back. Ramesses, however, gave his support to the usurper, and subsequently to his son Tudhaliya. Urhi-Teshub never succeeded in regaining his throne. But his (half-?)brother Kurunta, who had apparently also supported Hattusili and Tudhaliya, was awarded rule over the prestigious appanage kingdom Tarhuntassa in southern Anatolia. One of the most important recent discoveries from the Hittite capital Hattusa is a bronze tablet containing the text of a treaty drawn up by Tudhaliya with Kurunta as ruler of Tarhuntassa (**Chav.* 270–5, **CS* II: 100–6). It is possible that Kurunta may have eventually made his own bid for the Hittite throne, using Tarhuntassa as his base (see further under **Tarhuntassa**).

In spite of the establishment of an 'eternal peace' with Egypt, the last decades of C13 were marked by signs of increasing instability within the Hittite kingdom. A range of factors have been suggested for the kingdom's decline, including severe food shortages, pressure from outside forces, and factional strife among rival branches of the royal family. Early in C12, during the reign of Tudhaliya's son and second successor Suppiluliuma II, the kingdom collapsed, never to rise again. This occurred within the context of the general upheavals associated with the end of the Bronze Age and the decline, collapse, and disappearance of a number of the kingdoms and cities of the age. The defining event which marked the end of the Late Bronze Age kingdom of Hatti was the abandonment and destruction of the royal capital Hattusa (see under **Hattusa**). But remnants of Hittite civilization and the peoples who shared in it survived for some centuries to come. This was particularly the case in southeastern Anatolia and northern Syria, which from late M2 onwards provided a homeland for the so-called Neo-Hittite kingdoms (q.v.).

There are a number of references to Hittites in *OT* sources, in the forms *Het, ha-hittî, Hittîm*, and *hittiyyot*. What connection, if any, do the biblical Hittites have with the Hittites of the Late Bronze Age world? In one of the most recent discussions of this question, Singer (2006) distinguishes between two broad categories of biblical Hittites – 'inland' Hittites and 'outland' Hittites. References to the former in the *OT* indicate that they were a small Canaanite tribal group living in the hills of Palestine. On the other hand, there are five passages in which a much more extensive role is assigned to the Hittites. In these passages, the masculine plural form *hittîm* refers to the 'kings of the Hittites' or 'the land of the Hittites'. For example, in Joshua 1:4, the Hittite land is described as extending from the desert to Lebanon, and from the great river, the Euphrates, to the Great Sea on the west (i.e. the Mediterranean). There can be no doubt that the references in these passages are to the Neo-Hittite kingdoms of Syria and southeastern Anatolia. Singer discusses at some length the question of whether there is a connection between the so-called 'inland' and 'outland' Hittites. On the assumption that there is in fact no connection, he provides an explanation as to how the term 'Hittite' came to be applied to the Canaanite group. Most recently, Collins has discussed afresh the question of whether the biblical Hittites were linked with the Hittites attested in Late Bronze Age sources. She concludes that the former can in fact be identified with the latter, but not specifically with the Hittites living in Anatolia. 'Rather, the biblical authors had in mind those peoples living in Hittite-controlled areas directly to their north (in northern Palestine and Syria) who did not qualify already as Canaanite or Amorite, whatever their individual ethnic affiliation might have been' (Collins, 2007: 212).

Gurney (1990), Klengel (1999), Bryce (2002; 2005), Singer (2006), Collins (2007), Freu (2007).

Hivites In biblical tradition, one of the tribal groups occupying the hill country of central Palestine (other groups were the Amorites, Hittites, Perizzites, Canaanites, and Jebusites) (e.g. Exodus 3:8, 13:5, 23:23, 33:2). A number of biblical passages seem to indicate that the Hivites were identical with, or a branch of, the population group called the Horites (cf. e.g. Genesis 36:2, 20, 29). Outside *OT* sources, there is allegedly a reference to the Hivites (in the form *hwt*) in a topographical list of the C13 pharaoh Ramesses II (Görg, 1976), and a connection has also been suggested with the Iron Age country Que in southern Anatolia (Quwe → *Huwe → Hebrew *hiwwi*). A certain Awarikus is attested as king of Que in C8. In the Luwian version of a Phoenician–Luwian bilingual inscription found at mod. Çineköy (q.v.) within the region of Que, Awarikus calls his kingdom Hiyawa, an aphaeresized form of the name Ahhiyawa, which is used in a number of Late Bronze Age Hittite texts probably in reference to the contemporary Greek world. It has been suggested that the Hebrew form *hiwwi* derives from *Hiyawa* (see Collins, 2007: 201 with refs in n. 15).

Roberts (*HCBD* 436).

Hiyawa see Ahhiyawa, Que.

Horites In biblical tradition, a tribal group inhabiting Mt Seir in the region of Edom, south of the Dead Sea. It has been suggested that the group may have been a relic of the late Bronze Age Hurrians (q.v.) known from Hittite, Egyptian, and Akkadian texts. But despite the similarity of the names, there are no convincing grounds for linking the two peoples. A number of *OT* passages seem to indicate that the Horites were identical with, or a branch of, the Hivites (q.v.). The Horites are not attested outside biblical sources.

Roberts (*HCBD* 436).

Hubushkia (maps 13, 20) M1 royal city and country in the land of Nairi in mod. Kurdistan, to the south or west of Lake Urmia. Locations for it have been proposed on the upper course of the Greater Zab r. or further to the southeast in the Zagros mountain region (Salvini, 1995b: 43, Medvedskaya, 1997). Our information about Hubushkia comes primarily from Neo-Assyrian texts. After the reign of the Assyrian king Shalmaneser III (858–824), the names Hubushkia and Nairi seem to be used synonymously in these texts.

Hubushkia is first attested during a campaign in the Nairi lands by the Assyrian king Tukulti-Ninurta II (890–884) (**RIMA* 2: 180). Subsequently, Hubushkians were among the peoples conquered by Tukulti-Ninurta's son and successor Ashurnasirpal II (**RIMA* 2: 197) during a campaign which he conducted in his first regnal year (883). So too at the beginning of his reign, Shalmaneser III maintained Assyrian pressure on the region by conducting the first of a series of campaigns there. He destroyed the city of Hubushkia by fire, then ruled by a certain Kakia (also said to be king of the Nairi lands), and claims to have burnt one hundred other cities in its environs (**RIMA* 3: 8, 14). This particular campaign ended with Shalmaneser's defeat of the king of Nairi and his advance to the 'Sea of Nairi' (most likely Lake Urmia), where he erected an inscribed stele (**RIMA* 3: 8–9). Shalmaneser's campaigns in his third year again took him into Hubushkian territory, where he stormed, captured, and destroyed the stronghold Shilaia (**RIMA* 3: 21). In 844 he mounted a further brief campaign against Hubushkia, and in 829 and 828 operations against the country were conducted by his commander-in-chief Dayyan-Ashur. On these last two occasions, Hubushkia avoided destruction when its ruler, Datana, handed over tribute to the Assyrian (**RIMA* 3: 70). Shalmaneser's grandson Adad-nirari III conducted four campaigns against Hubushkia, in 801, 791, 785, and 784. In 715 its ruler, Ianzu, sent tribute to the Assyrian king Sargon II during the latter's campaign in Urartian territory (**ARAB* II: 29).

Hubushna see Hupisna.

Hudubilu Iron Age city on the middle Euphrates, north of Idu (mod. Hit). The Assyrian king Tukulti-Ninurta II encamped his forces there during his last recorded campaign (885) which took him through the middle Tigris and Euphrates regions (**RIMA* 2: 174).

Huhnur (map 12) Bronze Age city in western Iran, located between Susa and Anshan within the territory of Elam. First attested in texts of the Ur III period (C21), it has been identified from an inscription of Amar-Sin (2046–2038), third of the Ur III kings, with Tappeh (Tol-e) Bormi, near modern Ram Hormuz (Nasrabadi, 2005). Early in the Ur III period, Huhnur was among the eighty-one cities and regions which Puzur-Inshushinak, the last king of Awan's 'second dynasty' (according to the Susa King List), claims to have conquered (**DaK* 323; cf. Zadok, 1991: 227). It was also conquered by Amar-Sin and subsequently by Ibbi-Sin (2028–2004), last king of the Ur III dynasty, who went 'with massive power' to Huhnur and other cities in the region during his ninth regnal year. References are made to a 'king of Huhnuri' in C14 texts discovered at Haft Tepe (located 10 km southeast of Susa), which lay northwest of Huhnur.

RGTC 2: 768, D. T. Potts (1999: 332, index refs), Nasrabadi (2005).

Hulaya River Land Late Bronze Age country in southern Anatolia (probably to the southwest of mod. Konya), subject to Hatti. It was among the territories lost to the Hittites some time after the assassination of the Hittite king Mursili I (c. 1590), but regained by Telipinu (1525–1500), who located one of the Hittites' grain-storage depots there (*Hoffmann, 1984: 42–3). During the reign of Muwattalli II (1295–1272), the Hulaya River Land was incorporated as frontier territory into the newly created land of Tarhuntassa (Bryce, 2005: 453, n. 27). It provided troops and chariots for the Hittite army until exempted from this obligation by Hattusili III. This is indicated in a treaty which Hattusili drew up with Tarhuntassa's appanage king Ulmi-Teshub (**HDT* 109–10), identified by most scholars with Hattusili's nephew Kurunta. Hattusili's son and successor Tudhaliya IV also drew up a treaty with Kurunta, the famous bronze tablet discovered at Hattusa in 1986, in which he redefined the boundaries of Tarhuntassa and listed the cities belonging to Tarhuntassa's incorporated territory of Hulaya River Land (**HDT* 114–15, **CS* II: 100–1). Tudhaliya also reconfirmed in this treaty the Hulaya River Land's exemption from providing chariotry and infantry for the Hittite army (*HDT* 120, **CS* II: 104).

Hulun Iron Age city located to the south of Lake Van in eastern Anatolia. It lay on the route of the campaign conducted by the Assyrian king Ashurnasirpal II in his first year (883) against the lands to the northeast of Assyria (**RIMA* 2: 197). Ashurnasirpal advanced from Mt Kirruru to the interior of one of the regions called Habhu in Assyrian texts (see **Habhu (2)**), via the pass of Hulun. Liverani locates the pass in the Hakkari mountains.

Liverani (1992: 25).

Hulzu City located in the Kashiyari range (mod. Tur ʿAbdin) in northern Mesopotamia, attested in the records of the Assyrian king Ashur-bel-kala (1073–1056). Ashur-bel-kala conquered it during one of his campaigns against the Aramaeans (**RIMA* 2: 102).

Hume see Que.

Hunusu (Hanusa?) Fortified city of Qumanu, a land attested in Late Bronze Age and Iron Age Assyrian texts, in the borderlands between northeastern Mesopotamia and northwestern Iran. The Assyrian king Tiglath-pileser I (1114–1076) reports his conquest and destruction of the city after defeating and annihilating an army mustered from the entire land of Qumanu (**RIMA* 2: 24, 34). Hunusu may be identical with Neo-Assyrian Hanusa. The waters of Hanusa were among those brought to Nineveh by the aqueduct which Sennacherib constructed at Jerwan, according to the text inscribed on some of its stone blocks. Hanusa is perhaps to be identified with mod. Hinnis, close to Bavian at the head of the artificial watercourse (Jacobsen and Lloyd, 1935: 21)

Hupapanu M1 city and district in southeastern Elam (southwestern Iran). It was one of the Elamite lands in which the people of the Chaldaean tribe Bit-Yakin (q.v.) sought refuge, fleeing Babylonia with the Babylonian king Marduk-apla-iddina II (biblical Merodach-baladan) after the latter's defeat by the Assyrian king Sennacherib (see under **Babylonia**). In 694 Sennacherib 'crossed the sea in Hittite [i.e. Syrian] ships' and conquered the lands of Hupapanu, Nagitu, Hilmu, and Billatu, which he refers to as 'provinces of Elam' (**Sennach.* 38–9, **ABC* 78). He destroyed the cities of these lands, and then deported both their occupants and the Bit-Yakinite refugees to Assyria. Hupapanu later appears in a letter sent to the Assyrian king Ashurbanipal by his commander-in-chief Bel-ibni in southern Babylonia. This was in 649, during the conflict between Ashurbanipal and his brother Shamash-shum-ukin, Ashurbanipal's appointee to the throne of Babylon (see under **Babylon**).

Dietrich (*RlA* 4: 501).

Hupis(h)na (Hapisna, Assyrian **Hubishna/Hubushna, Hubushnu**, Classical **Cybistra**) (map 18) Late Bronze and Iron Age country in southern Anatolia. It lay in the region which the Hittites called the Lower Land, more specifically within the area of the Classical Tyanitis. Its chief city is probably to be identified with the site at Karahöyük near mod. Ereğli. According to the Hittite 'Telipinu Proclamation' (see glossary), Hupisna was among the cities or countries which the early C17 Hittite king Labarna conquered, thereupon appointing his sons to govern them (**Chav.* 230). It subsequently appears in the context of campaigns undertaken by the mid C16 Hittite king Ammuna in his attempts to re-establish Hatti's authority in subject states which had rebelled against its rule. After the collapse of the Hittite kingdom in early C12, Hupisna/Hubushnu became one of the states constituting the southern territories of the region called Tabal in Assyrian texts. Shalmaneser III of Assyria marched against it in 837 following his military operations in northern Tabal (**RIMA* 3: 79). At this time, its ruler was a man called Puhame. During the reign of the Assyrian king Tiglath-pileser III (745–727), Hupisna was ruled by a certain U(i)rimme, who is listed among Tiglath-pileser's five tributary-kings of Tabal (**Tigl. III* 68–9, 108–9). In 679 the Assyrian king Esarhaddon fought a battle against the Cimmerians here, defeating the Cimmerian leader Teushpa (**ARAB* II: 206).

Kessler/Levine (*RlA* 4: 500–1), **RGTC* 6: 117–19.

Huradu Iron Age royal city of the Chaldaean tribe Bit-Dakkuri in southern Mesopotamia. When the Assyrian king Shalmaneser III invaded the land of the Bit-Dakkuri during his second Babylonian campaign (850), he spared Huradu after Adinu, the tribe's ruler, voluntarily submitted to him and paid a substantial tribute (**RIMA* 3: 31).

Hurban (Ur(u)ban) Middle Bronze Age city in the region of Upper Suhum on the middle Euphrates south of Mari, between the cities Harradum and Hanat. In the reign of Zimri-Lim, king of Mari (1774–1762), the city was threatened by troops from Eshnunna whose ruler, Ibal-pi-El II, contested control over the region with Zimri-Lim. On this occasion the Eshnunnite forces withdrew when confronted by an army of Mariote troops assembled under the command of Zimri-Lim's representative Kibsi-Adad.

LKM 613 (refs).

Hurra Late Bronze Age city in western Mesopotamia, located in the kingdom of Hanigalbat. When Hanigalbat's ruler Wasashatta rebelled against Assyrian sovereignty, Hurra was among the cities conquered by the Assyrian king Adad-nirari I (1307–1275) as he crushed the rebellion (**RIMA* 1: 136).

Hurran Middle Bronze Age city in the middle Euphrates region, close to the city of Dur-Yahdun-Lim. Attested in the Mari archives (**LKM* 184), it is perhaps to be identified with Iron Age Haranu, a Laqean settlement, and with mod. Tell Handal on the east bank of the Habur r. near its confluence with the Euphrates.

Lipiński (2000: 93).

Hurrians (map 3) A large group of peoples, of uncertain origin, who from late M3 onwards began to spread through northern Mesopotamia, northern Syria, and eastern Anatolia. The Kura-Araxes region in Transcaucasia and eastern Anatolia have both been proposed as their original homeland. A common language, called Hurrian in written records, and common onomastic features, gave a loose cultural coherence to these peoples, enabling scholars to identify the various regions where they settled or with which they came in contact. The Hurrian language survives mainly in cuneiform inscriptions (though there are also a small number of texts in the alphabetic script of Ugarit), the longest of which is a letter in the mid C14 Amarna archive, written by the Mitannian king Tushratta to the pharaoh Amenhotep III (*EA 24). The language itself is not related to the Indo-European or the Semitic language groups, nor indeed to any other known language, with the possible exception of Urartian.

Hurrian states already existed in C23, for in this period they were incorporated into the Akkadian empire by Naram-Sin (2254–2218). After the empire's fall, Hurrian-speaking peoples established a number of small principalities through northern and eastern Mesopotamia. They were conquered by Shulgi (2094–2047), second ruler of the Ur III dynasty, during his triumphant military campaigns through the northern and eastern border regions of his kingdom. Large numbers of the conquered peoples who were taken as prisoners-of-war bore Hurrian names. In Anatolia, Hurrians make their first attested appearance as traders during the Assyrian Colony period (Middle Bronze Age; C20–18; see glossary), as illustrated by Hurrian names in the colony texts. By the end of C16 a number of small states with predominantly Hurrian populations had been amalgamated into a single political federation called the kingdom of Mitanni.

In the Late Bronze Age, Hittites and Hurrians fiercely contested control over the territories of northern Syria and eastern Anatolia, even before the creation of the Mitannian state. The Hittite king Hattusili I (1650–1620) was forced to cut short a campaign in Arzawan territory, western Anatolia, because of a Hurrian invasion of his homeland (**Chav.* 220), perhaps in retaliation for Hattusili's attacks on Hurrian states in northern Syria and eastern Anatolia. And Hattusili's successor Mursili I was attacked by Hurrian troops as he returned home from his conquest of Babylon c. 1595 (**Chav* 230; see Bryce, 2005: 416, n. 10). Yet again, in the reign of Mursili's assassin and successor Hantili I (1590–1560), Hurrians invaded the Hittite homeland, roaming through it and plundering it at will (**Chav.* 230). In southern Anatolia, the state of Kizzuwadna was probably created under Hurrian influence in C16, and contained a substantial Hurrian element in its population.

Long after the Hurrians had ceased to be a significant political power in western Asia, notably after the destruction of the Mitannian empire by the Hittite king Suppiluliuma I (1350–1322), many elements of Hurrian culture survived and flourished, particularly in the Hittite world. This is evident from Hurrian literary and religious traditions, preserved for us in Hittite texts and visual representations. Hurrian deities and religious practices were adopted with particular enthusiasm in C13 by Hattusili III and his Hurrian queen, Puduhepa, and subsequently by Hattusili's son and successor Tudhaliya IV. All three played a leading role in promoting the Hurrian pantheon in the Hittite world. This is most graphically illustrated by the parade of male and female deities, in Hurrian garb and with Hurrian names, carved on the walls of the Hittite rock sanctuary at Yazılıkaya.

Rulers with Hurrian names were still in evidence in northeastern Mesopotamia in C12. Indeed, Hurrian elements appear to have persisted in this region until at least mid M1.

Edzard, Kammenhuber/Mellink (*RlA* 4: 507–19), Wilhelm (1989; 1995).

Hursama One of the Late Bronze Age Hittite cult-centres in northern Anatolia destroyed by the Kaska people during the reign of the Hittite king Arnuwanda I in early C14. Other cult-centres in the region which suffered similar destruction in the same period included Nerik, Kastama, Serisa, Himuwa, Taggasta, and Kammama.

*ANET 399, Otten (RlA 4: 521), *RGTC 6: 126–7.

Hüseyindede Late Bronze Age Hittite cult-centre in northern Anatolia, located 30 km north of mod. Çorum. Excavations begun in 1998, under the direction of T. Yıldırım, T. Siparhi, and İ. Ediz, revealed the thickly plastered walls of what has been interpreted as a cult-building, dating apparently to the period of the Hittite Old Kingdom (C17–15). The building may have been dedicated to the worship of the storm god. Siparhi has also been investigating other closely linked Hittite sites at Fatmaören and Boyalı Höyük.

Burney (2004: 132); reports (in Turkish) by T. Yıldırım and T. Sipahi in *KST* from vol. 22, 2000, onwards.

Hu(wa)rsanassa Late Bronze Age country in western Anatolia, within or near the territory of the Lukka Lands. It was among the lands captured by the renegade Hittite vassal Madduwatta during his campaigns in western Anatolia (early C14). Attarimma and Suruta appear immediately before it in the list of Madduwatta's conquests (**HDT* 58). The three countries again appear together at the beginning of the Hittite king Mursili II's reign (1321), when they apparently joined an anti-Hittite rebellion in the west. Mursili responded by conducting a campaign against his western enemies during his third regnal year. In the course of this campaign, troops from Huwarsanassa, Attarimma, and Suruta fled before him and sought refuge in the kingdom of Arzawa Minor (**AM* 52–3, 58–9, **CS* II: 85).

Otten (*RlA* 4: 521–2).

Huzaza Iron Age city located in the Biqaᶜ valley, Lebanon, attested in letters addressed to the Assyrian king Sargon II (721–705) (e.g. **SAA* I: 136, no. 175). In the latter decades of C8 it was incorporated into the Assyrian empire as part of the province of which nearby Soba was the chief city. An identification has been proposed with Tell Gazza, a 250 m × 150 m settlement-mound in the central Biqaᶜ valley 5 km north of Kamid el-Loz (q.v.). During Sargon's reign, Arab merchants had engaged in trade with the city, and Sargon accused its governor Bel-liqbi of

Figure 51 Stamp seal of Hittite king Mursili II.

turning the city into a merchant-town. There were apparently restrictions on its rights to engage in trade. The king was particularly concerned at reports that the city was selling iron to the Arabs. Bel-liqbi protested that the only goods sold to these people were grapes and copper (*SAA I: 140–1, no. 179). Iron was sold only to deportees.

Lipiński (2000: 319, 327).

Huzirina (probably = ***Sultantepe***, Classical **Hostra**) (map 2) Settlement-mound of predominantly Iron Age date (though there are earlier, unexplored Bronze Age levels), 40 m high and 100 m in diameter, located in northwestern Mesopotamia 15 km east of mod. Urfa. Huzirina's name is known to us from Assyrian texts. Its identification with the site of Sultantepe is generally though not universally accepted (Lipiński, 2000: 112–14). It was one of the major cities, along with Harran and Dur-Qipani, of the Assyrian Province of the Commander-in-Chief (see glossary).

Excavation of Sultantepe was conducted in 1951 and 1952 by N. Gökçe on behalf of the Hittite Museum at Ankara and S. Lloyd for the British Institute of Archaeology at Ankara. Temples of the divine couple Zababa and Baba and the goddess Ishtar, and probably also a temple dedicated to the moon god, were erected on the site. A monumental entrance portico, whose remains are indicated by enormous basalt column bases, gave access to a walled enclosure on the summit where a number of public buildings were located. During the first season's excavations, a large hoard of tablets was brought to light, all except three unbaked. By the end of the second season, a total of c. 400 tablets and fragments had been unearthed. The three baked tablets consisted of a mathematical, an economic, and a medical text. All the other tablets were religious (hymns, prayers, and incantations), literary (including a version of the epic of Gilgamesh), medical, astronomical, or lexical in character. The excavators noted that the building outside which the tablets were found had the character of a private house, which came to be known as the 'House of Qurdi-Nergal'. The colophons of several of the tablets refer to Qurdi-Nergal, a priest of the gods Zababa and Baba, as the recipient of the tablets. Whether or not the house in question actually belonged to this man remains uncertain.

The Assyrian king Adad-nirari II records his capture of Huzirina during a campaign in Hanigalbat in 899 (*RIMA 2: 149–50). His successor, Tukulti-Ninurta II, encamped his forces there during his last recorded campaign (885) (*RIMA 2: 177). Tukulti-Ninurta's own son and successor Ashurnasirpal II visited Huzirina on his 866 campaign, and received there tribute from a number of lands, including Qipanu, Kummuhu, and Azallu (*RIMA 2: 219). Huzirina joined a widespread revolt against the Assyrian king Shalmaneser III (858–824), initiated by the king's son Ashur-da'in-apla towards the end of Shalmaneser's reign. The rebellion continued into the early regnal years of Shalmaneser's son and successor Shamshi-Adad V before it was finally crushed (*RIMA 3: 183).

Huzirina was destroyed and abandoned at the end of the Neo-Assyrian period. Its destruction was probably due to the Scythians and the Babylonians who ended the existence of the nearby city of Harran in 610. It remained virtually unoccupied through the succeeding Babylonian and Persian periods. There was, however, reoccupation by mid C2, in the Hellenistic period, represented by modest domestic architecture, and occupation continued through the Roman imperial period until C2 or C3

CE. In this last phase of its existence the settlement appears to have been confined to the area surrounding the base of the mound.

Lloyd and Gökçe (1953), Postgate (*RlA* 4: 535–6), Gurney (1998).

Hydae (Kydae) (*Damlıboğaz*) (map 5) M1 BCE–M1 CE city in Caria in southwestern Anatolia, 7 km west of Mylasa (mod. Milas). In C5, the city was a member of the Athenian Confederacy (see glossary), and in the Hellenistic period was part of a sympolity with Mylasa. The discovery on the site of a handmade jug dating to M3 suggests much earlier periods of occupation. Among the meagre Classical remains of the city are a circuit wall, several rock-tombs, and a very poorly preserved temple possibly dedicated to Apollo and Artemis.

Bean (1971: 49–50; *PECS* 399).

Hydis(s)us (*Karacahisar*) M1 BCE–M1 CE city in Caria, southwestern Anatolia, 20 km south of Mylasa (mod. Milas) (*BAGRW* 61 F3). Its origins date back at least to C5 when it is attested as a member of the Athenian Confederacy (see glossary), paying an annual tribute of one talent. Remains of its fortifications are of early Hellenistic date. Other remains, including an agora and a theatre, date to the Hellenistic and Roman periods. Coin issues from the latter period have also been found.

Bean (*PECS* 399–400).

Hyksos The name used of a line of Asiatic rulers who emerged from the Syro-Palestinian population group which settled in the Egyptian Delta during the Egyptian Middle Bronze Age. Some scholars believe that the immigrants were the cause of the breakdown of political control which brought the Egyptian Middle Kingdom to an end in mid C17. They may well have been a significant contributing factor. The name 'Hyksos' is a Greek rendering of the Egyptian term *hekau khasut*, which means 'rulers of foreign countries'. For perhaps as much as a century (c. 1650–1550) the Hyksos dominated Egypt. After first ruling from Memphis, they subsequently took up residence at Avaris (mod. Tell el-Dabʿa) in the eastern Delta. In the process, they reduced to vassal status the enfeebled Egyptian thirteenth dynasty, and its fourteenth dynasty offshoot in the Delta. The Hyksos thus became Egypt's fifteenth dynasty, one consisting of four or more foreign kings. Thebes in Upper Egypt finally emerged as a centre of resistance to them. Installed there, shortly after the Hyksos had subjugated the thirteenth dynasty, was a line of local kings constituting the seventeenth dynasty, following upon an earlier line of Theban rulers constituting the sixteenth dynasty. Kamose, the last of the seventeenth dynasty kings, launched a series of attacks on the Hyksos, wresting from their control all territory south of Memphis and carrying out a lightning raid on the seat of the foreigners' power in Avaris. This paved the way for the campaigns of his brother Ahmose. Ahmose captured Avaris, drove the Hyksos back to the lands whence their ancestors had come, inflicted further defeats upon them there, and reunited the whole of Egypt beneath his sway, becoming in 1550 the founder of the Egyptian New Kingdom.

**ANET* 173–5, Wolf (*RlA* 4: 537–9), Redford (1992: 98–122).

Hyope Attested by the C6–5 Greek geographer Hecataeus as a city of the people called the Matieni (q.v.). C. Sagona proposes a location in one of the valleys above the Kara Su in eastern Anatolia, most likely the Tortum valley.

C. Sagona, in Sagona and Sagona (2004: 48–9).

Hyrcania (map 16) M1 central Asian country, attested in both Persian and Classical sources, located south of the Caspian Sea, northwest of Parthia, and perhaps originally part of the land of Media prior to the conquests of the Persian king Cyrus II (559–530). According to Xenophon (*Cyropaedia* 1.1.4), Hyrcania voluntarily changed allegiance to Cyrus in the course of these conquests. But in the widespread rebellions against Cyrus' third successor Darius I at the beginning of his reign (522), it joined with Parthia in support of Phraortes, the rebel Median pretender to the Persian throne. Darius routed the forces of Phraortes at the battle of Kurundu in Media, while the Hyrcanian and Parthian rebel forces were crushed by Darius' father Hystaspes, satrap of Parthia, in battles fought at Vishpauzatish and Patigrabana (8 March and 12 July 521, respectively) (*DB 35–7). Thirty years later, in 481, a contingent of Hyrcanians under the command of Megapanus were among the forces assembled by the Persian king Xerxes for his invasion of Greece (Herodotus 6.92).

Vogelsang (1988).

I

Ialigu see Aligu.

Iasus (map 5) City located on a peninsula in Caria, southwestern Anatolia, opposite the mod. port of Güllük, with a history of occupation extending from the Neolithic to the Byzantine period. Excavations on the site were begun in 1960 and continued into the 1980s under the direction of D. Levi and C. Lavioso. The project was a collaborative one, with participation from the Universities of Bristol and Pisa and the Istituto per gli Studi Micenei et Egeo Anatolici of Rome, under the auspices of the Missione Archaeologica Italiana di Iasos. One of the site's earliest significant remains is a necropolis first used in the Early Bronze Age. Ninety-six rectangular and oval cist-tombs of this period were excavated, containing human skeletons in a contracted position, and in some cases a number of secondary burials. Locally made and imported Minoan pottery (Middle Minoan III) discovered at Iasus, and buildings of Minoan (Neopalatial) type, indicate the possibility of Minoan settlement there during the Middle Bronze Age, as at Miletus which lay to the north. In the Late Bronze Age, Minoan cultural elements gave way to Mycenaean, as also at Miletus. But while there is no doubt that Mycenaeans actually settled in Miletus, by the beginning of C13 at the latest, we have yet to find clear evidence that Iasus also became a Mycenaean settlement at this time. Its contact with the Mycenaean world may have been limited to trading activities.

According to Polybius (16.12), the inhabitants of M1 Iasus claimed that their city was originally a secondary colony of Argos (Peloponnese, southern mainland Greece), recolonized from Miletus at the invitation of its native inhabitants to make up the losses they had suffered in their war with the Carians. Indigenous groups had in fact occupied the site since at least the Early Bronze Age, and continued to form a significant proportion of the population after Greek settlement there (perhaps in C8 or C7). In C5 the city became a member of the Athenian Confederacy (see glossary), and was captured by the Peloponnesian fleet in 412 (Thucydides 8.28). Seven years later, it was destroyed by the Spartan commander Lysander (Diodorus 13.104.7). With the help of nearby Cnidus, the city was rebuilt, and subsequently came under the control of the Carian Hecatomnid dynasty. Following its liberation by Alexander the Great in 334, it remained independent through much of the Hellenistic period, but in 125 was incorporated into the Roman province of Asia.

Material remains of the site during the Greek, Hellenistic, and Roman phases of its existence include two circuit walls, sanctuaries dedicated to Zeus and Artemis, a theatre of C4 date, and a nymphaeum (fountain-house) and agora of the Roman imperial period. The city's necropolis, located on the mainland adjoining the peninsula, contained, in addition to the Early Bronze Age tombs referred to above, chambered tombs with both flat roofs and barrel vaults, and sarcophagi and funerary monuments of the Roman imperial period.

Laviosa (*PECS* 401–2), Kaletsch (*BNP* 6: 687).

Idalium (map 14) City kingdom of Cyprus, located 20 km south of Nicosia, with a history of occupation extending from the end of the Late Bronze Age (c. 1200) to the early Roman period (C1 CE). The site has been investigated and excavated a number of times during C19 and C20. The first of the C20 excavations were conducted by the Swedish Cyprus Expedition between 1927 and 1931, with the aim of firmly establishing a chronology for the site. Subsequently the Joint American Expedition to Idalium, directed by L. E. Stager and A. M. Walker from 1971 to 1980, carried out site-catchment analysis, in which they made an examination of the surrounding agricultural, mining, and settlement areas by means of surface survey and periodic sounding. In the 1990s M. Hadjicosti resumed excavations of the monumental buildings on the west acropolis, on behalf of the Dept of Antiquities of Cyprus. An important Phoenician archive was found here in a monumental building believed to have been erected on the foundations of the kingdom's Cypro-Archaic palace. Further American excavations in the 1990s under the directorship of P. Gaber concentrated on the domestic areas of the lower town.

The city consists of two acropoleis and a lower town, enclosed within a city wall of which traces still survive. On the west acropolis, a stronghold and cult-place were built in the first phase of the city's existence (C12), the cult-area subsequently becoming the location of a sanctuary dedicated to the goddess Athena. A sanctuary of Aphrodite was located on the summit of the east acropolis. Between the two acropoleis a sanctuary of Apollo, whom the Phoenicians identified with their god Resheph, was built. Excavations conducted in Aphrodite's and Apollo's sanctuaries in late C19 produced stone and terracotta sculptures dating to the Archaic, Classical, and Hellenistic periods. To the east of the city lies a necropolis with Late Bronze Age and Geometric (C8) tombs; to the west, a necropolis with tombs of the Archaic, Classical, Hellenistic, and Roman periods. A Late Cypriot III industrial area located on the lower slopes of Ampileri hill and an Early Geometric cemetery some 500 m to the northeast, both uncovered in 1997–8, provide important evidence for continuity of occupation from the Bronze to the Iron Age.

In written records, Idalium is first attested on the so-called prism of the Assyrian king Esarhaddon, dated to 673/672 (*Borger, 1956: 60 §27). Authority in the city appears to have been shared between a line of kings and a citizen-body (a unique arrangement on Cyprus). The former issued their own coins from shortly before 500. Several decades later, c. 470, Idalium was besieged and captured by a joint force of Persians and troops from Citium, the latter ruled by a Phoenician dynasty. This event can perhaps be linked to an archaeologically attested destruction of the fortified area on the west acropolis in mid C5. Thenceforth, Idalium came under the control of Citium. It continued to flourish during the Hellenistic and the early Roman periods. But to judge from Pliny the Elder (5.130) it had ceased to exist by C1 CE, since Pliny, who wrote in that period, places it in the category of 'former cities'.

Idalium was particularly noted for its cult of the Magna Mater goddess, syncretized with Greek Aphrodite and Roman Venus. The setting for the Classical myth of Venus and Adonis was located there.

Nicolaou (*PECS* 404), Stager and Walker (1989), Gaber (*OEANE* 3: 137–8), Hadjicosti (1999).

Ida-maras (map 10) The designation in the Middle Bronze Age Mari archives for the land comprising the western sector of the Habur triangle in northern Mesopotamia, extending roughly from Harran in the west to Shubat-Enlil in the east. It is frequently mentioned in the Mariote texts, in connection both with the Yaminite bedouin tribes and with a number of the petty kingdoms and cities of the region over which the Mariote king Zimri-Lim (1774–1762) exercised control, including Urkish, Kahat, Ashnakkum, and Nahur. Before Zimri-Lim's reign, the region had been subject to the Assyrian king Shamshi-Adad I (1796–1775), who had seized it from Zimri-Lim's father Yahdun-Lim. Zimri-Lim regained control of it after Shamshi-Adad's death. Numerous letters exchanged between the kings of Ida-maras have been discovered in the Mari archives. The Babylonian king Samsu-iluna (1749–1712) reports conquering the land 'from the border of Gutium to the border of Elam', then setting free its people after holding them captive for two months (**RIME* 4: 389–90).

Hawkins (*RlA* 5: 28–30), Lyonnet and Ziegler (*DCM* 403–4), *LKM* 613 (refs).

Idu see *Hit*.

Idumaea (map 8) Region in southern Palestine, south of Beersheba. Its name derives from the Iron Age kingdom of Edom in southern Transjordan. (Idumaea was the Greek name for Edom.) From late C7 until early C6, large numbers of Edomites appear to have migrated westwards from their homeland and resettled in the southern Judaean hill country. This westwards spread is implied in Ezekiel 36:5, and is archaeologically attested in the finds of Edomite pottery, seals, and inscriptions at a number of sites in the eastern Negev, with further westward expansion towards the Mediterranean coast by late C6 and C5. Idumaea was among the Syro-Palestinian lands that were absorbed into the Persian empire during the reign of Cambyses (530–522). After Egypt established its independence from Persia in 405, it became Persia's southern frontier region. In C3 Idumaea was one of the toparchies (external administrative districts) of the Ptolemaic empire, and in 40 it became a toparchy of Herod the Great, whose father Antipater had been a prominent Idumaean.

Graf (*OEANE* 3: 141–3).

Idyma (= Late Bronze Age **Utima**?) (map 5) M1 city in Caria in southwestern Anatolia, 18 km south of mod. Muğla. It is first attested as a member of the Athenian Confederacy (see glossary) in mid C5, when it was ruled by the tyrant Paktyes. During the Hellenistic period it became subject to Rhodes. Material remains include a city wall, within which is a small fort, and a number of rock-tombs, including several of the Ionic temple type, dating to c. 400.

Bean and Cook (1957: 68–72), Bean (*PECS* 405).

Ikakali Late Bronze Age city in eastern Anatolia or northern Syria, located north of Carchemish near the city of Urshu, west of the Euphrates r. It was among the cities which the Hittite king Hattusili I (1650–1620) attacked and destroyed on his march back to Hattusa at the end of his first(?) campaign in Syria (**Chav.* 220).

İkiztepe (map 2) Northern Anatolian site consisting of four mounds, located in the Pontic region west of the mouth of the Kızıl Irmak river. Human occupation first occurred in the late Chalcolithic period (M4) and continued without interruption into the Middle Bronze Age (early M2). Excavations at İkiztepe were begun in the 1970s by

Turkish teams, under the direction of B. Alkım and subsequently Ö. Bilgi, and have continued to the present day, with a total of over thirty campaign seasons. The site was used both for burial purposes and as a place of settlement for the living. In recent years work has concentrated on one of the mounds, Tepe I, where a sounding has revealed three separate levels of Early Bronze I date, the earliest on virgin soil. Above these were later Early Bronze levels, consisting of houses and workshops, and above these were the remains of an extensive Early Bronze III cemetery.

By the Early Bronze Age (M3), İkiztepe had become a relatively wealthy community, to judge from the artefacts, including weapons and figurines and handmade pottery, which were found in the cemeteries but mainly in the settlement itself. Bronze, lead, and gold were among the materials used in the manufacture of the artefacts. Possible trade links across the Black Sea and with regions extending south through Anatolia have been suggested as the basis for İkiztepe's wealth. Incursions by Kaska peoples may have led to the site's abandonment before the end of the Middle Bronze Age, though the Kaskans are not attested in written records before C15.

There is no evidence of later settlement at İkiztepe, though on Tepe I a monumental tomb dating to the Hellenistic period has been discovered, and late Iron Age remains have been found in the Bafra region.

Alkım *et al.* (1988), Bilgi (1999), reports (in Turkish) in *KST* from vol. 20, 1998, onwards, Yıldırım and Gates (2007: 294).

Ikkuwaniya (probably = Classical **Iconium**, ***Konya***) (map 3) Late Bronze Age city in southern Anatolia, subject to Hittite rule. The Hittite king Telipinu (1525–1500) established one of his grain storage depots there. In the C13 'bronze tablet' treaty drawn up between the Hittite king Tudhaliya IV and Kurunta, ruler of the land of Tarhuntassa, Ikkuwaniya is located among the countries bordering on the Hulaya River Land (**HDT* 120, **CS* II: 105). This land had been incorporated into Tarhuntassa as frontier territory. Ikkuwaniya is probably also to be identified with the place called Ikuna which appears next to Lukka in the so-called Südburg inscription (see glossary) among the lands conquered by the last Hittite king Suppiluliuma II (1207–) (*Hawkins, 1995: 22–3).

Hawkins (1995: 29, 51).

Iktanu, Tell (map 8) Settlement-mound in Transjordan northeast of the Dead Sea. Its history of occupation extends from the Early Bronze Age to the Ottoman period, with long intervals of abandonment in between. The most comprehensive investigations of the site were undertaken by K. Prag over a number of seasons between 1965 and 1990, initially within the context of the East Jordan Valley Survey and subsequently under the auspices of the British Institute at Amman for Archaeology and History.

First occupied in Early Bronze I, Tell Iktanu began life as a small farming community whose principal cereal crop was wheat. Abandoned at the end of this phase, the site was reoccupied and reached the peak of its development in Early Bronze IV, when it extended over 22 ha and had a population of 2,000–2,500 inhabitants. It was a well-planned settlement, featuring rectangular buildings and courtyards separated by unpaved lanes, which flourished on its mixed farming activities. But it survived for only a relatively short time before the site was again abandoned. There is no evidence for settlement in the Middle Bronze Age, and only meagre evidence for reoccupation in either the Late Bronze or Iron Age I periods. However, by Iron Age II (early M1) a large fort was constructed on the site, which continued in use until the Persian period (C6–4). Following this period, there is no further evidence of settlement at Tell Iktanu until Ottoman times.

Prag (1991; *OEANE* 3: 143–4).

Ikuna see **Ikkuwaniya**.

Ilaluha Late Bronze Hittite city in northern Anatolia listed in a prayer of the Hittite king Arnuwanda I among the cities sacked by the Kaskans in late C15–early C14, and thenceforth lying in Kaskan-occupied territory (*Singer, 2002: 42). It probably remained under Kaskan control until the Hittite prince Hattusili (later King Hattusili III) regained the region in which it lay in early C13, and repopulated it with Hittite subjects. Other countries/cities listed in the prayer and presumably lying in the same general region are Hursama, Kastama, Kammama, Zalpuwa, Katahha, Hurna, Dankusna, Tapapanuwa, Kazzapa, Tarugga, Zihhana, Sipidduwa, Washaya, and Parituya. The prayer refers to the Kaskans' sack of the temples in these places and the destruction of the gods' images.

Ilan-sura Small Middle Bronze Age city and kingdom in the Habur triangle, northern Mesopotamia, not far from Shubat-Enlil and perhaps to be identified with Tell Sharisi. Formerly subject to the Assyrian king Shamshi-Adad I (1796–1775), it was one of many principalities which established their independence from Assyria following Shamshi-Adad's death. Subsequently its king, Haya-Sumu, acknowledged Zimri-Lim, the new ruler of Mari (1774–1762), as his overlord. Haya-Sumu was clearly considered the most important and most trustworthy of Zimri-Lim's vassal rulers in the region, and served as an intermediary between him and the other vassals. His bonds with Zimri-Lim were strengthened by marriage alliances when he married, successively, two of Zimri-Lim's daughters. A number of letters written by the second of these, Kiru, to her father, highlight the chequered fortunes of her brief career as Haya-Sumu's consort, up to and including the time she had fallen out of favour with her husband. Her problems were perhaps caused, or exacerbated, by her rivalry with her sister Shimatum, whom Haya-Sumu had previously married.

LKM 613–14 (refs), *Mesop.* 194, 196.

Ildamusha M1 royal city of the land of Colchis, located on the eastern coast of the Black Sea. The Urartian king Sarduri II claims to have burnt it during the campaign which he conducted in Colchis (Urartian Kulhai) in 744 or 743. For this campaign, see under **Colchis**.

Ilion (Ilium) see **Troy**.

Illubru Iron Age city in southern Anatolia, (probably) belonging to the kingdom of Hilakku. Hilakku and the neighbouring kingdom of Que had become Assyrian provinces during the reign of the C8 Assyrian king Shalmaneser V or his successor Sargon II. But resistance to Assyrian rule, particularly in Hilakku, remained strong. In

696 Illubru's governor, Kirua, persuaded 'the men of Hilakku' and the cities of Ingira and Tarzi (Tarsus) to join him in a rebellion against Sargon's son and successor Sennacherib. The rebellion may in fact have spread through the whole of the region later known as Cilicia. But it was shortlived. An expeditionary force dispatched by Sennacherib against the rebels captured and plundered Ingira and Tarzi, and placed Illubru under siege (*Sennach. 61–2). The city eventually fell, and Kirua was deported to the Assyrian capital Nineveh, along with many other prisoners from the land of Hilakku and much booty in livestock. Sennacherib rebuilt the city, and resettled it with conquered peoples from other parts of his realm.

Kessler (*RlA* 5: 60), *CHLI* 1: 43.

Imgur-Enlil (*Balawat*) (map 13) M1 Assyrian city in northern Mesopotamia, 15 km northeast of Nimrud, covering 52 ha, including a main mound 230 m × 160 m. There is evidence of settlement already in the Chalcolithic Age (Ubaid and Uruk periods), but the chief period of occupation dates from C9 to C7. The site was apparently abandoned in late C7, at the time of the collapse of the main centres of Assyrian power. But some reoccupation took place in the Hellenistic period, as indicated by remains of this period on the mound. The first excavation was conducted in 1878 by H. Rassam for the British Museum. Further excavation was carried out by M. E. L. Mallowan from 1956 to 1957 for the British School of Archaeology in Iraq.

Rassam's excavation brought to light parts of a temple and a palace on the mound. One of the highlights of the excavation was Rassam's discovery of two sets of bronze bands used to decorate two of the palace's monumental doors. Such doors were a common feature of Assyrian public buildings. The bands, c. 27 cm high, are decorated with hunting and military scenes, the latter including depictions of campaigns, siege warfare, and camp life. Inscriptions on one set of bands provide a dating to the reign of the Assyrian king Ashurnasirpal II (883–859) (**RIMA* 2: 345–51), and on the other to that of his son and successor Shalmaneser III (858–824) (**RIMA* 3: 140–8). Shalmaneser's bands depict episodes from the campaigns which the king conducted in the first eleven years of his reign, as indicated by the cuneiform text above each scene. Mallowan discovered a third set of bronze door bands in the remains of the temple of Mamu (see below), with an inscription assigning them to the reign of Ashurnasirpal. The doors reached a height of almost 7 m. Though they themselves have long since perished, information from one of Ashurnasirpal's inscriptions indicates that they were made of cedar. A reconstruction of those from Shalmaneser's reign is now on display in the British Museum.

To Ashurnasirpal's reign can also be assigned stone foundation inscriptions from the temple, indicating that Ashurnasirpal had refounded the city, called it Imgur-Enlil, and built the palace and temple there, dedicating the latter to the god of dreams, Mamu. Excavations in the temple also produced an archive of forty economic and legal texts dating from late C8 to (in the case of most of the texts) the first decades of C7.

Imgur-Enlil was among the twenty-seven cities which rebelled against Assyria towards the end of the reign of Shalmaneser III and were subdued by his son and successor Shamshi-Adad V (823–811) (**RIMA* 3: 183). Some traces of Hellenistic occupation were recovered at the site.

Postgate (*RlA* 5: 66–7), J. E. Curtis (1982a), Frame (*OEANE* 1: 268), Curtis and Tallis (2008).

Figure 52 Reconstruction of Balawat gate.

Immerinu M1 city perhaps located between the Euphrates and the Balih rivers, near the Aramaean states Til-Abni and Bit-Adini. In 858 its ruler, Giri-Adad, along with other rulers in the region, paid a tribute consisting of silver, gold, tin, bronze, oxen, sheep, and wine to the Assyrian king Shalmaneser III during his first western campaign in his first regnal year (**RIMA* 3: 9, 15).

İmikuşağı Settlement located in eastern Anatolia on the east bank of the Euphrates, with thirteen occupation levels extending from the Middle Bronze Age to the mediaeval period. The site was excavated by V. Sevin on behalf of Istanbul University. Its most flourishing phase appears to belong to the Middle Bronze Age (early M2). Remains of this phase include a large, apparently public, building and a fortification wall with a tower at its south gate. A double wall enclosed the city during its Iron Age phase.

Sevin (1995), Burney (2004: 134).

İnandıktepe (map 2) Bronze and Iron Age site in north-central Anatolia, near the village of İnandık, 109 km north of Ankara. An identification with Hittite Hanhana (q.v.) has been suggested. The site was excavated in 1966 and 1967 by T. Özgüç on behalf of the Turkish General Directorate of Antiquities and Museums. It consists of two parts: a habitation mound (Termehöyük) and a natural hill opposite. The site's most flourishing phase dates to the period of the Hittite Old Kingdom (C17–15), when a large temple, 65 m × 45 m in extent and at least two storeys high, was built on the slopes and summit of the hill. It is the oldest known Hittite temple and displays many of the architectural features used in later Hittite temples, including the incorporation of recesses and projections instead of straight lines in its design, and the orientation of its chambers towards a central court. Cult-items found in the temple include a range of ceramic ware used as libation vessels or for other cultic purposes (small bowls, goblets, beaked pitchers, pilgrim flasks, and altars shaped like fruit stands), bull statuettes, and what appears to be a model of a shrine with a seated male god inside. The most striking of the temple finds is a vase decorated with four bands of reliefs depicting the various stages of a religious ceremony, apparently a sacred marriage. Excavations of the temple also produced one of the earliest known Hittite documents. Written on a clay tablet in the Akkadian language, it records a land grant which an official called Tuttulla made to his son-in-law and adopted son Ziti. The document is validated by the seal of the king. Built probably during the reign of the Hittite king Hattusili I (1650–1620), the temple was destroyed in a violent conflagration no later than the reign of Hattusili's successor, Mursili I (1620–1590). Its site was occupied by a number of small buildings, also destroyed by fire before the end of the Old Kingdom.

Occupation of the mound called Termehöyük extended from the Early Bronze Age to the Iron Age. A Hittite settlement was built there, contemporary with the temple on the hill. It appears to have been purely residential in character, with no evidence of any major buildings. The site was abandoned before the end of the Old Kingdom and remained uninhabited through the New Kingdom. A small Phrygian settlement occupied the site in C7–6, to judge from Phrygian sherds found there, but no architectural remains survive from this period. A more substantial settlement was built on the site in the Hellenistic period.

T. Özgüç (1988).

Ingira Iron Age city in southern Anatolia, near or within the kingdom of Hilakku. Probably during C8, it became subject to Assyrian overlordship along with Hilakku and the kingdom of Que. But in 696, it joined Hilakku and the city of Tarzi (Tarsus) in a rebellion against the Assyrian king Sennacherib, instigated by Kirua, ruler of the city of Illubru (q.v.) (**Sennach.* 61). The rebellion was crushed by an expeditionary force dispatched by Sennacherib, and Ingira, along with other rebel cities, was captured and plundered.

Ionia (map 4) Greek name for the central Aegean coastal region of Anatolia extending between the bays of Izmir and Bargylia and including the offshore islands Chios and Samos (map 5). It was settled by waves of refugee colonists, called Ionians, from the Greek mainland in the last two centuries of M2, following the collapse of the major centres of Late Bronze Age civilization in Greece and western Asia. The name Ionia is allegedly derived from the legendary Ion, son of the Athenian princess Creusa by the god Apollo. Though Athens' claim to be the mother city of all the Ionian colonists is clearly spurious, it was none the less believed that the city had strong kinship ties with the Ionian cities, most of whom worshipped Athene, Athens' patron goddess, as their chief deity. Athens' alleged ties with the Ionian cities provided a strong motive for the military support she gave to these cities in their rebellion against Persia in 499–494 (see below). However, according to Herodotus (1.146–7), the inhabitants of the Ionian cities were of mixed origin: their ancestors came from many different parts of the Greek mainland, and those from Athens, who considered themselves the noblest of all Ionians, married women of indigenous Carian stock after murdering their fathers, husbands, and children.

Herodotus also comments that irrespective of their origins, all the inhabitants of the region took great pride in the name 'Ionian', and adhered firmly to it. Probably in C9, the twelve chief Ionian cities formed a league called the Panionium (q.v.), which met initially in the sanctuary of Poseidon at the foot of Mt Mycale. In the early centuries of M1, Ionia developed into one of the most prosperous regions in the whole of the Greek world, and played a leading role in the development of Classical Greek culture, particularly in the fields of literature, science, and philosophy. In late C7 or early C6, the Ionian cities became part of the Lydian empire, except for Miletus whose independence was formally acknowledged in a treaty which the Lydian king Alyattes drew up with it. Subsequently, after the fall of the Lydian empire in 546, the Persian emperor Cyrus II established his sovereignty over the region. The Ionian cities bitterly resented their subjection to Persia, and rose up against Persian rule in 499. Initially, they had some significant military successes, including the capture and sack of part of the city of Sardis, the Persian headquarters in western Anatolia. But the rebellion was finally crushed by the Persians, who followed up their victory with brutal retaliation against the rebels.

Craftsmen from Ionia were among the stonemasons employed at Susa on the construction of the palace of the Persian king Darius I (522–486) (**DSf* 12, **DSz* 11).

J. M. Cook (1962), Gschnitzer (*BNP* 6: 907–8).

'Ira, Tell (map 8) Settlement-mound in the Negev desert, southern Judah, 18 km east of Beersheba. Its history of occupation extends from Early Bronze III (M3) to the Early Arab period (C7 CE), with long intervals of abandonment in between. Following surveys in the 1950s, the site was excavated by teams from the Institute of Archaeology, Tel Aviv University, between 1979 and 1987, mostly under the direction of I. Beit-Arieh. Nine occupation levels were identified. In the first of these (Early Bronze III), the settlement was relatively large but unfortified. It was apparently the southernmost settlement in Palestine at this time. After a long gap in occupation, the site was resettled by an Israelite population in late C10 or early C9 (VIII). There are no architectural remains of this period.

More substantial was the level VII Israelite city (first half of C7), which was protected by a 1.6 m thick wall and accessed by a four-entrance gateway with flanking towers. Examples of this (misleadingly called) 'Solomonic' gate are also known from Megiddo, Hazor, and Gezer. After this level was destroyed by fire, the city was rebuilt in the second half of C7 (VI). It was destroyed again after only a few decades at the end of C7 or early C6. Beit-Arieh suggests that its destruction may have been due to an Edomite attack. Remains of the Israelite city include, in addition to the fortifications, a large storage building, a necropolis containing twenty-five rock-cut bench tombs, and a number of rock-cut cisterns for water storage. Small finds include jewellery, figurines, and some jars bearing short inscriptions. Agriculture and sheep- and goat-herding provided the basis for the city's economy. Resettlement of the site occurred in the Persian period (V), apparently within the context of the liberation of the Jews from Babylonia (C6). A relatively large fortified city was built on the site during the Hellenistic period (IV), reusing some of the Iron Age fortifications. Though the city dwindled in size during the Roman period (III), it once again expanded in the Byzantine era (II). Its final occupation (I) dates to the Arab period.

Attempts to identify the site with a biblical city have proved inconclusive, despite the fact that it was clearly one of the most important cities of the Negev during Iron Age II.

Beit-Arieh (*NEAEHL* 2: 642–6; *OEANE* 3: 175–7).

Iranian A term used initially of several population groups believed to have arrived on the Iranian plateau c. mid M2 (or later), perhaps from a homeland east of the Caspian Sea. They were a branch of the Indo-European-speaking peoples who, over a period of several millennia from M3 onwards (if not earlier), dispersed in large numbers through many parts of western Asia and Europe. The Iranian branch of these peoples included speakers of the anc. Persian, Avestan, Scythian, and Median languages.

The name 'Iran' derives from Old Persian *ariyanam (khshathram)* – '(land) of the Aryans'. *ariyanam* comes from *ariya*, an Old Persian word meaning 'noble, lordly'. The Persian king Darius I (522–486) and his successors acknowledged in their inscriptions their Iranian or 'Aryan' origins, and in fact they called their language 'Aryan'. However, they maintained their core identity, and stressed their distinctiveness from other Aryan/Iranian groups, by identifying themselves with the region of southwestern Iran to which they had given their name – the land of Parsa (mod. Fars), which in Greek became *Persis*.

Ariya also provided the basis for the Middle Persian name *Eran*, from which in C3 CE the Sasanian kings adopted the political concept *Eranshahr* ('Empire of the Aryans'). (The term 'Aryan' has today become largely synonymous with a racist supremacist ideology, because of its misappropriation for this purpose in Nazi propaganda.) They did so 'because in order to legitimize their own power, they wanted to appear as the heirs of the ancient mythical Iranian kings, and also as the followers of the Zoroastrian faith, with its deep roots in Iran' (Wiesehöfer, 2001: xi).

From the Sasanian concept comes the name *Iranshar*, shortened to *Iran*, which was adopted (instead of Persia) as the mod. country's official name in 1935. The term 'Iranian' is today used as a broad, generic designation for the inhabitants of mod. Iran. The majority of these inhabitants are native speakers of Persian, and of Indo-European origin. But there are also large Turkic and Arabic ethnic groups in the Iranian population, along with Kurds, Lurs, Balochi, and Bakhtyari, and a number of minority groups including Armenians, Assyrians, and Jews. The mod. country of Iran extends over the high Iranian plateau (more than 1,500 m above sea level) from the Caspian Sea in the north to the Persian Gulf in the south. It shares land borders with Iraq and Turkey to the west, Armenia, Azerbaijan, and Turkmenistan to the north, and Afghanistan and Pakistan to the east.

Gnoli (1989), Brentjes (1995: 1003).

Irqata see **Arqa**.

Irridu (**Irrite**) Middle and Late Bronze Age city in northwestern Mesopotamia, probably located between Carchemish and Harran. A reference to it in a letter written by a king of Carchemish to Zimri-Lim, king of Mari (1774–1762), suggests that Irridu may for a time, in C18, have been subject to Carchemish. Subsequently it appears to have belonged to the kingdom of Yamhad in northern Syria, since it was captured by Abba-Il (Abban), king of Yamhad, after rebelling against him (**RIME* 4: 799–800). Abba-Il installed his brother Yarim-Lim on the throne of Alalah, which he had given him in exchange for Irridu – presumably indicating that Yarim-Lim had originally ruled in Irridu on Abba-Il's behalf.

During the final stages of the Hittite destruction of the Mitannian empire (third quarter of C14), Irridu was occupied by Hittite troops in their advance upon the Mitannian capital Washshukkanni (**HDT* 46). Irridu then became a regional centre of the kingdom of Hanigalbat. It was among the cities conquered by the Assyrian king Adad-nirari I (1307–1275) when Wasashatta, ruler of Hanigalbat, led an abortive rebellion against Assyrian rule (**RIMA* 1: 131, 136). Adad-nirari found members of Wasashatta's family and retinue in Irridu, including his wife and children, and took them back to Ashur. Irridu itself was put to the torch, and its site sown over with salty plants to indicate that it was never again to be resettled.

Hawkins (*RlA* 5: 171).

Irsia see **Erishu**.

Isauria (map 4) Classical name for the Taurus mountain region in central-southern Anatolia, bordered by Pisidia, Lycaonia, and Pamphylia. In the Late Bronze Age, Isauria served as a frontier-zone between the kingdom of Tarhuntassa and the Lukka Lands. In Classical sources, its mountain peoples were noted for their fierce resistance to external aggression, and for their banditry. The chief towns of the region were Isaura Vetus and Isaura Nova (Old and New Isaura respectively).

Mitchell (*OCD* 767–8).

Ishchali see **Nerebtum**.

Ishpilibria M1 fortified city in the Kashiyari range (mod. Tur ʿAbdin) of northern Mesopotamia. It belonged to the land of Nirbu, i.e. the Kashiyari plateau. In 882 the Assyrian king Ashurnasirpal II laid siege to the city on his return from military operations in the Nairi lands. The inhabitants of Nirbu had abandoned their cities on the approach of the Assyrian army and sought refuge within the walls of Ishpilibria. But neither fortifications nor the rugged terrain in which the city lay proved an obstacle to the Assyrian forces, who carried out a widespread massacre and deported the survivors to Assyria (**RIMA* 2: 203, 243–4). Ishpilibria is attested with the name Ishpallure in Neo-Assyrian documents; these indicate that it was located in Izalla, a wine-growing region (Radner, 2006: 295).

Ishtarate (in the toponym **Nerebu-sha-Ishtarate, 'Pass of the Goddesses'**) Iron Age pass in the Kashiyari mountain range (mod. Tur ʿAbdin) of northern Mesopotamia, leading north to the city of Matiate. The Assyrian king Ashurnasirpal II reports entering the pass following his passage through Kadmuhu in 879. He subsequently encamped his forces in the city of Kibaku, which paid him tribute in the form of livestock, wine, and bronze cooking vessels (**RIMA* 2: 208, 249). The same route was taken by Shalmaneser III on his way to conquer Matiate in 846 (**RIMA* 3: 39).

Radner (2006: 288).

Ishtu(a)nda Iron Age kingdom in southern Anatolia, located within the region of Tabal, and perhaps to be identified with Late Bronze Age Wasuduwanda (q.v.) attested in Hittite texts. It appears among the five kingdoms of Tabal which paid tribute to the Assyrian king Tiglath-pileser III in 738 and 732 (**ARAB* I: 276, 287, **Tigl. III* 68–9, 108–9), when its ruler was a man called Tuhamme. Around 710, during the reign of the Assyrian king Sargon II, Ishtuanda joined with its neighbour Atuna for an attack on the cities of Bit-Paruta (Bit-Burutash), the largest of the kingdoms of Tabal (**SAA* I: 6, no. 1). Its apparent proximity to the kingdom of Atuna, which almost certainly lay in the northwestern part of the land of Tabal in the vicinity of mod. Aksaray, provides a pointer to Ishtuanda's location in the same region.

Ishua see **Isuwa**.

Ishupitta Late Bronze Age country in north-central Anatolia. Though nominally subject to Hatti, it was long occupied by Kaska forces. The Hittite king Mursili II (1321–1295) claimed a successful military campaign against these forces (**CS* II: 84). But they were not finally dislodged from the land until the Hittite prince Hattusili, son of Mursili and later King Hattusili III (1267–1237), became ruler of the northern half of the Hittite homeland, drove the Kaskans from it, and resettled the region with a Hittite population (**CS* I: 200, 201). (See also **Hakpis(sa)** and **Turmitta**.) The city played an important role in the cult of the goddess Ishtar of Samuha.

**RGTC* 6: 146–7, Otten (*RlA* 5: 178–9).

Isin (*Ishan al-Bahriyat*) (map 11) City in southern Mesopotamia, c. 100 ha in area, located 27 km south of Nippur. Its history of occupation extends from the Ubaid (M4) through the Persian period (C6–4), though its principal periods of occupation date to the Early and Middle Bronze Ages. Excavations were carried out initially in 1924 by A. T. Clay and S. Langdon, and subsequently between 1973 and 1989 by archaeological teams from the University of Munich under the direction of B. Hrouda. The most important building unearthed was a temple dedicated to Gula, goddess of healing and Isin's chief deity, and her consort, Ninurta. This was located on the highest part of the mound. A staircase of nineteen steps, made of sundried bricks paved with clay, led up to the temple's main entrance. The temple itself was a rectangular building (c. 70 m × 50 m), containing two large courtyards and surrounded by a wall. It was probably first constructed in the Early Dynastic period (c. 2700), but only a few bricks from this phase, discovered beneath the walls of later levels, have survived. The temple was rebuilt several times, in the Old Babylonian (Middle Bronze Age), Kassite (Late Bronze Age), and Neo-Babylonian periods (the last time by the Babylonian king Nebuchadnezzar II early in C6). Its main period of use appears to have been under Kassite rule. Other material remains from the site include a necropolis of Early Bronze

Age date, a dog cemetery (c. 1000 BCE) with thirty-three graves located to the northeast of the temple (the dog was Gula's animal symbol), houses of the Old Babylonian period, an archive of eighty cuneiform tablets of the same period, several large buildings of the Kassite period (one of which may have been the city's palace), and a number of small finds, including cylinder seals, a mace-head from the reign of the Akkadian king Shar-kali-sharri (2217–2193), and terracotta reliefs of the Old Babylonian period.

Isin first rose to prominence in the last years of M3 when Ishbi-Erra, a high-ranking official of the last Ur III king Ibbi-Sin and governor of the city of Mari, established his authority over much of the region controlled by the Ur III dynasty before its collapse, and shifted the seat of his administration to Isin. He became the founder of the First Isin dynasty, which lasted for more than two centuries through the reigns of Ishbi-Erra and fourteen of his successors (c. 2017 to 1794). Though relatively long-lived, the dynasty was constantly threatened by rival kings, notably those of Larsa and Babylon. With Larsa in particular Ishbi-Erra's successors engaged in a series of bitter conflicts, in the course of which Isin suffered several major defeats. It none the less maintained its status as a major power in the region until the death of its tenth king, Enlil-bani (1860–1837), after whose reign it suffered steady and irreversible decline. Isin's status as an independent power came to an end with its conquest by Larsa in 1794, when the latter's throne was occupied by its last king, Rim-Sin. From then on Isin was incorporated into the kingdom of Larsa, and subsequently into the kingdom of Babylon when the Babylonian king Hammurabi brought the dynasty of Larsa to an end in 1763.

Through the Late Bronze Age Kassite period, Isin remained under Babylonian rule. But after the Kassite dynasty was ended by the Elamite invasion of Babylonia c. 1155, Isin may have regained its autonomy under a new ruling 'dynasty'. This has been concluded from the emergence of a line of rulers referred to in a Babylonian King List as the Second Dynasty of Isin (**RIMB* 2: 5–67). Lasting from 1154 until 1026, the so-called dynasty consisted of eleven kings, most of whom seem not to have been related to one another. Its name suggests that the political and administrative centre of Babylonia may have shifted south from Babylon to Isin for a time. But there is no actual evidence for such a shift, and it seems that most of the members of the 'dynasty' ruled from Babylon. The most famous of these rulers was the fourth king, Nebuchadnezzar I (1126–1105), who invaded Elam and sacked the city of Susa. He retrieved from the city the statue of the god Marduk, which the Elamites had taken during their invasion of Babylonia in mid C12.

Edzard/Brinkman/Hrouda (*RlA* 5: 181–92), Hrouda (1977–92; *OEANE* 3: 186–7).

Isinda (1) (map 15) M1 BCE–M1 CE city in Lycia in southwestern Anatolia, located on a hill with a poorly preserved circuit wall, 6 km northeast of mod. Kaş. The earliest remains, which date to the period between late C6 and C4, include three rock-cut tombs with sepulchral inscriptions in the Lycian language, and a pillar-tomb with relief sculptures. In Roman times, Isinda was a member of a tetrapolis (league of four cities), whose other three members were Apollonia, Simena, and Aperlae. Aperlae was the head of the tetrapolis.

Deltour-Levie (1982: 171–5).

Isinda (2) M1 BCE–M1 CE city in Pisidia in southern Anatolia, located near mod. Korkuteli on the route between Pamphylia and Caria (*BAGRW* 65 D3). Though the city is not attested before early C2, it was, according to its coinage, founded by colonists from Ionia (in western Anatolia). This claim might, if valid, take the city's origins back to C7. (A city called Isinda in Ionia is mentioned by the Byzantine scholar Stephanus of Byzantium.) Isinda's meagre remains, including the remnants of fortification walls and an uninscribed rock-tomb, do not pre-date the Hellenistic period.

Bean (*PECS* 417).

Ismerikka Late Bronze Age country in southern Anatolia, subject to Hittite rule and close to (and probably north of) Kizzuwadna. The early C14 Hittite king Arnuwanda I resettled some of Ismerikka's leading men (who appear to have been mostly of Hurrian stock) in six towns in Kizzuwadna – Zazlippa, Washshukanni, Arana, Terusa, Uriga, and Urushsha (= Urshu?) – where they were to carry out surveillance activities. He drew up with them a treaty or protocol (still extant), which required them to report on seditious and enemy activities in the region, take action in suppressing local uprisings, and provide troops for the Hittite king's standing army.

Kempinski and Košak (1970), Ünal (*RlA* 5: 197–8), Beal (1992b: 39–41), **HDT* 13–17.

Israel (map 8) Iron Age kingdom located in Palestine. If one accepts *OT* tradition, it reached its peak in C10, during the reign of King David. David allegedly exercised control over a large spread of territories extending from the Palestinian coastlands and plains northwards to the region of Damascus, and eastwards to the Euphrates. But attempts to reconcile this picture of the Israelite kingdom with information provided by archaeological and non-biblical sources have not been successful. (For a recently discovered Aramaic inscription which provides the first non-biblical evidence of a House of David, see **Dan**.) In *OT* tradition, the history of the Israelite nation begins with the migration of Abraham to the land of Canaan. Two generations after his arrival, Canaan suffered a severe famine which forced his grandson Jacob to migrate to Egypt, where he and his twelve sons settled. Here their descendants remained a race apart, and were eventually reduced to the status of slave labourers by the pharaoh. But under the leadership of Moses, they were liberated from their bondage, and left Egypt in search of the land promised to them by their god, Yahweh. Most scholars who accept the biblical tradition assign the exodus to the reign of the pharaoh Ramesses II (1279–1213), but earlier and later periods have also been proposed. After the Israelites had wandered forty years in the desert wilderness, Yahweh led them to the promised land, Canaan, where their patriarch Abraham had settled many generations earlier. The new arrivals became involved in numerous conflicts with the tribes already occupying Canaan, before they succeeded in bringing the whole of the country beneath their sway. By this time, they had organized themselves into twelve tribes, whose founders, according to tradition, were the twelve sons of Jacob.

There is little in either archaeological or contemporary written sources to corroborate *OT* accounts of the early history of the Israelites. Egyptian records, for example, contain no record of Israelite settlement in Egypt, of Israelites used as slave labour, or of an Israelite exodus from Egypt. The only reference to Israelites in Egyptian sources appears on a granite stele discovered in 1896 by W. F. Petrie in the mortuary temple of the pharaoh Merneptah (1213–1203) in Thebes (**ANET* 376–8). The people of Israel are included in a list of the pharaoh's conquests. This is, in fact, the earliest attestation we have of the name Israel. It indicates the existence of a population group so called at that time, though Israel as a nation-state seems not to have existed prior to M1. The hieroglyphic determinative accompanying the name Israel on the Merneptah stele indicates that the reference is to a people not to a land. According to Genesis 32:28, Jacob was renamed Israel after he had struggled with God. 'Israel' is in fact believed to be a personal rather than a tribal name, and means something like 'May God contend' or 'May God rule'. The two names Jacob and Israel have led some scholars to suggest that there were originally two separate tribal patriarchs, the double name perhaps reflecting an early process of tribal affiliation.

There is a trend in modern scholarship to identify the Israelites with a branch of the Late Bronze Age Canaanite population groups. According to this hypothesis, following the withdrawal of Egyptian sovereignty over the southern Canaanite city-states around mid C12, the 'Israelite branch' left the urban centres and founded new settlements, primarily in the hill country. There is, however, much debate and uncertainty over the historical processes involved. (J. Tubb, 2008: 23, has proposed that movements of disaffected people to the hill country regions may already have been under way during the restructuring of the Egyptian empire in the reigns of Seti I and Ramesses II.) On the basis of *OT* tradition, the Israelites subsequently expanded their territory westwards, absorbing Canaanite territory on the plains, and engaging in a series of conflicts with the Philistines along the coast. In *OT* tradition this marks the beginning of Israel as a nation-state, with the creation of a monarchy exercised by a ruler who would hold supreme authority over Israel's twelve tribes. It should be stressed that for the history of the 'united monarchy', and indeed for the very existence of such a monarchy, we have to rely almost entirely on biblical sources. Information provided by these sources cannot be independently verified. A. F. Rainey (2007), however, has recently concluded that the latest archaeological research supports the principal assumption of the biblical tradition that the Israelites migrated as pastoralists westwards from Transjordan. He comments that all the cultural features examined by W. G. Dever (2003b), in his discussion of the Israelites' origins, point to a radical change in the demography and settlement pattern of the hill country areas in early C12, compatible with a movement of an ethnic group, or groups, from the eastern steppe land. He believes that there is nothing among those cultural features that would suggest that this new population derived from the Late Bronze Age Canaanite areas on the coastal plains and valleys.

OT sources relate that the first king of the united monarchy was a man called Saul (c. 1020–1000). Saul suffered many setbacks and failures in his career as king and military leader of the Israelites, before finally committing suicide after a decisive defeat by the Philistines. He was succeeded by David, from the land of Judah in the south of the kingdom. Conflicts with the Philistines continued in David's reign, though David allegedly had considerable success against them. By the end of his reign the Philistines had lost their status as a significant power within the region. But David's greatest achievement was the establishment of a new capital of Israel, the city of Jerusalem. Under his son and successor Solomon (960–922), who organized the kingdom into twelve administrative districts, each under the authority of a governor, Israel reached the height of its cultural and commercial development. Solomon's promotion of close cultural and commercial links with foreign countries boosted his kingdom's prosperity, and brought to the royal court at Jerusalem a cosmopolitan flavour far removed from the ascetic lifestyle of the king's predecessors. Politically, however, Solomon's reign was less successful, and on his death, the tensions that had been brewing between the northern and southern tribes of Israel erupted into open conflict. Conflicts between the tribes led to the establishment of two separate kingdoms – Israel in the north, with its capital at Samaria, and Judah in the south.

Many scholars now argue that in the absence of either archaeological or written evidence to support it, the tradition of a united kingdom under Saul, David, and Solomon has no historical basis, and that these kings are essentially literary creations. (But for David, see under **Dan**.) The argument continues that it was not until the reign of Omri (876–869), allegedly the sixth king of Israel and founder of the so-called Omride dynasty, that a united kingdom was formed – with its capital at Samaria in central Palestine. In 853 Ahab, second ruler of the Omride dynasty, joined the military coalition which confronted and was defeated by the Assyrian king Shalmaneser III in the battle at Qarqar on the Orontes r. (**RIMA* 3: 23). The united kingdom supposedly founded by Omri came to an end with the death of Jehoram (Joram) (c. 842), traditionally considered the last ruler of Omri's dynasty (see glossary under **Omride dynasty**). Subsequently, the Israelite king Joash is listed among the Syro-Palestinian tributaries of the Assyrian king Adad-nirari III (810–783) (**RIMA* 3: 211). Assyria's king Tiglath-pileser III (745–727) made extensive conquests in Israel, mentioning Jehoahaz of Judah among his tributaries (**Tigl. III* 170–1), and under his successor Shalmaneser V (726–722) or his successor-but-one, Sargon II (721–705), the kingdom of Israel was brought to an end. Judah survived, but was forced to pay tribute to Assyria as the price of its survival.

After the fall of the Assyrian empire in late C7, Judah became for a time a vassal state of Egypt. But in 586 an expeditionary force dispatched by the Babylonian king Nebuchadnezzar II captured and destroyed its capital, Jerusalem. Judah was absorbed into the Babylonian empire, and (allegedly) almost all its population was deported (2 Kings 24:20–25:21). Thus began the period of the Israelite 'exile', lasting almost fifty years. It came to an end in 539, when the Persian king Cyrus II conquered Babylon. In the following year, the Israelites living in exile were allowed to return to their homeland. According to Ezra 2:64, 42,360 of them returned to Jerusalem. But many had made a good living in the land of their exile and chose to stay there, unwilling to abandon their possessions, according to the Jewish historian Josephus (*Jewish Antiquities* 11: 8).

We should note that the term 'Israel' has different connotations in different contexts. In its broadest sense, it designates an entire people rather than a land or nation-state. As we have seen, in its earliest attestation on the Merneptah stele, it refers to a population group, not a land. In *OT* tradition, it is the alternative name of the patriarch Jacob, and appears to be a personal rather than a tribal name in origin. It is used as the name of the united kingdom first ruled by Saul, and then in the period of the divided monarchy it is used of the northern kingdom, as distinct from the southern kingdom of Judah. After Sargon brought the northern kingdom to an end, 'Israel' was used also to refer to Judah. When the kingdom of Judah came to an end, the name persisted as a religious designation, to distinguish the worshippers of Yahweh from other contemporary peoples in the region.

McCarter (*HCBD* 466–70), Mitchell, chapters in *CAH* III.1 (442–510) and *CAH* III.2 (322–409), Miller and Hayes (1986), Redford (1992), Finkelstein and Silberman (2002), Dever (2003b), Rainey (2007), Tubb (2008), Ussishkin (2008).

Issus (map 4) M1 city on the southeastern Anatolian coast, just west of the Amanus range. First attested by Xenophon (*Anabasis* 1.2.24; 1.4.1), it was the site of a famous battle in which Alexander the Great defeated the Persian king Darius III in 333. The battle was fought by the Pinarus r. (= mod. Deli Çay or Payas).

Diodorus 17.33–4, Arrian, *Anabasis* 2.6–11, Plutarch, *Alexander* 20.

Istitina Late Bronze Age Hittite subject state in eastern Anatolia, in the region called the Upper Land (q.v.). It was seized by a Kaskan tribal chief called Pihhuniya during his attacks on the Upper Land in the seventh regnal year of the Hittite king Mursili II (c. 1315). Mursili restored Istitina to Hittite control and rebuilt it after his defeat and capture of Pihhuniya (**CS* II: 87). But two years later the country was ravaged by troops from the land of Azzi-Hayasa in a fresh invasion of the Upper Land. Istitina's (chief?) city Kannuwara was placed under siege (**CS* II: 89). Liberation of land and city was (doubtless) achieved by the Hittite commander Nuwanza when he was ordered by Mursili to attack and destroy the enemy forces occupying the Upper Land.

Isuwa (Ishua) (map 3) Late Bronze Age country in northern Mesopotamia, extending south of the Arsanias r. (mod. Murat Su) and east of the Euphrates towards and perhaps as far as the upper course of the Tigris. Its heartland lay within the region of mod. Elaziğ in Turkey and included the rich copper mines of Ergani Maden (q.v.). It thus occupied a position of considerable strategic significance between the Great Kingdoms of Hatti and Mitanni. Isuwa is first attested in the reign of the Hittite king Tudhaliya I/II, early C14, when it had apparently taken up arms against Hatti with the support of the king of Mitanni. Tudhaliya had crushed the rebellion, and re-established control over Isuwa, though a number of rebels escaped his authority and sought refuge in Mitanni (*Bryce, 2005: 127–8). Subsequently Hurrian troops invaded, sacked, and plundered Isuwa. Tudhaliya eventually re-established his control over the country, but it was to continue to be one of the most fractious of Hatti's subject territories, with strong leanings towards Mitanni. It was later to join the comprehensive invasions of the Hittite homeland which brought the kingdom of Hatti close to total destruction in the reign of Tudhaliya III, c. 1360 (*Bryce, 2005: 146).

Subsequently, Tudhaliya's son and successor Suppiluliuma I invaded Isuwa, in an attempt to regain control of it, and may have suffered a defeat at the hands of the Mitannian king Tushratta who came to Isuwa's support (Bryce, 2005: 156–7). This was one of the preliminaries to the one-year Syrian war fought between Hatti and Mitanni (c. 1344), in the course of which Suppiluliuma conquered Isuwa. Subsequently the country, originally perhaps controlled by a confederation of tribes, but later ruled by a monarchy, seems to have remained closely aligned with Hatti. In the reign of the Hittite king Hattusili III (1267–1237), the links between Hatti and Isuwa were further consolidated by the marriage of a Hittite princess, Kilusepa, to the king of Isuwa. The Assyrian king Tiglath-pileser I (1114–1076) reports his conquest of the city of Enzatu in the land of Isuwa (here attested in the form Ishua) (**RIMA* 2: 43). Three centuries later, the Assyrian king Shalmaneser III claimed to have conquered the entire land of Enzite in the third year of his reign (856) (**RIMA* 3: 19–20).

Klengel (1968; *RlA* 5: 214–16), Altman (2000).

Itabalhum (Itab/pal) Middle Bronze Age Turukkean kingdom in the northwestern Zagros mountain region, attested in the texts of Shemshara (Middle Bronze Age Shusharra). Its capital was the city of Kunshum. It was probably the most powerful of a number of kingdoms or polities of the western Zagros region, several of which, including Kusanarhum, Zutlum, and Shudamelum (as well as Itabalhum), formed a military coalition against the Gutians. The Elamites may also have sought an alliance with Itabalhum against the Gutians. Pishenden, one of Itabalhum's three known kings, appears in the Shemshara archive as the superior of Kuwari, who had been appointed as ruler of Shusharra early in C18. As letters from the archive indicate, Kuwari subsequently switched his allegiance to the Assyrian king Shamshi-Adad I.

*Eidem and Laessøe (2001: 26–7).

Ivriz (map 2) Iron Age rock relief in southern Anatolia, 17 km south of mod. Ereğli. The relief depicts two figures: on the left, a god wearing a horned cap, and holding ears of corn and a bunch of grapes in his left and right hands respectively; on the right, a smaller figure, wearing a fringed robe fastened with a fibula. A Luwian hieroglyphic inscription identifies the left-hand figure as the Luwian god Tarhunda, depicted apparently in the role of a fertility deity, and the right-hand figure as Warpalawas, ruler of the Iron Age kingdom of Tuwana in the region of southern Tabal (c. 740–705). The king is offering up prayer to the god. From Assyrian records, we know that Warpalawas (Assyrian Urballa) was a tributary of the Assyrian king Tiglath-pileser III (745–727), and continued to occupy his kingdom's throne through the reign of Tiglath-pileser's successor-but-one Sargon II (721–705). The Assyrian character of his headdress and robe in the Ivriz relief, in contrast to the Late Bronze Age Anatolian character of the god's depiction, is seen by Burney as reflecting the penetration of Assyrian cultural influence into the Neo-Hittite lands and the decline of the Hittite legacy to the Neo-Hittite principalities.

Bittel (1976: 289, 292, figs 269, 327–9; *RlA* 5: 224–5), Burney (2004: 139–40).

Iyalanda Late Bronze Age city in western Anatolia, perhaps to be identified with Classical Alinda (q.v.). Iyalanda appears to have been independent of, and sometimes hostile to, the kingdom of Hatti. Early in C14 it was one of several western Anatolian cities which the renegade Hittite vassal Madduwatta claimed by right of conquest (**HDT* 159). In mid C13 another anti-Hittite leader in the west, Piyamaradu, used it as a fortified stronghold against a Hittite army led by Hattusili III. The city finally fell to Hattusili, but only after heavy fighting. Piyamaradu himself escaped and fled to Milawata/Millawanda (Classical Miletus) (*Garstang and Gurney, 1959: 111–12).

Izalla (Azalla (2), Classical **Melabas,** ***Dibek Daği***) Iron Age land situated on the southeastern side of the Kashiyari mountain range (mod. Tur ʿAbdin), corresponding to the escarpment known as mod. Dibek Daği, between Nusaybin and İdil (Radner, 2006: 292–9, correcting previous studies which assumed a location in the western Kashiyari region). The region was renowned in Neo-Assyrian times as a wine-producing area. In 882 the Assyrian king Ashurnasirpal II received the tribute (including wine) of Izalla while staying at the source of the Supnat r. (**RIMA* 2: 201). Later on, vineyards in Izalla are mentioned in Neo-Assyrian land grants and sale documents. In 609 the Babylonian king Nabopolassar had to go up to Izalla and do battle there on his way to

Harran, where his garrison was under attack by the Egyptian allies of the last Assyrian king, Ashur-uballit II (*ABC* 96).
(H. D. Baker)

ʿIzbet Sartah (map 8) Small Iron Age I fortified village located in the hill country of Palestine, 16 km east of Tel Aviv and 3 km east of Tel Aphek. The site was excavated for four seasons from 1976 to 1978 by M. Kochavi on behalf of the Institute of Archaeology, Tel Aviv University, and the Dept for the Land of Israel Studies, Bar-Ilan University. Three occupation levels were identified, extending from late C13 or early C12 to C10. The earliest settlement was oval-shaped, and consisted of a continuous row of rooms built against the surrounding fortification wall, and forming part of the village's defences. Within the enclosure was a large open courtyard, where sheep and goats may have been kept. The rooms, whose walls were made of large stones, were accessed from the courtyard. The inhabitants of the village were part of a population which occupied hundreds of hill sites at this time. But the village's location on the hill country's western border also brought it into contact with the inhabitants of the plain. Ceramic evidence indicates that relations with them were sometimes peaceful. But conflict with the plain-dwelling Philistines, it has been suggested, may have led to the village's abandonment at the beginning of C11.

Its resettlement in the second half of C11 has been seen as a reflection of westward Israelite expansion, perhaps under King Saul, from the hill country to the plain – though this of course involves assumptions about the historical authenticity of the *OT* tradition. The new settlement, now extending over 0.4 ha, was double the size of its predecessor, and had a different layout. A series of small houses was built along the edge of the site. But the main feature of this level was a large, central four-room house. Around three of its sides a total of forty-three silos were dug, and lined with stones. One of them contained two fragments of an ostracon, with part of an inscription (eighty-six letters have survived) in the proto-Canaanite script – the longest known Proto-Canaanite inscription. The settlement was again abandoned later in C11, but by early C10 had once more been resettled. It has been suggested that this happened within the context of a resumption of Israelite westward expansion under King David. The new settlement was smaller than its predecessor, and the site was again abandoned, this time permanently, after only a brief occupation.
I. Finkelstein (1986), Watkins (*OEANE* 3: 198–9).

Izbia, Izzibia see *Ziwiyeh*.

Izeh (called ***Malamir*** until 1935) (map 11) Town and plain in the Bakhtiari mountains in southwestern Iran, located within the region of anc. Elam c. 150 km northeast of Susa. A preliminary survey of the plain, which covers c. 220 sq. km, has indicated that it contains numerous anc. sites, dating from M3 BCE to M1 CE. Though none of these sites has as yet been comprehensively investigated, a number of rock reliefs provide valuable information about the culture of the region in the Neo-Elamite and Parthian periods.

The Neo-Elamite reliefs appear on rock-faces in two areas, located on either side of the plain. Six reliefs were carved on the walls and boulders of a ravine now called Kul-e Farah. And at the site now known as Shikaft-e Salman, four reliefs were carved next to and within the entrance of a cave, near which was a spring. Processional, banqueting, and sacrificial scenes are represented in the Kul-e Farah reliefs. Those at Shikaft-e Salman depict nine human figures, including two women and two children, all of whom face towards a water source, in attitudes of prayer. Cuneiform inscriptions accompany both sets of reliefs.

At Kul-e Farah, the main inscription is a 24-line text which appears in a panel on the north wall of the ravine. It identifies the most important figure in the relief as a local ruler called Hanni, who has dedicated his image to the god Tirutur. Hanni identifies himself as the son of Tahhi, and the chief of Ayapir, presumably the city where he resided. The text also contains invocations to a number of Elamite deities, and a record of Hanni's exploits, including the suppression of a revolt, the capture of twenty rebellious chieftains, and the erection of a temple at Ayapir. Hanni was clearly an important local ruler who had a significant military force at his disposal. He seems, however, to have been the subordinate of a king called Shutur-Nahhunte, who is also mentioned in his inscription. Other figures in the relief panel are identified by short cuneiform labels inscribed next to them or on their garments. They include Hanni's arms-bearer and another official, three musicians, and four sacrificers. It has been suggested that Kul-e Farah was an open-air sanctuary used for occasional celebrations, some of which may have marked the beginning of the new year.

Hanni's name and filiation also appear in inscriptions which accompany the reliefs at Shikaft-e Salman. The main text appears to indicate a dedication by Hanni of himself and his family to the goddess Mashti. Tarrisha is named as the place where he intends to make images of himself and his wife and children, apparently to honour the goddess. The site may in fact have been called Tarrisha in the Elamite period, when it was

Figure 53 Kul-e Farah reliefs.

Figure 54 Kul-e Farah inscriptions.

perhaps venerated as a cult-place of the goddess Mashti. Caves and springs are often endowed with special cultic associations, and linked with particular deities.

Evidence provided by his inscriptions suggests that on linguistic grounds, Hanni is probably to be dated to C6, or C7 at the earliest. But with the exception of the inscribed panel at Kul-e Farah, all the reliefs at this site and Shikaft-e Salman belong stylistically to the reign of the Elamite king Shutruk-Nahhunte I (1185–1155), or to an earlier period – i.e. more than half a millennium before Hanni added his inscriptions to them. He must therefore have taken over these already anc. monuments for his own use, identifying them with himself by the inscriptions he put on them. The fact that he did so may well indicate that the sites had long been invested with a special significance, very likely religious in nature, which probably explains why the reliefs were carved there in the first place.

Vanden Berghe (1963), de Waele (1972), Calmeyer/Stolper (*RlA* 7: 275–87), Seidl (*OEANE* 3: 199–203).

Izirtu (Zirtu) Iron Age royal city in the country of the Mannaeans, located in mod. Iranian Kurdistan. Its ruling dynasty exercised relatively loose control over the confederation of Mannaean lands and tribes which occupied the lowlands south of Lake Urmia. Izirtu probably lay not far south of the lake. In 829 the Mannaean king Udaku fled the city when he received news of the approach of an army dispatched to the region by the Assyrian king Shalmaneser III, led by his commander-in-chief Dayyan-Ashur (**RIMA* 3: 70). It is unclear whether Izirtu suffered the fate of other Mannaean cities which Dayyan-Ashur plundered and put to the torch. In 716 the Assyrian king Sargon II seized and burned the city when the Mannaean throne was occupied by Ullusunu, an appointee of the Urartian king Rusa I, during a campaign in Mannaean territory.

Subsequently, when Ullusunu surrendered to him, Sargon allegedly repaired the damage to his land, including (presumably) the capital. He set up an inscribed statue of himself in Izirtu (**ARAB* II: 28–9). Izirtu's territory was subsequently invaded and ravaged by the Assyrian king Ashurbanipal (668–630/627) during his campaign in Mannaea, though the city itself appears not to have been captured on this occasion.

A place called Zatar, mentioned in an Aramaic inscription from Qalaichi Tappeh, south of Lake Urmia in Iranian Kurdistan, and presumably identifiable with it, may be the same as Assyrian Izirtu (Hassanzadeh, 2006).

Levine (*RlA* 5: 226).

J

Jaffa (Joppa) (map 8) Port-city on the coast of Palestine, located today in Israel in a suburb of Tel Aviv-Jaffa. The site's history of occupation is represented by eight archaeological strata, extending from Middle Bronze Age II to the Roman imperial period. It was excavated by P. L. O. Guy from 1945 to 1950 for the Israel Dept of Antiquities, by J. Bowman and B. S. J. Isserlin in 1952 for the University of Leeds, and by J. Kaplan from 1955 to 1974 for the Museum of Antiquities of Tel Aviv-Jaffa. There are material remains of all periods of its history, the most significant of which are a large Middle Bronze Age fortified enclosure with earth rampart, and a C13 citadel gate system with mudbrick walls and sandstone door jambs, the latter inscribed with titles and an inscription of Ramesses II (1279–1213).

Jaffa was conquered by the pharaoh Tuthmosis III in C15. It thenceforth became an important Egyptian stronghold and administrative centre, as attested in the mid C14 Amarna letters (see glossary), in the so-called Papyrus Anastasi I, dated to the reign of Ramesses II, and in a letter from Ugarit, found at Aphek, which refers to the city as the seat of an Egyptian official. In *OT* tradition it was allotted to the tribe of Dan (Joshua 19:46). *OT* sources also record its role as a port through which cedars from Lebanon were shipped for the construction of both the First and the Second Temples at Jerusalem (2 Chronicles 2:16, Ezra 3:7). In C8 Jaffa was apparently subject to the city of Ashkelon, until it was captured by the Assyrian king Sennacherib (according to the king's 'prism stele') in 701. In C6 it came under the control of the Persians, one of whose kings presented it, along with the city of Dor, to Eshmunazar, king of Sidon. During the Hellenistic period Jaffa was settled by Greeks. It was captured by the Seleucids in the Hasmonean period (c. 175–163), and fell to the Romans during Pompey's conquest of Palestine in 64.

In Greek mythological tradition, the sea off Jaffa was the setting for the story of Perseus and Andromeda.

Dessel (*OEANE* 3: 206–7).

Jawa (map 8) Early and Middle Bronze Age site in northeastern Jordan. Excavations were carried out in the 1970s by S. Helms for the British School of Archaeology in Jerusalem. The Early Bronze Age site consists of upper and lower settlements, both walled. The upper settlement had the more substantial fortifications, with access through them provided by a large, chambered gateway. Houses in the lower settlement were made of mudbrick on stone foundations, with mud and straw roofs on a timber framework. In the Middle Bronze Age, settlement took place within the fortifications of the Early Bronze Age upper area. The chief building of this period was a so-called citadel, consisting of a series of interconnected cells, and occupying the centre of the settlement. One of the main features of the site and its surrounding area is a complex water storage and distribution system, built in the Early Bronze Age and consisting of a network of canals, dams, and reservoirs. Ceramic ware found at Jawa in

Figure 55 Jaffa harbour-front.

both phases of its existence reflects cultural and commercial contacts with Syria and Palestine.

Betts (*OEANE* 3: 209–10).

Jaxartes r. (***Syr Darya***) (map 16) Central Asiatic river flowing northwestwards into the Aral Sea and forming part of the northeastern boundary of the Persian empire. In mid C6 Cyrus II, founder of the empire, established a series of fortified settlements along the river, including Cyropolis (Cyreschata), as part of his kingdom's frontier defence system.

Warmington and Spawforth (*OCD* 794).

Jebus A town in Canaan according to biblical tradition, equated on three occasions with Jerusalem (Joshua 15:8, 18:28, Judges 19:10), which is called a city of the Jebusites in Judges 19:11. A number of scholars have suggested that Jerusalem was in fact called Jebus before David's alleged conquest in C10. However, the name Jerusalem (Urusalim) occurs already in the mid C14 Amarna letters (see glossary). An alternative proposal locates Jebus near mod. Shaʿfat. In any case, Jerusalem appears to have been under Jebusite control in the pre-Davidic period, to judge from *OT* sources. There are numerous biblical references to Jebusites among other tribal groups (Amorites, Hittites, Perizzites, Canaanites, and Hivites) inhabiting the hill country of central Palestine (e.g. Exodus 3:8, 13:5, 23:23, 33:2). But neither Jebus nor Jebusites are otherwise attested in anc. sources.

Reid (*HCBD* 483–4).

Jemdet Nasr (map 17) Early Bronze Age settlement-mound in southern Mesopotamia, c. 26 km northeast of Kish, with occupation dating from M5 through to M3 (the Ubaid, Middle and Late Uruk, Jemdet Nasr, and Early Dynastic I periods). The site was excavated in 1926 and briefly in 1928 by a team led by S. Langdon, based at Kish. Excavations were resumed in 1988 by R. J. Matthews on behalf of the British School of Archaeology in Iraq, with subsequent seasons being conducted in 1989 and 1990. The name of the site has since been applied to the distinctive material culture assemblage which was first defined there, spanning the phase between the Late Uruk and Early Dynastic I periods (c. 3100–3000) in southern, central, and eastern Mesopotamia and corresponding to the Ninevite 5 phase in northern Mesopotamia (see under **Nineveh**). The Jemdet Nasr period is associated with distinctive types of polychrome painted pottery and seals, as well as archaic tablets of a kind also found in Level III at Uruk.

The site consists of three mounds, designated A, B, and C. The early excavations uncovered a substantial building measuring some 95 m × 40 m on the largest mound, B. However, its precise location and layout were never recorded with any satisfactory degree of accuracy. The excavations of this building recovered around 200 economic tablets of the Jemdet Nasr period (as subsequently defined); other, similar tablets deriving from illicit excavations have been thought to come from the site, but their provenance inevitably remains uncertain. On top of Mound A – a smaller mound to the southwest of Mound B – was a baked brick structure, possibly a fort of Parthian date. Beneath it, occupation of Middle Uruk date was attested. Surface finds of Ubaid pottery and artefacts were also recovered on Mound A. Mound C, which lay some distance to the east of Mound B, has not been investigated and appears to be unrelated, with surface sherds of Islamic date.

(H. D. Baker)
Matthews (1989; 1990; 2002).

Jemmeh, Tell (map 8) Settlement-mound in southern Palestine, 10 km south of Gaza. According to B. Mazar, it is to be identified with the town of Yurza, referred to twice in the mid C14 Amarna letters (see glossary) and also in New Kingdom Egypt topographical lists, and with Arsa, referred to in the inscriptions of the C7 Assyrian king Esarhaddon (see below). The site has a history of occupation beginning in the Chalcolithic period (M5–4), followed by abandonment during the Early Bronze and Middle Bronze I periods before settlement was resumed in Middle Bronze II–III. It continued thereafter until the early Hellenistic age.

Following earlier investigations in 1926 and 1927 by W. F. M. Petrie, the site was comprehensively excavated by G. Van Beek from 1972 to 1978, with subsequent 'problem-solving digs' in 1982, 1984, 1987, and 1990. Regular trade with Cyprus was a feature of the town's Middle Bronze Age phase. Its following Late Bronze Age phase was, according to Van Beek, an extraordinarily active period, as indicated by debris accumulated to a depth of 6 m. The most important architectural remains of this phase belong to a large C13 house, built on the western 'elite' side of the settlement. The house contained a public area with cobblestone floor and mud benches along the walls, and a domestic area with courtyard and ovens. An Iron Age Philistine settlement followed upon the Late Bronze Age phase. A casemate wall system, new buildings constructed on an Assyrian plan with vaulted mudbrick ceilings, and ceramic 'Assyrian Palace ware', all dated to C7, together with the obvious importance of the town in the Assyrian period, have provided circumstantial evidence for identifying Jemmeh with

Arsa in the texts of Esarhaddon. The town may have served as a military base for Assyrian troops. An enormous structure dated to C5–late C4 has been identified as a Persian fort. Twelve large circular storage buildings without house remains, dated to late C4–C3, have led the excavators to conclude that in the Hellenistic age, during the period of Ptolemaic rule, Jemmeh was converted into a vast grain storage depot, with most of the town's population relocated off the mound in the surrounding fields.

Van Beek (1984; *NEAEHL* 2: 667–74).

Jericho (*Tell es-Sultan*) (map 8) Settlement located in the Jordan valley, long identified with the 4 ha mound Tell es-Sultan 11 km northwest of the Dead Sea, c. 250 m below sea level. Its history of occupation extends from the Mesolithic (Epeopalaeolithic) period to the Iron Age (i.e. from c. 10,000 to 600), with numerous periods of abandonment in between; there is, for example, no evidence of settlement in the Chalcolithic period (M5–4). Well supplied by waters from a nearby spring called Elisha's Well or ʿAin es-Sultan (hence the site's mediaeval name Tell es-Sultan), it provided itself with a wide variety of crops and vegetables, and became famous for its gardens. Since mid M1 CE, the site's biblical associations have attracted a constant stream of travellers, many of them on religious pilgrimages. In *OT* tradition, Jericho was the first site west of the Jordan captured by the Israelites after they had crossed the river from the east and camped in the plains outside the city (Joshua 4:13). Under Joshua's command, the Israelites besieged the city for seven days, marching each day around its walls, blowing their trumpets, until on the seventh day the walls collapsed. The city and its inhabitants were destroyed, and Joshua placed a curse upon anyone attempting to rebuild it (Joshua 6).

The first excavations of the site were undertaken by C. Warren for the Palestine Exploration Fund in 1868. A second excavation was conducted from 1907 to 1909 and in 1911 for the Deutsche Orient-Gesellschaft by E. Sellin and C. Watzinger, who uncovered part of the Early Bronze Age city's walls, much of the Middle Bronze Age fortifications, and a number of the city's Iron Age domestic buildings. Further excavations were conducted from 1930 to 1936 by J. Garstang for the University of Liverpool and the British School of Archaeology in Jerusalem. These were partly intended to throw further light on questions concerning the dating and nature of the alleged Israelite conquest of the city. Although Garstang originally supported the *OT* tradition that the city had fallen to the Israelites, he later took the view that the city's destruction had occurred much earlier. The whole matter was revisited by K. M. Kenyon, who carried out new excavations on the site between 1952 and 1958 for the British School of Archaeology in Jerusalem, the Palestine Exploration Fund, and the British Academy, in collaboration with the American School of Oriental Research in Jerusalem (currently known as the Albright Institute) and the Royal Ontario Museum in Toronto. Kenyon's extensive excavations brought to light large areas of the city's Mesolithic and Neolithic phases, already revealed by Garstang, and contributed substantially to an overall understanding of the site's stratigraphy. As a result of Garstang's and Kenyon's excavations, it is clear that Jericho is one of the world's oldest settled communities. Already in 12,000 it was used as a campsite by hunters who erected a clay platform there, perhaps as the basis of a shrine. But there were numerous gaps in the site's history of occupation, thought to be due either to enemy destruction of the irrigation system, or to earthquake.

The Early Bronze Age phase of Jericho's existence began in late M4, when a new people arrived in the region. Their presence is reflected in the construction for the first time of rock-cut tombs (a practice which continued until much later times) and new pottery types. The settlement was protected by two parallel mudbrick walls, which enclosed a settlement of circular and oblong houses (the latter with curved ends), and later rectangular houses and mudbrick grain silos. It was in this period that the first artificial irrigation system was constructed, ensuring that the city's inhabitants enjoyed a constant and abundant food supply. None the less, for reasons unknown, the city was abandoned c. 2300. It was partially reoccupied from c. 2100 to 1950, in the transitional period between the Early and Middle Bronze Ages, before a Middle Bronze Age city was built, and substantially fortified. Much information about this level has come from the well-preserved tombs in its necropolis. The violent destruction of the city at the end of the Middle Bronze Age has been attributed either to earthquake or to enemy attack. Kenyon suggested that its destruction may have been due to the disturbance that followed the expulsion of the Hyksos (q.v.) from Egypt c. 1560. The site was then abandoned, and remained unoccupied for most of C15, before reoccupation, by 1400, in the Late Bronze Age.

Late Bronze Age Jericho (c. 1400–1325) has aroused the most interest and controversy of all the site's levels, because of its association with the attack and destruction by Joshua in *OT* tradition. Kenyon argued that there is no archaeological support for the tradition, since there is no evidence that Jericho had walls at this time. This has been disputed by several later scholars. But in any case, the destruction of the city in the last decades of C14 seems too early to associate it with the Israelites' arrival, though the following period of abandonment would not be inconsistent with biblical tradition.

There is a small amount of evidence for some reoccupation of Jericho in C11 or C10, during the Iron Age I phase. *OT* tradition ascribes its resettlement and fortification to Hiel the Bethelite, who lived in the reign of the C9 Omride king Ahab (1 Kings 16:34). But there was no major Iron Age settlement on the site until C7, a period in Jericho's history which has left quite extensive remains, including on the eastern slope of the mound a massive building with tripartite plan typical of a number of Iron Age II structures. Ceramic evidence indicates that this phase of Jericho's existence persisted until the Babylonian exile in 586. There is no trace of any further occupation after this, perhaps due partly to erosion. But settlement did continue from the Persian through the Byzantine periods on two nearby mounds.

Bartlett (1982), Bienkowski (1986), Kenyon (*NEAEHL* 2: 674–81), Holland (*OEANE* 3: 220–4).

Jerusalem (map 8) City in the land of Judah, southern Palestine, 56 km from the Mediterranean coast. Its name is generally thought to have been derived from that of the Canaanite deity Salem, known from C14 Ugaritic texts, and to mean 'Salem is its founder'. The site's history of occupation extends from a Chalcolithic settlement on the Ophel ridge (located to the south of the 'Old City's' eastern side and stretching between the Kidron and Tyropoeon valleys) through all succeeding ages until the present day. Its first written attestation is in the Middle Bronze Age Egyptian Execration texts (see glossary), where it appears as *Urushalimun*. The site has been excavated by a succession of archaeological teams from 1864 onwards, one of the more recent excavations being conducted by Y. Shiloh between 1978 and 1985 for the Hebrew University of Jerusalem and the City of David Society. Shiloh identified twenty-five occupational strata extending from the Chalcolithic to the mediaeval period. From an archaeological perspective, the city consists of three main sectors: the biblical City of David (on the hill of Ophel), located south of the Old City and the Temple Mount; the Old City, enclosed within C16 CE Ottoman walls; and the areas outside the walls, including the Mount of Olives.

Tombs and ceramic ware unearthed on the Ophel reflect occupation during the Early Bronze I and IV periods. However, it was not until the Middle Bronze II period (C18–17) that Jerusalem assumed the character of a city, when the settlement on the Ophel was fortified by a city wall. Excavations conducted by R. Reich, University of Haifa, in the 1990s have confirmed Jerusalem's status as a major city in the Middle Bronze Age. The city appears to have flourished also during the Late Bronze Age, when it is attested in a number of letters from the Egyptian mid C14 Amarna archive (see glossary), in the form *Urusalim* (**EA* 287, 289, 290). In this period it was the seat of a local king, appointed by the pharaoh, who received envoys from Egypt and sent gifts and tribute to his overlord. Although it was one of the lesser of the Syro-Palestinian states subject to Egypt, it became involved in the intrigues and power-plays of these states, and appears to have sought to expand its territories at the expense of its neighbours. One of the most notable material remains of the Late Bronze Age city is a monumental structure built on top of the southeastern hill in the City of David, and consisting of a series of terraces forming a large artificial mound. This is considered to be the work of Canaanite kings (though the ethnic composition of Jerusalem's population in this period is not altogether clear), who probably erected a citadel or palace on the podium thus created. In the period which *OT* tradition assigns to the reign of King David (C10), the podium supported an enormous stepped building, presumably the citadel of the City of David (referred to in 2 Samuel 5:7). It is the best-preserved structure of the Iron Age I city, whose material remains are otherwise very meagre.

According to *OT* sources, David's son and successor Solomon shifted the city's administrative centre north to the Temple Mount. No trace of this centre has been found because of the impossibility of excavation in the Temple Mount area. And no trace has been found of the most famous building of Solomon's period – the temple of Solomon, described in 1 Kings 6. It became the repository of the Ark of the Covenant (1 Kings 8) for an uncertain period of time – perhaps until the temple's destruction in 586 (see below), though this has been much debated (see Cline, 2007: 121–52). A description of Solomon's palace, constructed between the temple and the City of David, but also now completely lost, follows in 1 Kings 7. Two water systems are among the Iron Age city's most important material remains. Both involve the use of tunnels to bring water to the city from nearby springs. The first is conceivably of early Iron Age I date, and has been connected with the *OT* account of the entry of David's men into the city via a water shaft (2 Samuel 5:8). The second, dating to Iron Age II, has been associated with the late C8 Judaean king Hezekiah (though the evidence for the association is purely circumstantial), and thought to have been constructed in preparation for an attack on the city by the Assyrian king Sennacherib. The construction of a city wall in this period is also attributed to Hezekiah. He built it in response to the need to provide adequate defences for the city, at a time when its population had been expanded by refugees from the Assyrian conquests in Israel, and the city's limits had been extended by newly settled areas to its west. In 701 Sennacherib laid siege to Jerusalem (**CS* II: 302–3), blockading Hezekiah within it after allegedly conquering forty-six of his walled cities and surrounding towns. Jerusalem's new fortifications may have proved strong enough to withstand the Assyrian siege; contrary to the Assyrian record, the *OT* account of the conflict in 2 Kings 19:35 claims that the Assyrian army was defeated, and Sennacherib was forced to call off the siege and return to Nineveh.

According to 2 Kings 24:10–17, the Babylonian king Nebuchadnezzar II conquered Jerusalem (in 597), and deported to Babylon its king, Jehoiachin, along with 10,000 of its inhabitants, leaving behind only the poorest people of the land, and installing a puppet ruler Zedekiah on the kingdom's throne. But when eleven years later (586) Zedekiah rebelled against his overlord, Jerusalem was again attacked, and this time destroyed by the Babylonian forces; almost the entire population of Judah was removed from the land (2 Kings 24:20–25:21). Thus began the period of the Israelite 'exile', lasting almost fifty years. It came to an end in 539, when the Persian king Cyrus II conquered Babylon. In the following year, the Israelites living in exile were allowed to return to their homeland, and Cyrus issued a decree permitting them to rebuild the Temple in Jerusalem (Ezra 1:14, 6:2–5). The process of reconstructing Jerusalem thus began. The rebuilding of its walls is recorded in Nehemiah 3, and is generally dated to the reign of the Persian king Artaxerxes I (465–424), if this is the Artaxerxes referred to in Nehemiah 2:1. But the biblical account has yet to be confirmed by archaeological evidence. Almost nothing more is known of Jerusalem, from either written sources or the archaeological record, until the time of the Maccabaean rebellion against Seleucid rule in mid C2.

Biblical sources used in attempted reconstructions of Jerusalem's history begin with the city's alleged capture by Joab for his nephew David (2 Samuel 5:6–8, 1 Chronicles 11:4–6). *OT* tradition relates that the city was seized from its then occupants, the

Figure 56 Terrain between Jerusalem and Jericho.

Jebusites, and was in fact called Jebus at that time (but see **Jebus**). Seven years later, David transferred his royal capital from Hebron to Jerusalem. He also brought there the Ark of the Covenant, thus making Jerusalem the spiritual as well as the administrative and political centre of his kingdom. The name 'the City of David' came to be used of Jerusalem's citadel. *OT* sources report the massive building projects undertaken in the city by David's son and successor Solomon, and the hostility which Solomon's policies provoked, particularly among his northern subjects, who resented the centralization of power in Jerusalem. And all subjects alike resented the heavy burden of taxation made necessary by their king's grandiose building programme. The partitioning of the kingdom on Solomon's death saw a substantial reduction in the status of Jerusalem, which now became merely the capital of the tribal lands of Judah and Benjamin. *OT* accounts of the city's subsequent history are closely linked with the history of Israel and Judah as a whole. Biblical sources are complemented by Assyrian, Babylonian, and Persian sources contemporary with the events which they relate. The most notable of these events are the Assyrian and Babylonian conquests, the period of exile in Babylonia, and the repatriation of the Israelites to their homeland by the Persian king Cyrus II.

B. Mazar *et al.* (*NEAEHL* 2: 698–804), Bahat (1996), Bahat and Hurvitz (1996), Bahat (*OEANE* 3: 224–38), Geva (2000), Cline (2004).

Jezireh (Jezira, Jazira) Large grassland and semi-desert region located between the Euphrates and Tigris rivers, and extending through parts of northwestern Iraq, northeastern Syria, and southeastern Turkey. The name literally means 'island'. Watering by the Balih and Habur rivers makes the northern part of the region an agriculturally productive area.

Akkermans and Schwartz (2003: 5–6).

Jezreel, Tel (map 8) Settlement located in the eastern part of the Jezreel valley, overlooking a major route which passed from Egypt through Syria to Mesopotamia. There is evidence of occupation of the site from the Early Bronze Age through to the present day. Following earlier salvage operations by the Israel Dept of Antiquities in 1987 and 1988, the site was excavated from 1990 to 1996 as a joint enterprise by D. Ussishkin and J. Woodhead on behalf of their respective institutions – the Institute of Archaeology, Tel Aviv University, and the British School of Archaeology in Jerusalem. Pottery sherds dating to the Early, Middle, and Late Bronze Ages indicate the existence of a Canaanite settlement on the site during these periods. However, the most substantial remains are of Iron Age date. During this period, Jezreel reached its peak under the C9 Omride dynasty (see glossary) when, according to the excavators, the city became a royal centre of much importance in the kingdom of Israel. It has been suggested that Jezreel served as Israel's winter capital, complementing Samaria as the 'summer' capital. Its chief architectural feature is what the excavators describe as a 'royal enclosure', surrounded by a casemate wall, supported by a massive earthen rampart, with projecting towers at the corners. This fortress-settlement encompassed c. 6 ha. The excavators believe that the fortress was built by Omri (876–869) or his son and successor Ahab (869–850) (if we accept the dates traditionally assigned to these rulers) as a central military base for the royal Israelite army.

The Jezreel fortress is of major significance since it shows not only the expected close similarities with the architecture of Samaria, but also close similarities with monumental structures (gateways and public buildings) at Megiddo, Hazor, and Gezer, traditionally attributed to King Solomon. Since Jezreel is firmly anchored to the Omride dynasty, the supposedly Solomonic levels at these sites have had to be redated from C10 to C9, a process that has cast serious doubt upon the historical reality of an Israelite 'united monarchy', at least in C10 (see under **Israel**). Following the destruction of the fortress, perhaps at the end of the Omride dynasty, settlement continued on the site through the succeeding ages, as illustrated by remains from the Persian, Hellenistic, and Roman periods, and evidence of a densely populated city on the site in the Byzantine era. These post-Iron Age occupations have destroyed almost all trace of the buildings within the Iron Age fortress.

Jezreel appears in a number of *OT* sources – for example, in the story of Naboth who owned a vineyard in Jezreel close to the palace of Ahab (1 Kings 21). It is not attested in extra-biblical written sources.

Williamson (1991; 1996), Ussishkin and Woodhead (1994), Ussishkin (*OEANE* 3: 246–7), Negev and Gibson (2001: 270).

Jokneam see **Yokneam**.

Judah Iron Age kingdom in southern Palestine. See under **Israel**.

Judeideh, Tell el- (map 8) 2.5 ha hill settlement located in the Shephelah, southern Palestine, perhaps to be identified with biblical Moreshet-Gath (Micah 1:14), home of the prophet Micah. It was partly excavated by F. J. Bliss and R. A. S. Macalister in 1899–1900, with sponsorship provided by the Palestine Exploration Fund. Most of the material remains date to the Hellenistic and Roman periods, when the settlement, oval in shape, was enclosed by a 228 m long wall. The meagre evidence brought to light from earlier periods indicates settlement dating back to the Bronze Age, followed, perhaps, by a period of abandonment, with subsequent occupation during the Iron Age, when the site was apparently unfortified.

Broshi (*NEAEHL* 3: 837–8).

K

Kabnak (Kabinak) Late Bronze and Iron Age city in Susiana (region of mod. Khuzestan) in southwestern Iran. It is first attested as the seat of an Elamite governor called Athibu, subordinate of the C14 Elamite king Tepti-ahar, in seal impressions of Athibu discovered in the Late Bronze Age Elamite city now known as Haft Tepe (q.v.). Kabnak may therefore be the city's anc. name. Subsequently, it appears (in the form Kabinak) in the record of the Assyrian king Ashurbanipal's conquest of Susa and other cities in 646.

D. T. Potts (1999: 201–5).

Kabri, Tel (map 8) Settlement-mound covering, at its greatest extent, an area of c. 32 ha, and located in northern Palestine in the western Galilee region, 5 km north-east of mod. Nahariyah. Its history of occupation extends from the late Neolithic era through the Chalcolithic, Bronze, and Iron Ages, and the Persian, Hellenistic, and Roman periods. The site was discovered in the 1950s, and an initial survey was carried out by M. Prausnitz for the Israel Dept of Antiquities in 1957 and 1958. Subsequently, excavations were conducted from 1986 to 1993 by a team from the Institute of Archaeology, Tel Aviv University, under the direction of A. Kempinski. Kempinski describes Tel Kabri as 'a complex of archaeological sites clustered around the mound. . . . The lower city of the Middle Bronze Age II period extended north of the mound and the Neolithic and Early Chalcolithic settlements were located east of it.' The Early Bronze Age (EBA 1A–B) phase featured large oval houses with central pillars, and a number of graves. However, Kabri reached the peak of its development in the Middle Bronze Age, when it achieved its maximum size, expanding from the mound to the settlement of a lower city. Two sets of fortifications were built, the first in the Middle Bronze IIA phase (it is unclear whether the site was unoccupied in Middle Bronze Age I), and the second, on a massive scale, in the Middle Bronze IIB phase. During this phase, an impressive palace complex was built, the floor of whose main chamber, designated as a 'ceremonial hall', was plastered and decorated with an orange and yellow checkerboard pattern. A floral design was featured on the yellow plaster. The floral motifs bear a resemblance to the painted decoration of the contemporary Minoan civilization of Crete, and the fresco fragments have been compared with the frescos of Thera/Santorini. Recent excavations undertaken by A. Yasur-Landau and E. H. Cline, on behalf of the University of California at Santa Cruz and the George Washington University in Washington DC respectively, have determined that the palace complex was in fact twice as big as the previous excavators had thought. (The preliminary publication of Yasur-Landau's and Cline's work at Kabri is posted at http://digkabri.wordpress.com).

Despite its formidable defences, the city was destroyed at the end of its Middle Bronze IIB phase, c. 1600. The site appears to have been abandoned at the end of the Middle Bronze Age, but reoccupied in the Iron Age when Kempinski believes the city

Figure 57 Tel Kabri.

of Rehob, attested in Joshua 19:28, was located there. The Iron Age settlement was confined to the mound, and was no more than 2 ha in extent. It was destroyed, presumably by either the Assyrians or the Babylonians, at the end of its Iron Age phase, and rebuilt on a larger scale in the Persian period (C6–4). Occupation continued through the Hellenistic period. The Roman settlement, called Kabrita, was relocated on the site later occupied by the village Tel Kabri.

(in consultation with E. H. Cline)

Kempinski (*NEAEHL* 3: 839–41; 2002), Cline and Yasur-Landau (2007).

Kabsitu Iron Age city in northern Babylonia, located on the middle Euphrates r., near the cities of Rapiqu(m) and Rahimmu. The Assyrian king Tukulti-Ninurta II encamped his forces there during his last recorded campaign (885), which took him through the middle Tigris and Euphrates regions (**RIMA* 2: 174).

Kadesh see Qadesh.

Kadesh-Barnea see Qadesh-Barnea.

Kadmuhu (Katmuhu) (map 13) Country attested in M2 and M1 Assyrian texts, located in northern Mesopotamia in the eastern Kashiyari mountain region (mod. Tur ʿAbdin), west of the upper Tigris r. It is first mentioned in the reign of the Assyrian king Adad-nirari I (1307–1275) who reports the conquest of it, along with its allies the Ahlamu, Sutu, and Iuru, by his father and predecessor Arik-den-ili (1319–1308) (**RIMA* 1: 132). The country may have been lost to the Assyrians during Adad-nirari's own reign (if one can so judge from the lack of any reference to it among Adad-nirari's exploits), and was perhaps regained by his son and successor Shalmaneser I (1274–1245). But Kadmuhu had subsequently taken to plundering Assyrian territory and carrying off its inhabitants until Shalmaneser's successor, Tukulti-Ninurta I (1244–1208), conducted a campaign against it early in his reign, capturing five of its strongholds and transporting the spoils of battle and captives back to Assyria (**RIMA* 1: 235). In this same period, he conducted campaigns against a number of other small states in the region, over all of which he imposed or restored Assyrian control. They included Paphu, Bushu, Mummu, Amadanu, Nihanu, Alaya, Tepurzu, and Purukuzzu (Purulumzu) (**RIMA* 1: 236, 250 etc.).

There were further expeditions against Kadmuhu by later Assyrian kings. Most notable among these was the campaign conducted by Tiglath-pileser I in his accession year (1115). It was prompted by the alleged invasion and capture of Kadmuhu by a force, under the command of five kings, of 20,000 Mushki people. These people had hitherto occupied for some fifty years the lands of Alzu and Purulumzu as tributaries of the Assyrian crown (**RIMA* 2: 14–15). Tiglath-pileser responded to their expansion into Kadmuhu by leading an expedition into the country via the Kashiyari range. He defeated the Mushki in a pitched battle, in which more than two-thirds of their numbers were massacred. The 6,000 survivors thenceforth acknowledged the Assyrian king as their overlord. (For more on the Mushki, see under **Phrygia**.) The remaining inhabitants of Kadmuhu, who had fled eastwards over the Tigris, were pursued and defeated by Tiglath-pileser; Kadmuhu was thus restored to Assyrian control. It is apparent from the above account that Kadmuhu had continued to be hostile to Assyrian rule, and may well have welcomed the Mushki force as liberators from it. Tiglath-pileser refers to Kadmuhu as rebellious and refusing to pay tribute. His wholesale conquest, plunder, and destruction of the land and its cities indicate that his Kadmuhu campaign was a punitive one directed as much against its own people as against the Mushki occupying force. Nevertheless, the country continued to be rebellious, and within a year or so of his conquest Tiglath-pileser was obliged to conduct a further campaign against it (**RIMA* 2: 17). On this occasion he established his control more firmly over the country, attaching it as frontier territory to his kingdom.

However, Kadmuhu's relations with Assyria remained volatile. In C10, Ashur-dan II (934–912) reports its conquest and the capture of its king, Kundibhale, who was taken back to the city of Arbela and flayed alive (**RIMA* 2: 134). But in the reign of Ashurnasirpal II (883–859), Kadmuhu appears to have had had more peaceful relations with Assyria, or at least to have avoided conflict with it. On two or more occasions when Ashurnasirpal II's eastern campaigns took him through its territory (883 and 879), Kadmuhu apparently offered no resistance, escaping devastation by freely offering up tribute (**RIMA* 2: 198, 208). On the second of these occasions, Ashurnasirpal consecrated a palace in Til-uli, one of the cities of Kadmuhu. In 879 Kadmuhu was annexed, and two provinces, Shahuppa and Tille, were formed out of it (Radner, *RlA* 11: 53).

Postgate (*RlA* 5: 487–8).

Kahat (map 10) Middle and Late Bronze and Iron Age city in the Ida-maras region of northern Mesopotamia. It is perhaps to be identified with the site of Tell Barri on the Jaghjagh r. (Postgate, *RlA* 5: 287), though some scholars have expressed a preference for Tell Hamidiya. Kahat is attested in a number of letters from the Mari archive (*LKM* 614, refs) when Mari's throne was occupied by the Mariote king Zimri-Lim (1774–1762), who had captured the city early in his reign. It was a royal city, whose known kings in Zimri-Lim's reign were Akin-Amar, Kapiya, and Attaya. Kapiya was one of seventeen northern Mesopotamian rulers who received warning from Zimri-Lim of an imminent invasion of the region by the forces of Ibal-pi-El II, king of Eshnunna.

Some years later, after the fall of Mari in 1761, another king of Kahat, Yamsi-Hadnu, concluded a treaty with Till-Abnu, ruler of the land of Apum (whose capital was at Shubat-Enlil/Shehna). Kahat must later have been incorporated into the Mitannian empire, and after the Hittite conquest of Mitanni in the third quarter of C14, remained attached to the kingdom of Hanigalbat (the final remnant of Mitanni). Hanigalbat subsequently came under Assyrian control, and when the Hanigalbatean king Wasashatta rebelled against Assyrian sovereignty, Kahat was among the cities conquered by the Assyrian king Adad-nirari I (1307–1275) in the course of crushing the rebellion (**RIMA* 1: 136). It is later attested by the Assyrian king Tukulti-Ninurta II, who encamped his forces at Kahat, one night's march south of Nisibin, during his last recorded campaign (885) (**RIMA* 2: 177). Kahat joined a widespread rebellion against the Assyrian king Shalmaneser III (858–824), initiated by the king's son Ashur-da'in-apla. The rebellion continued into the early regnal years of Shalmaneser's son and successor Shamshi-Adad V before it was finally crushed (**RIMA* 3: 183).

Kailetu Iron Age city in the middle Euphrates region, between Harradu to the south and Hindanu to the north. The Assyrian king Tukulti-Ninurta II encamped his forces there during his progress up the Euphrates on his last recorded campaign (885) (**RIMA* 2: 175).

Kakkulatum Middle Bronze Age city located in central Mesopotamia on the banks of the Tigris. A river crossing was established there. In late C19 the city was captured by the Eshnunnite king Naram-Sin during a campaign which took him into north-western Mesopotamia. In the reign of the Mariote king Zimri-Lim (1774–1762), the Elamites were active in the region, on one occasion capturing the city and demolishing its walls as they retreated from Hiritum (**LKM* 459, 479, 511).

Röllig (*RlA* 5: 288–9), *Mesop.* 131.

Kakmum (Kakme?) Country and city located east of the Tigris r. in the northwestern Zagros mountains, attested in texts dating to the Early and Middle Bronze Age and Iron Age. First mentioned in the period of the Ur III dynasty (C21), it subsequently appears in correspondence from the Middle Bronze Age Mari and Shemshara archives (for the latter, see Eidem and Laessøe, 2001: 165, refs). One of the letters from Mari, dating to the reign of Zimri-Lim (1774–1762), refers to the defeat of a king of Qabra called Ardigandi by troops from Kakmum, whose king, Gurgurrum, attacked and plundered Qabra's territory (**LKM* 387). Kakme is attested in late C8, when it became involved in conflict with the Assyrian king Sargon II. However, Fuchs has suggested

that at this time Kakme was simply a term for 'Urartu' in the Mannaean language (*Sargon II* 440–1).
Röllig (*RlA* 5: 289).

Kalaly Gyr Large M1 Central Asiatic fortress settlement, 1000 m × 700 m, located in the country of Chorasmia, which lay south of the Aral Sea. A palace with hypostyle hall, reflecting strong Persian influence, has been excavated there (see Francfort, 1988: 181, fig 6). The settlement, dating to the end of the so-called Archaic Period (C6–4), is thought to have been the residence of a Persian official, possibly a satrap.

Kalasma One of the Late Bronze Age Hittite lands located on or near the Hittite frontier in northern Anatolia. In early C14, the Hittite king Arnuwanda I drew up pacts with his military commanders stationed in these lands, binding them by oath to maintain the security of the territories assigned to them (*von Schuler, 1956: 229). Subsequently, Kalasma appears in a prayer of the Hittite king Mursili II (1321–1295) among the countries which rebelled against Hittite rule during his reign while the Hittite kingdom was being ravaged by plague (*Singer, 2002: 52–3). According to Mursili's report of this (or possibly a later) rebellion in his Annals, Kalasma appears to have been subdued by the Hittite commander Nuwanza (**AM* 188–9). But rebellion broke out afresh several years later when a man of Kalasma called Aparru attacked the nearby Hittite state Sappa. Though Aparru was defeated and fled for his life, a further campaign the following year, by the Hittite commander Hutupiyanza, was needed to restore Kalasma fully to Hittite control.

Kalavasos-Ayios Dhimitrios (map 14) Late Bronze Age town, covering 11.5 ha, near the southern coast of Cyprus, between Limassol and Larnaca. Occupation of the area extends back to the Neolithic period (c. 4500), and there was significant settlement there during early M2 as well, to judge from sixty-one Middle Bronze Age tombs excavated in the mod. village. However, Ayios Dhimitrios reached the peak of its development in C13, in the Late Cypriot period, when it was almost certainly a centre for copper production and copper trading activities. Though much of the central part of the site has been destroyed by mod. highway construction, excavations conducted by A. South and I. A. Todd at its northern end uncovered an administrative complex built around a central courtyard. A particular feature of the complex, which may have been two storeys high, is a rectangular hall, whose roof was supported by a central row of stone pillars. The hall served primarily as a storage magazine for olive oil, as attested by fifty large pithoi with a total capacity estimated at c. 33,500 litres. The magazine may have been used for other commodities as well. The building's likely function as an administrative centre of the settlement, and perhaps of the region in which the settlement was located, may be reflected in the discovery, within and near the building, of a number of clay cylinders inscribed with symbols in the Cypro-Minoan script. Rock-cut chamber tombs were also found within the area of the settlement. The most important of the tombs, dated to c. 1375, may provide some indication of the wealth of the settlement, if one can so judge from the gold jewellery and other valuable grave goods which accompanied the deceased – in this case, three women, a child, and three infants. Much of the town's wealth probably came from its copper and olive oil industries. The site was abandoned at the end of the C13 and never resettled.

Figure 58 Kalavasos.

South (1992), Todd and South (*OEANE* 3: 262–5).

Kalhu see *Nimrud*.

Kalzu see Kilizu.

Kaman-Kalehöyük Predominantly Middle and Late Bronze Age urban settlement located in the Cappadocian region of eastern Anatolia between mod. Boğazkale (Boghazköy) and Kayseri. The site is currently being excavated by a Japanese team under the direction of S. Omura. To judge from both its architectural remains and the numerous seals and seal impressions found in them, Kaman-Kalehöyük appears to have been an important commercial and administrative centre of the Assyrian trading network during the Assyrian Colony period in eastern Anatolia (C20–18), and probably continued to be a settlement of some significance during the Hittite Old Kingdom (C17–15). Five enormous grain silos located around a building with massive stone walls have been dated to the latter period. They were perhaps part of the network of grain silos which extended through the territories controlled by the Hittites in the reign of Telipinu (1525–1500). By the Hittite New Kingdom (C14–early C12), the settlement appears to have lost much of its former importance, judging from the sparse material remains of this period. There is, however, evidence of later occupation during M1, including an Iron Age Phrygian residential area and traces of a Hellenistic settlement.

Omura (2005), Yıldırım and Gates (2007: 295).

Kamid el-Loz Settlement-mound located in the southern Lebanese Biqaʿ valley at the junction of two main roads: one from the upper Jordan valley into Syria, and another leading eastwards from the central Mediterranean coast (*OEANE* 5: 422, map). Its history of occupation extends, with gaps, from the Early Neolithic through the Roman period. No Chalcolithic remains have yet been found, and very little survives of the Early Bronze Age settlement, or of the Persian, Hellenistic, and Roman occupation levels, apart from their cemeteries. The site was excavated jointly, from 1963 to 1965, by teams from the Universities of Johana Gutenberg of Mainz, and Saarbrucken, under their respective directors A. Kuschke and R. Hachmann, and by the University of Saarbrucken alone between 1964 and 1981. During the Middle Bronze Age an important fortified urban centre occupied the site. Temples and a palace have been identified in this level, though they lie beneath a Late Bronze Age temple and palace and have not been excavated. The Late Bronze Age temple had a double court, the western one of which was paved with mudbrick blocks and had three rectangular plaster-lined basins, considered to have been used for sacrificial purposes. Both the temple and the palace located to its south were destroyed and rebuilt several times.

Kamid el-Loz has been identified with the city of Kumidi (Kumidu) attested in Late Bronze Age Egyptian sources. It was the seat of the resident commissioner of the Egyptian province Upi, as indicated in a number of letters from the mid C14 Amarna archive (see glossary), including one written to the pharaoh Akhenaten by its local ruler, Arashsha (**EA* 198). The city is probably also to be identified with the town called 'Ramesses the Settlement which is in the Valley of the Cedar', which lay on Ramesses II's campaign route to Qadesh in 1274 (*Gardiner, 1960: 8). The city was destroyed in late C12, and after a period of abandonment was occupied by a succession of Iron Age villages, with perhaps an Aramaean population.

Hachmann (*RlA* 6: 330–4, s.v. Kumidi), Badre (*OEANE* 3: 265–6).

Kammama Late Bronze Age Hittite city in northern Anatolia, listed in a Hittite prayer among the cities sacked by the Kaskans in late C15 (*Singer, 2002: 42), and thenceforth lying in Kaskan-occupied territory. While under Kaskan occupation, the city was destroyed by the Hittite king Suppiluliuma I (1350–1322) during a Hittite campaign in the region following his destruction of the Mitannian empire (**DS* 108). But it probably remained within Kaskan-controlled territory until early C13, when the Hittite prince Hattusili (later King Hattusili III) restored the region where it lay to Hittite control, and repopulated it with Hittite subjects.

Kammanu Iron Age country in eastern Anatolia, perhaps to be located in the plain of mod. Elbistan, and probably constituting the northern part of the kingdom of Melid/Malatya (see ***Arslantepe***). The name Kammanu is attested in the records of the Assyrian king Sargon II (721–705). The city of Til-garimmu (successor of Late Bronze Age Tegarama) appears to have belonged within its territory. After his occupation and conquest of Melid in 712, Sargon partitioned Kammanu off from the city of Melid and made it into a separate province under an Assyrian-appointed governor (**ARAB* II: 11–12, 30–1). He allocated the city of Melid to Mutallu, ruler of the kingdom of Kummuh. Kammanu was used as a place of resettlement for deportees from countries conquered by the Assyrians. The region appears to have regained its independence from Assyrian rule on the death of Sargon. (See also **Til-garimmu**.)

CHLI 1: 284, 285 with n. 45.

Kanesh (Nesa, *Kültepe*) (map 2) Settlement comprising a 20 m high mound (c. 550 m in diameter) and a lower city, located 21 km northeast of mod. Kayseri at the junction of several important routes connecting Mesopotamia and Syria with eastern Anatolia. The site's history of occupation on the mound, consisting of eighteen levels, extends from the Early Bronze Age through the Hellenistic and Roman periods. The history of the lower city is confined to the Middle Bronze Age, when Kanesh was the Anatolian headquarters of the Assyrian Colony trading network (see glossary). Excavation of the site began in 1948, under the direction of T. Özgüç on behalf of the Turkish Historical Foundation and the General Directorate of Monuments and Museums, and continued under Özgüç's direction until 2005. Mound and lower city were excavated simultaneously.

There are four major occupation levels at Kanesh. The first two (IV and III) belong to the Early Bronze Age. Level III was destroyed by fire in Early Bronze III. The Middle Bronze Age was the period of the Assyrian Colonies, represented archaeologically by two levels, II and Ib. During this period the mound was the site of an Anatolian settlement, capital of the kingdom of Kanesh, one of four known central-eastern Anatolian kingdoms of the Middle Bronze Age. (The other three were Hatti, Burushattum, and Wahsusana.) The palace of the Anatolian ruler was constructed on the top of the mound. At the mound's base, on its northern and northeastern sides, lay the Assyrian commercial centre, Karum Kanesh. It was not inhabited exclusively by Assyrian traders, but also included many Anatolians among its inhabitants. During the colony period, the city was protected by two concentric fortification systems.

Level II of the *karum*, or commercial centre (which was also protected by a fortification wall), lasted some sixty to seventy years, from relatively late in the reign of the Assyrian king Erishum I (1974–1935) until the end of the reign of Puzur-Ashur II (1880–1873). It ended in destruction by fire. The site was left unoccupied for a period of perhaps thirty years before resettlement took place in the Ib phase – the last phase of the merchant colonies. It is still not certain whether the settlement on the mound suffered destruction at the same time as the *karum*. Quite possibly it remained intact, since a number of the tablets found in the palace at Kanesh are to be ascribed to the intermediate period between levels II and Ib. Level Ib had a flourishing existence before it too was destroyed by fire. Roughly speaking, it extended from late C19 to about mid C18. In contrast to level II, from which more than 25,000 tablets have been unearthed, documentary evidence from Ib is sparse. This level has yielded no more than 250 tablets.

The great majority of the tablets are letters exchanged between merchants in the colonies and business associates and family members in Assyria involved in the trading operations at their home end. The letters throw much light on the nature of the goods imported into Anatolia – primarily tin and high-quality textiles – the mechanics of transportation and the personnel involved, the tolls and taxes to be paid, the dealings and contracts with the local Anatolian authorities, and the hazards and risks of the trading ventures. Of the twenty-one Assyrian trading colonies attested in the texts, Kanesh is only one of three to be located. The other two are Hattus (later the Hittite capital Hattusa) and the site now called Alişar (probably anc. Ankuwa). Small numbers of Assyrian merchant-tablets have come from both these sites.

A few of the letters also provide important information about political conditions in eastern Anatolia during the colony period. Above all, they reflect growing instability in the region as disputes broke out between the major kingdoms, sometimes sparked off by their subject towns in the border areas. One of these disputes led to hostilities between Nesa's successive kings, Inar and Warsama, and a man called Anum-hirbi, ruler of the large and wealthy kingdom of Mama (*Balkan, 1957). The best-known text originating from the colony period is the so-called Anitta inscription, which survives in three fragmentary copies from the Hittite period (**CS* I: 182–4, **Chav.* 216–19). It recounts the exploits of a king called Anitta whose father, Pithana, came from the city of Kussara lying to the southeast, and established Nesa as his capital. A dagger discovered in 1954 in the debris of a large building on the mound is inscribed with the words '(the property of) the palace of Anitta, the King' (T. Özgüç, 1956). The building was probably the residence of Anitta and his father. Nesa was Anitta's base for a series of campaigns which he launched against the other major kingdoms and cities located north and south of the (Classical) Halys r. (mod. Kızıl Irmak). His success in the campaigns resulted in the establishment of the first Anatolian empire, with Nesa as its centre. These events date to the Ib period of Kanesh/Nesa. Shortly afterwards, the fragile power structure built up by Anitta collapsed, and the Assyrian merchants, always apprehensive about trading in areas where conditions were unsettled, withdrew from Anatolia, bringing the Assyrian Colony period to an end (mid C18).

Towards the end of M2, in the early Iron Age, the city on the mound became the centre of one of the kingdoms of the land of Tabal, which extended southwards from the southern curve of the Halys r. into the region called the Lower Land in Hittite texts. This city was destroyed by the Assyrians toward the end of C8. There is evidence of reoccupation of the site in the Hellenistic and Roman periods.

Kanesh figures in a well-known Hittite legendary text, which tells the story of a queen of the city and her sixty offspring (**CS* 1: 181; see under Zalpa).

Veenhof/Orthmann/Porada (*RlA* 5: 369–89), T. Özgüç (1986; *OEANE* 3: 266–8), *Michel (2001).

Kapishakanish M1 city in the Central Asian country of Arachosia, mod. Afghanistan. It was among the eastern lands incorporated into the Persian empire by Cyrus II, probably some time after his conquest of Babylon in 539. In 521 Kapishakanish was the site of a battle fought between the Arachosian satrap Vivana, who supported the new Persian king Darius I, and a rebel army dispatched to Arachosia by the pretender to the Persian throne, Vahyazdata (who falsely claimed that he was Bardiya, brother of Cyrus' successor Cambyses) (**DB* 45). The battle was the most decisive of a number of engagements between the Arachosians and the rebel forces. (Other engagements were fought at Arshada in Arachosia and Ganduvata in neighbouring Sattagydia.) The rebels were soundly defeated, and their commander was captured and executed. Kapishakanish's location remains uncertain. Identifications have been proposed with Kandahar, the city called Capisa in Classical sources, and Qayqān in Baluchistan.

Kaprabu M1 fortified city belonging to the middle Euphrates Aramaean state Bit-Adini. Probably located near Bit-Adini's eastern frontier, it was one of its largest and most important cities. The Assyrian king Ashurnasirpal II besieged, captured, and destroyed the city after it refused to surrender to him, during his campaign in Bit-Adini c. 876. Ashurnasirpal claims to have carried off or slaughtered large numbers of its population, deporting 2,500 of its troops for resettlement in the Assyrian city of Kalhu (Calah) (**RIMA* 2: 216, 290).

Lipiński (2000: 188–9).

Karabel (maps 2, 3) Site of Late Bronze Age relief and inscribed monument in western Anatolia, located 28 km west of mod. Izmir, in a pass through the Tmolus mountain range. Of the original four reliefs, designated as Karabel A, B, and C1–2, only Karabel A now survives. It depicts a male human figure armed with bow and spear, and sword with crescent-shaped pommel. On his head is a tall peaked cap. A weathered inscription in Luwian hieroglyphs provides information about him. Herodotus, who visited the monument in C5, describes it (2.106) and provides an alleged translation of the inscription which, he declares, is written in the sacred script of Egypt: 'With my own shoulders I won this land.' He identifies the conqueror as 'Sesostris, king of Egypt'. But his information is entirely spurious. A recent re-examination of the inscription by J. D. Hawkins has enabled the figure adjacent to it to be identified as Tarkasnawa, king of the Arzawan land called Mira. This man had probably collaborated closely with the Hittite king Tudhaliya IV in reasserting Hittite authority in western Anatolia in the final decades of C13. The monument may mark the boundary between the kingdom of Mira and another Arzawan kingdom called Seha River Land, which lay to the north of Mira.

*Hawkins (1998b).

Karadağ see under ***Kızıldağ***.

Karagündüz (map 20) Settlement-mound and perhaps unrelated necropolis in eastern Anatolia, located 40 km northeast of Van city. The settlement's history of occupation extends from M3 to M1. When the rising waters of Lake Erçek threatened the mound and the necropolis which lay 1.5 km to its west, salvage excavations were commenced on the latter in 1992 and the former in 1994. The excavations were undertaken by a team from the Van Museum in collaboration with the Centre for Historical and Archaeological Researches in Van, Faculty of Letters, Istanbul University.

The necropolis, dating to the early Iron Age, contained a number of rectangular tomb-chambers for multiple burials, with between twenty to eighty burials in each chamber. Gifts of forged iron ornaments and ceremonial weapons were deposited in each tomb, along with food and drink offerings. As the tomb-chambers filled up, old interments were pushed aside to make way for new. The necropolis provides important information about the culture of the early Iron Age in eastern Anatolia, and demonstrates, according to the excavators, a cultural unity in the area north of Erçek Lake and Van Lake before the Urartian kingdom. The architecture of the tombs, the burial customs, the metal technology represented by the tomb-goods, and the ceramic ware all indicate close links between the culture which they reflect and that of the succeeding Urartian period.

Investigations of the mound revealed seven layers of settlement between M3 and M1. Level VII dates to M3. This is the thickest level. The excavators noted that of a total thickness of 8–9 m, VII on its own accounts for 6–7 m. The remains of a mudbrick structure of this period indicate that access to the building was via the roof. Only meagre remains survive from level VI, dating to the Middle–Late Bronze period. Level V represents the early Iron Age pre-Urartian period of settlement, whose artefacts show contemporaneity with the necropolis. Level IV is divided into several phases, of which IVB is contemporary with the kingdom of Urartu. Strong Urartian influence in this level is indicated by a building complex on the north side of the mound comparable, according to the excavators, with the classic covered courtyards of the Urartian civilization. The succeeding IVC phase postdates the collapse of the Urartian kingdom in the second half of C7, and is seen as reflecting significant changes throughout the Lake Van area leading to major overall decline. Level III, shown to be contemporaneous with level IIIa of Hasanlu in northwestern Iran, dates to the Persian period (C6–4). Levels II and I are of mediaeval date. Level I indicates use of the top of the mound as a cemetery.

Sevin and Özfırat (2001b).

Karahöyük (1) (map 2) Middle Bronze Age settlement-mound (with evidence of earlier occupation) in southern Anatolia near mod. Konya, covering an area of c. 600 m × 450 m. The site was excavated by S. Alp for the University of Ankara from 1953 onwards. Residential quarters and a number of large buildings, including one identified as a palace, have been unearthed. The settlement was fortified by a casemate wall. Seals and seal impressions were also found. The latter sometimes appeared on loom-weights, which may indicate that textile manufacture provided one of the sources of the city's income. Burials of both inhumation and cremation types were discovered. Unfortunately, there are no inscriptions to indicate the city's original name. However, it is now commonly identified with Purushattum (Hittite Purushanda) which is attested as the seat of a major kingdom in Middle Bronze Age texts of the Assyrian Colony period (C20–18). In the past, Purushattum had been identified with mod. Acem Höyük on the southern shore of the Salt Lake.

Alp (1972) (in Turkish); reports by Mellink in *AJA* 59, 1995, and subsequent vols; Burney (2004: 145–6).

Karahöyük (2) (map 2) Late Bronze and Iron Age settlement in south-central Anatolia near mod. Elbistan, excavated by T. and N. Özgüç in 1947. The city which it represents must have belonged to the Hittite kingdom prior to the kingdom's collapse in early C12. Subsequently it may have become part of the kingdom of Melid (Malatya). A stele found on the site, inscribed with a Luwian hieroglyphic text, has been dated to the later years of C12 (**CHLI* I: 288), and thus to the early decades of the Iron Age. Set up by a man called Armanani, the inscription records a visit to the city by a Great King, Ir-Teshub, who found it empty on his arrival. There is no indication in the inscription of the city's anc. name. The stele is now housed in the Museum of Anatolian Civilizations in Ankara.

T. Özgüç and N. Özgüç (1949), Burney (2004: 145).

Karahöyük (3) Late Bronze and Iron Age settlement located near mod. Ereğli (map 18) in southern Anatolia. It was probably the chief city of the country called Hupisna (q.v.) in Late Bronze and Iron Age texts, located in the region of the Hittite Lower Land (Classical Tyanitis).

CHLI I: 425.

Kar(a)kisa Late Bronze Age country in western Anatolia, mentioned several times in Hittite texts alongside the country of Masa. Like Masa, Karkisa was governed by a council of elders rather than a king, and remained independent of Hittite authority, sometimes collaborating with the Hittites, sometimes in conflict with them. It first appears as a member of the anti-Hittite Assuwan Confederacy (see **Assuwa**) defeated by the Hittite king Tudhaliya I/II early in C14 (*Bryce, 2005: 124–5). In late C14

Manapa-Tarhunda, the future king of the Arzawan state Seha River Land, sought refuge in Karkisa after a dispute with his brothers. The Hittite king Mursili II called upon the people of Karkisa to protect him – which they did, receiving a reward from Mursili in acknowledgement of their services (**AM* 68–71). In the battle of Qadesh, fought between the Hittite king Muwattalli II and the pharaoh Ramesses II in 1274, a contingent from Karkisa joined the Hittite side (*Gardiner, 1960: 8), probably in a mercenary capacity. There may be an etymological link between the names Karkisa and Caria. The latter was the name of a region in southwestern Anatolia in M1 BCE–M1 CE.

Karalla M1 region located on the western slopes of the Zagros mountains, between the headwaters of the Lesser Zab and Diyala rivers. At the time of Sargon II's accession to the Assyrian throne in 721, it was one of a number of countries lying within the land of Mannaea, which were allegedly still subject to Assyrian overlordship. However, under its ruler Ashur-le'u, it was induced by the Mannaean king Ullusunu to join a pro-Urartian alliance which engaged in conflict with the states that remained loyal to Assyria (**ARAB* II: 5). (One of the letters in Sargon's correspondence refers to a gift of five horses presented to Ashur-le'u by Ullusunu; **SAA* V: 155–6, no. 218). In 716, Sargon crushed the alliance, took Ashur-le'u back to Assyria in chains, and added Karalla to the neighbouring province of Lullumu which had maintained its allegiance to Assyria. But shortly afterwards Karalla rebelled once more, expelling its Assyrian-appointed officials and establishing its independence under Ashur-le'u's brother Amitashi. The uprising was crushed by Assyrian forces, and Karalla was now organized as a separate province. But it continued to defy Assyrian authority, and the Assyrians may have found it necessary to conduct further campaigns of pacification in the region – though we have no records of these.

Röllig (*RlA* 5: 405), Grayson (1991b: 93–4, 97).

Karana (probably = ***Tell er-Rimah***) (map 10) Small Bronze Age trading city located in northern Mesopotamia. If the identification with Tell er-Rimah is valid, the city lay 13 km south of mod. Tell ʿAfar, roughly midway between the Habur and Tigris rivers. Karana's wealth must have been due primarily to its location on a major east–west trade route that passed through northern Mesopotamia. No doubt tin figured prominently among the commodities in the merchant caravans that travelled this route. After being transported westwards across the Tigris at Ashur, from its place or places of origin, the metal was then conveyed northwestwards, along with other merchandise, via way-stations like Karana, and then due west to the Euphrates and regions beyond. An analysis of the personal names appearing in the tablets found at Tell er-Rimah suggests that the city's population was predominantly Hurrian, with an admixture of Akkadians and (in smaller numbers) Amorites.

The tablets, comprising c. 200 administrative records and letters, provide a number of details, supplemented by information contained in the Mari archives, about Karana's history during the early decades of C18. The city's first attested ruler, Samu-Addu, was a vassal of the Assyrian king Shamshi-Adad I (1796–1775). His fortunes were linked closely to those of his overlord, and with the beginning of the disintegration of the Old Assyrian kingdom on the death of Shamshi-Adad, Samu-Addu was overthrown by a usurper, Hatnu-rapi. This man had previously been ruler of the nearby city-state of

Qattara, but had fled the city when it was occupied by forces from Eshnunna, and had sought refuge in Karana. The circumstances of Hatnu-rapi's seizure of power in Karana are unknown. But upon his doing so, Samu-Addu and his family themselves became fugitives, and sought haven in Eshnunna. Hatnu-rapi allied himself with Zimri-Lim, who had seized the throne of Mari in 1774. However, one of Zimri-Lim's governors raised suspicions about his loyalties, alleging that he had entered into negotiations with Eshnunna's king, Ibal-pi-El II. Very likely reports such as these prompted Zimri-Lim to remove Hatnu-rapi from Karana's throne, replacing him with Ashkur-Addu, son of Samu-Addu. Karana seems to have flourished during Ashkur-Addu's reign. This was no doubt due to the benefits he enjoyed as a vassal of Zimri-Lim, who conferred a relatively long period of peace and stability upon northern Mesopotamia.

But Ashkur-Addu's kingship ended abruptly when his throne was seized by his brother-in-law Aqba-hammu. Aqba-hammu's action was apparently prompted by fresh interventions in northern Mesopotamia by the forces of Eshnunna, now ruled by a new king, Silli-Sin. The city of Razama (in the land of Yussan) was placed under siege by Eshnunnite troops, and it was clear that Karana was also under serious threat from the invaders. Though Zimri-Lim had dispatched forces to support Ashkur-Addu, they failed to protect his kingship. Aqba-hammu apparently believed that Mari had had its day as an overlord, and that regime change was necessary in Karana to ensure that it adapted to the newly emerging power structures in the region. In fact, it was the kingdom of Babylon, under its ruler Hammurabi, that now became the dominant power in northern Mesopotamia, after Hammurabi's destruction of Mari. Aqba-hammu acknowledged Hammurabi as his overlord, proclaiming himself on his seals 'servant of Hammurabi'.

The main group of tablets from Tell er-Rimah belongs to the reign of Aqba-hammu, whose consort was Iltani, daughter of Samu-Addu and sister of the deposed king Ashkur-Addu. Valuable information about this period is provided by the correspondence exchanged between Aqba-hammu and his wife. Aqba-hammu travelled widely during his reign, both inside and outside his kingdom, and it was probably under his rule that the territory over which Karana held sway reached its greatest extent. It included Qattara, Razama, perhaps Andarig, and also the land of Shirwunum. The territory of Shirwunum was thoroughly stripped by Aqba-hammu's forces – to the point where Aqba-hammu had to write to his wife for some suitable garments which could be handed over to the defeated king of Shirwunum, so that the latter had at least something to deliver up to Aqba-hammu by way of tribute.

Aqba-hammu's kingship may have ended within a few years of the end of Zimri-Lim's reign in 1762, though we have no details of this, nor of the immediate fate of his kingdom. But Karana continued to exist through the following centuries, as indicated by references to it in the Late Bronze Age archives of Nuzi. In this period, the city served as a major trading-post for merchants from Nuzi. The remains of Tell er-Rimah probably provide material evidence of Karana's prosperity during its Late Bronze Age phase. For the city's subsequent history (on the assumption that the identification with Tell er-Rimah is valid), see under ***Rimah, Tell er-***.

Dalley (*RlA* 5: 405–7; 1984), *LKM* 614–15 (refs).

Karania (Kirinu) Iron Age city located in the western part of the Kashiyari range (mod. Tur ʿAbdin), northern Mesopotamia. Lipiński suggests an identification with Tell

Harzem in the upper valley of the Zergan r. A king of Kirinu is one of twenty-three kings of Nairi listed in an inscription of Tiglath-pileser I (*RIMA 2: 21). During his campaign in the region in 866, the Assyrian king Ashurnasirpal II proceeded from the city of Karania to enter the pass of Mt Amadanu (q.v.) (*RIMA 2: 219–20).

Liverani (1992: 83), Lipiński (2000: 146).

Kar-Ashur City on a tell called Humut, east of the Tigris r., founded by the Assyrian king Tiglath-pileser III (745–727). Tiglath-pileser populated it with deportees from foreign lands which he had conquered (*Tigl. III 42–3, 122–3, 160–1). The city contained a royal palace.

Kar-Ashurnasirpal (*Zelebiya*?) One of two Iron Age fortresses built on opposite banks of the middle Euphrates by the Assyrian king Ashurnasirpal II during a campaign which he conducted in the region some time between 877 and 867 (*RIMA 2: 216). The fortress on the other (west) bank was called Nebarti-Ashur. Clearly, the fortresses were built to control an important ford on the river. Lipiński suggests that the ford was located at Tell Ashara (anc. Terqa/Sirqu). In Adad-nirari III's reign (810–783), Kar-Ashurnasirpal was among the cities and lands assigned to the governorship of an official called Nergal-erish (Palil-erish) (*RIMA 3: 209).

Röllig (*RlA* 5: 407–8), Lipiński (2000: 104).

Karatepe (= anc. **Azatiwataya**) (map 7) Iron Age Neo-Hittite site located above the Ceyhan valley in the Taurus region of Classical Cilicia, southern Anatolia, 100 km northeast of mod. Adana. Built as part of a system of frontier fortresses to protect the kingdom of Adana, it was named after its founder, Azatiwatas. The site was discovered by H. Bossert in 1946, and has been excavated and restored principally by H. Çambel under the auspices of the Institute of Archaeology at Istanbul.

Azatiwataya was a small, fortified hilltop city, c. 200 m × 400 m. Its most important finds are five inscriptions, two in Luwian hieroglyphs and three in Phoenician. They are parallel versions of a single text which commemorates the founding of the city. A fully preserved, 62-line Phoenician version (the longest known inscription in the Phoenician language) appears on the lower of the city's two gates, flanked by two stone lions. The inscription stretches in four columns across consecutive basalt orthostats (upright slabs) on the left side of the gate entrance, and ends on the adjoining lion. The accompanying Luwian version is haphazardly distributed between orthostats, bases, and gate sculptures to the right of the entrance. The orthostats are embellished with relief scenes, depicting a bear hunt, a man carrying a calf, a mother or nurse suckling a child, and entertainment provided at a royal banquet by musicians and dancing bears. Fragmentary, parallel Phoenician and Luwian versions of the inscription also appear in the area of the city's upper gate, and a third, slightly modified, Phoenician version is inscribed on a statue of the storm god (Luwian Tarhunza, Phoenician Baal). Stylistic features of the sculptures have raised doubts about the date of the remains and their inscriptions. It has been suggested that some of the reliefs may have been taken from the neighbouring site of (mod.) Domuztepe and later reused at Karatepe. However, palaeographic and historical considerations appear to favour a C8 date for Karatepe's remains.

The inscription indicates that the local ruler Azatiwatas who authored or commissioned it was subject to a king of Adanawa called Awarikus (Urikki) (the C8 king of

Que; see under **Que**), to whom he owed his elevation. Azatiwatas (perhaps to be identified with Sanduarri, king of Kundu and Sissu; see **Kundu**) claims to have fortified and extended the land of Adanawa, to have brought peace and prosperity to it, and to have established his overlord's family on its throne. He also links his name with the house of Muksas, MPŠ in the Phoenician version, as does Awarikus himself in the recently discovered Çineköy inscription (q.v.). The precise name-equation between Muksas/MPŠ in the Luwian–Phoenician bilinguals and Moxus/Mopsus in Classical texts has led scholars to link the remote ancestral figure of the Karatepe inscription with the legendary Greek seer and city founder Mopsus. An emigrant from western Anatolia to Cilicia, according to Greek tradition, Mopsus is associated with the foundation of a number of cities in southern Anatolia. More generally, the bilingual texts have contributed significantly to the decipherment of the Luwian hieroglyphic script, besides providing a valuable indication of the spread of Phoenician influence through southern Anatolia in the early centuries of M1.

Hawkins/Orthmann (*RlA* 5: 409–14), Winter (1979), **CHLI* I: 45–70, **CHLI* II, **CS* II: 124–6, 148–50.

Karduniash Geographical name frequently used of Babylonia (e.g. in the C14 Amarna letters and in Neo-Assyrian texts). The term was first used by the Late Bronze Age Kassites (q.v.). But its origin and meaning are uncertain.

Brinkman (*RlA* 5: 423).

Karkamish see Carchemish.

Karkar(a) (Kakru, *Tell Jidr*) M3–2 city probably to be identified with Tell Jidr, a site located in southern Mesopotamia between Adab and Umma, c. 25 km northwest of the latter. A cult-centre of the god Adad/Ishkur, Karkar is first attested in a pre-Sargonic text from nearby Adab. It was a station on the Urukean king Utu-hegal's campaign against the Gutians; he is said to have reached the city on the sixth day. Subsequently, the god Ishkur of Karkar is often mentioned in Ur III texts, when the city itself apparently belonged to the province of Umma. Karkar is known as late as the Middle Babylonian period (second half of M2), when it continued to be associated with the god Adad (*RGTC* 5: 156). In the early periods, the same cuneiform signs (IM^{ki}) are used to write the place-names Karkar, Ennegi, and Murum, resulting in a potential for confusion in some instances. In M1 sources, the same signs are likely to be read as Shatir rather than Karkar (despite the comments of Zadok, *RGTC* 8: 195). By this time, Karkar had most likely long been abandoned.

(H. D. Baker)
Powell (1980), Steinkeller (2001).

Karmir Blur see Teisheba City.

Kar-Tukulti-Ninurta (*Tulul al-ʿAqir*) (map 13) Late Bronze Age and Iron Age Assyrian city, covering c. 500 ha and located in northern Mesopotamia on the east bank of the Tigris, 4 km northeast of Ashur. Excavations on the site were first conducted by the German architect W. Bachmann in 1913–14. They were resumed in 1986 and 1989 under the direction of R. Dittmann, with sponsorship by the Deutsche Forschungsgemeinschaft. The city's dominant feature was its administrative quarter, which was divided into eastern and western sectors and separated by a fortification wall from the rest of the city. The eastern quarter has yet to be fully investigated and identified. The western quarter contained a sacred precinct, and a palace complex from which fragments of elaborate wall-paintings survive. Residential areas of the city may have been situated both north and south of the administrative quarter. The excavator notes that traces of large structures were found in the southern parts of the city, which he believes was the area where the king settled the different peoples deported there after his campaigns in neighbouring regions.

Kar-Tukulti-Ninurta, whose name means 'Harbour of Tukulti-Ninurta', was founded by the Middle Assyrian king Tukulti-Ninurta I (1244–1208) on a new site (**RIMA* 1: 270, 273–4, 276, 277–8). Alabaster tablets from his reign, discovered both here and in nearby Ashur, commemorate the city's foundation, and dedication as a cult-centre to the god Ashur. These tablets record Tukulti-Ninurta's construction of the sacred complex, which he called Ekurmesharra and dedicated to Ashur; inside the sanctuary, he built a great ziggurat (see glossary) as the god's cultic abode. The remains of this ziggurat (which has no obvious means of access) lie to the southeast of the palace complex. One or possibly two other temples lie to the north of the palace. From textual information, we know that the gods worshipped at Kar-Tukulti-Ninurta included (in addition to Ashur) Adad, Ishtar, Nergal, Ninurta, Shamash, and the Sebittu. Tukulti-Ninurta refers also to his construction of a canal, which irrigated the fields and brought abundant water to the city.

After the king's death by assassination, the new city may have been largely abandoned for a time, as indicated by both archaeological and documentary evidence. Reference is made to the partial demolition of a number of buildings in the one-year reign of Ninurta-Tukulti-Ashur (1133). There was, however, some reoccupation in C9, and official administrators of the city are attested in the period from the end of C9 to the second half of C8. There is no evidence of occupation of the site following the collapse of the Neo-Assyrian kingdom at the end of C7.

Dittman (1992), Freydank/Eickhoff (*RlA* 5: 455–9).

Kasapa (1) Middle Bronze Age city in the Jebel Sinjar region of northern Mesopotamia, attested in texts from the Mari archive during the reign of Zimri-Lim (1774–1762). It was apparently attached to the royal city of Kurda, serving frequently as a base and a residence for the kings of Kurda, notably Hammurabi. Hammurabi called an assembly of his land here (the assembly was made up of Kurda's Numha population) to deliberate on whether he should align himself with Mari or with Babylon.

LKM 615 (refs).

Kasap(p)a (2) M1 Neo-Assyrian city in northern Mesopotamia, probably to be located in the Assyrian province Kilizu. It has been identified with mod. Tell Keshaf, a settlement-mound on the Greater Zab r.

Postgate (*RlA* 5: 460).

Kasbuna (Kashpuna) Iron Age city in northwestern Syria, located in the northern part of the kingdom of Hamath. It is attested in a list of Hamathite cities and districts conquered by the Assyrian king Tiglath-pileser III (745–727). Kasbuna is described as being 'on the shore of the Lower Sea' (**Tigl. III* 60–1, 138–9, 176–7). The list was compiled within the context of a reorganization of the Assyrian provinces in the region in 738, following an anti-Assyrian rebellion there. Kasbuna was rebuilt by an Assyrian official, Qurdi-Ashur-lamur, who garrisoned it with thirty troops from nearby Siyannu, as indicated in a letter which the official sent to Tiglath-pileser (*ND* 2715).

*Saggs (1955: 127–30), Lipiński (2000: 287–9).

Kashiyari range (*Tur ʿAbdin*) (map 10) Mountain range in northern Mesopotamia, between the lands of Nairi to the north and Kadmuhu to the south. It is frequently mentioned in the records of Assyrian military campaigns in northern Mesopotamia, beginning with those of Adad-nirari I (1307–1275), who claims to have conquered the region in its entirety (**RIMA* 1: 131), as did his successor Shalmaneser I (1274–1245) (**RIMA* 1: 184). Tukulti-Ninurta I (1244–1208) makes a similar claim in his account of a campaign which he conducted against a coalition of rebel states there early in his reign (**RIMA* 1: 236–7). Further campaigns in the region were conducted by Ashurnasirpal II (883–859) during his early regnal years (**RIMA* 2: 209–10). Ashurnasirpal describes cutting a route through the mountain range for his troops and chariotry, an achievement accomplished with axes and picks over a period of six days. His son and successor Shalmaneser III records a campaign in the region in his fifth regnal year (854), in the course of which he captured eleven fortified cities (**RIMA* 3: 36).

Postgate (*RlA* 5: 460), Radner (2006).

Kaska (1) (map 3) Late Bronze Age region in the Pontic zone, northern Anatolia. Lying north of the Hittite homeland, it was inhabited by tribal groups, sometimes forming loose military confederations, who frequently invaded, laid waste, and occupied Hittite territory. Their capture of the Hittite holy city of Nerik in the reign of the C15 Hittite king Hantili II marks their first attested appearance in history. In the first half of C14, Kaska forces participated in the invasions which engulfed and almost destroyed the kingdom of Hatti, sweeping through and occupying the Hittite homeland to the southern bend of the Marassantiya (mod. Kızıl Irmak) r. in the reign of the Hittite king Tudhaliya III (*Bryce, 2005: 146). On this as on other occasions they were eventually driven back to their own lands. But while Hittite kings carried out extensive campaigns of retaliation in the Kaska lands, they never succeeded in imposing their authority over the Kaska peoples or subduing them for more than limited periods of time.

The Kaska menace continued to surface throughout Hittite history. Agreements occasionally concluded with groups of Kaska peoples, which granted some of them settlement and grazing rights within Hittite territory (*von Schuler, 1965: 109–40), were at best short-term expedients which could not be relied upon to give lasting security to the northern parts of the kingdom. And Kaskans may have been the first occupiers of what was left of the Hittite capital Hattusa after its fall early in C12. In the decades following the collapse of the Hittite empire, the Assyrian king Tiglath-pileser I (1114–1076) reports that 4,000 Kasku (and Urumu) warriors seized cities of the land of Subartu, which was then under Assyrian sovereignty. He claims that an expedition which he led to Subartu against the invaders resulted in their submission to him without resistance (**RIMA* 2: 17).

Little is known of Kaska administrative or social structures, or the relationships between the various tribes. They may have been ruled by tribal assemblies or councils, to judge from the remark which the Hittite king Mursili II made about one of their leaders: 'Thereafter, Pihhuniya did not rule like a Kaskan. When in Kaska there had never been a single ruler, suddenly this Pihhuniya ruled like a king' (*AM 88–9, here transl. *CS II: 87).

von Schuler (*1965; *RlA* 460–3).

Kaska (2) (Kasku) see **Ktk**.

Kassites An immigrant people in Babylonia, first attested in C18 Middle Bronze Age Babylonian texts. Their original homeland may have been in the Zagros mountains in the region of Elam, but other places of origin have also been proposed, including a homeland northwest of Babylonia. The name Kassite comes from the Akkadian word *kaššu*, though the Kassites' own word for themselves was *galzu*. The earliest references to them occur during the Old Babylonian period, in the reign of Hammurabi (1792–1750). Texts from Sippar, which lies north of Babylon, refer to both individuals and groups of Kassites hiring themselves out as farm labourers or soldiers. To begin with, there were military confrontations between the newcomers and the existing inhabitants of Babylonia. But the Kassites seem eventually to have settled into a peaceful existence in their new homeland. Many of them, reflecting their tribal origins, may have continued to live a semi-nomadic lifestyle as pastoralists and seasonal workers. But others rapidly adapted to a settled way of life.

By the time of Babylon's fall to the Hittites c. 1595 and the abrupt termination of the dynasty of Hammurabi, a group of Kassites was becoming a major political force within Babylonia. They established a dynasty which, after conquering the Sealanders in the south of the country, became the supreme power throughout Babylonia. The dynasty retained this position almost without interruption until the final years of the Late Bronze Age. They also maintained a presence in northern Mesopotamia, being attested in texts from Nuzi as well as in Middle Assyrian documents. Even after the fall of Babylonia to the Elamites c. 1155, which brought about the end of the dynasty, Kassites are attested as a significant presence in Babylonia until at least C9, and a number of them continued to hold high office in the land. After C9, they appear sporadically in our sources as warlike tribal groups in the hill country of eastern Mesopotamia and Iran. In the late 330s they may have provided troops for the Persians against Alexander the Great.

Under Kassite rule, Babylonia became once more a major international power, achieving the status of one of the Great Kingdoms of the Late Bronze Age. Of at least equal importance was Kassite cultural achievement. Not merely were the cultural traditions of Hammurabi's Babylon preserved and nurtured: under the patronage of the Kassite kings, the arts and sciences of the kingdom flourished as never before. Akkadian in its Babylonian dialect became the international language of diplomacy, used widely throughout western Asia.

Unfortunately, almost all our information about the Kassites comes from non-Kassite sources. We have nothing of their own language, which is related to no known language, beyond two Kassite–Akkadian 'dictionaries' which provide a list of personal and divine names and some basic vocabulary. We also have relatively little information about individual Kassite rulers, and most of what we do have again comes from foreign sources. Though the Babylonian King List records thirty-six Kassite kings, few are

Figure 59 C12 *kudurru* stone from Babylonia (see glossary).

more than names. Those about whom we do have some significant information, for example in letters written to and by them, belong to C14 (e.g. the Amarna letters – see glossary) and C13. For more specific information about these, see **Babylonia**.

Brinkman (*RlA* 5: 464–73), J. Oates (1986: 83–104), Kuhrt (1995a: 332–48), Sommerfeld (1995).

Kassiya (Gassiya, Kissiya) Late Bronze Age country in northern Anatolia, subject to the kingdom of Hatti. In C14 it was twice invaded and sacked by enemy forces from the nearby country of Arawanna (Bryce, 2005: 146, **AM* 78–9, **CS* II: 87), and repeatedly attacked by troops from the lands of Masa and Kammala (**DS* 65, **CS* I: 186). Though on every occasion the Hittites succeeded in re-establishing their authority in the country, and took severe retaliatory action against its oppressors, Kassiya remained vulnerable to enemy invasion. Early in C13, it was among the lands depopulated by incursions of Kaska tribes and other enemies from the north, and subsequently assigned by the Hittite king Muwattalli II to his brother Hattusili (later

King Hattusili III) when he appointed Hattusili ruler of the northern part of the Hittite homeland (**CS* I: 201) (see **Hakpis(sa)** and **Turmitta**).

Kastama Late Bronze Age Hittite cult-centre in northern Anatolia, also the seat of a Hittite administrative official during the period of the Hittite Old Kingdom (C17–16). It was plundered and occupied by the Kaska people from the Pontic zone early in C14, or perhaps already in C15. Other cult-centres in the region which suffered similar destruction in the same period included Nerik, Hursama, Serisa, Himuwa, Taggasta, and Kammama.

Ünal (*RlA* 5: 475–6), **RGTC* 6:193–4.

Katapa Late Bronze Age Hittite city in northern Anatolia. It had important cultic associations, appearing in a number of Hittite prayers and as the first place on the Hittite king's pilgrimage route to holy cities outside Hattusa for the celebration of the autumn *nuntarriyashas* festival (literally, 'festival of haste') (**RGTC* 6: 198). The city also served as a winter residence for the Hittite king. Mursili II spent a winter there while celebrating a religious festival (**CS* I: 211), and used it as a winter residence following his successful campaign against the Kaskan-occupied city of Timuhala (**AM* 170–1). Katapa was one of a number of lands in the northern Anatolian region which had been largely depopulated by enemy incursions. In early C13, the Hittite king Muwattalli II assigned these lands to the authority of his brother Hattusili (later King Hattusili III) when he appointed Hattusili ruler of the northern part of the Hittite homeland (**CS* I: 201) (see also **Hakpis(sa)** and **Turmitta**).

Otten (*RlA* 5: 486), **RGTC* 6: 197–201, Polit (1999).

Kayalıdere (map 20) Small Iron Age Urartian fortress settlement in eastern Anatolia 39 km north of Muş overlooking the upper Murat valley, and perhaps built within the territory of the country Dayenu (q.v.). No inscriptions have been found on the site, and neither its anc. name nor its founder is known. Excavations, limited to a single seven-week season in 1965, were conducted by S. Lloyd and C. Burney on behalf of the British Institute of Archaeology in Ankara. They brought to light a series of terraced structures, a 'tower-temple' with a cloister on one side and fronted by a paved courtyard, a storage magazine with large pithos vessels, and a multi-chambered rock tomb (at least seven chambers). All work was confined to the upper citadel, except for the tomb which was not fully excavated (only six chambers were cleared) due to the difficulties caused by the porosity of the rock and its deep fissures. A variety of small items was found scattered over the citadel's surface, including a bronze lion and other bronze items, arrowheads and quivers, and parts of furniture (e.g. three furniture legs with bull's-head feet). Burney suggests that the site, which apparently had only a brief existence, was destroyed during a Cimmerian attack in 714 or 707.

Burney (1966; 1998: 158–60), Burney and Lang (1971: 150–2), Orthmann (*RlA* 5: 541).

Kazallu (**Kasalluk**) (map 11) City in northern Babylonia attested in Early and Middle Bronze Age Mesopotamian texts. It appears first in these texts as a rebellious subject of the Akkadian empire. Following a campaign in Sumer, the Akkadian king Rimush (2278–2270) attacked and conquered the city, inflicting heavy casualties upon it, demolishing its walls and taking 5,862 prisoners, including its *ensi* (governor),

Ashared (**DaK* 192, 198–9, **RIME* 2: 48–51). Kazallu subsequently figures in letters of the Ur III period, during the reign of Ibbi-Sin (2028–2004), last king of the Ur III dynasty. From one of these letters, we learn that Ishbi-Erra, then governor of Mari and a subject of Ibbi-Sin, was sent to Isin and Kazallu to arrange grain supplies for Ur, now desperately short of food, and that he virtually held the royal capital to ransom by storing these supplies in Isin (*Jacobsen, 1953: 39–40). In another letter, written to Kazallu's governor Puzur-Numushda by Ibbi-Sin, the addressee is chastised for not using the troops at his disposal to help check the military advances of Ishbi-Erra, who was now in open revolt against Ibbi-Sin (**ANET* 480–1).

Kazallu subsequently figures in the list of cities which were devastated or occupied by the external enemies – Gutians, Elamites, and Subarians – who had dealt the death blow to the Ur III empire. But it emerged from this disaster to become for a time the dominant power in northern Babylonia, in effect sharing control over the southern Mesopotamian remnants of the Ur III empire with Ishbi-Erra's ruling dynasty at Isin in the south. As we know from tablets found there, the city of Kish was for a time subject to a king of Kazallu and Marad called Sumu-ditana. In 1878 another king of Kazallu, Halum-pi-umu (Halambu, Alumbiumu), perhaps Sumu-ditana's successor, provoked the wrath of the Babylonian king Sumu-la-El by seizing the city of Dilbat, at that time apparently a dependency of the kingdom of Babylon. Sumu-la-El responded by defeating the Kazallan king in battle later that year, thereby unifying Babylonia for a time. Five years later, Kazallu came into conflict with the kingdom of Larsa, whose seventh king, Sumu-El (1894–1866), inflicted a military defeat upon the city, perhaps then ruled by a man called Sumuatar. But through C19, Kazallu remained a significant force in the southern Mesopotamian scene, despite the apparent dominance of this scene by Isin and Larsa, and also by Babylon in the Isin dynasty's waning years. The city posed a constant threat to Larsa and Babylon, as illustrated by the activities of Yahzir-El, possibly a king of Kazallu, who repeatedly harassed their territories despite suffering several military defeats at their hands. Matters came to a head c. 1835, when Larsa's territory was occupied by armies from Kazallu and from the wider region of Mutiabal, of which Kazallu appears to have been the chief city. This occupation may have helped end the brief reign of Silli-Adad, last member of a long line of Larsan dynasts. But the occupation was shortlived, for soon afterwards a new leader called Kudur-Mabuk, son of Simti-Shilhak, established his control over Larsa, appointing his son Warad-Sin as king there. Kudur-Mabuk drove the invaders out of Larsa's territory, and pursued them to their own country, where he captured Kazallu and demolished its walls (**RIME* 4: 206).

Kazallu survived the Larsa onslaught, and seems to have maintained its independence under its own line of rulers, who presumably held sway over the whole land of Mutiabal. (We know of a late C19–early C18 king of Kazallu called Daganma-El.) But during the reign of the Babylonian king Hammurabi (1792–1750), Mutiabal was incorporated into the Old Babylonian kingdom. Mutiabalean troops were pressed into military service in Hammurabi's war with the Elamites. But they were unwilling conscripts, and many of them fled to Larsa. Others became prisoners-of-war of the Elamites. Among them was a Mutiabalean commander who informed his captors that his fellow countrymen were ready to rebel against Babylon (*Charpin, 2003: 72; *ARM *XXVI/2*: 166–8, no. 365). This persuaded the Elamite vizier to send him home to Kazallu with a secret message, which no doubt contained some form of encouragement – if not a promise of actual support – for an anti-Babylonian uprising. The rebellion broke out when the Mutiabaleans massacred a large number of the 6,000 Babylonians sent by Hammurabi to Kazallu to gather supplies and children for transport back to Babylon. Hammurabi responded by sending troops to Mutiabal. The rebels were comprehensively defeated, and their homes torn down and burnt. Subsequently Mutiabal was one of the regions which revolted against Hammurabi's successor Samsu-iluna (1749–1712) (*Mesop.* 341).

Edzard (*RlA* 5: 542–3), *LKM* 60–3, *320–1, *Mesop*. 87–9.

Kazel, Tell-el (map 7) Large, oval-shaped settlement-mound on the fertile Akkar plain in northern Syria, now 3.5 km from the Levantine coast. Its history of occupation extends from the Middle Bronze Age to the Islamic period. Excavations were carried out between 1960 and 1962 by M. Dunand, A. Bounni, and N. Saliby for the Syrian Directorate-General of Antiquities and Museums, and were resumed in the mid 1980s by a team from the American University of Beirut, under the direction of L. Badre. Material remains from the site include a Middle Bronze Age city wall, a Late Bronze Age palace dating to C14, a range of ceramic ware from Iron Age I and II, a monumental building and what may have been a Canaanite temple of the Persian period (C6–4), a large cemetery of the Hellenistic period, a tower of the Roman period, and ceramic ware from the Byzantine and Islamic periods.

Tell Kazel is commonly identified with anc. Sumur (q.v.), the chief city of the Late Bronze Age kingdom of Amurru, frequently attested in the mid C14 Amarna correspondence (see glossary). Sumur was probably the ancestor of Iron Age Simirra, a city belonging to the northern Syrian kingdom Hamath (before it was annexed by the Assyrian king Tiglath-pileser III in 738), and is referred to as Simyra in Greek texts.

Bounni (*OEANE* 3: 275–6).

Keisan, Tell (map 8) 6 ha settlement-mound in the Akko plain, mod. Israel, between Haifa and Akko, 8 km from the coast. A tentative identification has been proposed with biblical Achshaph, attested in Joshua (11:1, 12:20, 19:25). Though there is some evidence of Neolithic occupation, the site's history of settlement effectively begins with the Early Bronze Age and extends to the Byzantine age, with several periods of abandonment in between. Excavations were conducted by J. Garstang as director of the Neilson Expedition, by A. Rowe in 1935 and 1936, and subsequently by R. de Vaux, J. Prignaud, J. Briend, and J.-B. Humbert for the École Biblique et Archéologique Française in Jerusalem from 1971 to 1980.

In the Early Bronze Age, the settlement was fortified by a 5 m wide city wall, which was strengthened and made more elaborate during the succeeding Middle Bronze period. Three ocupational levels have been assigned to the Late Bronze Age, though this phase of the settlement's history has left only meagre remains. The violent destruction of the site in early C12 is generally attributed to the Sea Peoples. Its rebuilding, perhaps in mid C12, has been tentatively associated with one of the Sea Peoples' groups, perhaps the Sherden. Some Philistine bichrome ware found on the site also dates to this period. The succeeding occupation level, dated to late C12, indicates more substantial urban development. The destruction or abandonment which ended this level, perhaps early in C11, may indicate that Tell Keisan was one of the victims of the conflicts between Aramaeans, Israelites, and Philistines for control of the region. The next level reflected considerable foreign influence, its pottery showing a mixture of Mycenaean and Cypriot types. Large, well-planned, multi-roomed buildings laid out on a rectangular grid plan characterize the settlement in this phase of its existence. But it was apparently unwalled at this time. Its destruction c. 1000 is believed by the French excavators to have been due to local events rather than to a military campaign by the Israelite king David.

The site was reoccupied in Iron Age II. Throughout its three Iron Age II levels, Tell Keisan was remarkable for its strong cultural continuity. The French excavators regard the period as one of exceptional stability in the site's history. It came to an end with the settlement's destruction in the latter part of C8. While there is no indication that the Assyrians were responsible for this destruction, Assyrian influence became a prominent feature of Tell Keisan's material culture in the following two-phase Iron Age III period (as designated by the French excavators). This influence is reflected in Neo-Assyrian ceramic ware and Assyrian-style seals found on the site. In the second Iron Age III phase, elements of Phoenician culture are also present, as reflected particularly in the substantial Phoenician component within the settlement's pottery assemblage. Phoenician elements had first made their appearance in Tell Keisan in C8. In this period too, the settlement had apparently established commercial and cultural links with Cyprus. By the end of the second Iron Age III phase, trading links had expanded to other parts of the eastern Mediterranean and Aegean worlds, including Rhodes and the Greek Ionian states.

In mid C7 Tell Keisan once more suffered destruction, perhaps during the Assyrian king Ashurbanipal's expedition against Akko in 643. However, the site continued to be occupied through the Persian and for much of the Hellenistic period, prior to its abandonment (for unknown reasons) before the end of C2 BCE. In M1 CE a Byzantine village was established there.

Briend and Humbert (1980), Humbert (*NEAEHL* 3: 862–7), Dever (*OEANE* 3: 278–9).

Kerak (*al-Karak*) (map 8) Site in Transjordan east of the Dead Sea located at the junction of routes leading north–south through the Transjordanian plateau and east–west from the desert to the Dead Sea. Though now best known for its Crusader castle built in C12 CE, Kerak first flourished as an important centre of the kingdom of Moab, during the reign of the Moabite king Mesha. It is believed that the city is attested in a number of passages in the *OT* under the names Qir-Moab, Qir-Heres, and Qir-Hareset: see e.g. Isaiah 15:1, Jeremiah 48:31, and 2 Kings 3:25–7 respectively. In the third of these passages, Qir-Hareset was a fortress-settlement where Mesha made a last and unsuccessful stand in his rebellion against Israel. Kerak is later attested as an administrative centre of the Persian empire (C6–4), and subsequently appears to have flourished under Roman rule, particularly when the C2 CE Roman emperor Hadrian granted it the status of a polis.

Johns (*OEANE*: 280–3).

Kerkenes Dağ (map 4) Site of Iron Age mountaintop city in north-central Anatolia, on the northern periphery of the Cappadocian plain; perhaps = Hittite Mt Daha. The site was visited by J. J. G. Anderson in 1899, and investigated further by H. H. von der Osten, University of Chicago, in 1926, who identified it as an important Iron Age settlement, and F. H. Blackburn in 1927, who mapped the city's defences. In 1928

E. Schmidt dug a number of exploratory trenches on the site. In 1993 G. D. and M. E. F. Summers began what was to be a ten-year programme of remote sensing, using balloon photography, close-contour GPS survey, and large-area geophysical prospection.

The city is the largest Iron Age settlement on the Anatolian plateau. Seven gates gave access, through a curtain wall, to the 2.5 sq. km settlement. The entire fortification system, which was strengthened by towers and buttresses, ran for 7 km. Within lay a well-planned settlement divided into walled urban blocks, which must have served as residences for the population. Size and location distinguish the residences of the elite class from the common elements of the population. A separate, large, and similarly well-planned area contained the city's administrative quarter. Here, the excavators have tentatively identified what they believe were a palace complex, an administrative block, stables or storehouses, and a military area; they suggest that a large circular area may have been a camel pound. The so-called 'palace' was the city's most impressive building. Located on the high southern end of the site with commanding views, it was a huge complex, 200 m × 50 m, with an entranceway flanked by two towers. It may well have served as the residence of the city's ruler, although almost certainly it had official functions as well. Outside the walls was a large temple.

The city's prominence must in large measure have been due to its excellent strategic location, close by the main routes of communication linking the Black Sea regions with northern Syria via the Taurus mountains. It also had an abundant all-year-round water supply. Both features must have prompted the decision to build a city in this location. But who were its builders? G. D. Summers equated the site with Pteria (referred to by Herodotus 1.76), identifying it as a Median city which marked the western limit of the Median empire. He concluded, on the basis of this identification, that the city was built by the Medes shortly after the 'battle of the eclipse', fought in 585 by the Lydians and the Medes, and followed by a treaty which established the Halys r. as the boundary between the two kingdoms. It has been suggested that the Cappadocian mountain city was built to serve as the Medes' western capital. But Rollinger (2003a) has argued against the identification of Kerkenes as Pteria, or as a Median city, partly on the grounds that there is no independent archaeological evidence to support Summers' conclusion that Pteria was such a city, and partly on the grounds that the traditional concept of a Median empire, which extended as far west as the Halys r., cannot be sustained. Recent excavations have brought to light elements of Phrygian culture in the city, including architectural and sculptural elements, and inscriptions in the Phrygian language. This throws some doubt on both the date of the city's foundation and the identity of its founders. It also raises the question of what impact the Medes, once thought to be the city's founders, actually had on the city, both politically and culturally. In any event, the city had but a brief period of existence. Around mid C6 it was destroyed by fire, perhaps by the forces of the Lydian king Croesus.

Summers and Summers (1998; 2003; 2005; 2006), Rollinger (2003a), Kerkenes website (http://www.kerkenes.metu.edu.tr/kerk1/index.html).

Keteioi Obscure legendary people of the land of Mysia in western Anatolia. They are attested in Homer's *Odyssey* (11.521) as the subjects of Eurypylus, son of Telephus, who was slain by Achilles' son Neoptolemus. It has sometimes been suggested, implausibly, that the Keteioi were linked with the Late Bronze Age Hittites.

Kevenli Early M1 Urartian fortress covering an area of 9,000 sq. m, located in eastern Anatolia 10 km northeast of the Urartian capital Tushpa (which lay on the southeastern shore of Lake Van). The site has most recently been investigated by O. Belli and M. Salvini. The many cuneiform inscriptions found there at different times indicate that its fortress was built by the Urartian king Minua (805–788). One of these inscriptions commemorates Minua's construction of the fortress and a town 'where previously nothing had been built'. Kevenli was apparently one of the earliest, if not the earliest, of the settlements established by Minua. It was part of a series of fortresses built by him and his father Ishpuini for administrative and economic as well as military purposes. But it was apparently abandoned after Minua's reign.

*Belli and Salvini (2004).

Khãkbi M1 Lycian city in southwestern Anatolia, attested in C5 Lycian coin-legends and on the 255-line pillar inscription from Xanthus (**TAM* I: 44) (see under **Xanthus**). The coins were minted on the so-called light Lycian standard, which suggests that Khãkbi is to be located in western Lycia, as distinct from coins minted on the heavy standard which were produced in central Lycian mints. This has led some scholars to question the generally accepted identification of Khãkbi with the central Lycian city whose Greek name was Candyba.

Mørkholm (1964: esp. 72), Keen (1998: 143).

Khafajeh (**Dur-Samsu-iluna, Tutub**) (map 10) 216 ha complex consisting of four main settlement-mounds (A–D) located in the lower Diyala region of central Mesopotamia c. 80 km northeast of Baghdad, with a history of occupation extending from the Late Uruk period (c. 3300) until mid M2. The site was excavated between 1930 and 1938 under the direction of C. Preusser, P. Delougaz, and E. A. Speiser, working on behalf of the Oriental Institute of the University of Chicago and the University Museum of the University of Pennsylvania. Excavations concentrated primarily on Mound A, the largest of the four mounds, which was occupied from the Late Uruk period until its abandonment c. 2300 during the Old Akkadian period. The excavation on the mound of a temple traditionally but probably mistakenly associated with the moon god Sin revealed an unbroken succession of levels from the Jemdet Nasr (late M4) through the Early Dynastic period (c. 2900–2334). These levels not only provided valuable information about the chronology of the site itself, but have also contributed much to our understanding of Mesopotamian chronology in general. West and south of the temple, a twelve-level sequence of Early Dynastic private houses was uncovered. But the dominant building complex on Mound A was an Early Dynastic temple oval, consisting of a temple on a raised platform, a courtyard, and two enclosing mudbrick walls, between which a large building was constructed. The latter was presumably the administrative quarters of the temple, and may also have served as the residence of the chief priest. Three different levels of the temple were identified.

Remains from Mounds B and C, which probably formed a single settlement, date to the Old Babylonian period (Middle Bronze Age), perhaps continuing into the Kassite period (Late Bronze Age). The settlement was built as a fortress-city by the Old Babylonian king Samsu-iluna (1749–1712), son and successor of Hammurabi, and named Dur-Samsu-iluna ('Fort Samsu-iluna'). An inscription commemorating its construction by Samsu-iluna appears on several clay cylinders, two found under the floor of a gateway in the fortifications of Mound B, and a third in the city of Babylon (*Chav. 104–5). Settlement on the smallest of the mounds, Mound D, also dates to the Middle Bronze Age (Isin-Larsa and Old Babylonian periods). On this mound, the remains of a temple dedicated to the god Sin were uncovered. A tablet hoard found in the temple confirms its association with the god. This hoard, dating to the Old Babylonian period, enabled the site to be identified with the city called Tutub, whose name is already attested in the Akkadian period.

Delougaz (1940), Mallowan (1971: 246–57), Hansen (*OEANE* 3: 288–90).

Khaldeh (map 7) Site consisting of two promontories located on the Lebanese coast 12 km south of Beirut. Official excavations there were carried out in 1961 and 1962 by R. Saidah on behalf of the Lebanese Dept of Antiquities. The site's history of occupation is represented by Late Chalcolithic, Late Bronze, Persian, Hellenistic, and Roman levels. The meagre Late Bronze Age remains consist primarily of ceramic material located in the vicinity of the later Iron Age cemetery, whose construction probably accounted for the destruction of more substantial Late Bronze Age remains. During the Iron Age the site belonged to the Phoenician cultural sphere and has been identified with the city called Hilduya in Akkadian. It was attached to the city of Sidon, which lay to its south, but was annexed by the Assyrian king Esarhaddon in 677/676. The most prominent of the city's Iron Age remains is the cemetery, which consists of c. 422 graves. Inhumation and cremation were both practised. Cremated remains were interred in funerary urns.

Saidah (1966; 1967), Badre (*OEANE* 3: 291).

Khalil, el- see **Hebron**.

Kharaz, Tell Abu al- Settlement-mound covering c. 3.5 ha and located in the central Jordan valley, 5 km south of Pella. Its history of occupation extends from the Early Bronze Age through the Iron Age. The site was excavated between 1989 and 1998 by the Swedish Jordan Expedition under the direction of P. M. Fischer. Its Early Bronze Age phase is represented by well-preserved domestic structures enclosed within a city wall, and complete ceramic sequences. Trade links with Egypt are indicated by imported items of Egyptian provenance, including cylindrical jars and mace-heads. During the Middle and Late Bronze Ages, the city was fortified with a casemate wall. Remains from this period include domestic buildings, a small temple, and a range of ceramic material, notably chocolate-on-white ware, and pottery imported from Cyprus. Later domestic structures and towers date to Iron Age II. A building designated as the 'White Building', constructed partly of ashlar blocks and covered with white plaster, was erected on the summit of the site. Artefacts of this period indicate continuing trading links with Cyprus and Palestine.

Negev and Gibson (2001: 283).

Kheleifeh, Tell El- M1 fortified mudbrick settlement on a small, low mound located in southern Palestine at the northern end of the Gulf of Aqaba. F. Frank surveyed the site in 1933 and identified it with the biblical city Ezion-Geber. Subsequent excavations conducted by N. Glueck for the American Schools of Oriental Research between 1938 and 1940 uncovered, in the lowest of four occupation levels, a square fortress, with casemate walls, built of mudbrick, enclosing at its centre a large building which the excavator believed to be a citadel or a granary. The fortress was dated, on the basis of architectural similarities with the fortifications at Gezer and Hazor, to the reign of Solomon in C10, and seemed to support Frank's identification of the site with Ezion-Geber. However, the revised dating for the so-called 'Solomonic' levels at these sites makes the C10 dating of Tell el-Kheleifeh invalid, and in fact brings it into line with the observations of G. D. Pratico, who re-evaluated Glueck's excavations in 1993 and concluded that none of the pottery pre-dated C9. In these terms, it is possible that Ezion-Geber (assuming its identification with Kheleifeh is correct) was developed as a port by the C9 Israelite king Omri or his son and successor Ahab, or indeed by one of the later kings of Israel or Judah. Following the destruction of the fortress, a new and much larger fortified settlement was built on the site, surrounded by mudbrick walls, with access to the settlement provided by a four-chambered gate building. Ceramic ware indicates a dating from C8 to early C6 for the settlement. This dating is supported by stamp-impressions, on the handles of storage jars, whose script belongs to C7 or early C6. The excavator reports that the city was destroyed before the end of C6, but that a new industrial city which was built over its ruins lasted from late C6 to the end of C4. The material remains of this last period apparently indicate significant trade with Arabia, as in previous periods.

Glueck/Pratico (*NEAEHL* 3: 867–70), Pratico (1993).

Khorsabad see **Dur-Sharrukin**.

Kikalla Middle Bronze Age city in southern Mesopotamia near the city of Kish. The Babylonian king Samsu-iluna (1749–1712) claimed a decisive victory there over a Kassite army in his eighth or ninth regnal year. This marks the Kassites' first appearance in history as a significant military force.

Mesop. 339–40.

Kilise Tepe Settlement in southern Anatolia, located in the Göksü valley, 45 km northwest of mod. Silifke, with occupation levels extending through the Bronze and Iron Ages, Hellenistic and Roman periods, down to the middle Byzantine period (C5–7 CE). The site which stands on a flat promontory, 100 sq. m at its summit, was visited and described in the 1950s by J. Mellaart. But it was not until 1994 that systematic excavations began under the direction of J. N. Postgate for the British School of Archaeology at Ankara. Seven architectural sequences belonging to the Early Bronze Age were identified below the Middle Bronze Age strata. In the Middle Bronze Age, Kilise Tepe, though small, became a settlement of some importance, probably serving as an administrative centre for the district in which it was located. The two levels from this period (IVa and b) were both destroyed by fire. During the Late Bronze Age, Kilise was no doubt among the southern Anatolian cities that became subject to the kingdom of Hatti. Postgate comments that the Göksü valley must have been one of the principal routes to the sea, and Kilise an important way-station on that route. The settlement may well have provided the Hittites with one of their major links with the eastern Mediterranean world. Unfortunately, its meagre Late Bronze Age architectural remains provide little information about it during this phase of its existence.

Large quantities of painted pottery from the Iron Age levels (IIa–g) came to light during the excavators' initial surface clearance of the site. Postgate reports that the most distinctive vessels were one-handled jugs with elaborate black-painted targets and encircling bands. The discovery of identical types in Cyprus and at Al Mina, as well as in Tarsus, provides some indication of the spread of Kilise's commercial links at this time. One of the most prominent features of the settlement in its IId phase was a large building which focused on a central courtyard or hall, and was perhaps used for ceremonial purposes. In its Iron Age phase, Kilise may have been part of the kingdom of Tabal. But again, our knowledge of the Iron Age city is limited, mainly because much of the information about it has been obscured by continuing occupation, particularly in the Hellenistic and Byzantine periods.

Baker *et al.* (1995), Postgate (1998; 2008).

Kilizu (Kalzu, *Qasr Shemamok*) M2 and M1 city in northern Mesopotamia, 28 km west of mod. Arbil. Following initial investigations by A. H. Layard in C19, the site was briefly excavated in 1933 by an Italian team under the direction of G. Furlani. The remains of Neo-Assyrian buildings brought to light during the excavations contained bricks inscribed with the name of the Assyrian king Sennacherib (704–681). There were also remains of a later Parthian cemetery. Though no M2 levels were reached by the excavators, the city may be referred to in documentary sources dating to the Old Babylonian period (first quarter of M2). It is likely that the city and its immediate region were incorporated as a province into the Middle Assyrian kingdom during the reign of Ashur-uballit I (1365–1330), in the wake of the collapse of the kingdom of Mitanni. There are references to Kilizu in administrative texts of the Assyrian king Tiglath-pileser I (1114–1076), at the end of whose reign the region to which it belonged may have been invaded and occupied by Aramaean tribal groups.

In M1, Kilizu became the capital of a province of the Neo-Assyrian kingdom. Restoration work on the city appears to have been carried out by the Assyrian king Ashur-dan II (934–912) (**RIMA* 2: 140–1), and it was here that Ashurnasirpal II mustered his troops for his eastern campaigns against Zamua in 881 and 880 (**RIMA* 2: 204, 205). An important scribal centre was located in the city, which appears to have ranked among the major urban and administrative centres of Assyria until at least the reign of Esarhaddon (680–669). Kilizu may have been abandoned in late C7, when the Neo-Assyrian empire collapsed. There is no further evidence of its occupation before the Parthian period (C2 onwards).

Postgate (*RlA* 5: 591–3).

Kimash Early Bronze Age highland country of Iran, subject to Elam. Steinkeller suggests a location within the territory of the Gutians (q.v.). Along with Hu-urti (Hurtum), Kimash rose up against the Elamite-Awanite king Puzur-Inshushinak (early C21) who claims to have crushed the rebels (**DaK* 321). Kimash, Hu-urti, and Harshi were also the object of a military campaign by Shulgi (2094–2047), second ruler of the Ur III dynasty (**RIME* 3/2: 141). However, the so-called Messenger Texts, which make frequent reference to Kimash, indicate diplomatic relations between Kimash and the Ur III kingdom during the period when Kimash was at least theoretically still a subject state of Elam. Other references to Kimash indicate trading links with Mesopotamia. Cattle and copper figure among its items for trade. Gudea, king of

Lagash (late C22), claims to have imported copper from Abullat, a city or district which lay in the mountains of Kimash. It is uncertain whether Kimash actually had its own copper mines or acted merely as an intermediary in the copper trade. If the former, T. Potts suggests for Abullat a location near the mines of the Tiyari mountains north of Amadiyeh.

RGTC 2: 100–1, Edzard and Röllig (*RlA* 5: 593), T. Potts (1994: 24), Lafont (1996).

Kimuhu Iron Age city located in northwestern Mesopotamia on the west bank of the upper Euphrates near Carchemish. In the immediate aftermath of the fall of the Assyrian empire (late C7), control of the city was contested by Babylon and Egypt, in the broader context of their struggle for supremacy in the Syro-Palestinian region and other territories where the Assyrians had formerly held sway. In 607, the Babylonian prince Nebuchadnezzar sacked the city on his return from his Urartian campaign (**ABC* 98), apparently as a counter to Egyptian aggression in the region of Carchemish (during the reign of the pharaoh Necho II), and stationed a garrison there. But in the following year an Egyptian army captured the city and defeated its garrison after a four-month siege.

Kimuhu is almost certainly to be identified with Kummuh, capital of the Neo-Hittite kingdom of the same name (q.v.), and is therefore very likely to be located at mod. Samsat Höyük (Classical Samosata).

Wiseman (1991: 229–30), Hawkins (*RlA* 6: 340).

Kinabu M1 fortified city of Hulaya, ruler of the land of Halziluha in northern Mesopotamia during the reign of the Assyrian king Ashurnasirpal II (883–859) (**RIMA* 2: 201). For Hulaya's rebellion against Assyrian rule and its consequences, see **Halziluha**.

Kinalua (**Kunulua, Kinalia, Kunalia**; probably = ***Tell Tayinat***) Neo-Hittite city referred to in Assyrian texts as the capital of the kingdom of Unqi (the Assyrian name for Pat(t)in; q.v.) in northwestern Syria. The Assyrian king Ashurnasirpal II marched upon Kinalua during his western campaign in 870, and there intimidated the Patinite king Lubarna into submission without resistance. He took from the city large amounts of tribute and numerous hostages (including Lubarna's niece), and also infantry and cavalry forces to swell the ranks of his own army (**RIMA* 2: 217–18). In 831, when a second Patinite king called Lubarna was killed in an uprising by his own people, Ashurnasirpal's son and successor Shalmaneser III dispatched to Patin an Assyrian army under the command of the commander-in-chief Dayyan-Ashur, who pitched camp by Kinalua (**RIMA* 3: 69). Patin's new king, Surri, who had usurped the throne, died shortly after, and Dayyan-Ashur replaced him with his own appointee, a certain Sasi from the land of Kurussa. Before departing the land, Dayyan-Ashur set up a colossal statue of Shalmaneser in the temple of Kinalua.

In later years, when a pact of alliance with Assyria was breached by the last of the Patinite rulers, Tutammu (738), the Assyrian king Tiglath-pileser III removed Tutammu from power and incorporated his kingdom into the Assyrian empire (**Tigl. III* 56–7). Kinalua was converted into an Assyrian province. Along with other cities of the former Patinite kingdom, it became a place of resettlement for booty people deported there by Tiglath-pileser in the wake of his eastern campaigns. In Assyrian texts the province is attested under the name Kullani, apparently a dialectical variant of Kinalua.

Hawkins (*RlA* 5: 597–8; *CHLI* I: 361–3).

King's Highway Major route crossing the Transjordanian plateau, from Damascus to the Gulf of Aqaba. The Hebrew name for it is *derek hammelek* ('the royal way'). Most scholars now regard this expression as a specific designation for the Transjordanian road rather than simply as a generic term for a public highway. Along it lay a number of important towns, including Ashtaroth, Dibon, and Ezion-geber. In *OT* tradition, it was the route used by Moses to lead the Hebrews through Edom and Moab (e.g. Numbers 20:17).

Beitzel (1992).

Kinza see Qadesh.

Kipinu Iron Age Mesopotamian city in the land of Laqe, situated at a river-crossing on the middle Euphrates. Lipiński suggests a location at or near Deir ez-Zor (Dayr az-Zawr). It was the setting of a military confrontation, c. 877, between the Assyrian king Ashurnasirpal II and the troops of a Laqean leader, Azi-ilu (**RIMA* 2: 215). The latter had seized the crossing after Ashurnasirpal's victory over the combined forces of the kingdoms of Laqe, Hindanu, and Suhu. Azi-ilu's troops were routed, and their leader fled to Mt Bisuru (Mt Bishri, mod. Jebel Bishri).

Lipiński (2000: 97–8, 103).

Kipshuna (Kibshuna) Royal city of the land of Qumanu in northeastern Mesopotamia. The Assyrian king Tiglath-pileser I (1114–1076) reports surrounding the city after defeating and destroying an army mustered from the entire land. The city was spared when Qumanu's king submitted voluntarily to Tiglath-pileser, who ordered him to demolish his walls, hand over hostages, arrange the deportation of 300 families who refused submission to Assyria, and pay an increased tribute (**RIMA* 2: 24–5). In the reign of Shalmaneser III (858–824) the city was under the immediate authority of Shalmaneser's chief steward Iahalu, who governed Kipshuna and the lands of Qumanu, Mehranu, Uqu, and Erimmu (**RIMA* 3: 179). However, Kipshuna joined in a widespread rebellion against Shalmaneser late in his reign, initiated by the king's son Ashur-da'in-apla. The rebellion continued into the early regnal years of Shalmaneser's son and successor Shamshi-Adad V (823–811) before it was finally crushed (**RIMA* 3: 183). A legal document dated to C7 indicates that there were vineyards in the vicinity of Kipshuna (*Postgate, 1976: 85–6).

Röllig (*RlA* 5: 587–8).

Kirinu see Karania.

Kirruru (Kirriuru) (map 13) M1 mountain country located in northwestern Iran, to the southwest of Lake Urmia, in the upper reaches of the Greater Zab r. Lying close to Musasir (q.v.), it occupied an important strategic location between Assyria's northeastern frontier and the kingdom of Urartu. It is first attested in the reign of the Assyrian king Ashur-dan II (934–912), who records its conquest during a campaign which he conducted in the Greater Zab region (**RIMA* 2: 134), within the context of his Aramaean expeditions. In 886 the Assyrian king Tukulti-Ninurta II entered its passes in preparation for a campaign against the land of Ladanu, which was occupied by Aramaean and Lullumu tribal groups. This campaign took him through rugged terrain where, allegedly, none of his royal predecessors had ever ventured (**RIMA* 2: 172). He elsewhere refers to Mt Kirruru as marking one of the frontiers of his kingdom (**RIMA* 2: 180). In 883 his son and successor Ashurnasirpal II marched to Mt Kirruru following his conquests in the land of Tummu, and received there payments of tribute from a number of neighbouring or nearby lands, including Hubushkia and Gilzanu (**RIMA* 2: 197, 241). In 856 Ashurnasirpal's son and successor Shalmaneser III led his troops through the passes of Mt Kirruru after a campaign in Urartian territory, on his return to Assyria via Arbela (**RIMA* 3: 21).

Kirshu (*Meydancıkkale*) (map 4) M1 city located 700 m above sea level in Cilicia Tracheia/Aspera (Rough Cilicia), southern Anatolia, 10 km south of mod. Gülnar and 20 km from the coast. Its history of occupation extends from at least the end of C7 until the Hellenistic period, with subsequent reoccupation in Byzantine times. Excavations were undertaken in 1972 by a French team under the direction of E. Laroche. These revealed a well-fortified settlement, whose natural defences were strengthened by a built wall dating to the earliest known phase of Kirshu's history. Other remains of the city include a rampart and gate of the Persian period (C6–4); two reliefs of this period representing Persian-style processions; the foundations of a building of Persian type beneath a Hellenistic building dating to the Ptolemaic period; eight tombs, the earliest of which dates to C6; Byzantine residential quarters; and a hoard of 1,525 coins of Hellenistic date.

Written records from the site include two inscriptions in Aramaic and one in Greek, the last from the reign of Ptolemy III Euergetes (246–221). One of the Aramaic inscriptions is a fragmentary funerary text. The other, inscribed on a stone enclosure wall, contains the name of one of the four Persian kings called Artaxerxes (it is uncertain which one). References to Kirshu in the latter inscription have established that this was the site's anc. name. Kirshu was already known to scholars from Neo-Babylonian sources, where it is attested as a royal city of Appuashu, who ruled in mid C6 over the kingdom called Pirindu in Babylonian texts (Hilakku in Assyrian texts). Kirshu was said to lie six 'double-hours' from Ura, which was probably Appuashu's capital. The fact that Appuashu's ancestors had resided in Kirshu indicates the city's importance within the kingdom. A royal palace was built there. Further information about Kirshu's history is provided by a Babylonian chronicle (no. 6) from the reign of the Neo-Babylonian king Neriglissar, in the context of a military campaign which this king conducted against Appuashu in 557/556 (*Wiseman, 1956: 39–42, 86–8, **ABC* 103–4, **Chav.* 417–18). The chronicle reports that after his conquest of the neighbouring kingdom of Hume (called Que in Neo-Assyrian texts), Neriglissar embarked on a campaign against Appuashu. After capturing and pillaging Appuashu's royal capital Ura, Neriglissar proceeded to Kirshu, a difficult march across high mountains, and put the city to the torch.

When the region came under Persian domination, Kirshu was rebuilt as a fortified citadel by its Persian overlords, who clearly recognized the strategic value of its location. Davesne suggests that a Persian garrison may have been installed in the city, to provide surveillance of the region, control access to the sea, and facilitate the prompt levying of troops for military operations in Cyprus. He further suggests that the site may have served as the summer residence of the Persian satrap or a local governor. During the Hellenistic period, control over Kirshu and its region fluctuated between the successors of Alexander the Great. Ptolemaic sovereignty during the reign of Ptolemy III is indicated by a reference to this king in the Greek inscription referred to above.

Davesne *et al.* (1987), Davesne (*RlA* 8: 150–1).

Kish (maps 11, 17) Settlement in southern Mesopotamia, 15 km east of Babylon, consisting of several large mounds with occupation layers extending from the Jemdet Nasr period (M4) to mediaeval times. Following earlier French excavations in 1852 and 1912, a joint archaeological expedition of the Field Museum of Natural History of Chicago and the Ashmolean Museum, Oxford, worked for eleven seasons on the site, from 1923 to 1933, under the direction of S. Langdon. Further excavations were conducted in 1989 by Kokushikan University, Tokyo, under the direction of H. Fuji.

The site's most important mounds are those now called Ingharra (Sumerian Hursagkalama) and Uhaimir. The earliest occupation of the former is represented by ceramic ware of the Jemdet Nasr type. But it was in the subsequent Early Dynastic (ED) period of the Sumerian civilization (c. 2900–2334) that the site first came into prominence. There are remains on Ingharra of both domestic architecture, indicating a substantial residential quarter, and graves of the ED I period (c. 2900–2800). Several of the graves contained chariots or carts, of the type found at both Ur and Susa. But the most impressive buildings on this part of the site were two ziggurats (see glossary), evidenced by two enormous mudbrick platforms, and probably dating to the ED III period (c. 2600–2334). South of Ingharra, a mound designated 'A' by the excavators provided the location for a royal palace, built perhaps during the ED II period (c. 2800–2600). It is generally considered to be the most impressive of Early Dynastic Sumer's monumental buildings. However, it was abandoned before the end of ED IIIA (c. 2500), and its site was subsequently used as a cemetery, where 150 or more graves were sunk into the palace ruins. Another major building of the Early Dynastic period was located in what is called Area P, which lies to the north of Ingharra. Contemporary with the palace, it is commonly known as the Plano-Convex building because of the shape of the bricks used in its construction. It may have served as a large administrative building and storage complex.

Kish was clearly one of the most important cities of southern Mesopotamia during the Early Dynastic period, as attested also by the fact that Sumerian kings regularly used the title 'King of Kish' in their nomenclature, irrespective of their place of origin. This may indicate some form of traditional political and/or cultural hegemony enjoyed by Kish within the Sumerian world. Sargon, founder of the Akkadian empire, set out from Kish on the first stage of his imperial quest. But in later years, its king Iphur-Kish was the leader of the coalition of northern cities (there was also a coalition of southern cities) that rebelled against the Akkadian king Naram-Sin (2254–2218) in the so-called Great Revolt. Naram-Sin pursued Iphur-Kish to Kish itself, won a decisive battle against him outside the city's Ninkarrak gate, then seized the city and demolished its walls (**RIME* 2: 103–8).

In the centuries following the collapse of the M3 Mesopotamian kingdoms, Kish survived and prospered. It flourished during the Old Babylonian period (Middle

Bronze Age), when its continuing importance is reflected in the building of a ziggurat and temple complex on Tell Uhaimir, dedicated to the worship of the city's god Zababa. A scribal school of this period was also located on the mound. The ziggurat survived down to the Neo-Babylonian period in mid M1, undergoing a number of restorations over the centuries. Another feature of the city in the Neo-Babylonian period was a double temple built, or rebuilt, on Ingharra, probably by Nebuchadnezzar II (604–562). The city continued to be of some significance through the period of the Persian empire (C6–4) and in later ages (there was an important settlement there in the Sasanian period), until its final abandonment c. C6 CE.

Edzard/Gibson (*RlA* 5: 607–20), Hansen (*OEANE* 3: 298–300).

Kishesim M1 city in western Iran near the land of Parsua. It was among the cities which fell to the Assyrian king Sargon II during the campaign which he conducted in the land of Mannaea and other countries east of the Tigris in 716 (**ARAB* II: 29). Sargon plundered the city and carried off its ruler Bel-shar-usur to Assyria. He appointed an Assyrian governor in his place, renamed the city Kar-Nergal, set up his statue there, and added six neighbouring cities to its territory, now constituted as an Assyrian province.

Röllig (*RlA* 5: 453).

Kisirtu Fortified Iron Age city in the land of Zamua, located in the borderlands between northeastern Mesopotamia and northwestern Iran. It was conquered by the Assyrian king Ashurnasirpal II in 880, along with ten other cities in its environs, during Ashurnasirpal's third campaign against Zamua (**RIMA* 2: 206). Its ruler at the time was a man called Sabini.

Röllig (*RlA* 5: 622).

Kisiru Iron Age city in northeastern Mesopotamia in the Habur r. region, between Shadikannu to the north and Qatna to the south. The Assyrian king Adad-nirari II encamped his forces overnight there during his campaign in the region in 896 (**RIMA* 2: 153).

Kissik (**Kisiga, *Tell al-Lahm***) Southern Mesopotamian settlement occupied during M3–1, almost certainly to be identified with the site of Tell al-Lahm, c. 38 km southeast of Ur. It was originally (M3–2) a cult-centre of the goddess Inanna, and later (M1) of Ningal. The site was excavated briefly by J. E. Taylor in 1855, and again by R. C. Thompson in 1918. More extensive excavations were carried out by F. Safar in 1949, comprising soundings 1–6 on the main mound and soundings 7–11 on the nearby northeastern mound. An area of Neo-Babylonian housing was uncovered on the latter, with finds including some fragmentary tablets, some dated to the reign of the Persian king Darius I (522–486), and an inscribed cylinder of the Babylonian king Nabonidus (556–539) from the level below. Some of the cuneiform tablets indicate an association with the Ningal temple. The settlement must have been occupied already in the Neo-Assyrian period, since Kissik is one of the cities whose freedom the Assyrian king Sargon II claims to have established after his defeat of Marduk-apla-iddina II (biblical Merodach-baladan) (see under **Babylonia**). Many graves were also found on the surface, dating to the Neo-Babylonian and Persian periods, and perhaps also later.

(H. D. Baker)
Safar (1949).

Kissiya see Kassiya.

Kisuatnu Early Iron Age city in southern Anatolia belonging to the kingdom of Que. It was captured by the Assyrian king Shalmaneser III during his campaign against Que in 839 (**RIMA* 3: 55). The name is derived from the land called Kizzuwadna, Que's Late Bronze Age predecessor. Kizzuwadna was also the name of a city within the land of Kizzuwadna (see **Kummanni**), and it is possible that Kisuatnu was its Iron Age descendant.

Kisurra (*Abu Hatab*) (map 11) Southern Mesopotamian city, located 20 km southeast of Isin. First attested in C21 as part of the Ur III kingdom, it became in C20 a dependency of the kingdom of Isin. It was conquered by Gungunum (1932–1906), king of Larsa, but was subsequently regained by Isin's king Ur-Ninurta (1923–1896). Following the latter's death, Kisurra established its independence and was ruled by a line of its own kings, beginning with Itur-Shamash, for a period of c. thirty years. Excavations on the site of Abu Hatab, conducted by a German team in 1903, unearthed royal family archives dating to this period of self-rule. The city apparently then reverted to Larsa's control. During its independence, Kisurra may for a time have enjoyed a harmonious and perhaps cooperative relationship with Larsa, since one of its kings, Ibni-shadum, was married to a daughter of Sumu-El, king of Larsa. Other attested kings of Kisurra are Sallum, Ubaya, Zikru, and Manna-balti-El (father of Ibni-shadum). The history of their short reigns is unknown beyond references to their construction of temples and canals. Ibni-shadum is also noted for fortifying a town called Pi-naratim (q.v.). It is uncertain whether he did so on behalf of the Larsan king Sumu-El, his father-in-law, or as a protection against an attack by Larsa. Subsequently, during Larsa's ongoing conflicts with Isin, Kisurra came under the control of Isin's king Erra-imitti (1868–1861). It may later have been attached to the kingdom of Uruk, but was seized by Larsa's king Rim-Sin in 1802, the year Rim-Sin captured Uruk. In the reign of Hammurabi (1792–1750) Kisurra was incorporated into the Babylonian empire, and apparently prospered under later kings of Hammurabi's dynasty.

Kienast (*RlA* 5: 623–5), *Mesop.* 74–5, 426–7 (refs).

Kition see **Citium**.

Kızıldağ (maps 2, 3) Late Bronze Age hill settlement in south-central Anatolia. Remains of circuit walls are visible around the summit of the hill. On the west slope is an outcrop of rock bearing three Luwian hieroglyphic inscriptions and a seated human figure in relief. The figure is bearded and long-haired, and is wearing a peaked cap and long robe, and holding a bowl. The inscriptions refer to a Great King called Hartapus, son of Mursilis. However, the sculptured figure probably dates some four centuries after the inscriptions: J. D. Hawkins suggests that he may have been a C8 southern Anatolian king called Wasusarmas (see under **Tabal**), whose royal seat was possibly at Kululu (q.v.) near Kayseri. Two other inscriptions have also come to light at Kızıldağ. One of them refers to Hartapus as a great conqueror, beloved of the storm god. The other, on a fallen stele, refers to his father Mursilis. Hartapus also features in two rock-cut Luwian hieroglyphic inscriptions discovered in the mountaintop sanctuary Karadağ,

80 km to the southeast of Kızıldağ, and in another such inscription at Burunkaya, near mod. Aksaray. The Kızıldağ and Karadağ inscriptions were discovered in 1907, the former by W. M. Ramsay, the latter by G. Bell. Though they were once thought to date to early M1, primarily because of the Kızıldağ sculpture, they should probably be assigned to the last decades of the Late Bronze Age. Mursilis was very likely the Hittite king Urhi-Teshub (1272–1267), who adopted the throne-name Mursili(s) on his accession. He reigned for only a few years before being deposed and replaced on the Hittite throne by his uncle Hattusili III. It is possible that his displaced family line subsequently set up a rival kingdom in southern Anatolia (see under **Tarhuntassa**).

Bittel (1986), Hawkins (1992; **CHLI* I: 433–42).

Kızıltepe Fortified M1 hill site in Caria, southwestern Anatolia, 1.6 km southwest of Caunus. It is perhaps to be identified with Carbasyanda-by-Caunus, which figures in the Athenian Tribute Lists as a member of the Athenian Confederacy (see glossary) and was a deme (i.e. administrative district) of Caunus in the Hellenistic period.

Bean (*PECS* 458).

Kizzuwadna (map 3) Late Bronze Age country and kingdom in southern Anatolia. The territory it occupied was of considerable strategic importance, since through it passed major routes linking Anatolia with the states of northern Syria. First attested in the reign of the Hittite king Telipinu (1525–1500), Kizzuwadna was probably established as an independent kingdom during the upheavals which afflicted the Hittite world in the reign of Telipinu's predecessor-but-one Ammuna. The name of its earliest known king, Isputahsu, appears on a seal impression, discovered at Tarsus, with the inscription *Isputahsu, Great King, Son of Pariyawatri*. Isputahsu concluded with Telipinu the first known Hittite treaty, which survives in fragmentary form (*CTH* 21). One of the purposes of the treaty was apparently to formalize agreement on a border between Kizzuwadna and Hittite-controlled territory.

For a time Kizzuwadna fluctuated in its external alignments, allying itself in turn with the rival Great Kingdoms Hatti and Mitanni. In the second half of C15 its king, Pilliya, drew up a treaty with the Hittite king Zidanta (II), and a later treaty with Idrimi, who had been installed in the Syrian state Alalah as vassal ruler of the Mitannian king Parrattarna; the second of these treaties (**CS* II: 331–2, **Chav.* 174–5) indicates that Pilliya and Idrimi were, at that time, tributaries of Mitanni. But early in C14 Kizzuwadna became permanently attached to Hatti by a treaty which its king, Sunashshura, concluded with the Hittite king Tudhaliya I/II (**HDT* 17–26). Subsequently it was annexed to Hittite territory and placed under direct Hittite rule, perhaps while Tudhaliya still occupied the Hittite throne. It is possible that at this time Kizzuwadnan territory extended at least as far as the Euphrates, north of Carchemish. Several decades later, the Hittite king Suppiluliuma I made his son Telipinu priest in Kizzuwadna, an appointment which entailed important administrative and military as well as religious obligations.

Though Kizzuwadna became part of the kingdom of Hatti, its culture, from the earliest years of its existence, was predominantly Hurrian. The country was also in a Luwian as well as a Hurrian cultural zone, and its population was largely an admixture of Hurrian and Luwian elements. Its most important cities included Kummanni, the capital, and Lawazantiya. Both of these were major centres of Hurrian religion.

Kizzuwadna's Iron Age successor was the kingdom called Que (q.v.). The name Que may already have been in use by the time of the Sea Peoples' alleged onslaught on western Asia in the eighth regnal year of the pharaoh Ramesses III (1177) (see **Qode**).

Kümmel (*RlA* 5: 627–31), **RGTC* 6: 211–16, Beal (1986).

Kneidiğ, Tell (*Knēdiğ, Tall*) Small rural settlement in northeastern Syria, in the lower Habur valley, with Early Bronze Age, Iron Age, and Roman/Parthian levels. The site consists of an oval mound, 15 m high and 200 sq. m in area, and a 2 ha habitation area, built on a 2.5 m high plateau at the base of the mound's northeastern flank. A team from the Vorderasiatisches Museum, Berlin, conducted excavations here from 1993 to 1997. Their attention was focused on the Early Bronze Age levels, especially those of the first half of M3. There is no evidence of Middle or Late Bronze Age settlement on the site. Three Iron Age levels of the Neo-Assyrian period have been identified on the plateau. The settlement in this period was characterized by multi-roomed domestic architecture and what appears to have been an enclosed grain storage facility. These, together with the artefactual remains, make clear Tell Kneidiğ's rural and domestic character in this period. Burials, in which adults were interred in double pots and infants in single jars, were made beneath the floors of houses. A large cylindrical sarcophagus was uncovered amongst the burials.

Klengel-Brandt *et al.* (1998).

Kode see **Qode**.

Korucutepe (maps 2, 20) Settlement-mound in eastern Anatolia, 16 m high and c. 190 m in diameter, located 30 km east of mod. Elaziğ on the south bank of the Murad Su (anc. Arsanias r.). Its three seasons of excavation, from 1968, were directed by M. N. van Loon, under the sponsorship, principally, of the Oriental Institute, University of Chicago. The site was occupied from mid C5 in the Chalcolithic period through the Bronze and early Iron Ages. There is also evidence of settlement in later periods, until the site's final abandonment c. 800 CE. Some 140 occupation strata have been identified, extending over 5,000 years. During the Middle Bronze Age, Korucutepe was strongly fortified. Its defences were further developed in the Late Bronze Age, when it lay within the country of Isuwa, whose territory was invaded and fiercely contested by the kingdoms of Hatti and Mitanni. Burney suggests that the discovery of central Anatolian pottery in Korucutepe during the period of the Hittite Old Kingdom (C17–15), and its prevalence elsewhere in Isuwa, could imply the deliberate transplantation of people from the Hittite heartland, to counterbalance the pro-Mitannian sentiments of the local Hurrian population.

van Loon (1975–80), Ertem (1988), Burney (2004: 158–9).

Kourion see **Curium**.

Kromna Small M1 Greek city in Paphlagonia on Anatolia's Black Sea coast, first attested in Homer among Troy's Paphlagonian allies in the 'Trojan Catalogue' (Homer, *Iliad* 2.855). At the end of C4, Amastris, widow and successor of Dionysius, the former tyrant of Heraclea Pontica, formed a synoecism (see glossary) of four cities east of Heraclea, consisting of Tios, Sesamos, Kromna, and Kytoros (*BAGRW* 86 B2–C2).

Sesamos, renamed Amastris, was the nucleus of the amalgamated settlements. Kytoros lay c. 40 km to the east of it.

Strabo 12.3.10, Marek (*BNP* 3: 958).

Ktk (**Kaska (2), Kasku**) Small Iron Age Aramaean kingdom, with a capital city of the same name, in northern Syria, west of Carchemish. The treaties inscribed on the three Sefire stelae (see under **Sefire**) attest to its existence in C8. Identification of the kingdom and city has proved problematical, since in Aramaic the name appears simply as Ktk, without vowels. Fitzmyer (1995: 167–74) summarizes the proposals made by various scholars in their attempts to identify it. Most recently, Lipiński has argued that the capital (and also the kingdom) was called Kittik, which he equates with the site Yel Baba (11 km east of mod. ʿAzaz), called Kittika in the late Roman period.

Some time before the Assyrian king Tiglath-pileser III's conquest of the Aramaean kingdom of Arpad (Bit-Agusi) in 740, Bar-Gaʾyah, king of Ktk, drew up a treaty in Aramaic (documented on the Sefire stelae) with Matiʾilu, ruler of Arpad (**CS* II: 213–17). It is clear that Matiʾilu was the inferior partner in the pact, which the Assyrians, who supported Bar-Gaʾyah, had imposed upon him. In Assyrian texts, the name Ktk is vocalized as Kaska/Kasku. No doubt this form was adopted by Neo-Assyrian scribes because of its similarity to the name known to them from Late Bronze Age records (Ktk, Ksk). There is, however, no ethnic, cultural, or political connection between Aramaean Kaska/Kasku (Ktk) and the Late Bronze Age Pontic region so called. Lipiński believes that Kittik was annexed to Assyria by Sargon II, possibly in the same year, 711, as the annexation of Gurgum.

Hawkins (1982: 407–8), *Fitzmyer (1995), Lipiński (2000: 221–31).

Kukunu Iron Age city in the land of Dirru, on the north side of the Tigris r., roughly opposite the city of Tushhan. The Assyrian king Ashurnasirpal II conquered it during a campaign which he conducted in the region in his fifth regnal year (879); according to his account, Kukunu was situated at the entrance of the pass of Mt Matnu (**RIMA* 2: 210).

Kulhai see **Colchis**.

Kullani(a) see **Kinalua**.

Küllüboa Early Bronze Age settlement-mound covering 3.75 ha, located in central Anatolia in the province of mod. Eskişehir. The site has been excavated since 1996 by a Turkish team under the direction of T. Efe. Occupation dates from late M4/early M3, in the transitional period between the Late Chalcolithic and the Early Bronze Age. Already in its Early Bronze I phase, Küllüboa was an enclosed and fortified settlement, with houses opening onto a central courtyard. It reached the peak of its development towards the end of Early Bronze II (second half of M3), when it consisted of an upper fortified settlement and a lower settlement. In the former, buildings were laid out along streets in a linear plan, replacing the radial plan of the Early Bronze I settlement. The houses in the upper settlement were rectangular or square, and consisted of megaron units (see glossary) with smaller rooms attached. A large complex located opposite the gateway which gave access to the upper settlement may have served as the residence of the local ruler. Efe believes that the whole of the Early Bronze II settlement was encircled by a massive outer fortification wall. He concludes (2003: 276) that the plan of Küllüboa in this phase of its existence reflects its adaptation to meet the altering demands of a newly organized and more complex society now functioning under an administrative elite. The settlement's urban development was closely linked with its commercial development, and its prosperity was due to its location on what appears to have been the main caravan route between the Troad in northwestern Anatolia and Cilicia in the southeast. Small finds from the site, including many metal artefacts and a large assemblage of terracotta figurines, indicate that Küllüboa flourished for much of its existence, though it appears to have suffered a considerable reduction in size in its Early Bronze III phase (late M3).

Efe (2003), Yıldırım and Gates (2007: 288–9).

Kululu (map 18) Predominantly Iron Age settlement, with earlier M3 and M2 occupation levels, located in eastern Anatolia, 30 km northeast of Kayseri. It was a major centre, and may have been the capital, of the kingdom called Tabal which occupied the northern part of the Tabal region (see under **Tabal**). Kululu's Iron Age remains include carved orthostats and fragments of statues. But the most significant finds of this period are a series of inscriptions in Luwian hieroglyphs, which are carved on a number of stelae, several other stone fragments, and five lead strips, all dating to mid–late C8. The stele inscriptions are either funerary in character, or building foundation documents. The subject of three of them is a man called Ruwas, identified as 'servant of Tuwatis', who was the ruler of the kingdom of Tabal from c. 750 to 740, and the father of the next king, Wasusarmas. Ruwas was probably the ruler of a sub-kingdom within Tuwatis' realm. One of the stelae found in Kululu bears his funerary inscription. The lead strips are inscribed with economic texts, listing various persons, their towns of origin, and a record of gifts and payments, including livestock and human beings, made to or by them. Kululu's anc. name is unknown, but may have been Artulu (q.v.) or Tuna (q.v.).

**CHLI* I: 442–7, 485–91, 500–13, **CS* II: 127–8.

Kumidu (Kumidi) see ***Kamid el-Loz***.

Kummaha Late Bronze Age city in northeastern Anatolia, attested in Hittite texts. It lay in or near the country of Azzi-Hayasa. Towards mid C14, in the course of the Hittites' retaliatory campaigns against the enemies who had occupied their homeland (**DS* 66, **CS* I: 187), the Hittite prince Suppiluliuma (later King Suppiluliuma I) fought a battle near the city with the Hayasan king Karanni (or Lanni?). Kummaha should be distinguished from the later Iron Age kingdom of Kummuh, which lay further to the south.

**RGTC* 6: 220–1.

Kummanni (map 3) Late Bronze Age city, the most important religious centre of the country of Kizzuwadna in southern Anatolia. It is probably to be identified with Classical Comana Cappadociae, near mod. Şar. The city itself is sometimes called Kizzuwadna. It was dedicated to the worship of the Hurrian goddess Hepat and her consort Teshub. In the ninth year of his reign (c. 1313), the Hittite king Mursili II celebrated here a festival in honour of Hepat, completing an obligation which his father Suppiluliuma had left unfulfilled (*AM 108–9, *CS II: 88). The festival provided an opportunity for a meeting between Mursili and his brother Sharri-Kushuh (Piyassili), summoned from his viceregal post in Carchemish. Sharri-Kushuh fell ill and died while in Kummanni. A well-known ritual text from Mursili's reign indicates that a substitute ox was to be sent to Kummanni and burnt there, along with a wagonload of Mursili's personal possessions, in an attempt to cure the king of a speech affliction (*Beckman in Frantz-Szabó, 1995: 2010).

Kümmel (*RlA* 6: 335–6).

Kumme City in northeastern Mesopotamia, first attested in Middle Bronze Age texts from the Mari archives. It became famous in M2 as a cult-centre for the worship of the Hurrian god Teshub. However, it is best known as an Iron Age city located near the frontier of the kingdom of Urartu and bordering on one of the regions called Habhu in Assyrian texts (see **Habhu (3)**). The Assyrian king Adad-nirari II (911–891) came twice to its assistance, probably in response to attacks upon it by inhabitants of Habhu, whose cities he destroyed (**RIMA* 2: 152). Possibly Kumme was for a time subject to Urartian overlordship, but there is no clear evidence for this.

As a subject territory of the Assyrian empire, it was under the immediate rule of a certain Ariye during the reign of the Assyrian king Sargon II (721–705). Sennacherib, the Assyrian crown prince, reported to his father Sargon that good progress was being made on the construction of a fort in Kumme to strengthen the city's defences (**SAA* I: 28, no. 29). He also reported that he had received word from Ariye that information about the new fort had been sent by the king of the nearby city of Ukku to Assyria's enemy, the Urartian king, doubtless Rusa I. Ariye had further news for Sennacherib: Rusa had ordered a raid on Kumme, with the object of capturing the Assyrian king's officials from the Kummeans alive. He said that he would write again to the crown prince, once he had more details, requesting the urgent dispatch of troops to protect his city. Subsequently, however, Ashur-resuwa, an Assyrian official in Kumme, wrote to Sennacherib informing him that the danger had passed. We do not know whether Rusa did in fact make an abortive attack on the city, or simply directed his attention elsewhere.

It was perhaps in this same period that Ashur-resuwa wrote to the Assyrian official Tab-shar-ashur, informing him both of a visit to Urartu by a representative of the king of Ukku, and of a meeting between the Ukkaean king and Ariye (**SAA* I: 44, no. 41). The meeting took place in the Ukkaean city of Elizki, which lay in a mountain pass between the territories belonging to Ukku and Kumme. His suspicions aroused, Sargon demanded, through Tab-shar-ashur, an explanation from the Ukkaean king as to what he was about. The Ukkaean king did in fact provide a letter to Tab-shar-ashur (**SAA* I: 44–5, no. 42). But unfortunately only the opening words of this letter are preserved, and these give no indication of the substance of what the Ukkaean king said.

Some time after his accession to the throne of Urartu in 713, Argishti II wrote to the people of Kumme complaining of their failure to send representatives to his court, presumably to acknowledge his accession (**SAA* V: 76–7, no. 95). The Kummeans had explained this failure by stating that they were subjects of Assyria, which apparently meant that diplomatic missions of this kind to Urartu were forbidden. Even so, the Urartian complaint has been seen as an indication that Kumme may at this time have had at least a partially autonomous status, if only from the Urartian point of view (see *SAA* V: XXI–XXII). Whether or not its status *vis-à-vis* Assyria underwent some change during Sargon's reign remains unknown. In any case, its relations with the Assyrian administration seem generally to have been cooperative and submissive, though there were occasions when serious friction broke out between the Kummean populace and Assyria's royal delegates (**SAA* V: 83–4, nos 106–7).

Röllig (*RlA* 6: 336–7).

Kummuh (map 7) Neo-Hittite kingdom in eastern Anatolia, located between the kingdoms of Melid and Carchemish, and occupying roughly the area of the mod. Turkish province of Adıyaman. Its capital, also called Kummuh (very likely the city attested as Kimuhu in Neo-Babylonian texts), was probably the predecessor of Classical Samosata (mod. Samsat Höyük; q.v.), which lay on the west bank of the Euphrates. Excavations were conducted on this site in the 1980s by a Turkish team prior to the completion of the Atatürk Dam. Unfortunately, few Neo-Hittite remains were uncovered before the site was flooded.

Kummuh appears in Assyrian records from c. 870–605, in the Annals of the C8 Urartian king Sarduri II, and in Luwian hieroglyphic inscriptions of its own kings in the period c. 805–770. In C9 Kummuh's king Qatazilu paid tribute to the Assyrian king Ashurnasirpal II (883–859) (**RIMA* 2: 219) and to his son and successor Shalmaneser III (858–824) (**RIMA* 3: 15, 18–19, 23). (Qatazilu and subsequently Kundashpu are attested as rulers of Kummuh during Shalmaneser's reign.) In 805, the Assyrian king Adad-nirari III ordered a boundary stone to be erected between the kingdoms of Kummuh and Gurgum, ruled respectively by Ushpilulume and Qalparunda (III), the latter the son of Palalam. (See further under **Gurgum**. For the inscription on the boundary stone, the so-called Pazarcık stele, see **RIMA* 3: 205; see also Lipiński, 2000: 283–4.) Ushpilulume was at this time apparently a client ruler of the Assyrian king Adad-nirari III. He had sought Adad-nirari's support against a coalition of western states led by Attar-shumki I, ruler of Arpad (Bit-Agusi), in alliance with eight other kings. Gurgum's Qalparunda was almost certainly a member of the alliance, and in the wake of Adad-nirari's defeat of the coalition forces, the frontier between Kummuh and Gurgum was redefined. Almost certainly, the boundary stone reflected a reallocation of part of Gurgum's territory to Kummuh.

The new frontier between the two kingdoms was subsequently confirmed by the commander-in-chief Shamshi-ilu (see inscription on the reverse of the Pazarcık stele: **RIMA* 3: 240), one of the most powerful officials in the Assyrian kingdom in the first half of C8, when he put back in place the boundary stone which he had recovered during his attack upon Damascus in 773. The stone had apparently been seized on one of the campaigns which the Damascene king Bar-Hadad II had conducted against Kummuh and other states in the region. For a time in C8 Kummuh, under its king, Kushtashpi, became vassal territory of the kingdom of Urartu (along with the Neo-Hittite kingdoms Melid, Unqi, and Gurgum), then ruled by Sarduri II. But when an Urartian–Arpad military alliance, including Kummuh, was defeated by the Assyrian king Tiglath-pileser III in 743 (**ARAB* I: 272–3, 276, 281, 287, 292), Kushtashpi submitted voluntarily to Assyrian sovereignty. Sulumal and Tarhulara, the rulers respectively of Melid and Gurgum and also members of the anti-Assyrian alliance, did likewise. Pardons were evidently extended to them by their new overlord, for all three kings subsequently appear among Tiglath-pileser's tributaries (**ARAB* I: 276, 287, **Tigl. III* 68–9).

During the reign of Sargon II (721–705), Kummuh seems to have had favoured status in the region, due no doubt to the loyal support which Sargon received from its king, Mutallu. The latter was rewarded by having the city of Melid (Malatya) assigned to his control after the breakup of the troublesome kingdom of Melid. (It has been suggested that Sakçagözü, perhaps to be identified with the city of Lutibu in the kingdom of Sam'al, may also have been assigned to Mutallu in this period. Mutallu may be the ruler represented in the portrait-sculpture found on the site.) However, Mutallu subsequently fell out of favour with Sargon, who accused him of plotting with the Urartian king Argishti II. Bent on vengeance, Sargon dispatched an army against him. Mutallu himself managed to escape (**ARAB* II: 22–3, 32–3), but his land was occupied and plundered by the Assyrian forces, and his family and large numbers of the population of his land were deported, for relocation in Babylonia (**ARAB* II: 21, 35). The land was resettled by deportees from the Chaldaean tribe Bit-Yakin. Kummuh was annexed, and remained an Assyrian province until the fall of the Assyrian empire at the end of C7. Its territorial successor in later centuries was the kingdom called Commagene.

Hawkins (*RlA* 6: 338–40; **CHLI* I: 330–60).

Kundu Iron Age city in or near the country of Que in southern Anatolia. Along with the nearby city of Sissu, it seems to have formed a small sub-kingdom within Que, bordering on the Cilician plain. In early C7 it was ruled by a man called Sanduarri. As an ally of Abdi-milkutti, king of Sidon, Sanduarri apparently broke his allegiance to his Assyrian overlord Esarhaddon, and was pursued into the mountains by Esarhaddon's forces (**ARAB* II: 212). Though Abdi-milkutti seems to have gone to his aid, the fugitive was captured and beheaded (c. 675). It has been suggested (Winter, 1979: 146) that Sanduarri is to be identified with Azatiwatas, author of the Karatepe bilingual inscription (see **Karatepe**). Kundu has been tentatively located in the region of mod. Kozan, which lies to the northeast of Adana.

Hawkins (1982: 427–8; *CHLI* I: 43, 45).

Kunduru M1 city in Media, western Iran, site of the final military showdown, in 521, between the Persian king Darius I and the Median pretender to his throne, Phraortes (**DB* 31). The latter had joined the widespread rebellion against Darius at the beginning of his reign. Phraortes' forces were routed, with the loss of 34,000 troops, and the pretender himself was taken prisoner by Darius. He was later executed in the old Median city of Ecbatana.

Kunshum Middle Bronze Age city, attested in the texts of Shemshara (Middle Bronze Age Shusharra), in the western Zagros mountain region, in the area occupied by the Turukkeans. It was the capital of the kingdom of Itabalhum, probably the most powerful of a number of polities in the region during the Old Babylonian period. Letters from the Shemshara archive record an apparent sack of the city by the Gutians.

*Eidem (1985: 92–4), *Eidem and Laessøe (2001).

Kunulua see **Kinalua**.

Kurda (map 10) Middle Bronze Age royal city in the Jebel Sinjar region of northern Mesopotamia. Frequently attested in the Mari correspondence from the reign of Zimri-Lim (1774–1762), the city was ruled successively by three known kings during Zimri-Lim's reign: Simah-Ilane, Bunu-Eshtar, and Hammurabi. The third of these apparently became involved in territorial disputes with Atamrum, king of Andarig, which lay a short distance away. Terms of peace were negotiated between the two rulers, probably at the instigation of Zimri-Lim. In 1765 the Elamite king instructed Hammurabi (king of Kurda) to cease his communications with Babylon and Mari (*Charpin, 2003: 77). Kurda appears to have been subject to Andarig at this time. The latter's king, Atamrum, had declared his support for Elam against the Babylonian–Mariote alliance, which had been formed to drive the Elamite occupation forces from Mesopotamia. Later texts, discovered in one of the palaces at Shubat-Enlil/Shehna (Tell Leilan) and dated to the third quarter of C18, indicate an alliance between Ashtamar-Adad, then king of Kurda, Mutiya, king of the land of Apum (of which Shubat-Enlil was the capital), and a third king, Shepallu (whose kingdom is unknown). This alliance confronted a coalition formed by the kings of Andarig and Razama (in the land of Yussan). Subsequently Ashtamar-Adad drew up a treaty with Mutiya's successor Till-Abnu.

LKM 120, 615–16 (refs), *Mesop.* 350–1.

Kurussa Iron Age city in or near the kingdom of Pa(t)tin in northern Syria. A man called Sasi from this land was appointed ruler of Patin by the Assyrian commander-in-chief Dayyan-Ashur following the death of the previous ruler, Surri (**RIMA* 3: 69). For the circumstances, see under **Pat(t)in**.

Kurustama Late Bronze Age city in the northern or northeastern part of the kingdom of Hatti (i.e. northern or northeastern Anatolia). It figures in several Hittite texts: the biography of the mid C14 Hittite king Suppiluliuma I, written by his son and second successor Mursili II (**DS* 98, **CS* I: 191); a 'Plague Prayer' of Mursili (*Singer, 2002: 58, **CS* I: 158); and a few fragments of a text mentioning Kurustama, Hatti, and Egypt; the fragments have been collected as *CTH* 134. The first two texts refer to a pact between a king of Hatti and a king of Egypt, by the terms of which the former agreed to the transfer of persons from Kurustama to Egyptian territory and their resettlement there. At this time, a treaty was drawn up between Hatti and Egypt, in which an oath was sworn to the storm god of Hatti, to the effect that Hatti would never violate Egyptian territory. The treaty apparently remained in force until Suppiluliuma invaded Syria–Palestine during his campaigns against Mitanni and its subject and allied territories. According to Mursili's Plague Prayer, his attacks upon the Egyptian frontier land of Amka while conducting military operations in the region (1327) breached the treaty with Egypt, and provided one of the two reasons for the divinely inflicted plague which ravaged the land of Hatti for the next twenty years.

The text fragments gathered under *CTH* 134 have been interpreted by D. Sürenhagen as a type of farewell treaty to which the transferees from Kurustama were obliged to swear before they left home, and which imposed upon them obligations to both Hatti and Egypt. A more widely held view is that these fragments belong to the same Hittite–Egyptian treaty referred to twice by Mursili. That is to say, they stipulate the relocation of persons from Kurustama to Egyptian territory (in Syria–Palestine) as part of a mutual defence pact between Hatti and Egypt. The transferees were presumably intended to serve as an auxiliary force, perhaps forming a component of the troops garrisoning the Egyptian frontier. Where precisely they were located, and whether their resettlement was intended to be permanent or merely temporary, remain unknown. The date when the treaty was drawn up and the Kurustamans were transferred to Egyptian territory is also uncertain. We know the names of neither the Hittite nor the Egyptian signatories to the treaty. But on both philological and historical grounds, a late C15–early C14 date seems likely, with the co-signatories of the treaty perhaps to be identified with the Hittite king Tudhaliya I/II and the pharaoh Amenhotep II.

Ünal (*RlA* 6: 373–4), Sürenhagen (1985: 22–39), Singer (2004).

Kuşaklı see Sarissa.

Kussara (map 3) Middle and Late Bronze Age city in southern Anatolia, in the anti-Taurus region, on or near one of the main trade routes from Assyria and perhaps in the vicinity of mod. Şar (Classical Comana Cappadociae). In the second phase of the Assyrian Colony period (late C19–mid C18) (see glossary), Kussara was the seat of the dynasty of Pithana and his son Anitta, before Pithana's conquest and occupation of Nesa (**Chav.* 217; see also **Kanesh**). There may have been ethnic ties between the two cities, originating from a possible common Indo-European ancestry of many of their inhabitants. Kussara was apparently also the original seat of the Hittite royal dynasty before one of the early kings, probably Hattusili I (1650–1620), rebuilt Hattusa and made it the Hittite capital. But Kussara continued to be regarded as the ancestral home of the dynasty. It was in this city that the aged Hattusili delivered his famous 'Testament', perhaps on his deathbed, announcing the appointment of his grandson Mursili (I) as his successor, to an assemblage of the king's high-ranking subjects (**Chav.* 222–8). Kussara makes no further appearance in Hittite texts, apart from a reference to it in the genealogy and titulature of the C13 king Hattusili III.

**RGTC* 6: 230, Ünal (*RlA* 6: 379–84).

Kutalla (*Tell Sifr*) Middle Bronze Age city in southern Babylonia, located 14 km from the city of Larsa. It is attested as part of the kingdom of Larsa in the reigns of Gungunum (1932–1906), who built a temple in the city to the region's chief deity Lugalkiduna, and Rim-Sin (1822–1763). Tablets found on the site include land sale and land inheritance documents, which along with similar documents from other southern Babylonian sites (e.g. Larsa, Ur, Sippar) provide valuable information about land ownership in this period.

*Charpin (1980), Edzard (*RlA* 6: 383).

Kuwaliya Country in western Anatolia first attested in early C14 when its ruler Mazlawa served as an informant to the Hittite king Arnuwanda I on the activities of the renegade Hittite subject-ruler Madduwatta (**HDT* 158). It was subsequently attached to the Arzawan kingdom of Mira when the latter became a vassal state of Hatti in the reign of Mursili II (1321–1295) (**HDT* 74). Kuwaliya has been plausibly located by J. D. Hawkins near the headwaters of the Maeander r., its chief city perhaps to be identified with Beycesultan.

Heinhold-Krahmer (*RlA* 6: 397), Hawkins (1998b: 22–4).

Kydae see **Hydae**.

Kytoros (*Gideriz*) see **Kromna**.

L

Lab(a)dudu Iron Age Aramaean tribe in southeastern Mesopotamia, attested in Assyrian sources. The first reference to it dates to the reign of Adad-nirari III (810–783), when it was one of the tribal lands laid waste by the king's commander-in-chief Shamshi-ilu (**RIMA* 3: 232). Labdudu tribesmen were among the deportees from eastern Babylonia who were resettled in Assyria by Tiglath-pileser III c. 730 (*Tigl. III* 160–1). The tribe later figures in the list of Aramaean peoples conquered by Sargon II (721–705), and is last mentioned in correspondence from the reign of Ashurbanipal (668–630/627).

Lipiński (2000: 440–1).

Labaʾum (*Labwa*?) Bronze and Iron Age city in the central Biqaʿ valley, Lebanon. It is first clearly attested in Egyptian texts from the reigns of the pharaohs Tuthmosis III (C15) and Ramesses II (C13), though there may be an earlier reference to it in a text dating to Egypt's twelfth dynasty (1985–1773). Labaʾum appears in *OT* sources under the name *Lbʾ Hmt* or *Lbwʾ Hmt* – read as *Labwa Hamat* – indicating that the city had at one time been part of the Iron Age kingdom of Hamath; it was perhaps one of the territories of Hamath which, according to 2 Kings 14:25–8, fell to the C8 Israelite king Jeroboam II. Later in C8, it was incorporated into the Assyrian empire, as part of a province of which Soba (Assyrian Subutu) was the chief city. An identification has been proposed with mod. Labwa, located near the source of the Orontes r.

Röllig (*RlA* 6: 410), Lipiński (2000: 319–22).

Labraunda (Labraynda) (map 5) Religious sanctuary dedicated to the god Zeus Labraundus or Zeus Stratius (for the latter, see Herodotus 5.119), located in Caria, southwestern Anatolia, 48 km southeast of Miletus. The sanctuary was excavated, from 1948 onwards, by a Swedish team from the University of Uppsala. It was apparently first occupied in late C7. Built on a mountainside in a series of terraces, Labraunda was administered by the city of Mylasa, which lay 13 km to its south and was linked to it by a paved Sacred Way. Numerous rock-cut tombs, probably dating to C4, were built around the sanctuary and along the Sacred Way. L. Karlsson from Upssala University and current excavator of the site, reports that on top of the city's acropolis, 'a fortress with nine towers containing an inner fortress with two towers and barracks was documented as well as five freestanding towers on small hilltops in its vicinity. They appear to be part of a defensive system to protect the sanctuary in the late Hecatomnid period' (in Yıldırım and Gates, 2007: 319).

Labraunda's first cult-temple was probably constructed in C5, and in the following century the whole site was extensively redeveloped by members of Caria's ruling Hecatomnid dynasty, particularly Mausolus, who may have had a palace there. Little further development occurred until the early Roman imperial period when baths and other public buildings were added to the site. Labraunda continued to be occupied through the Byzantine period until its abandonment in C11 CE.

Bean (1971: 58–68), E. Akurgal (1973: 244–5), MacDonald (*PECS* 474–5), Karlsson (2006).

Lachish (*Tell ed-Duweir*) (map 8) 12 ha city located in the Judaean hill country in southern Palestine, 38 km southeast of Jerusalem. Its history of occupation extends from the Neolithic to the Hellenistic age, with several periods of abandonment in between. Identified as Lachish by W. F. Albright in 1929, the site was excavated successively by a British team under the direction of J. L. Starkey (1932–8), by Y. Aharoni on behalf of the Hebrew University of Jerusalem (1966–8), and by D. Ussishkin for Tel Aviv University (1973–87).

During the Early Bronze Age (M3), Lachish achieved the proportions of a substantial settlement, and in Middle Bronze II became one of the most important city-states of the region. A huge rampart and ditch or fosse enclosed the city in the latter period, and a large building complex constructed on the centre of the mound was probably the palace of the local ruler. It was destroyed by fire, but then apparently rebuilt and thenceforth used for domestic and industrial purposes. Rock-cut tombs contained a range of pottery, weapons, and scarabs. Already by the start of the Late Bronze Age, the imposing Middle Bronze Age defensive system had fallen into disuse, for above the debris which had accumulated in the ditch was erected, close to the northeast corner of the mound, a small temple which has become known as the Fosse Temple. In its earliest phase it consisted of a rectangular room, 15 m × 5 m, orientated north–south, with subsidiary rooms on the north and west. Against the south wall was the shrine or altar, consisting of a mudbrick bench with three projections, on and around which were found the apparatus of the cult. The temple went through two further phases, during which more chambers were added and the main cult room was enlarged and provided with additional benches.

The earliest written reference to Lachish occurs in a text from the reign of the pharaoh Amenhotep II (1427–1400). By C14 it had attained the status of one of Canaan's most important city-states. Its subjection to Egypt in this period is indicated by letters in the Amarna archive (see glossary) written to the pharaoh by its kings Yabni-ilu (**EA* 328), Zimreddi (**EA* 329), and Shipti-Baʿlu (**EA* 330–2), and by other references in the Amarna letters to its involvement in the disputes and conflicts among the pharaoh's vassal states. Destruction of the city (level VII) probably occurred around the end of C13. The last 'Canaanite' city (level VI), still under Egyptian control, was built shortly after this destruction. Its tax obligations to Egypt are indicated by inscriptions on votive bowls dating to the reign of the pharaoh Ramesses III (1184–1153).

Lachish did not escape the upheavals which afflicted many of the kingdoms and cities of the western Asian world in early C12. The level VI city was destroyed during these upheavals and the site was abandoned, not to be resettled until C10. The agents of destruction may have been groups of Sea Peoples. Alternatively, Lachish may have fallen to the Israelites, if their alleged destruction of the city and its inhabitants reported in Joshua 10:31–2 is historically valid and can be assigned to this period. The city's lack of fortifications during its Late Bronze Age phase no doubt facilitated its destruction. It remained unfortified after it was rebuilt (level V) in C10. This rebuilding marked the beginning of the Iron Age II phase of Lachish's existence (levels V–III;

c. 1000–587). But the city was again destroyed within a few decades, on this occasion during the campaign conducted by the pharaoh Sheshonq I (biblical Shishak) in the region c. 925. Yet again Lachish emerged from its ashes, this time as a large and massively fortified city, dominated by an enormous palace-fortress constructed within the centre of the city. There is an assumption that the new city, level IV, was constructed by one of the early kings of Judah (in the period late C10–early C9) within the context of the divided monarchy. Indeed Lachish now achieved a regional importance second only to that of Jerusalem.

The next archaeologically attested destruction, which levelled substantial parts of the city, including its palace, city gate, wall, and a residential area, has been attributed to environmental causes rather than to human agency. The earthquake reported in Amos 1:1 and Zechariah 14:5 in the reign of the Judaean king Uzziah (c. 760) may have been the culprit. But this remains speculative. In any case, the city's fortifications and palace-fortress were promptly rebuilt, the latter on a larger scale than previously, and the population also grew in size. But the level III city had a relatively short existence before it was destroyed, c. 701, by the Assyrian king Sennacherib, who deported its inhabitants and set up his camp there as a base for operations against Hezekiah, king of Jerusalem. Stone reliefs from Sennacherib's palace in Nineveh depict the conquest of the city.

Yet again Lachish was abandoned and yet again rebuilt and refortified, its level II phase being assigned to the period when Josiah was king of Judah (640–609). But it was now reduced in size, its palace-fortress was not rebuilt, its walls were less substantial, and parts of the centre of the city were left in ruins. A notable find dating to this level was a group of Hebrew ostraca now referred to as the Lachish letters, sent to or by an army commander stationed in Lachish. According to Jeremiah 34:7, Lachish was by now one of the few fortified cities left in Judah. The level II city was destroyed by the Babylonian king Nebuchadnezzar II c. 587, and once again abandoned. Its last designated phase, level I, began with its rebuilding as a centre of the Persian administration, the Persian governor being housed in a small government residency built over the remains of the former palace-fortress. Part of its population was made up of Judaean exiles liberated from Babylon by the Persians. The city survived into the Hellenistic period when, yet again, it was abandoned.

Weippert/Wright (*RlA* 6: 412–17), Ussishkin (*NEAEHL* 3: 897–911; *OEANE* 3: 317–23), Pardee (*OEANE* 3: 323–4, for the Lachish inscriptions), Ussishkin (2004), James (2007).

Ladanu Country in northeastern Mesopotamia, in the region of the Greater and Lesser Zab rivers, attested in the texts of the Assyrian king Tukulti-Ninurta II (890–884). Tukulti-Ninurta reports that the land was at that time occupied by Aramaean and Lullu(mu) tribes, and that he conquered and destroyed thirty of its cities (886) (**RIMA* 2: 172–3).

Lade (map 5) Small island off the southwestern coast of Anatolia near the city of Miletus. In 494 it was the scene of a naval engagement fought in defence of Miletus by the Ionian Greeks and their allies who, according to Herodotus, mustered 353 triremes against the 600 ships of the Persian fleet. The Greek forces were routed by the enemy. The Persians followed up their victory by blockading and capturing Miletus, and massacring or enslaving its inhabitants.

Herodotus 6.7–18, Bürchner (*RE* XII: 381).

Lagash (maps 11, 17) Early Bronze Age Sumerian city-state in southern Mesopotamia, occupying c. 300 ha and consisting of three urban centres: Lagash city (mod. al-Hiba), Girsu (mod. Telloh), and Nina-Sirara (mod. Zurghul), located c. 20 km apart. Lagash achieved prominence in Mesopotamia during the second half of M3, following the decline of two other leading Sumerian states, Uruk and Kish, and continued to play an important role in the political, military, and economic affairs of southern Mesopotamia until the collapse of the Ur III kingdom at the end of M3.

From royal inscriptions discovered on the site of Telloh during French excavations at the end of C19, a first royal 'dynasty' of nine kings has been assembled (the seventh and ninth of its members, Enentarzi and Urukagina, are thought to be interlopers) dated to the period c. 2520 to 2330. Under this dynasty, founded by Ur-Nanshe, Lagash dominated southern Mesopotamia for almost two centuries. It reached the peak of its power and development under its third king Eannatum, best known from the famous Stele of the Vultures monument. Now in the Louvre museum, the stele was found in a fragmentary state during the French excavations of Girsu (late C19). The surviving bas-relief and accompanying inscription record a battle between Lagash and its longstanding rival, Umma, located c. 56 km to the northwest. Boundary disputes led to frequent clashes between the states. The relief scenes on the Stele of the Vultures depict Lagash's tutelary deity Ningirsu entangling the Ummaite enemy in a net, and Eannatum in a chariot leading his infantry forces into battle. The inscription records Eannatum's victory, and the terms of the treaty subsequently concluded with Umma (**Chav.* 11–13). Other inscriptions give the impression that Eannatum extended his power and influence to Mari on the middle Euphrates and even further north into the region of Subartu in northern Mesopotamia, apparently after he had established by military force his control over the city-states of southern Mesopotamia, including Umma, Uruk, Ur, Kish, and Akshak. Unfortunately we have no independent sources of information for assessing whether Eannatum's achievements were as extensive as he claims.

Our knowledge of the First Dynasty of Lagash depends on 120 royal inscriptions found at Telloh, supported by information contained in almost 2,000 tablets dealing with the administration of the city's temple of the goddess Ba'u. The tablets date probably to the reigns of the last three members of the dynasty. Urukagina, the last member (and possibly a usurper), reigned for only eight years, at a time when Lagash had already become much weakened. His decisive defeat by Lugal-zage-si, the king of Umma, brought Lagash's status as a major Mesopotamian power to an end. But he is particularly remembered for introducing a series of social reforms, which were designed to eradicate the abuses perpetrated by officials and others in positions of power in his kingdom, and to provide adequate protection for the kingdom's less privileged inhabitants. These reforms served as an important forerunner to the later law codes of the Ur III king Ur-Nammu (late M3), of Lipit-Ishtar, king of Isin (early M2), and of the Babylonian king Hammurabi (C18).

Lagash was subsequently incorporated into the Akkadian empire founded by Sargon in 2334. Sargon's son and successor Rimush (2278–2270) reports the conquest and destruction of both Ur and Lagash, killing 8,040 men and taking 5,460 prisoners (**RIME* 2: 45–6). After the fall of this empire c. 2193, a new line of Lagash dynasts arose, who sought to restore their state to its former glory. The most distinguished member of this dynasty (its twelve members were apparently not confined to a single family) was its seventh king, Gudea, whose accession is dated to c. 2120. Under his reign in particular, Lagash appears to have enjoyed a renaissance, at least culturally and commercially. It became a flourishing centre for Sumerian art and literature, and established trading links as far afield as the Mediterranean coast and the Iranian plateau. Inscriptions on numerous stone statues of Gudea provide a wide range of information about the king's building exploits, his importation of luxury goods and commodities from distant regions, and the general prosperity of his reign; see *Edzard (1997), **Chav.* 45–51, **RIME* 3/1: 29–180.

Two decades or so later Lagash became part of the Ur III empire, founded by Ur-Nammu c. 2112. Under the Ur III regime it continued to play an important economic and political role in Mesopotamian affairs. In the final years of the Ur III kingdom, which came to an end c. 2004 in the reign of its last king, Ibbi-Sin, Lagash may have won a further brief period of independence, before coming under the control of the kingdom of Larsa during the so-called Isin-Larsa period. Thenceforth only a few scattered references attest to its continuing existence.

*Thureau-Dangin (1907), Bauer (*RlA* 6: 419–22), Lafont (*DCM* 453–6).

Lagash city (*al-Hiba*) One of the three urban centres comprising the Early Bronze Age Sumerian city-state of Lagash. The other two were Girsu (mod. Telloh) and Nina-Sirara (mod. Zurghul). Like both these sites, al-Hiba was first occupied in the Ubaid and Uruk periods. It has the distinction of being one of the largest archaeological sites in western Asia, covering at its maximum extent some 600 ha. The

Figure 60 Gudea, king of Lagash.

German archaeologist R. Koldewey conducted the first excavations there in 1887. The numerous burials within the houses he unearthed led him to conclude, wrongly, that al-Hiba was a necropolis. (He reached a similarly mistaken conclusion about Nina-Sirara.) Following brief regional surveys in the al-Hiba region in 1953 a d 1965, new excavations were conducted on the site, from 1968 onwards, by D. P. Hansen for the Institute of Fine Arts of New York University and the Metropolitan Museum of Art, New York. Inscriptions have identified al-Hiba's anc. name as Lagash. For a time, it was the capital of its city-state, probably in the first part of the Early Dynastic period (c. 2900–2334), before Girsu took on this role. Part of a large temple precinct called the Bagara has been unearthed. It was dedicated to Lagash's chief deity Ningirsu. A nearby building which appears to have been associated with this precinct has been identified as a brewery. Other buildings dating to the Early Dynastic III period include a temple complex dedicated to the goddess Inanna (the Ibgal of Inanna), located at the city's southwestern edge within an oval enclosure wall, and a large administrative building that contained tablets and sealings dating to the reigns of Eannatum and Enannatum I, third and fourth rulers of Lagash's first dynasty.

The large-scale abandonment of the city at the end of the Early Dynastic III period has been associated with the conquest of Lagash by its longstanding rival Umma. There was, however, some continuing occupation during the period of the Akkadian empire (2334–2193), to judge from a number of Akkadian texts found on the mound. Following the collapse of the empire, Gudea, king of a renascent Lagash, appears to have rebuilt the Bagara. Occupation continued through the following Ur III and Isin-Larsa periods. The latest attested evidence of the city's existence dates to the reign of the Larsan king Sin-iddinam (1849–1843).

Hansen (*RlA* 6: 422–30), Matthews (*OEANE* 2: 406–9).

Lahiru M1 city in the Diyala region, eastern Babylonia, near the Elamite frontier. The Assyrian king Adad-nirari II (911–891) claims that it marked one of the limits of the Babylonian territory which he annexed following his defeat of the Babylonian king Shamash-mudammiq (**RIMA* 2: 148). It was among the cities seized and destroyed by the Assyrian king Shalmaneser III in 850 during the second of his Babylonian campaigns (**RIMA* 3: 30). In 812 it was conquered by the Assyrian king Shamshi-Adad V, during his third Babylonian campaign (**ABC* 168). The Babylonian throne at this time was occupied by Baba-aha-iddina. Lahiru later fell to the Assyrian king Tiglath-pileser III (745–727), along with the nearby cities of Hilimmu and Pillutu and the territories of the Aramaean tribe Puqudu. Tiglath-pileser incorporated all these cities and lands into the Assyrian province of Arrapha (**Tigl. III* 160–1). Lahiru was the centre of a district variously called Yadburu, Yadibiri, Idibirina, and Dibirina in Assyrian texts. It served as a market-place for the wool which was purchased there by textile traders from Nippur, and as a collection centre for livestock (horses, mules, oxen, sheep, goats) brought by local sheikhs as tribute for the Assyrian king.

Brinkman (1968: 178), *Nippur IV*: 117, Lipiński (2000: 432–3).

Lahm, Tell al- see Kissik.

Laish see Dan.

Lalanda Late Bronze Age district in southern Anatolia, located in the Hittite region called the Lower Land (q.v.). Its inhabitants joined the forces from Arzawa when the latter invaded Hittite territory during the reign of the Hittite king Tudhaliya III (first half of C14). However, the Lalandans promptly renewed their allegiance to Hatti when Tudhaliya's son and successor Suppiluliuma I dispatched his military commander Hannutti to the Lower Land to reassert Hittite authority there (*Houwink ten Cate, 1966: 28–30). They again rose in rebellion in the reign of the C13 king Tudhaliya IV.
Frantz-Szabó and Ünal (*RlA* 6: 437), **RGTC* 6: 240–1.

La'la'tu M1 city belonging to the Aramaean state of Bit-Adini in northern Syria, and located near the capital, Til-Barsip (Tell Ahmar). In 858, when Bit-Adini was ruled by a man called Ahunu, La'la'tu was among the cities in the region conquered by the Assyrian king Shalmaneser III during his first western campaign (**RIMA* 3: 9, 15). Abandoned by its population, who fled at the approach of the Assyrian army, the city was seized by Shalmaneser and put to the torch.
Lipiński (2000: 174).

Lalluknu see Sukkia.

Lamena Iron Age mountainous land in southern Anatolia attacked by the Assyrian king Shalmaneser III, following his campaign in 833 against the kingdom of Que (**RIMA* 3: 68). The Assyrians captured the mountain peak where the population of the land had taken refuge, massacred their victims or took them prisoner, and plundered and burned their towns and villages before moving on to the conquest of Tarsus on the coast.

Lampsacus (map 5) M1 settlement in the Troad, northwestern Anatolia. Originally called Pityussa, it was an Ionian colony founded by settlers from either Miletus or Phocaea on Anatolia's western coast. It occupied a valuable strategic position on the southern shore of the Hellespont. The Greek geographer Strabo (13.1.18) speaks of its fine harbour. In C6 it was part of the Lydian empire, until 546 when the empire fell to the Persian king Cyrus II. In late C6 its inhabitants were involved in a dispute with the Athenian commander Militiades (I) over his domination of the Thracian Chersonesus, which lay close by to the north (Herodotus 6.37–8). Persian control was firmly established over Lampsacus by Darius I after he had crushed the Ionian rebellion in 494. Subsequently, Darius' grandson and successor-but-one Artaxerxes I assigned the city to the exiled Athenian commander Themistocles. The latter's travels after his banishment from Athens ended when he sought refuge with the Persians in western Anatolia and was appointed governor of the city of Magnesia on the Maeander (Magnesia ad Maeandrum). Apparently, Lampsacus kept Themistocles supplied with the wine for which it was famous (Thucydides 1.138). Later, the city became a member of the Athenian Confederacy (see glossary). Its prosperity at this time is indicated by its annual contribution to the Confederacy's treasury – the considerable sum of twelve talents. The city broke its ties with Athens in 412/411, when Athenian fortunes in the Peloponnesian War had reached a very low ebb (Thucydides 8.62). But Athens quickly re-established control over it. In 405 it was taken by the Spartan commander Lysander, and it remained under Spartan domination until it once more fell to the Persians. The city regained its independence c. 362, and remained free of outside control until it was taken by Alexander the Great in 334.

Schwertheim (*BNP* 7: 190–1).

Landa One of the small Late Bronze Age countries in southern Anatolia which the early Hittite king Labarna (C17) conquered and assigned to the governorship of his sons (**Chav.* 230). Later references to the city are confined to cultic contexts.

Ünal (*RlA* 6: 487–8).

Lapethos (Lapithus, ***Lampousa***) (map 14) Bronze and Iron Age settlement on the north-central coast of Cyprus, located 14 km west of mod. Kyrenia. Over 250 Early and Middle Bronze Age burials were excavated there in early C20 by J. L. Myres and M. Markides for the Dept of Antiquities, Cyprus, B. H. Hill for the University Museum of the University of Pennsylvania, and the Swedish Cyprus Expedition. The site was particularly important in the Middle Bronze Age, when large-scale consumption of metal is implied by the deposition of significant quantities of bronze weapons and implements in the tombs. This reflects a growing external demand for Cypriot copper and an increasing trade in this material from harbour-towns on the north coast. Lapethos may also have been a manufacturing centre for metal goods, drawing its copper from the Skouriotissa area in the northwestern Troodos. The settlement continued to be occupied, on a much reduced scale, in the Late Bronze Age.

The Iron Age town was founded, according to Greek tradition, by a certain Praxandrus from Laconia in southern mainland Greece. Although not among the local kingdoms listed in the prism inscription of the C7 Assyrian king Esarhaddon (Heidel, 1956), Lapethos appears to have enjoyed political autonomy, but very little is known of its history. Its coin issues, which date to C5 and C4, provide the names of some its kings. But otherwise, the earliest attestation of it in written sources occurs in a reference to it in the list of cities compiled in mid C4 under the name of the 'geographer' Pseudo-Scylax. The first historical reference to the city records the arrest by Ptolemy I Soter of its king, Praxippus (312), who was suspected of being in league with Ptolemy's rival Antigonus. In general, Lapethos appears to have enjoyed a prosperous existence through to the early Byzantine period, when it was the seat of a bishop. Decline set in after the first Arab invasions in 647, and the site was finally abandoned.

Nicolaou (*PECS* 482–3), Herscher (*OEANE* 3: 330–1).

Laqe (maps 7, 13) Iron Age land located on the middle Euphrates, including the confluence of the Euphrates and Habur rivers and the area to the south. It lay between the states of Bit-Halupe to the north and Hindanu to the south, the latter separating it from Suhu. Its population was made up of a mixture of Aramaean and northern Arabian tribal groups. As a cultural and political entity, its origins date back to the early years of M1. But Laqe was never united under a single ruler. Rather, it consisted of a loose confederation of states ruled by independent tribal chieftains. The Assyrian king Adad-nirari II (911–891) received tribute from its cities and the neighbouring land of Hindanu in his progress through the middle Euphrates region (**RIMA* 2: 153–4). Similarly, Tukulti-Ninurta II (890–884) received tribute from Laqean rulers called Mudadda, Hamataya, and Haranu while campaigning in the middle Euphrates region

(**RIMA* 2: 175–6). But in the reign of Ashurnasirpal II (883–859), Laqe and Hindanu joined with Suhu in an anti-Assyrian coalition, probably with the encouragement of Bit-Adini and Babylonia (c. 877). Ashurnasirpal crushed the coalition's forces, then set about destroying their cities and deporting large numbers of their populations (**RIMA* 2: 214–15). In a subsequent engagement at a crossing on the Euphrates, he routed the infantry and chariotry of Azi-ilu, one of the Laqean leaders whom he himself had installed as ruler of the city of Suru (**RIMA* 2: 199) (see **Suru (2)**). Azi-ilu survived the battle, fled to the hills, and apparently defied all the Assyrians' efforts to hunt him down.

In the reign of Adad-nirari III (810–783), Laqe was among the lands in the middle Euphrates region assigned to the governorship of a man called Nergal-erish (Palil-erish) (**RIMA* 2: 209, 211). In mid C8, when Laqe was being plundered by a force of 2,000 Hatallu (q.v.) tribesmen, its governor, Adad-da'anu, appealed to Ninurta-kudurri-usur, ruler of Suhu, for assistance. When he heard reports that the Hatallu were planning to set upon his own land as well, Ninurta-kudurri-usur responded to the appeal by attacking and annihilating the invaders while they were still in Laqean territory. He captured and killed their leader, Shama'gamni, then stripped off his skin and displayed it in front the gate of Al-gabbari-bani, one of the cities of Suhu (**RIMB* 2: 292–302).

Postgate (*RlA* 6: 492–4), Lipiński (2000: 77–108).

Larak Early Bronze Age Sumerian city-state in southern Mesopotamia, probably located near Nippur. According to the Sumerian King List, it was the third of five Sumerian cities to be granted kingship in Sumer before the great flood (**Chav.* 82). Written evidence indicates that the city was still occupied in M2 and in M1 down to the Persian period (C6–4).

Edzard (*RlA* 6: 494–5).

Larbusa Iron Age city located in the vicinity of Mt Nisir, in or near the land of Zamua on the edge of the Zagros mountain range. Larbusa and the cities belonging to it were conquered, plundered, and destroyed by the Assyrian king Ashurnasirpal II in 881 during his campaign against Zamua (**RIMA* 2: 204–5).

Laris(s)a Legendary city of the Pelasgians in Homeric tradition (*Iliad* 2.840–3). There are a number of cities of this name attested in Classical sources (Strabo 9.5.19 lists eleven). The Pelasgian city so called is probably to be located on the western coast of the Troad, in the region of Aeolis, though the listing of the Pelasgians next to Thrace in Homer's Trojan Catalogue (in the *Iliad*) could conceivably indicate a Thracian location for their city. If the city was in fact located in Aeolis, then it can perhaps be identified with the settlement on the hill above the mod. village of Buruncuk (28 km north of Izmir). An alternative identification has been proposed with the site at Yanık Köy, which lies a few km to the east. The Pelasgians of Larissa were apparently overcome by Aeolian Greek newcomers to the region in late C8. From then on Larissa became one of the most important Aeolian cities, and is generally assumed to have been the city attested by Herodotus (1.149), in the form Leris(s)ae, among the twelve original Aeolian communities.

Kaletsch (*BNP* 7: 254).

Larsa (*Tell Senkereh*) (map 11) City in southern Mesopotamia, covering more than 300 ha, located 20 km southeast of Uruk. Its history of occupation extends (probably) from the Ubaid period (M4) – though the earliest excavated remains date to M3 – to the Parthian period (C3 BCE–C3 CE). However, its main period of occupation falls within the Middle Bronze Age, in the first quarter of M2. Larsa was first identified with Tell Senkereh by W. K. Loftus in 1854. Since then, twelve excavation campaigns have been conducted on the site, the most important and most recent of which have been those of J.-C. Margueron in 1969 and 1970, and J.-L. Huot from 1976 until 1991.

The excavation, incomplete, of a large building dating to the Early Dynastic period (c. 2900–2334), indicates that Larsa was already a city of some importance at this time. However, it reached the height of its power and prosperity in the early years of M2, when it was one of the cities which sought to fill the vacuum left by the collapse of the Ur III empire c. 2004. Prior to this, a ruling dynasty had supposedly (according to the later 'Larsa King List') been established in Larsa by a man called Naplanum c. 2025. He was the first of a line of fourteen kings who held sway over the city and its territories through the first quarter of M2, until Larsa's independence was brought to an end in 1763 by the Babylonian king Hammurabi. The city's rise to prominence as the centre of a major kingdom began with the reign of its fifth king, Gungunum (1932–1906), who led Larsa into the first of a long series of conflicts with the rival kingdom Isin. Gungunum surrounded his city with a wall, seized the city of Ur from Isin's king Lipit-Ishtar, and temporarily 'liberated' the city of Kisurra and possibly also Uruk from Isin's domination. Military victories by Gungunum's successor-but-one Sumu-El (1894–1866) resulted in a northward expansion of the territories controlled by Larsa: Sumu-El conquered Kazallu and Kish, and also briefly gained sway over Kisurra and Nippur. However, his defeat at the hands of the Isin king Bur-Sin enabled Isin to regain control over Ur for awhile.

Sumu-El's successor Nur-Adad (1865–1850) is noted for his impressive building projects, at least according to his own inscriptions (**RIME* 4: 145–9). He claims to have rebuilt Larsa's city wall and a great palace in the city, and also to have ordered an extensive building programme in Ur (obviously now back under Larsa's control) and the restoration of the anc. sanctuary of Enki (Ea) in the city of Eridu. His palace in Larsa has in fact been identified, though it was apparently incomplete at the time of his death and was never occupied. This may have been due to political upheavals at the end of his reign – if we can so judge from an inscription of his son and successor Sin-iddinam (1849–1843), which seems to indicate an uprising in his father's reign but gives no details.

The last two independent rulers of Larsa, Warad-Sin (1834–1823) and Rim-Sin (1822–1763), were members of a new dynasty. The former was installed on Larsa's throne by his father, Kudur-Mabuk, an Amorite chieftain (following the expulsion of Silli-Adad, the last ruler of the previous dynasty). (For an account of Kudur-Mabuk's achievements, see **RIME* 4: 206–21.) Rim-Sin, brother of Warad-Sin, is one of the best known of the early Mesopotamian kings, with the distinction of having the longest reign of all of them: he occupied his kingdom's throne for sixty years. Rim-Sin conquered Uruk around 1802, thus putting an end to the local Sin-kashid dynasty. On his accession, the kingdom covered a 230 km strip of territory in western Babylonia, extending from Eridu and Ur in the south beyond Nippur in the north. During the first half of his reign, Rim-Sin pursued his kingdom's ongoing conflict with Isin. The result was a decisive victory for Rim-Sin in 1794, which resulted in Isin's incorporation as subject territory into the kingdom of Larsa. This triumph marked the high point of Rim-Sin's reign. The second half of the reign was characterized by increasingly strained relations with Babylon, then ruled by Hammurabi, who like his father and grandfather had formerly been a vassal of Rim-Sin. When Rim-Sin refused to join Hammurabi in a war against the Elamites, the Babylonian king used this as a pretext for attacking Larsa. He succeeded in capturing the city after a six-month siege, and took Rim-Sin and his son prisoner (1763). But Hammurabi spared the city, its buildings and its population, contenting himself simply with demolishing its fortifications. Initially, he sought to create the illusion of a partnership between the kingdoms of Babylon and Larsa, but this did little to disguise the reality of the absorption of Larsa into the Babylonian empire – along with Isin, Ur, and Uruk, which had formerly been under Larsa's control. (Much of the information about Larsa and its relations with Babylon in this period is provided by letters contained in the Mari archives; see e.g. **ARM XXVI/2*: 203–5, nos. 385, 386, *LKM* 616, refs.)

The territory previously controlled by Larsa was divided into a northern 'upper province' and a southern 'lower province', the former probably with Mashkan-shapir as its centre, the latter centred upon the city of Larsa. The name Yamutbal(um)/ Emutbal(um) was frequently applied to the region and also to the kingdom of Larsa, probably a reflection of the Amorite tribal origin of many of the region's inhabitants, including perhaps its kings (see under **Yamutbal(um)**). Along with other southern Mesopotamian cities, Larsa briefly regained its independence, under another leader called Rim-Sin, in the eighth(?) year of the reign of Hammurabi's successor Samsu-iluna (1749–1712). The rebellion was crushed by Samsu-iluna the following year, and Rim-Sin was killed (**RIME* 4: 387).

In Larsa, Hammurabi undertook a major building programme, most notably within the city's religious precinct, where the main buildings were a temple to the god Shamash, the Ebabbar, and a ziggurat (see glossary). Hammurabi commissioned a monumental new complex, which extended over 300 m and consisted of a succession of buildings and courtyards, the latter lined with chapels and workshops. The precinct was restored several times in the centuries following Hammurabi's reign, and remained in operation in that form until C11. The site has produced two important *kudurrus* (see glossary) of the Kassite period.

The Ebabbar was rebuilt in C6 by the Neo-Babylonian king Nebuchadnezzar II (604–562) (**CS* II: 308–9), as reflected in material remains of the period, and restored several decades later by the last Neo-Babylonian king, Nabonidus. The Ebabbar precinct clearly continued to provide a focus for religious activities within the city during the Neo-Babylonian, Persian, and Seleucid periods, according to tablets from the city.

Arnaud/Margueron/Huot (*RlA* 6: 496–506), Charpin (*DCM* 466–9), *Mesop*. 319–24.

Lasqum (map 10) City and mountain district in the middle Euphrates region, located above mod. Der ez-Zor (Dayr az-Zawr in Lipiński, 2000) and attested in the Middle Bronze Age Mari archives from Zimri-Lim's reign (1774–1762). It was used as a place of refuge by the inhabitants of a city on the Euphrates called Dunnum when the city fell victim to an epidemic. One of the Mari texts refers to the establishment of a large Yaminite encampment in Lasqum, which extended to the city of Manuhatan. The

Yaminite presence there provoked an attack upon the land by troops of the Hana people (q.v.), who in this case came from the region of Qattunan on the Habur r.

Durand (1988c: 125–6), *LKM* 616 (refs).

Latihu Iron Age city in northern Mesopotamia, in the lower Habur r. valley, between Qatnu and Shadikannu. The Assyrian king Tukulti-Ninurta II encamped his forces there during his progress up the Euphrates and Habur rivers on his last recorded campaign (885) (**RIMA* 2: 177).

Röllig (*RlA* 6: 511).

Lawazantiya (map 3) City in southern Anatolia, somewhere to the north of the Amanus range, attested in Middle and Late Bronze Age and Iron Age texts. It first appears, in the form Luhusaddia, in C18 Assyrian Colony texts (see glossary) (e.g. **CMK* 113, 166, 280–2, 298, 319). Subsequently, according to a well-known literary composition dating to the Hittite Old Kingdom, it provided winter quarters for a Hittite king who was laying siege to the city of Urshu (q.v.) (*Beckman, 1995: 26). In late C16, it was among the cities that took up arms against the Hittite king Telipinu (**Chav.* 232). Some time after this, Lawazantiya became part of the country of Kizzuwadna, and by C13 was acknowledged as one of Kizzuwadna's most important religious centres. The future Hittite king Hattusili III passed through it on his way back to Hatti from his Syrian command, and while in the city he met and married the Hurrian priestess Puduhepa (**CS* I: 202).

Lawazantiya has been identified with Lusanda, an Iron Age city which appears among the conquests of the Assyrian king Shalmaneser III during a campaign which he conducted into southern Anatolia in 839, against the kingdom of Que (**RIMA* 3: 55). If the identification is valid, then Lawazantiya must have been located in the region of Classical Cilicia, giving some support to its suggested equation with the site of Sirkeli (thus O. Casabonne), 40 km east of mod. Adana. However, it is difficult to reconcile a Cilician location for Lawazantiya with the references to it in the Late Bronze Age texts cited above.

Wegner (*RlA* 6: 435–6).

Lazpa see **Lesbos**.

Lebedus (map 5) Classical Greek city built on a peninsula on the Aegean coast of Anatolia, in the region called Ionia in M1, 36 km northwest of Ephesus. It was one of the twelve cities constituting the Ionian League (see **Panionium**). In C5 it became a member of the Athenian Confederacy (see glossary). In early C3 Lysimachus, former general of Alexander the Great, transplanted (at least some of) its inhabitants to his new city of Ephesus. Some years later, c. 266, Ptolemy II Philadelphus refounded the city, calling it Ptolemais. But its old name was soon reinstated. The peninsula on which Lebedus was located was fortified by an ashlar wall with four towers and three gates.

Bean (1966: 149–53; *PECS* 492–3).

Ledrae (**Ledroi, Ledra, Ledron,** ***Leukosia***) (map 14) City in north-central Cyprus in the vicinity of mod. Nicosia. Human settlement in the area dates back to the Chalcolithic period, and there is evidence also for extensive habitation from the Early

Bronze Age through the early Byzantine period. The first attested historical reference to the city comes from the prism inscription of the Assyrian king Esarhaddon (673/672) (*Borger, 1956 §27, Heidel, 1956), where the name Unasagusu, king of Ledir, appears – identified as Onasagoras(?), king of Ledrae. The next known reference to the city is found in early C4 graffiti from the temple of Anchoris at Karnak in Egypt, indicating the presence there of several persons from Ledrae. In C4 CE the city was the seat of a bishop.

Inscriptions attest to the worship of Aphrodite at Ledrae, but no trace of a sanctuary of the goddess has been found.

Nicolaou (*PECS* 494).

Lehun (map 8) 65 ha settlement in the region of Moab, central Jordan, with evidence of human activity extending back to the Palaeolithic Age and continuing to the Ottoman period. Excavations, sponsored by the Belgian Committee of Excavations in Jordan, were conducted from 1977 onwards under the successive directorships of P. Naster and D. Homès-Fredericq. The earliest evidence of actual habitation at Lehun goes back to the Early Bronze Age, when a large settlement was built on the site, with adjacent water reservoir. A later fortified agricultural village has been dated to the transitional Late Bronze–Iron Age period, between 1300 and 1000. Contact with Egypt is suggested by the discovery of a fine faience scarab, depicting a sphinx with ram's head, dated to Egypt's twentieth dynasty (1186–1069). Around 1000 the village was abandoned, and then succeeded, in Iron Age II, by a fortress settlement, c. 35 m × 43 m, believed to belong to a belt of military installations along the northern Moabite plateau. This is suggested by Homès-Fredericq, who notes the fortress' excellent strategic location, overlooking the whole region and controlling all traffic on the King's Highway (q.v.), with protection provided by the cliffs of northern Moab. The presence of fortified storage buildings in this level has suggested that the fortress-settlement served economic and agricultural as well as strategic purposes. A small, square temple dating to the Nabataean (late Hellenistic–early Roman) period was used, Homès-Fredericq suggests, by traders and caravaneers travelling one of the by-roads of the King's Highway.

Homès-Fredericq (*OEANE* 3: 340–1).

Leilan, Tell (Shehna, Shubat-Enlil) (map 10) Settlement with acropolis and lower town, its wall enclosing an area of 90 ha, located in northern Mesopotamia in the Habur triangle, with six main occupation levels extending from the Halaf period (M6) to the Middle Bronze Age (early M2). The region in which it lay was called Subir in M3 and Subartu in M2. Excavation of the site began in 1979 under the direction of H. Weiss. The first major urban development belongs to the phase designated Leilan IIId, c. 2600–2400, when the settlement increased sixfold, and extended from the original occupied area on the summit of the mound to a new lower town with a regular street layout. A public cultic quarter where sacrificial activities took place was constructed on the acropolis, in place of earlier domestic dwellings. In the Leilan IIa phase, c. 2400–2300, wealth and social differentiation are evident, with the construction of a fortification wall around the acropolis, which apparently divided off an administrative elite from the inhabitants of the lower, unfortified town. The excavator notes evidence of increasing economic and political connections with southern Mesopotamia in this period.

During the Leilan IIb phase, 2300–2200, the Subir region, including Tell Leilan, was conquered by Naram-Sin, thus coming under the domination of the Akkadian empire. The city, then called Shehna, became a centre of the Akkadian imperial administration, and the lower town was walled for the first time. With the collapse of the Akkadian empire c. 2193 the city was abandoned, along with many other settlements in northern Mesopotamia. This abandonment is attributed by the site's excavators to extreme climate change. The city remained derelict until early C18 when the Assyrian king Shamshi-Adad I (1796–1775) re-established it as his royal capital, with the name Shubat-Enlil, meaning 'the dwelling place of (the god) Enlil'. The city's new name has been identified from inscriptions found in the temple quarter on the acropolis, supplemented by inscriptional information unearthed in the two palaces of the lower town. Remains of the impressive public structures which were constructed both on the acropolis as well as in the lower town during this phase provide evidence of Shamshi-Adad's ambitious building programme. The excavator notes that the lower city's eastern palace covers an area of some 10 ha, and was therefore one of the largest early M2 palaces in northern Mesopotamia.

Among the rooms which led from the palace's central throne-room were a number containing cuneiform tablets and fragments, many hundreds in total. The contents of this archive include historical and administrative texts, treaties and letters, and a copy of the Sumerian King List. Many of the documents bear seal impressions of the king's palace staff. The historical information obtained from the texts relates to the period of Shamshi-Adad's successors (see below) at Shubat-Enlil. Excavations in the lower town palace (north) also brought to light a tablet archive, consisting of 590 tablets. But the contents of these are restricted to the documentation of beer production and disbursement.

Following Shamshi-Adad's death, Shubat-Enlil remained for a while under the control of one of his retainers, Samiya, but soon a dynasty from the local land of Apum (q.v.) gained control of the city. Thenceforth it became the capital of Apum, and was now commonly (though not invariably) referred to by its original name, Shehna. There are frequent references to Shubat-Enlil/Shehna in letters from the Mari archives during the period when Mari's throne was occupied by Zimri-Lim (1774–1762). These letters record the city's involvement in the complex and constantly changing power structures and political relationships of the period. Samiya supported the invading ruler of Eshnunna, Ibal-pi-El II, in a struggle against Turum-natki, king of Apum. However, Turum-natki died without being able to recapture Shehna, and was replaced by his son Zuzu. The Eshnunnites then departed from Shehna, leaving a garrison there under Yanuh-Samar and Zuzu; the latter became its ruler. Some time after the departure of the Eshnunnite army, Shubat-Enlil/Shehna was captured and pillaged by Hatnurapi, king of Qattara, and later king of nearby Karana. Subsequently it was occupied by an Elamite military commander called Kunnam when a king called Haya-Abum sat upon its throne. Kunnam claimed that he was the equal of this king, and regarded himself as a 'son of Zimri-Lim', like Haya-Abum (**LKM* 495). Atamrum, king of Andarig, sought to evict Kunnam from the city, allegedly acting on Zimri-Lim's behalf, but no doubt fearing that his own city was at risk of an Elamite occupation. Kunnam eventually left the city. We do not know whether his decision to do so was connected with any action taken by Atamrum, but the latter may eventually, for a time, have secured control of Shubat-Enlil/Shehna for himself. By 1762, when the Mari archives come to an end, the city was in the hands of Himdiya, Atamrum's successor at Andarig. When and how he came to exercise power over it, and for how long, remain unknown.

Thanks to the discovery of part of the city's royal archives during excavations in its eastern palace, we have some information about the last three kings of Shubat-Enlil/Shehna, in the period from c. 1750 to the city's fall twenty-two years later. Their names, in chronological order, are Mutiya, Till-Abnu, and Yakun-ashar (the last two were brothers). Texts from their reigns indicate the alliances they concluded with other kings in the region. Mutiya allied himself with Ashtamar-Adad, king of Kurda, and a third king, Shepallu (country unknown), against an alliance formed by Hazip-Teshub, king of Razama (in the land of Yussan), and Buriya, king of Andarig. External pressures eventually forced the two blocs to come to terms, as reflected in an extant treaty concluded between Mutiya and Hazip-Teshub. Mutiya's successor Til-Abnu (probably his nephew) concluded a treaty with Yamsi-Hadnu, king of Kahat, and also a commercial treaty with the city of Ashur. This latter document indicates the existence of an Assyrian trading colony at Tell Leilan, as do a number of other administrative documents found in the city.

The rule of Yakun-ashar, the last king of Apum, came to an end when the royal capital Shubat-Enlil/Shehna was conquered and destroyed by the Babylonian king Samsu-iluna in 1728. The city was thenceforth abandoned until it was resettled by Kurdish villagers early in C20 CE.

Weiss (1985; *OEANE* 3: 341–7), Charpin (1986), *LKM* 69–71, 83–6, 624 (refs), *Mesop.* 203, 348–51.

Lelegians Attested in Classical Greek sources as a pre-Greek population group of Greece and western Anatolia. In the Trojan War, a Lelegian contingent fought on the side of Troy (Homer, *Iliad* 10.429, 21.86). The Lelegians are associated with a wide variety of locations in both Greece and Anatolia, including (in Anatolia) the Troad, Pedasus on the Satnioeis r., Smyrna, Ephesus, Tralles, Miletus, Pisidia, and Caria. To judge from Greek tradition, Caria in particular appears to have become an important area of Lelegian settlement. It is possible that a Lelegian population group originally located in northwestern Anatolia, perhaps in the Troad, moved southwards during the upheavals at the end of the Bronze Age, and finally resettled in the southwest corner of Caria. But the Lelegians remain an elusive people.

Gschnitzer (*BNP* 7: 380–1).

Lesbos (maps 2, 3, 4, 5) Island off the northern Aegean coast of Anatolia, the third largest island in the Aegean Sea (after Crete and Euboea). In Late Bronze Age Hittite texts it is attested as Lazpa. It was a dependency in this period of the Arzawan kingdom called Seha River Land. A cult-idol from Lazpa was used in treating an illness of the Hittite king Mursili II.

In late M2 the island was settled by Aeolian migrants from mainland Greece. During the Classical period its chief city was Mytilene, which also possessed territory on the Anatolian mainland. In the second half of C6, Lesbos became a tributary of Persia, but joined the Ionian rebellion against Persia in 499. Subsequent to the allied Greek defeat of the Persians at the battle of Mycale (q.v.) in 479, Lesbos became a member of the Athenian Confederacy (see glossary). In 428/427 Mytilene made an abortive attempt to revolt from the alliance (Thucydides 3.1–50), following which Athens established a military colony of 2,700 Athenian settlers on the island. In 405

Lesbos came under Spartan control, but in C4 domination of it fluctuated between Sparta and Persia – except for two brief periods when it was again allied with Athens.
Paraskevaidis (*PECS* 502–3), Houwink ten Cate (*1985–6: 38–46).

Letoum (map 15) M1 BCE–M1 CE sanctuary in Lycia, southwestern Anatolia, near the west bank of the Xanthus r., 4 km southwest of Lycia's chief city, Xanthus. It was dedicated to the worship of the Letoids – the goddess Leto and her children Apollo and Artemis – and the nymphs. The site's history of known occupation extends from C8 through the Roman imperial period. From 1962 onwards, annual excavations have been conducted in the sanctuary by French teams, initially under the direction of H. Metzger, and currently under J. des Courtils and D. Laroche. (For accounts of the excavations in the last two decades, see reports in *An Ant* from vol. 6, 1988 onwards.)

According to the Roman poet Ovid's version of a well-known mythological tradition (*Metamorphoses* 6.316–81), Leto's association with Lycia began when the goddess sought to quench her thirst at a lake in the country, during her flight with her baby children Apollo and Artemis from the wrath of the goddess Hera. When the local peasants tried to drive her away, she rebuked them and turned them into frogs. The confrontation was almost certainly understood to have taken place on the site that became the sanctuary of the Letoids. None of the anc. sources explicitly states this, but Ovid's description of the scene – a small lake set in a deep valley amid grassy glades – is consistent with the low-lying marshy area where the Letoum was located.

It is likely that the sanctuary was first associated with the cult of an early Anatolian goddess of Luwian origin, called *ẽni mahanahi* ('mother of the gods') in Lycian inscriptions. Leto came to be identified with this deity, probably early in C4, at the time of increasing Greek influence on the native Lycian culture. Thenceforth, the cult of all three Greek deities gained in importance in Lycia through C4 and the Hellenistic period, as did the sanctuary itself where the cult was based. By the Roman imperial period, the Letoum was the religious focal point of the whole of Lycia. It was the cult-centre of all three Letoids, who were designated as the national gods of the country.

The sanctuary complex is dominated by three surviving temples, the most anc. of which dates to C5 or C4 and was almost certainly dedicated to the goddess Artemis. The other two temples, of Hellenistic date, are of unknown attribution but were presumably dedicated to one or more of the Letoids. In the southern part of the temple precinct are the remains of a monumental nymphaeum (fountain-house), generally dated to early C2 CE, but which may have been built later. It occupied the site of an earlier Hellenistic structure constructed around a natural water source. To the north of the precinct are the remains of a theatre of Hellenistic date.

One of the most important finds from the site is a stele, discovered in 1973, with a trilingual inscription – in Lycian, Greek, and Aramaic versions (**N* 320, **PE* 859–62, no. 33). Dated to 358, during the period when Lycia was subject to the Persian king Artaxerxes III, it contains regulations for the establishment of a new cult in the sanctuary. Apart from its content, the trilingual inscription has made a small but useful contribution to our knowledge of the still largely unintelligible Lycian language.
Bean (1978: 60–4), *Bryce (1978; 1983), Laroche (2006, report of most recent excavations).

Leucae (*Uç Tepeler*) Ionian city in northwestern Anatolia, located 30 km northwest of Izmir in the Gulf of Smyrna (*BAGRW* 56 D4). Pliny the Elder (5.119) refers to its

Figure 61 Letoum, temple.

situation 'on the promontory which was once an island'. According to Diodorus (15.18.1), it was founded in 383 by a Persian called Tachos, and contained a shrine of Apollo. Diodorus reports that after Tachos' death, control of Leucae was contested by the cities Clazomenae and Cyme. To avoid warfare between the contestants, the Pythian oracle decided that it should should be awarded to whichever of them first offered sacrifice in Leucae, with each side setting out from their city at dawn on an appointed day. Though Cyme was closer to Leucae, the Clazomenians won the contest through the stratagem of founding a city even closer to it, and sending their representatives from there. Coin issues of the city date exclusively to C4. There are some remains of Leucae's C5–4 fortifications, but the site now lies in a prohibited zone and cannot be visited.

Bean (1966: 125–7; *PECS* 505–6), Olshausen (*BNP* 7: 441–2).

Levant Term first used in mediaeval times, derived from the Latin verb *levare*, 'to raise', referring to a region or regions where, from a European perspective, the sun rises. The words Anatolia and Orient, of Greek and Latin origin respectively, are used in a similar way. All refer to lands lying to the east of Europe. The name 'Levant' is now applied particularly to the eastern Mediterranean coastal territories and hinterlands of Syria, Lebanon, Israel, and Palestine.

M. Sommer (2001).

Leviah Enclosure 9 ha site located in the land of Geshur, southern Golan Heights, northern Palestine, overlooking the Sea of Galilee. Its history of occupation extends from late M4 (c. 3300) to the end of M3. Following the site's discovery during the

1968 Golan Survey, excavations began in 1987 as part of the Land of Geshur Project, conducted by the Institute of Archaeology, Tel Aviv University. The term 'enclosure' was one used by early explorers of this and similar sites which they interpreted as 'places where nomads assembled with their flocks and herds in times of crisis, or as pens for livestock belonging to the Early Bronze Age towns in the valleys west of the Golan'. Thus Kochavi, who notes that the term is no longer apt. The excavations of the Leviah Enclosure, which during the Early Bronze Age developed into a strongly fortified urban settlement, have helped throw new light on the Early Bronze Age in the Golan. Kochavi comments: 'As early as M4, settlements sprang up with good natural defences. In the course of the Early Bronze Age, these settlements developed and became fully-fledged towns . . . The proximity of these towns . . . their size, massive fortifications, and long-lived existence attest to an intensive civilization that flourished in the Golan. . . . This urban civilization collapsed under the pressure of some besieging enemy.'

Kochavi (*NEAEHL* 3: 915–16).

Lidar Höyük (map 2) Settlement-mound in eastern Anatolia on the upper Euphrates, with a history of occupation extending from the beginning of the Early Bronze Age (M3) to the mediaeval period. There is some evidence also of habitation in the Chalcolithic period (Halaf, Ubaid, and Uruk phases). M3 occupation extended from the Early Dynastic II/III to the Akkadian/Ur III period. Excavation of the settlement, which reached its greatest extent in the Early Bronze Age, was conducted by H. Hauptmann from 1979 onwards, initially for the Institute of Near Eastern Archaeology, Free University of Berlin, and subsequently for the Heidelberg Institute for Prehistoric Archaeology. In its Early Bronze phase, Lidar was fortified by a 2 m wide mudbrick wall. Its acropolis covered an area of 200 m × 240 m, and the area of settlement, including the terraces, extended over a distance of 650 m. A necropolis of this period, located east of the mod. village of Lidar, contained over 200 burials.

Lidar Höyük apparently suffered violent destruction by fire early in the Late Bronze Age, but eventually recovered from this, as made clear by evidence of a substantial population on the acropolis during the latter half of the Late Bronze Age. The destruction was clearly caused by enemy attack, as indicated by the corpses found under the collapsed walls and in distorted positions in the entrances to several buildings, and by bronze arrowheads, one of which was found sticking in the plaster of the walls. Hauptmann concluded that the end of this phase of Lidar's existence is to be attributed to Hittite expansion, either under Hattusili I (1650–1620) or his grandson and successor Mursili I (1620–1590). M. Liverani (1988) has suggested that Lidar Höyük was the site of anc. Hahhum (q.v.), destroyed by Hattusili during his second Syrian campaign. But this identification has been disputed, and other locations have been proposed for Hahhum.

Among the important finds from the site are two seal impressions, dating to the period of the fall of the Hittite empire (early C12). They bear the name Kuzi-Teshub, son and successor of Talmi-Teshub, the last known Hittite viceroy at Carchemish. The presence of the sealings at Lidar may indicate that the city was and remained subject to the administration of Carchemish at the time of the Hittite empire's collapse. The fact that Ku(n)zi-Teshub styled himself 'Great King' suggests that the central Hittite dynasty based in Hattusa was now defunct, and that he saw himself as the successor of the Hittite royal line. Hauptmann suggests that Lidar was subsequently destroyed by the Assyrian king Tiglath-pileser I (1114–1076). Material remains of later periods include a Persian tomb dug into levels of C7–6 date, among whose contents was a bronze spatula-type object decorated with a male figure in Persian dress, and relics of Hellenistic and Roman occupation.

Hauptmann (1987; *RlA* 7: 15–16).

Limenia (*Limnitis*) (map 14) Town on the northwest coast of Cyprus, located to the west of the palace at Vouni. The town is attested in Strabo (14.6.3), though Strabo locates it inland. In 1899 the remains of a sanctuary were excavated at Limenia, containing sculptures and terracottas dating from the Archaic (C7–6) to the Hellenistic period.

Nicolaou (*PECS* 510).

Limyra (map 15) M1 BCE–M1 CE city in eastern Lycia, southwestern Anatolia, consisting of a fortified acropolis and lower city, located northeast of mod. Finike. Inscriptions in the native Lycian language, in which the city is called Zemu(ri), date its origins back to at least C5. In the first half of C4 it was the seat of the Lycian dynast Pericles, known both from inscriptions and coin issues, who extended his sway over much of Lycia and probably led his country's participation in the so-called satrap's revolt (see glossary). Pericles' tomb (heroon) is the most notable of Limyra's many sepulchral monuments. It was excavated and partly restored by a German team under the direction of J. Borchhardt. Portions of a frieze which originally decorated the walls of the cella depict Pericles in his chariot setting out for war, accompanied by mounted troops and foot soldiers. Its burial chamber was located in the foundations of the building. Built in the form of an Ionic temple, the monument was a clear assertion of Pericles' cultural affinities with the Greek world. Its caryatid porch (caryatids were columns in the form of draped women) was inspired by the similar porch of the Erechtheum on the acropolis in Athens, built several decades earlier. Further artistic inspiration for Pericles' tomb was provided by the so-called Nereid monument of Lycia's chief city, Xanthus.

Four large necropoleis at Limyra are considered by Borchhardt to provide material evidence of the city's wealth and power. Borchhardt notes that a third of all the known sepulchral inscriptions in the native Lycian language come from Limyra (see **TAM* I 98–148, **N* 316–17). Ten of the tombs, which include both cliff-chambers and free-standing structures, are decorated with reliefs. The most notable of the freestanding structures is identified by its inscriptions as the tomb of a certain Xñtabura, dating to mid C4. It is a two-storeyed building, whose lower chamber (*hyposorium*) is a Lycian house-type structure decorated with reliefs. One of these depicts the deceased standing before the judges of the next world. Above the *hyposorium* is an ogival sarcophagus, in which the tomb owner himself and the immediate members of his family were no doubt interred. Another inscribed and sculptured tomb, located in the necropolis west of the citadel, belonged to a man called Tebursseli. The reliefs depict him fighting alongside Pericles, and the inscriptions identify their opponent as a western Lycian ruler called Arttum̃para.

During the Hellenistic period, Limyra was subjected to Macedonian, Ptolemaic,

Figure 62 Limyra, house-tomb.

Seleucid, and Rhodian rule, before the Roman Senate declared its independence in 167. Gaius Caesar, grandson of Augustus, died here in 4 CE. The city prospered under Roman rule, with considerable development, beginning in the Hellenistic period, of the settlement at the foot of the citadel. It was the seat of a bishop in the Byzantine period, and was finally abandoned towards the end of M1 CE as a result of the Arab invasions.

Little remains of the city today apart from its tombs and a theatre of Hellenistic-Roman date. Inscriptions indicate that its chief deity, at least in later Greek and Roman times, was Olympian Zeus, in whose honour athletics contests were held. Pliny the Elder (31.22) reports that a fish-oracle was located at Limyra, where responses from the god were ascertained by the behaviour of fish – though some scholars have suggested that Pliny or his sources may have confused Limyra with the oracular centre at Sura.

Excavations concentrating on the 'West City' of Limyra and its pre-Hellenistic phases have recently been undertaken by T. Marksteiner.

Bean (1978: 142–5), Borchhardt (*PECS* 518), Marksteiner (2006).

Lissa M1 BCE–M1 CE city in Lycia in southwestern Anatolia, located on the western side of the gulf of Fethiye (anc. Telmessus) (*BAGRW* 65 A4). The date of the city's foundation is unknown, since the first evidence for its existence dates no earlier than C3 when its name is established in decrees from the reigns of Ptolemies II and III. No coins are known from the city. Material remains indicate that Lissa had an acropolis fortified by a wall and a tower. There are also a number of cist tombs and sarcophagi.

Bean (1978: 48; *PECS* 520).

Lita'u (Litamu) M1 Aramaean tribe, located in southeastern Babylonia. It is apparently first attested in a legal document from Nippur, dated c. 786, which refers to a man called Kabitu from Litamu (if the latter is an ethnic name). Later attested in the list of thirty-five so-called Aramaean tribes conquered by the Assyrian king Tiglath-pileser III (745) (**Tigl. III* 160–1, line 7), the tribe is attested elsewhere in Assyrian texts as being among the enemies on the banks of the Tigris against whom Sargon II (721–705) campaigned, as allies of the tribe Bit Yakin (**ARAB* II: 26, **Sargon II* 343). It also appears among the Aramaean enemies whom Sargon's son and successor Sennacherib conquered and carried off to Assyria (**Sennach.* 25, 49, 54, 57). In the reign of the Persian king Darius I (522–486), an area of countryside to the south of Babylon was known as Litamu (*RGTC* 8: 213).

Lipiński (2000: 467–8).

Figure 63 Arms-bearer of Tiglath-pileser III.

Lod (Lydda) (map 8) Settlement-mound in mod. Israel, located c. 15 km southeast of Tel Aviv near the southern bank of Nahal Ayalon (Wadi el-Kabir), and on a branch of the anc. Via Maris (q.v.). Its history of occupation extends from the Early Bronze Age to the Hellenistic, Roman, and Byzantine periods, with perhaps several periods of abandonment in between. Exploratory excavations were conducted on the site from December 1951 to January 1952 by J. Kaplan for the Israel Dept of Antiquities and Museums. Most of the site is today covered by mod. buildings.

Lod is first attested in written records as one of the Canaanite towns conquered by the pharaoh Tuthmosis III in C15. The first biblical reference to it occurs in 1 Chronicles 8:12, in the genealogical list of members of the Benjaminite tribe, where mention is made of its (re)settlement by the sons of Elpaal. This has led B. Mazar (cited by Kaplan) to conclude that the town remained abandoned for most of the Late Bronze and Iron Ages, and was not resettled until the reign of Josiah, a C7 king of Judah. Subsequently, in *OT* tradition, Lod was one of the sites resettled by the Israelites after their return from their Babylonian exile (e.g. Ezra 2:33). There are frequent references to the city in texts of the Hellenistic and Roman periods. It achieved its greatest important in the latter period, when the C2–3 CE emperor Septimius Severus bestowed upon it the status of a Roman *colonia* with the name Diospolis.

J. Schwartz (1990), Kaplan (*NEAEHL* 3: 917).

Loryma (map 5) M1 BCE–M1 CE coastal city of the Rhodian Peraea (see glossary) in Caria, southern Anatolia. First attested in Hecataeus (*FGrH* I F247), its location opposite the island of Rhodes led to its frequent use by naval forces in the Greek and Roman periods (see e.g. Thucydides 8.43.1, Diodorus 14.83.4).

Kaletsch (*BNP* 7: 815).

Lower Land (map 3) Late Bronze Age region in south-central Anatolia, extending in part through the Plain of Konya. It was incorporated into Hatti early in the period of the Hittite Old Kingdom (C17–15) and served as an important buffer zone between the Hittite homeland and the western and southwestern countries of Anatolia, especially the Arzawa Lands. During the comprehensive invasions of Hatti in the reign of Tudhaliya III (first half of C14), Arzawan forces swept through the Lower Land and established their frontier in the cities of Uda and Tuwanuwa, within striking distance of the Hittite heartland (*Bryce, 2005: 146). Tudhaliya's son Suppiluliuma led a counter-offensive against the occupation forces, driving them from the Lower Land and restoring the region to Hittite control. During his own reign, Suppiluliuma (I) (1350–1322) appointed his military commander Hannutti as governor of the Lower Land (*Bryce, 2005: 151), which may have served as a base for military operations against enemy countries in the west. A rebellion in the Lower Land during the reign of Tudhaliya IV (1237–1209) (Bryce, 2005: 299) reflects increasing unrest among Hatti's subject territories in the last decades of the Hittite kingdom. The rebellion may have been linked with possible insurrectionist activities by lineal descendants of Tudhaliya's uncle, Muwattalli II (1295–1272), in the kingdom of Tarhuntassa (see under **Tarhuntassa**). But this is purely speculative. In the first centuries of the Iron Age, the countries constituting the land of Tabal occupied much of the territory of the former Lower Land.

**RGTC* 6: 455 (s.v. Unteres Land), Bryce (1986–7: 97–9).

Luash (**Lugath, Luhuti**) (map 7) Iron Age country located in northwestern Syria, north of the kingdom of Hamath, in the region previously occupied by the Late Bronze Age Nuhashshi lands. Its capital was the city of Hatarikka/Hazrek (perhaps = Tell Afis). It appears in the records of the Assyrian king Ashurnasirpal II, in the context of the campaign which he conducted in 870 against the Syro-Palestinian states. After receiving the submission of Lubarna, ruler of the northern Syrian kingdom of Pat(t)in (Assyrian Unqi), in his capital Kinalua, Ashurnasirpal moved south along the Orontes r. and occupied the Patinite city of Aribua. Using this city as his base for military operations against Luhuti, which lay to its south, he claims to have conquered and destroyed Luhuti's cities and captured its soldiers, whom he impaled on stakes set up before their cities (**RIMA* 2: 218). Around 796 the country was incorporated into Hamath by the Hamathite king Zakur. This information is provided by the so-called Zakur stele found at Tell Afis (see under **Afis**) in 1903. J. D. Hawkins (1982: 389) suggests that Luash may already have formed the northern province of Hamath by the reign of the Assyrian king Shalmaneser III (858–824),or even earlier.

Hawkins (*RlA* 7:159–61), Lipiński (2000: 249–318).

Lubdu City in the east Tigris region of central/southern Mesopotamia, attested in sources of M2 (Old Babylonian, Middle Babylonian, Middle Assyrian, Nuzi) and M1 (Neo-Assyrian) date, especially in conjunction with the city of Arrapha. The Assyrian king Tiglath-pileser I (1114–1076) conquered it during a campaign in Babylonia (**RIMA* 2: 53). It marked one of the limits of former Babylonian territories which he now added to his kingdom. At some later time Lubdu reverted to Babylonian control, and became one of Babylonia's fortified frontier outposts. However, it fell to the Assyrian king Adad-nirari II (911–891) during his campaign in Babylonia, in the course of which he claims to have conquered Arrapha and Lubdu, then ruled by the Babylonian king Shamash-mudammiq (**RIMA* 2: 148). Lubdu joined in a widespread revolt against the Assyrian king Shalmaneser III (858–824), initiated late in his reign by the king's son Ashur-da'in-apla. The rebellion continued into the early regnal years of Shalmaneser's son and successor Shamshi-Adad V before it was finally crushed (**RIMA* 3: 183).

Lugath see **Luash**.

Luhuaiia see **Luhuatu**.

Luhuatu (**Lihuatu**) M1 tribe of possible North Arabian origin, probably to be located in northern Babylonia, east of the Tigris r. It appears to have been closely associated with the Ham(a)ranu tribe (q.v.), which it follows in the list of thirty-five Aramaean tribes conquered by the Assyrian king Tiglath-pileser III, probably in his first regnal year (745) (*Tigl. III* 158–9). The Luhuatu immediately precede the Aramaean tribe Hatallu (q.v.) in this list. They have been identified with the Luhuaiia (var. Minu'u) who are attested as a clan of the Hatallu tribe in an inscription of Ninurta-kudurri-usur, the mid C8 ruler of the middle Euphrates Aramaean state of Suhu (**RIMB* 2: 295).

Lipiński (2000: 427, 442–5).

Luhuti see Luash.

Lukka (map 3) The name of an ethnic group or groups belonging to the Luwian-speaking populations of western Anatolia, and attested in a number of Late Bronze Age written sources. They appear most frequently in Hittite texts, with an occasional reference to them in Egyptian records, and a late reference to Lukka in a text from Ugarit. Unlike many other Late Bronze Age Anatolian peoples, the Lukka people appear to have had no coherent political organization. We know of no Lukka kings, no Lukka states corresponding, for example, to those of the Arzawa complex, and no treaties of vassalhood between Lukka and the Hittite king; and no one person or city could act on behalf of Lukka as a whole. In other words, the term Lukka was used not in reference to a state with a clearly defined political organization, but rather to a conglomerate of independent communities, with close ethnic affinities and lying within a roughly definable geographical area. While it seems clear that there was a central Lukka region, a 'Lukka homeland', various elements of the Lukka population may have been widely scattered through southern and western Anatolia, and may in some cases have settled temporarily, or permanently, in states with formal political organizations. I. Singer (1983: 208) has defined the Lukka Lands as 'a loose geographical designation for southwestern Anatolia, used for a group of ethnically and culturally related communities and clans'.

From Hittite records, it is clear that 'Lukka people' became at least nominal subjects of the Hittite king, apparently from the time Hittite authority was extended over the Arzawan states. But we have the impression from the texts that these subjects were often fractious and difficult to control, and often openly hostile to Hatti, as indicated in one of the 'Plague Prayers' of Mursili II (*Singer, 2002: 49). Lukka people seem also to have had a reputation as seafarers who engaged in buccaneering enterprises in the waters and against the coastal cities of the eastern Mediterranean (e.g. **EA* 38), a clear indication that the territory which they occupied or from which they operated included a coastline. They were also listed in Egyptian records among the so-called Sea Peoples who attacked the coast of Egypt during the reign of the pharaoh Merneptah (1213–1203) (**ARE III*: §579). In early C12 Ammurapi, the last king of Ugarit, reported in a letter to the king of Alasiya that his entire fleet was stationed off the the coast of Lukka, no doubt part of the southwestern Anatolian coast (*Nougayrol *et al.*, 1968: 87–9, no. 24). On the basis of the above information, we can conclude that the term Lukka, or Lukka Lands (the plural form is not attested before C13), referred to a region extending from the western end of Pamphylia through Lycaonia, Pisidia, and Lycia (the later Classical names). It must, however, be said that a Lukka presence in these regions has yet to be confirmed by archaeological evidence.

Röllig (*RlA* 7: 161–3), Melchert (2003, *passim*; see index refs, 371).

Lullubu (Lullu, Lullumu) Mountain region and population group in northeastern Mesopotamia, first attested in records of the Akkadian empire (c. 2334–2193). It is likely that the group's geopolitical situation changed over time. On the basis of inscriptional evidence, their homeland is generally located on the western slopes of the Zagros mountains, between the headwaters of the Lesser Zab and Diyala rivers in the region of mod. Suleimaniya. They were among the peoples and lands incorporated into the Akkadian empire by its founder Sargon (2334–2279). In his famous victory stele, Sargon's grandson Naram-Sin (2254–2218) records a victory he won over the Lulluban king Satuni (or Sidu[r . . .]) (*RIME 2: 143–4). The Lullubu are depicted on the stele with short beards and braided hair, and clad in tunics with animal skins over their shoulders. They were apparently made up of a number of independent groups, each under its own 'king' or chieftain, which presumably banded together for military enterprises. The strength of the forces they could muster and the dangers they posed to the Akkadian empire are indicated by the (admittedly late and somewhat confused) 'Cuthean Legend' (*J. G. Westenholz, 1997: 310–15). According to this legend, they captured the cities of Purushanda in eastern Anatolia and Shubat-Enlil in northern Mesopotamia, and then embarked on a campaign of devastation through Gutian, Elamite, and Babylonian territory until they reached the Persian Gulf. These conquests are associated particularly with a Lulluban king called Annubanini. The king's rock relief found near mod. Zuhab links Annubanini with the goddess Inanna, who leads enemy prisoners before him. Archaeological evidence indicating a destruction of Naram-Sin's palace at Tell Brak has been connected with a supposed Lulluban attack upon the city.

The continuing threat posed by the Lullubu in later times, particularly to the kingdoms of Mesopotamia, is first indicated in the records of Shulgi (2094–2047), second ruler of the Ur III dynasty, who claims to have conducted nine campaigns against them: the year-name of his forty-fourth regnal year commemorates his ninth victory over Simurrum and Lullubu. The latter were to remain a major force in the western Asian world for many centuries to come. The Assyrian king Adad-nirari I (1307–1275) includes the Lullumu among the peoples whom he conquered (*RIMA 1: 131), as do his son and successor Shalmaneser I (*RIMA 1: 206, 207), and Shalmaneser's son and successor Tukulti-Ninurta I (*RIMA 1: 236–7). In C12 the Babylonian king Nebuchadnezzar I and the Assyrian king Ashur-resh-ishi I both report campaigns of conquest against the Lullubu/Lullumu (*RIMB 2: 34, *RIMA 1: 310–11). Ashur-resh-ishi's successor Tiglath-pileser I (1114–1076) also claims to have conquered the entire land of the Lullumu (*RIMA 2: 34). Almost certainly, these campaigns were provoked by attacks and raids mounted by the Lullubu/Lullumu against Babylonian and Assyrian territories. Although the campaigns were allegedly successful, they probably achieved little beyond temporary pacification of the Assyrians' aggressive eastern neighbours. Lullumu was one of the lands conquered by Adad-nirari II (911–891) during a campaign he conducted across the Lesser Zab (*RIMA 2: 157). Again, this campaign allegedly led to the subjugation of the enemy, as did Ashurnasirpal II's (883–859) confrontation with them (*RIMA 2: 221). But several decades later they were once more in conflict with the Assyrians, in the reign of Shalmaneser III (858–824).

By the beginning of Sargon II's reign (721), Lullumu was being used as an archaizing/literary term for the province of Mazamua (Zamua, q.v.) (Radner, *RlA* 11: 51–2), and as such it was one of the few eastern dependencies to remain loyal to Sargon in the early years of his reign. Its loyalty was rewarded when in 716 Sargon conquered the rebel states in the region which had attempted to align themselves with Urartu, and added one of them, Karalla, to Lullumu's territory.

Klengel (*RlA* 7: 164–8).

Luristan (maps 12, 16) Region in western Iran, associated with the production of thousands of anc. bronze weapons, tools, utensils, votive objects, and ornamental items.

A substantial number of these survive today. The bronzes first came to public attention when they began appearing on the antiquities market in the late 1920s. They had been illegally excavated by local tribesmen, and most were apparently grave goods recovered from anc. cist tombs and other burial places. Because of the clandestine nature of their recovery, specific provenances and contexts for the great majority of them are unknown. However, later official excavations have enhanced the information we have about the bronzes. In 1938 E. Schmidt investigated a number of Luristan sites, concentrating on Surkh Dum (map 13) which is located in the Zagros region, northwest of Susa. In 1965, the Belgian Archaeological Mission in Iran under the direction of L. Vanden Berghe resumed work at Surkh Dum, spending fifteen seasons there until 1978. Within a fifteen-roomed building complex, identified as a temple sanctuary and dated to C8–7, a total of 1,851 terracotta and bronze artefacts were found, including human and animal figurines. The bronzes also included depictions of deities, demons, and other supranatural figures. Of the cylinder seals among the finds, some were inscribed with the name of a goddess, and one depicted a mounted rider. The figures are represented both in relief and in the round. Their depictions are sometimes realistic, sometimes fantasized. 'Zoomorphic junctures and the coiling of body features are very characteristic' (Muscarella, 1995: 998). These figures, which appear on pinheads, axes, finials, and horse-bits, illustrate in a fairly comprehensive way the repertoire of classic Luristan bronzes. The period of the bronzes extends back as early as C10, but most of them belong to C8 and C7. They are readily distinguishable from M3 and M2 bronzes, as is evident from finds which came to light in the hundreds of burials unearthed by the Belgians during their excavations. (See also Haerinck and Overlaet, *RlA* 11: 121–4, for the excavations conducted by Vanden Berghe in the Pushti-i Kuh area of Luristan.) The dates of these burials range from M3 to M1. A few bronzes of the classic Luristan type were found among the M1 burials, but none from the earlier burials.

Though many thousands of the classic Luristan bronzes have now come to light, they provide very limited information about the people who produced them. Their abundance has been seen as evidence of a wealthy society, and their distinctive iconography as a reflection of a people who were both highly militaristic and highly spiritual. But such conclusions are vague and speculative. We know nothing of their producers' ethnic background (Cimmerian, Median, and Persian origins have all been suggested), the language or languages they spoke, the nature of their settlements, their way of life, or what brought their culture to an end, apparently in C7. We have neither inscriptional information about them, nor any significant archaeological remains apart from the bronzes, the great majority of which no longer have context. Of course, if those who produced them and were buried with them were essentially a nomadic people, we should not expect to find much surviving evidence of their places of settlement. Indeed, the nature of many of their artefacts (horse-trappings, portable objects) may be seen as supporting the view that their lifestyle was a nomadic one. On the other hand, the quality, variety, and sophistication of their artwork has led some scholars to argue that only a sedentary people would have been capable of such an achievement. It is of course possible that there were both sedentary and nomadic elements among them. But this too must remain speculative until further evidence comes to light.

Calmeyer (*RlA* 7: 174–9), Schmidt et al. (1989), Muscarella (1989; 1995: esp. 981–99).

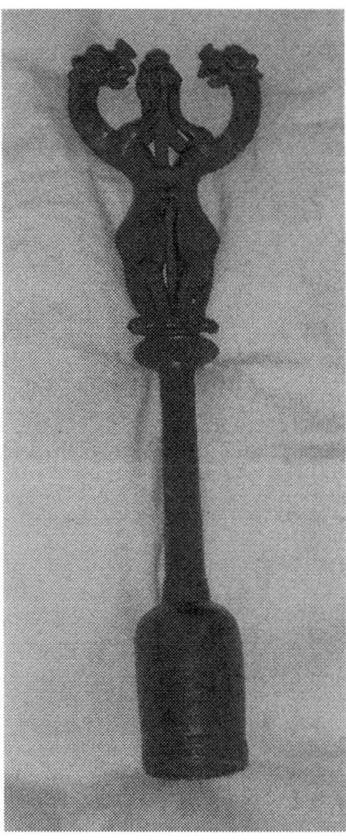

Figure 64 Luristan finial (C9–7)

Lusanda see **Lawazantiya**.

Lusna One of the small Late Bronze Age countries in southern Anatolia conquered by the early Hittite king Labarna (C17) and assigned to the governorship of his sons (**Chav.* 230). It was perhaps the forerunner of Classical Lystra (*BAGRW* 66 A1) in Lycaonia.

Lutibu Fortified Iron Age city belonging to the kingdom of Sam'al in southern Anatolia, perhaps to be identified with the site of Sakçagözü (q.v.), 21 km northeast of Zincirli. In 858, under the Sam'alite king Hayyanu, Lutibu joined a military coalition of northern Syrian–southeastern Anatolian states which confronted and was defeated by Shalmaneser III, the new king of Assyria, on his first western campaign (**RIMA* 3: 9, 16).

Luwians One of several Indo-European speaking peoples whose presence in Anatolia is attested in M2 written sources. There is no general consensus on where the original homeland of these peoples was, or how and when they first appeared in Anatolia. Most scholars date their arrival to a period or periods during the Early Bronze Age – though an entry date of c. 6000 has also been proposed. Nor do we know whether they came in a single large movement, or in a series of migrations spread through M3. In either case, their dispersal, probably soon after their arrival, led to marked differentiations in the languages they spoke. This has provided us with a basis for identifying, from M2 written records, three main Indo-European speaking groups in Bronze Age Anatolia:

the Hittite- (strictly Nesite-) speaking group of north-central Anatolia, the Palaic-speaking group south of the Black Sea in the region of later Paphlagonia, and the Luwian-speaking group, who by the Late Bronze Age had dispersed widely through Anatolia. Recently, I. Yakubovich has proposed that the core Luwian area was located in central Anatolia, in the region of the Konya plain, which in part extended over the region called the Lower Land (q.v.) in Hittite texts. In the final centuries of M2, after the collapse of the Hittite empire, and in the first centuries of M1, Luwian speakers may also have settled in parts of northern Syria (see below).

The Luwian language is attested in both cuneiform and hieroglyphic scripts. Passages in Luwian cuneiform, generally of a religious nature, occur in the archives of the Hittite capital Hattusa, where they have been incorporated into Hittite texts and are identified by the term *luwili* ('in the language of Luwiya'). Several hundred Luwian passages have been found inserted into Hittite festival, ritual, and incantation texts. The actual name 'Luwiya' is attested in very early versions of the Hittite laws (laws §§ 5, 19–21, 23a, **CS* II: 107, 108). The name is replaced by 'Arzawa' in subsequent versions of the laws, and 'Luwiya' thenceforth disappears from the texts, though the adverbial form *luwili* survived as a linguistic term. The explanation for the name replacement remains a matter for debate, particularly as the reading and interpretation of the passage in which it occurs (§5) are problematical. What does seem certain is that 'Luwiya' was never used as a geopolitical term to refer to a single political entity or an administratively unified territory. Rather, its connotations were purely ethno-geographical, indicating a general region whose inhabitants included large numbers of Luwian speakers, but without precise territorial limits. It may in fact have been a term of convenience used only by outsiders, and never, perhaps, by the inhabitants of 'Luwiya' themselves.

Most scholars believe that substantial numbers of Luwian speakers had spread into western Anatolia, particularly into the region of the Arzawa lands, by the Late Bronze Age. I. Yakubovich (2008) has opposed this view, arguing that what Luwian presence there was in the west may have been due, in part at least, to population deportation in the aftermath of Arzawan attacks upon the Lower Land. He believes that the predominant population of the Arzawa region was 'proto-Carian'. Yakubovich's arguments have yet to be fully assessed by other scholars, but they encourage a re-examination of the bases for the assumption that western Anatolia was politically dominated for much of M2 by Luwian speakers who formed a substantial part of the populations of the region.

On the other hand, it is quite clear that by the middle of M2, Luwian-speaking groups had occupied much of southern Anatolia, from the region of Classical Lycia in the west through Pamphylia, Pisidia, Lycaonia, and Isauria to Cilicia in the east. From the Luwian areas of southern Anatolia in the Late Bronze Age, several kingdoms or states came into being during the Hittite period. These included the kingdoms of Kizzuwadna, where Hurrian and Luwian elements were intermingled, and Tarhuntassa, perhaps a more exclusively Luwian state, which was apparently created by the Hittite king Muwattalli II in early C13. Almost certainly there were substantial numbers of Luwians settled in central Anatolia, including the region of the Hittite homeland, during the Late Bronze Age. This is indicated by Hittite military records which report the deportation of tens of thousands of persons from conquered states, including those of western and southern Anatolia, back to the homeland, for service with the Hittite king and his land-owning officers.

Figure 65 Luwian hieroglyphic inscription.

As noted above, the Luwian language was written in a hieroglyphic (as well as a cuneiform) script, made up largely of a series of pictographic symbols. The earliest known example of the script appears on a seal impression of C16, from the seal of Isputahsu, king of Kizzuwadna. But the majority of hieroglyphic texts date to C13 and (by far the larger category) to the period from c. 1100 to 700, i.e. the period of the Neo-Hittite kingdoms. Decipherment of the script was greatly facilitated by the discovery in 1946 of a C8 bilingual text, in Luwian hieroglyphs and Phoenician, at Karatepe in eastern Cilicia (see under ***Karatepe***). The language of the bilingual's Luwian version has been shown to be virtually identical with that of the Luwian cuneiform texts.

After the fall of Hattusa, the practice of writing cuneiform on clay tablets ceased. However, the surviving branches of the Hittite royal family in Syria and southern Anatolia continued to use the Luwian hieroglyphic script, primarily for monumental inscriptions on stone as in the past. But the script also appears in a small number of letters and economic texts, on leather and strips of lead, and on small votive objects. To what extent does this indicate the spread of Luwian population groups through northern Syria in the early centuries of the Iron Age? We should be careful not to make any *a priori* assumption that the language inscribed on the Iron Age hieroglyphic monuments and on other materials used as writing surfaces was in common use in the regions where they were found. The hieroglyphic tradition was a carry-over from Late Bronze Age Hittite royalty, and like the title 'Great King' was one of the trappings of kingship adopted by later and lesser kings. Of course, we can by no means exclude the possibility that the populations where the post-Bronze Age hieroglyphic inscriptions have been found had a significant Luwian component. It may be that Luwians came to these regions in increasing numbers in the post-Bronze Age centuries, spreading southeastwards from southern Anatolia. But this has yet to be demonstrated, since apart from the hieroglyphic inscriptions, there is no evidence to indicate a significant Luwian presence in Iron Age Syria. Of course, if a large number of Luwian personal names were to be found in the regions where the hieroglyphic inscriptions have come to light, this would greatly strengthen the likelihood that these regions had substantial Luwian populations.

Such was clearly the case in southern Anatolia, where the persistence of Luwian names through M1 indicates the survival of Luwian elements and, in some areas at least, the probable continuation of Luwian population groups down to the Hellenistic and Roman imperial periods. Luwian onomastic elements are found in the inscriptions of Lycia, Pisidia, Pamphylia, Isauria, Lycaonia, and Cilicia, with a particular concentration of Luwian names in Lycia and Cilicia Tracheia/Aspera (Rough Cilicia). These areas almost certainly continued to be inhabited by peoples of Luwian ethnic origin until at least early M1 CE.

Houwink ten Cate (1965), Laroche (*RlA* 7: 181–4), Melchert (2003).

Lycaonia (map 4) Classical name of the region in south-central Anatolia located south of the Salt Lake. Its western end was probably part of the Late Bronze Age Lukka Lands. In M1, as in the Bronze Age, Lycaonia occupied strategically important territory, for through it passed a major route linking western Anatolia with southeastern Cilicia and Syria. No doubt primarily for this reason control of the region was hotly contested by a succession of M1 powers, including Persia and the Seleucid and Attalid kingdoms.

Jones and Mitchell (*OCD* 894).

Lycia (maps 4, 15) M1 BCE–M1 CE country in southwestern Anatolia, covering part of the region called the Lukka Lands in Late Bronze Age Hittite texts. The name Lycia, of Greek origin, had various false etymologies assigned to it in Classical tradition; e.g. it was so called by the goddess Leto in honour of the wolves (*lykoi*) who had guided her there, with her baby children Apollo and Artemis, in her flight from the goddess Hera (Antoninus Liberalis 35.3). Unwittingly, Classical tradition may have preserved the authentic Bronze Age name Lukka. However, the Lycians themselves called their country Trm̃misa and themselves Trm̃mili, names which may reflect one of the country's early population groups. A tradition recorded by Herodotus (1.173) which tells of immigrants into Lycia from Crete called the Termilae perhaps has some basis in historical fact. The Lycian population may well have contained an Aegean element which intermingled with groups of Bronze Age Anatolian origin. In a tradition dating back at least to Homer, the Lycians under the leadership of Sarpedon were the most important of Troy's allies in the Trojan War. There are numerous references to Lycia in the *Iliad*, and to the prominent role of the Lycians in the conflict (see Bryce, 1986: 12–14). To Homer's period (C8) belongs the earliest M1 archaeological evidence for settlement in Lycia, unearthed in the country's most important city, Xanthus. More than forty other anc. cities have been found throughout Lycia.

About 540, the Persian commander Harpagus conquered Lycia, and thereupon it became part of the Persian empire ruled by Cyrus II. A local dynasty was established in Xanthus, which exercised authority over much of the country until the early decades of C4, except for several decades in mid C5 when Lycia became part of the Athenian Confederacy, (see glossary). The Xanthian dynasts along with the rulers of a number of individual Lycian cities issued coins which often bore their own and their cities' names as well as portrait-heads of themselves wearing Persian-type tiaras. In the 360s Lycia took part in the abortive satrap's revolt (see glossary). When the uprising was crushed, the country was restored to Persian overlordship and remained subject to Persia until Alexander the Great invaded it in 334/333. After Alexander's death in 323, Lycia came

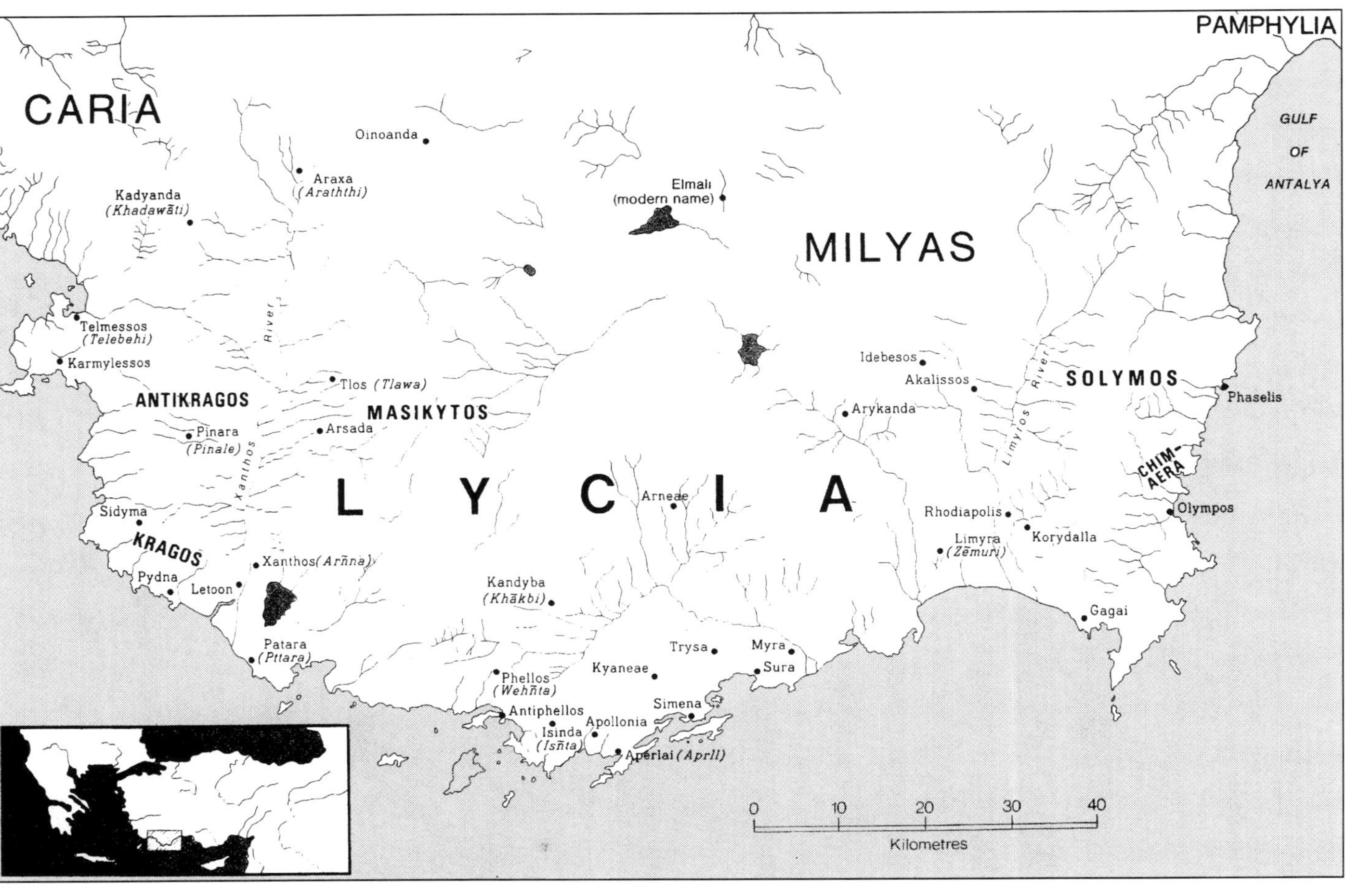
PAMPHYLIA
CARIA
GULF
OF
ANTALYA
MILYAS
L Y C I A
SOLYMOS
MASIKYTOS
ANTIKRAGOS
KRAGOS
CHIM-
AERA
Oinoanda
Araxa
(Araththi)
Kadyanda
(Khadawãti)
Elmalı
(modern name)
Telmessos
(Telebehi)
Karmylessos
Tlos (Tlawa)
Arsada
Pinara
(Pinale)
Xanthos River
Sidyma
Pydna
Letoon
Xanthos (Arñna)
Patara
(Pttara)
Kandyba
(Khãkbi)
Arneae
Phellos
(Wehñta)
Antiphellos
Isinda
(Isñta)
Apollonia
Aperlai (Aprll)
Simena
Kyaneae
Trysa
Myra
Sura
Idebesos
Akalissos
Arykanda
Limyros River
Rhodiapolis
Limyra
(Zẽmuri)
Korydalla
Gagai
Olympos
Phaselis
0
10
20
30
40
Kilometres

Map 15 Lycia.

first under the control of Antigonus of Macedon, and subsequently under Ptolemaic and Seleucid rule. However, with the defeat of the Seleucid king Antiochus III by the Romans at the battle of Magnesia in 190, Lycia was brought within the Roman sphere of influence. Early in C2 the Lycians formed a league amongst their cities which continued until C4 CE. It discussed and decided upon matters of war, conclusions of alliances, and diplomatic missions to foreign states. There were twenty-three member-cities of the league, ranked according to their size and importance. In 43 CE the emperor Claudius joined Lycia with the neighbouring country of Pamphylia and made it a Roman province.

The native language of Lycia is preserved in approx. 180 inscriptions, appearing mainly on rock-cut tombs which often replicate the façades of the wooden houses in which the Lycians lived. Both freestanding tombs and burial chambers cut into cliff-faces are found throughout the country. Many were used for multiple burials – for the tomb owners and their families, and sometimes also for the owners' friends and servants. Lycian inscriptions appear occasionally on steles, more commonly on coin legends, and, very rarely, as graffiti on metal and ceramic ware. The earliest of the inscriptions date to early C5, the latest to late C4. The language of the inscriptions belongs to the Indo-European language family and is closely related to Bronze Age Luwian. There are two dialects of Lycian, now referred to as Lycian A (by far the more common) and Lycian B. Apart from the highly formulaic sepulchral inscriptions and various words, phrases, and sentences in other texts, the language is still largely undecipherable. The inscriptions are written in a modified form of the Greek alphabet, derived from Rhodes. Greek inscriptions begin to appear at various Lycian sites in C5, and then from C4 onwards in increasing numbers. Over 1,200 Greek inscriptions have been recorded, primarily from the Roman imperial period (late C1 onwards), along with a small number of Latin inscriptions. The most prominent native Lycian deities

Figure 66 Lycian warriors.

were a mother goddess, called *ẽni mahanahi* ('mother of the gods'), and the storm god Trqqas (a descendant of the Luwian god Tarhunda), both of Bronze Age Anatolian origin. Greek deities also start to appear in inscriptions and on coins from C5 onwards. Subsequently, the Letoids (Leto, Apollo, and Artemis) achieved the status of the country's most important gods (see **Letoum**) as the Lycian civilization became increasingly Greek in character.

The following cities of Lycia are listed as separate entries: Antiphellus, Aperlae, Apollonia, Araxa, Arneae, Arsada, Arycanda, Cadyanda, Calynda (in Caria or Lycia?), Candyba, Choma, Corydalla, Crya (in Caria or Lycia?), Cyaneae, Gagae, Isinda (1), Khãkbi, Letoum, Limyra, Lissa, Myra, Patara, Phaselis, Phellus, Pinara, Rhodiapolis, Simena, Sura, Telmessus (2), Timiussa, Tlos, Trysa, Tyberissus, Xanthus.

**TAM* I, Bryce (1986), O. Masson (1991: 671–4), Keen (1998).

Lydda see **Lod**.

Lydia (maps 4, 16) Iron Age kingdom of western Anatolia, bordering on Phrygia in the east and the Ionian colonies in the west. According to Greek tradition, the kingdom's inhabitants were originally known as the Maeonians, but subsequently adopted the name of a legendary king of the region called Lydus. Lydia was later ruled by a dynasty allegedly founded by Hercules (Herakles), which in Greek tradition continued for 505 years, up to early C7. Candaules, the last member of this dynasty, was assassinated by one of his court favourites, a man called Gyges, who established a new dynasty – the so-called Mermnad dynasty – c. 685 (Herodotus 1.7–12). From his capital Sardis, Gyges (called Guggu in Assyrian texts) embarked on a programme of territorial expansion, continued by his successors, which made Lydia the dominant power in western Anatolia. But the Mermnad kings faced a formidable enemy in the Cimmerians, who had brought the Phrygian empire to an end in early C7, and now posed a serious threat to its Anatolian successor. On a number of occasions the Cimmerians attacked and invaded Lydian territory. Gyges secured some assistance against them from the Assyrian king Ashurbanipal. But he subsequently lost this assistance when he supported Egypt's rebellion against Assyria. Eventually he was killed in a Cimmerian onslaught, which also resulted in the destruction of part of the Lydian capital (c. 644). The struggles with the Cimmerians continued into the reign of the fourth ruler of the Mermnad dynasty, Alyattes (c. 609–560), who finally drove the invaders from Lydian territory (Herodotus 1.16).

Lydia's aggressive programme of expansion also brought it into conflict with the Ionian cities along Anatolia's western coast. The conflict ended with the incorporation of these cities into the Lydian empire, except for Miletus, whose independence was formally acknowledged in a treaty which Alyattes drew up with it (Herodotus 1.22). To the east, Alyattes was, according to Classical sources (esp. Herodotus), confronted with the westward expanding kingdom of the Medes, whose heartland lay in the Zagros mountain region of western Iran. A five-year conflict between the Lydians and the Medians culminated in the so-called 'battle of the eclipse', fought between Alyattes and the Median king Cyaxares on the banks of the Halys r. in north-central Anatolia (Herodotus 1.74, 103). The outcome was a treaty between the two kings which established the border between their kingdoms along the banks of the river. (For recently expressed doubts about the historicity of a Median 'empire' which stretched as far west

Figure 67 Account of Ashurbanipal's Egyptian campaigns and his reception of embassy from Gyges.

as the Halys r., see under **Medes**.) Lydia also appears to have been threatened to the east by the expansionist programme of the Neo-Babylonian empire. The Babylonian king Neriglissar, after his campaign of conquest in the kingdom of Pirindu in southern Anatolia (557/556), is reported to have started fires from the pass of Sallune (Classical Selinus in Cilicia Tracheia/Aspera) to the border of Lydia (**ABC* 104). But as far as is known, the Babylonians never consolidated their military penetration of the region with actual control over it.

Lydia reached the peak of its wealth and power under Croesus (560–546), the last member of the Mermnad dynasty. But with the rise of Persia under Cyrus II, the Lydian empire's days were numbered. Alarmed by the rapid expansion of Persian power westwards, Croesus led his troops across the Halys r. in an attempt to forestall a Persian invasion of his own territory. After a fierce but inconclusive encounter with Cyrus east of the Halys frontier (the 'battle of Pteria', spring 546; Herodotus 1.76), Croesus withdrew to the west where he was pursued by Cyrus' army and comprehensively defeated in a pitched battle outside Sardis (Herodotus 1.80). Croesus' royal capital fell to the Persians after a siege, and Croesus was taken prisoner (Herodotus 1.84–6). Lydia was now incorporated into the Persian empire, and Sardis became Persia's chief administrative centre in the west.

Under the Mermnad dynasty, Lydia became a powerful commercial and military empire, noted for its abundant mineral as well as agricultural resources. The mining of precious metals, especially silver and gold, accounted for much of the kingdom's

Figure 68 Lydian delegates at Persepolis.

wealth, and led to the invention of coined money in C6 – an invention which rapidly spread to the Greek world. The Lydian language survives in approximately sixty-four inscriptions, dating from C6 to C4 and found mostly on grave steles in Sardis. The language used in these inscriptions is Indo-European, but is imperfectly understood.

Neumann (*RlA* 7: 184–6), O. Masson (1991: 669–71), Mellink (1991: 643–55).

M

Maa (map 14) Late C13 and C12 fortified settlement on the west coast of Cyprus. The site is located at Palaeokastro on a small steep-sided promontory with a perennial spring and wide sandy bays on either side. It is defended by a Cyclopean fortification wall with a dog-leg entrance across the neck of the promontory and a second wall along the southern seaward limits. A number of late C13 buildings, excavated by V. Karageorghis and M. Demas for the Dept of Antiquities, Cyprus, from 1979 to 1986, provide evidence for olive oil and metallurgical production and storage. Two were equipped with communal halls and a central hearth. These buildings were destroyed by fire at the beginning of C12, and rebuilt on a reduced scale for a short period before the site was finally abandoned. Karageorghis has identified Maa as an early Aegean stronghold, established by an intrusive population unfamiliar with the Cypriot hinterland and concerned to secure the seaward approach. Other scholars suggest, alternatively, that both Maa and Pyla-Kokkinokremos (see **Pyla**) were indigenous strongholds, reflecting the unsettled conditions on the island in late C13 and C12. Internal activities at Maa are similar to those evident at other C13 settlements, such as Kalavasos, Maroni, and Alassa. The material culture shows both local and Aegean influences.

(J. M. Webb)
Karageorghis and Demas (1988), Steel (2004: 188–90).

Maacah Small state located in the northern Golan heights in northern Palestine, bordering the land of Geshur to its south. It may first be attested in the Middle Bronze Age Egyptian Execration texts (see glossary), but thenceforth only in biblical tradition. According to Joshua 13:13, the Israelites failed to drive out the people of Geshur and Maacah, both of whom maintained their independence. In C10 Maacah joined a coalition of Ammonites and Aramaeans who fought against David, and was presumably among the states which became subject to the Israelites following David's victory (2 Samuel 10:6–19). In C9 both Maacah and Geshur were probably incorporated into the Aramaean kingdom of Damascus.

B. Mazar (1986), Dorsey (*HCBD* 634).

Madaba (**Medeba**) (map 8) City in central Jordan, 30 km south of mod. Amman. Its material remains date back no earlier than the Roman and Byzantine periods (apart from a cave whose earliest burials go back to c. 1200). *OT* sources, however, record its seizure by the Israelites from the Amorite king Sihon (Numbers 21:30, Joshua 13:9–16). In C10, the Israelite army of King David did battle with a coalition of Ammonite and Aramaean forces outside the city, according to 1 Chronicles 19:7. A century later, in the second half of C9, the Moabite king Mesha recorded his liberation and rebuilding of the city in his well-known inscription on the so-called Moabite stone (see **Moab**). Before this, Mesha claims, the Israelites had occupied Madaba for forty years. In C2 the city figured in the Maccabaean revolt against Syria. Later in the century it fell to John Hyrcanus I (135/134–104) after a six-month siege, according to the C1 CE Jewish historian Josephus (*Jewish Antiquities* 13.9.1). It was subsequently handed over to the Nabataeans and remained under their control until its incorporation into the Roman empire as part of the province of Arabia. Among the city's Byzantine remains is the famous C6 CE mosaic pavement depicting the earliest known map of the Holy Land.

Piccirillo (*OEANE* 3: 393–7).

Madanu see Amadanu.

Madahisa Iron Age country probably to be located in the northwestern Zagros mountain region, south of Lake Urmia, in mod. Iranian Kurdistan. Dayyan-Ashur, commander-in-chief of the Assyrian king Shalmaneser III, received tribute from its cities during his progress through the region in 829 (**RIMA* 3: 70). His itinerary indicates that Madahisa lay between Hubushkia and Mannaea.

Madara (*Matar*) City located north of the Kashiyari range (mod. Tur ʿAbdin) in northern Mesopotamia, within the region called the Nairi land(s). Madara is first attested in a letter written by Yasmah-Addu, Assyrian viceroy of Mari in early C18, to his brother Ishme-Dagan (**LAPO* 16: 116–17, no. 27). It subsequently appears in Neo-Assyrian records as a heavily fortified city captured after a siege by the Assyrian king Ashurnasirpal II during his campaign in the region in 879 (**RIMA* 2: 209, 259). At that time, Madara was among the sixty cities said to have been ruled by Labturu, king of the land of Nirdun. Ashurnasirpal demolished the city but spared the lives of its inhabitants, taking some of their young men as hostages, upon their payment of a tribute to him. According to Ashurnasirpal's itinerary, the city lay between the Kashiyari range and Tushhan; it has long been identified with mod. Matar, located 1 km east of the Savur r.

Lipiński (2000: 140, 142).

Madaranzu Iron Age city in northern Mesopotamia, on the northern fringe of the Kashiyari mountain range (mod. Tur ʿAbdin) as it opens onto the Tigris valley. The Assyrian king Ashurnasirpal II conquered, plundered, and destroyed it, along with other cities, during his campaign in the region in 879 (**RIMA* 2: 209).

Madnasa (map 5) M1 city on the Myndus peninsula in Caria, southwestern Anatolia. In C5 it became a member of the Athenian Confederacy (see glossary). Pliny the Elder (5.107) reports that the city (which he calls Medmassa) was one of six Lelegian settlements assigned by Alexander the Great to the jurisdiction of Halicarnassus. (Their incorporation into Halicarnassus was in fact due to the mid C4 Carian satrap Mausolus prior to Alexander's campaigns.) Bean proposes an identification with the ruins on the hill above Türkbükü Bay and lower Göl. Remains of this site include an outer enclosure wall, at whose highest point is an ashlar tower, and within the enclosure half a dozen cisterns and numerous house foundations. At the northwest end of the site, a second tower was constructed. Nearby, a group of tombs was cut into the rock-face. Pottery sherds are of C5 and early C4 date.

Bean (1971: 115 map, 124).

Maeonia Legendary country in western Anatolia. The Trojan Catalogue in Homer's *Iliad* lists the Maeonians among Troy's allies immediately after the Phrygians (*Iliad* 2.864–6), and assigns them a homeland under Mt Tmolus (mod. Boz Daği) within the region of Lydia. Herodotus (7.74) claims that the Lydians were originally known as Maeonians, before they assumed their later name in commemoration of a legendary king, Lydus. It is possible that the name Maeonia is etymologically linked with Masa, a Late Bronze Age western Anatolian country frequently attested in Hittite texts.

Magan (map 12) Land attested in Mesopotamian Bronze and Iron Age texts and identified with the modern Sultanate of Oman and the United Arab Emirates, on the northeastern part of the Arabian peninsula. It was one of the three countries which in Mesopotamian tradition lay alongside the 'Lower Sea', i.e. the Persian Gulf and the Arabian Sea. The other two countries were Dilmun and Meluhha. In M3 Sumerian literary texts, Magan and Meluhha (the latter = the Harappan civilization, Indus valley?) both appear as distant lands, sources of a wide range of exotic goods. Other Mesopotamian texts confirm the importation of products from these lands: wood, copper, diorite, and semi-precious stones from Magan, black wood (ebony?), ivory, gold, silver, carnelian, and lapis lazuli from Meluhha. Most if not all of these goods were transported by water to their final destinations in Mesopotamia. During the reign of the Akkadian king Sargon (2334–2279), ships from Magan, Meluhha, and Dilmun docked at the royal capital Agade/Akkad. From the Akkadian period onwards, copper was the most sought-after commodity originating in the land of Magan. Evidence of anc. workings at numerous copper mines in Oman and Fujairah, in the northern United Arab Emirates, indicates that Magan was a major source of supply of the metal, which no doubt found its way to many of the cities of Mesopotamia, as attested already in the M3 literary texts. Magan was also the source of the hard black stone called diorite, which Gudea, a C22 king of Lagash, used for fashioning the many statues he commissioned of himself, to honour the city-state's patron deity Ningirsu.

Later Akkadian kings may have sought to obtain Magan's products by less peaceful means. For example, Sargon's grandson Naram-Sin (2254–2218) claims to have conducted a campaign against the country, capturing its king, Manium, and to have brought back booty from it (**RIME* 2: 117). His father, Manishtushu, probably also campaigned against Magan. Perhaps their hostility was prompted by commercial disputes with Magan and threats by it to cut off its exports. However, peaceful relations between Magan and Mesopotamia were restored by Ur-Nammu (2112–2095), founder of the Ur III dynasty. Magan resumed its trade with Mesopotamia, which continued, with Dilmun probably serving as intermediary on many occasions, through the Ur III period (c. 2112–2004) and the Middle and Late Bronze Ages. In return for the goods it exported to Mesopotamia, Magan received consignments of wool, hides, sesame oil, and plant products. From mid C18 onwards, however, there appears to have been some reduction in trading activity between Mesopotamia and the Gulf. This may be reflected in the material remains of Oman in this period. Bienkowski (*BMD* 218) notes that human occupation in Oman contemporary with the text references appears to reflect an oasis economy, with settlement characterized by mudbrick towers, either residences of local rulers or storage buildings, and stone-built tombs with hundreds of skeletons. He suggests that the numerous collective graves dating between c. 1800 and 1000, often without any apparent settlement nearby, may reflect a shift to a nomadic lifestyle.

The Iron Age saw a revival of urban settlement in Oman, which in Neo-Assyrian texts was called Qade. A king of Qade called Pade from the city of Izkie (= mod. Izki in Oman?) brought tribute to the Assyrian king Ashurbanipal in 640. But the name Magan did not entirely disappear. Ashurbanipal's predecessor Esarhaddon used it in his titulature, describing himself as 'king of the kings of Dilmun, Magan, and Meluhha'. No doubt he was following a tradition established by his own predecessors, which helped ensure the survival of the land's original name, at least in formal, ceremonial contexts, long after it had disappeared from everyday use. Magan is attested in Persian royal inscriptions as Maka (Old Persian) (q.v.), while in contemporary economic texts from Persepolis, written in Elamite, the name appears as Makkash.

Heimpel (*RlA* 7: 195–9), Zarins (*OEANE* 4: 184–7), D. T. Potts (1995: 1452–6).

Mag(a)risu Iron Age city in northwestern Mesopotamia, at or near the confluence of the Habur and Harmish rivers (possibly mod. Hassake). The city is first attested in the texts of the Assyrian king Ashur-bel-kala (1073–1056). It was the site of a battle fought by Assyrian and Aramaean forces during his reign (**RIMA* 2: 102). A further Assyrian–Aramaean confrontation took place in the same month near the city of Dur-Katlimmu on the Habur r. In 885 the Assyrian king Tukulti-Ninurta II encamped his forces in Magarisu while progressing up the Euphrates on his last recorded campaign (**RIMA* 2: 177). In 878 his son and successor Ashurnasirpal II also spent a night in the city, at the beginning of his expedition into the Habur/Middle Euphrates region (**RIMA* 2: 212).

Röllig (*RlA* 7: 199–200), Liverani (1992: 63–4).

Magnesia ad Maeandrum (map 5) M1 BCE–M1 CE western Anatolian city located near the Aegean coast, within the region called Ionia by the anc. Greeks, though not part of the Ionian League. According to Classical tradition, it was founded by Aeolian settlers from Magnesia in northern Greece. The city was captured by the Lydian king Gyges (680–652), and destroyed by a Cimmerian tribe called the Treres c. 650 (Strabo 14.1.40). It was rebuilt by the citizens of Miletus (which lay nearby to the southwest), but subsequently fell to Persia c. 530. In the late 460s, the Persian emperor Artaxerxes I presented the city to the former Athenian military commander Themistocles, ten years or so after his ostracism from Athens (Thucydides 1.138). Themistocles was greatly esteemed by the Magnesians, who gave him a lavish funeral on his death in 459, and set up a memorial to him in the agora. In 400 the Spartans captured Magnesia from the Persians. The victorious Spartan commander Thibron shifted the city to a new site (its original site has not been located) under Mt Thorax, formerly occupied by a village called Leukophrys ('White Eyebrowed') where a temple to the local goddess Artemis Leucophryene had been built (Strabo 14.1.40). In Magnesia's brief period under Spartan control (400–398), the temple of Artemis was refounded, and thenceforth the city became an important religious centre. During the Hellenistic period, it flourished under the rule first of the Seleucid and then of the Attalid kings, and subsequently enjoyed a prosperous, independent existence under the patronage and protection of Rome. In the Byzantine period it was the seat of a bishopric.

The most significant remains of the city are those of the temple of Artemis, a late C3 building in the Ionic order, erected on the site of an earlier temple dating to the period of Themistocles' residence in Magnesia. Excavations conducted in C19 brought to light other structures of Hellenistic and/or Roman date, among them a theatre, a stadium, and a number of buildings in the agora, which included a temple of the god Zeus (Sosipolis), an odeum, and a gymnasium. On the wall of a stoa in the agora, some seventy Hellenistic inscriptions were discovered. In these, various cities acknowledged Magnesia's territory as inviolate. Most of the results of C19 excavations are no longer visible, due to the site's annual flooding by the (Classical) Lethaius r.

E. Akurgal (1973: 177–84), Bean (*PECS* 544).

Magnesia ad Sipylum (*Manisa*) (map 5) M1 BCE–M1 CE city in western Anatolia, 32 km northeast of Izmir, within the country called Lydia in the first half of M1. The city was built in an excellent strategic location, in the fertile (Classical) Hermus r. valley at the junction of important communication routes. According to Classical tradition, it was founded by settlers from Thessaly in northern Greece after the Trojan War. In mid C6 it was captured by the Lydian king Croesus, but after the fall of the Lydian empire to the Persian king Cyrus II (546) it became subject to Persia. Thenceforth it remained under Persian sovereignty until its liberation by Alexander the Great (following his victory over the Persian forces at the Granicus r.) in 334.

During the Hellenistic period, Alexander's heirs and their successors contended for control over Magnesia. But the city is best known as the site of the famous battle between Rome and the Seleucid king Antiochus III in January 189. The confrontation ended in a decisive victory for the Roman general Lucius Cornelius Scipio, and marked the beginning of a new era in Rome's relations with the western Asian world. Despite one major setback when it was devastated by an earthquake in 17 CE, Magnesia flourished through the Roman imperial period, and continued to be an important city under Byzantine rule. No significant material remains of the anc. city survive.

MacDonald (*PECS* 544–5).

Mahiranu Country in northwestern Mesopotamia, attested in an inscription of the Assyrian king Ashur-bel-kala (1073–1056), and located in or near the land of Harran. At this time, the Harran area was occupied by large numbers of Aramaean tribal groups. Mahiranu was conquered by the Assyrians during one of Ashur-bel-kala's campaigns against the Aramaeans (**RIMA* 2: 102).

Maka (Maciya) Name of a country and people located in southern Iran and the Oman peninsula attested in M1 Persian sources. The name appears as Magan (q.v.) in Mesopotamian Bronze and Iron Age texts. Maka was among the eastern lands of the Persian empire listed several times in the inscriptions of Darius I (522–486), e.g. in his Bisitun inscription (**DB* 6), and also in the *daiva* inscription (see glossary) of his son and successor Xerxes (**XPh* 3). It also makes several appearances in the Persepolis Fortification tablets, where the name, written in Elamite, is Makkash (*Hallock, 1969:211, nos 679–80, 634, no. 2050, **PE* 875, no. 42 (i)). A kilted representative from Maka is depicted in one of the reliefs from Persepolis. The country has been identified with the land of the people called the Mykoi in Classical sources, located on the Oman peninsula (see *BAGRW* 95, inset). According to Herodotus (3.93), the Mykoi were part of the empire's fourteenth province (but see glossary under **satrapy**),and provided a contingent in the forces assembled by Darius' successor Xerxes for his invasion of Greece in 481, under the command of Darius' son Arsamenes (7.68).

D. T. Potts (1990: I.394–400), Wiesehöfer (*BNP* 9: 402).

Makaria (*Moulos*) (map 14) Site located on the northern coast of Cyprus, on the Moulos headland. Pottery sherds indicate settlement during the Late Bronze Age. The settlement apparently survived until the Byzantine period, but was gradually abandoned after the Arab invasions of 647. Apart from a passing reference in the C2 Greek geographer Ptolemy, there are no surviving written attestations of the settlement.

Nicolaou (*PECS* 546).

Malaha Iron Age city in southern Syria belonging to the kingdom of Aram-Damascus. The Assyrian king Shalmaneser III calls it a royal city of the Damascene king Hazael, and refers to booty he took from the city's temple of Sheru in the course of his campaigns in the region in 838 and 837 (**RIMA* 3: 62, 151). Lipiński suggests that Malaha is the early Aramaic name of the city of Hazor.

Lipiński (2000: 350–1).

Malamir see ***Izeh***.

Malatya see ***Arslantepe***.

Maldiya see ***Arslantepe***.

Malgium (map 11) Bronze Age city and city-state and Iron Age city in Babylonia, located on the Tigris south of its confluence with the Diyala, upstream from Mashkan-shapir. Though its history may have extended back to the Early Bronze Age, it is not clearly attested in written records before the Old Babylonian period (Middle Bronze Age). In this period, Malgium was the seat of a small kingdom. Three inscriptions provide us with the names of two of its kings, Takil-ilissu, son of Ishtaran-asu, and Ipiq-Ishtar, son of Apil-ilishu (**RIME* 4: 669–74). Two of the inscriptions were written on behalf of Takil-ilissu, one by Ipiq-Ishtar. All three record the construction of sacred buildings. (The dates of these kings' reigns are uncertain. For example, Charpin considers Ipiq-Ishtar a contemporary of the Babylonian king Hammurabi, Kutscher a contemporary of his successor Samsu-iluna.) Malgium evidently lay close to the territories controlled by Larsa, Babylon, and Elam. In C20 and C19 it suffered attacks by at least two of Larsa's kings, Gungunum (1932–1906) and Sin-iddinam (1849–1843). Warad-Sin (1834–1823), Larsa's penultimate ruler, may also have won a victory over an army from Malgium, if we can so judge from information provided by a date formula relating to the year 1831. But the reliability of this information is considered highly suspect (*Mesop*. 118–19). In 1777 the Babylonian king Hammurabi, acting in concert with Shamshi-Adad I and Ibal-pi-El II, the kings of Upper Mesopotamia and Eshnunna respectively, conducted a campaign against Malgium, destroying a number of its towns and placing its capital under siege. Faced with overwhelming odds, Malgium's ruler bought off the invaders with the substantial payment of fifteen talents of silver, which was shared equally among the coalition leaders (**LAPO* 17: 143, no. 544).

Malgium was used as a transit stop by Elamite messengers travelling between Susa and Hammurabi's court in Babylon. Subsequently it appears to have entered into an alliance with Elam, or else to have been subjected to Elamite control, for Hammurabi claims that in his thirtieth regnal year (1762) he defeated an army of Elamites, whose forces included contingents from Subartum, Gutium, Eshnunna, and Malgium (**Mesop.* 225). If Malgium had been obliged to fight against Hammurabi as a subject of Elam, then the Babylonian victory would have had the effect of liberating it from Elamite overlordship. Its ruler Ipiq-Ishtar concluded a treaty with the Babylonian king, and provided him with a contingent of 1,000 troops for his attack on the kingdom of Larsa, then ruled by Rim-Sin. For reasons unknown to us, relations between Babylon and Malgium turned sour soon afterwards. Hammurabi claims that in his thirty-third regnal year (1759) he won a victory over the armies of Mari and Malgium, which led to the imposition of his rule over the cities and countries in the region between the Tigris and the Euphrates (**Mesop.* 327). Two years later, he demolished the walls of Malgium's capital, and apparently deported a large part of the country's population to his own kingdom. Some thousands of people from Malgium are attested as inhabitants of the Babylonian kingdom in the reign of Hammurabi's successor Samsu-iluna.

Virtually nothing is known of Malgium's later history. It seems to have been an administrative district in the Middle Babylonian era (with its name now spelled Malgu). References to it as a settlement in several Neo-Assyrian sources (in the form Malaki or Maliki) in connection with the city of Der (3) indicate its continuing existence in M1 until at least the reign of the Assyrian king Ashurbanipal (668–630/627).

Kutscher (*RlA* 7: 300–4), *Mesop.* 31, 118–9, 183–4, 225, 318, 327–30.

Malyan, Tepe see Anshan.

Mama Middle Bronze Age kingdom in southern Anatolia, probably located in the mountainous region southeast of Nesa and in the region of mod. Elbistan or Maraş. Early in the second phase of the Assyrian Colony period (late C19–mid C18) (see glossary) Mama's king, Anum-hirbi, became involved in a dispute with Inar, king of Nesa/Kanesh, which culminated in an invasion of Mama's territory by Inar. Though peace was restored and a treaty concluded between the two kings, hostilities flared once more in the reign of Inar's son and successor Warsama. This was provoked by one of Warsama's vassal rulers, 'the man of Taisama', who had on his own initiative crossed into Mama and attacked and destroyed a number of its towns. Anum-hirbi wrote to Warsama complaining bitterly of his vassal's conduct, and urging him to keep a tight rein on the vassal in the future.

*Balkan (1957), Miller (2001a).

Mankisum (*Tell Kurr?*) (map 10) Middle Bronze Age city in central Mesopotamia, attested in Old Babylonian sources, located on or near the Tigris west or northwest of Eshnunna. It lay at the northern limit of the territory extending through the Tigris region from Upi northwards, annexed by the Babylonian king Apil-Sin (1830–1813). Shortly after this annexation, Mankisum together with Upi and a city called Shahaduni became attached to the kingdom of Eshnunna when it was ruled by Naram-Sin (late C19). Control over the region was now contested by a new player, Shamshi-Adad I (1796–1775), king of Assyria. Shamshi-Adad won possession of Mankisum, and established a boundary with Eshnunna between it and Upi to the south. The Eshnunnite king, now Dadusha, responded by assembling his forces at Upi in preparation for an attack on Mankisum. He invited Hammurabi, king of Babylon, to join forces with him, but the invitation was refused (**LAPO* 17: 132–5, no. 534). The Eshnunnites then entered Shamshi-Adad's territory, advancing towards a town called Mashkulliya, but withdrawing before a military confrontation took place. Mankisum subsequently fell to Dadusha. However, the Elamite seizure of Eshnunna in 1765 enabled Hammurabi to gain possession of Mankisum, and also the city of Upi. This infuriated the Elamite king, who sent an ultimatum to him, demanding that he return to him the cities formerly belonging to Eshnunna. When Hammurabi refused, the Elamites attacked and captured Mankisum, and then progressed downstream along the Tigris to lay siege to Upi (see under **Upi (1)**).

After the withdrawal of the Elamite troops from Mesopotamia in 1764, Hammurabi sought to resolve by diplomacy the question of sovereignty over Mankisum and other cities in the region, specifically Upi and Shahaduni, in treaty negotiations with the new Eshnunnite king Silli-Sin (1764–1762) (*Charpin, 2003: 80–1). He proposed two alternatives: either that all the cities be returned to Babylonian control, where they had been in the time of his grandfather Apil-Sin, or that Mankisum be conceded to the Eshnunnites, provided that they compensate him, Hammurabi, for the costs he had incurred in seeking to liberate the city from the Elamites. (The presence of Elamite troops in Mankisum is attested in a number of letters from the Mari archives.) The cities south of Mankisum were in either case to be confirmed as Babylonian territory. It appears that Silli-Sin initially rejected these proposals, but agreed to them a year or so later. Hammurabi's year formula for his thirty-second year (1760) commemorates a decisive victory over an Eshnunnite army at Mankisum, which he followed up by annexing Mankisum and the land on both banks of the Tigris as far as the country of Subartum (*Horsnell, 1999: 144–5).

Edzard (*RlA* 7: 339–40), *LKM* 616–17 (refs), *Mesop.* 115, 160–2, 227, 326.

Mannaea (Urartian **Mana**) (map 13) General name for what was originally a number of small Iron Age kingdoms, dating from early M1 and located south of Lake Urmia in mod. Iranian Kurdistan. The Urmia lowlands are referred to as the land of the Mannaeans in Assyrian texts, and as 'Mana, its land' in Urartian texts. When Dayyan-Ashur, commander-in-chief of the Assyrian king Shalmaneser III, campaigned in this region in 829 (**RIMA* 3: 70), the states or kingdoms located there were independent political entities. However, one of the kings of the region, Udaku, whose stronghold was the city of Izirtu (or Zirtu), may have exercised some form of hegemonic role over his neighbours. After plundering Mannaean territory at this time, the Assyrians apparently made no attempt to establish permanent authority there, though Shalmaneser's son and successor Shamshi-Adad V (823–811) reports receiving tribute from it during his third campaign in the Nairi lands (**RIMA* 3: 184).

Urartu adopted a different policy. In the decades following the Assyrians' departure, its repeated invasions of Mannaean territory culminated in the establishment of Urartian control over the Urmia lowlands, probably in 802/801, by the Urartian king Minua. Urartu's domination of the region continued into the reign of Minua's successor, Argishti I (787–766). But during Argishti's reign, Mannaea broke from Urartu and became a single united kingdom, whose frontiers extended all the way to the shores of Lake Urmia. This set the scene for a number of armed conflicts between Mannaea and Urartu, under Argishti and his successor Sarduri II (765–733), until the latter finally succeeded in reimposing Urartian control over Mannaean territory. But taking advantage of the ongoing contest between Urartu and Assyria, Mannaea once more regained its independence following a campaign into Urartian territory by the Assyrian king Tiglath-pileser III (745–727).

During the last decades of C8, under the rule of a king called Iranzu, Mannaea reached the peak of its power and prosperity. Its lands and those of its dependencies covered an extensive part of the Urmia basin, and perhaps included territories on both the eastern and western shores of the lake. But Iranzu was intimidated, by news of Assyrian conquests and annexations of neighbouring lands, into making his peace with Tiglath-pileser and paying him a substantial annual tribute (**Tigl. III* 98–100, 108–9). He subsequently pledged allegiance to the Assyrian king Sargon II (721–705). The benefits of doing so soon became evident. In 719, when Iranzu's position was threatened by several of his governors who supported the Urartian king Rusa I, Sargon intervened on his behalf, conducting a campaign of devastation against the dissidents and their cities (**ARAB* II: 3). Iranzu was thus made secure, and when he died shortly afterwards, Sargon put his son Aza on his throne (c. 716). But with the encouragement of the Urartian king Rusa, several Mannaean governors rebelled against the new king, taking him prisoner and executing him. (One of the rebellious governors, Daiukku, who was captured by Sargon in 715 and deported with his family to the city of Hamath in northern Syria, is commonly identified with Herodotus' Deioces, on whom see Panaino, 2003. For the problems of the identification, see Helm, 1981.) Rusa then replaced Aza on the Mannaean throne with his brother Ullusunu, who had (doubtless) pledged loyalty to the Urartian king, and handed over to him twenty-two of his fortresses as an earnest of this.

Sargon responded furiously. He invaded Mannaea, and seized and destroyed its capital Izirtu and the strongholds Izibia (Ziwiyeh) and Armit. He then proceeded to wreak havoc in other parts of the country. In the process he captured Bagdatti, the leader of the rebellion which had unseated Aza, and had him flayed alive. Ullusunu, who had fled his capital on the approach of the Assyrian forces, now returned and threw himself on Sargon's mercy. The outcome was perhaps better than he could have expected. Sargon forgave him, restored him to his throne, and returned to him the twenty-two Mannaean fortresses which he had seized back from the Urartian king Rusa (**ARAB* II: 27–9). In 714, the year of Sargon's great campaign against Urartu, Ullusunu reaffirmed his loyalty to the Assyrian king when the two met in Mannaean territory, and provided him with food supplies, horses, and cattle for his army. In turn, Sargon acknowledged Ullusunu as his ally, according him a place of honour at a special feast, and undertook to win back for him any of the remaining territories that he had lost to the Urartians (**ARAB* II: 75–8).

But the accord with Assyria was probably shortlived. Hostilities between Mannaea and Assyria, generally at the expense of the former, were much more characteristic of the relations between the two kingdoms. In the 670s Mannaea suffered another resounding defeat by Assyria when it formed an anti-Assyrian alliance with the Scythians. In 660–659 an attempt by the Mannaean king Ahseri to destroy an Assyrian force dispatched across the Zagros mountains also ended in failure. Ahseri was subsequently killed, along with most of his family, in an uprising of his subjects. His surviving son, Ualli, sought peace with the Assyrian king Ashurbanipal (668–630/627), and succeeded in forming an alliance with him. The Assyrian–Mannaean alliance proved a lasting one. It still remained in force in late C7, when the Babylonian king Nabopolassar (626–605) launched a series of campaigns into Assyrian territory, and in the course of these inflicted a defeat on Assyria's Mannaean allies.

Kingship in Mannaea seems to have been hereditary. The royal seat of the ruling dynasty was probably the city of Izirtu, which in all likelihood was located near the southern shore of Lake Urmia. The king was assisted and advised, and his power was probably circumscribed, by an aristocratic council of elders. Even after unification the Mannaean kingdom lacked a strongly coherent political structure. 'Provinces' of the kingdom were under the immediate authority of governors, who appear to have exercised a high degree of autonomy. The names of these provinces include Arsianshi, Ereshteiana, Messi, Subi, Surkiash, and Uishdish. Heads of families and communities seem also to have played important roles in the kingdom's administration. There may have been a core Mannaean population of perhaps Hurrian origin. But the overall population of the Mannaean lands was made up of a number of tribal groups of different ethnic origins. Included amongst the ones identified in Assyrian records were Dalians, Kumurdians, Messians, Sunbians, and Teurlians. Though these groups were loosely integrated into the kingdom of Mannaea, the tribal structure of Mannaean society remained strong. The basis of the kingdom's economy was agriculture. Wheat, barley, and wine figured amongst its principal crops. A variety of livestock was raised, including cattle, horse, sheep, camels, and donkeys.

Postgate (*RlA* 7: 340–2).

Mansuate Iron Age city in western Syria, first mentioned in the Assyrian Eponym Chronicles (see glossary). Reference is made there to a campaign conducted in 796 by Adad-nirari III 'as far as Mansuate' (*Millard, 1994: 57). The city later became a centre of the Assyrian administration, as indicated by references to it in Assyrian letters and administrative documents. Its status as the chief city of an Assyrian province may date back to the reign of Tiglath-pileser III (745–727), though its provincial status is not firmly attested until the beginning of the reign of Esarhaddon (680), when it was assigned to the Assyrian governor Dananu. Various identifications have been proposed for Mansuate's location. Most recently, Lipiński has equated it with mod. Masyaf, west of the Orontes.

Hawkins (*RlA* 7: 342–3), Lipiński (2000: 263 map, 304–10, with refs).

Manuhatan Middle Bronze Age city, attested in the Mari archives, probably to be located on the east bank of the Euphrates in the district of Saggaratum, an important city of the kingdom of Mari. It was fortified by the Yaminite leader Yagih-Adad, who was an enemy of the Mariote king Zimri-Lim (1774–1762). A large Yaminite encampment was established in the area extending between Manuhatan and Lasqum, which lay on the Euphrates to the north. The encampment was attacked by troops of the Hana people, from the district of Qattunan on the Habur r.

LKM 617 (refs).

Marabaya Late Bronze Age city in northern Syria belonging to the kingdom of Ugarit, and frequently attested in texts from Ras Shamra. The city [Ma-]raba, belonging to the Iron Age kingdom of Hamath and attested in a list of Hamathite cities and districts conquered by the Assyrian king Tiglath-pileser III (745–727) (**Tigl* III: 136), was probably its Iron Age successor. A location near the mod. coastal city of Latakia seems likely.

Lipiński (2000: 290, with refs).

Maracanda (*Samarkand*; archaeological site ***Afrasiab***, map 16) M1 BCE–M1 CE city located in the valley of the Zarafshan r. in mod. Uzbekistan, central Asia, on the northeastern edge of the Iranian highlands. It was the capital of the country called Sogdiana (Arrian, *Anabasis* 3.30.6). When Sogdiana was incorporated into the Persian empire, Maracanda probably became a regional centre of the Persian administration, and a royal palace may have been located there. In 329, Alexander the Great conquered the city and used it as his base for his two-year campaigns in the region. According to Curtius (7.6.10), Maracanda was a walled city of extensive proportions, dominated by a fortified citadel (which has now been identified by excavation). During the Hellenistic period the city probably became a colony of the Seleucid empire.

Sancisi-Weerdenburg (*OCD* 920–1), Brentjes (*BNP* 8: 278).

Marad (map 11) City in northern Babylonia located on the site of Wanna-wa-Sadum, midway between Babylon and Isin. Attested in sources spanning the period late M3–M1, it appears first in the reign of the Akkadian king Manishtushu (2269–2255). Subsequently it was governed by one of the sons of Manishtushu's successor Naram-Sin (2254–2218) (**RIME* 2: 112). Marad was later the centre of a province under the C21 Ur III administration, ruled on behalf of the administration by a series of governors (*ensis*). At the beginning of C19, its fortunes seem to have been linked closely with those of the city of Kazallu, which appears to have been located between Marad and the city of Kish. Kazallu became for a time the dominant power in northern Babylonia, in effect sharing control over the southern Mesopotamian remnants of the Ur III empire with Ishbi-Erra's ruling dynasty at Isin in the south. Marad and Kish were both subject to a king of Kazallu called Sumu-ditana. Subsequently, Marad and Kazallu were ruled by a king called Halum-pi-umu (variants Halambu, Alumbiumu), who seized the city of Dilbat, which apparently belonged to the kingdom of Babylon. In 1878 the Babylonian king Sumu-la-El responded by inflicting a defeat on the aggressor, and five years later Kazallu suffered a further military defeat at the hands of the Larsan king Sumu-El. In 1862, Sumu-la-El demolished the walls of Kazallu, and the following year Marad was incorporated into the kingdom of Babylon. This did not prevent its seizure by the kings of Isin and Larsa, but it was eventually recaptured by the Babylonian king Sin-muballit (1812–1793), who fortified its walls against further attack. It continued to make somewhat half-hearted attempts at regaining its independence during the reigns of Sin-muballit's successors Hammurabi and Samsu-iluna.

During the period of Kassite rule in Babylonia (Late Bronze Age), Marad was one of the more important cities of Babylonia, due partly to its status as a major religious centre. The city's chief deity was the god Lugal-Mar(a)da ('King of Marad'). At the end of the Late Bronze Age, when the Babylonian throne was occupied by the Assyrian-appointed Kassite king Adad-shuma-iddina (1222–1217), Marad was among the cities devastated by the Elamite king Kidin-Hutran during an Elamite invasion of

Babylonia (**ABC* 177). Several hundred years later, the Assyrian Eponym Chronicle (see glossary) entry for the year 770 refers to an expedition to Marad by the commander-in-chief Shamshi-ilu during the reign of the Assyrian king Ashur-dan III (772–755). Marad was one of a number of Babylonian cities (others included Borsippa, Kish, Sippar, Ur, and Uruk) whose temples Nebuchadnezzar II (604–562) rebuilt and decorated on a lavish scale.

Edzard (*RlA* 7: 351–3), *Mesop.* 87–8.

Marassantiya r. see **Halys r.**

Marathus (*Amrit*) (map 7) Phoenician city on the coast of Syria, serving as the continental port for the island of Arwad (Phoenician Ruad). Occupation of the site dates back to the end of M3, as indicated by ceramic ware of this period uncovered during excavations by M. Dunand, principally from 1954 onwards. Among the remains of later date were eight corbelled tombs (the so-called 'silo tombs') of the Middle and Late Bronze Age, whose contents included weapons and a range of incised and decorated ceramic ware, and in some cases the original human remains. An open-air colonnaded temple, cut in the side of a hill and now commonly referred to as the *Ma'abed*, was excavated in 1955 and 1957. Its covered portico with square pillars enclosed a large rectangular basin, 47 m × 39 m and over 3 m deep, in the centre of which was a cube-shaped chapel. The temple was probably dedicated to the gods Melqart of Tyre and Eshmun, and has been dated to the period of Persian expansion into Syria following Cyrus II's conquest of Babylon in 539. A second temple described by visitors to the site in 1697, 1743, and 1860 has now entirely disappeared. To the south of the city lies a cemetery dating to C4, the last century of the Persian period. It contains rock-cut tombs, three of which are surmounted by pyramidal- and cube-shaped funerary towers. They are among the most notable grave-monuments of the Phoenician world. The contents of the two-chambered 'pyramidal hypogeum', consisting of a cubic base on which stands a cylinder surmounted by an eight-sided pyramid (thus Saliby), indicates continuing use from C4 to C1. Excavations at Amrit have also brought to light the city's anc. harbour facilities, and a stadium of C4 date which remained in use in the early Hellenistic period. (For the surrender of Marathus to Alexander the Great in 333/332, see **Arwad**.) Settlement continued at Marathus until at least the end of this period. The city was in ruins in C1, according to Strabo (16.2.12). However, its continuing existence is indicated by references to it in later Classical writers (e.g. Pliny the Elder, 5.78).

Dunand and Saliby (1985), Saliby (*OEANE* 1: 111–13).

Mardaman Early and Middle Bronze Age city located in the eastern Habur region of northern Mesopotamia. The earliest reference to it allegedly dates to the reign of the Akkadian king Naram-Sin (2254–2218) when according to a later (Old Babylonian) tradition its ruler, Duhsusu, joined the 'Great Revolt' against Naram-Sin (**Chav.* 32). During its Middle Bronze Age phase Mardaman sent envoys to the court of Yahdun-Lim, king of Mari (1810–1794), and was subsequently one of the cities in the region captured by the Assyrian king Shamshi-Adad I (1796–1775), whose son Yasmah-Addu occupied the Assyrian viceregal seat at Mari.

The end of Shamshi-Adad's reign was followed after a brief interval by the seizure of

Figure 69 Marathus, temple.

Mari's throne by Zimri-Lim (1774–1762) (see **Mari**), who sought to win by diplomacy the support of Mardaman (along with a number of other northern Mesopotamian cities). At the very beginning of his reign, he wrote a letter to a certain Tish-Ulme, who later became king of Mardaman, proposing that Tish-Ulme and Mardaman's administrators hand the city over to him, with the promise that he would give it back to its 'rightful owner' – i.e. a local ruler loyal to him (**Chav.* 120–1). The letter was found still in its envelope in Mari, and was thus never dispatched. Other references to Mardaman during Zimri-Lim's reign indicate that its relations with Mari were hostile for at least part of this reign. The city came to the assistance of the land of Hadnum when the latter changed its alliance from Zimri-Lim to the city of Kurda, and in retaliation it was attacked and defeated by troops from Mari's ally, Karana (**LKM* 396). In another letter from the Mari archive, Zimri-Lim is informed that his allies Qarni-Lim and Sharraya, the kings of Andarig and northern Razama (see **Razama (2)**) respectively, had entered Mardaman and taken from it 1,000 prisoners (**LKM* 225).

Edzard (*RlA* 7: 357–8).

Margiana (**Margush**) (map 16) Central Asian country located west of the Oxus r. in the region of mod. Turkmenistan. From early in Cyrus II's reign (559–530) it was incorporated into the Persian empire as a dependency of the country of Bactria. It is listed in the Bisitun inscription among the states which rose in rebellion against Darius I shortly after his accession in 522 (**DB* 21). But its uprising under a king called Frada was shortlived. Darius' Bactrian satrap, Dardashish, crushed the Margian forces in a battle in December 522, in which 55,000 Margian troops were allegedly killed and a further 8,500 captured (**DB* 38). Alexander the Great built six forts in Margiana during the course of his eastern campaign in 328, and founded there one of his cities called Alexandria.

Wiesehöfer (*BNP* 8: 339).

Marhashi (Sumerian form of the name; Akkadian **Barahshum/Parahshum**, sometimes represented as **Warahshe**) (map 12) Important Early and Middle Bronze Age kingdom in Iran, bordering upon Elam. The mod. regions of eastern Fars or Kerman have been suggested as possible locations. (Tepe Yahya, q.v., whose anc. name is unknown, may have lain within its territory.) However, more easterly and more northerly locations have also been proposed (the former in the region of mod. Baluchistan). The kingdom is attested, either as B/Parahshum or Marhashi, in Mesopotamian texts of the Akkadian, Ur III, and Old Babylonian periods (i.e. second half of M3–early M2). It was independent of Elam but often allied with it. Indeed, there is a suggestion that up to the time of the eastern campaign of the Akkadian king Rimush (see below), Parahshum may have exercised some form of control, or at least strong influence, over Elam (Steinkeller, 1982: 257). By the end of the Old Babylonian period the kingdom had apparently ceased to exist as a separate political entity, though its name survived down to the very end of cuneiform literature in scientific and lexical texts.

The earliest references to Marhashi/Parahshum date to the reign of the Akkadian king Sargon (2334–2279), who conducted a major expedition into the highland regions of western Iran, and claimed to have conquered Parahshum and Elam (along with Awan, Susa, and other cities and states in the region). The conquered lands were incorporated into the Akkadian empire, with the probable exception of Parahshum, whose distance from the centre of Akkadian power made it impracticable for any form of permanent control to be established over it, by either the Akkadian rulers or the later Ur III kings. But it was not beyond the reach of military campaigns launched from southern Mesopotamia, as demonstrated by Sargon, and especially by his son and successor Rimush (2278–2270). Following Sargon's death, Parahshum had joined with Elam and Zahara (another of its neighbours) in an anti-Akkadian military alliance. Rimush responded with a devastating campaign of conquest, resulting in the greatest military triumph of his reign. After defeating Abalgamash, king of Parahshum, he attacked and defeated the combined forces of Zahara and Elam which confronted him within Parahshum's territory. According to his report of the campaign, he killed 16,212 of the enemy troops, and captured a further 4,216 (**DaK* 206–11, **RIME* 2: 52–67). Parahshum's general, Sidgau, was among the prisoners, as was the Elamite king Emahsini. But Abalgamash, who had led the alliance in partnership with Emahsini and Zahara's ruler Sargapi (who was also later captured), probably survived the battle and escaped. Rimush followed up his victory by establishing his sovereignty over Elam, though Zahara and Parahshum apparently retained their independence.

Parahshum is conspicuously absent from the records of Rimush's successor Manishtushu (2269–2255), who certainly campaigned in western Iran, and no doubt further strengthened his empire's control over Parahshum's neighbour, Elam. But it does appear on the extensive list of countries which rose up in the so-called 'Great Revolt' against Manishtushu's son and successor Naram-Sin (2254–2218) at the beginning of his reign (*Chav. 32) – though we have no details of the part it played in this uprising. In any case, by the end of Naram-Sin's reign, relations between Parahshum and Akkad must have taken a turn for the better, since either Naram-Sin's son Shar-kali-sharri travelled to Parahshum while he was crown prince to marry a local princess, or Shar-kali-sharri's son was sent there for this purpose.

Through the period of the Ur III empire (C21), Marhashi/Parahshum appears to have retained its independence and to have enjoyed close diplomatic links with at least some of the Ur III rulers. There were apparently regular diplomatic exchanges between the two royal courts, and on occasions the king of Marhashi may himself have visited Ur. If there were in fact a parity-type relationship between the kingdoms, this would indicate Marhashi's status as a major political, military, and probably economic power at this time. Such a relationship would no doubt have enabled Marhashi to serve as a valuable intermediary between the rulers of other lands in its region and the Ur III dynasty. Marhashi's own links with the dynasty were consolidated by a marriage alliance, when Shulgi (2094–2047), second of the Ur III rulers, gave one of his daughters in marriage to its king. (The relevant text refers to her as being 'raised to the ladyship of Marhashi'.) On the other hand, the fact that small detachments of troops from Marhashi served in the armed forces of the Ur III kingdom, during the reign of Amar-Sin (2046–2038) and under the overall command of one his own generals, may indicate that Marhashi played some sort of subordinate role in its relationship with Ur, but not necessarily. The provision of such troops may have been purely a goodwill gesture by the Marhashite king, or else part of a quid pro quo arrangement.

Following the collapse of the Ur III dynasty at the end of M3, conflicts appears to have broken out between Marhashi and other states on the Iranian plateau. This is suggested by inscriptions from the reign of Ilum-muttabbil, a ruler of the northern Babylonian city of Der in early M2 (Old Babylonian period), who claims to have 'smitten the heads of Anshan, Elam, and Shimashki', apparently as an ally of Marhashi. The last surviving reference to Marhashi/Paharshum, at least as a political entity, occurs in the year-formula of the Babylonian king Hammurabi for his thirtieth year (1762), which records a victory by Hammurabi over the Elamites.

Steinkeller (1982; *RlA* 7: 381–2).

Mari (*Tell Hariri*) (map 10) Early and Middle Bronze Age Mesopotamian city on the west bank of the middle Euphrates. Its history of occupation extends from the beginning of M3 until its destruction by the Babylonian king Hammurabi in 1762, with some evidence of later settlement on the site until the last centuries of M1. According to the Sumerian King List, it was the seat of the tenth postdiluvian (post-flood) dynasty. Excavations have been carried out at Tell Hariri by a succession of French teams from 1933 onwards, most notably by A. Parrot between 1951 and 1974, and by J.-C. Margueron from 1979 onwards. The chief phases of the city's existence, as identified by these excavations, belong successively to the Early Dynastic, Akkadian, Ur III, and Old Assyrian (Amorite) periods. In its Early Dynastic phase (c. 2900–2334), Mari was circular in plan (c. 1,900 m in diameter) and surrounded by a dyke to protect it from floodwaters. The Early Dynastic III sub-phase contained the remains of private houses, a porticoed market-place surrounding a square, a palace, and temples dedicated to Ishtar, Ninni-Zaza, and Ishtarat. By the middle of M3 Mari had become a wealthy city, due no doubt to its central position in a fertile strip of land along the Euphrates, and its involvement in the international trading operations that passed between Babylonia and Syria. But at some point during the period of the Akkadian empire (c. 2334–2193), the city suffered violent destruction, perhaps early in C23. The circumstances of this destruction are unknown.

Towards the end of the Akkadian period, Mari entered a new phase in its existence. For a brief time it was subject to Akkad, under the immediate authority of a military governor (Akkadian *shakkanakku*) installed by the Akkadian administration. This man became the first of a line of rulers constituting the so-called Shakkanakku dynasty, who presided over the city as an independent power through the period of the Ur III kingdom (last century of M3). Extensive building operations took place in the city during this period, including the construction of substantial fortifications of baked brick, the redevelopment of the temple quarter, to which new buildings were added, and the construction of a new palace over the ruins of the old. Laid out in a manner which became typical of Mesopotamian palaces of the Ur III and Old Babylonian periods, with multiple rooms grouped around open courts, it included among its main features a large courtyard (the so-called Court of the Palm) planted with palm trees and associated with two long rooms, one of which appears to have been the throne-room. A second, smaller palace is thought to have provided the local ruler with a temporary residence while the major palace was under construction. In the succeeding centuries the main royal palace was regularly restored, redeveloped, and enlarged, achieving its maximum extent in the reign of the Amorite king Zimri-Lim (1774–1762). At that time, it covered an area of over 2.5 ha, and contained at ground level almost 300 rooms. Evidence for a second storey suggests that this number could well be doubled. Apart from the royal living quarters, the complex included public reception halls, kitchens, administrative quarters, archive rooms, perhaps a scribal school, a market area, and a caravanserai. The throne-room, main courtyard, and other areas of the palace were decorated with wall-paintings, one of which depicted the investiture of the king in the presence of the gods.

We do not know when the Shakkanakku dynasty came to an end or the circumstances in which this occurred. After a period of obscurity, Mari again came into prominence with the accession of a king called Yahdun-Lim (1810–1794). From his royal seat, Yahdun-Lim exercised authority over a substantial amount of territory extending from Mari to the mouth of the Balih r. and including the cities of Terqa and Tuttul (**Chav.* 96–8). He also led an expedition to Lebanon, for the purpose of obtaining quantities of the prized timbers of the region. Presumably to try to secure himself against attack from his neighbours, he concluded a pact with the king of Yamhad (whose capital was Aleppo) in northern Syria. But the Yamhadite king, Sumu-epuh, became hostile when Yahdun-Lim subsequently formed an alliance with his powerful eastern neighbour Eshnunna, and sent troops to support a rebellion of several Yaminite kings against him (**CS* II: 260). Yahdun-Lim's son and successor Sumu-Yamam may have tried to repair relations with Aleppo, but his assassination after two years on the throne paved the way for the takeover of Mari c. 1792 by the Assyrian king Shamshi-Adad I (1796–1775). Following a major redevelopment and refurbishment of Mari's palace, Shamshi-Adad installed one of his sons, Yasmah-Addu, as viceroy in the city, giving him authority over the middle Euphrates region, and subsequently extending this authority to the city of Shubat-Shamash. (He appointed his other son, Ishme-Dagan, viceroy in the city of Ekallatum.) For eight years, Yasmah-Addu occupied the viceregal throne – though not with distinction, to judge from his father's correspondence with him, preserved in the Mari archives. In this correspondence, Shamshi-Adad frequently complains of the viceroy's fecklessness and neglect of his responsibilities.

The disintegration of the Old Assyrian kingdom, which began shortly after Shamshi-Adad's death in 1775, provided the opportunity for the return of a man called Zimri-Lim. Designated in official inscriptions as the son of Yahdun-Lim (who was in fact probably his grandfather or uncle), Zimri-Lim had fled Mari as a child when Yasmah-Addu was appointed viceroy there, and may have sought refuge in Aleppo. He returned to his homeland at the head of an army, captured the city of Tuttul in 1775 shortly before Shamshi-Adad's death, and several months later entered Mari in triumph after Yasmah-Addu's hasty flight from the city (though the Mariote throne may have been occupied for a brief time after Yasmah-Addu's departure by a certain Ishar-Lim; thus Dalley, 1984: 35, with n. 9). Zimri-Lim's thirteen-year rule in Mari (1774–1762) is the best attested of all periods of the city's history, thanks to the extensive documentation of his reign contained in the Mari archives (see below). Unfortunately, it is difficult to reconstruct a coherent history of the reign from these records. But Zimri-Lim's achievements included a successful campaign against the Yaminite princes early in the reign, and his establishment of alliances with his powerful neighbours, notably the Babylonian king Hammurabi, and Yarim-Lim, ruler of Yamhad. (For the former, see **ARM XXVI/2*: 364–6, no. 449.) Hammurabi in particular proved a valuable ally to Zimri-Lim in countering threats to his territories posed by both Eshnunna under its king Ibal-pi-El II (see e.g. under **Suhu(m)**) and Elam. But the threat from Eshnunna was considerably allayed when after much hesitation, and with strong reservations expressed by some of his own subjects and by oracles, Zimri-Lim finally concluded a treaty of alliance with Ibal-pi-El. All these alliances must have contributed significantly to the relatively high degree of peace and stability which Mari enjoyed under Zimri-Lim's rule, and the city prospered from its commercial enterprises (it had a flourishing textile industry) and the benefits derived from its location as a crossroads of international trading activities. The wealth that the city generated in this period enabled Zimri-Lim to complete Mari's great palace complex on a scale of unprecedented size and splendour.

But the brief years of peace and prosperity came abruptly to an end in 1762, when Hammurabi led his troops into Mari, occupied it for several months, plundered the palace of most of its contents for removal back to Babylon (though some were left in place where they were discovered during excavations), and later burnt all the city's monumental buildings. The reasons for this dramatic about-face in the relations between Babylon and Mari, which had previously enjoyed close, cordial relations, remain matters for speculation (see discussion in van de Mieroop, 2003: 64–78). But whatever the reasons, Hammurabi's comprehensive looting and destruction of the city left no doubt that he intended it never to rise again.

The cuneiform clay tablets excavated at Mari numbering more than 22,000 and consisting of both state and private archives (the latter belonging to palace personnel) came to light in a number of locations, but mainly in and around the great palace. Their contents include letters, administrative documents, and a few legal and religious texts. Though the total timespan covered by the archives extends from late M3 until 1762, the great majority of the tablets are confined to a quarter of a century at the very end of Mari's existence, from the period of the Assyrian viceroy Yasmah-Addu to the destruction of Mari by Hammurabi at the end of Zimri-Lim's reign. (Most of the tablets date to Zimri-Lim's reign.) They are a most valuable source of information on the daily life and administration of the kingdom of which Mari was the centre, and provide some important insights into the relations between the kingdoms and states of Mesopotamia and Syria in the period when the Old Assyrian kingdom was in terminal decline and the Old Babylonian state was on the rise.

Mari survived its destruction by Hammurabi, but was never again to play a major role in the western Asian world. During the Late Bronze Age it became part of the Middle Assyrian kingdom, and is listed among the thirty-eight districts and cities which the Assyrian king Tukulti-Ninurta I (1244–1208) conquered (**RIMA* 1: 273). Thenceforth it may have fluctuated between Assyrian and Babylonian control. A fragmentary text refers to the crushing of a rebellion in Mari by a Babylonian king (*Walker, 1982: 400–1). And in mid C11 resistance to the Assyrians by Mari's king, Tukulti-Mer, met with ruthless retaliation from the Assyrian king Ashur-bel-kala (**RIMA* 2: 89). (This Tukulti-Mer is thought to be identical with the king of Hana so called, who lived in the same period and has left a dedicatory inscription; **RIMA* 2: 111). Under the Assyrian king Adad-nirari III (810–783), Mari was among the cities and lands assigned to the governorship of a man called Nergal-erish (Palil-erish) (**RIMA* 3: 209). In the first half of C8 a certain Shamash-resha-usur, who may have been nominally subject to the Assyrian king (Ashur-dan III?), but who appears to have enjoyed a largely autonomous status, called himself governor of 'the land of Suhu and the land of Mari' (as did his son and successor, Ninurta-kudurri-usur). Information about his attempts to redevelop what was evidently a depressed and underpopulated region along the middle Euphrates is provided by an inscription on a stele commemorating his exploits (**RIMB* 2: 279–82). These exploits apparently did little to resurrect Mari's fortunes, though there is evidence that the city continued to exist, on a very modest scale, down to the Hellenistic period. Frame (*RIMB* 2: 275) comments that Mari was located in the land of Laqe at this time, that it is thus unlikely that Shamash-resha-usur actually controlled it, and that the term 'land of Mari' was employed in his title, along with Suhu, for historical reasons.

Kupper, Spycket, and Aynard (*RlA* 7: 382–418), Marguéron (*OEANE* 3: 413–17; 2004), **LAPO* 16–18, **LKM, Mesop.*, *passim.*

Marib (map 9) M1 BCE–M1 CE city in southern Arabia, capital of the kingdom of Saba (biblical Sheba), located on the north bank of the Wadi Dhanah in mod.Yemen. Covering an area of c. 23 ha, it is the largest known pre-Islamic settlement in southern Arabia. The site was first excavated by F. P. Albright for the American Foundation for the Study of Man in 1951 and 1953, with further excavations being conducted in the 1980s by the German Archaeological Institute, initially under the direction of J. Schmidt. Large numbers of South Arabian inscriptions were found on the site, dating from C8 onwards. These inscriptions, written in an alphabetic script, indicate that the language spoken by the Sabaeans belonged to a Northwest Semitic language sub-group. They provide important information about the dating of the site, and more generally about the kingdom of Saba, which was probably constituted no later than C10.

The most important of the city's architectural remains is the Awwam Temple, which was dedicated to the moon god, Marib's chief deity. This god also headed the pantheon of other South Arabian states, but was known by different names in different places. In

Marib he was called Ilumquh. The temple's principal feature was an entrance hall in the form of an open court surrounded by a roofed peristyle. The whole complex was enclosed within a casemated oval wall of limestone ashlar blocks. On its outer surface were carved seven inscriptions, which contain the names of the gods to whom particular parts of the wall were dedicated, and also the names of the kings who commissioned the building. The earliest of these inscriptions provide a mid C7 date for the wall, though its origins may go back to an earlier period. A mausoleum was built adjacent to the wall on its northwest corner. It contained sixty burial compartments arranged in tiers, and a number of underground burial chambers. Inscriptions on fragments of panels which closed the compartments contain the names of the deceased, including two kings. This has led to the building being dubbed the royal mausoleum. A group of mausolea lay 100 m to the south, dated to C8 by a boustrophedon inscription (see glossary) painted on one of the walls.

Van Beek (1974; *OEANE* 3: 417–18).

Marina Late Bronze Age and Iron Age city in northern Mesopotamia, probably the predecessor of the M1 Aramaean city Burmarina (Tell Shiyukh Fawqani) (q.v.). It is first attested in a C13 Assyrian letter found at Dur-Katlimmu, and subsequently on one of the bronze bands from a gate of the Assyrian king Ashurnasirpal II (883–859) at Balawat (see **Imgur-Enlil**) (**RIMA* 2: 345). The latter inscription locates it (like Burmarina) in Bit-Adini.

Cancik-Kirschbaum (1996: *96–7, 104), Lipiński (2000: 175–6).

Marion (*Polis*) (map 14) City built on two plateaus (thus an 'eastern' and a 'western' city) on the northwestern coast of Cyprus. Its name may first be attested, in the form Aimar, in an inscription from the funerary temple of the C12 Egyptian pharaoh Ramesses III at Medinet Habu. But there are no remains of any settlement on the site at this time. The origins of the settlement on the eastern plateau, known as *Peristeries*, have been dated, on the basis of archaeological evidence, to the Geometric period (C8). An important rural sanctuary and a large palatial building of the Cypro-Archaic period were excavated there by the Princeton University Archaeological Expedition in the 1980s and 1990s. A necropolis is located nearby, whose tombs date to the Geometric and Archaic (C7–6) periods. In mid C5, perhaps following the Athenian commander Cimon's arrival at Marion, the city was moved to the western plateau.

Very little is known of Marion's early history, beyond the fact that it was one of the kingdoms of Cyprus in the first half of M1, and the names of most of its C5 and C4 kings are known from coin issues. The king's name on these coins is accompanied by the designation *Marieus*. Marion's importance and affluence at the time apparently came from its exploitation of the copper mines nearby at Limne, and from its regular trade with Athens. It has been suggested that the hilltop palace at Vouni (q.v.) further east along the north coast may initially have been built, c. 500, as a royal summer residence by a king of Marion. But we have no hard evidence for this. The first clear reference to the city in historical records belongs to 449, when the Athenian general Cimon liberated it from the Persians, replacing its pro-Persian ruler with a pro-Greek one, who was then installed in the palace of Vouni.

Marion's last known king was a man called Stasiocus II, who in 312 made the unwise decision to support Alexander's former general, Antigonus, in his conflict with another of his generals, Ptolemy I Soter. The city was destroyed by Ptolemy and its inhabitants transported to Paphos, which lay south on Cyprus' southwest coast. It was, however, refounded c. 270 by Ptolemy II Philadelphus and renamed after his wife (and sister) Arsinoe. The city flourished in Hellenistic and Roman times, and was the seat of a bishopric in the Byzantine period. Remains of the Hellenistic, Roman, and Byzantine city of Arsinoe have been found on the ridge occupied by the mod. village of Polis.

Nicolaou (*PECS* 552), Smith (1997), Papalexandrou (2006).

Mariru Iron Age city in northern Mesopotamia, near the city of Damdammusa, possibly on the northwestern side of the Kashiyari mountain range (mod. Tur ʿAbdin) (Liverani, 1992: 37). It was conquered by the Assyrian king Ashurnasirpal II during a campaign in the region in his second regnal year (882) (**RIMA* 2: 201).

Marista Late Bronze Age country in northern Anatolia, first attested in Hittite texts as the site of one of the storage depots which the Hittite king Telipinu (c. 1525–1500) established in various parts of his realm. In the reign of Muwattalli II (1295–1272) its territory was ravaged by enemy forces from Kaska and other hostile northern countries, namely Pishuru and Daistipassa (**CS* I: 200). It was among the depopulated lands which Muwattalli assigned to his brother Hattusili (later King Hattusili III) when he appointed Hattusili ruler of the northern part of the Hittite homeland (**CS* I: 201) (see **Hakpis(sa)** and **Turmitta**).

**RGTC* 6: 262–3.

Marki (map 14) Early and Middle Bronze Age settlement and cemetery complex in central Cyprus, situated on the geological divide between the copper-bearing igneous foothills of the Troodos mountains and the agriculturally productive sedimentary soils of the central plain. Excavations here by D. Frankel and J. M. Webb from La Trobe University, Australia, between 1991 and 2001, exposed over 2000 sq. m of well-preserved domestic architecture, dating from the beginning of the Early Bronze Age to the middle years of the Middle Bronze Age. The settlement, which at its maximum extent covered 5 ha, was occupied for about 500 years. The population probably grew from several dozen in the earliest phase to over 300 before the village was gradually abandoned. A stone mould for casting copper ingots is among the earliest artefacts found at the site, testifying to the importance of metalworking from the settlement's foundation and suggesting that the site was located specifically to take advantage of nearby copper sources. The inhabitants were also engaged in agriculture and animal husbandry and the production of pottery and textiles for local use.

The excavators identified thirty-three house compounds and traced the evolution of domestic space over 500 years. House compounds with large courtyards and small interior rooms were the norm from first settlement. Artefacts suggest that the processing and small-scale storage of cereals and other commodities, spinning and weaving, chipped and ground stone tool production, and perhaps wood- and hide-working were routinely carried out in interior rooms, along with the preparation, serving, and consumption of food. Like other settlements of the period on Cyprus, Marki was not fortified, and there is no evidence for writing, sealing systems, centralized storage, communal buildings, cult-centres or major inequalities in wealth or status.

(**J. M. Webb**)

Frankel and Webb (2006).

Figure 70 Marki.

Maroni (map 14) Late Bronze Age settlement located on the low hillock of Vournes in the Maroni valley 500 m inland from the south coast, excavated by G. Cadogan for the University of Cincinnati. Both the Vournes hillock and an associated settlement on the coast at Tsaroukkas were in use from Late Cypriot (LC) IA (1650–1550). Evidence for copper-working at Vournes is visible from LC IIB (1375–1300). A number of buildings are of particular interest. These are the Basin Building, a 4.5 m square freestanding structure with a paved sunken basin erected in LC IIA (1450–1375) or IIB and abandoned in or after LC IIB, and the somewhat later Ashlar Building, constructed in LC IIC (1300–1200). The Ashlar Building is a tripartite structure measuring 30.5 m × 20 m and partly built of dressed ashlar blocks. It produced evidence of olive oil processing, cereal grinding, large-scale storage of staples, metalworking, weaving, and writing. It has been interpreted as an administration centre controlling food production and metalworking in the Maroni valley in C13.

(J. M. Webb)
Cadogan (1996).

Marqas (*Maraş*) (map 7) Iron Age city attested in the records of the Assyrian king Sargon II (721–705) as capital of the Neo-Hittite kingdom of Gurgum in southeastern Anatolia. After Sargon dethroned the last Gurgumite king, Mutallu, and deported him to Assyria (c. 711), Gurgum was incorporated into the Assyrian empire and thenceforth called Marqas, after its capital. Sargon boosted its population by settling deportees there (**SAA* I: 199, no. 257).

Parpola (1970: 239–40), Hawkins (*RlA* 7: 431–2).

Martu see **Amorites**.

Masa (map 3) Late Bronze Age country in western Anatolia, mentioned several times in Hittite texts alongside the country called Karkisa. Apparently governed by a council of elders rather than a king, Masa remained independent of Hittite control, but not beyond the reach of Hittite arms. When Mashuiluwa, rebel vassal ruler of Mira, fled his country and sought refuge in Masa during Mursili II's reign (1321–1295), Hittite forces invaded the country and demanded the surrender of the refugee (*Bryce, 2005: 212–14). Threatened with severe reprisals if they failed to comply, the people of Masa returned Mashuiluwa to Hittite authority. A contingent from Masa fought on the Hittite side in the battle of Qadesh, probably in a mercenary capacity (*Gardiner, 1960: 8). In the so-called Südburg inscription (see **Hattusa**), Masa appears among the western lands conquered and annexed by the last Hittite king Suppiluliuma II (1207–) (*Hawkins, 1995: 22–3). The name Masa has been linked, very conjecturally, with the Maeonians of Classical legendary tradition, whose homeland lay under Mt Tmolus (mod. Boz Daği) in the region of anc. Lydia.

**RGTC* 6: 264–5, Heinhold-Krahmer (*RlA* 7:441–2).

Masashuru Royal city of the Iron Age country Harna, which bordered upon the land of Mannaea in mod. Iranian Kurdistan (**RIMA* 3: 70).

Maşat see Tapikka.

Mashkan-shapir (*Tell Abu Duwari*)(map 11) Early and Middle Bronze Age site (with evidence of some occupation also in the Uruk period, M4) in southern Mesopotamia, a low mound rising 2–5 m above the surrounding plain, located east of Babylon and north of Nippur. Excavations began in 1987, following a survey of the Nippur region by R. McC. Adams, under the direction of E. C. Stone. First attested in correspondence from Nippur dating to the reign of the Akkadian king Sargon (2334–2279), Mashkan-shapir began life as a small rural settlement. It underwent some development in the period of the Ur III dynasty (C21), perhaps with the support of this dynasty, but remained relatively insignificant throughout the Ur III period, functioning primarily as the centre of a sheep-raising area. With the rise of the dynasties of Isin and Larsa early in M2, it became a frontier-post of the kingdom of Larsa, within the sub-region called the 'land of Yamutbal' (Yamutbal(um)/Emutbal(um)). This marked the beginning of its development into a major urban centre, becoming the second most important city in the kingdom of Larsa (see below). Its importance to Larsa was at least partly due to its strategic position which, Stone comments, enabled it to control trade moving from areas east and north of Babylonia into the southern heartland.

Larsa apparently lost control of Mashkan-shapir for a time, but Larsa's eighth ruler Nur-Adad recaptured it, and in the reign of his son and successor Sin-iddinam (1849–1843) Mashkan-shapir was fortified, or refortified, with an extensive wall. This enclosed an area of c. 72 ha, parts of which were only thinly populated. The wall was dedicated to the god Nergal, probably Mashkan-shapir's chief deity. A dedicatory inscription associated with one of its gates established the city's name. Mashkan-shapir was divided into sections by four major canals. Residential areas with manufacturing areas among them and a religious quarter have been identified. The manufacturing areas provide evidence of copper- and stone-working industries and pottery production. Within the religious quarter, baked- and mud-brick temple platforms have been unearthed, along with many fragments of terracotta life-size and half-size statues of lions, horses, and human figures. These may have served to guard the entrance to a temple. A walled-off area of the central mound was used as a cemetery in the last phase of the city's occupation. Funerary items scattered on the surface of this area include large burial jars, jewellery, and weapons.

Following Sin-iddinam's reign, Mashkan-shapir was again lost to and again regained by Larsa, and in the reign of Larsa's king Rim-Sin (1822–1763) reached the peak of its importance when it achieved the status of the kingdom's second capital (after the first capital, the city of Larsa). This is made clear by correspondence from the Assyrian viceroy Yasmah-Addu at Mari. The city was now governed by Rim-Sin's brother Sin-muballit, and was the base for Babylonian diplomatic missions to Larsa in the reign of the Babylonian king Hammurabi (1792–1750).

With the outbreak of war between Babylon and Larsa, following Rim-Sin's incursions into Babylonian territory, Hammurabi, in alliance with Mari, invaded Larsa, and launched the first attack of his campaign against Mashkan-shapir (Charpin, 2003: 84–5). The city fell after a siege, and Hammurabi went on to complete the conquest of Larsa. Under Hammurabi, Mashkan-shapir continued to be a city of some importance, though no longer with the status it had enjoyed during Rim-Sin's reign. Subsequently it became a victim of the Babylonian kingdom's decline under Hammurabi's successor Samsu-iluna (1749–1712). It was among a number of southern Babylonian cities which were abandoned during his reign. Many centuries later, the Parthians occupied the site – though only on a limited scale – for c. 500 years, from mid C3 BCE until the early decades of C3 CE.

Stone (*OEANE* 3: 430–2), *LKM* 617 (refs), Stone and Zimansky (2004a), Steinkeller (2004), *Mesop*. 319.

Mashqitu Iron Age city in the middle Euphrates r., in the region of Suhu, between the cities of Ana(t) and Haradu. During his last recorded campaign in 885, the Assyrian king Tukulti-Ninurta II spent the night in the city on his progress up the Euphrates (**RIMA* 2: 175). Haradu and Kailetu were other cities in this same region through which Tukulti-Ninurta passed on the same campaign.

Masos, Tel (Arabic ***Khirbet el-Meshash***) (map 8) Site in the northern Negev desert, Israel, 12 km east of Beersheba. Extending over both sides of a wadi, it consists of (a) a small tell, (b) a large village to the northeast of the tell, and (c) a fortified Middle Bronze Age enclosure on the wadi's southern bank. Occupation of one part or another of the site was spread over five periods. There were: a late Chalcolithic settlement continuing into the beginning of the Early Bronze Age (late M4–early M3; area a); a Middle Bronze Age fortified settlement built in two phases (early M2; area c); a relatively large Iron Age I village, c. 200 m × 150 m (1200–1000; area b); a fortified late Iron Age II settlement from which the tell was formed (C7; area a); and a Byzantine monastery (C7–8 CE; area a). The overall settlement pattern is one of brief periods of occupation with long intervals in between. Excavations were carried out from 1972 to 1975 by Y. Aharoni, V. Fritz, and A. Kempinski for the Institute of Archaeology, Tel Aviv University.

The two-phase Middle Bronze Age settlement (its first phase was demolished to make way for the second) has been seen by the excavators as an attempt by the cities in the southern Shephelah and along the Canaanite coast to control the route leading to the east. The Iron Age I settlement was progressively built up from a nomadic encampment to an urban centre by an ever-increasing population coming from apparently different cultural and ethnic backgrounds. The small finds from this period include a wide assemblage of imported ware, of Phoenician, Philistine, Midianite, and Egyptian origin. The site's cultural diversity is also reflected in a range of house types – predominantly four-room houses, but also three-room houses, broadroom houses, a courtyard house, and an Egypt-style 'Amarna house'. The settlement was abandoned c. 1000. Three hundred years later, a fortified Iron Age II settlement was built to its southwest. A large building in the centre of this settlement has been interpreted as a caravanserai. The settlement's shortlived existence (c. 50–70 years) was ended by a violent conflagration, perhaps the result of the Edomite invasion in early C6, around the time the kingdom of Judah was destroyed.

Attempts to identify Tel Masos with one of the many cities of the Negev listed in Joshua 15:21–32 have not been successful.

Kempinski (*NEAEHL* 3: 986–9), Fritz (*OEANE* 3: 437–9).

Massagetae (map 16) A group of M1 populations probably to be located in the region of mod. Kazakhstan. According to Herodotus (1.204), they occupied an immense tract of land east of the Caspian Sea. Herodotus reports that in their dress and lifestyle they were very like the Scythians whom, he alleges (4.11), they drove out of Asia across the Araxes r. Information about the Massagetae comes mainly from Greek sources (which are of limited reliability and often contradictory). Herodotus discusses them at some length (1.215–16), noting their reputation as fierce warriors who fought both on foot and on horseback. He portrays them as an essentially nomadic people who lived on fish and meat and milk; they knew nothing of agriculture, and though they had abundant quantities of bronze and gold, they had no knowledge of silver or iron; they shared their wives and ate the flesh of their dead elders as a mark of respect (cf. Strabo's account, 11.8.6–7). The Persian king Cyrus II (559–530) allegedly fought against the Massagetae during his final campaign in the east, in the region of the Oxus and Jaxartes rivers. According to Herodotus (1.205–14), Cyrus' forces were confronted by those of the Massagetae queen Tomyris. The Persian army was almost entirely destroyed, and Cyrus himself was killed in the conflict (Herodotus 1.214; but see under **Derbices**). His defeat was finally avenged by Darius I, who during his eastern campaign in 517 conquered the Massagetae and incorporated them into the Persian empire. In 329 the Massagetae allegedly fought against Alexander the Great under the leadership of the Persian commander Spitamenes, during Alexander's campaign across the Jaxartes r. After his army was defeated by Alexander, Spitamenes sought refuge with the Massagetae. A renewed uprising by Spitamenes against Alexander resulted in his death and the conquest of the Massagetae.

Hermann (*RE* XIV: 2123–30), Dandamaev (1989: 66–8), Vogelsang (1992: 181–3, 186–8).

Mastuma, Tell (= Ashtammaku?) (map 7) Early Iron Age settlement in Syria, 60 km southwest of Aleppo. The site, which also has remains of occupation from the Neolithic, Early, and Middle Bronze Ages, and the later Persian period (C4), was excavated by a Japanese team from the Ancient Orient Museum, Tokyo, for eight seasons between 1980 and 1995. The settlement-mound is oval-triangular in shape, 18 m high and 200 m in diameter. An area of c. 4,000 sq. m was uncovered, estimated to have been about 40 per cent of the site's total spread. The settlement was built on a terrace, and appears to have had a planned street system which divided it into housing blocks or *insulae*. The excavators suggest that its carefully organized layout arose from a need to adapt the settlement to the topography of the mound. They calculate that the total settlement may have contained up to one hundred housing units. So far, only one major residence has come to light, measuring c. 30 m × 16 m. It occupied one-third of a block and had three street-frontages. A number of the dwellings had storage jars sunk into the lime-plastered floors up to their mouths. Ovens were found in the courtyards. The fact that almost all the buildings are of domestic type is seen by the excavators as making a significant contribution to the study of the domestic architecture as well as the provincial lifestyle of Iron Age Syria.

Present indications are that the Iron Age settlement began in late C10 and was abandoned by the end of C8. It was probably located in the north of the kingdom of Hamath on the frontier between Hamath and Bit-Agusi, and was perhaps built, or later developed, as a garrison-settlement for the Hamath kingdom. This could explain its well-planned layout. However, the excavators comment that the site's small cooking pots and common standard-type dwellings may indicate that the nuclear family was the basic family unit at Mastuma. Perhaps the families who dwelt there belonged to the men who were (we may surmise) assigned to the settlement as garrison troops. The growth of the settlement, the excavators suggest, could have been due to a deliberate immigration policy intended to reinforce the region's military power; and the one great house found on the site was perhaps the residence of a military governor. Mastuma may have been part of a frontier defence system for the kingdom of Hamath. Such a system would have become particularly important in attempting to counter the threat of Assyrian penetration into northwestern Syria in C9, during the reign of the Assyrian king Shalmaneser III (858–824).

Tsuneki (1995), Wakita *et al.* (1995; 2000).

Masuwari see *Ahmar, Tell.*

Matiate (Mateiatu, ***Midyat***) Iron Age city in northern Mesopotamia in the Kashiyari mountain range (mod. Tur ʿAbdin), reached via the 'Pass of the Goddesses' (Ishtarate). The Assyrian king Ashurnasirpal II attacked and conquered the city during his progress through this region in his fifth regnal year (879) (**RIMA* 2: 208–9, 249). He had a statue of himself, inscribed with a record of his military victories, set up in the city. His son and successor Shalmaneser III reports conquering and plundering the city and massacring its inhabitants in his thirteenth regnal year (846) (**RIMA* 3: 39).

Kessler (*RlA* 7: 585–6), Radner (2006: 289).

Matieni (Matiani) Eastern Anatolian people whose land, according to Herodotus (1.202, 5.49, 52) lay east of Armenia and was the source of several rivers, including the Lesser Zab and the Araxes. Herodotus (3.94) claims that together with the lands of the Saspeires and the Alarodians it formed the eighteenth province of the Persian empire as reorganized by Darius I (522–486) (but see glossary under **satrapy**), and paid an annual tribute of 200 talents to the Persian administration. He also reports (7.72) that it contributed a contingent for Xerxes' invasion of Greece in 481. The Greek geographer Hecataeus names Hyope as a city of the Matieni.

Mazar, Tell el- (map 8) Small tell in the Jordan valley, near the junction of the Jordan and Jabbok rivers. Its history of occupation extends from C8 (early Iron Age II) to C4 (early Hellenistic period). Excavations were conducted by K. Yassine for Jordan University between 1977 and 1981. Five occupation levels were identified. In the earliest, C8 level (Early Iron Age II; Stratum V), the excavator uncovered a large paved courtyard surrounded by rooms containing loom-weights, grain storage jars, and animal bones. He suggests that the level's destruction was due to the Assyrian king Sennacherib's campaign in the region in 701. Yassine believes that the principal architectural remains of the succeeding Stratum IV (Iron Age II; C7) were those of private houses, in view of the modest walls and rooms of the buildings and the domestic utensils found in them. This level apparently ended peacefully. It was followed in late C7 (Late Iron Age II; Stratum III) by a settlement dominated by a large structure which Yassine designated as a palace-fort. Evidence of its destruction by fire suggested to him that it was a victim of the Babylonian campaign in the region in 582. Its C5 successor (Stratum II), dating to the Persian period (C6–4), was a meaner settlement than its predecessors, to judge from its ill-constructed mudbrick house- and courtyard complexes. In C4 (Stratum I) the site appears to have been used purely as a granary.

Associated with Tell Mazar was a small mound designated by Yassine as mound A, where the earliest stratum contained a tripartite structure, with mudbrick walls built on stone foundations. A 16 m wide courtyard was attached to it. Constructed in C11 and destroyed in C10, it preceded by two centuries the earliest level on Tell Mazar – though Yassine left open the possibility that the latter may contain earlier undiscovered remains beneath its C8 level. In C5 and perhaps also in early C4, mound A was used as a cemetery. Eighty-five graves have been recovered from this level, illustrative of several different kinds of burials. It was contemporary with Stratum II on the tell, and was evidently the burial ground for the occupants of the settlement in this phase of its existence.

Yassine (1989), McCreery and Yassine (*OEANE* 3: 443–4).

Mazuradum City in Ilan-sura, a Middle Bronze Age kingdom located in the Habur triangle, northern Mesopotamia. It was plundered by Hammurabi, king of Kurda, while the throne of Ilan-sura was occupied by Haya-Sumu, as reported by Haya-Sumu in a letter to his overlord Zimri-Lim, king of Mari (1774–1762) (**LKM* 502–3).

Medeba see Madaba.

Medes (map 16) Iron Age Indo-European-speaking population whose homeland, Media, lay in the central Zagros mountains in western Iran. It is first attested in mid C9 Assyrian texts, when the Assyrian king Shalmaneser III conducted a military campaign into the land of the Mada people in his twenty-fourth regnal year (835) (**RIMA* 3: 68). No separate texts written in the Median language have survived, and the language is known to us only from fragmentary survivals and loanwords found in texts written in the Old Persian language, to which Median is related. The term 'Median' came also to be applied to other neighbouring peoples whose lifestyle was similar to that of the original Medes, or who for one reason or another sought to identify themselves with them (Reade, 2003: 150).

Fragments of the history of the Medes can be pieced together from information contained in contemporary western Asian sources, including the records of campaigns conducted into Median territory during the reigns of the Assyrian kings Shalmaneser III (noted above), Tiglath-pileser III (**PE* 22, no. 1ii), Sargon II (**PE* 24–5, no. 2), and Esarhaddon (**PE* 26, no. 4), and the Babylonian Chronicles (see glossary). However, they are best known from the account of them provided by Herodotus in his so-called *Medikos Logikos* (*Histories* 1.95–106). According to Herodotus, the Medes originally comprised a number of independent tribal groups, living in villages, each ruled by a king. The tribes were eventually united (apparently in C7) into a single kingdom, with a royal capital established at Ecbatana (mod. Hamadan). This unification was, according to Herodotus (1.96–102), the achievement of a man called Deioces, son of Phraortes, who ruled for fifty-three years. Herodotus (1.101) lists the following tribes as components of the kingdom: the Busae, Paraetaceni, Struchates, Arizanti, Budians, and Magi. In his version of events, Deioces was succeeded by his son Phraortes, who expanded his kingdom by conquering the Persians and then various other Asian tribes until he was defeated and killed in battle by the Assyrians after a reign of twenty-two years (Herodotus 1.102).

Phraortes was succeeded by his son Cyaxares, who reorganized the Median army (Herodotus 1.103). Cyaxares has commonly been regarded as the true founder of the Median empire. Acceding to his country's throne c. 625, he ruled for forty years, during which time he conquered Assyria's traditional capital, Ashur, and subsequently formed an alliance with the Babylonian king Nabopolassar. This Median–Babylonian partnership effectively brought to an end the Neo-Assyrian empire, by its conquest and destruction of the Assyrian capital Nineveh in 612, as recorded in a Babylonian Chronicle (no. 3) (**ANET* 303–5, **ABC* 90–6, **PE* 30–2, no. 10). According to Herodotus, Cyaxares' Assyrian campaigns were interrupted for a time by the incursions of the Scythians into the western Asian world. The Scythians allegedly dominated this world for twenty-eight years (Herodotus 1.106), until their leaders were all massacred at a banquet arranged by Cyaxares.

In the latter years of his reign, Cyaxares expanded his territories progressively westwards, eventually into the eastern half of Anatolia. This brought him into conflict with the Lydians, overlords of an empire which extended through most of western Anatolia. A five-year conflict with the Lydian king Alyattes (Herodotus 1.74, 103) culminated in the so-called 'battle of the eclipse' fought between Cyaxares' and Alyattes' forces in 585 on the banks of the Halys r. in north-central Anatolia (1.74). The battle ended inconclusively, and was followed by a treaty which established the river as the border between the two empires. Peaceful relations between Media and Lydia were subsequently consolidated by a royal marriage alliance, when Alyattes wed his daughter to Cyaxares' successor Astyages. After thirty-five years of despotic rule, Astyages was attacked and overthrown by his 'grandson', the Persian Cyrus II (559), who went on to found the Persian empire. (For doubts about the alleged familial link between Cyrus and Astyages, see Brosius, 2006: 8.) Medes played an important role in the cultural and administrative activities of this empire, and in the defence of the realm. In this last capacity they served alongside Persians in the elite imperial guard, and were a prominent part of Persia's military forces. They remained a privileged people, acknowledged as the second most important ethnic group within the Persian empire. Indeed, the contemporary Greeks used the terms 'Persian' and 'Median' interchangeably.

The above reconstruction of Median history is based on a patchwork of information, much of which comes from Classical sources. These sources are now considered by many western Asian scholars to have little historical value, except for a few details in them which can be independently verified. Particularly suspect is any information for which Herodotus is our only source. Thus neither Deioces nor his son Phraortes is attested in any anc. texts, either Classical or Near Eastern, outside Herodotus (but on the former, see Panaino, 2003). More generally, a number of scholars have in recent years cast considerable doubt on, or almost completely rejected, the historicity of a Median empire as presented in Classical sources. Among the first scholars to do so were P. Helm (1981) and H. Sancisi-Weerdenburg (1988) who argued specifically against the validity of Herodotus' version of events. A comprehensive re-examination of the Median question was the focus of a conference held in Padua in 2001 (Lanfranchi *et al.*, 2003). Emphasis was placed throughout the conference on the absence of any archaeological evidence for the Herodotean account of Media, and a perceived lack of consistency between this account and contemporary treatments of the Medes in Assyrian and Neo-Babylonian documentary sources. With regard to the archaeological material, reference was made to excavations carried out in the 1960s and 1970s in what was apparently the core territory of Media, the region between Kermanshah and Hamadan. Information gathered from the most important sites so far uncovered in this region, Godin Tepe, Nush-i Jan, and Baba Jan, appears to indicate that while the Median civilization experienced significant material development during late C8 and C7, it suffered a major decline in the first half of C6. According to the Herodotean presentation of Median history, it was in the latter period that the civilization should have reached its height.

With regard to the contemporary documentary sources, the largest body of information comes from Assyrian texts, dating from mid C9 to mid C7 – from the reign of the Assyrian king Shalmaneser III (858–824) to that of Esarhaddon (680–669). Liverani (2003: 4) observes that in these texts the Medes appear as no more than 'a loose set of tribes, presenting no special features as compared to other Zagros tribes and devoid of political unity or even coordination'. He argues that the assumption about unification of the Median state during or after the reign of Esarhaddon's successor Ashurbanipal (668–630/627) has been made entirely in the absence of evidence to the contrary. On the other hand, as he notes, the subsequent Neo-Babylonian sources do have a couple of points of contact with Herodotus: first, in their account of the Median looting and destruction of the Assyrian capital Nineveh under the leadership of Cyaxares (Akkadian Umakishtar) (**ABC* 94 = **PE* 31, no. 10; cf. Herodotus 1.103, 106); and second, in their report of the defection of troops from the Median king Astyages (Akkadian Ishtumegu) to the Persian king Cyrus II, in 550 (**ABC* 106 = * *PE* 50, no. 1; cf. Herodotus 1.127). But Liverani stresses that this is where similarities between Herodotus and the Babylonian sources end. He claims that the latter present a quite different view of the Medians – as the plunderers and destroyers of the Assyrian cities, returning home once their 'dirty job' is completed and leaving to their Babylonian partners the role of reconstruction and political continuity. Other recent 'mimimalist' proposals, as summarized by Lanfranchi (2003: 117), portray the Medians who participated in the destruction of Assyria not as forces of a powerful independent kingdom, but as a major component of the Assyrian army who precipitated the fall of the last Assyrian king by rebelling against him.

In Liverani's view, Media's proximity to Assyria led to the transformation of the pastoral tribes in the Zagros region into the powerful chiefdoms which engaged in war and trade activities. Towards the end of C7, at the time of the fall of the Assyrian empire, Media's fortified manors and ceremonial centres were peacefully abandoned, and the Medes were confined to the Zagros region, which had already been lost to Assyria. Almost all the rest of Assyria's territory was inherited by Babylonia. Liverani develops arguments already advanced by Sancisi-Weerdenburg (1988) against the Herodotean tradition of Median expansion into central Anatolia, and by Kuhrt (1995b), who pointed out that the Assyrian heartland and its fringe territories, extending through Syria and southeastern Anatolia, were all absorbed into the Neo-Babylonian empire. Rollinger (2003b) also concludes that the extent of Neo-Babylonian power through Upper Mesopotamia, Syria, and southeastern Anatolia raises suspicion about the traditional view concerning Media's western frontier. He argues that there is considerable evidence that Herodotus' perception of the Halys r. as Media's western boundary in C6 is a mixture of post-C6 events and ideological constructs by the author. While he concedes that there must have been some kind of Median presence in eastern and central Anatolia in C6 – and contacts of some kind between Lydians and Medes in this period – he doubts that the Anatolian region remained long under Median control. But the evidence remains circumstantial, and Roaf (2003: 2) still maintains the possibility, which he believes is not inconsistent with this evidence, that the Median rulers, having acquired considerable wealth from the sacking of Assyria's heartland and having conquered the Assyrian provinces in the Zagros, expanded their rule until they held sway over territories stretching from Anatolia to the borders of Fars, and from central or eastern Iran to the foothills of the Zagros bordering on Babylonia. By implication, a common frontier in C6 between Media and Lydia on the Halys is still not out of the question.

In their summing up of the papers presented at the 2001 Padua conference, the editors of the conference proceedings (Lanfranchi *et al.*, 2003: 397–406) noted that recent re-examinations of the sources relating to Media have led to a radical reduction in the extent of the 'Median empire' before it was incorporated into the Persian empire. But they observed that opinions still vary between two extremes – a 'maximalist' and a 'mimimalist' view. The former 'might extend Median power from the west of the former kingdom of Urartu to the borders of Fars and from the western outliers of the Zagros mts on the plains of eastern Assyria to the fringes of the central Iranian desert beyond Rayy', while the latter 'would abandon the whole of the north, east and central western Iran to bands of nomads roaming freely over an extensive territory, and consider Median influence to be negligible'. The 'truth', the editors say, may well lie between these extremes.

Diakonoff (1985), Schmitt/Calmeyer, Brown (*RlA* 7: 617–23), Young (1988; *OEANE* 3: 448–50), Sancisi-Weerdenburg (1988), Lanfranchi *et al.* (2003), Liverani (2003), Roaf (2003), Rollinger (2003b), **PE* 19–46.

Megiddo (*Tell el-Mutesellim*) (map 8) 20 m high settlement-mound in northern Palestine at the westen end of the Jezreel valley, located in a strategically important position at a major intersection on the Via Maris (q.v.). It has been linked with biblical Armageddon where, according to Revelation 16:16, the apocalyptic conflict at the end of time will take place. The site's history of occupation, covering twenty major archaeological levels, extends from the Neolithic period (mid M9–mid M5) to the end of the

Persian period (C6–4). The first excavations were conducted by G. Schumacher, between 1903 and 1905, on behalf of the Deutsche Orient-Gesellschaft. Work on the site was resumed in 1925 and continued until 1939 under the (successive) directors C. S. Fisher, P. L. O. Guy, and G. Loud for the Oriental Institute, University of Chicago. The most recent series of excavations are those started in 1992 by D. Ussishkin and I. Finkelstein of the Institute of Archaeology, Tel Aviv University, and B. Halpern of Pennsylvania State University. One of the aims of these excavations has been to resolve a number of questions relating to the complex problems of the site's stratigraphy.

During the Early Bronze Age, the site was occupied by a large, initially unfortified settlement, whose proportions were later reduced in Early Bronze II–III when it was surrounded by a massive stone wall (Stratum XVIII). The settlement included a sanctuary compound in which was constructed a series of temples in successive layers. In the Middle Bronze Age, Megiddo developed into a major urban settlement which continued without a break through a number of occupation strata (XIII–VIIA) until its destruction at the end of the Late Bronze Age. The M2 city was heavily fortified, with a glacis (see glossary) and wall built on stone foundations with mudbrick superstructure. It was here that the pharaoh Tuthmosis III inflicted a defeat upon a coalition of Syrian states loyal to the kingdom of Mitanni during his first Asiatic campaign (c. 1479) (**ANET* 234–8). The significance of this victory was that it opened the way for Tuthmosis into the heartland of the kingdom of Mitanni. Megiddo itself fell to Tuthmosis after a seven-month siege, and thenceforth remained under Egyptian sovereignty until its destruction in C12. During the reign of the pharaoh Akhenaten (1352–1336), its involvement in the disputes and conflicts of Egypt's Syro-Palestinian vassal

Figure 71 Megiddo.

states is attested (as Magidda) in a number of letters from the Amarna archive. At that time it was ruled by a man called Biridya, some of whose letters to the pharaoh survive in the Amarna correspondence (**EA* 242–6). Material remains of the city's Late Bronze Age phase, represented archaeologically by Strata IX–VIIA, include a broad, paved roadway, a series of four superimposed palaces in one area (designated as area AA), and a second palatial complex in another (designated as DD). The final Stratum VIIA palace, unearthed in area AA, contained wall-paintings displaying Egyptian influence, and a room in which a collection of 382 carved ivories was discovered. Some were of local Canaanite type, others represented a variety of foreign provenances – Hittite, Aegean, Assyrian, and Egyptian. Scholars have suggested various explanations for the absence of a city wall in this period.

Following its destruction at the end of the Late Bronze Age, the city was rebuilt as a sizeable town (Stratum VIB), the life of which continued for a considerable period. Strata VIB and VIA were the city's first Iron Age levels. Ceramic ware of 'Philistine' type indicates contact with one of the Sea Peoples groups. Megiddo continued to be a Canaanite settlement until the destruction of Stratum VIA. In its new phase (Stratum V), the unfortified city was associated with the Omride dynasty (see glossary). In its subsequent Stratum IV phase, the city became a royal administrative centre fortified with a solid, 'inset-offset' wall, within which there were a palace and three large 'stable' complexes. These building projects are now dated to the later kings of Israel.

Subsequent to the conquest and annexation of northern Israel by the Assyrian king Tiglath-pileser III in 732, Megiddo became the administrative centre of the Assyrian province called Magiddu. Archaeologically, this phase of its existence is represented by Stratum III, which was a well-planned city with spacious residential quarters and two large public buildings. Stratum II is associated with the reign of the Judaean king Josiah (640–609), who may have gained independence from Assyria during the Assyrian empire's final years but was killed at Megiddo by the pharaoh Necho II, Assyria's ally. His death occurred when he tried to stop Necho's army at Megiddo on its march to Carchemish to support Assyria against Babylon (2 Kings 23:29–30; 2 Chonicles 35:20–4). The modest remains of the city of Stratum I (small houses and stone-built cist tombs) date from the Babylonian to the end of the Persian period. The city was abandoned in the last decades of C4, possibly at the time of Alexander's conquest of the region in 332.

Cogan/Wright (*RlA* 8: 12–20), Ussishkin (*OEANE* 3: 460–9), I. Finkelstein *et al.* (2000; 2006), Harrison (2004), Franklin (2006).

Mehru Country in northern Mesopotamia, attested in Late Bronze Age and Iron Age Assyrian texts. It was apparently noted for the high quality of its timber. The Assyrian king Tukulti-Ninurta I (1244–1208) conducted a campaign there, and used troops from the land of the Qutu to cut large beams from its forests to be used in the king's palace in Ashur (**RIMA* 1: 235). Mehru was one of the lands in the region which became regular tributaries of Tukulti-Ninurta (**RIMA* 1: 240, 244). Adad-nirari II (911–891) refers to his conquest of its cities on the banks of the Ruru r. in the context of his first campaign against the land of Qumanu (**RIMA* 2: 144), and claims further conquests in Mehru during his second campaign against Qumanu (**RIMA* 2: 148). His successor-but-one Ashurnasirpal II (883–859) claims also to have conquered the land, cutting timber from its forests for use in his new building projects in Nineveh (**RIMA* 2: 309).

Röllig (*RlA* 8: 31).

Meishta (*Tashtepe*?) (map 20) M1 city in the central western Zagros region of Iran. An inscription of the Urartian king Ishpuini (824–806) and his son and co-regent Minua records a campaign conducted by father and son in late C9 with an army of 106 chariots, 9,174 cavalry, and 2,704 infantry against Meishta and other cities in the region (**HcI* 40, no. 7). Horses and cattle were taken from these cities as booty. Meishta is generally identified with Tashtepe near Miyandowab (southeast of Lake Urmia) because of the discovery there of an inscription of Minua which refers to the city (**HcI* 59–60, no. 17).

Barnett (1982: 340).

Melid see *Arslantepe*.

Meluhha (map 12) Land attested in Mesopotamian Bronze and Iron Age texts, and generally identified with the Harappan civilization of the Indus valley. It was one of the three countries which in Mesopotamian tradition lay alongside the 'Lower Sea', i.e. the Persian Gulf and the Arabian Sea. The other two countries were Dilmun and Magan. The *floruit* of the Harappan civilization in late M3 corresponded to the period when Meluhha figures most prominently in Mesopotamian written sources. In M3 Sumerian literary texts, Meluhha and Magan both appear as distant lands, sources of a wide range of exotic goods and precious metals. Other Mesopotamian texts confirm the importation of products from these lands – gold, silver, carnelian, and a black wood (perhaps ebony) from Meluhha, and wood, copper, and semi-precious stones from Magan. Meluhha also exported lapis lazuli to Mesopotamia, as indicated by an inscription of Gudea, a C22 king of Lagash. Since this material was apparently not found in Meluhha, it must initially have been brought from elsewhere, probably from a source or sources in Afghanistan. Other goods exported from Meluhha may also have originated in other regions. Most if not all of the goods dispatched from Meluhha were transported by water to the Mesopotamian cities. During the reign of the Akkadian king Sargon (2334–2279), ships from Meluhha, Magan, and Dilmun docked at the royal capital Akkad/Agade.

Items of Harappan origin which have turned up in a number of southern Mesopotamian cities (e.g. Babylon, Kish, Nippur, and Ur) very likely reflect Mesopotamian commercial contacts with Meluhha. Included among these items are a number of inscribed square stamp seals. The inscription are in the Indus valley script, entirely different from Mesopotamian writing systems. Many hundreds of these stamp seals were found in the main urban centres of the Indus valley, and in smaller numbers at many other sites. The language too of Meluhha seems to have been unintelligible to the Mesopotamians, so that communication required the services of a translator. Harappan cuboid weights and ceramic ware found in Oman, the United Arab Emirates, Bahrain, and at Susa (where Harappan seals have also surfaced) probably indicate the presence of merchants from Meluhha in these places as well. Notable in this respect is the discovery of an assemblage of Harappan painted pottery at the site of Ras al-Janayz in the Oman peninsula, and, on one ceramic fragment, part of an incised

Harappan inscription. Trade between Meluhha and Mesopotamia may well have been direct on occasions, although much of this trade may have been conducted via Dilmun (mod. Bahrain), which played a prominent role as a commercial entrepôt in the international trading network, particularly during the Early and Middle Bronze Ages. Evidence for an actual presence of Mesopotamians in the Indus valley – which could indicate a trading colony – is very meagre. On the other hand, a 'village of Meluhha', attested in the territory of Lagash during the Ur III period (C21), may well indicate that settlers from Meluhha re-established themselves there, their way perhaps paved by merchants from their homeland who came to Mesopotamia for trading purposes.

After the fall of the Ur III kingdom at the end of M3, there is no further reference to Meluhha in the texts until the Assyrian king Tukulti-Ninurta I (1244–1208) calls himself 'king of Dilmun and Meluhha'. As far as this title has any validity, it probably signifies Assyrian control over the routes that led from these regions rather than control of the regions themselves. During the Iron Age Neo-Assyrian period, the name Meluhha again occasionally surfaces, e.g. in the titulature of the C7 Assyrian king Esarhaddon, who calls himself 'king of the kings of Dilmun, Magan, and Meluhha'. By this time, the names Magan and Meluhha are probably no more than fossilized relics of a past age, preserved in formal royal titles. They were, however, apparently used in reference to Egypt and Nubia, which supplied Assyria with a range of exotic goods as the Arabian peninsula and Indus valley had once done.

Heimpel (*RlA* 8: 53–5), D. T. Potts (1995: 1456–9).

Mersin (*Yümük Tepe*) (maps 2, 4) Anc. settlement, c. 250 m in diameter, located in the northwestern part of the mod. city of Mersin, in the Cilician plain of southeastern Anatolia. Its history of occupation extends from early Pottery Neolithic (c. 6000–5000) to the Islamic period. Initial soundings were made on the site in 1936 in the course of the Neilson Expedition to Cilicia, and excavations were carried out from 1937 to 1940 and in 1946–7, by J. Garstang for the British Institute of Archaeology at Ankara, and subsequently by I. Caneva. Thirty-three occupation levels were identified. Already in the Neolithic period there is evidence of trading connections with both the Anatolian plateau and the Levantine coast. Obsidian from central Anatolia found in Mersin illustrates the city's connection with the plateau. Commercial and cultural connections with Syria, Mesopotamia, and Anatolia continued through the Chalcolithic Age. In this period the settlement was fortified by a buttressed enclosure wall, and accessed through a gate which had an approach ramp and was flanked by two projecting towers. Mersin was a major settlement in the Middle Bronze Age, with extensive trading links, as in previous periods, with a number of regions of the western Asian world. In the Late Bronze Age it became a part of the Hittite empire, within the subject kingdom called Kizzuwadna. Its location on the southern Anatolian coast near the sea routes which brought grain and other imports to the Hittite world no doubt gave it considerable strategic value to the Hittites. It was heavily fortified in this period, with casemate walls and projecting square towers, typical of the fortifications of a number of Hittite sites. The Hittites may in fact have been responsible for its substantial fortifications, designed to protect it against enemy attack by sea as well as by land. In the Iron Age, Mersin continued its role as a trading city, when it had particularly close contacts with the Aegean world.

Garstang (1953), Esin (*RlA* 8: 66–73).

Mesopotamia (maps 1, 2, 3, 4, 10) Greek name meaning 'the land between the rivers', broadly used of the region encompassed by the Euphrates and Tigris rivers and their tributaries. Much of the region today belongs to Iraq, but it extends also into Syria and Turkey. Northern or Upper Mesopotamia (north of mod. Baghdad) was the homeland of the Akkadian (M3), Assyrian (M2 and M1), and Mitannian (M2) empires; southern Mesopotamia, often called Babylonia, was the homeland of the Sumerian city-states (M3) and the Babylonian empires of Hammurabi (early M2), the Kassites (later M2), and the Chaldaeans (M1) until the Persian conquest of 539.

Mesu M1 mountain city and land in western Zamua, northwestern Iran. The Zamuites established a garrison there in their retreat from the Assyrian king Ashurnasirpal II during his campaign in the region in 881 (**RIMA* 2: 208). Mesu was listed among the lands which Ashurnasirpal's son and successor Shalmaneser III entered after his campaign in Namri and Parsua in his twenty-fourth regnal year (835) (**RIMA* 3: 68). Other lands listed in this context include Media (Amadaiia), Araziash, and Harhar, along with the cities which Shalmaneser captured – Kuakinda, Hazzanabi, Esmaul, and Kinablila (and other cities in their environs). Shalmaneser's son and successor Shamshi-Adad V (823–811) conquered, plundered, and destroyed the cities of Mesu during his third campaign against the Nairi lands. He pursued inhabitants of the cities who had sought refuge in the mountains, and massacred many of them (**RIMA* 3: 184). Mesu again appears in the list of conquests of Shamshi-Adad's son and successor Adad-nirari III (810–783) (**RIMA* 3: 212). It is to be distinguished from the district of Missi (q.v), which was located in the southwest corner of Mannaea (Fuchs, 1994: 451, Zadok, 2002: 25).

Röllig (*RlA* 8: 95–6).

Me-Tur(r)an (Me-Turnat, Me-Turnu, *Tell Haddad*) (map 10) Bronze and Iron Age city located on the Diyala r. (at its furthermost navigable point) in eastern Mesopotamia. Its capture in mid C19 by Ipiq-Adad II, king of Eshnunna, paved the way for an eastwards expansion of Eshnunnite power. The city's remains have been uncovered in two adjacent settlement-mounds, Tell Haddad and Tell as-Sib (*Mesop.* 129). During rescue operations conducted on these sites prior to the construction of a dam, numerous cuneiform tablets came to light, whose contents include mathematical, literary, and ritual texts. First attested in Middle Bronze Age sources (early M2), the city is also mentioned in Middle Babylonian (Late Bronze Age) texts excavated at Tell Imlihiye. It reappears in 851, when it was besieged and captured by the Assyrian king Shalmaneser III on the first of his two Babylonian campaigns (**RIMA* 3: 30, 37). The city submitted to Shalmaneser's son and successor Shamshi-Adad V (823–811) during his fourth campaign, in which he led his forces into Babylonian territory (**RIMA* 3: 187). Several texts from the reign of Sargon II (721–705) refer to the city. One of these contains a report to Sargon of the murder of its mayor by an Assyrian military officer (**SAA* V: 47, no. 53). Inscribed bricks found at Tell Haddad report that the C7 Assyrian king Ashurbanipal (668–630/627) enlarged the courtyard of the temple Eshahula ('House of the Happy Heart'), a temple dedicated to the god Nergal 'lord of Sirara' at Me-Turran (**RIMB* 2: 229). Me-Turran is one of the cities east of the Tigris whose long-neglected cults the Persian conqueror Cyrus II claims to have restored, according to the so-called 'Cyrus Cylinder' (*Brosius, 2000: 11, no. 12, **Chav.* 429, **PE* 72, no. 21).

Röllig (*RlA* 8: 150), *Mesop.* 445–6.

Meydancıkkale see **Kirshu**.

Michal, Tel (map 8) Settlement spread over five hills in the southern part of the Sharon Plain, coastal Palestine, mod. Israel, north of the Yarkon r. estuary. Its history of occupation extends from Middle Bronze IIB (late C17) to the early Arab period. The main excavations on the site were conducted from 1977 to 1980 by a team from Tel Aviv University under the direction of Z. Herzog, in collaboration with a number of USA universities and Macquarie University in Australia. Seventeen occupation levels were identified. The excavators concluded that the first (Middle Bronze Age) city, located on the main mound, was a trading settlement connected with the maritime activities of the Hyksos people. This conclusion is based on the discovery of numerous 'Hyksos'-type scarabs (see **Hyksos**), Egyptian alabaster products, and a large quantity of Cypriot ware in the level. Its buildings were constructed on a large artificial platform which levelled the top of the mound. Destruction of the Middle Bronze Age settlement was followed by a Late Bronze Age community, which was accommodated by an artificial extension of the mound created by means of a massive earthen rampart. Houses and a small fort are among the meagre architectural remains of this level. It came to an end when the site was abandoned in C13.

After a gap of several hundred years, the site was reoccupied in C10, with settlement spreading from the main mound to the adjacent hills. Architectural remains of this phase, covering Strata XIV–XIII, include large domestic structures on the main mound, and what are apparently cultic structures on several of the hills. Near one of the hills, two wine presses were found, with adjacent wine storage facilities. Herzog believes that wine production may initially have been associated with the site's ceremonial needs, perhaps later developing into a commercial enterprise. He concludes that the site was settled as part of the expansion of Phoenician traders along the coast of the eastern Mediterranean, with the cultic chambers possibly reflecting the traders' ceremonial needs.

Another gap in occupation followed, prior to what the excavators concluded was Tel Michal's most prosperous phase, extending through the Persian to the early Hellenistic period, from c. 525 to 300 (Strata XI–VI). The discovery on the main mound of a large fort or administrative building, along with grain pits and a large silo, give support, they believe, to the view that Tel Michal was one of the stations along the coast that supplied the Persian army on its campaigns against Egypt. A dense array of housing on the settlement's northern hill, with an industrial area on its edges, further reflects the flourishing nature of this phase of Tel Michal's history. From a cemetery located on the hill's northern slope, 120 burials of different types were brought to light (pit-graves, cist tombs, and an infant jar burial), accompanied by jewellery, bronze bowls and fibulae, and iron tools. A temple unearthed on the northeastern hill contained numerous clay and stone figurines. Extensive overseas trading contacts are indicated by large quantities of luxury goods (made of clay, glass, alabaster, and bronze) originating from Cyprus, Egypt, Persia, and Greece. Herzog notes that the settlement's material remains in this period corroborate the picture of the political and commercial control of the region by the Phoenicians under Persian hegemony, as recorded in the inscription on the lid of a sarcophagus belonging to Eshmunazar, a late C6 (or early C5) king of Sidon (see under **Sidon**).

Herzog (*NEAEHL* 3: 1036–41; *OEANE* 4: 20–2), Herzog *et al.* (1989).

'Midas City' (map 4) Iron Age citadel located in the highlands of Phrygia, central Anatolia, between mod. Eskişehir and Afyon Karahisar. It was so named in the 1880s by W. M. Ramsay because of the location there of the structure commonly referred to as the Midas monument (see below), after the famous C8 king of Phrygia. Well known for its rock-cut buildings and monumental inscriptions, 'Midas City' was excavated by the French Institute of Archaeology at Istanbul, from 1937 to 1939 under C. H. E. Haspels as field director, and from 1948 to 1951 under the direction of H. Çambel. The first evidence of occupation dates to the Early Bronze Age, indicated by finds of pottery of the period on and east of the citadel, and by an Early Bronze Age cemetery at its base. In the Iron Age, gates with steep approaches gave entry to the citadel, with a ramp on its east side providing access for vehicles. Rock-cuttings and postholes suggest that the citadel was provided with man-made walls of stone, timber, and pisé (rammed mud and clay). Water supplies were accessed by staircases descending through tunnels, perhaps of C8 date, to cisterns at ground level. Rock-cut tombs of uncertain date, with chambers replicating the interiors of houses, were discovered along the eastern side and northern end of the citadel.

The monuments located on the citadel's edges and summit were apparently used for worship and religious ritual. The best known of these is the so-called Midas monument. It is a replica of a Phrygian temple façade, 16 m high, with central door niche, low gabled roof, and a decoration of geometric patterns in relief. There is an open square in front. Of the fifteen Phrygian inscriptions discovered in 'Midas City', one of the most important is a single-line text carved above the roof of this building. Though the precise interpretation of the text is uncertain, its subject is Midas and it may be a dedication to him. The inscription accords him the titles *lavag(e)tes* and *vanax*, which recall the similarly titled highest ranking officials in the Late Bronze Age Mycenaean world. The Midas monument has been dated to C8 on the basis of comparisons between its architecture and decorative elements, and similar features at Gordium. It was almost certainly intended as a place of worship for Phrygia's chief deity, the mother goddess Cybele. A statue of the goddess probably once stood in the door niche of the monument. The form in which she was originally depicted remains unknown. But a later image of her may survive in the lower part of a monumental female figure found on the site. Dated provisionally to the third quarter of C6, she is clad in a chiton and long veil.

From the period of its first settlement in C8, the citadel appears to have experienced no major disruption to its history or culture before its apparent end in the early decades of the Hellenistic age (late C4). Monuments and inscriptions were produced through C7 and C6, and the cult of Cybele probably persisted through the Persian period (C6–4). From C8 onwards, the citadel was very likely the most important religious sanctuary in the Phrygian highlands.

Haspels (1971, *passim*), Brixhe and Lejeune (1984: 1–29), Mellink (*RlA* 8: 153–6).

Midian(ites) Far-ranging Iron Age tribal groups, frequently referred to in *OT* sources, whose homeland seems to have lain in northwestern Arabia, immediately east of the Gulf of Aqaba. Their activities as raiders, caravaneers, grazers of flocks, and camel-herders account for their presence in many parts of southern and eastern Canaan in biblical tradition. Among the many *OT* references to Midian, some of the best known are the passages in Exodus, which refer to it as the place where Moses went as a fugitive from Egypt (2:15), married Zipporah, daughter of the Midianite priest Jethro (2:21), and was appointed by God to lead the Hebrews out of Egypt (3:1–15). Neither the land nor the people is attested in contemporary non-biblical sources.

Mattingly (*HCBD* 682–3), Parr (*OEANE* 4: 25).

Mikhmoret, Tell (map 8) Harbour settlement on the coast of mod. Israel, 8 km north of Netanya, consisting of a mound on the southern headland of a small bay and other areas of occupation spread around the bay. Its history of occupation extends from the Late Bronze Age (attested almost entirely by sherds) to mediaeval times. Excavations have been carried out in various areas of the settlement from the early 1950s, the most substantial being those on and around the southern headland, undertaken initially in 1978 by Y. Porath for the Israel Dept of Antiquities, and continued by the American directors S. M. Paley and R. R. Stieglitz between 1982 and 1984 under the auspices of the Emeq Hefer Archaeological Project. The Iron Age II period of the settlement's existence is also attested mainly by sherds. The excavators comment: 'If any historical importance is to be attributed to these Iron Age finds, it would seem that access to the harbour facility by the inhabitants of the local villages came about with King David's annexation of the Sharon coastal plain at the beginning of C10 and the establishment of a more secure political, social, and economic environment.' A large public building, covering more than 150 sq. m, has been interpreted as a fort, built in the time of Persian hegemony over the region. In 1960, during his excavations on the bay's shore and northern headland, B. J. Isserlin (University of Leeds) uncovered the remains of storage areas that had been destroyed at the end of the Persian period (C4). This, together with evidence of destruction within the abovementioned public building, has been taken to indicate that the settlement in this period was overrun c. 345 in the aftermath of the revolt against Persia by Tennes, king of Sidon (see under **Sidon**).

Porath, Paley, and Stieglitz (*NEAEHL* 3: 1043–6).

Milesia Region in Ionia on the Aegean coast of southwestern Anatolia, of fluctuating size. Its chief city was Miletus, but it also included the oracular sanctuary at Didyma (Branchidae) (Herodotus 1.46, 157), 16.4 km south of Miletus, and the town of Teichiussa (Thucydides 8.26), 26 km southeast of Miletus. The relationship between Classical Milesia and Miletus is perhaps comparable in some respects to that between their Late Bronze Age predecessors, the land and the city of Milawata.

Miletus (Bronze Age **Milawata/Millawanda**) (maps 3, 5) City in southwestern Anatolia, in the region called Milesia by Classical writers. Originally located on the Aegean coast (where it had four harbours), Miletus now lies in a plain 3 km inland. Its history of occupation extends from the late Chalcolithic period (second half of M4) through the Bronze Ages and the Archaic, Classical, Hellenistic, Roman, and Byzantine periods. There was also a later Ottoman settlement on the site. Excavations have been carried out since 1899 by a number of German archaeological teams. The first excavations, directed by T. Wiegand, were interrupted by the First World War. Work resumed under C. Weickert in 1938 was interrupted by the Second World War, but continued under Weickert's direction in 1955 and 1957. Subsequent excavations have been conducted by G. Kleiner, W. Müller-Wiener, V. von Graeve, and

P. Hommel, and are continuing today. Of particular interest are the ongoing excavations by W.-D. Niemeier of the Bronze Age settlements on the site.

In the last two decades, previously unknown Chalcolithic and Early and Middle Bronze Age phases of the site's history (designated as phases I–III) have come to light. Late Bronze Age occupation is divided into three further phases (IV–VI). Evidence for the first three phases has been found primarily in the vicinity of the later temple of Athena, built originally in the Archaic period in the southwest of the site. The Chalcolithic areas of settlement were located on two islands in the Latmian Gulf. Artefacts from the Early Bronze phase (Miletus II) – ceramic ware, figurines, including the head of a Cycladic marble statuette, and decorated spindle whorls – are seen as reflecting the unique position Miletus held between the Aegean and the Anatolian worlds, with the city participating in the intensive commercial activities of the Aegean region already in the second half of M3 (thus Niemeier). The site's commercially valuable strategic location between these worlds, as well as the access it gave to Anatolian metals, no doubt provided settlers from Minoan Crete with their chief incentive for occupying it during the Middle Bronze Age (c. 2000–1650; Miletus III). Minoan occupation in this period (with settlement still located on an island, in the area of the temple of Athena), has been inferred from the finds of Minoan pottery, including domestic ware, and a couple of Minoan-type seals and a seal impression. The domestic ware provides a clear pointer to settlement by those who made and used it, and the seals and sealing are considered by Niemeier to be a possible indication of a Minoan administration. In archaeological terms, the Miletus III phase extended from the Middle Minoan IA to the Middle Minoan IIB period, and ended with Miletus' destruction around the end of the Minoan 'First Palace' period (c. 1650).

Strong Minoan influence is again evident at Miletus in the first of its three Late Bronze Age phases (Miletus IV), almost certainly indicative of a second period of Minoan colonization, beginning early in the Minoan 'Second Palace' period (Middle Minoan III), which followed immediately upon the First Palace period. In the Late Bronze Age, the city apparently still occupied an island location in the area around the later Athena temple site. Minoan settlement is inferred from decorated Minoan-type ceramic ware, from Minoan-type kitchenware, including tripod cooking pots and large quantities of domestic pottery, and from a range of evidence for Minoan cult-practices. A further indication of a Minoan presence is indicated by fragments of frescoes, Minoan in both technique and content, from the wall of a building possibly used for cultic purposes.

The Minoan presence in Miletus survived two destructions of the city, but ended with a third, by fire, in the first half of C15 (Late Minoan II period). Niemeier has suggested that this destruction may have been caused by conquering Mycenaeans. In the subsequent phase (Late Helladic III; Miletus V), Mycenaean culture became dominant, as reflected in Mycenaean-type tombs and the abundance of Mycenaean-type pottery. Much of this pottery was imported from other parts of the Mycenaean world, but the discovery of seven kilns on the site indicates that Miletus itself became a major centre for the production of ceramic ware. The ratio of Mycenaean to local Anatolian pottery is now estimated at c. 95 per cent to 5 per cent. This is clearly indicative of very strong Mycenaean influence, though the excavators believe that the evidence for actual Mycenaean settlement in this period is less conclusive than that for Minoan settlement in the preceding periods.

The site was again destroyed, almost certainly by human agency according to the excavators, in the Late Helladic IIIA2 period or in the transition from Late Helladic IIIA2 to Late Helladic IIIB1. This particular destruction has been associated with a historical event recorded in the Annals of the Hittite king Mursili II (1321–1295). Late Bronze Age Hittite records contain a number of references to a western Anatolian land and city called Milawata (variant Millawanda). Milawata's precise location has long been debated, but there is now compelling (if still circumstantial) evidence to identify it with the land called Milesia in Greek texts, whose chief city was Miletus. Mursili reports that in the third year of his reign he dispatched an expeditionary force against Milawata, in response to its joining an anti-Hittite alliance on the side of the king of Ahhiyawa (almost certainly a Mycenaean kingdom of mainland Greece; see **Ahhiyawa**). According to Mursili, the city was captured and sacked (**AM* 36–7).

In its third and final Late Bronze Age phase (Miletus VI), Miletus/Milawata was rebuilt, and for the first time fortified. Its fortifications, which may have extended over 1,100 m, incorporated internal cross-walls and square towers, similar to and very likely modelled upon those of the Hittite capital Hattusa. Mycenaean-type pottery, domestic architecture, and burial practices seem to indicate that the city in this phase of its existence was predominantly a Mycenaean settlement. The burial practices are indicated by a cemetery of the period, located on the hill called Değirmentepe which lies 1.5 km southwest of the temple of Athena site. It contains Mycenaean-type tombs, with dromos (entrance passage) and stomion (doorway), in which a number of Mycenaean-type grave goods were discovered (though their contents also included swords of Hittite type). Mycenaean terracotta figurines, perhaps connected with cultic ceremonies, are adduced as further evidence of Mycenaean settlement. But although Mycenaean elements predominated on the site, there was also a significant admixture of Anatolian elements, indicating that the city was not wholly Mycenaean in character. It may, however, have come under the control of a Mycenaean king in late C14 or early C13, who used it as a base for the expansion of Mycenaean political, military, and commercial interests in western Anatolia. This is deduced from the fact that in mid C13 a Hittite king, probably Hattusili III, wrote a letter to the king of Ahhiyawa (commonly, though misleadingly, referred to as the 'Tawagalawa' letter), acknowledging his sovereignty over Milawata, but complaining that a prominent anti-Hittite insurrectionist had sought and received refuge there when pursued by a Hittite army (*Garstang and Gurney, 1959, 111–14). The immediate outcome of this letter is unknown. But from later Hittite documents, notably the so-called 'Milawata letter' (**HDT* 144–6; see Bryce, 2005: 306–8), it would appear that some time during the second half of C13, the Hittites regained sovereignty over Milawata. This was the only known base of Ahhiyawan/Mycenaean authority and activity in Anatolia, and with its loss, Mycenaean influence in the region was at an end.

Material evidence for settlement at Miletus in the centuries immediately following the collapse of the Bronze Age civilizations in C12 is confined almost entirely to pottery fragments on the site of the temple of Athena, until stone-built oval and rectilinear houses of C8 date begin making their appearance in the archaeological record. However, the city figures prominently in accounts of the Ionian migrations from the Greek mainland to the western coast of Anatolia, now dated to the last two centuries of M2. Miletus was the southernmost and most important of the colonies settled by the Ionian migrants. According to Herodotus (1.146), the colonists came from Athens, and took over the site from its native Carian inhabitants, murdering the adult males, and marrying their widows, sisters, and daughters. Miletus itself subsequently became a great colonizing city, dispatching settlers to found no fewer than ninety cities (according to Greek sources) at numerous locations on the shores of the Black Sea and Hellespont, and along the northern Aegean and Mediterranean coastlands.

During the Archaic period (c. 700–494), the most important part of the city appears to have been located on the summit and slopes of the fortified acropolis now called Kalabaktepe, lying to the south of the later city centre. On the south slope of Kalabaktepe, flat-roofed houses with courtyards were built. An industrial quarter may have been located on the mound. The main feature of the lower town, built on either side of the so-called Theatre Harbour, was the temple to the goddess Athena, one of a number of temples constructed in the city during this period. This area may also have contained the city's commercial centre. To the north the city extended to the harbour, whose entrance is still guarded on either side by lions of Hellenistic date. A sacred way running south from Miletus connected the city with the oracular sanctuary of the god Apollo at Didyma, 16.4 km away.

With an estimated population of 50,000 to 60,000, the city flourished as a centre of trade, commerce, and culture in C7 and C6, notably under the rule of the tyrant Thrasybulus (late C7–early C6). It was the home of several of the most eminent pre-Socratic philosopher-scientists, including Thales, Anaximenes, and Anaximander, and of the famous geographer-historian Hecataeus (fl. c. 500). Hippodamus, the greatest of all Greek town planners, was born here c. 500. Under Thrasybulus, Miletus held out against the armies of the Lydian empire, and retained its independence from Lydian control, as formally acknowledged in a treaty which the Lydian king Alyattes (610–560) drew up with it when the rest of the Ionian cities became part of the Lydian empire (Herodotus 1.22). The city seems also to have maintained a special status when the Lydian empire and all its possessions fell to the Persian emperor Cyrus II c. 546. None the less, it initiated and played a leading role in the Ionian rebellion which broke out against Persian rule in 499. When the rebellion ended with the total rout of the Ionian forces in a naval battle off the nearby island of Lade in 494, the Persians took their revenge on Miletus, following up their victory by blockading, capturing, and sacking the city, massacring or enslaving its inhabitants, and deporting the survivors to Susa. Herodotus (6.18–20) tells the story of the city's destruction. But the disaster may not have been as total as he suggests, for in 479 Milesians are listed among the allied Greek forces who confronted and defeated the Persians in the battle of Mycale (q.v.). In later years, Miletus became a member of the Athenian Confederacy (see glossary). But it was apparently a reluctant member, for in mid C5 Athens was obliged to place it under the control of a garrison – presumably because it had attempted to break away from the Confederacy. In 412 it did in fact succeed in defecting from Athens to Sparta, and was used by the Spartans as a base for naval operations in the region. However, in 386, by the terms of the 'King's Peace' (see glossary), it was handed over to Persia, and remained under Persian sovereignty until 334, when Alexander the Great campaigned in the region, and took the city by siege (Arrian, *Anabasis* 1.18–19, Diodorus 17.22).

Apart from the Bronze Age remains in the vicinity of the temple of Athena, and the Archaic remains unearthed at Kalabaktepe and Zeytintepe (the latter lay outside the circuit walls and was the location of a temple of Aphrodite), very little has survived of Miletus' pre-Hellenistic phases. This was due mainly to the Persian devastation of the site in 494, but partly also to the city's extensive redevelopment in the Hellenistic period. Miletus was rebuilt on a grand scale, its new public buildings including a number of temples, two agoras (market-places), a stadium, a bouleuterion (council house, consisting of propylon, colonnaded courtyard, and roofed auditorium), and a theatre. The Delphinium, sanctuary of the god Apollo, was the city's chief religious centre. Miletus became part of the Roman province of Asia in 129. Under Roman rule, the city's grid layout and many of its Hellenistic buildings remained in use. The theatre was considerably enlarged, and is today one of the city's most impressive features. Other noteworthy buildings of the Roman imperial period include an elaborately decorated nymphaeum (fountain-house), and the monumental baths built in honour of Faustina, wife of the C2 CE emperor Marcus Aurelius.

Greaves (2002), Niemeier (2005), von Graeve (2006).

Miqne, Tel see **Ekron**.

Mira (map 3) Late Bronze Age Hittite vassal kingdom in western Anatolia, one of the Arzawa Lands. The Hittite king Mursili II installed a man called Mashuiluwa on its throne in his fourth regnal year (c. 1318), shortly after conquering and dismantling the neighbouring kingdom of Arzawa 'Minor'. At that time, he probably increased Mira's size by allocating to it a substantial part – if not all – of the territory formerly belonging to Arzawa 'Minor'. He also attached another neighbouring land, Kuwaliya, to Mashuiluwa's kingdom (**HDT* 74). Mira was now almost certainly the largest and potentially the most powerful of the Arzawa Lands. An inscribed and sculptured rock monument in what is now called the Karabel pass, 28 km east of mod. Izmir (see **Karabel**), may have lain on the kingdom's northern frontier. In the south, the frontier probably extended along the coast to the borders of the land of Milawata (Classical Miletus) and perhaps inland along the Maeander valley to the river's headwaters.

In the twelfth year of Mursili's reign, Mashuiluwa staged a rebellion against his Hittite overlord, which was promptly crushed. Mursili deposed the rebel and had him deported to Hattusa. In his place, he installed Mashuiluwa's nephew and adopted son Kupanta-Kurunta as ruler of Mira, binding him to the Hittite crown with a (still extant) treaty (**HDT* 74–82, *Bryce, 2005: 212–14). Kupanta-Kurunta enjoyed a long reign in Mira, during which he appears to have remained loyal to his Hittite allegiance, if we can so judge from one attested instance of his support of Hittite interests in western Anatolia in the reign of Mursili's son and successor Muwattalli II (1295–1272) (*Houwink ten Cate, 1985–6: 39–40). He was still alive and active in the 1260s, following the seizure of the Hittite throne by Hattusili III c. 1267. This is indicated by a letter which the pharaoh Ramesses II wrote to him. The letter was in response to one written by Kupanta-Kurunta, who had asked the pharaoh whether he supported Hattusili or Hattusili's exiled nephew Urhi-Teshub, whose throne Hattusili had seized. Ramesses declared his support for Hattusili (**HDT* 130–1). Mira's last known ruler was a man called Tarkasnawa, who is depicted in the sculpture on the Karabel monument. He occupied Mira's throne in the final decades of C13, during the reign of the Hittite king Tudhaliya IV (*Hawkins, 1998b).

Mishlan (map 10) Middle Bronze Age Yaminite city located in the district of Mari on the west bank of the middle Euphrates. Attested in a number of letters in the Mari archive, particularly from the reign of Zimri-Lim (1774–1762), Mishlan was a prosperous settlement, deriving its wealth both from its commercial activities (in mid C19 its commercial status was equal to that of Mari), and its fertile, well-watered agricultural areas. At the end of the first year of his reign, Zimri-Lim was confronted with a major Yaminite uprising, which he crushed the following year. In the process, he seized the cities of Mishlan and Samanum, which had been the capitals of the chief rebel groups, and demolished their fortifications. Control of Mishlan and its farmlands provided Zimri-Lim with a substantial source of grain production for his kingdom.
Charpin (1989; 2000), *LKM* 617 (refs).

Mishrifeh see Qatna.

Missi (to be distinguished from the Zamuite city **Mesu**, q.v.) M1 district in the southwest corner of Mannaea, northwestern Iran. It lay on the route taken by the Assyrian king Sargon II during his famous eighth campaign in 714 (**ARAB* II 76–7, **Chav.* 338). While in Missi, Sargon met the Mannaean king Ullusunu in his fortress-city Surdakku. He received from him there supplies of flour and wine for his troops, tribute in the form of horses, cattle, and sheep, and Ullusunu's eldest son as a hostage, supposedly to ensure the son's succession to Mannaea's throne.

Mitanni (**Mittan(n)i**) (map 3) Late Bronze Age kingdom formed by the end of C16 from a number of small Hurrian states in Upper Mesopotamia, centred on the Habur region. The Egyptians and Canaanites used the West Semitic form Naharina or Naharima to designate the kingdom, which was also known as Hurri. In C15, it became one of the four Great Kingdoms of the western Asian world (the others at that time were Hatti, Babylon, and Egypt), and exercised control over a large expanse of territory extending from northern Mesopotamia through northern Syria and parts of eastern Anatolia. Its first royal capital was the city called Washshukkanni, yet to be located with certainty though commonly identified with the site of mod. Tell Feheriye (q.v.) in the Habur triangle. Later, after the destruction of Washshukkanni in the later C14, Taidu and then Irride were the most important royal seats. In Late Bronze Age texts, the kingdom is also referred to as Hurri and Hanigalbat (q.v.). Mitanni's formidable military might seems to have depended to a large extent on its élite class of warriors called the *maryannu*.

In the course of their expansion west of the Euphrates r., the Mitannians frequently clashed with the kingdom of Hatti, their chief rival for supremacy over the states and petty kingdoms of northern Syria. However, Mitanni's Syrian ambitions also brought it into conflict with Egypt, which similarly sought to extend its territorial enterprises through the Syro-Palestinian regions. The campaigns of the pharaoh Tuthmosis I (1504–1492) took Egyptian arms as far as the Euphrates, temporarily halting Mitannian ventures in the same region. But the shrinkage of Egyptian influence in Syria during Queen Hatshepsut's reign (1479–1458) very likely prompted the first major westward expansion of Mitanni's power across the Euphrates, in the reign of its king Parrattarna (second half of C15). Parrattarna established his sovereignty over the Syrian territories formerly controlled by the kingdom of Aleppo. He installed a man called Idrimi from Aleppo's royal dynastic line as his vassal ruler in the city of Alalah, and used him as an agent for the extension of Mitannian influence into southern Anatolia, notably the kingdom of Kizzuwadna which lay on the southeastern periphery of Hittite territory.

Mitannian territorial ambitions received a setback with the resurgence of Egyptian military enterprise under Tuthmosis III (1479–1425), who conducted numerous campaigns of conquest in Syria–Palestine. They suffered subsequently from renewed Hittite military campaigns in Syria under the Hittite king Tudhaliya I/II (early C14). But the Hittite claim that Tudhaliya destroyed the lands of the king of Mitanni is almost certainly an exaggerated one, since Mitanni continued to exercise sovereignty in northern Syria for many years to come. This sovereignty was consolidated by an agreement reached, also early in C14, between the Mitannian king Artatama I and his Egyptian counterpart Tuthmosis IV over a division of territory between them. The Egyptians conceded Mitannian territorial claims in northern Syria, while part of coastal and much of southern Syria were left within the Egyptian sphere of authority. Inland, the division of territory between the two kingdoms lay just to the north of the city of Qadesh on the Orontes r.

The scene was now set for a Hittite–Mitannian showdown over the territories in northern Syria subject to Mitannian overlordship. At this time, the Hittite and Mitannian thrones were occupied respectively by Suppiluliuma I and Tushratta, each of whom had come to power in a royal coup. The contest between the two resulted in the triumph of Suppiluliuma, and the destruction of the kingdom of Mitanni, whose last stronghold, Carchemish, fell to Suppiluliuma in 1327. Tushratta himself was later assassinated, and his son Shattiwaza was eventually installed as a Hittite ally and puppet ruler of the kingdom of Hanigalbat, the much reduced successor of the Great Kingdom of Mitanni. The name Mitanni, however, survived for some centuries after the collapse of the Mitannian empire, and is later attested in the records of the Assyrian king Tiglath-pileser I (1114–1076) (**RIMA* 2: 25).

Wilhelm (1989; 1995), Wilhelm/Stein (*RlA* 8: 286–99).

Mizpah (of Benjamin) Biblically attested city on the border between Judah and Israel. The entire Israelite army assembled there for their war against the Benjaminites (Judges 20:1–3). Asa, king of Judah (late C10–early C9), fortified the city during his war with Baasha, king of Israel (1 Kings 15:22). Following the conquest of Jerusalem by the Babylonian king Nebuchadnezzar II in 586, Mizpah became a provincial capital of the Babylonian empire. A man called Gedaliah, who was installed there as its governor by Nebuchadnezzar, was assassinated in the city by a Jewish nationalist, Ishmael, son of Nethaniah (2 Kings 25:25).

Most scholars now believe that Mizpah is to be identified with the site Tell en-Nasbeh (see ***Nasbeh, Tell en-***) which lies 12 km northwest of Jerusalem. Several interesting correlations can be established between this site and the Mizpah attested in biblical sources. Of particular interest is a seal from Tell en-Nasbeh belonging to a man called Jaazaniah, who is designated as 'servant of the king'. Conceivably, this is the Jaazaniah of 2 Kings 25:23, who was among the army officers who came before the abovementioned Gedaliah. Despite the correlations, the case for equating Mizpah and Tell en-Nasbeh remains circumstantial.

Drinkard (*HCBD* 691), Laughlin (2006: 188–91).

Mizpah (of Gilead) see **Gilead (Mizpah of)**.

Moab (map 8) Region and kingdom in Transjordan, located on the plateau east of the Dead Sea between the countries of Ammon to its north and Edom to its south, and occupying an area of c. 32,000 sq. km. In written sources, it is first attested in the inscriptions of the C13 pharaoh Ramesses II, who conducted campaigns in Moab and Edom, plundering a number of their cities. Across the eastern part of Moab passed the road known as the King's Highway (q.v.), from Damascus to the Gulf of Aqabah. In *OT* tradition, Moses used this road to lead his people through the lands of Edom and Moab (e.g. Numbers 20:17). According to Genesis 19:30–8, Abraham's nephew Lot was the ancestor of the Moabite people.

Archaeological surveys indicate that settlement on the plateau where Moab lay dates back at least to the Chalcolithic period (M6–4). Until the last decades of the Late Bronze Age (late C13–C12), the Moabite region seems to have been only sparsely populated. But from the end of the Late Bronze Age onwards the number of settlements appears to have increased steadily, and fortresses were built along the frontiers. There is no clear indication whether a kingdom of Moab had come into being at this time – i.e. in the early decades of the Iron Age. But such a kingdom is certainly in evidence in Iron Age II, when Moab reached the peak of its urban and political development. Its capital was the city of Dibon. Of particular importance for Moabite history was the discovery there in 1868 of a black basalt stele, commonly referred to as the Moabite Stone. On it appears a 34-line inscription in the Moabite language celebrating the military and building achievements of a C9 Moabite king called Mesha (**CS* II: 137–8, **Chav.* 311–16). This provides one of the best-known instances where contemporary historical sources and biblical tradition coincide, for Mesha was already known as a king of Moab from 2 Kings 3:4. The inscription records Mesha's success in establishing his country's independence from Israel, allegedly at the command of Moab's chief god, Kemosh. According to *OT* tradition, the (C10) Israelite king David had conquered the land and made it part of his kingdom (2 Samuel 8:2), after its earlier inconclusive conflicts with David's predecessor Saul (1 Samuel 14:47).

But Moabite independence was relatively shortlived. The Assyrians' western campaigns conducted in 734–732 by Tiglath-pileser III reduced Moab and other lands in Transjordan to Assyrian subject status. This is indicated by contemporary Assyrian texts, which also record the names of four other Moabite kings. During the period of Assyrian overlordship, Moab seems to have enjoyed a relatively peaceful existence, due largely to the protection it received from the Assyrians against predatory nomadic tribes. It is, however, possible that the kingdom was involved in an anti-Assyrian uprising c. 713, during the reign of Sargon II. This is suggested by a fragmentary prism text dating to Sargon's reign. Following the collapse of the Assyrian empire in late C7, Moab became part of the Babylonian empire, against which it mounted an unsuccessful rebellion. After the fall of the empire in Nabonidus' reign (556–539) it became subject to Persia. During the Hellenistic period Moab came under the control of the Nabataeans.

Labianca and Younker (1995), Weippert (*RlA* 8: 318–25), Routledge (2004).

Mopsuestia (Misis, *Yakapınar*) M1 BCE–M1 CE city in Cilicia in southern Anatolia, 37 km east of Adana at a strategically important crossing of the Pyramus

Figure 72 Moab from Mt Nebo.

(mod. Ceyhan) r. (*BAGRW* 67 B3). An identification has been suggested with the Iron Age city Pahru (q.v.), attested in records of the C9 Assyrian king Shalmaneser III as the royal capital of Kate, king of Que. According to Classical tradition, Mopsuestia was founded by the legendary Mopsus, who emigrated from western Anatolia to Cilicia and whose name is associated with the foundation of a number of cities in southern Anatolia. In late C6 Mopsuestia became subject to Persia, and remained under Persian overlordship until the campaigns of Alexander the Great in 334. It subsequently came under Seleucid control, and was renamed Seleucea-on-the-Pyramus in honour of the Seleucid king Seleucus IV Epiphanes. The city's material remains, dating almost entirely to the Roman period, include a Roman bridge, theatre, and gymnasium.

Gough (*PECS* 593–4), Bremmer (*OCD* 995), Kupper (*RlA* 8: 269–70).

Mor, Tel (map 8) Small settlement-mound located on the Via Maris (q.v.) on the coast of mod. Israel, 6 km north of Ashdod and probably serving as its port. Excavations were conducted by M. Dothan in 1959 and 1960 for the Israel Dept of Antiquities. Twelve occupation levels were identified, extending from the late Middle Bronze Age through the Hellenistic, Roman, and Byzantine periods. Within this time-frame, there were several long intervals when the site was abandoned. Small finds from the first of the levels indicate Middle Bronze Age trading contacts with Cyprus and Egypt. In the Late Bronze Age, Tel Mor was a prosperous settlement, material remains of which are provided by a large building identified as a fortress or storehouse. Its location on the Via Maris was no doubt reponsible for its importance in this period. The settlement's destruction in early C13 has been tentatively attributed to one of the campaigns conducted by the pharaoh Seti I in Canaan. But shortly afterwards it was rebuilt, with a new Egyptian-style multi-roomed fortress and courtyard complex. Large quantities of Mycenaean, Egyptian, and Cypriot ware found in the fortress are indicative of extensive overseas trading contacts. Dothan suggests that the destruction of this fortress may have occurred within the context of the pharaoh Merneptah's punitive raids against the rebellious cities of the Shephelah (q.v.); alternatively, its destruction may have been due to the Israelite tribes who devastated the coastal plain in that period without settling it. Reoccupation in late C13 or early C12 is attested by a small fort or tower. Egyptian pottery and scarabs among the small finds of this level have suggested to Dothan that an Egyptian governor still resided in the fortress during the reign of the pharaoh Ramesses III (1184–1153).

Following the withdrawal of the Egyptians from the Syro-Palestinian region, Tel Mor, like other coastal sites, was occupied by the Philistines – as indicated by the material culture of its two 'Philistine' levels (IV–III), which consisted mainly of early Iron Age agricultural structures, courtyards, silos, and a range of Philistine pottery. The destruction of level III is generally attributed to the Israelite king David's wars against the Philistines (C10). Abandonment of the site for several generations was followed by resettlement in C8, as represented by the remains of a fortress with casemate walls (level II). The destruction of this level has been attributed to the Assyrian king Sargon II (721–705), whose Annals record the king's conquest of Ashdod and its conversion into an Assyrian province. Tel Mor was again abandoned, and Ashdod's port was transferred to the site called Azotos in the Hellenistic period. Tel Mor itself was reoccupied in this period, when it appears to have become a centre of a purple-dye industry. Dothan notes that in the Roman–Byzantine period there was only a poor agricultural settlement on the site.

Dothan (*NEAEHL* 3: 1073–4).

Morphou (map 14) City near the northwest coast of Cyprus. A major settlement was founded there just north of the mod. village at Toumba tou Skourou at the end of the Middle Cypriot period. Following repeated episodes of bulldozing, which destroyed much of the site, excavations by E. T. Vermeule and F. Z. Wolsky for Harvard University from 1971 to 1973 uncovered pottery workshops, houses, and rich chamber tombs of Late Bronze Age date. Several huge stone blocks with ornamental bosses suggest the presence of a monumental building similar to those found in other Late Bronze Age centres, such as Alassa, Citium, and Enkomi. The settlement decreased in importance after C13, but survived until c. 700 when it was finally abandoned.

Occupation in the Morphou area is also indicated at Ambelia, close to the confluence of the Ovgos and Serakis rivers, where material dating from the Late Bronze Age to the Hellenistic period has been found. A small sanctuary of Aphrodite located opposite the earlier settlement at Toumba tou Skourou flourished from Archaic to early Christian times. It has been suggested that 'Morphou' may have taken its name from the cult of Aphrodite Morpho ('the Shapely'), who was also worshipped at Sparta. A nearby necropolis contains tombs ranging in date from the Geometric (C8) to the Hellenistic (C4–2) period. Among the finds in the necropolis was a funerary inscription of C4 date, written in the Cypriot syllabary.

(J. M. Webb)

Nicolaou (*PECS* 595–6), Vermeule and Wolsky (1990).

Mozan, Tell see **Urkesh**.

Mukish (map 3) Bronze Age region in northeastern Syria, north of Ugarit, first mentioned in tablets of the Ur III period (C21). In C16 it was incorporated into the kingdom of Aleppo, but later became subject to the Mitannian king Parrattarna when the latter established his rule over Aleppo (C15). In the second half of C15 Mukish, along with the states Niya and Ama'u, declared its support for Idrimi – son of Ilim-ilimma, the former king of Yamhad (Aleppo) – during his seven-year exile (see **Alalah**). When Idrimi was subsequently installed by Parrattarna on the throne at Alalah, he was formally recognized as the ruler of these states, no doubt in accordance with the sworn pact which he made with Parrattarna (*Greenstein, 1995: 2426, **CS* I: 479). In mid C14, Mukish was among the lands conquered by the Hittite king Suppiluliuma I during his one-year Syrian war (c. 1344) against Mitanni and its subject states (**HDT* 43–4). An anti-Hittite alliance which it joined in an attempt to break away from Hittite sovereignty was crushed by a Hittite expeditionary force. Suppiluliuma thereupon handed over a substantial part of its territory to his loyal subject-ally Niqmaddu II, king of Ugarit (*Bryce, 2005: 164–6).

Mulhan (map 10) Middle Bronze Age city in the middle Euphrates region called Suhu(m) which lay south of the kingdom of Mari. It was the northernmost city of Lower Suhum. In 1772, when Suhum was invaded by the forces of Ibal-pi-El II, king of Eshnunna, Mulhan was apparently under the command of a man called Buqaqum, otherwise known as governor of Sapiratum, another city in Suhum. Buqaqum wrote to Zimri-Lim, king of Mari and overlord of Suhum, warning him that unless a relief force arrived he would be forced to evacuate the city and abandon the entire region of Lower Suhum to the enemy (**LKM* 384).

Kupper (*RlA* 8: 414), *Mesop.* 197.

Munbaqa, Tall see **Ekalte**.

Munna Iron Age country located in the upper Diyala/Zagros region in the northeastern Mesopotamian–northwestern Iranian borderlands, near the lands of Zamua and Allabria. The Assyrian king Shalmaneser III conquered the land during his campaign in the region in his eighteenth regnal year (841) (**RIMA* 3: 40). It later appears in the list of conquests of Adad-nirari III (810–783) (**RIMA* 3: 212).

Murattash One of the small polities in northeastern Mesopotamia conquered by the Assyrian king Tiglath-pileser I (1114–1076) in the second year of his reign (**RIMA* 2: 19). The fortified city Murattash, lying east of the Lesser Zab in the Asania and Atuma mountain regions, was captured, plundered, and destroyed in a dawn attack. The nearby land of Saradaush also fell victim to the Assyrians in this campaign.

Murmuriga Late Bronze Age fortified settlement lying to the west of the middle bend of the Euphrates r., within the kingdom of Carchemish. The Hittite viceroy Telipinu, son of Suppiluliuma I, established a winter camp there in 1328, after conducting a military campaign against the countries of Arziya and Carchemish, at that time still subject to the Mitannian king Tushratta. Telipinu left a garrison of

600 troops and a chariot contingent at Murmuriga when he was summoned to Uda in the Hittite Lower Land for a meeting with his father. During his absence, Mitannian forces laid siege to the garrison. It was relieved the following spring when Suppiluliuma dispatched troops to the region in preparation for his final onslaught on Carchemish (**DS* 92, **CS* I: 189–90, **Chav.* 237).

Bryce (2005: 177).

Murat Su see **Arsanias r.**

Muru Fortified Iron Age city belonging to the Aramaean kingdom of Bit-Agusi in north-central Syria. Along with Arne and Apparazu, other cities of Bit-Agusi, Muru was captured by the Assyrians during the reign of Bit-Agusi's king Arame (858–c. 834). Arame lost Muru to the Assyrian king Shalmaneser III (858–824) while the latter was returning from a successful expedition in southern Anatolia against the kingdom of Que in his twenty-fifth regnal year. Shalmaneser claims that after capturing Muru, he rebuilt its gateways, and also constructed a palace within the city to serve as his royal residence (**RIMA* 3: 68) – an indication that thenceforth the city would be under permanent Assyrian control. Muru has been identified, tentatively, with ʿAin Dara (q.v.), on the right bank of the Afrin r.

CHLI I: 389, Lipiński (2000: 202).

Musanippa see **Muzunnum.**

Musasir (map 20) Small M1 state and city located in northeastern Mesopotamia between the middle course of the Greater Zab r. and the Zagros mountain range, and serving as a buffer zone between Urartian and Assyrian territory. It appears to have been an anc. tribal centre of the Urartian people before the formation of the kingdom of Urartu, and the original cult-centre for the worship of the god Haldi, later to become Urartu's chief deity. In the so-called Kelishin inscription, one of three Assyrian–Urartian bilingual texts found in the region (in this case it was set up in the Kelishin pass between Rowanduz and Lake Urmia), the Urartian king Ishpuini (824–806) and his son and co-regent Minua record their establishment of a new cult-centre at Musasir. Earlier in C9, Musasir appears to have had diplomatic relations with Assyria. This is indicated by the first attestation of it, which records an invitation for its representatives to join the celebrations associated with the consecration of the palace built by the Assyrian king Ashurnasirpal II (883–859) in Kalhu (Nimrud, biblical Calah), then the Assyrian capital (**RIMA* 2: 293). But several decades later, in 826, Dayyan-Ashur, commander-in-chief of Ashurnasirpal's son and successor Shalmaneser III, undertook a campaign against the land, during which he captured and destroyed its stronghold of Zapparia (Sapparia), along with forty-six other cities of Musasir (**RIMA* 3: 70).

Musasir's frontier location invested it with vital strategic significance in the ongoing conflicts between the Urartians and the Assyrians, as illustrated by events in the reigns of their respective kings Rusa I (732–714) and Sargon II (721–705). Musasir's king, Urzana, had become caught up in these conflicts, and gave his support to one side and then the other, no doubt on the basis of where he felt his best interests lay. In the period prior to Sargon's Urartian campaign in 714, he evidently believed that these lay with Assyria, and became openly hostile to Rusa. The Urartian king responded by promptly invading his former ally's kingdom. Urzana fled at his approach, seeking refuge in Assyria. But he failed to make good his escape and was apprehended by Rusa's forces, perhaps after he had already reached Assyrian territory. Despite Urzana's actions, Rusa reinstated him in Musasir as an Urartian vassal (*HcI 144–50, no. 122). Perhaps soon after, Cimmerian forces invaded Urartu, and the governor of the Urartian province of Waisi called upon Urzana for military support (*SAA V: 109–10, no. 145). Urzana may well have remained loyal to Rusa during Sargon's Urartian campaign in 714, for on his return journey from Urartu, Sargon suddenly and unexpectedly attacked Urzana's capital, Musasir (*Chav. 339). The Assyrian clearly rejected any notion that Musasir's apparent status as a sacred city should render it immune from attack. And after Urzana's alliance with Rusa, Musasir could hardly claim that it lay in neutral territory. Appeals to the gods by the city's panic-stricken citizens were of no avail. The city fell without resistance. Sargon then set about plundering it of its enormous wealth. Palace and temple were thoroughly looted, the latter yielding to the conqueror more than 333,500 precious objects. One of the reliefs (now lost) from Sargon's palace at Khorsabad depicted the looting of the palace. Over 1,000 kg of gold and 6,000 kg of silver were included in the spoil. One version of Sargon's Annals reports that when Rusa heard of the sack of Musasir, he took a dagger from his belt and ended his life.

A small group of letters from Sargon's correspondence have been tentatively assigned to the period immediately following Sargon's campaign (*SAA* V: XVII). One of these reports that troops had set out towards Musasir under the command of two Urartian governors (*SAA V: 72–3, no. 88), another is a letter from Urzana reporting the arrival of these governors in Musasir (*SAA V: 111–12, no. 147). If the suggested dating of these letters is correct, then Urzana clearly survived the Assyrian capture and plunder of Musasir in 714, and had in fact been reinstated once more as the city's ruler – this time under Assyrian overlordship.

Salvini/Boehmer (*RlA* 8: 444–50).

Mushani Iron Age region within the kingdom of Melid/Malatya in eastern Anatolia, referred to by the Urartian king Sarduri II in his invasion of the kingdom in the second year of his reign (late 760s) (*Kuhrt, 1995a: 556–7). It apparently marked the southern limit of Sarduri's campaign.

CHLI I: 284–5.

Mushki see **Phrygia**.

Musilanum Middle Bronze Age locality in the district of Talhayum, which belonged to the region called Ida-maras in the Habur triangle of northern Mesopotamia. It was noted for a special type of edible locust (*LKM 43).

Musri (1) Country east of the Tigris r., attested in M2 and early M1 Assyrian texts. In the earliest known reference to it, the country was conquered by the Assyrian king Ashur-uballit (1365–1330), perhaps in the context of his campaign against the Subarians, as reported by his third successor Adad-nirari I (*RIMA 1: 132). Following its conquest, Musri was incorporated into the Assyrian kingdom. But a rebellion in the reign of Shalmaneser I (1274–1245) prompted an Assyrian invasion of its territory and the capture and sack of its chief city, Arinu, which was razed to the ground (**RIMA* 1: 183). Further hostility in the reign of Tiglath-pileser I (1114–1076) led to a siege of Arinu, which was lifted when the people submitted to the Assyrians; regular tribute payments were imposed upon them (**RIMA* 2: 23). Other expeditions against Musri are attested in the reigns of Ashur-bel-kala (1073–1056; **RIMA* 2: 102) and Ashur-dan II (934–912; **RIMA* 2: 134). The region is certainly associated with the Mt Musri/ Musur which is attested in Neo-Assyrian texts. Sargon II claims to have built his new city, Dur-Sharrukin (Khorsabad), at the foot of Mt Musri, and using the springs there Sennacherib constructed his famous water-supply system for Nineveh.

Musri (2) Iron Age land and city in southern Anatolia or northern Syria. The occurrence of the name in a C8 Aramaic treaty found near Aleppo makes a northern Syrian location more likely, and an identification has recently been proposed with the kingdom called Masuwari (Aramaean Til-Barsip) in Neo-Hittite texts (Makinson, 2002–5). The centre of this kingdom was the city on the site of Tell Ahmar (q.v.), located on the east bank of the middle Euphrates.

Several references to Musri occur in the texts of the Assyrian king Shalmaneser III (858–824). It is the name, for example, of one of the participating states which fought against Shalmaneser in the battle of Qarqar (q.v.) in 853 (**RIMA* 3: 23), and of the country which sent Shalmaneser a tribute consisting of a range of exotic animals – including a rhinoceros(?), elephants, monkeys, apes, and a water buffalo (**RIMA* 3: 150). The former may well have been a Syrian country; the latter is commonly (though not universally) identified with Egypt (see Bunnens, 2006: 90, 92). (Musri was the name by which Egypt was commonly known in the western Asian world.)

Nashef (1982), Kessler (*RlA* 8: 497), Bunnens (2006: 88–96).

Mussian, Tepe (map 12) Settlement-mound encompassing an area of c. 14 ha, located on the Deh Luran plain (q.v.) in southwestern Iran, c. 90 km north west of Susa. It is the largest site on the plain. The site was excavated by J. E. Gautier and G. Lampre on behalf of a French mission to Iran in 1905, and briefly re-examined by E. Carter and J. Neely in 1969 during a survey of the Deh Luran plain. Tepe Khazineh and Tepe Ali Abad are other sites lying close to Tepe Mussian and commonly grouped with it under its name.

Tepe Mussian's history of occupation begins with a village settlement in M6 (late Neolithic), which continued until mid M4 (Chalcolithic period). The site was abandoned in the Uruk and subsequent Proto-Elamite periods (c. 3500 to 2800), but entered into a vigorous new phase c. 2800, when it grew rapidly in size, becoming the most important Early Bronze Age site on the Deh Luran plain. A distinctive feature of this period in the site's history is an assemblage of polychrome pottery, datable to the middle centuries of M3 (from perhaps as early as 2800 to c. 2400), and including large numbers of small jars painted black and red on a buff-coloured background with depictions of animal, plant, and geometric motifs. Archaeological surveys point to a population decline in the Deh Luran plain during the last centuries of M3, which inevitably affected Tepe Mussian. This became particularly marked during the early centuries of M2, and by the middle of M2 the site had been abandoned. There are very few architectural remains from any period of the site's existence, and no indication as to whether or not the settlement was ever fortified. Its anc. name is unknown, though an identification with the Elamite city of Urua (Arawa) has been suggested.

Gautier and Lampre (1905), de Miroschedji (*OEANE* 5: 186–7).

Mutalu Small Middle Bronze Age town in Babylonia, c. 25 km northeast of Kish (**RIME* 4: 658–9). Inscribed bricks found at mod. Ishan Dhahak tell of the building of the wall of Mutalu by a local ruler.

Mesop. 106.

Mutamutassa Late Bronze Age country in western Anatolia, within or near the territory of the Lukka Lands. It was among the countries captured by the renegade Hittite vassal Madduwatta during his campaigns in western Anatolia (early C14) (* *HDT* 158).

Mutiabal (Mutebal) Land/population group in northern Babylonia, centred on the city of Kazallu, and inhabited by a southern group of the Mutebal tribe. It is attested in Middle Bronze Age Mesopotamian texts, which record Mutiabal's hostilities with the kingdom of Larsa in C19, its involvement as a Babylonian subject state in Babylon's war with the Elamites (mid C18), and in this context its ill-fated rebellion against the Babylonian king Hammurabi (1792–1750). Subsequently it was one of the regions which revolted against Hammurabi's successor, Samsu-iluna. For further information on its activities, see under **Kazallu**. A northern Mesopotamian group of Mutebal are attested in the Mari archives from the reign of Zimri-Lim (1774–1762).

LKM 17, 61–3, 589 (refs).

Mutkinu Iron Age city in northwestern Mesopotamia, strategically located near an important river-crossing on the east bank of the Euphrates near its confluence with the Sajur. Tell Hamis near Qubba, 5 km east of Til-Barsip, has been suggested as a possible location. The city was established c. 1100 by the Assyrian king Tiglath-pileser I, but during the reign of Ashur-rabi II (1013–973) an Aramaean king seized control of it, along with the city of Pitru which lay on the the Euphrates' opposite bank. For the next 150 years Mutkinu remained under Aramaean control, becoming one of the cities in the Euphrates region attached to the Iron Age kingdom of Bit-Adini. In 856, when the kingdom was ruled by Ahuni, these cities were conquered by the Assyrian king Shalmaneser III. Following the restoration of Mutkinu to Assyrian control, Shalmaneser resettled it (as also Pitru) with an Assyrian population (**RIMA* 3:19).

Lipiński (2000: 163–8).

Muzunnum City in northwestern(?) Syria, first attested in the Middle Bronze Age Mari archives. It subsequently appears in the list of Syrian place-names recorded by the C15 pharaoh Tuthmosis III (in the form *M-ḏ-n*), and in a hieroglyphic Luwian inscription of Uratamis, a C9 king of Hamath (in the form Musanipa). Lipiński proposes a location c. 30 km southwest of Aleppo. The city is possibly to be identified with the site of Tell Maraq. Its name is of Hurrian origin.

Lipiński (2000: 249–50, 298).

Mycale, Mt Located on the Aegean coast of Anatolia north of Miletus, on a headland jutting out towards the island of Samos and overlooking the city of Priene

(*BAGRW* 61 E2). At the foot of the mountain, in the sanctuary of the god Poseidon Heliconius, representatives of the member states of the Ionian League assembled to formulate common policy (Herodotus 1.148) (see **Panionium**). In 479 the Mycale promontory provided the setting for the final land and sea engagement between the Persians and allied Greek forces, in the aftermath of Xerxes' abortive invasion of the Greek mainland. The battle resulted in the destruction of the Persian army and fleet (Herodotus 9.96–107). In Greek sources, Mycale is first attested in Homer (*Iliad* 2.869) as part of the Carian homeland at the time of the Trojan War.

Mykoi see **Maka**.

Mylasa (*Milas*) (map 5) M1 BCE–M1 CE city in Caria, southwestern Anatolia. The city is first attested in C7 when its ruler, Arselis, supported the Lydian Gyges' successful attempt to seize the throne of Lydia (c. 685). With the fall of the Lydian empire to

Figure 73 Mt Mycale, with temple of Athena (Priene) in foreground.

the Persian emperor Cyrus II c. 546, Mylasa along with the rest of Caria came under Persian control. In 500 its ruler was a man called Oliatus (Herodotus 5.37). Some time after the Greek defeat of the Persian forces in 479, Mylasa became a member of the Athenian Confederacy (see glossary). It returned to Persian control in 386, in accordance with the terms of the 'King's Peace' (see glossary). In this new period of Persian domination, Mylasa became the capital of Caria, under the immediate authority of a local ruling family called the Hecatomnid dynasty (Strabo 14.2.23). Mausolus (c. 377–353), the third ruler of this dynasty, probably shifted the capital to its location at mod. Milas from an original location at Peçin Kale, 5 km to the south. The remains of a temple on the latter site may be those of the temple of Carian Zeus, referred to by both Herodotus (1.171) and Strabo (14.2.23). Later in his reign, Mausolus made Halicarnassus (mod. Bodrum) his capital. Along with other cities subject to Persia, Mylasa was liberated by Alexander the Great in 334. Following Alexander's death, Mylasa was subject first to the Ptolemies, then to the Seleucids, and then to the Rhodians. Under Roman rule it became an important administrative centre of the province of Asia.

The city's Hellenistic and Roman remains include several temples (it once contained three temples dedicated to the god Zeus), a well-preserved arched gateway into the city (whose walls have now disappeared), a theatre, and numerous tombs. The finest of the tombs is a two-storeyed structure probably of C2 or C1 date, bearing a resemblance to, and perhaps influenced by, the Mausoleum of Halicarnassus.

Bean (1971: 31–44; *PECS* 601–2).

Myndus (map 5) M1 city in Caria, southwestern Anatolia, located 18 km west of mod. Bodrum (Halicarnassus). The original city, which was founded by Lelegian colonists, probably lay some 3 km southeast of the later city, on the hilltop site now called Bozdağ. Remains of a circuit wall can still be seen there. This first city was a member of the Athenian Confederacy (see glossary) in C5. Its annual contribution of one-twelfth of a talent to the Confederacy's treasury was a relatively small sum, giving clear indication of the city's lack of importance at this time. Then in C4 Mausolus, ruler of Caria, decided to enhance the city's status. He did so by refounding it in a new location and rebuilding it on a much grander scale. The site he chose for this enterprise is now called Gümüşlük. Its excellent harbour was no doubt a major factor in Mausolus' choice of the site. The new city was protected by a wall 3.5 km long, a large part of which still survives. The effectiveness of Myndus' defence system was put to the test within a couple of decades of its refounding, when the city came under attack from Alexander the Great. It stood the test well, for Myndus was one of the very few cities in Alexander's campaigns of conquest that successfully resisted the Macedonian's attempts to capture them.

Bean (1971: 116–19; *PECS* 602).

Myous (map 5) Classical Greek city located on the Aegean coast of Anatolia in the region of Ionia, a few km north of Miletus. In Classical tradition it was founded by a certain Cydrelus, bastard son of Codrus, a legendary king of Athens (Strabo 14.1.3). Myous was one of the twelve members of the Ionian League (see **Panionium**). In the 460s, the city was allegedly given by the Persian king Xerxes to the Athenian Themistocles after the latter had fled his homeland and sought refuge in western Anatolia (Strabo 14.1.10). Xerxes' purpose in presenting Themistocles with the city was, according to Strabo, to keep him supplied with fish. Myous subsequently became a member of the Athenian Confederacy (see glossary). Strabo also reports that due to the silting up of the Maeander r., the city lost its location on the sea. It also lost its independence, and subsequently its population, to Miletus. The site's scanty remains include parts of the foundations of two temples, one dedicated to the god Dionysus and dating back to mid C6, and the other a temple of Apollo Terebintheus, the city's chief deity.

Bean (1966: 244–6; *PECS* 602–3).

Myra (map 15) M1 BCE–M1 CE town in Lycia, southwestern Anatolia, 20 km west of mod. Finike. Monuments, coins, and inscriptions in the epichoric language date occupation of the site back to at least C5. A number of the inscriptions appear on the rock-cut tombs (though only a small minority of these are inscribed) which are carved in two groups, a western and an eastern group, into the cliff-face located to the west of the Roman theatre. The first and more impressive group consists predominantly of house-type tombs (i.e. tombs which replicate the main features of Lycian house-façades), but also includes more rudimentary burial chambers and a few structures whose façades are modelled on Greek temples, similar to the temple tombs at Telmessus in western Lycia and Caunus in Caria. A number of the tombs are embellished with relief carvings. The warrior motif sometimes features in these reliefs as elsewhere in Lycian relief sculptures. Two warriors carrying shields are depicted on one tomb, and on another a man is reclining on a couch with his wife sitting beside him and three warrior-like figures, perhaps his sons, standing to his left. In typical Lycian fashion, the tombs are intended for multiple burials, and contain couches, cut into the rock within the tomb-chambers, for the reception of the deceased. They are closed by sliding doors of stone, most of which have long since been smashed. One of the most noteworthy of the funerary monuments is the so-called Painted Tomb, a house-type structure on which appears a relief scene depicting eleven life-size human figures. The central figure is a reclining, bearded man who raises a wine-cup. The other figures are probably members of his family. While the overall interpretation of the composition is unclear, it may represent a scene from everyday family life rather than a funerary scene – thus nurturing an illusion that life after death continues as it did before death. The carvings were originally painted in red, blue, yellow, and purple colours, but practically all traces of paint have now disappeared.

Myra was among Lycia's largest and most important cities. During the period of the Lycian League, which operated from C2 BCE until C4 CE, it was one of six League members which had the privilege of three votes in the assembly – the highest number of votes that could be assigned to any League member.

Apart from the Lycian tombs, the most noteworthy material remains on the site date to the Roman period. These include the theatre, referred to above, and a granary with an inscription over the door which associates the building with the early C2 CE emperor Hadrian. In C4 CE Myra was the seat of the bishopric of (St) Nicholas, the remains of whose church are located at the western end of the village of Demre, 3 km from the Lycian site.

Bean (*PECS* 603–4; 1978: 120–30).

Myrina (map 5) City on the coast of Aeolis in western Anatolia, 37 km south of Pergamum. According to Greek legendary tradition, it was founded by an Amazon

Figure 74 Myra, rock-tombs.

queen called Myrrhine/Myrina (Diodorus 3.54–5). In C5 it was a member of the Athenian Confederacy (see glossary), and assessed at the relatively high sum of one talent as its annual contribution to the Confederacy. According to Xenophon (*Hellenica* 3.1.6), the Persian king (doubtless Xerxes) handed the cities Myrina and Grynium over to a Greek called Gongylus from the city of Eretria on the island of Euboea, as a reward for Gongylus' support of Xerxes' campaign against Greece in 481. (Gongylus had been exiled from his homeland for his treachery.) Nothing else is known of Myrina's history prior to the Roman imperial period. In 17 CE it was destroyed by earthquake and rebuilt with the assistance of the Roman emperor Tiberius. A large necropolis of over 4,000 graves was excavated between 1880 and 1882, but nothing of these can be seen today. Inscriptions and grave goods, including hundreds of terracotta figurines, date the necropolis to the late Hellenistic period.

Bean (1966: 106–10; *PECS* 604).

Mysia (maps 4, 5) M1 country located in northwestern Anatolia south of the Troad and extending to the Aegean coast, opposite the island of Lesbos (Herodotus 1.160). Strabo (12.4.4–5) located its northern limits between Bithynia and the mouth of the Aesepus r. in the Troad; it also shared a border with Phrygia. The Trojan Catalogue in Homer's *Iliad* (2.858) lists a contingent from Mysia, led by Chromis, among Troy's allies in the Trojan War. Mysia probably covered much of the territory occupied in the Late Bronze Age by the Arzawan kingdom called Seha River Land, though its boundaries fluctuated throughout its history. In Greek tradition, Mysia was close enough to Troy for the Greeks to land on its coast and begin plundering it, in the mistaken belief that they had actually reached Troy itself. Telephus, heir of the Mysian king Teuthras, succeeded in killing many of the invaders before he was finally driven into flight by Achilles. Herodotus claims that the Mysians were originally emigrants from Lydia (7.74), that the eponymous kings Lydus and Mysus were brothers (1.171), and that the Mysians were among the Anatolian peoples conquered by the Lydian king Croesus in C6 (1.28). A contingent of Mysians under the command of Artaphrenes, son of Artaphrenes, is listed by Herodotus (7.74) among the forces assembled by Xerxes for his invasion of Greece in 481. In 395 the Spartan king Agesilaus II invaded Mysia, with the intention of pressuring the Mysians into joining his campaign for the liberation of the Anatolian Greeks from Persian sovereignty (*Hellenica Oxyrhynchia* 21.1–3, 5–6; 22.1–3 = **PE* 374–5, no. 39). Some of the Mysians chose to join his army. But when others launched an attack on his forces, they were ambushed and suffered heavy casualties. Their alleged treachery prompted Agesilaus to carry out further reprisals against them.

N

Nabatu M1 tribal people, probably of North Arabian origin, located in eastern Babylonia. They are included in the list of thirty-five so-called Aramaean tribes conquered by the Assyrian king Tiglath-pileser III, probably in his first regnal year (745) (**Tigl. III* 158–9). The Nabatu are very likely to be identified with the Nabayatu tribe, attested in the reign of the Assyrian king Ashurbanipal (668–630/627). It is possible, but by no means certain, that they were forerunners of the Nabataean Arabs of the Hellenistic age, whose chief city was Petra in Jordan.

Lipiński (2000: 448–50).

Nabul(a) (Nabulu, Nabur, ***Girnavaz***) Late Bronze and early Iron Age city located in the northern Habur triangle, just to the north of Nusaybin. When the Hanigalbatean king Wasashatta rebelled against Assyrian sovereignty, Nabula was among the cities conquered by Adad-nirari I (1307–1275) in the course of crushing the rebellion (**RIMA* 1: 131). In C11 the Assyrian king Ashur-bel-kala (1073–1056) fought a battle with the Aramaeans there (**RIMA* 2: 102). Nabulu was among the twenty-seven cities which rebelled against the Assyrian king Shalmaneser III (858–824) towards the end of his reign (**RIMA* 3: 183). One of two Neo-Assyrian documents excavated at Girnavaz in 1984 mentions the anc. settlement name Nabul, thus vindicating Kessler's proposed location for the city at Girnavaz, 4 km north of Nusaybin (Kessler, 1980: 208–9; Lipiński, 2000: 139 map).

Röllig (*RlA* 9: 31), Lipiński (2000: 110–11, 152), Radner (2006: 299–300).

Nagar (Nawar) Bronze Age city and kingdom in the Habur r. region of northern Mesopotamia. The city is probably to be identified with the site of Tell Brak. It is first attested in texts from Ebla, dating to C24, which indicate the kingdom's close commercial links with Ebla. It is also mentioned in texts from mid M3 Tell Beydar. During C24, Nagar appears to have been the most important state in Upper Mesopotamia, its influence extending throughout the Habur region. The city was one of three major urban centres in the region at this time. Remains of the other two are the large mounds Tell Mozan (Urkesh) and Tell Leilan (Shehna, Shubat-Enlil). Both cities probably maintained their independence from Nagar, despite the latter's overall dominance of the region. Nagar's own status is uncertain during the Akkadian period (c. 2334–2193). But towards the end of M3, Nagar and Urkesh were linked as the two capitals of a Hurrian dynasty, under the rule of a king called Atal-sen.

Middle Bronze Age attestations of Nagar occur in texts from Mari dating to the reign of the Mariote king Yahdun-Lim (1810–1794). The city was apparently the site of a decisive battle between Yahdun-Lim and the Assyrian king Shamshi-Adad I (1796–1775), but otherwise appears to have been relatively insignificant in this period, when it was under the authority of the city of Kahat. There are no further occurrences of the name Nagar after the Middle Bronze Age (Old Babylonian period), but the city is probably to be identified with Nawar (or one of the cities so called), which was subject to Mitanni. (On the question of whether there were two cities called Nawar, one north and one south of Kahat, see Matthews and Eidem, 1993: 204–5. They suggest identifying the northern one with the later Nabula.)

Matthews and Eidem (1993), *Archi (1998), Eidem (*RlA* 9: 75–7).

Nagiate Iron Age city in the middle Euphrates region north of the city of Hindanu. During the course of his last recorded campaign in 885, the Assyrian king Tukulti-Ninurta II (890–884) spent the night in Nagiate on his progress up the Euphrates (**RIMA* 2: 175). He had to travel through rugged country to reach the city, which lay close to, but does not seem to have been a part of, the land of Laqe. Lipiński believes that Nagiate must refer to the islands in front of Abu Kamal, locating the city at Baguz aš-Šnamali close to the Iraqi–Syrian border, where there are large and small islands near both the right and left banks of the river.

Lipiński (2000: 94).

Nagibum Middle Bronze Age city in the south of the Jebel Sinjar, northern Mesopotamia, not far from Andarig. Zimri-Lim, king of Mari (1774–1762), encamped his troops there in preparation for his siege of Andarig (**LKM* 394). The presence of the Mariote forces at Nagibum prompted an army of Ibal-pi-El II, king of Eshnunna, to raise its siege of the city of Kurda, which lay to the north of Andarig, and proceed towards the Mariote king's encampment, presumably for a military showdown. Before confronting the Mariote army, however, Ibal-pi-El turned north, occupying the city of Shehna/Shubat-Enlil in the kingdom of Apum.

Mesop. 202–3.

Nagidus (map 4) M1 BCE–M1 CE city on the southeastern coast of Anatolia, in the region of Cilicia Tracheia/Aspera (Rough Cilicia). According to Pomponius Mela (1.77), it was founded by colonists from the island of Samos, which lay off Anatolia's western coast. An island called Nagidussa was associated with it (probably the small island which lies just offshore to the south; *BAGRW* 66 B4). The silver coinage of the city attests to its flourishing existence in C5 and C4. The most notable material remains of the site are those of a fragmentary circuit wall of mixed polygonal and ashlar masonry. It is possible that the city is to be identified with Late Bronze Age Nahita (q.v.).

Bean and Mitford (1970: 191–3), Bean (*PECS* 605).

Nagila, Tel (map 8) 4 ha settlement-mound on Israel's coastal plain 28 km east of Gaza. Its history of occupation extends from the Chalcolithic (M4) to the Mameluke period (C16 CE), with a number of gaps in between. The site was excavated in 1962 and 1963 by R. Amiran on behalf of the Institute for Mediterranean Studies in Jerusalem. Fourteen occupation levels were identified. The settlement's Early Bronze Age phase, represented by the remains of mudbrick houses on stone foundations, was followed by a period of abandonment lasting 600 to 700 years before the site was reoccupied in the Middle Bronze Age, c. 1750. The remains of residential architecture, two public buildings, and an elaborate defence system represent the material culture of this, the most prosperous period in the settlement's existence. Only meagre remains survive from Nagila's Late Bronze Age, Iron Age, and Hellenistic–Byzantine phases.

Amiran and Eitan (*NEAEHL* 3: 1079–81).

Nagitu Iron Age city in Elam, probably to be located (according to Frame) on an island in the marshes. Marduk-appla-iddina (biblical Merodach-baladan), the Chaldaean tribal leader who twice occupied the throne of Babylon, sought refuge here in 700, in his flight from the Assyrian king Sennacherib (see under **Babylon, Babylonia**). In 694 the city was captured and looted by Sennacherib's troops.

Frame (*RlA* 9: 80).

Nagsu Early Bronze Age Sumerian city in southern Mesopotamia belonging to the city-state of Umma. A military garrison was stationed there.

Lafont (*DCM* : 872).

Nahita Late Bronze Age city in southern Anatolia, attested in the fragmentary remains of the Annals of the Hittite king Hattusili III (1267–1237). It appears along with a number of other cities/lands in an account of military action undertaken by Hattusili in the region of the Lukka Lands. Identifications have been proposed with mod. Niğde (where the Iron Age city Nahitiya was located; q.v.) and the Classical city Nagidus (q.v.) on the coast of Cilicia Tracheia/Aspera (Rough Cilicia).

Hawkins (1995: 56), *Gurney (1997).

Nahitiya (*Niğde*) (map 18) Iron Age city in southern Anatolia, probably belonging to the kingdom of Tuwana which lay in the southern part of the region called Tabal. A Luwian hieroglyphic inscription found at Aktaş (formerly Andaval) was authored by a certain Saruwanis who styles himself 'the ruler, the lord of Nahitiya'. This man was apparently a C8 predecessor of Tuwana's king Warpalawas (thus *CHLI*), and his attestation as ruler of Nahitiya appears to indicate that Nahitiya was at this time part of the kingdom of Tuwana.

**CHLI* I: 514–15.

Nahlasi Iron Age city in northern Syria, located in the frontier region between the kingdoms of Arpad (Bit-Agusi) and Hamath. In early C8 these kingdoms were ruled respectively by Artta-shumki (I) and Zakur. Probably in 796, the Assyrian king Adad-nirari III and his commander-in-chief Shamshi-ilu defined, or redefined, the boundary between their kingdoms, stipulating the Orontes r. as the dividing line. Nahlasi and all its associated lands and settlements were allocated to Attar-shumki. The text which records this is inscribed on a stele, now commonly known as the Antakya stele, which was found near the Orontes r. not far from Antakya (**RIMA* 3: 203–4).

Naharina (Naharima) see **Mitanni**.

Nahur Northern Mesopotamian city located near one of the tributaries of the Habur r. in the vicinity of mod. Qamishli, attested in a Sargonic itinerary of late M3, as well as in M2 Mari texts and M2 and early M1 Assyrian texts. During the Middle Bronze Age, the city came under the control of Zimri-Lim, king of Mari (1774–1762), and was the centre of one of his kingdom's four administrative districts in the upper Ida-maras (q.v.) region. It figures in a number of letters in the Mari archives (*LKM* 618, refs), which indicate that it was used as a place of assembly by the kings of this region. The assembly was convened there for the kings to renew their allegiance to Zimri-Lim in the presence of their immediate superior Haya-Sumu, king of Ilan-sura (**LKM* 311, no. 26.347). Zimri-Lim's hold upon the city seems to have been fairly tenuous, to judge from an urgent letter sent to him by Shaknum, an official of Nahur, begging for troops to prevent the city liberating itself from Mariote control (*LKM 311, no. 26.348). In the Late Bronze Age, Nahur was conquered and plundered by the Assyrian king Adad-nirari I (1307–1275) (*RIMA 1: 159–60). Documents from the reign of Shalmaneser I (1274–1245) refer to a governor of Nahur. And the city (or at least a city called Nahur) may also figure among the conquests of Adad-nirari II (911–891) during a fourth campaign which the king conducted against the Nairi lands (*RIMA 2: 149) – but the reading *Nahur* in this passage is uncertain.

Kupper (*RlA* 9: 86–7), **Mesop.* 298.

Nairi (map 20) Mountainous region north of the upper Tigris r., stretching between mod. Diyarbakır and Lake Van and then to the southeast, to the region west of Lake Urmia. It was not a polity in its own right but contained numerous small principalities. Lying just beyond the northern and northeastern borders of Assyria, Nairi is attested primarily in Middle and Neo-Assyrian inscriptions of the Late Bronze Age and Iron Age.

In the former period, the Assyrian king Tukulti-Ninurta I (1244–1208) conducted a campaign against the fierce tribal groups which inhabited the Nairi lands; he claims to have fought forty kings and then imposed tax and tribute upon them (*RIMA 1: 244). Further Assyrian campaigns against Nairi were undertaken by Tiglath-pileser I (1114–1076), as recorded in his inscriptions (*RIMA 2: 21–2, 34, 52, **Chav.* 157–60). Tiglath-pileser states that he confronted and defeated a coalition of twenty-three kings (thirty in another account) under the leadership of Senu, king of Dayenu (q.v.). The lands of the coalition included Dayenu, Himua, Paiteru, and Tummu (*RIMA 2: 21). Following his victory, Tiglath-pileser plundered the lands and destroyed their cities. He captured their kings but subsequently released them, taking their sons as hostages for their good behaviour, and imposing a large tribute of horses and cattle upon them (*RIMA 2: 22). He brought back from the mountains of Nairi obsidian, *haltu* stone, and haematite to be deposited in the temple of the god Adad in Ashur (*RIMA 2: 29).

Subsequently, Adad-nirari II (911–891) led at least four campaigns against Nairi (*RIMA 2: 148). Between 889 and 886 the region was the object of Assyrian campaigns conducted by Tukulti-Ninurta II (*RIMA 2: 171–2, 180). His son and successor Ashurnasirpal II (883–859) carried out further operations in Nairi in his second and fifth regnal years, and received tribute from its kings in the city of Tushhan, which lay north of the Kashiyari range (mod. Tur ʿAbdin) (*RIMA 2: 202–3, 209–11).

From the reign of Ashurnasirpal's own son and successor Shalmaneser III, the term Nairi began to be used in a new sense. It was still on one occasion applied to the aforementioned region north of the upper Tigris: in his fifteenth regnal year (844), Shalmaneser marched into the Nairi lands, and erected a statue of himself on a mountain cliff at the source of the Tigris (*RIMA 3: 39). However, other passages in Shalmaneser's royal inscriptions indicate that the term now also denoted a specific region to the southwest of Lake Urmia, centred on the land of Hubushkia. Shalmaneser campaigned in this Nairi region in his first regnal year (858), and reports washing his weapons in the 'Sea of Nairi' (most likely Lake Urmia) where he erected an inscribed stele (*RIMA 3: 9, 15, 21). His son and successor Shamshi-Adad V (823–811) conducted at least three more campaigns in Nairi (*RIMA 3: 183–4). On his third campaign, he crossed the Greater Zab r. on his way to Nairi, where he received horses from the rulers of Hubushkia, Sunbu, Mannaea, Parsua, and Taurla; later on in the account he lists by name 'all the kings of the land Nairi' (*RIMA* 3: 184–6). Shamshi-Adad's son and successor Adad-nirari III claims to have conquered the whole of Nairi (*RIMA* 3: 211–12). Sargon II reports receiving the tribute of Ianzu, king of Nairi, in his fortified city of Hubushkia (*Sargon II* 452 for refs).

In C9 Urartian sources written in Assyrian, Nairi is used to denote Urartu itself, presumably reflecting the absorption of at least part of the former (northern) Nairi lands into the Urartian state. In C7 native Assyrian sources, Nairi is occasionally used in an archaizing manner to denote the province of Amedi (mod. Diyarbakır).

(H. D. Baker)
Salvini (*RlA* 9: 87–91).

Nami, Tel (map 8) Coastal settlement-mound in Israel, located on a peninsula 15 km south of Haifa. Remains of Middle and Late Bronze Age occupation have been uncovered there. Similar occupation levels have been unearthed at a site 100 m to the east of the mound, called Nami East. Thick layers of sand separated the levels in both cases. The sites' exposure to harsh elemental forces is held accountable for their shortlived existence. The fact that they were built there in the first place almost certainly indicates that the locations were considered beneficial for international trade. Small finds from the sites reflect trading contacts with Egypt, Crete, Cyprus, and the Mycenaean world. During Late Bronze IIB, changes in sea level leading to higher groundwater levels may have been responsible for the abandonment of Nami East as a living area, and its use in C13 as a necropolis. Many of the cemetery's grave goods were looted in antiquity. But those that escaped the tomb-robber give some indication of the wealth of the local inhabitants, which no doubt they derived from their commercial activities. Large quantities of bronze artefacts and jewellery, and many items of gold, silver, faience, and ivory, testify to an affluent society – especially since these are but the remnants of the original funerary goods plundered by the looters. Artzy, the site's excavator, observed that in the first years of C12, Nami served as an entrepôt for a trade network that combined maritime and desert routes via the valleys to Transjordan and beyond. (It is interesting to note in this respect that the necropolis contained several double-pithos burials similar to those uncovered in the cemetery at Tell es-Sa'idiyeh; q.v.) None the less, storms, sand, sea waves, and shifting sea levels with consequent damage to building foundations eventually prevailed over commercial considerations. Neither Tel Nami nor Nami East outlived its Bronze Age phases (though the tell was partially reoccupied many centuries later in the Byzantine age).

Following surveys in the 1960s and a brief excavation of Tel Nami in 1975 by M. Dothan, a comprehensive, multidisciplinary study of the site was undertaken in 1985 under the direction of M. Artzy for the University of Haifa. It involved geomorphological studies, further archaeological excavation, and land and underwater surveys.

Artzy (1990; *NEAEHL* 3: 1095–8).

Namri (Namru, Namar) (map 13) Land located in the region of the upper Diyala valley on the western fringes of the Zagros mountains. Namar is attested as early as M3, in geographical lists dating to the Early Dynastic period (c. 2900–2334). In a letter from Shemshara (q.v.) of the Old Babylonian period, it figures as a region located between Elam and the kingdom of Nikkum (Niqqu). It is also known from Middle Babylonian inscriptions; one source from this period refers to a governor of Namar and the land Halman.

Namri/Namru is known to us from Assyrian texts of M1, where it appears in a number of campaigns undertaken by Assyrian kings in the region. It is first attested in the Annals of Adad-nirari II (911–891), who reports on a campaign which took him beyond the Lesser Zab r. into the land of the Lullumu (Lullubu), into one of the regions called Habhu in Assyrian texts (see **Habhu (5)**), and into Zamua as far as the passes of Namru (***RIMA* 2: 148). In 843, Shalmaneser III won a battle against Marduk-mudammiq, king of Namri, plundered his lands, and deported his troops to Assyria. He set up a new king, Ianzu, as ruler of the land in place of Marduk-mudammiq, who escaped capture by fleeing to the mountains (***RIMA* 3: 40, 67). But Ianzu must have turned against his overlord, for in 834 Shalmaneser conducted a further campaign against Namri, while Ianzu was still king there, capturing, plundering, and destroying its cities (***RIMA* 3: 67–8). These included Sihishalah, Bit-Tamul, Bit-Shakki, and Bit-Shedi. Ianzu like his predecessor fled to the mountains, as did other refugees, from the havoc inflicted upon the land. But the refugees were flushed out and slaughtered. A further campaign against Namri was led by Shalmaneser's commander-in-chief Dayyan-Ashur in 828 (***RIMA* 3: 71). In 814 the land joined a military coalition in support of the Babylonian king Marduk-balassu-iqbi in his confrontation with the Assyrian king Shamshi-Adad V near Dur-Papsukkal (***RIMA* 3: 188). The Assyrian king Adad-nirari III conducted another campaign against Namri in 797, according to the Eponym Chronicle entry (see glossary) for that year (*Millard, 1994: 35, ***RIMA* 3: 212).

Continuing unrest and resistance to Assyrian overlordship were no doubt the prompts for further campaigns against Namri and other countries in the vicinity. One of these was conducted by Tiglath-pileser III in the second year of his reign (744) (***Tigl. III* 164–5); in this account, Namri is numbered among the 'provinces of the mighty Medes'. The new Assyrian king succeeded in asserting his control over the rebel states, and Namri appears to have remained submissive to Assyrian rule until perhaps the early years of the reign of Tiglath-pileser's grandson Sargon II (721–705). Some time during the first half of his reign, Sargon must again have campaigned in the region, for he reports that while he was in Parsua in 714, Namri was among three lands (the other two were Sangibuti and Bit-Abdadani) which sent representatives to him with a substantial tribute payment and a pledge of allegiance – mindful of the devastation he had inflicted upon them in a former year (***ARAB* II: 76). Namri thenceforth disappears from Assyrian records, and may in fact have been permanently lost to the Assyrians some time prior to the fall of their empire in late C7.

Kessler (*RlA* 9: 91–2).

Nappigu (Nanpigi, ***Manbiğ***) Iron Age city in northwestern Mesopotamia southwest of the confluence of the Euphrates and Sajur rivers (see Lipiński, 2000: 167 map). It was among the cities belonging to the Iron Age kingdom of Bit-Adini which in 856 (when the kingdom was ruled by Ahuni) were attacked and conquered by the Assyrian king Shalmaneser III during his military operations in the Euphrates region (***RIMA* 3: 19). The conquered towns (which included Aligu, Mutkinu, Pitru, and Rugulitu) were assigned new Assyrian names. Nappigu was thenceforth called Lita-Ashur, and a palace was established there as a royal residence. The military campaigns conducted by Shalmaneser in this year resulted in the total conquest of Bit-Adini and its absorption into the Assyrian empire. Nevertheless, Nanpigi was listed among Tiglath-pileser III's conquests in northern Syria in 738 (*Tigl.* III 102–3, 208–9, 234–5). A stone vessel with an inscription of a Persian king, Artaxerxes, was reportedly found at the site. Lipiński notes that Manbiğ, the original Aramaic form of the name, means 'spring-site', and Postgate observes that the town was famous in Classical times for its freshwater springs.

Postgate (*RlA* 9: 164), Lipiński (2000: 180).

Naqarabani see Aqarbani.

Naqsh-i Rustam (map 16) Cliff-site in southwestern Iran, 6 km north of Persepolis, containing four rock-cut tombs and a number of reliefs. The reliefs date to the M1 Neo-Elamite, mid M1 Persian, and mid M1 CE Sasanian periods. All four tombs belong to the Persian Achaemenid period (C6–4). The one surviving Elamite relief is largely obliterated by a scene carved over it in the reign of the C3 CE Sasanian king Bahram II. All that remains of the original is the depiction of an attendant who stands behind two seated deities. The Achaemenid period is represented by the tombs, along with the reliefs, of four kings. Only the earliest of these has an inscription, which enables it to be assigned to Darius I (522–486). The uninscribed tombs have been attributed to his successors Xerxes, Artaxerxes I, and probably Darius II. The façade of Darius' tomb, cruciform in shape (copied in the tombs of his successors), contains three registers. The bottom one is blank, the middle one depicts the front of a building – in fact a representation of the façade of Darius' palace at Persepolis – and the top one shows the king standing on a three-stepped podium and praying to the god Ahuramazda before an altar covered in flames. On either side of this scene, members of the royal court are represented – weapon-bearers and robed figures approaching the king to pay him homage. Supporting the platform on which king and god appear are two tiers of human figures, thirty in all, symbolizing all the lands over which Darius held sway. The symbolism is made clear in the tomb's main inscription, in which Darius acknowledges Ahuramazda's beneficence in granting this vast empire to him, as reflected in the personifications of the realm's thirty lands. The tombs were intended for the burial of the king and his closest family members. Darius' tomb contains a 19 m long corridor which gives access to three burial chambers, each with three burial cists intended for the reception of sarcophagi containing the deceased. All these spaces were carved out of the living rock. The cists were sealed with heavy stone lids.

A stone tower standing opposite the tombs and now known as the Kaba-i Zardusht closely resembles the so-called 'prison of Solomon' tower (Zendan-i Suleiman) at Pasargadae (q.v.), and presumably served the same purpose – whatever that was.

Eight rock reliefs were carved on the cliff-face during the Sasanian period.

Schmitt (1987; 1991), Seidel (*OEANE* 4: 98–101; *RlA* (9: 165–8).

Nasarum Middle Bronze Age city in southern Babylonia. In 1808 the city fell to Larsa's king Rim-Sin (along with Pi-naratim; q.v.), the year after he had defeated a coalition of enemy forces, including Uruk, Isin, and Babylon.

Charpin (*DCM* 724), *Mesop.* 113.

Figure 75 Naqsh-i Rustam, tombs of Darius I and Xerxes.

Nasbeh, Tell en- (map 8) 3 ha settlement-mound in southern Palestine, 12 km northwest of Jerusalem. Occupation dates initially to the Late Chalcolithic and Early Bronze I periods (the remains of which include tombs and several cave-dwellings), followed by a gap of many centuries before the site was resettled in the Iron Age. Excavations were conducted by W. F. Badè over five seasons between 1926 and 1935 for the Pacific School of Religion in Berkeley, California. Important work on the stratigraphy of the site was subsequently carried out by J. Zorn. Various identifications with biblically attested cities have been proposed for Tell en-Nasbeh. The most favoured is with Mizpah of Benjamin (see **Mizpah**), which lay on the border of Judah and Israel.

The site's earliest Iron Age level, probably of C12 date, is represented by Philistine and local pottery sherds, numerous cisterns and silos cut into the rock, and a wine press. Iron Age II houses uncovered on the site may have had their origins in this earlier period. The Iron Age II town was protected by a casemate wall, 660 m long and incorporating eleven towers. An outer and inner gate complex provided access to the settlement within the walls. The domestic structures of this level, with two or three long rooms (or a long room and a courtyard) and a broadroom across the back, were rebuilt and strengthened several times. Olive oil presses and storage facilities found in six of the buildings indicate the use of some of them for industrial purposes. Most houses had their own cisterns, and some were two storeys high. The settlement also extended outside the walls, as indicated by the remains of houses and agricultural installations in the extra-mural 'suburban' area. On the ridge north and west of the mound, the town's

Figure 76 Naqsh-i Rustam, close-up of Xerxes' tomb.

Iron Age cemetery was located; four of the tombs contained a total of almost 1,600 grave goods. Among the small finds from the site were numerous inscribed objects – ostraca, weights, and scarabs, a cylinder seal, and seal impressions. The most important of the seals belonged to a man called Jaazaniah, who is designated as 'servant of the king'. It has been suggested that this man is to be identified with the Jaazaniah of 2 Kings 25:23, who was among the army officers who came before Gedaliah, the Babylonian-appointed governor at Mizpah.

If Tell en-Nasbeh is in fact Mizpah, then the period of Neo-Babylonian domination (C6), when Mizpah became a provincial administrative centre of the Babylonian empire, was the most important phase in the site's history. The larger, more spacious dwellings of this period, including what may be a 'palace' building with paved, central courtyard, and the new orientation of the buildings, are seen as reflecting a change in the settlement's purpose from that of a border fortress to a minor provincial capital (thus Zorn). Remains of walls, two small kilns, fragments of late C6 to early C5 Greek pottery, and twenty-four seal impressions – all dating to the post-Babylonian period – make clear that settlement at Tell el-Nasbeh continued well into the Persian period (C6–4). There is also evidence (albeit meagre) of later occupation, during the Hellenistic, Roman, and Byzantine periods.

Zorn (*NEAEHL* 3: 1098–102). See also Zorn's website, www.arts.cornell.edu/jrz3/index.htm.

Nasibina see Nisibis.

Nawar see Nagar.

Neandria (map 5) M1 city in the Troad, northwestern Anatolia, located to the south of Troy on a ridge c. 500 m above sea level. The city is first attested in C5 as a member of the Athenian Confederacy (see glossary). In 399 it was among the cities assigned by the Persian satrap Pharnabazus to the governorship of a woman called Mania, after the death of her husband, Zenis. Following Mania's death, it came under the control of the Spartan military commander Dercylidas (Xenophon, *Hellenica* 3.1.16). In 310 Alexander the Great's former general, Antigonus, amalgamated Neandria with the nearby city of Antigoneia, later called Alexander Troas, and transferred its population there.

There are significant remains of Neandria's fortifications, which include recessed gates and eleven towers, dating back to C6 and C5. Houses of the Archaic (C7–6) and Classical (C5–4) periods have also been uncovered, and the site of a stadium has been identified, between the C5–4 houses and the city wall. A number of necropoleis have been found, with interments made between terracotta slabs, in pithoi, in slab caskets, and in monolithic and slab sarcophagi. A sanctuary of Zeus is attested in inscriptions, and the remains of a temple of Apollo have been discovered, whose columns were surmounted with Aeolian (proto-Ionic) capitals. Coin issues of the city, mostly in silver and featuring the head of Apollo, are dated between 430 and 310.

Bonacasa (*PECS* 613).

Neapolis (*Limassol*) (map 14) City on the south coast of Cyprus, whose remains now lie largely beneath the mod. city. There is evidence for occupation beginning by at least C8 (with indications of a Late Bronze Age settlement to the north of Limassol) and continuing until the Byzantine period, when the city perhaps reached the peak of its development. In this last period, it was also known as Theodosias or Theodosiana.

Nikolaou (*PECS* 613–14).

Negev (*Negeb*) (map 8) Name (meaning 'dryness' in Hebrew) given to the southern part of Judah, and now constituting the largest region of mod. Israel. It consists of three sub-regions, 'each with climatic, geologic, and topographical peculiarities that influence the type of settlement it attracted and the course of its history' (Cohen). Cohen defines the sub-regions as: (1) the northern Negev, whose most prominent area is the Beersheba basin, which flourished in the Chalcolithic period; (2) the Negev highlands, where settlement flourished in the Early Bronze Age, the Iron Age, and the Nabataean, Roman, and Byzantine periods; (3) the eastern Negev, the Arabah, which flourished principally in the Iron Age, Nabataean, Roman, and early Arab periods. The region as a whole has been described as 'forming an inverted triangle with its base roughly following a line from Gaza past Beersheba to the Dead Sea. The line then runs through the Wadi Arabah to the Gulf of Aqabah at Elath, and from there northwestward to Gaza' (Drinkard). Numerous surveys and excavations conducted in the Negev, particularly since mid C20, have thrown much light on the region's history and archaeology.

Human occupation dating back to the early Palaeolithic period had become quite extensive by the end of this period. During the Neolithic Age a number of settlements emerged, which in the Chalcolithic Age became increasingly widespread, with the Beersheba basin being the area of most intensive occupation. There were further increases in the number, size, and sophistication of settlements in the Early Bronze Age, as illustrated primarily by the fortified city of Arad. During the Iron Age, especially Iron Age II, many new villages and fortress-settlements were established through the whole Negev region. The fortresses were located particularly in Judah's southernmost areas, to protect the frontiers. Fortresses and other settlements were also built under Persian overlordship during the Persian period (C6–4). Beersheba served as an important centre of the Persian administration, as attested by ostraca with Aramaic inscriptions.

Despite the dry, parched nature of much of the Negev, there were many places within it where wells, springs, and oases provided sufficient water to support permanent human settlement. And despite the ruggedness of the region (particularly its central and southern parts), its location was such that several major north–south routes traversed it (e.g. one from Jerusalem and Hebron to Beersheba). The Via Maris (q.v.), passing from Egypt to Mesopotamia via Palestine and Syria, skirted its western edge. After the fall of Judah, and during the period of the Hebrews' Babylonian exile, the Negev came under the control of the Edomites. Through the Edomite period the population remained relatively small. But the Nabataean occupation of the region, during the Hellenistic period, resulted in an increase in the number of settlements as well as in the overall population. This was very largely the outcome of Nabataean commercial enterprise. To facilitate their spice trade with India and southern Arabia, the Nabataeans established a network of caravanserais and way-stations along the routes in the Negev, notably along the 'frankincense and myrrh route' which linked Gaza, near the Mediterranean coast, with Petra.

Drinkard (*HCBD* 745–6), Cohen (*OEANE* 4: 120–2).

Nemed-Ishtar Late Bronze and Iron Age city in the middle Euphrates region, to the south of the Jebel Sinjar. Nemed-Ishtar is attested as a provincial capital in a Middle Assyrian tablet excavated at Tell er-Rimah. It was among the cities and lands governed by Nergal-erish (Palil-erish) on behalf of the Assyrian king Adad-nirari III (810–783) (**RIMA* 3: 209). The cities included Ana-Ashur-uter-asbat (= Pitru), Anat, Apku, Dur-Duklimmu (= Dur-Katlimmu), Kar-Ashurnasirpal, Mari, and Sirqu (= Terqa). The lands included Hindanu, Laqe, Qatnu, Rasappa, and Suhu. The Assyrian king Sargon II (721–705) instructed his official Nabu-udammiq (Assyrian Nabu-de'iq) to extract cedar and cypress saplings from the land, presumably for replanting in other parts of his kingdom (**SAA* I: 177, no. 227). See also **Dur-Ishtar**.

Streck (*RlA* 9: 208).

Nemed-Tukulti-Ninurta Iron Age Assyrian city in northern Mesopotamia, so named by Tukulti-Ninurta II (890–884). It is uncertain whether it was a new foundation, or an earlier settlement with a different name, refounded and renamed by Tukulti-Ninurta. The city's location is unknown, but its existence is attested by an inscription on a stone slab discovered at Nineveh (**RIMA* 2: 179–80). The inscription provides a summary of Tukulti-Ninurta's military exploits.

Nemetti-Sharri Iron Age city in eastern Babylonia. In 813 the Babylonian king Marduk-balassu-iqbi fled there from his fortified city of Gannanate when the latter fell to the Assyrian king Shamshi-Adad V. Nemetti-Sharri was placed under siege by Shamshi-Adad, who breached its defences but apparently failed to capture it. Instead, he ravaged the surrounding countryside (**RIMA* 3: 190). Marduk-balassu-iqbi survived the Assyrian onslaught but was later captured, possibly in the city of Der (see **Der (3)**).

Nenassa Middle and Late Bronze Age city in central Anatolia, probably located just below the southern bend of the Halys (Hittite Marassantiya) r. In the Assyrian Colony period (C20–18) (see glossary), it lay on a caravan route passing from Assyria through Washaniya and terminating in Purushanda in south-central Anatolia. Early in the Hittite Old Kingdom, Nenassa was one of the lands which the first Hittite king, Labarna, assigned to his sons to govern (early C17) (**Chav.* 230). It was also among the lands that rebelled against Labarna's (probable) successor Hattusili I, and the first of the rebel cities to resubmit to Hattusili on the approach of his army (**Chav.* 220). In the reign of Tudhaliya III (first half of C14), it was the southernmost city to be occupied by the enemy forces which swept through the Hittite homeland (*Bryce, 2005: 146).

Wilhelm (*RlA* 9: 211).

Neo-Hittites Mod. term used to designate the Iron Age successors of the Late Bronze Age Hittites. The peoples so called inhabited the kingdoms and states which arose in southern and eastern Anatolia and northern Syria after the collapse of the Hittite empire, the Late Bronze Age kingdom of Hatti, in early C12. For the most part, the Neo-Hittite states were located within Hatti's former subject territories, particularly in the Taurus region and northern Syria, where the name Hatti continued to be used throughout the Iron Age, as attested in Neo-Assyrian, Urartian, and Hebrew texts. Some of the Neo-Hittite centres had their origins in Bronze Age cities and states; others appear to have been new foundations. All of them, however, preserved in modified form – for almost 500 years in some cases – many Hittite cultural traditions. In a number of the Neo-Hittite centres, these traditions were passed on directly by the Late Bronze Age inhabitants of these centres to their Iron Age successors.

Continuity is also illustrated by family links between the Bronze Age Hittite royal dynasty and a number of the Neo-Hittite rulers. Thus Talmi-Teshub, who was viceroy at Carchemish during the reign of the last Hittite king Suppiluliuma II, and great-great-grandson of Suppiluliuma I, was succeeded by his son Ku(n)zi-Teshub, whose grandsons were kings of Melid (see ***Arslantepe***). Kuzi-Teshub's title 'Great King' probably reflects his perception of himself as the legitimate successor of the 'Great Kings' of Late Bronze Age Hatti, though his kingdom extended over no more than part of the eastern territories of the former Hittite empire – along the west bank of the Euphrates from mod. Malatya through Carchemish to Emar.

Figure 77 Neo-Hittite relief from Malatya, depicting battle between the storm god and the dragon Illuyanka.

It is very likely that a number of groups from the old homeland, particularly the elite elements of Hittite society, found a new home for themselves in Carchemish. The continuity in Bronze Age Hittite cultural traditions in the Neo-Hittite world may well have been due partly to their preservation by these groups, who sought to maintain in their new environment whatever they could bring from their old. Carchemish was the most important of the Neo-Hittite kingdoms. Formerly a viceregal centre of the Hittite empire, it had survived the upheavals at the end of the Bronze Age relatively unscathed, despite Ramesses III's claim that it was one of the victims of the Sea Peoples' attacks. But it was not to continue for long in the form in which Kuzi-Teshub inherited it. Perhaps even in his lifetime it began to follow the pattern of fragmentation into smaller units that occurred elsewhere in the western Asian world. Other important Neo-Hittite kingdoms included Gurgum (mod. Maraş), Hamath (mod. Hama), Kummuh (later Commagene), Melid (mod. Arslantepe), and Til-Barsip (mod. Tell Ahmar).

While these and other Neo-Hittite states had many cultural features in common, they were never closely united politically. Their relative cultural coherence was also progressively weakened, as illustrated by the gradual replacement of the Luwian language (the Luwian hieroglyphic script now completely superseded the old cuneiform script in written records), originally the dominant language in the Neo-Hittite states, with Phoenician and Aramaic. Many of the distinctive features of the Neo-Hittite civilization began to yield to Aramaean influence as the Aramaean presence became ever more prominent in the region. And the more distinctive features of traditional Hittite art and architecture were increasingly modified by their intermixture with Syrian and Assyrian elements. (Specific examples of Neo-Hittite art and architecture are discussed under the headings of individual kingdoms and cities of the Neo-Hittite world.)

The storm god was the most prominent of the Neo-Hittite deities, though he may have owed this prominence as much to his importance in the western Asian world in general as to his status as one of the chief gods of the Bronze Age Hittite pantheon. At Hamath, his worship was shared with the Semitic goddess Baʿalat. There were temples to both deities in the city. At Carchemish, Kubaba had been the city goddess from at

Figure 78 Neo-Hittite stele depicting the goddess Kubaba.

least the Old Babylonian period (early M2). She continued to be one of the city's most important deities in the Neo-Hittite period as well.

Assyrian imperial expansion west of the Euphrates led to the eventual disappearance of the Neo-Hittite kingdoms, through their incorporation into the Assyrian empire. The last of the kingdoms fell to Sargon II between 717 and 708, though rulers in Tabal and Melid regained their independence in the following century.

Hawkins (1982; **CHLI* I), Collins (2007: 80–90).

Nerabu M1 city belonging to the western Aramaean kingdom of Bit-Agusi in north-central Syria. It is attested in inscriptions of the reign of the Assyrian king Tiglath-pileser III (745–727) (**Tigl. III* 146), and is perhaps to be located to the southeast of Aleppo.

Lipiński (2000: 203).

Nerebtum (*Ishchali*) (map 10) Central Mesopotamian city attested in Middle Bronze Age texts, located in the Diyala valley 25 km southwest of Eshnunna, and near the city of Tutub (Tell Khafaje). Its site, now known as Ishchali, was one of four major tells in the valley – the other three were Tell Asmar (Eshnunna), Khafajeh, and Tell Agrab. It was excavated by a team from the Oriental Institute, University of Chicago, between 1934 and 1936. In mid C19 Nerebtum was among the cities which lost their independence to the kingdom of Eshnunna when Eshnunna's king, Ipiq-Adad II, extended his authority over the Diyala valley. Nerebtum had until this time been under the control of a local king called Sin-abushu. The city's principal deity had been the god Sin, but Ipiq-Adad re-dedicated Nerebtum to his own patron deity, the goddess Ishtar-Kititum, and built a temple for her worship in the city (**CS* II: 254). Nerebtum was later seized by the Assyrian king Shamshi-Adad I (1796–1775) from his Eshnunnite counterpart Dadusha or the latter's successor Ibal-pi-El II (1779–1765). Ibal-pi-El apparently regained control of Nerebtum, but it was among the cities in the region destroyed by the Elamites following their capture of Eshnunna in 1765. A war between Nerebtum's king Hammidashur and Sumu-numhim, king of Shadlash (location unknown), was concluded by a peace treaty (*Greengus, 1979: 74–7, no. 326; *Wu Yuhong, 1994b), whose terms included an agreement on the prices to be paid for the ransoming of prisoners-of-war.

*Greengus (1986), Miglus (*RlA* 9: 211–14), *Mesop.* 97–100.

Nerik One of the most important cult-centres of the Late Bronze Age Hittite kingdom, dedicated to the worship of the storm god and located somewhere near the northern frontier of the Hittite homeland. A possible identification with the settlement-mound at Oymaağaç (q.v.) has recently been suggested. Nerik was captured by the Kaska people in the reign of the Hittite king Hantili II (C15), and though a later Hittite king, Mursili II (1321–1295), made a pilgrimage there to celebrate the festival of the storm god, it was not fully restored to Hittite control until the reign of Urhi-Teshub (1272–1267). The task of rebuilding the city was successfully undertaken by Urhi-Teshub's uncle, the future king Hattusili III (**CS* I: 202), who became chief priest of the storm god there. Nerik was one of Hattusili's two major power-bases in the northern part of the Hittite homeland, where Urhi-Teshub's father and predecessor Muwattalli II had appointed him as king. The other was his administrative centre at Hakpis. Growing tensions between Hattusili and Urhi-Teshub culminated in Urhi-Teshub's removal of both Nerik and Hakpis from his uncle's control. This sparked off a civil war, which ended in victory for Hattusili and his seizure of the Hittite throne (**CS* I: 203).

Haas (1970; *RlA* 9: 229–31), Cornil and Lebrun (1972), **RGTC* 6: 286–9, Gurney (1992: 214–15).

Nesa see **Kanesh**.

Nigimhu M2 mountain land in the Zagros region, close to the eastern frontiers of Assyria. The Assyrian king Arik-den-ili conducted a campaign against it in late C14, destroying its crops. Nigimhu's king, Esini, apparently retaliated, launching an attack on Assyrian territory with a contingent of thirty-three chariots. This prompted a further campaign by Arik-den-ili who placed Esini under siege in his city of Arnuna, and took the city by storm (**RIMA* 1: 126). As far as can be determined from the fragmentary text which reports these events, Esini surrendered to Arik-den-ili, and swore allegiance to him. Adad-nirari I, son of Arik-den-ili, declared that his father conquered the entire land of Nigimhu, and also Turukku, Qutu, and the land of Kadmuhu and its allies (**RIMA* 1: 132).

Streck (*RlA* 9: 312).

Nihriya (maps 3, 10) M2 settlement (and region) in northern Mesopotamia, possibly to be identified with Kazane Höyük on the west bank of the upper Balih r. (Charpin, *Mesop.* 181, following an idea of J. Miller). During the Assyrian Colony period (C20–18) (see glossary), Nihriya lay on the caravan route for Assyrian merchants travelling between Ashur and Kanesh, and is known to have housed a *karum* (trading-station) itself, as well as a palace. Later on, it fell within Mari's sphere of influence. In the Mari archives, it is attested in the context of military operations conducted in 1778 by the Assyrian king Shamshi-Adad I and his son Yasmah-Addu, viceroy at Mari, in the region called Zalmaqum (**LAPO* 17: 56–7, no. 477) which lay immediately to the south (if the abovementioned identification is correct). During the Middle Assyrian era, an Assyrian commander-in-chief is attested as governor of Nineveh, Katmuhu, and Nihriya.

According to a royal letter from Ugarit, probably sent to the king of Ugarit by the Assyrian king Tukulti-Ninurta I (1244–1208) (or perhaps his father, Shalmaneser I), the Hittite king Tudhaliya IV formed an alliance with the local rulers and fortified the land of Nihriya against the Assyrians (**RS* 34.165, rev. 6–13). When Tudhaliya refused a demand from Tukulti-Ninurta to withdraw his troops from the region, the Hittite and Assyrian forces clashed in a major battle somewhere between Nihriya and the Assyrian base at Surra. The result was, apparently, a resounding Assyrian victory. I. Singer suggests (1985) that this episode is to be identified with Tukulti-Ninurta's military defeat of the forty kings of Nairi, as recorded in his royal inscriptions (*RIMA* 1: 272, 275–6). However, this interpretation, and the implied identification of Nihriya with Nairi, is not universally accepted.

Subsequently, Nihriya was absorbed into the Hurrian-dominated realm. It has been suggested that Nihriya may be identical with Nihiriane, mentioned in an inscription of the C8 Urartian king Sarduri II as a royal city located in the province of Arme. However, since Arme was situated in the upper Tigris region, near Shubria, an identification of Urartian Nihiriane with Nihriya can only be sustained if Nihriya is located not in the upper Balih r. region but rather to the east, in the vicinity of Diyarbakır. (Some scholars have in fact preferred to locate Nihriya to the north or northeast of Diyarbakır.) Note also that if the location of Nihriya in the upper Balih r. region is accepted, then its identification with Nairi is certainly excluded.

(H. D. Baker)
Streck (*RlA* 9: 314–15).

Nikasamma M1 Assyrian province in western Iran near the land of Parsua. It was among the Assyrian subject territories in the region which rebelled against Sargon II (721–705) in the early years of his reign. Sargon conducted a campaign against the rebel states in 716, in the course of which he captured six of Nikasamma's cities and added them to the territory of Parsua, one of the few Assyrian provinces which had remained loyal to him (**ARAB* II: 29).

Nimrud (Assyrian **Kalhu**, biblical **Calah**; the name *Nimrud* comes from the *OT* king Nimrod) (map 13) Settlement located on the east bank of the Tigris r. in northern Mesopotamia, 30 km southeast of Mosul. Though the site was already occupied in the Halaf and Ubaid periods (M6 onwards), and continued to be inhabited until at least mid M1 CE, it is known mainly as an Iron Age Assyrian city and an early royal capital of the Neo-Assyrian kingdom. Excavations have concentrated primarily on Iron Age

Kalhu. The first were undertaken by A. H. Layard, from 1845 to 1847 and from 1849 to 1851. These brought to light large parts of several palaces, most notably the so-called Northwest Palace built by the C9 king Ashurnasirpal II. Layard explored the palace's state apartments, along with a number of its stone reliefs and colossal winged-bull statues guarding the entrances. He also carried out excavations in the Ninurta and Ishtar temples, two of the nine temples which Ashurnasirpal claims to have built in the city. One of Layard's most important finds was the famous black obelisk of Shalmaneser III (858–824), discovered in front of the so-called Central Building (probably another temple built by Ashurnasirpal II), and now in the British Museum. Subsequent excavations on the site were conducted first by Layard's former assistant H. Rassam for the British Museum (1877–9) and, after a long interval, by M. E. L. Mallowan (1949–58), D. Oates (1959–62), and G. Orchard (1963) for the British School of Archaeology in Iraq. In more recent years, the site has been excavated, successively, by a Polish team under the direction of J. Meuszyński (1974–6), an Italian team under the direction of P. Fiorina (1987–9), and a team from the British Museum under the direction of J. Curtis and D. Collon, beginning in 1989. Since 1956, the Iraq Dept of Antiquities has worked periodically on the site.

The Assyrian city of Kalhu was probably founded in early C13, in the last century of the Late Bronze Age, and to judge from C13 Assyrian texts, quickly became important.

Figure 79 Nimrud, guardian figure, palace of Ashurnasirpal II.

But its status as a royal capital was due to Ashurnasirpal II, whose major building programme in the city included massive new fortifications c. 7.5 km long, nine temples, and at least five palaces, the most important of which is the Northwest Palace referred to above. Four vaulted tombs were discovered beneath the palace by Iraqi archaeologists. Richly endowed with a range of gold jewellery and other valuable funerary goods, they are thought to have been the burial places of several Assyrian queens. In the so-called Governor's Palace, a major archive of administrative tablets was discovered. The most important of the temples was that of the god Nabu. The temple contained a large tablet archive, whose contents included a wide range of religious, ritual, and literary texts. The palaces and a number of the temples were built on Kalhu's citadel. Located in the city's southwest corner, the citadel encompassed an area of c. 20 ha, and had its own defensive wall. At its greatest extent, the greater walled city covered an area of c. 360 ha. Excavations in its southeast corner brought to light another large enclosure, some 30 ha in extent and separated by a wall from the rest of the city. Within the enclosure was a 5 ha palace complex, built originally by Shalmaneser III and subsequently renovated as a Review Palace or arsenal by the C7 Assyrian king Esarhaddon. The excavators have dubbed it 'Fort Shalmaneser'. It is an elaborate, multi-function complex, containing not only storerooms but also a block of state apartments. Most notable among its small finds, which included thousands of ivories, is a bronze and iron model of a turreted fortress on wheels, and the throne-base of Shalmaneser carved with scenes depicting events from his reign, with accompanying inscriptions.

Kalhu ceased to be Assyria's royal capital when Sargon II (721–705) shifted the royal seat to his new city, Dur-Sharrukin (Khorsabad). It none the less continued to be one of the Assyrian empire's most important cities, under the administration of a regional governor, and was extensively renovated by Sargon's grandson and second successor,

Figure 80 Nimrud, Assyrian hunting scene.

Esarhaddon. In the period 614–612 it was one of a number of Assyrian cities destroyed by the Medes during the empire's final years. There is evidence of some occupation in the Neo-Babylonian and Persian Achaemenid eras (C6–4), and during the Hellenistic period several small settlements were built in the southeastern area of the citadel.

Postgate and Reade (*RlA* 5: 303–23), Reade (1982a), Curtis (*OEANE* 4: 141–4), Oates and Oates (2001).

Nina-Sirara (mod. ***Zurghul***) One of the three major Early Bronze Age Sumerian cities constituting the city-state of Lagash in southern Mesopotamia (the other two were Girsu and Lagash). It consists of a settlement-mound covering c. 65 ha. The only excavations conducted there (in late C19) were those of the German archaeologist R. Koldewey, who concluded, wrongly, that the site was a necropolis. (He drew a similar mistaken conclusion about Lagash, mod. Al-Hiba.) Like Girsu and Lagash, Nina-Sirara has produced some evidence of occupation during the Ubaid and Uruk periods. The main occupation, however, dates to the Early Dynastic and immediately post-Akkadian periods. Construction work at the city was carried out by the rulers Enannatum I and Gudea, including a temple for the goddess Nanshe.

Matthews (*OEANE* 2: 406–9, s.v. Girsu and Lagash).

Nineveh (biblical Ninua; ***Mosul***) (maps 10, 13) Extensive settlement with lower town dominated by two high citadel-mounds, called Kuyunjik and Nebi Yunus, located on the east bank of the Tigris r. in northern Mesopotamia, within the mod. city of Mosul. Though it has a history of almost continuous occupation from M7 to the mediaeval period, Nineveh's main periods of occupation belong to the Bronze and Iron Ages, particularly from the Late Bronze Age onwards when it was an Assyrian city. The site was visited by the Spanish rabbi Benjamin of Tudela in C12 CE, and subsequently by a series of travellers, including C. J. Rich who mapped it in 1820. Following some preliminary diggings on Kuyunjik by P.-É. Botta, the French consul at Mosul, excavations of the site were undertaken by a series of British teams, directed firstly by A. H. Layard (1846–51) and finally by R. C. Thompson (1927–32). Thompson's work included an investigation of the site's prehistoric levels, conducted by M. E. L. Mallowan, which provided the first early pottery sequence for northern Mesopotamia. More recent excavations have been conducted by the Iraqi Dept of Antiquities and Heritage (1941, 1966–8), and by the University of California at Berkeley under the direction of D. Stronach (1987–90).

During the first half of the Early Bronze Age (c. 3000–2500), a substantial settlement grew up on the site, the so-called Ninevite 5 settlement, named after the northern Mesopotamian culture/period first defined on the basis of level 5 of the Nineveh deep sounding. The city may already have become an important cult-centre of the goddess Ishtar in this period. The longstanding renown of her temple in Nineveh is attested by the Assyrian king Shamshi-Adad I (1796–1775), who claims to have been the first ruler to renovate the temple since the reign of the C23 Akkadian king Manishtushu (**RIMA* 1: 51–4). However, the city is best known for its progressive development under the rulers of the Middle and Neo-Assyrian periods. From at least early M1, a substantial lower city developed to the north of the mound. This was greatly expanded in the reign of Sennacherib (704–681), who transferred the Assyrian royal capital to Nineveh from its previous location at Dur-Sharrukin (Khorsabad), the city built by his father Sargon II. Nineveh now covered an area of c. 750 ha. It was fortified by massive crenellated double walls, which extended over a distance of 12 km. At least fifteen gates provided access to the city through these walls. The most impressive of these was the so-called Nergal Gate, which was guarded by two winged colossi and faced southwards towards the Kuyunjik mound, where Sennacherib's palace was located. Lofty columns supported on the backs of striding bronze lions were one of the palace's most striking features.

Sennacherib's successors Esarhaddon (680–669) and Ashurbanipal (668–630/627) continued with a building programme on Nebi Yunus, where Sennacherib had established an arsenal. But overall building activity in the city was more limited than it had been in Sennacherib's reign. None the less, the so-called North Palace built by Ashurbanipal towards the northern end of Kuyunjik ranks as one of the greatest of all Assyrian architectural achievements. The splendid relief sculptures from the palace, epitomized by a famous lion-hunt scene, represent Mesopotamian art at its highest level. Another famous scene which depicts a royal park and elaborate irrigation system has contributed to the theory, proposed by S. Dalley (1994), that Nineveh not Babylon was the setting of the famous 'Hanging Gardens'. Within the palace, a library was discovered, consisting of two large chambers stacked with 24,000 cuneiform clay tablets. Its wide range of contents, including copies of literary texts which were gathered from all parts of the empire and whose originals in some cases dated back centuries before the foundation of the Neo-Assyrian kingdom, provide us with one of our most valuable sources of information on Mesopotamian history and culture.

The destruction of the city in 612 by a Babylonian–Median military alliance delivered the final death blow to the Assyrian empire. Several literary sources attest to this destruction. The first is a Babylonian Chronicle (no. 3; see glossary) which reports that Nineveh fell after a three-month siege to the Babylonian king Nabopolassar (626–605) (**ANET* 303–5, **ABC* 90–6, **PE* 30–2, no. 10), who allegedly held court in the royal palace. Rather more meagre information is provided by the Greek historian Herodotus, who refers to the advance upon the city (which he calls Ninus) by the Median army under the command of its king, Cyaxares (625–585) (1.103), and the Median capture of the city (1.106). (Herodotus promises to give details of this event elsewhere, but never gets around to doing so.) Diodorus (2.27) claims that the city fell (to the Median leader Arbaces) only after it had been besieged for more than two years, and then only when part of its walls had been destroyed by an inundation of the Euphrates (i.e. the Tigris).

Nineveh figures frequently in biblical sources, beginning with Genesis 10:11–12, where it appears as one of the cities founded by Noah's great-grandson Nimrod. Other biblical passages note that it was the royal seat of Sennacherib (2 Kings 19:36, Isaiah 37:37), and also the place where he was assassinated by his sons (2 Kings 19:37).

Russell (1996), Stronach (*OEANE* 4: 144–8), Reade/Veenhof (*RlA* 9: 388–434).

Nippur (Duranki, *Niffar/Nuffar*) (maps 11, 17) City serving as a major religious centre in south-central Mesopotamia, 150 km southwest of Baghdad. The site's history of occupation extends from early M6 to c. 800 CE, with periods of abandonment in between. Its history of excavation begins with a cursory two-week investigation by A. H. Layard in 1851, and proceeds, after four seasons on the site by the Babylonian Expedition between 1888 and 1900, through excavations conducted between 1948 and 1962 by teams from the University of Pennsylvania and the Oriental Institute of the University of Chicago, and continued by the Oriental Institute from 1963 to 1990.

Nippur reached the peak of its development in M3, growing in size throughout the millennium until it finally covered an area of 135–150 ha. It achieved a special status as Mesopotamia's most important religious centre. Here was the site of the Ekur, the temple of the supreme Mesopotamian deity Enlil. But the city never seems to have been ruled by kings who had secular ambitions, seeking to establish political and military dominance over their Mesopotamian neighbours. Rather, its special sacred character, and no doubt its political neutrality, prompted many M3 rulers of both Sumer and Akkad to seek divine endorsement for their regimes there. Resources for many of the city's public building projects, including its temples and fortifications, along with a stream of costly gifts for the temples, were provided by external benefactors, both states and individual kings. Undoubtedly M3 Nippur was a highly prosperous city, with well-endowed secular and sacred establishments.

During the first half of M2 the city's fortunes declined, due, it is thought, to a combination of politico-economic and environmental factors. It may have been abandoned almost entirely for a period of three centuries, between late C18 and the end of C15, before it received a fresh lease of life in C14 under the kings of the Kassite dynasty. Occupation continued through the remainder of M2 and through much of M1 until it again appears to have been abandoned for a time in mid C2. In C11 it was among the Babylonian cities which were afflicted by the Aramaean and Sutaean invasions of southern Mesopotamia during the reign of the Babylonian king Adad-apla-iddina (1069–1048) (**ABC* 180–1, **RIMB* 2: 73).

Though the worship of Enlil was Nippur's primary focus, the city contained the temples of a number of deities. The most notable of these temples was dedicated to the goddess Inanna. It has a sequence of twenty-two levels, extending from the middle Uruk through the late Parthian period. Its three levels of M3 Early Dynastic temples (IX–VII) produced a rich assemblage of sculptures and clay sealings. A further sequence of temples, extending from the end of the Ur III dynasty (late M3) through the Neo-Babylonian period, may have been dedicated to the healing goddess Gula, wife of Ninurta. Other buildings unearthed at Nippur include a ziggurat (see glossary), private houses dating to C19 and C18, a C13 palace built during the period of Kassite rule in Babylonia, and a so-called Court of Columns dating to late C3. Housing of the Neo-Babylonian and later periods has also been found. The city wall was rebuilt in C7.

Of great importance among the archaeological finds are 12,000 cuneiform clay tablets. The contents of large numbers of these are economic or lexical in nature. But they also include copies of the great majority of Sumerian literary compositions. The tablets were found mainly in private houses, and range in date from the Old Babylonian through the Kassite and later periods. Nippur was a centre for scribal education in the Old Babylonian period.

Ellis (1992), Zettler (*OEANE* 4: 148–52), Klein/Stol/Streck/Gibson, Hansen, Zettler (*RlA* 9: 532–65).

Nirbu Region attested in Iron Age Assyrian texts, located in the midst of the Kashiyari mountain range (mod. Tur ʿAbdin). The name means 'the Pass' or 'the Land of the Pass(es)' in Assyrian. In 882 the region was invaded and conquered by the Assyrian king Ashurnasirpal II (**RIMA* 2: 201–3). Liverani (1992: 37–9) believes that Nirbu is a generic appellation, probably referring to the plateau of the Kashiyari range. He also suggests that Urumu (q.v.) is another name for the same region.

(H. D. Baker)

Nirdun Iron Age kingdom in the Nairi lands, north of the Kashiyari range (mod. Tur ʿAbdin) of northern Mesopotamia, in the vicinity of Tushhan and to the southeast of that city. In 882 the Assyrian king Ashurnasirpal II received tribute from Labturu, ruler of the land of Nirdun, while staying in the city of Tushhan (**RIMA* 2: 202, 243). In 879 he again campaigned in the Nairi lands, conquering Madara, a fortress of Labturu. He went on to Tushhan, where he received tribute from Nirdun, and then proceeded to destroy sixty cities of Labturu at the foot of the Kashiyari range (**RIMA* 2: 209, 250, 259). Lipiński notes that Labturu's name is certainly not Semitic, and may in fact be Urartian in origin.

(H. D. Baker)
Liverani (1992: 40), Lipiński (2000: 140, 154).

Nisaya M1 district in Media, western Iran. It was the location of a fortress called Sikayauvatish, where in 522 the Persian military commander Darius overthrew and killed Gaumata, the 'false Bardiya', pretender to the Persian throne, before seizing the throne for himself (**DB* 11–13).

Nishtun Iron Age city located in one of the regions called Habhu in Assyrian texts (see **Habhu (2)**). It was among the cities of Habhu which were conquered by the Assyrian king Ashurnasirpal II in his first regnal year (883) (**RIMA* 2: 197–8). After Ashurnasirpal had flushed out the defeated troops from their mountain refuges, he took prisoner Bubu, grandson of the city ruler of Nishtun, and flayed him alive in the city of Arbil, draping his skin over the city walls.

Nisibis (Assyrian **Nasibina**, ***Nusaybin***) (map 13; see also maps in Lipiński, 2000: 113, 139) Predominantly Iron Age northern Mesopotamian city, located in the region of the upper Habur r., in the southern foothills of the Kashiyari range (mod. Tur ʿAbdin), within the territory of the former Late Bronze Age country called Hanigalbat. It lay on an important route linking northern Mesopotamia with the countries to the west. The Assyrian king Adad-nirari II claims to have conquered its king, Nur-Adad, from the Aramaean Temanite tribe, in two successive years, 901 and 900 (**RIMA* 2: 149). However, his victories appear not to have been conclusive, and he was obliged to conduct a further campaign against Nisibis in 896. On this occasion the city fell to him after a siege. It was annexed to the Assyrian empire, along with other cities in the region, and Nur-Adad and his troops were taken to Assyria as hostages (**RIMA* 2: 151). Nisibis also figures in the last recorded campaign of Adad-nirari's son and successor Tukulti-Ninurta II (890–884), as a place where Tukulti-Ninurta encamped his troops following his operations in the middle Euphrates region (**RIMA* 2: 177). Nasibina was incorporated into the Assyrian empire in the first half of C9 as part of the Province of the Commander-in-Chief (see glossary), and then became an independent province in 852 following the conquest of Bit-Adini (Radner, *RlA* 11: 52). A number of letters have survived from the correspondence addressed by Taklak-ana-Bel, governor of Nisibis in late C8, to the Assyrian king Sargon II (**SAA* I: 183–93, nos 235–49). In 612 the city was attacked and plundered by the Neo-Babylonian king Nabopolassar (**ABC* 94, **PE* 31, no. 10).

Nisibis then disappears from records until its re-emergence in the Hellenistic period, when it was for a time part of the Seleucid empire and briefly renamed Antioch

Mygdonia. However, its original name was later restored, and in C2 and C1 it became, successively, part of the Parthian and Armenian empires. Documentary sources attest to its continuing existence in the Roman and Byzantine periods.

Wiesehöfer (*OCD*: 1046), Streck (*RlA* 9: 185–6).

Niya (Nii) (maps 3, 6) Late Bronze Age kingdom in northern Syria, east of the Orontes r. In C16 it was one of several lands – including Ama'u (Amae) and Mukish – which were absorbed by the expanding kingdom of Aleppo. Subsequently, Niya established its independence from Aleppo, but shortly afterwards became a subject state of the kingdom of Mitanni (C15). In the second half of C15, Niya, Ama'u, and Mukish declared their support for Idrimi, the former king of Yamhad (Aleppo), during his seven-year exile (see **Alalah**). When Idrimi was subsequently installed by the Mitannian king Parrattarna on the throne at Alalah, he was formally recognized as the ruler of these states, no doubt in accordance with the treaty which he concluded with Parrattarna (cited in his inscription: *Greenstein, 1995: 2426, **CS* I: 479). In his one-year Syrian war (c. 1344), the Hittite king Suppiluliuma I seized control of all Mitanni's subject states between the Euphrates and the Mediterranean coast (as far south as the Damascus region), including Niya (**HDT* 43).

Klengel (1992: 151–6).

Norşuntepe (map 2) Settlement-mound in eastern Anatolia on the upper Euphrates r., 26 km southeast of mod. Elaziğ, with occupation levels extending from the Chalcolithic period through the Bronze and Iron Ages. Its final Chalcolithic phase shows close connections with the Uruk culture of southern Mesopotamia. During the Early Bronze Age, the settlement was fortified, and by the end of this phase of its existence a major building complex, perhaps a 'palace-centre', had been constructed. Copper production is in evidence on the site during the Chalcolithic period, and bronze production by the end of the Early Bronze Age. Destruction by fire has left little trace of the Middle and Late Bronze Age occupation levels; there are a few remains of rectangular and multiple-roomed dwellings belonging to the former and latter respectively, and a range of ceramic ware. In the Late Bronze Age Norşuntepe lay in the region called Isuwa in Hittite texts. During this period, it was fortified by a stone casemate wall, typical of the defensive architecture of a number of contemporaneous Anatolian sites. The regular layout of streets within the fortifications indicate some degree of town planning. Settlement continued through the early and middle Iron Ages, and in the latter period the site came under strong political and cultural influence from the kingdom of Urartu. In the middle Iron Age it lay within the frontiers of the Urartian kingdom, and was finally abandoned with the fall of this kingdom in late C7. The site was excavated from 1968 to 1974 by H. Hauptmann for the German Archaeological Institute in Istanbul, as part of the Keban Dam Rescue Project.

Hauptmann (*RlA* 9: 596–604).

Notium (map 5) M1 Greek city located on the Aegean coast of Anatolia, 55 km south of Smyrna. It lay near Colophon and was often closely associated with this city, serving as its harbour. In fact, in the Hellenistic period Notium was called Colophon on the Sea, or New Colophon. Thucydides (3.34) reports that refugees from Colophon settled in Notium around the time of the second Peloponnesian invasion of Attica (i.e.

c. 430). Notium had earlier become a member of the Athenian Confederacy (see glossary). Its small annual contribution to the Confederacy's treasury, one-third of a talent (cf. Ephesus which contributed six talents), reflects its relatively low status and income-producing capacity at this time.

The city extended over two summits of a hill overlooking the sea, and was enclosed by a fortification wall of Hellenistic or earlier date. Other material remains, which belong mainly to the Hellenistic and Roman periods, include a temple of Athena, two agoras, a council house, and a theatre.

Bean (1966: 185–90; *PECS* 629), E. Akurgal (1973: 133–6).

Nuhashshi lands (Nuhasse) (maps 3, 6) Middle and Late Bronze Age region of northern Syria, east of the Orontes r. The name first appears in the archives of Mari and Alalah (level VII) (C18 and C17 respectively). The Mari texts indicate that at the time of their composition the northern part of Nuhashshi belonged to the kingdom of Yamhad, and the southern part to the territory of Qatna. In C15 Nuhashshi was among the lands and cities conquered by the pharaoh Tuthmosis III during his eighth Syrian campaign. Later Hittite texts referring to the 'kings of Nuhashshi' indicate that the region was then (if not before) divided among a number of principalities or small kingdoms. Their rulers may have formed some kind of confederation in which one of them served as a *primus inter pares*. In early C14 Nuhashshi became embroiled in territorial disputes with the kingdom of Aleppo, and called upon both Mitanni and Hatti for support (Bryce, 2005: 141). By mid C14 it had become subject to Mitanni, then ruled by Tushratta. But prior to his 'one-year Syrian war' against Mitanni and its subject kingdoms (c. 1344), the Hittite king Suppiluliuma I concluded an alliance with one of the Nuhashshi kings, Sharrupshi (**HDT* 54–5). It seems that Sharrupshi subsequently abandoned his Hittite ties, and the region as a whole remained strongly hostile to Hatti until Suppiluliuma comprehensively defeated the forces of Tushratta, and established Hittite control over all the northern Syrian principalities formerly subject to Mitanni. The Nuhashshi lands now provided Suppiluliuma with a convenient base for menacing Egyptian subject territory in southern Syria, and negotiating with disloyal Egyptian vassal kings, who were persuaded or coerced into switching sides to Hatti.

In the reign of Suppiluliuma's son and (second) successor Mursili II (1321–1295), the people of Nuhashshi rose in rebellion against Hittite overlordship and urged other lands to join them (**PRU* IV: 54–5, *Bryce, 2005: 199–201). Their action was apparently prompted by the news of the death of Sharri-Kushuh (Piyassili), Hittite viceroy at Carchemish (c. 1313). Mursili responded by dispatching an armed force to the region under the command of the Hittite prince Kurunta, who restored Hittite control over Nuhashshi after destroying its crops and laying siege to its cities (**CS* II: 88–9). Nuhashshi later figures in the so-called Apology of the Hittite king Hattusili III. Around 1267, Hattusili seized the throne from his nephew Urhi-Teshub after a brief civil war, and exiled him to Nuhashshi (**CS* I: 203). It was there that the deposed king began his bid to regain his throne, secretly communicating with Babylon and Assyria, before fleeing to Egypt where he sought the protection and backing of the pharaoh Ramesses II.

Klengel (1992: 151–6; *RlA* 9: 610–11).

Nulia Iron Age city belonging to the Neo-Hittite kingdom of Pat(t)in (Assyrian

Unqi) in northern Syria. It was captured by the Assyrian king Shalmaneser III during his campaign against the cities of northern Syria in his first regnal year (858) (**RIMA* 3: 17).

CHLI I: 362.

Numha Amorite population group, attested in the Middle Bronze Age Mari texts, living in the hill country of northern Mesopotamia. Some of the Numha population inhabited the kingdoms of Karana and Kurda, located in the Jebel Sinjar region, and Ekallatum to the southeast. Numha troops figure frequently in the conflicts recorded in the Mari archives during Zimri-Lim's reign (1774–1762), sometimes on the side of Mari, sometimes in actions hostile to it. The assembly called by the Kurdaite king Hammurabi in Kasapa (see **Kasapa (1)**) consisted of Numha people.

LKM 17–18, 590 (refs).

Nurrugum Middle Bronze Age city and country located in northern Mesopotamia. According to J. Eidem (1985: 101, with n. 84), the country so called extended north of Ekallatum along the banks of the Tigris and included Nineveh. In his view, Nurrugum city probably lay east of the river. D. Oates, however (1968: 31, 39), placed it west of the river, in the region of the Jebel Sinjar. In the early decades of C18, Nurrugum was conquered by Ishme-Dagan, elder son of the Assyrian king Shamshi-Adad I and viceroy of Ekallatum. Subsequently the country became one of the administrative districts of the Old Assyrian kingdom, probably with Nurrugum city as its centre. Its governor was a man called Shashsharanum, who had served in the Assyrian campaign against Qabra and Nurrugum. Large numbers of recruits from Nurrugum were conscripted into the ranks of Shamshi-Adad's military forces. Fugitives arriving in Mari from Nurrugum were to be shared between Ishme-Dagan and his brother Yasmah-Addu, Assyrian viceroy in Mari.

**LAPO* 18: 206, no. 1034 (= **LKM* 280); 270–2, no. 1089, *Mesop.* 170.

Nush-i Jan Tepe (map 13) Small fortified Iron Age Median site (c. 100 m × 40 m) in western Iran, 70 km south of Hamadan (anc. Ecbatana). Built on a 30 m high outcrop of rock, primarily, it seems, as a religious centre, the site was established in mid C8 and abandoned c. 600. Excavations were carried out by D. Stronach for five seasons, between 1967 and 1977, on behalf of the British Institute of Persian Studies. The four main buildings brought to light in these excavations were identified as a central so-called 'fire temple' (C8), a 'fort', a western temple, and a columned hall (C7) perhaps used for ceremonial purposes. The complex was enclosed within a circular buttressed brick wall. Features of the architecture of the site, whose walls are preserved to a height of 7 m, include internal staircases and ramps to upper floors, mudbrick struts for arches and vaults, recessed buttresses and façades, and in the columned hall, stone bases which once supported wooden columns. This last feature is found at a number of Iron Age Iranian sites, including Hasanlu, Godin Tepe, and Baba Jan Tepe. It foreshadows one of the typical characteristics of later Persian Achaemenid architecture. The building identified as a fort included what was apparently a guardroom, four storage magazines, and arrow-shaped apertures in the buttress-reinforced walls. A silver hoard was unearthed on the site during the excavations. Many objects in this hoard are apparently of pre-Median origin.

With its commanding position overlooking the Malayer-Jowkar plain, Nush-i Jan Tepe has been interpreted as the headquarters of a Median ruler, with provision made for a retinue of nobles and royal guards. The buildings within the complex appear to have been designed exclusively for administrative, cultic, or defence purposes. There is no trace of a lower settlement on the plain. Dandamaev and Lukonin suggest that the structure of the settlement as a whole explains to some degree the character of the early Median state.

The site's monumental buildings were abandoned by early C6, followed by 'squatter occupation' during the first half of the century. Nush-i Jan's history of settlement has been influential in reshaping, in recent times, scholarly perceptions of the development, nature, and extent of the so-called Median empire (see under **Media**).

Stronach and Roaf (1978), Stronach (1985b; *RlA* 9: 624–9), Dandamaev and Lukonin (1989: 64–7).

Nuzi (*Yorgan Tepe*) (map 10) Site in northeastern Mesopotamia, consisting of a main mound (200 m × 200 m) and several smaller mounds, 10 km southwest of mod. Kirkuk. Occupation on the main mound began in the late Halaf period (M5) and continued until the Late Bronze Age (mid–late M2), when the site was under Mitannian and subsequently Assyrian domination. There was also some later occupation on a small scale during the Neo-Assyrian and the Parthian and subsequent early Sasanian periods (C3 BCE–C3 CE). The site was excavated by E. Chiera (1925–8), R. H. Pfeiffer (1928–9), and R. F. S. Starr (1929–31), with sponsorship provided by the Iraq Museum (initially), the American Schools of Oriental Research, the Fogg Art Museum, and the Harvard Semitic Museum. Twelve archaeological strata were identified. During M3 the settlement was called Gasur, as indicated by tablets found on the site dating to the Akkadian period (c. 2334–2193). The 222 tablets from this period are primarily business documents.

In the Late Bronze Age the settlement, now called Nuzi, experienced its most important and most prosperous phase, when it was an eastern provincial town of the Mitannian empire under the immediate authority of the city of Arrapha (mod. Kirkuk). At this time, it had a predominantly Hurrian population. Though relatively small, Nuzi was a thriving community, as indicated by its so-called palace and temple complex on the main mound, its finely constructed public buildings around this complex, and the residential quarters which were found in several sectors of the site. Wealthy landowners and administrative officials occupied houses outside the walled settlement. The 'palace' contained over one hundred rooms and courts, was supplied with a drainage system, had marble paving, and was decorated with wall-paintings reflecting Egyptian and Aegean influence. But well appointed though this complex was, the term 'palace' is considered to be a misnomer, since no reference is ever made to a king of Nuzi. The complex is more likely to have been the residence of a local governor, answering to the ruler installed at Arrapha.

The site also produced a range of fine, distinctive pottery, now known as Nuzi ware, typified by a white, often geometric pattern painted on a dark background. A number of such pieces were found in Babylonia and northern Syria, so that together with the contemporaneous glazed wares and glass and faience items found in Nuzi, it established the material assemblage for what is called the Nuzi period. But Nuzi is best known today for the large quantities of clay tablets which were unearthed from the site's Late Bronze Age phase, especially from Stratum II, and are dated roughly between mid C15 and mid C14. A total of over 5,000 tablets came from both public and private archives, and bear the seal impressions of their authors. Their contents include contracts, legal records, letters, and ration and personnel lists. They thus provide important information on the activities of a wide cross-section of the population of Nuzi and its surrounding areas, and valuable insights into Nuzi's social, economic, legal, and religious institutions. A number of the texts refer to Arrapha's royal family, and the city's principal temples. Written in a distinctive Akkadian dialect, with an admixture of Hurrian names, the tablets have been seen as indicative of declining socio-economic conditions in the region during the period of their composition. This is reflected in the references they make to an increase in military activity in the region, and to a decrease in the grain surplus and an increase in debts and litigation, with the wealth of the region being concentrated in the hands of a progressively smaller number of people.

The destruction of Nuzi in late C14 was probably due to the Assyrians who became the new power in northern Mesopotamia after the fall of the Mitannian empire.

Maidman (1995), Stein (*OEANE* 4: 171–5), Wilhelm/Stein (*RlA* 9: 636–47).

O

Olymus City in Caria, southwestern Anatolia, 8 km northwest of Milas (Classical Mylasa). It has been identified with Hylimus (*BAGRW* 61 F3), which appears in the C5 Athenian Tribute Lists as a member of the Athenian Confederacy (see glossary). Inscriptions indicate that a temple of Apollo and Artemis was once located on the site.
Bean (1971: 48; *PECS* 646).

Ophir In *OT* tradition, the name of a land and its inhabitants who were descended from Shem, son of Noah (Genesis 1:29, 1 Chronicles 1:23). Ophir was famous in biblical tradition for its abundant sources of gold. According to 1 Kings 9:28, ships dispatched to it by Solomon in a collaborative enterprise with Hiram, king of Tyre, brought back 420 talents of the precious metal. 1 Kings 10:11 reports that Hiram's ships also brought back cargoes of almug wood (red sandalwood?) which was used in the construction of Solomon's temple, and precious stones from Ophir. There is no certainty as to where (if anywhere) Ophir lay, the only clue being that it was accessible by ship. Anc. Greek and Roman sources placed it in India or on an island in the Red Sea. Mod. scholars have suggested locations in Sumatra, India, east Africa, and perhaps most plausibly, the southwestern corner of Arabia (Yemen).
Negev and Gibson (2001: 376), D. T. Potts (1995: 1460–1).

Opis see **Upi (1)**.

Ortaköy see **Sapinuwa**.

Orthocorybantes M1 population group of Central Asia attested in Herodotus (3.92) as forming part of the tenth province of the Persian empire (but see glossary under **satrapy**). An identification has been proposed with the Saka *tigrachauda* people (see **Saka**) who were probably located east of the Caspian Sea.
Hinz (*KP* 4: 365).

Oxus r. (*Amu Darya*) (map 16) River of Central Asia flowing northwestwards into the Aral Sea and marking the boundary between the M1 countries Sogdiana and Bactria. Herodotus (1.202) (and also Aristotle) confused it with the Araxes r., which flows eastwards through Armenia into the Caspian Sea. An assemblage of gold and silver objects discovered in 1877 on or near the Oxus (and thus known as the Oxus treasure) is now in the British Museum. The great majority of the items from the hoard, including rings and armlets, statuettes, bowls and plate, and a four-horse model chariot containing a Persian nobleman, are of C5–4 date. The hoard also contains coins of a later period.
Stein (*RE* XVIII: 2006–19), Warmington/Spawforth (*OCD* 1088). Re Oxus treasure: Curtis (*RlA* 10: 153–7).

Oymaağaç Höyük Bronze and Iron Age settlement-mound, 20 m high and c. 200 m × 180 m in area, located in northeastern Anatolia 7 km northwest of mod. Vezirköprü. Ceramic ware discovered on the surface of the mound indicates the settlement's time-span, from the Early Bronze Age to the late Iron Age. The Hittite period (Late Bronze Age) is not represented in the ceramic material. However, R. Czichon and J. Klinger, who in 2005 conducted a survey in the area to assess whether Oymaağaç could have been the site of the Hittite city of Nerik, report the discovery there of three tablet fragments and a bulla with the seal of a certain Sarini (Yıldırım and Gates, 2007: 300). A scribe of that name is known from Hattusa, the Hittite capital, and Tarsus. The remains of fortifications on the site including a postern may date to the Middle and Late Bronze Ages.

Dönmez (2002: 258–60), Karg (*RlA* 10: 158–9).

P

Paddira Iron Age fortified city located in the upper Diyala/Zagros region in the northeastern Mesopotamian–northwestern Iranian borderlands. The city fell to the Assyrian king Shalmaneser III during his campaign in the region in his sixteenth regnal year (843) (**RIMA* 3: 40). Shalmaneser refers to the city as a possession of Ianziburiash, ruler of Allabria (q.v.). In 827 a man of Paddira called Artasari paid tribute to Shalmaneser's commander-in-chief Dayyan-Ashur while the latter was campaigning in the region (**RIMA* 3: 70), thus saving Paddira from a further Assyrian attack. Shalmaneser's son and successor Shamshi-Adad V calls Paddira a city of the Nairi lands; it is one of the places cited by him in describing the furthest reaches of Assyria (**RIMA* 3: 183).

Padnu (Patnu?) Iron Age royal city in northeastern Babylonia destroyed by the Assyrian king Shamshi-Adad V in 813, during his second campaign in Babylonia, at that time ruled by Marduk-balassu-iqbi (**RIMA* 3: 190). Two other royal cities, Makurrete and Qai[. . .]na, are listed with Padnu among Shamshi-Adad's conquests in this campaign. Padnu may be identical with the place Padan which is known, in association with the cities of Zanban and Alman, from texts of the later M2 (*RGTC* 5: 213).

Pahhuwa Late Bronze Age Hittite vassal city, located in eastern Anatolia near the upper course of the Euphrates. Early in C14, during the reign of the Hittite king Arnuwanda I, Pahhuwa's king Mita committed a range of offences against his Hittite overlord, which included marrying the daughter of Usapa, a declared enemy of the Hittites. Arnuwanda sent an ultimatum to the city, demanding the extradition of Mita, his family, and all his possessions. In the event that Pahhuwa failed to accede to this ultimatum, Arnuwanda ordered its neighbours to attack it and begin a slaughter of its citizens, pending the arrival of a Hittite army to complete the city's punishment. The document which provides this information belongs to a small group of texts which were originally dated to the last decades of the Hittite kingdom, late C13, but were subsequently redated on philological and palaeographic grounds to the period of the first rulers of the Hittite New Kingdom, early C14.

*Gurney (1948), *RGTC* 6: 296, *HDT* *160–6.

Pahru Iron Age city in southern Anatolia, the royal capital of Kate, king of Que. It was attacked by the Assyrian king Shalmaneser III, possibly on his return from a campaign in the land of Tabal (thus J. D. Hawkins). Shalmaneser captured the city, then shut Kate up in it, carrying off his daughter and her dowry to the Assyrian capital, Nimrud (Calah) (**RIMA* 3: 119). The city is perhaps to be identified with Misis (Classical Mopsuestia).

CHLI I: 41.

Paiteru Country in the upper Euphrates region. Its ruler was listed by the Assyrian king Tiglath-pileser I (1114–1076) as one of twenty-three kings of the Nairi lands (**RIMA* 2: 21). It was among the lands conquered by Tiglath-pileser during his campaigns against a coalition of Nairi countries, which began in his third regnal year (**RIMA* 2: 37, 52).

Pala (map 3) Late Bronze Age country, subject to Hatti, lying in the mountainous region of Classical Paphlagonia, northwest of the Hittite homeland, and closely linked in Hittite texts with the neighbouring land of Tummanna. The inhabitants of the region spoke Palaic, an Indo-European language. Pala-Tummanna was one of the few Hittite subject states placed under the direct rule of a Hittite governor, no doubt in recognition of its strategically important location on the edge of the Kaska lands which lay to its east. Inevitably, attacks were made upon it by Kaska mountain tribes. During the reign of the Hittite king Mursili II (1321–1295), an attempt by one of Pala's cities, Wasumana, to establish its independence was aborted when Mursili sent his military commander, Nuwanza, to assist Hudupiyanza, governor of the region, with its recapture (**AM* 106–7). Pala was among the depopulated cities and lands which Mursili's son and successor Muwattalli II (1295–1272) assigned to his brother Hattusili (later King Hattusili III) when he appointed him ruler of the northern part of the Hittite homeland (**CS* I: 201) (see **Hakpis(sa)** and **Turmitta**).

**RGTC* 6: 297–8, van den Hout (*RlA* 10: 191–3).

Palestine A name originating from the Peleset, one of the groups of so-called Sea Peoples (q.v.), who in C12 settled in the southern coastal plain of the Levant, where they re-emerged in *OT* tradition as the Philistines (q.v.). Their land was called Philistia. Though in early C6 the Babylonians dealt the final death blow to their existence as a cultural and ethnic entity, Greek sources preserved their name in the geographical term *Palaistine Syria* (Palestinian Syria) (e.g. Herodotus 1.105). This gave rise to *Palaestina* as a standalone place-name covering the region of the Levant between Phoenicia and Egypt. The C1 CE Jewish historian Josephus was the first anc. writer who explicitly linked *Palaestina* with the Philistines. *Palaestina* was the abbreviated name that came to be used of the Roman province which the emperor Hadrian designated as *Provincia Syria Palaestina* in 135 CE (in place of the earlier *Provincia Iudaea*). In Arabic, the name was preserved in the form *Filastin*.

The term 'Palestine' has had a wide range of meanings throughout its history. In a geographical sense, it means different things at different times, its locations and its limits shifting, expanding, or contracting from one period to another. So too the adjective 'Palestinian' differs in meaning from one context to another, depending on whether it is used in an archaeological, a cultural, or a political sense. For surveys of Palestine's history through the ages, see *OEANE* 4: 207–34.

Palmyra see under **Tadmor**.

Pamphylia (map 4) Classical name for the region located on Anatolia's southern coastal plain between Lycia to the west and Cilicia to the east. 'Pamphylia' is a Greek name meaning 'place of all tribes'. According to Greek legendary tradition, it was settled by Greeks of mixed origin under the leadership of Amphilochus, Calchas, and

Mopsus some time after the Trojan War. The Pamphylians spoke a distinctive dialect of Greek, which was related to Cypriot and Arcadian and also contained an infusion of native Anatolian linguistic elements. Pamphylia no doubt became subject to Persian sovereignty c. 540 during the Persian commander Harpagus' campaigns along the southern Anatolian coast. But some time after the victory won by the Athenian commander Cimon over the Persian fleet at the Eurymedon r. in Pamphylia (c. 466), a number of its cities became members of the Athenian Confederacy (see glossary). The tribute assessment of the year 425 includes Aspendus, Perge, and Sillyum. Other important Pamphylian cities were Attaleia, Side, and Magydus. In C3 control over Pamphylia was contested by the Seleucid and Attalid kings, and in C2 by the Attalid kings and the Pisidians.

From textual evidence we know that in the Late Bronze Age the region formed the western coastal part of the kingdom of Tarhuntassa, and probably had a predominantly Luwian population. There is no evidence of Greek settlement in the region during the Bronze Age. However, the Pamphylian city of Perge, a Greek settlement according to Greek legendary tradition, was almost certainly the successor of Late Bronze Age Parha (q.v.), which lay just outside Tarhuntassa's western frontier.

Mitchell (*OCD*: 1102–3).

Panaru Mountain land in northeastern Mesopotamia, east of the Tigris, in the vicinity of Kadmuhu. Its capital, Urratinash, was captured by the Assyrian king Tiglath-pileser I in his accession year (1115), when the land was ruled by a certain Shadi-Teshub (**RIMA* 2: 15–16).

Panaztepe (map 5) Settlement located on the Aegean coast of western Anatolia on the north side of the Bay of Izmir. Its history of occupation extends, with apparent gaps, from the Late Bronze Age to the Ottoman period. The site has been excavated over a period of two decades by a Turkish archaeological team under the direction of A. Erkanal-Öktü. Four occupational levels dating to the Late Bronze Age have been identified. The earliest, containing a large building with broad walls and extending over seven phases, is contemporary with levels VIh–m at Troy (C13, Late Helladic IIIB). The last M2 level corresponds to Troy VIIb2 (C11, mid–late Late Helladic IIIC), a conclusion based on the artefacts unearthed in a large six-roomed rectangular building from this level. Later levels contain the remains of occupation dating to the Geometric and Archaic (C8–6), late Roman, Byzantine, and Ottoman periods.

Erkanal and Erkanal (1986), Erkanal-Öktü and Çınardalı-Karaaslan (2006), Yıldırım and Gates (2007: 291)

Panionium Meeting-place of the twelve members of the Greek Ionian League, probably founded in C9 (Herodotus 1.148). According to Herodotus (1.142), the cities comprising the league were Miletus, Myous, Priene, Ephesus, Colophon, Lebedus, Teos, Erythrae, Clazomenae, Phocaea, and the islands of Samos and Chios. Dedicated to the god Poseidon, the League first met in the sacred precinct associated with Poseidon (Heliconius) at the foot of Mt Mycale (*BAGRW* 61 E2), in the territory of the city of Priene. The mountain was located on the Aegean coast of Anatolia north of Miletus, on a headland jutting out towards the island of Samos. Representatives of the member states met here to formulate common policy. A League temple was built on the site, which also provided the venue for a festival called the Panionia. In C5 the League's meeting-place was shifted to Ephesus, apparently for security reasons, but was returned to Mycale the following century.

A survey of Mt Mycale conducted by H. Lohmann in 2004–5 identified a settlement with large fortification walls, 5 km north-northwest of Priene, as the site of the Panionium prior to its shift to Ephesus. Within the walls were the remains of a temple with a large chamber, possibly an assembly chamber. The temple, which may have been that of the Panionium, was used only for a short time, in the second half of C6. C7 ceramic ware and a group of terracotta warrior figurines indicate an earlier phase in the settlement's existence, prior to the construction of the temple and its sanctuary. (The above summary of Lohmann's survey has been adapted from Yıldırım and Gates, 2007: 321.)

Bean (*PECS* 670), Hornblower (1991: 527–9), Lohmann (2006).

Paphlagonia (map 4) Mountainous region in central-northern Anatolia, located south of the Black Sea between (the Hellenistic kingdom of) Pontus to the east and Bithynia to the west, and extending inland to Galatia on the Anatolian plateau. In Late Bronze Age Hittite texts, the region was called Pala. Herodotus (7.72) lists a contingent of Paphlagonians among the forces assembled by the Persian king Xerxes for his invasion of Greece in 481. In the Roman imperial period, a major route passed through it from Byzantium to the eastern Roman frontier.

Broughton, Mitchell (*OCD* 1107–8).

Paphos (Palaipaphos, ***Kouklia***) (map 14) City on the southwest coast of Cyprus, with a history of occupation extending from the Chalcolithic to the mediaeval period. Originally known simply as Paphos, it was renamed Palaipaphos ('Old Paphos') from late C4 onwards to distinguish it from the harbour town Nea Paphos ('New Paphos'), which lay 16 km to the northwest and was founded c. 320 by Nicocles, Paphos' last king.

The settlement at Paphos was established, according to Greek tradition, by Agapenor, king of Tegea, a city in Arcadia in the Peloponnese (southern mainland Greece). In one version of the foundation legend, Agapenor also founded the cult of Aphrodite in the city, in continuation of an indigenous fertility cult dating back at least to M3. According to Greek mythological tradition, Aphrodite first stepped ashore at Paphos after her birth from the sea foam. In another version of the foundation story, the goddess' cult was established prior to Greek settlement by Cinyras, a legendary king of Paphos, or of all Cyprus, who in Homer's *Iliad* (11.20) sent Agamemnon a corslet (a piece of armour covering the upper body) when he heard of his expedition against Troy. Cinyras continued to be revered by the later priest-kings of Paphos as the founder of their dynasty.

A monumental cult-building was constructed on the site c. 1200 with pillared hall and open temenos layout, reflecting western Asian architectural traditions. Within the hall a large conical stone, found many years ago in the vicinity, perhaps represented the deity in aniconic form (i.e. not bearing an image). Worship of the goddess Aphrodite in such a form during the Iron Age may represent a continuation of a long-established pre-Greek tradition. The Temple of Paphian Aphrodite, which replaced the earlier Bronze Age cult-building, was the most famous cult-place of the goddess in the anc. world.

The early Greek city was one of the largest and most prosperous in Cyprus. Its

Figure 81 Paphos, temple of Aphrodite, lustral basin(?).

intermixture of Cypriot, Aegean, and Levantine cultural elements produced thriving craft industries with the manufacture of a range of fine ceramic ware, ivories, and jewellery. But the city reached the peak of its prosperity in the Archaic (C7–6) and Classical (C5–4) periods, as far as we are able to judge from its (admittedly meagre) architectural remains and its tombs. The former include an impressive ashlar building of late C6 or early C5, thought to have been a royal residence, and a C4 'peristyle mansion'. The tombs indicate a large, wealthy elite in Paphos' mid M1 population. Unfortunately, later Roman remodelling has left little trace of Aphrodite's sanctuary as it would have appeared in the Archaic and Classical periods, though the survival of thousands of fragments of terracotta votive figurines from the temple, dating to the Geometric (C8), Archaic, and Classical periods, testify to the cult's continuing popularity throughout these periods.

A reference to Paphos in the inscription on the prism of the C7 Assyrian king Esarhaddon, dated to 673/672 (*Borger, 1956: 60 §27, Heidel, 1956), is one of the very few surviving historical attestations of the city. We do know, however, that in early C5 it joined the anti-Persian Ionian rebellion (499–494). There is substantial material evidence for fierce fighting at the northeast fortifications of the city, where the Persians raised a large mound in the course of their siege of the city and the Paphians responded with counter-siege works. In fact, it is possible to reconstruct in considerable detail the course of the siege and counter-siege, by examining the debris left in the aftermath of the conflict. This debris included hundreds of fragments of sculptures and votive monuments, which the Persians had plundered from a sanctuary outside the walls to use as material for building their siege ramp. The monumental sculptures recovered from this debris, obviously dating to the Archaic period, include kouroi (naked male statues) and fragments of lions and sphinxes. Egyptian, Phoenician, and Greek influence are all combined in the products of the Paphian school of sculpture.

Paphos went into decline when a large part of its population was transferred to the city of Nea Paphos. In 294 it lost its status as the capital of the kingdom of Paphos when the Ptolemies conquered Cyprus and abolished its local monarchies. Nevertheless, the old city remained an important centre of the worship of Aphrodite, whose cult continued to flourish through the Hellenistic and Roman periods.

Nicolaou (*PECS* 674–6), Maier and Karageorghis (1984), Iacovou (2002).

Paphu (Papanhu) Small Late Bronze Age and early Iron Age Hurrian(?) state in the upper Tigris region, northeastern Mesopotamia. It was among the countries conquered by the Assyrian king Tukulti-Ninurta I (1244–1208) early in his reign (see under **Alzu**) (**RIMA* 1: 250 etc.). In the accession year of the Assyrian king Tiglath-pileser I (1115) it rebelled against Assyrian rule, on this occasion in support of the land of Kadmuhu. Tiglath-pileser claims to have won a crushing victory, inflicting heavy casualties and carrying off its king, Kili-Teshub, and large numbers of his family and clan (**RIMA* 2: 15). The captured king's palace and capital were destroyed. But in the following year, Tiglath-pileser undertook a further campaign against the tribes of Paphu, and also the land of Haria. This took him deep into the mountains of northern Mesopotamia, where, he claims, no other Assyrian king had ever been (**RIMA* 2: 18). Passage through the rugged mountain terrains was impossible for his chariots, so he ordered his troops to carry them on their necks. He reports that the forces of the entire Paphu land were now massed against him. On this occasion, his slaughter of the enemy resulted, he says, in the hollows and plains of the mountains flowing with their blood. He also reports military operations against the tribes of Paphu in the context of his campaign in this same year against the land of Sugu, which was part of one of the regions called Habhu in Assyrian texts (see **Habhu (2)**) (**RIMA* 2: 19).

Wilhelm (*RlA* 10: 324–5).

Pappa see **Sukkia**.

Paqar(a)hubunu Iron Age city located on the west bank of the upper Euphrates in the region of mod. Pazarcık, near the border between the kingdoms of Kummuh and Gurgum, and in C9 belonging to the Aramaean kingdom of Bit-Adini, then ruled by Ahuni. It is attested in the Annals of the Assyrian king Shalmaneser III, who in his first regnal year (858) crossed the Euphrates and attacked the city, killing 1,300 of its troops and laying waste its towns and villages (**RIMA* 3: 15–16). This was a prelude to further successful campaigns by Shalmaneser against the cities of Bit-Adini, which ended with the absorption of the kingdom into the Assyrian empire. In his twelfth regnal year, 847, Shalmaneser again campaigned against Paqarahubunu (**RIMA* 3: 38, 66), which may then, J. D. Hawkins suggests (*CHLI* I: 175), have belonged to the kingdom of Carchemish. The city later provided a focus of resistance against Assyrian rule, and in 805 a major battle was fought there between a military coalition led by Attar-shumki (I), ruler of the Aramaean state of Bit-Agusi, and the forces of the Assyrian king Adad-nirari III (**RIMA* 3: 205). Though he defeated the coalition on this occasion, Adad-nirari failed to break it up, and it continued to challenge Assyrian sovereignty in the region for at least the next ten years.

Streck (*RlA* 10: 332).

Parabeste City, according to Pliny the Elder (6.92), belonging to the Central Asian land of Arachosia (in the region of mod. Afghanistan) which was among the eastern territories of the Persian empire (C6–4). The fact that there is only a single, late attestation of the city raises doubts about its authenticity. Conceivably, however, its name reflects that of the Persian province of Paropanisadae, which was originally part of Arachosia and is also mentioned by Pliny.

Paraetaceni Inhabitants of the mountainous region in southwestern Iran bordering on the territory of Susiana (mod. Khuzestan) in the southwest and Media in the north and east. They are attested by Herodotus as one of the tribes constituting the kingdom of Media (1.101) (cf. *Arrian, *Anabasis* 3.19.2). Their name is perhaps to be read in place of 'Paricani' (q.v.) in Herodotus' listing of the members of what he believed to be the tenth Persian province (3.92) (see glossary under **satrapy**). Strabo (16.1.17) refers to the country of Paraetacene as bordering on the land of Persis.

Treidler (*RE Suppl.* 10: 478–82).

Parahshum see **Marhashi**.

Parala Iron Age city belonging to the Neo-Hittite kingdom of Kummuh in eastern Anatolia. The Urartian king Sarduri II refers to it in his Annals as one of the royal cities which he captured, c. 750, from Kushtashpi, king of Kummuh (**HcI* 123–4, no. 103).

CLHI I: 332.

Parda M1 city, capital of the land of Zikirtu (q.v.) which was a sub-kingdom of the land of Mannaea in mod. Iranian Kurdistan. It was destroyed c. 716 by the Assyrian king Sargon II during his campaign against Zikirtu's governor, Mitatti. Mitatti had joined other Mannaean leaders in a rebellion against Assyrian sovereignty (**ARAB* II: 28).

Parga, Mt Mountain in Persis, southwestern Iran. It was the site of the final military showdown between Vahyazdata, a pretender to the Persian throne who had rebelled against Darius I, and Darius' military commander Artavadiya (522–521) (**DB* 42). Vahyazdata was decisively defeated and taken prisoner, and suffered death by impalement.

Parga (**Parqa**) City of the Iron Age kingdom of Hamath in northwestern Syria. It was among the three 'royal cities' which the Assyrian king Shalmaneser III captured from the Hamathite king Irhuleni (see **Hamath (1)**) during his sixth campaign (853) (**RIMA* 3: 23). (The other two cities were Adennu and Argana.) Its capture is recorded on one of the bronze bands from Balawat (see **Imgur-Enlil**) (**RIMA* 3: 144).

Lipiński (2000: 259–62), Radner (*RlA* 10: 336–7).

Parha (map 3) Late Bronze Age city in southern Anatolia located on the Kastaraya r., and almost certainly the ancestor of Classical Perge (which lay on the west bank of the Cestrus r. in Pamphylia). In the 'bronze tablet' treaty which the Hittite king Tudhaliya IV (1237–1209) drew up with his cousin Kurunta, appanage ruler (see glossary) of the kingdom of Tarhuntassa, Parha lay just outside the western boundary of Tarhuntassa, which was marked (at least in part) by the Kastaraya r. (**CS* II: 101). It also appears in a fragmentary Hittite text, which perhaps formed part of the Annals of Tudhaliya's father Hattusili III, within the context of a reference to the Lukka Lands (*Gurney, 1997).

Frantz-Szabó (*RlA* 10: 337).

Paricani Population group which according to Herodotus (3.94) formed, together with the Asiatic Ethiopians, the seventeenth Persian province. Herodotus (3.92) also refers to a *second* group of Paricanians who allegedly belonged to the tenth province, together with Ecbatana, the rest of Media, and the Orthocorybantes. But given the general unreliability of his account of the Persian provincial system (see glossary under **satrapy**), it is possible that he has mistakenly duplicated the Paricani's name. The name of the group supposedly belonging to the tenth province should perhaps be read as Paraetaceni, who are attested elsewhere in Herodotus as a people of southwestern Iran (see **Paraetaceni**). But there is no reason to doubt the historical reality of a group called the Paricani, located somewhere in Iran during M1 or further east in Central Asia, and it is conceivable that there were two such groups who were related but separately identifiable. Herodotus (7.68, 86) also reports the inclusion of a Paricanian force of infantry and cavalry in the army assembled by Darius' son and successor Xerxes for his invasion of Greece in 481. A city called Paricane, in Persis, is attested in a fragment from Hecataeus (*FGrH* 1 F 282).

Paripa see **Surunu**.

Parium (map 5) M1 city located on the southern shore of the Hellespont in northwestern Anatolia, near the entrance to the Propontis. Its name is perhaps derived from its putative eponymous founder Parium, son of Jason, who may have established a colony on the site with settlers from the mother city Erythrae. Alternatively, the city was a joint foundation of Miletus and Erythrae, and was named after the legendary Parilarians. Either way, the site was well chosen, and the city prospered as a result of its excellent strategic position. In the first half of C4 the sculptor Praxiteles carved a statue of the god Eros in the city.

During the Hellenistic period, Parium came under the control of the kingdom of Pergamum before being incorporated into the Roman empire in 133.

Bonacasa (*PECS* 676).

Paropanisadae A region of Central Asia, according to Pliny the Elder (6.92), north of and perhaps originally belonging to the land of Arachosia in Afghanistan. It occupied a key position on the route between Afghanistan and India. During his campaigns in the region in 327, Alexander the Great appointed a new satrap there, his father-in-law Oxyartes from the country of Sogdiana. The satrapy played a major role in the eastern frontier defence system of Alexander's empire.

Badian (1985: 468–9).

Parqa see Parga.

Parsa (1) (*Fars*) (map 16) M1 country in southwestern Iran, located to the east of the Persian Gulf, homeland of the Persian dynasty. The relationship between Parsa and the land in the central western Zagros mountains called Parsua (see below) in Neo-Assyrian texts remains a matter of debate. In Greek, the name Parsa was represented as Persis.
CAH IV: 902 (index refs s.v. Fars).

Parsa (2) = Dur-Kurigalzu (q.v.).

Parsua (Parsuash/Parsumash) (map 13) Iron Age land in the central western Zagros mountains of Iran, frequently attested in Neo-Assyrian records. Parsua appears to have consisted originally of a number of small polities, each under the rule of a king. The Assyrian king Shalmaneser III reports that it was among the lands and cities he destroyed during his campaign in the upper Diyala and Zagros regions in his sixteenth regnal year (843) (**RIMA* 3: 40, 54), and that twenty-seven of its kings voluntarily offered up tribute to him during his campaign in the region in 835 (**RIMA* 3: 68). When the Assyrian commander-in-chief Dayyan-Ashur was campaigning in Parsua on behalf of Shalmaneser in 828, he received a payment of tribute from its kings. But a number of Parsua's cities refused to accept Assyrian sovereignty. Dayyan-Ashur responded by conquering and plundering them (**RIMA* 3: 70). The following year he conducted a further campaign in Parsua, claiming to have captured and destroyed the fortified cities of Pushtu, Shalahamanu, and Kinihamanu, along with twenty-three other cities (**RIMA* 3: 71). Shalmaneser's son and successor Shamshi-Adad V reports receiving tribute from the people of Parsua during his third campaign in the Nairi lands (**RIMA* 3: 184).

In 781 Parsua was one of the countries against which the Urartian king Argishti I campaigned. The Assyrian king Adad-nirari III (810–783) lists Parsua among his conquests in northeastern Mesopotamia and northwestern Iran (**RIMA* 3: 212). However, the country appears to have remained largely independent of foreign control until the reign of the Assyrian king Tiglath-pileser III (745–727) who, during his campaign against Namri and other countries in the Zagros region, conquered and annexed it to his empire (**ARAB* I: 285–6, **Tigl. III* 132–3). Its capital was the fortified city of Nikkur. Kiguhtu and Kizahasi were other fortified settlements in the region of Nikkur (**SAA* XV: 37, no. 54). The former has been identified with the city of Ganguhtu, which Sargon II (721–705) annexed to Parsua in 716 (*Sargon II* 435). As an Assyrian province, Parsua held firm in its allegiance to Assyria through the difficult early years of Sargon II's reign, when many other Assyrian provinces in the region rebelled with the encouragement of Urartu. During his campaign in 716 against the rebel states, Sargon rewarded Parsua's loyalty by expanding its territory, adding to it rebel cities which he had conquered in the neighbouring lands, like Ganguhtu.

From then on, Parsua receives scant mention in Assyrian records. There is a brief reference to it in the 'Ashurbanipal Prism' (**PE* 53–4, no. 2) which records the dispatch of tribute to Ashurbanipal by Parsumash's king, Kurash (along with his eldest son as hostage), after Ashurbanipal's defeat of the Elamites in 653. Otherwise Parsua, like several other states in the region, disappears altogether from historical records
Fuchs (*RlA* 10: 340–2).

Parsuhanda see **Purushanda**.

Parthia (map 16) Central Asian country located in northeastern Iran, to the southeast of the Caspian Sea. Its capitals were Nysa and later Hecatompylos, possibly the site of Shahr-e Qumis near Mashhad (*BAGRW* 96 C4). 'Parthia' is a Greek form of the name *Parthava*, by which the country was known in both the Persian and the Hellenistic periods (the latter under Seleucid rule). It was probably incorporated into the Persian empire soon after the empire's foundation by Cyrus II (550). Herodotus (3.93) reports that Parthia formed part of the sixteenth Persian province, along with Chorasmia, Sogdiana, and Aria (but see glossary under **satrapy**). It was among the eastern lands of the Persian empire listed several times in the inscriptions of Darius I (522–486), e.g. in Darius' Bisitun inscription (**DB* 6), and also in the *daiva* inscription (see glossary) of his son and successor Xerxes (**XPh* 3). The Bisitun inscription records Parthia's participation in the widespread uprisings against Darius at the beginning of his reign (**DB* 21). The Parthians were supported by the Hyrcanians, with both peoples declaring their support for Phraortes, the Median pretender to the Persian throne. In battles fought at Vishpauzatish and Patigrabana (8 March and 12 July 521 respectively) (**DB* 35–7), the rebels were confronted and crushed by Darius' father Hystaspes, satrap of Parthia. Thenceforth, Parthia appears to have remained submissive to Persian rule. On the reliefs from the Audience Hall (Apadana) at Persepolis, its moccasin-shod representatives are depicted as Delegation XV, bringing tribute to Darius in the form of vessels and a two-humped camel. Herodotus (7.66) lists a contingent of Parthians under the command of Artabazus, son of Pharnaces, among the forces assembled by the Persian king Xerxes for his invasion of Greece in 481.

In the Hellenistic period, Parthia became a province of the Seleucid empire. But in 247 it entered upon a new era in its history with the emergence of a ruler called Arsaces (I), from an Iranian nomadic tribe called the Parni, who founded the so-called Arsacid dynasty. His reign coincided with the decline of Seleucid influence and power east of the Euphrates, and marked the beginning of the development of the Parthian empire (247 BCE–224 CE). At its peak, this empire held sway over territories extending eastwards from the Euphrates to the Indus r., and southwards from the Oxus r. (mod. Amu Darya) to the Indian Ocean.

Debevoise (1938), Keall (*OEANE* 4: 249–50), Streck/Curtis (*RlA* 10: 343–50).

Parzuta Iron Age city in southern Anatolia, attested in a Luwian hieroglyphic rock inscription found on the road between mod. Nevşehir and Aksaray near the village of Acıgöl (formerly Topada) (**CHLI* I: 451–61). The inscription features Wasusarmas, a C8 ruler of northern Tabal, and refers to hostilities between Wasusarmas, or one of his lieutenants, and a coalition of eight 'kings' whose base was the city of Parzuta. The hostilities involved the use of cavalry, and seem to have arisen, at least in part, out of a frontier dispute. Parzuta may therefore have been located near Wasusarmas' western frontier. This would be consistent with an identification between Parzuta and Bronze Age Purushanda (Hittite Parsuhanda) – if in fact Purushanda were located, as long believed, at mod. Acem Höyuk. However, the Hittite city is now commonly identified with the site of Karahöyük near Konya (see **Purushanda**).

Pasanda M1 BCE–M1 CE city in Caria, southwestern Anatolia, located in the vicinity of Caunus (*BAGRW* 65 A4). In C5, it was a member of the Athenian Confederacy (see glossary), paying an annual contribution of half a talent to the Confederacy's treasury. During the Hellenistic period it was apparently, for a time, a deme (i.e. administrative district) of Caunus.

Bean (*PECS* 679).

Pasargadae (Elamite **Baktrakatash**) (map 16) Persian royal capital, located in the Morghab plain of southwestern Iran in the province of Fars, 40 km northeast of Persepolis. The unwalled city was founded by Cyrus II in the late 540s, on the site, according to the Greek geographer Strabo (15.3.8), where Cyrus defeated the Median king Astyages. Excavations were carried out by E. Herzfeld for the University of Chicago (1928), A. Sami, for the Iranian Antiquities Service (1949–55), and D. Stronach, for the British Institute of Persian Studies (1961–3). Since 1999, a surface archaeological investigation of the site has been undertaken by the Iranian Cultural Heritage Organisation and a team from the Maison de l'Orient and CNRS (Centre Nationale de la Recherche Scientifique), France. The aim of this investigation has been to determine the limits of the occupied area in the Pasargadae plain and to understand better the layout of the city.

Cyrus' tomb, a freestanding structure with stepped podium, single chamber, and gabled roof, was erected on the site's southern edge. (For a description of the tomb and its contents, see Arrian, *Anabasis* 6.29.4–7 = **PE* 87, no. 29.) When Alexander the Great came here in 330, the lavishly furnished monument allegedly still contained Cyrus' body, interred in a gold sarcophagus. The tomb is located 1 km south of the city's palace area. A freestanding gatehouse, known as Gate R, appears to have provided the ceremonial entrance to the city. Originally adorned with colossal guardian bull statues of Assyrian type, the gate has only one remaining sculpture, a relief on the northeastern side door depicting a winged and bearded human figure, with hair arranged in the Elamite manner, wearing an Elamite royal robe and an Egyptian-type triple crown. The figure's purpose and meaning are a matter for speculation, though a common view is that it represents a genie with apotropaic function (see glossary).

Beyond the gateway lie the remains of two palaces, designated now as Palace S and Palace P. Both feature rectangular hypostyle (i.e. columned) halls, with surrounding porticoes. The columns are surmounted with capitals in the form of adjoining animal protomes – lions, hybrid lion monsters, and bulls – as at Susa and Persepolis. Both palaces border upon formal gardens, divided into four sections by still visible stone water channels. The palace and garden complex also contains two royal pavilions. Though begun by Cyrus, the complex as a whole could not have been completed until many years after his death, as indicated by a number of evolutionary changes in style and architecture in the period from its inception to its completion. Within the garden the so-called Pasargadae treasure, consisting of many gold and silver objects, was concealed, probably some time after 350.

One of Pasargadae's major features is a large stone platform, the Takht ('throne' in Persian), 66 m × 79 m in area, and rising 14.5 m above the plain. It was probably intended as the site of a palace, but was left unfinished at Cyrus' death in 530. Subsequently it was incorporated into a heavily fortified complex, perhaps by Darius I (522–486).

Most puzzling among the monuments from Cyrus' reign are the remains of a

Figure 82 Pasargadae, gatehouse.

roughly square tower, 14 m high with pyramidal roof, containing, halfway up, a single room accessed by an external staircase. Traditionally referred to as the 'prison of Solomon' (Zendan-i Suleiman), it has been variously identified as a tomb, a temple, or a storehouse for Zoroastrian religious paraphernalia. Urartian influence has been suggested, both in the plan of the building and in its use of blind windows in black stone.

Several trilingual (Old Persian, Elamite, and Babylonian) inscriptions in the name of Cyrus found in Pasargadae are believed to have been added during Darius' reign, in order to bolster the fiction that Cyrus was of the same, Achaemenid, line as Darius (whereas Cyrus' own inscriptions claim descent from Teispes).

Many of the architectural and sculptural features of the Pasargadae complex foreshadow developments which reappear in Darius I's new city of Persepolis, like the hypostyle halls with their animal-protome capitals, sculptured façades and doorjambs, and the raised platforms, accessed by double staircases, on which a number of the palaces and other monumental buildings were constructed. In the art and architecture of both cities, the influence of other civilizations is readily apparent, from the freestanding tomb of Cyrus, for which a Lydian model has been suggested (and which differs markedly from the later rock-cut royal Persian tombs), to the freestanding and relief sculptures, which reflect a range of Assyrian, Babylonian, Egyptian, Lydian, Ionian Greek, Elamite, and perhaps Urartian influences.

Stronach (1978; 1985a; *OEANE* 4: 250–3), Root (1995: 2616–20), Boucharlat (2002; *RlA* 10: 351–63).

Pashime (Bashime, Mishime) (map 12) Early Bronze Age country (whose history extends into C20) in southern Iran, possibly located on the eastern shores of the Persian Gulf. It is first attested c. 2400 in texts dating to the reign of the Sumerian ruler Eannatum, king of Lagash (Early Dynastic period). Eannatum claims that he conquered

Figure 83 Pasargadae, tomb of Cyrus.

the country while on a campaign in Elam. However, there is no evidence that Pashime became subject to Eannatum, or to any Mesopotamian overlord, before mid C23, when the Akkadian king Manishtushu installed a governor there. In C21 Shulgi, second ruler of the Ur III dynasty, became the first of three kings of this dynasty who married their daughters to local Iranian rulers. Shulgi's daughter, Taram-Shulgi, became the wife of Shuddabani, king of Pashime. These marriage unions may have been designed to strengthen the Ur III dynasty's alliances with the local Iranian dynasties in Marhashi, Anshan, and Zabshali and Pashime, to offset the coalition being built against Ur under the leadership of Shimashki. But it is likely that the marriage unions reflected a relationship between Mesopotamian overlord and vassal ruler rather than between peers. In either case, Pashime may subsequently have been annexed to the Ur III kingdom, to judge from its appearance among the lands directly governed by the Ur administration. But after the fall of the Ur III dynasty, c. 2004, Pashime was incorporated into, and formed part of the western boundary of, the kingdom of the Shimashki-Elamite king Kindattu. It probably shared a border to its north with the Elamite frontier town of Huhnur (Tol-e Bormi, near Ram Hormuz). It was attacked and destroyed by Gungunum, fifth king of the Larsa dynasty, in the third year of his reign (1930). Though the Elamite language was probably spoken in Pashime, the ethnic origins or affinities of its population remain unclear.

Steinkeller (1982: 240–3), T. Potts (1994: 18–19).

Patara (*Kelemiş*) (map 15) City on the coast of Lycia in southwestern Anatolia, 5 km east of the mouth of the Xanthus r., with a history of occupation extending from the Bronze Age to the Byzantine period. Its earliest remains include a stone axe dating to c. 2000, fortification walls, and pottery of Late Bronze Age date.

In M1 Patara became one of Lycia's major cities, and its most important port. According to Greek mythological tradition it was named after Patarus, a son of the god Apollo by the nymph Lycia. The city was famous in antiquity as an oracular centre of Apollo, who was believed to spend the winter there after ummering on the island of Delos. Herodotus (1.182) refers to the city's temple of Apollo, stating that a prophetess spends the night in the temple in communion with the god. The implication is that the responses she gave to her consultants came to her from the god in the form of dreams.

Though Patara is not attested in written sources before late C6 or early C5 (the Greek geographer Hecataeus is the first writer to make mention of it), settlement on the site, as noted above, dates back to a much earlier period. It may have a connection with a mountain called Patara, which a Late Bronze Age Luwian hieroglyphic inscription (the so-called Yalburt inscription; see **Yalburt**) indicates was located in the region. Inscriptions and coin legends inform us that the native form of the city's name was Pttara. There are no surviving refences to the city's history prior to its surrender (along with the rest of Lycia) to Alexander the Great in 333. During the Hellenistic period Patara was subject in succession to Macedonian, Ptolemaic, and Seleucid rule, and when the Lycian League was formed early in C2, it became one of the League's six major cities. It maintained this status through the Roman period, its importance enhanced when it became the seat of a provincial governor. In the early Byzantine period it achieved renown as the birthplace of Nicholas, who became bishop of Myra.

Patara's material remains – or at least those currently known to us – belong almost entirely to the Roman and Byzantine periods. However, excavations begun in 2003 on the Tepecik Acropolis at Patara, under the direction of F. Işık of Akdeniz University, have brought to light a building complex, thought to be a grain depot, and a large pottery assemblage dating back to the Archaic period of the city's history (particularly C7 and C6). (An up-to-date report of these excavations is to be published by G. Işın in *AS*.) To date, no trace has been discovered of the famous temple of Apollo where the oracle was located. But a large part of the anc. site has yet to be excavated.

Bean (1978: 82–91; *PECS* 679–80), Yıldırım and Gates (2007: 308).

Patishkun Iron Age city belonging to the Aramaean kingdom of Bit-Zamani, located in the upper Tigris region, northwest of the Kashiyari mountain region (mod. Tur ʿAbdin). It was among the cities which fell to the Assyrian king Tukulti-Ninurta II during his campaign against Ammi-Baʿal, ruler of Bit-Zamani, in 886 (**RIMA* 2: 171).

Pat(t)in (Luwian name, formerly read as 'Hattin'; = Assyrian **Unqi**) (map 7) Neo-Hittite state located in the Amuq plain of northern Syria on the territory of the Late Bronze Age kingdom of Alalah. Its capital was called Kinalua (Kunulua; probably = mod. Tell Tayinat) in Assyrian texts. Other cities of Patin referred to in Assyrian sources are Alimush(?), Aribua, Butamu, Hatatirra, Hazazu, Huzarra, Kulmadara, Nulia, Sagillu, Tae, Taia, Tarmanazi, and Urime. The history of the kingdom is known to us primarily from Assyrian sources, from the reign of Ashurnasirpal II (883–859) to that of Tiglath-pileser III (745–727), supplemented by meagre information provided by Patin's own poorly preserved records dating to C9 and C8. Ashurnasirpal invaded the country on his western campaign, c. 870, leading his troops first into Hazazu, and then across the Apre r. (mod. Afrin) into the capital, Kinalua (**RIMA* 2: 217–18).

Here he was paid a large tribute by Patin's king Lubarna (I), and took hostages, as well as contingents of infantry and cavalry which went with him on the rest of his western campaign. Envoys from Patin were present at the inauguration of Ashurnasirpal's new city of Kalhu (mod. Nimrud), and a number of Patin's inhabitants were resettled there. But when Ashurnasirpal's son and successor Shalmaneser III (858–824) launched an attack against the cities of northern Syria in the first year of his reign, the Patinite king Sapalulme, a successor of Lubarna, joined a coalition of northern Syrian, northern Mesopotamian, and southern Anatolian states against him. The coalition included Sam'al (ruled by Hayyanu), Bit-Adini (ruled by Ahunu), and Carchemish (ruled by Sangara). Shalmaneser won a decisive victory over their combined forces (**RIMA* 3: 9–10), and then proceeded across the Orontes r. to launch a further attack upon Sapalulme's fortified city of Alimush (Alishir). Sapalulme successfully called upon his former coalition partners to support him against the Assyrians, and the coalition was further swelled by troops provided by Kate, ruler of Que, Pihirim, ruler of Hilakku, Burannati, ruler of Yasbuq, and Adanu, ruler of Yahan(u) (for the last, see **Bit-Agusi**) (**RIMA* 3: 10, 17). Once again, the coalition was crushed by Shalmaneser's troops. His pacification of the region is reflected in the payments of tribute which he received on at least two occasions in subsequent years (857 and 853) from the Patinite and the other kingdoms which had joined the coalition.

Sapalulme was apparently succeeded during the second year of Shalmaneser's reign by a king referred to in the record of Shalmaneser's campaigns in 857 and 853 as 'Qalparunda the Unqite' and 'Qalparunda the Patinite' (**RIMA* 3: 11 and 18). He made a payment of tribute to Shalmaneser in these years. A Luwian hieroglyphic inscription bearing the name Halparuntiyas has been found beneath a palace floor at Tell Tayinat (**CHLI* I: 365–7). It is very likely that the man so named is to be identified with the Qalparunda attested in Shalmaneser's texts. (Three persons named Halparuntiyas are also included among the list of kings who ruled the contemporary Neo-Hittite kingdom of Gurgum.) Other attested rulers of the kingdom, mentioned in Shalmaneser's account of his exploits for the year 831, were Lubarna (II), Surri, and Sasi. At least the first of these was apparently a protégé of the Assyrian king. The names Sapalulme and Lubarna had a distinguished pedigree, for they were derived from two of the most famous names in the Bronze Age Hittite ruling dynasty – Suppiluliuma and Labarna. We do not know whether the Patinite kings were in any way linked with the Hittite royal family. But their adoption of the great names of Hittite royalty clearly reflects an ongoing memory of and reverence for their Bronze Age predecessors.

Lubarna II, a successor of Qalparunda, was killed in an uprising by his own people, who replaced him on the throne with a 'non-royal' person called Surri. In response, Shalmaneser dispatched an army to Patin under the command of his commander-in-chief Dayyan-Ashur, who pitched camp by the royal Patinite city Kinalua. But Surri died before a confrontation could take place, and his subjects, fearful of Assyrian reprisals for their overthrow and assassination of his predecessor, arrested his sons and soldiers, and delivered them to the Assyrian commander. Dayyan-Ashur had the soldiers impaled, and appointed a man called Sasi from the land of Kurussa as Patin's new ruler. These events date to Shalmaneser's twenty-eighth regnal year (**RIMA* 3: 69). The appointment was accepted by Patin's inhabitants, who handed over a large tribute to Dayyan-Ashur, as Shalmaneser's representative.

A pact of alliance was subsequently drawn up between the Assyrian and Patinite kings, which seems to have held until it was breached in 739 by Tutammu, the last of Patin's native rulers. The Assyrian king at the time, Tiglath-pileser III, responded by removing Tutammu from power and converting his kingdom, now renamed Kullanni(a) (a dialectal variant of the name Kinalua), into a province ruled by an Assyrian governor (**Tigl. III* 56–9). Large numbers of deportees from Tiglath-pileser's eastern conquests were settled in the cities of the former kingdom.

CHLI I: 361–3.

Pauza Iron Age city located in the upper Habur region of northern Mesopotamia at the foot of the Kashiyari mountain range (mod. Tur ʿAbdin), not far from Nusaybin. It is first attested in the reign of the Assyrian king Ashur-bel-kala (1073–1056), who fought a battle with the Aramaeans there (**RIMA* 2: 102). At the end of C10 it belonged to the territories ruled by the Aramaean chieftain Nur-Adad from his capital Nusaybin (Nisibis, Assyrian Nasibina). Pauza was conquered along with the other cities of Nur-Adad in the land of Hanigalbat, including Iaridu and Saraku, by the Assyrian king Adad-nirari II during his campaigns in the region in 901 and 900 (**RIMA* 2: 149).

Pedasa (Pidasa, *Gökçeler*) (map 5) M1 Carian city, of Lelegian (q.v.) origin, located in the Myndus peninsula, southwestern Anatolia. The city is referred to several times by Herodotus in his account of Persia's campaigns in the west. In his first reference (1.175), he notes that the Pedasians were the only people living in or around Caria who held out against the Persian commander Harpagus during his campaign in southwestern Anatolia c. 546. They caused the Persians major difficulties by building a stronghold on a hill called Lida. (Herodotus also states in this context that whenever disaster was about to strike the Pedasians or their neighbours, their priestess of Athena grew a long beard. This allegedly happened on three occasions.) In 499, the first year of the Ionian rebellion against Persia, Herodotus (5.121) reports that a Persian force was wiped out on the road to Pedasa as it was preparing a campaign against the cities of Caria. Five years later the Ionian rebellion was crushed, and the city of Miletus, which had led the rebel-states fell to the Persian army. According to Herodotus (6.20) the Persians occupied Miletus and the surrounding plain, but handed over the hill country to Carians from Pedasa. In G. E. Bean's view, this apparently means that a number of the Pedasians were transplanted to a new settlement, also called Pedasa, in the hills above Miletus, perhaps in an attempt to weaken potential centres of resistance against Persian rule in the future.

In C5, some time after the withdrawal of the Persians from the west, Pedasa became a member of the Athenian Confederacy (see glossary). Its annual payment of two talents was higher than that of Halicarnassus (one and two-thirds of a talent), which no doubt reflects the relative importance of the two cities in this period. In mid C4 Pedasa was incorporated into Halicarnassus by the Carian satrap Mausolus. (Pliny the Elder, 5.107, wrongly reports that it was one of six Lelegian towns which Alexander assigned to the jurisdiction of Halicarnassus. Their incorporation into Halicarnassus was in fact due to Mausolus prior to Alexander's campaigns.) Thenceforth the city was much reduced in size and status, but apparently continued to function as a military outpost.

Pedasa's material remains, on the site of Gökçeler, are typical of a Lelegian settlement.

They include a citadel, where traces of buildings can still be seen, a large outer enclosure wall fortified by towers, and beyond the fortified area a number of chamber tombs, dating in some cases to C7 or earlier.

Bean (1971: 115 map, 119–22; *PECS* 682).

Pelasgians A mythical people associated in Greek tradition with various parts of western Anatolia, Crete, and mainland Greece. The name has come to be used as a general term for the pre-Indo-European populations of the Greek and Aegean worlds. In Homer's *Iliad* (2.240–3), the Pelasgians are a specific population group listed among the allies of the Trojans, and are said to come from the city of Laris(s)a. Of the various cities so called, this one has been located either south of Troy, on the western coast of the Troad, or in Thrace. The former is more likely.

Peleset see **Philistines**.

Pella (*Tabaqat/Khirbet Fahl*) (map 8) City in Transjordan, located in the foothills of the eastern Jordan valley, 28 km south of the Sea of Galilee. The region's history of occupation extends from the Lower Palaeolithic period to the present day. Investigation of Pella itself, whose main archaeological feature is an oval mound, began with soundings made by R. Funk and N. Richardson in 1958 for the American Schools of Oriental Research. After the first major excavation was undertaken in 1967 by R. H. Smith for the College of Wooster, USA, the site was subsequently investigated, from 1979 onwards, by Smith with J. B. Hennessy and A. W. McNicoll, the latter two on behalf of the University of Sydney.

Evidence of settlement in the Early Bronze Age has been uncovered both on the principal mound, which lay on the north side of Wadi Jirm el-Moz, and on a dome-shaped natural hill called Tell es-Husn which lay on the south side. On the former, a large building dating to Early Bronze I has been discovered. It is likely that already in this early phase of its existence the settlement was protected by a fortification wall. The major architectural feature of Tell es-Husn in this period is a large stone platform dating to Early Bronze IIA.

Under the name Pihil/Pihilu, the city is attested in a number of Middle and Late Bronze Age Egyptian sources. It appears in the list of Asiatic conquests of the C15 pharaoh Tuthmosis III, and in two of the mid C14 Amarna letters, written by its king Mut-Bahlu to his overlord Akhenaten (**EA* 255, 256). The C13 Egyptian Anastasi Papyrus refers to it as one of the cities which supplied Egypt with chariot parts. Clearly, Pella was an important city during its Middle and Late Bronze Age phases, as indicated also by its material remains which place it firmly within a Canaanite cultural context. There appears to have been a smooth, uninterrupted progression from Middle to Late Bronze Age. The city's prosperity in these phases is indicated particularly by the contents of its tombs, which include many imported luxury items, such as inlaid ivory boxes, alabaster perfume bottles, and objects plated with gold. A combination of trade and manufacture has been suggested as the reason for the city's wealth. The tomb goods indicate trade and/or cultural contact with Egypt by the Middle Bronze II period, and also with Cyprus and the Aegean world in the Late Bronze Age. The city was at this time fortified by a substantial city wall, still used in the Iron Age.

By C13, Pella may have suffered some reduction in size, and though there was some degree of cultural continuity into the succeeding Iron Age, the city of this period was apparently smaller and poorer than its Middle and Late Bronze Age predecessors. Several scholars have commented on the absence of any reference to Pella in biblical sources. This may mean either that it was known to the Bible's authors under a different name, that it remained largely outside Israelite influence, or that the early C6 Babylonian conquest of the region resulted in the abandonment of the site. There are virtually no material remains that can be dated to the following Persian period (C6–4).

The anc. tradition that Pella was refounded by Alexander the Great in 332 and named after the Macedonian royal capital is now considered to be fictional. There is no evidence of resettlement on the site in the early Hellenistic period. However, by C2 the city had undergone a major revival with a substantial population increase, and was once more active in international trading enterprises.

Smith (*NEAEHL* 3: 1174–80), Hennessy *et al.* (1989).

Pergamum (map 5) M1 BCE–M1 CE city near the western coast of Anatolia, 110 km north of Smyrna and 24 km from the Aegean Sea. It was probably first settled by Aeolian Greeks in C8, but is not attested until 401 when it appears in Xenophon's *Anabasis*. On his return from Persia with his Greek mercenary forces after their abortive expedition to Persia in support of one of Darius II's sons, a pretender to the Persian throne called Cyrus the Younger, Xenophon arrived at Pergamum and sought food and shelter for his forces from the city's tyrant, Gongylus (*Anabasis* 7.8.8). He was hosted in the city by Gongylus' wife, Hellas. In C3 Pergamum came into high prominence as the seat of the Attalid dynasty (282–133), whose empire at the peak of its power extended over large parts of western and southern Anatolia.

E. Akurgal (1973: 69–111), Schäfer (*PECS* 688–92), Spawforth, Roueché (*OCD* 1138–9).

Perge (map 4) M1 BCE–M1 CE city in Pamphylia, southern Anatolia, 16 km northeast of Antalya. It was among the cities which, according to Greek legendary tradition, were established by Greeks of mixed origin under the leadership of Amphilochus, Calchas, and Mopsus after the Trojan War. In fact, some of the cities may not have been established until C7 or C6. But at Perge evidence has now been found for a Late Bronze Age settlement on the city's acropolis. This settlement is almost certainly to be identified with the city called Parha in Hittite texts, which lay just outside the western boundary of the kingdom of Tarhuntassa. Occupation appears to have continued at Perge without interruption from the Late Bronze Age through the early Iron Age. In C5 the city became a member of the Athenian Confederacy (see glossary). Along with two other Pamphylian cities, Aspendus and Sillyum, it appears in the Athenian Tribute Lists for the year 425. In 333 it provided Alexander the Great's army with a base of operations in Pamphylia. Following Alexander's death the city became subject to the kings of Pergamum, and was later incorporated into the Roman province of Cilicia.

Substantial remains of Perge's lower city survive, on the level ground extending south of the acropolis. Its walls date back to the Hellenistic period, but almost all the other remains, including colonnaded streets and stoas, a theatre, stadium, tombs, and baths, are of Roman date.

Bean (1968: 45–58; *PECS* 692–3), E. Akurgal (1973: 329–33), Yıldırım and Gates (2007: 308).

Persepolis (map 16) Persian royal capital, located in southwestern Iran in the

Figure 84 Pergamum, Hellenistic theatre.

province of Fars, on the eastern edge of the Marv Dasht plain, 47 km northeast of mod. Shiraz. 'Persepolis' is the name by which the city was known to the anc. Greeks (meaning 'city of Persis'). The Persians themselves called it Parsa (also the name of the Persian homeland). Founded by the Persian king Darius I (522–486) as a new royal seat to replace the former capital, Pasargadae (which lay 40 km to the north), Persepolis became the new administrative centre of the empire, and the place where coronations, royal burials, and other major ceremonies and festivals were held. It was to maintain its pre-eminent status for the remainder of the Persian empire (C6–4). The site was excavated by teams from the University of Chicago between 1931 and 1939. Later excavations carried out under the auspices of the Iranian Archaeological Service brought to light the layout of the remaining unexcavated portions of the site. An Italian restoration team working between 1964 and 1978, with the collaboration of other scholars, contributed important new information on the building techniques used at Persepolis and the various stages of its construction.

Directly west of a hill defended by a circuit wall lies the city's great stone terrace (the Takht, or 'throne' in Persian), some 455 m × 300 m in extent. On it were a series of monumental royal buildings constructed by Darius and his successors, particularly Xerxes, Artaxerxes I, and Artaxerxes III. Entry to these buildings was through the so-called All Nations Gate. This gate structure, which was built or completed by Darius' son and successor Xerxes (**XPa*), featured a pair of colossal stone bulls, and a second pair of winged, human-headed bulls, the two pairs guarding the outer and inner doorways respectively. The gatehouse was reached by ascending a double staircase, 14 m high. This provided the only formal access to the royal complex. Columned halls

Figure 85 Perge, colonnaded street, Roman period, with acropolis in background.

and porticoes were prominent architectural features of the complex, whose most notable buildings include the so-called Hall of 100 Columns (the throne-room?), the palaces of Darius and Xerxes, the so-called harem of Xerxes, and the Apadana, a great square Audience Hall covering an area of 60.5 sq. m (*apadana* is an old Persian term used for columned buildings, its use in Persian perhaps largely restricted to the most important of these buildings). The Apadana is one of several buildings that appear on raised platforms, providing scope for sculptural decoration on the retaining walls, such as the representations of files of palace guards and lion-and-bull-fighting scenes on the south side of Darius' palace. Also depicted are human figures climbing the double-reversed staircases which provide access to the palace, on its north and east sides. Both the staircases and the reliefs date to the reign of Artaxerxes III (359–338). Reliefs in other parts of the complex depict the king accompanied by the crown prince or other attendants, bulls, lions, griffins, sphinxes, and most notably, on the north and east sides of the Apadana, files of Median and Persian nobles, and tribute brought to the king by representatives from twenty-three regions throughout his realm. A number of freestanding stone statues, of bulls, ibexes, lions, and large dogs, have also survived. Columns throughout the complex are surmounted by the sculptured protomes of bulls, some human-headed, lions, hybrid lion monsters, and griffins. These served as capitals for supporting the ceiling beams, which were made of cedar. Much of the building and sculptural embellishment of the complex may have been carried out by craftsmen pressed into service from numerous parts of the kingdom, from as far afield as Lydia in western Anatolia. Smaller, private palaces were constructed in the southeast sector of

Figure 86 Persepolis, All Nations gate.

the terrace complex. No trace has yet been discovered of the city's residential quarter. Buildings in this quarter were no doubt constructed largely of mudbrick and timber.

A number of small finds came to light in the city during excavation. These include military equipment, seals, ceramic ware, gold jewellery, silver vessels, and bronze and lapis lazuli statuettes. Many of the finds were unearthed in the so-called Treasury, which once housed a vast array of works of art and other precious items, including booty and tributary gifts. A small tablet archive recording payments made by Treasury officials to workers (139 documents; see Cameron, 1948) came to light in this building. However, the most important tablets unearthed on the site are the 15,000–20,000 Fortification Tablets, so called because they were found in two rooms of the city's fortification system (*Hallock, 1969; for later refs, see *PE* 12). Dating from the thirteenth to the twenty-eighth year of Darius' reign (509–494), they are the earliest administrative documents we have of the Persian empire. (See most recently *PE* 763–70, *770–814.) They record food distributions made by Treasury officials from

Figure 87 Persepolis, palace of Darius I.

Figure 88 Persepolis, Treasury.

the imperial stores located around the capital to a large number of recipients (including members of the king's own family, priests, and workers in the employ of the royal court), supplies to travellers, and donations to the gods.

All these finds must represent only a tiny fraction of the city's contents at the time of its destruction. Persepolis was looted and put to the torch by Alexander the Great in 330. Diodorus (17.70), referring to Alexander's description of it as 'the most hateful of the cities of Asia', provides a graphic account of its destruction. He reports (17.71) that 120,000 talents of gold and silver were taken from the royal Treasury by Alexander; 3,000 camels and a vast number of mules were used to transport the bulk of this treasure to Susa.

Schmidt (1953, 1957, 1970), Root (1995: 2624–32), Stronach and Codella (*OEANE* 4: 273–7), Roaf (*RlA* 10: 393–412).

Persia(ns) (map 16) One of several Iranian population groups, who collectively formed a branch of the Indo-European-speaking peoples and are believed to have arrived on the Iranian plateau in the second half of M2, perhaps from a homeland east of the Caspian Sea. Two groups of Persians appear to be identifiable in the written sources: one of them occupied the land in the central western Zagros mountains called Parsua in Neo-Assyrian texts, and the second a region in southwestern Iran, to the east of the Persian Gulf, which was formerly part of the Elamite kingdom and came to be known as Parsa (mod. Fars). There is still debate about the possible relationship between the two groups – if they were in fact two separate groups. Do the names really refer to one and the same people? And if so, do they reflect a migration of these people from north to south? In any case, the Persians seem to have had a long association with the people called the Medes. It is uncertain whether, prior to mid C6, they were subordinate to the Medes, as Herodotus maintains, or of equal status with them.

Following the destruction of the Assyrian empire in late C7 by a Babylonian–Median military alliance, Mesopotamia and Assyria's former subject territories in the Syro-Palestinian region fell beneath the sway of the newly emergent Neo-Babylonian empire. The Medes, according to Classical sources, became the dominant power in western Iran under their king Cyaxares (625–585). (On the question of the reliability of these sources, see **Medes**). In mid C6 the Medes became subject to a new power which arose in the land of Parsa under the leadership of a man called Cyrus (II). Cyrus became the founder of the Persian empire, the most extensive of all anc. empires before the era of imperial Rome.

According to tradition, the city of Anshan in Parsa was the original home of the dynasty to which Cyrus belonged (but see under **Anshan**). The dynasty is commonly referred to as the Achaemenid dynasty. It is so called after the Persian king Darius I's (522–486) ancestor Achaemenes (Old Persian Haxamanish), attested by Darius in the Bisitun inscription (**DB* 2–3), by his successors, and by a number of Greek sources, notably Herodotus (7.11). (See further on this below.) Cyrus, who claimed to be a descendant of Teispes (not Achaemenes) (e.g. Cyrus Cylinder, **PE* 71, no. 21, line 21), succeeded to the dynastic seat in 559, in Anshan according to his own account. Herodotus (1.108–130) provides a vivid and largely fanciful account of his birth, childhood in exile (cf. Ctesias, *FGrH* 90 F66 = **PE* 97–8, no. 32), and subsequent rise to power. Elements of this account strikingly recall the circumstances surrounding the birth and upbringing of the M3 Akkadian king Sargon in Mesopotamian literary tradition, Moses in *OT* tradition, and Romulus and Remus in Roman tradition. There is also much doubt as to whether Cyrus' supposed familial link with the Median king Astyages (Akkadian Ishtumegu) (alleged to have been his maternal grandfather; thus Xenophon, *Cyropaedia* 1.2.1–3.2 = **PE* 98, no. 33) was anything more than 'a fictional

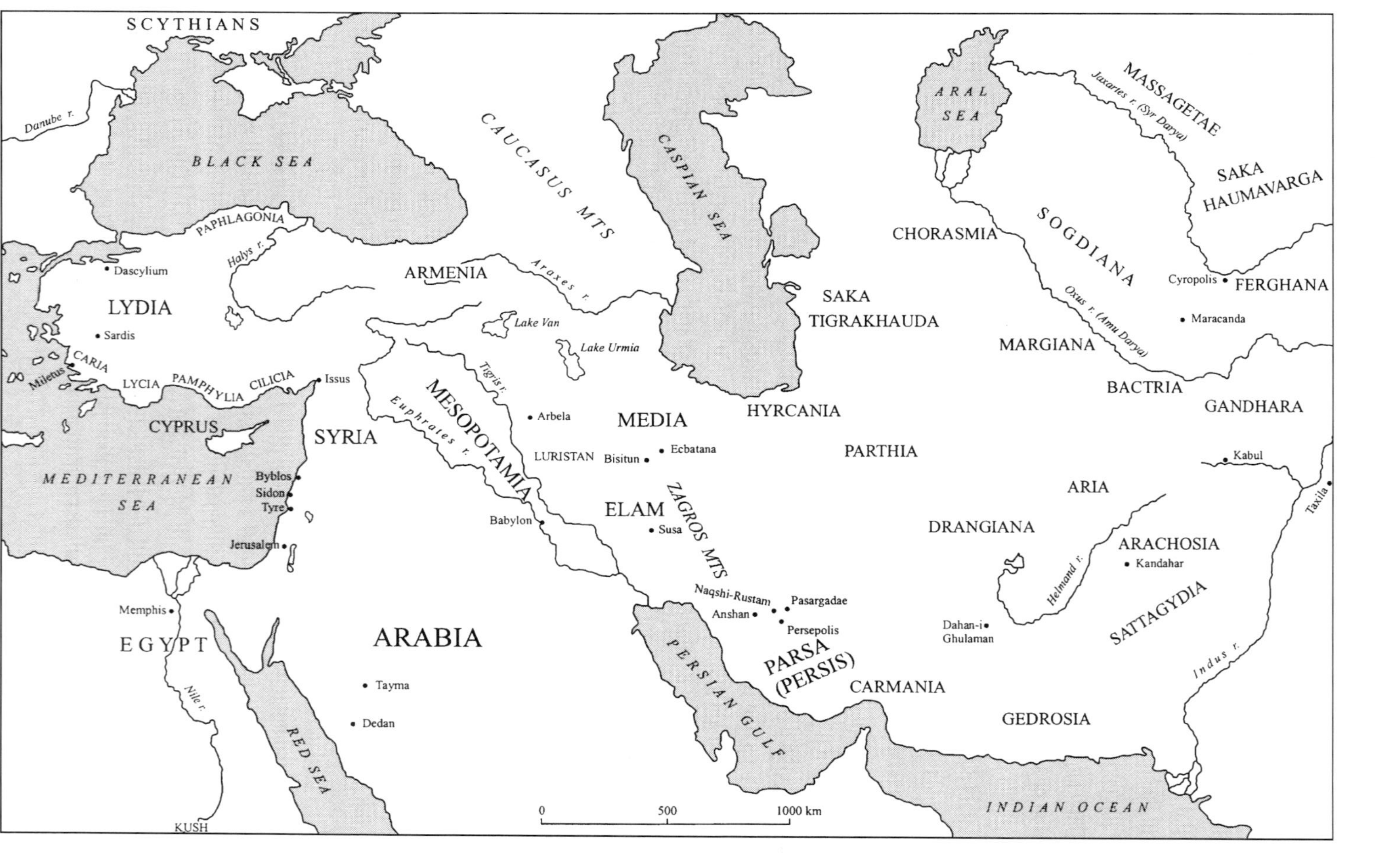

Map 16 The Persian empire.

addition to the story of conquest in order to legitimate Cyrus' rule in Media' (Brosius, 2006: 8). The C4 writer Ctesias categorically denied that Cyrus was in any way related to Astyages (*FGrH* 688 F9.1 = **PE* 58, no. 8).

In any case, Astyages' allegedly despotic and brutal regime provoked Cyrus, after uniting the Persian tribes, to lead an army of them into Media against his grandfather(?), where a military showdown took place. The battle resulted in a decisive victory for Cyrus, as reported in a Babylonian chronicle (no. 7), the so-called Nabonidus Chronicle (see glossary) (**ABC* 104–11, **Chav.* 418–19, **PE* 50–1, no. 1), and also by Herodotus (1.128). Cyrus' triumph was ensured by the defection of large numbers of Median troops to his side. According to the Nabonidus Chronicle, Astyages' rebellious troops actually handed over their king to Cyrus. In the battle's aftermath, Cyrus marched upon the royal Median city Ecbatana, plundered it, and carried off its spoils to Anshan (**ABC* 106). According to Ctesias (*FGrH* 688 F9.1 = **PE* 58, no. 8), Astyages had fled to Ecbatana after his defeat, but gave himself up to Cyrus' agents when the victorious Persian king arrived in the city. Cyrus allegedly set him free and 'honoured him as a father' (cf. Justin 1.6.16 = **PE* 59, no. 9). Thenceforth, the Medes were absorbed within Cyrus' fledgling empire. They were to play an important role within the empire, and were acknowledged as its second most important ethnic group. Indeed, the terms Persian and Median were used almost interchangeably by the contemporary Greeks. Cyrus' foundation of the Persian empire, whose homeland covered roughly the area of mod. Iran, dates to his defeat of Astyages in 550. According to Strabo (15.3.8), it was on the site of his victory that he established his new royal capital of Pasargadae.

The conquest of Media paved the way for Cyrus' conquests in the regions which lay to its north, including perhaps what still remained of the kingdom of Urartu. Far to

Figure 89 Persian archers.

the west, in Anatolia, the Lydian king Croesus, an ally and brother-in-law of the vanquished Astyages, became alarmed at the rise of the new power east of the Tigris. In an attempt to forestall a Persian invasion of his own country, Croesus led his army across the Halys r., the former boundary between Lydian and Median territory, where he confronted Cyrus' westward advancing Persian forces (Herodotus 1.75–7). Though the battle they fought was inconclusive, Croesus was forced to retreat to his own territory where the pursuing Cyrus inflicted a devastating defeat upon him on a plain outside the Lydian capital Sardis. Lydia was absorbed into the Persian empire, along with the Ionian Greek states located on the Aegean coast. These had formerly been subject to Lydia. Subsequently Cyrus turned his attention upon Babylonia, now a weak and divided kingdom under its then ruler Nabonidus (556–539). Disaffection amongst Nabonidus' subjects greatly facilitated Cyrus' conquest of Babylonia, Babylon itself falling to the Persian king in 539 without a battle (Nabonidus Chronicle: **ABC* 110, **CS* I: 468, **Chav.* 420, **PE* 51, no. 1; Cyrus Cylinder: **Chav.* 428–9, **CS* II: 315, **PE* 71, no. 21; cf. Herodotus 1.189–92). It was at this time, according to the *OT* sources Ezra 1: 1–4, 6: 2–5, that Cyrus issued a decree permitting the Jews to return to their homeland from their captivity in Babylon, and rebuild the Temple in Jerusalem.

Subsequently, Cyrus probably conducted a campaign into Central Asia, which resulted in the incorporation of a number of eastern lands into his empire, as reflected in the list of these lands appearing in Darius I's Bisitun inscription (**DB*), and his successor Xerxes' so-called *daiva* inscription (**XPh*) (see glossary). No contemporary record of such a campaign survives, but a later reference to it may be contained in Pliny the Elder's account (6.92) of Persia's eastern satrapies. Cyrus may now have set his sights on the conquest of Egypt. But he was diverted by uprisings on the eastern frontiers of his kingdom and was killed during a campaign against rebel forces in the region of the Oxus and Jaxartes rivers (mod. Uzbekistan and Kazakhstan). He had established a series of forts along the latter, which came to mark the Persian empire's northeastern frontier. There are, however, different versions in the Classical sources as

Figure 90 Persepolis, royal audience scene.

to who precisely was responsible for Cyrus' death. Herodotus (1.214), followed by most other sources, attributes his death in the field of battle to the Massagetae; Ctesias (*FGrH* 688 F9 = **PE* 101, no. 35) to the Derbices; and Berossus (*FGrH* 680 F10) to a Scythian tribe of western Central Asia called the Daai (Dahae). (See discussions by Dandamaev, 1989: 66–9, Vogelsang, 1992: 187–9.) According to Xenophon, however (*Cyropaedia* 8.7 = **PE* 102, no. 36), Cyrus died peacefully at home in his old age, surrounded by his family, friends, and governors.

Cyrus' son and successor Cambyses II (530–522) conquered Cyprus, and resumed his father's plans for the conquest of Egypt, leading a campaign there in 525. He defeated the pharaoh Psammetichus III in a battle outside Memphis (Herodotus 3.10–11), and thenceforth the whole of Egypt was incorporated into the Persian empire (*Autobiography of Udjahorresne(t)*, sec. c = *Brosius, 2000: 15, no. 20, **PE* 118, no. 11). The Persians also made further conquests in Nubia and northern Africa west of Egypt. Cambyses remained in Egypt for three years, before being recalled by news that a rebellion had broken out in his homeland, and that a usurper, perhaps his brother Bardiya, was attempting to seize his throne. (Bardiya is called Smerdis by Herodotus, and is probably to be identified with the Persian priest or magus called Gaumata in Darius I's Bisitun inscription; **DB* 10–14.) Cambyses' death in Syria on his return journey (Herodotus 3.64–6, Ctesias *FGrH* 688 F 13.11–15 = **PE* 163–4, no. 5) enabled Bardiya to claim the throne. But after a reign lasting only eight months, Bardiya was assassinated at the instigation of a rival claimant, Darius, formerly a commander in Cambyses' army and now the new occupant of the Persian throne.

Darius was certainly a member of the Persian aristocracy, but there is considerable doubt as to whether he was actually a member of the royal dynasty. He claimed descent from an ancestor called Achaemenes, whom he identified as the father of Teispes, great-grandfather of Cyrus II, thus linking his family with that of the founder of the Persian empire (see also **PE* 177, no. 19). But scholars have pointed out that none of the Persian records before Darius' reign, including the Cyrus Cylinder (see glossary), refers to an Achaemenes, and suggest that the link between Achaemenes and Cyrus may have been an invention on Darius' part to legitimize his succession (thus Brosius, 2006: 17–18). At all events, with the backing of a large part of the Persian nobility, Darius I (522–486) was installed as ruler of the empire. But in the first year of his reign there were uprisings against his authority throughout the kingdom, and a number of pretenders to the throne sought to remove him from power. He responded swiftly. According to the account he gives in his Bisitun inscription, he fought nineteen battles and took prisoner nine kings in a single year (**DB* 52). By the end of 521 he had crushed the rebellions, and then set his sights on expanding the empire's territories even further afield. Indeed, the empire reached its greatest extent during his reign, with new campaigns in the east, the conquest of parts of northern India, and the addition to the emperor's realm of the region Hindush or Sind along the banks of the Indus r.

Darius now prepared to expand his empire westwards into Europe. A campaign across the Bosporus against the Scythian tribes (perhaps in 513, but the date is disputed) paved the way for further expeditions on European soil, which resulted in the establishment of a Persian presence in Thrace and the northern Aegean. (The Greek sources for the Scythian campaign are collected in **PE* 193–203, nos 5–16.) Though the campaign ended inconclusively, and almost disastrously for the Persians, it paved the way for Darius' conflicts with the mainland Greek states. But it was the rebellion of a number of Ionian Greek states against Persian rule (499–494) that provided the actual catalyst for these conflicts. (For the Greek sources for the revolt and its aftermath, see **PE* 211–30, nos 31–49.) The rebels were supported by Athens and the small state of Eretria on the island of Euboea (which lay off the eastern coast of mainland Greece). Though Darius finally crushed the rebellion, he was, according to Herodotus, infuriated by Athens' and Eretria's intervention in the affair – which allegedly was the reason for his sending a punitive naval expedition against them in 490. The Persian fleet gained control of a number of Cycladic islands en route, captured Eretria through an act of treachery, and anchored in the bay of Marathon in preparation for an assault upon Athens, which lay 35 km away. But here on the Marathon plain, the Persians were resoundingly defeated by forces from Athens and Plataea (the latter lay in Boeotia in central Greece), and forced to abandon their Greek campaign (Herodotus 6.112–13, 115–17).

However, Darius' son and successor Xerxes I (486–465) made plans for a fresh assault upon the Greek mainland, preparing a massive force for a coordinated invasion by land and sea, under his personal command, via the coast of Thrace and Macedonia. The Persians advanced with little resistance through the Greek mainland until they reached Athens, which they captured and destroyed. But they were forced to abort their invasion when they suffered major defeats by the allied Greek forces in a sea battle in the strait of Salamis just off the coast of Attica (480) and a land battle the following year at Plataea. (For the sources, predominantly Herodotus, which record Xerxes' assault upon the Greek world, and the final Greek victories over his forces, see **PE* 250–85, nos 9–61.) Persia never again posed a direct threat to the city-states of the Greek mainland. However, a number of scholars are now inclined to see the repulse of Persia essentially in terms of a strategic withdrawal on Xerxes' part rather than a military debacle, noting that the Persian defeat and consequent loss of Greek territory to the Persians had no repercussions for the stability of the empire (thus Brosius, 2006: 25).

Xerxes was assassinated in a palace conspiracy in 465 (Ctesias *FGrH* 688 F13, Diodorus 11.69.1–2, Justin 3.1 = **PE* 307–9, no. 92 i–iii; see also **PE* 306, no. 90). His son Artaxerxes I followed him on the throne, after emerging triumphant from disputes with his brothers over the succession. When Artaxerxes died in 424, after forty years as king, contests for the throne broke out afresh, and were in fact to become a feature of every succession until the fall of the Persian empire to Alexander the Great in 330. Artaxerxes' successor Xerxes II occupied the royal seat for only forty-five days before he was assassinated. A contest for the succession between his brother Sogdianus and half-brother Ochus ended with victory for the latter, who assumed the throne as Darius II (424–404) (Ctesias *FGrH* 688 F125.48–50 = **PE* 332, no. 20). Following his death, civil war erupted between Darius' son and successor Artaxerxes II (Arsaces) (404–359) and another of his sons, Cyrus the Younger. The contest ended with Artaxerxes' victory at the battle of Cunaxa (401), a small town on the Euphrates. (The Greek sources relating to the conflict between Artaxerxes and Cyrus are collected in **PE* 353–67, nos 1–27). The end of Artaxerxes II's reign was marked by fresh palace conspiracies (Plutarch, *Artaxerxes* 30), as was the reign of his son and successor Artaxerxes III (Ochus) (359–338). The next king, Artaxerxes IV (Arses) (338–336) reigned for only two years before he too was assassinated, and his successor Darius III – who was defeated by Alexander – also met his death, in 330, by an assassin's hand (Arrian, *Anabasis* 3.21.1, 4–5, 10; 3.22.1).

Figure 91 Persepolis, griffin protomes.

Undoubtedly, the lack of clear, fixed principles of succession was a major cause of the disputes that broke out between rival pretenders to the Persian throne, almost every time the throne became vacant – and on many occasions even before it became vacant. Nevertheless, a number of those who did succeed in occupying the throne managed to remain there for a considerable time. Moreover, their reigns were sometimes marked by significant achievements. In early C4 the Persians under Artaxerxes II re-established their control over Cyprus and the Greek states in western Anatolia, which had been lost to them in 479, by the terms of a treaty called the King's Peace (386) (see glossary), drawn up with warring mainland Greek states. The Spartan Antalcidas was the most prominent negotiator on the Greek side. Artaxerxes III succeeded in reconquering Egypt, which had successfully rebelled against Persian rule in 405, as well as in putting down revolts in Cyprus and a number of Phoenician cities. And both Artaxerxes I and Artaxerxes III made significant contributions to the monumental architecture of Persepolis, the royal city founded by Darius I.

As with the imperial Roman world in C1 CE, we should be careful not to overestimate the impact of the palace conspiracies and coups on the operation of the Persian empire as a whole. The administrative organization set up primarily by Darius I provided, by and large, efficient and stable government for the vast realm which he and his predecessors had won by military force. Darius divided the empire into twenty provinces, called satrapies (the account of its organization given by Herodotus 3.89–97 is now not considered reliable; see glossary under **satrapy**). In most cases their governors, or satraps, were rulers of local origin who were allowed a large measure of autonomy.

Indeed, they enjoyed many of the trappings of monarchy in their own right, and were responsible directly to the emperor for the collection of tribute within their satrapy, the provision of levies for the Persian army, and just and efficient government in their satrapy. Communications between various parts of the empire were facili ated by the development of a network of major roads, the most famous of the communication routes being the 'Royal Road' which linked Susa with Sardis, a distant of c. 2,500 km. Darius also greatly improved travel and communication by sea, financing naval expeditions to seek out new trade markets, developing harbour facilities on the Persian Gulf, and cutting a canal between the Nile and the Red Sea (**DZc*). To stimulate agricultural productivity in the provinces, he financed irrigation projects and the building of underground water channels in areas where rainfall was meagre or unpredictable. And to facilitate commercial activities throughout the empire, he adopted from the Lydians the practice of minting coins. He issued both silver and gold coins (the latter commonly known as Darics), stamped with the royal insignia as a guarantee of their quality and weight.

While his policies were designed to promote stability throughout the empire by peaceful means, he created a powerful standing army of professional soldiers to ensure maintenance of his authority over the empire. This army could be increased substantially, when necessary, by levies from the satrapies. But the backbone of the army was an elite force of Persians and Medes known as the Ten Thousand Immortals, crack troops whose numbers were constantly replenished to offset casualties. For his

Figure 92 Persepolis, human-headed capital.

operations by sea, he had at his disposal a formidable navy, consisting initially of ships provided by Phoenician cities along the Syro-Palestinian seaboard.

The Persian empire fell to Alexander the Great in 330. Even allowing for Alexander's military genius, internal dissensions and upheavals within the empire's central power structure no doubt contributed significantly to its fall, especially in its final years. None the less, Cyrus and his successors built and maintained for more than two centuries what was arguably the greatest of all empires up to this time in human history. And the policy of Darius and his successors of employing craftsmen and artists from every part of the empire for their public works gave a rich, eclectic, cosmopolitan character to Persian material culture, to an extent unparalleled in any earlier or contemporary civilization.

Briant (1984b; 2002), Dandamaev (1989), Sancisi-Weerdenburg (1995), Wiesehöfer (2001), Schmitt/Wiesehöfer/Stausberg (*RlA* 10: 412–24), Allen (2005), Curtis and Tallis (2005), D. T. Potts (2005a), Brosius (2006), Koch *et al.* (2006), Kuhrt (2007b).

Phaselis (*Tekirova*) (map 15) M1 BCE–M1 CE town on the eastern coast of Lycia, southwestern Anatolia, 50 km southwest of Antalya. According to Greek tradition, it was founded c. 690 by colonists from Lindos on the island of Rhodes (though in another Greek tradition the city's founder came from Argos in mainland Greece). The site with its three harbours provided an excellent location for a commercial centre on the route between the Aegean world and the Syro-Palestinian coastlands. Around 630, it joined with other Greek cities of Anatolia and the islands off its coast in founding the Greek trading colony of Naucratis in the Nile Delta (Herodotus 2.178). Though today generally included in Lycian territory, its culture remained essentially Greek. Indeed, for much of its existence it was not reckoned part of Lycia, but of the neighbouring country of Pamphylia. In 540 it came under Persian domination, and remained so until the Athenian commander Cimon established his control over it during his campaign along Anatolia's southern coast in 469 (Plutarch, *Cimon* 12.3–4).

Initially, the Phaselitans remained loyal to their Persian allegiance and resisted Cimon. But they eventually came to terms with him, after suffering severely from a siege that he had mounted upon their city, and subsequently Phaselis became a member of the Athenian Confederacy (see glossary). Its relatively high annual contribution to the Confederacy's funds – three to six talents – is a reflection of its wealth, derived from its commercial enterprises. By the beginning of C4, Phaselis had once more come under Persian overlordship, where it remained (supporting the Carian satrap Mausolus against the Lycians in the satrap rebellion during the 360s) until its peaceful surrender to Alexander the Great in 333 (Arrian, *Anabasis* 1.24.5–6). It was at this time still clearly distinguished from Lycia. During the Hellenistic period it came under both Ptolemaic and Seleucid control. Following the battle of Magnesia in 189, Rome handed it over to Rhodes. In 167, however, it was granted independence by the Roman Senate. Around this time it became a member of the Lycian League, but its attachment to Lycia remained tenuous and sporadic.

Throughout its history, Phaselis was a flourishing city, due very largely to its commercial enterprises, which were greatly facilitated by its excellent harbours. The advantages of its location were to some extent countered by its allegedly unhealthy summer climate and disease-bearing marshes (Livy 37.23.2). To judge from Greek and Roman literary sources, the city acquired a highly unsavoury reputation. Its population were noted for mendacity and fraud, breach of faith in commercial contracts, and extreme litigiousness in the courts in actions covered by commercial laws. During the late Roman Republic, Phaselis established an alliance with the Cilician pirates (Strabo 14.5.7, Cicero, *Verrine Orations* 4.10.21), which led Cicero (*Verrine Orations* 4.10.23) to use the term Phaselis as a byword for plunder and extortion.

Phaselis' material remains date almost entirely to the Roman imperial period. They include the remnants of a city wall, three agoras (market-places), a paved main street, a theatre, baths, and a triple-arched gateway dedicated to the early C2 CE emperor Hadrian.

Bean (*PECS* 700–1), Keen (1998: 233–5).

Phellus (map 15) M1 BCE–M1 CE located near the central coast of Lycia, in southwestern Anatolia. Phellus is a Greek word meaning 'stony'. The city's native name was Wehñte, as attested in both inscriptions and coin legends probably dating to early or mid C4. Phellus is first attested c. 500 by the Greek geographer Hecataeus (*FGrH* 1 F258), who wrongly located it in Pamphylia. The city lay slightly inland, and used Antiphellus on the coast, 5 km away, as its port. M. Zimmermann concludes from a survey which he recently conducted at Phellus that the city reached the peak of its urban development in the period C6–C4. During the Hellenistic age it declined in importance and was eclipsed by Antiphellus, which became a major city in the region under Roman rule. Almost all the surviving remains of Phellus are sepulchral monuments, several of which date back to pre-Hellenistic times. Most notable is a freestanding tomb of Lycian house-type. Two inscriptions in the native Lycian language, whose use is attested in Lycia from late C6 to late C4, have also been found on the site.

Bean (*PECS* 701; 1978: 92–100), Zimmermann (2005).

Philistia see **Philistines**.

Philistines Iron Age population who in C12 occupied that part of the southern coastal plain of Palestine which came to be called Philistia, lying roughly between mod. Tel Aviv and Deir el-Balah. The Philistines are linked by most scholars with the Peleset, one of the groups of Sea Peoples who attacked the coast of Egypt in the eighth year of Ramesses III's reign (1184–1153), as recorded in the so-called Papyrus Harris (see glossary) (*Gertzen, 2008: 91), and in Ramesses' inscription on the walls of his mortuary temple at Medinet Habu. In the reliefs accompanying the latter, the Peleset are depicted among the captives, wearing tasselled kilts and what appears to be a feathered headdress, though the interpretation of the latter has been disputed.

In the context of the Sea Peoples' dispersal, the Peleset are generally believed to have settled in southwestern Palestine, where they re-emerged in *OT* tradition as the Philistines. Their original homeland is uncertain. An Aegean origin is commonly supposed, on the basis of a number of similarities between Philistine culture and the cultures of the Aegean world (see below). Attention is also sometimes drawn to an *OT* claim that the Philistines came from Caphtor, i.e. Crete (Amos 9:7), though it is not clear whether this is intended to be a reference to their actual homeland. Critics of an Aegean origin for the Peleset/Philistines stress the fact that in the Medinet Habu reliefs, the Peleset land force is accompanied by plough oxen and ox-carts; this, they argue, suggests an agriculture-based population in search of new lands to cultivate rather than a people from across the sea.

To judge from *OT* tradition, the Philistines apparently occupied their new homeland in coastal Palestine around the same time as the Canaanites occupied the inland plains, and the Israelites (now believed by some scholars to be a Canaanite sub-group) the hill country beyond. Five main cities, the so-called Philistine Pentapolis, provided the focal points of Philistine civilization. They were Ashdod, Ashkelon, Ekron, Gaza, and Gath (perhaps = Tell es-Safi). *OT* sources mention a number of smaller settlements as well, including Jabneh, Timnah, and Ziklag. A certain type of painted ceramic ware, derived from the decorative style of Mycenaean Late Helladic IIIC pottery, was one of the distinctive features of the Philistines' material culture. On the other hand, native Levantine influence is evident in a number of the shapes fashioned by Philistine potters, and in various stylistic features used by them in their painted designs. Cypriot and Egyptian influences are also apparent in the repertoire of Philistine ceramic ware. With regard to Philistine cult-practices, attention has been drawn to a number of apparent Aegean influences, illustrated by seated goddess figurines, ritual burial pits, offering benches, and hearthrooms. Another aspect of Philistine culture reflecting an Aegean origin is the use of rock-cut chamber tombs similar to those found at Mycenae.

The Philistines' evident prosperity derived largely from their participation in a thriving, widespread commercial network. Material remains and artefacts uncovered at a number of Philistine sites provide evidence of highly developed architectural, engineering, technological, and craft skills among Philistia's population. But while Philistine society had a strong urban orientation, its economy must have been boosted by a flourishing agricultural industry, which benefited much from the country's fertile coastal plain location. An indication of the importance of agriculture to the Philistines may be provided by the incorporation of the Semitic grain god Dagan into the Philistine pantheon, along with two other Semitic deities, Ashtaroth and Baal-zebub.

Figure 93 Philistine coffin lid, from Lachish.

Information about the history of the Philistine nation is largely dependent on *OT* sources, which contain more than 250 references to the Philistines and Philistia. To judge from these sources, the Philistines relatively early in their history sought to expand their territory eastwards, at the same time as the hill country Israelites began expanding their territories westwards. This inevitably led to conflicts between the two peoples, which culminated in the decisive defeat suffered by the Philistines at the hands of the Israelite king David early in C10. Though seriously weakened as a military power after this defeat, the Philistines continued to engage, with varying success, in sporadic conflict with the Israelites until the last decades of C8. (It has recently been argued, primarily on the basis of *OT* sources, that during Iron Age I the Philistine cities were united, perhaps in C10 under the *primus inter pares* leadership of Gath; this unified political structure persisted in Philistia through C10–9, but during C8–7 the existing Philistine cities became separate entities, each under its own ruler and with its own policies; Shai, 2006).

The Philistines had also to deal with a much more formidable power in the region, the kingdom of Assyria. Already by the end of C9, records of the Assyrian king Adad-nirari III (810–783) indicate that the Philistines were paying tribute to Assyria. Subsequently, a number of Philistine cities were destroyed by the Assyrians, as reported in both *OT* and Assyrian sources. A notable example is the destruction of the city of Ashdod by Sargon II (721–705), reported in Isaiah 20:1. Sargon himself described in his Annals his conquest of Ashdod and other cities of the Pentapolis, and depicted the siege of these cities in the reliefs in his palace at Khorsabad (Dur-Sharrukin). In fact, all of Philistia's cities must have suffered to a greater or lesser degree from the western campaigns conducted by Sargon and his two predecessors, Tiglath-pileser III and Shalmaneser V, which resulted in the imposition of Assyrian sovereignty over the entire Syro-Palestinian region to the borders of Egypt. Sargon's son and successor Sennacherib reported a conquest of the Pentapolis city of Ekron, and Philistine cities were called upon to provide building materials and troops to the Assyrians during the reigns of Sennacherib's successors Esarhaddon and Ashurbanipal.

With the fall of the Assyrian empire in late C7, Palestine's southern coastal cities came under Egyptian control. Shortly afterwards, Philistia fell victim to the newly emerging Neo-Babylonian empire. The campaigns which the Babylonian king Nebuchadnezzar II (604–562) conducted in the region resulted in the destruction of a number of Philistine cities, and the mass deportation of their populations. Some of the cities, including Ashdod, Askelon, and Gaza, survived and were reoccupied. But the Babylonians had effectively brought to an end the land and civilization of the people called the Philistines.

T. Dothan (1982; 1995), Görg/Maeir (*RlA* 10: 526–36), Laughlin (2006: 235–42), Gertzen (2008).

Phocaea (map 5) Greek city located on the northern Aegean coast of Anatolia. It was the northernmost member of the twelve cities of the Ionian League (see **Panionium**), but in fact lay in the region of Aeolis (q.v.). (Pottery evidence suggests that settlement in the area dates back to the Early Bronze Age.) According to Greek tradition, the earliest Phocaeans occupied land which they had received from the citizens of Aeolian Cyme. Ceramic ware dating to C9 suggests that these first inhabitants were of Aeolian stock. However, by the end of C9 (to judge from the Protogeometric pottery found on the site), settlers of Ionian origin had joined the original population.

According to Pausanias, these new settlers came from the cities of Teos and Erythrae. The Phocaeans were renowned for their coinage and their manufacture of purple dye. They had a high reputation for seafaring and trading, activities which paved the way for their engagement in a number of colonizing enterprises. Phocaea founded several new settlements on the shores of the Hellespont and the Black Sea. But the main areas which it colonized were in the lands of the western Mediterranean – southern Italy, Corsica, France, and Spain.

Phocaea's flourishing existence was abruptly ended in mid C6 when, along with other cities in the region, it was destroyed by the Persians. The colonies which its citizens had established in the western Mediterranean now provided new homelands for refugees from the devastated city (Herodotus 1.163–9). Some of the refugees may subsequently have returned, but the city never regained the status or level of prosperity it had enjoyed prior to its destruction. In C5 Phocaea became a member of the Athenian Confederacy (see glossary). But in 412 it joined other cities in rebelling against Athenian rule. In the Hellenistic period it was subject, successively, to the Seleucid and Attalid dynasties. In C1 Pompey the Great granted it independence.

Among the city's pre-Hellenistic remains are a temple of Athena, dated by ceramic evidence to 590–580, and fortification walls also of C6 date. Excavations are currently being conducted by a Turkish team under the direction of Ö. Özyiğit.

E. Akurgal (1973: 116–18; *PECS* 708–9), Özyiğit (2006).

Phoenicia(ns) (map 13) Classical name used to designate an Iron Age region, and the peoples who occupied it, extending along part of the Syro-Palestinian coast and inland to the Lebanon and anti-Lebanon ranges. (Scholarly opinions differ on where the region's precise limits should be set.) The name's most commonly accepted derivation is from the Greek word *phoinix*, meaning 'crimson-red' or 'purple'. This derivation may have been inspired by the copper colour of the hair and skin of the peoples so called, or by the famous purple dye extracted from the murex shellfish found in the region's coastal waters. But other explanations have been proposed. If the Phoenicians themselves did have a sense of a common identity, they probably referred to themselves generically as Canaanites, their direct Bronze Age ancestors.

The point at which these coastal Canaanites attained a specific identity and became Phoenicians is difficult to determine. But it can best be related to the reconfiguration of the political map of the region in C12. With the demise of the Hittite empire, the withdrawal of the Egyptian empire, and the corresponding ascendancy of the Aramaeans, Israelites, and Philistines, the only area left relatively unaffected by these changes was precisely that which would become known as Phoenicia. The reason why this area escaped the upheavals which caused the collapse of many Late Bronze Age centres elsewhere is not known for sure, but almost certainly resulted from a degree of collusion between the Canaanite inhabitants and invading Sea Peoples. The Phoenicians transmitted the purest ideals of Canaanite culture from M2 to M1, along with the Canaanite political configuration: Phoenicia consisted of a number of principalities or city-states, the most prominent of which were Sidon, Tyre, and Byblos. And like the Late Bronze Age Syro-Palestinian principalities, the Phoenician states became subject to one or other of the Great Kingdoms of their period.

With virtually no agricultural hinterland and little opportunity for territorial expansion within the Levant, the Phoenicians turned to the sea as a means of supporting and developing their economy. We know from early C11 Egyptian and Assyrian texts that they were already involved in maritime mercantile enterprises at this time. Trading links had been established with Cyprus, and *OT* sources indicate good commercial relations between Tyre and the early Israelite monarchy. The production of timber and purple dye featured among the Phoenicians' most important industries, along with the manufacture of a range of products fashioned from ivory, wood, stone, metal, wool, and linen. The distribution of these products throughout the Mediterranean world was in the hands of Phoenician merchantmen, who also acted as agents for the export and import of goods from other regions. Exotic items figured prominently among the merchandise brought back by Phoenician ships. They included ivory, ebony, precious stones, spices, aromatic substances, gold and silver, and a range of commodity metals.

The search for sources of these goods, especially silver (the main medium of exchange in the western Asian world at this time), took Phoenician trading expeditions to the western limits of the Mediterranean world, above all to western Italy, western Sicily, Sardinia, southern Spain, and the coast of Africa. This great westward expansion of Phoenician commercial enterprise began c. mid C8. Phoenician settlements and trading-posts were established in a number of the western Mediterranean countries. For the most part, these were no more than trading-posts or temporary encampments, which focused primarily on the exploitation of local resources and were abandoned once the reasons for their establishment no longer existed. But some settlements took on a more permanent character, especially in Spain, Sicily, and north Africa. Carthage, founded according to tradition by settlers from Tyre, is the prime example of a fully fledged Phoenician colonial enterprise. Established in late C9, it had already become a major urban centre with a large population by the first half of C8.

Phoenicia's wealth inevitably attracted the interest of the emerging Neo-Assyrian empire, beginning with the reign of the Assyrian king Ashurnasirpal II (883–859), who imposed tributary status on the Phoenician coastal cities. Though Phoenicia's commercial enterprises flourished and indeed expanded during the Neo-Assyrian period, the Assyrians' constant intervention in Phoenician affairs in the reigns of Ashurnasirpal's successors led to escalating tensions and conflicts, culminating in the Assyrian conquest of a number of Phoenician cities, most notably Sidon and Tyre, in the reigns of Sennacherib (704–681) and Esarhaddon (680–669). These cities regained their independence during the reign of Ashurbanipal (668–630/627), though subsequently, for a time, Egypt seems to have exercised some nominal control in the region. But Phoenicia's brief period of relative freedom came to an end in early C6 when it was forced into subjection by the Babylonian king Nebuchadnezzar II (604–562). With the rise of Persia following the fall of the Babylonian kingdom in the reign of Nabonidus (556–539), the Phoenician cities came under Persian rule, though they continued to enjoy a high degree of local autonomy. Sidon now became the administrative centre of Persia's fifth satrapy (Herodotus 3.94; but see glossary under **satrapy**). With Persian support, Phoenician trade and commerce continued to flourish. And in turn, the largely landlocked Persian kingdom benefited greatly from having a Phoenician navy at its disposal for its military operations conducted by sea. In the late 330s the Phoenician cities were forced to submit to Alexander the Great, Persia's conqueror, though Tyre did so only when it was besieged and sacked by Alexander's forces after offering fierce resistance. On Alexander's death, Phoenicia was contested by the Ptolemaic and Seleucid dynasties, succcumbing first to the former and then to the latter before regaining its independence. The region was finally absorbed into the Roman empire.

The Phoenician language, a descendant or later dialect of the West Semitic or Canaanite language, is preserved in a corpus of c. 6,000 inscriptions which were scattered throughout the lands where the Phoenicians had trading contacts and established settlements, as far west as Spain and Tunisia. The script used was alphabetic, consisting of twenty-two consonant symbols. This script was transmitted to the Greek world and became the basis of the Greek alphabet, though the date and manner of the transmission remain uncertain. The earliest surviving example of a Phoenician alphabetic inscription appears on a sarcophagus, the so-called Ahiram sarcophagus, discovered in Byblos and dating to late M2.

Our knowledge of Phoenician deities and religious practices is meagre. Though Phoenician cults derived most of their features from their Bronze Age Canaanite predecessors (including a shared focus on natural and cosmic phenomena, and the notion of divine assemblies), there were clearly some differences. These are reflected, for example, in the appearance of new deities, like Ba'al Hammon, Tanit, Melqart, and Eshmun. The overall picture of Phoenician religion is made more complex by the fact that each city-state appears to have had its own distinctive religious practices, and its own concept of the deities whom it worshipped.

Lipiński (1995), Ward/Guzzo/Markoe (*OEANE* 4: 313–31), Markoe (2000), Moscati (2001), Röllig/Gubel (*RlA* 10: 536–43).

Phrygia (map 4) Iron Age kingdom extending over much of central and western Anatolia. In Greek legendary tradition, the earliest Phrygians migrated into Anatolia

Figure 94 Phoenician figurine (C7–4), perhaps goddess Ashtarte.

from Macedon and Thrace. According to Homer, the Phrygians were already well established in their new homeland at the time of the Trojan War; they appear on seven occasions in the *Iliad*, and are listed by Homer among Troy's allies. But it is much more likely that Phrygian migration to Anatolia took place during the widespread upheavals associated with the collapse of many centres of western Asian civilization at the end of the Bronze Age. The last decades of M2 probably witnessed the formative stages of a Phrygian state, which was centred on Gordium, located on the Sakarya r. (Classical Sangarius) 100 km southwest of Ankara, and reached its peak in C8. By this time, Phrygian power extended eastwards across the Halys r. into what had been the homeland of the Late Bronze Age kingdom of Hatti.

At some point in their history, the Phrygians became associated with a people called the Mushki in Assyrian texts. Kossian (1997) regards 'Mushki' as a collective term designating numerous related tribes who during the second half of M2 were gradually infiltrating into different areas of the Armenian highlands. In documentary sources, the Mushki are first attested in the reign of the Assyrian king Tiglath-pileser I (1114–1076) when they invaded and captured, with a force of 20,000 troops commanded by their five kings, the Assyrian province of Kadmuhu in the Zagros region (**RIMA* 2: 14). (For the outcome of this episode, see **Kadmuhu**.) Tiglath-pileser elsewhere claims to have defeated a force of 12,000 Mushki troops, and to have added their land to the borders of his own territory (**RIMA* 2: 33). Two centuries later, the Assyrian king Tukulti-Ninurta II invaded and devastated Mushki territory in the course of his last recorded campaign (885) (**RIMA* 2: 177). His son and successor Ashurnasirpal II received tribute from the Mushki during a campaign in his first regnal year (883) which took Assyrian forces once more into the land of Kadmuhu (**RIMA* 2: 198). In late C9 or early C8, Shamshi-ilu, commander-in-chief of the Assyrian king Adad-nirari III, conquered the lands of both Mushki and Urartu (**RIMA* 3: 232).

The nature, date, and origins of the Phrygian–Mushki association are still matters for debate. However, a widely held view is that towards the end of C8 an amalgamation took place between Phrygian and Mushki groups, and that a Mushki king called Mita, better known by his Greek name Midas, was responsible for the union of the two groups. From his capital at Gordium, Mita/Midas (for his possible regnal dates, see DeVries, 2008: 30–1) ruled a kingdom which extended eastwards towards the Euphrates, southwards into the region later known as Cappadocia, and westwards as far as the Aegean Sea. He was also in contact with mainland Greece, where he made offerings to the god Apollo at Delphi. Though the historical Midas is to be distinguished from his legendary namesake, whose greed for gold caused everything he touched to be turned into the precious metal, it has been suggested that the king of legend may have lain behind the historical character.

The extent of Midas' territories, and especially the contacts which he established with other states in southern Anatolia, as far afield as the Neo-Hittite kingdom of Carchemish on the Euphrates, inevitably led to fresh tensions and conflicts with Assyria. For example, the Assyrian king Sargon II (721–705) accused Pisiris, ruler of Carchemish, of communicating with Midas, presumably with a view to forming an alliance with him (**ARAB* II: 4, **CS* II: 293). (For Sargon's retaliatory action, see under **Carchemish**.) In particular, Midas threatened the security of Assyria's western frontiers. He seized border territories of the kingdom of Que, which lay to the southeast of the Phrygian kingdom and was then under the control of an Assyrian governor.

Subsequently he sought to win local rulers in the country of Tabal away from their Assyrian allegiance, and appears to have had some success in doing so. Several of the Tabalic kings apparently switched their support to Midas, perhaps partly because of their relative proximity to his kingdom, which put them within close striking range of a Phrygian army. Such challenges to Assyrian authority in the region could not go unanswered. In 715, Sargon recaptured two border fortresses of Que which had been seized by Midas, and five years later his governor in Que, Ashur-sharru-usur, claims to have conducted three successful expeditions into Midas' territory.

Even so, Sargon was anxious to reach an accommodation with Midas, very likely to offset the danger of an alliance formed by Midas with Assyria's other great rival in the region, Urartu. Sargon did in fact succeed in making peace with Midas, as he reports in a letter which he sent from Nimrud to Ashur-sharru-usur (**SAA* I: 4–7, no. 1). He refers in the letter to a fourteen-man delegation dispatched to Urartu by Urikki (Luwian Awarikus), known to have been a king of Que already in the reign of the Assyrian king Tiglath-pileser III (745–727). The delegation had been intercepted by Midas and handed over to Ashur-sharru-usur. This action marked a dramatic change in Midas' relations with Assyria which up to this point had been emphatically hostile. Sargon welcomed his gesture, and responded by instructing Ashur-sharru-usur to return to Midas all the Phrygians whom he had detained in his court. (On the likely status of Urikki at this time, see under **Que**.) He no doubt saw a *détente* with Phrygia as a major step towards consolidating his control over a substantial part of Anatolia, notably the kingdoms of Tabal.

It is possible that there is a connection between Midas' about-face and the threat to his kingdom posed by the Cimmerians (cf. Hawkins, 1982: 420–1). In fact, within a few years of this improvement in Phrygian–Assyrian relations, Phrygia fell victim, c. 695, to an invasion from the north by the Cimmerians, who occupied large areas of Anatolia, and in the process destroyed Midas' kingdom. However, a number of Phrygian settlements, including Gordium, recovered from the invasions, and after the final withdrawal of the Cimmerians in late C7 or early C6, they regained some of their former prosperity as small principalities subject to the kings of Lydia. Following the collapse of the Lydian kingdom, Phrygia became part of the Persian empire, until in 333 it fell to Alexander the Great. Subsequently it was absorbed into the Seleucid empire, and in 133 the western part of the country was incorporated into the Roman empire.

The burial tumuli and sculptured rock façades, particularly those found at Gordium, provide the most notable surviving features of Phrygia's material civilization (see **Gordium**). Painted pottery depicting geometric and animal motifs is another distinctive feature of this civilization. Both the tumuli and the pottery indicate ongoing cultural influences from Thrace. Neo-Hittite elements also played an important role in the development of Phrygian culture. Cultural as well as political contacts between Phrygia and Carchemish may be reflected in the possible connection between the most prominent Phrygian deity, the mother goddess Cybele, and the goddess Kubaba, who had been the chief deity of Carchemish since the Old Babylonian period. Crafts and trades flourished in Phrygia, and Gordium in particular has yielded a fine range of artefacts of bronze, iron, wood, and ivory, as well as a wide assortment of ceramic ware.

The Phrygian language survives in two groups of inscriptions which are now only partly intelligible. Inscriptions of the first group are found mainly on the façades of rock-cut monuments dating from C8 to C3 (Brixhe and Lejeune, 1984); inscriptions of the second group, consisting mainly of curse formulae, date to C2 and C3 CE. Phrygian belongs to the Indo-European language family, and is written in an alphabetic script. It is very likely that this script was taken over from Greek, but a north Syrian origin is also a possibility.

Haspels (1971), Mellink (1991: 622–43), Masson (1991: 666–9), Sams (1995), Röllig (*RlA* 8: 493–5), Neumann/Strobel/Prayon (*RlA* 10: 543–55), Roller (2008).

Physcus (*Marmaris*) (map 5) M1 city in Caria, southwestern Anatolia. By mid C4 it had been incorporated into the state of Rhodes, as an attachment to the Rhodian city of Lindus. It became the most important possession of the Rhodian Peraea (see glossary), due, no doubt, to its excellent harbour facilities. The city's acropolis, located on a hill 2 km northwest of Marmaris, still has remains of fortifications of Classical and Hellenistic date. Nothing survives of the lower city, on the site of mod. Marmaris, beyond some inscriptions and sculptured blocks.

Bean (*PECS* 710).

Pina(li) Late Bronze Age city in southwestern Anatolia, attested in a cuneiform text commonly referred to as the 'Milawata letter' (**HDT* 146) and in a hieroglyphic inscription found at Yalburt (q.v.) (*Hawkins, 1995: 70–1), in both cases together with the city of Awarna (for details, see **Awarna**). An identification has been suggested between Pina(li) and the city of Pinara in Classical Lycia, though as yet there is no evidence of Bronze Age settlement at Pinara.

Pinara (**Pinale**, ***Minare***) (map 15) M1 BCE–M1 CE city in Lycia, southwestern Anatolia, located 17 km north of Xanthus. Pinara derives its name from Pina(li), a city attested in Bronze Age texts and perhaps Pinara's Bronze Age ancestor. According to the C4 writer Menecrates of Xanthus (in Stephanus of Byzantium, s.v. Artymnesus), Pinara was founded by colonists from Xanthus, and so called after a native Lycian word meaning 'round'. This proposed derivation clearly arose out of the town's original location on a rounded hill. Remains of the pre-Greek indigenous civilization of Lycia are well represented at Pinara by a number of rock-cut tombs, several inscribed with texts in the Lycian language. Some twelve Lycian inscriptions have survived (**TAM I*: 10–21). In the porch of one of the tombs are reliefs depicting fortified Lycian cities in which houses and tombs can be seen. Hundreds more rudimentary tombs are cut into the face of a 450 m high cliff, one of the site's most distinctive features. A well-preserved theatre reflects later Greek influence at Pinara. In Roman times, Pinara became one of the six most important cities of the Lycian League.

Bean (*PECS* 713; 1978: 82–91).

Pi-naratim (**'Mouth-of-the-Rivers'**) Middle Bronze Age city in southern Babylonia, perhaps in the vicinity of Cutha and Kish. Its conquest is commemorated in the name of the eighth regnal year of the Larsan king Sumu-El (1887). The king's son-in-law Ibni-shadum, ruler of Kisurra (q.v.), is reported to have built walls for the city, but scholars are uncertain whether he did so with the support of his father-in-law or to protect it against the armies of Larsa. In 1809 the city (along with Nazarum) fell to Larsa's king Rim-Sin, the year after he had defeated a coalition of enemy forces,

Figure 95 Pinara, round tower of rock honeycombed with tombs.

including Uruk, Isin, and Babylon. Pi-naratim is possibly identical with Pi-nari, which is known from later M2 (Middle Babylonian) texts.

Mesop. 75, 120, Streck (*RlA* 10: 566–7).

Pirindu see **Hilakku**.

Pirria and **Shitiuaria** Iron Age fortified cities in the western Zagros region near the land of Parsua. They were destroyed by Dayyan-Ashur, commander-in-chief of the Assyrian king Shalmaneser III, during his campaign in the region in 828 (**RIMA* 3: 71).

Pisidia (map 4) Classical name for the country occupying, in M1, the mountainous region of southwestern Anatolia inland from Lycia and Pamphylia. The rugged nature of the land, the strong defences of its cities, and the fierce character of its population presented a formidable obstacle to foreign aggressors. Pisidia remained independent of Persia during the period of the Persian empire (C6–4), and was never fully subjugated by the Persians' Hellenistic successors. But it eventually came under Roman control when it was incorporated into the Roman province of Galatia, created by Augustus in 25 BCE. From C4 onwards Pisidia's cities had become increasingly influenced by Greek civilization. But even under Roman domination a number of elements of the indigenous Pisidian culture persisted. This applied particularly to the country's language and religious cults, which continued to flourish in the region's rural areas.

Mitchell (*OCD* 1186).

Figure 96 Pinara, sliding door of tomb.

Pitane (map 5) M1 Greek city on Anatolia's Aegean coast, located northeast of Phocaea on a small peninsula near the mouth of the Caicus r. It is listed by Herodotus (1.149) among the eleven original Aeolian communities which remained after the twelfth, Smyrna, was taken over by the Ionians. Strabo (13.1.67) refers to a number of Pitane's features, noting that it had two harbours, that bricks floated on water there, and that the city was the home of Arcesilaus who became, c. 268, head of the Academy founded by Plato in Athens. E. Akurgal observes that Pitane is the only Aeolian site to have produced valuable archaeological material. Excavations conducted in C19 at the necropolis on the isthmus of the peninsula, to the west of the site, brought to light a Late Bronze Age Mycenaean octopus stirrup-jar and Greek Archaic pottery. The tombs in the necropolis were pit-graves. More recent excavations conducted in the necropolis have produced Protogeometric and Geometric pottery, pottery from Chios, orientalizing vases from the first half of C6, and an Archaic statue.

E. Akurgal (*PECS* 715), Mee (1978: 143–4).

Pitassa (map 3) Late Bronze Age Anatolian country in the region of Classical Lycaonia, east of the Salt Lake, and close to the northwestern frontier of Tarhuntassa (**HDT* 110, 114–15, **CS* II: 100). It was ruled by a council of elders. Located in a strategically important area near the Hittite Lower Land, Pitassa became a subject state of the kingdom of Hatti. But it was prone to insurrectionist activity, and on three known occasions in C14 it rebelled against its Hittite overlords – at least twice in collaboration with renegade Hittite subjects from other states (**HDT* 75, 158–9). In 1274, a contingent from Pitassa served in the Hittite army at the battle of Qadesh (*Gardiner, 1960: 8).

de Martino (*RlA* 10: 579).

Pitru (Assyrian **Ana-Ashur-uter-asbat**, ***ʿAwšar***) Iron Age city in northwestern Mesopotamia, strategically located, at mod. ʿAwšar (see Lipiński, 2000: 167 map), near an important river-crossing on the west bank of the Euphrates close to its confluence with the Sajur and not far from Til-Barsip (Tell Ahmar). Pitru was established c. 1100 by the Assyrian king Tiglath-pileser I, but during the reign of Ashur-rabi II (1013–973) an Aramaean king seized control of it, along with the city of Mutkinu which lay on the the Euphrates' opposite bank (**RIMA* 3: 19). (The city may also be mentioned in two fragmentary inscriptions of the early C11 king Ashur-bel-kala, who crossed the Euphrates in this area.) For the next 250 years, Pitru remained under Aramaean control, becoming one of the cities in the Euphrates region attached to the Iron Age kingdom of Bit-Adini. (It is uncertain whether the Aramaean king who seized Pitru from Ashur-rabi was an early ruler of Bit-Adini.) In 856, when the kingdom was ruled by Ahuni, these cities were conquered by the Assyrian king Shalmaneser III. Following the restoration of Pitru to Assyrian control, Shalmaneser renamed it Ana-Ashur-uter-asbat, meaning 'I seized and restored (it) to Ashur' (he claims that Pitru was the name which the people of the land of Hatti called it), and resettled it with an Assyrian population. It became incorporated into the newly formed 'Province of the Commander-in-Chief' (see glossary). In 853 Shalmaneser visited the city prior to embarking upon his next western campaign and received there tribute from the rulers of the kingdoms on the 'opposite' (i.e. western) bank of the Euphrates (**RIMA* 3: 23). Pitru was among the lands and cities which the Assyrian king Adad-nirari III (810–783) assigned to the governorship of a man called Nergal-erish (Palil-erish) (**RIMA* 3: 209, 211).

Lipiński (2000: 163–8, 193), Radner (*RlA* 10: 585–6).

Pittiyarik Late Bronze Age city in eastern Anatolia, subject to Hatti from at least the early years of the Hittite New Kingdom (early C14). It was linked by river transport with the city of Samuha, since grain was carried by boat from Pittiyarik to Samuha. Both these cities were therefore located on a river – probably the upper course of the Marassantiya (Classical Halys), though a Euphrates location for the cities has also been suggested. In any case, Pittiyarik lay near the city of Pahhuwa in the upper Euphrates region. Delegates from its council of elders attended an assembly of cities and countries called upon by the early C14 Hittite king Arnuwanda I to attack Pahhuwa in the event that Pahhuwa failed to hand over to the Hittites its rebel king, Mita.

**RGTC* 6: 319–20, **HDT* 162, 164.

Pitura (*Salat Tepe*?) Fortified Iron Age city in the land of Dirru north of the Kashiyari range (mod. Tur ʿAbdin), northern Mesopotamia, located on the east bank of the Tigris across the river from the city of Tushhan. It was attacked by the Assyrian king Ashurnasirpal II during a campaign which he conducted in his fifth regnal year (879) in the Kashiyari region (**RIMA* 2: 210, 260). Having left Tushhan, Ashurnasirpal crossed the Tigris and travelled all night to reach Pitura. The city's defences, which included a double wall and a lofty citadel, enabled it to withstand the Assyrian attack until dawn of the second day, when it fell to Ashurnasirpal. It was plundered and destroyed. Many of its defenders were captured and some were burnt alive. Ashurnasirpal built a pile of the living and the heads of those he slaughtered before the city gate. Seven hundred of the city's troops were also impaled there.

Liverani (1992: 60–1), Radner (*RlA* 10: 587–8).

Pontus (maps 2, 4) Region on the southern shores of the Black Sea, between the lands of Paphlagonia in north-central Anatolia and Colchis at the eastern end of the Black Sea, and extending southwards into Cappadocia. Its name comes from its location on the Pontus (literally meaning 'sea'), one of the anc. names for the Black Sea. Topographically, the region is dominated by mountain ranges separated by deep valleys. The rugged northernmost regions were the homes of a number of tribal groups. The harsh terrain in which they lived and their lack of any coherent political organization placed them largely beyond the control of the major anc. powers who dominated Anatolia. In the Late Bronze Age, the Kaska people (q.v.) of the Pontic zone were a constant threat to the Hittite homeland which lay to their south. Despite conducting a number of campaigns against them, in the process inflicting heavy casualties, the Hittites never succeeded in fully pacifying them. In the Hellenistic period, the Pontic sub-region lying on the southeastern shore of the Black Sea became the core territory of a kingdom called Pontus, ruled by a line of kings who bore the Persian name Mithridates (Mithradates).

Broughton, Mitchell (*OCD* 1220).

Posideion see ***Bassit, Ras el.***

Priene (map 5) M1 BCE–M1 CE city founded by Greek Ionian colonists near the anc. mouth of the Maeander r. (though its exact original location is unknown) on the southwestern coast of Anatolia, probably at the end of M2 or very early in M1. It was one of the twelve member states of the Ionian League, whose meeting-place, the Panionium (q.v.), lay in its territory at the foot of Mt Mycale. Bias, one of the Seven Sages of the Greek world, lived here in early C6. During C7 and C6 the city suffered devastation at the hands of several foreign invaders – Cimmerians, Lydians, and Persians. In 494 it provided twelve ships for the Ionians' naval engagement with the Persian fleet in the battle of Lade (q.v.). In the years following the repulse of Persia by the allied Greek states (479), it became a member of the Athenian Confederacy (see glossary), its annual contribution being assessed at the comparatively low sum of one talent. Around 350, the city was shifted to a new location 15 km southwest of mod. Söke. It was enclosed within a strong and still well-preserved city wall, built entirely of local marble. The city's port, Naulochus, lay on a harbour, which gradually disappeared because of the silting up of the Maeander r. Already by the Augustan age (late C1

BCE–early C1 CE) Priene was, according to Strabo (12.8.17), 40 stades (c. 7.4 km) from the sea, which now lies some some 13 km away.

Priene is particularly noteworthy today for its finely preserved Hellenistic and Roman remains. It provides an excellent example of a city built on the Hippodamian grid plan (see glossary), with streets intersecting at right angles. Most of its distinctive buildings date to the period C4–C2, including a temple of Athena (the building costs of which Alexander the Great subsidized), a sanctuary of the goddess Demeter, a temple of Olympian Zeus, a theatre, two gymnasia, a stadium, and an agora. E. Akurgal notes that despite Roman modifications, the essentially Greek character of Priene was largely preserved. Though the city had sunk into insignificance by the end of the Roman imperial period, it subsequently became the seat of an important diocese in the Byzantine age. The site was excavated between 1895 and 1898 by German archaeological teams under the successive directorships of C. Humann and T. Wiegand. Current excavations are being conducted by W. Raeck, of J. W. Goethe Universität, and W. Koenigs, Technische Universität (Munich).

E. Akurgal (1973: 185–206), Bean (*PECS* 737–9), Raeck (2006).

Propontis (*Sea of Marmara*) (maps 2, 3, 4, 19) Sea located between the straits of the Hellespont and the Bosporus, which link it respectively with the Aegean and the Black Seas. It is 225 km long and c. 64 km at its greatest width. The dimensions which Herodotus (4.85) gives are highly exaggerated. There are a number of islands within the sea, the largest of which, known as Proconessus in antiquity, is now called Marmara. This word, which means 'marble', has also been adopted as the mod. name for the Propontis. Four relatively large rivers empty into the sea on its south side: the Granicus, Aesepus, Macestus, and Rhyndacus. There are no significant rivers on its north side.

Bean (*OCD* 1259).

Pteria M1 city in north-central Anatolia. Herodotus (1.76) reports that the Lydian king Croesus established a camp there (in 546), after crossing the Halys r. in preparation for his confrontation with the Persian king Cyrus II. He comments that Pteria lay in the most impregnable region of Cappadocia. Croesus allegedly captured Pteria and enslaved its inhabitants. Cyrus took up a position opposite Croesus' camp at Pteria, which became the arena of an inconclusive battle between the Persian and Lydian armies. The city's actual location has yet to be firmly established. Though it was once commonly equated with the Iron Age settlement on the site of Hattusa, the Late Bronze Age Hittite capital, a number of scholars believe it should be identified with the large Iron Age mountain city on Kerkenes Dağ (q.v.). Against this identification, see most recently Rollinger (2003a: 322–6).

Puqudu (Piqudu) (map 11) Iron Age Aramaean tribe located in southern Babylonia and active in the area from Uruk in the west as far as Elam in the east, but especially around the Tigris r. Letters of the governor of Nippur in the early Neo-Babylonian period indicate the tribe's involvement in religious festivals in Nippur (e.g. **Nippur IV*: 88–9, no. 27) and in diplomatic alliances with other tribes, e.g. Bit-Amukani (with which the Puqudu later came into conflict). The tribe was probably brought under Assyrian control by Tiglath-pileser III (745–727), who claims to have defeated it

(*Tigl. III* 122–3) and to have attached its lands to the Assyrian province of Arrapha (*Tigl. III* 160–1). However, early in the reign of Tiglath-pileser's grandson Sargon II (721–705) it joined an anti-Assyrian coalition made up of Babylonians, Aramaeans, Chaldaeans, and Elamites, led by Marduk-apla-iddina (biblical Merodach-baladan) from the Chaldaean tribe Bit-Yakin, who was twice king of Babylonia (721–710, 703). In 710 Sargon added Puqudu to the newly formed province of Gambulu, and in the course of his campaigns from 709 to 707 against Dur-Yakin, capital of Bit-Yakin, the Puqudu tribesmen and their leaders were eventually hunted down and forced to surrender. But in the years 704 and 691 they again joined anti-Assyrian uprisings in the reign of Sargon's son and successor Sennacherib. Though apparently subdued and partly resettled in Assyrian territory proper, they continued to threaten Assyrian security and Assyrian interests in southern Mesopotamia. This is evident from letters written by Assyrian-appointed governors in Uruk and Ur during the reign of Ashurbanipal (668–630/627). The governors complained of hostile action by the Puqudu, and sought assistance from their overlord against them. There was also a complaint that the Puqudu had raided the land of the Bit-Amukani tribe, Assyria's faithful ally, and had even settled in their territory.

Although the texts regularly refer to the Puqudu collectively, they seem never to have been a united people, but rather were fragmented into a number of groups, each with its own leader or tribal sheikh. While these leaders may have formed temporary alliances in support of resistance movements against Assyrian sovereignty, there may have been occasions when their support was divided between opposing forces. Thus in the conflict between Shamash-shum-ukin and his brother Ashurbanipal, king of Assyria (see under **Babylon**), some Puqudaean clans may have remained loyal to the Assyrian king, while others joined forces with the rebel.

In the time of the Babylonian king Nebuchadnezzar II, the Puqudu were counted among the Babylonian peoples. In *OT* sources they are attested under the name Pekod (*Pqd*) (Jeremiah 50:21, Ezekiel 23:23).

Lipiński (2000: 429–537), Radner (*RlA* 10: 113–15).

Puranda Late Bronze Age Arzawan city in western Anatolia, perhaps to be identified with the hill now named Bademgediği tepe located a few km west of Torbalı. Hittite deportees sought refuge there (as also in Arinnanda) during the campaigns which the Hittite king Mursili II conducted against Arzawa in the third and fourth years of his reign (c. 1319–1318) (**AM* 62–5, **CS* II: 85–6). Mursili's capture of the city appears to have marked the end of Arzawan hostilities against Hatti for the rest of his reign.

Hawkins (*RlA* 11: 115).

Puruddum (Buruddum, Burunda, Burundum) Middle Bronze Age city and country probably to be located in the upper Tigris region of northern Mesopotamia. It is attested in the Old Assyrian merchant tablets from Kanesh, in the archives from Mari, on the victory stele of Dadusha, king of Eshnunna, and in the year-name for the thirty-third regnal year of the Babylonian king Hammurabi. It lay on the caravan route linking Ashur with eastern Anatolia, and subsequently became a vassal state of Mari in the reign of the Mariote king Zimri-Lim (1774–1762). According to the Dadusha stele, the land of Burunda was part of Subartu territory (q.v.) (**Chav.* 99). When Mari

was taken by Hammurabi in 1762, Burundum was among the many cities and countries of upper Mesopotamia which fell to the Babylonian king.
Michel (*RlA* 11: 116–18).

Purulumzu (**Purulimzu, Purukuzzu**) Country in northeastern Mesopotamia, attested in Late Bronze Age and early Iron Age Assyrian texts and probably located in the area between the Arsanias r. (mod. Murat Su) and the Kashiyari range (mod. Tur ʿAbdin). It apparently contained a famous cult-centre. Purulumzu joined a general rebellion in the region against Assyrian rule early in the reign of the Assyrian king Tukulti-Ninurta I (1244–1208). Subaru, Alzu, and Amadanu were among the principal rebel lands. In the course of his retaliatory campaign against the rebels, Tukulti-Ninurta captured Purulumzu's cult-centre, burnt its inhabitants alive, and took prisoner the surviving remnant of its army (**RIMA* 1: 236, 244). Assyrian sovereignty was imposed upon the country as upon the other rebel lands, and hostages were taken from these lands to ensure their future obedience. Subsequently Purulumzu, along with the land of Alzu, was occupied by settlers from Mushki (see under **Phrygia**). The settlers apparently remained on peaceful terms with the Assyrians by making regular payments of tribute, in effect acknowledging Assyria as their overlord. When Tiglath-pileser I acceded to Assyria's throne in 1115, the Mushki had reportedly been in Purulumzu and Alzu for fifty years (**RIMA* 2: 14). Perhaps emboldened by the change in kingship in Assyria, the Mushki embarked on further expansion, and a force of 20,000 of them, under the command of five kings, invaded and captured the land of Kadmuhu (for the outcome, see **Kadmuhu**). In the context of his campaign of conquest of the Subarian peoples, Tiglath-pileser reports that he reimposed Assyrian control over the lands of Alzu and Purulumzu, forcing them once more to pay tribute, a practice which they had apparently abandoned (**RIMA* 2:17).
Streck (*RlA* 11: 118).

Purushanda (**Purushattum, Parsuhanda**) Bronze Age city and kingdom in south-central Anatolia. It was perhaps located on the site of mod. Acem Höyük, to the southeast of the Salt Lake, 6 km northwest of mod. Aksaray, but is now more commonly identified with the site at Karahöyük, near mod. Konya (see ***Karahöyük (1)***). The city is attested in Middle Bronze Age Assyrian Colony texts (see glossary), in the form Burushattum (variant Purushattum), as one of the kingdoms, called *mātu*, which dominated central Anatolia during the Colony period (C20–18) and had regular commercial dealings with Assyrian merchants. Burushattum was linked to Assyria by a major trade route, which passed through the Anatolian cities Washaniya, Nenassa, and Ullamma. The designation of its ruler as a 'Great King' (*rubāʾum rabiʾum*) highlights its important status in the Colony period. Very probably the kingdom incorporated a number of communities, towns, and petty principalities.

Its wealth and power no doubt provided the major incentive for the campaign which Anitta, Great King of Nesa, launched against it after his conquests in other parts of central Anatolia. But when Anitta entered Purushandan territory, its king surrendered to him without resistance. Anitta took him back to Nesa, bestowed honours upon him, and may then have reinstated him as a vassal ruler in his own kingdom, or elsewhere in the territories now subject to Nesa (*Bryce, 2005: 38–9, **Chav.* 218). A tradition preserved in later times, in a text known as the 'King of the Battle' (*šar tamhāri*), relates that the Early Bronze Age Akkadian king Sargon (2334–2279) conducted a successful expedition against Nur-Dagan (Nur-Daggal), ruler of Purushanda, in response to an appeal from a delegation of oppressed Akkadian merchants in the city (*J. G. Westenholz, 1997: 118–27). If this tradition (which has been dismissed as a propagandistic fairy-tale) does in fact have an authentic historical basis, it indicates that there was already a kingdom of Burushattum (Purushanda) in the Early Bronze Age.

In the Late Bronze Age, Purushanda is mentioned (in the form Parsuhanda) as one of the territories which the Hittite king Labarna (early C17) assigned to his sons to govern (*Bryce, 2005: 64). It was subsequently the site of one of the storage depots which King Telipinu (1525–1500) established in various parts of his realm. The city then disappears from Hittite records, except for an occasional reference to it in religious texts. An identification with Parzuta (q.v.), attested in Iron Age Luwian hieroglyphic texts, has been suggested.

**RGTC* 6: 323–4, *CMK* 515–16 (index refs), Hecker (*RlA* 11:119–20).

Pushtu Iron Age fortified city of the land of Parsua in the central western Zagros mountains. Along with the fortified settlements Shalahamanu and Kinihamanu and twenty-three other cities in Parsua, it was captured and plundered by Dayyan-Ashur, commander-in-chief of the Assyrian king Shalmaneser III, during his campaign in the region in 828 (**RIMA* 3: 71).

Puzrish-Dagan (*Drehem*) Early Bronze Age city in southern Mesopotamia, located 10 km southeast of Nippur, and attested in texts of the C21 Ur III dynasty. Built by Shulgi (2094–2047), second ruler of the dynasty, it was a centrally located tax collection and redistribution centre of the Ur III administration, taxes being paid in the form of livestock by military personnel stationed in the empire's frontier settlements. Its location near Nippur is indicated by the statement that two officials of Shulgi were given leather shoes at Puzrish-Dagan for their journey from Nippur to Susa. Puzrish-Dagan appears to have reached the peak of its importance as an administrative centre of the Ur III dynasty during the reign of Shulgi's successor Amar-Sin (2046–2038). Detailed records were kept in its archives of the receipt and disbursement of goods, and the comings and goings of emissaries. The city served as a stopping-place for ambassadors on diplomatic missions to Mesopotamia from the east, e.g. from the western Iranian highland countries of Kimash and Marhashi. Food and drink, travel equipment, and gifts were bestowed upon the ambassadors. Some of the diplomatic emissaries spent a considerable period of time in the city, which leads M. Sigrist to wonder whether they might have lived there as hostages rather than as envoys (1992: 363). To judge from the Elamite names in the archives, large numbers of Elamites appear to have resided permanently in Puzrish-Dagan, as in other Mesopotamian cities. Puzrish-Dagan was abandoned in the third regnal year of the last Ur III king, Ibbi-Sin (2028–2004).

*Sigrist (1992), D. T. Potts (1999: 132, 138–9), Sallaberger (*RlA* 11: 125–8).

Puzurran Middle Bronze Age city in the middle Euphrates region, 12 km downstream from Mari, and just north of the region called Suhum in Middle Bronze Age texts. Originally a possession of the kingdom of Eshnunna, it was allegedly bought by the Mariote king Yahdun-Lim (1810–1794) from an Eshnunnite king, probably Iqish-Tishpak (late C19), for three talents of silver (c. 90 kg). A king of the city called Yaus-Addu is attested in a cylinder seal inscription.

Mesop. 131–3, 139–40.

Pyla (map 14) Late C13 fortified settlement in Cyprus, on the rocky plateau of Kokkinokremos 800 m inland from the northern part of Larnaka Bay, 10 km northeast of mod. Larnaka. The plateau dominates the surrounding plain and controls the pass connecting Larnaka Bay and the central plain. The site was excavated briefly by P. Dikaios in 1952 and by V. Karageorghis and M. Demas in 1981–2 for the Dept of Antiquities. Four complete domestic units and partial plans of three more were uncovered, all built at the same time against a defensive wall with casemates. The settlement was occupied for only twenty-five to thirty years, before being suddenly abandoned at the end of C13. Several hoards of gold jewellery, and bronze and silver, reflect this hasty abandonment and the unsettled conditions which prevailed on the island during late C13 and C12.

Karageorghis identified Pyla-Kokkinokremos as one of the earliest settlements established by Aegean colonists in Cyprus. Alternatively, it may represent a local stronghold established to secure movement of goods, in particular metals, between coastal towns and the hinterland (cf. ***Maa***). The inhabitants clearly enjoyed considerable wealth and wide-ranging contacts, as evidenced by the recovery of Egyptian alabaster vases and transport amphorae, imported Aegean pottery (including a chariot krater), copper and silver ingots, and sheet gold.

(J. M. Webb)

Karageorghis and Demas (1984), Steel (2004: 188–90).

Pyrgos (map 14) Early and Middle Bronze Age settlement in Cyprus, located below the mod. village of Pyrgos, 3 km from the south coast and 15 km northeast of Limassol. Current excavations by M. R. Belgiorno (Istituto per gli Studi Micenei ed Egeo-Anatolici, Rome) have uncovered a substantial Middle Bronze Age industrial and storage area. In it was a large room or courtyard with a series of large storage jars which originally contained olive oil. Adjacent spaces with furnaces and associated equipment were used for working metals. Other manufactured items – notably textiles – appear to have been produced in nearby areas. Unstratified material of earlier date indicates initial settlement here from the very beginning of the Early Bronze Age, while associated cemeteries have produced burials dating from the Early Bronze Age through to the Middle Bronze Age.

(J. M. Webb)

Belgiorno (2004).

Pyrnus (map 5) M1 BCE–M1 CE city of the Rhodian Peraea (q.v.) in Caria, southwestern Anatolia. It is attested in C5 as a member of the Athenian Confederacy (see glossary), and is later referred to by Pliny the Elder (5.104) as situated between Caunus and Loryma.

Bean (*PECS* 746).

Q

Qablitum r. River in western Iran, between Awan and Susa, attested in M3 Akkadian texts. Sargapi, ruler of the Zagros kingdom of Zahara, was captured there by the Akkadian king Rimush (**DaK* 207). This was after Rimush's victory in Parahshum (Sumerian Marhashi) (which probably lay east of Elam) over an anti-Akkadian military alliance consisting of troops from Elam, Parahshum, and Zahara (c. 2280). D. T. Potts suggests that the river is to be identified with the Saimarreh, a northern tributary of the Karun.

D. T. Potts (1999: 89, 105–6).

Qabra (Qabara) Middle Bronze Age northern Mesopotamian city and country, located in the vicinity of Arbela (Urbilum) in the plain lying between the Greater and Lesser Zab rivers east of the Tigris r. It was among the targets of a major Assyrian campaign to the Lesser Zab region led by the Assyrian king Shamshi-Adad I (1796–1775) (**RIMA* 1: 64). Qabra's troops were defeated in the confrontation, and its farmlands were laid waste. But the city itself remained unconquered, and provided a place of refuge for the population of the neighbouring town of Sarri, who had fled at the approach of the Assyrian forces. Shamshi-Adad's son Ishme-Dagan laid siege to the city, and was joined there by his brother Yasmah-Addu (**LKM* 286). For some weeks Qabra held out against its besiegers, now reinforced by troops sent by Dadusha, king of Eshnunna, who had previously concluded a peace agreement with Shamshi-Adad. The Eshnunnite troops were apparently placed under Ishme-Dagan's command, and the city finally fell, in the autumn of 1779. (Dadusha in fact claims direct credit for its conquest, stating that he had presented Qabra to Shamshi-Adad as a gift; **Chav.* 99). A letter from the Mari archives refers to the defeat of a king of Qabra called Ardigandi by troops from the city of Kakmum (**LKM* 387), whose King Gurgurrum attacked and plundered Qabra's territory. This event apparently occurred after Shamshi-Adad's death, when his son Ishme-Dagan ruled over the final remnants of the Old Assyrian kingdom. But the chronology is uncertain.

Eidem (1985), *LKM* 102–3, *Mesop.* 166–9, Streck (*RlA* 11: 139–40).

Qade Name in M1 Neo-Assyrian texts of the land of Magan, identified with the mod. Sultanate of Oman and the United Arab Emirates, on the southeastern part of the Arabian peninsula. In 640, a king of Qade called Pade from the city of Izkie (probably to be identified with mod. Izki) brought tribute to the Assyrian king Ashurbanipal. Inscriptions from the reign of the Persian king Darius I (522–486) equate Qade to Old Persian Maka (the name is apparently the successor of Akkadian Makkan).

D. T. Potts (1995: 1456).

Qadesh (Kadesh, Hittite Kinza, ***Tell Nebi Mend***; the city's name was probably pronounced Qidš(a), or the like, with 'Qadesh' being a misvocalization by mod.

scholars: thus *CS* II: 89, n. 46) (maps 3, 6, 7) Settlement-mound in Syria located on the Orontes r. 25 km south of mod. Homs, with occupations levels extending from the Pottery Neolithic (M7) to mid M1 CE. Excavations were carried out by a French Mandatory government expedition led by M. Pézard between 1921 and 1922, and subsequently by P. J. Parr for the University of London between 1975 and 1996. After a period of abandonment in M5 and M4, the site was reoccupied in M3 by a relatively substantial but apparently unwalled settlement. There may have been a further period of abandonment at the end of M3 prior to the building of a major, heavily fortified city in the Middle Bronze Age. This ended in destruction c. 1600. A new city, featuring large public buildings, was built shortly after, marking the beginning of Qadesh's most important historical phase.

In written records, Qadesh makes its first appearance as an ally of the Late Bronze Age Hurrian kingdom of Mitanni. It joined a coalition of Syro-Palestinian states that opposed and was defeated by the pharaoh Tuthmosis III at the battle of Megiddo (1479), during Tuthmosis' first Asiatic campaign. In one of Tuthmosis' subsequent campaigns, it was incorporated into Egyptian subject territory. Confirmation of its status as an Egyptian vassal was established in the accord reached between Mitanni and Egypt during the reign of Tuthmosis IV (1400–1390). Half a century later, the city became embroiled in territorial disputes between Egypt and the kingdom of Hatti. While the Hittite king Suppiluliuma I was in Syria campaigning against Mitanni's subject and allied states, c. 1340, Shuttarna (Shutatarra), king of Qadesh, launched an attack on his troops. Suppiluliuma promptly retaliated, conquering the city and deporting its king to Hatti, along with his children and leading citizens (**HDT* 44). Later, he allowed the king's son Aitakkama to return to Qadesh and occupy his father's throne, obviously believing that that this would best serve Hittite interests. Initially, Aitakkama may have made some show of allegiance to the

Figure 97 Qadesh.

pharaoh Akhenaten (*EA* 189; see Bryce, 2003b: 144, n. 33). But it is clear from the Amarna correspondence (see glossary) that he was effectively a vassal of the Hittite king – for the time being. In the reign of Suppiluliuma's son and (second) successor Mursili II (1321–1295), he broke his ties with Hatti and re-established his city's independence.

It was a shortlived independence. Hittite sovereignty over Qadesh was promptly restored when Aitakkama's eldest son, Niqmaddu, fearful of the consequences of Hittite retaliation (a Hittite army had just completed a punitive campaign against the rebel Nuhashshi lands which lay nearby), assassinated his father and declared his submission to Mursili (**CS* II: 89). But his action failed to prevent a Hittite attack upon Qadesh. It fell to the Hittite commander Kurunta, who arrested Niqmaddu and took him back to Hattusa. Niqmaddu was eventually installed as a Hittite vassal on his father's throne, despite Mursili's feelings of repugnance at his act of patricide (**AM* 112–13, **CS* II: 89–90). But sovereignty over the city remained a contentious issue, and shortly before his death in 1327 the pharaoh Tutankhamun sent troops there to wrest it back from Hittite control. Suppiluliuma responded by dispatching an expeditionary force against the Egyptians. They were driven out of the kingdom, and the Hittites followed up their success with a retaliatory attack on Egyptian territory in southern Syria (**CS* I: 190).

Tensions between Egypt and Hatti continued to simmer, and finally erupted into open conflict when Seti I (1294–1279), second ruler of Egypt's nineteenth dynasty, sought to recapture from the Hittite king Muwattalli II both Qadesh and the north-western Syrian state of Amurru. The battle, fought in the region of Qadesh, resulted in a decisive Egyptian victory (**ARE III*: §§ 72–3), and Amurru and Qadesh reverted to Egyptian control. Yet this was merely a prelude to the famous battle of Qadesh fought between Seti's son and successor Ramesses II and Muwattalli in 1274. A detailed account in word and picture of the battle itself and the Egyptian expedition leading up to it is recorded on the walls of five Egyptian temples (*Gardiner, 1960). Though Ramesses claims to have snatched victory from the jaws of defeat, the immediate outcome of the battle was a stalemate. None the less, one might judge the Hittites to be the ultimate victors, since subsequently all contested territory north of Damascus, including Qadesh, was ceded to them.

Qadesh was almost certainly among the Syro-Palestinian kingdoms and city-states which were destroyed during the upheavals associated with the Sea Peoples in early C12. It was, however, reoccupied in the Iron Age, and is mentioned in Assyrian administrative texts. An Assyrian garrison may have been stationed there. But it never again achieved the strategic importance which it had enjoyed, and from which it had suffered, during its Late Bronze Age phase. There is no evidence of occupation during the Persian period (C6–4). In Hellenistic times the site was occupied by the city of Laodicea (one of a number of Hellenistic cities of that name).

Parr (1983), Mathias and Parr (1989), Klengel (1992: 157–60), Klengel/Parr (*RlA* 11: 140–4).

Qadesh-Barnea (*Tell el-Qudeirat*) (map 13) Small Iron Age site located in the northern Sinai, on the southern border of Canaan and the western border of Edom. It was used as a camp by nomadic and semi-nomadic groups travelling in the Negev-Sinai desert regions. Following initial investigations in 1914 by C. L. Woolley and T. E. Lawrence, the site was excavated by M. Dothan on behalf of the Israel Dept of

Figure 98 Hittite warriors at Qadesh, temple of Ramesses II, Abydos, Egypt.

Antiquities in 1956, and by R. Cohen over ten seasons between 1976 and 1982. These excavations identified a sequence of three fortresses, the so-called Lower, Middle, and Upper Fortresses. The C10 Lower Fortress, consisting of casemate rooms surrounding a central courtyard in an elongated circle, was succeeded, many years after its destruction, by the rectangular C8 Middle Fortress, which had eight towers projecting from an outer wall and was endowed with substantial grain storage facilities. It was probably destroyed c. mid C7, and soon after replaced by the rectangular Upper Fortress, with casemate rooms replacing the outer wall. The destruction of this fortress is thought to have coincided with the Babylonian conquest of Judah in 586. The site was reoccupied in mid C5 by an unfortified settlement, built on the remains of the last fortress, following the repatriation of the Jewish exiles in Babylonia by the Persian king Cyrus II.

Qadesh-Barnea is referred to in a number of biblical passages, one of which, Genesis 14:7, gives En-mishpat as its alternative name. It plays an important role in the Exodus tradition as the place where the Israelites were encamped for a long period on their way to the Promised Land (Deuteronomy 1:46). It was from there that Moses sent spies into Canaan (Numbers 13:26) and made his unsuccessful bid to the king of Edom for permission to pass through his land (Numbers 20:14–21). However, biblical tradition cannot be reconciled with archaeological evidence, which gives no indication of settlement at Tell el-Qudeirat prior to C10. The lack of evidence for earlier settlement appears to provide support for the view that the Exodus narrative was devised in a later period, perhaps C7.

Cohen (*NEAEHL* 3: 843–7).

Qala'a (Qalawa) Iron Age region within the kingdom of Melid/Malatya, eastern Anatolia, referred to by the Urartian king Sarduri II in his invasion of the kingdom in the second year of his reign (late 760s)

*Kuhrt (1995a: 556), *CHLI* I: 284.

Qalatgah (map 20) Large Iron Age Urartian fortress overlooking the Ushnu-Solduz plain, near the southern shore of Lake Urmia in northwestern Iran. A badly worn inscription of the Urartian kings Ishpuini and Minua was discovered at the site in a secondary context in 1968, which, in combination with other epigraphic evidence from the Ushnu area, suggests a founding date of c. 800. The site is unexcavated and its anc. name is unknown, although Uasi (q.v.) and Ulhu have been suggested by various reconstructions of the itinerary of the Assyrian king Sargon II on his eighth campaign (714).

(P. Zimansky)
Kleiss (1971: 63–4).

Qalʿat al-Bahrain (map 12) 18 ha site located on the north coast of the main island of Bahrain in the Arabian Gulf, with a history of occupation extending from c. 2400 through M2, M1, and M1 CE levels. In C16 CE the Portuguese built a fortress there. Excavations on the site, first undertaken in 1954 by Danish teams from the University of Aarhus, continued until 1965, with a further season in 1970 (the excavation directors were P. V. Glob and subsequently T. G. Bibby). Later excavations were carried out by French teams, most recently from 1988 under the direction of P. Lombard.

From its origins in mid M3, Qalʿat al-Bahrain was the most important settlement of Bahrain which, along with the island of Falaika, has been identified with the land of Dilmun in Mesopotamian texts. The Danish excavators uncovered a sequence of five major levels on the site. The artefactual remains of the first two of these attest to Qalʿat al-Bahrain's far-reaching cultural and commercial links, extending northwards to southern Mesopotamia and eastwards as far as the Indus valley (the land of Meluhha?).

Figure 99 Qalatgah.

This is consistent with the general picture of Dilmun as a thriving commercial entrepôt within the networks of Early and Middle Bronze Age international trade. Levels I and II of the settlement's existence cover the periods 2400–2000 and 2000–1600 respectively, i.e. they extend through the four last centuries of the Early Bronze Age to the end of the Old Babylonian period (Middle Bronze Age). The most significant architectural remains of these early periods is a substantial city wall belonging to level II. It is 3.5 m thick and made of stone with rubble core.

Though Dilmun's importance diminished from mid C18, due to a reduction in trading activity between Mesopotamia and the Gulf, Qalʿat al-Bahrain retained its status as a major settlement during its level III phase (Late Bronze Age), when along with the rest of Dilmun it probably came under the control of Kassite Babylonia. A large building of this period is thought to have been a storehouse because of the thousands of burnt date-stones which it contained. The fire which destroyed the building also preserved cuneiform inscriptions on clay tablets, dating to C14. The tablets contain references to a temple, a Kassite king, and the palace of a local ruler. The settlement's most significant Iron Age remains (level IV) are those of a large residential building complex, dating to C7 or early C6, whose layout recalls Neo-Assyrian and Neo-Babylonian architectural concepts. The complex has sometimes been mistakenly identified as the palace of Uperi, attested as ruler of Dilmun at the time of the Assyrian king Sargon II's Babylonian campaign in 710–709. Dilmun was then a tributary of the Assyrian empire. There appears to be a gap in the history of Qalʿat al-Bahrain, and indeed in that of Dilmun in general, during the Persian period (C6–4). Level V of the city's existence dates to the Hellenistic, Parthian, and probably Sasanian periods. Level VI is the label applied to the site's later Islamic remains.

D. T. Potts (*OEANE* 4: 367–8).

Qaleh Ismail Agha (map 20) Major Iron Age Urartian fortress in northwestern Iran beside the Nazlu Çay, controlling access to the plain of Urmia from the east, 20 km northwest of the city centre of mod. Urmia. The fortified area of the site covers 9.3 ha and includes two citadels: a lower castle in the north and an upper castle in the south. Among the visible features in the ruins are two rock-cut tombs. The site was discovered and mapped by W. Kleiss in the early 1970s. But apart from an Italian expedition's brief season of archaeological survey and sounding in 1977 (Pecorella and Salvini, 1984: 215–28), it remains unexcavated. No inscriptions have been found at the site and its anc. name is unknown. However, its size and location on some reconstructions of the Assyrian king Sargon II's eighth campaign through Urartu (714) would make it a candidate for Uasi (q.v.), the strongest Urartian fortress encountered by Sargon.

(P. Zimansky)
Kleiss (1976: 19 map, 26–30).

Qarne Iron Age royal city located in the Diyala region of northeastern Mesopotamia. It lay across the Diyala r. (called the Turnat) from the city of Me-Turran/Turnat. The Assyrian king Shamshi-Adad V (823–811), reports destroying Qarne along with 200 cities in its environs during his fourth campaign, which he conducted into Babylonian territory (*RIMA 3: 187).

Qarqar (map 7) Iron Age Syrian city located on the Orontes r. within the kingdom of Hamath. In 853 it was the site of a battle fought between the Assyrian king Shalmaneser III and a coalition of anti-Assyrian states. Shalmaneser claims that an alliance of twelve kings had been formed against him, in which the Hamathite king Urhilina (Irhuleni in Assyrian texts) played a leading role. Other coalition leaders included Hadad-ezer (Adad-idri), king of Damascus, and Ahab, king of Israel. According to Shalmaneser's reckoning of the enemy forces, there were: 1,200 chariots, 1,200 cavalry, and 20,000 troops from Damascus; 700 chariots, 700 cavalry, and 10,000 troops from Hamath; 2,000 chariots and 10,000 troops from Israel; 500 troops from Byblos; 1,000 troops from the country called Musri (see **Musri (2)**); 10 chariots and 10,000 troops from the land of Irqata; 200 troops from the island-city of Arwada; 200 troops from the land of Usanatu; 30 chariots and [?]000 troops from the land of Shianu; 1,000 camels of Gindibu of the Arabs; and [?]000 troops provided by the Ammonite ruler Ba'asa (**RIMA* 3: 23–4). Though Shalmaneser claimed victory in the battle, capturing and destroying Qarqar itself (**RIMA* 3: 23, 145), the outcome of the conflict seems to have been inconclusive, for in later years (849, 848, 845) he was forced to engage in further conflicts with the same alliance. In 720 Qarqar was the setting for a battle fought between the recently enthroned Assyrian king Sargon II and another alliance of Syrian states, led by Yaubidi, king of Hamath. On this occasion, the outcome was more decisive. The alliance was conclusively defeated, Yaubidi was captured and flayed alive, and Qarqar was put to the torch (**CS* II: 293, 296). Hamath thenceforth became an Assyrian province.

Excavations carried out at Tell Qarqur (see ***Qarqur, Tell***) in the Orontes valley between 1993 and 1998 indicate that a significant Iron Age site was located there. It may in fact be the historically attested Qarqar, though a firm identification has yet to be established.

Lipiński (2000: 264–6), Weippert (*RlA* 11: 154–5).

Figure 100 Qarqur.

Qarqur, Tell (map 7) Predominantly early Iron Age site in the Orontes valley, consisting of a higher and a lower tell covering in total an area of approx. 22 ha. The site was excavated by J. Lundquist and subsequently by R. H. Dornemann, from 1983 to 1984 and 1993 to 1998 respectively, on behalf of the American Schools of Oriental Research. Human occupation began there in the Neolithic Age, and continued through the Bronze Age (there are remains, for example, of Late Bronze Age fortifications), Iron Age, Persian, Hellenistic, Roman, Byzantine, and mediaeval periods. The main period of settlement appears to have been in C9 and C8. Remains of this period include a gateway area giving access to a 2 m wide stone paved street, building foundations, and a range of ceramic ware of C9–8 Amuq Plain type. The higher tell may have served as a citadel at this time.

The site has been plausibly, though not conclusively, identified with the city of Qarqar (q.v.), located on the Orontes r. in the kingdom of Hamath, and the site of a well-known battle fought in 853 between the Assyrian king Shalmaneser III and a coalition of Syrian states (**RIMA* 3: 23–4).

Dornemann (2000; *RlA* 11: 155–6).

Qartihadasht (= 'New City') Cypriot Carthage, a Phoenician kingdom in Cyprus. Inscriptions indicate its subjection in C8 to Hiram, king of Tyre, and in C7 to the Assyrian kings Esarhaddon and Ashurbanipal. An identification has been suggested with Amathus (q.v.), capital of a small kingdom on Cyprus' southern coast. Alternatively, Qartihadasht has been identified with the Cypro-Phoenician kingdom of Citium (Kition).

Markoe (2000: 170–1).

Qasile, Tell (map 8) M1 BCE–M1 CE settlement-mound, c. 6 ha in extent, located in Palestine 1.5 km from the coast on the northern bank of the Yarkon r. It lies today in a suburb of Tel Aviv-Jaffa, Israel. The site was excavated by B. Mazar (1949–51, 1959) and A. Mazar (1971–4, 1982–92) for the Institute of Archaeology, Hebrew University of Jerusalem, and the Ha-aretz Museum, Tel Aviv. Tell Qasile was probably established by the Philistines in C12 during the Iron Age I period. This first phase of its existence was also its most important. Archaeologically, it is divided into three sub-phases (Strata XII–X), the third of which marked the peak of the settlement's urban development. In this, the last Philistine sub-phase, streets were laid out on a grid pattern separating blocks of buildings. Pillared square houses were constructed with central courtyards, and paved and roofed side spaces which were probably used for animal shelters. The most notable feature of the Iron Age I period is a religious sanctuary, which shows progressive development through the three Philistine strata from a small shrine in XII, to a more substantial stone-walled temple and courtyard complex in XI, to a rebuilding and enlargement of this complex in X. Ceramic cult-objects found in the sanctuary provide valuable information on the settlement's culture and ethnic composition. The material remains of the sanctuary and other buildings reflect a predominantly Philistine population and culture, though with a significant admixture of Canaanite elements.

The city was destroyed in C11 at the end of Stratum X, then partially rebuilt in C10 on a smaller and more modest scale. It was now less densely populated, with open paved spaces replacing earlier built-up areas. This phase of its existence has been associated with King David's incorporation of part of the Palestinian coast into the kingdom of Israel. The 'Israelite' settlement appears not to have lasted beyond the end of C9, its destruction perhaps due to the pharaoh Sheshonq I (*OT* Shishak) (945–924) in the course of his campaign in Israel. This may have occurred at the end of Stratum IX, followed by some rebuilding in C9. However, the site was apparently abandoned by the end of C9, and remained unoccupied until a small settlement was established there in late C7. It continued to be inhabited during the Persian period (C6–4; Stratum VI), perhaps suffering destruction by Alexander the Great in 333. There is further evidence of settlement on the mound in the Hellenistic and Roman periods (Strata V–III), and on and around the mound in the Byzantine period (Stratum II). A few remains also survive of later Arab occupation (Stratum I).

Mazar (*NEAEHL* 4: 1204–12).

Qataban (map 9) M2–1 state located in mod. Yemen, southern Arabia. It was one of the six kingdoms of pre-Islamic South Arabia. The other five were Saba (biblical Sheba), Hadhramaut, Ausin, Himyar, and Maʿin. Tangible evidence of human occupation in the Qataban region dates back no earlier than C11–10, though it is believed that there may have been settlement there at least a thousand years earlier. By late C7 or early C6, power in the state was centralized in the hands of a line of rulers, as attested in the South Arabic royal inscriptions of Hawfiʿamm Yuhanʿim, son of Sumhuʿalay, whose royal seat lay in the city of Timnah (see **Timnah (1)**). Qataban was for a time under the control of its neighbour, Saba. But by late C5 it had established its independence, and from this time onwards was one of the dominant powers of South Arabia, along with Hadhramaut and Maʿin. Ruled from its capital city, Timnah, Qataban remained a powerful and wealthy independent kingdom in its region until it lost part of its territory to the newly formed combined kingdom of Saba and Dhu-Rhaydan in late C2. But it continued to exist for another two centuries until it was incorporated, probably in late C1, into the kingdom of Hadhramaut.

Though it depended primarily on its agricultural activities, Qataban no doubt derived a significant part of its wealth from the merchant caravans which passed through its territory. Strabo (16.4.2–4) calls the land Cattabania, and specifically associates it with the merchant trade in incense. Pliny the Elder (32.153) refers to its inhabitants as the Gebbanitae, claiming that its capital Timnah (which he calls Thomna) contained sixty-five temples! The principal deity of the land was the moon god Anbay.

Van Beek (*OEANE* 4: 383–4).

Qatna (***Mishrifeh***) (maps 3, 6, 7) Central Syrian site, 100 ha in extent, located east of the Orontes r. and 18 km northeast of mod. Homs. It was occupied from the Early Bronze Age (M3) through the Neo-Babylonian period (late C7–6). The site was first excavated by R. du Mesnil du Buisson from 1924 to 1927. Cuneiform tablets unearthed during these excavations provided the identification of the city's anc. name. Excavations were resumed by the Syrian Dept of Antiquities in 1994, and have continued more recently with collaboration by teams from the universities of Tübingen and Udine. The site appears to have first been used by nomads during the Palaeolithic period. It rose to prominence early in M3 because of its strategic location on a trade route linking Syria with Mesopotamia. One of the richest finds of the Early Bronze Age city was a shaft-grave (designated as Tomb IV), which contained forty burials, over one hundred weapons and ornaments of copper and bronze, and a large quantity of pottery. The pottery finds indicate links with the Mesopotamian Ur III dynasty (C21). In early M2, Qatna was ruled by an Amorite dynasty, and became one of the most important Amorite kingdoms in Syria, rivalling the kingdom of Yamhad. Letters in the Mari archive indicate Qatna's diplomatic relations with the Assyrian king Shamshi-Adad I (1796–1775) and his son Yasmah-Addu, viceroy at Mari. Qatna also enjoyed peaceful relations with Alalah and Egypt in this period.

By late C16, however, it had fallen to the rapidly expanding Mitannian empire, and subsequently during the reigns of the C15 pharaohs Tuthmosis I and Tuthmosis III was subject to Egypt. In the following century it was one of the states conquered by the Hittites, c. 1340, during the Hittite king Suppiluliuma I's one-year Syrian campaign (**HDT* 43). But subsequently it broke from Hittite control under its local king, Akizzi, who had declared allegiance to the pharaoh Akhenaten (1352–1336). The Amarna archive (see glossary) contains several letters which Akizzi wrote to Akhenaten, complaining of hostile activity against his land by the Amurrite warlord Aziru, and more particularly by Aitakkama, ruler of Qadesh (**EA* 53–5). The latter had attacked Qatna, with Hittite backing, with the object of forcing it to rejoin the Hittite fold.

M2 Qatna had impressive fortifications, consisting of still surviving square ramparts, 15 m high on average and sometimes reaching a height of 20 m. Access to the city through the walls was provided by four triple-chambered gates. Excavations within the city brought to light a temple of Qatna's chief deity, the goddess Nin-Egal. The goddess's cella, where the image of the deity was originally housed, was located in the northeast corner of the temple's courtyard. To the east of the temple lay the royal

Figure 101 Qatna, rampart.

palace, originally founded in the Middle Bronze Age. It is here that the most important recent finds at Qatna have been made. During the German excavations in 2002, a hoard of sixty-seven tablets and fragments was unearthed, consisting of letters and judicial and administrative documents, dating to the Amarna period. The tablets confirm the existence of a major Hurrian element in Qatna's population – one which very likely dates back before the period of Mitannian domination of the region. The tablet hoard has been dubbed Idadda's (or Idanda's) archive. Idadda appears to have been Akizzi's predecessor on Qatna's throne. The names of Idadda and his three royal predecessors – Naplimma, Sînadu, and Adad-nirari – had already been identified from four inventory texts unearthed at Qatna during the earlier French excavations.

Within the confines of the palace, the 2002 excavations also uncovered an underground shaft which led to a royal tomb consisting of a main chamber and three side chambers. Two identical seated 'ancestor statues' made of basalt flanked the tomb entrance. Most of the burials were made in the main chamber, which appears to have been used also for ceremonial feasts. A basalt sarcophagus contained the remains of three secondary burials. Four other burials were indicated by traces of four wooden biers. Of the three side rooms, one has been interpreted as a possible banqueting chamber for the dead king, another has been identified as a room for primary burials, and the third as an ossuary.

In the Iron Age the city was apparently settled by Aramaeans, and enjoyed a flourishing existence as a trading centre during the Neo-Babylonian empire.

Abou Assaf (*OEANE* 4: 35–6), Novák and Pfälzner (2000–), Richter (2003; 2005), Pfälzner (2006), Richter/Pfälzner (*RlA* 11: 159–70).

Qatnu see Qattuna(n).

Qattara (map 10) Royal city in northeastern Mesopotamia, attested in the Old Assyrian texts from Karum Kanesh in Anatolia (see **Kanesh**), as well as in the Middle Bronze Age Mari archives and the tablets from Tell er-Rimah dating from the Old Babylonian (C18) and Middle Assyrian (late C13) periods. Qattara was ruled by a king called Hatnu-rapi during the reign of Zimri-lim, king of Mari (1774–1762). Hatnu-rapi's military exploits included the sacking and pillaging of the city of Shubat-Enlil (see ***Leilan, Tell***), formerly the capital of the Old Assyrian kingdom and since 1771 a protégé of the kingdom of Eshnunna. It was perhaps partly in retaliation for this action that Eshnunna's king, Ibal-pi-El II, dispatched an army to occupy Qattara. Hatnu-rapi was forced to flee his city and seek refuge in nearby Karana, where he seized the throne from its incumbent, Samu-Addu. At a later date, after the disappearance of Hatnu-rapi, Qattara came under the control of Ashkur-Adad, whom Zimri-Lim had installed on the throne of Karana. It probably remained subject to Karana under the latter's next king, Aqba-hammu, who had seized the throne from Ashkur-Adad, his brother-in-law, and now ruled the kingdom as a subject of Hammurabi, king of Babylon. Qattara is sometimes identified with the excavated site of Tell er-Rimah, for which an equation with Karana is also proposed. If the identification is valid, then Qattara received a new lease of life, under the name Zamahu (q.v.), in early M1 (see ***Rimah, Tell er-***).

Charpin and Durand (1987), *LKM* 619 (refs), *Mesop.* 200–1, Michel (*RlA* 11: 157–9).

Qattunan (Qatnu) (map 10) Middle and Late Bronze Age and Iron Age city located in northern Mesopotamia on the middle Habur r., probably on the east bank. Frequently attested in the Mari archives, Qattunan was the centre of one of the four chief administrative districts of the kingdom of Mari under the rule of Zimri-Lim (1774–1762). (The other three centres were Mari, Terqa, and Saggaratum.) It later marked the eastern limit of the kingdom of Hana, which rose in the wake of the end of the Mariote kingdom, and spanned the last part of the Middle and the first part of the Late Bronze Age. The city probably served as an important river port for Karana (q.v.), which lay to its northeast, and other cities in the semi-desert regions. It appears in Middle Assyrian texts under the name Qatun/Qatnu – e.g. on an itinerary from Dur-Katlimmu dated to the reign of Tukulti-Ninurta I (1244–1208).

Qatnu is attested in Iron Age Assyrian texts as a vassal state of Assyria. The Assyrian king Adad-nirari II visited the city during his campaign in the Habur region in 896, and received from its ruler Amil-Adad 'property from his palace', plus chariots, horses, wagons, and oxen (**RIMA* 2: 153). His successor Tukulti-Ninurta II also visited the city, on his last recorded campaign (885), which took him through the middle Euphrates region, and received tribute from it (**RIMA* 2: 177). Tukulti-Ninurta's son and successor Ashurnasirpal II did likewise, during a campaign in the region in his first regnal year (883) (**RIMA* 2: 199), and several years later in the course of another campaign in the region (**RIMA* 2: 213). Under the Assyrian king Adad-nirari III (810–783) Qatnu was among the cities and lands assigned to the governorship of a certain Nergal-erish (Palil-erish) (**RIMA* 3: 209, 211).

RGTC 3: 188–9, Birot (1993), *LKM* 619 (refs), Michel (*RlA* 11: 171–2).

Qirdahat (Kirdahat) Middle Bronze Age city, located in the Habur r. basin, northern Mesopotamia. It is first attested in the reign of the Assyrian king Shamshi-Adad I (1796–1775) when it was captured by the king's son, Ishme-Dagan, Assyrian viceroy at Ekallatum, after an eight-day siege (**ARM* I: 135). Qirdahat was the seat of one of four known petty kingdoms in the Upper Ida-maras (the others had their capitals at Ashnakkum, Tarmanni, and Shuduhum), whose kings visited Zimri-Lim, ruler of Mari (1774–1762), apparently on a joint diplomatic mission (**LKM* 418). Its ruler at this time was a man called Shub-Ram. The other kings were Sammetar (Ashnakkum), Tamarzi (Tarmanni), and Itur-Malik (Shuduhum).

Qirdahat is perhaps to be identified with the site of Chagar Bazar (q.v.), though the latter has also been equated with anc. Ashnakkum (q.v.).

Röllig (*RlA* 5: 604–5), *Mesop.* 185.

Qirghizia Central Asian country in the region of mod. Kyrgyzstan. It was probably among the lands incorporated by Cyrus II into the Persian empire during a campaign which he conducted into Central Asia some time after his conquest of Babylon in 539. It may have been occupied by one of the groups of Saka people (see **Saka**). The necropoleis of the region are suggestive of a nomadic population.

Francfort (1988: 184, 188, with refs).

Qiri, Tel (map 8) Settlement in northern Palestine, at the eastern end of a spur of the Carmel range, considered to be a satellite community of Tel Yokneam (Yoqneam), which lies 2 km to the northeast. Tel Qiri's history of occupation is represented by eleven archaeological strata, extending from the Late Neolithic (or Early Chalcolithic) period to the Byzantine age. But its main period of settlement was during the Iron Age, represented by five strata (IX–V) divided into twelve sub-phases. Whether there was settlement here during the Early and Late Bronze Ages, from which only a few sherds survive, remains uncertain. Excavations were undertaken between 1975 and 1978, as part of the Yoqneam Regional Project, under the direction of A. Ben-Tor for the Hebrew University of Jerusalem. During the Iron Age the settlement was an unfortified village consisting of well-constructed buildings in whose courtyards a large number of stone-lined storage silos were discovered, and in one case a large olive oil press. These features, along with seeds and faunal material, indicate an agriculturally based population which grew wheat, peas, vetch, and olives, and grazed sheep and goats. Ceramic ware from the site indicates continuous occupation down to C8 (Stratum V; Iron Age IIB), beginning with Philistine occupation in the early Iron Age (C12). The transition from Iron Age I to early Iron Age II (Strata VIII–VII) is marked by a significant change in the plan of buildings. Ben-Tor sees this as a possible reflection of the arrival of the Israelites. There appears to have been a break in occupation until the Persian period (C6–4), whose meagre remains include a cemetery and a few lengths of wall.

Ben-Tor (*NEAEHL* 4: 1228–9).

Qitar, El- (map 10) Predominantly Late Bronze Age mountain fortress-settlement (with evidence also of Early Bronze, Middle Bronze, and Hellenistic occupation), 6 ha in extent and located in eastern Syria on the west bank of the Euphrates, 60 km south of Carchemish. The site, consisting of upper and lower sections, was excavated by R. Dornemann for the Milwaukee Public Museum (1976), and subsequently by T. L. McClellan for the University of Melbourne (1982–5) and the University of Chicago (1986–7). Though little is left of the settlement's Middle Bronze Age phase, since it is covered by later buildings, the remains of what the excavators think may have been an official residence were revealed. It has been dubbed the Orthostat Building because its rooms were lined with orthostat slabs (see glossary). The settlement's main period of occupation dates to C15, when it was presumably under Mitannian control. After the Hittite king Suppiluliuma I destroyed the Mitannian empire in the third quarter of C14, El-Qitar was reoccupied and refortified, probably as a Hittite frontier-post. McClellan believes that its mountain setting identifies it as a fortress, while noting that neither its domestic architecture nor its artefacts hint at a military function. The upper and lower sections of the site were then connected by a rock-cut stairway. A Middle Assyrian cuneiform tablet found in the Late Bronze Age level and bearing a Luwian inscription with the name Til-Abnu may support identification of the site with the city of Til-Abni(m) (q. v.) known from Old Assyrian (Middle Bronze Age) and Aramaean Iron Age texts.

McClellan (1987).

Qode (*qdy*) Late Bronze Age country listed between Hatti and Carchemish by the pharaoh Ramesses III in his account of the Sea Peoples' onslaught upon the countries of western Asia in the eighth year of his reign (1177) (see **Sea Peoples**). It is commonly identified with the southern Anatolian country called Kizzuwadna in Hittite texts. Qode may correspond to Que, the name of Kizzuwadna's Iron Age successor in the region. If so, then Que may already have been used as a designation for this region by the early decades of C12.

CHLI I: 39 (with refs), Lebrun and De Vos (2006: 50–2).

Que (Qawe, Quwe, Adanawa, Hiyawa) (maps 7, 13) M1 kingdom in southern Anatolia, extending over much of the region of Late Bronze Age Kizzuwadna, including the Cilician plain and (originally) the mountainous region to the northeast of the plain. The kingdom is later referred to as Hume (i.e. *Khuwe) in Neo-Babylonian texts. Que is the name attested in Assyrian sources. In Luwian hieroglyphic inscriptions, the kingdom is called Adanawa. To the west of Que/Adanawa lay the kingdom of Hilakku. Both kingdoms fiercely resisted attempts by the Assyrians to impose their sovereignty upon them. In 858, under their respective kings Kate and Pihirim, Que and Hilakku sent contingents to join an alliance of northern Syrian states against the Assyrian king Shalmaneser III. But the alliance was no match for Shalmaneser's army, and its forces were decisively defeated (**RIMA* 3: 10, 16–17). It was, however, to be another twenty years before Shalmaneser invaded Que. In 839 he conducted an expedition across the Amanus range (q.v.) into the kingdom, and captured a number of its cities, including Lusanda, Abarnanu, and Kisuatni (**RIMA* 3: 55, 58). In 833, 832, and 831, he led further expeditions into Que (refs in *CHLI* I: 41, n. 45, including **RIMA* 3: 68), the third of which was followed by a temporary end to Assyrian military enterprises in Anatolia – perhaps an indication that the region remained submissive to Assyrian sovereignty for a time. Around 800, however, Que joined other states in the region, Gurgum, Patin (Unqi), and Melid, in another uprising against Assyrian rule. In the last decades of C8 it appears once again to have become submissive to Assyrian authority.

During its conflicts with Assyria, Que apparently suffered substantial loss of territory, and by the reign of the Assyrian king Tiglath-pileser III (745–727) its remaining lands had been confined largely to the Cilician plain. The seat of Que's power very likely lay in the city of Adana. From the well-known Luwian–Phoenician bilingual inscription found at Karatepe (q.v.), we learn that the inscription's author, Azatiwatas, was the subordinate of a king of Adanawa (Que's Luwian name) called Awarikus (Warikas, Awarikku). In the Phoenician version of the inscription, Awarikus is referred to as 'king of the Danunians'. He can be identified with the man called Urikki in Assyrian texts, king of Que, who was one of Assyria's tributary kings during Tiglath-pileser's reign (**Tigl. III* 68–9, 108–9), and apparently occupied Que's throne from c. 738 to 709, i.e. down to the final decade of the reign of Sargon II (721–705). We shall henceforth refer to him by his Luwian name, Awarikus.

More information about the relationship between Que and Assyria during Awarikus' reign is provided by a Luwian–Phoenician bilingual inscription discovered in 1997 at Çineköy, which lies 30 km south of Adana (*Tekoğlu and Lemaire, 2000). Awarikus is the author of the inscription. In the Luwian version, he calls his country Hiyawa (see under ***Çineköy***), and in the Phoenician version '(the land of) the Danunians' (see under **Adana**). It is perhaps from 'Hiyawa' that the name Que/Qaue/Quwe used for the country in Semitic sources is derived. (It has also been suggested that the Hebrew name *hiwwi* is derived from Hiyawa; see **Hivites**). We learn or are given the impression from the inscription that Que's relationship with Assyria at this time was one of alliance or partnership, in which, Tekoğlu and Lemaire suggest, the Assyrian king exercised the role of protector/suzerain, and probably had a treaty with Awarikus. Such a partnership, they believe, was essential to the success of Awarikus' long reign. Awarikus claims to have built fifteen fortresses, in both the east and the west of his kingdom, while occupying Que's throne. If, as seems likely, his inscription belongs to the final years of his reign, his overlord at the time of its composition must have been Sargon.

It was perhaps not long after the inscription was composed that Que and the neighbouring kingdom of Hilakku lost their status as client kingdoms and came under direct Assyrian rule. The first known governor of Que was a man called Ashur-sharru-usur, attested in a number of Sargon's letters. Precisely when and in what circumstances Ashur-sharru-usur was installed in Que remain unknown. But his Que-based appointment may also have given him authority over Hilakku and the Tabalic kingdoms of Bit-Burutash and Tuwana which lay to the north. Initially, the appointment may have taken place within the context of the new administrative arrangements which Sargon made for the region in 713, following his removal of Ambaris from the throne of Bit-Burutash (see under **Tabal**). Awarikus was presumably answerable to Ashur-sharru-usur as Sargon's representative in his country, and this may well have caused tensions between the local king and the Assyrian governor – which very likely prompted Awarikus to attempt to break his ties with Assyria. Ashur-sharru-usur reported to Sargon that Awarikus had sent a fourteen-man delegation to Urartu, presumably to conduct negotiations with the Urartian king. This must have been done secretly, and was undoubtedly an act hostile to Assyrian interests. But the delegation had been intercepted by Midas (Mita), king of Phrygia, and handed over to Ashur-sharru-usur (**SAA* I: 4–7, no. 1). Awarikus' death probably occurred not long after this episode, and may well have been a consequence of it.

Despite further rebellions against Assyria in southeastern Anatolia, Sargon's son and successor Sennacherib (704–681) probably maintained his authority over Que. But there is some uncertainty about the extent of Assyrian control there at this time. It may not have been until the reign of Sennacherib's son and successor Esarhaddon (680–669) that Assyrian authority was fully restored, with the re-establishment of Que as an Assyrian province, for which an Assyrian governor is attested in 675. Subsequently, Que appears to have remained submissive to Assyrian rule until at least the end of Ashurbanipal's reign (668–630/627).

In the early decades of C6 the Babylonians undertook several expeditions into Que, which they called Hume, and possibly also into Hilakku. Though there is no firm evidence that Babylon ever succeeded in establishing control over these regions, the Babylonian king Nebuchadnezzar II (604–562) claimed Hume amongst his conquests in Anatolia. A final reference to Hume occurs in a text from the reign of the last Babylonian king, Nabonidus (556–539), which records an expedition conducted by Nabonidus into Hume shortly after his accession.

**CHLI* I: 45–70, **CHLI* II, **CS* II: 124–6, 148–50, *Tekoğlu and Lemaire (2000), Lebrun and De Vos (2006).

Qumanu (Qum(m)enu, Uqumanu) Kingdom attested in Late Bronze Age and Iron Age Assyrian texts, located in the borderlands between northeastern Mesopotamia and northwestern Iran, to the north and east of the Alqosh plain. The city of Kipshuna is attested as its royal capital, or one of its capitals (**RIMA* 2: 24–5). The Assyrian king Tukulti-Ninurta I records a campaign against it in his accession year (1245), within the context of his military operations in the land of Qutu (q.v.) (**RIMA* 1: 234–5, 244). At this time, Qumanu was ruled by a certain Abule. Tukulti-Ninurta met with fierce resistance from the united forces of Qumanu, but retaliated ruthlessly, destroying their cities, massacring their inhabitants, and piling up the corpses at the city gates. The kingdom's local rulers were rounded up and deported in chains to Ashur. But they were allowed to return home after swearing an oath of allegiance to their conqueror.

Subsequently, troops from Qumanu came to the aid of the land of Musri when the Assyrian king Tiglath-pileser I (1114–1076) campaigned against it. Tiglath-pileser claims that after conquering the land of Musri (see **Musri (1)**), he confronted and defeated an army of 20,000 mustered from the entire land of Qumanu (**RIMA* 2: 23–4, 34). He followed up his victory by pursuing the remnants of their forces to Mt Harusa and massacring them there. Subsequently, he captured and destroyed Qumanu's chief cities. One of these was the city of Hunusu. Qumanu's royal capital, Kipshuna, was placed under siege by the Assyrians, but Tiglath-pileser spared it when its king submitted voluntarily. He was ordered to demolish his walls, hand over hostages, arrange the deportation of 300 families who refused submission to Assyria, and pay an increased tribute (**RIMA* 2: 24–5).

Qumanu was annexed to Assyria in the reign of Adad-nirari II (911–891). Adad-nirari claims to have conquered the country 'as far as the lands of Mehru, Salua, and Uratru (Urartu)', and to have captured its king, Iluia, within his palace. He took substantial booty from Qumanu back to Ashur, but peacefully resettled those of Qumanu's troops who had returned after initially fleeing the battle (**RIMA* 2: 143–4, 148). During the reign of Shalmaneser III (858–824) Qumanu was governed by a certain Iahalu, one of Shalmaneser's officials, who is described as governor of Kipshuna and the lands of Mehranu, Uqu, and Erimmu (**RIMA* 3: 179).

Radner (*RlA* 11: 206).

Qumran, Khirbet (map 8) M1 site located above the left bank of Wadi Qumran on the northwestern shore of the Dead Sea, and probably to be identified with the City of Salt listed among the six Judaean cities in Joshua 15:61–2. It was excavated from 1951 to 1956, and again in 1958, by a joint Franco-Jordanian team under the direction of R. G. de Vaux for the École Biblique et Archéologique Française, and G. L. Harding for the Dept of Antiquities of Jordan. These excavations followed upon the chance discovery of the Dead Sea scrolls in a nearby cave in 1947 and the excavation of the cave in 1949. (In subsequent years, from 1952 to 1956, scrolls and scroll fragments were discovered in ten more caves.)

In its first period of occupation, Khirbet Qumran was a fortified Israelite site, material remains of which include a rectangular building fronted by a courtyard containing a large round cistern. Pottery fragments along with a royal *lamelekh* seal (see glossary) and an ostracon (see glossary) bearing early Hebrew letters date the settlement to the period from C8 (beginning of Iron Age II) to early C6. Its destruction occurred at the time of the Babylonian conquest of Judah. Following several centuries of abandonment, the site was resettled in the Hellenistic period, and passed through several periods of development until its destruction by the Romans in 68 CE.

de Vaux and Broshi (*NEAEHL* 4: 1235–41), Donceel (*OEANE* 4: 392–7).

Qurayyah Site in northwestern Arabia, 63 km northwest of Tabuk, located near the main route connecting Yemen with the Levant. A survey of the site was undertaken by P. J. Parr in 1968 with a team from the University of London. Subsequent soundings were made by archaeologists from the Saudi Arabian Antiquities Dept. The site consists of a fortified citadel, at the foot of which are the remains of a small settlement surrounded by a stone wall. A number of fields delineated by traces of stone walls and crossed by stone irrigation channels lie to the east of the site. Parr sees all these remains as forming part of a single contemporary occupational context. Ceramic ware from the site, decorated with both naturalistic and geometric motifs derived from Egypt and the Aegean, and often termed 'Midianite Ware', has provided a tentative dating of c. 1300 to 1150 for the main period of occupation. Parr notes that this part of Arabia is usually identified with Midian, whose inhabitants are depicted in the *OT* as pastoralists and camel-raiders. But this appears to be inconsistent with the evidence from Qurayyah, whose walled settlement and adjacent fields suggest that its population was a largely sedentary farming one.

Parr (*OEANE* 4: 396–7).

Qutu (Quti) Name for one of the successor groups of the Gutians, attested in Assyrian texts of the Late Bronze and Iron Ages, in the region of Mannaea (Urartian Mana). The Qutu figure as one of the principal targets of a number of campaigns by Assyrian kings in the western Zagros mountain region. Adad-nirari I (1307–1275) included them among the peoples whom both he and his father, Arik-den-ili, conquered (**RIMA* 1: 131, 132). Shalmaneser I (1274–1245) refers to renewed revolts with which he had to deal in Qutu (**RIMA* 1: 184), and claims to have 'flattened like grain' its army (**RIMA* 1: 206, 207). Tukulti-Ninurta I marched against the Qutu at the beginning of his reign (c. 1244) (**RIMA* 1: 234–5), and also included the land in his list of conquests (**RIMA* 1: 241, 244). In the following century, Ashur-resh-ishi I (1132–1115) boasts his subjugation of Lullumu and all the Qutu (**RIMA* 1: 310–11). The Assyrian commander-in-chief Shamshi-ilu, who served under four Assyrian kings, from Adad-nirari III to Ashur-nirari V (i.e. from late C9 through the first half of C8), records his governorship of Qutu (here written Guti; see **Gutians**), along with the lands of Hatti and Namri (**RIMA* 3: 232). There is no evidence that the people so named had any political or ethnic links with their Gutian predecessors.

R

Rabbath-Ammon (*Amman*) (map 8) Transjordanian city, consisting of acropolis and lower city, capital of the Iron Age kingdom of Ammon, located on the Transjordanian plateau c. 40 km east of the Dead Sea. Its history of occupation extends from the Neolithic Age through succeeding ages to the Roman imperial period. After earlier preliminary surveys, the site was first excavated by an Italian team, under the direction of G. Guidi (1927) and subsequently R. Bartoccini (1929–33). Further excavations were undertaken after the Second World War, beginning with those of G. L. Harding in 1945, and J. B. Hennessy's exploration of a Late Bronze Age temple in 1966, near Amman airport. Excavations in more recent years have concentrated on the acropolis (Jebel Qala). Middle Bronze Age rock-cut tombs of roughly rectangular or semicircular shape were discovered near the summit of the acropolis. The remains of fortification walls on the summit itself appear to have been of both Middle Bronze Age (II) and early Iron Age (I) date. A circular Iron Age wall was also discovered at the southeastern corner of the lower city. In the southern part of the lower city, the remains of an extensive architectural complex, dating to C7, were unearthed. One of its chief features was a large courtyard with a high-quality polished white plaster floor. Tentatively designated as a palace, its architecture has been compared with that of the Neo-Assyrian palatial complexes at sites like Nimrud and Khorsabad.

Rabbath-Ammon is frequently attested in *OT* sources, sometimes under the name Rabbah or Rabbat. For example, in the course of Israelite hostilities with the Ammonites during King David's reign (C10), the king's nephew and military commander, Joab, captured Rabbah's royal citadel and water supply, paving the way for David's subsequent conquest and plunder of the whole city (2 Samuel 12:26–31). Only sparse information about the city is provided by extra-biblical sources. In 581 it was conquered by the Babylonian king Nebuchadnezzar II, and in the last decades of C6 must have been incorporated with the rest of Ammon into the Persian empire. The Ammonite monarchy became defunct under Persian rule, and Rabbath-Ammon itself came under the authority of the local pro-Persian Tobiad dynasty. It appears to have flourished in this period. During the Hellenistic age the city became part of the Ptolemaic empire. It was rebuilt by Ptolemy II Philadelphus in C3, and renamed Philadelphia after him, though the old name Rabbath-Ammon is still attested in C3 and C2.

Burdajewicz (*NEAEHL* 4: 1243–9).

Rab(b)ilu M1 Aramaean city and people in Babylonia, located probably in the region of the Diyala r. The city appears in the list of thirty-five so-called Aramaean tribes conquered by the Assyrian king Tiglath-pileser III (**Tigl. III* 158–9), probably in his first regnal year (745). Another text records the plundering of Rabbilu by Tiglath-pileser, along with the city of Hamranu (**ABC* 71). The settlement is subsequently mentioned in Babylonian texts of the Persian period (C6–4).

Lipiński (2000: 442, 446–7), Radner (*RlA* 11: 209).

Rabud, Khirbet (Debir?) (map 8) Settlement in the Judaean hill country 12 km south of Hebron. It is almost certainly to be identified with the Canaanite city of Debir (thus M. Kochavi), attested in *OT* sources and originally known as Kiriath-Sepher, 'city of the scribe'. This is *contra* W. F. Albright's proposed identification of Debir with Beit Mirsim. The site's history of occupation extends from the Chalcolithic to the Roman period. Excavations undertaken by Kochavi in 1968 and 1969 for the Institute of Archaeology, Tel Aviv University, revealed traces of only sporadic occupation in the Chalcolithic and Early Bronze Ages (M4–3). There appears to be no evidence of settlement in the Middle Bronze Age. In the Late Bronze Age, however, a walled city was built on the site, of which four phases have been distinguished. At this time, Khirbet Rabud/Debir extended over c. 6 ha. The site continued to be inhabited during the early centuries of the Iron Age, from C12 onwards, and reached the peak of its development under Israelite occupation probably in C9 when a substantial new city wall was constructed. The destruction of the city at the end of C8 is generally attributed to the Assyrian king Sennacherib in the course of his campaign in Judah in 701. The city was subsequently rebuilt, and fortified by a massive new city wall. But this failed to save it from destruction by the Babylonians during their campaign of conquest in Judah in early C6. Limited reoccupation occurred during the succeeding Persian period (C6–4), and the remains of a Roman lookout tower attest to continuing habitation, if on a very limited scale, in the Roman imperial period.

Kochavi (*NEAEHL* 4: 401), Negev and Gibson (2001: 426–7).

Raddana, Khirbet Small Iron Age I village (12–16 ha) in southern Palestine on the edge of mod. Ramallah, 16 km north of Jerusalem. There is also evidence, provided by ceramic ware, of a limited human presence on the site during the Early Bronze I and Byzantine periods. But Raddana is essentially a single-period site. Excavations were conducted between 1969 and 1974 by J. Callaway and R. Cooley for the Israel Dept of Antiquities. The excavators concluded that the site was inhabited by settlers of unknown origin in late C13 or early C12, who lived through two phases of village life before the settlement was violently destroyed and abandoned in mid C11. Its prime architectural feature was a cluster of houses, each consisting of a large room with roof supported by hewn pillars or stone piers, with a small room at the back. A hearth was located in the centre of the large room, and the houses were supplied with water cisterns and grain silos. The excavators noted the abundance of cereal food-processing tools found throughout the site, as well as evidence for primitive metalworking, including fragments of crucibles. One of the notable small finds was a jar handle inscribed with three letters in the Proto-Canaanite script.

Cooley (1975; *OEANE* 4: 401–2), Callaway (*NEAEHL* 4: 1253–4).

Rahimmu Iron Age city in northern Babylonia, located on the east bank of the Euphrates, opposite the city of Rapiqu(m), within three days' march of the city of Sippar. The Assyrian king Tukulti-Ninurta II encamped his forces there during his last recorded campaign (885) which took him through the middle Tigris and Euphrates regions (*RIMA 2: 174).

Ra'il Iron Age city located on an island in the middle Euphrates region, within the land of Suhu (*RIMB 2: 320). In the first half of C8, Suhu was governed by a certain

Shamash-resha-usur, who records planting date-palms in the courtyard of Ra'il's palace (*RIMB 2: 281). He built a new palace there to replace the old. He also planted date-palms in the palace courtyard of the city of Kar-Nabu, in the district of the city of Iaduru, and in the city of Ukalaia. Shamash-resha-usur's son and successor Ninurta-kudurri-usur reports that the people of Ra'il had staged a rebellion against his father. The rebellion was crushed, but the Ra'ilites once more rose in rebellion when Ninurta-kudurri-usur became governor of Suhu. He too succeeded in quashing the rebels. But he warned that the people of Ra'il should not in future be neglected (*RIMB 2: 292).

Na'aman (2007: 115–17).

Rakha M1 city in Persis in southwestern Iran. It was the site of a battle fought between the forces of Vahyazdata, a pretender to the Persian throne who had rebelled against Darius I on his accession in 522, and an army dispatched by Darius against him under the command of Artavadiya. Vahyazdata falsely claimed that he was Bardiya, brother of Cyrus' successor Cambyses. The rebel forces were defeated, but Vahyazdata escaped, and later mustered another army for a final showdown with Artavadiya. This took place at Mt Parga. Vahyazdata was again defeated, and this time captured along with his chief followers. All the prisoners were taken to a city called Uvadaicaya where they were crucified.

*DB 40–3.

Ramat Ra(c)hel (map 8) City in southern Palestine on the southern outskirts of Jerusalem, with a history of occupation extending from Iron Age IIC (C8–7) to the early Arab period (C7–8 CE). Excavations on the mound were undertaken over five seasons between 1954 and 1962 by Y. Aharoni on behalf of the Israel Dept of Antiquities, the Israel Exploration Society, the Hebrew University of Jerusalem, and the University of Rome. Further excavations were conducted in 1984 by G. Barclay for the Institute of Archaeology, Tel Aviv University, and have recently been resumed by R. Reich, University of Haifa, and O. Lipschits, Tel Aviv University. Five main occupation levels were identified in the course of Aharoni's excavations. In the earliest (Iron Age IIC) phase, a small citadel was constructed on the mound. It was replaced towards the end of the Iron Age, late C7–early C6 – the most important phase in the site's history – by an outer citadel with massive surrounding wall. The wall partly enclosed a smaller inner citadel, whose excellent construction has prompted its identification as the palace of a Judaean king, perhaps Jehoiakim. One of the most complete Iron Age royal citadels to be unearthed, the palace provides an important example of Israelite-Phoenician architecture. It was surrounded by a casemate wall, which incorporated on its eastern side a monumental double gateway of large ashlar blocks (see glossary). The excavators believe that the gateway may have been open only on festive occasions, while a narrower gateway to the south was used on a daily basis.

There are very few architectural remains of the Persian-Hellenistic period (C6–1) because of later building works on the site. The most important finds from this level are a large number of stamped jar handles with seal impressions, some bearing the name Jerusalem, or simply the word 'city', some the title 'governor', and some the names of governors, while others depict rosettes and animal figures. The next level has been dated to the Herodian period (C1 BCE–C1 CE), mainly on the basis of pottery and coins. The three succeeding levels spanned the late Roman to the early Arab period.

Aharoni (*OEANE* 4: 1261–7).

Ramoth Gilead Iron Age city in northern Transjordan. In *OT* tradition it was assigned to the Levite clan of Gad, and served as a place of refuge for those accused of murder (Joshua 21:38 etc.). Also according to biblical tradition, the Israelite king Ahab was killed there (1 Kings 22), and there too Jehu was anointed king of Israel by the prophet Elisha (2 Kings 9: 1–16). The city is probably to be identified with the site of Tell er-Rumeith (see ***Rumeith, Tell er-***) near Jordan's northern border. It has sometimes been identified with, but is probably to be distinguished from, the city of Gilead referred to by the Assyrian king Tiglath-pileser III and apparently destroyed by him c. 733.

Dearman (*HCBD* 913), Lipiński (2000: 354–5).

Raphia, Tell The southernmost city of Palestine, located on the Via Maris (q.v.) 35 km southwest of Gaza. It is first attested in Late Bronze Age Egyptian texts, where it appears in the record of Seti I's Syro-Palestinian campaigns (early C13). Assyrian records indicate that the later Iron Age city, which was part of the kingdom of Gaza, was called Rapihu. In late C8 the Assyrian king Sargon II defeated there a coalition of Egyptian forces and the army of Gaza's king, Hanunu (**CS* II: 296, 297, 298). Sargon burnt the city, and deported 9,033 of its inhabitants (**CS* II: 293). Reliefs depicting the siege of Raphia appear on the walls of Sargon's palace at Khorsabad. The city was rebuilt after its destruction, and during the Persian period (C6–4) grew into a relatively large and apparently unfortified settlement. A cult-site dating to this period, located 1,000 m from the city, may have been attached to it. Raphia subsequently appears in literary sources of the Hellenistic, Roman, and Byzantine periods.

Negev and Gibson (2001: 432–3).

Rapiqu(m) (*Tell Anbar*) (map 10) Northern Babylonian city and land on the middle Euphrates r., attested in texts ranging from the Ur III period until the reign of the Neo-Assyrian king Sargon II (Middle Bronze, Late Bronze, and Iron Ages). During the Ur III period (c. 2112–2004), Rapiqum had been the seat of a military governor, but thereafter it became an autonomous city-state. In the early decades of C18, control of the city fluctuated between Assyria under Shamshi-Adad I (1796–1775), Babylon under Hammurabi (1792–1750), and Eshnunna under Dadusha and Ibal-pi-El II (?–1780, 1779–1765 respectively), as indicated by information contained in the Mari archives and in Babylonian and Eshnunnite year-names. It was also part of a military coalition defeated by Rim-Sin (1822–1763), the last king of Larsa, in or after his fourteenth regnal year (**RIME* 4: 281). The city must have suffered from the fact that its location in the frontier region between Babylonia and Assyria made it a strategically valuable asset in the power play between the major kingdoms of the age. It fell to assaults by both Hammurabi and Ibal-pi-El. Hammurabi claimed that Shamshi-Adad had delivered it up to him after wresting it from Eshnunnite control (see *LKM* 620 for refs). His possession of it was confirmed in 1770 when Ibal-pi-El withdrew his occupation forces from the region of the Jebel Sinjar and the land of Suhum.

In the Late Bronze Age, the Assyrian king Adad-nirari I (1307–1275) claimed

Rapiqu among his wide-ranging conquests (**RIMA* 1: 131). Although Rapiqu is described at this time as 'of the land Karduniash (i.e. Babylonia)', this expression may be of geographical rather than political import. In the second half of C13, it was among the thirty-eight districts and cities which the Assyrian king Tukulti-Ninurta I (1244–1208) conquered (**RIMA* 1: 273), doubtless because of their commercial and strategic value. But fifteen years after Tukulti-Ninurta's death, the Babylonian king Adad-shuma-usur (1216–1187) liberated his country from Assyria, and Rapiqu presumably became once more part of Babylonian territory. The Elamite king Shilhak-Inshushinak (1155–1125) is known to have campaigned against it.

By the last century of M2, Rapiqu appears to have acquired a substantial Aramaean population. This is indicated by the Assyrian king Tiglath-pileser I's (1114–1076) inclusion of it in the report of his wide-ranging conquests of the Aramaean tribes – 'from the foot of Mt Lebanon . . . as far as Rapiqu of Kar(a)duniash' (**RIMA* 2: 38 and parallel passages). Tiglath-pileser's successor-but-one, Ashur-bel-kala (1073–1056), also refers to the city in his account of his extensive campaigns against the Aramaeans, from Anat in the land of Suhu to Rapiqu in Babylonia (**RIMA* 2: 98). Ashurnasirpal II (883–859) records his conquest of the city, along with the lands of Laqe and Suhu, in his summary account of his widespread conquests, from the Tigris r. westwards to Mt Lebanon and the 'Great Sea' (i.e. the Mediterranean) (**RIMA* 2: 304 etc.). 150 years later Rapiqu appears in a list of thirty-five so-called Aramaean tribes conquered by the Assyrian king Tiglath-pileser III probably in 745, the king's first regnal year (**Tigl. III* 158–9). (Lipiński (2000: 445), following Brinkman (1968: 271), suggests that the tribalization of the city may have been a fabrication of an Assyrian scribe.) Half a century later, the Assyrian king Sennacherib (704–681) included Rapiqu among the allies of Elam which he defeated at Halule (q.v.) (**Sennach.* 43), though there is no explicit indication of any involvement of the city in military activities during the Neo-Assyrian period.

Joannès (*RlA* 11: 243–6).

Raqamatu (Radammatu) see **Gidara**.

Rasappa (Rusapu) City and land located east of the Habur r. and south of the Jebel Sinjar, attested in M1 Assyrian and Babylonian sources. It was annexed to Assyria by Shalmaneser III (859–824) and was later among the lands assigned by Adad-nirari III (810–783) to the governorship of a man called Nergal-erish (Palil-erish) (**RIMA* 3: 209, 211). Around 770/760 Rasappa's governor, Sin-shallimanni, a successor of Nergal-erish, mustered his troops to help repel an incursion into the region by Aramaeans belonging to the Hatallu tribe (q.v.). But he was daunted by the size of the Aramaean force, which numbered 2,000, and hastily withdrew his troops (**RIMB* 2: 292–3, 296). The invaders were subsequently defeated by Ninurta-kudurri-usur, governor of the land of Suhu. In 611, troops of the Babylonian king Nabopolassar plundered Rasappa, bringing its people to the king at Nineveh (**ABC* 94, **PE* 31, no. 10). Neo-Babylonian and early Persian Achaemenid documents from Babylonia refer to herds being pastured in the Rasappa (Rusapu) region. The previous identification of Rasappa with Roman/Byzantine Resafa, located west of the Euphrates r., has to be rejected.

Radner (*RlA* 11: 52–3), Jursa (*RlA* 11: 254).

Ras Ibn Hani (map 2) Cape settlement on the Mediterranean coast of northern Syria, 4.5 km southwest of Ugarit. Its history of occupation extends from the Late Bronze Age, when it was undoubtedly a part of the kingdom of Ugarit, to the Byzantine period. The site has been excavated since 1975 by a joint Syrian and French expedition under the direction of A. Bounni and J. Lagarce.

Ras Ibn Hani must have played a valuable strategic role in the security of the Late Bronze Age kingdom of Ugarit, particularly in the last decades of C13 when threats of seaborne attacks against the kingdom became ever more serious. Jutting 2.5 km into the Mediterranean, the cape city was in an excellent position to control sea traffic in the area, and to provide advance warning of the approach of enemy ships. Its importance at this time is reflected in the construction of two C13 palace complexes, a 'Southern' and a 'Northern' Palace, covering 5,000 and 2,000 sq. m respectively. Along with other residency-type buildings of this period, the palaces would have been inhabited by members of the royal family of Ugarit and/or high-ranking officials installed in the city by the Ugaritic king.

Two groups of tablets were found among the city's Late Bronze Age remains. Most of them were written in the Ugaritic language, but some were in Akkadian, the international language of diplomacy in this period. The first group includes correspondence with the Ugaritic king, the queen mother, and royal officials, as well as administrative documents and a range of ritual, magical, and lexical texts. The texts in the second group are purely administrative; one of them may indicate that the city's anc. name was Biruti. It seems likely that both groups of texts should be assigned at least partly, if not entirely, to the reign of the Ugaritic king Ammistamru II (1260–1230). A clay sealing from this level is inscribed with Ammistamru's name. From other information contained in the inscriptions, it appears that the Northern Palace may have been the residence of Ammistamru's mother. But the many workshops found in this palace indicate that it was more than simply a royal residence.

Destruction of the city along with the entire Ugaritic kingdom in early C12 belongs within the context of the massive upheavals throughout the Near Eastern and eastern Mediterranean worlds which resulted in the collapse and disappearance of many of the centres of Late Bronze Age civilization. But unlike the Ugaritic capital, Ras Ibn Hani was reoccupied during the first two centuries of the Iron Age (C12–10). Though it suffered further destructions in its Iron Age phase, the excavators concluded that settlement continued there without interruption until at least early C5. During the Hellenistic period the site was occupied by a fortified city, which may have been built in C3 by Ptolemy III Euergetes. Subsequently the city came under Seleucid control.

Bounni and Lagarce (*OEANE* 4: 411–13).

Ras Shamra see Ugarit.

Razama (1) Middle Bronze Age northern Mesopotamian city belonging to the land of upper Yamutbal, perhaps on the Wadi Tharthar southeast of Qattara (map 8) and bordering upon the territories of the city of Ekallatum. (The latter was the seat of the Assyrian viceroy Ishme-Dagan and subsequently one of his important strongholds when he became king of Upper Mesopotamia, c. 1781). In early C18 Razama figured frequently in correspondence from the Mari archives, as a base or staging-post for military expeditions conducted by forces from Eshnunna, Ekallatum, Babylon, and

Turukkum, and also as a place for confining prisoners-of-war and storing grain. Ishme-Dagan visited Razama on a number of occasions, and on the death of its ruler, Sharrum-kima-kalima, who had occupied some of Ekallatum's territories, he took possession of his city and its lands (**LAPO* 17: 246, no. 592).

LKM 620–1 (refs), *Mesop.* 228.

Razama (2) (in the land of Yussan) Middle Bronze Age city probably to be located between the Tigris r. and the eastern end of the Habur triangle; an identification with the site of Tell el-Hawa has been proposed. Most of our information about the city comes from letters in the Mari archives dating to the reign of Zimri-Lim (1774–1762). From these we learn that while subject to Zimri-Lim, Razama was placed under siege by Atamrum, ruler of the city of Andarig. Supported by troops from Elam and Eshnunna, Atamrum had taken advantage of the fact that the city had been stripped of its own troops, which had been deployed for service with Zimri-Lim in Yamhad (Syria). Razama's king, Sharraya (Sharriya), appealed to Zimri-Lim for assistance, while at the same time entering into negotiations with Atamrum. But the terms Atamrum offered were unacceptable, and Sharraya continued to withstand the siege (**LAPO* 17: 158–9, no. 548). The messenger who reported this to Zimri-Lim urged him to march to the relief of Razama as quickly as possible, since it was likely that Atamrum would soon abandon the siege and thus deprive Zimri-Lim of the opportunity of winning fame for himself by liberating the city. Opinion is divided on whether Zimri-Lim actually reached the city in time to liberate it, or whether in fact it fell to Atamrum.

Following the end of the Mari archives in 1761, further references to Razama appear in texts discovered in Shubat-Enlil/Shehna (Tell Leilan), dating to the period 1750 to 1728. From these we learn that a king of Razama called Hazip-Teshshub allied himself with Buriya, king of Andarig, against a coalition formed by Mutiya and Ashtamar-Adad, kings of Apum (of which Shubat-Enlil/Shehna was the capital) and Kurda respectively, with a third king, Shepallu (capital unknown). External pressures eventually forced the two blocs to come to terms, as reflected in a treaty concluded between Hazip-Teshub and Mutiya.

LKM 32, no. 99 (for location), 558 (s.v. Šarraya, refs), 620 (refs), *Mesop.* 213–14, 350.

Rehob (Rehov) The name of several cities attested in biblical and Egyptian sources. These include:

Rehob (1) Late Bronze Age fortress-city, subject to Egypt, located in the Jezreel valley of northern Palestine a short distance from the Egyptian garrison centre at Beth Shean. This particular Rehob has been identified, though not conclusively, with the site of Tell Rehob (q.v.). From the inscription on a basalt stele of the pharaoh Seti I (1294–1279) discovered in Beth Shean, we learn that Beth Shean had been attacked by a military alliance from the nearby cities of Hamath and Pella, and that the enemy had confined the ruler of Rehob, who had remained loyal to the pharaoh, within his city (*Faulkner, 1947, **ANET* 253). Seti reports that he dispatched his 'first army of Amun' against the attackers, and thus relieved Beth Shean and presumably also Rehob.

Rehob (2) Iron Age city in the plain of Akko, northern Palestine, probably to be identified with the site of Tel Bira (q.v.). *OT* tradition relates that in the apportionment of former Canaanite territories to the Israelite tribes, Rehob was assigned to the tribe of Asher (Joshua 19:30, Judges 1:31).

Rehob, Bet see Soba.

Rehob, Tell (Arabic *Tell es-Sarem*) (map 8) 10 ha Canaanite settlement-mound, consisting of upper and lower tells, located in northern Palestine at the junction of the Jordan and Jezreel valleys, 5 km south of Beth Shean. It is perhaps to be identified with the Egyptian subject city of Rehob, attested in the reign of the pharaoh Seti I (1294–1279) (see **Rehob (1)**). The site was occupied through the Late Bronze and Iron Ages (with some evidence also of settlement in the Early Bronze Age), then abandoned until the early Islamic period. It was excavated over five seasons, between 1974 and 1980, by F. Vitto on behalf of the Israel Dept of Antiquities. Work on the site was resumed in 1997 by A. Mazar, for the Hebrew University of Jerusalem. The excavations have provided clear indications of a flourishing Canaanite culture during the city's Late Bronze Age and early Iron Age phases, though it appears to have suffered two destructions in this period. Mazar's study of the mound's stratigraphy has demonstrated that there was dense population there from C13 to C9, with continuity of urban life despite a number of destructions and rebuildings.

In C10, the new city built on the site appears to have come under Israelite occupation, and to have enjoyed a prosperous existence, with trading links with Phoenicia and Cyprus, until its destruction c. mid C9. This destruction has been linked to conflicts with the Aramaeans, following the death of the Israelite king Ahab c. 850. A new city built on the upper mound was apparently destroyed during a campaign in the region by the Assyrian king Tiglath-pileser III, c. 732. There may have been some reoccupation under Assyrian overlordship, but by the end of the Assyrian period the site had been abandoned. It was not to be resettled until the Islamic period, although a synagogue dating from C4–7 CE was discovered 1 km to the northwest.

Negev and Gibson (2001: 433–5).

Rhodiapolis (map 15) M1 BCE–M1 CE town in eastern Lycia, southwestern Anatolia, 6.5 km northwest of mod. Kumluca. Its name almost certainly means 'city of Rhodes', implying that it was founded by colonists from the island of Rhodes, though a legendary tradition recorded by the C4 Greek writer Theopompus ascribes its foundation to Rhode, daughter of the legendary Greek seer and city-founder Mopsus. It may have been settled in C7, around the time Rhodians colonized the coastal site of Phaselis. But there is no hard evidence for this. The surviving evidence for an indigenous Lycian presence at Rhodiapolis is limited to two rock-cut tombs inscribed with texts in the Lycian language, datable to C5 or early C4. Both inscriptions refer to the native Lycian goddess Maliya, with whom the Greek goddess Athena was identified. Athena's cult at Rhodiapolis, attested in Greek inscriptions found in the city, was probably imported from Rhodes by the settlers who colonized the site. Other material remains of the city are meagre and date almost entirely to the Roman imperial period. The most impressive of these are a relatively well-preserved theatre and a funerary monument to the city's most famous inhabitant, the C2 CE philanthropist Opramoas, benefactor of many Lycian cities. The texts on his tomb, recording the honours bestowed upon him, constitute the longest known inscription discovered in Lycia.

Bean (1978: 146–8), Keen (1998: 203).

Rhoeteum (map 5) Small M1 town in the Troad not far from Ilium (Troy). In C5 it became a member of the Athenian Confederacy (see glossary). According to Livy (38.39.10), the Romans added Rhoeteum and nearby Gergis to the territory of Ilium after their victory in the battle of Magnesia in 190.

Dörner (*KP* 4: 1424).

Ribanish Iron Age city in the Aramaean state of Suhu, located in the middle Euphrates region. In early C8 it was attacked by 400 warriors from the Aramaean tribe Tu'manu, but saved from destruction when the attackers were themselves attacked, pursued, and defeated by Shamash-resha-usur, ruler of Suhu (**RIMB* 2: 280). Shamash-resha-usur reports that he subsequently planted date-palms in the courtyard of the palace of Ribanish, and set up a throne and footstool there.

Rifaʿat, Tell (map 7) Settlement-mound in north-central Syria, 35 km north of Aleppo, with occupation levels ranging from the Chalcolithic (M5–4) to the Roman imperial period. It was perhaps the city called Arpad (q.v.) in Assyrian and *OT* sources, which became capital of the Iron Age Aramaean kingdom of Bit-Agusi. The site consists of a citadel with a surface area of 142 sq. m, and a lower city, now partially covered by mod. houses. The earliest excavations were conducted in 1924–5 by the Czech scholar B. Hrozný, who was the first to suggest an identification with Arpad. Subsequent though still limited excavations were conducted under the direction of M. V. Seton-Williams for the Institute of Archaeology, University of London, in 1956, 1960, and 1964. These excavations resulted in the identification of five occupation levels, extending from Chalcolithic to Roman times. A further survey of the area in which the settlement lay was carried out between 1977 and 1979 by J. Matthers. Remains from the site include a brick fortification wall whose origins date back to the Late Bronze Age, a large palace (923 m × 30 m) of M1 date with porch and paved courtyard, constructed on the western side of the mound, and a monumental limestone staircase of Graeco-Roman date which led through the fortifications. Stamp seals of the Neo-Assyrian, Neo-Babylonian, and Persian periods have also been unearthed. Other small finds include terracotta figurines of Late Bronze Age and Iron Age date, including many examples of 'Scythian' horsemen.

Seton-Williams (1967), Abou Assaf (*OEANE* 4: 427–8).

Rimah, Tell er- (M2 Karana or Qattara? Neo-Assyrian Zamahu) (map 10) Settlement-mound in northern Mesopotamia, 60 km west of Mosul. First occupied in prehistoric times, its main periods of occupation date from the beginning of M2 through the first half of M1, i.e. through the Middle and Late Bronze and Iron Ages. After an initial exploration by A. H. Layard in 1850, and a survey carried out by S. Lloyd in 1938, the site was excavated by D. Oates between 1964 and 1971. Its location on or near a caravan route from Assyria to central Anatolia no doubt provided the main reason for Tell er-Rimah's existence and apparent prosperity. In the Old Babylonian period, the city was fortified and contained a palace and temple, the latter with a courtyard accessed by a monumental staircase. A ziggurat (see glossary) was located on the western side of the temple. The earliest palace perhaps dates to the reign of the Assyrian king Shamshi-Adad I (1796–1775), while the one which replaced it contained a number of tablets of local rulers contemporary with Hammurabi of Babylon (1792–1750) and Zimri-Lim of Mari (1774–1762), including administrative records, sealings, and c. 200 letters. These documents, together with the Mari archives, attest the existence of four local rulers: Samu-Addu, Hatnu-rapi, Ashkur-Addu, and Aqba-hammu, whose collective reigns extended from the last years of Shamshi-Adad through the reign of Zimri-Lim, and part of the reign of Hammurabi. The fourth of these rulers, Aqba-hammu, became a vassal of Hammurabi, after the latter's destruction of the kingdom of Zimri-Lim. Aqba-hammu's queen, Iltani, figures in a number of the city's written records. For further details of Aqba-hammu and his predecessors, see under **Karana**. It is generally believed that Tell er-Rimah was part of a kingdom whose main cities were Karana and Qattara, and that it is in fact to be identified with one of these cities.

The city continued to be occupied and to prosper during the Late Bronze Age, to judge from the remains of a large administrative building, temples, and private houses constructed over the old palace area. In C14 or early C13 it came under Assyrian control. Written records indicating the city's business activities, especially to do with the production of barley and tin, date primarily to the reigns of the C13 kings Shalmaneser I and his son and successor Tukulti-Ninurta I. At the end of the Middle Assyrian period (late M2), the site was completely abandoned. But it was resettled under the Neo-Assyrian kings in early M1, with a population probably consisting largely of deportees brought from other areas conquered by the Assyrians. In the reign of Adad-nirari III (810–783) the city belonged to the Assyrian province of Rasappa; by this time it was called Zamahu (q.v.). A small temple to the god Adad was built by its governor Nergal-eresh (Palil-erish), who undertook the repopulation of the region on behalf of the Assyrian king.

D. Oates (1982a), Charpin and Durand (1987), Dalley (*NEAEHL* 4: 428–9).

Rimmon (En-Rimmon) Southern Judaean town attested only in *OT* sources. According to Nehemiah 11:29, it was one of the settlements occupied by the Jews on their return from their exile in Babylon. It is to be distinguished from the biblical town of the same name in Zebulun, which was given to the Levites (Joshua 19:13, 1 Chronicles 6:77). An identification has been proposed with the site of Tel Halif.

Weinstein (*HCBD* 936).

Risisuri Late Bronze and Iron Age city near the northern coast of Syria. In the Late Bronze Age, it is mentioned in a letter sent from Tyre to Ugarit, and apparently lay close to the latter. In the Iron Age it belonged to the kingdom of Hamath, as attested in a list of Hamathite cities and districts conquered and annexed by the Assyrian king Tiglath-pileser III (745–727) (**Tigl. III* 102–3, 136–7, 148–9). A location near the mod. coastal city of Latakia seems likely.

Lipiński (2000: 290–1).

Rogem Hiri (*Rujim el-Hiri*) (map 8) Megalithic monument consisting of a central tumulus with four concentric walls encircling it, with a total diameter of c. 140 m, located in the land of Geshur in the central Lower Golan region of northern Palestine. The site was studied over three seasons, from 1988 to 1990, as part of the Land of Geshur Project, Institute of Archaeology, Tel Aviv University, under the direction of Y. Mizrachi. Mizrachi reports that several research programmes were represented in the project: extensive excavations, a geophysical survey, a study of geometry and astronomy, and an aerial and ground survey of the site's environs. While Rogem Hiri's material remains extend from the Chalcolithic Age through the Roman and Byzantine periods to the present day, the data collected from the site appear to indicate that there were two main periods of utilization: M3 (Early Bronze Age) and late M2 (last phases of the Late Bronze Age) (thus Mizrachi and Zohar). But both the chronological history and the monument's purpose or purposes remain problematical. The site's most distinctive feature is a burial chamber, located in the central tumulus. A few gold earrings, bronze arrowheads, and some carnelian beads, found in the chamber itself and in the passageway leading to it, are among the small number of funerary gifts to survive the looting of the tomb. These objects, which can be dated to the second half of M2, raise the possibility that the structure was reused for burial purposes in the Late Bronze Age after initial use for this purpose in M3. The excavators suggest that the central cairn and the burial chamber, in their present form, may indicate Late Bronze Age building additions to an Early Bronze Age complex.

Rogem Hiri is seen as a multi-functional complex, 'with a distinction between primary and secondary functions within the framework of the region's changing cultural context'. In the excavators' view, a large ceremonial centre was erected on the site in M3, with perhaps the central cairn being built near the end of the millennium, and then extensively used and possibly rebuilt in late M2. All this may be reflective of a continuation of religious and cosmological traditions in later periods.

Mizrachi and Zohar (*NEAEHL* 4: 1286–7).

Ru'a M1 tribe perhaps of northern Arabian origin, located in southeastern Babylonia on the banks of the Tigris. First attested as one of the thirty-five so-called Aramaean tribes conquered by the Assyrian king Tiglath-pileser III (745–727) (**Tigl. III* 160–1, line 7), they appear among the enemies against whom several Assyrian kings campaigned in the region – Tiglath-pileser III (**Tigl. III* 122–3), Sargon II (**Sargon II* 195, 343), and Sennacherib (**Sennach.* 25, 43, 49, 57).

Lipiński (2000: 464–6).

Rug(g)ulitu (Rug(g)ulutu) Iron Age city on the middle Euphrates, near its confluence with the Sajur r. It was one of the cities belonging to the Iron Age kingdom Bit-Adini which in 856 (when the kingdom was ruled by Ahuni) were attacked and conquered by the Assyrian king Shalmaneser III during his military operations in the Euphrates region in his third regnal year (**RIMA* 3: 19). The conquered towns (which included Alligu, Nappigu, Rugulitu, Pitru, and Mutkinu) were assigned new Assyrian names. Rugulitu was thenceforth called Qibit-[Ashur?], and a palace was established there as a royal residence. The city is first attested by Shalmaneser's father and predecessor Ashurnasirpal II (883–859), who records his conquest of it on one of the bronze bands originally attached to a gate in the city of Imgur-Enlil (mod. Balawat) (**RIMA* 2: 347). In 611 Rugulitu was besieged – and its inhabitants subsequently massacred – by the Babylonian king Nabopolassar (**ABC* 95, **PE* 31, no. 10), probably on his way to attack Harran, the final stronghold of the last Assyrian king following the fall of Nineveh in 612.

Radner (*RlA* 11: 448–9).

Rumeith, Tell er- Settlement-mound in northern Transjordan with Iron Age fort, and later Hellenistic, Roman, Byzantine, and Arab remains east of the mound. The site was excavated in 1962 and more extensively in 1967 by P. W. Lapp with sponsorship by the American Schools of Oriental Research and the Pittsburgh Theological Seminary. Lapp identified eight archaeological strata, four of which (VIII–V) date to the settlement's Iron Age phases, the most important phases in its history. Lapp suggested that the earliest of these belonged to the time of Solomon (i.e. C10; but see under **Israel**) and was destroyed by the Aramaeans c. 885; the Aramaeans may then have occupied the site until their defeat by the Judaean king Joash at Aphek at the end of C9. The site is probably to be identified with biblical Ramoth Gilead (q.v.), which (*contra* Lapp) should be distinguished from the Gilead apparently destroyed by the Assyrian king Tiglath-pileser III c. 733 (see **Gilead (Mizpah of)**).

Lapp (*NEAEHL* 4: 1291–3).

Rummunina Iron Age city in the middle Euphrates region, belonging to the land of Laqe. During his last recorded campaign in 885, the Assyrian king Tukulti-Ninurta II approached the city and encamped his troops in its fields on his expedition along the Euphrates (**RIMA* 2: 176). Tukulti-Ninurta commented that the city lay on a canal of the Habur r. Lipiński identifies this with the Nahr ad-Dawwarin canal, which follows the left bank of the Habur and Euphrates for almost 130 km and certainly existed in the Neo-Assyrian period. He proposes an identification of Rummunina with mod. Tell Diban (3), which lies on the canal (see map, Lipiński, 2000: 81).

Lipiński (2000: 84–6, 100).

Rupu M1 Aramaean tribe attested in C8 Assyrian texts which, according to Lipiński, indicate locations first in Syria near the middle Euphrates, and later in south-eastern Babylonia. The earliest reference to the tribe dates to the reign of the Assyrian king Adad-nirari III (810–783), when the king's commander-in-chief Shamshi-ilu laid waste a number of tribal lands including those of the Rupu (**RIMA* 3: 232). The tribe later concluded agreements both with the governor of Nippur and with (Nabu-) Mukin-zeri, a sheikh of the Chaldaean Bit-Amukani tribe (**Nippur IV*: 48–9, no. 6), who subsequently became king of Babylon (731–729). Another Aramaean tribe called the Qamu 'went over' to – i.e. apparently amalgamated with – the Rupu during a meeting in Nippur (**Nippur IV*: 177–8, no. 83). Further references to the Rupu occur in texts from the reigns of the Assyrian kings Tiglath-pileser III (e.g. *Tigl. III* 122–3, 130–1) and Sargon II (**Sargon II* 343), spanning the last four decades of C8. At this time the Rupu were clearly located in southern Babylonia near the frontier with Elam.

Lipiński (2000: 439–40), Streck (*RlA* 11: 463–4).

Rusahinili (**Eidurukai**) (***Ayanis***) (map 20) Urartian fortress settlement in eastern Anatolia, located on the east shore of Lake Van, 25 km northwest of the Urartian capital, Tushpa (Van Kale). The citadel rises more than 200 m above the level of the lake and covers an area of at least 6 ha. Its anc. name, Rusahinili Eidurukai ('Rusahinili in front of Mt Eiduru'), distinguishes it from Rusahinili Qilbanikai ('Rusahinili before

Mt Qilbani') at Toprakkale. Dedicatory inscriptions found at the site record that it was constructed by the Urartian king Rusa II; this was in 673–672, according to Erdem and Batmaz (2008: 68), who conclude that it was the last Urartian fortress built by Rusa. Excavations carried out from 1989 onwards by A. A. Çilingiroğlu of Ege University (Izmir) brought to light the remains of porticoes with andesite pillar bases, a well-preserved temple, temple storerooms, several enormous magazines with pithos-jars buried to their shoulders, and a gateway of ashlar masonry. The courtyard of the temple was surrounded by a portico whose roof was supported by wooden beams. Large numbers of bronze artefacts were associated with the temple complex, including swords and shields which were apparently hung on the walls and pylons of buildings, helmets, quivers, large numbers of bronze and iron arrowheads, and a large cauldron. Many objects, including ceremonial bronze nails, cylinders, and a ceremonial lance known in Urartian as a *šuri*, were inscribed with cuneiform dedications by Rusa to the god Haldi. Other items among the small finds included clay bullae, inscribed clay tablets, gold ornaments, and fragments of gold leaf used for decorating artefacts of wood and bronze. The façade of the temple was decorated with the longest C7 Urartian inscription yet discovered. It records the dedication of the building, and lists Rusa's building projects and conquests. In the interior, walls of the cella were decorated with stone inlays of animals and genii, and an elaborately decorated alabaster platform at the rear of the room was the cultic focal point.

In the land around the citadel, Rusa resettled deportees from his conquered territories, if information provided by the inscription on the temple façade can be so interpreted. The remains of buildings outside the citadel's walls on all sides except the west are indicative of a relatively substantial extra-mural settlement. The citadel was largely surrounded by public buildings constructed on lower ground. While they indicate that Rusahinili exercised important administrative functions during its brief existence, Ayanis was but one of at least four fortress-settlements and administrative centres which Rusa built in the course of his reign. The city's primary residential quarter lay to the east of the citadel, extending over 12 ha on a ridge known as Güney Tepe. Here were located both elegant and poorly constructed houses, built at different levels along the slope's contours. The city had no outer wall, i.e. there were no fortifications to protect either the public building complexes or the residential areas outside the citadel.

McConchie (2004: 92, 117–18), Stone and Zimansky (2004b), Çilingiroğlu (2006), Erdem and Batmaz (2008).

Rusahinili (Qilbanikai) (*Toprakkale* 'earth castle') (map 20) Large C8–7 Urartian fortress-city in eastern Anatolia located on a spur extending over 2.6 ha, on the outskirts of mod. Van, and 6 km east of the Urartian capital Tushpa (Van Kale). After the construction of another Rusahinili (Eidurukai) at Ayanis, Toprakkale was sometimes referred to as Rusahinili Qilbanikai ('Rusahinili before Mt Qilbani'). Recent epigraphic discoveries near Keğiğ Göl, an artificial lake which supplied water to the area, have made it clear that the founder of the site was the Urartian king Rusa, son of Erimena, whose chronological placement is unclear. Certainly the city came into high prominence in Rusa II's reign, to which most of the inscribed artefacts found at the site date. Like most Urartian sites, Toprakkale was violently destroyed under unknown circumstances, probably in late C7.

Toprakkale has played an important if not entirely satisfactory role in the archaeological rediscovery of Urartu. It was the first Urartian site ever excavated and a

Figure 102 Van citadel, with Toprakkale in the background.

succession of archaeologists worked there, including H. Rassam (1880), C. F. Lehmann-Haupt and W. Belck (1898–9), I. A. Orbelli (1911–12), N. Y. Marr (1916), K. Lake (1938), and A. Erzen (1959–61), with new excavations undertaken in 1976 by A. Erzen. Little of the work of the early excavators was published and major structures, such as the temple and storerooms on the site, are known only from crude sketches. The finds of the Rassam excavations were brought to light only in the 1950s when they were published by R. D. Barnett of the British Museum. Lehmann-Haupt's excavations did produce a few cuneiform tablets, bullae with the king's seal impressions, and bronzes. Only a few stones survive of what was probably the city's most important building, the temple of the chief Urartian deity Haldi, in whose precinct a number of bronze shields and spears were unearthed.

Barnett (1950; 1954; 1972), Wartke (1990), Belli (2001c), McConchie (2004:126–8).

Rusai-URU.TUR (*Bastam*) (map 20) Large Iron Age fortress-city in the kingdom of Urartu, located in western Azerbaijan in the Aq Chay valley, 59 km southeast of Maku. It was excavated by W. Kleiss for the German Archaeological Institute, Tehran, from 1968 to 1978. Built by the Urartian king Rusa II (678–654), its anc. name, provided by inscriptions found on the site and in the nearby village, means 'Rusa's small city', though the city is in fact one of the largest known Urartian foundations. The massive citadel, which extends over 320,000 sq. m, is defended by fortifications built on several levels up a steep rock spur. On a platform cut from the rock near the citadel's summit, a temple presumably once stood, dedicated to the Urartian god Haldi. But all trace of the structure on the platform has now disappeared. Elsewhere on

Figure 103 Bastam.

the citadel there were extensive storage facilities containing large pithoi, and rooms packed with animal bones and bullae sealed with the king's seal. Although the citadel was thoroughly looted before it was destroyed by fire, several tablets and an important corpus of seal impressions have been found. A large lower town extended northward from the foot of the citadel and included a number of public buildings, stables, and private houses. A large rectangular enclosure to the citadel's east may have been a military camp.

Kleiss (1979; 1988), Zimansky (1998: 253–4).

S

Saar 2.5 ha settlement in the northwest of the main island of Bahrain, within the land of Dilmun attested in Bronze and Iron Age Mesopotamian texts. After preliminary excavations were undertaken by a joint Bahraini–Jordanian team in the 1980s, work was resumed on the site in 1990 by the London-Bahrain Archaeological Expedition under the direction of H. Crawford, R. Killick, and J. Moon. Their work brought to light what they see as a largely self-sufficient community, dependent on the sea and date-gardens for its subsistence. Large numbers of seal impressions (more than eighty) discovered in the houses of Saar, and originally used as stamps on bales and jars, appear to indicate a flourishing local economy, with much of the commerce conducted within Dilmun itself. At its highest point, Saar was dominated by a temple separated from the rest of the settlement by alleys and small streets. Town planning is evident from the layout of the streets which divide the settlement into blocks of up to five houses, built on a largely standardized plan. The settlement's regularity has suggested to the excavators that it may have been a workmen's village or a military barracks.

Crawford (1993; 1997).

Saba (biblical Sheba) (map 9) One of the six kingdoms of pre-Islamic southern Arabia, located in mod. Yemen. The other five kingdoms were Qataban, Hadhramaut, Ausin, Himyar, and Maʿin. Saba has the distinction of being the first of these kingdoms to be established, and the last to be extinguished. It probably came into existence as a territorial and cultural entity some time between C16 and C13, when it was occupied by immigrants thought to be of Levantine origin. By C10 it had been organized into a kingdom, which remained under monarchical rule until the Muslims brought it to an end in C7 CE. The city of Marib was its capital.

Under the name Sheba, Saba is frequently attested in *OT* sources, where it is best known because of the visit which its queen paid to the Israelite king Solomon in Jerusalem (1 Kings 10:1–13); she was accompanied by a great caravan, with camels carrying spices, large quantities of gold, and precious stones. Though the historicity of the biblical tradition is open to question, as indeed is the very existence of a queen of Sheba, the tradition does convey a reliable picture of the kingdom's wealth. Saba was located in a fertile area of southwestern Arabia, and agriculture provided the basis of its economy. But it was actively involved, like the other southern Arabian kingdoms, in lucrative merchant enterprises, trading principally in gold, spices, and incenses. Pliny the Elder (6.161) refers to the Sabaeans as the wealthiest of peoples, because of the fertility of their incense-bearing forests, their gold mines, their irrigated agricultural land, and their production of honey and wax. According to *OT* sources the Sabaeans also traded in slaves and engaged in robbery (Joel 3:8, Job 1:15).

In historical sources, Saba is first attested in C8, both in its own inscriptions (its language belonged to a Northwest Semitic language sub-group, written in an alphabetic script), discovered in Yemen, as well as in texts of the Assyrian kings Tiglath-pileser

III, Sargon II, and Sennacherib (C8–early C7). It was the dominant kingdom in southern Arabia for many centuries until its decline in C4, when it was eclipsed by Qataban, Hadhramaut, and Maʿin. It regained its dominance with the rise of Himyar in late C2, and subsequently formed with Himyar the kingdom of Saba and Dhu-Raydan. Decline once more set in with the reign of Constantine the Great in C4 CE, though the kingdom was to last another three centuries before its disappearance in C7 CE.

Van Beek (1974; *OEANE* 5: 18–19).

Sabi Abyad, Tell Settlement covering several mounds in the Balih r. valley of northern Syria, with evidence of occupation dating back to the Neolithic period. By 7000 a farming community had been established there, and by late M7 the site was occupied by a village consisting of large, closely spaced rectangular buildings surrounded by many small tholoi (see glossary). The settlement was excavated by P. M. M. G. Akkermans. Excavations uncovered a great many clay sealings of late M7 from a burnt storage building. On top of the Neolithic tell, a small Middle Assyrian (c. 1225–1120) settlement of c. 1 ha in extent was excavated. Called a *dunnu* ('fort') in Akkadian, the site consisted of a walled stronghold measuring 60 m square, with a massive square tower (c. 20 m × 23 m) at its centre. Adjacent to this was a 'palace', with central reception hall flanked by small private chambers and bathrooms. Outside the tower and palace were a number of administrative units, houses, workshops, and storage buildings.

Destruction of the settlement by fire preserved within it a number of artefacts, including weapons, jewellery, seals and sealings, and more than 300 cuneiform clay tablets. These tablets indicate that in the last century of the Late Bronze Age, Sabi Abyad was an economic and military centre of the Assyrian imperial administration on the empire's edge. It was probably built as a fortress during the reign of the Assyrian king Tukulti-Ninurta I (1244–1208). The written records identify it as the seat of a succession of local governors, of whom the last was a man called Ili-pada. Early in C12 the settlement was destroyed by fire, perhaps the result of Aramaean expansion in the region. Its subsequent reoccupation is indicated by numerous burials discovered near the ruins of the tower and palace, most notably the remains of two adults and a sheep found in a jar along with gold, bronze, and iron jewellery.

Akkermans and Rossmeisl (1990), Akkermans and Wiggermann (1999), Akkermans (*RlA* 11: 476–8).

Sabiritu see Sapiratu.

Sabum Settlement in southwestern Iran, attested in C21 texts of the Ur III administration. It was among the settlements located in the eastern peripheral territories of the Ur III empire (there were c. ninety such settlements), and was one of the largest and most important of them since a local governor (*ensi*) was installed there. (Susa and Urua had similar status.) As was the case with the other settlements, a provincial tax was imposed upon its military personnel. Its southwesterly location, in the region of Susiana, is indicated by the fact that one of its governors, Aburanum, passed through Lagash on his way to Nippur, which lay north of Lagash.

D. T. Potts (1999: 132, 135, 137).

Safut, Tell (map 8) Settlement-mound located in the central plateau of Transjordan. Works on the mod. highway between Amman and Jerash encroached partly on the mound, prompting a series of excavations begun in 1982 under the direction of D. Wimmer and jointly sponsored by Seton Hall University, New Jersey, USA, and the Dept of Antiquities of the Hashemite Kingdom of Jordan. Bulldozing for the new road on the edge of the mound apparently uncovered part of a Middle Bronze Age glacis (see glossary). But more significant remains date to the town's Late Bronze Age phase, and particularly to its late Iron Age phase. In the first half of M1, Tell Safut saw a considerable expansion of its population. At this time it belonged to the kingdom of Ammon. Its importance in the kingdom may have been due in part to its location on the main route leading to Rabbath-Ammon, capital of Ammon. It lay just 12 km to the north of the capital, so that in a strategic sense Tell Safut served as the capital's 'gatekeeper' (thus Wimmer). The well-watered location in which it lay enabled it to function as an agricultural as well as an administrative centre of the Ammonite kingdom. Small finds from the mound indicate that it continued to flourish under Assyrian and subsequently Babylonian sovereignty, with cultural continuity into the Persian period (C6–4). But it apparently went into sharp decline in the Hellenistic period (C4–1), to judge from the meagre remains of this period. None the less, it seems to have retained a modest population through Hellenistic and Roman times, and as late as the Byzantine period there was a small settlement there.

Wimmer (*OEANE* 4: 448–50).

Sagalassus M1 BCE–M1 CE city in Pisidia, north of Antalya (*BAGRW* 65 E2). Prior to its probable capture by Alexander the Great in 334, almost nothing is known of its history or material civilization. Its relatively significant remains date to the Hellenistic and Roman periods, when it was a well-planned city, laid out on a regular grid plan.

Bonacasa (*PECS* 781–2).

Sagartians Attested by Herodotus (1.125, 7.85) as a nomadic tribe of ethnic Persian origin. Herodotus (3.93) reports that the Sagartians were incorporated into the Persian empire's fourteenth province in Darius I's administrative reorganization of the empire (but see glossary under **satrapy**), and that they provided 8,000 horsemen for Xerxes' invasion of the Greek mainland in 481 (7.85). They allegedly used ropes with nooses as their principal weapon in battle, snaring and pulling the enemy towards them before dispatching them with their daggers.

Saggaratum (Iron Age **Sangaritu**) (map 10) River port in the middle Euphrates region, not far from the confluence of the Euphrates with the Habur r., attested in the Middle Bronze Age Mari archives (C18) as the third most important city of the kingdom of Mari, after Mari itself and Terqa. The archives contain frequent references to the city, particularly in the reign of the Mariote king Zimri-Lim (1774–1762), who records a victory he won there over the Yaminites. At that time, Saggaratum was governed by a certain Yaqqim-Addu. Following the Babylonian king Hammurabi's conquest of Mari in 1762, Saggaratum came under Babylonian control. The building programme which Hammurabi's son and successor Samsu-iluna (1749–1712) undertook in the city no doubt reflects the importance still attached to it at that time. The palace first built in the Mari period was no doubt restored and rebuilt as part of this programme. Saggaratum later appears, in the form Sangaritu, in the records of the

Assyrian king Ashur-bel-kala (1073–1056), who mentions it in the course of his campaign against the Aramaeans around the Lower Habur r. (**RIMA* 2: 102).

Lipiński (2000: 91–2), *LKM* 565 (s.v. Yaqqim-Addu 1, refs), 621 (refs).

Sagillu Iron Age city belonging to the Neo-Hittite kingdom of Pat(t)in (Assyrian Unqi) in northen Syria. It is mentioned in the Annals of the Assyrian king Tiglath-pileser III (745–727) as one of the cities where he resettled deportees from other parts of his kingdom (**ARAB* II: 276).

CHLI I: 362.

Sahab (map 8) Site in Transjordan 12 km southeast of Amman. Evidence of human activity dates back to the Neolithic/Chalcolithic periods, and thenceforth, after a 'transitional period' when no permanent occupation appears to have occurred, there was continuous settlement through the Bronze and Iron Ages. The site was excavated by M. Ibrahim between 1972 and 1980. Its Early and Middle Bronze Age levels are represented in the former case by a number of sherds without architectural context, and in the latter case by parts of a substantial fortification system. Ibrahim comments that Sahab was probably the closest of the Middle Bronze II fortresses to the desert area, and its location must have been significant in defending the high land against attacks from the desert. The Late Bronze Age city had an estimated lifespan of 200 or more years, from C15 to late C13. The C15 date is based on a seal impression found on a jar handle. Its depictions of seated sphinx with *ankh* (the Egyptian hieroglyphic symbol denoting 'life') in front, uraeus (snake), and god-beard are considered typical of the period of the pharaoh Tuthmosis III (1479–1425). The assemblage of pottery types includes, in addition to local products, Mycenaean or Mycenaean-imitation ware.

The settlement appears to have expanded during the early Iron Age (late M2), from which a number of examples of domestic architecture have survived. The general layout of the houses was one of rectangular rooms plastered in most cases with stones. In some instances the houses were constructed partly of materials reused from the Late Bronze Age fortifications. The walled Iron Age II settlement was apparently smaller than its predecessor, but better planned. Its main architectural feature was a large complex of rectangular rooms, the most prominent of which was a spacious, rectangular pillared chamber in the centre of the complex.

Sahab appears to have been abandoned after C6, and was not reoccupied until mediaeval times.

Ibrahim (*OEANE* 4: 450–2).

Sa'idiyeh, Tell es- (map 8) Large double settlement-mound, consisting of upper and lower tells, located in the central Jordan valley on the south bank of Wadi Kafranjeh. Tentatively identified with the biblical city of Zarethan, the site has a history of occupation extending from the Chalcolithic period (M4) to the early Islamic period (C7 CE). The first major excavations there were conducted over four seasons, between 1964 and 1967, by J. B. Pritchard for the University Museum of the University of Pennsylvania. New excavations were begun in 1985 by J. N. Tubb for the British Museum.

The site was first extensively occupied during the Early Bronze II period, with settlement predominantly on the lower tell, but probably also at the base of the upper tell. A large well-planned industrial/commercial complex of mudbrick on stone foundations features among the substantial architectural remains on the lower tell in this period. Settlement there was abandoned at the end of the Early Bronze Age. Subsequently, the site was used for an extensive cemetery. Over 500 graves and their contents have been excavated. They date predominantly to the end of the Late Bronze Age (late C13–early C12), with about 5 per cent assigned to the Late Iron Age–Persian periods. The wide variety of tomb types, burial methods and customs, and grave goods, suggest that Tell es-Saʿidiyeh's population was made up of elements from several different ethnic backgrounds. However, strong Egyptian influence is evident in the Late Bronze Age graves, both in the linen wrappings used to bind the deceased, and in the range of grave goods of Egyptian craftsmanship (e.g. seals, amulets, jewellery, and ivory artefacts) or Egyptian style.

Further indications that the settlement was under Egyptian control during the Late Bronze Age are provided by the large building constructed near the centre of the upper tell in this period – which was apparently the first period of occupation on this tell. The building's plan and method of construction make it very likely that it was the residence of an Egyptian governor during Egypt's twentieth dynasty. A second building complex unearthed on the western side of the tell and assumed to have been used for administrative purposes has been dubbed the 'Western Palace'. Also dating to this period is a finely constructed water system staircase, cut from the rock on the tell's northern slope. Tubb concludes that both the architecture of this level (designated as Stratum XII) and the contemporary cemetery indicate an Egyptian presence at Tell es-Saʿidiyeh in C12, with the city having the role of a major taxation centre or entrepôt, serving the needs of the Egyptian empire in its final phase under the twentieth dynasty pharaohs. Following the withdrawal of Egyptian rule in mid C12, the

Figure 104 Tell es-Saʿidiyeh, residency.

Figure 105 Tell es-Saʿidiyeh, staircase.

city of Stratum XII was maintained under local control for a further fifty or so years until it was destroyed by fire in late C12 or early C11. The lower tell cemetery fell out of use at this time also.

There appears to have been very limited occupation of the site during the succeeding four phases, covering the period from C11 to C9 (Strata XI–VIII). However, the next phase (Stratum VII) saw a substantially increased population and a marked expansion of the settlement, reflected in densely packed houses, workshops, industrial installations, and a well-planned intersecting grid of streets and alleyways. The settlement was once more fortified, for the first time since Stratum XII. Tubb suggests that these developments may have been connected with a renewed occupation of Transjordan at this time by the Israelite king Jeroboam II. But by the end of the first decade of C8, decline is once more evident. Though Stratum VII shows no indications of a violent end, its Stratum VI successor was much more limited in size. Whatever the reason for this, the city's fortunes revived in Stratum V, whose origins date to mid C8 when settlement once again expanded, a new city wall was built, and workshops and industrial installations once more appeared. In this level, as in VII, textile manufacture seems to have been the city's main industry.

Stratum V's destruction by fire c. 720 has been plausibly attributed to Assyria's intervention in this region in the early years of the Assyrian king Sargon II. In the succeeding Stratum IV, the site appears to have served essentially as a storage facility. A building which may have been a fortress was constructed on the summit of the tell during the Persian period (Stratum III; C6–4). As yet, no other occupation dating to this period has been identified. In the Hellenistic period (Stratum II) the Persian-period structure was replaced by a larger fortress. By the Roman period (Stratum I) the site seems to have been little more than a watchtower post.

Tubb (*NEAEHL* 4: 1297–1300; *OEANE* 4: 452–5; 1998: 40–8).

Saka (Greek Sacae) (map 16) The Iranian name for tribal groups occupying regions extending from Thrace across the steppes north of the Black Sea into Central Asia. In Classical sources, they are closely identified with the Scythians (q.v.). According to Herodotus (7.64), Sacae was the name used by the Persians for all Scythians. Persian inscriptions refer to various groups of Saka. These include the Saka *para Sugdam*, who have been tentatively located in Ferghana or east of the Pamir; the Saka *haumavarga*,who probably lived in the region of the Jaxartes r. (mod. Syr Darya); the Saka *tigrachauda* ('the pointed-hat Saka') located east of the Caspian Sea, in the region of Turkmenistan or Uzbekistan; and the Saka *paradraya* ('the Saka beyond the sea'), who probably lived in Thrace. An identification has been suggested between the Saka *tigrachauda* and the Orthocorybantes attested in Herodotus 3.92, and between the Saka *paradraya* and the Thracian Getae who, according to Herodotus (4.118), were conquered by the Persian king Darius I.

The Saka *para Sugdam* almost certainly lay beyond the eastern frontiers of the Persian empire. The Saka *haumavarga* are perhaps to be equated with the Scythians from Amyrgium who, Herodotus reports (7.64), provided troops alongside a contingent from Bactria for Xerxes' expedition against Greece in 481. They were under the command of Xerxes' brother Hystaspes. To judge from the C4 Greek historian Ctesias (*FGrH* 688 F 9.7–8 = **PE* 101, no. 35), this Saka group had first become Persian subjects in the reign of Cyrus II, and had provided Cyrus with 20,000 cavalry in his final ill-fated eastern campaign (530). The Saka *tigrachauda* were the object of a military campaign by Darius I in 520/519, following his suppression of the uprisings against him at the beginning of his reign. After 'crossing the sea', Darius inflicted a decisive defeat on the Saka enemy, capturing and executing their chief, and appointing another leader in his place (**DB* 74). Representatives from Saka appear as Delegation XI on the reliefs from the Apadana (Audience Hall) at Persepolis, bearing tribute to Darius in the form of bracelets, three-piece garments (trousers, tunic, and coat), and a stallion.

CAH IV: 921 (index refs).

Sakçagözü (map 7) M1 fortified settlement-mound, 70 m × 50 m, located on the western slopes of Kurd Dağ in southern Anatolia, 21 km northeast of Zincirli. Excavations were conducted there by J. Garstang in 1908 and 1911, and subsequently by M. V. Seton-Willams and J. Waecher in 1949. The settlement is surrounded by a wall, with access through a single gateway decorated with lion-hunt reliefs. Other reliefs found within a building of the *bit hilani* type (see glossary) include lions flanking the entrance, and a pair of human-headed sphinxes. A Neo-Hittite palace has been unearthed on the site.

Sakçagözü has been provisionally identified with the city of Lutibu (q.v.), which belonged to the Aramaean kingdom of Sam'al. A portrait sculpture found on the site is believed, on stylistic grounds, to be that of Mutallu, ruler of the Neo-Hittite kingdom of Kummuh during the reign of the Assyrian king Sargon II (721–705). Lipiński seeks to explain Mutallu's presence in Sakçagözü by suggesting that Sargon annexed the city to Kummuh at the same time as he assigned the city of Melid (Malatya) to Mutallu's control (712).

Du Plat Taylor *et al.* (1950), Hawkins (1982: 423), Lipiński (2000: 237–8, with refs in nn. 35–8), Burney (2004: 236).

Salamis (map 14) City on the east coast of Cyprus, 6.5 km north of mod. Famagusta, covering an area of c. 150 ha near the mouth of the Pediaeus r. Its history of occupation extends from its foundation in C11 to at least C8 CE and possibly as late as C12 CE. There have been numerous formal investigations of various parts of the site since 1880, beginning with the excavations of M. Ohnefalsch-Richter for the British Museum between 1880 and 1882. Regular, large-scale excavations were conducted between 1952 and 1974 by a number of teams under the auspices of the Cypriot Dept of Antiquities. According to Greek tradition the city was founded by Teucer, son of Telamon, who was king of the Greek island of Salamis in the Saronic Gulf and was among the Greek heroes who fought in the Trojan War. He founded Cypriot Salamis after he was banished from his homeland. The 'new Salamis' is considered to have been the successor of Bronze Age Enkomi, whose ruins lie 2 km inland to the southwest, when Enkomi was abandoned, probably because of the silting up of its harbour.

During the first half of M1, Salamis became the most important city and kingdom on Cyprus. Indeed, its C6 king Euelthon (560–525) claimed to exercise sway over the entire island. He was the first Cypriot king to issue coins. The so-called 'royal tombs', uncovered in the western necropolis and spanning the period from c. 800 to 500, provide some indication of the wealth of the city's elite, as well as reflecting the city's close ties with both the Greek and the Levantine worlds. But little is known of Salamis' history before the first years of C5. Its ruler at this time, Gorgus, grandson of Euelthon, supported the Persian king Darius I, and refused to join the anti-Persian Ionian rebellion which broke out in 499. His support for Persia led to his throne being seized by his younger brother Onesilus, who united all the other cities and kingdoms under his leadership (except the city of Amathus) for resistance against the Persians. This resistance ended in Onesilus' defeat and death in a battle with the Persians fought outside his city in 498. (For details of these events and their aftermath, see Herodotus 5.104, 108–15; see also **Amathus**.) The Cypriot cities again came under Persian control, though individual Cypriot rulers appear to have enjoyed a relatively high degree of autonomy.

The best known of all Salamis' kings, at least in the Greek world, was Evagoras I (435–374/373), who became ruler of the city in 411. Evagoras' cultural interests were emphatically Greek. He warmly welcomed Greek philosophers, artists, and musicians to his court, and used his links with Athens to promote Greek culture throughout Cyprus. He also sought to extend his political sway over the island, and won control over many of its cities by a combination of force and diplomacy. But several of Cyprus' cities, notably Amathus, Soli, and Citium, held out against him, and appealed to the Persian king Artaxerxes II for assistance (c. 391). To this point, Evagoras had maintained good relations with Persia, and had actually supported the revival of Persian sea power in the region. But Artaxerxes now established an alliance with his enemies, and prepared for war. The ensuing conflict lasted ten years. Initially Evagoras had some successes, including the capture of the Phoenician city of Tyre on the Levantine coast. But Persia had far superior resources at its disposal, and inevitably gained the upper hand. In 381 Evagoras was forced to appeal to Artaxerxes for peace, which he was granted on reasonable terms. Thereupon he continued to occupy his kingdom's throne, as a subject of Persia, until his assassination in 374/373. (The Greek sources which provide information about his career, especially his conflict with Persia, are collected in **PE* 382–90, nos 48–56.) Evagoras was succeeded by his son Nicocles, who was assassinated c. 360 and succeeded by (his son or brother) Evagoras II. After being deposed from his throne and replaced by a man called Pnytagoras, Evagoras became one of the two leaders (the other was the Athenian Phocis) appointed by the Carian dynast Idrieus to lead an assault against the cities of Cyprus which had rebelled against Persian rule (Diodorus 16.42). Idrieus was acting as the agent of the Persian king Artaxerxes III. The assault began with a siege of Salamis by land and sea. Evagoras had hoped that his support of Persia would regain him his throne. In fact, Pnytagoras surrendered willingly to the Persians, and by so doing ensured that he remained king of Salamis (Diodorus 16.46).

In the Hellenistic period, following the overthrow of the Persian empire by Alexander the Great, Salamis remained a prosperous city, though in C2 it was replaced by Paphos as the island's leading city. In the early Byzantine period it became the seat of a bishopric.

With the exception of the abovementioned 'royal tombs', most of the anc. city's significant remains date to the Hellenistic, Roman, and Byzantine periods. These include a temple of Olympian Zeus, a theatre, a set of baths, a gymnasium, and an agora. But much of the city has yet to be excavated.

Karageorghis (1969), Nicolaou (*PECS* 794–6), Iacovou (2002).

Salatiwara Middle Bronze Age city in south-central Anatolia on a road connecting the kingdoms of Wahsusana and Burushattum. Anitta, king of Nesa, conducted two campaigns against it (**Chav.* 218). On the first of these he defeated troops sent out from the city to confront him, and deported them to Nesa as prisoners-of-war. On the second, he stormed the city and put it to the torch.

Salıhadası M1 island settlement in Caria, southwestern Anatolia, located midway between Myndus and Bargylia. Its remains include portions of fortification and house walls, and a number of tiles and sherds which appear to date to C4. These remains have suggested that Salıhadası is to be identified with anc. Caryanda. The latter is attested by several anc. writers, most notably Strabo (14.2.20) who speaks of both an island and a harbour on the mainland of this name (*BAGRW* 61 E3, F3). The inhabitants of the island-settlement appear to have moved to the mainland in early C3, perhaps resettling on the shore of Lake Göl, where they became citizens of the city of Myndus.

Bean and Cook (1955: 155–60), Bean (*PECS* 798).

Sallahsuwa Middle and Late Bronze Age city in south-central Anatolia. In the Middle Bronze Age Assyrian Colony period (C20–18), it lay on or near a caravan route linking Assyria with central Anatolia via northern Syria. Subject to Hatti from early in the Hittite Old Kingdom, Sallahsuwa was one of the rebel cities destroyed by Hattusili I (1650–1620) during his campaigns of conquest south of the Hittite homeland (**Chav.* 220).

Sallapa Late Bronze Age city in central-western Anatolia on a route between Hatti and the Arzawa Lands. Variously located by scholars to the northeast, east, southeast, or southwest of the Salt Lake, Sallapa was among the cities and countries which rose up against Hatti in C16 prior to the reign of the Hittite king Telipinu (1525–1500) (**Chav.* 231). In the first half of C14, it was attacked and destroyed by the forces of Tudhaliya III, probably to prevent its use as a military base by the enemy from Arzawa (**DS* 60). When it was rebuilt, it became (or became once more) Hittite subject territory. In the third year of his reign, the Hittite king Mursili II (1321–1295) joined forces at Sallapa with his brother, Sharri-Kushuh (Piyassili), viceroy of Carchemish, for an expedition against the Arzawa Lands (**AM* 48–9). On a later occasion he demanded that his recalcitrant vassal Mashuiluwa, king of Mira, come to Sallapa for a meeting with him (**HDT* 75). Mashuiluwa refused. Some decades after this, Mursili's son Hattusili III (1267–1237) similarly demanded a meeting at Sallapa with a western Anatolian insurrectionist called Piyamaradu (*Bryce, 2005: 291). Once again, the Hittite demand was refused. For the contexts and consequences of these refusals, see Bryce (2005: 212–14, 291).

Sallatu (Babylonian **Shallatu**) Iron Age city in northern Babylonia, located on the east bank of the Euphrates within a day's march of the city of Sippar. The Assyrian king Tukulti-Ninurta II encamped his forces there during his last recorded campaign (885), which took him into northern Babylonia (**RIMA* 2: 174).

Sallawassi Late Bronze Age city in western Anatolia. It appears in the context of the abortive (and unauthorized) attack which the Hittites' western subject-ruler Madduwatta launched on the Arzawan leader Kupanta-Kurunta during the reign of the Hittite king Arnuwanda I (early C14) (Bryce, 2005: 131–2). Sallawassi provided a place of refuge for Madduwatta's family and possessions when Kupanta-Kurunta counter-attacked and invaded Madduwatta's own country, Zippasna (**HDT* 156). In the course of his invasion, Kupanta-Kurunta had seized and occupied Sallawassi. When Hittite troops subsequently drove the Arzawans back to their own land, they reinstated Madduwatta as ruler of Zippasna, and delivered to him both his own family and possessions, and those of Kupanta-Kurunta. The latter were also found in Sallawassi.

Sallune M1 city on the coast of Cilicia Tracheia/Aspera (Rough Cilicia) in southern Anatolia. The Neo-Babylonian king Neriglissar proceeded there after his campaign in Pirindu (see **Hilakku**) in 557/556. A Babylonian chronicle reports that before returning home after his campaign, Neriglissar started fires from the pass of Sallune to the border of Lydia (**ABC* 103–4). Sallune is probably to be identified with Selinus, a city on the Cilician coast attested in Classical sources from the Hellenistic and Roman periods (*BAGRW* 66 A4).

Bean (*PECS* 823), *RGTC* 8: 265.

Salua Late Bronze and Iron Age country probably located in the region to the southeast of Lake Van. It is first attested in the record of the Assyrian king Shalmaneser I's accession year (1275) as one of eight lands belonging to the country of Uruatri (Urartu) which Shalmaneser conquered, allegedly destroying fifty-one of their cities and carrying off their population and property (**RIMA* 1: 183). The other lands were Himme, Uatkun, Bargun (or Mashgun), Halila, Luha, Nilipahru, and Zingun. Tiglath-pileser I (1114–1076) claims to have conquered 'the land of Lullumu, the lands Salua, Qummenu, Katmuhu and Alzu' (*RIMA* 2: 42). Subsequently, the Assyrian king Adad-nirari II (911–891) refers to Salua when he claims conquest of 'the extensive land of Qumanu as far as the lands of Mehru, Salua, and Uratru (Urartu)' (**RIMA* 2: 148).

Sam'al (Yu'addi) (map 7) Small Aramaean city-state in southern Anatolia, located on the eastern slope of the Amanus range, west of mod. Gaziantep. Lipiński defines its territory as lying between the crest of the Amanus range to the west and the Kurd Dağ to the east, covering an area of c. 35 × 50 km. Sam'al is sometimes called Bit-Gabbari – 'the House of Gabbar' – by the Assyrian king Shalmaneser III (858–824) (**RIMA* 3: 18, 23). Its founder was very likely a certain Gabbar, probably a North Arabian or Aramaean chieftain, whose clan seized power in a predominantly Neo-Hittite area (thus Lipiński, 2000: 239) in the last decades of C10. Its capital was located on the site of mod. Zincirli, and its royal necropolis probably at mod. Gerçin, 7 km northeast of Zincirli.

Sam'al was one of a number of small city-states in southern Anatolia and Syria whose emergence reflects the revival of urbanism in these regions in the early Iron Age. The names of a number of Sam'al's kings are preserved in their inscriptions. The best known of these is a Phoenician inscription, dated c. 830–820, on a stele set up by a king called Kilamuwa (c. 840–815). (*Contra* the vocalization Kulamuwa, see Lipiński, 2000: 234, n. 11.) Kilamuwa succeeded his brother Sha'il on the Sam'alite throne, and was thus the second successor of his father Hayya(nu) (see below). His succession took place during the reign of Shalmaneser III (**CS* II: 147–8). From the Kilamuwa and later inscriptions, a list of eleven Sama'alite kings can be constructed (see Lipiński, 2000: 247). Some of the names on this list are of Semitic origin; others, like Kilamuwa and Panamuwa, are of Luwian origin. Lipiński (2000: 242) comments that this 'either reflects the ethnically and linguistically composite nature of the population of Sam'al or simply implies that Kilamuwa's mother was of Luwian stock'. We do not know whether all the kings were members of the same dynasty. The origins of their names are not a reliable guide to their ethnic origins. In general, the inscriptions of Sam'al reflect the kingdom's blend of Aramaean and Neo-Hittite cultural elements.

In Shalmaneser III's first regnal year (858), Sam'al joined a coalition of states in its region which twice confronted the Assyrian king during his first western campaign (**RIMA* 3: 10, 16–17; see under **Pat(t)in**). The first confrontation took place near the fortified city of Lutibu, on Sam'al's frontier. Hayyanu, father of Kilamuwa, was ruler of Sama'al at the time. Other members of the coalition included Patin (ruled by Sapalulme), Bit-Adini (ruled by Ahuni), and Carchemish (ruled by Sangara), joined for the second encounter by Que (ruled by Kate) and Hilakku (ruled by Pihirim). Shalmaneser claimed a decisive victory in each encounter (**RIMA* 3: 9–10, 16–17). The following year, during his second campaign in the region, he received a substantial tribute from Hayyanu. Hayyanu was also among the rulers of southern Anatolia and northern Syria from whom Shalmaneser received tribute early in the campaign he conducted in the west during his sixth regnal year (853).

From the reign of Kilamuwa onwards, Sam'al's rulers cultivated close links with Assyria, as protection against the threats posed to their kingdom by aggressive Luwian states in the region, notably Adana. Some time after Kilamuwa's reign (whether immediately after is uncertain), Sam'al's throne was occupied by a certain Qarli, whose non-Semitic name suggests that he may have been the founder of a new dynasty. The long and apparently prosperous reign of his son and successor Panamuwa I (c. mid C8) is indicated in a monumental inscription, in the 'Sam'alite' language (a local West Semitic archaic dialect of Aramaic), appearing on a statue of the god Hadad (**CS* II: 156–8). The success of his period on the throne may have been due in part at least to his kingdom's links with Assyria, which no doubt gave it some degree of protection against external aggression. But within Sam'al, disputes over the succession appear to have arisen towards the end of Panamuwa's reign, which resulted in the assassination of his first successor, Bar-Sur. Thanks to Assyrian support, Bar-Sur's son Panamuwa (II) survived the coup and was installed by the Assyrian king Tiglath-pileser III as ruler of Sam'al in the late 740s, thenceforth becoming a tributary of Tiglath-pileser (**Tigl. III* 68–9, 108–9). He remained loyal to Assyria throughout his reign, which ended when he was killed while taking part on Tiglath-pileser's side in the siege of Damascus (733–732). Details of his reign and death are known to us from an inscribed statue (in the Sam'alite language) dedicated to him posthumously by his son and successor Bar-Rakib (**CS* II: 158–60). The latter continued his father's allegiance to Assyria (**CS* II: 160–1) until his own death c. 713. At that time, Assyria's throne was occupied by Sargon II. Bar-Rakib claims that his reign was a time of great prosperity in his kingdom's history, making him the envy of all his brother-kings (**CS* II: 160–1). Remains of the impressive buildings and sculptures of the capital attributable to his reign suggest that his claim was not too greatly exaggerated.

Probably at the time of Bar-Rakib's death, or shortly after, Sam'al was converted into an Assyrian province. Lipiński comments that since no traces of a violent destruction of Zincirli can be attributed to this period, Assyria's annexation of Sam'al was probably a peaceful one. For the destruction of Zincirli's acropolis in the following century, see **Zincirli**.

CAH III.1: 1048 (index refs), Lipiński (2000: 233–47), Lemaire (2001).

Samanum (map 10) Middle Bronze Age port-city on the middle Euphrates, in the north part of the district of Terqa (probably a regional centre of the kingdom of Mari). Samanum was the site of a battle fought by the Mariote king Yahdun-Lim (1810–1794) against the Yaminites. At that time it was the chief city of the Upapru, one of the five main Yaminite tribal groups (see **Yaminites**). Samanum's King Laum, ruler of the Upapru, was a participant in the revolt against Yahdun-Lim. The latter claimed a decisive victory in the contest (**CS* II: 260, **Chav.* 97). In the Yaminite uprising against Zimri-Lim, king of Mari, at the end of the first year of his reign (1774), Samanum was one of the two chief cities of the rebels (the other was Mishlan). Zimri-Lim crushed the uprising the following year, seizing Samanum and Mishlan and demolishing their fortifications.

Charpin (2000), *Mesop.* 140–1, *LKM* 621 (refs).

Samaria (bilibical **Shomron**, Roman **Sebaste**) (map 8) City and region in the hill country of central Palestine. The city, strategically situated on the summit and slopes of a 100 m high hill above fertile valleys, overlooked the Via Maris (q.v.) and was located 56 km north of Jerusalem. It provided access to Jerusalem in the south, the Mediterranean coastal plain to the west, and Megiddo and the Jezreel valley to the north. The site has been excavated by several archaeological teams, under the direction of G. Schumacher (1908), G. A. Reisner and C. Fisher (1909–10), and J. W. Crowfoot (1932–5). The institutions involved at various times in these excavations include Harvard University, the Palestine Exploration Fund, the British Academy, the British School of Archaeology in Jerusalem, the Hebrew University, and the Dept of Antiquities of Jordan.

Though there is some evidence of Early Bronze Age occupation on the site, its history begins effectively in the Iron Age, when according to *OT* tradition the Israelite king Omri shifted the capital of the northern kingdom of Israel to it from Tirzah c. 870 (1 Kings 16:21–4). Omri allegedly purchased the site from a man called Shemer (hence the biblical name Shomron) for two talents of silver. Archaeological evidence supports the tradition, which credits Omri with building a new capital for himself at Samaria (see Kenyon, 1971: 73–82). The citadel of Omri and his successors consisted of a large rectangular enclosure protected by fortification walls. Within the citadel are the remains of a palace of *bit hilani* type (see glossary), with square rooms surrounding a central court, storerooms, several public buildings, and a large courtyard. The dynasty founded by Omri was brought to an end with the assassination of its last member, Jehoram, by Jehu (c. 841), according to *OT* tradition (2 Kings 9:24). Even so, the Assyrians continued to refer to Samaria as the House of Omri.

The city remained the political centre of power in Israel under a total of fourteen kings (beginning with Omri) until in 722 (**ABC* 73) it fell to the Assyrian king Shalmaneser V (though some decades prior to this, Samaria had appeared among the lands west of the Euphrates conquered by and made tributary to the Assyrian king Adad-nirari III). The Assyrians followed up their victory by deporting large numbers of Samaria's population, replacing them with deportees brought from other conquered territories, as reported in *OT* sources (see 2 Kings 17:6, 24) and Assyrian texts. But shortly afterwards, in the politically turbulent accession year of Shalmaneser's successor Sargon II (722), Samaria joined the rebellion of Syrian states against Assyria. The rebellion was shortlived. Within a year, Sargon had suppressed it, and in its aftermath he claims to have deported 27,290 people from Samaria, replacing them, in greater numbers, by new settlers from other lands he had conquered (**CS* II: 295–6; cf. **CS* II: 293). He then appointed one of his eunuch officials as the country's governor.

From its foundation by Omri, Samaria was a wealthy, cosmopolitan royal citadel and palace centre, to the point that, long after it had ceased to be the seat of the kings of Israel, the conservative Judaean writers of the Bible regarded the name as a byword for luxury, decadence, and idolatry. A large number of fragments of bone and ivory inlay, with some fragments of carved wooden ornament, probably of Phoenician manufacture, were found in deposits outside the citadel itself, and provide evidence of the decoration referred to in several biblical passages. These fragments have generally been dated to C9 and C8, but on the evidence of discoveries elsewhere, notably Nimrud, are probably later.

During its subjection to Assyrian overlordship, the citadel served as the centre of the Assyrian administration of the province of Samerina, and continued to be an administrative centre of its region under subsequent Babylonian (C6) and Persian rule (C6–4). Following its conquest by Alexander the Great in 332 it was rebuilt as a Greek city, and after its destruction in 108 by John Hyrcanus was once more rebuilt, on a magnificent scale, by Herod the Great (c. 30). Herod named the city Sebaste in honour of the Roman emperor Augustus (Greek *Sebastos*), a name which is preserved today in the form Sebastiyeh by which the mod. Arab village there is known.

Tappy (1992; *OEANE* 4: 463–7; 2001).

Samosata see *Samsat Höyük*.

Samsat Höyük (Classical Samosata) (map 2) Eastern Anatolian site located on the west bank of the Euphrates north of Carchemish, with occupation levels extending from the Late Bronze Age to the Roman imperial period. Though it was first visited as early as 1836, by W. F. Ainsworth, and a plan of it was produced by O. Puchstein in 1890, no excavation of the mound took place before the hasty and incomplete rescue operations conducted by a Turkish team prior to the flooding of the region by the Atatürk Dam in the 1980s. The remains of the city that have been investigated date almost entirely to the Roman period. Samosata was the capital of the kingdom called Commagene in Classical sources. Its predecessor was almost certainly the city attested in Neo-Assyrian texts as Kummuh (probably the city called Kimuhu in Neo-Babylonian texts), capital of the Neo-Hittite kingdom also called Kummuh (q.v.). (The name Commagene was derived from Kummuh.) In C3 Commagene was incorporated into the Seleucid empire. It subsequently enjoyed brief periods of independence before finally being annexed to Rome by the emperor Vespasian in 72 CE and attached to the Roman province of Syria.

Serdaroğlu (*PECS* 803–4), Jones, Hawkins, Spawforth (*OCD* 373, s.v. Commagene), Lipiński (2000: 176–7).

Samuha (map 3) Hittite cult-centre located either on the upper Marassantiya r. (Classical Halys, mod. Kızıl Irmak) or (less likely) the Euphrates, and dedicated to the worship of the goddess Ishtar (Hurrian Shaushka). An identification with mod. Kayalipinar has been suggested. Samuha served as the Hittite administrative centre of the Upper Land, and may have provided the Hittite royal court with a residence-in-exile when King Tudhaliya III was forced to abandon his capital during the comprehensive invasions of his homeland in the first half of C14. Subsequently, Tudhaliya and his son Suppiluliuma used it as their base of operations for driving the enemy forces from the homeland (**DS* 63, 64 etc.). The Hittite king Urhi-Teshub was taken prisoner there c. 1267 after being defeated by his uncle Hattusili in a brief civil war which led to Hattusili's seizure of the Hittite throne (**CS* I: 203).

**RGTC* 6: 338–41.

Samuru City on the Syrian coast, located 20 km from the island of Arwad. It is attested in the records of the Assyrian king Tiglath-pileser I (1114–1076), who travelled to it by boat from Arwad during his campaign in Amurru (**RIMA* 2: 37). Tiglath-pileser states that Samuru was a city of the land of Amurru. In this context, the name 'Amurru' is apparently used in its original, broad sense to refer to much of the region encompassed by mod. Syria (see **Amurru**), and extending to include the Levantine coastal cities.

Sanahuitta (map 3) Middle and Late Bronze Age city in northern Anatolia, located to the northeast of Hattusa. It first appears in a C18 Assyrian Colony text, in the form Sinahuttum (but see under **Shinuhtu**), among several cities, including Ankuwa and Kapitra, which rebelled against Hattus (Late Bronze Age Hattusa), capital of the land of Hatti in the Middle Bronze Age (*Larsen, 1972). Early in C17, Sanahuitta became a subject territory of the fledgling Hittite kingdom, and the first (clearly attested) Hittite king called Labarna appointed one of his sons as its governor. But the city rebelled and set up its own appointee, a man called Papahdilmah, as its ruler (**CS* II: 81). It apparently remained independent of Hittite authority until Labarna's grandson and successor, Hattusili I (1650–1620), ascended the throne. In his first recorded military campaign, Hattusili marched against Sanahuitta and plundered its territory. But he withdrew his forces before achieving the conquest of the city itself. Three years later he returned, placed the city under siege, and after an investment lasting six months, finally breached its defences (**Chav.* 219–20). The city was thus restored to Hittite sovereignty. It subsequently figured in the administrative network of the Hittite Old Kingdom, as the residence of an AGRIG, a keeper of one of the royal storehouses set up throughout the kingdom. But by the end of the Old Kingdom (c. 1400) it no longer played a significant role in the Hittite world, and except for occasional references to it in religious texts, it disappears at this time from our records.

RGTC 6: 342, Bryce (2005: 66–8, 75–6).

Sangaritu see Saggaratum.

Sapinuwa (***Ortaköy***) (maps 2, 3) Late Bronze Age Hittite provincial administrative centre, located in northern Anatolia 55 km southeast of mod. Çorum and 60 km northeast of Hattusa. It covered an area of c. 9 sq. km. The city is frequently attested in Hittite texts, playing an important role within the Hittite kingdom as a religious centre, a military base for Hittite armies (e.g. in the reign of the late C14 king Mursili II), and as an administrative centre near the Hittite homeland's northwestern frontier. Its administrative jurisdiction appears to have extended to a number of other cities, including perhaps Tapikka (q.v.; mod. Maşat). Excavations have been conducted at Sapinuwa from 1990 onwards by Turkish teams under the direction of A. Süel. Prominent among the city's architectural remains are two monumental buildings, designated as Buildings A and B, whose functions have yet to be firmly established. Building A has been tentatively identified as a palace, or an important administrative building. A palace at Sapinuwa is in fact attested several times in inscriptions from the archives in Hattusa. From the debris of Building A's upper storeys, over 3,000 clay tablets have come to light. As far as can presently be determined, they were divided into three archives. Many other tablets and tablet fragments were scattered widely through the building's debris at the time of its collapse, and more widely dispersed again by more recent farming activities. The ground floor of Building B appears to have served as a large storeroom. Two other structures, identified as Buildings C and D, belong to what is considered a ceremonial complex. The former, consisting of an open hall and pillared court, led to the latter, which had relief orthostats at its entrance and was apparently a temple.

We still await publication of the corpus of texts from the site. Advance information indicates that the majority of these texts are in Hittite, and include letters (the bulk of the texts), administrative documents dealing with political and military matters, and religious and omen texts. About 25 per cent of the texts are written in Hurrian. These texts are mostly ritual in character. They bear witness to the increasingly prominent role Hurrian elements were playing in Hittite culture in the second half of the Late Bronze Age. Other texts are written in Akkadian, the international language of diplomacy in the Late Bronze Age, and there are a few bilingual texts (Hittite–Hurrian, Hittite–Akkadian, and Hittite–Hattian). The letters consist almost entirely of correspondence between the Hittite king, the queen, and the king's officials from all parts of the Hittite world. The fact that they were found in Sapinuwa indicates that at least one of the Hittite kings used this city as a royal residence for at least part of his reign. Unfortunately, no documents from the site bear a royal sealing which might have identified the resident king (or kings). Based on content, palaeography, and other considerations, the tablets can be dated to the first half of C14, in what philologists sometimes call the 'Middle Hittite' period (in reference to C15–14 Hittite texts). For at least part of this time, the Hittite throne was occupied by Tudhaliya III, who was forced to evacuate the royal capital Hattusa, and set up a residence-in-exile (probably at Samuha) when enemy forces invaded the Hittite homeland across all its borders.

Though most of the tablets discovered at Sapinuwa date to the 'Middle Hittite period', there is no doubt that the city had a considerably longer lifespan, and probably continued to play an important role in the affairs of the Hittite kingdom until the kingdom itself collapsed in early C13.

A. Süel (2002), Süel and Süel (2006).

Sapiratum (Sab/piritu, ***Bejan***) (map 10) Middle Bronze Age and Iron Age city located on an island in the middle Euphrates, in the land of Suhu(m). The city has been identified with Bejan, where excavations by Polish (Warsaw) archaeologists recovered Middle Assyrian remains as well as part of a Neo-Assyrian fortress. In early M2 the region was subject to Zimri-Lim (1774–1762), king of Mari. Sapiratum is referred to in a number of letters of this period from the Mari archive, particularly in association with troop movements in the region. Its governor for at least the first part of Zimri-Lim's reign was a man called Buqaqum, who seems to have played a prominent role as an agent of Zimri-Lim in the region as a whole. Sapiratum was conquered by the Assyrian king Tiglath-pileser I (1114–1076) during a campaign which he conducted against Suhu (**RIMA* 2: 43, 53). Tukulti-Ninurta II encamped his forces between the island and the city of Zadidanu in the course of his last recorded campaign (885) which took him through the middle Tigris and Euphrates regions (**RIMA* 2: 174).

LKM 533 (s.v. Buqaqum, refs), 621 (refs), *Charpin (1997).

Sappa Late Bronze Age country in northern Anatolia, subject to Hatti. Early in C14 it was among the countries near the Hittites' northern frontier which were placed under the immediate authority of military commanders. The Hittite king Arnuwanda I drew up pacts with them which bound them on oath to maintain security within the districts under their authority (*von Schuler, 1956: 223–33). In the reign of Mursili II (1321–1295), Sappa was attacked by another of these countries, Kalasma, whose ruler Aparru had rebelled against Hittite overlordship (**AM* 188–9). A few years later

Sappa appears in a list of lands which had been depopulated by enemy incursions and were assigned by Muwattalli II to his brother Hattusili (later King Hattusili III) when he appointed Hattusili ruler of the northern part of the Hittite homeland (**CS* I: 201) (see **Hakpis(sa)** and **Turmitta**).

Saraga Höyük Settlement-mound, c. 200 m × 150 m, located in southeastern Anatolia on the west bank of the Euphrates, 5 km north of Carchemish. The site, whose occupation levels extend from late M4 through the Bronze and Iron Ages, was excavated in 1999 by the Ilisu-Karkamis Dam project team, prior to the flooding of the region. Remains of a monumental building and inhumation graves of Middle Bronze Age date were uncovered during the excavations, which concentrated on the M2 levels.

Kulakoğlu and Sertok (2001), Burney (2004: 237–8).

Sardis (*Sart*) (map 4) Western Anatolian city, located 100 km east of Izmir in the valley of the Hermus (mod. Gediz) r. at its confluence with the Pactolus and at the foot of Mt Tmolus (mod. Boz Dağı). The site's history of occupation effectively extends from the middle of the Late Bronze Age (C15) – though Neolithic and Early Bronze Age remains have also been discovered – until the Roman and Byzantine periods, with later Arab and Turkish occupations. From C15 CE onwards, Sardis was visited by many European and British travellers, and excavations have been carried out in various parts of the city since 1853. However, the first major, systematic explorations were those of the American Society for the Excavation of Sardis (whose members were mainly from Princeton University, USA), from 1910 to 1914, and in 1922, under the direction of H. C. Butler. Further excavations were undertaken, from 1959 onwards, by the Archaeological Exploration of Sardis project team, under the direction of G. M. A. Hanfmann, and subsequently by a team from Harvard and Cornell Universities under the direction of C. H. Greenewalt Jr.

The best-known and most important phase in Sardis' history dates to the Iron Age, especially the period from early C7 to the second half of C6. In this period, Sardis was the capital of the kingdom of Lydia, which held sway over the western half of Anatolia under a ruling family known as the Mermnad dynasty. It has been suggested that the discovery of late Mycenaean and Protogeometric pottery on the site, covering the period c. 1200–900, gives some credence to Herodotus' report (1.7) of an earlier dynasty founded c. 1190 by descendants of Hercules (Herakles). The Lydian empire came abruptly to an end in 546 when King Croesus, last of the Mermnad dynasts, was decisively defeated outside Sardis by the Persian king Cyrus II (Herodotus 1.84–6). Croesus' kingdom and its subject states, including the Ionian Greek cities along Anatolia's Aegean coast, were now incorporated into the Persian empire. Sardis became the administrative centre of the empire in the west, with overall responsibility for the Anatolian satrapies (see glossary under **satrapy**). It was also the western terminus of the Persian Royal Road, which ran eastwards to Susa (see Herodotus 5.52–4). But when the Ionian Greek states rose up in rebellion against Persian rule in 499, during the reign of the Persian king Darius I, Sardis was attacked by the Ionians' Greek allies Athens and Eretria which acted in concert with Aristagoras, the tyrant of Miletus. Sardis' lower city was burned to the ground (Herodotus 5.99–102). It was quickly rebuilt after the crushing of the Ionian rebellion in 494, and in 481 Darius' son and successor, Xerxes, spent the winter with his troops there before proceeding on his campaign to mainland Greece.

In 412–411 the exiled Athenian commander Alcibiades visited the court of the satrap Tissaphernes in Sardis. Six years later, in 405, the Spartan general Lysander also visited Sardis, for discussions with the satrap Cyrus the Younger, son of the Persian king Darius II. And in 401 Cyrus the Younger used Sardis as a mustering point for the 10,000 Greek mercenaries recruited for his abortive campaign against his brother, the Persian king Artaxerxes II, who had succeeded Darius in 404. The city remained subject to Persia until Alexander the Great liberated it in 334, restoring to its population their anc. customs and laws, according to Arrian (*Anabasis* 1.17.3–8). Following Alexander's death in 321, Sardis came under the control of a succession of Hellenistic rulers, beginning with Antigonus. The city was destroyed by earthquake in 17 CE, but promptly rebuilt with a massive grant from the Roman emperor Tiberius. It appears to have flourished under Roman rule, when it was noted for its prosperity and splendid architecture. It later became an important centre of Christianity.

At the peak of its development as a Lydian city in C6, Sardis probably covered an area of at least 115 ha, and perhaps much more. Its main components were an acropolis, on a northward projecting spur of the Tmolus range, and a lower city. The acropolis was defended by a triple fortification wall. The lower city was also fortified, with a 20 m thick wall of stone and adobe (sun-dried mudbrick), of which some fifty courses have been preserved. Arrowheads and other items of war found in the wall may reflect the Persian capture of it in 546. Ordinary residences within the lower city were made of mudbrick on a timber framework and roofed with thatch. The larger, more imposing structures were built of white limestone and marble, with terracotta roofs, whose revetment tiles were embellished with red, black, and white floral, figural, and abstract motifs – decorative elements which are clearly reflective of Greek influence. Industrial areas within the city, near an Archaic altar of the goddess Cybele, have produced evidence of gold-refining activities, which can be dated to the first half of C6. The market-place of the city when it was under Mermnad rule has come to light not far from the mod. highway, along with part of its surrounding stone wall. According to Herodotus (5.101), the gold-bearing Pactolus r., which had its headwaters in Mt Tmolus, flowed through the market-place on its way to the Hermus r. (the river is now some 100 m to the west of the market-place). Remains of the Persian period are represented by the so-called 'pyramid tomb', a stepped limestone platform lying east of the Pactolus, which bears some resemblance to Cyrus' tomb at Pasargadae. Craftsmen from Sardis were among the stonemasons and woodworkers employed at Susa on the construction of the palace of Darius I (**DSf* 12, 13, **DSz* 11). Gold was brought from both Sardis and Bactria for the project (**DSz* 9).

The most substantial surviving buildings at Sardis date to the Hellenistic, Roman, and Byzantine periods. Structures of the Hellenistic period include a large temple of Artemis and a theatre, and those of Roman and Byzantine date (after the destruction of the Hellenistic city in the 17 CE earthquake) include a stadium, gymnasium (one wing of which was converted into a synagogue in C3 CE), baths of both the Roman and the Byzantine periods, and a Byzantine church. The building remains on the acropolis are almost entirely of Byzantine date, with the principal exception of a marble tower which dates back to the Hellenistic period.

About 10 km to the north of Sardis, across the Hermus r. and south of the Gygaean

Lake (Lake Marmara), lies the cemetery of the Lydian kings and other elite members of Lydian society. Now known as Bin Tepe ('Thousand Hills'), the cemetery contains c. 100 cone-shaped burial mounds, under which tomb-chambers were constructed. Some of the tombs are provided with *dromoi*, or entrance passages, and some with antechambers. The tumuli of the kings were huge, the largest of them all, according to Herodotus (1.93), being the tomb of Alyattes, father of Croesus. The tumulus so identified is 355 m in diameter and 69 m high. Herodotus informs us that it was built by traders, artisans, and prostitutes. It is one of three tumuli located at the eastern end of the cemetery. They are the largest of all the burial mounds in the cemetery. The central tumulus in this group has been attributed to the Lydian king Gyges on the basis of inscriptional evidence.

Scott, Hanfmann (*PECS* 808–10), Hanfmann (1983), Greenewalt (*OEANE* 4: 484–8).

Sarduribinili (*Çavuştepe*) (map 20) Iron Age Urartian fortress in eastern Anatolia, 20 km southeast of mod. Van, built by the Urartian king Sarduri II, son of Argishti I, in the second half of C8. The site was excavated by a Turkish team under the direction of A. Erzen from 1961 to 1984. Consisting of upper and lower fortresses, Sardurihinili extends 900 m along a narrow ridge and covers an area of at least 6.25 ha. The smaller, upper fortress was built on a roughly square plan, and protected by finely dressed stone walls reaching 5 m in height. Its defences would have been completed by mudbrick walls, laid out in curtain-bastion form. These are estimated to have reached a height of 17–18 m. Within this fortress, on high ground overlooking a rock-cut platform, is a square temple assumed by the excavators to have been dedicated to the chief Urartian god Haldi, although no inscription is associated with it.

Figure 106 Çavuştepe.

The lower fortress contains a second temple, also of the square plan with reinforced corners known in Urartian as a *susi*. This temple is dedicated to the god Irmushini, as indicated by an inscription of Sarduri carved on two stone blocks near the temple's entrance. The inscription also mentions a sanctuary (É.BÁRA) of Haldi, and this, combined with the fact that it is unusual for a Urartian site to have two temples, suggests that Sardurihinili was an important cult-centre. Close by the temple of Irmushini is a two-storeyed building complex which the excavators have identified as a royal palace. Workshops on the west side of the complex indicate the range of crafts and trades practised in the fortress, including weaving, leather-tanning, and metalworking. Three large cisterns cut into the bedrock beneath the palace ensured a constant water supply for the fortress' inhabitants.

Sardurihinili was destroyed late in C7 under the same mysterious circumstances that brought down most of the other Urartian fortresses. The lower fortress was then completely abandoned. There was some reoccupation in the area of the upper fortress, until the small settlement established there was destroyed early in C6.

Zimansky (1998: 253–54), Belli (2001a), McConchie (2004: 118–19).

Sarepta (biblical **Zarephath**, ***Sarafand***) (map 8) Settlement-mound located in southern Lebanon, 50 km south of Beirut, between the cities of Sidon and Tyre. Written sources referring to the site indicate a history of occupation from (at least as early as) the Late Bronze Age until mediaeval times. Late Bronze Age references to Sarepta occur in C14 texts from Ugarit and C13 papyri from Egypt. Pottery sherds from this period, including ceramic ware imported from the Mycenaean world, provide material evidence of Sarepta's Late Bronze Age phase. However, the city probably reached the peak of its development in early M1 as an Iron Age Phoenician settlement. C8 Assyrian sources refer to it, and an *OT* tradition reports a visit to the city (called Zarephath) by the prophet Elijah, who performed two of his miracles there (1 Kings 17:8–24); at that time Sarepta apparently lay within the territory controlled by Sidon. Classical and subsequently Arab literary sources indicate the city's continuing existence through the Hellenistic, Roman, Byzantine, and mediaeval periods.

Following a series of earlier investigations, which extended back to 1861 and involved explorations of a number of burial places in the city's environs, including forty rock-cut tombs, J. B. Pritchard of the University of Pennsylvania excavated the site between 1969 and 1974. From a study of its successive levels, Pritchard concluded that the city enjoyed a peaceful existence in its Late Bronze Age phase, and a smooth transition, without destruction, from the Late Bronze Age to the Iron Age. For much of its history, Sarepta appears to have been a centre for the production of pottery (in one of Pritchard's two main soundings, twenty-two kilns were revealed) and metalware. The city may also have had a purple-dye industry. Outlets for its products were probably provided by overseas as well as local markets. The excavations also brought to light a port constructed in the Roman period.

Other discoveries included a C8 shrine (a later one was built over it) with benches and an offering table, which can be associated with the worship of the goddesses Tannit and Ashtart. A 32-letter Phoenician inscription incised on an ivory plaque contains a dedication to these deities. Numerous figurines, amulets, beads, and other small items discovered with the shrine were apparently intended as votive gifts. The dedicatory inscription is the longest of the twenty-one Phoenician inscriptions discovered on the site. For the most part, these inscriptions were incised or painted on jars or bowls. Of much earlier date (probably C13) is a Ugaritic inscription incised on the handle of an amphora.

Pritchard (1978), Khalifeh (*OEANE* 4: 488–91).

Sarissa (*Kuşaklı*) (map 2) Hittite provincial city located south of the Marassantiya r. (Classical Halys), 200 km southeast of the Hittite capital Hattusa in northern Anatolia. Founded in C16, it was conquered, plundered, and burnt in the first half of C14, no doubt during the comprehensive invasions of the Hittite homeland in the reign of Tudhaliya III (*Bryce, 2005: 146). With the restoration of Hittite control over the region before the end of Tudhaliya's reign, Sarissa was rebuilt, surviving until the collapse of the Hittite kingdom early in C12. There was partial reoccupation of the site in C12/11 before it was entirely abandoned. A small Iron Age fortress was erected on its acropolis in C7/6.

Excavations have been conducted on the site since 1992 by A. Müller-Karpe for Phillipps Universtät, Marburg. Its identification as Sarissa, a city long known from Hittite texts, was established during the second excavation season when a small tablet archive came to light, with fragments of the description of a spring festival held in Sarissa. The Hittite king himself participated in this festival. These fragmentary tablets were unearthed in the so-called archive room of the structure designated as Building A on the western edge of the acropolis. Other tablets which came to light in these excavations provide information primarily of a cultic nature, including procedures to be followed in oracle protocols, which were used to ascertain the divine will through consultation of bird oracles, lot oracles, and the like.

Covering an area of c. 18 ha, Sarissa consists of an acropolis, with settlement spreading over its terraces and slopes and flat areas at the bottom of the hill, and a lower hill lying to the south. The entire settlement is enclosed within an oval double casemate wall 1.5 km long and incorporating towers at 25 m intervals. The earthwork walls reinforced by timber were built on stone foundations. Four main gates in the walls provided access to the city. Several large buildings on the slopes of the acropolis have yet to be identified. The largest and most impressive of these is the building designated as Building C, an imposing, rectangular structure whose apartments surround an open central court. The complex covers an area 76 m × 61.5 m and occupies 2.5 per cent of the entire area within the walls. At least 110 rooms made up the complex. Its overall layout is similar to that of the known sacred buildings of the Hittite capital, leading the excavators to conclude that this too was a temple. Its monumentality and topographical prominence make it very likely that it was the temple of the Hittites' chief deity, the storm god. Among the small finds in the complex were two well-preserved 'Middle Hittite' letters ('Middle Hittite' is a designation used by philologists in reference to C15–14 Hittite texts) and a number of clay sealings, whose inscriptions read 'Seal of Tabarna, the Great King. Who changes it will die.' (Tabarna was one of the royal titles used by various Hittite kings.) On the north terrace of the city, another building has been identified as a temple, designated as Temple I. It is a 51-room complex, with central courtyard, covering an area of 36 m × 54 m.

Sarissa must have played an important strategic role as one of the Hittite kingdom's administrative centres on the homeland's periphery. It was no doubt intended to serve as a watchpost-settlement, on constant alert against enemy movements from the southeast, particularly from Mitanni. Archaeological evidence indicates that it was sustained by its agricultual produce. Crops of barley, millet, legumes, lentils, and peas were grown, with irrigation supplied by a series of stone drainage channels. A large central grain silo had a capacity of 820 tonnes of grain, sufficient to feed 5,000 people for a year. Sheep and cattle provided 80 per cent of the city's meat. Cattle were also bred for their dairy products, and textiles were manufactured from locally produced wool and flax.

Müller-Karpe (1995–; 2002).

Sarugu (1) (Saruga) M1 city probably located in the vicinity of Harran, northwestern Mesopotamia, and perhaps to be equated with mod. Suruç (see Lipiński, 2000: 167 map). It is to be distinguished from the Sarugu clan of the Hatallu tribe in Babylonia (see **Sarugu (2)**). The city is attested as a tributary of the Assyrian king Ashurnasirpal II (883–859) (**RIMA* 2: 347), and also of his son and successor, Shalmaneser III. The latter records receiving tribute from Sarugu's ruler Ga'unu during the western campaign which he conducted in his first regnal year (858) (**RIMA* 3: 15). Estates in the vicinity of Sarugu are among those listed in the so-called 'Harran Census' tablets, perhaps dating to the reign of Sargon II (e.g. **SAA* XI: 122, no. 101).

Lipiński (2000: 164, 174).

Sarugu (2) Sub-group within the warlike Aramaean tribe Hatallu located in southern Mesopotamia (Babylonia), to be distinguished from the city of the same name in the Harran region. In mid C8 the Sarugu appear in the records of Ninurta-kudurri-usur, ruler of the middle Euphrates Aramaean state of Suhu, as marauding tribesmen, along with the Minu'u (var. Luhuaiia) clan, who plundered and devastated the land of Laqe under their leader, Shama'gamni (**RIMB* 2: 292–3, 295, 297, 301, 313). In response to an appeal from Laqe's governor, Ninurta-kudurri-usur led a military expedition against the tribesmen and won a decisive victory over them. The Sarugan leader Shama'gamni was captured and killed.

Sasi Iron Age fortified city within the kingdom of Melid/Malatya, referred to by the Urartian king Sarduri II in his invasion of the kingdom during the second year of his reign (late 760s). Sarduri calls Sasi the royal city of the Melidite king Hilaruada. It was apparently used as a place of refuge from other parts of the kingdom during Sarduri's campaign of conquest. Sarduri laid siege to it and captured it after a battle. He plundered the city and took back with him booty people as part of the spoils of conquest.

*Kuhrt (1995a: 556–7).

Satkuru Iron Age city belonging to one of the regions called Habhu (see **Habhu (3)**) in Assyrian texts. It lay in the Assyrian–Urartian borderlands. The Assyrian king Adad-nirari II (911–891) reports its destruction during the second of two campaigns which he conducted against Habhu in 894 in support of the city of Kummu, which lay on Habhu's border and was at that time in conflict with it (**RIMA* 2: 152). Iasaddu, Kunnu, and Tabsia were other cities of Habhu destroyed by the Assyrians in this campaign.

Sattagydia (map 16) Central Asian country in the region of Pakistan, attested in M1 Iranian and Greek sources. It is listed several times among the eastern lands of the

Persian empire in the inscriptions of Darius I (522–486), e.g. in his Bisitun inscription (*DB 6), and also in the *daiva* inscription (see glossary) of his son and successor, Xerxes (*XPh 3). Sattagydia occupied an important strategic location in the empire's eastern frontier region. Darius records that it was one of the lands where rebellion broke out against him on his accession to the throne (*DB 21). According to Herodotus (3.91), it was a component of the empire's seventh province, which paid a total annual tribute of 170 talents of silver (but see glossary under **satrapy**). Representatives from Sattagydia are among the delegates from the eastern provinces who are named and depicted on the statue-base of Darius I from Susa (*Yoyotte, 1972), and a Sattagydian appears as a throne-bearer in the Hall of 100 Columns at Persepolis.

Sazabu Iron Age fortress-city belonging to the Neo-Hittite kingdom of Carchemish. It was besieged, conquered, and plundered by the Assyrian king Shalmaneser III during the campaign which he conducted across the Euphrates in his second regnal year (857) (**RIMA* 3: 18). The campaign was directed principally against the Aramaean kingdom of Bit-Adini, then ruled by Ahuni. At that time Sangara was king of Carchemish.

Sazana Iron Age city located in the Biqaʿ valley, Lebanon, attested in letters addressed to the Assyrian king Sargon II (721–705) (e.g. **SAA* I: 139, no. 177). In the latter decades of C8 it was incorporated into the Assyrian empire as part of the province of Soba, of which nearby Soba city was the capital. From references to the city in the Assyrian texts, I. Ephʿal (cited by Lipiński) concluded that Sazana lay on the highway north of Kamid el-Loz, probably near the junction of the Biqaʿ route and the Beirut–Damascus route. Possible identifications have been suggested with Tell Dayr Zanun and Tell Barr Elyas.

Lipiński (2000: 319, 328).

Scythians (see also Saka) Nomadic, horse-riding tribal groups, first attested in late C8 Assyrian texts from the reign of Sargon II (under the name Ashkuzi), and subsequently in Greek and Roman sources (notably Herodotus). They are also known by the name Sacae. Their homelands apparently lay within the regions stretching from eastern Europe through the steppes north of the Black Sea into central Asia. But information about their origins, history, and culture is extremely meagre. They sometimes appear in the same contexts as the Cimmerians who, according to Herodotus (1.15), entered the western Asian world after the Scythians drove them from their homeland, which apparently lay in the steppes of southern Russia. The Scythians themselves made numerous incursions into western Asia, particularly in late C7–early C6. They posed a serious threat to the Assyrians' subject lands, they attacked and plundered a number of Syro-Palestinian states when the Assyrians lost control over their western territories, and they destroyed a number of Urartian cities, like Teisheba City (mod. Karmir Blur) and Anzaf Kale (mod. name), in the final years of the kingdom of Urartu. Before the fall of their empire the Assyrians made numerous attempts to hold the invaders at bay by military action, with varying degrees of success.

Iran also suffered invasions by the Scythian hordes. But here, according to Herodotus, the Medes succeeded in driving the invaders back across the Caucasus. Herodotus (1.106) records the story of a massacre of their leaders by the Median king Cyaxares

(625–585), after he had invited them to a banquet and got them all drunk. The Persian king Darius I (522–486) includes Scythia among the lands subject to him at the beginning of his reign (**DB* 6), lists it among the lands which rebelled against him in his first regnal year (**DB* 21), and reports a crushing victory over Scythian forces as one of the achievements of his third regnal year (**DB* 74). Herodotus, on the other hand, gives a lengthy account of an expedition led by Darius across the Bosporus against the Scythians (in 513?), allegedly in retaliation for their invasion of Media (4.1–142). According to to his account, the enterprise ended inconclusively, and almost disastrously for the Persian forces. (See **PE* 193–203, nos 5–16 for a collection of the Greek sources relating to this enterprise.)

In C5 the Scythians were widely respected by Greeks and barbarians alike as a powerful military confederacy. Towards mid C4 they reached the height of their material prosperity, under a king called Atheas, whose authority extended as far as the Danube. The period during which he occupied the throne is generally considered to mark the golden age of Scythian art. But his reign ended abruptly when he was defeated and killed in battle by the Macedonian king Philip II. Some years later, in 331, Scythian forces were victorious over a large army commanded by Alexander the Great's general, Zopyrion.

The history of the Scythians continued until C3 CE, when disunity among them led to their displacement from their homelands and replacement by a range of other peoples, including the Huns, Alans, and Goths.

Prominent among Scythian material remains are the burial mounds called *kurgans* (see glossary), some of which, especially those around the Aral Sea, contained a range of valuable grave goods, including jewellery, weapons, furniture, and equipment for horses. The largest of the tombs are vast, in one case reaching a height of over 15 m from its subterranean floor to the top of the mound. It seems that both servants and horses were sacrificed to deceased members of the aristocracy.

Kretschmer (*RE* IIA: 923–46), Sulimirski (1985), Rolle (1989), Vogelsang (1992: 181–7), Braund (*OCD* 1375).

Sealand (map 11) Marshland region of southeastern lower Mesopotamia, attested in M2 Babylonian and M1 Babylonian, Assyrian, and Persian texts. Babylonian King Lists have provided the basis for reconstructing an early line of Sealand rulers, who held sway over the region from c. 1740 to 1475. They constituted what is known as the First Sealand Dynasty. However, attestations of this dynasty date no earlier than C15, and only five documents, found at Nippur, of a legal nature and giving year-names, can actually be attributed to the dynasty. The names of its members are known only from the Babylonian King Lists, and the C15 use of the term 'Sealand' for this dynasty may be anachronistic.

During the Late Bronze Age, by c. early C13, the Sealand became a province of Kassite Babylonia, and was later subject to the regime of the Second Dynasty of Isin (see under **Babylonia**). Subsequently, it regained its independent status under Simbar-shipak, the first ruler of the so-called Second Sealand Dynasty, who extended his ruler over large areas of Babylonia. The dynasty which he established, as attested in both contemporary inscriptions and Babylonian King Lists, began in 1026 but lasted only twenty-one years. Simbar-shipak ruled for eighteen of these years. He had only two successors, both of whom reigned briefly (five months and three years respectively) before the dynasty and the kingdom which he had built came to an end.

In Iron Age Neo-Assyrian texts, the Sealand is closely associated with the Bit-Yakin (q.v.), the most powerful of the Chaldaean tribes. At the time of Shalmaneser III's campaign in northern Babylonia in 850 in support of the Babylonian king Marduk-zakir-shumi I, the Sealand provided a base for the Bit-Yakin tribe, whose ruler Yakin was among the Chaldaean chiefs who dispatched splendid gifts to Shalmaneser, to save their lands from destruction by his forces. Yakin is referred to by Shalmaneser as 'King of the Sealand'. A later chief of Bit-Yakin, Marduk-apla-iddina (biblical Merodach-baladan), is similarly designated as king of the Sealand in the records of the Assyrian king Tiglath-pileser III (745–727). He too had saved his land from the Assyrians by paying a substantial tribute to Tiglath-pileser, following the latter's conquest of the Chaldaean Bit-Amukani tribe in 729.

Assyrian sources indicate that the association between the Sealand and Bit-Yakin continued through the first half of C7, when the region was under Assyrian sovereignty. Brinkman comments that the tribal affiliation became much less prominent in this period, perhaps due to a reduction in population levels caused by mass deportations. Rebellions by Bit-Yakinite rulers of the Sealand against Assyrian overlordship are recorded in the reigns of the Assyrian kings Esarhaddon and Ashurbanipal (see under **Bit-Yakin**). Ashurbanipal inflicted a defeat upon the Bit-Yakin chief Nabu-bel-shumati, ruler of the Sealand, who was forced to flee to Elam where he committed suicide. Under Nabu-bel-shumati's leadership, the Sealand had originally supported Shamash-shum-ukin, who had been installed by his brother Ashurbanipal on the throne of Babylon, but had rebelled against Ashurbanipal in 652. As Ashurbanipal began to gain the upper hand over the rebels, the Sealanders decided to switch their allegiance back to him. No doubt because it best served his own interests, Ashurbanipal took no punitive measures against them for the actions of their former leader Nabu-bel-shumati. A group of Babylonian allies with whom Ashurbanipal drew up a treaty may in fact have been the Sealanders (*SAA* II: XXXII–XXXIII, *64–8). The Assyrians maintained their sovereignty over the Sealand until the 620s when the region came under Babylonian control. During the period of the Neo-Babylonian empire (626–539), the Sealand appears to have retained its importance, particularly because of its economic value as a source of gold, grain, wool, and other commodities. The final known reference to it belongs to the reign of the Persian king Cambyses (530–522), when the Sealand is attested as a Babylonian province (Kessler, *RlA* 11: 40).

Brinkman (*RlA* 8: 6–10, s.v. Meerland).

Sea Peoples Large groups of peoples who, according to Egyptian records, swept across and devastated much of the Near Eastern world early in C12. The term 'Sea Peoples', coined by the C19 Egyptologist Gaston Maspero, is a misleading one since a number of the groups covered by it appear to have had neither an island nor a coastal origin. Nor indeed were their movements and activities confined to the sea or to coastal regions. They spread through many inland regions of the Near Eastern world as well. Already in the reign of the pharaoh Merneptah (1213–1203), groups of invaders called Sherden, Shekelesh, Ekwesh, Lukka, and Teresh had attacked the Egyptian Delta, in collaboration with a Libyan chieftain called Meryre (**ARE III*: §579). Merneptah succeeded in repelling the invaders. But their attacks on Egypt were merely the forerunners of the much more comprehensive invasions of the eastern Mediterranean countries during Ramesses III's reign (1184–1153). On the walls of his funerary temple at

Medinet Habu, Ramesses graphically records the trail of destruction left by the marauders from across the sea. According to the Medinet Habu inscription, they formed a confederation consisting of peoples called the Peleset, Tjekker, Shekelesh, Denyen, and Weshesh; the countries which fell before them included Hatti, Qode (Kizzuwadna?; see **Qode**), Carchemish, Arzawa, and Alasiya (**ARE IV*: §64, **ANET* 262, *Gertzen, 2008: 88–9). Their invasions of these lands were not merely military operations, but involved large masses of people seeking new lands to settle. To judge from Ramesses' account, their land forces were moving south along the Levantine coast and through Palestine when they were confronted and stopped by Egyptian forces at the Egyptian frontier in Djahi (in the region of later Phoenicia). Their ships, however, reached the coast of Egypt, where they were destroyed by the Egyptian navy.

But there is much doubt about the actual nature, extent, and duration of the Sea Peoples' activities. Almost certainly the assumption that they were participants in a concerted military operation has little basis in fact. It is more likely that the Sea Peoples were made up of largely independent groups, who banded together from time to time in their wanderings and sometimes joined forces for raids and, on occasions, more extensive military enterprises. Some scholars believe that the Egyptian representation of them as a united, organized enemy is a propagandistic distortion of the truth. Thus B. Cifola (1988) sees the graphic account of Ramesses' conflict with and triumph over his enemies as a 'narrative condensation of a continuous long-lasting process, consisting in small skirmishes and rebuffs of repeated attempts at assault

Figure 107 Sea Peoples.

and penetration, into a single great military event, to serve a precise propagandistic purpose'. In any case, the so-called Sea Peoples were almost certainly not responsible for the collapse of the Near Eastern centres of civilization at the end of the Bronze Age, but were rather among the victims of this collapse. They were not intruders into the Near Eastern world in this period, but peoples belonging to it, who were displaced by the massive upheavals – whether caused by drought, famine, earthquake, a general 'systems collapse', or a combination of some or all of these and other factors – and forced to take on a marauding aspect in their search for new homelands to settle.

The identity of the individual groups of Sea Peoples, their places of origin, and the places where they finally settled, are still matters for speculation. See the separate entries for each of these groups.

Sandars (1985), Redford (1992: 241–56), T. Dothan (1995), Oren (2000), Leahy (*OEAE* 3: 257–60).

Sefire (map 7) Site in north-central Syria, 25 km southeast of Aleppo, where three Aramaic inscriptions carved on basalt stelae were discovered in the late 1920s. Dated to mid C8, they are considered to be one of our most important sources of information on the Aramaic language in the first half of M1. Stelae I and II are now in the Damascus Museum, Stele III in the Beirut Museum. Together they comprise the oldest known Aramaic text so far discovered. The fragmentary nature of the inscriptions makes it uncertain what relationship, if any, they bear to one other. It is possible that one of them is an original text, of which one or both of the others are copies. The inscriptions contain the text of a treaty (or treaties) which Mati'ilu, ruler of the Aramaean kingdom Arpad (Bit-Agusi) (q.v.) concluded with Bar-Ga'yah, king of Ktk (q.v.), some time before the Assyrian king Tiglath-pileser III's conquest of Arpad/Bit-Agusi in 740. It is clear that Mati'ilu is the inferior partner in the pact, which the Assyrians, who supported Bar-Ga'yah, had imposed upon him.

Fitzmyer (*OEANE* 4: 512–13), **CS* II: 213–17, **Chav.* 299–305.

Seha River Land (map 3) Late Bronze Age Hittite vassal kingdom in northwestern Anatolia, one of the Arzawa Lands; the river itself is probably to be identified with the Classical Caicus (mod. Bakir) or the Hermus (mod. Gediz) r. Around 1318 the kingdom's ruler, Manapa-Tarhunda, rebelled against his Hittite overlord Mursili II, but resubmitted to Hittite authority to save his capital from sack and plunder when Mursili's army prepared to lay siege to it (**AM* 68–73, **CS* II: 86). Mursili accepted his submission, allegedly after Manapa-Tarhunda had sent to him a deputation consisting of his mother and other elderly citizens to plead for mercy. A treaty between overlord and vassal is still extant (**HDT* 82–6). The island of Lazpa (Lesbos) was a dependency of Seha River Land, whose territory Mursili further enlarged by adding to it a land called Appawiya. Manapa-Tarhunda was eventually removed from power by Mursili's son and successor Muwattalli II, who installed the vassal's son(?) Masturi in his place. Masturi later became the husband of Muwattalli's sister Massanauzi (Matanazi in Egyptian texts) (**CS* II: 99). After Masturi's reign, the kingdom's throne fell into the hands of a usurper, Tarhunaradu, probably with the support of the king of Ahhiyawa (q.v.). Timely intervention by the Hittite king Tudhaliya IV (1237–1209) ensured that the legitimate ruling family was promptly restored to power (*Bryce, 2005: 304).

Sela Iron Age fortress-city in the land of Edom in mod. Jordan, attested in *OT* tradition. The Hebrew word 'sela' means 'rock' or 'cleft of rock'. According to 2 Kings 14:7, the city was captured by the early C8 Judaean king Amaziah, who renamed it Joktheel. A once-proposed identification of Sela with the mountaintop settlement of Umm el-Biyara (q.v.) overlooking Petra is now considered untenable. An alternative identification has been suggested with mod. Sela near Buseirah in northern Edom. Sela was also the name of an Amorite border town mentioned in Judges 1:36 but of unknown location.

Achtemeier (*HCBD* 993), Negev and Gibson (2001: 454).

Selenkahiye, Tell (map 2) Small fortified city in the middle Euphrates region, with two major occupation levels, Early Bronze IVA and IVB, covering the last centuries of M3. The city's defences consisted of a mudbrick wall and rock-cut moat encompassing a central urban zone of c. 10 ha. It may have been the administrative centre of one of a number of small polities in the region. But to judge from its non-monumental graves and domestic architecture, and the lack of any evidence for 'palaces' or temples, it seems not to have been an important seat of power. The city was destroyed at the end of Early Bronze IVA, perhaps during the destructions carried out by the Akkadian king Sargon (2334–2279). In its new (IVB) phase, Selenkahiye's fortifications were considerably strengthened by incorporating within them rooms which were adjacent to the walls and filled with bricks. The densely packed houses lining the network of streets indicate that the small city flourished in this phase of its existence. Artefacts recovered from the houses, including lapis lazuli ornaments and votive stone statues, suggest a relatively affluent society. The most impressive building of this period was a seven-roomed structure which contained many jar-sealings and may have served as the city's administrative centre as well as a residence. Female figurines deposited beneath the floors of some of the houses are thought to have been used as foundation deposits intended to protect the houses from evil influences. Level IVB ended in destruction in a massive conflagration c. 2000. The city was perhaps a victim of the turbulent events surrounding the fall of the Ur III dynasty about this time. There was modest reoccupation following its destruction. But shortly afterwards, the site was abandoned and never resettled.

Van Loon (2001), Akkermans and Schwartz (2003: 250–1).

Selge M1 BCE–M1 CE city in Pisidia, southern Anatolia, located on the Eurymedon r. (mod. Köprüçayi) upstream of the city of Aspendus (*BAGRW* 65 F3). The country's mountainous terrain helped protect its population, descendants of colonists from Sparta, against outside aggression. Selge remained free of Persian domination in C6 and C5, and in 331 its inhabitants supported Alexander the Great against their Pisidian neighbours Sagalassus and Termessus, whom they saw as a threat to their independence. Selge's remains, which include a fortification wall, theatre, agora, stadium, and basilica, date almost entirely to the Roman imperial period.

Bonacasa (*PECS* 822–3).

Semites A term coined by a German scholar, A.C. Schlözer, in 1781 to refer to a wide range of peoples speaking closely related languages who inhabited various parts of the western Asian world, primarily from M3 through M1, especially the regions encompassed by the 'Fertile Crescent' (q.v.). However, 'Semite' also came to have much broader chronological and geographical applications. It is derived from the name Shem, one of the three sons of Noah. Biblical tradition records twenty-six of Shem's descendants. Many of the most prominent western Asian population groups are commonly referred to as Semitic, including the Babylonians, Assyrians, Canaanites, Phoenicians, Hebrews, and Arabs, because of certain similarities observable in their languages and cultures. However, it is impossible to define these peoples collectively on the basis of a comprehensive set of cultural, ethnic, or linguistic criteria. They had no common ethnic identity, and their origins for the most part remain obscure or debatable. The languages designated as Semitic fall into three main categories: East, West, and South Semitic. East Semitic includes the Akkadian language group, which is subdivided into dialects of Assyrian and Babylonian. West Semitic covers the Syro-Palestinian language family, which includes the M2 languages Amorite, Ugaritic, and Canaanite, and the M1 languages Phoenician, Aramaic, and Hebrew. The Arabic and Ethiopic languages belong to the South Semitic group, which thus extends the application of the term Semite into the African continent.

Dearman (*HCBD* 994–5), Gragg (*OEANE* 4: 516–27).

Seraʿ, Tel (*Tell esh-Shariʿa*) (map 8) Settlement-mound in the western Negev desert, southern Palestine, 20 km northwest of Beersheba, with a history of occupation extending through thirteen levels from the Chalcolithic (M4) to the Early Arab period (C7 CE). The site was excavated over six seasons between 1972 and 1979 by E. D. Oren for the Archaeology Division at Ben-Gurion University of the Negev in cooperation with the Israel Exploration Society. Tel Seraʿ is the most plausible of several candidates for which an identification with biblical Ziklag (q.v.) has been proposed.

Following brief occupations during the Chalcolithic and Early Bronze IV periods (Stratum XIII), a substantial town was built on the site in the late Middle Bronze Age (C17). This marked the beginning of Canaanite settlement there (Stratum XII). The remains of a large building, erected on an artificial platform and thought to have been a palace, date to the first phase of this period. Oren associates the Canaanite city, which may have been fortified by a system of earthen ramparts, with the intensive urban development in the northern Negev and coastal Philistia at this time. Architectural remains from the succeeding Late Bronze Age levels (XI–IX) include private and public buildings, the latter used for administrative or cult purposes. A building identified as an Egyptian-style residency was presumably associated with the city's administration. An apparent sacred precinct, with plastered benches, installations for libations, and favissae or sacrificial pits containing animal bones and cult objects, may have provided a focus for its religious activities.

After the destruction by fire of the last Canaanite settlement in mid C12, the site was reoccupied in Iron Age I (Stratum VIII), probably by Philistines. Remains of this period include a number of four-room houses with Philistine ceramics. The Iron Age settlement was further developed in Strata VII (C10–9) and VI (C8), characterized respectively by a well-organized town plan and an impressive building complex with ashlar masonry (see glossary), perhaps influenced by Phoenician architectural traditions. Oren notes that the transition from Stratum VIII to VII showed no signs of destruction and no gap in occupation. He concludes from this that because the Israelite settlement in C10 must have developed organically from the Philistine habitation, the ethnic nucleus of the town in Iron Age I–II was apparently Philistine. A major conflagration towards the end of C8 brought Stratum VI to an end. Assyrian campaigns in the region at this time may well account for the destruction. The succeeding Strata V–IV contained the remains of a large citadel that defended the southern approaches to the city. It has been dated on the basis of Assyrian palace-ware to C7, and may have served as the headquarters of an Assyrian military administration. Oren suggests that its destruction in the second half of the century occurred in the course of Saite expeditions from Egypt to the Palestinian coast. From Stratum III, dating to the Persian period (C6–4), the remains of another citadel came to light, above the ruins of the 'Assyrian citadel', along with many built silos and grain pits. Most notable among these storage facilities was a large, brick-lined granary, 5 m in diameter. Following the Persian period the site appears to have been abandoned, with occasional subsequent settlement on the summit of the mound.

Oren (*NEAEHL* 4: 1329–35).

Sesamos M1 BCE–M1 CE city in Paphlagonia on Anatolia's Black Sea coast, renamed Amastris in early C4 (see **Amastris**).

Sestus (map 5) M1 city located on the western shore of the Hellespont, in the Thracian Chersonnese peninsula, north of Abydus. The city is first attested in Homer's *Iliad* (2.836). Though Thracian in origin, it was colonized by Greek settlers from the island of Lesbos, probably early in M1. For most of the period from mid C6 to mid C4, it was under the control of Athens. The establishment of an Athenian naval base there enabled the Athenians to control sea traffic passing through the Hellespont, thus ensuring (among other things) their continuing access to the grain fields of the Black Sea region. In 481 Sestus came under the control of the Persian king Xerxes, who landed there after crossing the Hellespont in preparation for his invasion of mainland Greece. Two years later, Sestus was one of the first Greek cities to be liberated by the Athenians from Persian rule (Herodotus 9.114–18, Thucydides 1.89). Thenceforth, it became a member of the Athenian Confederacy (see glossary). Following Athens' defeat in the Peloponnesian War in 404, the city was subject to Sparta for a short time, before once more reverting to Athenian control. It had several changes of overlord during the Hellenistic period, and was finally declared a free city under Roman rule.

Borza (*OCD* 1396).

Shabireshu M1 city in northern Mesopotamia, on the route from central Assyria to Guzana (Tell Halaf). The city is attested in letters and documents from the reign of Adad-nirari III (810–783) onwards. An official of the Assyrian king Sargon II (721–705) went there to meet people and oxen brought to him from Guzana (**SAA* I: 102, no. 128). The city is perhaps to be identified with mod. Basorin, which lies on the left bank of the Tigris, near the juncture of the Turkish, Syrian, and Iraqi borders. Alternatively a location at Tell al-Uwaynat, to the east of Eski Mosul and north-east of the Jebel Sinjar, has been suggested.

Radner (*RlA* 11: 474–5).

Shabwa (Classical Sabota) (map 9) Fortified city in southern Arabia, in the land of Hadhramaut. Excavations were carried out by J. Pirenne in 1976 and 1977, under the auspices of the French Ministry of Foreign Affairs. Stratigraphic soundings identified fourteen occupation levels, extending from C16 to the first half of M1 CE. The city's name is attested in South Arabic inscriptions which indicate that by C4 (and probably much earlier) Shabwa had become the capital of the kingdom of Hadhramaut. It was one of the most important urban centres in the region. Several thousand hectares of irrigated land were attached to it, and it was probably a major station on the merchant caravan route. The city's impressive defence system, which eventually stretched 4,200 m, was extended and strengthened throughout Shabwa's history. The end of the anc. phase of this history came in late C3 CE when the kingdom of Hadhramaut was conquered by the kings of Saba (Sheba) and Dhu-Raydan.

Badre (*OEANE* 5: 13–14).

Shadikannu (*Tell Ajajah*) Iron Age city in northeastern Mesopotamia on the Habur r. (see Lipiński, 2000: 113 map). The Assyrian king Adad-nirari II entered the city during his campaign in the region in 894, and received from it tribute and tax plus chariots and gold (**RIMA* 2: 153). His son and successor Tukulti-Ninurta II likewise received tribute from the city when he visited it during his progress up the Euphrates on his last recorded campaign (885) (**RIMA* 2: 177), as did his own son and successor, Ashurnasirpal II, during campaigns which he conducted in his first regnal year (883) and subsequently in 878 (**RIMA* 2: 199, 212–13). Shadikannu's ruler in Ashurnasirpal's reign was a man called Samanuha-shar-ilani. His grandson, Mushezib-Ninurta, probably succeeded him late in Ashurnasirpal's reign, or early in the reign of Ashurnasirpal's successor Shalmaneser III (**RIMA* 2: 392–3). The Shadikanneans are represented in a letter written to Sargon II (721–705) by one of the local officials as a trustworthy people, who work for hire throughout the king's lands, fulfilling their obligations to the king and supplying recruits for his service (**SAA* I, 171–2, no. 223).

Shadlash Mesopotamian city in the Diyala valley, attested in Middle Bronze Age texts. Its precise location is unknown. During the Old Babylonian period, in early C19, a war between its king, Sumu-numhim, and Hammi-dashur, king of Nerebtum (mod. Ishchali), was ended by a peace treaty, whose terms included an agreement on the prices to be paid for the ransoming of prisoners-of-war. Subsequently, Shadlash was presumably among the cities which lost their independence to the kingdom of Eshnunna when its king, Ipiq-Adad II (1862–1818), extended his authority over the Diyala valley.

*Greengus (1979: 74–7, no. 326), *Wu Yuhong (1994b), *Mesop.* 97–9.

Shaduppum (*Tell Harmal*) Small Middle Bronze Age city in Babylonia, today located in a southeastern suburb of Baghdad. The 1 ha site was excavated for the Iraqi Department of Antiquities by T. Baqir and M.A. Mustafa during the period 1945–63, and then by L. Husseinn (Baghdad University) and P. Miglus (Deutsches Archäologisches Institut) in 1997 and 1998. Excavations have brought to light a series of courtyard houses packed closely together within the city walls, as well as a temple and public buildings; a number of cuneiform tablets were also found. The contents of the latter include many legal and administrative documents as well as a copy of the Eshnunna law code, scribal exercises, and a unique series of mathematical tablets. The earliest levels, VII–VI, were assigned to M3, while levels V–II were dated to the first quarter of M2, and level I was of Kassite date (second half of M2). The city of levels III–II represents a refounding, possibly by the C19 Eshnunnite king Ipiq-Adad II. The tablets found at the site cover the last 200 years prior to its destruction at the end of the reign of the Eshnunnite king Ibal-pi-El II (c. 1765).

Shaduppum was a small provincial centre of the kingdom of Eshnunna. Shortly before the accession of Ipiq-Adad II, the city had been seized by the Assyrian king Aminum. Ipiq-Adad succeeded in winning it back, after an initial defeat, and thenceforth the city (probably) remained under Eshnunnite control until Eshnunna's fall to the Elamites. Shaduppum was put to the torch, along with other cities of the Eshnunnite kingdom. The most recent excavators of the site have placed its destruction within the context of the Babylonian king Hammurabi's conquest of Eshnunna in 1762.

Baqir (1959), *Mesop.* 292 n. 1535, 345 n. 1798 (with refs in both cases), van Koppen (*RlA* 11: 488–91), Miglus (*RlA* 11: 491–)

Shahaduni Middle Bronze Age city in central Mesopotamia, located near the Tigris r. perhaps south of Upi (Opis). It was part of the Old Babylonian kingdom during the reign of Apil-Sin (1830–1813), but subsequently came under Eshnunnite control. Apil-Sin's grandson Hammurabi (1792–1750) negotiated with Silli-Sin, king of Eshnunna, for its return to Babylonian authority along with other cities in the Tigris border region between the kingdoms of Babylon and Eshnunna.

*Charpin (2003: 80–1), **Mesop.* 115, 227.

Sha-pi-Bel M1 city in southern Babylonia near the Elamite border. It was the traditional capital of the Aramaean tribe of Gambulu, which was converted into an Assyrian province by Sargon II following his conquest of the region c. 710. Sargon's grandson and second successor Esarhaddon referred to Sha-pi-Bel as the gateway to Elam (*Borger, 1956: 53), a clear indication of its strategic importance. The city was attacked and destroyed by Esarhaddon's son and successor Ashurbanipal (668–630/627) following Gambulu's participation in an anti-Assyrian military coalition with Elam early in the latter's reign. Though Ashurbanipal claims to have razed the city to the ground, it once more figures in military action during the rebellion (652–648) by the Assyrian prince Shamash-shum-ukin against his brother Ashurbanipal (see under **Babylon**).

Lipiński (2000: 473, 476, 479).

Shardana (Sherden) Late Bronze Age population group of uncertain but possibly northern Syrian origin. Shardana warriors are depicted in Egyptian reliefs wearing a horned helmet (with a spike between the horns surmounted by a disc) and short kilt. They carry a round shield and short stabbing spear or sword. The Shardana were present at Byblos in C14, and are also attested as seaborne raiders who attacked the coast of Egypt during the reigns of Amenhotep III (1390–1352) and Ramesses II (1279–1213) (*Kitchen, 1982: 40–1). Subsequently, some of them settled peacefully in Egypt, and a number of them joined the pharaoh's militia. Shardana warriors fought on the Egyptian side in the battle of Qadesh in 1274 (*Gardiner, 1960: 7). In the reign of Ramesses II's son Merneptah (1213–1203), the Shardana once more appeared as aggressors against Egypt, joining with other peoples from across the sea who attacked the Egyptian Delta in alliance with the Libyan chief Meryre (**ARE III*: §579). But other Shardana warriors fought for Merneptah – perhaps the descendants of those who had settled in Egypt during Ramesses II's reign. During the land and sea movements of the so-called Sea Peoples in Ramesses III's reign (1184–1153), Shardana fought as auxiliary troops in Syria on the Egyptian side. Possibly they served as mercenaries. But we know that in this period there were still Shardana families living in Egypt; and it may have been as the pharaoh's subjects rather than as mercenaries that their menfolk fought for Egypt. In the so-called Papyrus Harris (see glossary), Ramesses includes a Shardana group among the Sea Peoples whom he conquered, and refers to their subsequent deportation to and resettlement in Egypt (*Gertzen, 2008: 91). Dispersion of the Shardana people during the final two centuries of the Late Bronze Age – with some of them settling in new lands and taking on new allegiances and alliances – could well explain their apparently conflicting roles as warriors fighting both for and against Egypt.

As with other Sea Peoples, the ultimate fate of the Shardana is uncertain. Those who had already settled in Egypt may have remained there beyond the end of the Bronze Age. However, in the context of the Sea Peoples' dispersion after their apparently abortive attack on Egypt, other Shardana groups may first have settled on Cyprus and then subsequently travelled westwards, where they occupied the island of Sardinia. The island's name, first attested in C9, could conceivably have originated from the Late Bronze Age Shardana people. But the suggested connection remains very conjectural, in spite of archaeological evidence adduced in support of it.

Sandars (1985: 223, index refs), Knapp (1995: 1444).

Sharia, Tell es- Canaanite settlement-mound located in the western Negev desert 15 km northeast of Beersheba. Its thirteen levels of occupation extend from the Chalcolithic Age through the mediaeval period. An identification has been suggested with either Ziklag or Gerar, known from *OT* sources. Excavations were conducted by E. Oren for Ben-Gurion University of the Negev between 1972 and 1979. Among the remains uncovered was a sequence of public buildings of Middle and Late Bronze Age

Figure 108 Shardana warriors, temple of Ramesses II, Thebes, Egypt.

date. One of the buildings was a structure of the palace-courtyard type. An Egyptian governor's residence may also have been located there during the Late Bronze Age. After its destruction by fire in mid C12, the town was rebuilt and may have had a Philistine population, if we can so judge from Philistine ceramic ware found in level VIII (Iron Age I). It suffered further destructions in C8 and C7, but continued to be occupied through the Persian, Roman, Byzantine, and mediaeval periods.

Negev and Gibson (2001: 458–9).

Sharnida Late Bronze Age country probably to belocated in the borderlands between northeastern Mesopotamia and northwestern Iran, perhaps not far south of the Botan r. (*RGTC* 5: 104). The Assyrian king Tukulti-Ninurta I (1244–1208) conducted a campaign against it and the (presumably neighbouring) land of Mehru at the beginning of his reign (**RIMA* 1: 235). It was included among the countries in the region over which Tukulti-Ninurta established or restored Assyrian sovereignty (**RIMA* 1: 240, 244). Its history may well have extended into the Iron Age, but there is no attestation of it in this period.

Sharon (map 8) Plain in coastal Palestine extending c. 50 km between Mt Carmel in the north and the Yarkon r. in the south. *OT* references indicate that it was noted for its forests and rich pastures. The Via Maris (q.v.), linking Egypt with Palestine, Syria, and Mesopotamia, passed through it. A number of Phoenician settlements were located in the coastal strip, whose most impressive city was Caesarea, built by Herod the Great (c. 73–4).

Lapp (*HCBD* 1004–5).

Sharru-iddina Iron Age walled city built alongside the Assyrian capital Ashur on the Tigris r. Its name means 'The king has given to me'. It is thought to have been a foundation of the powerful Assyrian governor and commander-in-chief Shamshi-ilu (*regn.* c. 796–752 or longer), who served under four Assyrian kings from Adad-nirari III to Ashur-nirari V (**RIMA* 3: 235).

Sharuhen Late Bronze Age Hyksos settlement located in southwest Palestine. Identifications with the sites of Tell El-Ajjul, Tell el-Farah (South), and Tell Abu Hureirah (Tel Haror) have been proposed. Sharuhen was one of the Hyksos cities captured and destroyed by the pharaoh Ahmose (1550–1525) during his Asiatic campaigns after the expulsion of the Hyksos from Egypt. It was occupied by an Egyptian garrison at the time of Tuthmosis III's decisive defeat of a coalition of Syrian states at Megiddo c. 1479. The city is later attested in the list of places assigned by the Assembly of the Israelites to the tribe of Simeon following the Israelite conquests (Joshua 19:6).

Weinstein (*HCBD* 1005).

Shasila City attested in the texts of the Assyrian king Tukulti-Ninurta I (1244–1208), located in northeastern Mesopotamia south of the Lesser Zab r. Tukulti-Ninurta refers to it, and the territory lying between it and the city of Mashhat-sharri on the opposite bank of the river, within the context of the lands which he conquered early in his reign (**RIMA* 1: 236, 240, 250, 251, 252).

Shasiru City in western Mesopotamia, attested in the records of the Assyrian king Ashur-bel-kala (1073–1056) as the site of a battle between Assyrian and Aramaean forces (**RIMA* 2: 101).

Shasu (Shosu) A name used in Late Bronze Age Egyptian texts to refer to nomadic or semi-nomadic groups of people, who appear variously in these texts as tent-dwelling pastoralists, brigands, mercenaries, anti-Egyptian rebels, refugees, and social outcasts. Like the Habiru peoples, they lived on or outside the fringes of settled societies, and often posed a serious threat to the security of these societies. They had no common ethnic identity (the name assigned to them may simply mean 'wanderer' or 'plunderer'), nor a common homeland. One of the main areas of Shosu occupation was the Palestinian region called Seir-Edom, which lay south of the Dead Sea. But Shosu are also attested in other regions of Palestine and Syria, as well as in the Negev desert, and even in Nubia. Hostilities are recorded on several occasions between Egyptian and Shosu forces. The pharaoh Seti I was obliged to conduct a campaign against them in Palestine during the first year of his reign (1294), in response to an anti-Egyptian rebellion instigated by their tribal chiefs. The campaign ended in victory for the pharaoh (see Murnane, 1990: 40–2). Twenty years later, the Shosu figure in a famous deception of Seti's son Ramesses II. As Ramesses was approaching the Syrian city of Qadesh for his military showdown with the Hittite king Muwattalli II (see **Qadesh**), two Shosu bedouins misled him into believing that the forces of his adversary were far to the north, whereas in fact the entire Hittite army was in a concealed position just behind Qadesh, and ready to attack. In the years immediately following Qadesh, Shosu forces conducted raids into Canaan, sensing a slackening of Egyptian control in the region. Ramesses responded by driving them out of Canaan, following up his victory with conquests in Edom-Seir. Tent-dwelling Shosu from Edom also appear among the enemies conquered by the pharaoh Ramesses III (1184–1153) in the context of his victories over the Sea Peoples, recorded in a document now referred to as the Papyrus Harris (see glossary). (For the relevant passage, see *Gertzen, 2008: 91.)

Sandars (1985: 223, index refs), Murnane (1990: 40–2, 45–8), Redford (1992: 269–80).

Sheba see Saba.

Shebeteria (maps 2, 20) M1 city in eastern Anatolia, probably to be identified with mod. Palu on the Arsanias r. (mod. Murat Su). A stele discovered there of the Urartian king Minua (805–788) records its author's occupation of Shebeteria, which he used as a base for his campaigns across the Euphrates into the region of the Neo-Hittite kingdoms (**HcI* 25). Minua also built a temple in Shebeteria dedicated to Haldi, Urartu's chief deity.

Shechem (Shakmu, *Tell Balatah*) (maps 6, 8) M2 and M1 Canaanite and subsequently Israelite city, located in central Palestine between the Jezreel valley and the Plain of Sharon, 60 km north of Jerusalem. Excavations were carried out initially by an Austro-German team under the direction of E. Sellin, from 1913 to 1914 and from 1926 to 1928, and subsequently by G. E. Wright in the course of eight campaigns between 1956 and 1969. Wright's excavations were sponsored by Drew University, McCormick Theological Seminary, and Harvard University, with assistance from the

American Schools of Oriental Research. Twenty-four occupation levels were identified on the main settlement-mound, the earliest two extending back to the Chalcolithic period (mid M4). The site was apparently unoccupied during the Early Bronze Age (M3), with resettlement taking placing in the Middle Bronze Age, c. 1900, when the first major city was built. The earliest references to the city occur in Egyptian sources, from the reign of the C19 pharaoh Senusret III and in the Middle Bronze Age Execration texts (see glossary) found at Saqqara.

From mid C18, Shechem was protected by earthwork fortifications (on stone foundations), which between mid C17 and mid C16 were replaced by a great Cyclopean (see glossary) stone wall with large north and east entrance gates. A complex constructed just inside the wall, consisting of a two-storey palace and fortress-temple and rebuilt during the mid C14 Amarna period, was the city's dominant feature. The fortress-temple was a huge tripartite structure with entrance hall, corridor, and cella (inner sanctuary) of the so-called *migdal* type. (The Hebrew term *migdal* refers to a military defensive tower within a city.) Shechem's destruction in mid C16 has been linked to the Asiatic expeditions launched by the pharaoh Ahmose, founder of the Egyptian New Kingdom, following his expulsion of the Hyksos (q.v.) from Egypt. The city was abandoned for a century or more before being rebuilt in mid C15. During this phase of its existence it was an Egyptian subject state. But despite its ties to Egypt, we learn from the Amarna letters (see glossary) that particularly under its king Lab'ayu, its aggressive expansionist ambitions posed a serious threat to its neighbours, who were also subjects of Egypt (**EA* 237, 244–5, 250, 252–5, 280, 287). Lab'ayu made his city the nucleus of a small empire – while still declaring his allegiance to the pharaoh Akhenaten – by invading and conquering the territories of his neighbours on his northern and western borders. He was eventually taken prisoner, by the pharaoh's men or his local agents, and probably executed. But his sons, who joined forces with the Habiru (q.v.), proved no less serious a threat to Egyptian subject territories in the region.

Shechem figures prominently in *OT* sources. In Patriarchal tradition, it was the city where Abraham had his first encounter with the inhabitants of Palestine (Genesis 12: 1–7). Elsewhere, Shechem is attested as the earliest religious centre of the Jewish tribes; it was the city where the tribes were assembled by Joshua so that their leaders could swear or renew their allegiance to God. And it became the first capital of the Northern Kingdom of Israel, under a new king Jeroboam (I), when Israel's ten northern tribes assembled there after the death of Solomon and renounced their allegiance to Judah.

There have been many attempts to link biblical sources with archaeological and contemporary historical evidence relating to Shechem during its Iron Age phases. For the most part, the links (some of which are referred to below) remain highly speculative. To judge from its material remains, the city seems to have made a peaceful transition from the end of the Late Bronze Age to the early Iron Age (early C12), though remains dating to the latter period are seen as reflecting economic decline and political instability in its Iron Age I phase. The end of this phase has been linked to the biblically attested destruction of the city by Abimelech, son of the judge Jeribaal by a Shechemite concubine, reported in Judges 2:42–9. Shechem was rebuilt in C10, supposedly during the relatively stable period of the alleged united monarchy of David and Solomon. It was again destroyed, probably before the end of the century if this destruction can be associated with the campaign which the pharaoh Sheshonq I (biblical Shishak) (945–924) conducted in the region. An alternative scenario for its destruction places it within the context of the conflicts associated with the dissolution of the united monarchy. 1 Kings 12:25 attributes Shechem's subsequent rebuilding to Jeroboam I, who made the city his capital. But this phase of its existence was also shortlived, ending in destruction in late C9. Two further rebuildings and destructions have been connected with Assyrian military campaigns in the northern kingdom of Israel. The second of these destructions can probably be linked to the Assyrian campaign in the region late in Shalmaneser V's reign, which ended with the capture of nearby Samaria (722/721). The city which emerged in the wake of this destruction apparently struggled for its survival, and was probably abandoned altogether in the early decades of C5.

Resettlement occurred in the wake of Alexander the Great's campaigns in the region, some time after 331, when the city became a place of resettlement for refugees expelled by Alexander from Samaria. In its early Hellenistic phase Shechem was a secure, well-fortified settlement. At this time, a prosperous residential quarter was established at the foot of Mt Gerizim, on which the city's temple was now located. But in C3 Shechem suffered from the conflicts between the Seleucids and the Ptolemies, and the decline which began in this period continued in C2 when the city was under Seleucid rule. Its final destruction in 107 was probably due to John Hyrcanus during his conquest of Samaria, of which Shechem had become the religious centre.

Campbell (*NEAEHL* 4: 1345–54), Toombs (*HCBD* 1006–8), Seger (*OEANE* 5: 19–23).

Shehna see ***Leilan, Tell.***

Sheikh Hamad, Tell see **Dur-Katlimmu.**

Shekelesh Late Bronze Age population group, possibly of Anatolian origin, listed as one of the so-called Sea Peoples in Egyptian records. The Shekelesh first appear among the invaders who joined the Libyans for an attack on the Egyptian Delta during the reign of the pharaoh Merneptah (1213–1203), as recorded on the east wall of Merneptah's temple at Karnak (**ARE III*: §579). Subsequently they are included in the list of peoples who, according to the inscription on the walls of the temple of Ramesses III (1184–1153) at Medinet Habu, destroyed many of the centres of Bronze Age civilization in Anatolia and Syria before attacking the coast of Egypt (**ARE IV*: §§65–6, **ANET* 262, *Gertzen, 2008: 88–9). The reliefs at Medinet Habu may contain a depiction of a Shekelesh warrior among the prisoners taken by Ramesses. The figure is bearded and wears turban-type headgear. But the inscription identifying it is fragmentary, and the attribution remains conjectural. Very probably, the Shekelesh are to be identified with a group described as 'the people of Shikila who live on ships' in a letter written by the Hittite king to a king of Ugarit, probably Ammurapi (**RS* 34.129 = *Malbran-Labat, 1991: 38–40, no. 12, *Gertzen, 2008: 87–8).

As with other Sea Peoples, the ultimate fate of the Shekelesh remains uncertain, following the Sea Peoples' abortive attack on Egypt in Ramesses III's reign. At least some of them may have travelled westwards, settling first in southern Italy and subsequently in Sicily. Greek colonists, on their arrival in Sicily in C8, encountered in the southeast of the island a population called Sikels, from which the name Sicily was derived. It is conceivable, though not provable, that the ancestors of these Sikels were the Shekelesh people who may have found a new homeland in the west in the last centuries of M2.

Sandars (1985: 223, index refs).

Shemshara, Tell (map 10) Settlement called Shusharra in the Old Babylonian period (Middle Bronze Age), located in the Dokan valley of northeastern Iraq on the right bank of the Lesser Zab, near where it enters the Rania plain. The site consists of a mound 19 m high and a 6 m high southern extension, covering a total area of c. 3 ha. Excavations were carried out by the Danish Dokan Expedition under the direction of H. Ingholt and J. Laessøe in 1957, and an Iraqi team under the direction of A. al-Qadir al-Tekriti in 1958 and 1959. The excavations were prompted by the Iraqi government's decision in 1950 to build a dam across the Lesser Zab at Dokan, which subsequent archaeological surveys revealed would flood about forty anc. sites.

The main excavations on the northern mound revealed a total of sixteen levels, the earliest of which (16–9) indicate occupation in the Hassuna period (late M7/early M6). Five later levels (8–4) belong to the Middle Bronze Age (first centuries of M2). These constitute the 'Hurrian period' of the site's history, so called because onomastic material in the lower town's palace archive (see below) indicates Hurrian affiliations. The site then appears to have been abandoned for three millennia before resettlement took place in the Islamic period, represented by levels 3–1 (C12–14 CE). Excavations on the southern extension of the mound revealed that in this area there was also settlement in M4 and M3, thus considerably shortening the gap in occupation following the Hassuna period. Almost certainly Shusharra can be identified with the town called Shash(sh)urum/Shashrum in texts of the Ur III period (C21), when it was the target of a number of military expeditions dispatched from Ur.

The principal Middle Bronze Age remains on the high mound are a number of graves containing funerary goods (bronze weapons etc.), and a mudbrick platform, which may once have supported a small temple. From the contemporary settlement on the lower mound (level 5 in this area), the only surviving building has been identified as a palace. Important information about Shusharra in this period is provided by an archive, discovered by the Danish team in one of its rooms. The archive consists of 250 complete and fragmentary clay tablets – letters, administrative documents, and sealings. (A few additional administrative texts were discovered by the Iraqi team during its further excavations of the palace.) If the total size of the settlement was at this time only a few hectares, then it was probably no more than a fortress outpost or small administrative centre. However, if the mounds in the surrounding region also belonged to the site, then it may well have been a city of some size and significance during the Middle Bronze Age.

Most of the letters found in the palace archive were written to Shusharra's ruler, Kuwari, at a time when the town was becoming caught up in the conflicts between the warring major and petty kingdoms of Mesopotamia, particularly during the reign of the Assyrian king Shamshi-Adad I (1796–1775). Kuwari was apparently a man of Turukkean origin and a native of a city called Zukula. He had been appointed as administrator of Shusharra by Pishenden, ruler of the kingdom of Itabalhum. Pishenden apparently held sway over at least part of the western Zagros region where Shusharra lay. The earlier group of letters contained in the palace archive consists of communications with Pishenden and other rulers and officials in this region. Subsequently, Kuwari switched his allegiance to Shamshi-Adad, despite the appeals of his Turukkean associates. The later correspondence, to which the great majority of the letters belong, consists of communications sent to Kuwari by Shamshi-Adad, his son Ishme-Dagan (Assyrian viceroy in Ekallatum), and various Assyrian officials. This correspondence can be dated to the mid 1780s. In this period, Shamshi-Adad conducted campaigns in the region lying between the Greater and Lesser Zab rivers. These resulted in the conquest of a number of cities in the region, including Qabra, which fell to a combined assault by Assyrian and Eshnunnite forces following upon an alliance which Eshnunna's king, Dadusha, had concluded with Shamshi-Adad.

The palace of Shusharra was destroyed by fire c. 1783, i.e. within a couple of years of Kuwari's switch of allegiance to Shamshi-Adad. The agents of its destruction are unknown. Later text-evidence may indicate that Shusharra continued to be occupied for some time after this destruction. But there is no archaeological confirmation of this.

*Eidem (1992), *Eidem and Laessøe (2001).

Shephelah Hebrew term used for the low hills (c. 300 m high) located in western Palestine between the coastal plains and the hill country to the east. It was an intermediate zone between Philistia and the kingdom of Judah. Its strategic value prompted both states to seek control of it.

Negev and Gibson (2001: 463).

Sherden see Shardana.

Shereshshu Fortified city attested in the records of the Assyrian king Tiglath-pileser I (1114–1076), located in northeastern Mesopotamia on the east bank of the Tigris. It was used as a stronghold by fugitives from the nearby land of Kadmuhu, west of the Tigris, a rebellious Assyrian subject state, following a campaign of conquest and destruction in the land by Tiglath-pileser in his accession year (**RIMA* 2: 14–15). The Assyrian king pursued the fugitives, capturing Shereshshu and massacring its defenders.

Shikshabbum Middle Bronze Age city in northern Mesopotamia, capital of the Assyrian vassal kingdom of Ahazum (q.v.).

Shilaia M1 stronghold in the land of Hubushkia, part of the territory of Nairi in mod. Kurdistan. The Assyrian king Shalmaneser III stormed, captured, and destroyed it during his campaign in the region in his third regnal year, 856 (**RIMA* 3: 21). Its ruler at the time was a man called Kaki.

Shiloh (***Khirbet Seilun***) (map 8) In its most important phase, an early Iron Age Israelite religious sanctuary in northern Palestine west of the Jordan r. Its history of occupation extends from Middle Bronze Age II (c. 1750–1650) through Middle Bronze Age III, Late Bronze Age, Iron Age, Hellenistic, Roman, Byzantine and early Arab periods. After a preliminary investigation by A. Schmidt in 1915, the site was excavated by Danish teams under the direction of H. Kjaer between 1926 and 1932, and subsequently by teams from Bar-Ilan University under the direction of I. Finkelstein,

S. Bunimovitz, and Z. Lederman between 1981 and 1984. Eight settlement strata were identified. Beginning life as a small unfortified village, Shiloh had by Middle Bronze Age III developed into a relatively large, strongly fortified town, c. 1.5 ha in extent, before its first destruction c. 1550. During the Late Bronze Age there was probably no more than a small cult-place on the site, which was abandoned by the end of the age. The resettlement which occurred in late C12 or early C11 is commonly associated with the arrival of the Israelites. Several columned public buildings and more than twenty grain silos are among the material remains of this phase of Shiloh's existence. Its destruction in C11 has been attributed to the Philistines. Shiloh then appears to have been left in ruins for a brief period until a small village was built there in Iron Age II (early M1). There are a few remains of occupation in the Hellenistic period. In Roman and Byzantine times Shiloh became a much more substantial settlement, and continued to be occupied until the early Arab period.

In *OT* tradition, Shiloh was the most important religious and administrative centre of the Israelites after their arrival in the 'Promised Land'. It was here that they set up the tabernacle (the 'Tent of Meeting') (Joshua 18:1). Here too they apportioned the land by lot among the seven tribes who had not yet received their inheritance (Joshua 18:2–10), and allocated cities to the Levites (Joshua 21). Religious festivals took place in Shiloh every year (Judges 21:19). The Ark of the Covenant was originally housed in the temple of Shiloh, until its capture by the Philistines following their defeat of the Israelites at the battle of Ebenezer; the Israelites had brought the Ark to the battle-site in the hope that it would give them victory (1 Samuel 4). The destruction of Shiloh, attested in Jeremiah 7:12–14, is commonly attributed to the Philistines in the aftermath of their triumph at Ebenezer. As noted above, archaeological evidence also indicates a destruction around this time. Though Shiloh was later rebuilt, and probably continued to be venerated as a holy place, it never again regained the status and prestige it had enjoyed during the first period of Israelite settlement.

I. Finkelstein (1985), Kempinski and Finkelstein (*NEAEHL* 4: 1364–70).

Shimashki Highland region and kingdom in western Iran, attested in Mesopotamian and Elamite written sources from C21 until c. 1900. Texts of the Ur III period (C21) list a number of lands making up the region, including Zabshali (the most important of them), Sigrish, Nibulmat, Alumiddatum, Garta, and Shatilu (e.g. **DaK* 348). In spite of the geographical information which these texts provide, there is still uncertainty as to where precisely Shimashki lay and how extensive it was. In the course of C21, the mountain peoples who inhabited the region were united into a kingdom whose territories, at the peak of its power in late C21, may have stretched from the land of Anshan westwards into Luristan and northwards towards the Caspian Sea (thus T. Potts, 1994: 34). However, a more easterly location for Shimashki, around the region of mod. Kerman, has also been proposed.

The formation of the kingdom was linked with the establishment c. 2040 of a ruling Shimashki dynasty whose kings bore Elamite names. Information about these kings comes from an early M2 Old Babylonian school-text from Susa. The text records two lists of rulers, twelve in each list, referred to respectively as 'kings of Awan' and 'kings of Shimashki'. Though questions have been raised about the text's reliability as a historical source, the historicity of the Shimashki kings recorded in the second list is confirmed by references to them in contemporary Mesopotamian texts of the Ur III

(C21) and Isin-Larsa (C20–18) periods. The earliest of these kings can be securely dated to the reigns of the third and fourth kings of the Ur III dynasty, Amar-Sin (2046–2038) and Shu-Sin (2037–2029). It has been suggested that the dynasty may have originated in Anshan. But the kingdom over which its rulers held sway should probably be regarded as a component of a broader Elamite world, what we might call a 'Greater Elam', to distinguish it from a core Elamite region centred on Anshan. Though clearly an integral part of Elam, at least in this broader sense, Shimashki was separately identified from it in Elamite royal titulary, as illustrated by the fact that later kings used the joint title 'king of Elam and Shimashki'.

During the Ur III period, Shimashki was invaded several times, by Puzur-Inshushinak, the king of Awan, a rival Elamite confederacy, and by (at least) two of the Ur III kings. Puzur-Inshushinak claims to have received the submission of Shimashki during an expedition which he led, early in C21, against the Elamite states Kimash and Hu-urti. Later, Shimashki was conquered and plundered by Shulgi, second ruler of the Ur III dynasty (2094–2047), and again by Shu-Sin (2037–2029) (**DaK* 348), probably in the campaign which he conducted in the seventh year of his reign. D. T. Potts suggests that uprisings in which the Shimashkians played a major role must have helped provoke these campaigns. There seem also to have been relatively long interludes of peace between Shimashki and the Ur III rulers, which were marked by regular diplomatic exchanges.

Nevertheless, Shimashki must have felt under constant threat from its western neighbour. This may have provided the incentive for the lands of which Shimashki was composed to join together in a political and military confederacy under the leadership of a ruling dynasty. Eventually, Shimashki gained the upper hand in its conflicts with the Ur III kingdom. According to Sumerian tradition, it was a man called Kindattu who delivered the death blow to this kingdom, by conquering its last ruler, Ibbi-Sin (2028–2004). Under Kindattu, Shimashki reached the peak of its power and influence in the western Asian world. And by establishing his rule over Anshan and Susiana, the core region of Elam (probably after driving the last remnants of Ibbi-Sin's forces from the region), Kindattu became the supreme ruler of the Elamites. For a brief time, southern Babylonia and Ur itself came under Shimashki rule. But the dynasty's lease of power in western Asia was shortlived. After the fall of Ur, Kindattu came into conflict with Ishbi-Erra, founder and first ruler (2017–1985) of the First Dynasty of Isin. He was defeated by Ishbi-Erra, and forced to flee for his life. Relations may have improved between Shimashki's remaining kings and Ishbi-Erra's successors in Isin. We can perhaps see a reflection of this in the marriage contracted between Tan-Ruhurater, eighth king of Shimashki (according to the Susa King List), and the daughter of the governor of the city of Eshnunna (thus D. T. Potts, 1999: 149), which was then under Isin's control.

But the Shimashki dynasty was now in irreversible decline. When conflicts broke out, c. 1980, between the Elamites and the kingdom of Marhashi (which bordered on Elamite territory to the east or northeast), Ilum-muttabbil, ruler of the northern Babylonian city of Der, intervened as an ally of Marhashi, and claims to have 'smitten the heads of Anshan, Elam, and Shimashki'. By the last years of C20, the line of Shimashki kings had come to an end, perhaps due to campaigns in the region by Gungunum (1932–1906), founder of the ruling dynasty of Larsa. It was replaced by another royal line, the so-called *sukkalmah* dynasty. The members of this dynasty, based in Anshan, were probably of the same royal stock, or came from the same extended family, as their Shimashki predecessors. Under their rule, Elam entered into a further period of power and prosperity which was to last for another 300 years.

T. Potts (1994: 30–4), D. T. Potts (1999: 130–59).

Shimron (Shim ʿon) Bronze Age Canaanite city in the western Jezreel valley, identified with the site of Khirbet Sammuniyeh (Tell Shimron). Apart from references to it in *OT* sources (e.g. Joshua 11:1, 19:15), the city maybe attested in the Egyptian Execration texts (C19–18; see glossary), the list of Syro-Palestinian conquests of the pharaoh Tuthmosis III (C15), and the Amarna letters (mid C14; see glossary). But the identifications in these cases (e.g. with Shamhuna in the Amarna letter **EA* 225:4) remain uncertain.

Negev and Gibson (2001: 463–4).

Shinamu(m) (Shinabu, Sinabu = ***Pornak**?*) City on the upper Tigris r., first attested in the Middle Bronze Age Mari archives (first half of C18) as an ally of Mari and the city of Tushhum (Tushhan) (see **LAPO* 17: 50, no. 473). The town was conquered by the Assyrian king Shamshi-Adad I c. 1782 as part of his expansion into Upper Mesopotamia. In the Late Bronze Age, the Assyrian king Shalmaneser I (1274–1245) built a fortified stronghold on the site of Shinabu to serve as an Assyrian garrison centre on the frontier with the Nairi lands, according to a later account of Ashurnasirpal II (**RIMA* 2: 261). It was subsequently captured by Aramaeans and became part of the Aramaean kingdom of Bit-Zamani. The Assyrian king Ashur-bel-kala (1073–1056) fought a battle with Aramaean forces there at the time the region was ruled by a certain Lishur-sala-Ashur (**RIMA* 2: 102). In 879 Sinabu was among the cities in the region recaptured by the Assyrian king Ashurnasirpal II, and resettled with Assyrians. Ashurnasirpal constructed storage depots here and in other cities for the grain which his troops harvested from the Nairi lands (**RIMA* 2: 261).

Radner and Schachner (2001: 756).

Shinar, Plain of Biblical name for southern Mesopotamia (Sumer and Akkad, later Babylonia). According to Genesis 10:10, the first centres of the kingdom ruled by Nimrod – Babylon, Erech (Uruk/Warka), and Akkad – were located in the land of Shinar, whence Nimrod went north to Assyria to build Nineveh and other cities. Genesis 11:2 relates that migrants from the east settled in the Plain of Shinar and built the Tower of Babel there. In other biblical contexts, Shinar is equated with Babylon under Chaldaean rule (mid M1). Daniel 1:2 reports that God delivered up Jehoiakim, king of Judah, to the Babylonian king Nebuchadnezzar II, who took him to Shinar, i.e. to Babylon. This event is confirmed by Nebuchadnezzar's historically attested siege and capture of Jerusalem followed by the removal of King Jehoiakim along with his family and courtiers to Babylon in 597. Other references to Shinar as Chaldaean Babylon appear in Isaiah 11:11 and Zechariah 5:11. The origin of the name is disputed.

Baly (*HCBD* 1016).

Shi(ni)gishu Iron Age city in northern Mesopotamia, on the northern fringe of the Kashiyari mountain range (mod. Tur ʿAbdin). The Assyrian king Ashurnasirpal II (883–859) encamped his forces for the night there during his second campaign against the Nairi lands (*RIMA 2: 209). It was his first stop on leaving the Kashiyari, before moving on to Madara and then Tushshan.

Shinuhtu (probably ***Aksaray***) (map 18) Iron Age city in southern Anatolia in the region called Tabal in Neo-Assyrian texts. Its location is based on the likely identification of a ruler called Kiyakiyas, whose name appears in a hieroglyphic inscription on a stele discovered at Aksaray (**CHLI* I: 476), with a certain Kiakki, attested in Assyrian texts from the reign of Sargon II (721–705) as a king of Shinuhtu. Shinuhtu had been a tribute-paying state of Assyria, but when Kiakki breached his oath of allegiance and withheld the tribute, perhaps at the instigation of the Phrygian/Mushki king Mita (Greek Midas), Sargon took his city by storm in 718, and deported him, along with his family, warriors, and (allegedly) 7,350 of his city's inhabitants, to Assyria. Kiakki himself was executed by being burned alive (**ARAB* II: 4, 27, 61). Sargon then handed over Shinuhtu to Kurti, king of Atuna, a Tabalic land which must have been located relatively close by. To judge from the fragmentary Aksaray inscription, Shinuhtu was a flourishing state at this time. Some scholars have suggested that it is to be identified with the city called Sinahuttum in texts of the Assyrian Colony period (C20–18), which would thus extend its history back at least to the Middle Bronze Age. But unless there is more than one place of this name, Sinahuttum is more likely to be equated with Sanahuitta (q.v.) attested in Late Bronze Age Hittite texts.

CHLI I: 431.

Shipri Late Bronze Age fortified Syrian city located on the west bank of the middle Euphrates within the kingdom of Carchemish (**HDT* 45).

Shirihum (Sherihum) Early Bronze Age city or region in southwestern Iran, attested in Old Akkadian texts. The Akkadian king Sargon (2334–2279) lists it among the cities and lands against which he campaigned in the east. Subsequently, Sargon's son and second successor Manishtushu (2269–2255) conquered it along with Anshan (**DaK* 76–7, 220–2), which presumably lay close by, before crossing the Persian Gulf. Shirihum is perhaps to be identified with the coastal region of Fars.

Steinkeller (1982: 256).

Shirwunum Middle Bronze Age royal city and land in northern Mesopotamia to the east or southeast of the Jebel Sinjar, near the city of Karana. In a letter from the Mari archives, Zimri-lim, king of Mari (1774–1762), was warned by Yasim-El, his agent in Karana, that Shirwunum's king, Arrapha-Adal, was preparing to lay siege to the city of Adallya in the Jebel Sinjar region – apparently on the orders of Atamrum, king of Andarig (**LKM* 347). A siege actually took place, but it was conducted by Atamrum himself, and there was some doubt as to whether he received any assistance at all from Arrapha-Adal (**LKM* 348). After the fall of Zimri-Lim's kingdom to the Babylonian king Hammurabi, Shirwunum was conquered and plundered by Aqba-hammu, who had seized the throne of nearby Karana from his brother-in-law Ashkur-Addu and now ruled Karana as a subject of Hammurabi. Shirwunum thenceforth became a vassal state of Karana. But so thoroughly had its territory been plundered by Karana's forces that Aqba-hammu himself had to supply its king with the gifts which he was required to present to his new overlord (*Dalley, 1984: 42–3).

Shit(t)amrat Mountain in northern Mesopotamia on the right bank of the middle Euphrates, perhaps to be located at the site of the mediaeval fortress at Rumkale (see Lipiński, 2000: 167, map). In 856 Bit-Adini's ruler, Ahuni, sought refuge there, with a force of infantry, chariotry, and cavalry, from the Assyrian king Shalmaneser III after the latter had captured his royal capital, Til-Barsip. The following year, Shalmaneser surrounded his mountain stronghold and defeated his forces in a pitched battle within the stronghold itself (*RIMA 3: 29–30). The survivors of the battle were deported to the Assyrian royal capital Ashur for resettlement. Ahuni himself was among the deportees. It is not certain whether Bit-Adini extended as far north as the area where Shitamrat must have been located, or whether Shitamrat was rather in the land of Kummuhu.

*Taşyürek (1979: 47–53), Lipiński (2000: 174–5).

Shitullum (map 10) Middle Bronze Age city in northern Mesopotamia, located on the west bank of the Tigris south of Ashur. It lay within the southern border region of the Old Assyrian kingdom in the reign of Shamshi-Adad I (1796–1775). Due to its strategic location between the kingdoms of Eshnunna and Assyria, Shitullum became a target of Eshnunnite military expeditions on their route from Eshnunna into the territories of Upper Mesopotamia and Mari. The city served also as an important clearing-house for intelligence reports on Eshnunna and Babylon, brought by messengers, spies, and informers, for transmission to the Mariote king Zimri-Lim (1774–1762).

LKM 623–4 (refs).

Shosu see Shasu.

Shuandahul M1 city within the land of Zikirtu, which formed part of the kingdom of Mannaea (in mod. Iranian Kurdistan). In 716 it was one of the cities destroyed by the Assyrian king Sargon II when he campaigned in Mannaea against the kingdom's pro-Urartian rebels, including Zikirtu's King Mitatti (*ARAB* II: 28). Zurzukka was another of the cities of Zikirtu destroyed by Sargon during this campaign.

Shubartum see Subartu.

Shubat-Enlil see ***Leilan, Tell.***

Shubat-Shamash Middle Bronze Age city in northwestern Mesopotamia, probably to be located on the left bank of the Euphrates downstream from mod. Birecik, on the caravan route from Aleppo to Harran (thus Durand, *LAPO* 17: 76–7, n. e). Charpin suggests that it may be the Middle Bronze Age city on the site of Tell Ahmar (*Mesop.* 174, n. 818), known later, in M1, as Til-Barsip. The city is mentioned in a number of letters from the Mari archive, particularly in connection with events in 1779. Unrest in the country of Zalmaqum at this time had prompted the Assyrian king Shamshi-Adad I to urge his son Yasmah-Addu, viceroy at Mari, to proceed with his troops to Shubat-Shamash; other forces would join him there, including one led by his brother Ishme-Dagan, viceroy at Ekallatum, for military operations in the region. The catalyst for this action appears to have been a revolt by Larim-Numaha, king of the city of Aparha. For the outcome, see **Aparha**.

Mesop. 174 (with refs).

Shubria (map 20; cf. Kessler 1980: 121, Karte V) M1 country north of the upper Tigris r. across from Tushhan, to the east of the land of Dirru, south of mod. Muş and extending eastwards towards Lake Van, to the frontiers of the kingdom of Urartu. Shubria also lay close to the northern frontier of the Assyrian empire, thus providing the Assyrians in C7 with a useful buffer zone against the Cimmerians. A number of fortresses are attested as belonging to Shubria, including Uppumu and Kulimmeri.

In 854, Shubria was attacked by the Assyrian king Shalmaneser III, who confined its king, Anhitti (Ili-hite), to his city and received tribute from him (**RIMA* 3: 36, 52, 65). Anhitti had previously rendered tribute in the city of Tushhan to Shalmaneser's predecessor, Ashurnasirpal II (**RIMA* 2: 202, 243); in a summary account, Ashurnasirpal refers to Shubria by the older form Shubaru (**RIMA* 2: 221). Shubria occupied a difficult position, sandwiched between two powerful states, Assyria and Urartu. This is reflected in a letter to the Assyrian king Sargon II (721–705) from the governor of Tushhan, who complains of a pro-Urartian bias displayed by the king of Shubria in his treatment of deserters from Urartu, whom he fails to hand over to the Assyrians as expected (**SAA* V:29–30, no. 35). In another letter, the Shubrians are accused of attacking and seizing an Assyrian military cohort sent on a mission to apprehend Assyrian deserters, who had presumably sought refuge in Shubrian territory (**SAA* V: 25–6, no. 32).

In early C7, when fugitives from Assyria, perhaps conspirators involved in the assassination of the Assyrian king Sennacherib (681), sought asylum in Shubria, Sennacherib's son and successor Esarhaddon wrote to Shubria's ruler demanding their extradition. After negotiations had failed to deliver them up, Esarhaddon invaded Shubria in 673, laid siege to its capital, Uppumu, and captured and plundered it (**ABC* 84, 127, *Borger, 1956: 86, 102–7). The fugitives were caught and mutilated. Esarhaddon rebuilt the city and settled deportees there. Shubria was now annexed to Assyria, being incorporated into the new provinces of Uppumu and Kulimmeri (Radner, *RlA* 11: 63) under the governorship of two of Esarhaddon's eunuchs. The fact that it had harboured fugitives no doubt provided Esarhaddon with a welcome pretext for invading and annexing the country. In 657, during the reign of Esarhaddon's successor Ashurbanipal, the Urartians attempted to regain control of Shubria. The attempt failed. The Urartian force was defeated by Ashurbanipal's troops, and its leader was beheaded.

(H. D. Baker)

Kessler (1980: 106–9), Parker (2001: 230–46), Eph῾al (2005).

Shuda Middle Bronze Age royal city in northern Mesopotamia, attested in the Mari texts from the reign of Zimri-Lim (1774–1762). At this time, it was part of the land of Zalmaqum (which consisted of a number of principalities), and was ruled by a king called Sibkuna-Addu. Qattunan's governor, Zakira-Hammu, reports that 800 troops dispatched by Sibkuna-Addu had arrived in his city, apparently en route to Mari for service with Zimri-Lim (**LKM* 438).

Shudu see Sudu.

Shuduhum Middle and Late Bronze Age city in west or central Ida-maras, in the Habur triangle of northern Mesopotamia, first attested in the Mari archives from the reign of Zimri-Lim (1774–1762). At this time, it was ruled by a king called Itur-Malik, who joined with three other kings of the Ida-maras region (Sammetar of Ashnakkum, Tamarzi of the Tarmannians, and Shub-Ram of Kirdahat/Qirdahat) on what was apparently a diplomatic mission to Zimri-Lim (*LKM 418). The city later appears among the conquests of the Assyrian king Adad-nirari I (1307–1275) (*RIMA 1:131).

Shuhpad Middle Bronze Age city in northern Mesopotamia attested in the Mari archives from the reign of Zimri-Lim (1774–1762). It was located near the city of Shubat-Enlil and close to the kingdom of Ilan-sura, whose ruler, Haya-Sumu, claimed possession of Shuhpad. His claim was contested by Atamrum, king of Andarig, who sought to resolve the matter by seizing Shuhpad and installing one of his officials, Mannum-balu-Inana, as its regent. (Perhaps at this time Atamrum also controlled Shubat-Enlil, which lay not far east on one of the Habur's eastern tributaries.) Haya-Sumu complained bitterly to Zimri-Lim, his overlord, about Atamrum's action. Zimri-Lim responded by seeking advice on the matter from his agent in Andarig, a man called Yasim-El. In support of Atamrum, Yasim-El accused Haya-Sumu of making false statements, and reported that the citizens of Shuhpad wanted Atamrum confirmed as their new ruler. He further stated that Atamrum had actually made terms of peace with the city, swearing not to harm or deport any of its inhabitants, while they in turn undertook not to harm Atamrum's regent, or to attempt to restore their city's former king, Haya-Sumu. (At least, this is the version of events reported by Yasim-El to Zimri-Lim; *LKM 349–51.) Though he was already in possession of the city, Atamrum was anxious to maintain his current good relations with Mari, and apparently declared that he was happy to leave to Zimri-Lim a final decision on who Shuhpad's rightful ruler was. The latter called his bluff. It seems that in spite of the recommendations of his Andarig envoy, and the allegedly peaceful overtures of Atamrum, Zimri-Lim did in fact recognize Haya-Sumu's claim to Shuhpad, and wrote to Atamrum telling him to return the city to its former ruler. Atamrum must have been slow to respond. Haya-Sumu subsequently wrote to Zimri-Lim, urging him to ensure that Atamrum complied with his order, and reminding him of earlier undertakings given by Zimri-Lim which had not been fulfilled (*LAPO 16: 484–5, no. 307 = *LKM 502–3).
LKM 115–16.

Shuppu City in the vicinity of Harran in northwestern Mesopotamia, attested in the texts of the Assyrian king Ashur-bel-kala (1073–1056). At this time, Harran was occupied by large numbers of Aramaean tribal groups, and Shuppu was conquered by the Assyrians during one of Ashur-bel-kala's campaigns against the Aramaeans (*RIMA 2: 102). The reading of the place-name is uncertain; Ruppa is also possible.

Shurgadia M1 city in western Iran in the Assyrian province of Nikasamma. In 716 it was one of six of Nikasamma's cities captured by Sargon II, in response to the province's participation in a rebellion against him (*ARAB II: 29). Sargon incorporated the city into the neighbouring province of Parsua, which had remained loyal to Assyria.

Shurnat Middle Bronze Age royal city in central Ida-maras, located in the eastern part of the Habur triangle, northern Mesopotamia. During the reign of Zimri-Lim, king of Mari (1774–1762), its ruler was a man called Zu-Hadni. During his kingship the city was attacked by a force of 2,000 troops dispatched by Hammurabi, king of Kurda. The attackers captured the surrounding countryside and many of its inhabitants, but the townspeople themselves found safe refuge in Shurnat's citadel (**LKM* 360–1). Some years later (third quarter of C18), Till-Abnu, the future king of Apum, resided in Shurnat while his predecessor (and uncle?) Mutiya occupied the throne in the royal capital Shehna/Shubat-Enlil.

Mesop. 350.

Shuru (Shura) Late Bronze Age and Iron Age city in the kingdom of Hanigalbat, identified with mod. Savur to the northeast of Mardin in the Kashiyari range (mod. Tur ʿAdin) (*RGTC* 5: 254). When the Hanigalbatean king Wasashatta rebelled against Assyrian sovereignty, Shuru was among the cities conquered by the Assyrian king Adad-nirari I (1307–1275) in the course of crushing the rebellion (**RIMA* 1: 136). Later, the Assyrian king Ashur-bel-kala (1073–1056) claims to have depopulated the town of Shuru in Hanigalbat while campaigning against the Aramaeans (**RIMA* 2: 102) Ashurnasirpal II (883–859) records a payment of tribute from 'Shura of Hanigalbat' during a campaign in the region in his fifth regnal year (879) (**RIMA* 2: 209). Shura is also attested in later documents (late C8 and possibly also C7).

Radner (2006: 292).

Shurun Late Bronze Age fortified Syrian city located on the west bank of the middle Euphrates within the kingdom of Carchemish. It is listed among the conquests of the Assyrian king Adad-nirari I (1307–1275) (**HDT* 45, **RIMA* 1:131).

Shuruppak (*Fara*) (map 17) Early Bronze Age Sumerian city, extending over 220 ha, in southern Mesopotamia, northeast of Uruk. The site was visited by W. K. Loftus (1850) and W. H. Ward (1885), and later excavated by H. V. Hilprecht (1900), R. Koldewey (1902–3) for the Deutsche Orient-Gesellschaft, and E. Schmidt (1931) for the University of Pennsylvania. It was first settled in the Jemdet Nasr period (end of M4), and thereafter continuously occupied until the end of M2. Already in the Early Dynastic I period (c. 2900–2800), Shuruppak had achieved substantial proportions. Scholars are therefore surprised that its kings are not included among the Early Dynastic III dynasties recorded in the Sumerian King List (**Chav.* 82). It does, however, appear among the five antediluvian cities in this list. During the Ur III period (2112–2004) the city was ruled by a local governor (*ensi*) on behalf of the Ur III administration.

The most important finds from the site are a total of over 800 cuneiform tablets and 1,300 seal impressions. The tablets, discovered in a number of mudbrick buildings across the mound, date to the Early Dynastic IIIA period (mid M3). They are bureaucratic documents, reflecting the complexity of the city's administration in this period, which included the organization of a workforce consisting of thousands of labourers. More generally, the tablets throw valuable light on the social and economic organization of Sumerian society. In literary tradition, Shuruppak was the home of Utnapishtim, the 'Babylonian Noah', who after surviving the great flood took up residence in Dilmun. Gilgamesh visited him there, in his quest for the secret of eternal life.

Shuruppak's end seems not to have come about through violent destruction. Scholars believe that its abandonment at the end of M3 may have been due to environmental factors – above all, a change in the course of the Euphrates. After the Ur III period, it is only mentioned in syllabaries, geographical lists, and literary texts, though a very small amount of evidence for Isin-Larsa period settlement was recovered.

Schmidt (1931), Martin (1988).

Shusharra see *Shemshara, Tell.*

Sibda see Side (2).

Side (1) (*Selimiye*) (map 4) M1 BCE–M1 CE city in Pamphylia, on the central-southern Anatolian coast. It was the region's most important port-city prior to the founding of Attaleia by Attalus II Philadelphus in mid C2. According to Classical tradition, it was established by settlers from Cyme (an Aeolian city on Anatolia's northwestern coast), probably in C7 or early C6. (In fact, the C3 CE scholar Eusebius dates its foundation many centuries earlier, which would in effect take its origins back to the Late Bronze Age. But there is no trace of any settlement of Bronze Age date to support this.) Arrian (*Anabasis* 1.26.4) reports that on their arrival at the site, the colonists forgot their native language and began to speak a strange tongue of their own. Scholars consider this to be a reflection of the indigenous language of Pamphylia, which survives in Sidetan coin legends (C6) and inscriptions (C3) but is not otherwise known. The language, which has yet to be satisfactorily deciphered, apparently disappeared elsewhere in Pamphylia as a result of Greek settlement.Virtually nothing is known of Side's history prior to its voluntary surrender to Alexander the Great in 333. In the late Hellenistic period, it acquired an unsavoury reputation as a base for Cilician pirates and provided a slave market for the sale of their prisoners. The material remains of the city date to the Roman and Byzantine periods.

Bean (1968: 78–100; *PECS* 835–6).

Side (2) M1 Carian city, of Lelegian origin, located in the Myndus peninsula, southwestern Anatolia. It is referred to among the six Carian towns which according to Pliny the Elder (5.107) were assigned by Alexander the Great to the jurisdiction of Halicarnassus. (Their incorporation into Halicarnassus was in fact due to the mid C4 Carian satrap Mausolus prior to Alexander's campaigns.) The city is not otherwise attested in Classical sources unless it can be identified with the city of Sibda referred to by the C6 CE scholar Stephanus of Byzantium. Bean proposed an identification with the remains of the Lelegian-type settlement on the mountain site of Karadağ in the Myndus peninsula.

Bean (1971: 124–6).

Sidon (maps 6, 7) Canaanite and Phoenician city located on the Lebanese coast 43 km south of Beirut. The area was occupied from the late Chalcolithic period (M4, to which the remains of round or oval stone houses belong) through late Roman times. Investigation of the anc. city has been limited by the fact that mod. Sidon overlies much of it, and its two anc. harbours (inner and outer), protected by a breakwater, are now silted up. Following earlier excavations, in the last decades of C19 and early C20 (the latter by G. Contenau of the Louvre Museum), the site was most comprehensively investigated by M. Dunand for the French Archaeological Institute of Beirut from 1924 onwards, and most recently from 1963 to 1968. By the end of the 1968 season, it was estimated that still only a quarter of the anc. city had been brought to light. In 1998, the Directorate-General of Antiquities of Lebanon authorized the British Museum to begin excavations in the city of Saida on an area of land expropriated for archaeological research. Under the directorship of Dr. C. Doumet-Serhal, this excavation has for the first time been revealing the continuous stages in the development of the city from M3 to M1.

First attested in late M3 Babylonian sources, Sidon came under Egyptian control in the Late Bronze Age. It figures prominently in the mid C14 Amarna letters (where it is called Siduna; see Moran, 1992: 391, index refs), particularly within the context of the constant squabbles and conflicts among the pharaoh's Syro-Palestinian vassals. The letters are full of complaints about Sidon's ruler, Zimredda, whom Abi-Milku, the king of Tyre (which lay 40 km to the south), accused of aggression against his own city, and of collaborating with the pharaoh's enemies, most notably Aziru, ruler of the kingdom of Amurru.

The fate of both Sidon and Tyre at the end of the Bronze Age remains uncertain. A later Classical tradition that Tyre was refounded and settled by colonists from Sidon might suggest that either or both cities succumbed to the C12 upheavals which accompanied the collapse of the Bronze Age civilizations. But there is no archaeological evidence to support such an assumption. In any case, both cities were, or had become, flourishing centres of trade and commerce by the end of M2, and were among the most prosperous of the Iron Age Phoenician cities. The Assyrian king Tiglath-pileser I (1114–1076) reports receiving tribute from Sidon (and also from Byblos and Arwad) in the context of his campaign in the west against the land of Amurru (*RIMA*

Figure 109 Sidon harbour.

2: 37, 53). The C11 Egyptian *Tale of Wenamun* text refers to fifty merchant ships in Sidon's harbour (**CS* I: 91). Indeed, Sidon was probably the first of the Phoenician cities to engage in overseas merchant enterprises. These, coupled with the highly sought products of the city's weavers and gold-, silver-, and copper-smiths, accounted for much of Sidon's wealth. The Sidonians appear to have been the first Phoenicians to establish trading contacts with the Greek world. Homer refers to the elaborately wrought robes which the Trojan prince Paris brought back from the land of Sidon (*Iliad* 6.289–92). By early M1 Sidon had become one of the most important Phoenician cities, rivalling even if subordinate to Tyre. It was the mother city of many commercial colonies established along the Mediterranean coastlands.

Inevitably Sidon, together with other Phoenician cities, attracted the attention of the Assyrians. The region came under Assyrian domination for a second time in the reign of Ashurnasirpal II (883–859), who exacted tribute from all the Phoenician cities. Adad-nirari III (810–783) also records receiving tribute from both Sidon and Tyre (**RIMA* 3: 211, 213). But the Sidonians, like the inhabitants of many other Syro-Palestinian cities and kingdoms, constantly rose up against their overlords, and their city was the object of a number of campaigns by later Assyrian kings, including Shalmaneser V, Sennacherib, and Esarhaddon. The last of these destroyed Sidon, captured and beheaded its king, Abdi-milkutti, and deported many of its people to other parts of his realm, replacing them with new settlers from the east (**ARAB* II: 211–12). Sidon revived and regained its prosperity, only to be conquered again by the Babylonian king Nebuchadnezzar II (605–562).

Following the fall of Babylon, Sidon once more revived and prospered, this time under Persian sovereignty. The territory it controlled was expanded, and it now surpassed Tyre in importance, due no doubt to the fact that it proved more amenable to Persian overlordship. An apadana-style (see glossary) Persian building may have been erected in the city, if one can so judge from the discovery there in C19 CE of a double-bull capital, which is a typical feature of Persian royal architecture. Sidon may have been one of the Phoenician cities which provided forces for the Persian king Cambyses' Egyptian campaign in 526. A sarcophagus intended originally for an Egyptian general and acquired presumably by plunder was used for the interment of a king of Sidon called Tabnit, who probably ruled briefly during the second quarter of C5 (see *CS* II: 182, n. 1). The sarcophagus, which contained Tabnit's mummified remains, bore an eight-line Phoenician inscription, beneath the earlier Egyptian hieroglyphic text, identifying Tabnit and warning against violation of his tomb (**CS* II: 181–2).

Sidon finally turned against its Persian overlords, rebelling against Artaxerxes III on his accession in 359. The city's ruler, Tennes, led the rebellion (Diodorus 16.42). As Persian retaliation became imminent, Tennes lost his nerve and betrayed his city to the Persians (Diodorus 16.43, 45). Sidon was put to the torch, but yet again rose from its ashes, in time to support Alexander the Great twenty years later in his siege and conquest of Tyre. It is not surprising that Sidon, still not fully recovered from the Persian sack, should welcome the opportunity to gain ascendancy over its long-time rival Tyre. After Alexander's death, the city came first under Ptolemaic and subsequently under Seleucid control. In 64, it was granted autonomy by the Roman general Pompey the Great. In the Hellenistic and Roman periods Sidon enjoyed a resurgence of its prosperity, becoming famous during the former period as a centre of glass production.

The various excavations in and around the anc. city have brought to light a number of cemeteries, tombs, and sarcophaguses dating to the Middle and Late Bronze Ages, and from Babylonian to late Roman times. The best-known funerary monument from the city is the so-called Alexander sarcophagus (actually the coffin of a local ruler with scenes featuring Alexander carved upon it), now in the Istanbul Archaeological Museum. Of particular interest is the black basalt sarcophagus, discovered in 1855, of the Sidonian king Eshmunazar II (mid C5), son of Tabnit. It came to light in the cemetery at Magharat Abloun, which lay to the southeast of Sidon. From a 22-line Phoenician inscription on the sarcophagus (**CS* II: 182–3, **PE* 663–4, no. 45), we learn that Sidon was granted possession of the cities of Dor and Joppa, which lay to the south of Tyre. Eshmunazar also claimed to have built temples for the goddess Astarte in Sidon, and a temple for Eshmun, the Phoenician god of healing. A temple dedicated to Eshmun was in fact discovered 4 km north of Sidon on the bank of the el-Awali r. It was first investigated by Maqridi Bey in 1901 and 1902, and subsequently by G. Contenau and M. Dunand respectively. Contenau discovered a funerary grotto, a stone sarcophagus, a Greek inscription, and three Phoenician inscriptions. The inscriptions indicate that the temple was built for Eshmun by the Sidonian king Bodashtart. It continued in use as a centre of healing into the early Christian period (C5 CE). An earthquake in the following century (551 CE) appears to have left Sidon largely in ruins.

Dunand (1966; 1967; 1969), Khalifeh (*OEANE* 5: 38–41), Doumet-Serhal (1998–9).

Sidqum Middle Bronze Age city located in the kingdom of Karana in northeastern Mesopotamia, near Karana's border with (northern) Yamutbal. A peace treaty was concluded here between Ashkur-Addu and Atamrum, the kings of Karana and Andarig respectively during the reign of Zimri-Lim, king of Mari (1774–1762) (**LKM* 343–6). There was another city called Sidqum which lay relatively close by in the Mt Saggar (Jebel Sinjar) region.

LKM 133–5.

Sigeum (map 5) M1 Aeolian Greek city located in the Troad in northwestern Anatolia. Its location near the Hellespont gave it considerable strategic significance, and in C7 it became Athens' first overseas possession. Athens subsequently lost control over it to the city of Mytilene on the island of Lesbos. But the Athenian tyrant Pisistratus (560–527) regained it by force of arms, and placed it under the rule of his illegitimate son Hegesistratus (Herodotus 5.94–5). Subsequently, Sigeum served as a place of refuge for Hippias, son and successor of Pisistratus (Thucydides 6.59.4), who was forced to flee from Athens in 510 after the Spartan king Cleomenes invaded Attica. In C5 the city became a conspicuously loyal member of the Athenian Confederacy (see glossary), initially paying an annual tribute of 1,000 drachmas, which by 418 had increased sixfold to one talent. In C3 Sigeum was conquered by Alexander the Great's former general, Lysimachus, and was later, according to Strabo (13.1.39), destroyed by Ilium.

Hornblower (*OCD* 1406).

Sikayauvatish M1 fortress in Media, western Iran, in the district of Nisaya. Here, in 522, the soon-to-be Persian king Darius (I) overthrew and killed the priest (magus)

Gaumata who, on the pretence that he was Bardiya, brother of the previous king Cambyses II, had occupied the Persian throne for six months (March/April–September 522) (*DB* 11–13).

Sikkan (Sikanu) see ***Feberiye, Tell.***

Sikkur Late Bronze Age and Iron Age city in northern Mesopotamia, attested along with the city Sappanu in the inscriptions of the Assyrian king Adad-nirari II (911–891). During the Late Bronze Age, both cities had been subject to Assyria, but had withheld tribute and taxes since the reign of Tukulti-Ninurta I (1244–1208), according to Adad-nirari. Owing to their location in rugged mountain terrain, their defiance of Assyrian authority had remained unpunished until Adad-nirari led a campaign against them in 896, following one of his expeditions earlier in the year into the land of Hanigalbat. The cities were placed under siege, conquered, and plundered, along with all other cities in the region (**RIMA* 2: 152). Adad-nirari thus restored Assyrian sovereignty over the recalcitrant cities, and imposed heavy new taxes and dues upon them.

Sillyum M1 BCE–M1 CE city in Pamphylia, southern Anatolia, located on a 210 m high flat-topped hill 28 km northeast of Antalya (*BAGRW* 65 E4). To judge from the name Mopsus which was discovered on a statue base in the city, Sillyum was one of a number of settlements in southern Anatolia whose foundation was associated with the legendary Mopsus. It was probably settled in C7 or C6, by Greek colonists of mixed origin. In C5 it became a member of the Athenian Confederacy (see glossary), appearing in the Athenian Tribute Lists for the year 425. In 333 it defended itself successfully against the army of Alexander the Great – and was in fact the only Pamphylian city to resist Alexander.

Sillyum's material remains, which include fortifications, a poorly preserved city gate, a small temple, a theatre and an odeum (a small, roofed theatre used for musical performances), domestic architecture, and simple rectangular tombs, date almost entirely to the Hellenistic, Roman, and Byzantine periods.

Bean (1968: 59–66; *PECS* 840).

Simena (***Kale***, formerly ***Kekova***) (map 15) Small M1 BCE–M1 CE hill city overlooking the central coast of Lycia, southwestern Anatolia, 11 km west of Myra. Its origins date back at least to early C4, since one of its tombs bears a text in the native Lycian language. (The language is attested in inscriptions dating to C5 and early C4.) Most of Simena's remains, which include baths, numerous tombs, a small rock-cut theatre, and a stoa, are of Hellenistic or Roman date. A portion of the city's anc. fortifications, made up of sections of polygonal masonry, can be seen on the southern part of the site. On the northern part are the remains of a well-preserved mediaeval castle.

Bean (1978: 116–17; *PECS* 841).

Simesi Mountain land in the border region between northeastern Mesopotamia and northwestern Iran. The Assyrian king Shalmaneser III passed through and received tribute from it at the beginning of his northern campaign against Hubushkia, the Nairi lands, and Urartu in his accession year (859) (**RIMA* 3: 8, 14).

Simirra District and city belonging to the Iron Age northern Syrian kingdom of Hamath and located on the Levantine coast. It was among the Hamathite cities which the Assyrian king Tiglath-pileser III claims to have annexed in 738 (*Tigl. III* 186–7), and was used by Tiglath-pileser as a place of resettlement for Assyrian deportees from the east (**Tigl. III* 66–7). But it did not readily accept Assyrian overlordship. In 721, on the accession of the Assyrian king Sargon II, it joined the cities Arpad, Damascus, and Samaria in a rebellion against Assyrian rule, under the leadership of the last known Hamathite king, Yaubidi (**CS* II: 293, 296). The rebellion was crushed by Sargon in the following year. Yaubidi was captured and flayed alive.

Simirra is probably the Iron Age descendant of Late Bronze Age Sumur (q.v.), well known from the mid C14 Amarna correspondence and commonly identified with the site of Tell Kazel at the mouth of the mod. Nahr el-Kabir r. (Classical Eleutheros). The city is attested as Simyra in Classical sources.

CHLI I: 401 (with refs), Lipiński (2000: 287).

Simurrum Early Bronze Age city in northeastern Mesopotamia, located, as recently proposed by D. R. Frayne, on the upper course of the Diyala r. W. W. Hallo observes that it represents the gateway to Hurrian territory 'from the Mesopotamian point of view'. First attested in the record of the eastern campaigns of the Akkadian king Sargon (2334–2279), it was conquered by Sargon's third successor Naram-Sin (**DaK* 51), and subsequently came into conflict with rulers of the Ur III dynasty (2112–2004), no doubt because of its valuable strategic location east of the Tigris. One of the regnal years of the Ur III dynasty's second ruler Shulgi is called 'the year Simurrum was destroyed for the third time' (**RIME* 3/2: 104–5). Hallo suggests that this may have involved Shulgi's crowning achievement. In the period just after the Ur III dynasty fell (late C21), Simurrum was ruled by a king called Iddi-Sin, a contemporary of Ishbi-Erra who founded the Isin dynasty. Iddi-Sin was succeeded in Simurrum by his son Zabazuna (**RIME* 4: 707–16). In later lexical tradition, Simurrum is equated with Zabban (q.v.), which places it firmly on the Diyala r.

Hallo (1978), Frayne (1997a).

Sinabu see **Shinamu(m)**.

Sinnuwanta Late Bronze Age frontier settlement in southern Anatolia, perhaps to be identified with mod. Sinanti. Sinnuwanta and the cities of Zunahara and Adaniya are listed in consecutive lines in a fragmentary text which records a campaign undertaken by the Hittite king Arnuwanda I in southern Anatolia in early C14 (*Carruba, 1977: 167). In the following century, a treaty drawn up between the Hittite king Hattusili III and Ulmi-Teshub (Kurunta), ruler of the appanage Hittite kingdom of Tarhuntassa, locates Sinnuwanta in the border zone between Hatti and the Hulaya River Land (**HDT* 110, 115).

Sinope (map 4) Greek colony founded on the south shore of the Black Sea in mid C8 by settlers from Miletus. Its founder, Habrondas (Abron), was allegedly killed by the Cimmerians (Pseudo-Skymnos 986–7). According to Herodotus (4.12), the Cimmerians themselves settled the site after their flight into Asia from the Scythians in the second half of C8. Milesians subsequently resettled there in 631. The above chronology, which follows Classical sources, is disputed by some scholars who date Sinope's original foundation by Milesian colonists to late C7. The promontory on which the colony was located was fertile and easily defensible. It was well known for its excellent fishing grounds (tunny fish were particularly abundant), though the region's rich metal deposits are now thought to have been the prime motive for Greek settlement. Cinnabar (Sinopic earth) was one of the items for which merchants from Anatolia and other lands traded. Sinope established many colonies of its own along the Black Sea coast. In 437 the Athenian military commander Pericles helped rid the city of its tyrant, Timesilaus, and arranged for the settlement of 600 Athenians there (Plutarch, *Pericles* 20). Except for a brief period in C4 when it was captured and occupied by the Persian satrap Datames (c. 375), Sinope seems to have maintained its independence until its occupation by Pharnaces I, king of Pontus, in 183.

Broughton, Mitchell (*OCD* 1412).

Sipirmena Iron Age city in the land of Zamua, which was located in the borderlands between northeastern Mesopotamia and northwestern Iran, to the east of the upper Diyala r. (Liverani, 1992: 54, and map, fig. 5). The Assyrian king Ashurnasirpal II reports receiving tribute from it during his third campaign against Zamua in 880 (**RIMA* 2: 207). He comments that the inhabitants of the land 'do their hair like women'.

Sippar (*Abu Habbah, Tell*) (maps 10, 11, 17) City in northern Babylonia, located on the east bank of the Euphrates at its closest approach to the Tigris. Within the walled city are two mounds, a southwestern one joined to a much smaller northeastern one, covering a total area of c. 100 ha. The nearby site of Sippar-Amnānum (Tell ed-Der) was also sometimes known simply as Sippar. Abu Habbah's history of occupation extends from M4 (Uruk period) until C2 CE. It enjoyed particular prominence in the Sumerian (M3), Old Babylonian (early M2), and Neo-Babylonian (esp. C6) periods. There have been a number of excavations on the site, some of the earliest of which, in C19, brought to light many thousands of cuneiform tablets, now housed in the British Museum. In more recent years, excavations were conducted by an Iraqi team from the University of Baghdad, beginning in 1978, under the direction of Walid al-Jadir, and continuing through the 1980s. A sounding was made on the city wall in 1972–3 by a team excavating at nearby Tell ed-Der. In 2000, German archaeologists working on behalf of the Deutsches Archäologisches Institut participated in a joint excavation with the University of Baghdad. The city wall – unusually, but like that of nearby Tell ed-Der – took the form of a continuous earthen rampart, with no apparent gates. It has been suggested that it was built this way to serve as a defence against flooding.

In M3, Sippar was the centre of an important Sumerian city-state. According to the Sumerian King List, it was the fourth of five cities upon which kingship was bestowed by heaven in the period before the great flood (**Chav.* 82). During the Early Dynastic period (c. 2900–2334), it was one of only fourteen major cities listed in the sources for the whole of Sumer and Akkad. Excavations revealed that Sippar's main secular quarter occupied the site's northeastern mound, while the southwestern mound contained Sippar's religious quarter, where temples and a ziggurat (see glossary) were located. The dominant temple, the Ebabbar ('White Temple'), was dedicated to the city's chief god, Shamash. During the Old Babylonian period (early M2) the city was noted for its *gagûm*, a cloister which provided quarters for a special 'chaste' group of women called *nadītu*, who were devoted to the worship of Shamash. Hammurabi's law code (C18) indicates that these women also occupied quarters outside the cloister, perhaps some of the two-roomed houses dating to the period C19–17 which came to light during the Iraqi excavations.

These excavations also uncovered, in the temple of the god Shamash, a library of Persian date (C6), containing 60,000–70,000 tablet fragments. Hundreds of tablets were found in their original pigeonholes. Most of the texts were literary in character, and include Standard Babylonian recensions of 'classics' like the Atrahasis myth, as well as a historical text purportedly written in the name of the C23 Akkadian king Manishtushu but actually composed much later, and texts of Hammurabi's reign. The earliest *dated* text belongs to the reign of Adad-apla-iddina (1069–1048), eighth king of the Second Dynasty of Isin. Sippar was among the Babylonian cities which were afflicted by the Aramaean and Sutaean invasions of southern Mesopotamia during his reign (**ABC* 180–1, **RIMB* 2: 73). The Elamite king Shutruk-Nahhunte I (1185–1155) claims to have carried off from Sippar a stele with an inscription of the Akkadian king Naram-Sin on it, which he replaced with an inscription of his own, dedicating the stele to his god Inshushinak (**DaK* 92).

In early C11 Sippar was among the Babylonian cities captured by the Assyrian king Tiglath-pileser I (other captured cities were Dur-Kurigalzu, Opis, and Babylon itself) (**RIMA* 2: 43). It was also one of the Babylonian cities to suffer from the devastating raids inflicted on southern Mesopotamia by Aramaean/Sutaean tribal groups in early M1 (as well as in late M2). The invaders were eventually overthrown and driven from the land by the Babylonian king Nabu-apla-iddina (888–855). A decade or so before this, the Assyrian king Tukulti-Ninurta II encamped his troops outside the city during his last recorded campaign (885) which took him into northern Babylonia and the middle Euphrates region (**RIMA* 2: 174). Elsewhere, Tukulti-Ninurta includes Sippar among the cities and countries which he subjugated during his reign (**RIMA* 2: 180).

In the course of his own long reign, the Babylonian Nabu-apla-iddina provided for the restoration on a lavish scale of Sippar's cult establishments. A new statue of the god Shamash was made and duly consecrated, to replace the statue of the god which had been lost during the upheavals from which the city had suffered two centuries earlier. Thenceforth, Sippar maintained its traditional status as one of southern Mesopotamia's most important religious centres. An Elamite army occupied the city in 675, but withdrew shortly after, probably on receipt of news that the Elamite king Humban-haltash II had died. Shamash-shum-ukin (son of the Assyrian king Esarhaddon), who occupied the Babylonian throne from 667 to 648, restored the city's walls and its Ebabbar temple (**RIMB* 2: 249–51). The Ebabbar was again rebuilt in mid C6 by Nabonidus, the last of the Neo-Babylonian kings. According to the Nabonidus Chronicle (see glossary), the Persian king Cyrus II marched upon the city and captured it without a battle, following his victory over the forces of Nabonidus at Opis on the Tigris r. in 539 (**ABC* 109, **CS* I: 468, **Chav.* 420, **PE* 51, no. 1). Sippar continued to be occupied into the Hellenistic era and is occasionally mentioned in chronicle texts of that time.

Gasche and Janssen (*OEANE* 5: 47–9).

Sippar-Amnānum see *Der, Tell-ed.*

Sipylus (*Manisa Dağ*) (map 5) Mountain range in western Anatolia, located in the mod. Turkish province of Manisa, 30 km northeast of Izmir. In the Late Bronze Age it lay within the Arzawan kingdom called Mira, and in M1 was part of the kingdom of Lydia. According to Homer (*Iliad* 24.615–16), Sipylus was a resting place of the nymphs. A noteworthy survival from the Late Bronze Age is a much weathered rock relief, with accompanying hieroglyphic inscription, which is generally interpreted as a seated goddess, perhaps the Luwian mother goddess (E. Akurgal, 1976: plate XXII). She (or he – the figure may be male) appears to be wearing a headdress shaped like a walled city. Stylistic comparisons with other rock reliefs at Karabel, Yazılıkaya, and Fraktin indicate a C13 date for the monument. Collins (2007: 128) notes that the monument is unique among Hittite sculptures in presenting a deity fully frontal and in high relief. According to Classical tradition, it depicted the princess Niobe, whose sons and daughters had been killed by Apollo and Artemis. Niobe, consumed with grief, was transformed into a rock on Mt Sipylus, which was forever moist with tears. The anc. Greek travel writer Pausanias (1.21.3) observes that though the rock is a natural phenomenon, it does in fact bear a resemblance to a weeping woman.

Sirani Iron Age city in the middle Euphrates kingdom of Masuwari. G. Bunnens suggests an identification with Middle Bronze Age Ziranum, attested in the Mari archives and located in the region of Carchemish, and with mod. Serrin, opposite Qalaat Nejem on the east bank of the Euphrates.

Bunnens (2006: 94).

Sirkeli (map 2) Predominantly Late Bronze Age Hittite city, dominated by a 30 m high oval-shaped mound, located on the Ceyhan r. in southeastern Anatolia (Classical Cilicia), 40 km east of mod. Adana. The site is currently being excavated by Eberhard Karls Universität, Tübingen, and the Çannakale Onsekiz Mart Üniversitesi, under the joint direction of K. Volk and M. Novák (from the former) and E. Kozal (from the latter). One of the objectives of these excavations is a complete reconstruction of Sirkeli's settlement system and its chronological and historical development. Occupation of the site extended back to the Chalcolithic Age (M5–4), and then continued through the Bronze and Iron Ages and the Hellenistic period. The Hittite city covered an area of c. 300 m × 400 m. It appears to have reached the peak of its development in the first half of C13. To this period belong two rock reliefs, located close to each other. The better preserved one depicts the Hittite king Muwattalli II (1295–1272). We know his identity from the accompanying hieroglyphic inscription. The king wears priestly garb consisting of close-fitting skull cap and long robe, and he carries the *kalmus*, the curved staff which symbolizes his religious office. It is the oldest Hittite rock relief so far known. The identity of the figure in the second relief (mutilated already in antiquity) is uncertain, though he is thought to represent one of Muwattalli's two known sons, Kurunta or Urhi-Teshub (Mursili III). An assemblage of pits or basins found near the reliefs is believed by the current excavators to form part of a cultic installation for the Hittite king. Other finds from the site include a column base, dating probably to C10 (and thus of the Neo-Hittite period) in the form of two lions, a Middle Bronze Age figurine of north Syrian style, a Phrygian bronze fibula dating to c. 700, and seals and sealings of various periods. A cemetery of Hellenistic date has been located in the west of the settlement.

Bittel (1976: 174–5, figs. 195, 197), Hrouda (1997), http://www.sirkeli-project.info/en/index.html (for current excavations).

Sirqu see Terqa.

Sissu Iron Age city in or near the country of Que in southern Anatolia. Along with the nearby city of Kundu, it seems to have formed a small sub-kingdom within Que, bordering on the Cilician plain. In early C7 it was ruled by a man called Sanduarri who allied himself with Abdi-milkutti, ruler of Sidon, in a rebellion against the Assyrian king Esarhaddon (**ARAB* II: 212) (see **Kundu**). Sissu and Kundu have been tentatively placed within the region of mod. Kozan (formerly Sis), where the site of Classical Sisium is located, to the northeast of Adana. Sissu is perhaps to be identified with Sisium.

Hawkins (1982: 427–8; *CHLI* I: 43).

Siyannu and Ushnati Closely linked Late Bronze Age kingdoms on the coast of northern Syria, dependencies of the kingdom of Ugarit. Siyannu and Ushnati were also the names of the chief cities in their kingdoms, which included a number of smaller towns and communities. In accordance with the terms of a treaty drawn up by the Hittite king Mursili II (1321–1295) with Niqmepa, king of Ugarit, a substantial portion of Ugarit's territory, including the kingdom of Siyannu, was assigned to the Hittite viceregal kingdom of Carchemish (**PRU* IV: 71–81). This was apparently in response to an appeal from Siyannu's king, Abdianati, who had sought to sever his country's links with Ugarit in favour of an attachment to Carchemish. Mursili also used the treaty to resolve disputes over a number of towns in the border region between Ugarit and Siyannu by formally assigning these towns to Ugarit. It is not clear from the texts whether Siyannu and Ushnati continued to be linked, and if not, what the eventual fate of Ushnati was after Siyannu was reassigned to Carchemish.

But both cities re-emerge in Iron Age Assyrian texts. In 853 they supplied troops to the coalition army which confronted, and was defeated by, the Assyrian king Shalmaneser III in the battle of Qarqar (q.v.) (**RIMA* 3: 23). They are again attested in the list of cities and districts of the kingdom of Hamath conquered by the Assyrian king Tiglath-pileser III (745–727) (**Tigl. III* 148–9). And they appear in Tiglath-pileser's Annals (Ushnati in the form Usnu) among the cities where the king resettled deportees from other parts of his kingdom (**Tigl. III* 66–7).

Ushnati/Usnu has been identified with Tell Daruk, 9 km north of Banyas, where in 1959 P. J. Riis, on behalf of the Carlsberg Expedition to Phoenicia, undertook a sounding to bedrock. The results showed a long history of occupation from the Chalcolithic period (M5) to mediaeval times. Siyannu is most probably to be identified with Tell Sianu, situated inland, approximately halfway between Latakia and Tartous. Excavations conducted there since 1990 by A. Bounni and M. Al-Maqdissi for the Syrian Dept of Antiquities have uncovered important Bronze and Iron Age remains, including a large fortified citadel dating to C8.

Oldenburg and Rohweder (1981), Al-Maqdissi (1995: 159–63).

Smyrna (*Bayraklı*) (map 5) City on the gulf of Smyrna, located on the western coast of Anatolia, 4 km north of mod. Izmir. Its history of occupation extends from the beginning of M3 through the Roman imperial period. The site was settled by colonists from mainland Greece in the last century of M2, within the context of the Aeolian and Ionian migrations to Anatolia's Aegean coastlands. The earliest surviving remains of Greek settlement are those of private houses dating back to early C9. Smyrna is one of seven towns believed by the anc. Greeks to be the birthplace of the epic poet Homer. According to Herodotus (1.16), it was settled by colonists from Colophon, which lay 40 km to the south. But it remained little more than an agricultural village until mid C7, when it became a fortified city with well laid out streets. The remains of private residences of megaron type, consisting of a porch and two rooms, belong to this period. Small finds unearthed from these houses include bird bowls, vases, and bronze, ivory, and terracotta figurines. Smyrna's prosperity in this period was due in part to its international trading contacts, as indicated by the discovery on the site of statuettes of Cypriot and Syrian origin, and after 580 by black-figure pottery from Attica in mainland Greece. A first temple dedicated to the goddess Athena was built in the city in the third quarter of C7. It was destroyed along with much of the rest of Smyrna by the Lydian king Alyattes c. 600, who forced the population to abandon the city and live in villages outside it.

Over the next two decades, the population gradually returned, and rebuilt their houses and the temple, enlarging the latter's precinct. The rebuilding programme is also illustrated by M. Akurgal's recent excavations of a necropolis dating to the first half of C6. These have revealed, outside an earlier city wall (c. 640–620), a second city wall of polygonal masonry built in 600–590 shortly after the Lydian attack. But further devastation followed c. 545, when the Persians attacked the city, destroying once more the temple of Athena. Through the next two centuries of Persian rule, Smyrna remained a small and insignificant city. But in the period following Alexander the Great's conquests in 334, it benefited from the urban development of the western Anatolian region under various Hellenistic rulers. Old Smyrna now proved too small to accommodate its rapidly increasing population, so a new, larger city was established on the slope of Mt Pagus. According to Greek tradition, Alexander himself chose this as the site for the new city, after he was instructed to do so in a dream he had while sleeping under a plane tree on the mountain. By the time of the Greek geographer Strabo (14.1.37), who wrote in the early Roman imperial period, Smyrna was the most beautiful of the Ionian cities. It was largely destroyed in an earthquake in 178 CE, but was reconstructed with the help of the Roman emperor Marcus Aurelius.

E. Akurgal (1973: 119–24; *PECS* 847–8), M. Akurgal (2006).

Soba (Aram-Zobah, Bet Rehob) (map 7) Iron Age Aramaean city and kingdom located in the Biqaʿ valley, Lebanon, between the Lebanon and Antilebanon ranges and the kingdoms of Hamath and Damascus. Lipiński suggests that the kingdom came into existence in early C10, when it was founded by the clan or dynasty of Rehob in the Biqaʿ valley. This provides an explanation for the existence of the two names Soba and Bet Rehob, *contra* the assumption of two originally separate Aramaean states which eventually amalgamated. The location of Soba's chief city (also called Soba) has yet to be precisely determined. Called Subutu in Assyrian records, it was in the early decades of C8 part of the kingdom of Hamath, after having perhaps become a vassal state of Hamath in mid C9. Before the end of C8 it had been incorporated into the Assyrian empire and became the administrative centre of an Assyrian province, as attested in the

Eponym Chronicle (see glossary). Other cities which lay within the province were Labau (Labwa), Sazana, and Huzaza (**SAA* I : 138–41, nos 176–9).

In *OT* tradition, Zobah became an arch rival of the early kingdom of Israel. Already in the reign of the Israelite king Saul, it was among Israel's enemies whom Saul fought and defeated (1 Samuel 14:47). But it was in the reign of Saul's successor David that Zobah posed the most serious threat to Israel. At that time, its throne was occupied by a king called Hadadezer who built his kingdom into a powerful state by annexing territories in eastern Syria across to the Euphrates r. In a military showdown fought between Israel and Zobah near the Euphrates, David defeated Hadadezer's forces, captured 1,000 of his chariots, 7,000 charioteers, and 20,000 infantry. He then plundered Zobah's subject territories and allies, reducing many of them to tributary status (2 Samuel 8:3–12). This effectively put an end to Zobah as a significant political and military power in the Syro-Palestinian region. None of these events is attested in extra-biblical sources.

Kuhrt (1995a: 400, 451, 456), King (*HCBD* 1247), Lipiński (2000: 319–45, with refs).

Socoh Iron Age city in northern Judah, attested in *OT* tradition. The Philistines assembled there for war with Israel (Samuel 17:1). In late C10 it was conquered by the pharaoh Sheshonq I (biblical Shishak) (945–924), but was subsequently restored to the kingdom of Judah. In C8, however, during the reign of the Judaean king Ahaz (735–715), it was among the towns of southern Judah which fell to the Philistines, according to 2 Chronicles 28:18. An identification has been suggested with Khirbet Abbad, a fortified Iron Age settlement located above the Elah valley.

Another site called Socoh is attested in *OT* tradition in the hill country of southern Judah (Joshua 15:48).

Negev and Gibson (2001: 475).

Sodom City attested only in *OT* sources where it is a byword for wickedness and depravity. According to Genesis and Deuteronomy, it was one of the five destroyed 'Cities of the Plain'. Genesis 13:12 relates that prior to their destruction, Abraham's nephew Lot chose to live among them, pitching his tents near Sodom. A quasi-historical reference to the city occurs in Genesis 14:1, which relates that Bera, king of Sodom, joined forces with other kings in the region for a war against the Elamite king Chedorlaomer. There is a common belief that Sodom's remains lie somewhere to the south of the Dead Sea or under the southern end of the sea, but attempts to locate these remains have proved unsuccessful. A late M3 or early M2 date has been proposed for the city, primarily on the basis of patterns of urban settlement to the east and south of the Dead Sea in this period, but also because of the traditional chronology assigned to the patriarchal narratives. The historical authenticity of the city remains highly doubtful. Some scholars have suggested an identification with Bab edh-Dhra (q.v.), an Early Bronze Age city in Jordan, on the plain near the southeastern end of the Dead Sea. An alternative suggestion is that it is located at Tall el Hammam in Jordan, currently being excavated by S. Collins of Trinity Southwest University College, USA.

Dearman (*HCBD* 1046), Cline (2007: 39–60).

Sogdiana (Subdastan) (map 16) Country, attested in M1 Iranian and Greek texts, located between the Oxus and Jaxartes rivers in the region of mod. Uzbekistan and

Kazakhstan, Central Asia. It was among the eastern lands of the Persian empire listed several times in the inscriptions of Darius I (522–486), e.g. in his Bisitun inscription (**DB* 6), and also in the *daiva* inscription (see glossary) of his son and successor Xerxes (**XPh* 3). Lapis lazuli and carnelian were brought from Sogdiana for use in the construction of Darius' palace at Susa (**DSf* 10, **DSz* 9). Herodotus (3.93) lists the country as one of the components of the Persian empire's sixteenth province (but see glossary under **satrapy**). Cyrus II (559–530), founder of the empire, established the city of Cyropolis (Cyreschata) in Sogdiana, on the banks of the Jaxartes. But the country's chief city was Maracanda (mod. Samarkand), situated in the valley of the Zarafshan r. A Persian royal palace was probably located there. Sogdians appear in the Persepolis Fortification Tablets (see under **Persepolis**; **PF* 325, no. 1118; 338, no. 1175) among the labour force recruited by the Persian Great King from all parts of his empire, and also among the troops recruited by Xerxes (486–465), according to Herodotus (7.66), for his invasion of Greece in 481. The conquest of Maracanda by Alexander the Great in 329 has been suggested as the chief reason for the diaspora of the Sogdians, and their establishment of trading colonies along the caravan routes between China and the west.

Soli (1) (map 14) City on the northwest coast of Cyprus, on the Bay of Morphou, consisting of an acropolis and lower city. Its history of occupation probably extends back at least to the Late Bronze Age (though the earliest attested remains are those of early Iron Age, C11, pottery) and continues until the Arab conquests in C7 CE. For much of this period a considerable portion of the city's income was derived from the exploitation of the copper mines which lay in the mountains to the south of the city. Excavations on the site were conducted initially by E. Gjerstad in 1926 for the Swedish Cyprus Expedition, with subsequent excavations by Laval University, Quebec, from 1964 to 1974, commenced under the direction of J. des Gagniers.

According to a legendary tradition recorded by Plutarch (*Solon* 26), Soli was founded by Demophon, son of the Athenian hero Theseus. Plutarch further states that the city was originally called Aipeia, until the C6 Athenian statesman Solon visited it and persuaded its king, Philocyprus, to shift it closer to the sea. Solon allegedly took charge of the re-establishment of the city, making it so attractive that new settlers flocked to it. Out of gratitude for Solon's services, Philocyprus renamed his city after him. In historical records the city is first attested at the beginning of C5, when its king, Aristocyprus, joined other local rulers under the hegemony of Onesilus, king of Salamis, in an uprising against Persia at the time of the Ionian rebellion which broke out in 499 (Herodotus 5.113). The Cypriot alliance was decisively defeated by the Persians in a battle outside the city of Salamis in 498. Both Onesilus and Aristocyprus were killed in the conflict. The Persians subsequently laid siege to Soli, now a well-fortified city, which held out for five months before it was finally taken.

Little else is known of Soli's history. It very likely remained under Persian domination until its liberation by Alexander the Great, after which it became part of the Ptolemaic empire. Ptolemy abolished all the kingdoms of Cyprus except Soli, where the king Pasicrates reigned at this time. He had only one successor, Eunostus, probably his son. From inscriptions, we know the names of two other kings of Soli, Stasias and Stasicrates. Both probably reigned in C4.

The city's material remains include an Archaic (C6) Greek temple on the acropolis, and several buildings dating back to the Archaic period in the lower city. In the city's eastern necropolis, several tombs of the Cypro-Geometric period – the oldest structures so far discovered in Soli – have come to light. Tombs of Archaic date have also been discovered. However, most of the city's remains, including the theatre on the acropolis, belong to the Hellenistic and Roman periods. In the latter period Soli reached the peak of its development, its prosperity then due very largely to full exploitation of the copper mines. The city continued to prosper into the Byzantine period, to judge from the imposing Christian basilica built there, even though by this time mining activity had diminished and the city's harbour had largely silted up.

Gjerstad (*SCE* III: 399–582), Nicolaou (*PECS* 850–1), Ginouvès (1989).

Soli (2) (map 4) M1 BCE–M1 CE city on the coast of Cilicia Pedias/Campestris (Smooth Cilicia), southeastern Anatolia, 11 km west of Mersin. According to Greek sources, it was founded in C8 by colonists from Argos in the Peloponnese, mainland Greece, and from Lindos on the island of Rhodes. However, a Late Bronze Age level has been identified beneath the Iron Age and later Hellenistic levels. The mound on this level was the focus of excavations begun in 1999 by a Turkish team under the direction of R. Yağcı. In the course of these excavations, a large assemblage of imported ceramic ware of Cypriot and Mycenaean origin was uncovered, along with local Late Bronze Age II ceramic ware said to be characteristic of the Hittite empire. A Luwian hieroglyphic seal impression found on a cup on the site names a certain Targasnawa as lord of the city. Remains of a fortification wall dating to the Hittite period have also been uncovered. The Late Bronze Age city is perhaps to be identified with Ura (see **Ura (1)**), attested in Hittite texts; the site would subsequently have become known as Soli when it was refounded by the Greeks.

In 333 Alexander the Great fined Soli 200 talents for supporting the Persian king Darius III. In 67 the city was renamed Pompeiopolis in honour of the Roman general Pompey, who resettled it with ex-pirates after much of its earlier population had been deported to Tigranocerta by the Armenian king Tigranes II ('the Great').

Gough (*PECS* 851), Yağcı (2006).

Solymians Legendary or semi-legendary people of southwestern Anatolia, associated particularly, in Greek literary tradition, with the countries of Lycia and Pisidia. They make their first appearance in Homer's *Iliad*, where they are one of the three enemies of Lycia slaughtered by the Greek hero Bellerophon (*Iliad* 6.178–86). (The other two are the Amazons and the fire-breathing monster Chimaera.) According to Herodotus (1.173), they were an indigenous population of Lycia, later known as the Milyans. Their association with Pisidia is first attested in Strabo (13.4.16), who claims that the inhabitants of the Pisidian city of Termessus were called Solymians, and notes that the mountain at whose foot the town lay was known as Mt Solymus. Stephanus of Byzantium equated the Pisidians as a whole with the early Solymians. But Strabo seems to regard the latter as a separate ethnic group, speaking a language different from that of the Pisidians. It is possible that in the region of Termessus certain elements of the old Solymian culture survived in later times. Some of these elements may have been reflected in the cult of Zeus Solymeus, which is attested at Termessus in the Roman imperial period.

Bryce (1986: 19–20).

Soreg, Tell (map 8) Small agricultural settlement located in the land of Geshur in the southern Golan Heights (Nahal ʿEn Gev area) of northern Palestine. The site was occupied from the Middle Bronze Age to the Hellenistic period. Following its discovery and survey by D. Ban-Ami in 1980, Tell Soreg was excavated between 1987 and 1989 as part of the Land of Geshur Project, conducted by the Institute of Archaeology, Tel Aviv University. Material remains include a large quantity of painted ceramic ware dating to the Middle Bronze Age, and a number of burials, discovered in a cave accessed by a rock-cut corridor, ranging in date from the Middle Bronze to the Iron Age. Iron Age remains also include silo pits, and from Iron Age II the remains of private dwellings containing a large number of agricultural tools. In C9 and C8, a small casemate fort was established on the mound's northeastern corner. Its construction has been associated with the wars between the Israelites and the Aramaeans, when the road through Nahal ʿEn Gev assumed considerable strategic significance. There was resettlement of the site in the Persian period (C6–4), with continuing occupation into the Hellenistic age.

Kochavi (*NEAEHL* 4: 1410).

Sotira Early Bronze Age settlement and cemetery at Kaminoudhia in Cyprus, near the mod. village of Sotira, located inland from the south coast 15 km west of Limassol. An Early Bronze Age tomb was excavated there by P. Dikaios in 1947, and large-scale excavation of both settlement and cemetery was undertaken by S. Swiny and G. R. Rapp for the Cyprus American Archaeological Research Institute from 1981. The burial evidence suggests continuous occupation through the Early Bronze Age. The excavated architectural remains date to the last phase of the Early Bronze Age and are domestic in character. They produced numerous lithic, ceramic, and occasional metal finds. Finished and unfinished items of picrolite, an easily carved coloured stone found in the nearby Kouris river-bed and used in the production of ornaments, were recovered throughout the site, indicating widespread household production. The excavators suggest that Sotira was a centre of transit and exchange related to a regional trade in this material.

(J. M. Webb)
Swiny *et al.* (2003).

Subartu(m) (Shubartu(m), Subir, Subar(u)) Subartu and the related toponyms Shubartu and Subir refer to a geopolitical entity which cannot be tied down to a single area but whose configuration changed over time, as did its ethnic/cultural associations. Its people were often called the Subaru/Shubaru ('Subarians'). At times, also, the conception of Subartu depended on the perspective of those using the term: for the occupants of southern Mesopotamia, for example, 'Subarians' might simply refer to the occupants of the north.

Subartum/Subir is first attested in pre-Sargonic sources, namely, in inscriptions of Eannatum of Lagash. Subartum was one of the enemies which Eannatum defeated after they invaded the territory of Lagash. During the Sargonic era, some sources indicate a location for the land east of the Tigris, while others point to a location near to the (Hurrian-named) city of Azuhinnum which may have been located in the upper Habur region. Inscriptions of Naram-Sin suggest that Subartum extended westwards from the eastern Tigris region as far as the Mediterranean. For the Ur III period there are no

Figure 110 Sotira.

contemporary sources, but later (Old Babylonian) versions of the Royal Correspondence mention Subir in connection with Simurrum (east of the Tigris, in the Jebel Hamrin). Other Old Babylonian copies of Ur III period texts suggest that Subir figures either as a general term for 'north' or denotes the northeastern highlands to the north of Elam.

From early M2 on, Subartum/Shubartum is better attested. At this time it was one of the principalities of Upper Mesopotamia, prior to the unification of the region under the Assyrian king Shamshi-Adad I (1796–1775) and also following the collapse of the Upper Mesopotamian kingdom after his death. A location in the area between the Tigris r. and the eastern end of the Habur triangle has been proposed (*Mesop.* map). Around 1771, following his conquest of Shubat-Enlil/Shehna, the Eshnnunite king Ibal-pi-El II claims to have defeated the forces of Shubartum: these included the kings of Razama, Azuhinnum, and Hurasan. Shubartum also figured on several occasions among the conquests of the Babylonian king Hammurabi (1792–1750). In the texts which record these conquests, as also in the Mari archives when the throne of Mari was occupied by Zimri-Lim (1774–1762), Shubartum is virtually synonymous with what later became Assyria. When Zimri-Lim raised a coalition against the Elamites, it is said to have included 'Ekallatum, Atamrum, and the upper country, the land of Shubartum'.

In M2, Shubartu(m) is often assumed to refer to the Hurrian peoples and, by extension, to the entire Habur region which then formed the Hurrian heartland. However, the language spoken by its people is of uncertain origin and it is not clear that it bore any affinity with Hurrian (Gragg, 1995: 2162). An Old Babylonian period text written in an unknown language is entitled 'incantation in the tongue of Subartum'.

In Late Bronze Age Assyrian texts, following the destruction of the Hurrian kingdom of Mitanni by the Hittite king Suppiluliuma I in the third quarter of C14, the term Shubaru ('Subarians') is used in reference to the remnant peoples of the former Mitannian empire, inhabiting the region of the upper Tigris valley. A number of Middle Assyrian kings claimed victories over the Subarians, including Adad-nirari I, Shalmaneser I, and Tukulti-Ninurta I. Despite these conquests, anti-Assyrian uprisings continued among the Subarian peoples, as indicated by a campaign which the Assyrian king Tiglath-pileser I (1114–1076) conducted against the 'insubmissive Shubaru' early in his reign (**RIMA* 2: 17). The king reports that at this time cities in the land of Shubartu had been seized by 4,000 Kasku and Urumu troops from the land of

Hatti – who, he claims, submitted peacefully to him on his arrival in Shubartu. Here Shubartu is associated with the lands of Alzu and Purulumzu.

In M1, the land of **Shubria** (q.v.) and the people called Shubaru (re-)emerge in later Neo-Assyrian texts, representing the legacy of Shubartu, in the region south of mod. Muş and extending eastwards towards Lake Van. The Shubaru (meaning here the inhabitants of Shubria) are included among the list of lands and peoples which the Assyrian king Ashurnasirpal II claims to have conquered (**RIMA* 2: 221). In M1 Babylonian texts the names Subartu and Subarian are used to designate Assyria and the Assyrians (e.g. **RIMB* 2: 137).

(H. D. Baker)
Michalowski (1986; 2001).

Subutu see **Soba**.

Sudu (Shudu) Late Bronze Age fortress-city in northern Mesopotamia, located in the kingdom of Hanigalbat. When the Hanigalbatean king Wasashatta rebelled against Assyrian sovereignty, Sudu was among the cities conquered by the Assyrian king Adad-nirari I (1307–1275) while he was crushing the rebellion (**RIMA* 1:131). Lipiński (2000: 143–4, with map, 139) supports an identification between Sudu and the site of Tell Bisme, south of mod. Derik. Sudu is probably to be equated with Middle Assyrian Shudu, which features in texts, listing different administrative districts, from the reign of Tiglath-pileser I (1114–1076). Nashef (*RGTC* 5: 234–5) suggests that Shudu and Shuduhu(m) may be identical.

Sugu see **Habhu**.

Sugunia M1 royal Urartian city in eastern Anatolia, one of the strongholds (the other was Arzashkun) of the mid C9 Urartian king Arame, perhaps to be located to the south or southwest of Lake Van. The city was destroyed by the Assyrian king Shalmaneser III during the campaign which he conducted into Urartian territory in his accession year (859). Shalmaneser followed up his victory by erecting a tower of the heads of the slaughtered in front of Sugunia, before burning another fourteen cities in the region and then moving on to 'wash his weapons' in the sea of the land of Nairi (most likely Lake Urmia) (**RIMA* 3: 8–9, 14–15). His capture of Sugunia is also recorded on one of the bronze bands from Balawat (**RIMA* 3: 140) (see **Imgur-Enlil**). The city lay close to the city (and land) of Hubushkia, since Shalmaneser proceeded directly to it after his capture of Hubushkia.

Salvini (1995b).

Sugziya Late Bronze Age city, probably located in the Euphrates region in southeastern Anatolia, north of the city of Urshu (which lay north of Carchemish). Originally subject to Hatti, it was occupied by the Hurrians during the reign of the Hittite king Hantili I (early C16). Hantili's queen, Harapsili, and his two sons were captured by the Hurrians and held prisoner in Sugziya where they died, perhaps victims of the local queen (**CS* I: 195). Sugziya was among the cities recaptured by the Hittite king Telipinu (1525–1500). It became the site of one of the grain storage depots which Telipinu installed throughout his kingdom.

*Helck (1984), *Soysal (1990).

Suhma (Zuhma) Late Bronze Age country in eastern Anatolia, subject to Hatti from at least the early years of the Hittite New Kingdom (early C14). It lay near the city of Pahhuwa in the upper Euphrates region. Delegates from its council of elders attended an assembly of cities and countries called upon by the Hittite king Arnuwanda I to attack Pahhuwa in the event that Pahhuwa failed to hand over its rebel king Mita to the Hittites (**HDT* 164). It was perhaps the Bronze Age predecessor of the Iron Age land called Suhme (q.v.) which lay in the same region.

Garstang and Gurney (1959: 35), *RGTC* 6: 516 (s.v. Zuhma).

Suhme/Suhne (= Late Bronze Age **Suhma**?) Country attested in late M2 and early M1 Assyrian texts, located in southeastern Anatolia, across the Arsanias r. (mod. Murat Su) from the land of Enzite in Isuwa (Assyrian Ishua). Its chief city was perhaps the fortified stronghold called Uashtal. The Assyrian king Tiglath-pileser I (1114–1076) reports his conquest of it during his military operations in Hatti and Isuwa (**RIMA* 2: 43). In 856 Shalmaneser III conquered and ravaged its territories prior to his advance further east into the heartland of the Urartian kingdom (**RIMA* 3: 20). In 844 the land suffered further devastation from Shalmaneser in the course of another of his campaigns into Urartian territory and the lands further west (**RIMA* 3: 39).

Suhu(m) (maps 7, 10) Region on the middle Euphrates south of Mari, with an attested history extending from the Middle Bronze Age through the Iron Age. In the Middle Bronze Age it was divided into two sub-regions, Upper and Lower Suhum. The city of Hanat was the capital of the former, Yabliya of the latter. Other cities in the region included Mulhan (the northernmost city of Lower Suhum), Ayabu (Ayyabe), Harbe (1), Nashir (Nishir), Qasa, and Sapiratum. In late C19, the Eshnunnite king Naram-Sin annexed the entire region during a military campaign. Subsequently it was incorporated into the kingdom of Upper Mesopotamia in the reign of the Assyrian king Shamshi-Adad I (1796–1775), who assigned it to his son Yasmah-Addu, viceroy at Mari. But the viceroy's authority over Suhum remained tenuous, and conditions there became increasingly unsettled. This was at least partly due to the movements and military operations of Babylonian forces in the region, which may well have helped precipitate uprisings by a number of cities in Lower Suhum. The easing of tensions between Shamshi-Adad and the Babylonian king Hammurabi no doubt took some of the pressure off Yasmah-Addu's southern territories. But Eshnunna had not abandoned its territorial ambitions in the middle Euphrates region. Two successive military expeditions dispatched by its king, Dadusha, were sufficient to bring the land of Suhum once more under Eshnunnite control (1782). Hostilities between the Upper Mesopotamian and Eshnunnite kingdoms came to an end when Shamshi-Adad launched a counter-attack against the Eshnunnites and Dadusha was forced to conclude a peace with him.

But control of Suhum was again contested by Eshnunna when Mari's throne was occupied by Zimri-Lim (1774–1762) and Eshnunna's by Ibal-pi-El II (1779–1765). Letters sent to Zimri-lim by Yasim-El, his agent based in Andarig, and Buqaqum, mayor of Sapiratum (q.v.), warned that the Eshnunnite military commander Shallurum had set his sights on the conquest of the whole of Suhum, after occupying and fortifying the city of Harbe in Lower Suhum with 15,000 troops; further, an advance force of 5,000 Eshnunnite troops had been sent to occupy Yabliya, the regional capital (**LKM* 383–4). Suhum also attracted the attention of another of the major powers, Elam. This is indicated in another letter received by Zimri-Lim, which warned that the Elamites were likely to send 10,000 troops to the region to start an uprising there (*LKM 478–9). With the support of Hammurabi, who had maintained an active interest and presence in Suhum, Zimri-Lim regained possession of the occupied territories, his control of them confirmed in a peace accord concluded with Ibal-pi-El in 1770. However, the Babylonians also continued their presence in the region, and after Zimri-Lim's death Suhum came firmly under Babylonian control, where it remained until the fall of the Old Babylonian kingdom in 1595.

During the Iron Age, Suhu was a wealthy Iron Age Aramaean state lying between the kingdom of Bit-Adini to the north and Babylonia to the south. Its wealth was probably due, in part at least, to its apparently close commercial ties with Babylonia. It is first attested in the inscriptions of the Assyrian king Tiglath-pileser I (1114–1076), who conducted several campaigns against it (*RIMA 2: 23, 43). Adad-nirari II (911–891) reports receiving tribute from it (*RIMA 2: 149). In 885 it was among the states which rendered tribute to the Assyrian king Tukulti-Ninurta II, in the form of provisions and costly gifts, during Tukulti-Ninurta's progress around the southern and western limits of his kingdom (*RIMA 2: 174–5). Several years later its ruler Ilu-ibni, who had paid a large tribute to Tukulti-Ninurta, was coerced into paying a further substantial tribute to his successor Ashurnasirpal II (*RIMA 2: 200), to secure his family's safety. But in 878 Suhu's new ruler, Kudurru, rose up against Ashurnasirpal, with the support of Babylonian troops, when the Assyrian was campaigning in the Habur and middle Euphrates region. According to Ashurnasirpal, this was the first resistance he encountered in the course of his campaign. Kudurru made his stand in his fortified city of Suru, which Ashurnasirpal took by storm, plundering and destroying it (*RIMA 2: 213–14). But little more than a year later, Suhu joined the neighbouring states of Laqe and Hindanu in a fresh rebellion against Assyrian rule (*RIMA 2: 214–15), probably with the encouragement of Bit-Adini and Babylonia (c. 877). In spite of Ashurnasirpal's claim to have crushed the rebel states, destroying their armies and laying waste their cities, anti-Assyrian uprisings persisted throughout the middle Euphrates region.

In the third quarter of C9, Suhu appears to have enjoyed semi-independent status. At this time, its ruler was Marduk-aplar-usur, who paid tribute to the Assyrian king Shalmaneser III, but was also in communication with Rudamu (Urtamis), king of Hamath (*Parpola, 1990). Subsequently, in late C9 or early C8, a governor of Suhu called Tabnea was assassinated while in Assyria to render tribute to and have an audience (with the Assyrian king?) (*RIMB 2: 307, 315). In the first half of C8 Suhu was governed, along with the land of Mari, by a certain Shamash-resha-usur – probably at the time the Assyrian throne was occupied by Ashur-dan III (772–755). This information is provided by an inscription on a stele commemorating the deeds of Shamash-resha-usur, who was attempting to redevelop what was evidently a depressed and underpopulated region along the middle Euphrates (*RIMB 2: 279–82). The inscription also records a military victory won by Shamash-resha-usur over the Aramaean Tumanu tribe. To judge from the inscriptions of Shamash-resha-usur's son and successor Ninurta-kudurri-usur, who also claims to have won a victory over another Aramaean tribe, the warlike Hatallu, Suhu may have achieved full independence from Assyrian rule in this period (for the texts of Ninurta-kudurri-usur, see *RIMB 2: 291–323) before it once more came under firm Assyrian control in the reign of

Tiglath-pileser III (745–727). In 616, Suhu and Hindanu became tributaries of the Babylonian king Nabopolassar (626–605), but three years later, in 613, Suhu rebelled against Nabopolassar, prompting a retaliatory campaign by the Babylonian king into its territory (**ABC* 91, 93, **PE* 30–1, no. 10).

Lipiński (2000: 680, refs), *Mesop.* 161–3, 172–3, 369–70, Na'aman (2007).

Sukas, Tell (map 7) City on the northern Syrian coast, 37 km south of Latakia, attested as Suksu in Late Bronze Age Egyptian, Ugaritic, and Hittite texts. In the Late Bronze Age it lay on the southern frontier of the kingdom of Ugarit, and was one of the kingdom's important port-cities. It had both northern and southern harbours. The site has a long history of occupation, extending from the Neolithic (M7) to the mediaeval period. Excavations were carried out between 1958 and 1963 by the Danish archaeologist P. J. Riis under the auspices of the Carlsberg Foundation. These excavations indicated that the city was partially destroyed at the end of the Late Bronze Age, though the devastation there was apparently less than in the city of Ugarit itself, which was completely obliterated. The succeeding Iron Age was divided by the excavator into two phases – 'Phoenician I' (c. 1170–850) and 'Phoenician II' (c. 850–675), with destruction by the army of the Assyrian king Shalmaneser III marking the transition between the two phases. Material evidence of the period is relatively meagre. However, vegetable and animal remains from a storage area within the city indicate that the population's diet included a range of agricultural products, fish and molluscs, and the meat of cattle, sheep and goats. This period also saw the development of trading links with Cyprus and the Aegean world.

A further Assyrian destruction of the city in 677 or 671, during the reign of the Assyrian king Esarhaddon, was followed by rebuilding and reoccupation, with Greek settlers making up the bulk of the population. The remains of a number of houses and temples date to this phase. Ceramic ware from the site indicates further trade and cultural contacts with Cyprus and the east Greek world, though the city's inhabitants seem to have been primarily agriculturalists. Settlement continued through part of the Persian period, beginning in mid C6, but the town appears to have been destroyed at the beginning of C5, and remained unoccupied until c. 380, when a neo-Phoenician settlement was built on the site. This city survived into the late Hellenistic period, and perhaps until 69, when the excavator suggests that it was destroyed by earthquake. In the Byzantine and mediaeval periods, the mound was occupied by a fortress.

Riis *et al.* (1970–86), Abou Assaf (*OEANE* 5: 90–1).

Sukita Iron Age city belonging to the Neo-Hittite kingdom of Kummuh and located on the middle Euphrates. It is attested in Luwian hieroglyphic inscriptions of Panamuwatis, wife of Suppiluliumas (who is probably the Kummuhite king Ushpilulume attested in Assyrian sources dated to 805 and 773), and a man called Atayazas, subject of Suppiluliumas' son and successor Hattusilis (**CHLI* I: 336–7, 341–2).

Sukkia One of the cities of the kingdom of Mannaea which rebelled against Assyrian sovereignty early in the reign of the Assyrian king Sargon II (721–705), with the encouragement of the Urartian king Rusa I. In 719 Sargon conducted a campaign of conquest against the rebel leaders and their cities (see **Mannaea**), the latter including Sukkia, Bala, Abitikna, Pappa, and Lalluknu (**ARAB* II: 29). The populations of these cities were deported to the west and resettled in Damascus and other parts of Syria (in the region which the Assyrians called Hatti).

Sultanhan (map 18) Iron Age settlement-mound in south-central Anatolia, located within the kingdom of northern Tabal (Assyrian Bit-Burutash). A stele with a 51-line inscription in Luwian hieroglyphs (**CHLI* I: 463–72) was discovered there in 1939. The inscription contains a dedication by a man called Sarwatiwaras to the god Tarhunzas of the Vineyard, and a list of offerings for the god. Sarwatiwaras identifies himself as a subject of the Tabalic Great King Wasusarmas. The stele is now housed in the Kayseri Museum.

Sultantepe see **Huzirina**.

Sumer, Sumerians (map 17) The name 'Sumer' is conventionally applied to southern Mesopotamia through much of M3 (the Early Bronze Age), while the derived term 'Sumerians' conventionally denotes the inhabitants of the region in M3 and early M2. It is derived from *Shumerum*, an Akkadian name (of unknown origin) for the region. The occupants themselves called their country Kengir, and referred to them-

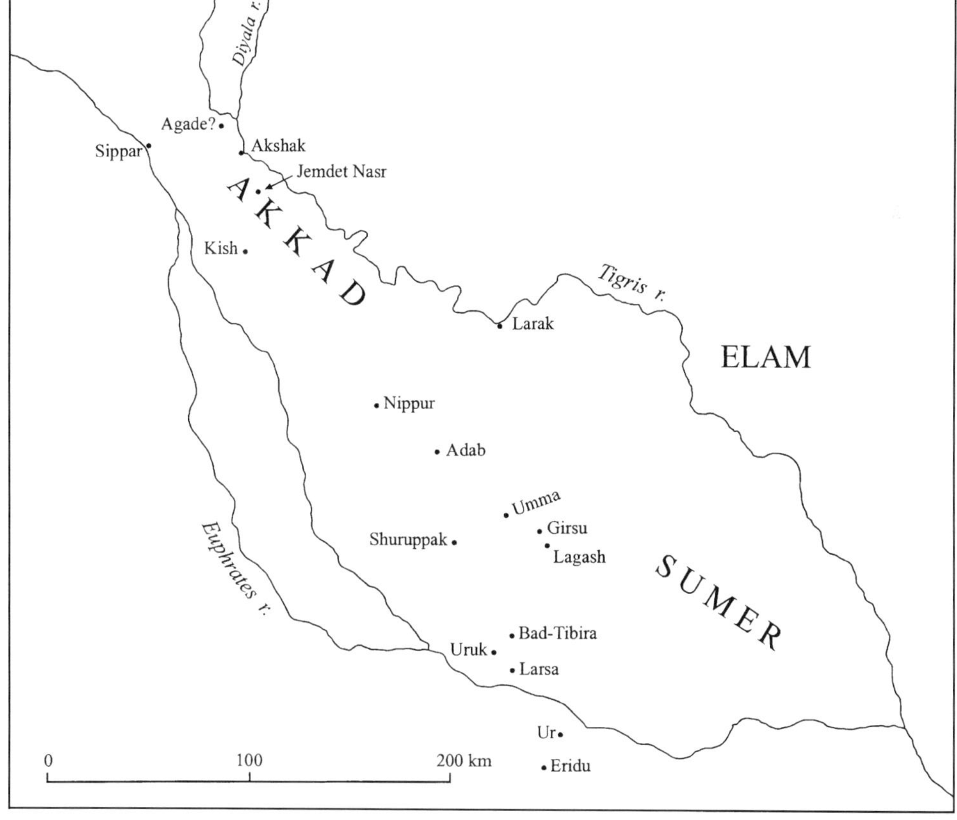

Map 17 Sumer and Akkad.

selves as the Saggiga, 'the black-headed people'. They are first attested in history early in M3. But there has been much debate about who precisely they were – whether they were a race of newcomers who arrived in Mesopotamia at the end of M4, whether they evolved out of the indigenous peoples of the region, and whether they mingled or came into conflict with other groups who entered and settled in the same region, most notably population groups of Semitic stock. It is indeed likely that the so-called Sumerians were, like the so-called Hittites, a population of mixed ethnic origins. An original 'proto-Sumerian' population with a common ethnic origin is perhaps indicated by the distinctive 'Sumerian' language, unrelated to any other known language, which became the dominant tongue of southern Mesopotamia in the Early Bronze Age. But probably from the time of their first appearance in history, the Sumerian-speaking occupants of this region coexisted and intermingled with population groups of Semitic origin. Out of this ethnic mix, the so-called Sumerian civilization of Early Bronze Age southern Mesopotamia evolved. The city of Nippur, seat of Enlil, the chief god of the Sumerian pantheon, came to provide a religious focus for this region.

The most important administrative unit within the Sumerian world was the city-state, consisting of an urban centre along with peripheral rural areas, where villages and farmlands were located. Generally, there were three main parts of a city-state: (a) a walled inner city containing temples, palaces, official administrative quarters, and some domestic dwellings; within the city centre lay the temple enclosure, generally surrounded by an oval wall; (b) the *kar*, a business district located on the canal banks to facilitate trading operations between cities linked by southern Mesopotamia's waterways; (c) a suburban area (*uru-bar-ra*), which included outlying rural districts. Fourteen city-states are known to us: Sippar, Kish, Akshak, Larak, Nippur, Adab, Shuruppak, Umma, Lagash, Bad-tibira, Uruk, Larsa, Ur, and Eridu. These are attested in sources of what is known as the Early Dynastic period, c. 2900–2334 – i.e. the period of Sumerian history which ended with the rise of the kingdom of Akkad. The supreme monarch of each city-state was a patron deity, whose earthly representative was a ruler known as an *ensi* ('lord') or *lugal* ('great man'). Initially, the ruler's importance seems to have been fairly limited, since much of the city-state's power was exercised by a wealthy temple-priesthood. But later in the Early Dynastic period there was a growing separation between religious and secular authority. In a number of states, certain kings emerged as powerful absolute rulers, who sometimes extended their authority over neighbouring city-states by military force. Such was the case with a king of Lagash called Eannatum, who in C25 or C24 expelled the Elamite invaders from southern Mesopotamia and also conquered the city-states of Ur, Uruk, and Kish.

According to the Sumerian King List, a document which dates to early M2 i.e. some centuries after the end of the Early Dynastic period (**Chav.* 81–5), the city-states throughout their history did in fact form some kind of confederation in which one state enjoyed a measure of political hegemony over the others; in the course of time, this hegemony passed from one state to another. Another feature of the King List is that it divides Sumerian history into pre-flood (antediluvian) and post-flood (postdiluvian) eras. But the document contains many distortions and gross exaggerations, particularly with regard to the prodigious lengths of a number of kings' reigns. And it treats as sequential many ruling dynasties which, if they did exist, must have been contemporaneous. Further, the degree of political unity which it bestows upon the network of Early Dynastic city-states is almost certainly influenced by later imperial administrative systems, like those of Akkad and the Ur III dynasty. Nevertheless, the document clearly contains some elements of historical truth, besides providing interesting grounds for speculation on the origins of the great flood tradition.

The city-states placed much emphasis on practical skills, efficient organization, and the importance of large-scale cooperation on community projects, such as the building and maintenance of complex irrigation systems. Highly developed practical and organizational skills were essential in mastering the harsh natural environment in which the Sumerians lived. Indeed the name 'Sumerian' is associated with many new developments, particularly in the area of practical skills, in the history of human civilization. One of the most notable of these is the development of the world's first written script. The Sumerian writing system is now known as cuneiform, so called from the Latin word *cuneus* meaning 'wedge'. The written symbols were produced by pressing the ends of wedge-shaped reeds, which grow in profusion along the banks of the Mesopotamian rivers, into soft clay. Tens of thousands of cuneiform clay tablets have been unearthed from the Sumerian cities. Of these, the great majority are administrative records, business contracts, lists of commodities, and the like. But in addition, a small number of literary texts have come to light. These include poems about a king of Uruk called Gilgamesh. Such poems provided material for the famous Epic of Gilgamesh, composed early in M2.

The Sumerian language continued in common use, through the Early Dynastic,

Figure 111 Sumerian figurine.

Akkadian, and Ur III periods, until the end of M3, though the Sumerian civilization itself, as commonly defined, ended with the Akkadian domination of southern Mesopotamia in C24. (The expression 'Neo-Sumerian' or 'Sumerian renaissance' sometimes applied to the Ur III period is a misleading one.) By (or very early in) M2, Sumerian had given way to Akkadian as the region's most widely spoken language. By mid C17 it had probably ceased to be used in any spoken contexts, even as a formal language used on ceremonial occasions. On the other hand, as a language learnt in scribal schools and used for religious and literary compositions, it survived until the very end of the cuneiform tradition in late M1 and perhaps even into early M1 CE.

Sigrist and Westenholz (1996), Michalowski (*OEANE* 5: 95–101), Crawford (2004).

Sumua The name of a well in the middle Euphrates region where Ninurta-kudurri-usur, ruler in mid C8 of the Aramaean kingdom of Suhu, mustered his troops for a showdown with 2,000 marauding tribesmen from the Aramaean Hatallu tribe who had invaded and plundered the land of Laqe (**RIMB* 2: 293, 296–7 etc.). Here, and in the area extending from the well Makiru to the wells Gallabu and Suribu, Ninurta-kudurri-usur wiped out the invaders, and subsequently displayed the skin of their leader Shama-gamni on the gate of the city called Al-gabbari-bani.

Sumur (*Tell Kazel*?) (map 6) Late Bronze Age fortress-city on the Levantine coast at the mouth of the Nahr el-Kabir r., probably to be identified with middle Assyrian Sumri, Iron Age Simirra, and Classical Simyra. Subject to Egypt, Sumur occupied a position of considerable strategic importance close to the northern periphery of Egyptian vassal territory in Syria. In the reign of the pharaoh Amenhotep III (1390–1352) it was captured by Abdi-Ashirta, ruler of the northwestern Syrian state of Amurru, during the absence of its resident Egyptian commissioner, Pahhanate. Abdi-Ashirta used the city as a base for his future military operations, while maintaining a semblance of allegiance to the pharaoh. For reasons which remain unclear, Egypt's ally, Tushratta, king of Mitanni, visited Sumur during its occupation by Abdi-Ashirta. After Abdi-Ashirta's capture and death the city reverted to Egyptian control and was fortified by garrison troops. But shortly afterwards it fell to Abdi-Ashirta's son Aziru, who like his father claimed loyalty to the pharaoh, now Akhenaten (1352–1336), and complained of the hostility towards him of the pharaoh's local officials. Aziru promised to rebuild Sumur after his siege and occupation left it in a ruined state. But his promise was never fulfilled.

Moran (1992: 391, index refs).

Sunbu Iron Age country in or near the Nairi lands, situated in the western Zagros range, perhaps in the region of mod. Suleimaniya. The Chief Eunuch of the Assyrian king Shamshi-Adad V (823–811) conquered it as he was returning from his second campaign in the Nairi lands, and Shamshi-Adad himself received tribute from its people during his third campaign in Nairi (**RIMA* 3: 184).

Supa M1 city in the upper Euphrates valley, on the east bank of the river opposite Malatya, Iron Age predecessor of Classical Sophene. It was conquered by the Urartian king Minua (805–788), along with the city Huzana, prior to Minua's campaign across the Euphrates into the territory of the Neo-Hittite kingdoms of northern Syria and eastern Anatolia (**HcI* 63–4, no. 25).

Supru(m) Mesopotamian city in the middle Euphrates region, attested in Middle Bronze Age texts from Mari and in Iron Age Neo-Assyrian inscriptions. It is perhaps to be identified with Tell Abu Hasan, located 12 km upstream from Mari. During the Middle Bronze Age, Suprum was an important garrison centre in the region along the Euphrates which was subject to Yasmah-Addu, son of the Assyrian king Shamshi-Adad I (1796–1775) and viceroy in Mari. When the forces of Zimri-Lim, the man who was to seize his throne, bore down upon his kingdom soon after Shamshi-Adad's death, Yasmah-Addu sought to maintain his hold on Suprum by strengthening its defences, as also the defences of Mari, while sending an urgent appeal for assistance to his brother, Ishme-Dagan, viceroy in Ekallatum. Shortly afterwards he wrote again to his brother with news that Suprum had fallen to the enemy after a siege, its population taking refuge in Mari (**LAPO* 17: 129–30, no. 533).

In the Iron Age, Suprum was among the cities of the land of Laqe (q.v.). The Assyrian king Tukulti-Ninurta II received tribute there from Hamataya, one of the rulers of Laqe, during his campaign along the middle Euphrates and Habur rivers in 885 (**RIMA* 2: 176). His son and successor Ashurnasirpal II also received tribute from the city on a similar campaign in 878 (**RIMA* 2: 213).

Mesop. 134, 189–90 (with refs).

Sura (map 15) Small M1 BCE–M1 CE town in Lycia, southwestern Anatolia, 4 km west of the city of Myra to which it belonged. The site contains a number of rock-cut house-tombs of Lycian type. There are also two inscriptions in the native Lycian language (attested from late C6 to C4), one a burial inscription on a house-tomb (**TAM* I 84), the other a lengthy but very fragmentary inscription on a statue base (**N* 304). Sura is best known as the site of a temple and oracle of Apollo. The relatively well-preserved but small temple is built close to the edge of a marsh and a water spring which is associated with a famous fish oracle. Here priests sought advice from the god on behalf of their clients by observing the behaviour, or species, of fish which appeared when food was thrown into a freshwater spring or seawater whirlpool. According to Pliny the Elder (32.17) the fish were summoned by a pipe. If they tore at the meat tossed to them it was a good omen, but if they cast the flesh aside with their tails, the omen was bad. As described by Greek and Roman writers, the hydrological features of the site – if not the eccentric behaviour of the fish – can still be seen today.

Bean (*PECS* 868; 1978: 130–3).

Surih (or Zurih?) M1 Mesopotamian city in the land of Laqe, perhaps to be identified with Tell Suwwar on the west bank of the Habur r., 18 km south of Dur-Katlimmu. The Assyrian king Adad-nirari II encountered it on his entry into Laqe during his campaign along the Habur in 894 (**RIMA* 2: 153). At that time it was under the control of Baratara, a ruler of the Aramaean tribal state Bit-Halupe, from whom Adad-nirari received a payment of tax and tribute.

Lipiński (2000: 82–3).

Surkh Dum (map 13) Predominantly Iron Age settlement in western Iran, located in the Zagros region northwest of Susa, excavated by E. Schmidt in 1938 and subsequently by a Belgian team under the direction of L. Vanden Berghe between 1965 and 1978. The most significant remains on the site are those of a seventeen-room building complex, from which a total of 1,851 artefacts were unearthed. Among these were items made of terracotta, including human and animal figurines, faience, bone, and stone. But the most important of the finds were bronzes of the classic Luristan type. For details of these, see **Luristan**. Cylinder seals inscribed with a goddess' name, bronze representations of what appear to be deities, and a number of apparently votive objects, provide the basis for identifying the building as a religious sanctuary, dating to C8 and C7. During the course of their excavations, the Belgians uncovered hundreds of tombs ranging in date from M3 to M1.

Schmidt *et al.* (1989), Muscarella (1995: 997–8).

Suru (1) Iron Age fortified city belonging to the Aramaean land of Suhu, located south of Anat in the middle Euphrates region. The Assyrian king Tukulti-Ninurta II encamped his forces near the city during his last recorded campaign (885), which took him through the middle Tigris and Euphrates regions (**RIMA* 2: 174). In 878 Suhu's governor, Kudurru, rebelled against his overlord, the Assyrian king Ashurnasirpal II, with the support of 'Kassite' (i.e. Babylonian) troops, and made his stand in his capital, Suru, against the Assyrian forces. Ashurnasirpal took the city by storm, then plundered and destroyed it, massacring many of its defenders and taking prisoner the Babylonian troops who survived. Kudurru and seventy of his forces escaped capture by fleeing the city (**RIMA* 2: 213–14). To celebrate his conquests in the region, Ashurnasirpal set up a victory stele in Suru.

Suru (2) Iron Age Mesopotamian city located on the lower Habur r., within the Aramaean land of Bit-Halupe. Lipiński (2000: 89, with map, 81) suggests an identification with mod. Al-Busayra on the west bank of the Habur near its confluence with the Euphrates. During his last recorded campaign in 885, the Assyrian king Tukulti-Ninurta II approached the city and received rich tribute there from Hamataya, one of the rulers of Laqe, including his two sisters accompanied by a substantial dowry (**RIMA* 2: 176). But in 883 Tukulti-Ninurta's son and successor Ashurnasirpal II received news that its inhabitants had rebelled, killing its governor, Hamataya, and replacing him with an appointee of their own, Ahi-yababa, from the land of Bit-Adini. Ashurnasirpal responded by leading an expeditionary force along the Habur to the city, where he was met by its nobles and elders who begged for mercy and delivered up to him the rebel governor. The city was plundered, and those who had taken part in the rebellion were ruthlessly punished. The new governor was deposed and taken back to Nineveh, where he was flayed alive. Ashurnasirpal replaced him in Suru with his own appointee, a man called Azi-ilu (**RIMA* 2: 198–9). Subsequently, when the people of Laqe, Suhu, and Hindanu revolted, Ashurnasirpal went to Suru and built boats there, and then made his way to the Euphrates (*RIMA* 2: 214).

Surunu Fortified Iron Age city in northern Syria, west of the middle Euphrates, belonging to the Aramaean kingdom of Bit-Adini. It was one of six such cities attacked, captured, and plundered by the Assyrian king Shalmaneser III, after his troops had crossed the Euphrates on rafts made of inflated goatskins, during the campaign he conducted against Bit-Adini's king Ahuni in his second regnal year (857) (**RIMA* 3: 18). The other five cities were [. . .]ga, Tagi[. . .], Paripa, Til-Bashere (= Tilbeshar), and (the most important) Dabigu. Surunu has been identified with mod.

Sawran, 5 km northwest of Tell Dabiq and, more plausibly, with Sazgın, 15 km southeast of Gaziantep.

Lipiński (2000: 178).

Suruta Late Bronze Age country in western Anatolia, within or near the territory of the Lukka Lands. It was one of the countries captured by the renegade Hittite vassal Madduwatta during his campaigns in western Anatolia (early C14). The Hittite king Arnuwanda I lists Suruta, along with Attarimma and Hu(wa)rsanassa, among Madduwatta's conquests in the region (**HDT* 158). The three countries again appear together at the beginning of the Hittite king Mursili II's reign (1321), when they apparently joined an anti-Hittite rebellion in the west. Mursili responded by conducting a campaign against his western enemies in his third regnal year. During this campaign, troops from Huwarsanassa, Attarimma, and Suruta fled before him and sought refuge in the kingdom of Arzawa 'Minor' (**AM* 40–1, 52–9, **CS* II: 85).

Susa (biblical **Shushan**, mod. ***Shush***) (maps 13, 16) 550 ha site comprising several mounds, located in southwestern Iran on the northwestern edge of the mod. province of Khuzestan, and on the left bank of the Shaur r. Its history of occupation extends from the Chalcolithic Age (c. 4200) to the period of the Mongol invasions in C13 CE. Initial investigations of the site by the British archaeologist W. K. Loftus from 1843 to 1845 were followed by a series of French missions undertaken between 1884 and 1979; the earliest of these was led by M. Dieulafoy (1884–6), and the most recent by J. Perrot (1968–79), who concentrated on the stratigraphy of the site and its surrounding district, Susiana.

The material remains of Susa's earliest period of habitation (late M5 to mid M4,

Figure 112 Susa, chateau, headquarters of French archaeological mission.

designated as Susa I), including a huge 12 m high stepped platform, indicate that already in this period the city had become the chief centre of the region which in M2 was incorporated into the kingdom of Elam, first attested in M3 Mesopotamian texts. In its following two phases (Susa II and III, c. 3500–2700), the city may have suffered some decline in its size and status, due to the emergence (in the Susa II phase) of other urban centres in Susiana, Chogha Mish (which had already in M6 and M5 been the dominant site in the region before being abandoned towards the end of M5) and Abu Fanduweh. But by the end of phase III, Susa appears to have reasserted its dominance. From this level of the city's existence, some 1,500 tablets have been unearthed. Written in a pictographic script, and still undecipherable, they have traditionally been designated 'Proto-Elamite', on the assumption that they were the ancestors of the 'Old Elamite' inscriptions dating to later M3 and early M2. It is now clear, however, that there is no connection between the two, and that the term 'Proto-Elamite' is thus an inappropriate and misleading one.

The rise of the first Mesopotamian empires in the second half of M3 put an end to Susa's independence. The city became subject in succession to the Akkadian and the Ur III empires. Both empires were, however, relatively shortlived, and after the destruction of the latter by an alliance led by the Elamite Shimashki dynasty under King Kindattu at the end of M3, Susa became an integral part of the Elamite kingdom. It now entered upon a period when it enjoyed high political prominence and prosperity, firstly under the rule of the Shimashki dynasty, and subsequently under that of the sukkalmah kings; these royal houses were based respectively in Luristan (probably) and Anshan in Fars. Susa was established as one of the royal seats of the Elamite kingdom during this period, with a population estimated at more than 20,000. During the middle centuries of M2 Elam experienced a relatively long period of decline, reaching one of its lowest points in late C14 when the Babylonian king Kurigalzu II (1332–1308), a member of the ruling Kassite dynasty, invaded and devastated Susiana, captured Susa, set up a statue of himself in one of the city's temples, and declared himself the conqueror of Susa and Elam. But by C13 Elam was again emerging as a major power, though Susa's power and influence at this time were initially limited by the rise of other administrative centres in its region, notably Al-Untash-Napirisha (mod. Chogha Zanbil), a new religious and ceremonial royal city built by the Elamite king Untash-napirisha (1275–1240).

The restoration of Susa's ascendancy under the rulers of the Shutrukid dynasty, founded by Shutruk-Nahhunte I (1185–1155), ushered in a new phase in the city's history, during which it once more exercised political supremacy over its region, and also played a major role in renewed Elamite campaigns against the west, particularly against Babylonia. Among the spoils of conquest brought back to Susa from one of these campaigns were the famous victory stele of the C23 Akkadian king Naram-Sin and the law code of the C18 Babylonian king Hammurabi. These were placed in the sanctuary of Susa's chief deity, Inshushinak. There was much new construction activity in Susa during this period, with the restoration of both sacred and secular public buildings on the acropolis. Mudbrick as a building material was replaced by glazed and baked brick. The city also became a major centre of science, arts and crafts, trade and industry.

The early Neo-Elamite period (c. 1100–539) witnessed another period of political turmoil in Susa, beginning with the destruction of the city c. 1110 by Nebuchadnezzar

I, fourth king of the Second Dynasty of Isin. However, there was a revival of the city's fortunes in late C8, no doubt associated with a brief resurgence of Elamite power at this time. In 646 Susa fell to and was destroyed by the Assyrian king Ashurbanipal, despite Elamite and Babylonian efforts to contain Assyrian military expansion. It later came under the control, for a time, of the Neo-Babylonian king Nebuchadnezzar II (604–562). But in the last decades of C6, the city entered upon one last period of florescence when Elam became subject to the fledgling Persian empire. The fourth member of the ruling Achaemenid dynasty, Darius I (522–486), carried out an extensive rebuilding programme in Susa, constructing there a summer palace for himself and making the city the centre of his administration (*DSf*). Susa's location at the terminus of the Persian Royal Road, which ran west to Sardis in western Anatolia (see Herodotus 5.52–4), helped give the city a strongly cosmopolitan character.

Most of the Persian remains on the site belong to the reign of Darius or to a later Achaemenid ruler, Artaxerxes II (404–359). There were three main components of the Achaemenid city: the acropolis, which is the highest part of the site, the *apadana* mound, where the royal audience hall and palace complex were located, and the so-called 'royal city' (Ville Royale), which in fact contains the mudbrick remains of a number of periods. Numerous inscriptions from the site dating to Darius' reign, including fragments of trilingual inscriptions (in Elamite, Akkadian, and Old Persian), provide valuable information on the construction of the city under Darius, the rebellions which Darius put down, and the extent of the empire which he ruled. This last is made clear by the king's description of the materials and the craftsmen brought from the furthest parts of his realm for the construction of his palace. Darius' son and successor Xerxes continued to develop the site after his father's death in 486, but the most significant later remains are those of a small palace built across the river by Artaxerxes II. In keeping with Achaemenid royal architectonic tradition, the palace was embellished with carved stone reliefs, wall-paintings, and glazed bricks.

Though Susa lost its royal status following the conquest of the Persian empire by Alexander the Great in 330 (for its surrender to Alexander, see Arrian, *Anabasis* 3.16.6–7), it seems to have prospered as a regional centre during the Hellenistic period (to judge from the expansion of settlement in this period) when it was renamed Seleucia-on-the-Eulaios. It was also a flourishing city under Parthian rule (C3 BCE–C3 CE), and once more assumed its traditional name, Susa. It survived with varying fortunes through the following centuries until it was finally abandoned in C13 CE.

*Malbran-Labat (1995), Vallat (1995), Perrot and Ladiray (1996), Pittman (*OEANE* 5: 106–10), D. T. Potts (1999: 488, index refs).

Susiana (map 12) Region in southwestern Iran, covering roughly the area of the mod. province of Khuzestan, with a history of settlement extending back to M8. In M6 and M5 its most important settlement was Chogha Mish, which was apparently abandoned in late M5 when the site of Susa was first occupied. Susa thenceforth became the chief city in Susiana. It maintained this status, very largely, until the second half of M1, although already in late M4 (Susa II period) its supremacy was challenged for a time by the emergence of two other centres in the region, at Chogha Mish (once more)

Figure 113 Susa, column capital.

and Abu Fanduweh. In the final centuries of M3, Susiana became subject to the Akkadian and Ur III empires in succession. In M2 it was incorporated into the kingdom of Elam, and Susa became one of the royal Elamite capitals. In the middle centuries of M2 Elam suffered a relatively long period of decline, during the course of which, in late C14, Susiana was invaded and conquered by the Babylonian king Kurigalzu II. But Babylonian sovereignty over the region was shortlived. By early C13, when Elam was once more emerging as a major power, Susiana had regained its independence. New settlements were built in the region, the most notable of which was Al-Untash-Napirisha (mod. Chogha Zanbil), a religious and ceremonial royal city built by the Elamite king Untash-napirisha (1275–1240), though never completed. Around 1110, Nebuchadnezzar I, fourth king of the Second Dynasty of Isin, invaded and plundered Susiana, and destroyed Susa. Neo-Elamite, Persian, and Seleucid settlement is also well attested on the plain.

Vallat (1995).

Sutu (Sutaeans) A confederation of nomadic tribes, probably of Amorite origin, located west of the middle Euphrates, inhabiting regions of Syria and Palestine between Mari and Qatna. They are first attested with certainty during the Middle Bronze Age in the Egyptian Execration texts (C19–18) in the form *Šwtw*, and in letters from the Mari archives (C18). In the latter, their relations with Mari are sometimes peaceful, but generally hostile. A small number of Sutaeans also appear to have been active in Babylonia at this time, and there is a possible (but very conjectural) reference in Egyptian sources to a Sutaean presence in the eastern Delta of Egypt. Sutaeans figure frequently in the Late Bronze Age Amarna letters (mid C14; see glossary) as dangerous bands of marauders and cut-throats (e.g. **EA* 16:37–42, 122:34). In these letters, as in earlier Babylonian documents, the term 'Sutu' was probably used in a broad general sense to designate all groups of predatory nomads. Later in C14, Sutu is listed among the allies of the land of Kadmuhu in northeastern Mesopotamia, who were conquered (along with Kadmuhu) by the Assyrian king Arik-den-ili (1319–1308) (**RIMA* 1: 132). Several centuries later, the Sutu appear along with Aramaeans as sackers of a number of southern Mesopotamian cities, including Der, Nippur (Duranki), Sippar, and Dur-Kurigalzu (Parsa), during the reign of the Babylonian king Adad-apla-iddina (1069–1048). Their incursions into Babylonian territory at this time, reported in several sources – including an inscription of the Sealand king Simbar-Shihu (1025–1008), a Babylonian Chronicle (no. 24) (**ABC* 180–1), and the Babylonian Erra Epic – appear to have been merely hit-and-run raiding operations rather than a prelude to occupation of a more permanent nature. Aramaeans and Sutaeans also appear together, in eastern Syria around the middle Euphrates region, in a fragmentary inscription of the Assyrian king Ashur-bel-kala (1073–1056).

Babylonia appears to have suffered further Aramaean/Sutaean incursions in the course of the next two centuries, until the reign of Nabu-apla-iddina (888–855), who claims to have driven the Sutaeans from the land. By this time, Sutaeans and Aramaeans, separately identified in the inscriptions recording their attacks on Babylonian cities in Adad-apla-iddina's reign, had become virtually indistinguishable.

Brinkman (1968: 285–7), Heltzer (1981), **LAPO* 17: 505–11, nos 744–9, Lipiński (2000: 38–40, 409–12), *LKM* 25–8.

Syangela (Theangela) (map 5) M1 BCE–M1 CE city in Caria in southwestern Anatolia. Strabo (13.1.59), citing Callisthenes, notes that it was one of the two cities of Lelegian origin (see **Lelegians**) which the C4 Carian ruler Mausolus did not incorporate into his new capital Halicarnassus. Previously, in C5, it had been a member of the Athenian Confederacy (see glossary), along with its dependency Amynanda, under the rule of a Carian dynast called Pigres. Mausolus refounded the city, enlarging it and probably shifting it to a new site, with a new Greek-sounding name, Theangela. It occupied a hilltop location above the mod. village of Etrim, which lies 14 km northeast of Bodrum. Scholars disagree as to whether this was in fact the site of the original city. Two alternative locations have been proposed for Syangela, one on the site of Alazeytin, the other on Kaplan Dağ. The former, principally occupied in the period C7–4, lies 5 km southwest of Etrim. It was a fortified Lelegian settlement whose remains include private dwellings, several sanctuaries and public buildings, and an agora. The latter settlement was of similar size and lies 3 km to the west of Etrim. A fort forming part of its substantial defences is thought to have served as a place of refuge. Other remains of the site include six burial tumuli with dromos entrances (see glossary). If one of these sites was in fact anc. Syangela, then it is possible that the city was destroyed by the Persians in early C5, and that subsequently its population took refuge on the hill above Etrim where Mausolus later built the new city.

The city which Mausolus founded, or refounded, covered three summits, extending over an area of c. 1300 m × 250 m. It was encompassed by a wall, built mainly in the Lelegian style and including a strong fort, with a tower on each corner, erected on top of the city's western summit. Access to the city was provided by several gates, the most important of which lay on the south side of the settlement near its western end. A cross-wall divided the city into two sections. It is thought that this may have had something to do with reducing the city's size so that it could more easily be manned. Other remains include public buildings, a well-preserved three-roomed Lelegian house with corbel-vaulted roof, and several water cisterns. There is now no trace of the temple of Athena attested in inscriptions, but several Archaic Greek statues which apparently belonged to Athena's sanctuary have been unearthed. The site's most impressive feature is an excellently preserved 7 m long tomb with corbelled roof. It contained a number of skeletal remains and some pottery dating to the second half of C5. The discovery of about forty stone balls (c. 15 cm in diameter) on the tomb's roof suggests that there was once an artillery emplacement there. The tomb may have been the final resting place of the local C5 dynast Pigres, who is known to have been still alive in 427. Pottery of mid and late C4 date indicates that the city was occupied for at least the first part of the Hellenistic age. However, it appears to have been abandoned during the Roman period, with perhaps some reoccupation in later times.

Bean (1971: 128–34; *PECS* 869).

Syria A name first attested in Herodotus, and commonly believed to be a Greek derivative of 'Assyria'. The derivation has long been debated. But Rollinger (2006) has recently demonstrated its likely validity, on the basis of information supplied by a Luwian–Phoenician bilingual inscription discovered in 1997 at Çineköy (q.v.) in southeastern Anatolia (Tecoğlu and Lemaire, 2000). It appears from this inscription that 'Syria' and 'Assyria' were the Greek forms of the names 'Sura/i' and 'Asura/i', which by C8, when they were first encountered by the Greeks, were used interchangeably for the same region. Rollinger (2006: 286) concludes from the inscription that 'the original linguistic and historical context (for the abbreviation Sura/i) was not a Greek or an Assyrian one but the multilingual milieu of southern Anatolia and northern Syria at the beginning of the Iron Age'.

For most Bronze and Iron Age scholars, 'Syria' covers a region extending southwards from southeastern Anatolia through the territories of Israel and Palestine, and eastwards from the Mediterranean littoral to the Euphrates. Some scholars would prefer to reduce and others to extend these limits. In any case, use of the term in a Bronze and Iron Age context is by and large a modern convention. The region to which it is applied never had a high degree of cultural or ethnic coherence in these early periods, and did not become a single political entity, or part of such an entity, until it was incorporated into the administrative systems of the Persian, Seleucid, and Roman empires, from the second half of M1 onwards.

Syria–Palestine 'Often used in archaeological and historical studies, the term *Syria-Palestine* designates ancient Canaan, although the correspondence is inexact because its geographic and political boundaries varied from period to period. In practical usage, the term is usually employed archaeologically to designate central and southern Canaan (*not* "Greater Canaan"), or to incorporate the modern boundaries of coastal and south-central Syria (south of the bend of the Orontes r.), Lebanon, Israel, Jordan, and part of Egypt's Sinai Desert.' Dever (*OEANE* 5: 147).

Syrna (*Bayır*) (map 5) M1 BCE–M1 CE city in Caria, southwestern Anatolia, southwest of mod. Marmaris on the Loryma peninsula. According to a legendary tradition recorded by Stephanus of Byzantium, its founder was Podaleirius (son of Asclepius, god of healing), who named it after his wife, Syrna. A sanctuary of Asclepius at Syrna is attested in inscriptions, but all trace of it has now disappeared.

Bean (*PECS* 874).

T

Taanach (map 8) Canaanite city built on a mound, c. 6 ha in extent, located in northern Palestine at the southern end of the Jezreel valley, 8 km southeast of Megiddo. Its history of occupation extends from the Early Bronze Age (c. 2700) until C18 CE. Excavations were carried out by E. Sellin for the University of Vienna from 1902 to 1904, and by P. W. Lapp, leader of a joint expedition of the American Schools of Oriental Research and Concordia Seminary, St Louis, from 1963 to 1968.

In the Early Bronze Age, Taanach was a fortified settlement which lasted some 300 years, from c. 2700 to 2400 (Early Bronze Age II–III). It was then abandoned until C18, when it began life again as a modest settlement, developing over the next two centuries into a prosperous urban centre (Middle Bronze Age IIC), with massive fortifications of casemate construction. An Akkadian text found on the site provides evidence of a metallurgical industry. A range of burial practices is indicated by the discovery of c. sixty intramural burials, including childburials, in sub-floor locations.

Around the end of C16, the city suffered a major destruction. Though it was rebuilt soon afterwards, as attested by a C15 building complex (Late Bronze Age I) and a number of Akkadian cuneiform tablets, it fell to the pharaoh Tuthmosis III when he defeated a coalition of Syrian states in the battle of Megiddo (c. 1479), and probably destroyed Taanach. There is little material evidence for occupation of the site in the next two centuries, though scholars draw attention to an eighteenth dynasty Egyptian text which indicates that Taanach provided warriors, called *maryannu*, for the Egyptian court. And there is a possible (but far from certain) reference to it, in the form Tahnaka, in one of the C14 Amarna letters (**EA* 248:14). The site was, however, occupied in C12, as attested by the remains of several large buildings of this period, and a cuneiform tablet referring to a shipment of grain.

Destruction of the C12 level c. 1125 was followed by an Iron Age city, noted for its assemblage of cultic material. A number of *OT* sources refer to the city in this phase of its existence. Its king was allegedly among those conquered by Joshua (Joshua 12:21), though other *OT* sources deny an Israelite conquest. In reality, it may have remained under Canaanite control until the establishment of the Israelite monarchy in C9. This is implied by the inclusion of Taanach in the list of cities conquered by the pharaoh Sheshonq I (*OT* Shishak) in late C10. Its destruction is depicted in a relief in the pharaoh's temple at Karnak. Only sparse remains of the city have survived from its later phases, in the Iron Age II, Persian, Hellenistic, Roman, and Byzantine periods. However, the C4 CE bishop of Caesarea, Eusebius, indicates in his *Onomasticon* the existence of a large community on the site in his time.

Lapp (1967), Glock (*OEANE* 5: 149).

Tabal (biblical Tubal) (map 18) Iron Age country (so designated in M1 Neo-Assyrian texts) in southern Anatolia, extending southwards from the southern curve of the Halys r. (mod. Kızıl Irmak) into the region called the Lower Land (q.v.) in Late Bronze Age

Hittite texts. Originally, Tabal was made up of a series of mainly small, independent kingdoms. The Assyrian king Shalmaneser III claims to have received gifts from twenty-four kings of Tabal during a campaign which he conducted in the region in 837 (**RIMA* 3: 67; twenty kings, according to **RIMA* 3: 79). In the following year, he received further tribute from these kings while he was campaigning in the land of Melid.

A century later, five kings from the Tabal region were listed among the tributaries of the Assyrian king Tiglath-pileser III (745–727): Wassurme (Luwian Wasusarmas),

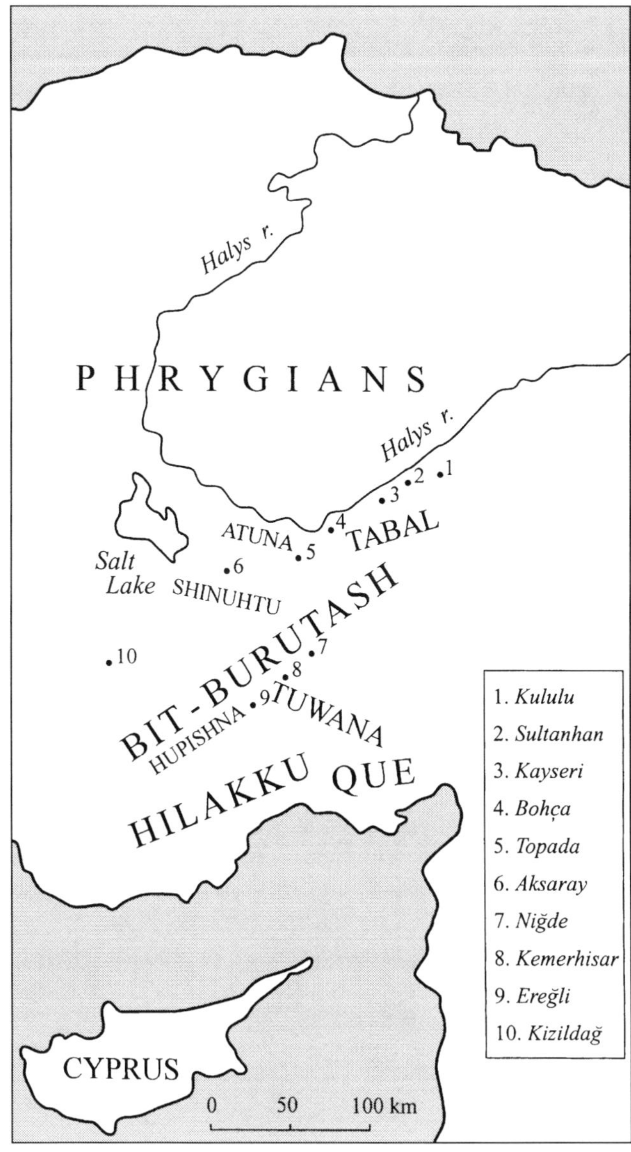

Map 18 Tabal.

Ushhiti, Urballa (Luwian Warpalawas), Tuhamme, and Uirime (*Tigl. III* 68–9, 108–9). They were the rulers, respectively, of the kingdoms of Tabal, Atuna, Tuwana (Assyrian Tuhana), Ishtuanda, and Hupisna (see entries on each of these). Only Wassurme (henceforth Wasusarmas) is explicitly identified as a king of Tabal. In a broad sense, the term Tabal may have been used by the Assyrians as a generic designation for all the kingdoms that lay within the territories delineated above. But in a specific political sense, it appears to have been used, prior to the reign of Sargon II, exclusively of the northernmost of these kingdoms, over which Wasusarmas had held sway during Tiglath-pileser's reign. Wasusarmas' kingdom was almost certainly the largest of the kingdoms of Tabal, and probably incorporated a number of the small Tabalic principalities to which Shalmaneser had referred a century earlier. It is sometimes now referred to by scholars as 'Tabal Proper'. Extending southwards from the Halys r., it corresponded roughly to the mod. provinces of Kayseri and Niğde (Hawkins, 1982: 376). Its capital may have been located on the site of mod. Kululu (q.v.), which lies 30 km northeast of Kayseri. Another of its cities was discovered at Sultanhan (q.v.), a few km west of Kululu.

A long hieroglyphic inscription from Wasusarmas' reign records a battle in which the king or one of his subordinate commanders engaged against a coalition of eight enemy rulers (**CHLI* I: 452–4) near the city of Parzuta (q.v.). Wasusarmas claims to have had the support of three 'friendly kings': Warpalawas, Kiyakiyas (probably Kiakki, king of Shinuhtu in Assyrian texts), and Ruwatas (otherwise unknown). Whether or not these kings actually took part in the conflict, which may have arisen out of a dispute over frontiers, Wasusarmas defeated the coalition forces, and no doubt took the opportunity to extend his frontiers at their expense. He styled himself 'Great King', son of another 'Great King', Tuwatis, and was accused by Tiglath-pileser of acting as if he were his overlord's equal. The suspicions which his attitude and conduct roused in the Assyrian court were to prove his undoing. A tablet from Nimrud indicates that Tiglath-pileser had him deposed, replacing him on his throne with a commoner called Hulli, a 'son of nobody' (**ARAB* I: 288, **Tigl. III* 170–1). But Hulli too seems to have fallen foul of his Assyrian overlord, for he and his son Ambaris were taken off to Assyria by Tiglath-pileser's successor Shalmaneser V (726–722). They were, however, repatriated by Shalmaneser's successor Sargon II (721–705), who subsequently placed Ambaris on the throne once occupied by his father, married his daughter to him, and gave him the country of Hilakku (q.v.) as a dowry (**ARAB* II: 11).

Sargon claims to have 'widened the land' which he assigned to Ambaris. The new name, Bit-Burutash (Bit-Paruta), by which Ambaris' kingdom was called, almost certainly reflects a significant expansion southwards of the former kingdom of northern Tabal ('Tabal Proper'), probably to the northern border of Hilakku. Perhaps in the face of increasing threats to the region posed by the Phrygian king Mita, better known by his Greek name Midas, from the west (see below) and the Urartian king Rusa I from the east, Sargon sought to establish a more centralized authority within Tabal, under a local ruler whom he believed he could trust. But if so, his trust was misplaced. Ambaris later fell out of favour with Sargon, who accused him of plotting with Phrygia and Urartu, and deported him along with his family and chief courtiers to Assyria in 713 (**ARAB* II: 27). Bit-Burutash along with Hilakku was placed under the administration of an Assyrian governor. (Bit-Burutash was settled with deportees brought from other regions which fell to Assyrian conquests.) That is the first clear indication we have of direct Assyrian rule being imposed over Tabal. Prior to this, the Assyrian kings had exercised their authority in the region through the imposition of an annual tribute upon the local rulers, and the requirement that they pay homage in person to the Assyrian king.

The union of the Phrygian and Mushki peoples under Midas towards the end of C8 led to the emergence of a major new rival to Assyrian supremacy in eastern Anatolia. Tabal now became contested territory between the two Great Kings Midas and Sargon. Midas set out to win over the local Tabalic rulers from their Assyrian allegiance, and several of these rulers apparently switched allegiance to him. But Sargon promptly reasserted his authority in the region, deporting the rebel leaders to Assyria (**ARAB* II: 7, 11, 27). He handed over their cities to other local leaders who had remained loyal to him. He further consolidated his authority in the Tabalic and adjacent regions by settling Assyrians and other foreigners in Tabal, and establishing Assyrian governors in the neighbouring countries of Hilakku and Que. (It is possible that the one governor, Ashur-sharru-usur, was assigned authority over all three regions.) Hostilities between Assyria and Phrygia were finally resolved when a *détente* was established between Sargon and Midas (**SAA* I: 4–7; see under **Phrygia**).

In the last year of his reign (705), Sargon undertook an expedition into Tabal (**ABC* 76), and was probably killed in the course of this campaign, perhaps while fighting the Cimmerians. This almost certainly marked the end of direct Assyrian authority in the region. For a time, however, Tabal continued to figure in Assyrian activities in southern Anatolia. The Assyrian king Esarhaddon (680–669) engaged in military operations there, from his base in Que, against the Cimmerians, defeating the Cimmerian leader Teushpa in the territory of Hubushna (Hupisna) (**ABC* 125). During Esarhaddon's reign, a Tabalic leader called Ishkallu apparently joined forces with Mugallu, a king of Melid, against whom the Assyrians had conducted a campaign in 675. There is also in this period a Tabalic king called Mugallu who established diplomatic relations with Esarhaddon's son and successor Ashurbanipal early in his reign (668–630/627), sending an embassy to him and paying him a yearly tribute. The Tabalic Mugallu is almost certainly the same man as the king of Melid. His association with two countries very likely indicates an extension of his power from Melid to Tabal by the beginning of Ashurbanipal's reign. Fear of the Cimmerians may have been the cause of Mugallu's realignment with Assyria, though his son subsequently broke with Assyria and joined forces with the intruders led by Lygdamis (Dugdamme) (on whom see Kuhrt, *RlA* 7: 186–9). This was an act of treachery, which, according to an Assyrian Ishtar temple-text dating to c. 640, brought the wrath of the gods upon its perpetrator (*Thompson and Mallowan, 1933: 88–9, 96–7). It also brings to an end references to Tabal in Assyrian sources. It is quite possible that the kingdom and its culture ended during the Cimmerian invasions. The country appears in later texts under the name Cappadocia.

**CHLI* I: 424–531.

Tabatum (Assyrian **Tabetu (1)**, ***Tell Taban***?) Middle Bronze Age and Iron Age city in the district of Qattunan, in the Habur r. region, northwestern Mesopotamia. It is frequently attested in the Mari archives from the reign of Zimri-Lim (1774–1762), generally in contexts relating to its cultivable lands and to travel and the transport of goods through it. These sources place it between Magarisu to the north and Shadikannu to the south.

LKM 626 (refs).

Tabitu/Tabetu (2) Iron Age city located in the Habur region of Upper Mesopotamia, at the confluence of the Wadi Radd and the Jaghjagh r. (Liverani, 1992: 63). After crossing the Tigris from east to west, the Assyrian king Ashurnasirpal II first encamped for the night at Tabitu before continuing along the banks of the Harmish r. on his way through the Habur region in 878 (*RIMA* 2: 212).

Tadmor (Roman **Palmyra**) (maps 7, 10) City located in the Syrian desert 235 km northeast of Damascus, with a history of occupation extending from late M3 until the Islamic period. The site was explored by a succession of visitors from C17 CE onwards, and has been extensively excavated since 1924. Throughout its history, Tadmor was an important caravan city, due to its location in an oasis on a major east–west caravan route. In written records, it is first attested in C19 (Middle Bronze Age) Assyrian merchant texts found at Kanesh in north-central Anatolia. Other references to it appear in texts from Middle Bronze Age Mari, and Late Bronze Age Emar. According to the Annals of the Assyrian king Tiglath-pileser I (1114–1076), it belonged to the country of Amurru (**RIMA* 2: 38). (The name 'Amurru' is apparently used here in its original broad sense; see under **Amurru**.) The city reached the peak of its development in the Roman imperial period, when it was called Palmyra, 'City of Palms'. To this period it owes its importance today as one of the best-known and best-preserved cities of the anc. world.

Bounni (*OEANE* 4: 238–44).

Tadum (*Tell Farfara*?) City documented already in mid M3, but best known as a Middle Bronze Age royal city in the eastern Habur region of northern Mesopotamia, in the vicinity of Ilan-sura, attested in the Mari archives from the reign of Zimri-Lim (1774–1762). Zimri-Lim had installed a man called Ibni-Addu as its king. But when his subjects removed him from power, Ibni-Addu went to Shehna (Shubat-Enlil) seeking assistance from Kunnam, the Elamite military commander then occupying the city, in his bid to regain his throne. Kunnam promised Ibni-Addu his support, but appears to have provided him with no more than token assistance. Tadum's inhabitants once more rejected their king, though they stopped short of killing him as Haya-Sumu, king of Ilan-sura, had urged them to do. Ibni-Addu then returned to Kunnam, probably hoping to gain more substantial support from him in yet another attempt to be reinstated on his throne (**LKM* 294, no. 26.310). However, he was seized, probably at the instigation of Haya-Sumu, and attempts to extradite him to Mari failed; Haya-Sumu may have had him executed in order to install his own son in Tadum as ruler. Tadum is usually identified with the settlement later known as Taidu (see **Taidu (1)**).

LKM 77–8, 86–7.

Tae Iron Age city belonging to the Neo-Hittite kingdom Pat(t)in (Assyrian Unqi) in northern Syria, mentioned in the Annals of the Assyrian king Tiglath-pileser III (745–727) as one of the cities where he resettled deportees from other parts of his kingdom. Tarmanazi was another city of Patin used for this purpose (**ARAB* II: 276, **Tigl. III* 66–7).

CHLI I: 362.

Taia Iron Age city belonging to the Neo-Hittite kingdom of Pat(t)in (Assyrian Unqi)

in northern Syria. It was captured by the Assyrian king Shalmaneser III during his campaign against the cities of northern Syria in his first regnal year (858) (**RIMA* 3: 17).
CHLI I: 362.

Taidu (1) (*Tell Farfara*?) Middle and Late Bronze Age city in the Habur region of Upper Mesopotamia. Its location in this area is assured by a Middle Assyrian itinerary text found at Dur-Katlimmu, which covers the journey between Taidu and Dur-Katlimmu, and also by a Mitanni-period tablet excavated at Tell Brak which mentions 'Nawar (probably Tell Brak) in the district of Taidu'. An identification has been suggested with the site of Tell Hamidiya (q.v.) in the Habur triangle, where a sequence of palaces was constructed on top of the 20 ha mound (thus Wäfler). However, this location has been rejected by Guichard (1994: 244), who prefers to identify Taidu with Tell Farfara, based on the Mari evidence. In any case, an identification of this Taidu with earlier M2 Tadum (q.v.) seems secure.
(H. D. Baker)
Eichler and Wäfler (1989/90), Guichard (1994).

Taidu (2) City in northern Mesopotamia, first attested in Late Bronze Age texts as the eastern capital of the C14–13 kingdom of Hanigalbat, rump state of the former Mitannian empire. When the Hanigalbatean king Wasashatta attempted to break away from Assyrian sovereignty, the Assyrian king Adad-nirari I (1307–1295) captured and burnt Taidu (**RIMA* 1: 131, 136). He then apparently restored it (**RIMA* 1: 137), and established a royal residence there after incorporating Hanigalbat into his kingdom. Subsequently, however, Wasashatta's son and successor Shattuara II gained control of Taidu and the neighbouring areas. But he and his coalition were defeated by Shalmaneser I (1274–1245), who fought him and captured cities 'from Taidu to Irride, all of Mt Kashiyari to the city Eluhat' (**RIMA* 2: 184).

This Taidu has often been identified with Taidu (1) and was conventionally located in the upper Tigris region, at the site of later Tidu (q.v.) (Kessler, 1980: 85–121). However, publication of the Dur-Katlimmu itinerary (s.v. **Taidu (1)**) made it clear that there was definitely a settlement called Taidu in the Habur region. A possible solution is to assume that there were two places called Taidu: (1) in the Habur region, identical with earlier Tadum; (2) in the upper Tigris, later known as Tidu.
(H. D. Baker)

Talbish (Talmish) Iron Age city located on an island in the middle Euphrates r., near the city of Suru (see **Suru (2)**), which lay in the Aramaean land of Suhu. The Assyrian king Tukulti-Ninurta II encamped his forces nearby during his last recorded campaign (885) which took him through the middle Tigris and Euphrates regions (**RIMA* 2: 174).

Talhayum Middle Bronze Age city, capital of Yapturum, one of four districts in the northern part of the Ida-maras region, northern Mesopotamia. In late C19 Talhayum was subject territory, along with other cities and kingdoms in the region, of Yahdun-Lim, king of Mari (1810–1794). Subsequently Zimri-Lim, who occupied Mari's throne in 1774 after the Assyrian viceroy Yasmah-Addu fled the city, installed Yawi-Ila upon Talhayum's throne. To judge from a letter written to Zimri-Lim by Sammetar, king of Ashnakkum, Yawi-Ila was among the local rulers loyal to Zimri-Lim who became the targets of pro-Elamite groups. Most of them seem to have been assassinated. But Yawi-Ila apparently escaped this fate. He is otherwise known to us because of letters he wrote to Zimri-Lim about a conflict he had with Bunuma-Adad, king of Nihriya, allegedly in defence of Zimri-Lim's interests in the region (**LAPO* 16: 527–8, no. 338; **LAPO* 17: 269–70, no. 606). At the end of Zimri-Lim's twelfth year, Yawi-Ila lost his throne in unknown circumstances, and was replaced by a man called Asdi-Nehim.

*Durand (1988b), *Mesop.* 220.

Tamassus (***Politiko***) (map 14) City kingdom in central Cyprus, located 22 km southwest of Nicosia, listed under the name Tamesu among the ten M1 kingdoms of the island in an inscription of the Assyrian king Esarhaddon, the so-called Esarhaddon prism, dated to 673/672 (*Borger, 1956: 60 §27; Heidel, 1956). Evidence provided by tombs indicates that settlement on the site extends back at least to the Middle Bronze Age. Much of the city's wealth throughout its existence must have been derived from its exploitation of the nearby copper mines. Tamassus consisted of both acropolis and lower town, with a large necropolis extending to the south and southeast. In the inscriptions of Esarhaddon, its king appears to have been a man called Atmesu (Greek Admetus) (**ARAB* II: 266, 341). The city is not attested in Greek sources until mid C4, when we learn that its then ruler, Pasicyprus, sold his kingdom for fifty talents to Pumiathon, king of Citium, and thereupon went to Amathus where he spent his old age. Tamassus was subsequently taken from Pumiathon by Alexander the Great and handed over to Salamis' king Pnytagoras.

Figure 114 Tamassus, male worshipper, sanctuary of Apollo.

The city appears to have prospered through the various phases of its existence, from the Archaic period (C7–6) onwards, and became a bishopric in the Byzantine period. Prior to this, it was a centre for the worship of Apollo and the Mother of the Gods. The sanctuaries of both these deities have been tentatively identified. Cults of other deities – Aphrodite, Dionysus, Asclepius, and Artemis – are also known from written sources to have been practised in the city. Among the very few remains to be excavated are a temple dedicated to Aphrodite, part of the city's fortifications, installations for the production of copper, and two well-preserved 'royal built tombs', which date to the Archaic period. Both tombs show extremely fine workmanship, in the structures themselves as well as in their architectonic decorations. Six unique Cypro-Archaic statues depicting recumbent lions and sphinxes were accidentally discovered near the tombs in 1997.

Nicolaou (*PECS* 875–6), Solomidou-Ieronymidou (2001), Iacovou (2002).

Tamina Late Bronze Age country in southwestern Anatolia. It was one of the cities/countries conquered by the last Hittite king, Suppiluliuma II (early C12), during his campaigns in southern and southwestern Anatolia, as recorded in the so-called 'Sudbürg inscription' recently discovered in the Hittite capital, Hattusa (*Hawkins, 1995: 22–3).

Tanakun Fortified Iron Age city, probably to be located in or near the land of Que in southern Anatolia. The city's ruler, Tullu, surrendered to the Assyrian king Shalmaneser III in the course of or immediately following a campaign which Shalmaneser had conducted in Que in his twenty-sixth regnal year (833) (**RIMA* 3: 68). Shalmaneser took hostages from the city, and a tribute of gold, silver, iron, oxen, and sheep.

Tapikka (*Maşat*) (maps 2, 3) City located in northern Anatolia, with a history of occupation extending from late M3 to early C13. At its greatest extent, it covered 10 ha. Its most distinguished phase dates to the Late Bronze Age, when it became an important regional administrative, military, and economic centre of the Hittite kingdom. Lying in the frontier-zone of the Hittite homeland, 116 km northeast of the Hittite capital Hattusa and close to the region of the Kaska peoples, its location gave it considerable strategic significance. The city reached the peak of its development in the first half of C14, probably during the reign of the Hittite king Tudhaliya III. Kaska invaders were almost certainly responsible for its destruction during the comprehensive invasions of the Hittite homeland towards the end of Tudhaliya's reign. After the Hittites regained their lost territories, Tapikka was rebuilt, probably by Tudhaliya's son and successor Suppiluliuma I (1350–1322). In the last decades of the Late Bronze Age, it was again destroyed by fire. The Phrygians reoccupied it in the early Iron Age, building a small settlement on the citadel.

Excavation of the site began in 1973, under the direction of T. Özgüç, and continued until 1984. The site consists of a citadel, which rises 29 m above the surrounding plain, and a lower city adjacent to the citadel's southeast side. Of the five levels dating to the Hittite period, level III was the largest and most important. At this time Tudhaliya III almost certainly occupied the Hittite throne. The most prominent feature of level III was a building erected on the citadel covering an area of almost 4,500 sq. m. Commonly referred to as a palace, it was clearly the headquarters of the regional administration. There are remains of north and east wings of the palace, and an inner colonnaded courtyard. The only significant remains of the lower city belong to a temple, of which a 50 m long south wing and part of an east wing and inner court survive.

A range of artefacts was unearthed from both palace and temple, including seals and inscribed bullae, bull and stag figures (apparently symbols of divinity), and animal-shaped drinking vessels. But the most significant find in this level was a tablet archive, housed in two adjoining rooms in the palace. Ninety-six of the 116 texts brought to light are letters. These include correspondence exchanged between the Hittite king and his deputies in Tapikka, between officials based in Tapikka and their colleagues in Hattusa, and between officials in Tapikka and other cities of the Hittite kingdom. The communications between the king and his officials have much to do with the security of the region. They include reports to the king on enemy movements and raids on grain lands, requests from officials for reinforcements, and instructions from the king about the relocation of populations in territories threatened by the enemy and the treatment to be accorded to defectors or enemy prisoners taken in battle. The entire surviving corpus may date to a period of no more than a few months before Tapikka was destroyed. Texts of a cultic nature were also found in Tapikka, dating to the last phase of its existence as a Hittite city in C13.

Alp/Özgüç (*RlA* 7: 442–6), *Alp (1991a; 1991b), T. Özgüç (2002), **CS* III: 45–51, Bryce (2003b: 170–81).

Tappassanda Late Bronze Age city in central Anatolia subjected to Hittite rule by the Hittite king Hattusili I (1650–1620). Hattusili appointed his son Huzziya as its governor. Subsequently, the city's inhabitants induced Huzziya to lead an uprising against his father. Hattusili evidently crushed the rebellion and removed his son from office (**CS* II: 80, **Chav.* 225–6).

Tarava (*Tarum*) M1 city in Vautiya, a district in southern Persis, southwestern Iran. A pretender to the Persian throne called Vahyazdata rose up in rebellion there, with the support of local Persian forces, against the Persian king Darius I on the latter's accession in 522 (**DB* 40–1). Vahyazdata falsely claimed that he was Bardiya, brother of Cyrus II's son and successor Cambyses. See also **Rakha**.

Tarhuntassa (map 3) Late Bronze Age kingdom in southern Anatolia. It was probably created by the Hittite king Muwattalli II early in C13, though Tarhuntassa as a geographical entity may have existed much earlier. Around 1280, Muwattalli transferred the seat of the Hittite administration there from Hattusa (**CS* I: 200, 201). Scholars debate whether he made the shift for strategic reasons, in order to have a base closer to his forthcoming military operations in Syria against the pharaoh Ramesses II, or whether his action was motivated primarily by religious or personal considerations. Though he clearly intended the move to be a permanent one, his son and successor Urhi-Teshub (Mursili III) (1272–1267) transferred the capital back to Hattusa shortly after occupying the throne. Subsequently, Tarhuntassa became an important appanage kingdom of Hatti. Urhi-Teshub's successor Hattusili III appointed his nephew Kurunta (=Ulmi-Teshub, according to most scholars), son of Muwattalli and (half-?)brother of Urhi-Teshub, as its ruler (**CS* I: 204), and Hattusili's son Tudhaliya IV renewed the appointment. Both Great Kings conferred numerous privileges and favours upon Kurunta, as indicated by still extant treaties which they concluded with him (**HDT*

109–13, 114–24, **CS* II: 100–6). Tudhaliya's treaty is inscribed on the famous bronze tablet discovered at Hattusa in 1986. Included among its provisions is a definition of the boundaries of Tarhuntassa. From this and other information, we can conclude that the kingdom extended along the southern coast of Anatolia through the regions of Classical Cilicia and Pamphylia. It incorporated the territory called the Hulaya River Land, and bordered the country of Kizzuwadna to its east. Its western boundary was marked in part by a city called Parha (Classical Perge) and a river called the Kastaraya (Classical Cestrus). Both Classical names indicate a western Pamphylian location for this boundary, or at least the southernmost part of it.

Hieroglyphic inscriptions discovered at mod. Hatip, Kızıldağ, Karadağ, and Burunkaya (**CHLI* I: 433–8; see **Hatip** and **Kızıldağ**) may indicate that by the last decades of C13, Tarhuntassa's territory extended northwards into Classical Lycaonia and Cappadocia. It is possible that Muwattalli's lineal descendants, including Kurunta, established Tarhuntassa as a breakaway kingdom from Hatti – until such time as the Hittite throne, seized by Muwattalli's brother Hattusili (III), could be restored to its rightful heirs. Tarhuntassa does in fact appear to have broken its ties with Hatti some time after the treaty recorded on the bronze tablet, since it appears in the so-called 'Südburg inscription' at Hattusa, dating to the reign of the last Hittite king Suppiluliuma II (1207–), as one of the enemy countries reconquered by the Hittites (*Hawkins, 1995: 22–3). Control of Tarhuntassa was vital to the Hittite kingdom in

Figure 115 The Hittite king Suppiluliuma II, from 'Südburg', Hattusa.

the last years of its existence, since the port of Ura, through which imported grain was transported to the Hittite homeland, lay in or near its territory.

Otten (1988), Dinçol *et al.* (2000), Bryce (2007), Melchert (2007), Taracha (2007).

Tarnip Middle Bronze Age city located within the western part of the Ida-maras region of the Habur triangle, northern Mesopotamia. In late C19 it was captured, along with the city of Ashnakkum, by the Eshnunnite king Naram-Sin during his campaign of conquest in the Habur triangle.

Mesop. 131.

Tarsus (Tarzi in Assyrian texts) (maps 2, 4) City located in the Cilician plain in southern Anatolia, with a history of occupation from the Neolithic (M6 or earlier) to the Roman imperial period. It was excavated by H. Goldman from 1934 to 1939. Investigations of the site were resumed in 2001 by an international, interdisciplinary team, with participants from Boğaziçi University, Bryn Mawr College, and other institutions, under the overall direction of A. Özyar.

In the Early Bronze Age, the site was occupied by a large fortified settlement with extensive trading contacts. Situated as it was on Anatolia's southeastern coast, it provided an important link between the Anatolian region and the countries lying further to the east. The *depas amphikypellon* type of pottery (see glossary) found at Tarsus indicates trading contacts with Troy II (M3), and there was also an abundance of pottery on the site originating from Cyprus, Syria, and Mesopotamia. Impressive private dwellings, probably two-storeyed in some cases, constructed at the peak of the city's Early Bronze Age development, reflect the existence of an elite class which had almost certainly built its wealth on commerce. In spite of its strong defences, the city was destroyed by enemy action on at least two occasions in its Early Bronze phase. Settlement continued, however, through the Middle and Late Bronze Ages, and in the latter period Tarsus became subject to the kingdom of Hatti. At this time it lay within the territory of the Hittite vassal state Kizzuwadna. Like nearby Mersin, its location on the coast near the sea routes which brought grain and other imports to the Hittite world no doubt made it of considerable strategic value to the Hittites.

After a period of apparent abandonment at the end of the Late Bronze Age, Tarsus was reoccupied in the early Iron Age, and was conquered by the Assyrian king Shalmaneser III in his twenty-sixth regnal year, 833 (**RIMA* 3: 68–9). Shalmaneser appointed a certain Kirri, brother of Kate, king of the land of Que, as ruler of Tarsus and other cities and peoples he had conquered in the region. Tarsus later joined a rebellion against the Assyrian king Sennacherib c. 696, and was captured, plundered, and destroyed (**ARAB* II: 137). Again rebuilt, it became subject to Persia in the second half of C6. But along with the rest of Cilicia, it appears to have enjoyed a relatively high degree of autonomy during the Persian period (C6–4), under a line of local kings called by the title Syennesis. The dynasty's seat of power may have been located in Tarsus. In 333 the city was captured by Alexander the Great, and was subject to the Seleucid dynasty during the Hellenistic period. Under Roman rule, it became the capital of the Roman province of Cilicia. The apostle Paul was said to be a native of Tarsus.

Goldman (1956), Özyar (2005).

Taruisa Late Bronze Age city or small country in northwestern Anatolia. It was the last place, following Wilusiya, in the list of countries forming the anti-Hittite Assuwan Confederacy, as recorded by the Hittite king Tudhaliya I/II (see **Assuwa**). Many scholars believe that the names Wilusiya and Taruisa correspond to (W)ilios and Troia (Ilios and Troy), which are used interchangeably for the same city in the *Iliad*. Conceivably, Wilusiya and Taruisa were originally separate but adjoining countries which subsequently merged, with local tradition preserving the latter's name until it resurfaced in the form Troia as an alternative to Ilios in Homeric tradition. Taruisa is only once more attested – in a hieroglyphic inscription carved on a silver bowl of unknown provenance, now in the Museum of Anatolian Civilizations in Ankara. The inscription, in Luwian hieroglyphics, records the conquest of a place called Tarwiza (presumably the hieroglyphic form of Taruisa) by a king called Tudhaliya (*Hawkins, 1997).

Taşci (map 2) Site of Late Bronze Age rock-carved sculptures, dating to C13, located in central Anatolia, in the region of Classical Cappadocia. The site was discovered by H. Rott in 1906. The sculptures consist of a single figure, whose nature and role are uncertain, and a row of three other figures identified either as gods, or as worshippers in an attitude of prayer. Luwian hieroglyphic inscriptions accompany both compositions.
Bittel (1976: 184–5), Burney (2004: 267).

Tashiniya Late Bronze Age city in eastern Anatolia or northeastern Syria, located north of Carchemish near the city of Urshu, west of the Euphrates r. It was among the cities which the Hittite king Hattusili I (1650–1620) attacked and destroyed on his march back to Hattusa at the end of his first(?) campaign in Syria (**Chav.* 220), perhaps because it was a subject or ally of the kingdom of Aleppo.

Tawilan (map 13) Iron Age II settlement in Jordan north of Petra in the anc. kingdom of Edom, dating predominantly to C7–6. It is perhaps to be identified with the biblically attested city of Teman (q.v.). Following an initial survey by N. Glueck in 1933, the site was excavated by C.-M. Bennett from 1968 to 1970 and in 1982, for the British School of Archaeology in Jerusalem and subsequently for the British Institute at Amman for Archaeology and History. These excavations revealed that Tawilan was an unfortified agricultural settlement, whose principal period of occupation was C7. Among the small finds was an assemblage of painted 'Edomite' ceramic ware, currently dated to C7–6, though it may be earlier, and a seal depicting an altar and a star and crescent, symbols of the moon god Sin and the goddess Ishtar.

The last season of excavation produced a treasure hoard consisting of eighteen gold rings and earrings and 334 carnelian beads. The most recent studies have suggested a date of C9–8 for the hoard, whose gold jewellery is the first such anc. assemblage to be unearthed in Jordan. The 1982 season of excavation also produced the first cuneiform tablet recovered from Jordan. Drawn up in Harran in northern Mesopotamia, it is a legal document which concerns a dispute over a sale of livestock. There is no precise archaeological context for the document. But a reference within it to the accession year of a King Darius (there were three Persian kings of this name) suggests that Tawilan continued to exist through at least part of the Persian period (C6–4).

There followed a period of apparent abandonment of the site until it was reoccupied probably in C1–2 CE when part of it was used as a cemetery. It was again occupied during the Mameluke period (C13–16 CE).

P. Bienkowski (1990: 95–101; *OEANE* 5: 156–8).

Tawiniya Late Bronze Age Hittite city and cult-centre, probably Hattian in origin, in north-central Anatolia. Alaca Höyük and the Celtic city of Tavium, capital of Roman Galatia, are among several proposed identifications for the city. Located on one of the festival routes from Hattusa, one day's journey from the capital, it played an important role in the festival of the Hattian goddess Teteshapi, and also had close associations with the Hattian god Telipinu.

**RGTC* 6: 416–18.

Taxila (map 16) Central Asian city attested in Classical texts, located in northwestern Pakistan, east of the Indus r. and northwest of the mod. city of Rawalpindi. It was originally part of the country of Gandhara, but apparently separate from it during the period of the Persian empire (C6–4). It lay at the intersection of trade routes passing between India and the Asian lands lying to the west. By the time of Alexander the Great's campaigns in the east, it had become the dominant city of the region between the Indus and Jhelum rivers. Taxiles, the ruler of this region at the time, came to terms with Alexander prior to the latter's crossing of the Indus in 326, and succeeded in maintaining his position on Taxila's throne, as a subject of Alexander under the immediate authority of a Macedonian satrap (Arrian, *Anabasis* 5.3.6, 7.2.2, Strabo 15.1.28). In the western world, Taxila was reputed to be a splendid and powerful city. In India, it was noted as a seat of learning and a centre for Buddhist worship.

Hermann (*RE* VA: 75–8).

Taya, Tell Settlement in northern Mesopotamia, consisting of a central mound and surrounding settlement, one of four major sites in the northeastern corner of the Sinjar-Tell Afar plain, covering at its peak in M3 a total area of c. 160 ha. The site was excavated by J. E. Reade over three seasons, 1967, 1968–9, and 1972–3, for the British School of Archaeology in Iraq. The earliest evidence for settlement, in the form of ceramic ware, dates back to the Ubaid period (up to early M4). In the second half of M3 a substantial urban centre had developed on the site, probably the most important centre in its region. Its so-called Inner Town on the mound was fortified by an oval wall which enclosed some 5 ha, with a 2 ha extension to the southwest. But the settlement extended well beyond this, to a densely settled, unwalled Outer Town covering c. 65 ha, and beyond that a further area of less dense settlement covering c. 90 ha. Inside the Inner Town a circular citadel was built, with stonework 1.6 m thick and 3 m high and a mudbrick superstructure of at least 2 m. The Outer Town contained many courtyard houses, and a number of chapels or shrines and industrial installations.

After a period of c. 100 years of abandonment, the central mound was reoccupied c. 1900 (Middle Bronze Age). Sherds of early 'Habur ware' and a rectangular house or shrine are among the meagre remains of this first period of reoccupation. It was followed, also in the Middle Bronze Age, by a settlement with a new layout. Remains of this phase indicate that Tell Taya had now assumed the character of a large farming community. The finds from it include two cuneiform tablets bearing the seal of an official of the Assyrian king Shamshi-Adad I (1796–1775), indicating that at this time the town was part of the Old Assyrian kingdom. Virtually nothing more is known about the settlement until the Iron Age II period. Above the early M2 remains, a Neo-Assyrian settlement occupied the site, in the period c. 850–750. In this phase of its existence, a large stone terrace encircled the (probably fortified) central mound. Subsequent remains date to M1 CE when the site apparently came under Parthian and Sasanian control.

Reade (1982b; *OEANE* 5: 158–60).

Tayinat, Tell (map 7) Settlement-mound, with Early Bronze Age and Iron Age occupation levels, located in northwestern Syria, 25 km from Antakya and 800 m from Tell Atchana (Bronze Age Alalah). The site is very likely to be identified with Kinalua, capital of the Iron Age Neo-Hittite kingdom of Pat(t)in (Assyrian Unqi) which was located in the Amuq plain. Tell Tayinat was excavated in the 1930s by a team from the Oriental Institute, University of Chicago, with new excavations being undertaken from 2004 onwards by an expedition from the University of Toronto under the direction of T. Harrison. During the Early Bronze Age (M3), Tell Tayinat became an important urban centre, but in M2 it was abandoned in favour of nearby Alalah. The destruction of Alalah in C12 left a vacuum in the immediate region, which a renewed settlement at Tell Tayinat eventually filled, almost certainly as Kinalua, Patin's capital.

The city was dominated during its Iron Age phase by a royal citadel, in which two main periods have been identified. The complete plan of a palace of the *bit hilani* type (see glossary) belonging to the first of these periods has been uncovered. It has been designated Building XIII. Above it, a citadel was constructed in a second building phase. The earlier complex can be dated back at least to C10. Its destruction occurred around the middle of C9. This has been determined by the discovery, beneath the palace floor, of a fragmentary Luwian hieroglyphic inscription on the podium of a statue, bearing the name Halparuntiyas (**CHLI* I: 366). Very likely, the man so named is to be identified with the local ruler Qalparunda whom the Assyrian king Shalmaneser III (858–824) refers to as the Patinite and the Unqite (**RIMA* 3: 11, 18 respectively), and as paying tribute to him on at least two occasions (857 and 853). He was, apparently, successor to a man called Sapalulme, who was himself successor (or a successor) to Patin's first attested king, Lubarna (I). Unfortunately, Qalparunda's inscription and statue are too fragmentary for any further significant information to be gained from them. Several more building phases occurred in the city before it was destroyed by Assyrian forces during the last three decades of C8. The Assyrians built a new citadel on the site, incorporating Assyrian architectural features, in the southern part of the mound. The focal point of the citadel complex was a central courtyard, accessed via a gate building. A temple adjoined the complex on its south side. Remains of a number of frescoes which decorated both the palace and temple buildings have been found in the course of the excavations.

Traces of Early Bronze Age remains have also been uncovered on the mound. Subsequent excavations are expected to bring more of these to light.

Haines (1971: 37–66), Harrison *et al.* (2006), Yıldırım and Gates (2007: 305–6).

Tayma (biblical Tema) (map 16) Caravan-centre in northwestern Saudi Arabia (cf. **Dedan**). The presence there of so-called Qurayyah painted pottery provides evidence of the earliest known occupation of the site, in late M2. Tayma, in the form

Tema, is attested in a number of *OT* sources (Job 6:19, Isaiah 21:14, Jeremiah 25:23). However, it is first attested in historical records in the texts of the Assyrian king Tiglath-pileser III who conquered the Arab tribes in the region c. 733 (**Tigl. III* 168–9). There has been some debate as to whether Tayma was by this time already a walled, permanently occupied settlement, since the relevant archaeological evidence is apparently equivocal or inconclusive. In general terms, nomadic pastoralism was the defining feature of the northern Arabian populations in this period.

However, in mid C6 Tayma achieved particular prominence in its region when the Babylonian king Nabonidus (556–539) spent ten years there, fortifying the settlement and building a palace for himself (**PE* 76–7, no. 23). Various reasons have been suggested for his shift from Babylon to Tayma, including a desire to escape plague and famine, to establish a forward base for expeditions to the south by his troops, or to gain control over the highly profitable Arabian trade in incense and gold. But most scholars believe that the reason was primarily a religious one. Nabonidus was a devotee of the moon god Sin, and Tayma was a centre of the god's worship. The top portion of a stele depicting Nabonidus with symbols of the sun, the moon, and a star has recently been unearthed in an official building on top of the main mound at Tayma. Below the sculpture is part of a cuneiform inscription, the first such inscription to be discovered in Saudi Arabia. The surviving part of it refers to semi-precious stones, including lapis lazuli and carnelian.

Following the fall of the Neo-Babylonian empire, Tayma continue to prosper in the Persian period (C6–4), when it was perhaps nominally under Persian rule. But like the northwestern Arabian caravan-centre Dedan, it was eclipsed, in C1, by the Nabataean city of Hegra, and thenceforth went into decline.

Parr (*OEANE* 5: 160–1).

Tegarama (map 3) Late Bronze Age predecessor of the Iron Age city Til-garimmu (q.v.) in east-central Anatolia, located on the main route between Carchemish and Hattusa. Though the city is commonly identified with mod. Gürün, J. D. Hawkins (*CHLI* I: 285, n. 45) favours a location in the plain of Elbistan. The city was sacked by forces from the land of Isuwa, which lay to its east, during the comprehensive invasions of Hittite territory in the first half of C14 (*Bryce, 2005: 146). In 1327 the Hittite king Suppiluliuma I marched to Tegarama, where he held a general review of his infantry and chariotry before proceeding to the Euphrates and the conquest of Carchemish (**DS* 93, **CS* I: 190).

Teichiussa (map 5) M1 Ionian city on a low mound, located on the Aegean coast of southwestern Anatolia, 26 km southeast of Miletus. It is first attested in a C6 Greek inscription carved on the statue base of a certain Chares, called ruler of Teichiussa. In the Athenian Tribute Lists, the city is designated as a dependency of Miletus. A year after Miletus' defection to Sparta in 412, Teichiussa was used by the Spartans as a base for mounting an attack on Iasus, which lay further down the coast (Thucydides 8.28). Teichiussa's meagre remains include a poorly preserved fortification wall, probably of C5 date.

Bean (*PECS* 890–1).

Teisheba, City of (***Karmir Blur***) (map 20) Iron Age Urartian fortress and city in eastern Anatolia on the outskirts of mod. Erevan. Its anc. name, derived from the Urartian storm god Teisheba to whom the city was dedicated, is indicated by a cuneiform inscription dating to Rusa II's reign (678–654). Excavation of the site, under the direction of B. B. Piotrovskij for the Hermitage Museum and the Armenian SSR Academy of Science, began in 1939 and continued into the 1960s. The settlement's first Urartian phase dates to the reign of Minua (805–788). Finds from this phase include a number of pointed helmets, decorated with sacred trees and genii and inscribed with cuneiform texts. Subsequently, the city was rebuilt by Rusa II, as indicated by two long cuneiform inscriptions on blocks of stone discovered among the foundations of a temple. It was the first fortress constructed by Rusa (see Erdem and Batmaz, 2008: 66–7). The new city contained a fortified citadel some 4 ha in area, and a lower settlement extending over c. 40 ha. A number of streets and public buildings have been uncovered in the lower settlement. The fortifications which surrounded the city were apparently never completed. Inside the citadel are the remains of a large 150-room building complex. Provisionally identified as a residential palace, it may have served as an administrative centre for the surrounding region as well as providing storage for animal and agricultural produce and items produced by local craftsmen. The workshops of potters and metalsmiths were found outside the citadel. Inscriptions from the site, in addition to those mentioned above, include a number of letters and decrees of the Urartian king and his officials. They refer to such matters as land distribution, inheritance issues, the collection of tribute, and the movement of animals and peoples.

Teisheba city is noted for the richness and abundance of its small finds, particularly those unearthed in the large citadel building. They include statuettes of warrior gods, large numbers of bronze vessels, a great variety of finely made pottery, an enormous brass sacrificial cauldron, and an extensive range of bronze, silver, and gold jewellery. Here too were preserved some of the treasures brought from Erebuni (q.v.), including fourteen decorated and inscribed bronze shields. These finds, together with the royal correspondence, serve to illustrate Teisheba city's status as a flourishing regional centre of the Urartian kingdom in mid C7. The citadel was violently destroyed at the end of Urartu's history and not reoccupied.

Piotrovsky (1969: 135–80), Zimansky (1998: 267–8), McConchie (2004: 124).

Tela M1 city in the Kashiyari range (mod. Tur ʿAbdin) of northern Mesopotamia, in the land of Nerbu. The Assyrian king Ashurnasirpal II laid siege to the city during his campaign in the region in 882 (**RIMA* 2: 201). Though it was protected by a triple wall and defended by a substantial number of troops, it fell to the Assyrians. Ashurnasirpal massacred and mutilated many of its inhabitants, deported others, then plundered the city and put it to the torch; from there he moved on to Tushshan.

Radner (2006: 290–1)

Telloh see Girsu.

Telmessus (1) (Telmissus) (map 5) M1 Lelegian (q.v.) city on the Myndus peninsula in Caria, southwestern Anatolia. Cicero (*De divinatione* 1.42.94) comments on the fertility of its surrounding countryside. The city apparently lay c. 10 km from Halicarnassus. According to Pliny the Elder (5.107), Telmisum (*sic*) was one of six Lelegian towns assigned by Alexander the Great to the jurisdiction of Halicarnassus.

But its incorporation into Halicarnassus, along with seven other Lelegian cities, was in fact due to the Carian satrap Mausolus (377–353) prior to Alexander's campaigns. Many of the city's inhabitants were at that time resettled in Halicarnassus. The city's actual location remains uncertain. Bean suggests an identification with a Lelegian site near Gürice, 3 km west of Müsgebi. Gürice has a number of characteristic Lelegian features, its remains including a citadel, an outer enclosure, a large, square ashlar tower, and several rock-tombs, among them a vaulted chamber tomb.

Telmessus achieved considerable fame as an oracular centre of the god Apollo. Here the priests were concerned primarily with the interpretation of omens, prodigies, and dreams experienced by their consultants. Herodotus (1.78) reports that the Lydian king Croesus sought an explanation from the oracle for a curious event that occurred in the outskirts of his capital, Sardis: prior to the Persian king Cyrus II's advance on Sardis, snakes swarmed in the outer part of the city and were devoured by horses who preferred the reptiles to their own pasturage (so the story goes). On another occasion, the oracle was consulted by Gordius, a man of humble origins but later to become the father of the Phrygian king Midas (Arrian, *Anabasis* 2.3.3). After the transplantation of the majority of its population to Halicarnassus in C4, Telmessus appears to have been reduced to little more than a religious community dedicated to the worship of Apollo. But its reputation as an oracular centre persisted through the Hellenistic and Roman periods, even though it never achieved the prominence of the oracle at Patara, which lay further to the southeast on the coast of Lycia.

Bean (1971: 122–3; *PECS* 892), Bryce (1986: 200–2).

Telmessus (2) (***Fethiye***, formerly ***Makri***) (map 15) M1 BCE–M1 CE city on the western coast of Lycia, southwestern Anatolia. Though five native Lycian inscriptions were discovered there, the city was not originally considered to be part of Lycia. It was clearly distinguished from it at the time of the C5 Athenian Tribute Lists, which listed Lycia and Telmessus separately as members of the Athenian Confederacy (see glossary). Despite its evident cultural links with Lycia, it may not have become politically attached to the country until the first half of C4, when a Lycian leader called Pericles (see **Limyra**) gained control of the city by military conquest. Several decades later, Telmessus submitted without resistance to Alexander the Great during the Macedonian's campaign along Anatolia's southern coast (334/333) – though one of Alexander's 'Companions', Nearchus the Cretan, had to retake the city by a stratagem after a certain Antipatrides had established his control over it (Polyaenus 5.35). In the Hellenistic period, Telmessus became subject first to the Ptolemies and subsequently to the kings of Pergamum. When the Pergamene kingdom ended in 133, it was incorporated into the Roman province of Asia.

Telmessus' remains are today confined to its tombs, of various periods. Two theatres of Hellenistic and/or Roman date, one of which was apparently in a good state of preservation in mid C19, have now entirely disappeared. The main group of tombs was cut into a hillside located just east of the city. Of these the most notable is dated to C4 and identified by its inscription as belonging to a certain Amyntas, son of Hermapias. Its façade is in the form of an Ionic Greek temple, complete with pediment and acroteria (ornaments generally placed above the three angles of the pediment). Inside, a single burial chamber has been carved from the rock, with benches around the walls. Other similar tombs are located close by. A freestanding double-storeyed sarcophagus tomb, richly embellished with relief sculptures, and now located next to Fethiye's municipal building, is among the finest examples of its type in the whole of Lycia.

Telmessus was apparently a centre for the practice of divination, though many of the stories of Telmessian seers should probably be attributed to the nearby Carian city of the same name. One of these stories concerns Alexander's consultation of a Telmessian seer called Aristandrus, when he sought from him the interpretation of a dream which he had had in the course of his siege of Halicarnassus.

Bean (1978: 38–41; *PECS* 892).

Tema see Tayma.

Teman M1 district and city in Edom, a country which lay to the south of the Dead Sea. According to Genesis 36:34, a man called Husham of the land of the Temanites (to be distinguished from the Aramaean Temanites who occupied the Habur region in northern Mesopotamia; see Lipiński, 2000: 109–10) became king of Edom after the death of the previous ruler Joab. (On the highly questionable validity of the Edomite King List, see under ***Buseirah***.) Also in *OT* tradition, Teman figures in a prophecy of Ezekiel (25:13), who declared that the land of Edom would be destroyed from Teman to Dedan. This reference suggests that the cities and districts in question lay at either end of the kingdom of Edom. Teman has yet to be located, though Tawilan (q.v.) north of Petra is a possibility. Dedan (q.v.) was a northwestern Arabian caravan-centre, located at the site of al-Khuraybah in the al-ʿUla oasis in Saudi Arabia.

de Vaux (1969), Negev and Gibson (2001: 497).

Figure 116 Telmessus, Amyntas tomb.

Teman(n)ites Large Aramaean tribe occupying (probably from C10 onwards) the upper Habur region of northern Mesopotamia. Their name is derived from Aramaic *tymn*, which means 'south', 'southern'. To be distinguished from the Temanites who in *OT* tradition (e.g. Genesis 36:34) lived in the land of Edom, they are attested in the reign of the Assyrian king Adad-nirari II (911–891); Adad-nirari claims to have defeated three Temanite kings, Nur-Adad, Mamli, and Muquru, during his campaigns in the region of Hanigalbat in 901 and 900 (**RIMA* 2: 149–52). Nur-Adad ruled the city of Nisibis (q.v.) and its attached territories. It is unlikely that the Temanites ever formed a united kingdom.

Lipiński (2000: 109–17).

Teos (map 5) Greek city located on the Aegean coast of Anatolia, in the region called Ionia in M1, 40 km southwest of Smyrna. According to Classical tradition, it was founded by Minyans from Orchomenus in northern Greece. It was one of the twelve cities of the Ionian League (see **Panionium**). When Teos was conquered by the Persian commander Harpagus c. 540, its population refused to accept Persian sovereignty and sailed to Thrace, where they founded the city of Abdera (Herodotus 1.168, Strabo 14.1.30). But many of them returned home shortly after. In C5, Teos became a member of the Athenian Confederacy (see glossary). The city's scanty material remains include harbour works, some poorly preserved fortifications on the acropolis, and below the acropolis the remnants of a theatre, odeum (a small, roofed theatre used for musical performances), gymnasium, and temple of Dionysus. Most of these remains belong to the Hellenistic and Roman periods.

E. Akurgal (1973: 139–42), Bean (*PECS* 893–4), Moustaka *et al.* (2004).

Teresh Late Bronze Age population group, possibly of western Anatolian origin, listed as one of the so-called Sea Peoples in Egyptian records. The Teresh first appear among the invaders who joined with the Libyans for an attack on the Egyptian Delta during the reign of the pharaoh Merneptah (1213–1203), as recorded on the east wall of Merneptah's temple at Karnak (**ARE III*: §579). They may also have been among the invaders who attacked the coast of Egypt during Ramesses III's reign (1184–1153), to judge from the inclusion of a Teresh chieftain among the enemy captives depicted on the walls of Ramesses' mortuary temple at Medinet Habu. They are not listed among the invading groups in the accompanying inscription, but elsewhere, in an inscription from Deir el Medineh, Ramesses claims that they were one of the groups of foreigners coming from the midst of the sea whom he trampled down. The similarity of their name to Taruisa, which figures in Hittite texts as a country or city in the region of the Troad, has suggested a possible northwestern Anatolian origin for the Teresh. Alternatively, they have been linked with the Tyrsenoi or Tyrrhenians, who according to Herodotus (1. 94) migrated from Lydia in central western Anatolia and resettled in western Italy, where allegedly they became the founders of the Etruscan civilization. It is conceivable that this tradition reflects one of the supposed westward migrations of several of the Sea Peoples after their unsuccessful attack on the Egyptian coast in Ramesses III's reign (see also **Shekelesh** and **Shardana**). However, most scholars now believe that the Etruscans were an indigenous Italian population group.

Sandars (1985: 224, index refs).

Termera (*Asarlık*) (map 5) M1 city in Caria in southwestern Anatolia, 15 km southwest of mod. Bodrum. Founded by the Lelegians (q.v.) according to Classical tradition, the city is first attested in coin legends of late C6 or early C5, in association with the name Tymnes, probably to be identified with the tyrant of Termera referred to by Herodotus (5.37, 7.98). In C5, the city was a member of the Athenian Confederacy (see glossary), originally paying two-and-a-half talents per year as its contribution to the Confederacy's treasury, but after 447 only one-fifth of this amount. In the course of C4, the city appears to have undergone a considerable decline. Its role at that time was perhaps no more than a guardpost, and it was used as a prison. Material remains of the site include a citadel wall surrounded by an outer wall, the latter of polygonal masonry and apparently dating to C5. Several tombs built in different styles and of uncertain date are located on the site.

Bean (*PECS* 895–6).

Termessus (map 4) M1 BCE–M1 CE city in Pisidia near Anatolia's southern coast, located 1,000 m above sea level, 30 km northwest of Antalya. Its inhabitants identified themselves in their inscriptions with a semi-legendary people called the Solymians (q.v.), who first appear in Homer's *Iliad* (6.184–5). Writing in the early Roman imperial period, Strabo (13.4.16–17) noted that the Termessians still at that time called themselves Solymians, and distinguished the language they spoke from the Pisidian tongue. It is likely, however, that the Solymian language or dialect had died out well before the Hellenistic period. Alexander the Great decided not to proceed with a planned attack on the city following his conquests in Pamphylia in 333, probably because of its strongly protected mountaintop site, which offers spectacular views over the Taurus range. Its well-preserved remains, including a theatre, agora, bouleuterion (council house), gymnasium, temples, and avenues of tombs, date almost entirely to the Hellenistic and Roman periods. In C3, Termessus founded a colony of the same name in neighbouring Lycia, near the city of Oenoanda.

Bean (1968: 119–37; *PECS* 896–7), E. Akurgal (1973: 325–9).

Termilae see **Lycia**.

Terqa (*Tell Ashara*) (map 10) Settlement mound located on the west bank of the Euphrates, 50 km north of Mari. The site was identified in 1910 by E. Herzfeld, who found there a cuneiform tablet referring to the construction of a temple of Dagan in Terqa. Its history of occupation extends from early M3 until M1, followed by a long period of abandonment until reoccupation in the mediaeval period. Investigation of Terqa's remains has been limited by the fact that mod. settlement overlies a large part of the anc. site, leaving only about 25 per cent of the 10 ha mound available for excavation. The lack of any trace of a lower city has been attributed to its being swept away by floods or covered by alluvium. Tell Ashara has been studied in a series of excavations, the earliest of which was conducted in 1923. From 1976 onwards, work on the site was directed by G. Buccellati and M. Kelly-Buccellati, and from 1985 onwards the excavations have been carried out by O. Rouault. A number of institutions have sponsored these excavations, including the International Institute for Mesopotamian Area Studies, the University of California, and California State University at Los Angeles.

Figure 117 Termessus.

Settlement at Terqa in M3 is indicated by several well-appointed shaft-graves, and especially by the remains of the city's fortifications consisting of three substantial mudbrick concentric walls, 20 m in total width, originally dating to this period and continuing in use until mid M2. During the Middle Bronze Age (early M2), Terqa was probably a regional centre of the kingdom of Mari. From an administrative building dating to the Shakkanakku period (see under **Mari**) and continuing in use during the period of the Amorite dynasty at Mari, a number of bureaucratic texts and clay door-sealings have been unearthed. The building appears to have housed a scribal school, to judge from items of furniture and equipment appropriate to scribal activity which were found within it. These included a jar and a bin containing tablets and located near another container in which fine clay had been deposited.

After Mari was conquered by the Babylonian king Hammurabi in 1762, an independent dynasty was established at Terqa. Probably towards the end of the Middle Bronze Age, Terqa became either the capital or one of the major centres of a kingdom now commonly referred to as the kingdom of Hana (q.v.). Among the city's architectural remains of this period were those of a temple dedicated to Ninkarrak, goddess of healing. The temple was a long, narrow building containing four rooms, a bent-axis entry, and rabbeted doorways (niched doorjambs). Hyksos-type scarabs were found within it. Tablets from the site refer to clashes with the land of Hatte/Hattu, very likely a reference to early conflicts with the Hittites, whose Old Kingdom ruler Hattusili I (1650–1620) campaigned in and east of the Euphrates region (see also Klengel, 1999:

Figure 118 Euphrates at Tell Ashara (Terqa).

66, Singer, 2000: 638–9, who refer to the discovery of a Hittite Old Kingdom seal on the site). Subsequently, by c. 1500, the city had come under Mitannian domination and remained so until the Mitannian empire was destroyed by the Hittite king Suppiluliuma I in the third quarter of C14. At this time it lay within the kingdom of Ashtata (*HDT 45–6), hitherto subject to Mitanni.

Terqa was abandoned towards the end of the Late Bronze Age. There is a small amount of both archaeological and written evidence (including an inscribed stele of the early C9 Assyrian king Tukulti-Ninurta II – see **RIMA* 2: 188) for reoccupation in M1, when Terqa is referred to as Sirqu in Assyrian records. Both Adad-nirari II (911–891) and Ashurnasirpal II (883–859) received tribute from it during their campaigns in the region (**RIMA* 2: 153, 213). But in this period, it is likely that the city was relatively small and insignificant.

Another settlement called Terqa is attested east of the Tigris in the Diyala r. region from M3 on, and there may have been yet another Mesopotamian settlement of that name, of unknown location (see Luciani, 1999, for refs and discussion).

Buccellati and Kelly-Buccellati (*OEANE* 5: 188–90), Roualt (1998).

Thamanaeans M1 Central Asian population group attested by Herodotus (3.93) as a component of the fourteenth Persian province following the reorganization of the Persian administration by Darius I shortly after his accession in 522 (but see glossary under **satrapy**). Herodotus locates the Thamanaeans in the eastern part of the empire in the same general region as the Chorasmians, Parthians, Hyrcanians, and Sarangae (3.117).

Theangela see Syangela.

Tidu (*Kurkh/Uctepe*) City on the upper Tigris r., attested in Neo-Assyrian royal inscriptions. An identification with mod. Kurkh (Kerh), as proposed by Kessler (1980: 117), seems likely. Kessler's identification of Tidu with the Late Bronze Age Mitannian settlement Taidu (see **Taidu (2)**) has been rejected by most scholars in favour of a location for the latter in the Habur region. Recently, however, Radner and Schachner (2001: 756–7) have supported the identification of Tidu with Taidu, while noting that there may have been more than one settlement of that name in later M2. Shalmaneser I (1274–1245) built a fortified stronghold at Tidu, and another at Shinabu, to serve as an Assyrian garrison centre on the frontier with the Nairi lands, according to a later account of Ashurnasirpal II. In the intervening period, the two forts had been occupied by Aramaeans, but Ashurnasirpal recaptured them and expelled the Aramaean garrisons. In 879 Tidu was one of the cities in which he constructed storage depots for the grain which his troops harvested from the Nairi lands (**RIMA* 2: 261). Later on, Tidu was among the twenty-seven cities which revolted against Shalmaneser III towards the end of his reign, and were subdued by his son Shamshi-Adad V (*RIMA* 3: 183).

(H. D. Baker)

Radner and Schachner (2001: 754–7).

Tigunanum see Tikunani.

Tikunani (map 3) Middle and Late Bronze Age city and kingdom in northern Mesopotamia, between the upper Tigris and Euphrates rivers. Its capital lay close to the Tigris, probably on its east bank, c. 40 km downstream from mod. Diyarbakır (*Mesop.* 177). It is first attested, in the form *Tigunanum*, in letters from the Mari archive, early C18, which Ishme-Dagan, son of the Old Assyrian king Shamshi-Adad I and viceroy at Ekallatum, wrote to his brother, Yasmah-Addu, viceroy at Mari, about attacks upon Tigunanum by the Turukkeans (**LAPO* 16: 128–9, no. 31; **LAPO* 17: 98–100, nos 505–6).

A recently published letter written by the Hittite king Hattusili I (1650–1620) to a king of Tikunani called Tunip-Teshub, also known as Tuniya, has thrown important new light on the Mesopotamian kingdom and its relations with the relatively young Hittite kingdom (*Salvini, 1994; 1996). Hattusili addresses Tuniya as his servant, and calls on his support for an attack upon the city of Hahhum, whose territory adjoined or lay close to Tikunani. In preparation for his campaign across the Euphrates (known also from the king's Annals), Hattusili had apparently contracted an alliance with Tunip-Teshub, promising him protection and material rewards in return for his support against Hahhum, whose relations with Tikunani were probably already hostile. Despite the letter's terminology, it seems most unlikely that Hittite subject territory extended as far east as Tikunani. It is more likely that Tunib-Teshub's relationship with Hattusili was that of a junior partner in a *pro tem* military alliance, rather than a vassal.

Salvini (1994; 1996; 1998), Miller (2001b).

Til-Abni(m) City in northern Syria, attested in Middle Bronze and Iron Age texts. It lay within the bend of the Euphrates r., and is probably to be identified with the site of Tell el-Qitar (see ***Qitar, El-***). In the Middle Bronze Age it lay in or near the land of Zalmaqum, becoming involved in the anti-Assyrian uprising which broke out in the region in 1778, during the reign of the Assyrian king Shamshi-Adad I. The king's son, Yasmah-Addu, viceroy at Mari, captured the city, but refrained from slaughtering its male population. For this his father heaped praise upon him, declaring that his act of mercy was worth ten talents of gold (**LAPO* 17: 52, no. 475).

In M1, Til-Abni was a small Aramaean state bordering on the land of Bit-Adini. The Assyrian king Ashurnasirpal II received tribute (including gold, silver, tin, bronze, linen garments, and cedar logs) from its ruler Habinu during campaigns which he conducted in the middle Euphrates region between 877 and 867 (**RIMA* 2: 216, 217). His son and successor Shalmaneser III (858–824) also reports receiving tribute from the same ruler during his first western campaign in his first regnal year (**RIMA* 3: 9, 15). On these occasions, the Assyrians apparently spared the city's capital (also called Til-Abni) because tribute was voluntarily offered. However, Habinu may shortly afterwards have joined an uprising in the region against Shalmaneser, for in his seventh regnal year (852) the Assyrian king attacked and destroyed the capital along with other cities in its environs (**RIMA* 3: 37, 46 etc.). Towards the end of Shalmaneser's reign, Til-Abni joined in a widespread revolt against him, initiated by the king's son, Ashur-da'in-apla. The rebellion continued into the early regnal years of Shalmaneser's son and successor Shamshi-Adad V before it was finally crushed (**RIMA* 3: 183).

Lipiński (2000: 164), *Mesop.* 181.

Til-Bari Iron Age city in east-central Mesopotamia, located east of the Tigris along the upper course of the Lesser Zab r. The Assyrian king Tukulti-Ninurta II (890–884) lists the city among the lands which he subjected (**RIMA* 2: 180). His son and successor Ashurnasirpal II cites it to denote the farthest (northeasterly) extent of his territory (**RIMA* 2: 309). Liverani (1992: 47) suggests that Til-Bari may be connected with the city and polity of Bara, near Dagara (also in the eastern Tigris region).

Til-Barsip see ***Ahmar, Tell.***

Til-Bashere see **Tilbeshar**.

Tilbeshar Early and Middle Bronze Age settlement in northern Mesopotamia, with later periods of occupation in M1, located in the basin of the Sajur r., a western tributary of the Euphrates, 20 km southeast of mod. Gaziantep (see Lipiński, 2000: 167, map). After an initial survey of the site in 1994 and 1995, excavation has been carried out by C. Kepinski under the auspices of the Gaziantep Museum from 1996 on. Covering at its greatest extent an area of 56 ha, the site consisted of upper and lower cities, whose boundaries fluctuated throughout the periods of its existence. Though there is evidence of occupation extending back to the late Neolithic period, significant development began in the Early Bronze Age, with settlement limited in the first phases of this period (designated TILB III A1 and A2: c. 3100–2700) to the citadel and covering an area of c. 6 ha. Population growth may have prompted the expansion of the settlement to the foot of the citadel in the following phase (TILB III B1 and B2: c. 2700–2500).

In the next phase (TILB III C: c. 2500–2300), Tilbeshar reached its maximum size. It had the character of a prosperous urban settlement, which like many other cities in the region no doubt derived much of its wealth from its participation in a network of long-distance as well as more local trading activity. Diversity of funerary practices evident from the burials in the city is seen as reflecting a mixed population of different ethnic origins. At the end of the final phase of the Early Bronze Age (TILB III D: c. 2300–2100), the city was suddenly abandoned. The reasons for this are unknown, but unsettled political conditions in northern Mesopotamia and southeastern Anatolia around the time of the fall of the Akkadian empire may have been a significant factor. There was subsequent reoccupation in the Middle Bronze Age (TILB IVA: c. 2000–1800). By the end of this period, the settlement had probably spread over the entire area occupied by the city at the height of its prosperity in the second half of M3. The site was again abandoned at the end of the Middle Bronze Age. In C9, it is listed (in the form Til-Bashere) among the six fortified cities west of the Euphrates belonging to the Aramaean kingdom of Bit-Adini (then ruled by Ahuni), and attacked, captured, and plundered by the Assyrian king Shalmaneser III in his second regnal year (857) (**RIMA* 3: 18). During the Persian and Byzantine periods, there was further occupation, though only of a limited and irregular nature.

Kepinski (2005).

Til-garimmu Iron Age Neo-Hittite city, successor of Late Bronze Age Tegarama (q.v.), probably to be located in the plain of mod. Elbistan in east-central Anatolia. According to the Assyrian king Sennacherib (704–681), it lay on the border of the kingdom of Tabal (**Sennach.* 62). Prior to the campaign which Sennacherib's father and predecessor Sargon II conducted against the kingdom of Melid in 712, it appears to have belonged to the land of Kammanu (q.v.), which probably constituted the northern part of Melid (see ***Arslantepe***). Sargon refers to it as a royal city of Melid, whose ruler at the time was a man called Tarhunazi. When Tarhunazi switched his support to the Phrygian king Midas, Sargon invaded his land, forcing Tarhunazi to seek refuge in Til-garimmu. Here he was captured, and deported to Assyria, along with his family and 5,000 of his troops, according to Sargon (**ARAB* II: 11–12, 30–1). Sargon then claims to have rebuilt the city, which no doubt had suffered some destruction from the Assyrian attack upon it, placed it under the control of an Assyrian governor, and settled it with deportees from other parts of his kingdom. None the less, Til-garimmu appears to have broken its ties with Assyria soon after, probably at the time of Sargon's death in 705, and reasserted its independence under a new king called Gurdi. It was to be ten years before action was taken against it, in 695, by Sennacherib, who claims to have captured and destroyed the city (**ARAB* II 138 = **Sennach.* 62–3; for update from new prism inscription, see *CHLI* I: 285, n. 51, citing *Heidel, 1953: 150–1, lines 29–52). But there is no indication that Til-garimmu thenceforth reverted to Assyrian control.

CHLI I: 285.

Tiliura Late Bronze Age Hittite city in north-central Anatolia located within the Hittite–Kaska frontier zone. The city was abandoned in the reign of Hantili II (C15), due to Kaska incursions in the region, and eventually rebuilt by Mursili II in late C14. Mursili used deportees from conquered territories as its new inhabitants. But the task of restoring the city remained unfinished at his death. His son, Hattusili III, claimed credit for fully re-establishing Tiliura, by transferring to it the remaining descendants of its original population. Hattusili wanted to ensure that Tiliura had a substantially Hittite population, clearly distinguishable from the deportees, and particularly from the Kaska people who were now banned from settling in or even entering the city. He stipulated this in a treaty, still extant in fragments, which he drew up with Tiliura's inhabitants.

*Garstang and Gurney (1959: 119–20), **RGTC* 6: 421–2.

Tilla (Middle/Neo-Assyrian **Tille**, also Neo-Assyrian **Til-uli**?) Middle Bronze Age royal city in the southern Ida-maras district of northern Mesopotamia, attested in the archives of Mari from the reign of Zimri-Lim (1774–1762). It was the first station on the route between Shubat-Enlil and Saggaratum. During this period, when it was ruled by a king called Samsi-Erah, it was attacked by troops from Andarig and Karana, then ruled (respectively) by Himdiya and Aqba-Hammu. On another occasion, the city was occupied by troops from Eshnunna. Tilla may have joined in attacks upon the kingdom of Ilan-sura in the Habur triangle, since Haya-Sumu, ruler of Ilan-sura, had requested support from his overlord Zimri-Lim for action against the city.

The M1 city Til-uli, which belonged to the land of Kadmuhu, is generally held to be identical with the better attested Tille. The Assyrian king Ashurnasirpal II consecrated a palace in Til-uli during his campaign in Kadmuhu in 879 (**RIMA* 2: 208). Later, Tille was the principal city of the Assyrian province which incorporated the southern part of what had formerly been the land of Kadmuhu.

Liverani (1992: 57), *LKM* 137, 626 (refs).

Tille Höyük Settlement-mound in eastern Anatolia, located in the province of Adıyaman on the west bank of the Euphrates north of Carchemish. It was continuously occupied from the Late Bronze Age through the succeeding Iron Age and the Babylonian, Persian, Hellenistic, Roman and mediaeval periods. Ceramic material indicates that there was also settlement on the mound in the Chalcolithic Age (M5 or M4) and Early Bronze Age (M3). The site was excavated by D. French on behalf of the British School of Archaeology at Ankara between 1978 and 1990. Its excavation belongs within the context of the archaeological rescue projects undertaken at various sites in the Euphrates floodplain prior to the completion of the Atatürk Dam and the consequent inundation of the region. It was the only one of these sites to yield Late Bronze Age remains. Twelve building levels dating to this period have been unearthed. Settlement was confined to the mound (as indeed it continued to be up to the Hellenistic period) and covered an area of no more than 100 m in diameter. It was, however, surrounded by a very large casemate wall with entrance gate whose impressive proportions, it has been suggested, reflected the strategic significance of the settlement's location at an important crossing on the Euphrates. Four springs kept it well supplied with fresh water. Tille's anc. name is unknown, but it was almost certainly an outlying post of the Hittite empire, under the rule of a local vassal or Hittite garrison commander.

Though Tille survived the fall of the Hittite empire in early C12, it was destroyed by fire seventy or more years later, perhaps in an Assyrian raid across the Euphrates. But it was built afresh shortly after, and subsequently became a frontier-post of the Neo-Hittite kingdom of Kummuh. A rebuilt entrance gate, and well-planned building complexes and streets, evidence of efficient central organization, were features of the new settlement. The phases in the settlement's history from late M2 to the Hellenistic period are designated as levels I–X, proceeding from the earliest to the latest phase. Tille's Neo-Hittite phase is represented archaeologically by levels IV–VII (levels I–III belong to C11 and at least part of C10), extending from C9 (or perhaps C10) to C8. The phase terminates with the conquest of Kummuh by the Assyrian king Sargon II in 708. In the final two levels (VI and VII) of its Neo-Hittite phase, the settlement seems to have gone into decline, and was perhaps abandoned for a time.

With the Assyrian annexation of Kummuh after Sargon's conquest, Tille gained a fresh lease of life, with new constructions in level VIII (probably extending through much of C7) which shows clear signs of Assyrian influence. A large building complex was the most prominent feature of level IX. This level dates to the last years of the Assyrian empire or the early years of the Neo-Babylonian empire (late C7). But it was in the Persian period that Tille appears to have reached the peak of its development, to judge from the relatively well-preserved architectural remains of this period (level X) at the time of their excavation. A feature of the period, extending through the second half of C6 and early C5, was a substantial building complex which gave clear evidence of Persian architectural influence. Part of the walls of the complex were still over 2 m high when uncovered by the excavators.

During the Hellenistic and early Roman imperial periods, from late C4 to C1 CE, settlement at Tille spread for the first time to the plain at the bottom of the mound. Three building levels were identified. In 72 CE Tille was annexed into the Roman empire, and became part of the empire's eastern frontier-defence system.

Summers (1993), Blaylock (1998).

Tillima (*Tl'ym*) Iron Age district belonging to the Aramaean state Ktk (q.v.) in northern Syria. It had been occupied by the ruler of the neighbouring kingdom of Arpad (Bit-Agusi), but was restored to Ktk (perhaps c. 754), in accordance with the terms of a treaty concluded between the two states as recorded on Stele III from Sefire (q.v.).

Lipiński (2000: 223, 231).

Tilmen Höyük M2 settlement mound in southern Anatolia, located within the Turkish province of Gaziantep. Excavation of the site between 1959 and 1972 by a Turkish team, under the direction of U. B. Alkım, brought to light palaces of the Middle and Late Bronze Ages. Alkım's excavations demonstrated that Tilmen was conceived as a smaller version of its southern neighbour, Alalah (q.v.), its public buildings mirroring Alalah's plans and construction techniques (thus Yıldırım and Gates, 2007: 303). In 2003, excavation was resumed by a Turkish–Italian team under the direction of N. Marchetti. The investigation of four areas along the southern edge of the acropolis provided new information about the city's monumental architecture, as revealed during the earlier campaigns, including the so-called Royal Palace A. Only one inscription, a sealing with a short Akkadian cuneiform inscription, has so far been discovered at Tilmen, whose anc. name remains unknown. The city is considered to have been the capital of a vassal kingdom, subject first to Yamhad and then to Mitanni during the Middle Bronze Age II and Late Bronze Age I periods respectively. Marchetti comments that 'Tilmen Höyük represents one of the main sites for extensively investigating the urban structure of an ancient capital, and for reconstructing the scale and mode of contacts between Anatolia and Syria during the second millennium B.C.'

There is evidence of limited reoccupation of the site in the Hellenistic period.

Duru (2003), Marchetti (2004), Yıldırım and Gates (2007: 303–4).

Til-sha-Turahi Iron Age city located in the Balih r. valley of northwestern Mesopotamia. It was among the places captured and plundered by the Assyrian king Shalmaneser III during his campaign along the Balih r. in his sixth regnal year, 853 (**RIMA* 3: 22 and parallel passages). Fearful at his approach, the cities of the region seized and assassinated their overlord, Giammu. Though the precise location of Til-sha-Turahi is unknown, its name has been related to Terah, father of Abraham in *OT* tradition (e.g. Genesis 11:24–8). On this basis, a location near the city of Harran, the city to which Terah migrated from Ur, is considered likely.

Lipiński (2000: 127–8).

Til-sha-Zabdani Iron Age city in the Assyro-Babylonian borderlands, east of the Tigris r. It was among the cities and lands which the Assyrian king Ashurnasirpal II (883–859) incorporated into the southeastern frontier territory of his kingdom (**RIMA* 2: 309). Til-sha-Abtani on the Diyala r. near Me-Turnu (Me-Tur(r)an) was another of these cities, which are listed by the king as 'fortresses of Karduniash (Babylonia)'.

Til-uli see Tilla.

Timiussa (Teimioussa, *Üçağız*) M1 BCE–M1 CE city on the central coast of Lycia, southwestern Anatolia (*BAGRW* 65 C5). Its origins date back at least to early C4, since two of its tombs bear texts in the native Lycian language, which is attested in inscriptions from late C6 to C4. One of these texts refers to a man called Pericles (**TAM* I 67), a well-known Lycian dynast who extended his sway over much of Lycia during the first half of C4 (see under **Limyra**). Almost nothing survives of Timiussa beyond its numerous tombs, mostly sarcophagi, the majority of which have Greek inscriptions dating to the Hellenistic and Roman periods. The persons in these inscriptions refer to themselves as citizens of Cyaneae or Myra, which suggests that Timiussa came under the jurisdiction of one of these cities.

Bean (*PECS* 891; 1978: 115–16).

Timnah (1) (*Hajar Kohlan*) (map 9) M1 city in southern Arabia, capital of the kingdom of Qataban. The site was excavated in 1950 and 1951 by W. F. Albright for the American Foundation for the Study of Man. Excavations were concentrated on the so-called South Gate area, the temple site, and the cemetery. The first of these contained the remains of a small public square, two streets, and several large buildings, as well as the South Gate itself, which consisted of a stone-paved passageway flanked by two towers. The names of three of the buildings are known from inscriptions on them – Yafash House, Yafʿam House, and Hadath House. The temple complex consisted of the temple itself, a courtyard, and a series of what were probably storerooms. A large stone water tank was located next to the courtyard. The cemetery, covering an area of c. 2,550 sq. m, lay on a hill 500 m north of the city. Its contents included three buildings identified as mortuary chapels (the earliest of mudbrick, the later two of stone) and a mausoleum complex. The latter, as described by the excavators, was made up of square rubble burial structures fronting on to a central aisle, each divided by partition walls into two or three vertical chambers for individual burials. Associated with a number of the burials were stone boxes with an alabaster head depicting the deceased or a relief bearing the deceased's personal and family names. These apparently marked out elite members of Timnah's society. Cremation and inhumation were both in evidence. The surviving funerary gifts include many imported from a wide range of homelands, indicative of the large international trading network of which Timnah was a part, and otherwise 'provide a view of a wealthy culture that stresses the arts of sculpture, architecture, and writing' (thus Van Beek). Much of the city's wealth may have come from its strategically advantageous location on a major merchant caravan route. Strabo (16.4.2) refers to Timnah (in the form Tamna) as the royal seat of the Cattabanians, who are noted for their involvement in the incense trade (16.4.4) According to Pliny the Elder (6.153), Timnah (in the form Thomna) was endowed with no fewer than sixty-five temples. Probably in late C1 CE, the city was destroyed in a great conflagration, at the time that Qataban was conquered and subsequently incorporated into the kingdom of Hadhramaut.

Van Beek (*OEANE* 5: 215–17).

Timnah (2) (*Wadi Meneiyeh*) Valley in the Negev desert, southern Palestine, extending over c. 70 sq. km, and located 30 km north of the Gulf of Aqaba. The region has been mined, from the Chalcolithic Age through the Roman and Islamic periods, for its copper-ore deposits. Following a number of explorations by C19 and early C20 investigators, it was comprehensively surveyed and excavated between 1959 and 1990 by B. Rothenberg for the Haaretz Museum, Tel Aviv University. The mines themselves are described as 'deep vertical shafts extending as deep as 35 m – narrow, horizontal galleries driven deep into the rock, sometimes branched, and saucerlike depressions in the hillsides' (Dever). The region was most intensively occupied and exploited under Egyptian rule towards the end of the Late Bronze Age, particularly during Egypt's nineteenth and early twentieth dynasties. In this period, a number of Egyptian mining expeditions were dispatched to the region, and Egyptian garrisons were stationed there. The eleven smelting camps found in the valley belong mainly to the period of Egyptian control.

One of the most notable discoveries in the valley, made by Rothenberg in 1966, is a mining sanctuary at the foot of what are known as 'Solomon's Pillars' – two enormous Nubian sandstone formations at the southwestern end of the Timnah massif and located almost in the centre of Timnah's copper-mining area. Two square pillars with representations of the Egyptian goddess Hathor have prompted the naming of the sanctuary as the temple of Hathor. The Egyptian building, whose two phases (Strata III and II) date to the reigns of the C13 pharaohs Seti I and Ramesses II, was constructed over Chalcolithic remains. Small finds include quantities of ceramic ware, votive offerings in a range of materials, animal and Hathor figurines, jewellery, scarabs, seals, and a small sphinx. Earthquake apparently brought the sanctuary's second Egyptian phase to an end. A large quantity of heavy red and yellow cloth found in the sanctuary has been assigned to its final phase (Stratum I), after the Egyptians abandoned the region in mid C12. The cloth is considered to have been part of a tent used in this final phase when, it has been suggested, the sanctuary was associated with the Midianites of *OT* tradition.

Rothenberg (*NEAEHL* 4: 1475–86), Dever (*OEANE* 5: 217–18).

Timnah (3) Iron Age Judaean-Philistine city on Judah's northern border, attested only in *OT* sources, but now generally identified with Tel Batash. For further details, see ***Batash, Tel.***

Timnah (4) Iron Age town in the hill country of Judah, attested only in Joshua 15:57. It has not yet been identified with any known archaeological site.

Timuhala Late Bronze Age city in northern Anatolia, perhaps not far from the Hittite cult-centre of Nerik. It was occupied by Kaska peoples when the Hittite king Suppiluliuma I (1350–1322) marched against it during his campaigns in the region. The submission of its population saved it from destruction by Suppiluliuma's forces, and it was restored to Hittite overlordship (**DS* 110, **CS* I: 191). It subsequently broke its ties with Hatti, during the reign of Suppiluliuma's son and second successor Mursili II (1321–1295). Mursili gives us a fairly detailed account of the expedition which he conducted against the city (**AM* 166–71). It was difficult of access because it lay in a mountainous, thickly wooded region, and the king and his army were forced to approach it on foot. But when they reached the city they found it deserted, its occupants having already fled to mountain retreats. The approach of winter prevented Mursili from pursuing the refugees. But before withdrawing from the city, he put it to the torch and forbade any future settlement on it.

**RGTC* 6: 423–4.

Timur Fortified Iron Age city in southeastern Anatolia belonging to the kingdom of Que. In 833 it was placed under siege, captured, and plundered by the Assyrian king Shalmaneser III, during the first of three expeditions which he conducted against Que, then ruled by a king called Kate (**RIMA* 3: 68).

Tios (Tieium) Small M1 Greek city in Paphlagonia (though sometimes assigned to Bithynia) on Anatolia's Black Sea coast, between Heraclea Pontica and Amastris (*BAGRW* 86 C2). According to a tradition recorded by Strabo (12.3.5), the city was founded by the Cauconians, who were of Scythian, Macedonian, or Peslasgian stock. At the end of C4, Amastris, widow and successor of Dionysius, the former tyrant of Heraclea Pontica, formed a synoecism (see glossary) of four cities east of Heraclea, consisting of Tios, Sesamos, Kromna, and Kytoros. Sesamos, renamed Amastris, was the nucleus of the amalgamated settlements. According to Strabo (12.3.10), Tios soon broke free of the amalgamation.

Tipiya Late Bronze Age country in north-central Anatolia, located in territory occupied by the Kaska peoples. Attested in Hittite texts, Tipiya first appears among the enemy lands against which the Hittite king Ammuna campaigned in C16. Later references to it occur in the Annals of the Hittite king Mursili II, who records a campaign against it in his second regnal year (c. 1320), when it had become hostile to him and had ceased supplying him with troops (**AM* 26–9, **CS* II: 84). For some time prior to this, Tipiya must have been subject to Hittite control. Mursili's campaign evidently failed to restore this control, for the king reports that in his seventh year, Tipiya was the base of a Kaska tribal chief called Pihhuniya. From Tipiya, Pihhuniya repeatedly attacked the Upper Land (q.v.), looting it and carrying off the spoils of victory, including Hittite subjects, to Kaska. Thereafter, Mursili says, Pihhuniya did not rule in the usual Kaska manner but like a king (*AM 88–9, *CS II: 87). When he refused a demand from Mursili to hand back the Hittite subjects he had taken, Mursili attacked and destroyed the land of Tipiya, capturing Pihhuniya in the process.

Tirzah According to *OT* tradition, one of the Canaanite cities west of the Jordan r. defeated by Joshua (Joshua 12:24). 1 Kings 14:17 reports that it became the capital of the northern kingdom of Israel in the reign of Jeroboam I (traditionally dated 922–901); however, it lost this status fifty years later, when Omri, Israel's sixth king, shifted the royal seat to his new city, Samaria (1 Kings 16:23–4). The city is not attested outside *OT* sources, but is commonly identified with the site of Tell el-Farah (North) (see ***Farah, Tell el- (North)***), which lies 10 km northeast of mod. Nablus.

Campbell (*HCBD* 1156–7).

Tjekker Late Bronze Age population group listed among the so-called Sea Peoples who swept through western Asia and attacked Egypt by land and sea in the reign of the pharaoh Ramesses III (1184–1153) (**ARE IV*: §§65–6, **ANET* 262). It has been suggested that the Tjekker's original homeland lay in the Troad, on the basis of a supposed link between their name and Teucer, ancestor in Greek literary tradition of the Troad people known as the Teucri. But this is purely speculative. In the aftermath of the Sea Peoples' attack on Egypt and their defeat by Ramesses' forces, the Tjekker appear to have settled on the coast of Palestine in the region around Dor, located on the coast 21 km south of mod. Haifa. Evidence for this comes from Egyptian literary tradition. In a well-known Egyptian tale of early C11 (and thus almost contemporary with the Sea Peoples), a sea merchant of Egypt called Wenamun incurs the wrath of the Tjekker prince Beder, ruler of Dor, during a trading expedition along the Syro-Palestinian coast. Tjekker ships pursue him to the harbour-city of Byblos, but the ruler of Byblos refuses the Tjekker demand for his arrest (**CS* I: 90, 92–3).

Sandars (1985: 224, index refs).

Tlos (Lyc. Tlawa, near mod. Düver) (map 15) M1 BCE–M1 CE city in Lycia, southwestern Anatolia, located in the Xanthus valley, 20 km north of the city of Xanthus. Though the site was almost certainly occupied in the Bronze Age (= Late Bronze Age Dalawa?), the earliest material evidence for settlement dates back no earlier than C5 (but see the discussion of Raimond, 2002). A wall built by the indigenous inhabitants and two groups of rock-cut tombs feature among the oldest remains of Tlos. The city's most impressive feature is an acropolis which overlooks the site from the northwest. Later Roman and subsequently Byzantine remains include a stadium, theatre, gymnasium, baths, market-place, and church. Recent excavations of the necropolis of Tlos, conducted by H. I. Işık, have brought to light a hitherto unknown and undisturbed Lycian rock-cut tomb, whose door has been dated by an inscription to 340–250. The tomb's contents cover a period from early C3 to C1 (Adak and Şahin, 2004).

Politically, Tlos was one of Lycia's most prominent cities. It was an important coin-minting centre in C4, and in C2 enjoyed the status of one of the six principal members of the newly formed Lycian League. In legendary tradition, Tlos is closely associated with the Greek hero Bellerophon, who was allegedly buried in the city; a tomb with a relief depicting him on his winged horse, Pegasus, and reputedly his burial place actually dates to the second half of C4. One of the city's demes (administrative districts) was named after him, and a cult in his honour appears to have been established in the city.

Bean (*PECS* 927; 1978: 65–8), Raimond (2002).

Toprakkale see **Rusahinili (Qilbanikai)**.

Tralles (*Aydın*) (map 5) M1 BCE–M1 CE city in western Anatolia, north of the Maeander r. According to a tradition recorded by Strabo (14.1.42), it was founded by a mixed population from Argos in the Peloponnese (southern mainland Greece) and a barbarian tribal group called the Tralleis from Thrace. Diodorus (14.36.2) records an unsuccessful attempt by the Spartans to wrest the city from Persian control in 400. When Alexander the Great arrived in Ephesus in 334, Tralles sent a delegation to offer him their city's submission. In 313 the city was captured by Antigonus, one of Alexander's heirs (Diodorus 19.75). But in 301 it was incorporated into the Seleucid kingdom, and was thereafter known as Seleuceia. All that remains of the anc. city are three arches which once formed part of a Roman gymnasium, and an arched entrance which belonged to the city's Roman theatre.

Bean (1971: 208–11; *PECS* 931).

Trapezus (*Trebizond*) (map 4) Colony founded by Sinope on the Black Sea coast of northern Anatolia in 756 (according to Classical tradition). It was intended essentially as a trading settlement, providing access to the metal sources of the eastern Black Sea region, especially the land of Colchis, and to trade with the kingdom of Urartu. Its failure to develop in M1 into a city of any significance has been attributed to its mediocre harbour and the inhospitability of its neighbours. In the late Hellenistic period, Trapezus became part of the kingdom of the Pontine ruler Mithradates VI, and in 64 CE was annexed by Nero to the Roman empire.

Broughton, Mitchell (*OCD* 1547).

Tripolis M1 BCE–M1 CE city on the coast of Lebanon (*BAGRW* 68 A5), 65 km north of Beirut, founded by Phoenician colonists from Tyre, Sidon, and Aradus (the island Arwad), as reflected in the three separate sectors of the city. The Council of the Phoenicians met here, and in 351 voted to rebel against the Persian king Artaxerxes III (Ochus). After the battle of Issus (q.v.) in 333, 4,000 Greeks from Darius III's army fled via Tripolis to Cyprus and Egypt.

Bean (*PECS* 935).

Troas (Troad) (maps 4, 19) Classical name for the mountainous region in northwestern Anatolia, bounded on three sides by water – the Propontis and Hellespont to the north and northwest, and the Aegean Sea to the west and southwest. Its chief rivers are the Simois and the Scamander, near whose confluence Troy was located, and the Granicus and Aesepus, which drain into the Black Sea. The Mt Ida range marks part of the region's southern boundary. The name Troas reflects the Classical view that the whole region was once dominated by Troy.

J. M. Cook (1973).

Troy (Troia, ***Hisarlık***) (maps 2, 19) Bronze Age and Graeco-Roman city, in the region of the Classical Troad, northwestern Anatolia. In the Late Bronze Age it was probably the royal seat of the kingdom called Wilusa in Hittite texts. The site was occupied almost continuously from the beginning of M3 (Early Bronze Age) through M1 CE. Three main series of excavations have been conducted there: (1) seven campaigns by Heinrich Schliemann between 1871 and 1890, followed by two further campaigns by Schliemann's associate Wilhelm Dörpfeld (1893 and 1894); (2) campaigns by Carl Blegen on behalf of the University of Cincinnati, 1932–8; (3) campaigns by Manfred Korfmann of the University of Tübingen, 1988–2005. By the end of Schliemann's final season, nine major levels had been identified, each of which were divided into a number of sub-levels (forty-one or more) with a total height of more than 20 m.

Troy I was a small fortified settlement, less than 100 m in diameter, containing ten sub-levels extending from c. 3000 to 2500. Troy II covered a period of some 200 years, from c. 2500 to 2300. It was the most distinguished of the Early Bronze Age settlements at Troy, as reflected in its impressive stone fortifications, monumental ramp, and what is left of its residential architecture. Wheel-made pottery and advanced metallurgical skills were features of the technology of this level, which Schliemann believed was the city of King Priam of Homeric tradition. His alleged discovery in the city wall of a large cache of objects, many made of precious materials, reinforced his belief.

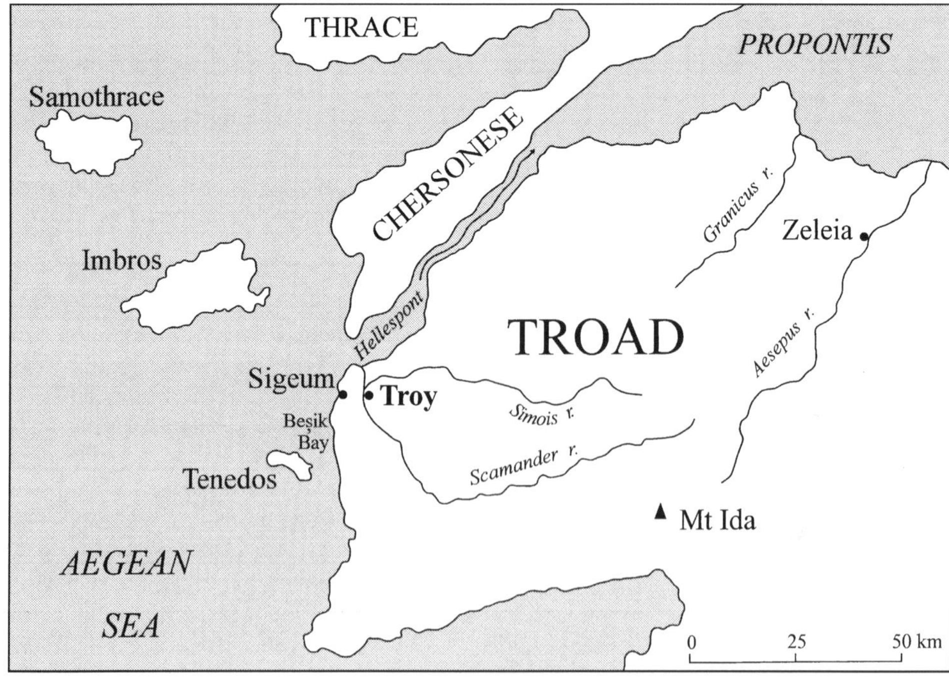

Map 19 The Troad.

Figure 119 Schliemann monument, Athens.

Figure 120 Troy, trench cut by Schliemann.

Troy II was destroyed by fire and followed by three relatively undistinguished levels, III to V, extending from c. 2300 to 1700. The last of these levels was again destroyed by fire, and succeeded by Troy VI, c. 1700–1280, the most impressive of Troy's Bronze Age cities. Remains of the citadel of this period provide evidence of imposing fortifications, including watchtowers, five gates, and a great northeast bastion. The buildings within the citadel were constructed on a series of terraces rising up towards the centre of the site. There were spacious, freestanding, two-storeyed houses, with solid stone walls and a pillared megaron. Evidence of a royal palace which may once have been constructed on the summit of the citadel is now irretrievably lost, both because of Schliemann's excavations and the clearing of the site in Graeco-Roman times to make way for a temple to the goddess Athena. Troy VIh is generally considered the most likely candidate for Homeric Troy, the city of King Priam and the Trojan War, if the tradition has any historical basis. The city ended in a major conflagration, but we cannot prove whether this was due to human agency or earthquake. The fragmentary Hittite texts which refer to Wilusa are also inconclusive in terms of possible evidence for a specific 'Trojan War' (see Bryce, 2006: 182–6).

Troy VIIa (sometimes called Troy VIi) immediately followed VIh, with no perceptible break in the population or the basic culture. However, the smaller, humbler structures which were now crowded within the citadel are indicative of significant material decline in this level, which also succumbed to destruction by fire. The final phase of Troy VII is divided into two sub-phases: VIIb1 and VIIb2. The former continued the culture of its predecessors, but the latter is marked by the appearance of a coarse ceramic knobbed ware referred to as *Buckelkeramik*, perhaps reflecting the arrival of an immigrant population group from southeastern Europe. Troy VIIb2 also ended in destruction by fire, some time between 1050 and 1000. Korfmann's excavations in the VIIb1 level brought to light a biconvex bronze seal, inscribed on both sides in the Luwian hieroglyphic script, the earliest example of writing discovered in Troy. One side of the seal gives the name of a man, and his profession as scribe, the other side the

Figure 121 Troy, sloping walls of level VI.

name of a woman. Probably the pair are husband and wife. The inscriptions are among the very last of the Anatolian Bronze Age.

Korfmann has identified a 'lower city' at Troy, extending to the south and east of the citadel. Basing his findings partly on magnetometer surveys, he concluded that the lower city spanned levels VI and VIIa, and was enclosed by a defence system consisting of a mudbrick wall marking the city's perimeter, and beyond it two ditches serving as initial lines of defence. His proposals if correct would increase the known area of Troy tenfold – from c. 20,000 to 200,000 sq. m, with a population estimated between 4,000 and 10,000. But opinion is divided on the authenticity of these findings. Korfmann's critics claim that he has misinterpreted what evidence is available, and dismiss much of his reconstruction of the lower city as mere imagination. On the other hand, the overall validity of his methodology and conclusions has been strongly endorsed by a number of distinguished Anatolian archaeologists.

Following VIIb2, Troy became all but derelict until it was resettled by Aeolian Greeks in late C8. It may have been then that the name Ilion was first used for the site, in what is now designated as the Level VIII phase of its existence. In 480, the Persian emperor Xerxes I visited Ilion just before his invasion of the western Greek world (Herodotus 7.43), and in 334 Alexander the Great made a pilgrimage there after his victory over the Persians at the Granicus r. (q.v.) (Strabo 13.1.26). Alexander gave orders that Ilion was to be accorded special status, and promised that its most important institution, the temple of Athena, would be rebuilt – a promise which his general, Lysimachus, eventually fulfilled. In 85 Ilion was captured and allegedly destroyed by the Roman commander Fimbria (Strabo 13.1.27, Appian, *Mithridatic Wars* 12.53). Though there is no clear archaeological corroboration for this destruction, it is generally seen as marking the end of level VIII in the city's history. Level IX – the Roman city 'New Ilium' – had a flourishing existence, particularly during the first two centuries of the Roman empire (27 BCE onwards), due initially to the patronage of the emperor Augustus, who made provision for major new public buildings. Athena's temple was now extensively restored. The work involved levelling and terracing the citadel's surface, destroying much of what still remained of the earlier levels. Other constructions during Augustus' reign included a Roman bath with fine mosaics, and subsequently a concert theatre and a council chamber (bouleuterion). Aqueducts were built to pipe water to what was now becoming a thoroughly Roman city. In the Byzantine period, the city sank slowly into obscurity, the empress Eudoxia, wife of Theodosius II (421–444 CE), remarking that in her day it was a complete ruin. It did not entirely disappear, however, and even in C10 the emperor Constantine VII Porphyrogenitus mentions a bishop of Ilium. Five hundred years later, the Turkish sultan Mehmet II, conqueror of Constantinople in 1453 CE, visited the site and declared that by punishing the descendants of those who had destroyed Troy, he had at last paid the debt they owed the people of Asia.

Latacz (2004), Bryce (2006), Korfmann (2006).

Trysa (map 15) M1 BCE–M1 CE hillside city in central Lycia, southwestern Anatolia, near the village of Gölbaşı. Trysa is not attested in anc. writers, but appears among the cities listed in the 255-line inscription on the 'Inscribed Pillar' in Xanthus (late C5–early C4; see **Xanthus**). A pillar-tomb with relief-decorated grave chamber, located on the city's small acropolis and dating to the last quarter of C6, is among the oldest surviving examples of Lycia's material culture. The reliefs depicting warriors or riders are considered to represent either a historical event or a funeral procession. On the upper of two terraces east of the citadel there once stood a rectangular heroon, a funerary monument in honour of a dead hero or ruler. The heroon consists of a sarcophagus, cut from the rock and located in a 20 m sq. enclosure. The walls of the enclosure are covered with relief scenes depicting episodes from Greek mythology, e.g. scenes from the Trojan War, the battles of the Greeks and the Amazons, Bellerophon's struggle with the Chimaera, the exploits of Theseus, and the battle between the lapiths and the centaurs. The monument is in the tradition of late C5–early C4 Lycian monuments, bearing much resemblance in concept to the so-called Nereid monument erected in Xanthus in early C4. The Trysa monument has been dated to the first half of C4. Its builder and no doubt its chief (if not exclusive) occupant must have been a member of a local ruling dynasty. Like the contemporaneous dynasty at Xanthus, Trysa's ruling family would have held power under Persian patronage, though the iconography of the heroon, like the Nereid monument and other similar heroa, is emphatically Greek in style. This dynasty's lease of power may have extended back to C6, when Persia established its sovereignty over Lycia. The chief occupant of the pillar-tomb referred to above may have been one of the dynasty's early members.

On the lower terrace below the heroon, another relief-decorated sarcophagus, belonging to Deireimis and Aeschylus, was originally located, along with three more Lycian-type funerary monuments of C4 date. Both the Trysa monument and the heroon on the lower terrace are now in the Kunsthistorisches Museum in Vienna. Other remains of the city include numerous sarcophagi of the Hellenistic and Roman periods, portions of a wall dating back to C5, a small temple, and a number of cisterns.

Borchhardt (*PECS* 937–8), Bean (1978: 112–14), Oberleitner (1993).

Tugliash Iron Age country within the land of Namri, located in the region of the upper Diyala valley in the borderlands of northeastern Mesopotamia and northwestern Iran, near the western verge of the Zagros mountains. Its cities Shumurza, Bit-Nergal, and Niqqu were abandoned by the Namrite king Marduk-mudammiq after he was defeated by the Assyrian king Shalmaneser III in 843, and fled from his land (**RIMA* 3: 40, 54).

Tuka M1 city belonging to the western Aramaean kingdom of Bit-Agusi in north-central Syria. It is attested in inscriptions from the reign of the Assyrian king Tiglath-pileser III (745–727) (**Tigl. III* 146–7), and is perhaps to be identified with mod. Toqat (Toqad), 24 km west of Aleppo.

Lipiński (2000: 203).

Tukrish Country attested in Middle Bronze Age texts, probably to be located on the Iranian plateau north of Elam (though D. Charpin prefers a more westerly location). The Assyrian king Shamshi-Adad I (1796–1775) reports receiving tribute in Ashur from Tukrish's kings and from the king of the 'Upper Country', perhaps in the Elamite region (**RIMA* 1: 50). Shamshi-Adad's contemporary Hammurabi, king of Babylon, campaigned against Tukrish, Elam, Gutium, and Subartum, and records his conquests of these countries on a stele which he set up in Ur (*Gadd and Legrain, 1928: 44–5, no. 146).

Mesop. 190–1.

Tukulti-Ashur-asbat Iron Age city in the land of Zamua, which was located in the borderlands of northeastern Mesopotamia and northwestern Iran. The Assyrian king Ashurnasirpal II mentions it in connection with his campaigns in Zamua in 881 and 880 (**RIMA* 2: 205, 207). He notes that the city was called Arrakdu by the Lullumu people. This was apparently its original name. The new name indicates that it was refounded or restored by the Assyrians, perhaps during the reign of Tukulti-Ninurta II (890–884), Ashurnasirpal's father.

Tu'manu (Tu'muna, Tu'na) Iron Age Aramaean tribe in northern Babylonia. It is first attested in an inscription of Shamash-resha-usur, a C8 ruler of the Aramaean state of Suhu on the middle Euphrates. Shamash-resha-usur reports pursuing and defeating a force of 400 Tu'manu warriors at a place called Qaqqaru-aradatu after they had attacked the city of Ribanish. He claims to have killed 350 of the Tu'manu tribesmen, then released the remaining fifty so that they could spread the news of their victor's triumph (**RIMB* 2: 280). Later references to the Tu'manu tribe occur in the inscriptions of the Assyrian kings Sargon II (721–705), who refers to his deportation of Tu'muna tribesmen, and Sennacherib (704–681). At this time, the land of the tribe 'seems to have been a large territorial entity, governed by men who had close relations with Chaldaea' (Lipiński). Note that Brinkman (1968: 219) rejected the identification of the Tu'manu with the Tu'muna of Sargon's time.

Lipiński (2000: 425).

Tumeshki Iron Age castle belonging to the kingdom of Melid/Malatya in eastern Anatolia. It was one of nine such establishments which the Urartian king Sarduri II claims to have added to his own kingdom following his conquests in Melid in the second year of his reign (c. 764). The other eight were Hazani, Yaurahi, Wasini, Maninui, Arushi, Qulbitarrini, Tashe, and Meluiani (**HcI* 130–2, no. 104, *Kuhrt, 1995a: 556–7). Hawkins notes (*CHLI*) that Sarduri's conquest of Tumeshki, which lay on an important crossing of the Euphrates, opened up the way for his domination of Syria.

*van Loon (1974), *CHLI* I: 284–5.

Tummanna (map 3) Late Bronze Age country, subject to the kingdom of Hatti (though not consistently), lying in the mountainous region of Classical Paphlagonia, northwest of the Hittite homeland, and closely linked in Hittite texts with the neighbouring land of Pala. Tummanna was lost to the Hittites during Tudhaliya III's reign (first half of C14), and although Tudhaliya's son and successor Suppiluliuma I sought to re-establish it as Hittite territory (**DS* 110, **CS* I: 189), his campaigns in the region apparently had no lasting impact. The country was not fully restored to Hittite control until Suppiluliuma's son Mursili II conducted a decisive military operation against it c. 1300 (**AM* 160–1). Tummanna was among the depopulated cities and lands which Mursili's son Muwattalli II (1295–1272) assigned to his brother Hattusili (later King Hattusili III) when he appointed him ruler of the northern part of the Hittite homeland (see **Hakpis(sa)** and **Turmitta**).

**RGTC* 6: 437–8.

Tummu (Tumme) Country in northeastern Mesopotamia, whose ruler was numbered by the Assyrian king Tiglath-pileser I (1114–1076) among the twenty-three kings of the Nairi lands (*RIMA 2: 21). It was conquered by Tiglath-pileser during his campaigns in these lands, which began in his third regnal year (*RIMA 2: 34, 37, 52). The Assyrian king Ashurnasirpal II records conquering Tummu and its cities in his accession year and first regnal year (884–883). These cities included Libe, Surra, Abuqu, Arura, and Arube (*RIMA 2: 196–7). Liverani (1992: 19) suggests a location in the upper basin of the Lesser Zab r., perhaps more specifically in the Rania plain.

Tuna Iron Age city in southeastern Anatolia, within the region of northern Tabal. It figures prominently in one of the lead-strip inscriptions from Kululu (q.v.) (*CHLI I: 506–9), where a distinction is made between an Upper and a Lower Tuna. Hawkins comments (CHLI I: 431–2) that it is uncertain whether this indicates different parts of the same town or different towns, perhaps widely separated. He further suggests that Tuna may be the anc. name of Kululu (alternatively identified with Artulu). But this is purely speculative. In any case, Tuna should be distinguished from the kingdom of (A)tuna, another of the kingdoms of Tabal which probably lay in the region of mod. Aksaray (see **Atuna**).

Tunip (maps 3, 6) Late Bronze Age city in central Syria on the west bank of the middle course of the Orontes r. The pharaoh Tuthmosis III (1479–1425) secured this former ally (or subject) of the kingdom of Aleppo for Egypt during his Syrian campaigns. By the mid C14 Amarna period, it had become one of Egypt's three major strongholds in the northernmost part of the pharaoh's subject territories (the other two were Sumur and Ullassa). In one of the Amarna letters the citizens of Tunip, left leaderless by the death of their king, Aki-Teshub, appealed to the pharaoh Akhenaten (1352–1336) to return to them Aki-Teshub's son, who had been taken to Egypt for 're-education', so that he could assume his father's throne (*EA 59). They also expressed grave concern that their city would fall victim to the Amurrite warlord Aziru (see **Amurru**). Their fears were realized when Aziru seized and occupied Tunip, and thenceforth used it as one of his residences. It provided him with an excellent base for his subsequent negotiations with the Hittites, which resulted in his switching allegiance from Egypt to Hatti. Tunip may now also have become an ally or subject of Hatti, if a fragmentary treaty between a Hittite king (Suppiluliuma I?) and the people of Tunip can be assigned to this period (*Weidner, 1923: 136–47). In the years following the battle of Qadesh (1274), Tunip was one of the cities captured by Ramesses II during his eighth and ninth campaigns in Syro-Palestinian territory. An identification has been proposed with the site of Tell ʿAšarne.

Lipiński (2000: 259–60), Bryce (2005: 553, index refs).

Turira Late Bronze Age city in western Mesopotamia, located on the Assyrian–Hittite frontier in C13 and formerly part of the kingdom of Hanigalbat. In mid C13, the inhabitants of Turira had taken to raiding the neighbouring kingdom of Carchemish, which belonged to Hittite territory. Concerned that these raids could escalate into a major conflict between Hittite and Assyrian forces, the Hittite king Hattusili III had written to his Assyrian counterpart Adad-nirari I asking him to do one of two things: take punitive action against Turira if he claimed sovereignty over it, or else declare that it was not his territory; such a declaration would enable Hattusili to attack the hostile city without risking war with Assyria (*HDT 148).

Turmitta (Durmitta) Middle and Late Bronze Age city and country in north-central Anatolia, site of a *karum* (Assyrian merchant-colony) called Duhurmid in the Assyrian Colony period (C20–18). In the Late Bronze Age, it was among the Hittite homeland cities and lands occupied by the Kaska people, and was the object, c. 1320, of military campaigns conducted against the occupying forces by the Hittite king Mursili II (**AM* 22–5, **CS* II: 84). The city was finally recaptured from the Kaskans by his son Hattusili (later King Hattusili III) in early C13. It became part of the northern kingdom which the Hittite king Muwattalli II assigned to Hattusili (his brother), to buffer the Hittite homeland against enemy invasion and occupation, particularly from the Kaska lands (**CS* I: 200–1). The territory ruled by Hattusili, which incorporated the countries depopulated as a consequence of enemy action – Ishupitta, Marista, Hissashapa, Katapa, Hanhana, Darahna, Hattena, T/Durmitta, Pala, Tummanna, Gassiya, Sappa, and the Hulana River Land – extended from Classical Paphlagonia across the northern half of the Marassantiya (Classical Halys) river basin to the region of mod. Sivas.

**RGTC* 6: 442–4.

Turukkum A region attested in Old Babylonian (Middle Bronze Age) texts, probably to be located in the Urmia basin and the valleys of the northwestern Zagros mountains (see Dalley, 1984, 21, map). It appears to have consisted of a group of kingdoms whose populations were of mixed stock, perhaps predominantly Hurrian but with a significant Semitic component. The Turukkeans were long considered to be a semi-nomadic tribal people who repeatedly raided the cities and kingdoms of northern Mesopotamia. But according to Eidem and Laessøe, evidence provided by the Shemshara (q.v.) archives indicates that Turukkum was made up of a number of polities with a relatively complex political organization and systems of noble lineage sharing territorial power. The kingdom of Itabalhum seems to have been the most important of these polities.

The Turukkeans were a constant threat to the security of the Old Assyrian kingdom during the reign of Shamshi-Adad I (1796–1775) and his son and successor Ishme-Dagan. Shamshi-Adad conducted a number of military operations against them, with mixed results, though he apparently succeeded in establishing his sovereignty over part of the Zagros piedmont, which was occupied by Turukkean settlements. But under the leadership of a local chieftain called Lidaya, a number of Turukkean cities in the Zagros piedmont revolted against Assyrian rule in 1779, apparently in response to Shamshi-Adad's conclusion of a pact with the Turukkeans' traditional enemies the Gutians, who also dwelt in the central Zagros region.

Whatever the outcome of this uprising, Shamshi-Adad's son Ishme-Dagan, at that time Assyrian viceroy at Ekallatum, subsequently wrote to his brother Yasmah-Addu, viceroy at Mari, in response to a letter from him about Shusharra (Shemshara, on the right bank of the Lesser Zab r.). Ishme-Dagan stated that it was impossible to maintain Assyrian control over the region because of Lidaya's activities, and that he was evacuating its population to Arrapha and Qabra (**LAPO* 17: 126, no. 531). His generals laid siege to the Turukkeans who had entrenched themselves in the city of Amurzakkum, which lay to the northwest of Shamshi-Adad's capital, Shubat-Enlil (Shehna). The Turukkeans were forced to abandon the city and to flee north, with Ishme-Dagan's forces in hot pursuit. Their progress impeded by bad weather, they decided to kill the weaker of their companions, and to abandon many of their chariots. But they reached and crossed the Tigris r. before their pursuers caught up with them, and then proceeded to ravage the country of Tigunanum (*LAPO 16: 128–9, no. 31; *LAPO 17: 98–100, nos 505–6).

The Mari letters report frequent and sometimes devastating attacks by Turukkeans against Mesopotamian cities, particularly in the period after Shamshi-Adad's death when the mantle of kingship was assumed by Ishme-Dagan. One of the most prominent Turukkean rulers with whom Ishme-Dagan had to deal was a man called Zaziya (Sasiya). In what has been considered a desperate attempt to end a prolonged war with Zaziya, Ishme-Dagan drew up a non-aggression pact with him, consolidated by a marriage between Zaziya's daughter and Ishme-Dagan's son and successor, Mut-Ashkur (*LAPO 17: 264, no. 602). However, Ishme-Dagan's relationship with Zaziya remained contentious. At one point 4,000 troops of Zaziya were reported to have crossed the Tigris on their way towards Ekallatum (*LKM 401, no. 26.522). Ishme-Dagan suffered a defeat at the hands of 5,000 Turukkeans when he attempted to rescue his subjects from them (*LKM 394–5, no. 26.510), and on another occasion the Turukkeans seized one of his cities and sent the head of its ruler to him as a taunt (*LKM 396, no. 26.511). The Babylonian king Hammurabi also sought to conclude an alliance with Zaziya (*LAPO 16: 531, no. 340). Almost certainly, the Turukkeans contributed to the disintegration of the Old Assyrian kingdom, which finally fell to Hammurabi in 1763.

In the Late Bronze Age, Turukkum appears in the list of conquests of the Assyrian king Adad-nirari I (1307–1275) (*RIMA 1: 132).

*LAPO 17: 80–100, Eidem and Laessøe (2001: 25–9), *Mesop.* 174–8.

Tushha(n) (Tushhum, *Ziyaret Tepe*) City in the upper Tigris region, attested in Middle Bronze Age and Iron Age texts, probably to be identified, on the basis of cuneiform tablet finds, with the site of Ziyaret Tepe (q.v.). It first appears in the Middle Bronze Age Mari archives as an ally of the cities Eluh(h)ut and Shinamum. In the early Iron Age, it lay within the territory of the Aramaean state of Bit-Zamani before its occupation by the Assyrian king Ashurnasirpal II in 882. Following his campaign in the land of Nirbu (q.v.), Ashurnasirpal entered Tushha, which had fallen into a state of disrepair. He demolished the old fortifications and built new ones, constructed a palace as a royal residence, and commissioned a white limestone statue of himself, with an inscription extolling his achievements. The city thus became a local headquarters of the Assyrian administration. While Ashurnasirpal was there, he received tribute from the kings of the neighbouring lands – Bit-Zamani, Shubru, Nirdun, Urumu, and the Nairi lands – in the form of chariots, horses, mules, oxen and sheep, wine, and objects of gold, silver, and bronze (*RIMA 2: 202, 210). He resettled the city with Assyrian inhabitants, and established straw and grain storage depots there, as receptacles for produce taken from Nirbu and the Nairi lands (*RIMA 2: 202, 211). During the reign of Shalmaneser III, Tushhan was amalgamated with Amedu to form the Province of the Chief Cupbearer. But in the reign of Adad-nirari III it became an independent province again (Radner, *RlA* 11: 53). Subsequently, the Assyrian king Tiglath-pileser III resettled deportees from his western conquests there (*Tigl. III 62–3). In late C7 a man called Bel-iqbi was known variously as governor of Tushhan and of Bit-Zamani (i.e. Amedu), which indicates that by this time the two provinces had again been united.

LAPO 16: 117; 17: 50.

Tushpa (Assyrian Turushpa, *Van Kale*) (map 20) M1 Urartian fortress and settlement in eastern Anatolia, located 5 km east of mod. Van, close to the southeastern shore of Lake Van. Named after the Urartian goddess Tushpea, it was founded by the Urartian king Sarduri I (832–825) – on a site which shows evidence of occupation dating back to M3 – as the first capital of the Urartian empire. The site played a key role in the rediscovery of Urartu, as both rock-cut tombs and numerous cuneiform inscriptions carved in the citadel have always been visible – although local traditions ascribed these to the Assyrians. In the late 1820s, F. E. Schulz copied many of the inscriptions, which have played an important role in introducing the Urartian language to mod. scholarship, as well as in the decipherment of cuneiform generally. Brief and largely unpublished excavations were carried out by Russians during World War I, and by an American expedition in 1939. Subsequently, between 1987 and 1991, the fortress was more systematically explored by M. Taner Tarhan. It extends for more than a kilometre along the east–west-running rock ridge of the Van massif, and rises 90 m above the surrounding plain at its summit. Settlement areas apparently lay both north and south of the citadel rock.

Tushpa's strategic location at the junction of major communication routes in the Van region no doubt provided the chief incentive for its establishment as the administrative centre of the Urartian kingdom. But another important incentive was the fertility of the surrounding plain, whose food-producing capacity was greatly increased by the construction of a major water storage and distribution system, consisting of dams, canals, and subterranean water channels. Much useful information about the city's building activities is provided by the inscriptions found on the site. These were carved into the citadel rock (as noted above) and on stelae and column bases. Written records from the site also include a number of 'display inscriptions', notably two sets of royal annals, which extol the achievements of various Urartian kings.

The oldest datable structure of the citadel complex is a large rectangular platform, 47 m × 13 m, made of enormous blocks of limestone, located at the citadel's northwestern foot and known as the Sardurisburg or Mudur Buluç. It is inscribed with six copies of an inscription of Sarduri I, written in the Akkadian language and borrowing the titulary of Neo-Assyrian kings. The remains of a building uncovered at the highest point of the inner fortress are considered by the excavators to be those of Tushpa's earliest temple. Typical in size and layout of the square tower-temples found elsewhere in the Urartian kingdom, it also contains two cellas, one of which was probably dedicated to Urartu's chief deity, Haldi, and the other perhaps connected with ancestor cult. Other remains close by are thought to belong to Tushpa's oldest palace. A later palace, probably to be assigned to the Urartian king Argishti I (787–766), was constructed at the western end of the massif outside the upper citadel.

Immediately below the temple are Tushpa's earliest royal tombs (hence the view that the temple may have been connected with ancestor cult). The tomb complexes consisted of large platforms or halls, where religious ceremonies presumably took place, and adjoining them the tombs of the kings and their families. Access to each complex was provided by steps leading from a stone platform to the tomb entrance, whose façade was carved out of the living rock and accompanied by stone pedestals. Beyond it lay the burial chambers for the king and his family. Niches cut into the walls made provision for tomb-gifts and cremation vessels. The kings who were interred in these tombs, as identified by the tomb inscriptions, included Sarduri I, Ishpuini and Minua

Figure 122 Van citadel (Tushpa), tomb of Argishti I.

(father-and-son co-regents), Sarduri II, and Argishti I. Rock-cut tomb complexes are found in a number of locations within the citadel. The settlement's main necropolis is located a few km north of the citadel.

The Assyrian king Tiglath-pileser III (745–727) claims to have inflicted a defeat upon Sarduri II in the region of Kummuh, and subsequently to have blockaded him in Tushpa. After defeating Sarduri once more in a battle before the city's gates, Tiglath-pileser set up a statue of himself on the site of his victory (**Tigl. III* 124–5). None of Sarduri's successors carved any inscriptions on the Van citadel, although Urartian rulers claimed the title 'Ruler of Tushpa' until the last days of the kingdom. It is unclear whether or not the city continued to serve as Urartu's administrative capital. But it continued to play an important role, at least in a ceremonial sense, because of its strong associations with the origins of the united Urartian kingdom and its importance as the burial place of the great Urartian kings. In this respect, Tushpa bears some comparison with Ashur, which continued to be the place where Assyrian kings were crowned and buried long after the city itself had ceased to be the administrative centre of the Assyrian empire.

Even after the fall of the kingdom, Tushpa's citadel continued to be used as a fortress. There is evidence of occupation of the site by a number of later peoples, including Medes, Persians, Parthians, Byzantine Greeks, and Ottoman Turks. Xerxes carved a large trilingual inscription on the south face of the citadel (in Old Persian, Elamite, and Akkadian), and in mediaeval times a castle was built over the Urartian city's remains.

Zimansky (1985: 78–9), Tarhan (1994; 2001), Salvini (2005).

Figure 123 Niches in Van citadel.

Tuttul (*Tell Bi'a*) (map 10) Early and Middle Bronze Age settlement-mound in western Mesopotamia, located at the confluence of the Balih and Euphrates rivers, and covering an area of 35–40 ha. Excavations conducted by E. Strommenger, from 1980 onwards, revealed a sequence of occupation levels extending from M3 to the early centuries of M2. The fortified city, whose anc. name Tuttul was identified in texts of the Old Assyrian period (Middle Bronze Age), was dedicated to the god Dagan, and probably had the status of a major religious centre. One of its most noteworthy archaeological features is a set of six three-roomed mudbrick tombs, built above ground. Dating to c. 2500, these structures have been compared with the elite tombs in the royal cemetery of Ur, and presumably served as burial places for local rulers and their families. Later M3 occupation levels revealed what appears to be a large administrative building, which contained numerous seal impressions. Pottery kilns and round storage silos were also found, along with a number of burials, including shaft-grave burials, which provide further indications of a wealthy elite class. Commercial and trading activities almost certainly accounted for the city's prosperity, which continued through the Middle Bronze Age. In this period, Tuttul served as an administrative centre of the Old Assyrian kingdom under the immediate authority of Yasmah-Addu, viceroy at Mari, as indicated by texts found in the city's palace, built or rebuilt shortly before the reign of the Assyrian king Shamshi-Adad I (1796–1775). The excavation of the palace brought to light in its early phase an underground vault containing the remains of eighty persons who had evidently died violently, perhaps as the result of a massacre.

The palace of Yasmah-Addu at Tuttul was destroyed, and thereafter Tuttul was used as a base for operations against the Assyrian viceroy. It was here that Zimri-Lim organized his coalition prior to taking Mari, and a tablet found there bears the year formula 'Year when Zimri-Lim entered Tuttul'. Eventually Tuttul, like Mari, was conquered by the Babylonian king Hammurabi.

Occupation of the site in a much later period is indicated by two mosaic pavements dating to C6 CE and bearing Syriac inscriptions which refer to the building of a Christian monastery.

Strommenger and Kohlmeyer (2000), Akkermans and Schwartz (2003: 255, 287, 313).

Tutub see ***Khafaje***.

Tuwana (Assyrian Tuhana, ***Kemerhisar***) (map 18) Iron Age kingdom in southern Anatolia, in the region called Tabal in Neo-Assyrian texts. It occupied the territory of the Classical Tyanitis, extending southwards to the Cilician Gates. Deriving its name from Late Bronze Age Tuwanuwa (q.v.), Tuwana was the largest and most important of the southern Tabalic kingdoms, encompassing within its boundaries a royal capital and a number of peripheral settlements. Its capital is commonly identified with the site of Classical Tyana (mod. Kemerhisar), 20 km southwest of mod. Niğde.

In C8, Tuwana was ruled by a king called Warpalawas (Assyrian Urballa/Urpalla) (c. 740–705), son of Muwaharanis (I). Warpalawas is first attested among the five Tabalic kings who paid tribute to the Assyrian king Tiglath-pileser III (745–727) (see **Tabal**). His occupation of Tuwana's throne until the last decade of C8, when the Assyrian throne was occupied by Sargon II, is indicated by a letter written by Sargon in 710–709 to Ashur-sharru-usur, the Assyrian governor in Que (**SAA* I: 6, no. 1). From this letter, it is evident that Warpalawas' kingdom had come under pressure because of its location between the kingdom of the Mushki/Phrygian king Mita/Midas, and the territory controlled by Ashur-sharru-usur. Sargon may in fact have assigned wider authority to Warpalawas in Tabal in 713, after he had deposed Ambaris, king of Bit-Burutash, and removed him to Assyria (see **Tabal**). This is suggested by Ashur-sharru-usur's report that the people of the Tabalic city-states Atuna and Ishtuanda had taken cities of Bit-Burutash away from Warpalawas. The implication seems to be that at least part of Bit-Burutash's territory was ruled by Warpalawas at this time. Hawkins (1982: 421) suggests that the king's long reign was probably due to a policy of ostensible cooperation with the Assyrians, and notes the strongly Assyrianizing style of sculpture on his surviving monuments. His dynastic line continued for at least one more generation after his death, for he was succeeded by his son, Muwaharanis (II), whose name is attested on a stele found at Niğde.

Classical Tyana was a fortified city built on a mound beneath mod. Kemerhisar. It is mentioned in a number of Greek and Roman literary texts and inscriptions of the Hellenistic, Roman, and Byzantine periods.

Hawkins (*OEANE* 5: 246–7; *CHLI* I: 425–6, *516–26).

Tuwanuwa (Classical Tyana, ***Kermerhisar***) (map 3) Late Bronze Age city in south-eastern Anatolia, in the northern part of the Hittite Lower Land. It is first mentioned in the so-called Telipinu Proclamation (late C16; see glossary) among the lands governed by the sons of the first Hittite king called Labarna (**Chav.* 230). Later references indicate that it was an important cult-centre. Together with the nearby city of Uda, it became the frontier of the Arzawan occupation forces who swept through the Lower Land during the reign of the Hittite king Tudhaliya III (first half of C14) (*Bryce, 2005: 146). Tudhaliya's son, Suppiluliuma (later King Suppiluliuma I), clashed with the Arzawan forces around Tuwanuwa in the campaign which he conducted on behalf of his father to drive these forces from the Lower Land (**DS* 76, **CS* I: 187). His recapture of Tuwanuwa provided him with a base for further operations against the Arzawan enemy, leading to their expulsion from the region. For Tuwanuwa's Iron Age successor, see **Tuwana**.

**RGTC* 6: 447–9.

Tyana see Tuwana.

Tyberissus Small M1 BCE–M1 CE hill city on the central coast of Lycia, south-western Anatolia, 15 km west of Myra (*BAGRW* 65 C5). Its origins date back at least to early C4, since two of its tombs bear texts in the native Lycian language (**TAM* I 75, 76), attested on sepulchral and other monuments of C5 and C4. The tombs are Lycian house-type structures. The relief on one of them suggests on stylistic grounds a date of c. 400. Nothing is known of the city's history. Sarcophagi and 'pigeonhole-tombs' on the site are dated by their inscriptions to the Hellenistic or Roman periods. There was originally a Doric temple in the city, probably dedicated to Apollo Tyberisseus, whom inscriptions identify as the city's principal deity.

Bean (*PECS* 942–3; 1978: 117–18).

Tyre (maps 6, 7) Site originally consisting of two islands (sandstone reefs) located 2 km off the coast of southern Lebanon, 40 km south of Sidon. Its history of occupation extends from mid M3 (Early Bronze Age) through the later Bronze and Iron Ages, and the Persian, Hellenistic, Roman, and Byzantine periods. According to Josephus (*Against Apion* 1.17), the Tyrian king Hiram I (969–936) linked the islands into a single fortified settlement. Excavations at Tyre, beginning in the 1830s, were long concentrated on the upper Byzantine and Roman levels. However, renewed investigations, carried out by P. Bikai from 1973 to 1974 for the Lebanese Dept of Antiquities, established the site's earliest settlement, c. 2700, and a cultural sequence extending over two millennia, from c. 2700 to 700. A gap of 400 years in this sequence, from c. 2000 to 1600, suggests that the city may have been abandoned during the Middle Bronze Age.

Despite alleged references to Tyre in the M3 Ebla texts and the C18 Egyptian Execration texts, there are no clear attestations of the island-city before the Late Bronze Age tablet archives of Ugarit and Amarna. In the mid C14 Amarna period, Tyre (called Surru in the Amarna letters) was one of Egypt's Syro-Palestinian vassal states. Tyre's ruler at this time was a man called Abi-Milku. The letters which he wrote to the pharaoh Akhenaten (**EA* 146–55) provide first-hand information about the conflicts which constantly broke out among the pharaoh's Syro-Palestinian vassals. Abi-Milku complained particularly about Sidon's ruler, Zimredda. He accused him of planning an attack upon Tyre, cutting off its food and water by seizing the mainland city of Ushu which provisioned it, and collaborating with the pharaoh's enemies, most notably the feared warlords of the country of Amurru to the north. The city eventually joined forces with the Amurrites after its citizens had assassinated their ruler, along with the sister of the king of Byblos (Gubla) and her children (*_EA_ 89), who had been sent to Tyre in the mistaken belief that they would find safe haven there.

Tyre survived the political instability of the Amarna period, and continued as an Egyptian vassal until the end of the Bronze Age. But its fate after that remains uncertain. A later Classical tradition – that it was refounded and settled by colonists from Sidon – may indicate that it had been a victim of the C12 upheavals which accompanied the collapse of the Bronze Age civilizations. But there is no archaeological evidence for a destruction of Tyre at this time. In any case, it had clearly gained a new lease of life by the last century of M2, when it became a thriving centre of trade and commerce. Trading links with Cyprus were established, and the city may at this time have set up a colony on Cyprus at Citium (Kition). By C10 it was clearly the most important of the Phoenician cities. Together with Sidon, it pioneered western Phoenician commercial enterprises as far afield as north Africa and Spain. Its best-known western colony was Carthage, on the African coast in Tunisia, which it established early in C9. According to Classical tradition, the founder of Carthage was Dido, queen of Tyre, who fled her city when her brother Pygmalion seized the throne after her husband's death. In another Greek tradition reported by Herodotus (2.49), Cadmus of Tyre led a group of Phoenicians to Boeotia in mainland Greece, where they established a settlement and introduced the Phoenician alphabet to the Greeks. Within the context of the Phoenician presence in Cyprus from the late C9 onwards, Na'aman (1998) has argued that Tyre, while a vassal state of Assyria, enjoyed a hegemonic role in the island at least until the end of C8.

Tyre also figures prominently in _OT_ tradition, particularly under King Hiram, who provided the Israelite king David with cedars and craftsmen (e.g. 2 Samuel 5:11), and his son and successor Solomon with assistance in building his temple in Jerusalem (e.g. 1 Kings 7:13–46). From C9 to C7, Tyre and other Phoenician cities were client states of Assyria. So long as these cities acknowledged Assyrian overlordship and paid the tribute demanded of them, they continued to prosper and were spared Assyrian occupation and the brutalities inflicted upon other Syro-Palestinian states. It was of course in Assyria's interest to allow cities like Tyre to maintain and increase their wealth through commercial enterprises in a peaceful, stable environment, because of the substantial revenue this brought into Assyrian coffers. But refusal to meet tribute obligations or any attempt to resist Assyrian authority met with prompt and harsh retaliation – as happened several times in the case of Sidon. In C7, the Assyrian king Esarhaddon (680–669) crushed a coalition of rebel forces led by Baal, king of Tyre. And though he subsequently drew up with the defeated king a treaty giving back to him the various territories which Tyre had formerly controlled (_SAA_ V: XXIX, *24–7), Baal again rose up against Assyria in the reign of Esarhaddon's successor Ashurbanipal (668–630/627). On this occasion, resistance ended when the Assyrians starved the city into submission by cutting off its food supplies from the mainland, presumably after seizing the city of Ushu.

At the end of C7, Assyrian domination in the region was replaced by that of the newly emerging Neo-Babylonian empire. The Babylonian king Nebuchadnezzar II (604–562) laid siege to Tyre after his capture of Jerusalem. The siege allegedly lasted thirteen years, at the end of which Nebuchadnezzar had still not subdued the island. None the less, Tyre decided to accept his sovereignty, and Babylonian officials were installed in the city. The Egyptians seem also to have involved themselves in the affairs of the region around this time, if we can so judge from Herodotus (2.161), who reports that the pharaoh Apries (589–570) attacked Sidon and fought a sea battle against the king of Tyre.

With the fall of the Babylonian empire in 539, Persia became the new overlord of Syria–Palestine. Amongst the Phoenician cities, the Persian king Cyrus II favoured Sidon over Tyre, making it the administrative seat of his fifth Persian satrapy, whose territories included Cyprus and Egypt. Thus, under Persian patronage, Sidon finally superseded its longstanding rival Tyre as Phoenicia's pre-eminent city. In C4 the loyalties of a number of Phoenician cities, including Tyre, fluctuated between Greece and Persia. But when Alexander the Great came to the region in 332, Tyre stuck firm to its Persian allegiance and held out against the Macedonian invader (Diodorus 17.40–6; see also Curtius 4.2.24–3.1). It was only after a seven-month siege, and the construction of a causeway to the island-fortress, that Alexander eventually managed to capture the city. Following the Macedonian conquest, Tyre entered a new era of growth and development. The city prospered under Seleucid rule, and in the Roman imperial period it became one of the most important commercial centres along the eastern Mediterranean coast. Its anc. remains today date predominantly to the Roman and Byzantine periods.

Joukowsky (1992), Katzenstein (1973/1997), Ward (*OEANE* 5: 247–50).

U

Uashtal M1 fortified city in the land of Suhme (q.v.) in eastern Anatolia. In 856 it was captured and destroyed by the Assyrian king Shalmaneser III during his conquest of Suhme (**RIMA* 3: 20). The city's ruler at the time was a man called Sua.

Uasi (Waisi, Uaiais, Uazai, Uesi) Iron Age city and provincial capital on the frontier of the kingdom of Urartu, eastern Anatolia. Its location can be roughly deduced from its proximity to Musasir (see below), and its position as the last Urartian fortress which the Assyrian king Sargon II encountered, and attacked, before returning to Assyria at the end of his eighth campaign in 714. But a specific site for the city has yet to be determined. Most recent interpretations of Sargon's eighth campaign would put it somewhere immediately west of Lake Urmia; the Assyrian king's claim that it was the strongest of the Urartian fortresses suggests either Qalatgah or Qaleh Ismail Agha as sites of the appropriate size (see map 20). Uasi's importance at this time is reflected in Assyrian espionage reports, which record that its governor requested military support from Urzana, the king of Musasir (**SAA* V: 109–10, no. 145), that it was the site of a rebellion against the king of Urartu which briefly placed a usurper on the Urartian throne (**SAA* V: 71–2, no. 87), and that its governor was killed by the Cimmerians when they inflicted a disastrous defeat on the Urartian king Rusa I (**SAA* I: 31, no. 30).

*Thureau-Dangin (1912: 46–7), Barnett (1982: 354–5).

Ubulu M1 Aramaean tribe in southeastern Babylonia, first attested in two letters from the mid C8 Nippur archive, addressed to the governor of Nippur (**Nippur IV*: 96, no. 32; 204–5, no. 98). One of the letters involves a case of alleged theft of some dromedaries from the people of Uruk; the second concerns a dispute between the sheikh of the Ubulu tribe and the letter's author. The Ubulu are included in the list of thirty-five so-called Aramaean tribes conquered by the Assyrian king Tiglath-pileser III, probably in his accession year (745) (**Tigl. III* 160–1).

Lipiński (2000: 460–1).

Ubumu (Ibume, Uppumu) City belonging to the Iron Age country of Shubria, located in eastern Anatolia west or southwest of Lake Van. An inscription on one of the bronze bands from Balawat (see **Imgur-Enlil**) refers to the city's conquest in 854 by the Assyrian king Shalmaneser III, when Shubria was ruled by a man called Anhitti (**RIMA* 3: 143–4). Anhitti was confined to the city by the Assyrian king, and paid him tribute there (**RIMA* 3: 104). Uppumu was later captured and sacked by the Assyrian king Esarhaddon during his campaign against Shubria in 672 (*Borger, 1956: 104).

Uda (1) (Classical Hyde? For location, see *BAGRW* 66 D2) Late Bronze Age city in

southern Anatolia, in the northern part of the Hittite Lower Land (q.v.). Together with Tuwanuwa, Uda became the frontier of the Arzawan occupation forces which swept through the Lower Land during the reign of the Hittite king Tudhaliya III (first half of C14) (*Bryce, 2005: 146). Tudhaliya's son and successor Suppiluliuma I (1350–1322) held a meeting in Uda with his own son, Telipinu, viceroy of Aleppo, while Suppiluliuma was celebrating religious festivals in the city (**DS* 92, **CS* I: 189). The purpose of the meeting may have been to discuss military developments in Syria, where Hittite military operations were being conducted in the war against Mitanni.
**RGTC* 6: 466–7.

Uda (2) Iron Age fortified city in the Kashiyari range (mod. Tur ʿAbdin) of northern Mesopotamia, first attested in a letter reportedly written by the son of Amme-Baʿala, ruler of Bit-Zamani, to the Assyrian king Tukulti-Ninurta II in early C9 (**RIMA* 2: 171). In 866, the Assyrian king Ashurnasirpal II captured Uda after a siege, impaled its troops alive on stakes around the city, and deported part of its population to Assyria (**RIMA* 2: 220). At the time of the Assyrian campaign, Uda was among the (alleged) sixty cities ruled by Labturu, king of the land of Nirdun.
Lipiński (2000: 139–40).

Uetash/Uita Iron Age city in southeastern Anatolia, located on the border between the Neo-Hittite kingdoms of Melid (Malatya) and Kummuh. In 836 it was captured by the Assyrian king Shalmaneser III during a campaign in Melid, and was at that time referred to as a fortified city of the Melidite king Lalla (**RIMA* 3: 67). The Urartian king Sarduri II mentions it in his Annals as one of the royal cities which he captured from Kushtashpi, king of Kummuh (c. 750).
CHLI I: 331, n. 11, 332 with n. 29.

Ugarit (*Ras Shamra*) (maps 3, 6) Bronze Age city located on the coast of northern Syria. Its history of occupation actually begins in the Neolithic Age and includes brief periods of settlement in Persian (C6–4) and Roman times. But its most important occupation phases belong to the Bronze Ages. During the Late Bronze Age, the city reached the peak of its development, as the capital of the kingdom of Ugarit. Excavations at Ras Shamra have been conducted since 1929 by a series of French teams for the Mission Archéologique Française under the direction successively of C. F.-A. Schaeffer (1929–70), H. de Contenson (1971–4), J. Margueron (1975–7), and M. Yon (since 1978). Urban development began on the site c. 3000, and in the course of M3 (Early Bronze Age) a substantial settlement grew up there, before the site was abandoned c. 2200. After a gap of c. 100 years, the Middle Bronze Age phase of Ugarit's existence began with occupation by Semitic-speaking nomadic groups, some of whom seem rapidly to have adapted to a sedentary lifestyle, as reflected in the expansion of settlement over the entire mound. The Middle Bronze Age city was substantially fortified. Diplomatic contacts with Mesopotamia in this period are indicated by the record in the Mari texts of a visit by Mari's king Zimri-Lim (1774–1762) to the city (*LAPO* 17: 165, 384). Commercial and possibly political contacts with Egypt are indicated by the presence on the site of Egyptian artefacts and hieroglyphic inscriptions of the period.

Ugarit seems to have declined into relatively obscurity at the end of the Middle

Bronze Age (c. mid C17). But by mid C14, it had re-emerged to become the centre of one of the most important and most prosperous of all the kingdoms in the Syro-Palestinian region. Much of its wealth derived from the fact that the kingdom it controlled was a valuable timber-producing area, and its rich, fertile steppes and plains were excellent for grazing purposes and for the production of a wide range of goods, including grain, wine, oil, and flax. Ugarit was also the centre of thriving manufacturing industries, where the arts of bronzesmiths and goldsmiths flourished and a wide range of linen and woollen goods were produced for export. Its 50 km coastline contained four or more seaports, making it an important link between the Mediterranean world and the lands stretching to the Euphrates and beyond. And through its territory passed some of the major land routes of Syria, north through Mukish to Anatolia and east through Aleppo to Mesopotamia. It was, however, never a militarily strong state, and preferred to pay a substantial annual tribute to the Hittites when they established their dominance over it in C14 rather than provide troops for their armies.

The city's dominant building complex in its Late Bronze Age phase was the royal palace, constructed in several phases and at its greatest extent covering some 10,000 sq. m. Shut off from the rest of the city by its external wall, the palace contained multiple rooms built around open courtyards, and in its final development one or more upper storeys accessed by a dozen staircases. Areas for administration, official functions, and private living are distinguishable in the palace's floor plan. The private apartments were luxuriously appointed, and in one area of the palace opened on to a large garden. Two large temple-towers, perhaps of Middle Bronze Age origin, were built on the city's acropolis. They were dedicated (separately) to the gods Baal and Dagan. Nearby on the acropolis were blocks of houses divided off by narrow streets. This was one of the city's several residential areas, which consisted of houses of various sizes, generally built along narrow, winding streets and often provided with their own wells. A large quantity of small finds, many of precious materials, have come to light during the excavations. They include jewellery, weapons, figurines, golden bowls, and faience and alabaster vases – reflecting both the high level of local craftsmanship as well as the extensive foreign commercial and cultural contacts which Ugarit enjoyed, with Egypt, Cyprus, the Aegean world, Anatolia, and Babylonia. Its port served as one of the most important international emporia of the anc. western Asian world.

Detailed information about Ugarit's dealings and relations with other states is provided by the city's archives. These constitute one of our most valuable sources of information on international relations in the Late Bronze Age. (The majority of the documents are written in a local version of the Akkadian language. But some are written in Ugaritic, and several other languages are also represented in the archive, e.g. Hittite.) A wide range of letters written to foreign rulers, administrative and legal documents, and ritual, medical, and literary texts have been unearthed from six palace archives, from the so-called High Priest's House between the two temples on the acropolis, and from several private houses. One of the most important of the 'private archives' consists of 335 tablets of varying content unearthed in a large residence owned by one of Ugarit's most important citizens, a scribe called Rapanu, and located not far from the palace. In 1994, excavations brought to light another private archive, consisting of more than 400 tablets and fragments, in the house of a man called Urtenu, another high-ranking dignitary of Ugarit in C13.

Figure 124 Ugarit, gateway.

But the earliest surviving Ugaritic document belongs to the mid C14 Amarna archive (see glossary) found in Egypt. It is a letter which the Ugaritic king Ammistamru I wrote to the pharaoh Amenhotep III, or his successor Akhenaten in his first years, declaring his allegiance to the Egyptian crown (**EA* 45). Shortly after Ammistamru's death, the Hittite king Suppiluliuma I approached his son and successor Niqmaddu II, as revealed in a letter he wrote to him, found in the palace archives in Ugarit (**HDT* 125–6), and succeeded in winning him over to the Hittite side. But Niqmaddu's decision to ally himself with Hatti met with prompt reprisals from a coalition of Syrian kingdoms whose overtures he had rejected. Ugarit was invaded and plundered (**PRU IV*: 49). Perhaps belatedly, a Hittite expeditionary force was dispatched to the region to drive out the invaders and return to Niqmaddu the booty taken from him. Subsequently, Suppiluliuma delivered up to him a substantial portion of the invaders' territories, which may have resulted in a fourfold increase of his own lands. But Ugaritic territory was later reduced, by Suppiluliuma's son and (second) successor Mursili II, to two-thirds of its former size, when Mursili assigned a slice of it to the Hittite viceregal kingdom of Carchemish. This is indicated in the terms of a treaty which Mursili drew up with Niqmaddu's son and (second) successor Niqmepa (**PRU IV*: 84–101). Niqmepa's immediate predecessor, his brother Arhalba, had apparently refused to recognize Hittite sovereignty, and had been deposed by Suppiluliuma for this reason. Otherwise, Ugarit appears to have remained loyal to its Hittite allegiance until the end of the Bronze Age, in spite of an apparent attempt by Tukulti-Ninurta

I, king of Assyria, to win it over to the Assyrian side during the reign of the Hittite king Tudhaliya IV (1237–1209).

In these final decades of the Late Bronze Age, the Hittites were increasingly unable to protect their subject territories against outside attacks, particularly those associated with the Sea Peoples. Letters dating to the final months of Ugarit's existence highlight the city's plight. An urgent communication sent by the last Ugaritic king, Ammurapi, to the Hittite viceroy in Carchemish requesting assistance against an imminent seaborne invasion received the reply that Ugarit would have to rely on its own resources to defend itself (*Nougayrol *et al.*, 1968: 85–6, no. 23). And when the king of Alasiya (Cyprus) sent a desperate appeal to Ammurapi begging for assistance against the enemy from the sea, Ammurapi replied that his own land had been ravaged by the enemy, and that he had no ships to spare since they were engaged elsewhere in fighting the enemy (**RS* 20.238 = Nougayrol *et al.*, 1968: 87–9, no. 24). The letter was found in the house of Rapanu; that is to say, it was never dispatched – graphic evidence of the city's sudden, violent end. Ugarit was looted and abandoned, perhaps already some years before the fall of the Hittite capital Hattusa in early C12. The city had no Iron Age successor.

We should note, by way of postscript, that while a large number of the tablets found in Ugarit relate to the kingdom's political and military dealings with its neighbours, there are others that record interactions of a different kind, indicating, for example, regular activity of a peaceful commercial nature between the local Syrian states. Letters exchanged between the kings of Ugarit and Sidon, and the king of Beirut and a high official in Ugarit, testify to close, cordial relations between the Levantine coastal states in the Bronze Age's final decades. And Ugarit seems also to have had close links with Emar on the Euphrates. Commercial interaction between the two states is reflected in the establishment of a Ugaritic trading office in Emar, early in C12, where Dagan-belu was installed as Ugarit's representative and manager of its trading operations. From Emar he wrote to Shipti-Baʿal, agent and husband of the daughter of the Ugaritic king Ammurapi, assuring him that all was well, asking for news from home, and sending along with his messenger some plants for Shipti-Baʿal. In return, he asked that if a messenger were to come from Shipti-Baʿal, he would be grateful if he could bring with him some oil and a large linen garment of good quality, for Dagan-belu's own use (**RS* [Varia 26] = *Arnaud, 1991: 66–7, no. 30). As the epigraphist P. Bordreuil comments, these letters display in full light the high degree of 'cosmopolitanism' that characterized the world of Ugarit and its neighbours in these

Figure 125 Ugarit, alphabet.

final decades. There is little hint in them of the great catastrophe that was so soon to engulf Ugarit and its neighbours.

A. Curtis (1985), *Bordreuil (1991), Yon *et al.* (1995), Singer (1999b), Lackenbacher and Malbran-Labat (2005), Vidal (2005), Yon (2006).

Uishdish Province of the M1 kingdom of Mannaea, bordering to the north the kingdom of Urartu. In 716, its pro-Urartian ruler Bagdatti joined a rebellion against the Mannaean king Aza, newly installed on the Mannaean throne by his Assyrian overlord Sargon II. Aza was overthrown and executed. Sargon responded by conducting a campaign in Mannaean territory, during which he captured Bagdatti and had him flayed alive (**ARAB* II: 28). In the following year, Sargon returned to Uishdish, which had been occupied by the Urartian king Rusa I, and launched an attack upon his army on Mt Uaush (Mt Sahen, south of Tabriz?), where the Urartians had set up camp. Sargon won a resounding victory, and Rusa barely escaped with his life (**ARAB* II: 78–83). Sargon subsequently seized back from Urartian control the whole of the province of Uishdish, then demolished the fortifications of its cities and allowed his troops to plunder its food lands (**ARAB* II: 84).

Ukku Iron Age city at the foot of Judi Dağ, mod. Kurdistan, in Assyrian frontier territory near Urartu. In a letter to his father, the Assyrian king Sargon II (721–705), Sennacherib reports that the ruler of Ukku has informed Urartu's king (Rusa I) that Assyrian governors were building a fort in Kumme (q.v.) (**SAA* I: 28–9, no. 29). Sennacherib had received this news from a messenger of Ariye, ruler of Kumme. The fort was presumably intended to strengthen the city's defences against an Urartian attack. Kumme lay close to Ukku, probably to its north. For further details of the Ukkean king's activities, including a meeting he held with Ariye, see **Kumme**.

Ukulzat Late Bronze Age city in Nuhashshi in Syria. Following his conquest of Nuhashshi c. 1340, the Hittite king Suppiluliuma I appointed a local man, Takibsharri, as ruler of the city (**HDT* 43).

Ullamma (Ulma) Middle and Late Bronze Age city in central Anatolia, located somewhere in the vicinity of mod. Aksaray. It was the southernmost city conquered by Anitta, a C18 king of Nesa (see **Kanesh**), during his first series of campaigns against the lands which lay within or near the Kızıl Irmak basin (**Chav.* 217, **CS* I: 183). Early in the Hittite Old Kingdom (C17), Ullamma was the seat of a Hittite governor. However, it was among the rebel cities which rose up against the Hittite king Hattusili I (1650–1620). It twice confronted the king in battle and was twice defeated by him (**Chav.* 220). To prevent a third uprising, Hattusili ordered its total destruction and its site to be sown with weeds as a sign that it was never to be resettled.

Ullassa Late Bronze Age city on the Levantine coast near the southern frontier of Amurru. In mid C14 it was occupied by the Amurrite warlord Abdi-Ashirta, who claimed to be protecting it on behalf of the pharaoh Amenhotep III (**EA* 60). After Abdi-Ashirta's capture (see under **Amurru**), Ullassa was among the cities which were liberated by Egyptian troops, but reoccupied soon after (along with Ardata, Wahliya,

Ampi, Shigata, and Arwada) by Abdi-Ashirta's sons (**EA* 104, 105). Egyptians resident in Ullassa fled south from the city and sought refuge in the kingdom of Gubla (Byblos).

Ulluba M1 country in northeastern Mesopotamia, within the frontier regions of Urartu and Assyria, c. 100 km north of Nineveh (see Parpola and Porter, 2001: 4, map). An inscribed rock relief discovered at mod. Mila Mergi helps fix Ulluba's location, as well as providing information about the campaign which the Assyrian king Tiglath-pileser III conducted against it in 739 (*Postgate, 1973 *Tigl. III* 111–16). The campaign was in response to a planned invasion by Ulluba of Assyrian territory, probably with Urartian encouragement and support. It resulted in the subjugation of Ulluba and its incorporation into the Assyrian empire (**Tigl. III* 166–7). But a further Assyrian campaign was needed, in 736, to ensure that Ulluba was fully pacified. Thereafter the country played an important role as a buffer-zone on Assyria's north-eastern frontier. Tiglath-pileser set up a provincial capital there, called Ashur-iqisha (**ARAB* I: 282, 292, **Tigl III* 124–7), expanded the province's territories by the addition of a number of cities to it, and increased its population by resettling deportees there from his western conquests (**Tigl. III* 62–3).

Uluburun (map 2) Cape on Anatolia's southern coast in the country of Lycia, 8.5 km southeast of mod. Kaş. In 1982, a Late Bronze Age shipwreck was discovered by a sponge diver 400 m from the tip of the cape. Tree-ring analysis of the logs in the cargo (see below) provides a tentative date of c. 1316 for the disaster which befell the ship. The site was excavated by the Institute of Nautical Archaeology at Texas A&M University, under the direction of G. Bass and C. Pulak, from 1984 to 1994.

The ship's main cargo consisted of ten tonnes of Cypriot copper, in the form of four-handled, two-handled, pillow-shaped, and plano-convex 'bun' ingots. It also included a tonne of four-handled and bun-shaped tin ingots, of unknown origin. The two metals would have been offloaded together at one or more of the vessel's ports of call, where they would have been combined to produce bronze. As Bass notes, the 10:1 ratio of the copper and tin components of the cargo reflects the proportions in which the metals were mixed to produce bronze. In addition to the metals, the ship's cargo was made up of a number of manufactured items and raw materials. The former included more than 150 discoid glass ingots (in cobalt blue, turquoise, and lavender colours), ten large pithoi (storage jars), faience goblets in the shape of rams' heads and in one case a woman, silver bracelets and gold pendants from Canaan, duck-shaped ivory cosmetics boxes, copper cauldrons and bowls, a trumpet carved from a hippopotamus tooth, and a large range of bronze weapons, tools, and weights. The foodstuffs identified among the finds – almonds, figs, olives, grapes, pomegranates, wheat, barley, and the spices cumin, sumac, and coriander – may have been intended partly as cargo, partly for on-board consumption. Raw materials in the cargo included 'ebony' (the Egyptian name for blackwood) and cedar logs from tropical Africa, ivory in the form of elephant tusks and hippopotamus teeth, tortoise carapaces, and ostrich eggshells. Of particular interest to a number of scholars is the discovery of a folding wooden writing tablet with ivory hinges and recessed surfaces once covered with wax. It recalls the folding tablet used for the letter which Bellerophon brought to Lycia, as related by Homer (*Iliad* 6.169) – the only reference to writing in the Homeric epics. It is clear that while merchant ships like the Uluburun vessel traded primarily in commodity items, metals above all, they also conducted what must have been a lucrative trade in luxury items. These were no doubt eagerly sought after by the wealthy elites of the countries which benefited from the sea-trading network.

The origin of the Uluburun wreck, as also of the smaller and later Gelidonya wreck (q.v.), remains uncertain. Though most of the ship's cargo may have come from Cyprus or the Syro-Palestinian region, this in itself provides no indication of the ship's place of origin. However, its twenty-four anchors are of a type found off the coast of Israel, and thus make a Syro-Palestinian origin likely. The crews could have been drawn from many parts of the Aegean and Near Eastern world. Almost certainly the vessel carried a number of passengers, including merchants and emissaries from various lands. There is evidence that several high-ranking Mycenaeans were among these passengers.

Pulak and Bass (*OEANE* 5: 266–8), Yalçın *et al.* (2005).

Umalia Iron Age fortified city located in the Amadanu mountain region which lies to the west of the Kashiyari range (mod. Tur ʿAbdin) of northern Mesopotamia. Another fortified city, Hiranu, lay close by. The Assyrian king Ashurnasirpal II destroyed both cities during his 866 campaign, massacring or deporting their inhabitants (**RIMA* 2: 219).

Liverani (1992: 83).

Umeiri, Tell el- (*West*) (map 8) Fortified site on the Transjordanian plateau 15 km north of Amman. It belongs to a group of three tells in the locality (the other two are called Tell-el Umeiri East and Tell el-Umeiri North) which developed around a spring. Tell el-Umeiri's history of occupation extends from at least the Middle Bronze Age to the Roman period. Excavations have been carried out on the site since 1984, and continue to the present day, within the context of the Madaba Plains project. The current directors are D. R. Clark, La Sierra University, and L. G. Herr, Canadian University College.

From the city's Late Bronze Age phase, a well preserved temple/palace complex has emerged, and is still being investigated. Excavation in recent years has also concentrated on the city's early Iron Age I phase, whose remains spread over much of the mound. It has been suggested that the destruction at the end of Iron Age I (C11) was due to the Ammonites. Subsequently, the city must have been incorporated into the kingdom of Ammon, whose capital, Rabbath-Ammon (mod. Amman), lay only a few km to the south. Recent finds from the period of supposed Ammonite occupation include a cobbled courtyard (dating to C11), thought to be a religious area because of several ceramic shrine-models found there. The courtyard contained a line of stone benches and a wooden shelter on one side of it. Above this courtyard was another, dating to C10–9. Summary reports of recent excavations appear in *AJA*. The latest to hand, for the 2006 season, is in Savage and Keller (2007: 532–3). The original overall director of the project, L. T. Geraty, comments that 'Umeiri West is the best preserved Iron Age I city (c. 1200) so far uncovered in Jordan, . . . and has the largest, most coherent defensive system in Palestine from this period.'

When Ammon was absorbed within the Persian empire in late C6, Tell Umeiri appears to have become a local centre of the Persian administration, to judge from about forty seals and seal impressions discovered in a building complex of this period.

Some of these bear the names and titles of the last members of the Ammonite monarchy, and of officials of the Persian administration. They apparently lived in a residential quarter located to the north of the administration complex, and were responsible for supervising the agricultural estates in the surrounding region and ensuring that production targets were met.

Geraty (*OEANE* 5: 273–4).

Umma (map 17) Early Bronze Age (M3) Sumerian city and city-state in southern Mesopotamia, located 30 km northwest of its long-term rival Lagash. Umma's continuing existence in early M2 is attested by texts and material remains from the Old Babylonian period (C19–early C16). Clay tablets uncovered during clandestine excavations from the beginning of C20 led to an identification of this city with Tell Jokha, where a temple of the Old Babylonian period (early M2), perhaps dedicated to Umma's tutelary deity, Shara, has come to light. The temple was unearthed during the course of official Iraqi excavations, which were also carried out at the site of Umm al-Aqarib, 7 km southwest of Tell Jokha. At Umm al-Aqarib, levels dating to the Sumerian Early Dynastic period (c. 2900–2334) contained a monumental building variously identified as a temple, a palace, or a necropolis. Umm al-Aqarib is now considered to be the original site of Umma, with Tell Jokha to be identified with the city called Gisha (Kissa) in M3 texts. Both sites belonged to the city-state of Umma.

Information about Umma comes from a range of cuneiform sources, dating from c. 2600 to the Old Babylonian period (Middle Bronze Age). A number of Early Dynastic texts refer to conflicts between Umma and Lagash over the boundaries which lay between them. The best known of these conflicts is recorded in the famous Stele of the Vultures monument found in a fragmentary state during the French excavations at Girsu, capital of the city-state of Lagash. It records, in word and bas-relief, a victory over Umma by Eannatum, king of Lagash (C25) (**Chav.* 11–13).

From the records of both Umma and Lagash as well as from other sources, we know the name of a number of Umma's kings, the most famous of whom was Lugal-zage-si, who came to power c. 2340. He decisively defeated Urukagina, the last of Lagash's 'first dynasty' rulers, and destroyed Lagash's capital, Girsu (c. 2330). He also conquered the city-states of Ur and Uruk and established his authority over the whole of Sumer, declaring himself 'king of Uruk and the country (of Sumer)' (**Chav.* 15). This declaration was apparently made while Lugal-zage-si's conflict with Lagash was still in progress (see A. Westenholz, *RlA* 7: 156–7). But whatever the sequence of events, there is no doubt that Lugal-zage-si was the first king to succeed in uniting the Sumerian city-states under a single rule, foreshadowing (in the opinion of some scholars) the enterprises of Sargon (2334–2279), founder of the Akkadian empire. Sargon's defeat of Lugal-zage-si (**CS* II: 243) brought to an abrupt end the latter's brief lease of power over the Sumerian world. Umma now became part of the kingdom of Akkad. It apparently tried to re-establish its independence during the reign of Sargon's successor Rimush, who reports his defeat of an army from Umma, with heavy casualties, the capture of Umma, and the demolition of its walls (**DaK* 202–3).

Despite this setback, Umma continued to prosper, as a subject state first of the Akkadian empire and subsequently of the empire of the Ur III dynasty (2112–2004), as indicated by large numbers of administrative texts from both periods, especially the latter (which has produced some 15,000 texts from the Umma region). These texts indicate that for administrative purposes, Umma was now divided into two districts, one centred upon the cities of Gisha and Umma, the other upon the city of Apishal. Within the former district lay two other cities, Nagsu, where a military garrison was located, and Zabala(m). The Ur III texts make clear that Umma played a major role in the Ur III empire, no doubt due partly to its strategic location on the route between Nippur and Ur.

The city of Umma's continuing existence in the early centuries of M2 is attested by a small number of texts of the Old Babylonian period. But it was probably abandoned during or at the end of this period.

Lafont (*DCM* 870–2).

Umm al-Aqarib see Umma.

Umm el-Biyara (map 13) 6 ha Iron Age II unfortified settlement located on a mountain summit overlooking Petra in Jordan in the land of Edom. The site was excavated by C.-M. Bennett over three seasons, 1960, 1963, and 1965, following earlier work there by P. J. Parr for the British School of Archaeology in Jerusalem. Bennett's aim was partly to prove or disprove the identification of the site with *OT* Sela (which she was unable to do; the identification is now generally considered untenable), and partly to obtain a corpus of stratified Edomite pottery. Her excavations extending over 700 sq. m, less than one-third of the site, uncovered a group of dry-stone domestic dwellings, with long corridors and small rooms attached to them. Their contents included a number of looms and spindle whorls. The site, and hence the Edomite pottery which it contained, was able to be dated on the basis of a seal impression found in one of the houses. Its inscription, as restored, refers to a king of Edom called Qos-Gabr. This king was already known from Assyrian inscriptions dating to 673/672 in the reign of Esarhaddon, and to 667, early in the reign of his successor Ashurbanipal. Thus the settlement at Umm el-Biyara can be securely assigned to the first half of C7, and appears not to have extended either back before this period or after it. (The seal impression has also proved of considerable importance in dating Edomite sites in general.) Subsequent occupation by the Nabataeans (Hellenistic and early Roman periods) is indicated by a Nabataean temple on the edge of the plateau.

Bienkowski (1990: 91–5; *NEAEHL* 4: 1488–90; *OEANE* 5: 274–6).

Umm el-Marra, Tell (= anc. Tuba?) (map 2) 25 ha site in northern Syria, located between Aleppo and Emar on a major east–west route connecting Mesopotamia with western Syria. Its history of occupation extends through Early, Middle, and Late Bronze Age phases, and Persian-Hellenistic and Roman phases, thus spanning a total of more than 3,000 years, from c. 2700 BCE to 400 CE. Excavation of the site was begun in 1994 by a team from Johns Hopkins University. Its primary aim was to investigate the major developmental episodes in the history of urban life at Umm el-Marra and its region. The Early Bronze Age remains include sequences of domestic architecture and a two-chambered kiln. An important recent discovery is a small tomb which contained the remains of eight persons in three layers: two young women each with a baby, and three adult males and another baby. That this was an elite burial group is indicated by the gold, silver, and lapis lazuli ornaments worn by the women. The men are more modestly adorned. The depositing of female figurines beneath house floors at Umm el-Marra, as also at the site of Selenkahiye (q.v.), may have had an apotropaic purpose – i.e. to protect the house from evil influences. The community in this period was protected by an earthen enclosure wall.

In the Middle Bronze I period (c. 2000–1800), the site appears to have suffered partial abandonment. Palaeobotanical evidence may indicate that this was due to environmental factors, e.g. a sequence of drought years. The excavators have noted that a number of other sites in the region were deserted in the same period. But the city took on a new lease of life in Middle Bronze II (c. 1800–1600), when new fortifications and new domestic residences were built, and there is evidence of economic development. The excavators suggest that these developments coincided with the rise of the kingdom of Yamhad (q.v.), to which Umm el-Marra very likely became subject. In its Late Bronze Age phase (c. 1600–1200), following the destruction of Yamhad, the city was probably absorbed within the Mitannian and the Hittite empires in turn. Finds from this period include central-room houses and luxury items such as alabaster and glazed ceramic vessels. There is no trace of a defensive wall. The excavators report that survey data show a substantial reduction in the number of sedentary communities in the region at this time.

No information is available as yet from later periods of Umm el-Marra's existence.

G. Schwartz *et al.* (2000a; 2000b).

Unqi see **Pat(t)in.**

Upi (1) (**Opis**) (map 10) Bronze and Iron Age city in northern Babylonia, thought to lie on the east bank of the Tigris r. near its junction with the Diyala r. and just south of mod. Baghdad. An identification has been proposed with the site of Tell Bawi, just east of Ctesiphon, or alternatively with Tulul al-Mujaili. The city is first clearly attested in Middle Bronze Age texts. Apil-Sin, king of Babylon (1830–1813), refers to his annexation of it, along with other territories in the Tigris region north to Mankisum. Shortly after this annexation Upi, together with Mankisum and a city called Shahaduni, became attached to the kingdom of Eshnunna when it was ruled by Naram-Sin (late C19). Control over the region was now contested by a new player, the Old Assyrian king Shamshi-Adad I (1796–1775), ruler of Upper Mesopotamia. Shamshi-Adad won possession of Mankisum, and established a boundary with Eshnunna between the city and Upi to the south. The Eshnunnite king responded by assembling his forces at Upi in preparation for an attack on Mankisum. He invited Hammurabi, king of Babylon, to join forces with him, but the invitation was refused. The Eshnunnites then entered Shamshi-Adad's territory, advancing towards a town called Mashkulliya, but withdrawing before a military confrontation with the Assyrian forces took place. Mankisum subsequently fell to the Eshnunnite king Dadusha.

But in 1765, when an Elamite army seized Eshnunna, Hammurabi took the opportunity to seize both Mankisum and Upi for himself. This infuriated the Elamite king, who sent an ultimatum to the Babylonian, demanding that he return to him the cities formerly belonging to Eshnunna. When Hammurabi refused, the Elamites attacked and captured Mankisum, and then progressed downstream along the Tigris to Upi. The city was placed under siege by Elamite forces, who established a military encampment nearby (**LKM* 319, 321). This may have been in preparation for an attack on Babylon itself, which lay on the Euphrates just a few km to the southwest.

Babylonian troops were mustered on the west bank of the Tigris for an apparent counter-offensive against the invaders. But as far as we know, no such action took place, and for reasons unknown the Babylonians were subsequently evacuated. The Elamites left a garrison at Upi while the main body of their troops returned to Eshnunna, which was still occupied by the Elamite king (**LKM* 323–4).

After the withdrawal of the Elamite troops from Mesopotamia in 1764, Hammurabi sought to resolve by diplomacy the question of sovereignty over Upi and other cities in the region, specifically Mankisum and Shahaduni, in treaty negotiations with the new Eshnunnite king Silli-Sin (see under **Mankisum**). In accordance with the terms of the treaty, Upi would revert to Babylonian control. It appears that Silli-Sin initially rejected these proposals, but agreed to them a year or so later.

During the Late Bronze Age, Opis was a province of the Babylonian Kassite state. In C12, it was one of the northern Babylonian cities conquered and looted by the Elamite king Shutruk-Nahhunte I (1185–1155). In C11 it was caught up in the conflicts between Assyria and Babylon, and was finally conquered, along with Babylon and Dur-Kurigalzu, by the Assyrian king Tiglath-pileser I (1114–1076) (**RIMA* 2: 43), when Babylon's throne was occupied by Marduk-nadin-ahhe (1100–1083). It was for a time a part of the Neo-Assyrian province of Dur-Sharukku (Radner, *RlA* 11: 65). The governor of Ashur wrote to the Assyrian king Sargon II (721–705) requesting that his boat should come to Opis in order to bring straw and fodder (**SAA* I: 80–1, no. 94). In 539 Opis was the site of a fierce and bloody battle between the Persian and Babylonian armies, under their respective kings Cyrus II and Nabonidus. The latter was defeated and fled for his life, while Cyrus plundered Opis and massacred its inhabitants (**ABC* 109, **CS* I: 468, **Chav.* 420, **PE* 51, no. 1). He then proceeded to Sippar, and shortly afterwards his victorious troops entered Babylon.

Further references to Opis occur in texts dating as late as the second year of the reign of Cambyses (c. 529), Cyrus II's son and successor. It is also mentioned in Xenophon's description of the homeward March of the Ten Thousand Greek mercenary troops in 401. Xenophon (2.4.25) indicates that a bridge had been built across the Tigris at this point (almost certainly by the Persians). In a late text discovered in Nippur, a customs official from Opis is mentioned; he may have been responsible for this same bridge. In 324 Opis was the venue of a spectacular feast organized by Alexander for both Macedonians and Persians (Arrian, *Anabasis* 7.12), following the great Macedonian–Persian marriage ceremony in Susa in the spring of that year.

LKM 60–1, Streck (*RlA* 10: 113–16), *Mesop.* 115–16 (with refs).

Upi (2) (Aba, Apina, Upu) (map 6) Late Bronze Age region in Syria south of the plain of Homs, whose main urban centre was the city of Damascus. A number of letters in the mid C14 Amarna archive record disputes in which its ruler Biryawaza became embroiled with his neighbours, particularly Aitakkama of Qadesh (Moran, 1992: 381, index refs s.v. Biryawaza). At that time, Upi was subject to the pharaoh Akhenaten. Around 1340 it was captured by the Hittite king Suppiluliuma I during his one-year Syrian campaign against Mitanni and its Syro-Palestinian subjects. However, Upi lay within the border area of Egyptian territory, and Suppiluliuma probably relinquished control of it, in the interests of maintaining peace with the pharaoh, shortly after the Syrian campaign. In 1274 Upi was retaken by the Hittites in the aftermath of the battle of Qadesh, fought between the Hittite king Muwattalli II and the pharaoh

Ramesses II. For a time, it was placed under the command of Muwattalli's brother Hattusili (later King Hattusili III) (*Bryce, 2005: 240), before eventually being handed back to Egypt.

Upper Land (map 3) Late Bronze Age Hittite region in northern Anatolia extending over much of the territory between the upper Kızıl Irmak r. (Hittite Marassantiya, Classical Halys) and the northwestern bend of the Euphrates. It served as an important eastern buffer zone for the Hittite homeland. The Kaska region bordered it to the northwest and the country of Azzi-Hayasa to the northeast. It was invaded and occupied a number of times by enemies from both these regions – for example, in the seventh regnal year of the Hittite king Mursili II (c. 1315), when it was attacked and looted by a Kaskan tribal chief called Pihhuniya (*AM* 88–9, *CS* II: 87). From at least the time of Mursili, the Upper Land was administered by a governor appointed by the Hittite king. Samuha may have been its administrative centre. Governorship of the region was one of the earliest appointments conferred by King Muwattalli II upon his brother Hattusili (**CS* I: 200), later King Hattusili III.

**RGTC* 6: 293–4, Bryce (1986–1987: 89–90).

Uqair, Tell Settlement in southern Mesopotamia, south of Baghdad, with occupation levels ranging from the Ubaid period, when it was extensively inhabited, through the Uruk, Jemdet Nasr, Sumerian, and Akkadian periods (i.e. from M5 to the end of M3). Excavations were conducted by S. Lloyd and F. Safar in the 1940s, and more briefly by M. Müller-Karpe in the 1970s. One of the site's most prominent architectural features is the so-called Painted Temple, dating to the Late Uruk period. The structure consisted of platform and temple, the latter's walls decorated with paintings which depict human figures in skirts, feline and other animals, and polychrome geometric patterns. The remains of a small temple of the Jemdet Nasr period (late M4–early M3) have also been unearthed. Tablets inscribed with proto-cuneiform script suggest that the site's anc. name may have been Urum. Excavations on Mound B have revealed graves and walls dating to the Early Dynastic III (c. 2600–2334) and the Akkadian periods (C24–22).

Lloyd and Safar (1943), Green (1986), Matthews (*BMD* 308–9).

Uqumanu see Qumanu.

Ur (*Tell el-Muqayyar*) (maps 11, 17) Southern Mesopotamian city located on a former (now dried-up) branch of the Euphrates r., with a history of occupation from the Ubaid period (mid M5) to the late Persian Achaemenid period (mid M1). The site was first identified by H. C. Rawlinson on the basis of inscriptions discovered there in 1854 by J. E. Taylor, the British consul at Basra. It was most extensively excavated by C. L. Woolley over twelve seasons, between 1922 and 1934, on behalf of the University Museum of the University of Pennsylvania and the British Museum. The Ubaid level, which reached c. 10 ha in extent, lay beneath what Woolley believed was a flood deposit, which he related to the *OT* tradition of a great flood. This deposit has subsequently been attributed either to one of a number of localized floods in the region, or to the remains of a wind-created dune.

Ur was one of the more important towns in its region during the Ubaid period, and its importance continued in the succeeding Uruk and Jemdet Nasr periods (c. 4000–2900). From the Uruk phase of its existence, remains of a temple platform have survived, located within the temenos or sacred precinct where the later ziggurat (see glossary) of Ur was constructed. The platform was rebuilt at least twice during the (Sumerian) Early Dynastic period (c. 2900–2334). A number of graves belonging to a large cemetery, dated from the Uruk through the Early Dynastic II period, contained bodies lying on their sides in a foetal position. They were accompanied by a range of funerary gifts including beads, and stone, ceramic, copper, and lead vessels. However, the most impressive funerary remains discovered at Ur were those of the so-called Royal Cemetery, which contained c. 2,000 graves, dating from the Early Dynastic III period through and beyond the Akkadian period (i.e. from c. 2600 to 2100). The designation 'Royal Cemetery' arises from sixteen of the graves belonging to the Early Dynastic III period. They consisted of chambers made of brick or stone, and contained numerous human burials, the majority of which are believed to have been the remains of attendants interred along with the graves' principal inhabitants to serve them in the afterlife. The distinctive structure of these graves, the apparent evidence of human sacrifice, and the richness of the grave goods – which included jewellery made of gold and silver and semi-precious stones, along with an assortment of weapons, musical instruments, furniture, and other items – have led to the conclusion that they were the burial places of royalty. Whether or not the major tomb occupants were in fact Early Dynastic kings and queens remains uncertain. None of the names inscribed on seals or other objects are those of kings or queens known from other sources, including the Sumerian King List.

Ur continued to be an important city through the period of the Akkadian empire (though the second Akkadian king, Rimush (2278–2270), claimed to have conquered and destroyed it; **RIME* 2: 45–6). But it achieved its greatest prominence as the capital of the Ur III dynasty, which lasted one hundred years from c. 2112 to 2004. In this period, the city expanded to cover an area of 50 or more hectares. Vast numbers of administrative documents inscribed on clay tablets indicate an extensive and complex bureaucracy used in the administration of the Ur III empire. The official language of

Figure 126 'Standard of Ur', c. 2600.

Figure 127 Ur, copy of helmet of Meskalamdug, c. 2600.

the Ur III administration was Sumerian. Ur-Nammu (2112–2095), founder of the dynasty, embarked on an ambitious building programme in the city, particularly within the area of its sacred precinct, where a great ziggurat was constructed on the remains of the earlier temple platforms. The precinct was dedicated to the moon god Nanna and his consort, Ningal. It is very likely that their main temple stood on top of the ziggurat. Within the temenos, remains of a number of other buildings were unearthed, including what was probably a palace, a series of storage chambers, and a building where priestesses resided and were buried. Another of the important monuments of this period is a stele of Ur-Nammu, found in fragments and depicting Ur-Nammu receiving orders to build the temple of Nanna. Ur-Nammu was also the promulgator of the earliest collection of laws yet discovered (**ANET* 523–5). A text dealing with the death of Ur-Nammu survives in a number of Old Babylonian copies found in the cities of Nippur and Susa (**Chav.* 61–5).

Ur-Nammu had four dynastic successors, beginning with his son Shulgi who was followed by Amar-Sin, Shu-Sin, and Ibbi-Sin. The empire which he had built came under serious threat from the Amorites during Shu-Sin's reign (2037–2029). But the final death blow to it was delivered by the Elamites, who attacked, plundered, and burnt the city of Ur, and took back to their homeland the last Sumerian king, Ibbi-Sin, in 2004. Poetical accounts of Ur's destruction, along with that of Sumer's other major cities (Nippur, Eridu, and Uruk), are preserved in texts dating to the early Old Babylonian period (early M2), the so-called 'Lamentations' (**Chav.* 66–75). Shortly afterwards, Ur was rebuilt by the kings of Isin, who represented themselves as the

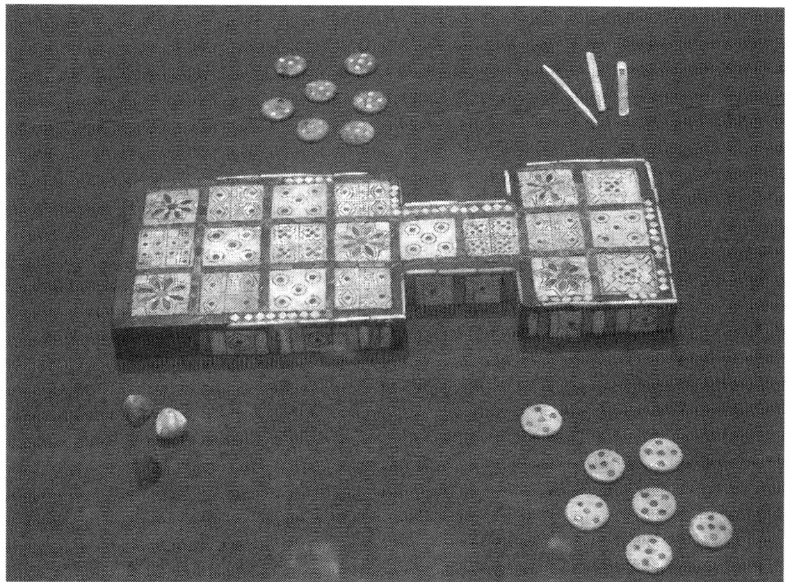

Figure 128 Ur, gaming-board.

legitimate successors of the Ur III dynasty. Throughout the so-called Isin-Larsa period (c. 2000–1800), Ur remained an important religious and commercial centre, reaching a size of c. 60 ha. There was much rebuilding within the temenos, and large residential areas were constructed. Houses were built around open courtyards, and were separated by narrow, winding streets. Numerous burials were made beneath the house floors, in pits, clay coffins, and brick tombs, with a range of ceramic ware and jewellery as grave goods. Ur declined in importance during the peak period of the Old Babylonian state in C18. Its city wall and many of its major buildings were destroyed in the aftermath of the rebellion of a number of southern Mesopotamian cities against Babylonian sovereignty (c. 1740). Nevertheless, it continued to be occupied in the centuries which followed, and experienced a resurgence of building activity in the reign of the early C14 Kassite king Kurigalzu I, particularly within its sacred precinct.

During M1, Ur's revered traditional status as a religious centre was reflected by further restoration and rebuilding programmes within this area, e.g. by a C7 Assyrian governor called Sin-balassu-iqbi (**RIMB* 2: 230–47), and most notably during the Neo-Babylonian period by the Babylonian kings Nebuchadnezzar II (604–562) and Nabonidus (556–539). These kings were responsible for rebuilding Ur's ziggurat as well as other temples and the temenos wall which enclosed them. Private housing dating from this period was also excavated, but during the Persian period the city declined, and Ur's days as a major commercial and administrative centre were now past. The city was finally abandoned around the end of C4.

In *OT* tradition, Ur appears on four occasions as the birthplace and first home of Abram (later to become Abraham, 'Father of Many') before his father took his family from the city and resettled them in Harran (e.g. Genesis 11:28). Abram lived in Harran until he was seventy-five, when he finally migrated to Canaan. The fact that

Abram's birthplace in this tradition is referred to as 'Ur of the Chaldees' has prompted some scholars to suggest that it may be a different city from the one attested in historical and archaeological sources.

Woolley et al. (1927–76), Woolley (1963; 1982), J. G. Westenholz (1996c), Pollock (*OEANE* 5: 288–91), Sallaberger (1999).

Ura (1) (map 3) Late Bronze Age and Iron Age city on Anatolia's southeastern coast, probably located at or near mod. Silifke, or further west at Gilindere. In the Late Bronze Age, it almost certainly belonged to the kingdom of Tarhuntassa (*contra* this, see de Martino, 1999, and Melchert, 2007: 510). Important information about its location is provided by the Chronicle of the C6 Babylonian king Neriglissar (**ABC* 103–4, **Chav.* 417–18). The text refers to Neriglissar's capture and sack of the city during his pursuit of Appuashu, king of Pirindu. Ura appears to have been the capital of Pirindu (the Neo-Babylonian name for the kingdom called Hilakku in Neo-Assyrian texts).

In the Late Bronze Age, Ura served as a major port for goods shipped into Anatolia from Egypt and Ugarit. From this disembarkation point, the goods were conveyed overland by donkey caravans to the heartland of the kingdom of Hatti. The transport of merchandise from the coast to the Hittite homeland seems to have been largely in the hands of merchants of Ura. Hatti's growing dependence on grain shipments from Egypt and the Levant during the last century of the Late Bronze Age greatly increased the importance of Ura's role in the provisioning of the Hittite world. This is reflected in an urgent letter sent from the Hittite court to one of the last kings of Ugarit demanding a ship and crew for the transport of 2,000 *kor* of grain (c. 450 tonnes) to Ura (**RS* 20.212, 17-–26-; *Bryce, 2005: 331). The necessity of ensuring that Ura was firmly under Hittite control may have been one of the prime reasons for the Hittite conquest and annexation of Tarhuntassa during the reign of the last Hittite king Suppiluliuma II (1207–), after Tarhuntassa had earlier (apparently) broken its ties with Hatti.

The practice by merchants of Ura of investing in the property market in Ugarit while waiting there for new consignments of goods led to disputes with the local populace. Niqmepa, king of Ugarit, referred the matter for arbitration to his overlord Hattusili III, who forbade any further speculation by the merchants in Ugaritic real estate (**PRU IV*: 103–5).

Ura is perhaps to be identified with the site of Soli (later Pompeiopolis; see **Soli (2)**), founded by Greek colonists on the Mediterranean coast in C8.

Beal (1992a), Lemaire (1993), de Martino (1999).

Ura (2) Late Bronze Age fortress settlement on the frontier of Azzi in northeastern Anatolia. It was captured by the Hittite king Mursili II during the campaigns which he conducted in his seventh year (c. 1315) (**AM* 98–9, **CS* II: 88).

Urammu (= Ulammu?) Iron Age city on the frontier between Elamite and Assyrian territory. The Assyrian king Sargon II (721–705) dispatched orders for an Assyrian army to camp on the plain there (**SAA* I: 15, no. 13). Since access to it from Elam was limited to a difficult mountain pass, it was well protected against attack by an Elamite army.

Uranium (map 5) M1 city on the Myndus peninsula in Caria, southwestern Anatolia. According to Diodorus (5.23), it was founded by Carians who had originally occupied Syme, a small island off Anatolia's southwestern coast, after the Trojan War. The settlers had been forced by a series of droughts to abandon their island homeland. In C5, Uranium became a member of the Athenian Confederacy (see glossary). Pliny the Elder (5.107) reports that it was one of six Lelegian (q.v.) towns assigned by Alexander the Great to the jurisdiction of Halicarnassus. (The incorporation of these towns into Halicarnassus was in fact due to the mid C4 Carian satrap Mausolus prior to Alexander's campaigns.) Uranium is almost certainly to be identified with mod. Burgaz, a Lelegian site on the Myndus peninsula with a citadel, two towers, and remains of an outer polygonal wall. The pottery is of Archaic and Classical date. Several chamber tombs have been discovered in the vicinity.

Bean (1971: 126; *PECS* 172, s.v. Burgaz).

Urartu (map 20) Iron Age kingdom in the highland regions of eastern Anatolia, reaching the peak of its political and military development in C8 and early C7. At that time, it was one of the most powerful states of the western Asian world. Urartu is the Assyrian name for the kingdom. Its own inhabitants called their country Bianili, from which the mod. name Van is derived. Urartu, in the form Uruatri as a geographical term, is already attested in C13, in the inscriptions of the Assyrian king Shalmaneser I. In this period, the name designated a region near Lake Van, which was occupied by a number of small independent principalities. Shalmaneser apparently claimed sovereignty over them, for he reports a rebellion by Uruatri against him, and the conquest of its eight lands and fifty-one cities in three days (**RIMA* 1: 183). Uruatri is later attested on the campaign itinerary of the Assyrian king Ashur-bel-kala (1073–1056) (**RIMA* 2: 91, 97). And a later Assyrian king, Adad-nirari II (911–891), reports conquests extending as far as Urartu during military operations which he conducted against the easternmost of the regions called Habhu in Assyrian texts (see **Habhu (1)**; **RIMA* 2: 148). But it was not until the second half of C9 that Urartu's lands and cities were consolidated into a single political entity. In this period, a united Urartian kingdom was established under a royal dynasty based in the city of Tushpa (mod. Van). The dynasty was founded by Sarduri I (832–825). (On the regnal dates of the Urartian kings, see Appendix III.)

The union of Urartian states may initially have been formed to counter constant incursions by the Assyrians, of the kind launched by Shalmaneser III (858–824), who claims to have conducted five campaigns in Urartu. But whether or not defence of their lands was the prime reason for the union of Urartian states, the kingdom quickly assumed an aggressor's role. Sarduri and his successors embarked on a programme of territorial expansion which extended Urartu's frontiers northwards into Armenia, eastwards to the Araxes r., southeastwards to the shores of Lake Urmia, and southwestwards to the western bend of the Euphrates. The greatest period of expansion occurred in the reign of King Minua (805–788), grandson of Sarduri I, and son and co-regent of Ishpuini. For administrative purposes, Urartu was divided into a number of provinces. Each was assigned to a governor, who may have enjoyed a high degree of local autonomy, given the topographically fragmented nature of the kingdom.

The reign of Minua's successor Argishti I (787–766) has been seen as the period when Urartu reached 'its virtual zenith in extent, prestige, and power' (Barnett, 1982:

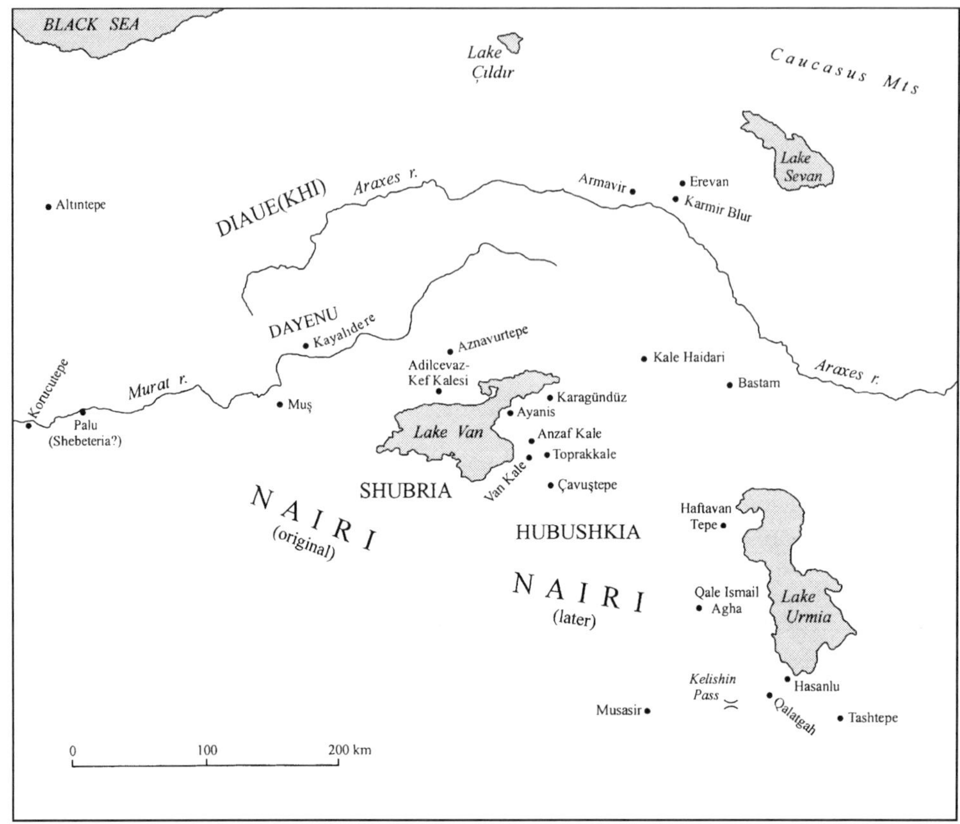

Map 20 Urartu.

347). At its height, the kingdom covered substantial areas of eastern Anatolia, northwestern Iran, and Transcaucasia. But inevitably, Urartu's expansionist programme led to fresh conflicts with Assyria, which by the second half of C9 had recovered from a period of relative weakness, and was once more playing a dominant role in western Asian affairs. The Assyrian commander-in-chief Shamshi-ilu clashed with the forces of Argishti in the land of the Qutu in the western Zagros region, and Shamshi-ilu claims to have inflicted a defeat on Argishti and captured his camp (**RIMA* 3: 232–3). This Assyrian military success has been assigned to the reigns of both Adad-nirari III (810–783) and his successor, Shalmaneser IV (782–773). But the outcome of the confrontation was probably less conclusive than Shamshi-ilu's record would suggest. In any case, tensions between Assyria and Urartu continued to mount, no doubt largely prompted on the Assyrian side by the threat Urartu posed to its northern territories.

In 743, the Assyrian king Tiglath-pileser III defeated a coalition of forces from Urartu and the Aramaean city of Arpad (q.v.). The king refers to the defeat he inflicted upon Sarduri II in the battle, fought in the region of Kummuh. In 735, Tiglath-pileser led an expedition into Urartu where he blockaded Sarduri in his capital Tushpa, and defeated him in a battle fought before the city's gates (**Tigl. III* 124–5). Subsequently, the rivalry between the two kingdoms culminated in a military showdown between the Assyrian king Sargon II (721–705) and his Urartian counterpart Rusa I (732–714).

Figure 129 Urartian helmet.

This occurred in 714 while Sargon was campaigning in the northern Zagros mountain region. Following his victory over Rusa's forces, Sargon invaded and plundered part of his kingdom (**Chav.* 338–40). The fact that Urartu had been weakened at this time by internal dissension, as reflected in a number of letters written to Sargon by his officials (e.g. **SAA* V: 74, no. 91; 124, no. 166) and an invasion by the Cimmerians from the north (**SAA* V: 109–10, no. 145), no doubt facilitated Sargon's victory over the kingdom. Other letters report that in this same year an army led by Rusa against the Cimmerians was routed, with the loss of eleven of the king's provincial governors and a substantial number of the troops under their command; his commander-in-chief and two more of his governors were taken prisoner (**SAA* I: 29–32, nos 30–2). Rusa himself escaped from the battle, but died shortly afterwards. According to Sargon, he did so after receiving news of the sack of his city of Musasir (q.v.) by the Assyrians (**Chav.* 339). But despite this disastrous series of events, Urartu was far from a spent force.

Rusa's successor Argishti II (713–679) did not leave many inscriptions, but the few that survive show him campaigning further to the northeast than any other Urartian ruler. His successor, Rusa II, was the most energetic builder the kingdom ever saw, and apparently restructured the kingdom by building the massive centres of Ayanis, Adilcevaz, Karmir Blur, and Bastam. (For the chronological sequence of their construction, see Erdem and Batmaz, 2008: 65–8.) These are the largest Urartian sites known outside Van, and the ones from which most Urartian objects with a secure archaeological context have been recovered. While it may be an accident of recovery, all of the known cuneiform tablets and seal impressions come from Rusa II's reign and not earlier, so the possibility of bureaucratic reform must be considered. Rusa's Annals, if they were ever written, have not been found, but his standard building inscriptions from Ayanis and other sites claim military conquests of all the surrounding lands, including Assyria. While the latter claim is clearly an exaggeration, there is no doubt that a certain tension prevailed between the two great empires. Relations may well have taken a turn for the worse when the Assyrian king Esarhaddon (680–669) invaded and conquered Urartu's western neighbour Shubria (q.v.). In the reign of Esarhaddon's successor Ashurbanipal (668–630/627), an unsuccessful attempt was made by an Urartian force to seize Shubria from the Assyrians.

We have little further information about Urartu. Rusa II was the last Urartian king to leave any building inscriptions, and the last datable reference to an Urartian king occurs in an inscription from the reign of Ashurbanipal, who refers to a diplomatic mission sent to his court by 'Ishtar-duri' – Sarduri III or IV. By the end of the century, Assyria had fallen to a coalition of Medes and Chaldaeans. The Urartian kingdom came to a violent end around the same time, or a few decades earlier, reflected in the destruction by fire of almost all Urartian sites. But their destructions cannot be precisely dated. Because of the paucity of records after Rusa II, we have no clear indication of who the destroyers were or when the destructions took place.

In C6, the region occupied by the Urartian kingdom came under the control of the Medes and later the Persians. The name Urartu survived as a geographical designation, but the region was now inhabited by the Armenians, who were of different ethnic stock from their Urartian predecessors. It is possible, however, that a remnant of the original Urartian population lived on in peoples known to Greek authors as Chaldians, Alarodians, and Carduchians, some of whom were encountered by Xenophon's troops in the region bordering Armenia on their way home from their disastrous Persian expedition (early C4). The name Urartu survives today in the form Ararat, a transformation brought about by the addition of vowels to biblical texts by scholars who no longer knew the original pronunciation.

Written records, which provide the basis of our knowledge about Urartian history, begin with the reign of Sarduri I, founder of the Urartian dynasty. At this time Urartian scribes used the Assyrian language and cuneiform script. But in the reign of subsequent Urartian kings, all surviving inscriptions, except for a few bilinguals, were written in the Urartian language (though the formulaic expressions of the Assyrian royal titulary continued to be used), a language closely related to Hurrian. Urartian texts, carved on stone, provide information about the kingdom's building programmes, religious activities, and military enterprises. Inscriptions which record the military enterprises are carved, throughout the subject territories, on cliff-faces, stelae, and the stone blocks used in the construction of major public buildings. Royal Annals, with year-by-year accounts of conquests and booty lists of human captives and animals taken, survive at Van for two kings, Argishti I and Sarduri II. The construction projects are also commemorated in a number of brief dedicatory inscriptions which appear on various artefacts, including bronze bowls, shields, helmets, arrowheads, and quivers. But the historical information that can be gleaned from native Urartian sources is mostly piecemeal and fragmentary. Assyrian texts, particularly from the cities of Nimrud and Nineveh, provide our most important source of information on Urartian history.

State-sponsored religion seems to have played a major role in maintaining unity within the kingdom's core regions as well as in its conquered territories. The chief Urartian deity was Haldi, who was regularly invoked at the beginning of military campaigns and in the dedicatory inscriptions of buildings. The chief centre of his cult, which may have been imported into the kingdom at the end of C9, lay in the city of Musasir, but temples to Haldi were erected within most royal citadels all over the kingdom. Ranking below Haldi were the storm god (Teisheba) and sun god (Shiuni), prominent figures in the Hurrian pantheon, followed by numerous local deities and mountain gods.

The kingdom's mountainous terrain provided it with formidable barriers against invading enemy forces. The effect of these natural defences was reinforced by the massive fortresses which Urartian kings built on great outcrops of rock. The fortresses were strategically located to control the plains and valleys which lay between the rugged highland mountains. They contained palaces and administrative centres, temples to the state gods, and great warehouses to store the produce of the plains. The most impressive achievements of Urartian architecture, which features buildings constructed from stone blocks, sometimes partly carved out of the living rock, with mudbrick superstructures, amply justify the claims made by Urartian kings to have been great builders. Large-scale irrigation works, consisting of great canals and dams, provide further evidence of their building achievements. The greatest of these works was an aqueduct and canal built by King Minua, which watered the plain of Van. Much of

Figure 130 Embankment of Minua canal at Edremit, 8 km south of Van.

Urartu's wealth may have been derived from its mineral resources, most notably from its copper and iron mines. A wide range of metal and stone artefacts have been unearthed at various sites, reflecting a high level of skill among the kingdom's artists and craftsmen. Assyrian influence is, however, clearly evident in the style and iconography of much Urartian art, which has been assessed as innovative and distinctive to begin with, though later becoming repetitive and stereotyped.

Kleiss (1976), Kleiss and Hauptmann (1976), Barnett (1982), Zimansky (1985; 1998), Salvini (1995a), Smith and Thompson (2004), Tarhan (2004).

Urbil(um) see Arbela.

Ugar-sallu City and district in eastern Mesopotamia, on the east bank of the Tigris just south of the Lesser Zab r. The Assyrian king Adad-nirari I (1307–1275) reportedly fought the Kassite ruler Nazi-maruttash in Ugar-sallu, and a later Assyrian king, Ashur-dan I (1179–1134), captured it and nearby cities (**ABC* 160–2). Tiglath-pileser I (1114–1076) also reports his conquest of one its cities, Arman, during a campaign in Babylonia (**RIMA* 2: 53). It was subsequently part of the territory annexed by Adad-nirari II (911–891), following his conquest of northern Babylonia during the reign of the Babylonian king Shamash-mudammiq (**RIMA* 2: 148).

Urime Iron Age city belonging to the kingdom of Pat(t)in (Assyrian Unqi) in northern Syria, destroyed by the Assyrian king Shalmaneser III during his campaign against the northern Syrian cities in his first regnal year (858) (**RIMA* 3: 25). At that time, Urime was a stronghold of the Patinite king Lubarna.

Urkesh (*Tell Mozan*) (map 10) Settlement located in the Habur plains of Syria, with occupation levels extending from the beginning of M6 (Halaf period) to mid M2. The most important occupational strata date to the second half of M3. After a brief exploratory season by M. Mallowan in 1934, the site has been regularly excavated since 1984 by G. Buccellati and M. Kelly-Buccellati. Its identification with Urkesh, well known from Hurrian mythology (where it was the residence of the god Kumarbi), was established by large numbers of inscribed seal impressions. Throughout its Bronze Age phase, Urkesh was a major centre of Hurrian civilization – and indeed the only M3 city yet known that can be identified with the Hurrians. Further confirmation of its Hurrian ethnic identity comes from the foundation inscription of a king of Urkesh called Tish-atal (whose name is associated with the famous bronze lions of Urkesh) and approx. 300 inscribed seal impressions attributable to another king, Tupkish, to the king's wife, and to other members of the royal court. Dating to the last centuries of M3, these inscriptions provide us with the earliest surviving examples of the Hurrian language. Tupkish, who ruled during the ascendancy of the Akkadian empire (C24–22), assumed the title 'king of Urkesh and Nawar'. The current excavators of Urkesh see his use of the Hurrian term *endan* (king) as an expression aimed at emphasizing Hurrian distinctiveness at a time when the Akkadian empire was expanding. But the ruling dynasty in Urkesh (we know of eight kings of this dynasty) was not unreceptive to Akkadian influence. Tupkish's wife, Uqnitum, had an Akkadian name. And the probable marriage of a later king of Urkesh to Tar'am-Agade, daughter of the Akkadian king Naram-Sin, suggests the development of close personal links between Akkad and

Urkesh's royal families. More generally, Kelly-Buccellatti believes that what makes the culture of Urkesh intriguing and unique during the later part of M3 is the juxtaposition of Hurrian and Akkadian cultural traditions.

Urkesh consists of two parts – a citadel mound extending over c. 18 ha, and an outer city of c. 135 ha. A temple and a palace were the most prominent features of the walled inner city on the mound. The temple was built c. 2450, 250 years or so before the palace. Its interior measured 9 m × 16.5 m, and access to it was via a monumental entrance approached by a long stone ramp. Presumably, a statue of the god Kumarbi was housed in the building. The current excavators believe that a single monumental building complex combining palace and temple may have occupied the entire western and central part of the mound, extending across a vast distance of 250 m; it would thus have been one of the most impressive M3 architectural complexes in Syro-Mesopotamia. The obvious prosperity of the M3 city must have been due very largely to its location at the hub of major trade routes, and its relative proximity to the copper mining region which lay to its north.

The palace which was built c. 2200 (c. 250 years after the temple) lasted only a century or so before it was abandoned. A series of residential settlements was constructed over its ruins, and an area set aside for communal burials. Rectangular and vaulted structures have been interpreted as miniature houses for the dead. In the first half of the Late Bronze Age, Urkesh became a city of the Mitannian empire, without ever achieving again the status it had enjoyed at the height of its development in the last centuries of M3.

Buccellati and Kelly-Buccellatti (*OEANE* 4: 60–3; *RlA* 8: 386–93; 2005), Buccellati (2005), Kelly-Buccellati (2005).

Urratinash (or Urrahinash?) Fortified city in the mountain land of Panaru, north-eastern Mesopotamia, east of the Tigris r. It is attested in the records of the Assyrian king Tiglath-pileser I (1114–1076), who marched upon the city after his victorious campaign against the land of Paphu in the first year of his reign (**RIMA* 2: 15–16). Before the arrival of the Assyrian army, the city's population had fled to mountain refuges. But its king, Shadi-Teshub, surrendered to Tiglath-pileser, and his life was spared on the promise that he would pay a substantial tribute to his overlord. Members of his family were taken hostage to guarantee this. The city's name has alternatively been read as Urrahinash (*RGTC* 5: 274).

Urshu (Warshuwa) (map 3) Middle and Late Bronze Age city in eastern Anatolia, located west of the Euphrates r. and north of the city of Carchemish. It is first attested in a letter from the C18 archives at Mari, during the period of the Old Assyrian kingdom, and is listed in the archives from Alalah (level VII) among the states and cities which were subject to or allied with the kingdom of Aleppo/Yamhad in C17. It also figures among the cities which the Hittite king Hattusili I (1650–1620) attacked and destroyed on his march back to Hattusa at the end of his first(?) campaign in Syria (**Chav.* 220). His attacks on these subject or allied cities of Aleppo may have been designed to weaken the Aleppan kingdom in preparation for further Hittite campaigns against it in later years. Urshu is best known from a literary composition, commonly referred to as the *Siege of Urshu*, which describes a protracted and incompetent siege operation, lasting six months, conducted by Hittite troops against the city. The text records the (unnamed) Hittite king's fury at his officers' ineptitude in conducting the siege. It is generally assigned to the reign of Hattusili I, but although it provides useful information about Hittite siege operations, it is of dubious value as a historical source of information. A highly questionable identification has been proposed between Urshu and Urushsha, one of the towns of Kizzuwadna which figures in the treaty drawn up by the Hittite king Arnuwanda I with the men of Ismerikka (q.v.).

*Beckman (1995), *Bryce (2005: 72–3).

Urua Elamite city (probably = Arawa) attested in Early Bronze Age Mesopotamian texts, and located between southern Babylonia and Susa, perhaps in the region of northwest Khuzestan. An identification with the site of Tepe Mussian (q.v.) has been suggested. Due to its strategic position on the route from Babylonia into the Susiana plain, Urua seems to have been a commercially important city, and to have enjoyed close economic ties with Lagash and other southern Mesopotamian cities. It was also involved in military conflicts with the kingdoms of southern Mesopotamia in the second half of M3, and fell victim to campaigns launched from this region, first by Eannatum, king of Lagash (c. 2450), and subsequently by the Akkadian king Sargon (2234–2279). The latter's capture of the city may have paved the way for his conquest of the whole of Elam. Urua later became a province of the Ur III kingdom (2112–2004), under the immediate authority of a local governor whose responsibilities included the collection of a provincial tax levied on the city. This tax had been imposed on the ninety or so settlements located in the Ur III kingdom's peripheral territories. Urua was one of the most important of these settlements.

Steinkeller (1982: 244–6), Vallat (1993).

Uruk (*Warka,* biblical **Erech**) (maps 11, 17) Southern Mesopotamian site, located on an old course of the Euphrates r. Its history of occupation extends from the Late Ubaid period (M5) until or shortly before the period of the Arab invasions in C7 CE. After early investigations by W. K. Loftus in 1849 and 1853, excavations were conducted spasmodically by a number of German teams from 1912 onwards, and were resumed in 1980 under the direction of R. M. Boehmer. The site consisted originally of two settlements, Uruk and Kullab: the former was in the area later to be called Eanna (a Sumerian term meaning 'house of heaven'), the precinct dedicated to the goddess Inanna, and the latter lay in the religious complex dedicated to the supreme Mesopotamian god Anu.

In M4 (if not earlier) the settlements were combined into the single city of Uruk, which became the most important political, administrative, cultural, and religious centre in the whole of Mesopotamia. Its significance is reflected in the fact that the term 'Uruk' is now used as a general designation for the cultural phase which spanned much of M4 in Mesopotamia, between the Ubaid and Jemdet Nasr periods. The most prominent architectural feature of the city in this period was a series of monumental buildings, religious and/or administrative in function. Uruk has been seen at this time as the central power in an economic and political empire which reached up the Euphrates into northern Syria and Anatolia as well as into Iran in the east (thus R. Matthews, *BMD* 313). Excavators who work on contemporary sites in northern Mesopotamia tend to reject such a south-centred view. Uruk is also considered the birthplace of writing in Mesopotamia, in view of the discovery there of clay tablets containing the first evidence of a pictographic script and numerical notation, dating to c. 3100.

Uruk's importance continued in the Early Dynastic (ED) period of the Sumerian civilization (c. 2900–2334). In fact, the city was now more intensively settled, in ED I, than in any of its earlier phases. It was enclosed by a 9.5 km long mudbrick fortification wall, which Mesopotamian literary tradition ascribed to Uruk's legendary king, Gilgamesh. After a period of apparent decline in ED II, the city seems to have enjoyed another flourishing phase of its existence in ED III, the end of this period being marked by the supremacy which its king, Lugal-zage-si, established over the whole of southern Mesopotamia. Lugal-zage-si had begun his career as ruler of the Sumerian city-state of Umma, subsequently extending his power over other Sumerian states (and in the process defeating his arch rival, Urukagina of Lagash), and declaring himself 'king of Uruk and the country (of Sumer)' (**Chav.* 15). Thenceforth, his main title became 'king of Uruk' (though in Lagash texts he was still referred to as 'lord (*ensi*) of Lagash'). An ambitious building programme was undertaken within Uruk under his rule. But his career came abruptly to an end when he was defeated in battle c. 2334 by Sargon, founder of the Akkadian empire. Sargon followed up his victory by demolishing Uruk's walls and taking Lugal-zage-si prisoner (**CS* II: 243). Uruk's consequent decline in size and importance was followed by another brief resurgence of power after the destruction of the Akkadian empire by the Gutians, c. 2193. This resurgence was attributed to Uruk's king Utu-hegal (2123–2113) who expelled the Gutians from Sumer (**RIME* 2: 284–7) and established his dominance over it – until his rule ended with the rise of the Ur III dynasty founded by Ur-Nammu (c. 2112). Uruk continued to prosper under the rule of the Ur III kings. Ur-Nammu himself commissioned an extensive building programme in the city, which included the construction of a ziggurat (see glossary).

Figure 131 Kurill, an official of Uruk, c. 2500.

With the collapse of the Ur III dynasty at the end of M3, Uruk once more went into decline. After the fall of Ur, it became attached first to the kingdom of Isin, and subsequently to the kingdom of Larsa. After a short period of independence it was once more subjected to Larsa's sovereignty when Sumu-El, king of Larsa, established his authority over it in 1891. Several decades later, c. 1864, a man called Sin-kashid regained Uruk's independence from Larsa and established a new dynasty in the city. His reign (c. 1864–1833) was marked by ambitious new building projects (**RIME* 4: 440–63). These included the construction of a new palace and temples to a number of deities, most notably to Uruk's patron goddess Inanna/Ishtar. Under the new dynasty, Uruk became the centre of a small kingdom which included the nearby cities of Durum (formerly subject to the Ur III dynasty, Isin, and Larsa in succession), Bit-Shu-Sin, Nasarum, and Usarpara. Bolstered by an alliance with Babylon, which was cemented by marriage ties, the dynasty continued to maintain Uruk's independence. However, relations between Uruk's king Anam and his Babylonian counterpart Sin-muballit (1812–1793) were sometimes strained, to judge from an acrimonious exchange of correspondence between them (**Chav.* 127–30). Around 1802, Uruk fell to Larsa's king Rim-Sin (**RIME* 4: 287–8). (Seven years previously, Uruk had been part of a military coalition, whose other members were Isin, Babylon, Rapiqum, and Sutium, which had been defeated by Rim-Sin; **RIME* 4: 281. Uruk's king Ìr-ne-ne was captured during the battle.) It thenceforth remained subject to Larsa until the latter fell to the Babylonian king Hammurabi in 1763.

Uruk was now incorporated into the Babylonian empire. When it joined a rebellion against Babylon in the reign of Hammurabi's successor Samsu-iluna (1749–1712), the Babylonian king responded with a crushing defeat of the rebel cities, in the process capturing Uruk and demolishing its walls. The city was probably abandoned at this time, remaining derelict for more than two centuries. However, c. mid C15 the Kassite king Kara-indash undertook another rebuilding programme in Uruk's religious quarter, which initiated a new phase in the city's history. Through the first half of M1, a succession of kings – both Neo-Assyrian and Neo-Babylonian – undertook building and restoration programmes in Uruk, especially within its sacred precincts. But by the later Persian period, the great Eanna temple dedicated to Ishtar had fallen into disuse. In the Hellenistic period, when the region came under Seleucid control, Uruk was the seat of several governors, and two great new temple precincts were built: the Resh, dedicated to the sky god Anu, and the Eshgal (sometimes read Irigal), the temple of the goddesses Ishtar and Nanaya. Thereafter, under Parthian and Sasanian rule, the city suffered steady decline until its final abandonment by C7 CE.

Boehmer (*OEANE* 5: 294–8), Stein (1999: 82–116), Rothman (2001), Charpin, Joannès, Sauvage (*DCM* 890–6).

Urumu Iron Age country located in northern Mesopotamia, probably in the vicinity of the Kashiyari range (mod. Tur ʿAbdin). It is first attested by the Assyrian king Tiglath-pileser I (1114–1076), who reports that 4,000 Kasku and Urumu forces, described as 'insubmissive troops of Hatti', had seized the cities of the land of Shubartu; but on the approach of his army, they had submitted without resistance (**RIMA* 2: 17). Two centuries later, the Assyrian king Ashurnasirpal II (883–859) recorded his conquest of Urumu (**RIMA* 2: 243, 309), and the receipt of tribute from it while he was residing in the nearby city of Tushha(n). Liverani (1992: 40–1) suggests that Urumu is the mountain region also known as Nirbu (q.v.), since the two toponyms occur in the same context; in that case, we may be dealing with the plateau of the Tur ʿAbdin.

Uruniash City in the Late Bronze and Iron Age land of Himme, which was located in the borderlands between northeastern Mesopotamia and northwestern Iran, probably to the south of Lake Van. Uruniash was captured and destroyed by the Assyrian king Ashur-bel-kala (1073–1056), after a siege by his infantry forces in the second of his two campaigns against Himme (**RIMA* 2: 92–3, 94). Its location in the heart of the mountains made it inaccessible to the Assyrian chariotry.

Usala (*Tell Namliya?*) Iron Age city in the middle Euphrates region, belonging to the land of Laqe and situated between Suru and Dur-Katlimmu. During his last recorded campaign in 885, the Assyrian king Tukulti-Ninurta II (890–884) approached the city, received tribute from it, and encamped his army in its fields, on his expedition through the middle Euphrates region (**RIMA* 2: 176).

Lipiński (2000: 83).

Usarpara (or **Uzarpara**) Southern Mesopotamian city near Uruk, referred to in Early and Middle Bronze Age texts. During the period of the dynasty which Sin-kashid established c. 1864 at Uruk (q.v.), Usarpara was part of the small kingdom of Uruk – until 1804, when Larsa's king Rim-Sin seized control of it, two years before his conquest of Uruk itself. Durum, Nasarum, and Bit-Shu-Sin were other cities attached to Uruk during the Sin-kashid dynasty.

Mesop. 109, 120.

Ushnati, Usnu see **Siyannu and Ushnati**.

Ushu Mainland city on the coast of southern Lebanon, attested in M2 Egyptian and M1 Assyrian texts, opposite the island-city of Tyre. Throughout its history, Ushu was closely attached to Tyre, generally in a subordinate role, and served as an important source of food and water for the island-settlement. The capture of Ushu in mid C14 by Zimredda, king of Sidon, as attested in the Amarna letters (e.g. **EA* 149: 49), posed a serious threat to Tyre's survival. In C7 the Assyrian king Ashurbanipal (668–630/627) starved the rebellious Tyrians into surrender by cutting off their food and water, presumably by seizing Ushu (*Streck, 1916: 80–1). The city's remains probably lie under mod. habitation, though identifications with the sites of Tell Rashidiyeh and Tell Mashouk have been suggested.

Utians M1 people of western Iran (?) attested in Herodotus (3.93) as forming part of the fourteenth province of the Persian empire (but see glossary under **satrapy**). According to Herodotus, other members of this province were the Sagartians, Sarangians, Thamanaeans, Mycians, and the inhabitants of the islands of the Erythraean Sea (see glossary). Utians provided a contingent for the army of Xerxes for his invasion of Greece in 481, under the command of Arsamenes, son of Darius I (Herodotus 7.68). An identification has been proposed between the Utians and the land called Vautiya (Yautiya), located in southern Persis and attested in Darius I's Bisitun inscription (**DB* 40).

Utima (= Classical **Idyma**?) (map 5) Late Bronze Age city in southwestern Anatolia. The so-called 'Milawata letter' (see **Miletus**), generally assigned to the Hittite king Tudhaliya IV (1237–1209), refers to the seizure by the addressee's father of hostages – Hittite subjects – from Utima and the nearby town of Atriya (**HDT* 145–6). The addressee, who was now being asked to return the hostages, is unknown, but may have been Tarkasnawa, ruler at that time of the Arzawan kingdom of Mira (see Hawkins, 1998b: 19).

Utu' (Itu') M1 Aramaean tribe located in central Mesopotamia on the west bank of the Tigris r. In 885, the Assyrian king Tukulti-Ninurta II captured and plundered its encampments and villages and massacred its inhabitants (**RIMA* 2: 173). Though the tribe was subsequently placed under the control of the governor of the Assyrian province of Ashur, the need for repeated Assyrian campaigns against it in the first half of C8 no doubt indicates the tenuous nature of Assyrian authority in the region through this period. Utu' was among the tribal lands laid waste by Shamshi-ilu, commander-in-chief of the Assyrian king Adad-nirari III (810–783) (**RIMA* 3: 232). But it was not until 745 that Assyrian sovereignty over it was fully established. In this year, a campaign mounted by Tiglath-pileser III resulted in the final subjugation of the Utu' and a number of other Aramaean tribes in the region between the two rivers. Some of the Utu' tribespeople along with deportees from other tribes may then have been resettled in Tiglath-pileser's new city of Kar-Ashur, located east of the Tigris. The Utu' subsequently figured prominently among the resettled peoples who provided contingents for the Assyrian army.

Lipiński (2000: 437–8).

Uvadaicaya M1 city in Persis, southwestern Iran. Vahyazdata, a pretender to the Persian throne who had rebelled against Darius I, was crucified there after his forces were defeated by Darius' military commander Artavadiya in a battle at Mt Parga (522–521) (**DB* 43).

'Uza, Horvat (*Khirbet Ghazzeh*) (map 8) Iron Age Israelite fortress and settlement 8 km southeast of Arad in the Negev desert region, mod. Israel. Strategically, it occupied a commanding position overlooking the Nahal Qina, thereby giving it control over the route passing from this region to Edom and the Arabah. The site was jointly excavated by the Institute of Archaeology, Tel Aviv University, and Baylor University, Waco, Texas, under the direction of I. Beit-Arieh and B. Cresson in 1982, 1983–6, and 1988. Its most distinctive feature is a large, rectangular C7 fortress surrounded by a wall with ten square outer towers. The settlement built downstream from the fortress, and from which the remains of houses built on terraces were unearthed, is believed to have been connected with the fortress, and perhaps provided housing for the families of the garrison installed in it.

A number of inscriptions were found during excavations, including twenty-nine ostraca (twenty-seven from the fortress and two from the settlement), and an inscribed jar. The inscriptions deal with a range of military, logistical, and administrative matters, reflecting 'Uza's importance as a frontier settlement and garrison-centre in the Judaean Negev's border region. The pottery from both the settlement and the fortress is typical of the Negev at the end of the First Temple period, thus providing part of the evidence for the dating of the sites. There is also evidence, from an Edomite letter, that the fortress fell into the hands of the Edomites around this time, or a little later. Subsequently the site was abandoned for four centuries, with reoccupation occurring in the Hellenistic period under the sovereignty of the Seleucid kings.

Tatum (1991), Beit-Arieh (*NEAEHL* 4: 1495–7).

Uze M1 fortified city in the land of Dagara, a district of Zamua in the central Zagros region which fell to the Assyrian king Ashurnasirpal II during his conquest of these lands in his third regnal year (881). Birutu and Lagalaga were other fortified cities in Dagara conquered by Ashurnasirpal, allegedly along with one hundred other unspecified cities (**RIMA* 2: 203).

V

Van Kale see Tushpa.

Vautiya (Yautiya) M1 region in southern Persis, southwestern Iran. Within it lay the city of Tarava (mod. Tarum), where Vahyazdata, a pretender to the Persian throne, rose up in rebellion against the Persian king Darius I on his accession in 522, with the support of local Persian forces (**DB* 40). An identification has been proposed between Vautiya and the people called the Utians (q.v.), attested in Herodotus.

Via Maris The Latin name (meaning 'Way of the Sea') for the coastal road connecting Mesopotamia with Egypt via the Mediterranean coastline, and passing through Palestine and coastal Syria before turning east and crossing the Euphrates to Babylon. Under Roman rule, it was paved and marked with milestones. A branch-line of the Via Maris, linking Gaza, Ashdod, Jaffa, and Aphek, was known as the 'Way of the Land of the Philistines'.

Vishpauzatish M1 central Asian city in Parthia, perhaps to be identified with the site of El'ken Tepe. It was the setting of one of the two battles fought in 521 by the Parthian satrap Hystaspes against rebel forces from Parthia and Hyrcania who had joined the widespread uprisings against the Persian king Darius I at the beginning of his reign (Hystaspes was Darius' father) (**DB* 35). The other battle was fought four months later at Patigrabana (**DB* 36). Both engagements resulted in decisive victories for Hystaspes.

Vouni (map 14) Hilltop palace settlement, built initially in early C5, on the northwest coast of Cyprus, 6.5 km northwest of Soli. Surrounded by a wall, the complex is believed to have been constructed by a Cypriot king (of Marion? q.v.) to serve as a fortified summer royal residence, or as a base for a military garrison. The site was excavated between 1927 and 1931 by E. Gjerstad on behalf of the Swedish Cyprus Expedition. Two main building periods were identified: c. 500–450 and c. 450–380. The complex in the first of these periods was essentially Near Eastern in plan. It consisted of a series of state and private apartments built around a colonnaded court. Access to the court from the state apartments was provided by a monumental staircase. A sacred precinct with an altar court was incorporated within the complex. Numerous limestone votive figures and terracotta figurines were deposited in various parts of the precinct. In the second building period the palace was expanded, and its layout substantially reorganized along Greek lines. A temple of the goddess Athena, constructed on the terrace above the palace, has been dated to this period. Its main architectural features are a square cella, which opened on to a large court, and beyond that a smaller forecourt. On the floor of the cella, which the excavators identified as a later addition to the sanctuary, a number of bronzes were found, including a small, solid bronze cow and representations of two lions attacking a bull. Three connected treasuries lay along the south side of the temple complex. The peripheral settlement area, which no doubt housed many of the palace personnel, extended down the slope of the hill towards the sea. Rock-cut tombs belonging to the second palace period were discovered on the hill's northern slopes between the palace and the settlement.

Attempts have been made to place the two palace periods in a historical context. For example, its original Near Eastern character has led to the suggestion that it was first built by a pro-Persian Cypriot king around the time of the anti-Persian Ionian rebellion at the beginning of C5, and that its later rebuilding in a 'Greek' style was due to a pro-Greek local ruler. This remains purely speculative. So too does the theory that destruction and abandonment of the palace c. 380 is attributable to a pro-Persian administration in the nearby city of Soli.

Gjerstad (*SCE* III: 76–339), Nicolaou (*PECS* 990), Gaber (*OEANE* 5: 321–2).

Vounous (*Vounoi*) see ***Bellapais***.

W

Wadi Tharthar (map 10) A natural depression cutting into the plateau of the Jazira on a north–south course between the Euphrates and Tigris rivers, originating to the south-east of the Jebel Sinjar and terminating at its southern end in a salty marsh, Lake Tharthar. The Wadi is attested in the last recorded campaign of the Assyrian king Tukulti-Ninurta II (885). After departing with his army from Ashur, Tukulti-Ninurta marched westwards to the Wadi across the desert, then travelled south along its banks for four days. After pitching camp at its mouth on the evening of the fourth day, he headed east to the Tigris r., where he attacked the settlements of the Aramaean-occupied land of Utu before moving south along the river to Dur-Kurigalzu (**RIMA* 2: 173).

Wahsusana Middle Bronze Age kingdom (called a *mātum* in Assyrian texts) in southeastern Anatolia, to the west of the kingdom of Burushattum/Purushanda, and perhaps in the region of mod. Niğde. An Assyrian *kārum* (merchant-colony) was located there. Political unrest in Wahsusana (as well as in neighbouring Burushattum) at the end of the first phase of the Assyrian Colony period (second half of C19) forced an Assyrian merchant Idi-Ishtar to postpone a visit to the kingdom where he was to arrange for the dispatch of a consignment of copper held in storage there. Perhaps the unsettled conditions to which he refers in a letter to one of his merchant colleagues led to the decline and disappearance of Wahsusana as an important commercial centre and political power in the region. There is no further mention of it in the second and last phase of the Colony period, and it may have become part of the territory of Burushattum/Purushanda.

*Larsen (1976: 249), *Bryce (2005: 24–6, 33).

Wallarimma Late Bronze Age western Anatolian country lying in or near the Lukka Lands. It was one of the countries captured by the renegade Hittite vassal Madduwatta during his campaigns in western Anatolia (early C14) (**HDT* 158).

Walma Late Bronze Age country in southwestern Anatolia. Its northern limit is generally located near Classical Holmi southeast of mod. Afyon (Melchert, 2003: 37 map). It is uncertain how far south the country extended. (For various proposals regarding its location, see *RGTC* 6: 473, and Melchert, 2003: 6). The Hittite king Mursili II (1321–1295) reports that early in his campaign against the Arzawa lands (1319–1318), he fought a battle on the Astarpa r. in Walma with Piyama-Kurunta, son of the Arzawan king Uhhaziti (**AM* 50–1, **CS* II: 85, *Bryce, 2005: 194). After defeating Piyama-Kurunta's forces, he invaded Uhhaziti's kingdom and occupied his chief city, Apasa. The Astarpa r. has been identified with both the mod. Akar Çay (inland Classical Cayster) and the upper course of the Maeander. It subsequently formed part of the boundary of the Arzawan state of Mira-Kuwaliya. Walma is mentioned in the fragmentary Annals of Mursili's son and third successor Hattusili III (1267–1237) as one of the lands adjoining the Hulaya River Land (q.v.) repeatedly invaded by an enemy (*Gurney, 1997: 131). Hattusili again mentions it as bordering upon this land in a treaty he drew up with Ulmi-Teshub, probably his nephew Kurunta (**HDT* 110). Hattusili's son and successor Tudhaliya IV refers to it as a border city on the frontier with the kingdom of Tarhuntassa, which then incorporated the Hulaya River Land (**HDT* 115, **CS* II: 101).

Warahshe see **Marhashi**.

Warsiyalla Late Bronze Age city in western Anatolia. The Hittite king Muwattalli II (1295–1272) referred to it as a possible base for a Hittite campaign in the region (**HDT* 90).

Washaniya Middle Bronze Age city in southern Anatolia, on a major trade route between Assyria and Burushattum/Purushanda during the Assyrian Colony period (C20–18). It was the seat of a (presumably minor) king (*rubā'um* in the Assyrian texts), who wrote to the Assyrian merchants at nearby Wahsusana, advising them that he had succeeded to his father's throne and wished to renew a treaty with them. A small Assyrian settlement called a *wabartum* was associated with the city.

*Larsen (1976: 249–50), *Bryce (2005: 26).

Washshukkanni (**Washshuganni, Washshukanni**) Capital of the Late Bronze Age kingdom of Mitanni. Its location is unknown, though it is perhaps to be identified with mod. Tell Feheriye in the Habur r. triangle, northern Mesopotamia (but see ***Feheriye, Tell***). A city called Washshukkanni is attested as belonging to the country of Kizzuwadna in southeastern Anatolia early in C14, when the Hittite throne was occupied by Arnuwanda I (**HDT* 16). Arnuwanda's predecessor and co-regent Tudhaliya I/II claimed to have conquered the land of Hanigalbat (Mitanni) in the course of a campaign against the kingdoms of Aleppo and Hanigalbat (*Bryce, 2005: 140), and it is just possible that the Hanigalbataean/Mitannian capital Washshukkanni was captured on this campaign and allocated to the territory of Kizzuwadna. More likely, it is to be distinguished from the homonymous Kizzuwadnan city.

If Washshukkanni was in fact captured by Tudhaliya, the Mitannians soon regained it, and it continued to function as Mitanni's royal capital until it was occupied and plundered by the Hittite king Suppiluliuma I c. 1340 in the course of his 'one-year' Syrian campaign (**DS* 84–5, **HDT* 43, **CS* I: 189). The political vacuum left by Suppiluliuma's destruction of the Mitannian kingdom (the last Mitannian stronghold, Carchemish, fell to Suppiluliuma in 1327) was rapidly filled by Assyria. A contest arose between Hatti and Assyria for control over Washshukkanni. Though initially the Hittite viceroy Sharri-Kushuh (Piyassili) succeeded in imposing his authority upon the city (**HDT* 50–1), it soon fell to Assyria and was reduced to Assyrian vassal status. It was one of a number of Mitannian cities which rebelled against Assyrian rule during the reign of Adad-nirari I (1307–1275), but the rebellion was promptly crushed by Adad-nirari and the rebel states were then fully annexed into Assyrian territory (**RIMA* 1: 131, 136).

Wasuduwanda Late Bronze Age Hittite city in southern Anatolia, perhaps to be identified with the Iron Age city Ishtuanda (q.v.) attested in Neo-Assyrian texts. A shrine of the goddess Hepat was located there.

RGTC 6: 480.

Wawiyat, Tell el- (map 8) Small settlement-mound located in the Lower Galilee region, mod. Israel, 12 km north of Nazareth. Its history of excavation extends from the Middle Bronze to the Iron Age. Excavations were conducted in 1986 and 1987 by B. A. Nakhai, J. P. Dessel, and B. L. Wisthoff for the University of Arizona, in cooperation with the William F. Albright School of Archaeological Research in Jerusalem and the American Schools of Oriental Research. Six levels of occupation were identified. Evidence of human activity in the Middle Bronze Age (Stratum VI; C17–16) was confined to two child jar-burials, and in the Late Bronze Age (Strata V–IV; C15–13) almost entirely to pottery assemblages (with a few meagre architectural remains from Stratum IV). However, the large quantity of imported ceramic ware in this level (C14–13), coming particularly from Cyprus but also from the Aegean world, indicates the settlement's contacts with the world of international trade and its apparent prosperity. The excavators consider it likely that during this period the village served as a way-station supplying food and accommodation to travellers crossing the Lower Galilee.

The site's first Iron Age (IA) level (Stratum III; late C13–early C12) contain its earliest significant architectural remains, in the form of two large multi-roomed building complexes, with some evidence of continuity in both architectural and ceramic traditions from the preceding Late Bronze Age level. One of these complexes apparently had cultic purposes, the other seems to have been primarily of a domestic nature. The excavators concluded that in its first Iron Age phase, Tell el-Wawiyat was a farming hamlet, with complex economic and social activities. In Stratum II (Iron Age IB; C11), buildings from the previous level were reused, but modified by constructing walls to divide up their formerly spacious rooms. The excavators interpret this as representing an indigent squatters' reuse of the site, perhaps reflecting an Israelite occupation of a previously abandoned village.

Nakhai, Dessel, Wisthoff (*NEAEHL* 4: 1500–1).

Weshesh Late Bronze Age population group, listed among the so-called Sea Peoples who attacked the coast of Egypt during Ramesses III's reign (1184–1153) (**ARE IV*: §64, **ANET* 262, *Gertzen, 2008: 88–9). They may have been of northwestern Anatolian origin, if their name can be linked with Wilusa, a northwestern Anatolian kingdom attested in Hittite texts. But the suggested link is very dubious. In the so-called Papyrus Harris (see glossary), Ramesses records the capture of Weshesh and Shardana groups of Sea Peoples, and their deportation to Egypt (*Gertzen, 2008: 91).

Sandars (1985: 224, index refs).

Wilusa (map 3) Hittite vassal kingdom in northwestern Anatolia, generally considered to be one of the Arzawa Lands (q.v.) (though some scholars dispute this). It first appears in Hittite texts (in the form Wilusiya) as the penultimate name in the list of western Anatolian countries forming the anti-Hittite Assuwan Confederacy (c. 1400; see under **Assuwa**) (*Bryce, 2005: 124–5). The last name in the list is

Taruisa. Subsequently, Wilusa's relations with Hatti appear to have been generally peaceful, and at some undetermined time it became one of Hatti's vassal states. In the early decades of C13 its king, Alaksandu, concluded a (still extant) treaty with his Hittite overlord Muwattalli II (*HDT* 87–93). To judge from other fragmentary texts, Wilusa may have been occupied by enemy forces on at least one occasion during C13, and/or destabilized by uprisings within its own population (*Bryce, 2006: 184). It was also the cause of a dispute, perhaps even military conflict, between the kings of Ahhiyawa and Hatti, as recorded in the so-called Tawagalawa letter (see Güterbock, 1986: 37). In the final decades of C13 its last known ruler, Walmu, appears to have been driven from his throne, but was restored to it by the Hittite king Tudhaliya IV (**HDT* 145).

Most scholars now believe that Wilusa/Wilusiya is the Bronze Age equivalent of Ilios (originally Wilios) in Greek epic tradition, and that the Late Bronze Age settlement at Hisarlık in the Troad was the seat of the kingdom of Wilusa. (In Homer's *Iliad*, the name Ilios is used interchangeably with Troia (Troy), the latter commonly equated by scholars with Taruisa.) Recent studies of the political geography of western Anatolia provide additional support for this view, by strengthening the case for locating Wilusa in the northwest corner of Anatolia.

*Latacz (2004: esp. 75–100), *Bryce (2006: 107–12, 117–21, 182–6).

Wiyanawanda The name of (probably) several cities in Late Bronze Age Anatolia, the most clearly attested of which lay in the southwest, within or near the Lukka Lands, and on the frontier of the Arzawan kingdom of Mira-Kuwaliya (**HDT* 76). It appears in the so-called Yalburt inscription (q.v.) in the same context as Lukka, among the lands conquered by the Hittite king Tudhaliya IV (1237–1209) (*Hawkins, 1995: 68–9). It subsequently appears along with Lukka among the lands in southern Anatolia conquered by Tudhaliya's son, Suppiluliuma II (1207–) (*Hawkins, 1995: 22–3). An identification with the Lycian city of Oenoanda (32 km northwest of mod. Elmalı, map 15) has been suggested. However, Oenoanda is not attested before the late Hellenistic period, and is probably too far south to be compatible with a location for the Bronze Age Wiyanawanda which lay on the border of Mira-Kuwaliya.

X

Xanthus (Lycian Arñna, *Kɪnɪk*) (map 15) M1 BCE–M1 CE city in Lycia in southwestern Anatolia, the largest and most important city in its region. It is located on the Xanthus r. 12 km north of the river's mouth. Remains on its walled 'Lycian' acropolis, which lies at the southwestern end of the site (there is another acropolis, of Hellenistic and Roman date, at the site's northern end), date the city's origins back to late C8 (though a Chalcolithic axe discovered in a recent sounding may indicate much earlier settlement). Xanthus continued to be occupied through the Persian, Hellenistic, Roman, and Byzantine periods, until the Arab invasion in C7 CE. The English explorer Charles Fellows first investigated and described the site in 1838. From 1950 onwards it was excavated by French archaeological teams, whose first two directors, successively, were P. Demargne and H. Metzger. French excavations continue on the site, currently under the direction of J. des Coutils (see his annual reports in *An Ant*, the most recent of which is indicated below).

The most impressive remains of the indigenous Lycian civilization at Xanthus are the city's sepulchral monuments, which date to the period C6–4. They include a number of house-type and pillar-tombs. The latter, no doubt intended for the families of elite members of Lycian society, were surmounted by small grave chambers (or perhaps spirit-houses?). One of the oldest of these tombs is the 'Lion Pillar', which dates to the second quarter of C6. It was originally topped by a sarcophagus, decorated with a frieze depicting a reclining lion and a warrior-horseman. The sarcophagus is now in the British Museum. Two of the most conspicuous pillar-tombs are situated in the area that later became the Roman agora. They are the so-called Harpy Tomb (early C5) and Inscribed Pillar (late C5–early C4). The former is so named because the winged females who are depicted on it carrying off diminutive human figures were once thought to be harpies. They are now generally believed to be sirens conveying the spirits of the dead to their afterlife. The Inscribed Pillar is so called because it has a 255-line inscription carved on it – 243 lines in the Lycian language (in two dialects), and a twelve-line Greek epigram (**TAM* I: 44). It is the longest surviving inscription in the Lycian language. Though only a few words and phrases of the Lycian text can be understood (the Lycian language is still largely undeciphered), we can deduce from these as well as from information contained in the Greek epigram that the inscription belongs to a man called Kheriga, member of a ruling Lycian dynasty based in Xanthus. The inscription contains (among other things) a record of the dynasty's exploits, and two genealogical lists of its leading members. The upper part of the pillar is much damaged, though the many fragments of it which the French have recovered indicate that its funerary chamber was decorated with a relief depicting the dynast's victory over his enemies. There is also evidence that a statue, probably of the dynast himself, once stood atop the tomb. Another sepulchral monument lying close to the Harpy Tomb consists of a sarcophagus with ogival roof set upon a chamber formed of upright slabs. A burial found intact in this chamber can be dated by its accompanying pottery

Figure 132 Xanthus river.

to C3. However, it once contained a relief slab reused from a C6 monument (and now in the Istanbul Archaeological Museum) depicting, apparently, funeral games. (For recently discovered tombs in Xanthus, see Cavalier, 2003).

Just by the entrance to the city, where the arch of the C1 Roman emperor Vespasian still stands, are the remains of another of the important monuments dating to the period of Lycia's indigenous inscriptions (late C6–C4). This is the so-called Nereid monument, most of which was taken in sections to London by Charles Fellows, where it was reassembled (probably inaccurately), and is still on display in the British Museum. Built in early C4 entirely of marble, it is the most magnificent and elaborate of all Lycian tombs, and was probably the burial place of a man called Erbbina, the last known member of the Xanthian dynasty. The monument is in the form of a Greek Ionic temple, and derives its mod. name from the statues of female figures (who may or may not be Nereids) placed between its columns. Recent finds from the city's pre-Classical phase include 'a large wall of Lesbian masonry at least 10 m in length and two blocks with reliefs featuring bulls in an orientalizing Neo-Hittite and Phrygian style, similar to reliefs found a decade earlier in the same area' (thus reported by Yıldırım and Gates, 2007: 314, from des Courtils, 2005: 454–7).

Xanthus was destroyed c. 540 by the Persian commander Harpagus during his campaign of conquest along the southern Anatolian coast. Herodotus (1.176) records the city's last defiant but futile stand against the Persians. Subsequently it became subject, with the rest of Lycia, to Persian overlordship, when Lycia was included in the states which formed the first Persian satrapy (see glossary under **satrapy**). It was probably at this time that a local dynasty emerged in Xanthus which was to hold sway

Figure 133 Xanthus, pillar-tomb and house-tombs.

over much of Lycia, on behalf of the Persians, until early C4, except during the middle decades of C5 when Lycia became part of the Athenian Confederacy. By the 420s, Persia had re-established control over Lycia, and the Xanthian dynasty continued to rule the country on its behalf, as attested in the many coin issues of the period, which depict the Xanthian dynasts wearing Persian-type tiaras. But the dynasty came to an end in early C4, and Xanthus may have participated with other Lycian cities in the satrap rebellion which broke out in the 360s against the Persian king Artaxerxes II. The rebel forces were defeated some years later (c. 360?). Xanthus, along with the rest of Lycia, once more reverted to Persian control, until 334/333, when the country was invaded and conquered by Alexander the Great.

Xanthus continued to exercise a dominant role in Lycia through the Hellenistic and Roman periods. It was destroyed by the Roman Brutus in 42 during the civil war which followed the assassination of Julius Caesar. But it was rebuilt and flourished

Figure 134 Xanthus, 'Harpy Tomb' relief.

Figure 135 Xanthus, Nereid monument.

under Roman rule. One of the more substantial remains of the Roman period is a relatively well-preserved C2 CE theatre. During the Byzantine period, Xanthus' walls were repaired, and the city became the seat of a bishop. A Byzantine basilica was built on the site of the Hellenistic and Roman acropolis.

Bean (*PECS* 996; 1978: 49–60), Toksöz (1986: 31–73), des Courtils (2005; 2006a; 2006b: these are the most recent reports to hand of the current excavations).

Y

Yabliya (map 10) Middle Bronze Age city in the middle Euphrates region called Suhum which lay south of the kingdom of Mari. Yabliya was the capital of Lower Suhum. Hammurabi, king of Babylon (1792–1750), and Zimri-Lim, king of Mari (1774–1762), apparently both claimed possession of the city, along with the cities of Hit and Harbe (**ARM XXVI/2*: 336–7, no. 449), all of which lay in the frontier region between Babylonia and Mari. The governor of Lower Suhum, who was based at Yabliya, was a man called Hammanum. He had occupied the governorship from the time Suhum was subject to Yasmah-Addu, the Assyrian viceroy at Mari (1782–1775). Military operations conducted in Suhum by forces from Eshnunna early in Zimri-Lim's reign resulted in the capture of the city of Harbe by the Eshnunnite commander Shallurum, who dispatched a force of 5,000 troops from there to occupy Yabliya (**LKM* 383–4, nos 26.479 and 26.480). These operations were intended to pave the way for Eshnunna's seizure of the entire land of Suhum. Reinforcements sent to Yabliya to fortify it failed to prevent the city from eventually falling to the Eshnunnites, along with the nearby cities of Ayabu and Mulhan. With the support of Hammurabi, king of Babylon, Zimri-Lim regained possession of the occupied territories. His control of them was confirmed in a peace accord concluded with the Eshnunnite king Ibal-pi-El II in 1770. Possession of the cities of Yabliya, Harbe, and Hit was eventually conceded by Hammurabi to Zimri-Lim when the Babylonian and Mariote kings shared out the territories of Suhum following the retreat of the Eshnunnite forces from the region.

LKM 627 (refs), *Mesop*. 161–2, 196–7.

Yadnana The name commonly used for Cyprus in Assyrian royal inscriptions (e.g. **CS* II: 297).

Yahan(u) see **Bit-Agusi**.

Yahya, Tepe (map 12) Settlement-mound in southeastern Iran, covering c. 3 ha at its base and almost 20 m high, located 220 km south of mod. Kerman, perhaps within the region of the country called Marhashi (in Sumerian) or Parahshum (in Akkadian) in late M3 Mesopotamian texts. Its history of occupation extends, with intervals of abandonment, through ten major phases, from M7 (late Neolithic period) to the first half of M1 CE (Parthian and Sasanian periods). The site was discovered in 1967, and excavated from 1967 to 1971, and in 1973 and 1975, by a joint expedition of the Peabody Museum (Harvard University) and the Archaeological Service of Iran, under the direction of C. C. Lamberg-Karlovsky.

In its prehistoric phases, Tepe Yahya was occupied by a series of Neolithic villages (levels VII–VI; c. 5500–4500), from which the remains of many domestic dwellings have been unearthed, followed by further occupation in the Chalcolithic period (levels VI–VA; c. 4500–3200). The distinguishing feature of its subsequent 'Proto-Elamite' phase (level IVC; c. 3100–2800) was a building complex of over 500 sq. m, from which twenty-five tablets inscribed in the so-called Proto-Elamite script came to light (but see **Elam**), along with many cylinder sealings, and ceramic ware of a type also found at Susa and Tal-e Malyan (Anshan). At the end of this phase, the settlement was apparently abandoned until c. 2400, when a new level of occupation becomes evident, extending through the final centuries of the Early Bronze Age into the early centuries of the Middle Bronze Age (level IVB; c. 2400–2000). In this period, Tepe Yahya may have been the centre, or at least a part, of the kingdom of Marhashi, attested in texts of the C21 Ur III dynasty. Large numbers of bowls and other artefacts made from locally mined chlorite (and engraved with a range of animal and geometric motifs) were one of the distinguishing features of this period, though they are found in other periods as well. Tepe Yahya was very probably a centre for trade in goods made of this material. Architectural and ceramic features of the subsequent occupation level (IVA), extending from the Middle Bronze Age into the first centuries of the Late Bronze Age (c. 1800–1400), suggest a cultural break with the preceding period.

The site then appears to have been abandoned until at least early M1. Two phases of occupation during M1, from 800 to 500 and 500 to 275 (levels III and II respectively), are represented by complexes of large houses, and in the latter case by ceramic ware with parallels to Persian Achaemenid pottery. Level I, represented by some poorly preserved architectural remains and pottery of Parthian-Sasanian type, is datable to the period 200 to 300 CE.

Lamberg-Karlovsky (*OEANE* 5: 187–8), D. T. Potts (2004).

Ya'ilānum Tribal group, probably of Amorite origin, living in the Zagros foothills of northeastern Mesopotamia, near Qabra. It is attested in the Middle Bronze Age Mari archives from the reign of the Assyrian king Shamshi-Adad I (1796–1775). After unsuccessful attempts to establish an alliance with the tribe, Shamshi-Adad ordered his son, Yasmah-Addu, viceroy at Mari, to execute the Ya'ilānum hostages who were in his custody (**LAPO* 17: 414–16, no. 679). Ya'ilānum's ruler in this period was a certain Bina- (or Mar-)Addu, who was defeated and killed by Ishme-Dagan, brother of Yasmah-Addu and Assyrian viceroy at Ekallatum, in a battle at Tutarrum (Tutarwe) (**LAPO* 17: 122–3, no. 527), one of the cities of the Ya'ilānum. This occurred during an Assyrian campaign launched against the northern Mesopotamian country Qabra,

Figure 136 Tepe Yahya IVC sealing.

with the assistance of Dadusha, king of Eshnunna. Himara and Dur-Ya'ilānim were among other cities belonging to the territory of the Ya'ilānum. The first of these was conquered by Shamshi-Adad five days after his victory over the king of Qabra, at the beginning of the autumn of 1779.

Eidem and Laessoe (2001: 23), *Mesop.* 167–8.

Yalburt (map 2) Late Bronze Age site near the village of Ilgin in the district of Konya in south-central Anatolia. Excavation of the site, accidentally discovered in 1970 during a bulldozing operation, began in 1971 under the direction of T. Özgüç for the Turkish General Directorate of Antiquities and Museums. On the location of a spring, a Late Bronze Age rectangular stone basin lined with stone walls was unearthed. Three of the water basin's sides bear a Luwian hieroglyphic inscription carved in high relief on twenty large limestone blocks. The inscription, which is the longest known hieroglyphic text of the Hittite empire, records a military campaign conducted by the Hittite king Tudhaliya IV (1237–1209) against the Lukka Lands in southwestern Anatolia. It provides an important source of information on the history of the Hittite world during the kingdom's final decades.

T. Özgüç (1988), *Poetto (1993), *Hawkins (1995: 66–85).

Yalihum Middle Bronze Age town in the middle Euphrates region near Saggaratum. A letter from the Mari archives indicates that Saggaratum's governor considered it a suitable place in his neighbourhood for stationing a garrison of troops (**LAPO* 17: 437–9, no. 694).

Yamhad (map 10) Middle and (early) Late Bronze Age Amorite kingdom in northern Syria. Its royal seat was located at Aleppo. By the beginning of C18, Yamhad had replaced Ebla as the dominant power in the region, exercising sovereignty over a number of cities and petty kingdoms between the Euphrates and Orontes rivers. Nine kings of Yamhad are known, whose collective reigns spanned a period of two centuries (c. 1800–1600). Its first known ruler was Sumu-epuh, a contemporary of Yahdun-Lim (1810–1794), king of Mari, who had married a princess of Aleppo. Despite the marriage alliance, relations between the two kingdoms became hostile, as evidenced by military support provided by Sumu-epuh to the Yaminite tribes (q.v.) in their conflicts with Mari during Yahdun-Lim's reign. Yamhad subsequently became embroiled in hostilities with Shamshi-Adad I (1796–1775), ruler of the Old Assyrian kingdom, who formed an alliance with Qatna against it. In the course of these hostilities, Sumu-epuh was killed in action against Shamshi-Adad, and his throne passed to his son, Yarim-Lim I.

The disintegration of the Old Assyrian kingdom and the seizure of the throne of Mari, hitherto a viceregal seat of the kingdom, by Zimri-Lim (1774–1762), paved the way for a period of sustained peace and cooperation between Yamhad and Mari. Zimri-Lim married a daughter of Yarim-Lim, and gifts were exchanged between the royal courts. Yamhad's relations also improved with Qatna in this period, and Yarim-Lim concluded an alliance with Babylon. His successor, Hammurabi, sent troops to the Babylonian king, also called Hammurabi, to assist in the latter's capture of the kingdom of Larsa. Yamhad became one of the great political and military powers of the Middle Bronze Age, holding sway over some twenty subject rulers (*Charpin, 1995: 816).

It continued to exercise dominance over northern Syria for another century, until the reign of Yarim-Lim III in the second half of C17. In this period (for which we have information about the kingdom from the archives of Alalah and the Hittite capital Hattusa), the Hittite king Hattusili I (1650–1620) conducted a series of campaigns against the northern Syrian city-states which were subject to or allied with Yamhad. He succeeded in capturing and destroying a number of these states, and seriously weakened the kingdom in the process. But he failed to take its capital, Aleppo. It was left to his successor, Mursili I, to deliver the *coup de grâce* by conquering and destroying the city c. 1595 (see under **Aleppo**). Aleppo itself was to rise again, for a time as the capital of an independent kingdom. But after Mursili's conquest there are no further references to the kingdom of Yamhad.

Klengel (1992: 44–83), Lion (*DCM* 30–3), *Mesop.* 211–12.

Yaminites ('Sons of the Right', i.e. the south when facing the rising sun? The name was formerly translated as 'Benjaminites' on the assumption of a close link with the Benjaminites of *OT* tradition) Confederation of Amorite nomadic and semi-nomadic tribes, attested in the Middle Bronze Age archives of Mari. The tribes were spread over large areas of Mesopotamia and northern Syria, especially in the region between Suhum and the borders of Yamhad. There were five known major tribal sub-groups: the Amnanu/Awnan, the Rabbu, the Upapru, the Yahruru, and the Yarihu. The Simalites (Bensamilites; 'Sons of the Left', i.e. the north) appear to have been a related tribal group, made up of about a dozen sub-groups. To judge from their names, the basic distinction between Yaminites and Simalites appears to have been geographical rather than ethnic. The designation of the Yaminites as 'southerners' and 'northerners' probably reflects their original homelands, more so than their geographical distribution at the time of the Mari archives. At this time, Yaminites were widely distributed through both northern and southern Mesopotamia and are also attested as inhabiting regions between the Euphrates and the Mediterranean coast. The Simalites are attested in the Lower Habur region and along the Euphrates downstream to the Delta. But they may also have had considerable penetration into regions inhabited by Yaminites. Yaminites and Simalites are in some contexts represented as branches of an ancestral tribal entity called the Hana. Together they probably made up a large part of the population of the kingdom of Mari. The Mariote king Zimri-Lim (1774–1762) was of Simalite origin.

The Yaminites' encampments were located principally along the Euphrates r., with urban centres at Terqa and Tuttul. But their constant need to find suitable grazing lands for their livestock meant that they moved regularly through the steppe-lands lying both east and west of the river. Each of their tribes was led by a sheikh, and sometimes, in addition, a war leader. Their movements inevitably brought them into conflict with settled populations in the regions where they grazed their livestock. They attacked cities in these regions and made travel between them unsafe. Hostilities with the kingdom of Mari in particular are recorded in texts dating to the reigns of the Mariote kings Yahdun-Lim (1810–1794) and Zimri-Lim (1774–1762). Yahdun-Lim reports a decisive victory over the Yaminites at the city of Samanum on the Euphrates (**Chav.*97). He later appears to have established an accord with them, which in effect gave him control over their transit territories between the Euphrates and the Mediterranean coast. But they continued to threaten cities in or near the lands through which they moved, both during the reign of the Assyrian king Shamshi-Adad I, when the king's son Yasmah-Addu was viceroy in Mari (1782–1775), and especially in the period when the Mariote throne was occupied by Zimri-Lim. Alliances with Eshnunna and other local kings undoubtedly enhanced the dangers they posed to the security of Zimri-Lim's kingdom. None the less, Zimri-Lim had his successes against them, including a resounding victory which he won over their forces in a battle near the city of Saggaratum on the middle Euphrates. An accord which he established with the Yaminite leaders c. 1770 probably led to at least a temporary cessation of hostilities between the kingdom and the tribal groups, if not to a lasting peace.

Dossin (1939), Durand and Charpin (1986), Whiting (1995: 1238), *LKM* 15–17, 603–4 (refs), *Mesop.* 140–2, 195–6, 204–6.

Yamutbal(um) (Emutbal(um)) (maps 10, 11) Amorite tribal groups attested in the Middle Bronze Age archives from Mari in the reign of Zimri-Lim (1774–1762). They apparently had two main areas of settlement: one in northern Mesopotamia centring upon the city of Andarig (map 10), and one in southern Mesopotamia along the Tigris r. with the city of Mashkan-Shapir as its focus (map 11). Sovereignty over northern Yamutbal seems to have fluctuated between Atamrum, king of Andarig, and Zimri-Lim, who was Atamrum's father-in-law (**LKM* 492). In early M2, southern Yamutbalum was part of, or was incorporated into, the kingdom of Larsa, its territories including the cities of Mashkan-Shapir and Razama (1). Charpin (*Mesop.* 32) observes that the name Yamutbalum/Emutbalum seems sometimes to designate the region around Mashkan-Shapir, and sometimes the entire territory of the former kingdom of Larsa after its conquest by the Babylonian king Hammurabi in 1763. He cites Steinkeller's proposed rationalization of this apparent anomaly: (Yamutbalum)/Emutbalum was the name of an Amorite tribe originally installed around Mashkan-Shapir, but the name came to be used in a progressively broader sense to encompass Larsa, reflecting the fact that the kings of this city had an Emutbalean tribal origin.

Following the outbreak of hostilities between Hammurabi and Rim-Sin, Larsa's king, Babylonian troops invaded Larsa and seized the city of Mashkan-Shapir. The welcome they allegedly received from the whole land of Yamutbal (**LKM* 331) may simply have been a calculated diplomatic gesture towards the region's potential new overlord, rather than an expression of disaffection with Rim-Sin's rule.

Mesop. 70, 116–17, 318–19, *LKM* 18, Steinkeller (2004).

Yaraşlı Late Bronze Age fortified city in central Anatolia, north of the Salt Lake. Discovered by W. M. Calder and subsequently by M. Ballance and A. Hall in 1957, the site covering approx. 500 m × 200 m is enclosed by a rubble wall. There are remains of an entrance gate, a possible postern tunnel, a citadel, and a lower town. J. Mellaart proposed identifying the site with the Hittite city of Sallapa (q.v.).

Macqueen (1968), Burney (2004: 317–18).

Yarmut, Tel (map 8) 16 ha site consisting of a small acropolis and large lower city (both fortified in the Early Bronze Age), located in the Shephelah in western Palestine, 25 km southwest of Jerusalem. Its history of occupation extends from Early Bronze I (second half of M4) to the early Byzantine period, with a long period of abandonment after its Early Bronze phase. From 1980 onwards, excavations were conducted on the site by P. de Miroschedji for the Centre du Recherche Français de Jérusalem and the Hebrew University of Jerusalem.

During the Early Bronze Age, the city reached the peak of its development. Its fortifications protected a relatively large settlement of as many as 3,000 inhabitants, who produced a wide range of crops, vegetables, fruit, and olives, and grazed sheep, goats, and cattle. The city was dominated by several monumental public buildings. These included what was probably a sanctuary, whose main feature was a plastered and columned broadroom hall, and a 6,000 sq. m palace complex, the largest of all such Levantine complexes dating to the Early Bronze Age. Interconnected rooms, small courtyards, numerous corridors, and storerooms made up the complex. A large array of small finds, including a comprehensive assemblage of ceramic ware, many human and animal figurines, and a wide variety of other objects made of stone, bone, and terracotta, has given Tel Yarmut the status of a type-site for the material culture of southern Palestine in this period. Not long after mid M3, at the height of its prosperity, the city was unaccountably abandoned. There is no evidence that this was due to violent destruction of the site. It was reoccupied 1,000 years later, in Late Bronze II, though settlement was now limited to the small acropolis. Occupation was thenceforth fairly continuous, through the succeeding Iron Age and later phases until the Byzantine age, when a small village was built on the northeast side of the acropolis.

An identification has been proposed between Tel Yarmut and the biblical city of Yarmut attested in several *OT* sources. Joshua 10:3–5 reports that Yarmut's ruler, Piram, joined in a coalition of four kings in response to an appeal from Adoni-Zedek, the Amorite king of Jerusalem, for an attack on Gibeon, because it had formed an alliance with Joshua and the Israelites. Another possible reference to the city, under the name Yaramu, may occur in a letter of mid C14 date discovered at Tell el-Hesi (see under ***Hesi, Tell el-***) near the border of the Shephelah and the Negev desert.

Miroschedji (*OEANE* 5: 369–72; reports in *IEJ* from vol. 31, 1981, onwards).

Yaruwatta Late Bronze Age city in northern Syria in the frontier-zone between the kingdoms of Barga and the Nuhashshi lands, and probably to be located on the east bank of the middle Orontes. Control over the city was contested by the above kingdoms, and resolved by the Hittite king Mursili II (c. 1315) in favour of Nuhashshi. See also **Barga**.

* Klengel (1963), Lipiński (2000: 259–60), Bryce (2005: 199–200).

Yasbuq M1 northern Arabian tribe, located in the lower Orontes r. valley. In 858 it participated under its chief, Burannati, in the coalition of northern Syrian and south-eastern Anatolian kingdoms (together with the northwestern Mesopotamian kingdom of Bit-Adini) which opposed, but was defeated by, the Assyrian king Shalmaneser III (**RIMA* 3: 10, 17). The name has been related to *OT* Ishbak, one of Abraham's five sons by Keturah (Genesis 25:2).

Lipiński (2000: 192).

Yasubigalli M1 tribal group in the Zagros mountains, attacked by the Assyrian king Sennacherib during his campaign in the region in 702 (*Sennach.* 26–7, 58, 67, 86). The tribe apparently had a long history of resistance to Assyrian rule.

Yavneh-Yam (map 8) M2 BCE–M1 CE coastal city located in mod. Israel on the northwestern border of Judaea, 16 km south of Tel Aviv-Jaffa. Its history of occupation extends from the Middle Bronze Age to the Byzantine period, with a long period of abandonment in between. The site was excavated from 1967 to 1969 by J. Kaplan on behalf of the Tel Aviv-Jaffa Municipal Museum. Subsequent rescue operations were conducted in 1980–7 to save one of the city's building complexes from sea erosion. In its Middle and Late Bronze Age phases, Yavneh-Yam consisted primarily of a square enclosure, 800 sq. m in extent, bounded by a rampart. The site was abandoned during the first part of the Late Bronze Age, after periods of intermittent occupation, and not resettled until the Persian period (C6–4), when it was attached to Idumaea (q.v.), an administrative district of the Persian empire. The city expanded considerably during its Persian and Hellenistic phases, and in the subsequent Roman and Byzantine periods it was one of the Palestinian coastal region's major ports.

Dessel (*OEANE* 5: 374–5).

Yazılıkaya (Turkish for 'inscribed rock'; anc. name unknown) Late Bronze Age rock-sanctuary in north-central Anatolia, 1 km northeast of the Hittite capital Hattusa. Its principal natural features are two open-air rock-chambers, designated as A and B, and a number of niches, crevices, and small caves. Although in use since M4 or earlier, the rock outcrop appears to have been left largely in its natural state until c. 1500, when a wall was built, shutting off the main chamber (A) from the outside world. From at least mid M2, Yazılıkaya appears to have been used for cultic purposes, though it may in fact have served this purpose since the Chalcolithic period. Its first building phase continued through C14 into early C13. During the reign of the Hittite king Hattusili III (1267–1237), a gatehouse and temple complex with interior court and inner sanctuary were constructed across the front of the site, replacing the earlier wall and shutting off direct access into the sanctuary's two natural chambers. The excavator of the complex, K. Bittel, observed that the buildings were erected in a strikingly careless manner, with their foundations hardly anywhere going down to bedrock. This suggested to him that use of the sanctuary was limited to a few special occasions in the year.

The walls of the rock-chambers behind the building complex were embellished, during the reign of Hattusili's son and successor Tudhaliya IV, with a number of relief sculptures. The most impressive group of reliefs consists of two files of deities, male on the left and female on the right (with one exception in each case), apparently approaching each other. The deities are identified by names inscribed next to them in the Luwian hieroglyphic script (though many of the inscriptions are now badly weathered to the point of obscurity, or entirely lost). It is clear both from the arrangement of the figures and from the names associated with them that the Hurrian pantheon of deities is represented here. The depiction of these deities reflects the strong influence of Hurrian culture, especially Hurrian religion, on Hittite civilization, particularly during C13. The deities leading the two files are, on the left, the Hurrian god Teshub, and facing him his consort Hepat. On the opposite wall, a 3 m high relief of King Tudhaliya is carved, dressed and equipped as a Hittite priest.

Behind chamber A is a narrow passage, guarded by a pair of winged and lion-headed demons with human bodies, which leads into the 3 m wide chamber B, with a subsidiary chamber opening off its northeast corner. On the right of the chamber as one

Figure 137 Yazılıkaya, 'running gods'.

enters, twelve identical gods are depicted. They appear to be running, or marching, and are carrying sickle-shaped swords. On the opposite wall are two closely linked figures. The larger figure is Tudhaliya's patron god Sharrumma, son of Teshub and Hepat. Sharrumma extends his arm around the smaller figure, his protégé Tudhaliya. The so-called 'dagger-god' is also carved on this wall. The top part of the relief consists of a human head (evidently that of a god, since it wears a conical cap), underneath which are the foreparts of two lions, and beneath them two lion-skins hanging head down. All this forms the 'hilt' of the dagger. The lower part of the relief is in the form of a double-edged blade with a distinct midrib. The bottom half of the blade is not visible, and almost certainly the relief as a whole is intended to represent a dagger plunged into the ground. A number of scholars believe that the dagger-god and the twelve running/marching gods have underworld associations.

The precise purpose and function of the sanctuary remains unclear. But it has long been suggested that Yazılıkaya was the principal place where the Hittite New Year festival was celebrated, in the presence of all the chief deities of the land. The site's apparent netherworld associations would not be inconsistent with this. Death and new life were commonly juxtaposed in the anc. world, for in the cyclic pattern of things, decay and death are followed by new beginnings, new growth, new life. In the Hittite kingdom's last decades, Yazılıkaya may also have served as a mortuary chapel, a place of ancestor worship where the royal family paid homage to its dead. The prominence of the reliefs of Tudhaliya IV, the only human figure depicted at Yazılıkaya, suggests that chamber B may have been his tomb.

Bittel *et al.* (1975), Macqueen (1986: 123–32).

Figure 138 Yazılıkaya, Sharrumma and Tudhaliya.

Yin'am, Tell (map 8) Site located in the Yavne'el valley in the eastern Lower Galilee region, with a history of occupation extending from the Neolithic to the late Roman period. The site was excavated by H. A. Liebowitz for the University of Texas, from 1976 to 1981 and from 1983 to 1989. A circular platform structure identified as a *bamah* (a high place where Jews worshipped) was the main architectural feature surviving from the Early Bronze Age level. During the Middle Bronze Age, a fortress was built on the site. From this period too an electrum figurine of a standing goddess came to light. (Electrum is a mixture of gold and silver.) After a period of abandonment, Tell Yin'am was reoccupied during the latter half of the Late Bronze Age, when the settlement was dominated by a large, ten-room building complex identified as the residence of the local ruler. Small finds from the complex included cylinder seals, a stamp seal, and a range of jewellery. Other buildings dating to C13 adjoined this complex. The Late Bronze Age city ended in violent destruction, but was followed shortly after by the first Iron Age level (Iron Age I). Well-built houses and high quality ceramic ware were features of this level. Occupation continued into Iron Age IIA (C10), from which we have the remains of two houses, in one of which was an olive oil press, an olive-cracking device, and stone weights, suggestive of cottage industry.

Figure 139 Yazılıkaya, 'dagger god'.

In another room, forty-five loom-weights were discovered. The settlement's Iron Age IIC phase produced a range of cooking pots, jugs, and storage jars. Evidence of occupation during the Persian period (C6–4) included assemblages of both local and imported ceramic ware, and some architectural remains, including a building (probably a house) with ovens and grain silos. There is no evidence of occupation during the Hellenistic period, but the site was certainly resettled in Roman times.

Liebowitz (*OEANE* 5: 379–81).

Yocantepe Eastern Anatolian early Iron Age fortress settlement and necropolis, located 9 km southeast of mod. Van on a conical hill, 2051 m above sea level. Identified during a survey in 1995 in the course of a search for Urartian dam and irrigation systems, it is to date the highest excavated site in Turkey. The excavations, conducted jointly by Istanbul University and the Van Museum, under the direction of O. Belli since 1997, cover three areas: the acropolis, lower settlement, and necropolis. The fortress occupies an area of 600 sq. m on the highest part of the site. Its walls are carefully constructed with an admixture of earth and slab-stones. It was part of an architectural complex which spread through the entire excavated area. The necropolis contains numerous grave-chambers, all oriented in a north–south direction, and some with a front dromos (see glossary). The tops of the graves were covered with huge slab-stones. Each grave contained numerous human remains, thirty-five skeletons in one case. Burial practices follow those of other Early Iron Age necropoleis, in which bones were heaped together on the grave floors, and sometimes crushed, when the chambers were full, to make way for fresh interments. But the skulls were carefully placed in bowls. Grave goods included pottery typical of early Iron Age ceramic ware (e.g. carinated, flat-based, wheel-made bowls), and large numbers of iron ornaments and ceremonial weapons. A few pieces of jewellery, such as a pair of gold pendulum ear-rings, were also found among the graves' contents. The site is considered important for a study of cultural transfer from M2 to the early Iron Age and then to the Urartian period.

Belli and Konyar (2001).

Yokneam (*Tel Yokneam/Joqneam; Tel Qeimum*) (map 8) Canaanite city in Palestine located on a 4 ha mound in the western Jezreel valley above the junction between the Via Maris (q.v.) and the route which passed across the Carmel range. Its history of occupation, covering twenty-seven archaeological strata, extends from the Early Bronze Age to the Ottoman period. The site was excavated by A. Ben-Tor on behalf of the Hebrew University of Jerusalem between 1977 and 1988, as part of the Yokneam Regional Project. Yokneam first appears in written records among the Syro-Palestinian conquests of the pharaoh Tuthmosis III in C15. There are frequent references to it in *OT* sources: e.g. its ruler was one of thirty-one kings defeated by Joshua (Joshua 12:22), and it was subsequently one of the cities assigned to the Levites (Joshua 21:34). The city was first fortified during the Middle Bronze Age, but left unfortified in subsequent phases of its Bronze Age history, up to its destruction at the end of the Late Bronze Age. It was reoccupied and refortified in the early Iron Age. However, its defence system was apparently abandoned at the end of C8, perhaps in the context of the Assyrian conquests in the region. During the Persian period (C6–4) an unwalled settlement occupied the site. Hellenistic remains dating to C2 and C1 include a small square watchtower.

Ben-Tor (*NEAEHL* 3: 805–11).

Yorgan Tepe see Nuzi.

Yurza Late Bronze Age Canaanite city-state subject to Egypt, attested in the mid C14 Amarna archive (see glossary) and in Egyptian New Kingdom topographical lists. The pharaoh Tuthmosis III refers to it as the southernmost city to have rebelled against Egypt during his reign (1479–1425). Scholars now generally accept B. Mazar's identification of it with the site of Tell Jemmeh (q.v.), 10 km south of Gaza. Two of the Amarna letters are written to the pharaoh Akhenaten by Yurza's ruler Pu-Baʿlu, who assures the pharaoh that he is faithfully fulfilling his role as guardian of the city on his overlord's behalf (**EA* 314 and 315). Yurza-Tell Jemmeh has also been equated with the city called 'Arsa (Arza) near the brook of Egypt' in the texts of the Assyrian king Esarhaddon (680–669). The city (if it is Tell Jemmeh) was refortified and refurbished by Esarhaddon, doubtless to provide his troops with a military base.

Van Beek (*OEANE* 3: 213–14, s.v. *Jemmeh, Tell*).

Z

Zabala(m) Early Bronze Age city in southern Mesopotamia, belonging to the Sumerian city-state of Umma. It was apparently destroyed during the reign of the Akkadian king Rimush (2278–2270), who reports that he fought a battle with Zabala and the nearby city of Adab, killing 15,718 of the enemy's troops and taking 14,576 of them prisoner, including the cities' governors; he then demolished the walls of both cities (**DaK* 200–1, **RIME* 2: 41–2). But Zabala (like Adab) was subsequently rebuilt. Temples dedicated to its tutelary deity, Ishtar, were built or rebuilt by a number of rulers, including Naram-Sin (2254–2218) (George, 1993: 115, no. 664), his successor Shar-kali-sharri (**RIME* 2: 192) and, in the Old Babylonian period, Hammurabi (George, 1993: 160, no. 1245). The goddess Ishtar of Zabalam was also worshipped in other cities, i.e. in the temples built for her in Nineveh and Babylon by Naram-Sin (**DaK* 86, **RIME* 2: 138–40).

Zabban (Zanban, Zamban) Iron Age country on the Assyro-Babylonian border, in the region of the upper Diyala r. It was one of the lands which Ashurnasirpal II (883–859) incorporated into the northeastern frontier territory of Assyria (**RIMA* 2: 309). Ashurnasirpal's son and successor Shalmaneser III offered sacrifices in the city to its god, Adad, shortly after setting out in 851 on the first of his two Babylonian campaigns (**RIMA* 3: 30). Zabban joined a widespread revolt against Shalmaneser, initiated by the king's son Ashur-da'in-apla. The rebellion continued into the early regnal years of Shalmaneser's son and successor Shamshi-Adad V before it was finally crushed (**RIMA* 3: 183). Note that lexical tradition equates Zabban with earlier Simurrum (q.v.) (Frayne, 1997a).

Zabshali Elamite country located in western Iran within the region of the kingdom of Shimashki. Attested in late M3 and early M2 Mesopotamian texts, it was one of the most important lands making up this kingdom. Shu-Sin (2037–2029), fourth king of the Ur III dynasty, conducted campaigns against it, capturing its ruler, Indasu (e.g. **DaK* 348–50). Ibbi-Sin (2028–2004), fifth and last king of the dynasty, married his daughter to an unnamed ruler of the land. Zabshali appears in an early M2 context in a hymn to Ishbi-Erra (2017–1985), founder of the Isin dynasty, as a land bordering upon the kingdom ruled by the Shimashki-Elamite king Kindattu.

*Edzard (1959–60: 8–11, nos 2–4).

Zadidanu Iron Age city on the middle Euphrates r. The Assyrian king Tukulti-Ninurta II encamped his forces between the city and Sabiritu, an island-city in the Euphrates, during the course of his last recorded campaign (885) which took him through the middle Tigris and Euphrates regions (**RIMA* 2: 174).

Zafit, Tel (*Safi, Tell es-*) (map 8) Settlement-mound located in western Palestine in the border region between the Shephelah and Iron Age Philistia, with evidence of continuous occupation extending probably from the end of the Chalcolithic or beginning of the Early Bronze Age to the present day. The site was excavated by F. J. Bliss and R. A. S. Macalister under the sponsorship of the Palestine Exploration Fund for two seasons in 1899, with renewed excavations being undertaken from 1997 onwards by A. Maeir of Bar-Ilan University. The tell's Iron Age I and II levels appear to represent its most flourishing period. They followed upon a Late Bronze Age Canaanite city, which was destroyed c. 1200. The relatively large Iron Age city, covering up to 40 ha, reflects many aspects of Philistine culture. This has prompted an identification with the city of Gath, one of the members of the Philistine Pentapolis (see glossary). It has been suggested that the archaeologically attested destruction of Tel Zafit in late C9 or early C8 may have been due to Hazael, king of Aram-Damascus, whose attack upon and capture of Gath is recorded in 2 Kings 12:17.

The name es-Safi is that of an Arab village which first occupied the site in the mediaeval period.

Stern (*NEAEHL* 4: 1522–4), Maeir and Ehrlich (2001).

Zahara Small highland country in the Zagros mountain region, southwestern Iran, adjacent to or near the frontiers of Elam and Parahshum (Marhashi). It is attested only in texts of the (Early Bronze Age) Akkadian period, beginning with the reign of the Akkadian king Rimush (2278–2270). An anti-Akkadian military alliance which it formed with Elam and Parahshum prompted a campaign by Rimush into the highland regions of western Iran. Here, Rimush claims to have defeated Abalgamash, king of Parahshum, before attacking and conquering the combined forces of Zahara and Elam which confronted him within Parahshum's territory. He allegedly killed 16,212 of the enemy troops, and captured a further 4,216, including Sargapi (Sargabi), ruler of Zahara and leader of the Zaharan forces, and the Elamite king Emahsini (**DaK* 206–11, **RIME* 2: 52–3). Sargapi apparently escaped the battle itself, for Rimush reports that he was captured 'between Awan and Susa by the river Qablitum'. (D. T. Potts, 1999: 106, suggests that the river is to be identified with the Saimarreh, a northern tributary of the Karun, implying a location in the Pusht-i Kuh.) Rimush followed up his victory by establishing his sovereignty over Elam, but Zahara and Parahshum seem to have retained their independence. Zahara and Elam subsequently formed a coalition against the last Akkadian king, Shar-kali-sharri (2217–2193), and fought a battle against him near Akshak in northern Akkad. Shar-kali-sharri claims to have won the battle (**DaK* 54).

T. Potts (1994: 18, 100–2, 118).

Zallara One of the small Late Bronze Age countries in southern Anatolia which the early Hittite king Labarna (C17) conquered and assigned to the governorship of his sons (**Chav.* 230). It probably lay in or near the territory of Classical Lycaonia.

Zallu (Azallu) Iron Age land located around the upper reaches of the Balih r. in northwestern Mesopotamia close to Harran and Huzirina, between the Aramaean states of Bit-Bahiani to the east and Bit-Adini to the west. At least part of the land was occupied by members of the Aramaean clan of Bit-Yahiri (q.v.). In 882, a Zallean ruler belonging to Bit-Yahiri gave tribute to the Assyrian king Ashurnasirpal II (**RIMA* 2:

203). While crossing the region from east to west during his ninth campaign (between 875 and 867), Ashurnasirpal received tribute from Adda-'imme, the Zallean ruler, in (A)zallu (**RIMA* 2: 216). In 866 he again crossed the region, passing through the land of Qipanu to reach Huzirina, where the Zallean ruler Itti was among those who paid tribute (**RIMA* 2: 219). The land was later incorporated into the Province of the Commander-in-Chief (see glossary), most likely by Shalmaneser III (858–824) in his provincial reorganization. 'Zallu and Balihu' were among the places said to be under the governorship of the commander-in-chief Belu-lu-balat, according to his official titulary (**RIMA* 3: 178).

(H. D. Baker)
Radner (2006: 298).

Zalmaqum (map 10) Middle Bronze Age country in northern Mesopotamia. It was apparently divided into a number of petty kingdoms whose rulers sometimes collaborated on military enterprises (see e.g. **LKM* 189, no. 26.24). The Old Assyrian king Shamshi-Adad I conducted a major campaign in the country, probably in the summer and early autumn of 1778. Cities in or near Zalmaqum which became involved in this campaign (as indicated by letters from the Mari archive) included Aparha, Hamsha, Hanzat, Harran, Heshshum, Mammagira, Shatupanazim, Shuda, and Til-Abnim. After the fall of the Old Assyrian kingdom, the rulers of Zalmaqum engaged in diplomatic communications with Zimri-Lim, who in 1774 occupied the city of Mari after the flight from the city of the former Assyrian viceroy Yasmah-Addu. Zalmaqum's kings promised military support to Zimri-Lim, assuring him that they had not provided troops to Babylon (**LAPO* 16: 407, no. 260 = **LKM* 494, no. 14.76).

RGTC 3: 258–9, *LKM* 95–7, *Mesop.* 174, 180–3.

Zalpa (Zalpuwa) One of five known kingdoms which collectively exercised sway over a large part of eastern Anatolia during the Middle Bronze Age, in the Assyrian Colony period (C20–18). Its centre was probably located on or near the mouth of the Kızıl Irmak (Classical Halys) r. on the Black Sea coast. Under its king Uhna, Zalpa attacked, conquered, and plundered the city of Nesa/Kanesh, carrying off the statue of its chief god (**Chav.* 217). Nesa/Kanesh was located at mod. Kültepe just south of the Kızıl Irmak (see **Kanesh**). Subsequently, after the installation of a new dynasty in Nesa, the second king of this dynasty, Anitta, carried out a retaliatory attack on Zalpa. He retrieved the statue of Nesa's god, captured Zalpa's king, Huzziya, and brought him to Nesa in chains.

Zalpa and Kanesh also figure in a legend preserved in a later Hittite text (**CS* I: 181–2). The legend relates that a queen of Kanesh gave birth to thirty sons, all at once, and placed them in baskets which she set afloat on a river. The baskets travelled downstream until they reached the sea in the land of Zalpuwa. Here the children grew to adulthood. They returned to Kanesh, but were not recognized by their mother, who arranged for their marriage to her thirty daughters. The text becomes very fragmentary at this point. But after the fairytale nature of its first twenty lines, it takes on a more historical character as it relates various conflicts in which the people of Zalpa subsequently engaged.

The C17 Hittite king Hattusili I records his conquest of a city called Zalpa (variants Zalbar, Zalwar) in the first of six campaigns recorded in his Annals (**Chav.* 219). But it is now generally believed that the Zalpa in question was a different city from that which lay on the southern coast of the Black Sea. The Zalpa of the Annals has been located at Tilmen Höyük in northwestern Syria. However, the Black Sea Zalpa is almost certainly the city which became involved in a rebellion against Hattusili later in his reign. Hattusili had appointed his son Hakkarpili as governor of the city, and it is likely that the rebellion was in support of a bid by Hakkarpili for his father's throne. No record survives of the outcome of the rebellion. But Hattusili was presumably successful in crushing it. Thereafter Zalpa ceases to appear in historical contexts, though it continues to figure in a number of Hittite cultic contexts.

**RGTC* 6: 490–2.

Zalpah Middle and Late Bronze Age city located on the Balih r. in northwestern Mesopotamia. It lay on a major trade route connecting Assyria with its merchant colonies in northern Syria and eastern Anatolia during the Assyrian Colony period (C20–18). It may have been linked with the city of Tuttul, which lay to the south at the confluence of the Balih and Euphrates rivers.

RGTC 3: 259–60, *LKM* 628 (refs).

Zamahu City in northern Mesopotamia on the site of Tell er-Rimah (see ***Rimah, Tell er-***). Zamahu was the Neo-Assyrian name of the city. (The earlier settlement on the site has been identified with either Karana or Qattara, cities attested in M2 texts.) Finds from the site include a stele of Neo-Assyrian date which bears a dedicatory inscription to the god Adad 'who dwells in the city Zamahu' (**RIMA* 3: 211). According to this stele, Zamahu belonged to the Assyrian province of Rasappa, which King Adad-nirari III (810–783) assigned to the governorship of a certain Nergal-erish (Palil-erish). The latter undertook the task of repopulating the region on behalf of the king.

Dalley (*NEAEHL* 4: 429).

Zamba Iron Age country located in northern Mesopotamia to the northwest of the Kashiyari range (mod. Tur ʿAbdin). Its cities were captured and burnt by the Assyrian king Ashurnasirpal II during his campaign in the region in 866 (**RIMA* 2: 220).

Zamru Iron Age royal city in the land of Zamua, which was located in the borderlands between northeastern Mesopotamia and northwestern Iran. In 880, the withholding of tribute from Assyria by Zamru's ruler, Ameka, and another Zamuan king, Arashtua, prompted the third campaign against Zamua undertaken by the Assyrian king Ashurnasirpal II. Zamru, along with Ameka's other cities (including Arasidku, Ammaru, Parsindu, Iritu, and Suritu) were plundered and destroyed by the Assyrian army (**RIMA* 2: 205–7). Ameka himself escaped and fled to various hiding places in the mountains, defying all attempts by the pursuing Assyrians to capture him, though they massacred many of his troops.

Zamua (Mazamua) (map 13) Country attested in M1 Neo-Assyrian texts (also called Lullumu in Sargon II's reign – **ARAB* II: 74), located in the borderlands between northeastern Mesopotamia and northwestern Iran. It extended north of the headwaters of the Diyala r., from the western slopes of the Zagros mountains to the Shahrizor plain around the mod. Iraqi city of Sulaymaniyeh. Zamua comprised a number of geopolitical regions, each containing a number of cities which were each ruled by a local king.

By the beginning of C9, the entire land had come under Assyrian control, probably during the reign of Adad-nirari II (911–891), who reports its conquest (**RIMA* 2: 148). But in the reign of Adad-nirari's grandson, Ashurnasirpal II, the land rebelled several times against Assyria, twice in 881 (**RIMA* 2: 203–5) and again in 880 (**RIMA* 2: 205–8). On at least the first occasion, the leader of the rebellion was a man called Nur-Adad, ruler of Dagara, one of the petty kingdoms within Zamua. All three rebellions prompted Assyrian campaigns under Ashurnasirpal and ruthless retaliation against the rebels. On the second occasion, Ashurnasirpal marched deep into Zamuan territory, completing his campaign with the conquest and destruction of Nur-Adad's cities and garrisons. But it needed a third campaign before Zamua was brought completely to heel. On this occasion, Ashurnasirpal records further extensive conquests in the land before finally receiving the submission of all its kings in the city of Tukulti-Ashur-asbat (called Arrakdu by the Lullumu people) (**RIMA* 2: 207–8).

Zamua was attacked again, in 843, by Ashurnasirpal's son and successor Shalmaneser III during his campaign in the upper Diyala and Zagros regions (**RIMA* 3: 40). At this time it became a province of the Assyrian empire (Radner, *RlA* 11: 52). In 714 the Assyrian king Sargon II passed through the region on his eighth campaign (**ARAB* II: 74), which was directed primarily against the kingdom of Urartu. Several references to Mazamua appear in letters to Sargon from his officials in the region (e.g. **SAA* V: 164,

Figure 140 Zagros mountains.

no. 227). Troops from Mazamua were deployed in Babylonia during Ashurbanipal's struggle against his rebellious brother Shamash-shum-ukin (c. 652–648).

Liverani (1992: 45–50), Greco (2003: 72–5).

Zanziuna Iron Age city in eastern Anatolia, belonging (probably) to the kingdom of Urartu. It voluntarily surrendered to the Assyrian king Shalmaneser III during his campaign in Urartian territory in his third regnal year, 856, and was spared destruction on payment of a tribute of horses, cattle, and sheep (**RIMA* 3: 21).

Zapparia (Sapparia) Iron Age fortified city of the land of Musasir, northeastern Mesopotamia, on the edge of the Zagros mountains. It was captured along with forty-six other cities of Musasir by Dayyan-Ashur, commander-in-chief of the Assyrian king Shalmaneser III, during his campaign in the region in 828 (**RIMA* 3: 70).

Zaqqu City in northeastern Mesopotamia, attested in the texts of the Assyrian king Adad-nirari II (911–891), who established Assyrian control over it and made it a fortified frontier city of the Assyrian kingdom (**RIMA* 2: 149).

Zaralulu (Uzarlulu, *Tell al-Dhibai*) M2 Babylonian city identified with Tell al-Dhibai, a site which now lies within the mod. city of Baghdad, close to Tell Harmal. Yadkur-El, attested as one of its kings, is perhaps to be identified with Yazkur-El, referred to in the Assyrian King List as the grandfather of Shamshi-Adad I (1796–1775). The city is referred to in a C17 Babylonian text as part of the land of Eshnunna. Excavated remains include domestic dwellings, a temple, an administrative building, and c. 600 cuneiform tablets. Among the latter was a mathematical text which has been identified as a proof of the theorem of the C6 Greek philosopher Pythagoras, 2,000 years before his own lifetime.

Wu Yuhong (1994a: 62–3, 66), *Mesop.* 444.

Zarangians see **Ariaspae** and **Drangiana**.

Zaranu (Aramaic **Azran**) Iron Age city of the Aramaean kingdom Bit-Bahiani in the upper Habur valley, northern Mesopotamia. (Zaranu is the Assyrian form of the name.) In mid C9 it was one of the cities governed by Hadd-yitʿi (Adad-itʾi), ruler of Guzana (Gozan, Tell Halaf), the capital of Bit-Bahiani. This information is provided by an Aramaic–Assyrian bilingual inscription carved on a statue which Hadd-yitʿi erected in Sikkan (Assyrian Sikanu, mod. Tell Feheriye) (**RIMA* 2: 389–91), another of the cities of Bit-Bahiani which he governed. At this time, Bit-Bahiani was subject to the Assyrian king Ashurnasirpal II (883–859), whose control over it was, however, rather loose.

Zarethan Biblically attested city in the Jordan valley. It belonged to one of the administrative districts of Israel during Solomon's reign (1 Kings 4:12). An identification has been proposed with several sites in the Jordan valley. Tell es-Saʿidiyeh (q.v.) is the most favoured of these.

McClellan (*HCBD* 1236).

Zaruar Middle(?) and Late Bronze Age city, located near the city of Urshu and attested in the Hittite *Siege of Urshu* text (see **Urshu**). Urshu lay in eastern Anatolia, west of the Euphrates r. and north of the city of Carchemish. In the *Siege* text, generally assigned to the reign of the C17 Hittite king Hattusili I, Zaruar appears as an ally of Urshu against the Hittites. The reading of the city's name is not altogether certain, and it has sometimes been read as Aruar; but the form Zaruar is now generally preferred. The Middle Bronze Age city Zaruar attested in the C18 Mari archives may be the same as the Zaruar of this text.

RGTC 6: 41, s.v. Aruar, Beckman (1995: *26–7, 30).

Zaruna (*Akkadian* **Zarunti**) Late Bronze Age city in northern Syria not far from Alalah. It was destroyed by the Hittite king Hattusili I (1650–1620) early in his second Syrian campaign, during his march eastward to the Euphrates (**Chav*. 220).

Zazabuha Iron Age city in northern Mesopotamia in the eastern part of the Kashiyari mountain range (mod. Tur ʿAbdin), between Matiatu and Irsia. The Assyrian king Ashurnasirpal II encamped his troops for the night in the city and received tribute there from one of the regions called Habhu in Assyrian texts (see **Habhu (4)**), as he progressed through the region in his fifth regnal year (879) (**RIMA* 2: 209).

Radner (2006: 287–8).

Zeleia (map 5) M2–1 city in northwestern Anatolia located in the Troad on the Aesepus r. (mod. Gönen Çayi) at the edge of the foothills of Mt Ida. Homer's Trojan Catalogue lists Zeleia among the allies who fought alongside Troy in the Trojan War (*Iliad* 2.824–7).

Zeror, Tel (map 8) 6 ha settlement mound located on the Via Maris (q.v.) in the northern Sharon plain, coastal Palestine. Its history of occupation extends from the Middle Bronze Age to the early Roman period, with periods of abandonment in between. The site was excavated by K. Ohata for the Japanese Society for Near Eastern Research from 1964 to 1966 and in 1974. Middle Bronze Age Zeror was enclosed within walls of mudbrick on stone foundations. The city reached the peak of its development at the beginning of the Middle Bronze IIA phase (C20–19). Its site was subsequently deserted, and remained unoccupied through the first part of the Late Bronze Age. When resettlement occurred, perhaps under Egyptian influence, the new city which developed on the site was left unwalled. A large public building on the mound's southern spur is the chief remaining architectural feature from this period. Evidence of a copper-smelting industry and a large proportion of Cypriot ceramic ware in the pottery assemblage suggest close links with Cyprus, almost certainly the source of the copper used in the local industry. M. Kochavi believes that a community of coppersmiths of Cypriot origin had installed themselves in the city at this time. Other material remains of Late Bronze Age Zeror include a number of burials of C14–13 date. The graves, intended for single interments, were cut into the soil and sometimes lined with stones. The site was again abandoned at the end of the Late Bronze Age. Kochavi conjures up a picture of its inhabitants fleeing the unwalled city and seeking refuge in neighbouring fortified settlements along the Via Maris.

There are only meagre remains of the first Iron Age settlement at Tel Zeror, dated to

C12. Information about it comes mainly from refuse pits. The settlement's destruction by fire was due possibly to the Philistines. In C11, a small fort with casemate walls was built on the mound. Nine family graves in stone-lined pits date to this period. The wealth of the persons interred in these graves is indicated by the funerary goods, which included Philistine pottery, bronze bowls, and terracotta works of art (a lioness-shaped rhyton, the nude figurine of a goddess, etc.). In C10, warehouses containing large numbers of storage jars were built over the ruins of the earlier citadel. While the settlement's location on the Via Maris placed it in an excellent strategic position in terms of trading activities, it also exposed it to the ravages of military campaigns. Kochavi notes that it suffered a series of destructions in C9 and C8 during the campaigns of the Aramaeans and the Assyrians along the Via Maris. The end of its Iron Age phase has been associated with the Assyrian conquest of the Israelite kingdom in the second half of C8. Evidence of some reoccupation in later times is provided by pottery from the Persian period (C6–4) found in large pits, a farmhouse from the Hellenistic period, and a watchtower from the early Roman period.

Ohata (1966–1970), Kochavi (*NEAEHL* 4: 1524–6, *OEANE* 5: 389–90).

Zibia see ***Ziwiyeh***.

Zikirtu M1 sub-kingdom in the land of Mannaea, in mod. Iranian Kurdistan. In the last decades of C8 its ruler Mitatti, a Median prince, was one of the pro-Urartian Mannaean governors who rebelled against the Assyrian-backed Mannaean king Iranzu (c. 719). Close relations between Zikirtu and Urartu are indicated in several letters written to the Assyrian king Sargon II by his officials in the region (e.g. **SAA* V: 123, no. 164; 125, no. 169). Sargon responded with a campaign of devastation against Zikirtu and the other rebel lands and cities (**ARAB* II: 3). After the death of Iranzu, Mitatti again joined a rebellion against Assyrian overlordship, which overthrew Iranzu's son and successor Aza in favour of his pro-Urartian brother Ullusunu (c. 716). Once more Sargon responded with a retaliatory campaign against the rebels, forcing Mitatti to flee for his life and burning his chief city, Parda, and other cities in the region (**ARAB* II: 28). But in the following year, Mitatti again rallied the troops of Zikirtu who joined with an Urartian army, under the command of the Urartian king Rusa I, for a further confrontation with Sargon on Mt Uaush in the Mannaean land of Uishdish. Catching the enemy forces off guard, Sargon inflicted a resounding defeat on them. Rusa escaped the conflict, but Mitatti was apparently captured and killed (**ARAB* II: 78–83).

Ziklag Iron Age town in southwestern Palestine, on Judaea's southern border, attested in *OT* sources. According to 1 Samuel 27:1–7, at the time of King Saul the town belonged to the Philistines, who handed it over to David when he sought refuge with them from Saul; thenceforth it remained in the possession of the kings of Judah. Identifications have been suggested with several sites, including Tell el-Hesi (see ***Hesi, Tell el-***), Khirbet el-Meshash (see ***Masos, Tel***), Tel es-Seba' (see **Beersheba**), and Tell Khuweilifeh (see ***Halif, Tel***). However, the most favoured candidate is Tell esh-Shari'a (see ***Sera', Tel***) in the western Negev, an identification which has recently received fresh support from J. A. Blakely.

Negev and Gibson (2001: 553–4), Blakely (2007).

Zincirli Höyük (map 7) Capital of the small, predominantly Aramaean state of Sam'al in southern Anatolia, located on the east slope of the Amanus range, west of mod. Gaziantep. The site, whose foundation by the Aramaeans dates to late C10, was excavated by C. Humann, F. von Luschan, and R. Koldewey between 1888 and 1902. The settlement was roughly circular in shape, and was fortified by a double wall surmounted by towers. There were three gates in the walls, the southernmost of which gave access to the citadel. The citadel itself was surrounded by a wall with a single gate, upon whose orthostats guardian bulls and lions were carved. Inside was yet another protective wall and gate. This provided further protection for the citadel's buildings, which included two palaces of the *bit hilani* type (see glossary). Sculptural features of the site indicate a mingling of Luwian and Aramaean cultural traditions, and strong Assyrian influence becomes evident in C8. The city's predominantly Aramaean character is indicated by its many Aramaic inscriptions – about half of all the known inscriptions in this language. But Sam'al's epigraphic tradition includes Phoenician and Luwian elements as well. A Phoenician presence is indicated by a stele with an inscription in a Phoenician–Aramaic script (there are also remnants of a Luwian hieroglyphic script), dating to the second half of C9.

Some time during C7, the acropolis of Zincirli was destroyed. No precise date can be assigned to the destruction, but Lipiński (2000: 246–7) suggests that it may have been a consequence of the Assyrian king Esarhaddon's unsuccessful campaign against Mugallu of Melid in 675, and of the latter's expansionist policy in the region.

Sam'al's royal necropolis was probably located at mod. Gerçin, 7 km northeast of Zincirli.

von Luschan *et al.* (1893–1943), Lipiński (2000: 233–47), Lemaire (2001).

Zippalanda Late Bronze Age city and major Hittite cult-centre in north-central Anatolia, dedicated primarily to the worship of the storm god, and possibly of Hattic origin. A number of important religious festivals were celebrated in Zippalanda, including the spring AN.TAH.SUM ('crocus') and *purulli* ('of the earth') festivals, and the autumn(?) KI.LAM ('gatehouse') festival. Hittite texts indicate that Zippalanda contained a temple of the storm god, and a royal residence which provided lodgings for the king during his religious pilgrimages to the city. The city was an administrative as well as a religious centre of the Hittite kingdom. It was governed by a council of elders, perhaps theocratically based. In the Hittite Old Kingdom, a number of persons living in Zippalanda and other holy cities were granted exemption from various services which other subjects of Hatti were required to perform for their king. The exemptees included not only members of the priestly class, but also certain craftsmen and their families. It seems that the number of persons accorded these privileges was later substantially reduced.

Some scholars have suggested identifying Zippalanda with the site now called Alaca Höyük, which lay just to the north of the Hittite capital Hattusa. But Alaca is probably the holy city of Arinna. More plausibly, Zippalanda has been located to the north of Alişar not far from the mountain now called Kerkenes Dağ. R. Gorny has identified it with the site of Çadir Höyük, a 30 m high mound in the mod. province of Yozgat. Gorny is currently directing excavations at Çadir Höyük for the Oriental Institute, University of Chicago. He suggests that a complex of rooms discovered on the site in 2005 may be part of a temple (presumably the temple of the storm god).

The shattered vessels in this building are dated early in the period of the Hittite Old Kingdom (first half of C17). On the north slope of the mound, there is a monumental gate dating to the Hittite New Kingdom (C15–12), but continuing in use during the succeeding Iron Age. If Zippalanda's identification with Çadir Höyük is valid, the city clearly survived the fall of the Hittite empire in early C12.

In Hittite texts a Mt Daha, 'beloved of the storm god of Zippalanda', is attested as lying between Zippalanda and Ankuwa. It has been identified by some scholars with Kerkenes Dağ. Gorny, however, believes that Mt Daha is the mountain now called Çaltepecan, which lies close to Çadir Höyük. He reports that the walls of several large structures are visible on the surface of the mountain and could be associated with the Hittite period. He believes that a 40 m × 80 m enclosure just below the summit may represent the temple area, approached by a gated courtyard compound (a Hittite *hilammar*) to its east. 'These discoveries correspond closely to how the Hittite texts describe Zippalanda and nearby Mount Daha, where a mountain-top edifice served as counterpart to the storm god's city-temple during his stay on the mountain for the various Hittite festivals' (Gorny, in Yıldırım and Gates, 2007: 294).

**RGTC* 6: 506–9, Paley (2006).

Zippasna Late Bronze Age city in the Euphrates region, probably north of Carchemish and close to Hassuwa and Hahhum. It was one of the cities attacked by Hattusili I during his second Syrian campaign (mid C17), and destroyed by him in a night assault (**Chav*. 221).

Zippor, Tel (map 8) Small settlement-mound on the coastal plain of mod. Israel, with evidence of occupation extending from the Middle Bronze Age until the early Iron Age. The site was excavated by A. Biran and O. Negbi between 1963 and 1965 for the Israel Dept of Antiquities and Museums. Its most flourishing phase, called the Philistine period, occurred between mid C12 and mid C11. There was continuity from this period into the settlement's final phase, which ended with its abandonment in late C11 or early C10.

Biran (*NEAEHL* 4: 1526–7).

Zirtu see **Izirtu**.

Z(i)uquni Iron Age city and small kingdom located on the northern shore of Lake Van in eastern Anatolia, within the territories comprising the land of Urartu. The city was one of thirty-two captured in the course of an expedition launched against the Urartian region by the Assyrian king Ashur-bel-kala (**RIMA* 2: 91) in mid C11. Ziuquni has been identified with Late Bronze Age Zingun, one of eight lands belonging to the country of Uruatri (the earlier form of the name Urartu) conquered by the Assyrian king Shalmaneser I (1274–1245) (**RIMA* 1: 183; see also **Himme**). In the second quarter of C7, the Urartian king Rusa II founded a city dedicated to Urartu's chief deity, Haldi, on the site now known as Kef Kalesi (see ***Adilcevaz***) in the land of Ziuquni.

Ziwiyeh (**Izbia, Izzibia, Zibia**) (map 13) M1 fortified settlement in Kurdistan, northwestern Iran, 40 km east of Saqqez, located on or near the northern frontier of

Media or the frontier of the land of Mannaea. The site was first surveyed in 1964, and excavations were subsequently carried out by Iranian archaeologists in 1976 and 1994. In the course of these, a large fortified building approached by a rock-cut staircase was revealed. It has been dated to C7. Prior to the official investigations of the site, there were reports, in the 1940s, of the discovery there of a royal tomb with a bronze sarcophagus, which contained a range of precious gifts including gold and ivory plaques, fibulae, and gold and silver swords. (The reports were followed by publications, in 1950 and 1951, by A. Godard of the 'treasure' allegedly found at Ziwiye.) Depicted on the sarcophagus were tribute-bearers wearing peaked hats. Many artefacts subsequently appearing on the antiquities market allegedly came from the tomb. If this was in fact their provenance, then the stylized animal figures which decorated a number of them (lions, stags, ibises etc.) may indicate that the tomb owner was a Scythian or Median prince. But there is no clear proof of their origin, and there is also a suspicion that some of them may be forgeries. The official excavations produced no evidence that might have helped authenticate the material.

In M1 Neo-Assyrian records, Izbia appears as an important stronghold of the Mannaean kingdom. It was one of the fortresses captured by the Assyrian king Sargon II in 716, during his campaign against the Urartian-appointed Mannaean king Ullusunu (**ARAB* II: 28). It subsequently fell to the Assyrian military commander Nabusarrusur in 660–659, in the course of his campaign against the Mannaean king Ahseri. The Assyrian throne was at that time occupied by Ashurbanipal.

Muscarella (1977), Sulimirski (1985: 171–3).

Ziyaret Tepe (map 2) 32 ha settlement located in the upper Tigris region, to the north of the Kashiyari range (mod. Tur ʿAbdin) on the south bank of the Tigris, 60 km east of mod. Diyarbakır. It is probably to be identified with anc. Tushha(n) (q.v.). The settlement consists of a mound, with occupation levels extending from the Early Bronze Age to the Islamic period, and a lower town, settled only in the Iron Age (mid-late Assyrian period). The site is currently being excavated by T. Matney for the University of Akron. In the Early Bronze Age levels (on which the 2004 excavation season concentrated), grain storage pits and the foundations of a mudbrick wall, thought to be the encircling wall for the Early Bronze citadel, were uncovered. The lower town contained several late Assyrian 'official' buildings with large pebble-mosaic courtyards. One of the buildings, perhaps part of a temple complex dedicated to the goddess Ishtar of Nineveh, contained storage jars and twenty-seven cuneiform tablets and fragments dealing with grain receipt, storage, and redistribution. From the year eponyms which they bear, the tablets can be dated to 613 and 611, that is, at the time of (and even immediately after) the final collapse of the Assyrian empire. The lower town was defended by a fortification wall, probably of early Iron Age date.

Matney and Rainville (2006), Yıldırım and Gates (2007: 301–2).

Zizzilippa Late Bronze Age city in southeastern Anatolia or northern Syria, located probably in the Euphrates region north of Carchemish and relatively close to Lawazantiya and Hassuwa. These latter two cities along with Zizzilippa lay in the border zone between Hatti and Kizzuwadna (q.v.). The Hittite king Telipinu undertook an expedition against them in late C16 in his attempt to restore control over Hatti's lost territories (**Chav.* 231). Zizzilippa and Lawazantiya later became part of Kizzuwadna's territory. The former is probably to be identified with Zazlippa, one of the six towns in Kizzuwadna in which the Hittite king Arnuwanda I settled men from Ismerikka for surveillance purposes and to suppress local uprisings (see **Ismerikka**).

Zobah see Soba.

Zuhma see Suhma.

Zukula (Zigula) Middle Bronze Age Turukkean town in the western Zagros region, attested in the Shemshara archive. It was the home town of Kuwari, who was later installed as ruler of Shusharra (mod. Shemshara) by his overlord Pishenden, king of the land of Itabalhum.

*Eidem and Laessøe (2001: 105–6, 129–30).

Zumanti Late Bronze Age western Anatolian country lying in or near the Lukka Lands. It was one of the lands captured by the renegade Hittite vassal Madduwatta during his campaigns in western Anatolia (early C14) (**HDT* 158).

Zurghul see **Nina-Sirara**.

Zurubban Mesopotamian city attested in the Middle Bronze Age Mari archives, located in the middle Euphrates region on the west bank of the Euphrates, in the borderland between Mari and Terqa. It was one of the cities from which Kibri-Dagan, governor of Terqa, recruited troops for his army during the reign of Zimri-Lim, king of Mari (1774–1762), who was overlord of the region. Other cities from which Kibri-Dagan drew recruits were Hanna, Himaran, and Hishamta.

LKM 629 (refs).

Zurzukka see **Shuandahul**.

Appendix I

GENERAL CHRONOLOGY

(The dates for the Neolithic, Chalcolithic, Bronze, and Iron Ages are broad approximations, and vary from one region to another)

Neolithic Age	mid M9 – mid M5
Chalcolithic Age	mid M5 – late M4
Early Bronze Age	late M4 – c. 2000
Middle Bronze Age	c. 2000 – C17/16
Late Bronze Age	C17/16 – early C12
Iron Age	C12 – late C7
Neo–Babylonian period	late C7 – C6
Persian (Achaemenid) period	mid C6 – 330
Hellenistic period	330 – end of C2
Roman period	C1 BCE – mid C4 CE
Byzantine period	mid C4 CE – C7 CE
Arab period	C7 – C11 CE

Appendix II

THE MAJOR ROYAL DYNASTIES

(NB The dates indicated below are in most cases conjectural; see Introduction)

EARLY BRONZE AGE

Akkad

Sargon 2334–2279
Rimush 2278–2270
Manishtushu 2269–2255
Naram-Sin 2254–2218
Shar-kali-sharri 2217–2193

Ur III

Ur-Nammu 2112–2095
Shulgi 2094–2047
Amar-Sin 2046–2038
Shu-Sin 2037–2029
Ibbi-Sin 2028–2004

MIDDLE BRONZE AGE

Assyria

Puzur-Ashur I (c. 2000)
Shalim-ahum ?–?
Ilu-shumma ?–?
Erishum I 1974–1935
Ikunum 1934–1921
Sargon I 1920–1881
Puzur-Ashur II 1880–1873
Naram-Sin 1872–?

Erishum II ?-1807

Shamshi-Adad I 1796–1775
Ishme-Dagan 1775–1735

Babylon

Sumu-Abum 1894–1881
Sumu-la-El 1880–1845
Sabium 1844–1831
Apil-Sin 1830–1813
Sin-muballit 1812–1793
Hammurabi 1792–1750
Samsu-iluna 1749–1712
Abi-eshuh 1711–1684
Ammi-ditana 1683–1647
Ammi-saduqa 1646–1626
Samsu-ditana 1625–1595

Isin (First Dynasty)

Ishbi-Erra 2017–1985
Shu-ilishu 1984–1975
Iddin-Dagan 1974–1954
Ishme-Dagan 1953–1935
Lipit-Ishtar 1934–1924
Ur-Ninurta 1923–1896
Bur-Sin 1895–1874
Lipit-Enlil 1873–1869
Erra-imitti 1868–1861
Enlil-bani 1860–1837
Zambiya 1836–?
Iter-pisha ?–?
Ur-Dukuga ?–1828
Sin-magir 1827–1817
Damiq-ilishu 1816–1794

Larsa

Naplanum 2025–2005
Yamsium 2004–1977
Samium 1976–1942
Zabaya 1941–1933
Gungunum 1932–1906
Abi-sare 1905–1895

Sumu-El 1894–1866
Nur-Adad 1865–1850
Sin-iddinam 1849–1843
Sim-eribam 1842–1841
Sin-iqisham 1840–1836
Silli-Adad 1835
Warad-Sin 1834–1823

Rim-Sin 1822–1763

Rim-Sin II 1741–1736

Mari

Yahdun-Lim 1810–1794
Sumu-Yamam 1793–1792
Yasmah-Addu (from Assyrian royal line) 1782–1775
Zimri-Lim 1774–1762

LATE BRONZE AGE

Assyria

Eriba-Adad I 1392–1366
Ashur-uballit 1365–1330
Enlil-nirari 1329–1320
Arik-den-ili 1319–1308
Adad-nirari I 1307–1275
Shalmaneser I 1274–1245
Tukulti-Ninurta I 1244–1208
Ashur-nadin-apli 1207–1204
Ashur-nirari III 1203–1198
Enlil-kudurri-usur 1197–1193
Ninurta-apil-Ekur 1192–1180
Ashur-dan I 1179–1134
(*with continuity into Iron Age*)

Babylonia (Kassite dynasty)

Agum II c. 1570
Burna-Buriash I c. 1530
six kings late C16–early C14
Kadashman-Enlil I 1374–1360
Burna-Buriash II 1359–1333
Kara-hardash 1333
Nazi-Bugash 1333
Kurigalzu II 1332–1308
Nazi-Maruttash 1307–1282
Kadashman-Turgu 1281–1264
Kadashman-Enlil II 1263–1255
Kudur-Enlil 1254–1246
Shagarakti-Shuriash 1245–1233
Kashtiliash IV 1232–1225
Enlil-nadin-shumi 1224
Kadashman-Harbe II 1223
Adad-shuma-iddina 1222–1217
Adad-shuma-usur 1216–1187
Meli-shipak 1186–1172
Marduk-apla-iddina 1171–1159
Zababa-shuma-iddina 1158
Enlil-nadin-ahi 1157–1155

Hatti

Labarna ?–1650
Hattusili I 1650–1620
Mursili I 1620–1590
Hantili I 1590–1560
Zidanta I
Ammuna } 1560–1525
Huzziya I
Telipinu 1525–1500
Alluwamna
Tahurwaili
Hantili II } 1500–1400
Zidanta II
Huzziya II
Muwattalli I
Tudhaliya I/II (*start of New Kingdom*)[1]
Arnuwanda I
Hattusili II? } 1400–1350
Tudhaliya III
Suppiluliuma I 1350–1322
Arnuwanda II 1322–1321
Mursili II 1321–1295
Muwattalli II 1295–1272
Urhi-Teshub (Mursili III) 1272–1267
Hattusili III 1267–1237
Tudhaliya IV 1237–1209
Arnuwanda III 1209–1207
Suppiluliuma II 1207–?

Mitanni/Hanigalbat

Kirta C16

Shuttarna I C16
Parrattarna I C15
Parsatatar C15
Saushtatar C15
Artatama I C14
Shuttarna C14
Artashumara C14
Tushratta C14
Artatama II C14
Shuttarna III C14
Shattiwaza C14 (ruler of Hanigalbat)
Shattuara I C13
Wasashatta C13
Shattuara II C13

IRON AGE

Assyria

Ninurta-tukulti-Ashur 1133
Mutakkil-Nusku 1133
Ashur-resh-ishi I 1132–1115
Tiglath-pileser I 1114–1076
Ashared-apil-Ekur 1075–1074
Ashur-bel-kala 1073–1056
Eriba-Adad II 1055–1054
Shamshi-Adad IV 1053–1050
Ashurnasirpal I 1049–1031
Shalmaneser II 1031–1020
Ashur-nirari IV 1019–1014
Ashur-rabi II 1013–973
Ashur-resh-ishi II 972–968
Tiglath-pileser II 967–935
Ashur-dan II 934–912
(*start of Neo-Assyrian empire*)
Adad-nirari II 911–891
Tukulti-Ninurta II 890–884
Ashurnasirpal II 883–859
Shalmaneser III 858–824
Shamshi-Adad V 823–811
Adad-nirari III 810–783
Shalmaneser IV 782–773
Ashur-dan III 772–755
Ashur-nirari V 754–746
Tiglath-pileser III 745–727
Shalmaneser V 726–722
Sargon II 721–705
Sennacherib 704–681
Esarhaddon 680–669
Ashurbanipal 668–630/27
Ashur-etil-ilani 630/27–625
Sin-shum-lishir 626–625
Sin-sharra-ishkun 624–612
Ashur-uballit II 612–610

Babylonia

Second Dynasty of Isin
(see under **Babylonia**) 1154–1026
Eleven kings, the most notable of whom were:
Nebuchadnezzar I 1126–1105
Marduk-nadin-ahhe 1100–1083

Second Sealand Dynasty
(see under **Sealand**)
Simbar-shipak 1026–1009
Ea-mukin-zeri 1009
Kashu-nadin-ahi 1008–1006

Bazi Dynasty
Eulmash-shakin-shumi 1005–989
Ninurta-kudurri-usur I 988–986
Shirikti-Shuqamuna 986

Mar-biti-apla-usur
(*Elamite king*) 985–980

'Dynasty of E' 979–732
Many kings, the most notable of whom were:
Nabu-mukin-apli 979–944
Nabu-apla-iddina 888–855
Eriba-Marduk 769–761
Nabu-nasir (Nabonassar) 747–734

Elam (Neo-Elamite kingdom)
Humban-tahra I ?–?

Humban-nimena II ?–743
Humban-nikash I 743–717
Shutruk-Nahhunte II 716–699
Hallushu 699–693

Kutir-Nahhunte II 693
Humban-nimena III 692–689
Humban-haltash I 688–681
Humban-haltash II 680–675
Urtaku 674–664
Te-Umman 664–653
Humban-nikash II 652–649?
Inda-bigash 649–648
Humban-haltash III 648–642?
? – 539

Urartu

(see Appendix III)
Sarduri I 832–825
Ishpuini 824–806
Minua 805–788 (independent reign)
Argishti I 787–766
Sarduri II 765–733
Rusa I 732–714
Argishti II 713–679
Rusa II 678–654
Sarduri III (includes 640)
later Urartian kings?[2]

NEO-BABYLONIAN AND PERSIAN (ACHAEMENID) PERIODS

Babylonia

Nabopolassar 626–605
Nebuchadnezzar II 604–562
Amel-Marduk 562–560
Neriglissar 560–556
Labashi-Marduk 556
Nabonidus 556–539

Persia

Teispes c. 650–620
Cyrus I c. 620–590
Cambyses I c. 590–559
Cyrus II 559–530
Cambyses II 530–522
Bardiya 522
Darius I 522–486
Xerxes I 486–465
Artaxerxes I 465–424
Xerxes II 424
Darius II 424–404
Artaxerxes II (Arsaces) 404–359
Artaxerxes III (Ochus) 359–338
Artaxerxes IV (Arses) 338–336
Darius III 336–330

Notes

1. It is uncertain whether there were one or two early New Kingdom rulers of this name.
2. Another Urartian king called Rusa (son of Erimena) is also attested, but we do not known when he reigned. See Appendix III.

Appendix III

A NOTE ON URARTIAN CHRONOLOGY

(P. Zimansky)

While the history of the Kingdom of Van played out within a reasonably well-defined chronological frame, specific dates can only be assigned on the basis of a small number of synchronisms in Assyrian records. We cannot confidently give beginning or end dates to the reign of any Urartian ruler, and in some cases we are even uncertain of the sequence in which they ruled. The end of the kingdom is particularly obscure, with putative dates for its demise ranging over more than half a century.

Urartian royal documents regularly give the patronymic as well as the name of the king in whose name they were composed, and by linking names of fathers and sons it is possible to put together a chain of rulers spanning more than a century. This begins with Sarduri, son of Lutipri, whom Shalmaneser III (858–824) mentions in 830, and ends with Sarduri, son of Argishti, mentioned by Tiglath-pileser III in 735. What chronological information we have on these kings is summarized in the table below:

King	*Son of*	*Synchronisms*	*Notes*
Sarduri (I)	Lutipri	830	There is no evidence that Lutipri ruled as king.
Ishpuini	Sarduri	c. 818	
Minua	Ishpuini		There are many inscriptions in the name of Minua and Ishpuini together, suggesting a co-regency of some sort. Minua's son Inushpua is also mentioned in one of these, but there is no evidence he ever ruled
Argishti (I)	Minua	774	Argishti's Annals, carved on the Van citadel outside a royal tomb, recount eighteen annual campaigns. Some scholars have linked the Assyrian synchronism with one of his campaigns against Assyria
Sarduri (II)	Argishti	743, 735	

After Sarduri II, there is less certainty. Three different kings named Rusa left royal inscriptions, and the Assyrians do not give their patronymics, so in some cases it is unclear to which king the synchronism should be assigned. Until quite recently, the accepted sequence of 'later rulers' was:

King	*Son of*	*Synchronisms*	*Notes*
Rusa	Sarduri	numerous 719–714	Antagonist of Sargon II of Assyria in his eighth campaign
Argishti	Rusa	708	
Rusa	Argishti	673, perhaps 655	Numerous building projects suggest a long reign
Rusa	Erimena	perhaps 655	Erimena did not rule

No other Urartian king left inscriptions, although individuals whose names appear to be royal – Rusa, son of Rusa, and Sarduri, son of Sarduri – are mentioned on the legends of seal impressions on bullae and tablets discovered in archaeological context in sites founded by Rusa, son of Argishti. The final Assyrian synchronism is provided by the Annals of Ashurbanipal, which mentions a Sarduri c. 640. There is no solid evidence for the existence of a unified Urartian kingdom after this, although there is a reference to the kingdom of Ararat in the book of Jeremiah (51:27), ostensibly dated to 594.

Recently, it has been demonstrated that the 'traditional' scheme is almost certainly wrong, but there is no consensus on a new one. A newly discovered stele shows that Rusa, son of Erimena, created irrigation works for the city of Rusahinili Qilbanikai (Toprakkale), and we know that city was in existence in the time of Rusa, son of Argishti. Thus Rusa, son of Erimena, cannot come at the end of the sequence of Rusas, and it is possible that he may stand at the beginning. Art associated with him is closer in style to that of Sarduri II than Rusa, son of Argishti, and it is not ruled out that he is the Rusa against whom Sargon campaigned in his celebrated eighth campaign of 714. Moving him to late C8 would make it almost certain that Rusa, son of Argishti, was the Rusa mentioned by Ashurbanipal in 655, and the last effective ruler of Urartu.

Appendix IV

GREEK AND ROMAN AUTHORS

(Italicized names are the titles of works by these authors cited in this volume.)

Antoninus Liberalis C2 CE Greek mythographer, *Metamorphoses* ('Transformations').
Appian C2 CE Greek historian, *Mithridatic Wars*.
Arrian C2 CE Greek historian, *Anabasis*.
Berossus C3 Babylonian scholar (writing in Greek), *Babyloniaca*.
Cicero C1 Roman orator and philosopher, *Verrine Orations*, *De divinatione*.
Ctesias C4 Greek historian, *Persica*.
Curtius (Quintus Curtius Rufus) C1 CE Roman historian, *History of Alexander*.
Diodorus Siculus C1 Greek historian, *Bibliotheke* ('Library').
Ephorus C4 historian, *Historiae*.
Eusebius C3–4 CE Greek chronicler and biblical scholar, *Chronicles*.
Hecataeus C6–5 Greek geographer and mythographer; fragments of geographical and mythographical works survive.
Hellenica Oxyrhynchia Two sets of C2 papyrus fragments found at Oxyrhynchus in Egypt.
Herodotus C5 Greek historian, *Historiae*.
Hesiod C7 Greek poet, *Theogony* ('Genealogy').
Hierocles' *Synekdemos* C5(?) CE list of cities of the eastern Roman empire.
Homer C8 Greek epic poet, *Iliad* and *Odyssey*.
Homeric Hymns Greek poems (probably of C7 date) composed in the epic metre, by unknown authors, honouring various deities.
Josephus C1 CE Jewish historian, *Against Apion*, *Jewish Antiquities*.
Justin C2, C3, or C4 CE Roman historian, *Epitome* (i.e. abridged version) of the *Historiae Philippicae* ('Philippic Histories') of Pompeius Trogus.
Livy C1 BCE–CE Roman historian, *Ab urbe condita libri* ('Books from the Foundation of the City').
Menecrates of Xanthus C4 Greek historian, *Lykiaka* ('Lycian Matters').
Ovid C1 BCE–CE Roman poet, *Metamorphoses*.
Pausanias C2 CE Greek travel writer, *Description of Greece*.
Pliny the Elder C1 CE Roman encyclopaedist, *Naturalis Historia*.
Plutarch C1–2 CE Greek philosopher and biographer, *Lives of Alexander*, *Artaxerxes II*, *Cimon*, *Pericles*, *Solon*.
Polyaenus C2 CE Greek rhetorician, *Strategemata* ('Stratagems').
Polybius C2 Greek historian, *Historiae*.
Pomponius Mela C1 CE Roman geographer, *Chorographia* ('Description of Regions').

Pseudo-Scymnus Fragment of a C1 geographical composition (*periegesis*), associated with the name of the C2 Greek geographer Scymnus.
Ptolemy C2 CE Greek scholar (at Alexandria), author of many works on mathematics, astronomy, and geography.
Stephanus of Byzantium C6 CE Greek scholar, *Ethnica*.
Strabo C1 BCE–C1 CE Greek geographer, *Geographia*.
Tacitus C1 CE Roman historian, *Annals*.
Theopompus C4 Greek historian; fragments of historical works survive.
Thucydides C5 Greek historian, *History of the Peloponnesian War*.
Virgil C1 Roman poet, *Aeneid*.
Vitruvius C1 Roman architect and engineer, *De architectura*.
Xenophon C5–4 Greek soldier and writer on many topics (notably philosophy and history), *Agesilaus*, *Anabasis*, *Cyropaedia*, *Hellenica*.

GLOSSARY

Achaemenid The name commonly used by scholars to refer to the first Persian empire, founded by Cyrus II in 550 and destroyed by Alexander the Great in 330. Achaemenes was allegedly an ancestor of Cyrus and the founder of the Persian royal line. But the claim of a family link between Cyrus and Achaemenes, first made by Cyrus' third successor Darius I (522–486), was almost certainly false (see under **Persians**). It none the less became an established part of Persian dynastic tradition, as attested in the inscriptions of Darius' successors as well as in Classical sources.

acropolis Highest area of a city built on, or partly on, a mound or mountain site, and often fortified separately from the rest of the city. It was generally the area where the palace of the city's ruler was built.

Akkadian language Akkadian as a written language had fully evolved by the end of M3. Its main development no doubt took place during the period of the Akkadian empire (c. 2334–2193). Through much of M2, Akkadian was used widely throughout the western Asian world as an international language of diplomacy. Two main varieties of the language were recognized by its first decipherers – Assyrian and Babylonian. There were also a number of regional variants of the language, as illustrated, for example, by the Amarna letters.

Amarna archive A cache of clay tablets, now 382 in number, discovered in 1887 on the site of Tell el-Amarna (anc. Akhetaton) in Egypt, 300 km south of Cairo. Of the tablets 350 are letters, or copies of letters, exchanged by the pharaoh Amenhotep III (1390–1352) or his successor Amenhotep IV/Akhenaten (1352–1336) with foreign rulers or with the pharaoh's vassal subjects in Syria–Palestine. The remaining thirty-two tablets consist of syllabaries, lexical lists, and mythological texts. With the exception of two pieces of correspondence in Hittite, one in Assyrian, and one in Hurrian, the Amarna documents are written in Akkadian. The total number of tablets actually discovered is unknown, since some of them were secretly sold off to private buyers soon after their discovery. It is estimated that the surviving tablets represent about 75 per cent of the original number found.

aniconic Not bearing an image.

antediluvian Mod. term meaning 'before the flood', used in reference to the 'great flood' attested in *OT* (Genesis 7, 8) and Mesopotamian sources. The Sumerian King List divides the allocation of the seat of kingship among the southern Mesopotamian city-states into two main periods, antediluvian and postdiluvian, i.e. the periods before and after the flood.

apadana A Persian term for a columned building. Its use in Persian is perhaps largely confined to the most important of these buildings, notably the columned halls which formed part of the Achaemenid palace complexes. The best-known and best-preserved apadana is the great square Audience Hall at Persepolis.

aphaeresize Remove a letter or syllable from the beginning of a word.

apotropaic Having the power to ward off evil spirits or influences.

appanage Used in this book in reference to a sub-kingdom on whose throne a supreme king has installed a member of his family. Thus the C14 Hittite king Hattusili III appointed his nephew Kurunta to the throne of the Hittite sub-kingdom of Tarhuntassa in southern Anatolia.

ashlar masonry Walls built from precisely cut square or rectangular blocks of stone.

Assyrian Colony period Term commonly used of the period in early M2 (C20–18) when the Assyrians established a series of merchant-colonies between Ashur and central and northern Anatolia. The headquarters of the merchant-colony network was the city of Kanesh/Nesa, located just south of the Kızıl Irmak (Classical Halys) r.

Athenian Confederacy Alliance of Greek states formed in 477, under the leadership of Athens, following the abortive invasion of Greece by the Persian king Xerxes. The aim of the Confederacy was to provide a permanent defence for the Greek world against any further threat from Persia. The alliance is today commonly referred to as the Delian League, since its treasury was originally housed on the island of Delos in the Aegean. In 454 the treasury was transferred to Athens. The allied Greek states contributed ships to the Confederacy's forces, or, in by far the larger number of cases, made an annual cash payment into the Confederacy's treasury. From 454 onwards, the states paying cash contributions, and the amounts they paid, were recorded in what are called the Athenian Tribute Lists.

Avesta Corpus of M1 Iranian religious texts associated with the worship of the god Ahuramazda. According to tradition, the writings were revealed by the prophet Zoroaster (628–551). But only seventeen hymns, from the earliest part of the corpus, can be attributed to him.

Babylonian Chronicles Records of the Neo-Babylonian and Late Babylonian periods (extending from 747 to C2) contained in fifteen tablets or fragments, ed. and transl. in *ABC*, and in *Chav.* 407–26 (in the latter case, nos 1–7, the Neo-Babylonian Chronicles). Though the information they contain is often piecemeal and fragmentary, the chronicles are particularly important sources for the periods which they cover, since there are no royal annals of Babylonia to document these periods. They also contain useful supplementary information about Babylonia's neighbours, notably Assyria and Elam, and their relations and conflicts with Babylonia.

bit hilani The term used of public buildings, commonly found in Iron Age Syrian cities, in which a columned portico provides entry to a rectangular central room. (For further details, see Akkermans and Schwartz, 2003: 368–70.)

boustrophedon Term derived from Classical Greek, literally meaning 'as the ox turns (in ploughing)'. It is used with reference to inscriptions whose lines run alternately from right to left and left to right.

bulla (plur. **bullae**) Lump of clay stamped with seal impression and attached to a document, as a label, certificate of authentication, etc.

cartouche Oval frame containing the names and titles, in hieroglyphs, of Egyptian kings. The device was sometimes used by other peoples, including the Hittites.

caryatid Greek term used of columns sculpted in the form of draped women. The concept is of Near Eastern origin. In the Greek world, the earliest examples date to mid C6.

casemate wall Double fortification wall with partitioned sections in between.

cella The inner sanctuary of a temple, where the statue of the deity was generally located.

chogha see **tell**.

cuneiform A modern designation for the script used in the western Asian world, primarily on clay tablets but also on other writing surfaces, over a period of several millennia. Cuneiform symbols were most commonly produced by pressing the triangular ends of reeds, cut from the banks of the Mesopotamian and other rivers, into soft clay. The term, meaning 'wedge-shaped', is derived from the Latin word *cuneus*, 'wedge'.

Cyclopean Archaeological term used of fortifications and other structures made of very large, unworked, or only roughly worked, stones or boulders. The name was inspired by the giants of Greek mythological tradition called the Cyclopes, considered in myth to be the builders of the Greeks' prehistoric citadels.

Cyrus Cylinder Clay cylinder found in Babylon in 1879 and now housed in the British Museum. Its text, written in Akkadian, was commissioned by Cyrus II and composed by a Babylonian priest or royal scribe. It deals principally with Cyrus' conquest of Babylon. (For translations, see Brosius, 2000: 10–11, no. 12, *Chav.* 428–9, *PE* 70–2, no. 21.)

***daiva* inscription** (*XPh*) A trilingual inscription, in the Old Persian, Babylonian, and Elamite languages, inscribed on stone tablets and found in various copies in Persepolis and Pasargadae. It records the countries over which the Persian king Xerxes I (486–465) held sway, and pays homage to the god Ahuramazda. The name by which the inscription is commonly known comes from a reference which it makes to 'demons' (*daivas*) whose sanctuary was destroyed by Xerxes and replaced by a sanctuary to Ahuramazda. (For translations, see Brosius, 2000: 89, no. 191, *PE* 304–5, no. 88.)

depas amphikypellon Homeric term meaning 'double cup', used in reference to a vessel shaped as a cup at both top and bottom. The term has been adopted into archaeological terminology to designate this distinctive type of pottery.

dromos Entrance passageway to a burial chamber which has been built underground or cut into a hillside.

Early Dynastic period The name commonly used to designate the Sumerian period in Mesopotamian history, which began with the emergence of the Sumerian city-states c. 2900 and ended with the rise of the kingdom of Akkad c. 2334. Scholars generally divide the period into three main phases: ED I (c. 2900–2800), ED II (c. 2800–2600), and ED III (c. 2600–2334).

Eponym Lists and Eponym Chronicles (see Millard, 1994) The term 'eponym' refers to the Assyrian dating system whereby a year is named after the official who held the office of *līmu* (q.v.) in that year. This system, which relied on the keeping of lists of consecutive eponym officials (Eponym Lists), was in use in Assyria from C19 until the end of the Assyrian empire in late C7. However, the coverage of this period by surviving Eponym Lists is by no means complete. For M1, a consecutive list of eponyms survives only for the period 910 to 649. From

648 on, eponym officials are known only from date-formulae in legal and administrative documents and their precise sequence is still disputed; the eponyms of this period are known as 'post-canonical'. A related series of tablets, the so-called Eponym Chronicles, gives the name of the eponym official and his title, and mentions a significant event which took place during his eponymy.
(H. D. Baker)

Erythraean Sea Literary name for the Red Sea. In Herodotus (3.93) the term includes both the Arabian Gulf and the Indian Ocean.

Execration texts Texts found at Saqqara in Egypt, dating to late C19 and C18. They were inscribed on clay figurines of prisoners or on pottery vessels, and contained the names of the persons and cities regarded as the pharaoh's enemies. The ritual breaking of them was believed to bring about the destruction of the persons or cities so named.

extispicy Examination of animal entrails as a means of predicting the future.

favissa Pit or underground repository for cultic objects and sacrificial remains.

glacis A rampart of earth sloping down from the exterior walls of a number of cities and forming part of their fortifications.

Hecatomnid dynasty C4 Carian ruling family, whose power was backed by Persia. Its most notable member was Mausolus (377–353), son of Hecatomnus, who styled himself Persian satrap in his inscriptions.

Helladic Archaeological term used to designate the Bronze Age civilizations of mainland Greece.

Hippodamian The term used for a city layout which featured parallel intersecting streets forming a grid or chequerboard pattern. Hippodamus was born c. 500 in the city of Miletus on Anatolia's western coast, and played a major role in the planning of a number of cities in the Greek world, including the Peiraeus, the port of Athens. He was not, however, the inventor of the street layout with which his name is so closely associated.

hypogeum A subterranean chamber (e.g. burial chamber) of an anc. building.

King's Peace Negotiated end to the Corinthian War (395–386), fought against Sparta by an alliance of other Greek states and Persia. In accordance with the terms of the peace imposed by the Persian king Artaxerxes II, the Greek cities in Asia were ceded to Persia, along with Clazomenae (which had been relocated on an island in the Gulf of Smyrna) and Cyprus (Xenophon, *Hellenica* 5.1.31 = **PE* 381, no. 47).

kudurru Babylonian term conventionally used by scholars to refer to a particular class of inscribed upright stones, often embellished with reliefs, which are traditionally thought to have served as boundary markers for the privately held land whose title of ownership they recorded. In fact, it appears that the Babylonians themselves did not use the term *kudurru* to refer to these monuments; moreover, they most likely did not serve as boundary markers but were rather set up in temples. Approx. 160 Babylonian *kudurrus* have come to light in Babylonia and Susa (where they were taken following Elamite raids). They date from C14, during the period of Kassite rule, to C7. The majority of *kudurrus* of the Kassite period record grants of land conferred by the king on officials for services rendered to the crown.

kurgan Russian term primarily meaning 'fortress', but commonly used in a Russian archaeological context to refer to barrows or burial-mounds, which overtop subterranean grave chambers. The term has been adopted as a cultural designation for a group of Indo-European peoples from southern Russia who used this form of burial. There is a theory that some of these peoples migrated into north-central Anatolia towards the end of M3 and established their dominance over the local Hattian population. It has been suggested that the Early Bronze Age 'royal tombs' unearthed at Alaca Höyük may reflect an immigrant Kurgan culture.

lamelekh Term literally meaning 'belonging to the king', and used, generally in a Syro-Palestinian archaeological context, to refer to royal seals or seal impressions.

līmu, limmu Term for a one-year office held by a high official or the king, whose name was then used to designate that particular year. For example, 'eponymy of Nabu-sharru-usur, governor of Marqasa' in the date-formula of a legal contract (**SAA* XIV: 46–7, no. 45) indicates that the tablet was draw up in the year 682, when Nabu-sharru-usur held the office of eponym. This method of dating relies upon the keeping of lists giving the sequence of named eponym officials (see **Eponym Lists and Eponym Chronicles**).

(H. D. Baker)

Linear B The term used by Sir Arthur Evans to designate the script written on clay tablets (and in a few cases on vases) found in a number of Late Bronze Age Mycenaean palaces on the Greek mainland (particularly Pylos), and at Cnossus in Crete, dating to the period of Mycenaean occupation of the site (beginning c. 1400). By far the largest number of Linear B tablets – c. 3,000 – was unearthed at Cnossus. In the early 1950s, M. Ventris demonstrated that the script was an early form of Greek. This paved the way for Ventris' decipherment of the inscriptions, which for the most part contain inventories of a range of items and personnel. The Linear A script which preceded Linear B was apparently used to write the Minoan language. Only a few hundred Linear A inscriptions, generally short and distributed over nine or more sites, have been discovered. They have yet to be deciphered.

megaron Term for an architectural complex, attested in Homer and most commonly used to designate the main component of a Mycenaean palace. In a Mycenaean context, the megaron consisted of three parts: a portico or columned porch, a vestibule, and a main rectangular room with central hearth. The megaron no doubt served as the palace's principal reception area. Prototypes of the megaron are found in a number of Near Eastern settings, both in houses and in public buildings. Their main feature is a large, rectangular room accessed through a columned porch.

Minoan Archaeological term coined by the archaeologist Sir Arthur Evans to designate the Bronze Age civilizations of mainland Crete. It was adopted from the name of the legendary king of Crete called Minos.

Mizpah Hebrew term meaning 'watchtower', associated with a number of places attested in *OT* sources. The place specifically referred to in each case is generally indicated by a city or regional name attached to the term: e.g. Mizpah of Benjamin, Mizpah of Gilead, Mizpah of Judah.

Mycenaean Term commonly used to designate the Late Bronze Age civilization of Greece. It was adopted by the C19 archaeologist Heinrich Schliemann from the name Mycenae, home of Agamemnon, leader of the Greek forces in the Trojan War.

Mycenae was the first major Late Bronze Age Greek site to be excavated, and has proved the richest of these sites in terms of its archaeological remains.

Nabonidus Chronicle The seventh in the Babylonian Chronicle series (q.v.), so named because of its coverage of events during the reign of the last Babylonian king, Nabonidus, from his accession in 556 to the destruction of the Neo-Babylonian kingdom by the Persian king Cyrus II in 539. For translations of the document, see *ABC* 104–11, *Chav.* 418–20, *PE* 50–1, no. 1.

necropolis Burial complex. The name literally means 'city of the dead'.

Omride dynasty In *OT* tradition, a ruling dynasty of the kingdom of Israel, founded by Israel's (alleged) sixth king Omri c. 876. Though the traditional view is that the dynasty lasted only c. thirty-five years, through the reigns of Omri and three of his descendants (Ahab, Ahaziah, and Jehoram/Joram), the Assyrians continued to refer to Israelite kings for the next hundred years as sons of Omri, and Israel itself as belonging to the house of Omri. A number of scholars argue that if there was ever a united kingdom of Israel, it should be assigned to the period of the Omride dynasty, and not to the reigns of Saul, David, and Solomon as in *OT* tradition (see under **Israel**). There is, however, no certainty about the dates or the length of the Omride dynasty.

orthostats Large, upright rectangular slabs of stone commonly used to revet the bases of city walls and public buildings, and sometimes decorated with relief sculptures.

ostracon (pl. **ostraca**) Piece of broken pottery used as a surface for writing and drawing.

palaestra Wrestling school or ground, place of training for athletes.

Papyrus Harris The longest known papyrus from Egypt, with some 1,500 lines of text, covering the entire reign of the pharaoh Ramesses III (1184–1153). The papyrus was discovered in a tomb near Deir el-Medineh, and named after its collector, A. C. Harris. It was compiled by Ramesses III's son and successor Ramesses IV, and provides one of our two chief sources of information on the Sea Peoples' onslaught on Egypt during Ramesses III's reign. (The inscriptions on the walls of Ramesses' temple at Medinet Habu provide the other source.)

Peloponnesian War The name commonly used for the war which broke out in 431 between the Greek states Athens and Sparta, supported by their respective allies. The war ended with Sparta's victory in 404.

Pentapolis Greek term meaning 'five cities'. It is used in an *OT* context to refer to a league of five Philistine cities, each with its own ruler – the 'five lords'. The cities were Gaza, Ashdod, Ashkelon, Gath, and Ekron (Joshua 13:3).

Peraea 'Territory opposite, and controlled and often economically exploited by, an island' (*OCD*). The Rhodian Peraea consisted of territories which the island of Rhodes controlled on the Anatolian mainland opposite.

peristyle A courtyard surrounded by a roofed colonnade.

postdiluvian see **antediluvian**.

protome Sculpture depicting the forepart of an animal.

Province of the Commander-in-Chief Neo-Assyrian designation. From the time of the Assyrian king Shalmaneser III (858–824) onwards, a number of Assyrian provinces are attested which were attached to some of the highest offices of the land (the officials themselves are sometimes called the 'magnates', hence collectively the 'provinces of the magnates'). Probably this arose out of a reform of the provincial system by Shalmaneser III himself. These new provinces were all in key border regions. Therefore 'Province of the Commander-in-Chief' indicates the province attached to the commander-in-chief. Postgate has described these provinces as: '*ex officio* governorates, provinces which were habitually attached to the major offices of the state'.

(H. D. Baker)

Sargonic period Referring to the reign of the Akkadian king Sargon (2234–2279).

satrap's revolt An uprising in the 360s by a number of Persia's western Anatolian satraps against Persian rule, during the reign of Artaxerxes II (404–359). The rebellion, one of a number of satrapal uprisings in C4, is attested by Diodorus (15.90–1). Its duration remains uncertain (366 to 360?).

satrapy For administrative and revenue-gathering purposes, the Persian Achaemenid (q.v.) empire was divided into a number of provinces, called satrapies. The term comes from Old Persian *xšaçapāvan*, which designates the governor or satrap, literally 'the protector of the realm', who administered the satrapy on behalf of the Persian king. One of the satrap's tasks was to gather the annual tribute assessed for each satrapy and payable by it to the king. In addition to the tribute, the king also received annual gifts from the satrapies, as depicted by the procession of gift-bearers on the Grand Staircase of the Audience Hall (Apadana) at Persepolis. States and peoples on the periphery of the Persian empire who enjoyed a semi-autonomous status may have been exempted from tribute payment, their contributions to the royal treasury limited to annual gift payments. Persis, the core region of the empire, was also exempted from tribute payments, but was obliged to pay tax to the king. The inscriptions of Darius I list on five occasions the lands constituting the Persian empire at the time of his accession in 522. The earliest of the lists (**DB* 6) names twenty-three countries (see Brosius, 2000: 78 for the list). The other lists have small variations on this. Unfortunately, none of the Persian sources indicates which lands paid tribute or how high their payment was. Hence some importance has been attached to the list of 'satrapies' provided by the C5 Greek historian Herodotus (3.89–94), who groups the states and peoples of the empire into twenty provinces and states the amount each pays either as tribute or as gifts. But a number of scholars have pointed out that the Herodotean list is misleading and historically unreliable, and that it refers not to the satrapies of the empire but to administrative and fiscal districts within it. There are omissions from the list when compared with Persian sources, and it groups together into provinces various peoples and lands which are separately listed in Darius' inscription at Bisitun.

Shishak The *OT* name of the Egyptian king Sheshonq (Shoshenq) I (945–924), founder of Egypt's twenty-second dynasty.

stele (pl. **stelae**) Upright stone slab or pillar, on whose surface inscriptions and relief sculptures were generally carved.

Südburg inscription Late Bronze Age Luwian hieroglyphic inscription carved in the interior of one of the chambers of a two-chambered cult complex discovered in the Hittite capital Hattusa in 1988. The inscription records the military exploits in southern Anatolia of the last Hittite king Suppiluliuma II (1207–). It is accompanied by reliefs depicting the king and a deity. (For a translation, see Hawkins, 1995: 23.)

sukkalmah Term first attested in M3 Mesopotamian texts as the title of a high-ranking official (sometimes equated to a 'grand vizier'), most notably in documents of the Ur III administration (C21). It was subsequently the name used of the members of a royal dynasty – the so-called sukkalmah dynasty – which came to power in Anshan in early M2 and ruled Elam for several hundred years.

synoecism Term adopted from Classical Greek to indicate the process whereby a number of small settlements in a region are amalgamated into a single administrative unit with an urban centre.

talent Originally a Persian weight measure which was adopted by the Greeks and used in their monetary systems. Several different weight standards were in operation in the Greek world, the principal ones being the Attic-Euboic standard, in which the talent weighed 25.86 kg, and the Aeginetic standard, in which it weighed 37.80 kg. The talent was the largest monetary unit used by the Greeks. Smaller units were the mina (one-sixtieth of a talent) and the drachma (one-hundredth of a mina). The actual monetary value of a talent depended on the metal of which it was composed, generally silver. Contributions made by most members of the Athenian Confederacy (q.v.) to the Confederacy's treasury were assessed in silver talents.

'Tawagalawa' letter Letter written in mid C13 by a Hittite king to a king of Ahhiyawa. Neither the author's nor the addressee's name has survived. Most scholars believe that the former is Hattusili III. The letter is concerned primarily with the activities of a certain Piyamaradu, responsible for causing major disruptions in the Hittites' subject territories in western Anatolia. Tawagalawa is attested briefly in the letter as the brother of the Ahhiyawan king. Scholars long ago dubbed the document the Tawagalawa letter on the mistaken assumption that Tawagalawa played a major role in the events recorded in the letter.

Telipinu Proclamation The name given by scholars to a decree issued by the Hittite king Telipinu (1525–1500), proclaiming fixed principles for the royal succession. The relevant clauses are preceded by a lengthy preamble which summarizes the history of the Hittite monarchy from the time of its earliest kings.

tell Arabic word for an artificial mound containing one or more levels of an anc. settlement. The Turkish equivalent is *höyük*, the Iranian *chogha*.

temenos Sacred walled precinct enclosing one or more temples.

theriomorphic Having the form of an animal.

tholos (pl. **tholoi**) Term used, most commonly in a Classical Greek architectural context, for a circular building. In a Mycenaean context, tholos is used to designate a stone-built tomb, sometimes freestanding and sometimes cut into a hillside, with a circular base and domed roof.

Ubaid The name given by the Mesopotamian archaeologist C. L. Woolley to a prehistoric culture phase in Mesopotamian history, extending roughly from mid M6 to the end of M5. Woolley adopted the name from the site in southern Mesopotamia now known as Ubaid, located on the Euphrates r. 6 km west of Ur. Painted ceramic ware unearthed on the site was also found at a number of other sites in both northern and southern Mesopotamia. Ubaid thus became a type-site for the period and the culture which its pottery represents.

Udjahorresnet Egyptian official working for the Persian administration in Egypt during the reigns of the Persian kings Cambyses II and Darius I. Formerly serving as a naval commander in the Egyptian fleet prior to the Persian conquest of Egypt, he wrote an autobiography which was inscribed on a statue of himself. The statue is thought to have been set up originally in the temple of Osiris at Saïs in the western Delta of Egypt. It is now in the Vatican Museum in Rome. The autobiography provides an account of Udjahorresnet's career in the service of his Persian overlords. (For translations of the text, see Brosius, 2000: 15, no. 20, *PE* 118, no. 11.)

wadi Generally dry watercourse which becomes swampy or waterlogged in wet seasons.

ziggurat The term, Akkadian in origin, used of the stepped, pyramidal-type structures, with square or rectangular bases, found at a number of sites in Mesopotamia. Each was a solid brick structure, surmounted by a temple dedicated to a particular deity. Access to the summit was via an external (sometimes triple) staircase or a ramp. The earliest ziggurat dates to c. 2200, the latest to c. 550. Ziggurats were first built by the Babylonians and later by the Assyrians. The best-preserved example was constructed by Ur-Nammu, founder of the Ur III dynasty, c. 2110. Ziggurats were not confined to Mesopotamia. There is also a well-preserved Late Bronze Age example, dating to C13, on the site of the Elamite city now known as Chogha Zanbil in southwestern Iran.

GENERAL BIBLIOGRAPHY

(For the abbreviations used for journal names and frequently cited works, see pages xviii–xxiii.)

Abou Assaf, A. (1968), 'Tell Aschtara in Südsyrien. Erste Kampagne 1966', *Annales Archéologiques Arabes Syriennes* 18: 103–22.

—— (1969), 'Tell Aschtara in Südsyrien. 2. Kampagne 1967', *Annales Archéologiques Arabes Syriennes* 19: 101–8.

—— (1990), *Der Tempel von* ʿAin Dara, Mainz am Rhein: Philipp von Zabern.

Abou Assaf, A., Bordreuil, P., and Millard, A. (1982), *La statue de Tell Fekheriye et son inscription bilingue assyro-araméenne*, Paris: Éditions Recherche sur les Civilisations.

Achtemeier, P. (ed.) (1996), *The HarperCollins Bible Dictionary*, New York: HarperCollins, cited as *HCBD*.

Adak, M. and Şahin, S. (2004), 'Neue Inschriften aus Tlos', *Gephyra* 1: 85–105.

Adams, R. McC. (1965), *Land Behind Baghdad. A History of Settlement on the Diyala Plains*, Chicago: University of Chicago Press.

Akkermans, P. M. M. G. and Rossmeisl, I. (1990), 'Excavations at Tell Sabi Abyad, Northern Syria: A Regional Centre on the Assyrian Frontier', *Akkadica* 66: 13–60.

Akkermans, P. M. M. G. and Wiggermann, F. (1999), 'La fortresse de Tell Sabi Abyad – sentinal de l'empire assyrien', *Archéologia* 358: 56–65.

Akkermans, P. M. M. G. and Schwartz, G. M. (2003), *The Archaeology of Syria: From Complex Urban Societies to Early Urban Societies (c. 16,000–300 BC)*, Cambridge: Cambridge University Press.

Akurgal, E. (1973), *Ancient Civilizations and Ruins of Turkey*, Istanbul: Türk Tarih Kurumu Basimevi.

—— (1976), *Die Kunst der Hethiter*, Munich: Hirmer.

Akurgal, M. (2006), 'Alt-Smyrna', in Radt, 373–82.

Alkım, U. B., Alkım, H., and Bilgi, Ö. (1988), *İkiztepe I. The First and Second Seasons' Excavations (1974–1975)*, Ankara: Türk Tarih Kurumu Basimevi.

Allen, L. (2005), *The Persian Empire*, London: British Museum Press.

Al-Maqdissi, M. (1995), 'Chronique des activités archéologiques en Syrie II', *Syria* 72: 159–63.

Alp, S. (1972), *Konya Civarinda Karahöyük Kazılarında Bulunan Silindir ve Damga Mühürleri*, Ankara: Türk Tarih Kurumu Basimevi.

—— (1991a), *Hethitische Briefe aus Maşat-Höyük*, Ankara: Türk Tarih Kurumu Basimevi.

—— (1991b), *Hethitische Keilschrifttafeln aus Maşat-Höyük*, Ankara: Türk Tarih Kurumu Basimevi.

Alparslan, M., Doğan-Alparslan, M., and Peker, H. (eds) (2007), *Festschrift in Honor of Belkıs and Ali Dinçol*, Istanbul: Ege Yayınları, cited as *Fs B. and A. Dinçol*.

Altman, A., (2000), 'The Isuwa Affair in the Sattiwaza Treaty (CTH 51: A, obv. 10–24) Reconsidered', *Ugarit-Forschungen* 32: 11–21.

Archi, A. (1986), 'The Archives of Ebla', in Veenhof, 72–86.

—— (1998), 'The Regional State of Nagar According to the Texts of Ebla', *Subartu* IV/2: 1–22.

Armstrong, J. A. (1995), 'Surface Survey at Tell al-Deylam', *Sumer* 47: 28–9.

Arnaud, D. (1986), *Recherches au pays d'Aštata. Emar VI.3: Textes sumériens et accadiens*, Paris: Éditions Recherche sur les Civilisations.

—— (1991), 'Une correspondance d'affaires entre Ougaritains et Emariotes (nos. 30–36)', in Bordreuil, 65–78.

Artzy, M. (1990), 'Nami Land and Sea Project', *IEJ* 40: 73–6.

Åström, P. (1986), 'Hala Sultan Tekke: An International Harbour Town of the Late Cypriote Bronze Age', *Opuscula Atheniensia* 16: 7–17.

Bachelot, L. (1999), 'Tell Shiouk Faouqâni (1994–1998)', in del Olmo Lete and Montero Fenollós, 143–62.

—— *et al.* (1997), 'La 4e campagne de fouilles à Tell Shioukh Faouqani (Syrie)', *Orient Express* 1997/3: 79–85.

Badian, E. (1985), 'Alexander in Iran', *CHI* 2: 420–501.

Bahat, D. (1996), 'Jerusalem – Capital of Israel and Judah', in J. G. Westenholz (1996b), 307–26.

Bahat, D. and Hurvitz, G. (1996), 'Jerusalem – First Temple Period: Archaeological Exploration', in J. G. Westenholz (1996b), 287–306.

Baker, H. D. *et al.* (1995), 'Kilise Tepe 1994', *AS* 45: 139–91.

Bakır, T. (2006), 'Daskyleion', in Radt, 61–71.

Balkan, K. (1957), *Letter of King Anum-Hirbi of Mama to King Warshama of Kanish*, Ankara: Türk Tarih Kurumu Basimevi.

—— (1960), 'Ein urartäisches Tempel auf Anzavurtepe bei Patnos und hier entdeckte Inschriften', *Anatolia* 5: 99–131.

—— (1973), *Eine Schenkungsurkunde aus der althethitischen Zeit Gefunden in İnandık, 1966*, Ankara: Türk Tarih Kurumu Basimevi.

Bammer, A. (1988), *Ephesos: Stadt an Fluss und Meer*, Graz: Akademische Druck- u. Verlagsanstalt.

Banks, E. J. (1912), *Bismya, or, The Lost City of Adab*, New York and London: G. P. Putnam's Sons.

Baqir, T. (1959), *Tell Harmal*, Baghdad: Directorate General of Antiquities.

Barnett, R. D. (1950), 'The Excavations of the British Museum at Toprak Kale, Near Van', *Iraq* 12: 1–43.

—— (1954), 'The Excavations of the British Museum at Toprak Kale, Near Van – Addenda', *Iraq* 16: 3–22.

—— (1972), 'More Addenda from Toprak Kale', *AS* 22: 163–78.

—— (1982), 'Urartu', *CAH* III.1: 314–71.

Bartlett, J. R. (1982), *Jericho*, Guildford: Lutterworth Press.

Bass, G. F. (1967), *Cape Gelidonya: a Bronze Age Shipwreck*, Transactions of the American Philosophical Society, New Series vol. 57, Part 8, Philadelphia: American Philosophical Society.

Beal, R. H. (1986), 'The History of Kizzuwatna and the Date of the Sunaššura Treaty', *Or* 55: 424–45.

—— (1992a), 'The Location of Cilician Ura', *AS* 42: 65–73.

—— (1992b), *The Organisation of the Hittite Military*, Heidelberg: Carl Winter.

Bean, G. E. (1949), 'Notes and Inscriptions from Lycia', *JHS* 69: 40–58.

—— (1966), *Aegean Turkey*, London: Ernest Benn.

—— (1968), *Turkey's Southern Shore*, London: Ernest Benn.

—— (1971), *Turkey Beyond the Maeander*, London: Ernest Benn.

—— (1978), *Lycian Turkey*, London: Ernest Benn.

Bean, G. E. and Cook, J. M. (1955), 'The Halicarnassus Peninsula', *BSA* 50: 85–171.

—— (1957), 'The Carian Coast III', *BSA* 52: 68–72.

Bean, G. E. and Mitford, T. B. (1970), *Journeys in Rough Cilicia 1964–1968*: Vienna: Böhlau.
Beaulieu, P.-A. (1995), 'King Nabonidus and the Neo-Babylonian Empire', *CANE* II: 969–79.
Beckman, G. (1995), 'The Siege of Uršu Text (*CTH* 7) and Old Hittite Historiography', *JCS* 47: 23–34.
—— (1999), *Hittite Diplomatic Texts* (2nd edn), Atlanta: Scholars Press, cited as *HDT*.
Beitzel, B. (1992), 'Roads and Highways', *Anchor Bible Dictionary*, New York: Doubleday, 5: 776–82.
Belgiorno, M. R. (2004), *Pyrgos Mavroraki: Advanced Technology in Bronze Age Cyprus*, Nicosia: Department of Antiquities.
Belli, O. (1999), *The Anzaf Fortresses and the Gods of Urartu*, Istanbul: Arkeoloji ve Sanat Publications.
—— (2001a), 'Çavuştepe (Sardurihinili) Excavations', in Belli (2001d), 173–8.
—— (2001b), 'Excavations at the Upper and Lower Anzaf Urartian Fortresses', in Belli (2001d), 165–72.
—— (2001c), 'Excavations at Toprakkale (Rusahinili), Second Capital of the Urartian Kingdom', in Belli (2001d), 184–9.
—— (ed.) (2001d), *Istanbul University's Contributions to Archaeology in Turkey, 1932–2000*, Istanbul: Istanbul University.
—— (2003), 'Excavations at Van-Lower and Upper Anzaf Urartian Fortresses: An Intermediary Evaluation (1991–2002)', *Colloquium Anatolicum* 2: 1–49.
—— (2004), 'An Early Iron Age and Urartian fortress in the Van region: Aliler', *SMEA* 46: 5–14.
Belli, O. and Konyar, E. (2001), 'Excavations at Van-Yocantepe Fortress and Necropolis', *Tel Aviv* 28: 169–212.
Belli, O. and Salvini, M. (2004), 'The Urartian Fortress of Kevenli and the Cuneiform Inscriptions of King Minua Found There', *SMEA* 46: 155–74.
Ben-Ami, D. (2001), 'The Iron Age I at Tel Hazor in Light of the Renewed Excavations', *IEJ* 51: 148–70.
Ben Tor, A. (1997), 'The Yigel Yadin Memorial Excavations at Hazor, 1990–93: Aims and Preliminary Results', in Silberman and Small, 107–27.
Benveniste, E. (1943–5), 'La ville de Cyreschata', *Journal Asiatique* 234: 163–6.
Berg Briese, M. and Pedersen, P. (2005), 'Halicarnassos 2003', in Olşen *et al.*, 1: 401–14.
Beyer, D. (1982), *Meskéné-Emar, Dix ans de travaux 1972–82*, Paris: Éditions Recherche sur les Civilisations.
Berlin, A. (1979), *Enmerkar and Ensuhkešdanna: A Sumerian Narrative Poem*, Philadelphia: University Museum.
Bienkowski, P. (1986), *Jericho in the Late Bronze Age*, Warminster: Aris & Phillips.
—— (1990), 'Umm el-Biyara, Tawilan, and Buseirah in Retrospect', *Levant* 22: 91–109.
—— (ed.) (1992), *Early Edom and Moab. The Beginning of the Iron Age in Southern Jordan*, Sheffield Archaeological Monographs 7, Sheffield: J. R. Collis.
Bienkowski, P. and Millard, A. (eds) (2000), *British Museum Dictionary of the Ancient Near East*, London: British Museum, cited as *BMD*.
Bilgi, Ö. (1999), 'İkiztepe in the Late Iron Age', *AS* 49: 27–54.
Birot, M (1993), *Correspondance des gouverneurs de Qattunân. Archives Royales de Mari XXVII*, Paris: Éditions Recherche sur les Civilisations.
Bittel, K. (1976), *Die Hethiter*, Munich: C. H. Beck.
—— (1986), 'Hartapus and Kızıldağ', in J. V. Canby, E. Porada, B. S. Ridgway, and T. Stech (eds), *Ancient Anatolia: Aspects of Change and Cultural Development (Essays in Honor of Machteld J. Mellink)*, Madison: University of Wisconsin Press, 103–111.
—— *et al.* (1975), *Das hethitische Felsheiligtum Yazılıkaya*, Berlin: Gebr. Mann.
Bivar, A. D. H. (1988), 'The Indus Lands', *CAH* IV: 194–210.

Blakely, J. A. (2007), 'The Location of Medieval/Pre-Modern and Biblical Ziklag', *PEQ* 139: 21–6.

Blaylock, S. (1998), 'Rescue Operations by the BIAA at Tille Höyük, on the Euphrates, 1979–1990', in R. Matthews (1998), 111–26.

Boardman, J. (1980), *The Greeks Overseas*, London: Thames and Hudson.

—— (2002), 'Al Mina: The Study of a Site', *Ancient West and East* 1.2: 315–31.

Bordreuil, P. (ed.) (1991), *Une bibliothèque au sud de la ville. Les textes de la 34ᵉ campagne (1973)* (Ras Shamra-Ougarit VII), Paris: Éditions Recherche sur les Civilisations.

Borger, R. (1956), *Die Inschriften Asarhaddons Königs von Assyrien, AfO* Beiheft 9, Graz.

Börker-Klahn, J. (1982), *Altvorderasiatische Bildstelen und Vergleichbare Felsreliefs*, Baghdader Forschungen 4, Mainz am Rhein: Philipp von Zabern.

Boucharlat, R. (2002), 'Pasargadae', *Iran* 40: 279–82.

Breasted, J. H. (1906), *Ancient Records of Egypt*, vols III and IV, Chicago: University of Chicago Press, cited as *ARE III* and *IV*.

—— (1944), *Ancient Times: A History of the Early World*, Boston, New York, and Chicago: Ginn.

Brentjes, B. (1995), 'The History of Elam and Achaemenid Persia: An Overview', *CANE* II: 1001–21.

Briant, P. (1984a), 'La Perse avant l'empire', *Ir Ant* 19: 71–118.

—— (1984b), *L'Asie Centrale et les Royaumes Proche-Orientaux du Premier Millénaire (c. VIIIᵉ–IVᵉ siècles avant notre ère)*, Paris: Éditions Recherche sur les Civilisations.

—— (2002), *From Cyrus to Alexander: A History of the Persian Empire* (transl. P. T. Daniels), Winona Lake: Eisenbrauns.

Bridges, R. (1974), 'The Mycenaean Tholos Tomb at Kolophon', *Hesperia* 43: 264–6.

Briend, J. and Humbert, J.-B. (1980), *Tell Keisan, 1971–1976: Une cité phénicienne en Galilée*, Fribourg: Éditions Universitaires.

Brinkman, J. A. (1968), *A Political History of Post-Kassite Babylonia 1158–722 B.C.*, Rome: Pontificium Institutum Biblicum.

—— (1984), *Prelude to Empire: Babylonian Society and Politics, 747–626 B.C.*, Philadelphia: Occasional Publications of the Babylonian Fund, 7.

—— (1991), 'Babylonia in the shadow of Assyria (747–626 B.C.)', *CAH* III.2: 1–70.

Brixhe, C. and Lejeune, M. (1984), *Corpus des Inscriptions Paléo-Phrygiennes* (2 vols), Paris: Éditions Recherche sur les Civilisations.

Brosius, M. (2000), *The Persian Empire from Cyrus II to Artaxerxes I*, London: London Association of Classical Teachers.

—— (2006), *The Persians*, London: Routledge.

Bryce, T. R. (1978), 'A Recently Discovered Cult in Lycia', *Journal of Religious History* 10: 115–27.

—— (1983), 'The Arrival of the Goddess Leto in Lycia', *Historia* 32: 1–13.

—— (1986), *The Lycians in Literary and Epigraphic Sources*, Copenhagen: Museum Tusculanum Press.

—— (1986–7), 'The Boundaries of Hatti and Hittite Border Policy', *Tel Aviv* 13–14: 85–102.

—— (1989), 'Ahhiyawans and Mycenaeans – An Anatolian Viewpoint', *Oxford Journal of Archaeology* 8: 297–310.

—— (1992), 'The Role of Telipinu, the Priest, in the Hittite Kingdom', *Hethitica* 11: 5–18.

—— (2002), *Life and Society in the Hittite World*, Oxford: Oxford University Press.

—— (2003a), 'History', in Melchert (2003), 27–127.

—— (2003b), *Letters of the Great Kings of the Ancient Near East*, London: Routledge.

—— (2005), *The Kingdom of the Hittites* (new edn), Oxford: Oxford University Press.

—— (2006), *The Trojans and their Neighbours*, London and New York: Routledge.

—— (2007), 'The Secession of Tarhuntassa', in D. Groddek and M. Zorman (eds), *Tabularia Hethaeorum. Hethitologische Beiträge Silvin Košak zum 65. Geburtstag*, Wiesbaden: Harrassowitz, 119–29.

Buccellati, G. (1988), 'The Kingdom and Period of Khana', *BASOR* 270 (May 1988): 43–61.
—— (2005), 'The Monumental Urban Complex at Urkesh: Report on the 16th Season of Excavations, July–September 2003', in Owen and Wilhelm, 3–28.
Buccellati, G. and Kelly-Buccellati, M. (2005), 'Urkesh as a Hurrian Religious Centre', *SMEA* 47: 27–59.
Bunimovitz, S. and Lederman, Z. (2000), 'Tel Beth-Shemesh, 1997–2000', *IEJ* 50: 254–8.
—— (2001), 'The Iron Age Fortifications of Beth-Shemesh: A 1990–2000 Perspective', *IEJ* 51: 121–47.
—— (2006), 'The Early Israelite Monarchy in the Sorek Valley: Tel Beth-Shemesh and Tel Batash (Timnah) in the 10th and 9th Centuries BCE', in Maeir and de Miroschedji, 402–27.
Bunnens, G. (ed.) (1990), *Tell Ahmar 1988 Season*, Abr-Nahrain Supplement Series 2, Leuven: Publications of the Melbourne University Expedition to Tell Ahmar 1.
—— (1993–4), 'Tall Ahmar/Til Barsip 1988–1992', *AfO* 40/41: 221–5.
—— (1995), 'Hittites and Aramaeans at Til Barsib: A Reappraisal', in K. van Lerberghe and A. Schoors (eds), *Immigration and Emigration within the Ancient Near East: Festschrift E. Lipiński*, Leuven: Uitgeverij Peeters en Departement Orientalistiek, 19–27.
—— (ed.) (2000a), *Essays on Syria in the Iron Age*, Ancient Near East Studies, Supplement 7, Louvain, Paris, and Sterling: Peeters.
—— (2000b), 'Syria in the Iron Age. Problems of Definition', in Bunnens (2000a), 3–19.
—— (ed.) (2006), *A New Luwian Stele and the Cult of the Storm-God at Til Barsib-Masuwari (Tell Ahmar II)*, Louvain, Paris, and Dudley, MA: Peeters.
Burke, M. (1961), '*Ganibâtim*, ville du Moyen Euphrate', *RA* 55: 147–51.
Burney, C. (1966), 'A First Season of Excavations at the Urartian Citadel of Kayalıdere', *AS* 16: 55–111.
—— (1970, 1972, 1973, 1975), 'Excavations at Haftavan Tepe', *Iran* 8: 157–71; 10: 127–42; 11: 153–72; 13: 149–64.
—— (1998), 'The Kingdom of Urartu (Van): Investigations into the Archaeology of the Early First Millennium BC within Eastern Anatolia (1956–65)', in R. Matthews (1998), 144–62.
—— (2004), *Historical Dictionary of the Hittites*, Lanham, MD, Toronto, and Oxford: Scarecrow Press.
Burney, C. and Lang, D. M. (1971), *The Peoples of the Hills: Ancient Ararat and Caucasus*, London: Phoenix.
Büyükkolanci, M. (2000), 'Excavations on Ayasuluk Hill in Selçuk/Turkey: A Contribution to the Early History of Ephesus', in F. Krinzinger (ed.), *Die Ägäis und das Westliche Mittelmeer. Beziehungen und Wechselwirkungen 8. bis 5. Jh. v. Chr.* (*Archäologischen Forschungen* Bd 4), Akten des Symposions, Vienna, 24–27 March 1999, Vienna: Österreichische Akademie der Wissenschaften, 39–43.
Cadogan, G. (1996), 'Maroni: Change in Late Bronze Age Cyprus', in P. Åström and E. Herscher (eds), *Late Bronze Age Settlement in Cyprus: Function and Relationship*, Studies in Mediterranean Archaeology pocket-book 126, Jonsered: Paul Åströms Förlag, 15–22.
Callaway, J. A. (1972), *The Early Bronze Age Sanctuary at Ai (et-Tell)*, London: Quaritch.
—— (1980), *The Early Bronze Age Citadel and Lower City at Ai (et-Tell)*, Cambridge, MA: American Schools of Oriental Research.
Çambel, H. (1999), *Corpus of Hieroglyphic Luwian Inscriptions*, vol. II: *Karatepe-Aslantaş: The Inscriptions*, Berlin and New York: de Gruyter, cited as *CHLI* II.
Cameron, G. G. (1948), *Persepolis Treasury Tablets*, Chicago: OIP 65, University of Chicago Press.
Cancik-Kirschbaum, E. (1996), *Die mittelassyrische Briefe aus Tall Šeh Hamad* (Berichteder Ausgrabungen Tall Šeh Hamad/Dur-Katlimmu Band 4), Berlin: Dietrich Reimer Verlag.
Carruba, O. (1977), 'Beiträge zur mittelhethitischen Geschichte: I – Die Tuthalijas und die Arnuwandas', *SMEA* 18: 137–74.
Cavalier, L. (2003), 'Nouvelles tombes de Xanthos', *An Ant* 11: 201–14.

Cecchini, S. and Mazzoni, S. (eds) (1998), *Tell Afis (Siria): Scavi sull'acropoli 1988–1992 (The 1998–1992 Excavations of the Acropolis)*, Pisa: Edizioni ETS.
Charpin, D. (1980), *Archives familiales et propriété privée en Babylonie ancienne: étude des documents de 'Tell Sifr'*, Geneva: Librairie Droz.
—— (1986), 'Les Elamites à Šubat-Enlil', in De Meyer *et al.*, 129–37.
—— (1989), 'Mari et Mišlan au temps de Sumu-El', *NABU*, 76–7.
—— (1990), 'Une mention d'Alasiya dans une lettre de Mari', *RA* 84: 125–7.
—— (1995) 'The History of Ancient Mesopotamia: An Overview', *CANE* II: 807–29.
—— (1997), Sapiratum, ville du Suhûm', *MARI* 8: 341–66.
—— (2000), 'La date de la destruction des murailles de Mišlan et Samanum', *NABU*, 57.
—— (2003), *Hammu-rabi, Roi de Babylone*, Paris: Presses Universitaires de France.
Charpin, D. and Durand, J.-M. (1987), 'Le nom antique de Tell Rimah', *RA* 81: 125–46.
Charpin, D. and Ziegler, N. (1997), 'Mekum, Roi d'Apišal', *MARI* 8: 243–7.
Charpin, D. *et al.* (eds) (1988) *Archives Épistolaires de Mari* 1/2, Paris: Éditions Recherche sur les Civilisations, cited as *ARM XXVI 1/2*.
Charpin, D., Edzard, D. O., and Stol, M. (2004), *Mesopotamien. Die altbabylonische Zeit*, Göttingen: Vandenhoeck & Ruprecht, cited as *Mesop.*
Chavalas, M. W. (ed.) (2006), *The Ancient Near East: Historical Sources in Translation*, Oxford: Blackwell, cited as *Chav.*
Cifola, B. (1988), 'Ramesses III and the Sea Peoples: A Structural Analysis of the Medinet Habu Inscriptions', *Or* 57: 275–306.
Çilingiroğlu, A. (2006), 'An Urartian Fortress in Front of Mount Eiduru: Ayanis', *AJNEAS* 1: 135–42.
Çınaroğlu, A. and Çelik, D. (2006), '2004 Yılı Alaca Höyük ve Alaca Höyük Hitit Barajı Kazıları', in Olşen *et al.* 1: 1–6.
Cline, E. H. (1996), 'Assuwa and the Achaeans: the "Mycenaean" Sword at Hattusas and its Possible Implications', *BSA* 91: 137–51.
—— (2004), *Jerusalem Besieged, from Ancient Canaan to Modern Israel*, Ann Arbor: University of Michigan Press.
—— (2007), *From Eden to Exile*, Washington, DC: National Geographic Society.
Cline, E. H. and Yasur-Landau, A (2007), 'Poetry in Motion: Canaanite Rulership and Aegean Narrative at Kabri', in S. P. Morris and R. Laffineur (eds), *EPOS: Reconsidering Greek Epic and Aegean Bronze Age Archaeology*, Aegaeum 28, Liège: Université de Liège, 157–65.
Cogan, M. (2002), 'Locating *māt Hatti* in Neo-Assyrian Inscriptions', in E. D. Oren and S. Ahituv (eds), *Aharon Kempinski Memorial Volume: Studies in Archaeology and Related Disciplines*, Beersheba 15, Beersheba: Ben Gurion University of the Negev, 86–92.
Cohen, S. (1973), *Enmerkar and the Lord of Aratta*, Philadelphia: University Microfilms International.
Cole, S. W. (1996), *Nippur IV: The Early Neo-Babylonian Governor's Archive from Nippur*, Chicago: OIP 114, University of Chicago Press, cited as *Nippur IV*.
Cole, S. W. and Gasche, H. (1998), 'Second- and First-Millennium BC Rivers in Northern Babylonia', in H. Gasche and M. Tanret (eds), *Changing Watercourses in Babylonia – Towards a Reconstruction of the Ancient Environment in Lower Mesopotamia*, Ghent: University of Ghent and OIP, 1–64.
Coleman, J. E., Barlow, J. A., Mogelonsky, M. K., and Schaar, K. W. (1996), *Alambra: A Middle Bronze Age Settlement in Cyprus – Archaeological Investigations by Cornell University 1974–1985*, Studies in Mediterranean Archaeology vol. CXVIII, Jonsered: Paul Åströms Förlag.
Collins, B. J. (2007), *The Hittites and Their World*, Atlanta: Society of Biblical Literature.
Cook, B. F. (2005), *Relief Sculpture of the Mausoleum at Halicarnassus*, Oxford and New York: Oxford University Press.
Cook, J. M. (1962), *The Greeks in Ionia and the East*, London: Thames and Hudson.

—— (1973), *The Troad: An Archaeological and Topographical Study*, Oxford: Clarendon Press.
Cook, J. M. and Plommer, W. H. (1966), *The Sanctuary of Hemithea at Kastabos*, Cambridge: Cambridge University Press.
Cooley, R. E. (1975), 'Four Seasons of Excavation at Khirbet Raddana, in Bireh', *Near Eastern Archaeological Society Bulletin*, no. 5: 5–20.
Cooper, J. S. (1983), *The Curse of Agade*, Baltimore and London: Johns Hopkins University Press.
Cornil, P. and Lebrun, R. (1972), 'La restauration de Nérik', *Hethitica* 1: 15–30.
Córdoba, J. M. (1990), 'Tell es-Seman = Ahuna? Stationen einer babylonischen Reiseroute durch das Balih-Tal', *AoF* 17: 360–78.
Corsten, T. (1988), 'Daskyleion am Meer', *Epigraphica Anatolica* 12: 53–76.
Courbin, P. (1986), 'Bassit', *Syria* 63: 175–220.
Courtils, J. des (2005), 'Xanthos: Rapport sur la campagne de 2004', *An Ant* 13: 449–66.
—— (2006a), 'Excavations and Researches at Xanthos in 2005', *News of Archaeology from Anatolia's Mediterranean Areas*, 4: 31–5.
—— (2006b), 'La campagne 2005 à Xanthos', *An Ant* 14: 275–91.
Courtois, J.-C, Lagarce, J., and Largace, E. (1986), *Enkomi et le Bronze récent à Chypre*, Nicosia: Imprimeri Zavallis.
Crawford, H. (1993), 'London-Bahrain Archaeological Expedition: Excavations at Saar, 1991', *Arabian Archaeology and Epigraphy* 4: 1–19.
—— (1997), 'The Site of Saar: Dilmun Reconsidered', *Antiquity* 273: 701–8.
—— (2004), *Sumer and the Sumerians* (2nd edn; 1st edn 1991), Cambridge: Cambridge University Press.
Curtis, A. (1985), *Ugarit (Ras Shamra)*, Cambridge: Lutterworth Press.
Curtis, J. E. (1982a), 'Balawat', in Curtis (1982c), 113–19.
—— (1982b), 'Chagar Bazar', in Curtis (1982c), 79–85.
—— (ed.) (1982c), *Fifty Years of Mesopotamian Discovery: The Work of the British School of Archaeology in Iraq, 1932–1982*, London: British School of Archaeology in Iraq.
Curtis, J. E. and Tallis, N. (2005), *Forgotten Empire: The World of Ancient Persia*, London: British Museum Press.
—— (eds) (2008), *The Balawat Gates of Ashurnasirpal*, London: British Museum Press.
Cryer, F. H. (1995), 'Chronology: Issues and Problems', in Sasson, 651–64.
Dales, G. (1977), *New Excavations at Nad-i Ali (Sorkh Dagh), Afghanistan* (Research Monograph 16), Berkeley: Centre for South and South East Asia Studies, University of California.
D'Alfonso, L., Cohen, Y., and Sürenhagen, D. (eds) (2008), *The City of Emar among the Late Bronze Age Empires: History, Landscape, and Society* (Proceedings of the Konstanz Emar Conference, 25–26 April 2006), Münster: Ugarit-Verlag (*AOAT* 349).
Dalley, S. (1984), *Mari and Karana: Two Old Babylonian Cities*, London and New York: Longman.
—— (1994), 'Nineveh, Babylon, and the Hanging Gardens: Cuneiform and Classical Sources Reconciled', *Iraq* 56: 45–58.
—— (2000), 'Shamshi-Ilu, Language and Power in the Western Assyrian Empire', in Bunnens (2000a), 79–88.
Dalton, O. M. (1964), *The Treasure of the Oxus, with Other Examples of Early Oriental Metal-work* (3rd edn), London: British Museum.
Dandamaev, M. A. (1989), *A Political History of the Achaemenid Empire* (transl. W. J. Vogelsang), Leiden, New York, Copenhagen, and Cologne: Brill.
Dandamaev, M. A. and Lukonin, V. G. (1989), *The Culture and Social Institutions of Ancient Iran*, Cambridge: Cambridge University Press.
Davesne, A., Lemaire, A., and Lozachmeur, H. (1987), 'Le site archéologique de Meydancıkkale (Turqie): du royaume de Pirindu à la garnison ptolémaïque', *CRAI*:359–83.
Debevoise, N. C. (1938), *A Political History of Parthia*, Chicago: University of Chicago Press.
Del Monte, G. F. and Tischler J. (1978), *Répertoire Géographique des Textes Cunéiformes Bd. 6: Die*

Orts- und Gewässernamen der hethitischen Texte (suppl. 6/2, 1992), Wiesbaden: Ludwig Reichert, cited as *RGTC* 6.

Delougaz, P. (1940), *The Temple Oval at Khafajah*, Chicago: OIP 53, University of Chicago.

Delougaz, P. and Lloyd, S. (1942), *Pre-Sargonic Temples in the Diy.·la Region*, Chicago: OIP 58, University of Chicago Press.

Delougaz, P. and Kantor, H. (1996–), *Chogha Mish, vol. I: The First Five Seasons of Excavations 1961–1971*, Chicago: University of Chicago Press.

Deltour-Levie, C. (1982), *Les Piliers Funéraires de Lycie*, Louvain-la-Neuve: Université Catholique de Louvain.

De Meyer, L. *et al.* (eds) (1986), *Fragmenta Historiae Elamicae. Mélanges offerts à M. J. Steve*, Paris: Éditions Recherche sur les Civilisations.

Dever, W. G. (2003a), 'Visiting the Real Gezer: A Reply to Israel Finkelstein', *Tel Aviv* 30: 259–82.

—— (2003b), *Who Were the Early Israelites and Where Did They Come From?*, Grand, MI and Cambridge, UK: William B. Eerdmans.

DeVries, K. (2008), 'The Age of Midas at Gordion and Beyond', *ANES* 45: 30–64.

Diakonoff, I. M. (1985), 'Media', *CHI* 2: 36–148.

Dietrich, M. (2003), *The Babylonian Correspondence of Sargon and Sennacherib* (State Archives of Assyria, vol. XVII), Helsinki: Helsinki University Press, cited as *SAA* XVII.

Dinçol, A. M. (1998), 'Die Entdeckung des Felsmonuments in Hatip und ihre Auswirkungen über die historischen und geographischen Fragen des Hethiterreichs', *TÜBA-AR* 1: 27–35.

Dinçol, A. M., Yakar, J., Dinçol, B., and Taffnet, A. (2000), 'The Borders of the Appanage Kingdom of Tarhuntassa – a Geographical and Archaeological Assessment', *Anatolica* 26: 1–29.

Dion, P. E. (1995), 'Aramaean Tribes and Nations of First-Millennium Western Asia', *CANE* II: 1281–94.

Dittmann, R. (1992), 'Aššur und Kar Tukulti-Ninurta', *AJA* 96: 307–12.

Dönmez, Ş. (2002), 'The 2nd Millennium BC Settlements in Samsun and Amasya Provinces, Central Black Sea Region, Turkey', *Ancient West and East* 1.2: 243–93.

Donner, H. and Röllig, W. (1966–9), *Kanaanäische und aramäische Inschriften I–III* (2nd edn), Wiesbaden: Harrassowitz.

Dornemann, R. H. (1985), 'Salvage Excavations at Tel Hadidi in the Euphrates River Valley', *BA* 48: 49–59.

—— (2000), 'The Iron Age Remains at Tell Qarqur in the Orontes Valley', in Bunnens (2000a), 459–85.

Dossin, G. (1939), 'Benjaminites dans les textes de Mari', in *Mélanges syriens offerts à Monsieur R. Dussaud*, Paris: Paul Geuthner, 981–96.

—— (1950), *Correspondance de Šamši-Addu et de ses fils*, Paris: Imprimerie Nationale, cited as *ARM I*.

Dothan, M. *et al.* (1967, 1971, 1982, 1993), Reports of Ashdod excavations, published in ʿAtiqot vols 7, 9–10, 15, and 23.

Dothan, T. (1982), *The Philistines and their Material Culture*, New Haven: Yale University Press.

—— (1995), 'The "Sea Peoples" and the Philistines of Ancient Palestine', *CANE* II: 1267–79.

Doumet-Serhal, C. (1998–9), 'First Season of Excavation at Sidon: Preliminary Report', *Bulletin d'Archéologie et d'Architecture Libanaises* 3: 181–224.

Drower, M. S. (1971), 'Syria Before 2200 B.C.', *CAH* I.2: 315–62.

Dunand, M. (1937–73), *Fouilles de Byblos*, Paris: P. Geuthner.

—— (1966, 1967, 1969), 'Rapport préliminaire sur les fouilles de Sidon', *Bulletin du Musée de Beyrouth* 19: 103–5; 20: 27–44; 22: 102–7.

Dunand, M. and Saliby, N. (1985), *Le Temple d'Amrith dans la perée d'Aradus*, Paris: Librairie Orientaliste Paul Geuthner.

Du Plat Taylor, J., Seton-Williams, M. V., and Waecher, J. (1950), 'The Excavations at Sakçe Gözü', *Iraq* 12: 53–138.

Durand, J.-M. (ed.) (1988a), *Archives Épistolaires de Mari* 1/1, Paris: Éditions Recherche sur les Civilisations, cited as *ARM XXVI 1/1*.

—— (1988b), 'Les Anciens de Talhayûm', *RA* 82: 97–113.

—— (1988c), 'Missions Diverses sur l'Euphrate', *ARM XXVI 1/1*: 119–38.

Durand, J.-M. and Charpin, D. (1986), ' "Fils de Sim'al": Les origines tribales des rois de Mari', *RA* 80: 141–83.

Duru, R. (2003), *Tilmen – A Forgotten Capital City*, Istanbul: Tursab.

Dyson, R. H. and Voigt, M. M. (eds) (1989), 'East of Assyria: The Highland Settlement of Hasanlu', *Expedition* 31/2–3.

Easton, D. F., Hawkins, J. D., Sherratt, A. G., and Sherratt, E. S. (2002), 'Troy in Recent Perspective', *AS* 52: 75–109.

Edel, E. (1994), *Die Ägyptisch-hethitische Korrespondenz aus Boghazköy*, vol. I, Opladen: Westdeutscher Verlag, cited as *ÄHK*.

Edwards, I. E. S. (1982), 'Egypt, from the Twenty-Second to the Twenty-Fourth Dynasty', *CAH* III.1: 534–81.

Edzard, D. O. (1959–60), 'Neue Inschriften zur Geschichte von Ur III unter Šusuen', *AfO* 19: 1–32.

—— (1997), *The Royal Inscriptions of Mesopotamia: Early Periods*, vol. 3/1: *Gudea and His Dynasty*, Toronto, Buffalo, and London: University of Toronto, cited as *RIME* 3/1.

Edzard, D. O. and Farber, G. (1974), *Répertoire Géographique des Textes Cunéiformes Bd. 2: Die Orts- und Gewässernamen der Zeit der 3. Dynastie von Ur*, Wiesbaden: Ludwig Reichert, cited as *RGTC* 2.

Efe, T. (2003), 'Küllüboa and the Initial Stages of Urbanism in Western Anatolia', in M. Özdoğan, H. Hauptmann, and N. Başgelen (eds), *From Villages to Towns: Studies Presented to Ufuk Esin*, Istanbul: Arkeoloji ve Sanat Publications, 265–82.

Eichler, S. and Wäfler, M. (1989–90), 'Tall al-Hamidiya', *AfO* 36/37: 246–51.

Eichler, S., Wäfler M. *et al.* (1985–2003), *Tall al-Hamidiya* (4 vols), Orbis Biblicus et Orientalis, Series Archaeologica, Fribourg: Academic Press; Göttingen: Vandenhoeck & Ruprecht.

Eidem, J. (1985), 'News from the Eastern Front: The Evidence from Tell Shemshara', *Iraq* 47: 83–107.

—— (1992), *The Shemshāra Archives, vol. 2: The Administrative Texts*, Copenhagen: Kongelige Danske Videnskabernes Selskab (Royal Danish Academy of Sciences and Letters).

Eidem, J. and Laessøe, J. (2001), *The Shemshāra Archives, vol. 1: The Letters*, Copenhagen: Kongelige Danske Videnskabernes Selskab.

Elayi, J. (2000), 'Les sites phéniciens de Syrie au Fer III/Perse. Bilan et perspectives de Recherche', in Bunnens (2000a), 327–48.

Ellis, M. D. (ed.) (1992), *Nippur at the Centennial* (Papers read at the 35th Rencontre Assyriologique Internationale, Philadelphia, 1988), Philadelphia, PA.

Emberling, G. and McDonald, H. (2001), 'Excavations at Tell Brak 2000: Preliminary Report', *Iraq* 63: 21–54.

—— (2003), 'Excavations at Tell Brak 2001–2002: Preliminary Report', *Iraq* 65: 1–75.

Ephʿal, I. (2005), 'Esarhaddon, Egypt, and Shubria: Politics and Propaganda', *JCS* 57: 99–111.

Erdem, A. Ü. and Batmaz, A. (2008), 'Contributions of the Ayanis Fortress to Iron Age Chronology', *ANES* 45: 65–84.

Erim, K. T. (1986), *Aphrodisias: City of Venus Aphrodite*, London: Muller, Blond, and White.

Erkanal, A. and Erkanal, H. (1986), 'A New Archaeological Excavation in Western Anatolia: Panaztepe', *Turkish Review Quarterly Digest* 1: 67–76.

Erkanal-Öktü, A. and Çınardalı-Karaaslan, N. (2006), 'Panaztepe 2004 Yılı Kazıları', in Olşen *et al.*, 1: 309–18.

Ertem, H. (1988), *Korucutepe I*, Ankara: Türk Tari Kurumu Basimevi.

Esin, U. (1993–7), 'Mersin', *RlA* 8: 66–73.

Faist, B. and Finkbeiner, U. (2002), 'Emar', *KatHet*: 190–5.

Falconer, S. E. and Magness-Gardiner, B. (1989), 'Tell el-Hayyat', in Homès-Fredericq and Hennessy, 254–61.

Fales, F. M. (1999), 'The Tablets from Tell Shiouk Fawqani/Burmarina in the Context of Assyro-Aramaic Studies', in del Olmo Lete and Montero Fenollós, 625–36.

Fales, F. M. and Postgate, J. N. (1995), *Imperial Administrative Records, Part II* (State Archives of Assyria, vol. XI), Helsinki: Helsinki University Press, cited as *SAA* XI.

Fales, F. M., Bachelot, L., and Attardo, E. (1996), 'An Aramaic Tablet from Tell Shioukh Fawqani (Syria)', *Semitica* 46: 81–121.

Faulkner, R. O. (1947), 'The Wars of Sethos I', *Journal of Egyptian Archaeology* 33: 34–9.

Finkelstein, I. (ed.) (1985), 'Excavations at Shiloh 1981–1984: Preliminary Report', *Tel Aviv* 12: 123–80.

—— (1986), *ʿizbet Sartah: An Early Iron Age Site near Rosh Haʿayan, Israel*, Oxford: British Archaeological Reports, International Series, no. 299.

—— (2002), 'Gezer Revisited and Revised', *Tel Aviv* 29: 262–96.

Finkelstein, I. and Silberman, N. A. (2002), *The Bible Unearthed*, New York, London, Toronto, and Sydney: Simon and Schuster.

Finkelstein, I., Ussishkin D., and Halpern, B. (2000), *Megiddo III: The 1992–1996 Seasons*, Tel Aviv: Monograph Series of the Institute of Archaeology of Tel Aviv University no. 18.

—— (2006), *Megiddo IV: The 1998–2002 Seasons* (2 vols), Tel Aviv: Emery and Claire Yass Publications in Archaeology.

Finkelstein, J. J. (1953), 'Cuneiform Texts from Tell Billa', *JCS* 7: 111–76.

Fitzmyer, J. A. (1995), *The Aramaic Inscriptions of Sefire* (rev. edn), Rome: Pontifical Editrice Pontificio Istituto Biblico.

Frame, G. (1992), *Babylonia 689–627 B.C.: A Political History*, Istanbul: Nederlands Historisch-Archaeologisch Instituut te Istanbul.

—— (1995), *The Royal Inscriptions of Mesopotamia: Babylonian Periods*, vol. 2: *Rulers of Babylonia From the Second Dynasty of Isin to the End of Assyrian Domination (1157–612)*, Toronto, Buffalo, and London: University of Toronto Press, cited as *RIMB* 2.

Francfort, H.-P. (1988), 'Central Asia and Eastern Iran', *CAH* IV: 165–93.

Frankel, D. and Webb, J. M. (2006), *Marki Alonia: An Early and Middle Bronze Age Settlement in Cyprus – Excavations 1995–2000*, Studies in Mediterranean Archaeology CXXIII: 2, Sävedalen: Paul Åströms Förlag.

—— (2007), *The Bronze Age Cemeteries at Deneia in Cyprus*, Studies in Mediterranean Archaeology CXXXV, Sävedalen: Paul Åströms Förlag.

Franken, H. J. (1992), *Excavations at Tell Deir* ʿAlla, the Late Bronze Age Sanctuary, Louvain: Peeters.

Franklin, N. (2006), 'Revealing Stratum V at Megiddo', *BASOR* 342: 95–111.

Frantz-Szabó, G. (1995), 'Hittite Witchcraft, Magic, and Divination', *CANE* III: 2007–19.

Frayne, D. R. (1990), *The Royal Inscriptions of Mesopotamia: Early Periods*, vol. 4: *Old Babylonian Period (2003–1595 BC)*, Toronto, Buffalo, and London: University of Toronto, cited as *RIME* 4.

—— (1992), *The Early Dynastic List of Geographical Names*, New Haven: American Oriental Society.

—— (1993), *The Royal Inscriptions of Mesopotamia: Early Periods*, vol. 2: *Sargonic and Gutian Periods (2334–2113 BC)*, Toronto, Buffalo, and London: University of Toronto, cited as *RIME* 2.

—— (1997a), 'On the Location of Simurrum', in G. D. Young, M. W. Chavalas, and R. E. Averbeck (eds), *Crossing Boundaries and Linking Horizons: Studies in Honor of Michael C. Astour on His 80th Birthday*, Bethesda: CDL Press, 243–69.

—— (1997b), *The Royal Inscriptions of Mesopotamia: Early Periods*, vol. 3/2: *Ur III Period (2112–2004 BC)*, Toronto, Buffalo, and London: University of Toronto, cited as *RIME* 3/2.

Freu, J. (2007), *Des origines à la fin de l'ancien royaume hittite. Les hittites et leur histoire*, Paris: l'Harmattan.

Fuchs, A. (1994), *Die Inschriften Sargons II. aus Khorsabad*, Göttingen: Cuvillier Verlag, cited as *Sargon II*.

—— (1998), *Die Annalen des Jahres 711 v. Chr.* (State Archives of Assyria, vol. VIII), Helsinki: Helsinki University Press, cited as *SAA* VIII.

—— (2000), 'Mat Habhi', in J. Marzahn and H. Neumann (eds), *Assyriologica et Semitica: Festschrift für Joachim Oelsner anlasslich seines 65. Geburtstages am 18. Februar 1997, AOAT* 252, Münster: Ugarit-Verlag, 73–94.

Fuchs, A. and Parpola, S. (2001), *The Correspondence of Sargon II, Part III* (State Archives of Assyria, vol. XV), Helsinki: Helsinki University Press, cited as *SAA* XV.

Furtwängler, A. (2006), 'Didyma', in Radt, 73–80.

Gadd, C. J. (1926), 'Tablets from Kirkuk', *RA* 23: 49–161.

—— (1971), 'The Dynasty of Agade', *CAH* I.2: 417–63.

Gadd, C. J. and Legrain, L. (1928), *Ur Excavations Texts I: Royal Inscriptions*, London: British Museum.

Gardiner, A. (1960), *The Kadesh Inscriptions of Ramesses II*, Oxford: Ashmolean Museum.

Garstang, J. (1953), *Prehistoric Mersin, Yümük Tepe in Southern Turkey*, Oxford: Clarendon Press.

Garstang, J. and Gurney, O. R. (1959), *The Geography of the Hittite Empire*, London: British Institute of Archaeology at Ankara.

Gasche, H., Armstrong, J., and Cole, S. W. (1998), *Dating the Fall of Babylon, a Reappraisal of Second-Millennium Chronology*, Chicago: University of Chicago Press.

Gautier, J. and Lampre, G. (1905), 'Fouilles de Tépé Moussian', *Mémoires de la Délégation en Perse* 8: 59–149.

Gelb, I. J. and Kienast, B. (1990), *Die altakkadischen Königsinschriften des dritten Jahrtausends v. Chr.*, Stuttgart: Freiburger altorientalische Studien 6, cited as *DaK*.

Genière, J. de la (1996), 'Bilan sommaire des decouvertes recentes à Claros', *An Ant* 4: 303–9.

George, A. R. (1993), *House Most High: The Temples of Ancient Mesopotamia*, Mesopotamian Civilizations 5, Winona Lake: Eisenbrauns.

Gertzen, T. L. (2008), ' "Profiling" the Philistines: Some Further Remarks on the Egyptian Depictions of Philistine Warriors at Medinet Habu', *ANES* 45: 85–101.

Geva, H. (ed.) (2000), *Ancient Jerusalem Revealed* (expanded edn), Jerusalem: Israel Exploration Society.

Ghirshman, R. (1966–8), *Tchoga Zanbil (Dur Untash)*, vol. 1: *La ziggurat*; vol. 2: *Téménos, temples, palais, tombes*, Mémoires de la Mission Archéologique en Iran, vols 39–40, Paris: Paul Geuthner.

Giannotta, M. E., Gusmani, R., *et al.* (eds) (1994), *La Decifrazione del Cario*, Atti del 1⁰ Simposio Internazionale Roma, 3–4 maggio, 1993.

Gibson, J. C. L. (1975), *Textbook of Syrian Semitic Inscriptions, II: Aramaic Inscriptions*, Oxford: Clarendon Press, cited as *TSSI II*.

Gibson, M. *et al.* (2002). 'First season of Syrian-American investigations at Hamoukar, Hasekeh Province', *Iraq* 64: 45–68.

Ginouvès, R. (1989), *Soloi, dix campaignes de fouilles*, vol. 2: *La ville basse*, Sainte-Foy, Quebec: Presses de l'Université Louval.

Gjerstad, E. *et al.* (1934–48), *The Swedish Cyprus Expedition: Finds and Results of the Excavations in Cyprus, 1927–1931* (4 vols), Stockholm: Swedish Cyprus Expedition, cited as *SCE*.

Gnoli, G. (1989), *The Idea of Iran: An Essay on its Origin*, Rome: Serie Orientale Roma LXII.

Goddeeris, A. (2005), 'The Emergence of Amorite Dynasties in Northern Babylonia during the early Old Babylonian Period', in van Soldt, 138–46.

Goetze, A. (1933), *Die Annalen des Mursilis, MVAG* 38, Leipzig (repr. Darmstadt, 1967), cited as *AM*.

—— (1940), *Kizzuwatna and the Problem of Hittite Geography*, New Haven: Yale University Press.

Goff, C. (1968, 1969, 1970, 1977, 1978, 1985), 'Excavations at Baba Jan . . .', *Iran* 6: 105–34; 7: 115–30; 8: 141–56; 15: 103–40; 16: 29–65; 22: 1–20.

Goldman, H. (1956), *Excavations at Gözlü Kule, Tarsus 2: From the Neolithic through the Bronze Age*, Princeton: Princeton University Press.

Görg, M. (1976), 'Hiwwiter im 13. Jahrhundert v. Chr.', *UF* 8: 53–5.

Graeve, V. von (2006), 'Milet', in Radt, 241–62.

Gragg, G. B. (1995), 'Less-Understood Languages of Ancient Western Asia', *CANE* IV: 2161–79.

Grayson, A. K. (1972–6), *Assyrian Royal Inscriptions*, i–ii, Wiesbaden: Harrassowitz.

—— (1975), *Assyrian and Babylonian Chronicles*, New York: J. J. Augustin, cited as *ABC*.

—— (1982), 'Assyria: Ashurdan II to Ashur-Nirari V (934–745 B.C.)', *CAH* III.1: 238–81.

—— (1987), *The Royal Inscriptions of Mesopotamia: Assyrian Periods*, vol. 1: *Assyrian Rulers of the Third and Second Millennium BC (to 1115 BC)*, Toronto, Buffalo, and London: University of Toronto, cited as *RIMA* 1.

—— (1991a), 'Assyria: Sennacherib and Esarhaddon (704–679 B.C.)', *CAH* III.2: 103–41.

—— (1991b), 'Assyria: Tiglath-pileser III to Sargon II (744–705)', *CAH* III.2: 71–102.

—— (1991c), *The Royal Inscriptions of Mesopotamia: Assyrian Periods*, vol. 2: *Assyrian Rulers of the Early First Millennium BC I (1114–859 BC)*, Toronto, Buffalo, and London: University of Toronto, cited as *RIMA* 2.

—— (1992), 'History and Culture of Babylonia', in D. N. Freedman (ed.), *Anchor Bible Dictionary* (6 vols), New York and London: Doubleday, 4: 756–77.

—— (1995), 'Assyrian Rule of Conquered Territory in Ancient Western Asia', *CANE* II, 959–68.

—— (1996), *The Royal Inscriptions of Mesopotamia: Assyrian Periods*, vol. 3: *Assyrian Rulers of the Early First Millennium BC II (858–745 BC)*, Toronto, Buffalo, and London: University of Toronto, cited as *RIMA* 3.

Greaves, A. M. (2002), *Miletos: A History*, London and New York: Routledge.

Greco, A. (2003), 'Zagros Pastoralism and Assyrian Imperial Expansion: A Methodological Approach', in Lanfranchi *et al.*, 65–78.

Green, M. (1986), 'Urum and Uqair', *Acta Sumerologica* 8: 77–83.

Greenberg, M. (1955), *The Hab/piru*, New Haven: American Oriental Society.

Greengus, S. (1979), *Old Babylonian Tablets from Ishchali and Vicinity*, Istanbul: Nederlands Historisch-Archaeologisch Instituut te Istanbul.

—— (1986), *Studies in Ishchali Documents*, Bibliotheca Mesopotamica 19, Malibu: Undena Publications.

Greenstein, E. L. (1995), 'Autobiographies in Ancient Western Asia', *CANE* IV: 2421–32.

Groneborg, B. (1980), *Répertoire Géographique des Textes Cunéiformes 3: Die Orts- und Gewässernamen der altbabylonischen Zeit*, Wiesbaden: Ludwig Reichert, cited as *RGTC* 3.

Guichard, M. (1994), 'Au pays de la Dame de Nagar', in M. Birot, D. Charpin, and J.-M. Durand (eds), *Florilegium Marianum II: Recueil d'études à la mémoire de Maurice Birot*, Paris: SEPOA, 235–72.

Gurney, O. R. (1948), 'Mita of Pahhuwa', *LAAA* 28: 32–47.

—— (1990), *The Hittites*, London: Harmondsworth.

—— (1992), 'Hittite Geography: Thirty Years On', *Fs Alp* 213–21.

—— (1997), 'The Annals of Hattusili III', *AS* 47: 127–39.

—— (1998), 'Sultantepe and Harran', in R. Matthews (1998), 163–76.

Güterbock, H. G. (1934), 'Die historische Tradition und ihre literarische Gestaltung bei Babyloniern und Hethitern bis 1200', *ZA* 42: 1–91.

—— (1956), 'The Deeds of Suppiluliuma as Told by his Son, Mursili II', *JCS* 10: 41–68, 75–98, 101–30, cited as *DS*.

—— (1986), 'Troy in Hittite Texts? Wilusa, Ahhiyawa, and Hittite History', in Mellink (1986), 33–44.

Haas, V. (1970), *Die Kult von Nerik: ein Beitrag zur hethitischen Religionsgeschichte*, Rome: Päpstliches Bibelinstitut.

Hadjicosti, M. (1999), 'Idalion before the Phoenicians: The Archaeological Evidence and its Topographical Distribution', in M. Iacovou and D. Michaelides (eds), *Cyprus: The Historicity of the Geometric Horizon*, Nicosia: Archaeological Research Unit, University of Cyprus, 35–43.

Hadjisavvas, S. (1996), 'Alassa: A regional centre of Alasia?', in P. Åström and E. Herscher (eds), *Late Bronze Age Settlement in Cyprus: Function and Relationship*, Studies in Mediterranean Archaeology pocket-book 126, Jonsered: Paul Åströms Förlag, 23–38.

Haggi, A. (2006), 'Phoenician Atlit and its Newly-Excavated Harbour: A Reassessment', *Tel Aviv* 33: 43–60.

Haider, P. W. (1997), 'Troia zwischen Hethitern, Mykenern und Mysern. Besitzt der Troianische Krieg einen historischen Hintergrund?', in H. D. Galter (ed.), *Troia. Mythen und Archäologie*, Graz: Grazer Morgenländische Studien 4: 99–140.

Haines, R. C. (1971), *Excavations in the Plain of Antioch, vol. II: The Structural Remains of the Later Phases (Çatal Hüyük, Tell Al Judaidah, and Tell Tayinat)*, Chicago: OIP 95, University of Chicago Press.

Hallo, W. W. (1978), 'Simurrum and the Hurrian Frontier', *RHA* 36: 71–83.

—— (2005), 'New Light on the Gutians', in van Soldt, 147–61.

Hallo, W. W. and Younger, K. L. (eds) (1997, 2000, 2002), *The Context of Scripture* (3 vols), Leiden, New York, and Cologne: Brill, cited as *CS* I–III.

Hallock, R. T. (1969), *Persepolis Fortification Tablets*, Chicago: University of Chicago Press.

Hanfmann, G. M. A. (1983), *Sardis from Prehistoric to Roman Times: Results of the Archaeological Exploration of Sardis 1958–1975*, Cambridge, MA: Harvard University Press.

Harrison, T. P. (2004), *Megiddo 3: Final Report on the Stratum VI Excavations*, Chicago: OIP 127, University of Chicago Press.

Harrison, T. P., Batiuk, S., and Snow, H. (2006), '2004 Yılı Tayinat Höyük Kazıları', in Olşen *et al.*, 2: 353–62.

Haspels, C. H. E. (1971), *The Highlands of Phrygia: Sites and Monuments* (2 vols), Princeton: Princeton University Press.

Hassanzadeh, Y. (2006), 'The glazed bricks from Bukan (Iran): New insights into Mannaean art', *Antiquity* 80/307; available at http://antiquity.ac.uk.

Hauptmann, H. (1987), report on Lidar Höyük, in *AS* 37: 203–6.

Hawkins, J. D. (1982), 'The Neo-Hittite States in Syria and Anatolia', *CAH* III.1: 372–441.

—— (1992), 'The Inscriptions of the Kizildağ and the Karadağ in the Light of the Yalburt Inscription', *Fs Alp* 259–75.

—— (1995), *The Hieroglyphic Inscription of the Sacred Pool Complex at Hattusa (SÜDBURG)* (*StBoT* Beiheft 3), Wiesbaden: Harrassowitz.

—— (1997), 'A Hieroglyphic Luwian Inscription on a Silver Bowl in the Museum of Anatolian Civilizations, Ankara', Ankara: Anadolu Medeniyetleri Musezi, 1996 Yilliği.

—— (1998a), 'Hittites and Assyrians at Melid (Malatya)', Proceedings of the 34th Rencontre Assyriologique Internationale, Istanbul, 1987, Ankara: Türk Tarih Kurumu Basimevi, 63–77.

—— (1998b), 'Tarkasnawa King of Mira: "Tarkondemos", Boğazköy Sealings and Karabel', *AS* 48: 1–31.

—— (2000), *Corpus of Hieroglyphic Luwian Inscriptions*, vol. I: *Inscriptions of the Iron Age*, Berlin and New York: de Gruyter, cited as *CHLI I*.

Heidel, A. (1953), 'The Octagonal Sennacherib Prism in the Iraq Museum', *Sumer* 9: 117–88.

—— (1956), 'A New Hexagonal Prism of Esarhaddon', *Sumer* 12: 9–37.

Heimpel, W. (2003), *Letters to the King of Mari*, Winona Lake: Eisenbrauns, cited as *LKM*.

Heinhold-Krahmer, S. (1977), *Arzawa, Untersuchungen zu seiner Geschichte nach den hethitischen Quellen*, Heidelberg: Carl Winter.

Helck, W. (1984), 'Die Sukzija-Episode im Dekret des Telepinus', *WO* 15: 103–8.

Hellmuth, A. (2008), 'Chronological Setting of Cimmerian and Early Scythian Material', *ANES* 45: 102–22.

Helm, P. (1981), 'Herodotos' *Medikos Logos* and Median History', *Iran* 19: 85–90.

Heltzer, M. (1981), *The Sutaeans*, Naples: Istituto universitario orientale.

Henkelman, W. (2003), 'Persians, Medes and Elamites: Acculturation in the Neo-Elamite Period', in Lanfranchi *et al.* 181–231.

Hennessy, J. B. *et al.* (1989), 'Pella', in Homès-Fredericq and Hennessy, 406–42.

Henning, W. B. (1978), 'The First Indo-Europeans in History', in G. L. Ulmen (ed.), *Society and History: Essays in Honor of Karl August Wittfogel*, The Hague, Paris, and New York: Mouton, 215–30.

Herzog, Z. (2002), 'The Fortress Mound at Tel Arad', *Tel Aviv* 29: 3–109.

Herzog, Z. *et al.* (1989), *Excavations at Tel Michal, Israel*, Tel Aviv: Publications of the Institute of Archaeology 10, Tel Aviv University.

Hinz, W. (1967), 'Elams Vertrag mit Naram-Sin von Akkade', *ZA* N.F. 24: 66–96.

Hoffmann, I. (1984), *Der Erlass Telipinus*, Heidelberg: Carl Winter.

Holt, F. L. (1988), *Alexander the Great and Bactria: The Formation of a Greek Frontier in Central Asia*, Leiden, New York, Copenhagen, and Cologne: Brill.

Homès-Fredericq, D. and Hennessy, J. B. (eds) (1989), *Archaeology of Jordan II*, Leuven: Peeters.

Hornblower, S. (1991), *A Commentary on Thucydides, vol. I: Books I–III*, Oxford: Clarendon Press.

Horsnell, M. J. A. (1999), *The Year-Names of the First Dynasty of Babylon, vol. 2: The Year-Names Reconstructed and Critically Annotated in Light of their Exemplars*, Hamilton: McMaster University Press.

Hout, Th. P. J. van den (1995), *Der Ulmitešub-Vertrag* (*StBoT* 38), Wiesbaden: Harrassowitz.

—— (ed.) (2006), *The Life and Times of Hattusili III and Tudhaliya IV: Proceedings of a Symposium held in Honor of J. de Roos, 12–13 December, 2003, Leiden*, Leiden: Nederlands Instituut voor Het Nabije Oosten.

Houwink ten Cate, Ph. H. J. (1965), *The Luwian Population Groups of Lycia and Cilicia Aspera during the Hellenistic Period*, Leiden: Brill.

—— (1966), 'A New Fragment of the "Deeds of Suppiluliuma as told by his Son Mursili II" ', *JNES* 25: 27–31.

—— (1971), *Records of the Early Hittite Empire*, Istanbul: Nederlands Historisch-Archaeologisch Instituut in Het Nabije Oosten.

—— (1985–6), 'Sidelights on the Ahhiyawa Question from Hittite Vassal and Royal Correspondence', *JEOL* 28: 33–79.

Hrouda, B. (ed.) (1977, 1981, 1987, 1992), *Isin-Išan Bahriyat. Die Ergebnisse der Ausgrabungen*, Munich: Bayerische Akademie der Wissenschaften. (The 4 vols in the series report results of excavations conducted from 1973 to 1984.)

—— (1997), 'Vorläufiger Bericht über die Ausgrabungsergebnisse auf dem Sirkelihöyük Südtürkei von 1992–1995', *Kazı Sonuçları Toplantısı* 18: 291–312.

Iacovou, M. (2002), 'From ten to naught: formation, consolidation and abolition of Cyprus' Iron Age polities', in *Hommage à Marguerite Yon. Actes du colloque internationale 'Le temps des royaumes de Chypre, XIII–IV s. av. J.-C.'*, Cahier du centre d'études chypriotes 32: 73–87.

Ivantchik, A. I. (1993), *Les Cimmériens au Proche-Orient*, Orbus Biblicus et Orientalis 127, Göttingen: Vandenhoeck & Ruprecht.

Jacobsen, T. (1953), 'The Reign of Ibbi-Suen', *JCS* 7: 36–47.

—— (1987), *The Harps That Once . . .*, New Haven and London: Yale University Press.

Jacobsen, T. and Lloyd, S. (1935), *Sennacherib's Aqueduct at Jerwan*, Chicago: OIP 24, University of Chicago Press.

James, P. (2007), review of Ussishkin (2004), *PEQ* 139: 213–30.

Jenkins, I. (1999–), *Anatolian Archaeology* 5– (annual reports of excavations on Cnidus).

Jidejian, N. (1971), *Byblos through the Ages* (2nd edn), Beirut: Dar el-Machreq Publishers.

Joannès, F. (ed.) (1992), 'Histoire de Harâdum à l'époque paléo-babylonienne', in Kepinski-Lecomte, 30–6.

—— (ed.) (2001), *Dictionnaire de la Civilisation Mésopotamienne*, Paris: Éditions Robert Laffont, cited as *DCM*.

Jones, A. H. M. (1971), *Cities of the Eastern Roman Provinces* (2nd edn., rev. M. Avi-Yonah *et al.*), Oxford: Clarendon Press.

Joukowsky, M. S. (ed.) (1992), *The Heritage of Tyre: Essays on the History, Archaeology, and Preservation of Tyre*, Dubuque: Kendall/Hunt.

Kahn, D. (2007), 'The Kingdom of Arpad (Bīt Agūsi) and "All Aram": International Relations in Northern Syria in the Ninth and Eighth Centuries BCE', *ANES* 44: 66–89.

Karageorghis, V. (1969), *Salamis in Cyprus: Homeric, Hellenistic, and Roman*, London: Thames and Hudson.

—— (1976), *Kition: Mycenaean and Phoenician Discoveries in Cyprus*, London: Thames and Hudson.

—— (1982), *Cyprus: From the Stone Age to the Romans*, London: Thames and Hudson.

—— (ed.) (1985), *Archaeology in Cyprus, 1960–1985*, Nicosia: A. G. Leventis Foundation.

Karageorghis, V. and Demas, M. (1984), *Pyla-Kokkinokremos: A Late 13th Century BC Fortified Settlement in Cyprus*, Nicosia: Department of Antiquities.

—— (1988), *Excavations at Maa-Palaeokastro 1979–1986*, Nicosia: Department of Antiquities.

Karlsson, L. (2006), 'Labraunda, 2004', in Olşen *et al.*, 1: 101–4.

Katala, L. and Whiting, R. (1995), *Grants, Decrees and Gifts of the Neo-Assyrian Period* (State Archives of Assyria, vol. XII), Helsinki: Helsinki University Press, cited as *SAA* XII.

Katzenstein, H. J. (1973), *The History of Tyre, From the Beginning of the Second Millennium B.C.E. until the Fall of the Neo-Babylonian Empire in 538 B.C.E.*, Jerusalem: Schocken Institute for Jewish Research of the Theological Seminary of America (rev. edn Beersheba, 1997).

Kealhofer, L. (ed.) (2005), *The Archaeology of Midas and the Phrygians: Recent Work at Gordion*, Philadelphia: University of Pennsylvania Museum of Archaeology and Anthropology.

Keen, A. G. (1998), *A Political History of the Lycians and their Relations with Foreign Powers, c. 545–362 B.C.*, Leiden, Boston, and Cologne: Brill.

Kelly-Buccellati, M. (2005), 'Urkesh and the North: Recent Discoveries', in Owen and Wilhelm, 29–40.

Kelso, J. L. (1968), *The Excavations of Bethel 1934–1960*, Cambridge, MA: American Schools of Oriental Research.

Kempinski, A. (ed. N. Scheftelowitz and R. Oren) (2002), *Tel Kabri: The 1986–1993 Excavation Seasons*, Tel Aviv: Emery and Claire Yass Publications in Archaeology.

Kempinski, A. and Košak, S. (1970), 'Der Išmeriga-Vertrag', *WO* 5: 191–217.

Kenyon, K. (1971), *Royal Cities of the Old Testament*, London: Barrie & Jenkins.

Kepinski, C. (2005), 'Tilbesar – A Bronze Age City in the Sajur Valley (Southeast Anatolia)', *Anatolica* 31: 145–59.

Kepinski-Lecomte, C. (ed.) (1992), *Haradum I. Une nouvelle ville sur le Moyen-Euphrate (XVIIIe–XVIIe siècles av. J.-C.)*, Paris: Éditions Recherche sur les Civilisations.

Kessler, K. (1980), *Untersuchungen zur historischen Topographie Nordmesopotamiens nach keilschriftlichen Quellen des I. Jahrtausends v. Chr.*, Beihefte zum Tübinger Atlas des Vorderen Orients B/26, Wiesbaden: Dr. Ludwig Reichert Verlag.

Kitchen, K. A. (1982), *Pharaoh Triumphant*, Warminster: Aris & Phillips.

Kleiss, W. (1971), 'Bericht über Erkundungsfahrten in Iran im Jahre 1970', *AMI* 4: 51–111.

—— (1976), 'Urartäische Plätze in Iran (Stand der Forschung Herbst 1975)', *AMI* N.F. 9: 19–43.

—— (1979), *Bastam I. Ausgrabungen in den Urartäischen Anlagen 1972–1975*, Berlin: Gebr. Mann.

—— (1988), *Bastam II. Ausgrabungen in den Urartäischen Anlagen 1977–1978*, Berlin: Gebr. Mann.

Kleiss, W. and Hauptmann, H. (1976), *Topographische Karte von Urartu, Verzeichnis der Fundorte und Bibliographie* (*AMI* Ergänzungsband 3), Berlin: Reimer.

Kleiss, W. and Calmeyer, P. (eds) (1996), *Bisutun. Ausgrabungen und Forschungen in den Jahren 1963–1967* (Tehraner Forschungen VII), Berlin: Gebr. Mann.

Klengel, H. (1963), 'Der Schiedsspruch des Mursili II. hinsichtlich Barga und seine Übereinkunft mit Duppi-Tešup von Amurru (KBo III 3)', *Or* 32: 32–55.

—— (1968), 'Die Hethiter und Isuwa', *OA* 7: 63–76.

—— (1976), 'Untersuchungen zu den sozialen Verhältnissen im altbabylonischen Dilbat', *AoF* 4: 63–110.

—— (1992), *Syria: 3000–300 B.C.: A Handbook of Political History*, Berlin: Akademie Verlag.

—— (1999), *Geschichte des Hethitischen Reiches* (Handbuch der Orientalistik, 1, 034), Leiden: Brill.

Klengel-Brandt, E. *et al.* (1998), 'Vorläufiger Bericht über die Ausgrabungen des Vorderasiatischen Museums auf Tall Knediğ/NO-Syrien, Zusammenfassung der Ergebnisse 1993–1997', *MDOG* 130: 73–82.

Knapp, A. B. (1995), 'Island Cultures: Crete, Thera, Cyprus, Rhodes, and Sardinia', *CANE* III: 1433–49.

Koch, A. *et al.* (2006), *Pracht und Prunk der Grosskönige – Das persische Weltreich*, Stuttgart: Historisches Museum der Pfalz Speyer, Konrad Theiss Verlag.

Kochavi, M. (1981), 'The History and Archaeology of Aphek-Antipatris, a Biblical City in the Sharon Plain', *BA* 44: 75–86.

König, F. W. (1955), *Handbuch der chaldischen Inschriften, AfO* Beiheft 8, Graz, cited as *HcI*.

Korfmann, M. (ed.) (2006), *Troia. Archäologie eines Siedlungshügels unde seiner Landschaft*, Mainz am Rhein: Philipp von Zabern.

Koşay, H. Z. and Akok, M. (1966), *Ausgrabungen von Alaca Höyük. Vorbericht über die Forschungen und Entdeckungen von 1940–1948*, Ankara: *TTKY*, Series V, no. 5.

—— (1973), *Alaca Höyük Excavations: Preliminary Report on Research and Discoveries 1963–1967*, Ankara: *TTKY*, Series V, No. 28.

Kossian, A. V. (1997), 'The Mushki Problem Reconsidered', *SMEA* 39: 253–66.

Kühne, H. (1983–4), 'Tall Šeh Hamad/Dur-katlimmu 1981–1983', *AfO* 31: 166–78.

—— (1989–90), 'Tall Šeh Hamad/Dur-katlimmu 1985–1987', *AfO* 36/37: 308–23.

—— (1993–4), 'Tall Šeh Hamad/Dur-katlimmu 1988–1990', *AfO* 41: 267–72.

Kuhrt, A. (1995a), *The Ancient Near East c. 3000–330 BC* (2 vols), London: Routledge.

—— (1995b), 'The Assyrian Heartland in the Achaemenid Period', in P. Briant (ed.), *Dans les pas des Dix-Mille: peuples et pays du Proche Orient vus par un grec (Actes de la Table ronde internationale organisé à l' initiative du GRACO, Toulouse 3–4 février)*, Toulouse: Presses Universitaires du Mirail, 239–54.

—— (2007a), *The Persian Empire: A Corpus of Sources from the Achaemenid Period* (2 vols), Abingdon: Routledge, cited as *PE*.

—— (2007b), 'The Persian Empire', in Leick (2007), 562–76.

Kuhrt, A. and Sancisi-Weerdenburg, H. (eds) (1988), *Achaemenid History III: Method and Theory* (Proceedings of the London 1985 Achaemenid History Workshop), Leiden: Nederlands Instituut voor Het Nabije Oosten.

Kulakoğlu, F. and Sertok, K. (2001), 'Saraga Höyük', *AJA* 105: 492–3.

LaBianca, Ø. S. (1989), 'Hesban', in Homès-Fredericq and Hennessy, 261–9.

LaBianca, Ø. S. and Younker, R. W. (1995), 'The Kingdoms of Ammon, Moab, and Edom: The Archaeology of Society in Late Bronze/Iron Age Transjordan (ca. 1400–500 BCE)', in T. E. Levy (ed.), *The Archaeology of Society in the Holy Land*, London: Leicester University Press, 399–415.

Lacambre, D. (1997), 'La bataille de Hirîtum', *MARI* 8: 431–54.

Lackenbacher, S. (1982), 'Nouveaux documents d'Ugarit', *RA* 76: 141–56.

—— (1988), 'L'affaire de Hît', *ARM XXVI 1/2*: 451–7.

Lackenbacher, S. and Malbran-Labat, F. (2005), 'Ugarit et les Hittites dans les archives de la "Maison d'Urtenu" ', *SMEA* 47: 227–40.

Laessøe, J. and Jacobsen, T. (1990), 'Šikšabbum Again', *JCS* 42: 127–78.

Lafont, B. (1996), L'extraction du minerai de cuivre en Iran à la fin du IIIe millénaire', in Ö. Tunca and D. Deheselle (eds), *Tablettes et images aux pays de Sumer et Akkad*, Leuven: Peeters, 87–93.

Lambert, W. G. (1961), 'The Sultantepe Tablets, VIII: Shalmaneser in Ararat', *AS* 11: 143–58.

Lanfranchi, G. B. (2003), 'The Assyrian Expansion in the Zagros and the Local Ruling Elites', in Lanfranchi *et al.*, 81–118.

Lanfranchi, G. B. and Parpola, S. (1990), *The Correspondence of Sargon II, Part II* (State Archives of Assyria, vol. V), Helsinki: Helsinki University Press, cited as *SAA* V.

Lanfranchi, G. B., Roaf, M., and Rollinger, R. (eds) (2003), *Continuity of Empire(?) Assyria, Media, Persia*, History of the Ancient Near East Monographs V (Proceedings of a conference held in Padua, 26–28 April 2001), Padua: S.a.r.g.o.n. Editrice e Libreria.

Lapp, P. W. (1965), 'Tell el-Ful', *BA* 28: 2–10.

—— (1967), 'Taanach by the Waters of Megiddo', *BA* 30: 2–27.

Laroche, D. (2006), 'Rapport sur les travaux de la mission archéologique de Létoon en 2005', *An Ant* 14: 293–308.

Larsen, M. T. (1972), 'A Revolt Against Hattusa', *JCS* 24: 100–1.

—— (1976), *The Old Assyrian City-State and its Colonies*, Copenhagen: Akademisk Forlag.

Latacz, J. (2004), *Troy and Homer*, Oxford: Oxford University Press.

Laughlin, J. C. H. (2006), *Fifty Major Cities of the Bible*, London and New York: Routledge.

Lebeau, M. and Suleiman, A. (eds) (1997), *Tell Beydar, Three Seasons of Excavations (1992–1994): A Preliminary Report* (Subartu III), Turnhout: Brepols.

—— (2003), *Tell Beydar: The 1995–1999 Seasons of Excavations: A Preliminary Report* (Subartu X), Turnhout: Brepols.

—— (2007), *Tell Beydar: The 2000–2002 Seasons of Excavations, the 2003–2004 Seasons of Architectural Restoration: A Preliminary Report* (Subartu XV), Turnhout: Brepols.

Lebrun, R. and De Vos, J. (2006), 'A Propos de l'inscription bilingue de l'ensemble sculptural de Çineköy', *An Ant* 14: 45–64.

Lehmann, G. (2001), 'Phoenicians in Western Galilee: First Results of an Archaeological Survey in the Hinterland of Akko', in A. Mazar (ed.), *Studies in the Archaeology of the Iron Age in Israel and Jordan*, Journal for the Study of the Old Testament Supplement Series 331, Sheffield: Sheffield Academic Press, 65–112.

Lehmann, G. and Schneider, T. J. (2000), 'Tell el-Farah (South), 1999 and 2000', *IEJ* 50: 258–61.

Leick, G. (2003), *The Babylonians*, London and New York: Routledge.

—— (ed.) (2007), *The Babylonian World*, London and New York: Routledge.

Lemaire, A. (1993), 'Ougarit, Oura et la Cilicie vers la fin du XIIIe s. av. J.-C.', *Ugarit-Forschungen* 25: 227–36.

—— (2001), 'Les langues du royaume Sam'al aux IXe–VIIIe av. J.-C. et leurs relations avec le royaume de Qué', in E. Jean, A. M. Dinçol, and S. Durugönül (eds), *La Cilicie: espaces et pouvoirs locaux, 2e millénaire av. J.-C. – 4e siècle ap. J.-C.* (Actes de la table ronde internationale d'Istanbul, 2–5 November 1999), Paris: De Boccard.

Levine, L. D. (1982), 'Sennacherib's Southern Front: 704–689 B.C.', *JCS* 34: 28–55.

Lichtheim, M. (1976), *Ancient Egyptian Literature: A Book of Readings*, Berkeley, Los Angeles, and London: University of California Press.

Lipiński, E. (1994), *Studies in Aramaic Inscriptions and Onomastics II*, Leuven: Leuven University Press, cited as *SAIO* II.

—— (1995), 'The Phoenicians', *CANE* II: 1321–33.

—— (2000), *The Aramaeans, their Ancient History, Culture, Religion*, Louvain, Paris, and Sterling: Peeters.

Liverani, M. (1988), 'The Fire of Hahhum', *OA* 27: 165–72.

—— (1992), *Studies on the Annals of Ashurnasirpal II, vol. 2: Topographical Analysis (Quadernidi Geografia Storica* 4), Rome: Università di Roma 'La Sapienza'.

—— (2003), 'The Rise and Fall of Media', in Lanfranchi *et al.*, 1–12.

—— (2005), *Israel's History and the History of Israel* (transl. C. Peri and P. R. Davies), London and Oakville: Equinox.

Lloyd, S. (1967), *Early Highland Peoples of Anatolia*, London: Thames and Hudson.

—— (1989), *Ancient Turkey: A Traveller's History of Anatolia*, London: British Museum.

Lloyd, S. and Safar, F. (1943), 'Tell Uqair: Excavations by the Iraq Government Directorate of Antiquities in 1940 and 1941', *JNES* 2: 131–58.

Lloyd, S. and Gökçe, N. (1953), 'Sultantepe', *AS* 3: 27–51.

Lohmann, H. (2006), 'Survey of Mykale (Dilek Dağları) 3rd Campaign: The Discovery of the Archaic Panionion', in Olşen *et al.*, 1: 241–52.

Loon, M. N. van (1974), 'The Euphrates Mentioned by Sarduri II of Urartu', in. K. Bittel *et al.* (eds), *Anatolian Studies Presented to Hans Gustav Güterbock on the Occasion of his 65th Birthday*, Istanbul: Nederlands Historisch-Archaeologisch Instituut in Het Nabije Oosten, 187–94.

—— (1975–80), *Korucutepe: Final Report on the Excavations of the Universities of Chicago, California (Los Angeles) and Amsterdam in the Keban Reservoir, Eastern Anatolia, 1968–1970* (3 vols), Amsterdam, New York, and Oxford: North-Holland Publishing Company.

—— (ed.) (2001), *Selenkahiye: Final Report on the University of Chicago and University of Amsterdam Excavations in the Tabqa Reservoir, Northern Syria, 1967–1975*, Istanbul: Nederlands Historisch-Archaeologisch Instituut in Het Nabije Oosten.

Loretz, O. (1984), *Habiru-Hebräer. Eine sozio-linguistische Studie über die Herkunft des Gentiliziums ʿibrî vom Appellativum habiru*, Berlin: de Gruyter.

Luciani, M. (1999), 'Zur Lage Terqas in Schriftlichen Quellen', *ZA* 89: 1–23.

Luckenbill, D. D. (1924), *The Annals of Sennacherib*, Chicago: University of Chicago Press (repr. Wipf & Stock Publishers, Eugene, OR, 2005), cited as *Sennach.*

—— (1928), *Ancient Records of Assyria and Babylonia* (vols I and II), Chicago: University of Chicago Press (repr. Greenwood Press, New York, 1968), cited as *ARAB*.

Lumsden, S. (2002), 'Gavurkalesi: Investigations at a Hittite Sacred Place', in Yener and Hoffner, 111–25.

Luschan, F. von, *et al.* (1893–1943), *Ausgranbungen in Sendschirli I–V*, Berlin: Mitteilungen aus den orientalischen Sammlungen der Königlichen Museen zu Berlin 11–15.

McClellan, T. (1987), 'A Syrian Fortress of the Bronze Age: El-Qitar', *National Geographic Research* 2: 418–40.

McClellan, T. and Porter, A. (1997), 'Banat', in H. Weiss (ed.), 'Archaeology in Syria', *AJA* 101: 97–148.

—— (1999), 'Survey of Excavations at Tell Banat: Funerary Practices', in del Olmo Lete and Montero Fenollós, 107–16.

McConchie, M. (2004), *Archaeology at the North-East Anatolian Frontier, vol. V: Iron Technology and Iron-making Communities of the First Millennium BC.*, Ancient Near Eastern Studies Supplement 13, Louvain, Paris, and Dudley, MA: Peeters.

McEwen, C. *et al.* (1958), *Soundings at Tell Fakhariyah*, Chicago: OIP 79, University of Chicago Press.
McMahon, A., Tunca, Ö., and Bagdo, A.-M. (2001), 'New Excavations at Chagar Bazar, 1999–2000', *Iraq* 63: 201–22.
McMahon, A., Colantoni, C., and Semple, M. (2005), 'British Excavations at Chagar Bazar, 2001–2', *Iraq* 67: 1–16.
Macqueen, J. G. (1968), 'Geography and History in Western Asia Minor in the Second Millennium B.C.', *AS* 18: 169–85.
—— (1986), *The Hittites and their Contemporaries in Asia Minor*, London: Thames and Hudson.
Maeir, A. M. and Ehrlich, C. S. (2001), 'Excavating Philistine Gath. Have We Found Goliath's Hometown?', *BAR* 27.6: 22–31.
Maeir, A. M. and Miroschedji, P. de (eds) (2006), *'I Will Speak the Riddles of Ancient Times': Archaeological and Historical Studies in Honor of Amihai Mazar on the Occasion of His Sixtieth Birthday* (2 vols), Winona Lake: Eisenbrauns.
Maidman, M. P. (1995), 'Nuzi: Portrait of an Ancient Mesopotamian Provincial Town', *CANE* IV: 931–7.
Maier, F. G. and Karageorghis, V. (1984), *Paphos: History and Archaeology*, Nicosia: A. G. Leventis Foundation.
Majidzadeh, Y. (2003), *Jiroft, the Earliest Oriental Civilization*, Tehran: Cultural Heritage Organization.
Makinson, M. (2002–5), 'Muṣru, Maṣuwari and MṢR: From Middle Assyrian Frontier to Iron Age City', *State Archives of Assyia Bulletin* 20: 33–62.
Malbran-Labat, F. (1991), in Bordreuil, 15–64, 127–30.
—— (1995), *Les inscriptions royales de Suse: Briques de l'époque paléo-élamite à l'Empire néo-élamite*, Paris: Éditions de la Réunion des musées nationaux.
Mallowan, M. E. L. (1971), 'The Early Dynastic period in Mesopotamia', *CAH* I.2: 238–314.
Marchetti, N. (2004), 'The 2003 Joint Turkish-Italian Excavations at Tilmen Höyük', *KST* 26.2: 129–36.
Margueron, J.-C. (1995), 'Emar, Capital of Aštata in the Fourteenth Century BCE', *BA* 58: 126–38.
—— (2004), *Mari, Métropole de l'Euphrate au IIIe et au début du IIe millénaire av. J.-C.*, Paris: Éditions A. et J. Picard.
Markoe, G. E. (2000), *Phoenicians*, London: British Museum Press.
Marksteiner, T. (2006), 'Limyra', in Radt, 179–86.
Martin, H. P. (1988), *Fara: A Reconstruction of the Ancient City of Shuruppak*, Birmingham: Chris Martin.
Martino, S. de (1999), 'Ura and the Boundaries of Tarhuntassa', *AoF* 26: 291–300.
Masson, E. (1979), 'Les inscriptions louvites hiéroglyphiques d'Emirgazi', *Journal des Savants* 3–49.
Masson, O. (1991), 'Anatolian Languages', *CAH* III.2: 666–76.
Mathias, V. T. and Parr, P. J. (1989), 'The Early Phases at Tell Nebi Mend', *Levant* 21: 13–32.
Matney, T. and Rainey, L. (2006), 'Eighth Preliminary Report on Excavations at Ziyaret Tepe (Diyabakır Province), 2004 Season', in Olşen *et al.*, 1: 117–30.
Matthews, D. and Eidem, J. (1993), 'Tell Brak and Nagar', *Iraq* 55: 201–7.
Matthews, R. (1989), 'Excavations at Jemdet Nasr, 1988', *Iraq* 51: 225–48.
—— (1990), 'Excavations at Jemdet Nasr, 1989', *Iraq* 52: 25–39.
—— (ed.) (1998), *Ancient Anatolia: Fifty Years' Work by the British Institute of Archaeology at Ankara*, London: British Institute of Archaeology at Ankara.
—— (2000), 'Fourth and Third Millennia Chronologies: The View from Tell Brak, North-East Syria', in C. Marro and H. Hauptmann (eds), *Chronologies des Pays du Caucase et de l'Euphrate aux IVe–IIIe Millénaires*, Paris: De Boccard, 65–72.

—— (2002), *Secrets of the Dark Mound: Jemdet Nasr 1926–1928*, Warminster: Aris & Phillips.
Matthews, T. J., Matthews, W., and McDonald, H. (1994), 'Excavations at Tell Brak, 1994', *Iraq* 56:177–94.
Matthiae, P. (1980), *Ebla: An Empire Rediscovered* (transl. C. Holme), New York: Garden City.
—— (1985), *I tesori di Ebla*, Rome: Editori Laterza.
Mayer, M. (1983), 'Sargons Feldzug gegen Urartu – 714 v. Chr.', *MDOG* 115: 65–132.
Mazar, A. (1997a), 'The Excavations at Tel Beth-Shean During the Years 1989–94', in Silberman and Small, 144–64.
—— (1997b), *Timnah (Tel Batash) I: Stratigraphy and Architecture: Text*, Qedem 37, Jerusalem: Hebrew University.
—— (2006), *Excavations at Tel Beth-Shean 1989–1996, vol. I*, Jerusalem: Hebrew University.
Mazar, A. and Panitz-Cohen, N. (2001), *Timnah (Tel Batash) II: The Finds from the First Millennium BCE*, Qedem 42, Jerusalem: Hebrew University.
Mazar, B. (1986), 'Geshur and Maachah', in. S. Ahituv and B. A. Levine (eds), *The Early Biblical Period: Historical Studies*, Jerusalem: Israel Exploration Society, 113–25.
Medvedskaya, I. (1997), 'The Localization of Hubuškia', in Parpola and Whiting, 197–206.
Mee, C. (1978), 'Aegean Trade and Settlement in Anatolia', *AS* 28: 121–56.
Megaw, A. H. S. (1981), 'Excavations at Ayios Philon, the Ancient Carpasia, II', *RDAC* 209–50.
Melchert, H. C. (ed.) (2003), *The Luwians*, Handbuch der Orientalistik 68, Leiden: Brill.
—— (2007), 'The Borders of Tarhuntassa Revisited', in *Fs B. and A. Dinçol*, 507–13.
Mellaart, J. (1998), 'Beycesultan', in R. Matthews (1998), 61–8.
Mellink, M. J. (ed.) (1986), *Troy and the Trojan War: A Symposium held at Bryn Mawr College, October, 1984*, Bryn Mawr: Bryn Mawr College.
—— (1991), 'The Native Kingdoms of Anatolia', *CAH* III.2: 619–65.
—— (1998), *Kızılbel: An Archaic Painted Tomb Chamber in Northern Lycia*, Philadelphia: University Museum, University of Pennsylvania.
Meyers, E. M. (ed.) (1997), *The Oxford Encyclopedia of Archaeology in the Near East* (5 vols), Oxford: Oxford University Press, cited as *OEANE* .
Michalowski, P. (1977), 'Durum and Uruk during the Ur III Period', *Mesopotamia* 12: 83–96.
—— (1986), 'Mental Maps and Ideology: Reflections on Subartu', in H. Weiss (ed.), *The Origins of Cities in Dry-farming Syria and Mesopotamia in the Third Millennium B.C.*, Guilford, CT: Four Quarters, 129–56.
—— (2001), 'Sumer Dreams of Subartu. Politics and the Geographical Imagination', in K. Van Lerberghe and G. Voet (eds), *Languages and Cultures in Contact: At the Crossroads of Civilizations in the Syro-Mesopotamian Realm* (Proceedings of the 42th [*sic*] Rencontre Assyriologique Internationale, Louvain, 1995), Leuven: Orientalia Lovaniensia Analecta 96, 305–16.
—— (2007), 'Observations on "Elamites" and "Elam" in Ur III Times', *JCS* 59: 1–14.
Michel, C. (2001), *Correspondance des marchands de Kanish au début du II*[e] *millénaire avant J.-C.*, Paris: Cerf, cited as *CMK*.
Mieroop, M. van de (2005), *King Hammurabi of Babylon*, Oxford: Blackwell.
Milano, L. *et al.* (2004), *Third Millennium Cuneiform Texts from Tell Beydar (Seasons 1996–2002)* (Subartu XII), Turnhout: Brepols.
Millard, A. R. (1994), *The Eponyms of the Assyrian Empire: 910–612 BC* (State Archives of Assyria Studies 2), Helsinki: Neo-Assyrian Text Corpus Project.
Miller, J. L. (2001a), 'Anum-Khirbi and his Kingdom', *AoF* 28: 65–101.
—— (2001b), 'Hattusili's Expansion into Northern Syria in Light of the Tikunani Letter', in Wilhelm (2001), 410–29.
Miller, J. M. and Hayes, J. L. (1986), *A History of Ancient Israel and Judah*, London: SCM Press.
Moran, W. L. (1992), *The Amarna Letters*, Baltimore and London: Johns Hopkins University Press.

Mørkholm, O. (1964), 'The Classification of Lycian Coins before Alexander the Great', *Jahrbuch für Numismatik und Geldgeschichte* 14: 65–76.
Moscati, S. (ed.) (2001), *The Phoenicians*, London: I B Taurus (previously published by Bompiani, Milan, 1988).
Moustaka, A. E. *et al.* (eds) (2004), *Klazomenai, Teos, and Abdera: Metropoleis and Colony* (Proceedings of the International Symposium Held at the Archaeological Museum of Abdera, Abdera, 20–21 October 2001), Thessaloniki: University Studio Press.
Müller-Karpe, A. (1995–), 'Untersuchungen in Kuşaklı', *MDOG* 127– (annual reports of excavations).
—— (2002), 'Kuşaklı-Sarissa', *KatHet* 176–88.
Murnane, W. (1990), *The Road to Kadesh* (2nd edn), Chicago: Chicago University Press.
Muscarella, O. W. (1977), ' "Ziwiye" and Ziwiye: The Forgery of a Provenience', *Journal of Field Archaeology* 4: 197–219.
—— (1989), 'Bronzes of Luristan', *Encyclopaedia Iranica* 4: fasc. 5.
—— (1995), 'Art and Archaeology of Western Iran in Prehistory', *CANE* II: 981–9.
Na'aman, N. (1998), 'Sargon II and the Rebellion of the Cypriote Kings against Shilta of Tyre', *Or* 67: 239–47.
—— (2007), 'The Contribution of the Suhu Inscriptions to the Historical Research of the Kingdoms of Israel and Judah', *JNES* 66: 107–22.
Nashef, K. (1982), *Répertoire Géographique des Textes Cunéiformes Bd. 5: Die Orts- und Gewässernamen der mittelbabylonischen und mittelassyrischen Zeit*, Wiesbaden: Ludwig Reichert, cited as *RGTC* 5.
Nasrabadi, B. M. (2005), 'Eine Steininschrift des Amar-Suena aus Tappeh Bormi (Iran)', *ZA* 95: 161–71.
Nassouhi, E. (1924–5), 'Prisme d'Assurbânipal daté de sa trentième année, provenant du temple de Gula à Babylone', *Archiv für Keilschriftforschung* 2: 97–106, cited as *AP*.
Negev, A. and Gibson, S. (2001), *Archaeological Encyclopedia of the Holy Land*, New York and London: Continuum.
Neumann, G. (1979), *Neufunde lykischer Inschriften seit 1901*, Vienna: Österreichischen Akademie der Wissenschaften (cited as *N*).
Neve, P. (1993), *Hattusa. Stadt der Götter und Tempel*, Mainz am Rhein: Philipp von Zabern.
Niemeier, W.-D. (2005), 'Minoans, Mycenaeans, Hittites, and Ionians in Western Asia Minor. New Excavations in Bronze Age Miletus-Milawata', in A. Villing (ed.), *The Greeks in the East*, London: British Museum, 1–36.
Northedge, A., Bamber, A., and Roaf, M. (1988), *Excavations at* ʿAna, Qalʿ*a Island*, Warminster: Aris & Phillips.
Nougayrol, J., Laroche, E., Virolleaud, C., and Schaeffer, C. F. A. (1968), *Ugaritica* V (Mission de Ras Shamra Tome XVI), Paris: Klincksieck.
Novák, M. and Pfälzner, P. (2000–), 'Ausgrabungen in Tall Mišrife-Qatna', *MDOG* 132– (annual reports of excavations).
Oates, D. (1968), *Studies in the Ancient History of Northern Iraq*, London: Oxford University Press.
—— (1982a), 'Tell al Rimah', in J. E. Curtis (1982c), 86–98.
—— (1982b), 'Tell Brak', in J. E. Curtis (1982c), 62–71.
Oates D. and Oates, J. (1997), *Excavations at Tell Brak, vol. II: Nagar in the Third Millennium B.C.*, Cambridge: McDonald Institute for Archaeological Research.
—— (2001), *Nimrud: An Assyrian Imperial City Revealed*, London: British School of Archaeology in Iraq.
Oates, D., Oates, J., and McDonald, H. (1997), *Excavations at Tell Brak, vol. I: The Mitanni and Old Babylonian Periods*, London: British School of Archaeology in Iraq.
Oates, J. (1986), *Babylon*, London: Thames and Hudson.
Oberleitner, W. (1993), 'Die Neuaufstellung des Heroons von Trysa', *Antike Welt* 24: 133–47.

Ohata, K. (ed.) (1966–70), *Tel Zeror* (3 vols), Tokyo: Society for Near Eastern Studies in Japan.

Oldenburg, E. and Rohweder, J. (1981), *The Excavations at Tall Darūk (Usnu?) and ʿArab al-Mulk (Paltos)*, Publications of the Carlsberg Expedition to Phoenicia 8, Copenhagen: Munksgaard.

Olmo Lete, G. del and Montero Fenollós, J.-L. (eds) (1999), *Archaeology of the Upper Syrian Euphrates: The Tishrin Dam Area* (Proceedings of the International Symposium held at Barcelona, 28–30 January 1998), Barcelona: Editorial AUSA.

Olşen, K. F., Bayram, F., and Özme, A. (eds) (2006), *27. Araştırma Sonuçları: 30 Mayıs-3 Haziran 2005, Antalya* (2 vols), Ankara: Kültür ve Turizm Bakanlığı DÖSİMM Basimevi.

Omura, S. (ed.) (2005), *Kaman-Kalehöyük*, vol. 14, Tokyo: Middle Eastern Culture Center in Japan.

Oppenheim, M. F. von (1933), *Tell Halaf: A New Culture in Oldest Mesopotamia*, London and New York: G. P. Putnam's Sons.

Oren, D. (ed.) (2000), *The Sea Peoples and their World: A Reassessment*, Philadelphia: University of Pennsylvania.

Osten, H. H. von der (1937), *The Alishar Hüyük Seasons of 1930–1932*, Chicago: OIP 30, University of Chicago Press.

Otten, H. (1973), *Eine althethitische Erzählung um die Stadt Zalpa* (*StBoT* 17), Wiesbaden: Harrassowitz.

—— (1981), *Die Apologie Hattusili III* (*StBoT* 24), Wiesbaden: Harrassowitz.

—— (1988), *Die Bronzetafel aus Boğazköy: ein Staatsvertrag Tuthalijas IV.*, Wiesbaden: Harrassowitz.

Owen, D. I. and Wilhelm, G. (eds) (2005), *Studies on the Civilization and Culture of Nuzi and the Hurrians*, vol. 15: *General Studies and Excavations at Nuzi 11/1*, Bethesday, MD: CDL Press.

Özgüç, N. (1966), 'Excavations at Acemhöyük', *Anadolu (Anatolia)* 10: 29–52.

—— (1980), 'Seal Impressions from the Palaces of Acemhöyük', in E. Porada (ed.), *Ancient Art in Seals*, Princeton: Princeton University Press, 61–86.

Özgüç, T. (1956), 'The Dagger of Anitta', *Belleten* 20: 29–36.

—— (1966, 1969), *Altıntepe* I–II, Ankara: Türk Tarih Kurumu Basimevi.

—— (1971), *Kültepe and its Vicinity in the Iron Age*, Ankara: Türk Tarih Kurumu Basimevi.

—— (1986), *Kültepe-Kanish II: New Researches at the Trading Center of the Ancient Near East*, Ankara: Türk Tarih Kurumu Basimevi.

—— (1988), *İnandıktepe, An Important Cult Center in the Old Hittite Period*, Ankara: Türk Tarih Kurumu Basimevi.

—— (2002), 'Maşathöyük', *KatHet* 168–71.

Özgüç, T. and Özgüç, N. (1949), *Türk Tarih Kurumu Tarafından Yapilan Karahöyük Hafriyatı Raporu 1947. Ausgrabungen in Karahöyük*, Ankara: Türk Tarih Kurumu Basimevi.

Özgüç, T. and Temizer, R. (1993), 'The Eskiyapar Treaure', in M. J. Mellink, E. Porada, and T. Özgüç (eds) (1993), *Aspects of Art and Iconography: Anatolia and its Neighbours. Studies in Honor of Nimet Özgüç*, Ankara: Türk Tarih Kurumu Basimevi, 613–28.

Özyar, A. (ed.) (2005), *Field Seasons 2001–2003 of the Tarsus-Gözlükule Interdisciplinary Research Project*, Istanbul: Ege Yayınları.

Özyiğit, Ö. (2006), 'Phokaia', in Radt, 303–14.

Paley, S. M. (2006), 'The Excavations at Çadır Höyük, 2004', in Olşen *et al.*, 1: 351–66.

Palmieri, A. (1981), 'Excavations at Arslantepe (Malatya)', *AS* 31: 101–19.

Panaino, A. (2003), 'Herodotus I, 96–101: "Deioces" Conquest of Power and the Foundation of Sacred Royalty', in Lanfranchi *et al.*, 327–38.

Papalexandrou, N. (2006), 'A Cypro-Archaic Public Building at Polis Chrysochou, 1999–2003: Preliminary Report', *Report of the Department of Antiquities, Cyprus*, 222–37.

Parker, B. J. (2001), *The Mechanics of Empire: The Northern Frontier of Assyria as a Case Study in Imperial Dynamics*, Helsinki: Helsinki University Press.

Parpola, S. (1970), *Neo-Assyrian Toponyms* (Alter Orient und Altes Testament 6), Neukirchen-Vluyn: Butzon and Bercker Kevelaer.

—— (1987), *The Correspondence of Sargon II, Part I* (State Archives of Assyria, vol. I), Helsinki: Helsinki University Press, cited as *SAA* I.

—— (1990), 'A Letter from Marduk-apla-usur of Anah to Rudamu/Uratamis, King of Hamath', in P. J. Riis and M. L. Buhl (eds), *Les Objets de la période dite syro-hittite (l'Âge du Fer), Hama II/2*, Copenhagen: Carlsberg Foundation, 257–65.

—— (1995) 'The Construction of Dur-Šarrukin in the Assyrian Royal Correspondence', in A. Caubet (ed.), *Khorsabad, le palais de Sargon II, roi d'Assyrie: actes du colloque organisé au musée du Louvre par le Service culturel les 21 et 22 janvier, 1994*, Paris: Documentation Française, 47–77.

Parpola, S. and Watanabe, K. (1988), *Neo-Assyrian Treaties and Loyalty Oaths* (State Archives of Assyria, vol. II), Helsinki: Helsinki University Press, cited as *SAA* II.

Parpola, S. and Whiting, R. M. (eds) (1997), *Assyria 1995* (Proceedings of the 10th Anniversary Symposium of the Neo-Assyrian Text Corpus Project, Helsinki, 10–11 September 1995), Helsinki: Neo-Assyrian Text Project, Department of Asian and African Studies, University of Helinski.

Parpola, S. and Porter, M. (2001), *The Helsinki Atlas of the Near East in the Neo-Assyrian Period*, Helsinki: Casco Bay Assyriological Institute.

Parr, P. J. (1983), 'The Tell Nebi Mend Project', *Les annales archéologiques arabes syriennes* 33/2: 99–117.

Parrot, A. (1948), *Tello, vingt campagnes de fouilles (1877–1933)*, Paris: Albin Michel.

Pecorella, P. E. and Salvini, M. (1984), *Tra lo Zagros e l'Urmia: Richerche storiche ed archeologiche nell'Azerbaigiano Iranico*, Incunabula Graeca, vol. 78, Rome: Edizioni dell'Ateneo.

Perrot, J. and Ladiray, D. (1996), 'The Palace of Susa', in J. G. Westenholz (1996b), 237–54.

Pfälzner, P. (2006), 'Syria's Royal Tombs Uncovered', *Current World Archaeology* 15: 12–22.

Pinnock, F. (2001), 'The Urban Landscape of Old Syrian Ebla', *JCS* 53: 13–33.

Piotrovsky, B. B. (1969), *Urartu* (transl. J. Hogarth), London: Barrie and Rockliff, The Cresset Press.

Pitard, W. (1987), *Ancient Damascus*, Winona Lake: Eisenbrauns.

Poetto, M. (1993), *L'iscrizione luvio-geroglifica di Yalburt. Nuove acquisizioni relative alla geografia dell'Anatolia sud-occidentale (Studia Mediterranea 8)*, Pavia: G. Iuculano.

Polit, A. (1999), 'Die Stadt Katapa im Lichte hethitischer Keilschrifttexte', *Hethitica* 14: 81–96.

Posener, G. (1940), *Princes et Pays d'Asie et de Nubie*, Brussels: Fondation Égyptologique Reine Élisabeth.

Postgate, J. N. (1973), 'The Inscription of Tiglath-pileser III at Mila Mergi', *Sumer* 29: 47–59.

—— (1976), *Fifty Neo-Assyrian Legal Documents*, Warminster: Aris & Phillips.

—— (1998), 'Between the Plateau and the Sea: Kilise Tepe 1994–97', in R. Matthews (1998), 137–9.

—— (2008), 'The Chronology of the Iron Age seen from Kilise Tepe', *ANES* 45: 166–87.

Potts, D. T. (ed.) (1983), *Dilmun: New Studies in the Archaeology and Early History of Bahrain*, Berliner Beitrage zur Vorderen Orient Bd 2, Berlin: Dietrich Reimer Verlag.

—— (1989), 'Seleucid Karmania', in L. De Meyer and E. Haerinck (eds), *Archaeologica Iranica et Orientalis: Miscellanea in Honorem Louis Vanden Berghe*, Gent: Peeters, 581–603.

—— (ed.) (1990), *The Arabian Gulf in Antiquity* (2 vols), Oxford: Clarendon Press.

—— (1995), 'Distant Shores: Ancient Near Eastern Trade with South Asia and Northeast Africa', *CANE* III: 1451–63.

—— (1999), *The Archaeology of Elam*, Cambridge: Cambridge University Press.

—— (2004), 'Tepe Yahya', *Encyclopaedia Iranica*, available online at www.iranica.com.

—— (2005a), 'Cyrus the Great and the Kingdom of Anshan', in V. S. Curtis and S. Stewart (eds), *Birth of the Persian Empire*, London: I. B. Tauris, 7–28.

—— (2005b), 'Exit Aratta: Southeastern Iran and the land of Marhashi', *Name-ye Iran-e Bastan* 6: 1–11.

—— (2006), 'An Ass for Ares', *Bulletin of the Asia Institute* 16: 103–15.

Potts, T. (1994), *Mesopotamia and the East: An Archaeological and Historical Study of Foreign Relations, 3400–2000 BC*, Oxford: Oxford University Committee for Archaeology.

Powell, M. A. (1980), 'Karkar, Dabrum and Tall Ǧidr: an unresolved problem', *JNES* 39: 47–52.

Prag, K. (1991), 'Preliminary Report on the Excavations at Tell Iktanu and Tel al-Hammam, Jordan, 1990', *Levant* 23: 55–66.

Pratico, G. D. (1993), *Nelson Glueck's 1938–1940 Excavations at Tell el-Kheleifeh: A Reappraisal*, Atlanta: Scholars Press.

Pritchard, J. B. (1969), *Ancient Near Eastern Texts relating to the Old Testament* (3rd edn), Princeton: Princeton University Press, cited as *ANET*.

—— (1978), *Recovering Sarepta, a Phoenician City: Excavations at Sarafand, Lebanon, 1969–1974, by the University Museum of the University of Pennsylvania*, Princeton: Princeton University Press.

Radner, K. (2006), 'How to Reach the Upper Tigris: the Route Through the Tūr ʿAbdīn', *State Archives of Assyria Bulletin* 15: 273–305.

Radner, K. and Schachner, A. (2001), 'From Tushhan to Amedi: Topographical Questions concerning the Upper Tigris Region in the Assyrian Period', in N. Tuna, J. Öztürk, and J. Velibeyoglu (eds), *Salvage Project of the Archaeological Heritage of the Ilisu and Carchemish Dam Reservoirs: Activities in 1999*, Ankara: ODTÜ/METU,752–76.

Radt, W. (ed.) (2006), *Stadtgrabungen und Stadt-forschung im westlichen Kleinasien: Geplantes und Erreichtes, Internationales Symposium 6./7. August 2004 in Bergama (Türkei)*, Byzas 3, Istanbul: Ege Yayınları.

Raeck, W. (2006), 'Priene', in Radt, 315–24.

Raimond, E. (2002), 'Tlos, un centre de pouvoir politique et religieux de l'Age du Bronze au IVe s. av. J.-C.', *An Ant* 10: 113–29.

Rainey, A. F. (2007), 'Whence Came the Israelites and their Language?', *IEJ* 57: 41–64.

Reade, J. E. (1982a), 'Nimrud', in J. E. Curtis (1982c), 99–112.

—— (1982b), 'Tell Taya', in J. E. Curtis (1982c), 72–8.

—— (2003), 'Why Did the Medes Invade Assyria?', in Lanfranchi *et al.*, 149–56.

Redford, D. B. (1992), *Egypt, Israel, and Canaan in Ancient Times*, Princeton: Princeton University Press.

—— (ed.) (2001), *Oxford Encyclopedia of Ancient Egypt* (3 vols), Oxford: Oxford University Press, cited as *OEAE*.

Reyes, A. (1994), *Archaic Cyprus: A Study of the Textual and Archaeological Evidence*, Oxford: Clarendon Press.

Reynolds, F. (2003), *The Babylonian Correspondence of Esarhaddon* (State Archives of Assyria, vol. XVIII), Helsinki: Helsinki University Press, cited as *SAA* XVIII.

Richter, T. (2003), 'Das "Archiv des Idanda": Bericht über Inschriftenfunde der Grabungskampagne 2002 in Mišrife/Qatna', *MDOG* 135: 167–88.

—— (2005), 'Qatna in the Late Bronze Age. Preliminary Remarks', in Owen and Wilhelm, 109–26.

Riis, P. J. *et al.* (1970–86), *Sukas: Publications of the Carlsberg Expedition to Phoenicia* (8 vols), Copenhagen: Kongelige Danske Videnskabernes Selskab.

Roaf, M. (1974), 'The Subject Peoples on the Base of the Statue of Darius', *Cahiers de la délegation archéologique française en Iran* 4: 73–160.

—— (1996), *Cultural Atlas of Mesopotamia and the Ancient Near East*, Oxford: Andromeda.

—— (2003), 'The Median Dark Age', in Lanfranchi *et al.*, 13–22.

Robert, L. and Robert, J. (1989), *Claros I. Décrets hellénistiques*, Paris: Éditions Recherche sur les Civilisations.

—— (1992), 'Décret de Colophon pour un Chresmologue de Smyrne appelé à diriger l'oracle de Claros', *BCH* 280–91.

Rolle, R. (1989), *The World of the Scythians* (transl. G. Walls), London: Batsford.

Roller, L. (2008), 'Early Phrygian Sculpture: Refining the Chronology', *ANES* 45: 188–201.

Röllig, W. (1978), 'Dur-Katlimmu', *Or* 47: 419–30.

Rollinger, R. (2003a), 'Kerkenes Dağ and the Median "Empire" ', in Lanfranchi *et al.*, 321–6.

—— (2003b), 'The Western Expansion of the Median "Empire": A Re-examination', in Lanfranchi *et al.*, 289–319.

—— (2006), 'The Terms "Assyria" and "Syria" Again', *JNES* 65: 283–7.

Römer, W. H. Ph. (1985), 'Zur Siegesinschrift des Königs Utuhegal von Unug (+/-2116–2110 v. Chr.), *Or* 54: 274–88.

Roobaert, A. and Bunnens, G. (1999), 'Excavations at Tell Ahmar-Til Barsib', in del Olmo Lete and Montero Fenollós, 163–78.

Roos, P. (1969), 'Topographical and Other Notes on South-eastern Caria', *Opuscula Atheniensia* 8: 59–93.

Root, M. C. (1995), 'Art and Archaeology of the Achaemenid Empire', *CANE* IV: 2615–37.

Rose, C. B. and Körpe, R. (2006), 'The Granicus River Valley Survey Project, 2004', in Olşen *et al.*, 1: 323–32.

Rossner, E. P. (1988), *Die hethitischen Felsreliefs in der Türkei* (2nd edn), Munich: E. P. Rossner.

Rothman, M. S. (ed.) (2001), *Uruk Mesopotamia and Its Neighbours: Cross-cultural Interactions in the Era of State Formation*, Oxford: James Currey; Santa Fe: School of American Research Press.

Rouault, O. (1984), *L'archive de Puzurum (Terqa Final Reports no. 1)*, Bibliotheca Mesopotamica 16, Malibu: Undena Publications.

—— (1998), Récherches récentes à Tell Ashara-Terqa (1991–1995)', *Subartu* IV/1: 313–30.

Routledge, B. (2004), *Moab in the Iron Age*, Philadelphia: University of Pennsylvania Press.

Roux, G. (1980), *Ancient Iraq* (2nd edn), Penguin: London.

Russell, J. M. (1996), 'Nineveh', in J. G. Westenholz (1996b), 153–70.

Safar, F. (1949), 'Soundings at Tell Al-Lahm', *Sumer: A Journal of Archaeology in Iraq* 5: 154–72.

Safar, F., Mustafa, M. A., and Lloyd, S. (1981), *Eridu*, Baghdad: Ministry of Culture and Information.

Saggs, H. W. F. (1955), 'The Nimrud Letters, 1952 – Part II. Relations with the West', *Iraq* 17: 126–60.

—— (1984), *The Might that was Assyria*, London: Sidgwick and Jackson.

—— (1995), *Babylonians*, London: British Museum Press.

Sagona, A. (ed.) (2004), *A View from the Highlands: Archaeological Studies in Honour of Charles Burney*, Ancient Near Eastern Studies Supplement 12, Herent: Peeters, cited as *Fs Burney*.

Sagona, A. and Sagona, C. (2004), *Archaeology at the North-East Anatolian Frontier, I: An Historical Geography and a Field Survey of the Bayburt Province*, Ancient Near Eastern Studies Supplement 14, Louvain, Paris, and Dudley, MA: Peeters.

Saidah, R. (1966, 1967) 'Fouilles de Khaldeh', *Bulletin du Musée de Beyrouth* 19: 51–90; 20: 155–80.

Sallaberger, W. (1999), 'Ur-III-Zeit', in Sallaberger and Westenholz (eds), 121–390.

Sallaberger, W. and Westenholz, A. (eds) (1999), *Akkade-Zeit und Ur III-Zeit*, Göttingen: Vandenhoeck and Ruprecht; Freiburg: Universität Freiburg.

Salvini, M. (1994), 'Una Lettera di Hattusili relativa alla spedizione contro Hahhum', *SMEA* 34: 61–80.

—— (1995a), *Geschichte und Kultur der Urartäer*, Darmstadt: Wissenschaftliche Buchgesellschaft.

—— (1995b), 'Some Historic-Geographical Problems Concerning Assyria and Urartu', in M. Liverani (ed.), *Neo-Assyrian Geography*, Rome: Università di Roma 'La Sapienza',

Dipartimento di Scienze storiche, archaeologiche e antropologiche dell'Antichità Qaderni di Geografica Storica 5: 43–53.

—— (1996), *The Habiru Prism of King Tunip-Teššup of Tikunani*, Documenta Asiana Vol III, Rome: Istituti editoriali e poligrafici internazionali.

—— (1998), 'Un royaume hourrite en Mésopotamie du Nord à l'époque de Hattusili I', *Subartu* IV: 305–11.

—— (2005), 'Some Considerations on Van Kalesi', in A. A. Çilingiroğlu and G. Darbyshire (eds), *Anatolian Iron Ages 5* (Proceedings of the Fifth Anatolian Iron Ages Colloquium held at Van, 6–10 August 2001), London: British Institute at Ankara Monograph 31, 145–155.

Sams, G. K. (ed.) (1994–5), *The Gordion Excavations, 1950–1973: Final Reports* (4 vols), Philadelphia: University of Pennsylvania.

—— (1995), 'Midas of Gordion and the Anatolian Kingdom of Phrygia', *CANE* II: 1147–59.

Sams, G. K. and Goldman, A. L. (2006), 'Gordion', in K. Olşen, H. Dönmez, and A. Özme (eds), *27 Kazı Sonuçları Toplantısı: 30 Mayıs – 3 Haziram 2005, Antalya* 2, Ankara: Kültür ve Turizm Bakanlığı DÖSİMM Basımevi, 43–56.

Sancisi-Weerdenburg, H. (1988), 'Was There Ever a Median Empire?', in Kuhrt and Sancisi-Weerdenburg, 197–212.

—— (1995), 'Darius I and the Persian Empire', *CANE* II: 1035–50.

Sandars, N. K. (1985), *The Sea Peoples* (rev. edn), London: Thames and Hudson.

Sarraf, M. R. (2003), 'Archaeological Excavations in Tepe Ekbatana (Hamadan) by the Iranian Archaeological Mission between 1983 and 1999', in Lanfranchi *et al.*, 269–79.

Sasson, J. M. (ed.) (1995), *Civilizations of the Ancient Near East* (4 vols), New York: Charles Scribner's Sons, cited as *CANE*.

Savage, S. H. and Keller, D. R. (2007), 'Archaeology in Jordan, 2006 Season', *AJA* 111: 523–51.

Scerrato, U. (1966), 'Excavations at Dahan-i Ghulaman (Seistan-Iran): First Preliminary Report (1962–1963)', *East and West* 16: 9–30.

Schmidt, E. F. (1931), 'Excavations at Fara, 1931', *University of Pennsylvania Museum Journal* 22: 193–235.

—— (1953, 1957, 1970), *Persepolis* (3 vols), Chicago: University of Chicago Press.

Schmidt, E. F., Loon, M. N. van, and Curvers, H. H. (1989), *The Holmes Expeditions to Luristan*, Chicago: OIP 108, University of Chicago Press.

Schmitt, R. (1987), 'Bīsotūn', *Encyclopaedia Iranica* 4: 289–305.

—— (1990), 'Carmania', *Encyclopaedia Iranica* 4: 822–3.

—— (1991), *The Bisitun Inscriptions of Darius the Great: Old Persian Text*, London: School of Oriental and African Studies.

—— (1995), 'Drangiana', *Encyclopaedia Iranica* 5: 535–7.

Schniedewind, W. M. (1998), 'The Geopolitical History of Philistine Gath', *BASOR* 309: 69–77.

Schramm, W. (1983), ' "Uša" = Sama'al', *Or* 52: 458–60.

Schuler, E. von (1956), 'Die Würdenträgereide des Arnuwanda', *Or* 25: 209–40.

—— (1965), *Die Kaškaer*, Berlin: De Gruyter.

Schwartz, G., Curvers, H., and Stuart, B. (2000a), 'A Third Millennium B.C. Elite Tomb from Tell Umm el-Marra, Syria', *Antiquity* 74: 771–2.

Schwartz, G. *et al.* (2000b), 'Excavation and Survey in the Jabbul Plain, Western Syria: The Umm el-Marra Project 1996–1997', *AJA* 104: 419–62.

Schwartz, J. (1990), 'Once More on the "Boundary of Gezer" Inscriptions and the History of Gezer and Lydda at the End of the Second Temple Period', *IEJ* 40: 47–57.

Seeher, J. (2000), 'Getreidelagerung in unterirdischen Großspeichern: zur Methode und ihrer Anwendung im 2. Jahrtausend v. Chr. am Beispiel der Befunde in Hattuša', *SMEA* 42: 261–301.

—— (2001), 'Die Zerstörung der Stadt Hattusa', in Wilhelm (2001), 623–34.

—— (2002), *Hattusha Guide: A Day in the Hittite Capital*, Istanbul: Ege Yayınları.
—— (ed.) (2006a), *Ergebnisse der Grabungen an den Ostteichen und am mittleren Büyükkale-Nordwesthang in den Jahren 1996–2000*, Mainz am Rhein: Philipp von Zabern.
—— (2006b), 'Hattuša-Tuthalia-Stadt? Argumente für eine Revision der Chronologie der hethitischen Haupstadt', in van den Hout (2006), 131–46.
Serdaroğlu, Ü (1995), *Assos*, Istanbul: Archaeology and Art Publication.
Seton-Williams, M. V. (1967), 'The Excavations at Tell Rifaʿat, 1964: Second Preliminary Report', *Iraq* 29: 16–33.
Sevin, V. (1995), *İmikuşağı I*, Ankara: Turk Tarih Kurumu Basimevi.
Sevin, V. and Özfırat, A. (2001a), 'Van-Altintepe Excavations', in Belli (2001d), 179–83.
—— (2001b), 'Van Karagündüz Excavations', in Belli (2001d), 140–4.
Shai, I. (2006), 'The Political Organization of the Philistines', in Maeir and de Miroschedji, 347–59.
Sigrist, M. (1992), *Drehem*, Bethesda: CDL Press.
Sigrist, M. and Gomi, T. (1991), *The Comprehensive Catalogue of Published Ur III Tablets*, Bethesda: CDL Press, cited as *CC*.
Sigrist, M. and Westenholz, J. G. (1996), 'The Neo-Sumerian Empire: Its History, Culture and Religion', in J. G. Westenholz (1996b), 31–49.
Silberman, N. A. and Small, D. (eds) (1997), *The Archaeology of Israel: Constructing the Past, Interpreting the Present*, Sheffield: Sheffield Academic Press.
Singer, I. (1981), 'Hittites and Hattians in Anatolia at the Beginning of the Second Millennium B.C.', *JIES* 9: 119–34.
—— (1983), 'Western Anatolia in the Thirteenth Century B.C. according to the Hittite Sources', *AS* 33: 205–17.
—— (1985), 'The Battle of Nihriya and the End of the Hittite Empire', *ZA* 75: 100–23.
—— (1991), 'A Concise History of Amurru', in S. Izre'el, *Amurru Akkadian: A Linguistic Study* (vol. ii), Atlanta: Scholars Press, 135–95 (Appendix III).
—— (1999a), 'A New Letter from Emar', in L. Milano, S. de Martino, F. M. Fales, and G. B. Lanfranchi (eds), *Landscapes, Territories, Frontiers and Horizons in the Ancient Near East* (Proceedings of the 44th Rencontre Assyriologique Internationale, Venice, 1997, vol. II, *Geography and Cultural Landscapes*), Padua: History of the Ancient Near East/Monographs III, 65–72.
—— (1999b), 'A Political History of Ugarit', in W. G. E. Watson and N. Wyatt (eds), *Handbook of Oriental Studies* (Handbuch der Orientalistik, Abt. 1, *Der Nahe und Mittlere Osten: Bd 39*), Leiden, Boston, and Cologne: Brill, 603–733.
—— (2000), Review of Klengel (1999), *BiOr* 57: 636–43.
—— (2002), *Hittite Prayers*, Atlanta: Society of Biblical Literature.
—— (2004), 'The Kuruštama Treaty Reconsidered', in D. Groddek and S. Rössle (eds), *Šarnikze. Hethitologische Studien zum Gedenken am Emil Orgetorix Forrer*, Dresden: Technischen Universität.
—— (2006), 'The Hittites and the Bible Revisited', in Maeir and de Miroschedji, 723–56.
Smith, A. T. and Thompson, T. T. (2004), 'Urartu and the Southern Caucasian Political Tradition', *Fs Burney*: 557–77.
Smith, J. (1997), 'Preliminary Comments on a Rural Cypro-Archaic Sanctuary in Polis-Peristeries', *BASOR* 308: 77–98.
Smith, R. R. R. and Ratté, C. (2006), 'Aphrodisias 2004', in Olşen *et al.*, 2: 19–32.
Soldt, W. H. van (ed.) (2005), *Ethnicity in Ancient Mesopotamia* (Proceedingss of the 48th Rencontre Assyriologique Internationale, Leiden, 1–4 July 2002), Leiden: Nederlands Instituut voor Het Nabije Oosten.
Solomidou-Ieronymidou, M. (2001), 'The discovery of Six Unique Cypro-Archaic Statues at Tamassos', *Report of the Dept of Antiquities, Cyprus*, 165–182.
Sommer, F. (1932), *Die Ahhijavā Urkunden*, Munich: Bayerischen Akademie der Wissenschaften (repr. Hildesheim, 1975), cited as *AU*.

Sommer, M. (ed.) (2001), *Die Levante. Beiträge zur Historisierung des Nahostkonflikts*, Freiburg: Arnold Bergstraesser Institut.
Sommerfeld, W. (1995), 'The Kassites of Ancient Mesopotamia: Origins, Politics, and Culture', *CANE* II: 917–30.
South, A. K. (1992), 'Kalavasos-Ayios-Dhimitrios 1991', *Report of the Dept of Antiquities, Cyprus*, 133–46.
Soysal, Ö. (1990), 'Noch einmal zur Sukziya-Episode im Erlass Telipinus', *Or* 59: 271–9.
Spek, R. van der (1977–8), 'The Struggle of King Sargon II of Assyria against the Chaldaean Merodach-baladan (710–707)', *JEOL* 25: 56–66.
Stager, L. E. and Walker, A. M. (eds.) (1989), *American Expedition to Idalion, Cyprus, 1973–1980*, Chicago: OIP, University of Chicago Press.
Steel, L. (2004), *Cyprus Before History: From the Earliest Settlers to the End of the Bronze Age*, London: Duckworth.
Stein, G. J. (1999), *Rethinking World Systems: Diasporas, Colonies and Interaction in Uruk Mesopotamia*, Tucson: University of Arizona Press.
Steinkeller, P. (1982), 'The Question of Marhaši: A Contribution to the Historical Geography of Iran in the Third Millennium', *ZA* 72: 237–64.
—— (2001), 'New Light on the Hydrology and Topography of Southern Babylonia in the Third Millennium', *ZA* 91: 22–84.
—— (2004), 'A History of Mashkan-shapir and its Role in the Kingdom of Larsa', in Stone and Zimansky (2004a), 26–42.
Stern, E. (ed.) (1993), *The New Encyclopedia of Archaeological Excavations in the Holy Land* (4 vols), New York, London, Toronto, Sydney, Tokyo, and Singapore: Simon and Schuster, cited as *NEAEHL*.
Steve, M.-J. (2001), 'La tablette sumérienne de Šuštar (T. MK 203*)', *Akkadica* 121: 5–21.
Stillwell, R. (ed.) (1976), *The Princeton Encyclopedia of Classical Sites*, Princeton: Princeton University Press, cited as *PECS*.
Stone, E. C. and Zimansky, P. (eds.) (2004a), *The Anatomy of a Mesopotamian City: Survey and Soundings at Mashkan-shapir*, Winona Lake: Eisenbrauns.
—— (2004b), 'Urartian City Planning at Ayanis', *Fs Burney*: 233–43.
Streck, M. (1916), *Assurbanipal und die letzeten assyrischen Könige bis zum Untergange Ninevehs* (3 vols), Leipzig: J. C. Hinrich.
Strommenger, E. and Kohlmeyer, K. (2000), *Die Schichten des 3. Jahrtausends v. Chr. im Zentralhügel E (Ausgrabungen in Tall Biʿa/Tuttul)*, Saarbrücken: Saarbrücker Druckerei und Verlag.
Stronach, D. (1978), *Pasargadae: A Report on the Excavations Conducted by the British Institute of Persian Studies from 1961 to 1963*, Oxford: Clarendon Press.
—— (1985a), 'Pasargadae', *CHI* 2: 838–55.
—— (1985b), 'Tepe Nush-i Jan: The Median Settlement', *CHI* 2: 832–7.
—— (2003), 'Independent Media: Archaeological Notes from the Homeland', in Lanfranchi *et al.*, 233–48.
Stronach, D. and Roaf, M. (1978), 'Excavations at Nush-i Jan', *Iran* 16: 1–28.
Süel, A. (2002), 'Ortaköy-Shapinuwa', in Yener and Hoffner, 157–65.
Süel, A. and Süel, M. (2006), 'Ortaköy/Şapinuwa 2004', in Olşen *et al.*, 2: 1–8.
Sulimirski, T. (1985), 'The Scyths', *CHI* 2: 149–99.
Summers, G. D. (1993), *Tille Höyük: The Late Bronze Age and the Iron Age Transition*, London: British Institute of Archaeology at Ankara.
Summers, G. D. and Summers, F. (1998), 'The Kerkenes Dağ Project', in R. Matthews (1998), 177–94.
—— (2003), 'The Kerkenes Project', *Anatolian Archaeology* 9: 22–4.
—— (2005), 'Kerkenes 2005', *Anatolian Archaeology* 11: 34–6.

—— (2006), 'Aspects of Urban Design at the Iron Age City on the Kerkenes Dağ as Revealed by Geophysical Survey', *An Ant* 14: 71–88.

Sürenhagen, D. (1985), *Paritätische Staatsverträge aus hethitischer Sicht*, Pavia: G. Iuculano.

Swiny S., Rapp, G., and Herscher, E. (eds) (2003), *Sotira Kaminoudhia: An Early Bronze Age Site in Cyprus*, American Schools of Oriental Research Archaeological Reports, no. 8/CAARI Monograph Series, vol. 4, Boston: American Schools of Oriental Research.

Tadmor, H. (1958), 'The Campaigns of Sargon II of Assur (Conclusion)', *JCS* 12: 77–100.

—— (1994), *The Inscriptions of Tiglath-Pileser III, King of Assyria: Critical Edition with Introduction, Translation, and Commentary*, Jerusalem: Israel Academy of Sciences and Humanities, cited as *Tigl. III*.

Talbot, R. J. A. (2000), *Barrington Atlas of the Greek and Roman World*, Princeton: Princeton University Press, cited as *BAGRW*.

Tappy, R. (1992), *The Archaeology of Israelite Samaria, volume I: Early Iron Age Through the Ninth Century BCE*, Atlanta: Scholars Press.

—— (2001), *The Archaeology of Israelite Samaria, volume II: The Eighth Century BCE*, Winona Lake: Eisenbrauns.

Taracha, P. (2007), 'The Capital Hattusa and Other Residential Cities of Hittite Great Kings', *Fs B. and A. Dinçol*, 755–9.

Tarhan, M. T. (1994), 'Recent Research at the Urartian Capital Tushpa', *Tel Aviv* 21: 22–57.

—— (2001), 'Tushpa-Van Fortress: Researches and Excavations at the Mysterious Iron Age Capital', in Belli (2001d), 157–64.

—— (2004), 'Diverse Perspectives on the Anatolian Highlands', *Fs Burney*: 335–42.

Taşyürek, O. A. (1979), 'A Rock Relief of Shalmaneser III on the Euphrates', *Iraq* 41: 47–53, with Pl. XV–XVI (transl. by J. D. Hawkins).

Tatum, L. (1991), 'King Manasseh and the Royal Fortress at Horvat 'Usa', *Biblical Archaeologist* 54: 136–45.

Taylor, J. D. P. *et al.* (1980), 'Excavations at Ayios Philon, the Ancient Carpasia, I', *RDAC* 152–216.

Tekoğlu, R. and Lemaire, A. (2000), 'La bilingue royale louvito-phénicienne de Çineköy', *CRAI*: 961–1007.

Thalmann, J.-P. (2006), *Tell Arqa 1: Les niveaux de l'âge du Bronze*, Beirut: Bibliothèque Archéologique et Historique 117, IFPO.

Thareani-Sussely, Y. (2007), 'The "Archaeology of the Days of Manasseh" Reconsidered in the light of Evidence from the Beersheba Valley', *PEQ* 139: 69–77.

Thompson, R. C. and Mallowan, M. E. L. (1933), 'The British Museum Excavations at Nineveh, 1931–32', *Annals of Archaeology and Anthropology*, University of Liverpool, 20: 71–186.

Thureau-Dangin, F. (1907), *Die sumerischen und akkadischen Königsinschriften*, Leipzig: J. C. Hinrich.

—— (1912), *Une relation de la huitième campagne de Sargon*, Paris: Paul Geuthner.

—— (1931), *Arslan-Tash*, Paris: Paul Geuthner.

Toksöz, C (1986), *Ancient Cities of Lycia*, Istanbul: Hankur Matbaacilik.

Tsuneki, A. (1995), 'Neolithic and Early Bronze Age Layers of Tell Mastuma', *Bulletin of the Ancient Orient Museum* 16: 75–107.

Tubb, J. (1998), *Canaanites*, London: British Museum Press.

—— (2008), 'Israel's First Kings. How Archaeology is Rewriting the Bible', *World Archaeology* 31: 18–28.

Ussishkin, D. (2004), *The Renewed Excavations at Lachish (1973–1994)* (5 vols), Tel Aviv: Emery and Claire Yass Publications.

—— (2008), 'The Chronology of the Iron Age in Israel: The Current State of Research', *ANES* 45: 218–34.

Ussishkin, D. and Woodhead, J. (1994), 'Excavations at Tel Jezreel, 1992–1993: Second Preliminary Report', *Levant* 26: 1–48.

Vallat, F. (1993), *Répertoire Géographique des Textes Cunéiformes 11: Les noms géographiques des sources suso-élamites*, Wiesbaden: Ludwig Reichert, cited as *RGTC* 11.

—— (1995), 'Susa and Susiana in Second-Millennium Iran', *CANE* II: 1023–33.

Van Beek, G. W. (1974), 'The Land of Sheba', in J. B. Pritchard (ed.), *Solomon and Sheba*, London: Phaidon, 40–63.

—— (1984), 'Archaeological Investigations at Tell Jemmeh, Israel', *National Geographic Society Research Reports: 1975 Projects*, Washington, DC, 675–96.

Vanden Berghe, L. (1963), 'Les reliefs élamites de Malamir', *Iranica Antiqua* 3: 22–39.

Vaux, R. de (1969), 'Téman, ville ou région d'Édom?', *Revue Biblique* 76: 379–85.

Veenhof, K. R. (ed.) (1986), *Cuneiform Archives and Libraries* (Proceedings of the 30th Rencontre Assyriologique Internationale, Leiden, 1983), Leiden: Brill.

Vermeule, E. T. and Wolsky, F. Z. (1999), *Toumba tou Skourou: A Bronze Age Potters' Quarter on Morphou Bay in Cyprus*, Cambridge, MA: Harvard University Press.

Vidal, J. (2005), 'Beirut and Ugarit in the 13th Century BCE', *SMEA* 47: 291–8.

Vogelsang, W. J. (1988), 'Some Observations on Achaemenid Hyrcania', *Achaemenid History* III: 121–35.

—— (1992), *The Rise and Organisation of the Achaemenid Empire: The Eastern Iranian Evidence*, Leiden: Brill.

Waele, E. de (1972), 'Shutruk-Nahunte II et les reliefs rupestres dits néo-élamites d'Iseh/ Malamir', *Revue des Archéologiques et Historiens d'Art de Louvain* 5: 17–32.

—— (1976), 'Remarques sur les inscriptions élamites de Šekaf-e Salman et Kul-e Farah près Izeh I. Leur corrélation avec les bas-reliefs', *Le Muséon* 89: 441–50.

Wakita, S. *et al.* (1995), 'Tell Mastuma: A Preliminary Report of the Excavations at Idlib, Syria, in 1994 and 1995', *Bulletin of the Ancient Orient Museum* 16: 1–73.

Wakita, S., Wada, H., and Nishiyama, S. (2000), 'Tell Mastuma. Change in Settlement Plans and Historical Context during the First Quarter of the First Millennium B.C.', in Bunnens (2000a), 537–57.

Walker, C. B. F. (1982), 'Babylonian Chronicle 25: A Chronicle of the Kassite and Isin II Dynasties', in G. van Driel *et al.* (eds), *Zikir Šumim, Assyriological Studies presented to F. R. Kraus on the Occasion of his Seventieth Birthday*, Leiden: Brill, 398–417.

Wartke, R.-B. (1990), *Toprakkale*, Berlin: Akademie Verlag.

Waterman, L. (1930), *Royal Correspondence of the Assyrian Empire Part I*, Ann Arbor: University of Michigan Press.

Weidner, E. F. (1923), *Politische Dokumente aus Kleinasien*, Leipzig: J. C. Hinrichs'sche Buchhandlung; repr. Hildesheim, New York: Georg Olms Verlag, 1970.

—— (1957–8), 'Die Feldzüge und Bauten Tiglatpilesers I', *AfO* 18: 342–60.

Weisberg, D. (1996), 'The Neo-Babylonian Empire', in J. G. Westenholz (1996b), 221–33.

Weiss, H. (1985), 'Tell Leilan on the Habur Plains of Syria', *BA* 48: 5–34.

Werner, P. (1998), *Tall Munbaqa: Bronzezeit in Syrien*, Neumünster: Wachholtz Verlag.

Westenholz, A. (1999), 'The Old Akkadian Period: History and Culture', in Sallaberger and Westenholz, 17–117.

Westenholz, J. G. (1996a), 'Babylon – Place of the Creation of the Great Gods', in J. G. Westenholz (1996b), 197–220.

—— (ed.) (1996b), *Royal Cities of the Biblical World*, Jerusalem: Bible Lands Museum.

—— (1996c), 'Ur – Capital of Sumer', in J. G. Westenholz (1996b), 3–30.

—— (1997), *Legends of the Kings of Agade*, Winona Lake: Eisenbrauns.

—— (ed.) (2000), *Cuneiform Inscriptions in the Collection of the Bible Lands Museum, Jerusalem: The Emar Tablets*, Groningen: Styx.

Whiting, R. M. (1995), 'Amorite Tribes and Nations of Second-Millennium Western Asia', *CANE* II: 1231–42.

Wiesehöfer, J. (2001), *Ancient Persia, from 550 BC to 650 AD*, London and New York: I. B. Tauris.

Wilhelm, G. (1989), *The Hurrians*, Warminster: Aris & Phillips.

—— (1995), 'The Kingdom of Mitanni in Second-Millennium Upper Mesopotamia', *CANE* II: 1243–54.

—— (ed.) (2001), *Akten IV. Internationalen Kongresses für Hethitologie. Würzburg, 4-8 Oktober 1999* (*StBoT* 45), Wiesbaden: Harrassowitz.

Williamson, H. G. M. (1991), 'Jezreel in the Biblical Texts', *Tel Aviv* 18: 72–92.

—— (1996), 'Tel Jezreel and the Dynasty of Omri', *PEQ* 128: 41–51.

Winter, I. J. (1979), 'On the Problems of Karatepe: The Reliefs and their Context', *AS* 29: 115–51.

Wiseman, D. J. (1952), 'A New Stela of Aššur-nasir-pal II', *Iraq* 14: 24–44.

—— (1956), *Chronicles of Chaldean Kings (626–556 B.C.) in the British Museum*, London: British Museum.

—— (1991), 'Babylonia 605–539 B.C.', *CAH* III.2: 229–51.

Woolley, C. L. (1955), *Alalakh: An Account of the Excavations at Tell Atchana in the Hatay, 1937–1949*, London: Society of Antiquaries.

—— (1963), *Excavations at Ur: A Record of Twelve Years' Work*, London: Ernest Benn; New York: Barnes and Noble.

—— (1982), *Ur of the Chaldees: The Final Account. Excavations at Ur* (rev. and updated by P. R. S. Moorey), London: Herbert Press.

Woolley, C. L. *et al.* (1927–76), *Ur Excavations and Ur Excavation Texts* (19 vols), Publications of the Joint Expedition of the British Museum and of the Museum of the University of Pennsylvania to Mesopotamia.

Wright, H. T. (ed.) (1981), *An Early Town on the Deh Luran Plain: Excavations at Tepe Farukhabad*, Ann Arbor: University of Michigan.

Wu Yuhong (1994a), *A Political History of Eshnunna, Mari, and Assyria during the Early Old Babylonian Period (from the End of Ur III to the Death of Šamšī-Adad)*, Changchun: Institute for the History of Ancient Civilizations.

—— (1994b), 'The Treaty between Shadlash (Sumu-Numhim) and Neribtum (Hammi-dushur)', *JAC* 9: 124–36.

Yağcı, R. (2006), 'Excavations at Soli/Pompeiopolis in 2005', *Anadolu Akdenizi Arkeoloji Haberleri/News of Archaeology from Anatolia's Mediterranean Areas* 4: 57–60.

Yakubovich, I. (2008), 'Sociolinguistics of the Luvian Language', available online at http://oi.u-chicago.edu/pdf/yakubovich_diss_2008.pdf.

Yalçın, Ü., Pulak, C., and Slotta, R. (2005), *Das Schiff von Uluburun. Welthandel vor 3000 Jahren. Katalog der Ausstellung des Deutschen Bergbau-Museums Bochum vom 15. Juli 2005 bis 16. Juli 2006*, Bochum: Deutsches Bergbau Museum.

Yassine, K. (1989), 'Mazar', in Homès-Fredericq and Hennessy, 381–4.

Yener, K. A. and Hoffner, H. A. (eds) (2002), *Recent Developments in Hittite Archaeology and History: Papers in Memory of Hans G. Güterbock*, Winona Lake: Eisenbrauns.

Yıldırım, T. and Gates, M.-H. (2007), 'Archaeology in Turkey, 2004–2005', *AJA* 111: 275–356.

Yıldırım, T. and Sipahi, T. (2000), 'Hüseyindede Kazısı', *KST* 22.1: 349–54 (in Turkish).

Yon, M. (2006), *The City of Ugarit at Tel Ras Shamra*, Winona Lake: Eisenbrauns.

Yon, M., Sznycer, M., and Bordreuil, P. (eds) (1995), *Le Pays d'Ougarit autour de 1200 av. J.-C.* (Actes du Colloque Internationale, Paris, 1993), Paris: Éditions Recherche sur les Civilisations.

Young, T. C. (1988), 'The Early History of the Medes and the Persians and the Achaemenid Empire to the Death of Cambyses', *CAH* IV: 1–52.

Young, T. C. and Devine, L. D. (1974), *Excavations at the Godin Project: Second Progress Report*, Toronto: Royal Ontario Museum.

Yoyotte, J. (1972), 'Une statue de Darius découverte à Susa: Les inscriptions hiéroglyphiques. Darius et l'Égypte', *Journal asiatique* 260: 253–66.

Zaccagnini, C. (1995), 'War and Famine at Emar', *Or* 64: 92–109.

Zadok, R. (1985), *Répertoire Géographique des Textes Cunéiformes 8: Geographical Names According to New- and Late- Babylonian Texts*, Wiesbaden: Ludwig Reichert, cited as *RGTC* 8.

—— (1991), 'Elamite Onomastics', *Studi Epigrafici e Linguistici sul Vicino Oriente* 8: 225–37.

—— (2002), *The Ethno-Linguistic Character of Northwestern Iran and Kurdistan in the Neo-Assyrian Period*, Jaffa: Archaeological Center Publications.

Zevit, Z. (1985), 'The Problem of ʿAi: New Theory Rejects the Battle as Described in Bible but Explains how Story Evolved', *BAR* 11.2: 58–9.

Zimansky, P. E. (1985), *Ecology and Empire: The Structure of the Urartian State*, Studies in Ancient Oriental Civilization no. 41, Chicago: OIP, University of Chicago Press.

—— (1998), *Ancient Ararat: A Handbook of Urartian Studies*, Delmar/New York: Caravan Books.

Zimmermann, M. (2005), 'Eine Stadt und ihr kulturelles Erbe. Vorbericht über Feldforschungen im zentral-lykischen Phellos 2002–2004', *IstMitt* 55: 215–70.

Zoroğlu, K. L. (2006), 'Excavations and Repair Work at Kelenderis in 2005', *News of Archaeology from Anatolia's Mediterranean Areas* 4: 25–30.

INDEX I: PEOPLES AND PLACES

(Page nos in bold indicate specific entries. mr. = mountain range, r. = river.)

INDEX II: PERSONS

an. = ancestor, b. = brother, Byz. = Byzantine, d. = daughter, dyn. = dynasty, Eg. = Egyptian, emp. = emperor, f. = father, found. = founder, Gk = Greek, grands. = grandson, l. = leader, leg. = legendary, m. = mother, Maced. = Macedonian, m.c. = military commander, merch. = merchant, neph. = nephew, off. = official, p'cess = princess, Pers. = Persian, p. = prince, philos. = philosopher, pret. = pretender, q. = queen, rep. = representative, Rom. = Roman, r. = ruler*, s. = son, sat. = satrap, w. = wife.
(*term used generically to refer to kings, chieftains, tyrants, governors)

INDEX III: DEITIES